Advanced Accounting

The Willard J. Graham Series in Accounting

Consulting Editor   Robert N. Anthony   *Harvard University*

ADVANCED ACCOUNTING

Leopold A. Bernstein, Ph.D., CPA

Professor of Accounting
Baruch College
of the City University of New York

Calvin Engler, Ph.D., CPA

Professor of Accounting
Iona College

 1982

RICHARD D. IRWIN, INC.   Homewood, Illinois   60430

ISBN 0-256-02456-1

Library of Congress Catalog Card No. 81–82998

Printed in the United States of America

1 2 3 4 5 6 7 8 9 0 RRD 9 8 7 6 5 4 3 2

To our wives, Cynthia and Phyllis

Preface

Authors of an advanced accounting text for the 1980s and beyond face a number of significant challenges. First, the considerable complexity of the subject matter does cause serious learning difficulties to many students. At the same time, larger than usual enrollments and class sizes require now, more than ever, that the writing style and the exposition of the text be as helpful to individual study effort as possible. Second, the subject matter to be covered is growing at an unprecedented rate, and many traditional as well as new topics vie for inclusion in this often terminal course of the accounting sequence. Third are the pedagogical considerations which determine the optimal blend of theory and practice and of concepts and procedures.

As to the first challenge, the authors have endeavored to follow in each chapter a step-by-step approach which explains to the student the underlying theory as well as the why and the how of the subject matter. Widespread use is made of examples and detailed illustrations. Each chapter begins with an overview section of the subject matter and ends with a series of questions which should be helpful to the student in testing study coverage and comprehension. The basic approach is to expose the student to a gradual development of the subjects covered in a comprehensive yet easy to follow and to absorb manner.

The second challenge is met by including in the text not only the traditional subjects associated with the advanced accounting area, but also newer areas such as SEC accounting and accounting for a wider variety of nonbusiness organizations. An earnings per share chapter, whose coverage is consistent with an advanced-level text, is included because this subject often cannot be accommodated in the already overburdened intermediate level courses. The watchword here is *flexibility*. The selection of topics and their organization affords instructors the maximum leeway in teaching an advanced course consisting of subject matter configurations best suited to their students' objectives. To this end, specialized or difficult subject matter has been moved to appropriate end-of-chapter appendixes, thus affording the instructor the easiest choice for their inclusion or exclusion.

The third challenge was met by what the authors believe is a good blend of emphasis on theory and practice. Throughout the text we have endeavored to explain the theory behind procedures as well as a variety of viewpoints, while always clearly identifying the generally accepted accounting standards in current use. To heighten student interest, the text is illustrated with a variety of treatments used in published financial statements.

Every effort was made to render this text as up to date as possible. All chapters incorporate the latest professional pronouncements. Thus, the chapter on accounting for foreign operations incorporates the latest approach reconsidered by the FASB in June 1981 while retaining the presently authoritative *SFAS No. 8* in an appendix. There is a rich mix of exercises and problems to cover both approaches. As the expected shift from *SFAS No. 8* to the new approach occurs, the instructor will find that the teaching focus can be changed with ease.

The chapters on accounting for state and local governments as well as other nonbusiness organizations reflect the latest pronouncements by the Financial Accounting Standards Board, the Municipal Finance Officers Association of the United States and Canada, the National Council on Governmental Accounting, and the American Institute of Certified Public Accountants.

The chapter on SEC accounting includes the provisions of the SEC's new 1980 integrated disclosure system as well as an appendix which illustrates comprehensive financial statements included in filings with the commission. Chapter 20, Corporate Reorganizations and Liquidations, contains a modern version of the realization and liquidation account which replaces the now-archaic T-account version. This chapter also contains the provisions of the recently enacted Bankruptcy Act.

The first 11 chapters contain a comprehensive discussion of business combinations and consolidated statements. The current trend in accounting for investments by parent companies is to use what we call the "complete equity" method. When this method is used, the parent company records on its books all of the entries that affect consolidated net income. These entries are reflected in the carrying value of the Investment in Subsidiary account. Thus, the parent company's net income is the same as consolidated net income. This method of accounting for investments in subsidiaries gives the reader a preview of all of the adjusting entries that will be required in the preparation of consolidated working papers. Accordingly, we use this method for all illustrations contained in the consolidation chapters.

Other methods used in practice, principally the "cost" method and the "modified equity" method (we prefer the designation of "incomplete equity" method) are also covered in this text. To provide the user of this text with the greatest degree of flexibility, we provide parallel treatments for these methods by using the same illustrations used for the "complete equity" method. The "cost method" is contained in a separate appendix at the end of each chapter, where appropriate. Similar treatment—a separate appendix—is given the "incomplete equity" method, thus enabling users to select either method or both.

To provide additional flexibility for the users of this text, the chapter content was designed to exclude the more complex areas from the chapter and to provide these areas as self-contained appendixes. Thus, separate appendixes are provided for (1) tax aspects of mergers; (2) elimination entries on a net-of-tax basis when consolidated income tax returns are filed; (3) elimination entries on a net-of-tax basis when separate income tax returns are filed; (4) income tax requirements for filing consolidated income tax returns; (5) fractional elimination; (6) alternate methods of attributing gains and losses on the purchase of intercompany bonds; (7) trial balance working papers; and (8) "push down" theory. The latter theory has recently received some attention by the Accounting Standards Executive Committee of the AICPA.

Also provided in the consolidation chapters are published Consolidated Statements of Changes in Financial Position. The published statements illustrate the treatment of minority interest net income, dividends received by the parent company, equity in earnings of investees, and other matters. A discussion of these items and how they affect the preparation of the statement is also included.

Following this major area are a variety of specified topics which can be used by the instructor in any sequence that is desired. In our treatment of partnership accounting, we cover the tax basis of a partnership interest and the taxable gain or loss on the sale of a partnership interest. These matters are presented in a self-contained appendix, since we believe that some users prefer to cover this topic while others do not.

The exercises and problems which follow most chapters and are designed to reinforce the learning process have been class-tested; they reflect a variety of levels of complexity. A significant number of exercises and problems are based on recent CPA examinations.

Acknowledgments

While there are many to whom we are indebted for the encouragement and assistance rendered to us which enabled us to undertake and complete this project, our first and foremost debt is to Distinguished University Professor Emanuel Saxe. We were both privileged to have been students of his and we both count him as one of our dearest friends. Those who have benefited from his constructive and analytical reviews can fully appreciate the impact of Professor Saxe's review of portions of this work.

Naming everyone who assisted us in this project would make this section unwieldy. However, there are those who must be singled out. Among those to whom we wish to express our sincerest appreciation for reading portions of this manuscript are Robert N. Anthony, Harvard University; Martin Mellman, Harry Davis, Abraham N. Tawil, Hugo Nurnberg and Victor Pastena of Baruch College of the City University of New York; Terry Arndt, Ball State University; Roy E. Baker, University of Missouri; Galen D. Hadley, University of South Dakota; Orville Keister, University of Akron; Abdel M. Agami, Old Dominion University; Abraham J. Simon, Queens College of the City University of New York; Fred Spindel, partner, Coopers & Lybrand; Michael L. Ferrante, partner, Ernst and Whinney; and E. Raymond Simpson, project director, Financial Accounting Standards Board.

The authors are also greatly indebted to the American Institute of Certified Public Accountants for granting permission to use problems from the certified public accountant examinations and to quote material from its publications; the Municipal Finance Officers Association of the United States and

Canada for permitting us to reproduce exhibits and financial statements for state and local governments; the National Association of College and University Business Officers for granting permission to use some of their material; the United Way of America for permitting the reproduction of illustrations from *Accounting and Financial Reporting: A Guide for United Ways and Not-For-Profit Human Service Organizations;* and the American Law Institute and the National Conference of Commissioners on Uniform State Laws for allowing us to reproduce the Uniform Partnership Act.

Finally, we wish to express our appreciation to our wives, Cynthia and Phyllis, for their patience and understanding while this was being written and for their valuable editorial assistance. Our children, Debbie and Jeffrey and Linda and Mitchell, rendered assistance with various stages of typing and proofreading of the manuscript.

We sincerely solicit comments and suggestions for improving this text from users and others.

Leopold A. Bernstein
Calvin Engler

Contents

1. **An introduction to accounting for multi-unit enterprises: Home office and branch accounting** 2

Agencies. Branch operations: *Shipments to branch—at cost. Shipments to branch—billed price in excess of cost. Financial statements. Reconciliation of reciprocal accounts. Interbranch freight charges.*

2. **Business combinations** 26

Reasons for combinations. Legal forms of business combinations: *Statutory merger. Statutory consolidation. Acquisition.* Directional and antitrust considerations: *Horizontal combinations. Vertical combinations. Conglomerate combinations. Circular combinations.* METHODS OF ACCOUNTING FOR BUSINESS COMBINATIONS. Purchase accounting. Pooling accounting. Historical development of pooling accounting. Revised opinions on accounting for business combinations: *Conditions for the pooling of interests method. Application of the purchase method. Pro forma supplementary disclosure.* Costs and expenses of consummating the combination. Taxable versus nontaxable exchanges. Illustration of accounting mechanics: Purchase versus pooling accounting. Dissenting shareholders. Application of the 90 percent rule. Operating results.

    Appendix: Tax aspects of business combinations, 47

3. **Consolidated statements—date of acquisition** 60

Reasons for consolidated statements. Purchase of a wholly owned subsidiary at book value. Purchase of a wholly owned subsidiary at other than book value. Negative goodwill. Purchase of a partially owned subsidiary at book value. Purchase of a partially owned subsidiary at other than book value.

4. **Consolidated statements—subsequent to date of acquisition** 90

Equity method. Cost method. Unconsolidated subsidiaries. CONSOLIDATION PROCEDURES SUBSEQUENT TO DATE OF ACQUISITION. Partially owned subsidiary using the complete equity method. Minority interest. Intercompany transactions.

    Appendix 4–A: Income tax implications between parents and subsidiaries, 108
    Appendix 4–B: Incomplete equity method, 110
    Appendix 4–C: Cost method—partially owned subsidiaries, 114
    Appendix 4–D: Trial balance working papers, 118

5. **Consolidated statements—intercompany profits on inventories** 138

Billing above cost. Unconfirmed (unrealized) profits—sales by parent company (downstream): *First year. Second year.* Unconfirmed profits—sales by subsidiaries (upstream): *First year. Second year.* Inventories—unconfirmed profits—comprehensive illustration. Sales between subsidiaries of one affiliated group—lateral sales. Reductions of inventories—lower of cost or market write-downs. Gross profit versus net profit. Disclosure of consolidation policies.

Appendix 5–A: **Income tax considerations for consolidated financial statements, 158**

Appendix 5–B: **Partial (fractional) elimination of intercompany profits—inventories, 162**

Appendix 5–C: **Incomplete equity method—intercompany profit on inventories, 166**

Appendix 5–D: **Cost methods—intercompany profit on inventories, 173**

6. **Consolidated statements—intercompany profit on plant asset transfers and other related matters 192**

Sales of plant assets by subsidiaries subsequent to the date of acquisition. Intercompany sales of plant assets. Plant asset sale by parent company—downstream sale. Intercompany sale of manufacturing equipment. Sale of equipment prior to expiration of useful life. Sale by parent of nondepreciable assets. Plant assets—sale by subsidiaries—upstream sale. Sales of assets at other than end of a year—upstream sale. Balance sheet only working papers.

Appendix: **Consolidated statements—provision for income taxes on consolidated income tax returns involving intercompany profits on asset transfers, 211**

7. **Consolidated statements—transactions in intercompany bonds and preferred stock 234**

Overview of accounting for the retirement of treasury bonds. Purchase of intercompany bonds. Treatment of gain or loss on consolidated statements. Subsidiary purchases parent's bonds. Parent purchases subsidiary's bonds. Purchase between interest dates. PREFERRED STOCK. Investments in preferred stock. Allocation of retained earnings. Income apportionment.

Appendix 7–A: **Gain or loss on purchase of intercompany bonds attributable to issuer—complete equity method, 258**

Appendix 7–B: **Intercompany bond transactions—cost method, 261**

8. **Consolidated statements—increases in parent's percentages of ownership by purchases of stock 248**

Piecemeal acquisitions. Conversion from cost method to equity method. Purchase of shares from a subsidiary. Purchases of stock at interim dates—purchase accounting. Preferred stock purchases on interim dates. POOLING ACCOUNTING. Acquisition on an interim date. Intercompany transactions.

Appendix: **Preacquisition income—cost method, 301**

9. **Consolidated statements—decreases in parent's (investor's) share of ownership and other related matters 322**

Sale of shares by subsidiary to third parties: *At book value. At a price in excess of book value. At a price below book value.* Sales by investors of investee's stock—equity method. Sales by an investor of part of its investment in a subsidiary or affiliate. Treasury stock transactions—subsidiary's purchase of shares from third parties. Stock dividends.

Appendix: **Decreases in parent's ownership percentage—cost method, 334**

10. **Consolidated statements—complex affiliation structures 350**

Lineal structures. MUTUAL HOLDINGS. Treasury stock approach—equity method. Indirect holdings of less than 50 percent—consolidated statements.

Appendix: **Reciprocal holdings—algebraic solution, 365**

11. **Consolidated statements—consolidation theories and other topics 382**

The entity method. *Discussion. Entity method—date of acquisition. Entity method—subsequent to date of acquisition.* Limitations of consolidated statements: *Minority interest stockholders. Creditors of subsidiary companies. Creditors of the parent company. Financial statement ratios. Consolidated retained earnings.* Consolidated statement of changes in financial position.

Appendix: **Push-down theory, 396**

12. **Accounting for foreign operations . . . 410**

Foreign accounting practices. Efforts to develop

worldwide accounting standards. Transactions in foreign currencies: *Import and export transactions. Conducting foreign operations. Measured versus denominated. Conversion versus translation. Currency exchange rates.* Accounting for foreign currency transactions: *Unsettled transactions in foreign currency. Forward exchange contracts. Accounting for forward exchange contracts. Accounting for a hedge on a foreign currency net asset or liability position. Accounting for a hedge of an identifiable foreign currency commitment. Transaction gains and losses to be excluded from determination of net income. Accounting for gains and losses on speculative forward exchange contracts.* Translation of foreign currency financial statements: *Evolution of the accounting for foreign exchange translation.* Statement of Financial Accounting Standards 52: *Basic objectives. Major provisions. Accounting for investment by parent company. Accounting when an investment in subsidiary is sold or liquidated. Disclosure requirements. Exposure to foreign exchange losses.*

Appendix: The temporal method of translation (the methodology of SFAS 8) 430

13. Segment reporting by diversified enterprise **452**

The evolving interest in segmental reporting. SEC reporting requirements. FASB *SFAS 14,* "Financial reporting for segments of a business enterprise." Objectives of segment disclosure. Applicable accounting standards. Unconsolidated investments. Areas covered by segmental disclosures. Operations in different industries: *Revenue test. Operating profit test. Asset test. Evaluation of reportable segments. Dominant segments. Operation in different industries—criteria for disclosure.* Foreign operations: *Disclosure requirements. Export sales. Major customers. The SEC's position on segmental reporting. Problem areas of segmental reporting.*

14. Interim financial reporting **470**

The need for interim reports. Problem areas. Two divergent views. *APB Opinion 28.* Standards for interim reporting of revenues, costs, and expenses: *Illustration of the application of the lower of cost or market rule to interim reporting.* Income taxes in interim statements: *Illus-*

tration of the computation of interim statement tax provision. Illustration of interim tax provision when losses occur. Reporting of accounting changes and extraordinary and other nonoperating items. Disclosure of summarized interim financial data. SEC disclosure requirements.

15. Earnings per share **486**

Evolution of the earnings per share computation. Major provisions of *APB Opinion 15. Simple capital structure. Computation of weighted average of common shares outstanding.* Complex capital structure: *Primary EPS.* Options and warrants: *Fully diluted EPS. Illustration of the computation of primary and fully diluted EPS.* More complex aspects of the computation of earnings per share: *Illustration of classification of contingently issuable shares. Illustration of option agreements in the computation of EPS. Computations involving changing conversion rates or exercise prices. Examples of EPS computations in a period during which a business combination occurs. EPS computations of investor companies with affiliates. Illustration of EPS computation involving an affiliate. Restatement of prior period EPS. Illustration of prior period EPS restatement. Requirements for additional disclosures in conjunction with the presentation of EPS data.* Alleged weaknesses of APB Opinion 15.

16. Partnerships—formation and operation **516**

Definitions and features of partnerships: *Mutual agency. Unlimited liability. Assignment of partner's interest. Limited life. Taxation.* Entity versus proprietorship theories. Initial contributions to capital. Written partnership agreements. DIVISION OF OPERATING RESULTS. Salaries to partners. Interest on capital and loan accounts. Division of income in capital ratio. Bonus to partners. Financial statements.

Appendix 16–A: Selected principles of partnership taxation and basis of partnership interests, 528

Appendix 16–B: Uniform Partnership Act, 530

17. Partnerships—changes in ownership . 546

Changes in the profit and loss ratios. Admission of a partner—purchase from existing partners. Admission of a partner—investment into the partnership. Admission of a partner—investment at other than book value—profit and loss ratio and capital ratio coincide. Admission of a partner—profit and loss ratios and capital ratios are different. Retirement of a partner. Death of a partner. Incorporation of a partnership.

18. **Partnerships—liquidation and dissolution** **568**

Rights of partners in liquidation. LIQUIDATION IN ONE TRANSACTION. Partners' capital and loan accounts sufficient to absorb losses. Partners' capital and loan accounts insufficient to absorb losses. Marshaling of assets. LIQUIDATION IN INSTALLMENTS. Advance cash distribution plans. Loan balances.

19. **Accounting for estates and trusts** . . . **588**

Estate planning. Legal aspects of estate administration: *Inventory of assets. Claims against the estate. The settlement of an estate.* The classifications of legacies. Accounting aspects of estate administration: *The distinction between principal and income.* Depreciation and depletion. Accounting and reporting for estates: *Accounts relating to principal. Accounts relating to income. Reporting.* Accounting for an estate—an illustration. Legal and accounting aspects of trusts.

20. **Corporate reorganizations and liquidations** **606**

Enterprises in financial difficulty. Insolvency. Enterprises in financial difficulty—available options: *The nonjudicial route. The judicial route.* Bankruptcy Reform Act of 1978. Reorganizations. Accounting for a reorganization. Liquidations. Trustee in bankruptcy. Distribution of the estate in bankruptcy. Accounting and reporting for a liquidation. The statement of affairs: *Statement of affairs format. Illustration of the statement of affairs.* Statement of realization and liquidation: *Illustrative example.*

21. **Accounting for nonbusiness organizations: State and local governments—general fund** **626**

Conceptual matters. Dichotomy of nonbusiness accounting. FUND ACCOUNTING—STATE AND LOCAL GOVERNMENTS. Definition and types of funds. Number of funds. Accounting for fixed assets and long-term liabilities. Valuation of fixed assets. Depreciation of fixed assets. Basis of accounting—accrual basis in governmental accounting. Budgeting, account classification, terminology, and financial reporting: *Budgeting, budgetary control, and budgetary reporting. Transfer, revenue, expenditure, and expense account classifications. Common terminology and classification. Interim and annual financial reports.* BUDGETING, CONTROL, AND REPORTING. Budgeting. Encumbrances and expenditures. Comprehensive illustration—general fund. Inventory of supplies. Financial statements.

22. **Accounting for state and local governments—special funds** **656**

Special Revenue Funds. Capital Projects Fund. Debt Service Fund. Special Assessment Funds. Internal Service Funds. Enterprise Funds. Fiduciary Funds. Agency Funds. Trust Funds: *Accounting for Nonexpendable Trust Funds.* General fixed assets account group. General long-term debt account group.

Appendix: Financial statements for a state or local government, 680

23. **Accounting for colleges, hospitals, and welfare organizations** **712**

Colleges and universities: *Illustrative entries. Current Fund—restricted. Closing entries. Depreciation. Loan Funds. Endowment and similar funds. Annuity and Life Income Funds. Financial statements.* Hospital accounting: *Revenues. Expenses. Depreciation. Journal entries. Financial statements.* Accounting for voluntary health and welfare organizations: *Funds. Revenues. Donated services. Expenses. Depreciation. Closing entries. Financial statements.*

24. **Regulation of accounting by the SEC** **758**

Origins of the SEC. Organization of the SEC. Principal acts administered by the SEC: *The Securities Exchange Act of 1934. Accountant involvement. Accounting Series Releases. The principal registration statement—Form S–1. Reporting and disclosure requirements.* The SEC's influence on accounting theory and practice: *The SEC's position on the promulgation of accounting standards. Leadership in promoting change in financial accounting and reporting. Reporting of leases. Leadership of the SEC in requiring analytically oriented data.*

Appendix 24–A: **Selected pages from joint proxy statement of Mattel,** **Inc., and Western Publishing Company, Inc., 773**

Appendix 24–B: **Galveston Houston Company—Management's discussion and analysis of financial condition and results of operation, 791**

Index **795**

Advanced Accounting

1

An introduction to accounting for multi-unit enterprises: Home office and branch accounting

OVERVIEW

Most large business enterprises operate in a multi-unit mode. The most popular form of multi-unit operation is that of one or more corporations owning a majority interest in one or more other corporations. This form of operation is referred to as a parent-subsidiary relationship.

Another form of multi-unit operation is that of a home office with one or more branches. In this type of operation, one corporation encompasses all units, instead of separate corporations as in a parent-subsidiary relationship.

Regardless of which form of operation is used, the financial statements of each separate unit is combined with that of the controlling unit which then results in a single set of financial statements for the economic entity as a whole.

Except for small, localized business organizations, businesses usually have operations in more than one location. A vertically integrated business is one that engages in more than one level of activity, such as mining, refining, fabricating, wholesaling, and retailing. A horizontally integrated business is one that has more than one location on the same level of operations, such as a series of retail stores as in a supermarket chain. A business organization can be both vertically integrated and horizontally integrated. Many oil refineries have multiple locations for refining operations as well as multiple retail gasoline filling stations.

Forms of ownership may vary. When separate corporate existence prevails, the corporation owning the shares of other corporations in an affiliated group of companies is called the *parent* company, and a parent-subsidiary relationship exists between the companies. For this purpose, a controlling interest of more than 50 percent is required. Another form of ownership is one where all locations, including the main location, are part of one legal entity, usually a corporation. In organizations of this type, one location is usually the dominant one and is referred to as the *home office.* The remaining locations are either referred to as *agencies* or *branches,* depending upon the function and mode of operation of each location.

A major emphasis of this text is on the preparation of consolidated financial statements for a parent company and its subsidiary or subsidiaries. The most common form of corporate organization found in practice is that of parent and subsidiary companies rather than that of home office and branch(es). Portions of this text are also devoted to ancillary problems concerning multinational ownerships (foreign subsidiaries and branches) and segment reporting by multiproduct companies.

The procedures used in the preparation of consolidated working papers are often complex. Many problems are present in parent-subsidiary relationships that require sophisticated problem-solving techniques not usually required in home office and branch relationships. Examples include: less than 100 percent owned subsidiaries (the noncontrolling stockholders are referred to as *minority interests*); sales of additional shares by subsidiaries; purchases of a parent company's stock by a subsidiary (referred to as *mutual* or *reciprocal* holdings); and others. The development of the theories and problem-solving techniques associated with consolidation accounting (parent-subsidiary relationships) usually requires 10 or more chapters while the accounting for branches and agencies rarely requires more than one chapter. The distinction between agencies and branches, and the accounting for them, will form our beginning discussion since they do provide a good introductory framework to the principles of consolidation accounting.

AGENCIES

Agencies and branches are entirely different types of operations. An agency is merely an office in which orders are taken and then transmitted to the home office for processing, billing, and the actual shipment of the merchandise. The agency office usually is limited to a samples inventory and does not carry any merchandise for shipment. Usually, the number of employees working in an agency office are few. The agency very rarely collects cash from customers; rather, the funds are normally remitted by customers directly to the home office. An example of an agency operation might be that of a dress manufacturer whose offices and factory are located in a midwestern state. The manufacturer might have a showroom in the garment center of New York City. Buyers would visit the showroom office in New York and purchase selected garments from the samples; shipment as well as billing would emanate from the factory and offices located in the midwestern state. In an operation such as this one, the agency would possess some furniture, some samples, and possibly a small amount of cash to take care of daily out-of-pocket expenses such as freight, postage, fares, and other small expenditures. If we assume that the Superior Dress Manufacturing Company, Inc., operates the Able Agency in New York City, typical entries on the books of the Superior Dress Manufacturing Company, Inc. (hereinafter referred to as the home office), might appear as follows:

Furniture and Fixtures (Able Agency)	20,000	
Cash		20,000
Samples Inventory (Able Agency)	10,000	
Merchandise Inventory		10,000
Working Capital Fund (Able Agency)	1,000	
Cash		1,000
Accounts Receivable	150,000	
Sales (Able Agency)		150,000
Rent Expense, Etc. (Able Agency)	30,000	
Cash		30,000
Cost of Goods Sold (Able Agency)	60,000	
Merchandise Inventory		60,000
Transportation Costs, Etc. (Able Agency)	350	
Cash		350

To reimburse the Able Agency for out-of-pocket expenditures.

From the foregoing illustrative entries it can be seen that the operations of the agency will be recorded on the books of the home office. The home office will usually segregate the transactions that pertain to the agency throughout the year; and then at year's end, it will have, in effect, a summary of the sales generated by the agency as well as the costs associated with making those sales. This will enable the home office to evaluate the success of the operation of the agency office.

BRANCH OPERATIONS

A branch office is quite different from that of an agency office. A branch office usually carries a complete inventory of its own from which it delivers merchandise to its customers. In addition, the branch usually keeps records of its own accounts receivable, collects funds from its customers, and deposits the funds in a bank account. It will pay its vendors, and it will remit to the home office amounts not needed for continuing operations.

There are two approaches that can be used to account for a branch's accounting function. One method is to have the branch summarize all of its transactions on a daily basis and remit these summaries to the home office. The home office will then be responsible for the record-keeping function of the branch. The other method is to have the branch keep its own set of accounting and bookkeeping records. Under this approach, the branch would record all of its entries as if it were a separate accounting entity. However, certain entries will interact with the books of the home office, and for this reason it is necessary to create a set of reciprocal accounts. Therefore, on the books of the branch an account will be opened labeled Home Office Control. On the home office books, however, the reciprocal account will be labeled Branch Control (in the actual account title, the word "Office" is often omitted). Whenever a transaction involves both sets of books, the reciprocal accounts will be used in the following fashion:

Home Office Books

Branch Control	20,000	
Cash		20,000
To record a cash advance to the Better Branch.		

Branch Books

Cash	20,000	
Home Office Control		20,000
To record the receipt of a cash advance from the home office.		

From the above entries it is evident that not only should the reciprocal accounts always be in balance but this format will also facilitate the integration of the home office and branch trial balances by canceling out these reciprocal accounts. By a comprehensive example we will now illustrate the use of the two sets of books when the branch does its own bookkeeping on an autonomous basis.

Shipments to branch— at cost

Shipments by a home office to a branch can be made at different prices. The possibilities are:

1. Shipments to the branch at the branch's selling price.
2. Shipments to the branch at the home office's cost.
3. Shipments to the branch at a price in excess of cost (hereinafter the *billed price*).

The first category *(selling price)* is not one in wide use since it allows for no gross profit for the branch. When this approach is used, the branch operation will always operate at a loss, and the amount of the loss will always be equal to the operating expenses of the branch. This approach provides very little useful information from a control or management viewpoint. For this reason we will not illustrate this method. The other two approaches are used extensively in practice. The third approach *(billed price in excess of cost)* involves complexities not found in the second method and, therefore, will be discussed in a later section of this chapter.

Illustration 1–1 contains representative summary entries of the second method *(billed at cost)*. The closing entries for the home office are assumed

Illustration 1–1
SUPERIOR DRESS MANUFACTURING COMPANY, INC.
Journal Entries
During the Year Ended December 31, 19x1

Home Office Books			*Branch Books*		
(1)			**(1)**		
Branch Control	50,000		Cash	50,000	
Cash		50,000	Home Office Control		50,000
(2)			**(2)**		
Branch Control	150,000		Shipments from Home Office	150,000	
Shipments to Branch		150,000	Home Office Control		150,000
(3)			**(3)**		
No entry.			Purchases	20,000	
			Accounts Payable		20,000
(4)			**(4)**		
No entry.			Accounts Receivable	290,000	
			Sales		290,000
(5)			**(5)**		
No entry.			Cash	280,000	
			Accounts Receivable		280,000
(6)			**(6)**		
No entry.			Expenses (various)	100,000	
			Cash		100,000
(7)			**(7)**		
No entry.			Accounts Payable	15,000	
			Cash		15,000
(8)			**(8)**		
Branch Control	12,000		Expenses (insurance, depreciation)	12,000	
Unexpired Insurance		6,000			
Accumulated Depreciation . . .		6,000	Home Office Control		12,000
(9)			**(9)**		
Cash	160,000		Home Office Control	160,000	
Branch Control		160,000	Cash		160,000
(Closing Entries)			**(Closing Entries)**		
(10a)			**(10)**		
Shipments to Branch	150,000		Sales	290,000	
Sales	1,000,000		Inventory (12/31/x1)	30,000	
Inventory (1/1/x1)		200,000	Purchases		20,000
Purchases, Etc.		600,000	Shipments from Home Office .		150,000
Expenses		200,000	Expenses (various)		112,000
Income Summary		150,000	Home Office Control		38,000
(10b)					
Branch Control	38,000				
Branch Net Income		38,000			
(11)			**(11)**		
Branch Net Income	38,000		No entry.		
Income Summary		38,000			

except for those that integrate with the branch entries. A review of the illustration will reveal the following:

1. Whenever an entry is made on one set of books affecting the reciprocal accounts, a corresponding entry for the same amount is required on the other set of books.

2. In this example, shipments between the home office and branch office have been segregated into special "shipments to" and "shipments from" accounts. In some firms, however, the shipments are recorded as sales or purchases as if they were transactions between unrelated parties. This approach is acceptable, provided that the intracompany sales and purchases are eliminated on the working paper when the trial balances are combined for financial statement purposes. If not, the resulting combined trial balance would contain a double counting of sales and purchases. In Illustration 1–2, a working paper that combines the trial balances of the Superior Dress Manufacturing Company, Inc., and its Better Branch, it can be noted that the "shipments to" and "shipments from" are eliminated and double counting is thereby avoided.

3. It is obvious that some entries affect one set of books only. When this occurs, a reciprocal entry on the other set of books is not required.

4. When a branch office requires insurance coverage, it will usually be advantageous for the home office to purchase a blanket insurance policy covering all branches. When this occurs, the home office will make an entry debiting Unexpired Insurance and crediting Cash. An apportionment of the insurance premium will be made for each branch; and as the insurance policy expires, a journal voucher will be made notifying the branch of its pro rata charge for insurance coverage. This entry can be seen as part of entry (8).

When a branch acquires equipment or assets of a capital nature, the usual procedure is to keep the equipment ledger on the books of the home office, regardless of who purchases the equipment. Thus, if the home office purchases the equipment, the entry on the home office books would be a debit to Equipment—Branch and a credit to Cash. No entry is necessary on the branch office books since the home office paid for the equipment in that particular case. Alternatively, if the branch purchased the equipment, the entries on the home office and branch books would be as follows:

Home Office Books

Dr. Equipment	30,000	
Cr. Branch Control		30,000
To record equipment purchased by branch.		

Branch Books

Home Office Control	30,000	
Cash		30,000
To record the purchase of equipment.		

In either case the Equipment account is maintained on the home office books. When the entry for depreciation expense is to be made, it will appear

Illustration 1–2
SUPERIOR DRESS MANUFACTURING COMPANY, INC.
Home Office and Branch Combined Statement Working Papers
For the Year Ended December 31, 19x1

	Home Office (per books)		Branch (per books)		Eliminations Dr.	Eliminations Cr.	Combined	
Income Statement								
Sales		1,000,000		290,000				1,290,000
Shipments to branch		150,000			(1) 150,000			–0–
Total		1,150,000		290,000				1,290,000
Cost of goods sold:								
Inventory, 1/1/x1	200,000		–0–				200,000	
Purchases, etc.	600,000		20,000				620,000	
Shipments from home office			150,000			(1) 150,000	–0–	
Total	800,000		170,000				820,000	
Inventory, 12/31/x1	300,000	500,000	30,000	140,000			330,000	490,000
Gross margin		650,000		150,000				800,000
Expenses		400,000		112,000				512,000
Net income—carried forward		250,000		38,000				288,000
Retained Earnings Statement								
Retained earnings, 1/1/x1		500,000						500,000
Net income—brought forward		250,000		38,000				288,000
Retained earnings, 12/31/x1—carried forward		750,000		38,000				788,000
Balance Sheet								
Cash		78,000		55,000				133,000
Accounts receivable		150,000		10,000				160,000
Inventory, 12/31/x1		300,000		30,000				330,000
Branch control		52,000				(2) 52,000		–0–
Other assets		470,000						470,000
Total assets		1,050,000		95,000				1,093,000
Liabilities		200,000		5,000				205,000
Common stock		100,000						100,000
Retained earnings—brought forward		750,000		38,000				788,000
Home office control				52,000	(2) 52,000			–0–
Total liabilities and stockholders' equity		1,050,000		95,000				1,093,000

as previously shown in Illustration 1–1 as part of entry (8). In this entry, it can be seen that the home office debits Branch Control and credits Accumulated Depreciation. A journal voucher is then issued to the branch notifying it of its share of depreciation expense, and the branch office debits Depreciation Expense and credits Home Office Control.

The closing entries on the respective sets of books are illustrated by entries (10) through (11). Since each set of books must be in balance, the net income of the branch will be reflected on both sets of books, as seen by entries (10, (10a), and (10b). Particular attention should be paid to the closing process of the shipments accounts. These accounts are closed individually on each set of books because of the necessity of maintaining the balance of each set of books independently. However, after reviewing Illustration 1–2, the working paper of these trial balances, it is noted that the shipments accounts are eliminated on the working paper. This occurs because the trial balances on the working paper reflect account balances before closing entries have been posted on the respective sets of books.

A study of Illustration 1–2 will reveal that the elimination entry to shipments coincides with the net effect of closing entry (9) on both sets of books, since the elimination on the working paper and the closing of these accounts are compatible. However, the elimination entry of the reciprocal accounts, Home Office Control and Branch Control, is necessary on the working paper, although these accounts are not closed on the respective books. In essence, the reciprocal accounts represent the investment by the home office in the branch at any given point in time. An analogy can be made between the Home Office Control account and the stockholders' equity section of the balance sheet. The dollar amounts of each would be the same. This will become clearer when the financial statements of a branch are prepared. It will be seen that the *equity section* of the branch's balance sheet is equal to the Home Office Control account balance.

Shipments to branch—billed price in excess of cost

In both vertically integrated and horizontally integrated companies, branch managers are usually offered some form of incentive compensation. This is usually done by offering the branch manager a percentage of the branch's net income. This results in motivation to maximize profits for the firm since this will also maximize the bonus. Examples of this type of business organization are a petroleum company that operates retail gasoline outlets and national brand clothing manufacturers which operate company-owned retail stores. For these types of businesses, the home office must select a price at which the branch will be billed for its merchandise shipments. The price selected must be one that is fair to both the home office and the branch manager. If the home office were to ship merchandise to the branch at its cost price, the branch manager would reap a windfall since the gross operating margin would include both the retailing and manufacturing margins. The latter margin properly belongs on the books of the home office. Accordingly, many companies bill the branch manager for shipments at the same price charged to other retailers who are not a part of the business organization. In this manner, the manufacturing margin will be earned by the home office and the retail trading margin will appear on the books of the branch. When this approach is used, the home office is placed in the position of billing merchandise shipments to the branch at a price in excess of its cost. Not only is this procedure fair, but it also provides very useful information to the home office from the standpoint of control and evaluation of the profitability of various branches.

While billing a branch at a price in excess of cost is the most useful procedure from a management viewpoint, it is not an acceptable approach for purposes of external financial reporting. The business organization is then placed in the position of keeping its books on a basis that is most useful for internal management purposes; yet, this basis is not in accordance with generally accepted accounting principles (GAAP). Manufacturing margin from intracompany shipments is not considered as "earned" in accordance with GAAP until the intracompany merchandise is sold to third parties by the branch office. Therefore, any inventory on hand at the branch office at the end of any accounting period will contain unconfirmed[1] (unrealized) manufacturing profits on the books of the home office. This unconfirmed profit must be removed from the combined financial statement of the home office and the branch whenever financial statements are prepared for external use. Illustration 1–3 demonstrates this technique (using periodic inventories) by using illustrative journal entries for both sets of books to show how each profit (manufacturing margin and retail trading margin) is recorded on the respective sets of books. Additionally, working paper combination procedures are demonstrated in Illustration 1–4 showing how the unconfirmed profit is removed on the working paper for the purpose of preparing financial statements for external use. Illustration 1–5 demonstrates these same procedures for the second year of branch operations.

A review of illustration 1–3 reveals the following:

1. In entry (2), the branch records its shipments from the home office at the *billed price*. The branch manager is usually not aware of the home office's cost; and, therefore, the only figure available is the billed price. However, the home office records the shipment at its cost and sets up an allowance for unrealized profit which is reflected in the "Allowance for Overvaluation of Branch Inventory account.

2. In entry (10), the branch records its retailing net income at $58,000. Incentive compensation, if any, will be based on this amount. However, the home office must make entry (12) to record the realized manufacturing margin on sales made by the branch. Assuming that the branch inventory consists entirely of merchandise purchased from the home office, the calculations follow:

$$\text{Unconfirmed profit} \times \frac{\text{Goods sold}}{\text{Goods shipped}} = \text{Confirmed profit}$$

or

$$\$60,000 \times \frac{\$250,000}{\$300,000} = \$50,000$$

---

[1]*Unconfirmed* and *unrealized* are used interchangeably by accountants.

Illustration 1–3

HEART MARCS SUIT MANUFACTURING COMPANY, INC.
Journal Entries
During the Year Ended December 31, 19x2

Home Office Books			*Branch Books*		
(1)			**(1)**		
Branch Control	100,000		Cash	100,000	
Cash		100,000	Home Office Control		100,000
(2)			**(2)**		
Branch Control	300,000		Shipments from Home Office	300,000	
Shipments to Branch		240,000	Home Office Control		300,000
Allowance for Overvaluation of					
Branch Inventory		60,000			
(3)			**(3)**		
No entry.			Purchases	60,000	
			Accounts Payable		60,000
(4)			**(4)**		
No entry.			Accounts Receivable	600,000	
			Sales		600,000
(5)			**(5)**		
No entry.			Cash	560,000	
			Accounts Receivable		560,000
(6)			**(6)**		
No entry.			Expenses (various)	200,000	
			Cash		200,000
(7)			**(7)**		
No entry.			Accounts Payable	45,000	
			Cash		45,000
(8)			**(8)**		
Branch Control	32,000		Expenses (insurance, depreciation)	32,000	
Unexpired Insurance		16,000	Home Office Control		32,000
Accumulated Depreciation		16,000			
(9)			**(9)**		
Cash	380,000		Home Office Control	380,000	
Branch Control		380,000	Cash		380,000
Closing Entries			**Closing Entries**		
(10)			**(10)**		
Sales	1,000,000		Sales	600,000	
Inventory (12/31/x2)	100,000		Inventory (12/31/x2)	50,000	
Shipments to Branch	240,000		Purchases		60,000
Purchases, Etc.		600,000	Shipments from Home Office		300,000
Inventory (1/1/x2)		150,000	Expenses (various)		232,000
Expenses		300,000	Home Office Control		58,000
Income Summary		290,000			
(11)			**(11)**		
Branch Control	58,000		No entry.		
Branch Net Income		58,000			
(12)			**(12)**		
Allowance for Overvaluation of			No entry.		
Branch Inventory	50,000				
Branch Net Income		50,000			
(13)			**(13)**		
Branch Net Income	108,000		No entry.		
Income Summary		108,000			

Illustration 1–4
HEART MARCS SUIT MANUFACTURING COMPANY, INC.
Home Office and Branch
Combined Statement Working Papers
For the Year Ended December 31, 19x2

	Home Office (per books)		Branch (per books)	Eliminations Dr.	Eliminations Cr.	Combined	
Income Statement							
Sales		1,000,000	600,000				1,600,000
Shipments to branch		240,000	–0–	(1) 240,000			–0–
Total		1,240,000	600,000				1,600,000
Cost of goods sold:							
Inventory 1/1/x2	150,000		–0–			150,000	
Purchases, etc.	600,000		60,000			660,000	
Shipments from home office	–0–		300,000		(1) 300,000	–0–	
Total	750,000		360,000			810,000	
Inventory, 12/31/x2	100,000		50,000	(2) 10,000		140,000	
Cost of goods sold		650,000	310,000				670,000
Gross margin		590,000	290,000				930,000
Expenses		300,000	232,000				532,000
Net income—carried forward		290,000	58,000				398,000
Retained Earnings Statement							
Retained earnings, 1/1/x2		300,000	–0–				300,000
Net income—brought forward		290,000	58,000				398,000
Retained earnings, 12/31/x2— carried forward		590,000	58,000				698,000
Balance Sheet							
Cash		120,000	35,000				155,000
Accounts receivable		180,000	40,000				220,000
Inventory, 12/31/x2		100,000	50,000		(2) 10,000		140,000
Branch control		52,000			(3) 52,000		
Other assets		448,000					448,000
Total assets		900,000	125,000				963,000
Liabilities		150,000	15,000				165,000
Allowance for overvaluation of branch inventory		60,000		(1) 60,000			–0–
Common stock		100,000					100,000
Retained earnings— brought forward		590,000	58,000				698,000
Home office control			52,000	(3) 52,000			–0–
Total liabilities and stockholders' equity		900,000	125,000				963,000

Illustration 1–5
HEART MARCS SUIT MANUFACTURING COMPANY, INC.
Home Office and Branch Combined Statement Working Papers
For the Year Ended December 31, 19x3

	Home Office (per books)	Branch (per books)	Eliminations Dr.	Eliminations Cr.	Combined
Income Statement					
Sales	1,200,000	700,000			1,900,000
Shipments to branch	300,000	–0–	(2) 300,000		–0–
Total	1,500,000	700,000			1,900,000
Cost of goods sold:					
Inventory, 1/1/x3	100,000	50,000		(1) 10,000	140,000
Purchases, etc.	700,000	100,000			800,000
Shipments from home office	–0–	375,000		(2) 375,000	–0–
Total	800,000	525,000			940,000
Inventory, 12/31/x3	200,000	125,000	(3) 25,000		300,000
Cost of goods sold	600,000	400,000			640,000
Gross margin	900,000	300,000			1,260,000
Expenses	350,000	250,000			600,000
Net income—carried forward	550,000	50,000			660,000
Retained Earnings Statement					
Retained earnings, 1/1/x3	698,000				698,000
Net income—brought forward	550,000	50,000			660,000
Retained earnings, 12/31/x3— carried forward	1,248,000	50,000			1,358,000
Balance Sheet					
Cash	250,000	25,000			275,000
Accounts receivable	300,000	60,000			360,000
Inventory, 12/31/x3	200,000	125,000		(3) 25,000	300,000
Branch control	135,000			(4) 135,000	–0–
Other assets	748,000				748,000
Total assets	1,633,000	210,000			1,683,000
Liabilities	200,000	25,000			225,000
			(2) 75,000		
Allowance for overvaluation of branch inventory	85,000		(1) 10,000		
Common stock	100,000				100,000
Retained earnings— brought forward	1,248,000	50,000			1,358,000
Home office control		135,000	(4) 135,000		–0–
Total liabilities and stock-holders' equity	1,633,000	210,000			1,683,000

An alternate calculation would be:

Balance of unconfirmed profit $60,000
Less: Unconfirmed profit in closing inventory:
Inventory × Percent of profit on billed price

or

$50,000 × $\dfrac{\$60,000}{\$300,000}$ =   10,000

Realized profit $50,000

3. After closing entry (12), the Allowance for Overvaluation of Branch Inventory account will appear as follows:

Allowance for Overvaluation of Branch Inventory

19x2			19x2		
Dec. 31	GJ	50,000	Shipments		60,000
			Balance	10,000	

The balance in the account can be verified by multiplying the branch closing inventory ($50,000) by the profit percentage on billed price (20 percent) or $10,000. If the profit percentage were given on cost (25 percent), it can be converted to the billed price profit margin by adding the numerator of this fraction to the denominator as follows:

$$25\% \text{ or } \frac{1}{4} \text{ becomes } \frac{1}{4+1} = \frac{1}{5} \text{ or } 20\%$$

A review of Illustrations 1–4 and 1–5 reveals the following:

1. The elimination of the intracompany shipments requires the complete elimination of the allowance for overvaluation account. In the first year of operations this requires only one entry because there is no opening inventory. In the second year of operations the allowance for overvaluation is also eliminated in full, but this is done in two parts. The first part reflects intracompany shipments, and the second part involves an adjustment to the opening inventory. It should be noted that although the allowance for overvaluation account has a balance on the home office books *after* closing entries are posted, it is nevertheless eliminated completely on the working papers. This occurs because the $10,000 balance in the account (previously illustrated) appears on the *home office books* and the related inventory (which is overstated by $10,000) appears on the *branch books.* While the individual books of account retain these balances, on the working papers the elimination entries result in a zero balance in the combined column which is the source from which financial statements for external users are prepared.

2. The branch inventory is carried at billed price on the branch's books but is reduced to cost on the working papers prepared by the home office. The entries that appear on the *working papers* as elimination entries do *not* appear on either set of books, nor are they ever recorded on the books. They are adjustments made for purposes of preparing financial statements for external users.

3. It should be noted that the net income is carried forward to the retained earnings statement and the ending retained earnings is carried forward to the balance sheet. In Illustration 1–2, the net income of the home office and the net income of the branch could be added together to arrive at the combined net income. This is possible because the shipments to the branch were at cost. In Illustration 1–4, however, the combined net income cannot be arrived at in this way. It can be gotten by subtracting the combined expenses from the combined gross margin. Similarly, the combined ending retained earnings of the two entities cannot be arrived at by the mere addition of the respective retained earnings accounts.

Illustration 1–5 is a working paper that extends the preceding working paper to the second year of operations. The major difference between this illustration and the preceding one is found in the entries used to eliminate the Allowance for Overvaluation of Branch Inventory account. Two entries are required as discussed previously. However, it should be noted that the balance in the allowance for overvaluation account is $85,000 and would appear on the books of the home office as follows:

Allowance for Overvaluation of Branch Inventory

	19x3	
	Jan. 1 Balance	10,000
	Shipments	75,000

The adjustment which should be made to the account on the home office's books as of December 31, 19x3, would depend on the composition of the branch's closing inventory. If it is assumed that it all represents shipments from the home office and a first-in, first-out inventory flow is used, the computations are as follows:

Balance of unrealized profit, December 31, 19x3 . . .	$85,000
Less: Unrealized profit in closing inventory	
($125,000 × 20%)	25,000
Adjustment required	$60,000

This can also be reconciled as follows:

Profit in beginning inventory which is now realized	
(unrealized in 19x2)	$10,000
Profit realized from 19x3 shipments to branch	
sold in 19x3—20% ($375,000 − $125,000)	50,000
Total realized	$60,000

The entry on the home office's books would then be:

Allowance for Overvaluation of Branch Inventory	60,000	
Branch Net Income		60,000

If we assume, however, that the branch closing inventory consisted of $100,000 of home office merchandise and $25,000 of other merchandise, the adjustment would have been $65,000 instead of $60,000 ($85,000 − $20,000), and entry (3) in Illustration 1–5 would have been for $20,000 (20% × $100,000) instead of $25,000.

Financial statements

When a separate set of financial statements are to be prepared for the branch office, two possibilities exist. They can be prepared on a billed price basis or they can be prepared on a cost basis. If they are to be prepared on a billed price basis—as would be the case if they were prepared by the branch manager—the income statement would appear as is shown in the branch columns in Illustration 1–5. The balance sheet would also appear as is shown in these columns except that the equity section would appear as follows:

Equity:
Home office $185,000

The retained earnings and the home office control are combined into one amount.

If the statements are to be prepared on a cost basis—as would be the case if they are prepared for some facets of home office use—the income statement would appear as in Illustration 1–6.

Reconciliation of reciprocal accounts

Occasionally, the Branch Control and Home Office Control accounts will have different balances when the combined statement working papers are prepared. This will arise whenever there are transactions in transit between the home office and branch office. If, for example, the branch has shipped funds to the home office on December 30, 19x2, and the home office receives them on January 3, 19x3, the accounts will not agree as of December

Illustration 1–6
HEART MARCS SUIT MANUFACTURING
COMPANY, INC.—CALIFORNIA BRANCH
Income Statement—Cost Basis
For the Year Ended December 31, 19x3

Sales		$700,000
Cost of sales:		
Inventory, January 1, 19x3	$ 40,000	
Purchases	100,000	
Shipments from home office	300,000	
Merchandise available for sale	440,000	
Inventory, December 31, 19x3	100,000	340,000
Gross margin		360,000
Expenses		250,000
Net income		$110,000

Note: Branch net income consists of $50,000 of branch operating net income and $60,000 of income earned by the home office on shipments to the branch.

31, 19x2. The simplest procedure is to take these items in transit and make adjusting entries for them on the working paper *only*. This will enable the preparer of the working paper to complete the combination without disturbing the normal bookkeeping procedure. The items in transit will in due course clear on the individual sets of books. The entry needed to adjust for the example above on the working papers would be:

```
Cash . . . . . . . . . . . . . . . . . . . . . . . . . . . . . . . . . . . . . . . . .   XXX
        Branch Control . . . . . . . . . . . . . . . . . . . . . . . . . . . . . .          XXX
```

Interbranch freight charges

Sometimes a home office ships merchandise to one branch and later discovers that a different branch has a need for this merchandise. The home office may direct the branch that has the excess merchandise to ship it directly to the branch requesting the merchandise. When this occurs, the disposition of the second freight charge can either be treated as an expense or as freight-in depending on the circumstances. To illustrate the principles applicable to this situation, the following assumptions are made:

1. Branch A purchased $1,000 of merchandise from the home office and paid $50 freight on the shipment. It reshipped the merchandise to branch B prepaying $20 of freight charges.
2. The normal freight charge for this merchandise from the home office to branch B is $35.

The entries to record excess freight charges would be:

Branch A Books

Shipments from Home Office	1,000	
Freight-In	50	
Home Office Control		1,000
Cash		50

To record the purchase of merchandise from the home office.

Home Office Control	1,050	
Shipments from Home Office		1,000
Freight-In		50

To record the shipment of merchandise to branch B.

Home Office Control	20	
Cash		20

To record freight charge prepaid.

Branch B Books

Shipments from Home Office	1,000	
Freight-In	35	
Home Office Control		1,035

To record receipt of merchandise from branch A.

Home Office Books

Shipments to Branch A	1,000	
Shipments to Branch B		1,000

To record shipment from branch A to branch B.

Branch Control—Branch B	1,035	
Interbranch Freight Expense	35	
Branch Control—Branch A		1,070

To charge branch B for shipment and to record excess freight on interbranch shipment.

It should be noted that the total freight expended was $70 ($50 + $20), but only the normal freight charge of $35 is considered as part of freight-in with the balance of $35 charged to Interbranch Freight Expense.

QUESTIONS

1. Agencies and branches are different types of operations. What is an agency and how does it operate?

2. What is a branch and how does it operate?

3. Does a branch usually have its own set of books? If so, what is the equity portion of its balance sheet called? How does this account relate to the home office?

4. When a home office ships merchandise to a branch, there are three possible transfer prices that may be used. What are they? Which of the three is unrealistic and why?

5. In order for the home office–branch reciprocal accounts to maintain reciprocity, certain procedures must be followed. What are they? Use an example to illustrate how the reciprocity is maintained.

6. How does the home office record the income or loss reported by a branch? Use an example for a hypothetical amount of net income reported by a branch.

7. What procedure(s) does a home office use to prepare financial statements for external use?

8. Are the reciprocal accounts closed on the

books of the home office and branch? Are the reciprocal accounts eliminated on the working paper? Explain each of your answers.

9. Is it customary to make shipments to a branch in excess of a home office's cost? Why?

10. How is this excess amount treated on the home office's books? Why?

11. If any of the shipments to a branch in excess of cost is unsold at the end of an accounting period, how is the inventory handled on the branch's books? How is the amount in excess of the home office's cost handled on the home office's books? How is it handled on the working paper?

12. Does the home office do anything about the excess on inventory that is sold to third parties? What does the home office do? Use an example to illustrate the journal entry that is required.

13. Financial statements that are prepared for external use must be prepared on one basis only, while statements prepared for internal use can be prepared on more than one basis. Discuss each case.

14. Occasionally, a home office may ship merchandise to one branch which is then reshipped in turn to another branch. When this occurs, excess freight charges may be incurred. What is the proper treatment of excess freight charges and how are they calculated?

EXERCISES

Exercise 1–1. The Block Corporation located in Closter, New Jersey, opened a branch on January 1, 19x2, in New Rochelle, New York. The transactions of the branch for 19x2 are summarized as follows:

1. Received cash of $40,000 from the home office.
2. Received merchandise from the home office amounting to $100,000. (This merchandise was shipped at the home office's cost.)
3. Purchased merchandise on account from a local vendor in the amount of $10,000.
4. Sales on account amounted to $180,000.
5. Returned $5,000 of merchandise to the home office.
6. Collected $160,000 from sales on account.
7. Paid $8,000 on account of purchases in 3 above.
8. Incurred the following expenditures during the year (all paid in cash):

   a. Salaries $20,000
   b. Rent   10,000
   c. Utilities   5,000
   d. Other operating   15,000

9. Received a journal voucher from the home office for the following charges:

   a. Depreciation expense . . . . $ 3,000
   b. Allocated advertising   4,000
   c. Insurance   2,000

10. Remitted $95,000 to the home office for merchandise shipments.
11. A customer paid $5,000 directly to the home office. The home office is keeping the funds.
12. Closed the income summary accounts. The closing inventory amounted to $20,000.

Required:

Prepare the necessary journal entries on the books of the branch and the home office.

Exercise 1–2. Given:

[Relates to Exercise 1–2]

Home Office Control (Branch Books)

19x2			19x2		
Dec. 1	Cash remitted to home office	30,000	Jan. 1	Balance	10,000
28	Cash remitted to home office	12,000	Feb. 5	Shipments from home office	80,000
28	Merchandise returned to home office	8,000	Dec. 28	Expenses from home office	18,400
			Balance 58,400		

Branch Control (Home Office Books)

19x2			19x2		
Jan. 1	Balance	10,000	Dec. 1	Cash received from branch	30,000
Feb. 4	Shipments to branch	80,000	28	Collection from branch customer	6,000
Dec. 28	Expense allocation	14,800			
28	Shipments to branch	20,000			
28	Supplies purchased for branch and shipped directly to branch	2,000			
Balance 90,800					

Except for the error by the branch in recording its share of allocated expenses, all differences are timing differences.

Required:

a. Prepare a reconciliation to arrive at the correct balances.

b. Prepare summary entries on the home office's books and the branch's books to correct the accounts so that a combined working paper can be prepared.

Exercise 1–3. The Mitchell Corporation has two branches, branch X and branch Y. The home office shipped $3,000 of merchandise to branch X and prepaid the freight charges of $40. A short time thereafter, branch X was instructed to reship this merchandise to branch Y at a prepaid freight cost of $60. Freight charges for this merchandise normally cost $70 when shipped from the home office directly to branch Y. (Reciprocal accounts between branches is *not* permitted.)

Required:

a. Prepare the necessary entries on the books of branch X.

b. Prepare the necessary entries on the books of branch Y.

c. Prepare the necessary entries on the books of the home office.

Exercise 1–4. The following information was extracted from the books and records of Lind Corporation and its branch. The balances are at December 31, 19x2, the second year of the corporation's existence.

	Home office dr. (cr.)	Branch dr. (cr.)
Sales		$(400,000)
Expenses		100,000
Shipments to branch	$(200,000)	
Allowance for overvaluation of branch inventory	(57,500)	

The branch purchases all of its merchandise from the home office. The home office ships this merchandise at 125 percent of its cost. The ending inventory of the branch is $40,000 at the billed price.

Required:

a. Compute the beginning inventory of the branch at the billed price.

b. Compute the net income as reflected on the books of the branch.

c. Prepare the entries on the books of the home office to record the true income of the branch.

Exercise 1–5. The following information was extracted from the books and records of Phil Corporation and its branch. The balances are at December 31, 19x3, the third year of the corporation's existence.

	Home office dr. (cr.)	Branch dr. (cr.)
Sales		$(600,000)
Expenses		200,000
Shipments from home office .		360,000
Allowance for overvaluation of branch inventory	$(72,500)	

The branch purchases all of its merchandise from the home office. The inventories of the branch at billed prices are as follows:

January 1, 19x3	$75,000
December 31, 19x3	84,000

Required:

a. Compute the percentage of profit on *cost* that the home office uses to ship merchandise to the branch.

b. Compute the balance in the Shipments to Branch account before closing entries are posted.

c. Prepare the entries on the books of the home office to record the true profit of the branch.

Exercise 1–6. The following information was ex-

tracted from the books and records of Philip Corporation and its branch. The balances are at December 31, 19x4, the fourth year of the corporation's existence.

	Home office dr. (cr.)	Branch dr. (cr.)
Sales		$(200,000)
Shipments to branch	$(60,000)	
Shipments from home office .		80,000
Purchases		30,000
Expenses		60,000
Inventory, January 1, 19x4 . . .		20,000
Unrealized profit in branch inventory	(24,000)	

There are no shipments in transit between the home office and the branch. Both shipments accounts are properly recorded. The closing inventory at billed prices includes merchandise acquired from the home office in the amount of $20,000 and $6,000 acquired from vendors for a total of $26,000.

Required:

a. How much of the beginning inventory, at billed price, was acquired from "outsiders?"

b. Prepare the closing entry on the books of the branch.

c. Prepare the entries on the books of the home office to record the true branch net income.

PROBLEMS

Problem 1–7. The Hat Corporation has a branch in a nearby city. The respective trial balances on December 31, 19x3, are given as follows:

HAT CORPORATION
Trial Balances
December 31, 19x3

	Home office	Branch
Debits		
Cash	$ 20,000	$ 4,000
Accounts receivable	30,000	16,000
Inventory, January 1, 19x3	25,000	10,000
Branch control	40,000	
Equipment (net)	50,000	
Purchases	300,000	
Shipments from home office		80,000
Expenses	50,000	10,000
Totals	$515,000	$120,000

	Home office	Branch
Credits		
Accounts payable	$ 15,000	$ 2,000
Home office control		40,000
Capital stock	30,000	
Retained earnings, January 1, 19x3	80,000	
Sales	310,000	78,000
Shipments to branch	80,000	
Totals	$515,000	$120,000
Inventory, December 31, 19x3 . . .	$ 60,000	$ 40,000

Required:

a. Prepare closing entries for the branch.

b. Prepare closing entries for the home office including the entry to record the branch net income.

c. Prepare a combined working paper.

Problem 1–8. The Deb Corporation operates a branch in a nearby city. Trial balances for the branch and the home office at December 31, 19x5, are as follows:

Home Office Trial Balance

	Debit	Credit
Cash	$ 20,000	
Accounts receivable	30,000	
Inventory, January 1, 19x5	25,000	
Fixtures (net)	50,000	
Branch control	40,000	
Accounts payable		$ 15,000
Unrealized profit in branch inventory		18,000
Capital stock		30,000
Retained earnings		78,000
Sales		310,000
Shipments to branch		64,000
Purchases	300,000	
Selling expenses	20,000	
Administrative expenses	30,000	
Totals	$515,000	$515,000

Branch Trial Balance

	Debit	Credit
Cash	$ 4,000	
Accounts receivable	16,000	
Inventory, January 1, 19x5	10,000	
Accounts payable		$ 2,000
Home office control		40,000
Shipments from home office	80,000	
Sales		78,000
Selling expenses	4,000	
Administrative expenses	6,000	
Totals	$120,000	$120,000

All merchandise shipped to the branch by the home office was shipped at 125 percent of cost. The closing inventories are home office, $30,000; and branch, $12,000.

Required:

a. Prepare closing entries for the branch.

b. Prepare closing entries for the home office including the entries necessary to record the true branch net income.

c. Prepare a combined working paper.

Problem 1–9. The Best Corporation operates a branch in a nearby city. The home office ships mer-

chandise to the branch at 125 percent of its cost. Selected information from the December 31, 19x4, trial balances is as follows:

	Home office dr. (cr.)	Branch dr. (cr.)
Sales	$(600,000)	$(300,000)
Shipments to branch	(200,000)	
Purchases	350,000	
Shipments from home office .		250,000
Inventory, January 1, 19x4 . . .	100,000	40,000
Allowance for overvaluation of branch inventory	58,000	
Expenses	120,000	50,000

Closing inventories at December 31, 19x4, are:

Home office	$30,000
Branch	60,000

Required:

a. Prepare a branch income statement for managerial use at billed prices.

b. Prepare a branch income statement at cost for the purpose of combining it with a home office income statement.

c. Prepare a combined income statement for issuance to stockholders.

Problem 1–10. The Most Corporation operates a branch at a distant city. The home office ships merchandise to the branch at 120 percent of its cost. The trial balances of the corporation and its branch at December 31, 19x5, are as follows:

[Relates to Problem 1–10]

MOST CORPORATION
Trial Balances
December 31, 19x5

	Home office Dr.	Home office Cr.	Branch Dr.	Branch Cr.
Cash	$ 20,000		$ 16,000	
Accounts receivable	80,000		15,000	
Inventory, January 1, 19x5	25,000		12,000	
Branch control	34,000			
Equipment (net)	160,000		5,000	
Accounts payable		$ 40,000		$ 10,000
Unrealized profit in branch inventory		19,000		
Home office control				18,000
Capital stock		50,000		
Retained earnings		21,000		
Sales		400,000		160,000
Shipments from home office			90,000	
Purchases	200,000			
Shipments to branch		85,000		
Advertising	40,000		3,000	
Utilities	16,000		2,000	
Other expenses	40,000		45,000	
Totals	$615,000	$615,000	$188,000	$188,000

Additional information:

1. Merchandise billed at $12,000 was shipped on December 30, 19x5, by the home office. This has not yet been received by the branch.
2. The branch shipped $4,000 of cash to the home office on December 31, 19x5.
3. The closing inventory of the branch is $9,000 at billed prices.
4. The closing inventory of the home office is $15,000.

Required:

a. Prepare a reconciliation of the reciprocal accounts.

b. Prepare a combined working paper. The adjusting entries necessary from (a) above may be posted directly to the working paper. Do *not* adjust the trial balances.

c. Prepare a complete set of financial statements (income statement, retained earnings statement, and balance sheet).

Problem 1–11. You are engaged to audit the records of Pacific Import Company which have not previously been audited. The trial balance as of December 31, 19x6, follows:

PACIFIC IMPORT COMPANY
Trial Balances
December 31, 19x6

	Home office	Branch
Debits		
Cash	$ 15,000	$ 2,000
Accounts receivable	20,000	17,000
Inventory, December 31, 19x6	30,000	8,000
Branch control	44,000	
Fixed assets (net)	150,000	
Cost of sales	220,000	93,000
Expenses	70,000	41,000
Totals	$549,000	$161,000
Credits		
Accounts payable	$ 23,000	
Mortgage payable	50,000	
Accrued expenses		$ 2,000
Home office control		9,000
Capital stock	100,000	
Retained earnings, January 1, 19x6	26,000	
Sales	350,000	150,000
Totals	$549,000	$161,000

Additional information:

1. The branch receives all of its merchandise from the home office. The home office bills goods to the branch at 125 percent of cost. During 19x6, the branch was billed for $105,000 on shipments from the home office.

2. The home office credits Sales for the selling price of good shipped to the branch.
3. On January 1, 19x6, the inventory of the home office was $25,000. The branch books showed a $6,000 inventory.
4. The home office billed the branch for $12,000 on December 31, 19x6, representing the branch's share of expenses paid at the home office. The branch has not recorded this billing.
5. All cash collections made by the branch are deposited in a local bank to the account of the home office. Deposits of this nature included the following:

Amount	Date deposited by branch	Date recorded by home office
$5,000	12/28/x6	12/31/x6
3,000	12/30/x6	1/2/x7
7,000	12/31/x6	1/3/x7
2,000	1/2/x7	1/5/x7

6. Expenses incurred locally by the branch are paid from an imprest bank account which is reimbursed periodically by the home office. Just prior to the end of the year, the home office forwarded a reimbursement check in the amount of $3,000 which was not received by the branch office until January 19x7.
7. It is not necessary to make provisions for federal income tax.

Required:

a. You are to prepare a columnar worksheet for the company and its branch with columns for Trial Balance, Adjustments and Eliminations, Branch Income Statement, Home Office Income Statement, and Balance Sheet. Complete the worksheet and key and explain all adjustments and eliminations. (The income statements should be on a *cost* basis.)

b. Prepare a reconciliation of branch office and home office current accounts showing the *corrected* book balances. (AICPA adapted)

Problem 1–12. The preclosing general ledger trial balances at December 31, 19x5, for the Baltimore Wholesale Company and its Atlanta branch are shown below.

BALTIMORE WHOLESALE COMPANY
General Ledger Trial Balances
December 31, 19x5

	Home office dr. (cr.)	Branch dr. (cr.)
Cash	$ 36,000	$ 8,000
Accounts receivable	35,000	12,000
Inventory—home	70,000	
Inventory—branch		15,000
Fixed assets (net)	90,000	
Branch control	20,000	
Accounts payable	(36,000)	(13,500)
Accrued expenses payable	(14,000)	(2,500)
Home office control		(9,000)
Capital stock	(50,000)	
Retained earnings	(45,000)	
Home office:		
Sales	(440,000)	
Purchases	290,000	
Expenses	44,000	
Branch:		
Sales		(95,000)
Purchases		24,000
Purchases from home office		45,000
Expenses		16,000
Totals	–0–	–0–

Your audit disclosed the following:

1. On December 23, the branch manager purchased $4,000 of furniture and fixtures but failed to notify the home office. The bookkeeper, knowing that all fixed assets are carried on the home office books, recorded the proper entry on the branch records. It is the company's policy not to take any depreciation on assets acquired in the last half of a year.
2. On December 27, a branch customer erroneously paid his account of $2,000 to the home office. The bookkeeper made the correct entry on the home office books but did not notify the branch.
3. On December 30, the branch remitted cash of $5,000 which was received by the home office in January 19x6.
4. On December 31, the branch erroneously recorded the December allocated expenses from the home office as $500 instead of $1,500.
5. On December 31, the home office shipped merchandise billed at $3,000 to the branch, which was received in January 19x6.

6. The entire beginning inventory of the branch had been purchased from the home office. Home office 19x5 shipments to the branch were purchased by the home office in 19x5. The physical inventories at December 31, 19x5, excluding the shipment in transit, are home office, $55,000 (at cost); and branch, $20,000 (comprised of $18,000 from home office and $2,000 from outside vendors).
7. The home office consistently bills shipments to the branch at 20 percent above cost. The Sales account is credited for the invoice price.

Required (disregard income taxes):

Prepare a worksheet showing Adjustments and Eliminations, Home Office Income Statement, Branch Income Statement, and Combined Balance Sheet. The branch income data should be on the basis of home office cost. Number your worksheet adjusting and eliminating entries. (Formal entries are not required. Supporting computations, including the computation of the ending inventories, should be in good form.)   (AICPA adapted)

Problem 1–13. The trial balances of the home office and branch office of the Azure Company appear below:

AZURE COMPANY
Trial Balances
December 31, 19x3

	Home office	Branch
Debits		
Cash	$ 17,000	$ 200
Inventory—home office	23,000	
Inventory—branch		11,550
Sundry assets	200,000	48,450
Branch current account	60,000	
Purchases	190,000	
Purchased from home		105,000
Freight in from home		5,500
Sundry expenses	42,000	24,300
Totals	$532,000	$195,000
Credits		
Sundry liabilities	$ 35,000	$ 3,500
Home current account		51,500
Sales	155,000	140,000
Sales to branch	110,000	
Allowance for markup in branch inventory	1,000	
Capital stock	200,000	
Retained earnings	31,000	
Totals	$532,000	$195,000

The audit at December 31, 19x3, disclosed the following:

1. The branch office deposits all cash receipts in a local bank for the account of the home office. The audit worksheet for the cash cutoff revealed:

Amount	Date deposited by branch	Date recorded by home office
$1,050	12/27/x3	12/31/x3
1,100	12/30/x3	1/2/x4
600	12/31/x3	1/3/x4
300	1/2/x4	1/6/x4

2. The branch office pays expenses incurred locally from an imprest bank account that is maintained with a balance of $2,000. Checks are drawn once a week on this imprest account, and the home office is notified of the amount needed to replenish the account. At December 31, an $1,8000 reimbursement check was mailed to the branch office.
3. The branch office receives all its goods from the home office. The home office bills the goods at cost plus a markup of 10 percent of cost. At December 31, a shipment with a billing value of $5,000 was in transit to the branch. Freight costs are typically 5 percent of billed values. Freight costs are considered to be inventoriable costs.
4. The trial balance opening inventories are shown at their respective costs to the home office and to the branch office. The inventories at December 31, excluding the shipment in transit, are:

Home office, at cost	$30,000
Branch office, at billing value	10,400

Required (disregard income taxes):

Prepare a columnar worksheet for the company and its branch with columns for Trial Balance, Adjustments and Eliminations, Branch Income Statement, Home Income Statement, and Combined Balance Sheet. The branch income statement should be prepared on the basis of home cost. (Formal journal entries are not required. Supporting computations must be in good form.) Number your worksheet adjusting and eliminating entries.   (AICPA adapted)

2

Business combinations

OVERVIEW

During the past 25 years, there has been an increased tendency for unrelated business organizations to combine their operations by means of mergers and acquisitions. There are many broad economic factors that contributed to this phenomenon as well as the antitrust environment, the accounting treatments of mergers, and tax considerations.

Two methods of accounting for business combinations are used in practice. One method, purchase accounting, *requires that the fair market value of the consideration given (the price paid for the acquired company) be the measure for recording the business combination. The other method,* pooling accounting, *requires that the book value of the acquired company's net assets be the measure for recording the business combination while the fair market value of the consideration given is ignored. These methods are not elective, as in inventory pricing or in depreciation accounting, and the appropriate method must be used in a given set of conditions. The resulting combined financial statements may be radically different depending on the method of accounting used.*

The combination of business entities is not a new phenomenon on the business scene. In fact combinations escalate and decline in accordance with economic conditions, the legal climate, and other causitive conditions. The cyclical aspect of business combination activity can be seen from Illustration 2–1. The history of business combinations as we know them today can be traced back to the 1890s.

REASONS FOR COMBINATIONS

There are, of course, many legitimate reasons for *external* business expansion, that is, expansion by means of business combinations under which two or more entities are brought under common control. These reasons include: (1) acquisition of sources of new materials, productive facilities, production know-how, marketing organizations, and established shares of a market; (2) the acquisition of financial resources; (3) the acquisition of competent management; (4) savings of time in entering new markets; and (5) achieving economies of scale and acquiring tax advantages such as those relating to tax-loss carryovers.

LEGAL FORMS OF BUSINESS COMBINATIONS
Statutory merger

A statutory merger is one where two (or more) companies merge into one surviving company. Although the requirements vary among the different states, in many states it is necessary for two thirds of the stockholders of each constituent corporation to approve the merger.

Statutory consolidation

A statutory consolidation is similar to a statutory merger except that instead of one of the constituent corporations surviving, a new corporation is formed to conduct the combined businesses of the constituents who dissolve and cease to exist.

Acquisition

Although the term *acquisition* is used in an imprecise manner, it is generally used to mean that one corporation acquires a *majority* of the shares of an-

Illustration 2–1: Manufacturing and mining mergers and acquisitions, 1920–1975*

Years	Number
1920–24	2,235
1925–29	4,583
1930–34	1,687
1935–39	577
1940–44	906
1945–49	1,505
1950–54	1,424
1955–59	3,365
1960–64	4,366
1965–69	8,213
1970–74	4,749

*While this is the latest data available, a new wave of merger activity is emerging in the early 1980s with many of these mergers involving net asset exchanges of billions of dollars.

Source: U.S. Bureau of the Census, *Statistical Abstract of the United States: 1978*, (99th ed.) (Washington, D.C., 1978).

other corporation and both companies continue in existence as separate legal entities in a parent-subsidiary relationship.

The above can be summarized as follows:

	Constituents	Survivors
Statutory merger	A and B	A or B
Statutory consolidation	A and B	C
Acquisition	A and B	A and B

DIRECTIONAL AND ANTITRUST CONSIDERATIONS
Horizontal combinations

These combinations are between parties that are in the same type of business on the same level of activity and usually compete with one another. An example would be if Exxon and Mobil Oil, both integrated oil companies, were to combine.

Vertical combinations

These combinations are between parties in the same type of business but at different levels of activity. The combination can be between a mining company, a manufacturer, a wholesaler, and a retailer, or a combination of them. An example of this type of combination would be if Brown Shoe Company (basically a manufacturer of shoes) would combine with G. R. Kinney Company (basically a retailer of shoes).

Conglomerate combinations

These combinations are not necessarily horizontal or vertical; rather, they are entered into for the purpose of diversification into new markets or industries. An example of this type of combination is when International Telephone and Telegraph Company acquires companies in the car-leasing field and/or in the insurance field.

Circular combinations

A circular combination is different in that although it entails some diversification, it is not as drastic a departure in operation as is involved in conglomeration. Practitioners of this type of diversification attempt to increase the utilization of existing productive facilities and/or marketing channels. An example of this type of diversification is when Beatrice Foods combined its yoghurt business with an orange juice business by acquisition of Tropicana Products.

Various governmental agencies such as the Anti-Trust Division of the Department of Justice and the Federal Trade Commission (FTC) have had a modest amount of success in enforcing antitrust statutes. The principal enforcement statutes that are available are the Sherman Act of 1890 and the Clayton Act of 1914 amended through 1955. In addition, in 1976 the Hart-Scott-Rodino amendments were enacted that require premerger notification of an anticipated combination. Such notification must be given to both the Anti-Trust Division and the FTC. Various guidelines are available setting forth the permissible limits for horizontal and vertical combinations. The guidelines take into account the market shares of the constituents, concentration (oligopoly, monopoly, etc.), barriers of entry into the industry, imminence of entry, and other economic considerations and restraints of trade. Prior to 1976, enforcement activities were after the fait accompli, and they had to overcome the burden of the hardships created by breaking up the combination. The premerger notification requirement permits the enforcement agencies to evaluate the economic implications prior to the consummation of the combination.

METHODS OF ACCOUNTING FOR BUSINESS COMBINATIONS

Presently two methods of accounting for business combinations are sanctioned by generally accepted accounting principles (GAAP). One method, called purchase accounting, involves a new basis of accountability (the book values of the seller are ignored in recording the combination) and thus requires that the transaction be recorded at its fair value. This method is generally used where cash, debt, and/or securities other than common stock are used, or if these are used in conjunction with common stock in effecting the acquisition.

The second method of accounting for a business combination, the pooling of interests method, is used where at least 90 percent in common stock is used to effect the combination and 11 other criteria (discussed later) are met. When pooling accounting is used, a new basis for accountability does *not* arise. In pooling, the *book values* of the assets and liabilities of the parties to the combination are combined for reporting purposes, and this contrasts to the fair market values used in purchase accounting. A discussion of both accounting methods follows.

PURCHASE ACCOUNTING The treatment of a business combination as a purchase is compatible with the treatment of the acquisition of any asset by a business entity; the fair value of the transaction is the basis of recording the exchange. When purchase accounting is used—

1. The parties have bargained in good faith using fair values rather than book values in determining the acquisition price.
2. The transaction is recorded at the fair value of the price paid (cash, debt, preferred stock, etc., or combinations of these with common stock) or the value of the net assets acquired, whichever is more clearly evident.
3. The components of the assets acquired will be recorded at their respective fair values. Any excess of cost over the fair values of total identifiable net assets will be assigned to intangibles.
4. The retained earnings of the former owners shown on the balance sheet of the acquired company is not carried forward to the books of the acquiring corporation.
5. The revenues generated subsequent to acquisition by the acquired assets

are matched with the expired costs, using the fair values assigned to the assets rather than the book values of the selling corporation.

POOLING ACCOUNTING

The accounting for a business combination by the pooling method represents a special case of accounting. This treatment must be used when the attributes of the business combination meet certain specified criteria which are discussed later. A major attribute is that the business combination be effectuated by an exchange of common stock (90 percent or more of the selling stockholders must accept common stock). When common stock is exchanged for common stock, arguments have been advanced to support the pooling concept. Proponents of pooling maintain that—

1. A pooling of interests is a transaction taking place between the stockholder groups of the parties to the combination. The entities have not changed; the stockholder interests have merely been realigned.
2. The stockholders have pooled their risks and resources so that each stockholder group now shares the risks of the other while continuing to share a part of its former risks and resources.
3. No assets or liabilities of the firms are altered. Common stock is not an asset, and consequently no assets have been disbursed.

The principle differences between pooling and purchase accounting are that for pooling accounting—

1. The retained earnings of the combinee is carried forward and becomes part of the retained earnings of the surviving combined or consolidated entity.
2. Restatement of the financial statements is required. Regardless of the date of acquisition, earnings prior to the date of a pooling are combined with the survivor's earnings as if the constituents were always combined. In the case of purchase accounting, only the post-acquisition earnings of the acquired entity are combined with the surviving entity's earnings.
3. Market values of individual assets and liabilities are ignored, and only the book values of the combinee are used in recording the combination. Consequently, no goodwill ever arises in a pooling regardless of the number of shares issued to effect the combination.
4. The aggregate dollar amount at which the combination is recorded is the same regardless of how many shares are exchanged to effect the combination. The same does not apply to purchase accounting. In the latter case the greater the number of shares exchanged, the greater the dollar value at which the combination is recorded.

HISTORICAL DEVELOPMENT OF POOLING ACCOUNTING

With the exception of some brother-sister poolings (different corporations owned by the same stockholders) in the 1920s, the first significant pooling made its debut shortly after World War II. The chair of the American Institute of Certified Public Accountants (AICPA) Committee on Co-operation with the Securities and Exchange Commission published a paper about a petition his firm filed with the SEC regarding the merger of the Celanese Corporation and Tubize Rayon Corporation.[1] The paper was concerned with the following:

1. The merger was consummated because the two firms would operate more efficiently under one management.
2. Since the firms had actually pooled their operations and resources, it seemed unfair that the earned surplus of Tubize Rayon Corporation should be capitalized and not be available for dividends.
3. A large goodwill account would be created if purchase accounting were used, and since it appeared that the combined entity had little or no goodwill, it would require an immediate write-off of the goodwill account to surplus.

It was not too long (three years) after the Celanese brief that the Committee on Accounting Procedure of the AICPA issued *Accounting Research Bulletin (ARB) No. 40* (September 1950). This bulletin attempted to differentiate the criteria to be used in accounting for pooling of interests versus purchase accounting. Although *ARB 40* was later codified as chapter 7, section C, of *ARB 43*, implementation problems of the relative-size concept contained in *ARB 43* required clarification. This was attempted in 1957 by the issuance of *ARB 48*.

Between 1957, when *ARB 48* was issued, and 1970, when *Accounting Principles Board (APB) Opinion 16* was issued, several astute academicians and practitioners commented on various kinds of abuses of the pooling accounting concept. The eminent accountant George C. May called attention to some potential abuses in his article "Business Combinations: An Alternative View."[2] Other practitioners saw some of the pitfalls of pooling, but it was Prof. Abraham J. Briloff who apprised the academic and financial communities of the seriousness of the pooling abuses in his article "Dirty Poolings."[3] Various kinds of abuses emerged during this period, the more notable being:

1. *Retrospective pooling*—combining with a company after the close of the fiscal year but before a report is issued. A company with a loss could combine with a company showing a profit, and the loss could be buried in the combined (restated) report. This treatment was mandated at the time by *APB Opinion 10*, issued in December 1966.
2. *Part purchase/part pooling*—using cash and securities and treating each as a separate transaction. The cash portion (purchase accounting) was applied to cash, receivables, and other assets whose book values were stated at fair market values. The stock portion (pooling accounting) was applied to inventories and plant assets whose book values were significantly below fair market values, and these assets could then be carried forward at book value.

---

[1] William M. Black, "Certain Phases of Merger Accounting," *The Journal of Accountancy* 83 (March 1947): 214–20.

[2] George O. May, "Business Combinations: An Alternate View," *The Journal of Accountancy* 103 (April 1957): 33–36.

[3] Abraham J. Briloff, "Dirty Pooling," *Accounting Review,* 42 (July 1967): 489–96.

3. *Instant earnings*—combining with a company having low book values for certain assets (marketable securities, LIFO inventories, amortized assets) and then selling these at substantial gains after the combination. Since the fair market value of these assets was not booked at the time of the business combination, the reporting of a gain was virtually assured.

4. *Funny money*—using securities which are not common stock but which had common stock characteristics (e.g., warrants) which did not affect the earnings per share (EPS) statistic, prior to the issuance of *APB Opinions 9* and *15*.

5. *Contingent payouts*—issuing additional shares of stock after the combination is completed. The number of additional shares of stock would be contingent upon the earnings of the seller and/or the market price per share of the purchaser.

6. *Treasury stock*—acquiring treasury stock either before or after a combination. If one considers this a *step transaction*, then the combination was actually effectuated with cash, the two steps being:
   a. Using cash to acquire the treasury stock.
   b. Using the stock to combine as a pooling of interests.

With the growth in these abuses, the chorus of criticism grew, and this resulted in a call by many for the abolition of pooling of interests accounting. Instead, members of the APB compromised and issued *Opinion 16*, which, as we shall see, established stricter and more specific conditions for use of this method of accounting in the future.

REVISED OPINIONS ON ACCOUNTING FOR BUSINESS COMBINATIONS

In an attempt to improve the accounting for business combinations, the APB issued in 1970 *Opinions 16* and *17*. However, in late 1976 the FASB issued a voluminous Discussion Memorandum on the subject which was designed to lead to public hearings in 1977 and to a reconsideration of the entire subject. At this writing the reconsideration has been placed on an inactive status pending the outcome of deliberations of a "Conceptual Framework" for accounting.

APB Opinion 16[4] concluded that if a business combination meets the 12 specific criteria enumerated in it, it must be accounted for as a pooling of interests. Otherwise it must be accounted for as a purchase.

Conditions for the pooling of interests method

There are 12 conditions which must be met under the provision of *APB Opinion 16* before a business combination may be accounted for as a pooling of interests. These can be grouped under three main categories:

I. Attributes of the combining companies.
II. Manner of combining interests.
III. Absence of planned transactions.

---

[4]Copyright © (1970) by the American Institute of Certified Public Accountants, New York.

I. Attributes of the combining companies

    A. Each of the combining companies should be autonomous and not have operated as a subsidiary or division of another company within two years before the plan of combination is initiated. An exception to this condition concerns the divestiture of assets which was ordered by a governmental or judicial body. A subsidiary which is divested under an order or a new company which acquires assets disposed of under such an order is considered autonomous for this condition.

    B. Each of the combining companies must be independent of each other. That means that no combining company or group of combining companies can hold as an intercompany investment more than 10 percent of the outstanding voting common stock of any other combining company. To illustrate the 10 percent requirement, let's assume that company A plans to issue its voting common stock to acquire the voting common stock of companies B and C. If companies A and B each own 7 percent of company C's outstanding common stock, A can pool with B, but the combined entity cannot subsequently pool with C since more than 10 percent of company C's outstanding stock would have been held by the other combining companies.

II. Manner of combining interests

    C. The combination should be effected in a single transaction or should be completed in accordance with a specific plan within one year after the plan is initiated. The *Opinion* provides an exception to this one-year rule when the delay is beyond the control of the combining companies because of proceedings of a governmental authority or pending litigation.

    D. The combination should involve the issuance of voting common stock only in exchange for substantially all of the voting common stock interest of the company being combined. "Substantially all" in this context means at least 90 percent of the voting common stock interest of the company being combined. Thus, the issuer may purchase for cash or other nonvoting common stock consideration up to 10 percent of the voting common shares of the company to be pooled. Such a cash outlay may be necessary to eliminate fractional shares or to pay dissenting stockholders. The rationale of this criterion is that substantially all of the voting common stock interest in each party to a pooling should be carried forward as a voting common stock interest in the issuer in the pooling. The payment of cash, debt, or an equity instrument which does not satisfy this test destroys the most fundamental basis of a pooling. If the company being combined has securities other than voting stock, such securities may be exchanged for common stock of the issuing corporation or may be exchanged for substantially identical securities of the issuing corporation.

E. None of the combining companies should change the equity interest of their voting common stock in contemplation of effecting the combination. This restriction applies during the period from two years preceding the date the plan is initiated through the date the plan is consummated. Changes in the equity interest of the voting common stock which may violate this condition include distributions to shareholders, additional issuance or exchange of securities, and the retirement of securities. The purpose of this rule is to disallow changes in equity interests prior to a combination because such changes indicate a sale rather than a combining and sharing of risks.

F. Each combining company may reacquire shares of voting common stock only for purposes other than business combinations, and no company may reacquire more than a normal number of shares between the date the plan of combination is initiated and consummated.

G. The ratio of the interest of an individual common stockholder to those of other common shareholders in a combining company should remain the same as a result of the exchange of stock to effect the combination. This condition insures that no common stockholder is denied his potential share of a voting common stock interest in a combined corporation.

H. The stockholders of the resulting combined corporation cannot be deprived of, nor restricted in, their ability to exercise their voting rights on common stock of the combined corporation. For example, establishing a voting trust to hold some of the shares issued in the combination disqualifies the combination as a pooling of interests.

I. The combination must be resolved at the date the plan is consummated, and there must be no contingent arrangements for the issuance of additional securities or other consideration. All consideration to be given to effect the combination of the companies, must be determinable as of the date the plan of combination is consummated. The only exception to this would be a provision to adjust the exchange ratio as a result of a subsequent settlement of a contingency such as an existing lawsuit.

III. Absence of planned transactions

J. The combined corporation should not agree directly or indirectly to retire or reacquire any of the common stock issued to effect the combination.

K. The combined corporation cannot enter into other financial arrangements for the benefit of the former stockholders of a combining company, such as a guarantee of loans secured by stock issued in the combination. This financial arrangement may require the payment of cash in the future which would negate the exchange of equity securities, and thus the combination would not qualify for pooling of interests treatment.

L. The combined corporation may not intend to dispose of a significant part of the assets of the combining companies within two years after the combination. Some disposal of assets may be effected within the two-year period provided the disposals would have been in the ordinary course of business of the formerly separate companies or if the disposals were to eliminate duplicate facilities or excess capacity.

If a combining company remains a subsidiary of the issuing corporation after the combination is consummated, the combination could still be accounted for as a pooling of interests, as long as all the conditions for a pooling are met. Any business combination which meets all the above conditions *must* be accounted for under the pooling of interests method.

Application of the purchase method

As we have seen in the foregoing discussion, under purchase accounting the business combination is viewed as the acquisition of one entity by another.

Problem of valuation of the consideration. One of the major problems in accounting for a purchase is to determine the total cost of an acquired entity. The same accounting principles apply whether determining the cost of assets acquired individually, in a group, or in a business combination. It is the nature of the transaction which determines which accounting principles apply in arriving at the total cost of assets acquired.

There usually is no problem in determining the total cost of assets acquired for cash, since the amount of cash disbursed is the total cost of the acquired assets. The difficulty is, however, in the proper allocation of the total cost to the individual assets acquired.

If assets are acquired by incurring liabilities, total cost of the assets is the present value of the amounts to be paid in the future. The present value of a debt security is the fair value of the liability. If the debt security has been issued at an interest rate which is substantially above or below the present effective rate for a similar security, the appropriate amount of premium or discount should be recorded. In some cases the characteristics of a preferred stock may be so similar to a debt security that it should be valued in the same manner.

If assets are acquired in exchange for stock, the general rule for determining the total cost of the assets acquired would be that it is the fair value of the stock given or the fair value of the assets received, whichever is more clearly evident.

The fair value of securities traded in the market is normally more clearly evident than is the fair value of the acquired company. Quoted market price should serve as a guide in determining total cost of an acquired company after considering market fluctuations, the quantities traded, issue costs, and so forth.

If the quoted market price is not a reliable indicator of the value of stock issued, it is still necessary to determine the fair value of the assets received, including goodwill, even though this valuation is difficult.

In these cases the best means of estimation should be used, including a detailed review of the negotiations leading up to the purchase and the use of independent appraisals.

Contingent additional consideration.   The amount of any additional contingent consideration payable in accordance with the purchase agreement is usually recorded when the contingency is resolved and the consideration is to be issued or becomes issuable. Two of the most common types of contingencies are based on either earnings or security prices.

The following guides to the accounting for such contingent additional consideration are contained in *APB Opinion 16:*

1. A contingent issuance of additional consideration should be disclosed but should not be recorded as a liability or shown as outstanding securities unless the outcome of the contingency is determinable beyond a reasonable doubt.
2. A contingent issuance of additional consideration based on future earnings should be recorded as an additional cost of the acquisition when the contingency is resolved. In this case the total amount of consideration representing cost was not determinable at the date of acquisition.
3. A contingent issuance of additional consideration which is based on future security prices should be considered as an adjustment of the amount originally recorded for the securities at the date of acquisition.

Allocation of total cost.   Once the total cost of an acquired entity is determined, it is then necessary to allocate this total cost to the individual assets received. All identifiable assets acquired and liabilities assumed in a business combination should be assigned a portion of the total cost, normally equal to their fair value at date of acquisition. The excess of the total cost over the amounts assigned to identifiable assets acquired, less liabilities assumed, should be recorded as goodwill. Such goodwill must be amortized over a period not to exceed 40 years.

It may be possible in some cases that the market or appraisal values of identifiable assets acquired, less liabilities assumed, exceeds the cost of the acquired company. In those cases, the values otherwise assignable to non-current assets acquired (except long-term investments in marketable securities) should be reduced by a proportionate part of the excess. Negative goodwill should not be recorded unless the value assigned to such long-term assets is first reduced to zero. If such allocation results in an excess of net assets over cost, it should be classified as a deferred credit and should be amortized systematically to income over the period estimated to be benefited but not in excess of 40 years.[5]

North American Philips Corporation provides the following example of a *bargain purchase* acquisition:

> *Note 2: Acquisitions.* Effective October 1, 19x4, a subsidiary of NAPC acquired approximately 84 percent of the common stock of The Magnavox Company (Magnavox) for an aggregate cash purchase cost of approximately $142 million. The transaction has been accounted for as a purchase and

[5]APB, *"Business Combinations,"* APB Opinion No. 16 (New York: AICPA, August 1970), par. 91.

accordingly the operations of Magnavox are included in the consolidated statement of income from October 1, 19x4. The equity in the net assets of Magnavox exceeded acquisition cost by $18,977,000. Of such amount, $12,552,000 was assigned to specific assets and liabilities and $6,425,000 was allocated to remaining noncurrent assets acquired on a pro rata basis in accordance with the provisions of *Accounting Principles Board Opinion No. 16. . . .*

Guidelines for valuation of assets and liabilities. *APB Opinion 16* established general guides for assigning amounts to individual assets and liabilities assumed, except goodwill, as follows:

1. Marketable securities should be recorded at current net realizable values.
2. Receivables should be recorded at the present values of amounts to be received, determined at appropriate current interest rates, less allowances for uncollectibility and collection costs, if necessary.
3. Inventories:
    a. Finished goods should be recorded at selling prices less cost of disposal and reasonable profit allowance.
    b. Work in process inventories should be stated at estimated selling prices of finished goods less the sum of the costs to complete, costs of disposal, and a reasonable profit allowance for the completing and selling effort of the acquired corporation.
    c. Raw materials should be recorded at current replacement costs.
4. Plant and equipment to be used in the business should be stated at current replacement costs for similar capacity unless the expected future use of the assets indicates a lower value to the acquirer. Replacement cost may be determined directly if a used asset market exists for the assets acquired. Otherwise, replacement cost should be approximated from replacement cost new, less estimated accumulated depreciation.
5. Indentifiable intangible assets should be valued at appraised values.
6. Other assets, such as land, natural resources, and nonmarketable securities, should be recorded at appraised values.
7. Accounts and notes payable, long-term debt, and other claims payable should be stated at present values of amounts, to be paid, determined at appropriate current interest rates.

An acquiring corporation should not record as a separate asset goodwill previously recorded by an acquired company, and it should not record deferred income taxes previously recorded by an acquired company. Amounts assigned to identifiable assets and liabilities should recognize that their value may be less, if part or all of the assigned value is not deductible for income taxes. However, the acquiring corporation should not record deferred tax accounts for the tax effect of these differences at the date of acquisition.

Treatment of goodwill. *APB Opinion 17* provides that for the intangible assets acquired in a business combination, the method of allocating the total cost of the acquired company depends on whether or not the asset is identifiable, such as a patent, or unidentifiable, such as goodwill. The cost of an identifiable intangible asset should be based on the fair value of the asset. The cost of an unidentifiable intangible asset is measured by the difference between total cost and the amount assigned to other assets acquired and liabilities assumed.

The cost of an intangible asset should be amortized based on the estimated life of that specific asset; the period of amortization, however, should not exceed 40 years. The straight-line method of amortization should be used unless the company can demonstrate that another systematic method is more appropriate. The method and period of amortization should be disclosed in the financial statements.

Pro forma supplementary disclosure

Under the purchase method, notes to the financial statements of the acquiring corporation for the period in which a business combination occurs should include as supplemental information the following results of operations on a pro forma basis:

1. Combined results of operations for the current period as though the companies had combined at the beginning of the period unless the acquisition was at or near the beginning of the period.
2. If comparative financial statements are presented, combined results of operations for the immediately preceding period should be reported as though the companies had combined at the beginning of that period.

This supplemental pro forma information should, as a minimum, show revenue, income before extraordinary items, net income, and earnings per share.

COSTS AND EXPENSES OF CONSUMMATING THE COMBINATION

Different types of costs and expenses are incurred during the search phase, the investigative phase, and the consummation phase of a business combination. They can be grouped into:

A. *Costs to acquire the combination candidate.* These include:
    1. Finder's fees.
    2. Accounting fees for a preacquisition audit.
    3. Legal fees in connection with the contract to acquire the candidate.
B. *Costs to finance the combination.* These include:
    1. Accounting and legal fees in connection with an SEC registration statement.
    2. Cost of printing stock certificates.
    3. Registration costs.

The above list is not all-inclusive.

The costs in category A would be incurred regardless of the mode of financing, i.e., cash, common stock, debt, and so on. Thus, in purchase accounting where a new basis of accountability prevails, these costs are capitalized as part of the cost of the investment. This treatment is no different from preacquisition costs (commissions, legal, etc.) of acquiring real property or machinery. The costs in category B, however, arise only when the mode of financing is other than cash. Therefore, these costs arise from the financial aspects of issuing additional securities or debt and, accordingly, are treated as a reduction of the proceeds of the financing and they are *not* capitalized when purchase accounting is used.

For pooling accounting, however, both categories are treated as *expenses* in the period in which they are incurred. Since there is no new basis of accountability for pooling accounting, book values must be used and they cannot be increased by these expenditures. Further, since the issuance of the additional shares of common stock used in the combination is viewed as merely an exchange arrangement between the stockholders of the constituent companies, they are not viewed as consideration given as in purchase accounting. Therefore, there are no "proceeds" from which to deduct the category B costs.

TAXABLE VERSUS NONTAXABLE EXCHANGES

Business combinations can be either taxable or nontaxable exchanges. Generally, nontaxable exchanges tend to be accounted for as *poolings* and taxable exchanges tend to be accounted for as *purchases*. However, this need not always be the case since the requirements for a nontaxable exchange are not the same as the requirements for a pooling. In fact, many purchases are nontaxable exchanges. Tax implications of business combinations are discussed in the appendix at the end of this chapter.

ILLUSTRATION OF ACCOUNTING MECHANICS: PURCHASE VERSUS POOLING ACCOUNTING

We turn now to the mechanics of recording business combinations. It is now assumed that—

1. The post-closing trial balance of Baker Corporation on December 31, 19x2, is as presented in Illustration 2–2.

Illustration 2–2
BAKER CORPORATION
Post-Closing Trial Balance
December 31, 19x2

	Debit	Credit	Fair Market Value
Cash	$ 100,000		
Marketable securities (cost)	50,000		$ 70,000
Accounts receivable	80,000		
Allowance for doubtful accounts		$ 3,000	75,000
Inventories	150,000		180,000
Machinery and equipment	800,000		
Accumulated depreciation		200,000	700,000
Patent	5,000		100,000
Accounts payable		102,000	
Notes payable		80,000	
Common stock ($10 par value)		100,000	
Additional paid-in capital		50,000	
Retained earnings		650,000	
Totals	$1,185,000	$1,185,000	

Note: Operating results for the year 19x2 are omitted for ease of illustration. The treatment of operating results is covered later in this chapter.

2. Able Corporation and Baker Corporation have agreed to a statutory merger effective December 31, 19x2. During the negotiation and consummation phases, Able Corporation incurred the following expenditures:
   a. Finder's fee, $30,000.
   b. Legal and accounting fees in connection with the acquisition, $40,000.
   c. SEC registration costs, $50,000.
3. Able Corporation's stockholders' equity on December 31, 19x2, consisted of:
   a. Common stock—$50 par value—40,000 shares outstanding, $2,000,000.
   b. Additional paid-in capital, $200,000.
   c. Retained earnings, $1,000,000.
4. Able Corporation's stock was trading at $200 per share on a national stock exchange on December 31, 19x2.

Four cases will now be illustrated. They are:

A. Eight thousand shares of Able's common stock are issued for 100 percent of Baker's outstanding shares. Included in the merger agreement is a plan whereby Able agrees to repurchase in the future the shares issued to Baker's stockholders. (*Hint:* Purchase accounting must be used.)
B. All conditions in A above are the same except that 6,000 shares of Able's common stock are issued instead of 8,000 shares.
C. Eight thousand shares of Able's common stock are issued for 100 percent of Baker's outstanding shares and all conditions for a pooling have been met.
D. The same as C above except that 6,000 shares of Able's common stock are issued.

The following is a brief outline of a methodology that is useful for problem solving in a variety of circumstances. The methodology for *purchase* accounting is:

1. Ascertain the identifiable net assets (assets minus liabilities) of the acquired company at *fair market value* and compare this with the fair market value of the consideration given. The resulting difference, if any, if positive, will be the goodwill implicit in the combination. Goodwill is increased by capitalized expenditures (finder's fees, etc.). A negative amount must be prorated over a long-term assets other than investments in marketable securities and is illustrated in Chapter 3, Illustration 3–7.
2. Since a new basis of accountability is present in purchase accounting, fair market values of individual assets and liabilities form the basis of the merger journal entries. Accumulated depreciation is *not* carried forward to the acquirer's books; the fair market values of the assets are used instead. The same holds true for accounts receivable—the fair market value is used. However, since it is not possible to write off specific re-

ceivables prior to the time they become uncollectible, the gross amount of accounts receivable is used and an allowance for doubtful accounts is created for the difference between the gross amount and the fair market value of the receivables.

The methodology for *pooling* accounting is:

1. Ascertain the net assets of the combinee at *book value* and use this amount as the debit to Investment in X Company. This amount will be used in *all cases* regardless of how many shares are issued. If less than 100 percent is acquired, a parent and subsidiary relationship usually results—the debit equals net assets multiplied by the owned percentage.
2. The credit to Common Stock is for the number of shares issued multiplied by the par value or stated value per share. If stock with no-par and stated value is used, the credit to Common Stock is the balancing amount after Retained Earnings is credited (see item 3 below).
3. The amount of retained earnings to be carried forward to the combinor's books is limited to the amount on the combinee's books. In no event can this amount be exceeded. However, in some cases a lesser amount might be used. If the upper limit plus the amount credited to Common Stock exceeds the debit to Investment in X Company, the balancing debit is to the combinor's (survivor's) Additional Paid-In Capital (APIC) account to the extent that it is available. If this amount is insufficient to balance the entry, then the amount of retained earnings carried forward is reduced in order to balance the entry. If less than 100 percent of the combinee's stock is acquired, the upper limit of retained earnings to be carried forward is the combinee's amount multiplied by the percentage of ownership.
4. If a credit is required to balance the entry when the upper limit of retained earnings is reached, the credit is to APIC without limit as to amount.
5. When a merger entry is made, the individual assets and liabilities replace the Investment in X Company account which equals the amount of net assets.

From the foregoing, it can be seen that a pooling is accounted for as if the two companies combine their resources with carrying amounts remaining intact including their respective retained earnings balances. The only shift that is possible in a pooling is a change in the components of stockholders' equity, but not in its total.

The entries on Able's books for each of the above cases would be:

Able's Books—Purchase Accounting

	Case A		Case B	
	Dr.	Cr.	Dr.	Cr.

(1)

Investment in Baker Corporation	70,000		70,000	
Cash		70,000		70,000

To record payment of finder's fee and legal and accounting fees.   Same

(2)

Additional Paid-In Capital	50,000		50,000	
Cash		50,000		50,000

To record payment of SEC registration costs for combination with Baker Corporation.   Same

(3)

Investment in Baker Corporation	1,600,000		1,200,000	
Common Stock		400,000		300,000
Additional Paid-In Capital		1,200,000		900,000

To record issuance of 8,000 shares at $200 fair market value and $50 par value per share for 100 percent of Baker Corporation.

To record issuance of 6,000 shares at $200 fair market value and $50 par value per share for 100 percent of Baker Corporation.

(4)

Cash	100,000		100,000	
Marketable Securities	70,000		70,000	
Accounts Receivable	80,000		80,000	
Inventories	180,000		180,000	
Machinery and Equipment	700,000		700,000	
Patent	100,000		100,000	
Goodwill	627,000		227,000	
Allowance for Doubtful Accounts* . .		5,000		5,000
Accounts Payable		102,000		102,000
Notes Payable		80,000		80,000
Investment in Baker Corporation . . .		1,670,000		1,270,000

To record the merger of Baker Corporation into Able corporation.   Same

*Note: The allowance is computed as:

Gross amount of accounts receivable	$80,000
Less: Fair market value	75,000
Necessary allowance	$ 5,000

Able's Books—Pooling Accounting

	Case C		Case D	
	Dr.	Cr.	Dr.	Cr.
(5)				
Investment in Baker Corporation	800,000		800,000	
Additional Paid-In Capital	200,000		150,000	
Common Stock		400,000		300,000
Retained Earnings of Pooled Company		600,000		650,000

To record issuance of 8,000 shares of common stock for 100 percent of Baker Corporation.

(Case D) To record issuance of 6,000 shares of common stock for 100 percent of Baker Corporation.

	Case C		Case D	
	Dr.	Cr.	Dr.	Cr.
(6)				
Expenses	120,000		120,000	
Cash		120,000		120,000

To record payment of finder's fees, legal and accounting fees, and SEC registration costs. *(Case D)* Same

	Case C		Case D	
	Dr.	Cr.	Dr.	Cr.
(7)				
Cash	100,000			
Marketable Securities	50,000			
Accounts Receivable	80,000			
Inventories	150,000			
Machinery and Equipment	800,000			
Patent	5,000			
Allowance for Doubtful Accounts		3,000		
Accumulated Depreciation		200,000		
Accounts Payable		102,000		
Notes Payable		80,000		
Investment in Baker Corporation		800,000		

To record merger of Baker Corporation into Able Corporation. *(Case D)* Same

Regarding the above entries, the following observations are noteworthy:

1. Goodwill is affected by the number of shares issued in the business combination. See entries (4) under case A and (4) under case B.

2. Accumulated depreciation is carried forward for pooling accounting but not for purchase accounting. See entries (7) and (4).

3. In entry (5) under case D, Baker's retained earnings are carried forward in full ($650,000), whereas in entry (5) under case C, only $600,000 could be carried forward. The reason for this is that Able's APIC is $200,000 and is completely used up in the pooling entry. The remaining $50,000

necessarily reduces the retained earnings amount that is carried forward. This can be reconciled as follows:

Common stock issued (8,000 shares @ $50 par value)		$400,000
Less: Baker's capital to be eliminated—common stock . . .	$100,000	
Baker's—APIC	50,000	
Able's—APIC	200,000	350,000
Balance—retained earnings reduction		$ 50,000*

*Note: In actual practice this is sometimes recorded as negative APIC (debit) and is shown as a deduction in the stockholders' equity section of the balance sheet. If positive APIC arises in subsequent years, this amount is then offset.

DISSENTING SHAREHOLDERS

Some states permit mergers when 95 percent or more of the outstanding shares of an acquiree are held by the acquirer. The usual case when this occurs is not a merger but a parent-subsidiary relationship. If the requirements for a merger are met and a merger is to be implemented, a liability to dissenting stockholders is set up on the acquirer's books for the fair value of the untendered shares. A challenge in the courts is usually available to the dissenting shareholders if the offered price does not coincide with their expectation of fair value. This right is known as *appraisal rights.*

Special rules exist for pooling accounting. Since only 90 percent of the combinee's stock is necessary for a pooling, up to 10 percent of the combinee's shares can be acquired for cash. However, there are instances when 100 percent must be acquired to effect a pooling. A shareholder must tender *all* shares; partial dissenting is not permitted. Thus, in diagram A 100 percent exchange of stock is necessary for a pooling, and in diagram B both R and S must tender shares if a pooling is to be effected while T can dissent.

Using the same information as presented in Illustration 2–2 and the information presented in case D, i.e., 6,000 shares are issued for a pooling, it is now assumed that only 90 percent of Baker's outstanding shares are exchanged for the 6,000 shares of Able's common stock. Since a merger is not possible, a parent-subsidiary relationship will result from the transaction.

The entry to record the acquisition on Able's books would be:

Able's Books—December 31, 19x2

(1)

Investment in Baker Corporation	720,000	
Additional Paid-In Capital	165,000	
Common Stock		300,000
Retained Earnings of Pooled Subsidiary		585,000

To record the acquisition of 90 percent of Baker
Corporation in a pooling as follows:

Net assets: 90 percent x $800,000 = $720,000.
Retained earnings: 90 percent x $650,000 = $585,000.
Common stock: 6,000 shares x $50 = $300,000.

(2)

Expenses	120,000	
Cash		120,000

To record payment of finder's fee, legal and accounting fees,
and SEC registration costs.

APPLICATION OF THE 90 PERCENT RULE

When an exchange of common stock is required, such as in a pooling, business combination agreements contain what is known as an *exchange ratio.* The ratio is usually specified in a fashion such as .25 for 1. If Able and Baker are the constituent companies and Able is issuing its shares for Baker's, this means that Able will issue one-fourth share for each share of Baker that is tendered.

The following assumptions will be used to demonstrate the application of the 90 percent test:

	Shares
Able Corporation:	
Issued and outstanding	5,000,000
Investment in Baker Corporation	50,000
Baker Corporation:	
Issued	600,000
Treasury stock	6,000
Investment in Able Corporation	3,000
Exchange ratio = .25 for 1.	

The calculations for the 90 percent test are:

Required shares:	
Baker's shares issued	600,000
Less: Treasury shares	6,000
Shares outstanding	594,000
Amount required—90 percent of above	534,600
Possible shares:	
Baker's shares outstanding	594,000
Less: Baker's shares owned by Able	50,000
Total	544,000
Less: Able's shares owned by Baker converted into an equivalent number of Baker shares (3,000 ÷ .25)	12,000
Maximum possible	532,000

Since a minimum of 534,600 shares must be obtained for a pooling, the above example would not qualify for pooling treatment.

If, however, a business combination of less than 100 percent does qualify for pooling treatment, and later on the parent company is able to acquire the remaining shares outstanding (minority interests), the accounting treatment to be accorded to these shares must be purchase accounting.

OPERATING RESULTS

As noted previously, when purchase accounting is used, only the acquiree's operating results subsequent to the date of the business combination would appear on the acquirer's books. Thus, only a post-closing trial balance should be used for purchase accounting regardless of the effective date of the business combination. For pooling accounting, however, the combinee's results of operations prior to the date of acquisition are included in the combinor's results of operations as if the combination took place at the beginning of the year. Accordingly, an interim or year-end trial balance of the combinee would include revenue and expense accounts and these accounts are transferred to the combinor's books as part of a merger accounted for as a pooling.

Appendix: Tax aspects of business combinations

A business combination can be (1) a taxable event in which case the seller has a recognized gain or loss for tax purposes, and the purchaser's tax basis is the consideration given (market value); (2) a nontaxable reorganization which permits the seller to treat the shares of stock received as an exchange, and the seller's basis of the shares received is the seller's basis of the shares surrendered while the purchaser's basis is generally the seller's basis of the property; or (3) a combination of a taxable event and a tax-free reorganization when some cash is used.

Nontaxable reorganizations

If, as is frequently the case, the market value of the shares received by the seller greatly exceeds the tax cost (basis) of the property sold, the seller may not wish to incur an immediate tax liability, especially if he or she is interested in holding on to the shares received from the purchaser. For estate-planning reasons or because an up-front tax payment means holding fewer shares as an investment, a seller usually insists that the business combination be structured so as to qualify as a tax-free reorganization. This usually will conflict with the purchaser's interests. If the price paid (market value) for the seller's shares greatly exceeds the tax basis of the underlying net assets of the acquired company, the purchaser will desire a stepped-up basis of the net assets because this results in larger tax deductions in subsequent years. However, such stepping up in basis normally leads to a taxable transaction. This conflict must be resolved in the negotiation phase if the business combination is to be consummated.

Types of reorganizations

Although there are technically six types of nontaxable reorganizations, two types—an E type and an F type[6]—do not require elaboration since they concern themselves with a "recapitalization" and a "change in identity, form, or place of organization," respectively, which are merely internal organizational matters. The remaining four types (A, B, C, and D)[7] will be the focus of this appendix.

A type. An A type reorganization is one that meets state requirements as a statutory merger or a statutory consolidation. It should be noted that some cash consideration (boot) is permissible and that *none* of the 12 conditions for pooling accounting are specified in connection with A type reorganizations. Thus, while a statutory merger is nontaxable, its accounting treatment is dictated by *APB Opinion 16*. Many A type reorganizations are accounted for as poolings, but they need not necessarily be accounted for in this manner.

B type. A B type reorganization involves an exchange of voting stock *only* for all or part of the voting stock of another corporation and usually results in a parent-subsidiary relationship. After the exchange, the acquiring corporation must have control of at least 80 percent of the acquiree's shares. Cash consideration (boot) is *not* permitted in this type of reorganization. Moreover, the 80 percent control need not be acquired in one transaction. Thus, if two exchanges occur, the first for 70 percent and the second for 10 percent, the first does not qualify as a B type but the second one does qualify. Although this type of reorganization involves an exchange of voting stocks—which conforms to the pooling concept—it permits "creeping control" and also defines control as 80 percent ownership which are conditions that violate the accounting concept of pooling. Neverthe-

---

[6]Internal Revenue Code, sec. 368 (a)(1).
[7]Ibid.

47

less, many B type reorganizations qualify as poolings and are accounted for as such.

C type. Under this type of reorganization, the acquiring corporation must acquire *substantially all* of the properties of the acquiree and it must issue voting stock for *at least 80 percent of the properties.* The valuation of the properties is critical if cash is used. For example, if the properties are valued at $100 and cash of $20 is used with voting stock for the balance, and if it is later determined that the properties were really worth only $90, the reorganization will not qualify as a C type. The treatment of the liabilities of the acquiree (assumption versus liquidation) can affect this type of reorganization, and the definition of "substantially all" involve complexities that are beyond the scope of this text.

D type. This type of reorganization is referred to as a divisive type. Thus, if corporation A owned two businesses and forms two new corporations (corporation B and corporation C) to which it transfers these each to the new corporations respectively, the requirements of a D type have been met and it qualifies as a nontaxable reorganization.

Boot—use of cash

Some boot is permissible in both an A-type and a C-type reorganization. The recipient of boot may have a taxable gain to the extent that he or she has a realized gain. Information on the variety of possible tax consequences to the recipients of boot can be found in federal income tax course texts.

Judicial doctrines

Over the years, taxpayers have attempted, through a variety of schemes, to disguise taxable sales and dividend transactions as nontaxable reorganizations. Many of these schemes have been litigated, and as a result there evolved three judicial doctrines pertaining to reorganizations.

Business purpose. In structuring transactions, many taxpayers attempt to structure a transaction in a manner that conforms to a particular section of the Internal Revenue Code (IRC). However, if the transaction lacks a business purpose or if the substance of the transaction, as opposed to its form, violates the particular section of the IRC, the taxpayer's structure of the transaction may not prevail.

Step transaction. Here too, substance and form are intertwined with this doctrine. If a series of steps are taken within a reasonable time and if the individual steps do comply with a section(s) of the IRC but the cumulative effect of the steps *do not,* then the cumulative effect of this step transaction will usually be relevant for purposes of deciding compliance with the IRC. Thus, for example, if a corporation, wishing to avoid the taxation of its accumulated earnings as a dividend upon distribution, effects a dissolution (where these earnings become taxable as capital gains) followed by a reincorporation of the same business (minus the accumulated earnings), this will be classified as a step transaction if the reincorporation takes place within a short time (usually less than one to two years). The net effect of these transactions would be that the distribution of the earnings will be considered as a taxable dividend and the dissolution-reincorporation scheme would be disregarded.

Continuity of interest. This doctrine deals with the recipients of shares issued in an acquisition, i.e., selling shareholders as opposed to the disposing corporation. The doctrine has two aspects. One aspect pertains to the type and amount of consideration, especially in an A-type reorganization. Thus, cash for 70 percent and voting stock for 30 percent of the total consideration would not qualify as an A type, but the reverse—70 percent stock and 30 percent cash—would so qualify. The second aspect pertains to the retention of the shares received by the investors. If there is a plan to dispose of the shares soon after they are received (a bailout), this would not qualify as a reorganization. While no required specific time period for the retention of the shares is mentioned, the IRS accepts five years without reservation. Shorter periods are also acceptable depending on the circumstances. Interestingly, prior to *APB Opinion 16,* this aspect of this doctrine, i.e., retention of interest, was a condition for pooling accounting. However, *APB Opinion 16* has no continuity of interest requirement.

QUESTIONS

1. What are some of the reasons for external growth (mergers and acquisitions)?

2. Define:

a. Statutory merger.

b. Statutory consolidation.

c. Acquisition.

3. Differentiate between:

a. Horizontal combinations.

b. Vertical combinations.

c. Conglomerate combinations.

d. Circular combinations.

4. Discuss the underlying philosophies of pooling accounting as contrasted with those of purchase accounting.

5. What are some of the abuses of the pooling concept that was practiced prior to 1970 when *APB Opinion 16* was issued?

6. There are 12 conditions that must be met before pooling accounting is used. Briefly outline the 12 conditions.

7. Can one of the parties to a pooling remain as a subsidiary of the issuing corporation? Explain.

8. How should contingent consideration be handled in a business combination? (*Hint:* Purchase accounting is required.)

9. In a business combination accounted for as a purchase, how should the total cost of the acquired entity be treated?

10. According to *APB Opinion 17*, how should goodwill be calculated? When goodwill, so calculated, is positive, how should it be treated in years subsequent to the business combination?

11. Costs and expenses incurred in connection with business combinations fall into two categories. What are they? Give examples to demonstrate each type. For each category, indicate the appropriate treatment in a purchase. In a pooling.

12. How are the retained earnings of the acquiree corporation treated in purchase accounting? In pooling accounting? Explain.

13. Can dissenting shareholders tender some shares for exchange in a pooling and refuse to tender the remaining shares? Explain.

14. On the date of a business combination that occurs in an interim period, will the interim operating data affect the subsequently published financial statements when purchase accounting is used? For pooling accounting? Explain.

Questions for Appendix:

15. A business combination can be either a *taxable exchange* or a *nontaxable reorganization*. What is meant by these terms?

16. What is meant by an A type of reorganization, a B type, a C type, and a D type?

17. There are three judicial doctrines pertaining to reorganizations. Discuss each of them.

EXERCISES

Exercise 2–1.

1. Which of the following is a potential abuse that can arise when a business combination is accounted for as a pooling of interest?

a. Assets of the investee may be overvalued when the price paid by the investor is allocated among specific assets.

b. Liabilities may be undervalued when the price paid by the investor is allocated to the specific liabilities.

c. An undue amount of cost may be assigned to goodwill, thus potentially allowing for an overstatement of pooled earnings.

d. Earnings of the pooled entity may be increased because of the combination only and *not* as a result of efficient operations.

2. Which of the following transactions related to a business combination would require that the combination be accounted for as a purchase?

a. The combination is to be completed within 12 months from the date the plan was initiated.

b. Ninety-two percent of one company's common stock is exchanged for only common stock in the other company.

c. The combined company is to retire a portion of the common stock exchanged to effect the combination within 12 months of the combination.

d. The combined company will dispose of numerous fixed assets representing duplicate facilities subsequent to the combination.

3. In a business combination accounted for as a pooling of interests, the combined corporation's retained earnings usually equals the sum of the retained earnings of the individual combining corporations. Assuming there is *no* contributed capital other than capital stock at par value, which of the following describes a situation where the combined retained earnings must be increased or decreased?

a. Increased if the par value dollar amount of the outstanding shares of the combined corporation exceeds the total capital stock of the separate combining companies.

b. Increased if the par value dollar amount of the outstanding shares of the combined corporation is less than the total capital stock of the separate combining companies.

c. Decreased if the par value dollar amount of the outstanding shares of the combined corporation exceeds the total capital stock of the separate combining companies.

d. Decreased if the par value dollar amount of the outstanding shares of the combined corporation is less than the total capital stock of the separate combining companies.

On December 1, 19x6, company B was merged into company A, with company B going out of existence. Both companies report on a calendar-year basis. This business combination should have been accounted for as a pooling of interests, but it was mistakenly accounted for as a purchase.

4. As a result of this error, what was the effect upon company A's net earnings for the year ended December 31, 19x6?

a. Overstated if B had a net loss from December 1, 19x6, to December 31, 19x6.

b. Understated if B had a net loss from January 1, 19x6, to November 30, 19xᶠ

c. Overstated if B had net earnings from December 1, 19x6, to December 31, 19x6.

d. Understated if B had net earnings from January 1, 19x6, to November 30, 19x6.

5. What was the effect of this error upon company A's asset valuations at December 1, 19x6?

a. Overstated under any circumstances.

b. Understated under any curcumstances.

c. Overstated if the fair value of B's assets exceeded their book value.

d. Understated if the fair value of B's assets exceeded their book value.   (AICPA adapted)

Exercise 2–2. When a business combination is effected by an exchange of common stock, the transaction is accounted for as a purchase or as a pooling of interests, depending on the circumstances. The methods are not optional, and each yields significantly different results as to financial position and results of operations.

Required:

Discuss the *supportive* arguments for each of the following:

a. Purchase method.

b. Pooling of interests method.

Do *not* discuss in your answer the rules for distinguishing between a purchase and a pooling of interests.   (AICPA adapted)

Exercise 2–3.

1. Ethel Corporation issued voting common stock with a stated value of $90,000 in exchange for all of the outstanding common stock of Lum Company. The combination was properly accounted for as a pooling of interests.

The stockholders' equity section of Lum Company at the date of the combination was as follows:

Common stock	$ 70,000
Capital contributed in excess of stated value	7,000
Retained earnings	50,000
	$127,000

What should be the increase in stockholders' equity of Ethel Corporation at the date of acquisition as a result of this business combination?

a. $0.

b. $37,000.

c. $90,000.

d. $127,000.

2. The Action Corporation issued nonvoting preferred stock with a fair market value of $4,000,000 in exchange for all of the outstanding common stock of Master Corporation. On the date of the exchange, Master had tangible net assets with a book value of $2,000,000 and a fair value of $2,500,000. In addition, Action issued perferred stock valued at $400,000 to an individual as a finder's fee in arranging the transaction. As a result of this transaction, Action should record an increase in net assets of—

a. $2,000,000.
b. $2,500,000.
c. $2,900,000.
d. $4,400,000.   (AICPA adapted)

Exercise 2–4. Items 1 and 2 are based on the following information:

On June 30, 19x5, Axel, Inc., acquired Belle, Inc., in a business combination properly accounted for as a pooling of interest. Axel exchanged six of its shares of common stock for each share of Belle's outstanding common stock. June 30 was the fiscal year-end for both companies. There were *no* intercompany transactions during the year. The balance sheets immediately before the combination follow:

stock of which 1,600,000 were issued and outstanding. On December 1, 19x8, Kim issued 250,000 additional shares of its $10 par value voting common stock in exchange for all 100,000 shares of Terry Company's outstanding $20 par value voting common stock in a business combination appropriately accounted for by the pooling of interest method. The market value of Kim's voting common stock was $30 per share on the date of the business combination. What is the total *consolidated* common stock issued and outstanding for Kim and its subsidiary, Terry, at December 31, 19x8?

a. $17,000,000.   c. $22,500,000.
b. $18,500,000.   d. $55,500,000.

[Relates to Exercise 2–4]	Axel	Belle	
	Book value	Book value	Fair value
Current assets	$ 40,000	$ 30,000	$ 45,000
Equipment (net)	150,000	120,000	140,000
Land	30,000	—	—
Totals	$220,000	$150,000	$185,000
Current liabilities	$ 35,000	$ 15,000	$ 15,000
Notes payable	40,000	—	—
Bonds payable	—	100,000	100,000
Common stock ($1 par)	75,000	—	—
Common stock ($5 par)	—	50,000	—
Retained earnings	70,000	(15,000)	—
Totals	$220,000	$150,000	

1. What was the retained earnings balance on the combined balance sheet at June 30, 19x5?

a. $45,000.
b. $55,000.
c. $70,000.
d. $80,000.

2. How should the combined net income for the year be computed?

a. Use only Axel's income because the combination occurred on the last day of the fiscal year.

b. Use only Belle's income because the combination occurred on the last day of the fiscal year.

c. Add together both companies' incomes even though the combination occurred on the last day of the fiscal year.

d. Add together both companies' incomes and subtract the annual amortization of goodwill.

(AICPA adapted)

Exercise 2–5.

1. On December 31, 19x7, Kim, Inc., had 2,000,000 shares of authorized $10 par value voting common

2. The Troy Corporation was organized to consolidate the resources of Able Company and Baker, Inc., in a business combination appropriately accounted for by the pooling of interest method. On January 1, 19x0, Troy issued 65,000 shares of its $10 par value voting stock in exchange for all of the outstanding capital stock of Able and Baker. The equity account balances of Able and Baker on this date were:

	Able	Baker	Total
Par value of common stock	$150,000	$450,000	$600,000
Additional paid-in capital	20,000	55,000	75,000
Retained earnings	110,000	210,000	320,000
Totals	$280,000	$715,000	$995,000

What is the balance in Troy's Additional Paid-In Capital account immediately after the business combination?

a. $0.   c. $75,000.
b. $25,000.   d. $395,000.

(AICPA adapted)

Exercise 2–6. Effective December 31, 19x4, Able proposes to issue additional shares of its common stock in exchange for all of the assets and liabilities of Baker and Cain, after which the latter two corporations will distribute the Able shares to their shareholders in complete liquidation and dissolution. The plan complies with all of the criteria for a pooling of interests. Balance sheets for each of the three companies immediately prior to the merger are given below. The common stock exchange ratios were each negotiated to be 1:1.

	Able	Baker	Cain
Current assets . . .	$ 2,000,000	$ 500,000	$ 25,000
Fixed assets (net) .	10,000,000	4,000,000	200,000
Totals	$12,000,000	$4,500,000	$225,000
Current liabilities .	$ 1,000,000	$ 300,000	$ 20,000
Long-term debt . .	3,000,000	1,000,000	105,000
Common stock			
($10 par)	3,000,000	1,000,000	50,000
Retained earnings .	5,000,000	2,200,000	50,000
Totals	$12,000,000	$4,500,000	$225,000

Required:

a. Prepare Abel's journal entries to record the combination of Able, Baker, and Cain.

b. Assume that the combination fails to meet the criteria for a pooling of interests because Baker and Cain have not been autonomous entities for two years prior to the combination. The identifiable assets and liabilities of Baker and Cain are all reflected in the balance sheets (above), and their recorded amounts are equal to their current fair market values. Able's common stock is traded actively and has a current market price of $45. Prepare Able's journal entries to record the combination. (AICPA adapted)

Exercise 2–7. After Corporation initiated a plan to acquire 100 percent of the outstanding voting common stock of Jamestown Corporation on July 1, 19x5. The following information was available as at the initiation date:

	Jamestown Corporation's Books
Issued common stock	500,000 shares
Treasury stock—common	40,000
Investment in After Corporation— common stock	5,500

The exchange ratio is .25 to 1 (i.e., one share of After Corporation's common stock will be issued for each four shares tendered by the stockholders of Jamestown Corporation). On July 1, 19x5, After Corporation owned 10,000 shares of Jamestown Corporation common stock. On July 15, 19x5, After Corporation purchased 15,000 shares Jamestown Corporation common stock and the business combination is to be consummated on September 1, 19x5.

Required:

If After Corporation acquires all of the remaining outstanding shares of Jamestown, can the combination be accounted for as a pooling of interests? Show your calculations. (Assume any other conditions required for pooling accounting have been met.)

Exercise 2–8. On January 2, 19x4, Pam Company acquired all of the outstanding shares of Sam Company by issuing 8,000 of its shares to the stockholders of Sam Company. Trial balances of the companies on that day, together with other pertinent information, are as follows:

[Relates to Exercise 2–8]

	Book values — Pam Company	Book values — Sam Company	Sam Company fair market values
Cash	$ 300,000	$ 50,000	$ 50,000
Accounts receivable	200,000	100,000	100,000
Inventory	150,000	60,000	90,000
Land		70,000	120,000
Equipment (net of accumulated depreciation) .	600,000	470,000	600,000
Patents	950,000		
Totals	$2,200,000	$750,000	
Accounts payable	$ 100,000	$ 50,000	50,000
Common stock—Pam Company ($50 par)	600,000		
Common stock—Sam Company ($10 par)		200,000	
Additional paid-in capital—Sam Company		100,000	
Retained earnings—Pam Company	1,500,000		
Retained earnings—Sam Company		400,000	
Totals	$2,200,000	$750,000	

The common stock of Pam Company trades regularly on a stock exchange, and it traded at $125 per share at the time of the acquisition.

Required:

a. Prepare the journal entry (entries) on the books of Pam Company if Sam Company is dissolved (merger) and the combination qualifies as a pooling of interests.

b. Repeat (a) above except that the requisites for a pooling were not met and purchase accounting is to be used.

c. Repeat (a) above except that Sam Company is to be maintained as a subsidiary.

d. Repeat part (c) above except that purchase accounting is to be used.

PROBLEMS

Problem 2–9. P Company acquired 100 percent of the outstanding common stock of S Company on January 2, 19x4, by issuing 6,000 of its shares to the stockholders of S Company.

In connection with this combination, the following costs were incurred:

Finder's fee	$20,000
Accountant's fee for preacquisition audit	40,000
Legal fee for contract of business combination .	80,000
Legal and accounting fees for SEC registration .	60,000
Printing cost of stock certificates issued to S Company shareholders	3,000

Trial balances of the companies on that date, together with other pertinent information is as follows:

Required:

a. Prepare the journal entries to record the *merger* of S Company into P Company if pooling of interests accounting is used. Include in your entries the payment of the additional costs incurred.

b. Repeat (a) above except that purchase accounting is to be used.

c. Repeat (a) above except that S Company is to remain a subsidiary of P Company.

d. Repeat (b) above except that S Company is to remain a subsidiary of P Company

Problem 2–10. Using the information provided in Problem 2–9, assume now that T Company, a newly formed corporation, issues 15,000 shares of its

[Relates to Problem 2–9]

	Book values		S Company fair market values
	P Company	S Company	
Cash	$ 400,000	$100,000	$100,000
Accounts receivable	200,000	150,000	150,000
Inventory	150,000	130,000	140,000
Land	50,000	80,000	120,000
Equipment (net of accumulated depreciation) .	300,000	200,000	180,000
Patents	242,000		
Long-term investments in marketable securities	100,000	125,000	140,000
Totals	$1,442,000	$785,000	
Accounts payable	175,000	115,000	115,000
Common stock—P Company ($50 par)	400,000		
Common stock—S Company ($10 par)		200,000	
Additional paid-in capital—P Company	200,000		
Retained earnings—P Company	667,000		
Retained earnings—S Company		470,000	
Totals	$1,442,000	$785,000	

The common stock of P Company trades regularly on a stock exchange, and it traded at $125 per share at the time of the acquisition.

$50 par value common stock to the shareholders of P Company and 8,500 shares of its $50 par value common stock to the shareholders of S Company for all of the outstanding shares in the respective corporations. The expenses incurred are to be treated as accrued liabilities.

The individual assets and liabilities of P Company have book values approximately equal to their respective fair market values.

It is estimated that the common stock of T Company has a fair market value of $90 per share.

Required:

a. Prepare the journal entries to record the consolidation of P Company and S Company into T Company if pooling of interests accounting is to be used.

b. Repeat *(a)* above except that purchase accounting is to be used.

c. Repeat *(a)* above except that P Company and S Company are to remain subsidiaries of T Company.

d. Repeat *(b)* above except that P Company and S Company are to remain subsidiaries of T Company.

Problem 2–11. On January 2, 19x3, P Company acquired 100 percent of the outstanding shares of S Company. On that date each of the assets and liabilities of S Company had book values approximately equal to their respective fair market values. Balance sheets of the companies on January 2, 19x3, are as follows:

	P Company	S Company
Cash	$ 600,000	$100,000
Accounts receivable	400,000	50,000
Inventory	300,000	80,000
Land	100,000	—
Equipment (net of accumulated depreciation)	200,000	120,000
Patents	340,000	
Totals	$1,940,000	$350,000
Accounts payable	$ 400,000	$ 50,000
Common stock—P Company ($50 par)	200,000	
Common stock—S Company ($10 par)		100,000
Additional paid-in capital—P Company	100,000	
Retained earnings—P Company	1,240,000	
Retained earnings—S Company		200,000
Totals	$1,940,000	$350,000

For each of the following cases, pooling accounting is to be used.

Case	Number of P Company shares issued to S Company stockholders
A	1,000
B	3,000
C	5,000
D	10,000

Required:

a. For each case, prepare the journal entry (entries) to record the combination if it is to be treated as a merger.

b. Repeat *(a)* above for each case but assume that S Company will remain a subsidiary of P Company.

Problem 2–12. Using the information provided in Problem 2–11, it is now assumed that only 90 percent of the outstanding shares of S Company were acquired in each case, for the number of shares indicated. All conditions for a pooling have been met.

Required:

a. Prepare the journal entry (entries) for each case if S Company is to remain a subsidiary of P Company.

b. What conclusions have you reached regarding the number of shares issued in a business combination accounted for as a pooling? Discuss.

Problem 2–13. On December 31, 19x1, P Company acquired 100 percent of the outstanding shares of S Company by issuing 10,000 of its shares to the stockholders of S Company. All conditions for a pooling have been met. S Company is to be dissolved and merged into P Company.

Trial balances for the companies for the year ended December 31, 19x1, are as follows:

	P Company	S Company
Debits		
Cash	$ 200,000	$ 100,000
Accounts receivable	150,000	50,000
Inventories	100,000	40,000
Land		150,000
Building (net of accumulated depreciation)		200,000
Equipment (net of accumulated depreciation) .	700,000	450,000
Investments in long-term marketable securities	808,800	
Cost of sales	400,000	150,000
Expenses	200,000	100,000
Provision for income taxes . .	160,000	100,000
Dividends paid	100,000	50,000
Totals	$2,818,800	$1,390,000
Credits		
Accounts payable and accrued expenses	$ 124,000	$ 190,000
Bonds payable	400,000	
Bond premium	2,000	
Common stock ($50 par; $10 par)	200,000	300,000
Additional paid-in capital . . .	400,000	
Retained earnings	600,000	400,000
Sales	1,000,000	500,000
Dividend income	92,800	
Totals	$2,818,800	$1,390,000

Required:

a. Prepare the journal entry (entries) to record the business combination.

b. Prepare financial statements for P Company at December 31, 19x1, *after* the above entry is (entries) reflected on the books of P Company.

Problem 2–14. Blue Corporation was merged into Ace Corporation on August 31, 19x4, with Blue Corporation going out of existence. Both corporations had fiscal years ending on August 31, and Ace Corporation will retain this fiscal year. The enclosed worksheet contains a balance sheet for each corporation and a combined balance sheet as of August 31, 19x4, immediately prior to the merger and net income figures for each corporation for the fiscal year ended August 31, 19x4. You have obtained the following additional information as of the date of the merger:

1. The fair value of the assets and liabilities on August 31, 19x4, of Ace Corporation and Blue Corporation was as follows:

	Ace	Blue
Current assets	$ 4,950,000	$ 3,400,000
Plant and equipment (net)	22,000,000	14,000,000
Patents	570,000	360,000
Market research	150,000	40,000
Total assets	27,670,000	17,800,000
Liabilities	(2,650,000)	(2,100,000)
Net assets	$25,020,000	$15,700,000

2. Ace Corporation capitalized its fiscal year 19x4 market research costs and has always amortized them over five years beginning with the year of expenditure. All market research costs of Ace have been appropriately capitalized and amortized for the current and preceding years. Blue Corporation incurred $50,000 of market research costs which were expensed during the fiscal year ending August 31, 19x4. Blue did not have any market research costs in any year before 19x4. Blue will adopt Ace's method of accounting for market research costs.

3. Internally generated general expenses incurred because of the merger were $25,000 and are included in the current assets of Ace as a prepaid expense.

4. There were no intercompany transactions during the year.

5. Before the merger, Ace had 3,000,000 shares of common stock authorized; 1,200,000 shares issued; and 1,100,000 shares outstanding. Blue had 750,000 shares of common stock authorized, issued, and outstanding.

Required:

Prepare the balance sheet and determine the amount of net income under each of the following independent situations. Include explanations of adjustments on the worksheet. Cross-reference the explanations to the adjustments. *Do not prepare formal journal entries.*

a. Ace Corporation exchanged 400,000 shares of previously unissued common stock and 100,000 shares of treasury stock for all the outstanding common stock of Blue Corporation. All the conditions for pooling of interests accounting enumerated in *APB Opinion 16* ("Business Combination") were met.

b. Ace Corporation purchased the assets and assumed the liabilities of Blue Corporation by paying $3,100,000 cash and issuing debentures of $16,900,000 at face value.

[Relates to Problem 2–14]

ACE CORPORATION AND BLUE CORPORATION
Worksheet for Pooling of Interests and Purchase Accounting
August 31, 19x4

	Ace Corpor-ation	Blue Corpor-ation	Com-bined	(a.) Adjustments Dr.	(a.) Adjustments Cr.	Pool-ing of Inter-ests	(b.) Adjustments Dr.	(b.) Adjustments Cr.	Pur-chase
Current assets	$ 4,350,000	$ 3,000,000	$ 7,350,000						
Plant and equipment (net)	18,500,000	11,300,000	29,800,000						
Patents	450,000	200,000	650,000						
Market research	150,000	—	150,000						
	$23,450,000	$14,500,000	$37,950,000						
Liabilities	$ 2,650,000	$ 2,100,000	$ 4,750,000						
Common stock $10 par value	12,000,000	—	12,000,000						
Common stock $5 par value	—	3,750,000	3,750,000						
Paid-in capital in excess of par	4,200,000	—	4,200,000						
Paid-in capital in excess of par	—	3,200,000	3,200,000						
Retained earnings	5,850,000	—	5,850,000						
Retained earnings	—	5,450,000	5,450,000						
	24,700,000	14,500,000	39,200,000						
Less treasury stock, at cost, 100,000 shares	1,250,000	—	1,250,000						
	$23,450,000	$14,500,000	$37,950,000						
Net income (no extraordinary items) for fiscal year ended August 31, 19x4	$ 2,450,000	$ 1,300,000							

(AICPA adapted)

Problem 2–15. On January 2, 19x5, Asch Corporation paid $1,000,000 cash for all of Bacher Company's outstanding stock. The recorded amount (book value) of Bacher's net assets on January 2 was $880,000. Both Asch and Bacher have operated profitably for many years, both have December 31 accounting year-ends, and each has only one class of stock outstanding. This business combination should be accounted for by the purchase method in which Asch should follow certain principles in allocating its investment cost to the assets acquired and liabilities assumed.

Required:

a. Describe the principles that Asch should follow in allocating its investment cost to the assets purchased and liabilities assumed for January 2, 19x5, consolidated balance sheet. Explain.

b. Independent of your answer to *(a)* above, assume that on January 2, 19x5, Asch acquired all of Bacher's outstanding stock in a stock-for-stock exchange and that all other conditions prerequisite to a pooling of interests were met. Describe the principles that Asch should follow in applying the pooling of interests method to this business combination when combining the balance sheet accounts of both companies in the preparation of a consolidated balance sheet on January 2, 19x5.   (AICPA adapted)

Problem 2–16. Hanover Company and Case Company, both of whom have only voting common stock, are considering a merger whereby Hanover would be the surviving company. The terms of the combination provide that the transaction would be carried out by Hanover exchanging one share of its stock for two shares of Case's stock. Prior to the date of the contemplated exchange, Hanover had purchased 5 percent of Case's stock which it holds as an investment. Case, at the same date, owns 2 percent of Hanover's stock. All of the remaining outstanding stock of Case will be acquired by Hanover in this contemplated exchange. Neither of the two companies has ever had any affiliation as a subsidiary or division of any other company.

Required:.

a. Without enumerating specific criteria, how is a determination made as to whether a business combination is accounted for as a pooling of interests or as a purchase?

b. Based only on the facts above discuss the specific criteria which would qualify or disqualify this business combination as being accounted for as a pooling of interests.

c. What additional requirements (other than those discussed in [b] above) must be met in order to account for this business combination as a pooling of interests?   (AICPA adapted)

Problem 2–17. The boards of directors of Kessler Corporation, Bar Company, Cohen, Inc., and Mason Corporation are meeting jointly to discuss plans for a business combination. Each of the corporations has one class of common stock outstanding; Bar also has one class of preferred stock outstanding. Although terms have not as yet been settled, Kessler will be the acquiring or issuing corporation. Because the directors want to conform to generally accepted accounting principles (GAAP), they have asked you to attend the meeting as an advisor.

Required:

Consider each of the following questions independently of the others and answer each in accordance with GAAP. Explain your answers.

a. Assume that the combination will be consummated August 31, 19x3. Explain the philosophy underlying the accounting and how the balance sheet accounts of each of the four corporations will appear on Kessler's consolidated balance sheet on September 1, 19x3, if the combination is accounted for as a —

1. Pooling of interests.

2. Purchase.

b. Assume that the combination will be consummated August 31, 19x3. Explain how the income statement accounts for each of the four corporations will be accounted for in preparing Kessler's consolidated income statement for the year ended December 31, 19x3, if the combination is accounted for as a —

1. Pooling of interests.

2. Purchase.

c. Some of the directors believe that the terms of the combination should be agreed upon immediately and that the method of accounting to be used (whether pooling of interests, purchse, or a mixture) may be chosen at some later date. Others believe that the terms of the combination and the method to be used are very closely related. Which position is correct?

d. Kessler and Mason are comparable in size; Cohen and Bar are much smaller. How do these facts affect the choice of accounting method?

e. Bar was formerly a subsidiary of Tucker Corporation, which has no other relationship to any of the four companies discussing combination. Eighteen months ago Tucker voluntarily spun off Bar. What effect, if any, do these facts have on the choice of accounting method?

f. Kessler holds 2,000 of Bar's 10,000 outstanding shares of preferred stock and 15,000 of Cohen's 100,000 outstanding shares of common stock. All of Kessler's holdings were acquired during the first three months of 19x3. What effect, of any, do these facts have on the choice of accounting method?

g. It is almost certain that Mrs. Victor Mason, Sr., who holds 5 percent of Mason's common stock, will object to the combination. Assume that Kessler is able to acquire only 95 percent (rather than 100 percent) of Mason's stock, issuing Kessler common stock in exchange.

1. Which accounting method is applicable?

2. If Kessler is able to acquire the remaining 5 percent at some future time—in five years, for instance—in exchange for its own common stock, which accounting method will be applicable to this second acquisition?

h. Since the directors feel that one of Mason's major divisions will not be compatible with the operations of the combined company, they anticipate that it will be sold as soon as possible after the combination is consummated. They expect to have no trouble in finding a buyer. What effect, if any, do these facts have on the choice of accounting method? (AICPA adapted)

Problem 2–18. On December 31, 19x6, Cole Company and Bond Company entered into a business combination appropriately accounted for as a pooling of interests. As a result of this combination, a new company, Gold Corporation, was formed with 500,000 authorized shares of no-par, $1 stated value common stock. The management of Gold did *not* intend to retain either Cole of Bond as subsidiaries.

On December 31, 19x6, Gold issued its common stock in exchange for all of the outstanding common stock of Cole and Bond as follows:

Cole: 300,000 shares of Gold common stock for all 10,000 outstanding shares of Cole's $5 par value common stock.

Bond: 200,000 shares of Gold common stock for all 4,000 outstanding shares of Bond's $10 par value common stock.

There were *no* intercompany transactions between these companies.

Presented below were condensed financial statements of Cole and Bond for the year ended December 31, 19x6, prior to the pooling of interests.

Balance Sheets

	Cole Company	Bond Company
Assets		
Current assets	$260,000	$235,000
Property, plant, and equipment		
(net)	410,000	320,000
Other assets	90,000	65,000
Total assets	$760,000	$620,000
Liabilities and Stockholders' Equity		
Current liabilities	$167,000	$124,000
Long-term debt	300,000	—
Common stock	50,000	40,000
Capital in excess of par value . .	10,000	160,000
Retained earnings	233,000	296,000
Total liabilities and stockholders' equity . .	$760,000	$620,000

Statements of Income and Retained Earnings

	Cole Company	Bond Company
Net sales	$1,600,000	$2,200,000
Cost and expenses:		
Cost of sales	1,120,000	1,560,000
Operating and other expenses	330,000	480,000
	1,450,000	2,040,000
Net income	150,000	160,000
Retained earnings, January 1, 19x6	83,000	136,000
Retained earnings, December 31, 19x6	$ 233,000	$ 296,000

Cole values its inventory using the Fifo method; Bond uses the Lifo method for its inventory. Bond agreed to change its method of inventory valuation from Lifo to Fifo prior to the business combination.

Bond began operations on January 1, 19x5, and data relevant to Bond's inventory are as follows:

	Lifo Method	Fifo Method
Inventory, December 31, 19x5	$42,000	$62,000
Inventory, December 31, 19x6	$55,000	$85,000

Required:

a. Prepare the adjusting journal entry with the appropriate explanation and supporting calculations to be made by Bond Company on December 31, 19x6, to change its inventory from Lifo cost to Fifo cost.

Income taxes should *not* be considered in your solution.

b. Prepare a schedule computing pooled retained earnings of Gold Corporation as of December 31, 19x6.

c. Prepare the December 31, 19x6, journal entry on the books of Gold Corporation to record the business combination as a pooling of interests.

(AICPA adapted)

Problem 2–19 (related to Appendix A, Chapter 24). Using the Mattel, Inc., pro forma balance sheet and related notes in Appendix A, Chapter 24, prepare the journal entry (entries) if —

a. Western is to be *merged* into Mattel, Inc., and the price paid is as given. (*Hint:* Use purchase accounting.)

b. Instead of perferred stock and debt, the consideration for the Western shares was 10,000,000 shares of Mattel common stock with a $1 par value, and all of the conditions for a pooling have been met. Western is to be merged into Mattel, Inc.

3

Consolidated statements—date of acquisition

Just as in branch accounting it is necessary to combine a home office's trial balance with those of its branches whenever a financial statement is prepared for external use, a parent corporation is generally similarly obligated to combine its financial statements with those of its subsidiaries. However, additional problems are encountered in combining a subsidiary's financial statements with those of its parent company.

A parent company rarely acquires shares of a subsidiary at book value. Thus, when the reciprocal accounts—the Investment in Subsidiary account on the parent's books and the subsidiary's stockholder's equity accounts on its books—are eliminated, a difference between them usually arises. This difference can be due to:

1. *A difference between the fair market value and the book value of individual assets and liabilities of the subsidiary.*
2. *The payment for intangibles at amounts other than reflected on the subsidiary's books.*

The above-mentioned differences must be allocated to specific assets and liabilities whenever consolidated financial statements are prepared.

Another facet of consolidated statements not present in home office statements is the existence of minority interests when a parent company purchases less than 100 percent of the outstanding shares of a subsidiary.

REASONS FOR CONSOLIDATED STATEMENTS

In the discussion of organization forms in Chapter 1, we saw that a business organization may choose to operate part of its business through one or more branches. In this case, each branch's trial balance (or financial statements) is integrated with the home office's trial balance (statements) to arrive at the entity's combined trial balance (statements). This is required in order to reflect economic reality, since a branch is merely an artificial subdivision from an entity viewpoint. Carrying this concept one step further, the same treatment would be required if a business were to incorporate its branch office. The mere legal separation of corporate existence does not change the underlying reality of the entity's overall operations, i.e., in essence that of home office and branch. From an accounting standpoint, the separate trial balances are still combined, except that the term *consolidated* is used to denote the combined trial balances (statements) when one corporation owns a majority of the outstanding shares of another corporation (parent-subsidiary relationship.)[1] It is true that some of the account titles are different from those found in the home office–branch relationship, but the consolidation procedures of subsidiaries are similar to the combination procedures of branches. Consolidation procedures will be illustrated in this and succeeding chapters.

To simplify the procedures, Illustration 3–1 presents home office and branch trial balances at the beginning of 19x1. The elimination entry and the combined balances are handled in the same manner as in Chapter 1.

Assuming that the branch is incorporated on January 1, 19x1, and the

Illustration 3–1
HOME SERIAL COMPANY, INC.
Combined Trial Balance Working Paper
January 1, 19x1

	Home Office	Branch	Elimination Dr.	Elimination Cr.	Combined
Debits					
Cash in bank	10,000	3,000			13,000
Accounts receivable	20,000	6,000			26,000
Inventories	12,000	4,000			16,000
Branch control	10,000			(1) 10,000	
Equipment	40,000				40,000
Totals	92,000	13,000			95,000
Credits					
Accounts payable	8,000	2,800			10,800
Allowance for doubtful accounts	400	200			600
Accumulated depreciation—equipment	8,000				8,000
Home office control		10,000	(1) 10,000		
Common stock	20,000				20,000
Retained earnings	55,600				55,600
Totals	92,000	13,000	10,000	10,000	95,000

---

[1] Consolidated statements are also prepared when indirect holdings are less than a majority and control is achieved. See Chapter 10.

capital stock issued is equal to $10,000, the entries to record the incorpora-
tion can be condensed into the following:

Home Office Books

Investment in Branch, Inc.	10,000	
Branch Control		10,000

Branch Books

Home Office Control	10,000	
Common Stock		10,000

The consolidated working paper after giving effect to the above entries appears in Illustration 3–2. It should be noted that the consolidated balances
in Illustration 3–2 are identical with the combined balances in Illustration
3–1, as they should be from an entity viewpoint. The only difference between the two illustrations is the nomenclature of the reciprocal accounts,
i.e., Branch Control and Home Office Control as opposed to Investment in
Branch, Inc., and Common Stock. In essence, the entire stockholders' equity
of a subsidiary (common stock, additional paid-in capital, and retained earnings) is a reciprocal balance of the investment account of the parent, and
these accounts are eliminated when consolidated statements are prepared.
These reciprocal balances are equal to each other only when a parent corporation organizes a new subsidiary or when it purchases 100 percent of
the common stock of an existing subsidiary at book value. In most cases,
however, a parent corporation will purchase a subsidiary at other than book
value, and these reciprocal balances will not be equal.

The treatment of these differences will be discussed later in this chapter.

Illustration 3–2
HOME SERIAL COMPANY, INC.
Consolidated Working Paper
January 1, 19x1

	Home Serial Co., Inc.	Branch, Inc.	Eliminations		Consol- idated
			Dr.	Cr.	
Debits					
Cash in bank	10,000	3,000			13,000
Accounts receivable	20,000	6,000			26,000
Inventories	12,000	4,000			16,000
Investment in Branch, Inc.	10,000			(1) 10,000	
Equipment	40,000				40,000
Totals	92,000	13,000			95,000
Credits					
Accounts payable	8,000	2,800			10,800
Allowance for doubtful accounts	400	200			600
Accumulated depreciation—equipment	8,000				8,000
Common stock:					
Home Serial Co., Inc.	20,000				20,000
Branch, Inc.		10,000	(1) 10,000		
Retained earnings	55,600				55,600
Totals	92,000	13,000	10,000	10,000	95,000

PURCHASE OF A WHOLLY OWNED SUBSIDIARY AT BOOK VALUE

If, instead of incorporating a branch as a subsidiary, a corporation purchases 100 percent of the common stock of an existing corporation (newly formed), the entry to record the purchase of stock will be as follows:

Investment in Branch, Inc.   10,000
    Cash   10,000

Assuming that the trial balance of Branch, Inc., on the date of acquisition is as appears in Illustration 3–2, the consolidated working paper would be the same as Illustration 3–2.

Instead of a newly formed corporation, let us consider now the purchase of stock in a corporation that has been operating for a period of time. In purchasing the stock of another corporation, the purchaser's focus is on the net assets (assets minus liabilities) of the acquiree and not on the composition of its stockholders' equity. The individual balances in the Capital Stock and Retained Earnings accounts are not of interest to the purchaser; rather, the *total* stockholders' equity (net assets) is the focal point. To illustrate this concept, it is now assumed that Branch, Inc., has the same trial balance on January 1, 19x1, as indicated in Illustration 3–2 except that common stock is $6,000 instead of $10,000 and retained earnings is $4,000. If Home Serial Company Inc., purchases 100 percent of the outstanding shares of Branch, Inc., at book value, i.e., net asset value, the entry to record the purchase on Home's books is as follows:

Investment in Branch, Inc.   10,000
    Cash   10,000

The elimination entry on the working paper would then be:[2]

Common Stock—Branch, Inc.   6,000
Retained Earnings—Branch, Inc.   4,000
    Investment in Branch, Inc.   10,000

Notice that the elimination entry eliminates all of the subsidiary's stockholder equity balances. If there were other accounts, such as Additional Paid-In Capital, they would also be eliminated in the same manner as common stock and retained earnings. It is worth noting that the consolidated column in Illustration 3–2 would be the same even if Branch, Inc., had an additional paid-in capital, a deficit instead of retained earnings, or any other combination of stockholders' equity accounts. It is also worth noting that the consolidated column contains *only* the parent's common stock and retained earnings balances. Subsidiary stockholder's equity balances are never extended to the consolidated column.

PURCHASE OF A WHOLLY OWNED SUBSIDIARY AT OTHER THAN BOOK VALUE

Only rarely will shares of stock be purchased at book value. Since shares of stock are purchased at market values and accounting records are prepared and kept in accordance with generally accepted accounting principles (GAAP), most purchases of subsidiaries will produce an investment account

---

[2]Note: It is important to understand the difference between entries which appear on *books of entry* and entries which *appear only on working papers*. Entries which appear only on working papers are *shaded* in this text.

on the parent's books that differs from the net assets of the subsidiary. When this is the case, the question arises as to the disposition of this difference. Consider the following:

Illustration 3–3
BRANCH, INC.
Trial Balance
January 1, 19x1

	Book Values
Debits	
Cash in bank	$ 13,000
Accounts receivable (net of estimated uncollectibles)	26,000
Inventories	14,000
Land	10,000
Building (net of depreciation)	50,000
Equipment (net of depreciation)	30,000
Totals	$143,000
Credits	
Accounts payable and other liabilities	$ 30,000
8% bonds payable due January 1, 19x6	50,000
Unamortized bond premium	2,000
Capital stock—common	40,000
Additional paid-in capital	12,000
Retained earnings	9,000
Totals	$143,000

The following assumptions are made pertaining to Illustration 3–3:

1. The fair market value of each of the assets and liabilities is approximately equal to their respective book values as shown in the trial balance.
2. Chrome Serial Company Inc., paid $157,000 for 100 percent of the net assets (assets minus liabilities) of Branch, Inc. The purchase was accomplished by purchasing all of the outstanding shares of Branch, Inc.
3. Since cash was used to purchase the shares, purchase accounting is to be used to account for the acquisition.

The entry to record the acquisition would be:

Chrome Serial Company, Inc., Books

Investment in Branch, Inc.	157,000	
Cash		157,000

To record the acquisition of 100 percent of the outstanding shares of Branch, Inc.

If a consolidated working paper is to be prepared on the date of acquisition, it is first necessary to ascertain the amount of the difference between the price paid for the shares and the underlying book value of the net assets of the subsidiary. Once this difference is ascertained, it then must be allocated to the appropriate account(s). Since there are no differences between the fair market values and the book values of the individual assets and liabilities, a positive difference is allocated entirely to goodwill or excess of cost over net assets of acquired companies. The calculation is made as follows:

Price paid	$157,000
Less: 100% of net assets acquired ($143,000 − $82,000)	61,000
Goodwill	$ 96,000

The consolidated working paper can now be prepared, and it appears in Illustration 3–4. The working paper elimination entry is:

Illustration 3–4
CHROME SERIAL COMPANY, INC.
Consolidated Working Paper
January, 19x1

100 Percent Subsidiary
Date of Aquisition
Positive Goodwill

	Chrome Serial Co., Inc.	Branch, Inc. (100%)	Eliminations Dr.	Eliminations Cr.	Consolidated
Assets					
Cash in bank	80,000	13,000			93,000
Accounts receivable (net of estimated uncollectibles)	50,000	26,000			76,000
Inventories	60,000	14,000			74,000
Land	70,000	10,000			80,000
Building (net of depreciation)	120,000	50,000			170,000
Equipment (net of depreciation)	200,000	30,000			230,000
Goodwill			(1) 96,000		96,000
Investment in Branch, Inc.	157,000			(1) 157,000	
Totals	737,000	143,000			819,000
Liabilities and Stockholders' Equity					
Accounts payable and other liabilities	60,000	30,000			90,000
8% bonds payable ($50,000)		52,000			52,000
Common stock:					
Chrome Serial Co., Inc.	200,000				200,000
Branch, Inc.		40,000	(1) 40,000		
Additional paid-in capital		12,000	(1) 12,000		
Retained earnings:					
Chrome Serial Co., Inc.	477,000				477,000
Branch, Inc.		9,000	(1) 9,000		
Totals	737,000	143,000	157,000	157,000	819,000

(1) To eliminate parent's investment in Branch, Inc., and to eliminate Branch, Inc.'s stockholders' equity.

(1)		
Common Stock—Branch, Inc.	40,000	
Additional Paid-In Capital	12,000	
Retained Earnings—Branch, Inc.	9,000	
Goodwill	96,000	
Investment in Branch, Inc.		157,000

A review of Illustration 3–4 will reveal that:

1. The parent's investment in Branch, Inc., is eliminated.
2. The stockholder's equity of Branch, Inc. (common stock, additional paid-in capital, and retained earnings), is eliminated.
3. Goodwill in the amount of $96,000 (as previously calculated) has to be booked if the elimination entry is to balance.
4. The assets and liabilities of Branch, Inc., are combined with those of the parent company to arrive at a consolidated balance sheet.
5. Only the parent's equity capital accounts appear in the consolidated column.

In actual practice, the book values of specific assets and liabilities are rarely all equal to their respective fair market values. Thus, to expand the illustration to a more realistic level, it is now assumed that the book and market values of the assets and liabilities of Branch, Inc., are as indicated in Illustration 3–5.

Illustration 3–5
BRANCH, INC.
Trial Balance and Market Values
January 1, 19x1

	Book values	Market values
Debits		
Cash in bank	$ 13,000	$ 13,000
Accounts receivable (net of estimated uncollectibles)	26,000	26,000
Inventories	14,000	30,000
Land	10,000	20,000
Building (net of depreciation)	50,000	70,000
Equipment (net of depreciation)	30,000	20,000
Patents	–0–	10,000
Totals	$143,000	$189,000
Credits		
Accounts payable and other liabilities	$ 30,000	$ 30,000
8% bonds payable due January 1, 19x6	50,000	
Unamortized bond premium	2,000	42,000
Capital stock—common	40,000	
Additional paid-in capital	12,000	117,000*
Retained earnings	9,000	
Totals	$143,000	$189,000

*This amount represents the difference between total assets ($189,000) and liabilities ($30,000 + $42,000) at *fair market values;* sometimes referred to as "net assets at market value."

If Chrome Serial Company, Inc., paid $157,000 for 100 percent of the net assets (assets minus liabilities) of Branch, Inc., then allocation of the purchase price to specific assets can be accomplished as in Illustration 3–6.

Illustration 3–6
BRANCH, INC.
Allocation of Purchase Price
January 1, 19x1

Purchase price paid	$157,000
Less: Net assets at book value ($40,000 + $12,000 + $9,000) or ($143,000 −	
$82,000) × 100%	61,000
Unallocated excess of cost	96,000

Allocation of excess:

	Fair market value	−	Book value	=	Differ- ence
Inventories	$ 30,000		$14,000		$16,000
Land	20,000		10,000		10,000
Building	70,000		50,000		20,000
Equipment	20,000		30,000		(10,000)
Patent	10,000		–0–		10,000
Bonds payable	(42,000)		(52,000)		10,000
Totals	$108,000	−	$52,000	=	$56,000

Parent's percentage of ownership	×	100%
Allocated excess of cost		$ 56,000
Cost in excess of net assets of purchased subsidiaries (goodwill) . .		$ 40,000

    From this allocation of the purchase price to specific assets and liabilities, the following should be noted.

1. When the market value of an asset exceeds its book value, this difference *reduces* the unallocated portion of the purchase price paid. When the reverse is true, i.e., book value is higher, the difference *increases* the unallocated purchase price.

2. Although the bonds payable have a maturity value of $50,000 and a carrying value of $52,000 (including a premium of $2,000), the market value of the bonds is only $42,000. This may be because the market rate of interest at the time of the business acquisition is higher the 8 percent rate which these bonds carry. In allocating the difference of $10,000 ($52,000 − $42,000), it should be noted that liabilities are treated as the opposite of assets, and therefore the $10,000 is a reduction of the unallocated purchase price.

    Illustration 3–7 contains the necessary working paper with the following elimination entry:

(1)		
Common Stock—Branch, Inc.	40,000	
Additional Paid-In Capital	12,000	
Retained Earnings—Branch, Inc.	9,000	
Inventories	16,000	
Land	10,000	
Building	20,000	
Patents	10,000	
Goodwill	40,000	
Bonds Payable	10,000	
Investment in Branch, Inc.		157,000
Equipment		10,000

A published example of this elimination entry can be found in Appendix A to Chapter 24. The pro forma consolidated balance sheet of Mattel and Western Publishing reflects the adjustment of the assets and liabilities of Western Publishing to fair market values. In addition, the elimination of the capital stock, additional paid-in capital, and retained earnings can also be seen in that pro forma working paper.

Illustration 3–7
CHROME SERIAL COMPANY, INC.
Consolidated Working Paper
January 1, 19x1

100 Percent Subsidiary
Date of Acquisition
Positive Goodwill

	Chrome Serial Co., Inc.	Branch, Inc. (100%)	Eliminations Dr.	Eliminations Cr.	Consolidated
Assets					
Cash in bank	80,000	13,000			93,000
Accounts receivable (net of estimated uncollectibles)	50,000	26,000			76,000
Inventories	60,000	14,000	(1) 16,000		90,000
Land	70,000	10,000	(1) 10,000		90,000
Building (net of depreciation)	120,000	50,000	(1) 20,000		190,000
Equipment (net of depreciation)	200,000	30,000		(1) 10,000	220,000
Patents			(1) 10,000		10,000
Goodwill			(1) 40,000		40,000
Investment in Branch, Inc.	157,000			(1) 157,000	
Totals	737,000	143,000			809,000
Liabilities and Stockholders' Equity					
Accounts payable and other liabilities	60,000	30,000			90,000
8% bonds payable ($50,000)		52,000	(1) 10,000		42,000
Common stock:					
Chrome Serial Co., Inc.	200,000				200,000
Branch, Inc.		40,000	(1) 40,000		
Additional paid-in capital		12,000	(1) 12,000		
Retained earnings:					
Chrome Serial Co., Inc.	477,000				477,000
Branch, Inc.		9,000	(1) 9,000		
Totals	737,000	143,000	167,000	167,000	809,000

(1) To eliminate parents' investment in Branch, Inc.; to eliminate Branch, Inc.'s stockholders' equity; and to adjust the latter's book values to reflect the market values (price paid) of specific assets and liabilities as computed in Illustration 3–6.

A consolidated balance sheet as of January 1, 19x1, can be prepared from the consolidated working paper shown in Illustration 3–7. The trial balance for Chrome Serial Company, Inc., is given as of January 1, 19x1. The working paper elimination entry (1) accomplishes three things. It *(a)* eliminates the Investment in Branch, Inc., account against Branch's stockholders' equity accounts (reciprocal balances); *(b)* it adjusts the book values of certain assets and liabilities of Branch, Inc., to their respective market values; and *(c)* it records as goodwill the amount computed in Illustration 3–6.[3] The consolidated column of Illustration 3–7 reflects the *book* values of Chrome Serial Company, Inc. (except for its investment in Branch, Inc.) plus the *market* values of *Branch's assets and liabilities* plus the implicit goodwill account previously noted.

NEGATIVE GOODWILL

In some cases, a corporation may acquire the shares of another corporation at a "bargain purchase" price, i.e., at an amount which is less than the fair market value of the net assets of the acquired company. In this case the parent corporation will again record an excess account except that the account will now be called, Excess of Net Assets Acquired Over the Cost of Purchased Subsidiary. This excess must be "allocated to reduce proportionately the value assigned to noncurrent assets (except long-term investments in marketable securities) in determining their fair values."[4]

Referring back to Illustration 3–5, it is now assumed that instead of paying $157,000 for 100 percent of the shares of Branch, Inc., Chrome Serial Company, Inc., paid only $93,000 for the shares. Using the same market values as in Illustration 3–5, the allocation of the price paid can be computed as shown in Illustration 3–8.

Illustration 3–8
BRANCH, INC.
Allocation of Purchase Price
January 1, 19x1

Purchase price paid		$93,000
Less: Book value—100% × ($143,000 − $82,000)		61,000
Unallocated excess of cost		32,000
Less: Differences between market values and book values (see Illustration 3–6):		
Inventories	$16,000	
Land	10,000	
Building	20,000	
Equipment	(10,000)	
Patent	10,000	
Bonds payable	10,000	56,000
Excess of net assets acquired over the cost of purchased subsidiary		$24,000

Since the net assets acquired exceed the purchase price paid, this excess must proportionately reduce noncurrent assets (using fair market values). These noncurrent assets must be reduced to zero before any amount can be allocated to a negative excess account, sometimes referred to as *negative goodwill.* If a negative excess does materialize, it should be amortized to income over a period of time not to exceed 40 years.

---

[3]Working paper elimination entries are *not* journalized on either set of books of original entry. In fact, portions of one working paper entry affect both sets of books and, therefore, *cannot* be journalized without causing each set of books to be out of balance.

[4]APB, "Business Combinations," *APB Opinion No. 16* (New York: AICPA, August 1970), par. 91.

Illustration 3–9 shows how the $24,000 of "excess net assets over cost" is proportionately assigned to noncurrent assets. Illustration 3–10 shows how the working papers would appear after incorporating the allocation from Illustration 3–8 and the proration from Illustration 3–9. The working paper in Illustration 3–10 is similar to the one in Illustration 3–7 except for the $24,000 apportionment of negative excess. The elimination entries on Illustration 3–10 appear as follows:

(1)

Investment in Branch, Inc.	24,000	
Land		4,000
Building		14,000
Equipment		4,000
Patents		2,000

(2)

Common Stock—Branch, Inc.	40,000	
Additional Paid-In Capital	12,000	
Retained Earnings—Branch, Inc.	9,000	
Inventories	16,000	
Land	10,000	
Building	20,000	
Patents	10,000	
Bonds Payable	10,000	
Investment in Branch, Inc.		117,000
Equipment		10,000

Illustration 3–9
CHROME SERIAL COMPANY, INC.
Proration of Branch, Inc., Excess of Net Assets
January 1, 19x1

	Market value	Percent of total	Excess	Apportionment
Noncurrent assets:				
Land	$ 20,000	16 $^2/_3$	$24,000	$ 4,000
Building	70,000	58 $^1/_3$	24,000	14,000
Equipment	20,000	16 $^2/_3$	24,000	4,000
Patent	10,000	8 $^1/_3$	24,000	2,000
	$120,000	100		$24,000

It is worth noting that if there were long-term investments in marketable securities on the books of Branch, Inc., they would be revalued to fair market value for purposes of consolidation but they would not be subject to downward adjustments for purposes of determining negative goodwill.

Under the circumstances, it is possible that the apportionment process will reduce all noncurrent assets to zero with some excess of net assets over cost still remaining. When this happens, the parent corporation will *not* reduce current assets below their fair market value, but instead will create a credit balance of excess which is amortized to income over a period not to exceed 40 years. As noted earlier this excess is sometimes referred to as *negative goodwill* or *bargain purchase credit*.

Illustration 3–10
CHROME SERIAL COMPANY, INC.
Consolidated Working Paper
January 1, 19x1

100 Percent Subsidiary
Date of Acquisition
Negative Excess

	Chrome Serial Co., Inc.	Branch, Inc. (100%)	Eliminations Dr.	Eliminations Cr.	Consolidated
Assets					
Cash in bank	144,000	13,000			157,000
Accounts receivable (net of estimated uncollectibles)	50,000	26,000			76,000
Inventories	60,000	14,000	(2) 16,000		90,000
Land	70,000	10,000	(2) 10,000	(1) 4,000	86,000
Building (net of depreciation)	120,000	50,000	(2) 20,000	(1) 14,000 (2) 10,000	176,000
Equipment (net of depreciation)	200,000	30,000		(1) 4,000	216,000
Patents			(2) 10,000	(1) 2,000	8,000
Investment in Branch, Inc.	93,000		(1) 24,000	(2) 117,000	
Totals	737,000	143,000			809,000
Liabilities and Stockholders' Equity					
Accounts payable and other liabilities	60,000	30,000			90,000
8% Bonds payable ($50,000)		52,000	(2) 10,000		42,000
Common stock:					
Chrome Serial Co., Inc.	200,000				200,000
Branch, Inc.		40,000	(2) 40,000		
Additional paid-in capital		12,000	(2) 12,000		
Retained earnings:					
Chrome Serial Co., Inc.	477,000				477,000
Branch, Inc.		9,000	(2) 9,000		
Totals	737,000	143,000	151,000	151,000	809,000

(1) Apportionment of negative excess. (See Illustration 3–7.)

(2) Elimination of parent's investment account and allocation of differences between book values and market values (as was shown in Illustration 3–7).

A published example of the booking of such as excess can be seen in Illustration 3–11 which shows Gulf United Corporation's acquisition of Southwestern Drug Corporation and the resulting pro forma consolidated balance sheet. The computation of negative goodwill is shown in Illustration 3–12. Especially noteworthy is elimination entry (B) on the balance sheet wherein Southwestern's property and equipment ($2,558,000) is reduced to zero and negative goodwill of $1,746,000 is created. The note in Illustration 3–12 indicates that the negative goodwill will be amortized to income over 20 years.

Illustration 3–11
GULF UNITED CORPORATION AND SOUTHWESTERN DRUG CORPORATION
Condensed Pro Forma Combined Balance Sheet (Unaudited)
($000)

	Gulf United December 31, 1978		South-western historical May 31, 1979	Pro Forma Adjust-ments add (deduct)	Pro Forma Combined
	Historical	Pro forma			Combined
Assets					
Investments:					
Bonds	$ 453,298	$ 599,156			$ 599,156
Stocks	110,145	148,680			148,680
Mortgage loans on real estate	368,986	437,046			437,046
Policy loans, real estate and other	180,825	158,404	$ 299		158,703
Cash	12,028	13,942	1,274		15,216
Property and equipment	46,582	46,806	2,558	$(2,558)(B)	46,806
Deferred policy acquisition costs	158,012	216,759			216,759
Excess cost and broadcast licenses	67,856	67,856			67,856
Receivables, etc.	51,425	56,614	16,857	(383)(B)	73,088
Inventories			21,030		21,030
Totals	$1,449,157	$1,745,263	$42,018		$1,784,340
Liabilities					
Policy reserves	$ 738,471	$ 918,083			$ 918,083
Policy claims payable and funds held for policyholders	95,760	98,406			98,406
Notes payable	150,864	181,983	$11,871	$ (697)(B) 2,400 (B)	195,557
Accounts payable, accrued expenses, etc . . .	47,950	52,765	8,707	850 (B) 797 (B) 1,746 (B)	64,865
Income taxes	62,962	64,157			64,157
Totals	1,096,007	1,315,394	20,578		1,341,068
Preferred stock:					
Series A (aggregate liquidation and redemption value, $38,032,000)	28,239	28,239			28,239
Series B (aggregate liquidation and redemption value, $84,293,000)		77,550			77,550
Total	28,239	105,789			105,789
Common stockholders' equity:					
Net assets of Southwestern			21,440	(21,440)(B)	
Common stock	22,898	22,898		916 (B)	23,814
Additional paid-in capital	85,171	85,171		12,487 (B)	97,658
Unrealized investment gains (losses)	(19,762)	(20,593)			(20,593)
Retained earnings	245,466	245,466			245,466
Treasury stock	(8,862)	(8,862)			(8,862)
Common stockholders' equity	324,911	324,080	21,440		337,483
Totals	$1,449,157	$1,745,263	$42,018		$1,784,340

PURCHASE OF A PARTIALLY OWNED SUBSIDIARY AT BOOK VALUE

In many cases a parent company may purchase less than 100 percent of a subsidiary's outstanding shares. This will result in the creation of minority interests that can be accounted for in a variety of ways. The alternative accounting treatments of partially owned subsidiaries will now be considered.

Let us first clarify the treatment of the subsidiary's assets and liabilities

Illustration 3–12

For the purposes of the pro forma combined balance sheet, Southwestern's net assets have been adjusted to reflect the preliminary estimated fair value of its tangible assets and liabilities at May 31, 1979, as follows ($000):

Net assets as shown in Southwestern's balance sheet	$21,440
Adjustment of notes payable (including capital lease obligations) to reflect present values at appropriate current interest rates	697
Elimination of intangible assets	(383)
Reflection of the excess of value of vested pension benefits over plan assets and related balance sheet accruals	(850)
Subtotal	20,904
Cost of Gulf United's investment in Southwestern	16,600
Remainder	4,304
Reduction of property and equipment to zero value	2,558
Excess of Gulf United's equity in the underlying net assets of Southwestern over cost (negative goodwill)	$1,746

The negative goodwill is amortized in the pro forma combined summary of earnings over a 20-year period on a straight-line basis. A final determination of the negative goodwill will be made based on the financial position of Southwestern as of the effective date of the merger, the fair value of Southwestern's net tangible assets and liabilities at that date, and other relevant factors.

C. The pro forma combined summary of earnings gives effect to the adjustments described below, based on the assumption that the proposed merger had been consummated at the beginning of the period and the balance sheet adjustments described in Note B had been made at that date.

(1) Elimination of the provision for income taxes of Southwestern (taxable income of Southwestern during the period would have been offset by Gulf United's excess deductions).

(2) Amortization of discount on notes payable and capital lease obligations arising from the adjustment to reflect present values at appropriate current interest rates.

(3) Elimination of amortization of intangible assets and depreciation of property and equipment.

(4) Amortization of the negative goodwill over 20 years.

(5) Additional interest expense of Gulf United assuming that the cash portion of the acquisition had been financed since January 1, 1978.

---

on the parent's consolidated balance sheet. If a parent company acquires 80 percent of a subsidiary's outstanding shares, do 80 percent or 100 percent of the assets and liabilities get consolidated with the parent's assets and liabilities? It is generally agreed that since an 80 percent subsidiary is considered a *part of the consolidated entity,* *all* of the assets and liabilities are consolidated. This then gives rise to an auxiliary question. How should the interests of the 20 percent minority be disclosed on the parent's consolidated balance sheet? Technically, minority interests are not liabilities since there is no payment obligation to anyone. However, in practice, minority interests are occassionally shown as liabilities in the parent's consolidated balance sheets, but the usual practice is to show minority interests between liabilities and stockholders' equity (see Illustration 3–14).

Referring to Illustration 3–13, assume that Sun Serial Company, Inc., purchased 80 percent of Branch, Inc., for $14,800. The consolidated working paper appears in Illustration 3–14. In this illustration it is also assumed that book values are equal to their respective fair market values. The working paper elimination entry is as follows:

(1)

Common Stock—Branch Inc.	4,800	
Additional Paid-In Capital—Branch, Inc.	2,400	
Retained Earnings—Branch, Inc.	7,600	
Investment in Branch, Inc.		14,800

Illustration 3–13
BRANCH, INC.
Trial Balance
January 1, 19x1

Debits

Cash in bank	$ 3,000
Accounts receivable	6,000
Inventories	4,000
Land	10,000
Total	$23,000

Credits

Accounts payable	$ 4,000
Allowance for doubtful accounts	500
Capital stock—common	6,000
Additional paid-in capital	3,000
Retained earnings	9,500
Total	$23,000

The following should be noted:

1. Although only 80 percent of the shares of Branch, Inc., are owned, 100 percent of its assets and liabilities are consolidated with those of Sun Serial Company, Inc.
2. The net assets of Branch, Inc., are $18,500 ($23,000 − $4,500).
3. The minority interest is $3,700, which is 20 percent of the net assets.

There are several ways to show the minority interests on a consolidated balance sheet. One method that is theoretically sound is to show them as a *single* amount in the equity section as a separate item from the parent's equity regardless of how many subsidiaries are owned by the parent company. Another method, less correct, theoretically, but used extensively in practice, is either to show minority interests in a section of the balance sheet between liabilities and stockholder's equity as mentioned earlier. The creation of a no-man's land between liabilities and equity as an unclassified category may serve to confuse the reader of the balance sheet. Illustration 3–15 is an example of the presentation of a consolidated balance sheet with minority interest shown as part of stockholder's equity. Illustration 3–16 is an example of a method that is widely used in practice.

Illustration 3–14
SUN SERIAL COMPANY, INC.
Consolidated Working Paper
January 1, 19x1

80 Percent Subsidiary
Date of Acquisition

	Sun Serial Co., Inc.	Branch, Inc. (80%)	Eliminations Dr.	Eliminations Cr.	Minority Interest	Consol- idated
Debits						
Cash in bank	10,000	3,000				13,000
Accounts receivable	20,000	6,000				26,000
Inventories	12,000	4,000				16,000
Investment in Branch, Inc.	14,800			(1) 14,800		
Land		10,000				10,000
Equipment	40,000					40,000
Totals	96,800	23,000				105,000
Credits						
Accounts payable	8,000	4,000				12,000
Notes payable	10,000					10,000
Allowance for doubtful accounts	400	500				900
Accumulated depreciation—equipment	8,000					8,000
Common stock:						
Sun Serial Co., inc.	20,000					20,000
Branch, Inc.		6,000	(1) 4,800		1,200	
Additional paid-in capital:						
Sun Serial Co., Inc.	30,000					30,000
Branch, Inc.		3,000	(1) 2,400		600	
Retained earnings:						
Sun Serials Co., Inc.	20,400					20,400
Branch, Inc.		9,500	(1) 7,600		1,900	
Minority interest					7,300	3,700
Totals	96,800	23,000	14,800	14,800		105,000

To eliminate the parent's investment and 80 percent of each element of Branch, Inc.'s stockholders' equity.

Illustration 3–15
SUN SERIAL COMPANY, INC.
Consolidated Balance Sheet
January 1, 19x1

Assets

Current assets:			
Cash in bank		$13,000	
Accounts receivable	$26,000		
Less: Allowance for doubtful accounts	900	25,100	
Inventories		16,000	$54,100
Long-term investments:			
Land			10,000
Property, plant, and equipment:			
Equipment		$40,000	
Less: Accumulated depreciation		8,000	32,000
Total assets			$96,100

Liabilities

Current liabilities:			
Notes payable		$10,000	
Accounts payable		12,000	$22,000

Stockholders' Equity

Paid-in capital:			
Common stock	$20,000		
Premium on common stock	30,000	$50,000	
Retained earnings		20,400	
Total majority interests		$70,400	
Minority interest		3,700	
Total stockholders' equity			74,100
Total liabilities and stockholders' equity			$96,100

Illustration 3–16
STANDARD BRANDS INCORPORATED AND SUBSIDIARY COMPANIES
Consolidated Balance Sheet
December 31
($000)

	1978	1977
Assets		
Current assets:		
Cash	$ 8,887	$ 17,708
Marketable securities, at cost which approximates market . . .	58,565	23,399
Receivables, less allowances of $7,311 in 1978 and $5,195 in 1977	229,106	222,376
Inventories, principally at lower of average cost or market . .	406,358	397,130
Prepaid expenses	14,099	8,298
Total current assets	717,015	668,911
Investments and notes receivable	13,685	10,258
Property, plant, and equipment, at cost:		
Land	10,596	10,677
Buildings	172,090	169,541
Machinery and equipment	529,895	489,222
	712,581	669,440
Less: Accumulated depreciation	284,211	261,457
Total property, plant, and equipment	428,370	407,983
Assets under capitalized leases–net	20,566	21,017
Other assets	15,022	11,494
Intangibles, including brand names, trademarks, and goodwill . .	69,608	76,476
Total assets	$1,264,266	$1,196,139
Liabilities and Stockholders' Equity		
Current liabilities:		
Notes and loans payable	$ 66,427	$ 96,094
Current maturities—long-term debt	8,901	7,523
Accounts payable and accrued expenses	247,651	230,332
United States and foreign taxes on income	48,002	41,311
Total current liabilities	370,981	375,260
Long-term debt	229,789	215,128
Deferred income taxes	63,268	50,970
Other liabilities	33,259	28,980
Capital lease obligations	23,037	23,892
Minority interests	3,987	3,067
Stockholders' equity:		
Preferred stock	20,000	20,000
Common stock	28,216	27,968
Capital surplus	29,369	26,925
Retained earnings	468,683	430,370
	546,268	505,263
Less: Capital stock held in treasury, at cost	6,323	6,421
Total stockholders' equity	539,945	498,842
Total liabilities and stockholders' equity	$1,264,266	$1,196,139

See notes to consolidated financial statements.
Source: Standard Brands Incorporated Annual Report, 1978.

PURCHASE OF A PARTIALLY OWNED SUBSIDIARY AT OTHER THAN BOOK VALUE

When a company purchases more than 50 percent but less than 100 percent of another company's shares of stock, and the amount paid for the shares is other than book value, a new allocation problem is created. If a wholly owned subsidiary has book values of assets that differ from their respective fair market values, it is clear that 100 percent of these differences are allocated as demonstrated previously in this chapter. However, what allocation is appropriate if, for example, only 80 percent of the subsidiary's shares are owned by the parent? Unfortunately, the answer to this question is not a simple one. At present, two generally accepted methods are used in practice. Under the *parent method* only the parent's share of the differences between market and book values are reflected in the consolidated financial statements. This method is most frequently used in practice and will, therefore, be used in this and succeeding chapters. Under the second method, known as the *entity method,* 100 percent of the differences between market and book values are reflected in the consolidation, and this causes the minority interests to be shown at the market prices implicit in the business combination. The illustration of this method will be deferred until Chapter 11.

To demonstrate the application of the parent method it is now assumed that Chrome Serials Company, Inc., purchased 80 percent of the outstanding capital stock in Branch, Inc., for $153,600 on January 1, 19x1. The book and market values are as shown in Illustration 3-5. The allocation of the purchase price paid would be as shown in Illustration 3–17.

Illustration 3–17
BRANCH, INC.
Allocation of Purchase Price
January 1, 19x1

Purchase price paid $153,600
Less: Net assets at book value—($61,000) × 80% 48,800

Unallocated excess of cost $104,800
Less: Allocation of excess:

	Fair market value	−	Book value	=	Differ-ence	×	Per cent	=	Alloca-tion
Inventories	$ 30,000		$14,000		$16,000	×	80	=	$12,800
Land	20,000		10,000		10,000	×	80	=	8,000
Building	70,000		50,000		20,000	×	80	=	16,000
Equipment	20,000		30,000		(10,000)	×	80	=	(8,000)
Patent	10,000		–0–		10,000	×	80	=	8,000
Bonds payable	(42,000)		(52,000)		10,000	×	80	=	8,000
Totals	$108,000		$52,000		$56,000	×	80	=	$44,800

Allocated excess of cost 44,800
Goodwill . . . . $ 60,000

This allocation is similar to the method used in Illustration 3–6 and can be compared to it. A proof of the calculation of goodwill is as follows:

Price paid $153,600
Less: 80% of the net assets acquired at market value (80% × $117,000) 93,600
Goodwill . . . . $ 60,000

The elimination entry on the working paper appears in Illustration 3–18 and is reproduced as follows:

(1)		
Common Stock—Branch, Inc.	32,000	
Additional Paid-In Capital	9,600	
Retained Earnings—Branch, Inc.	7,200	
Inventories	12,800	
Land	8,000	
Building	16,000	
Patents	8,000	
Goodwill	60,000	
Bonds Payable	8,000	
Investment in Branch, Inc.		153,600
Equipment		8,000

Illustration 3–18
CHROME SERIAL COMPANY, INC.
Consolidated Working Paper
January 1, 19x1

80% Percent Subsidiary
Date of Acquisition

	Chrome Serial Co., Inc.	Branch, Inc. (80%)	Eliminations		Minority Interest	Consolidated
			Dr.	Cr.		
Assets						
Cash in bank	83,400	13,000				96,400
Accounts receivable (net of estimated uncollectibles)	50,000	26,000				76,000
Inventories	60,000	14,000	(1) 12,800			86,800
Land	70,000	10,000	(1) 8,000			88,000
Building (net of depreciation)	120,000	50,000	(1) 16,000			186,000
Equipment (net of depreciation)	200,000	30,000		(1) 8,000		222,000
Patents			(1) 8,000			8,000
Goodwill			(1) 60,000			60,000
Investment in Branch, Inc.	153,600			(1) 153,600		
Totals	737,000	143,000				823,200
Liabilities and Stockholders' Equity						
Accounts payable and other liabilities	60,000	30,000				90,000
8% Bonds payable ($50,000)		52,000	(1) 8,000			44,000
Common stock:						
Chrome Serial Co., Inc.	200,000					200,000
Branch, Inc.		40,000	(1) 32,000		8,000	
Additional paid-in capital		12,000	(1) 9,600		2,400	
Retained earnings:						
Chrome Serial Co., Inc.	477,000					477,000
Branch, Inc.		9,000	(1) 7,200		1,800	
Minority Interest					12,200	12,200
Totals	737,000	143,000	161,600	161,600		823,200

(1) To eliminate parent's investment in Branch, Inc., and to adjust the latter's book values to reflect 80% of the market values (price paid) of specific assets and liabilities.

Except for the allocation of only 80 percent of the under/overvaluations and the minority interest of 20 percent, Illustration 3–18 is similar to Illustration 3–7.

When the price paid produces "negative goodwill" and less than 100 percent of the outstanding shares is acquired, a slightly different calculation is required. Using assumed data, Illustration 3-19 demonstrates the appropriate procedure.

Illustration 3–19: Allocation of purchase price—negative goodwill (date of acquisition)

Price paid	$ 142,000
Less: 90% of the net assets at book value (90% × $300,000)	270,000
Negative excess	$(128,000)

Less: Allocation of differences between book values and fair market values:

	Fair Market Value	−	Book value	=	Differ- ence	×	Percent	=	Allo- cated amount
Inventory	$ 50,000		$ 40,000		$10,000	×	90	=	$ 9,000
Equipment	100,000		70,000		30,000	×	90	=	27,000
Patent	25,000		–0–		25,000	×	90	=	22,500
Totals	$175,000		$110,000		$65,000	×	90	=	$ 58,500
Allocated negative excess									$(186,500)

The proration of the negative excess in accordance with paragraph 91 of *APB Opinion 16* would be:

	Fair market value	Per- cent	Prorated negative excess—limited to 90% of fair value
Equipment	$100,000	80	$ 90,000
Patent	25,000	20	22,500
Totals	$125,000	100	$112,500
Negative goodwill			74,000
Total			$186,500

If the prorated negative excess were not limited to the parent's share (90 percent) of the fair market value, the negative excess proration to patents would have been $25,000 instead of the $22,500 shown above. This would have created a $2,500 negative balance in the patent amount as follows:

Book value	$ –0–
Allocation	22,500
Proration	(25,000)
Total	$ (2,500)

By limiting the proration to $22,500, a zero balance results. In essence, when this procedure is used, only the minority interest's share of the book value is carried to the consolidated column. Thus, for Patents the amount is 20% × $0 = $0. For equipment the calculation would be:

Book value	$70,000
Allocated amount	27,000
Total	97,000
Less: Prorated negative excess	90,000
Amount carried to the consolidated statement (10% × $70,000)	$ 7,000

QUESTIONS

1. It is well established that a home office must combine its branch(s)'s trial balance with its own whenever financial statements are prepared for external use. Is there a similar requirement between a parent company and its subsidiaries? Explain.

2. Reciprocal accounts exist between a home office and its branch. These accounts are eliminated whenever the trial balances are combined. Does a similar reciprocity exist between a parent company and its subsidiary? If so, provide an example of the accounts involved.

3. When a parent company purchases the outstanding shares (or a portion of them) of another company, is it usual to purchase them at book value? If not, why not?

4. If a parent company purchases its investment at other than book value, what disposition is made of the difference between book value and the price paid for the investment?

5. What does the term *negative goodwill* mean and how is it arrived at?

6. What disposition is made of negative goodwill?

7. What is meant by the term *minority interests?* Why does it arise?

8. There are three places to show minority interests on the balance sheet. Where are they? Briefly, discuss the theoretical, or lack of theoretical, justification for each one. Which method is used most often in practice?

9. When a parent company purchases less than 100% (but more than 50%) of the outstanding common stock of another company and the purchase is made at an amount other than book value, how is the difference between book value and the price paid treated? Is there more than one method used to account for this difference? If so, which one is most prevalently used?

10. What is meant by the parent method? Use an example to illustrate the method.

EXERCISES

Exercise 3–1.

1. In a business combination what is the appropriate method of accounting for an excess of fair value assigned to net assets over the cost paid for them?

a. Record as negative goodwill.

b. Record as additional paid-in capital from combination on the books of the combined company.

c. Proportionately reduce values assigned to non-monetary assets and record any remaining excess as a deferred credit.

d. Proportionately reduce values assigned to non-current assets and record any remaining excess as a deferred credit.

2. Which of the following is the best theoretical justification for consolidated financial statements?

a. In form the companies are one entity; in substance they are separate.

b. In form the companies are separate; in substance they are one entity.

c. In form and substance the companies are one entity.

d. In form and substance the companies are separate.

3. Consolidated financial statements are prepared when a parent-subsidiary relationship exists in recognition of the accounting concept of—

a. Materiality.

b. Entity.

c. Objectivity.

d. Going concern.   (AICPA adapted)

Exercise 3–2.

1. On April 1, 19x9, the Jack Company paid $800,000 for the issued and outstanding common stock of Ann Corporation in a transaction properly accounted for as a purchase. The recorded assets and liabilities of Ann Corporation on April 1, 19x9, follows:

Cash	$ 80,000
Inventory	240,000
Property and equipment (net of accumulated	
depreciation of $320,000)	480,000
Liabilities	(180,000)

On April 1, 19x9, it was determined that the inventory of Ann had a fair value of $190,000 and the property and equipment (net) had a fair value of $560,000. What is the amount of goodwill resulting from the business combination?

a. $0.
b. $50,000.
c. $150,000.
d. $180,000.

2. On June 30, 19x9, Needle Corporation purchased for cash at $10 per share all 100,000 shares of the outstanding common stock of Thread Company. The total appraised value of identifiable assets less liabilities of Thread was $1,400,000 at June 30, 19x9, including the appraised value of Thread's property, plant, and equipment (its only noncurrent asset) of $250,000. The consolidated balance sheet of Needle Corporation and its wholly owned subsidiary at June 30, 19x9, should reflect—

a. A deferred credit (negative goodwill) of $150,000.
b. Goodwill of $150,000.
c. A deferred credit (negative goodwill) of $400,000.
d. Goodwill of $400,000.

3. On November 30, 19x8, Eagle, Incorporated, purchased for cash at $25 per share all 300,000 shares of the outstanding common stock of Perch Company. Perch's balance sheet at November 30, 19x8, showed a book value of $6,000,000. Additionally, the fair value of Perch's property, plant, and equipment on November 30, 19x8, was $800,000 in excess of its book value. What amount, if any, will be shown in the balance sheet caption "Goodwill" in the November 30, 19x8, consolidated balance sheet of Eagle, Incorporated, and its wholly owned subsidiary, Perch Company?

a. $0.
b. $700,000.
c. $800,000.
d. $1,500,000.   (AICPA adapted)

Exercise 3–3. Items 1 and 2 are based on the following information:

The Nugget Company's balance sheet on December 31, 19x6, is as follows:

Assets

Cash	$ 100,000
Accounts receivable	200,000
Inventories	500,000
Property, plant, and equipment	900,000
Total assets	$1,700,000

*Liabilities and
Stockholders' Equity*

Current liabilities	$ 300,000
Long-term debt	500,000
Common stock (par $1 per share)	100,000
Additional paid-in capital	200,000
Retained earnings	600,000
Total liabilities and stockholders' equity	$1,700,000

On December 31, 19x6, the Bronc Company purchased all of the outstanding common stock of Nugget for $1,500,000 cash. On that date, the fair (market) value of Nugget's inventories was $450,000 and the fair value of Nugget's property, plant, and equipment was $1,000,000. The fair values of all other assets and liabilities of Nugget were equal to their book values.

1. As a result of the acquisition of Nugget by Bronc, the consolidated balance sheet of Bronc and Nugget should reflect goodwill in the amount of—

a. $500,000.
b. $550,000.
c. $600,000.
d. $650,000.

2. Assuming that the balance sheet of Bronc (unconsolidated) at December 31, 19x6, reflected retained earnings of $2,000,000, what amount of retained earnings should be shown in the December 31, 19x6, consolidated balance sheet of Bronc and its new subsidiary, Nugget?

a. $2,000,000.
b. $2,600,000.
c. $2,800,000.
d. $3,150,000.   (AICPA adapted)

Exercise 3–4.

1. On July 31, 19x9, Light Company purchased for cash of $8,000,000, all of the outstanding common stock of Shirk Company when Shirk's balance sheet showed net assets of $6,400,000. Shirk's assets and liabilities had fair values different from the book values as follows:

	Book value	Fair value
Property, plant, and equipment, net	$10,000,000	$11,500,000
Other assets	1,000,000	700,000
Long-term debt	6,000,000	5,600,000

As a result of the transaction above, what amount, if any, will be shown as goodwill in the July 31, 19x9, consolidated balance sheet of Light Company and its wholly owned subsidiary, Shirk Company?

a. $0.
b. $100,000.
c. $1,200,000.
d. $1,600,000.

2. During 19x8, the Henderson Company purchased the net assets of John Corporation for $800,-000. On the date of the transaction, John had no long-term investments in marketable securities and had $100,000 of liabilities. The fair value of John's assets when acquired were as follows:

Current assets	$ 400,000
Noncurrent assets	600,000
	$1,000,000

How should the $100,000 difference between the fair value of the net assets acquired ($900,000) and the cost ($800,000) be accounted for by Henderson?

a. The $100,000 difference should be credited to retained earnings.

b. The noncurrent assets should be recorded at $500,000.

c. The current assets should be recorded at $360,000, and the noncurrent assets should be recorded at $540,000.

d. A deferred credit of $100,000 should be set up and then amortized to income over a period not to exceed 40 years.

3. Companies A and B have been operating separately for five years. Each company has a minimal amount of liabilities and a simple capital structure consisting solely of voting common stock. Company A, in exchange for 40 percent of its voting stock, acquired 80 percent of the common stock of Company B. This was a "tax-free" stock for stock (type B) exchange for tax purposes. Company B assets have a total net fair market value of $800,000 and a total net book value of $580,000. The fair market value of the A stock used in the exchange was $700,000. The goodwill on this acquisition would be—

a. Zero, this would be a pooling of interest.
b. $60,000.
c. $120,000.
d. $236,000.   (AICPA adapted)

Exercise 3–5. Items 1 and 2 are based on the following information:

Apex Company acquired 70 percent of the outstanding stock of Nadir Corporation. The separate balance sheet of Apex immediately after the acquisition and the consolidated balance sheet are as follows:

	Apex	Consolidated
Current assets	$106,000	$146,000
Investment in Nadir (cost) . . .	100,000	—
Goodwill	—	8,100
Fixed assets (net)	270,000	370,000
Totals	$476,000	$524,100
Current liabilities	$ 15,000	$ 28,000
Capital stock	350,000	350,000
Minority interest	—	35,100
Retained earnings	111,000	111,000
Totals	$476,000	$524,100

Ten thousand dollars of the excess payment for the investment in Nadir was ascribed to undervaluation of its fixed assets; the balance of the excess payment was ascribed to goodwill. Current assets of Nadir included a $2,000 receivable from Apex which arose before they became related on an ownership basis.

The following two items relate to Nadir's separate balance sheet prepared at the time Apex acquired its 70 percent interest in Nadir.

1. What was the total of the current assets on Nadir's separate balance sheet at the time Apex acquired its 70 percent interest?

a. $38,000.
b. $40,000.
c. $42,000.
d. $104,000.

2. What was the total stockholders' equity on Nadir's separate balance sheet at the time Apex acquired its 70 percent interest?

a. $64,900.
b. $70,000.
c. $100,000.
d. $117,000.   (AICPA adapted)

Exercise 3–6. For each of the following independent cases, prepare the working paper elimination entry for P Company and its subsidiary S Company. Assume that purchase accounting is to be used and that all of the assets and liabilities of S Company have fair market values approximately equal to their respective book values. (Hint: Calculate excess prior to preparing entry.)

[Relates to Exercise 3–6]

			S Company balances		
Case	Price paid	Percent of stock acquired	Capital stock	Additional paid-in capital	Retained earnings (deficit)
A	$1,300,000	100	$500,000	$200,000	$600,000
B	1,500,000	100	500,000	—	800,000
C	640,000	80	500,000	300,000	(200,000)

Exercise 3–7. On January 1, 19x2, P Company purchased an 80 percent interest in S Company for $140,000. On that date the assets and liabilities of S Company had book values equal to their fair values. S Company's balance sheet on January 1, 19x2, was as follows:

Assets

Cash	$ 50,000
Accounts receivable	30,000
Inventory	20,000
Long-term investments in marketable securities	40,000
Plant and equipment (net of accumulated depreciation)	240,000
Land	120,000
Total assets	$500,000

Liabilities and Stockholders' Equity

Liabilities	$100,000
Common stock	100,000
Retained earnings	300,000
Total liabilities and stockholders' equity	$500,000

Required:

Prepare the working paper elimination entry for P Company as of January 1, 19x2. (Hint: Calculate excess prior to preparing entry.)

Exercise 3–8. On January 1, 19x3, P Company purchased an 80 percent interest in S Company for $464,000. On that date the book values and fair market values of S Company were as follows:

Assets

	Book values	Fair market values
Cash	$ 50,000	$ 50,000
Accounts receivable	30,000	30,000
Inventory	20,000	50,000
Plant and equipment (net of accumulated depreciation)	300,000	400,000
Patents	–0–	50,000
Total assets	$400,000	$580,000

Liabilities and Stockholders' Equity

Liabilities	$ 50,000	$ 50,000
Common stock	100,000	
Retained earnings	250,000	
Total liabilities and stockholders' equity	$400,000	

Required:

Prepare the working paper elimination entry for P Company on January 1, 19x3.

Exercise 3–9. Using the data provided in Exercise 3–8, assume P Company purchased the investment (80 percent) for $244,000. All other information is unchanged.

Required:

Prepare the working paper elimination entry for P Company on January 1, 19x3.

Exercise 3–10. On January 1, 19x3, P Company purchased an 80 percent interest in S Company. On that date the book values and fair market values of S Company's assets and liabilities were the same. A *consolidated* balance sheet prepared on that date appeared as follows:

P COMPANY AND SUBSIDIARY
Consolidated Balance Sheet
January 1, 19x3

Assets

Current assets	$200,000
Plant assets (net of accumulated depreciation) .	500,000
Goodwill	250,000
Total assets	$950,000

Liabilities and
Stockholders' Equity

Current liabilities	$150,000
Common stock	200,000
Retained earnings	500,000
Minority interest	100,000
Total liabilities and stockholders' equity	$950,000

Required:

Calculate the following:

a. Common stock of P Company.

b. Retained earnings of P Company.

c. The identifiable net assets of S Company at book value.

d. The price paid by P Company for its 80 percent investment in S Company.

PROBLEMS

Problem 3–11. On July 1, 19x1, P Company purchased 100 percent of the outstanding common stock of S Company for $340,000 payable in cash. On that date each of the assets and liabilities of S Company had book values approximately equal to their respective fair market values. Balance sheets of the companies on July 1, 19x1, are as follows:

	P Company	S Company
Cash	$ 600,000	$100,000
Accounts receivable	400,000	50,000
Inventory	300,000	80,000
Land	100,000	—
Equipment (net of accumulated depreciation) .	200,000	120,000
Investment in S Company . .	340,000	
Totals	$1,940,000	$350,000
Accounts payable	$ 400,000	$ 50,000
Common stock—P Company	200,000	
Common stock—S Company		100,000
Additional paid-in capital—P Company	100,000	
Retained earnings—P Company	1,240,000	
Retained earnings—S Company		200,000
Totals	$1,940,000	$350,000

Required:

a. Prepare an allocation schedule to compute goodwill.

b. Prepare a consolidated working paper.

Problem 3–12. Using the balance sheets that appear in Problem 3–11, assume that only 80 percent of the outstanding stock of S Company was acquired by P Company for $340,000 payable in cash. All other information in the problem is unchanged.

Required:

a. Prepare an allocation schedule to compute goodwill.

b. Prepare a consolidated working paper.

Problem 3–13. On January 2, 19x2, P Company purchased 100 percent of the outstanding common stock of S Company for $950,000 payable in cash. On that date the assets and liabilities of S Company had fair market values as indicated below. Balance sheets of the companies on January 2, 19x2, are as follows:

[Relates to Problem 3–13]

	Book values		S Company fair market values
	P Company	S Company	
Cash	$ 300,000	$ 50,000	$ 50,000
Accounts receivable	200,000	100,000	100,000
Inventory	150,000	60,000	90,000
Land		70,000	120,000
Equipment (net of accumulated depreciation) .	600,000	470,000	600,000
Investment in S Company	950,000		
Totals	$2,200,000	$750,000	
Accounts payable	$ 100,000	$ 50,000	50,000
Common stock—P Company	600,000		
Common stock—S Company		200,000	
Additional paid-in capital—S Company		100,000	
Retained earnings—P Company	1,500,000		
Retained earnings—S Company		400,000	
Totals	$2,200,000	$750,000	

Required:

a. Prepare an allocation schedule to compute goodwill.

b. Prepare a consolidated working paper.

Problem 3–14. Using the balance sheets that appear in Problem 3–13, assume that only 90 percent of the outstanding stock of S Company was acquired by P Company for $950,000 payable in cash. All other information in the problem is unchanged.

Required:

a. Prepare an allocation schedule to compute goodwill.

b. Prepare a consolidated working paper.

Problem 3–15. On January 2, 19x3, P Company purchased 100 percent of the outstanding common stock of S Company for $500,000 payable in cash. On that date, the assets and liabilities of S Company had fair market values as indicated below. Balance sheets of the companies on January 2, 19x3, are as shown below:

Required:

a. Prepare an allocation schedule to compute goodwill.

b. Prepare a consolidated working paper.

Problem 3–16. Using the balance sheets that appear in Problem 3–15, assume that only 80 percent of the outstanding stock of S Company was acquired by P Company for $500,000 payable in cash. All other information in the problem is unchanged.

[Relates to Problem 3–15]

	Book values		S Company fair market values
	P Company	S Company	
Cash	$ 300,000	$ 50,000	$ 50,000
Accounts receivable	200,000	100,000	100,000
Inventory	200,000	80,000	100,000
Land	100,000	50,000	60,000
Building (net of accumulated depreciation) . . .	600,000	400,000	350,000
Equipment (net of accumulated depreciation) .	800,000	200,000	140,000
Investment in S Company	500,000		
Totals	$2,700,000	$880,000	
Accounts payable	$ 150,000	$ 60,000	60,000
8% bonds payable (face amount $300,000)		290,000	240,000
Common stock—P Company	1,500,000		
Common stock—S Company		100,000	
Additional paid-in capital—S Company		200,000	
Retained earnings—P Company	1,050,000		
Retained earnings—S Company		230,000	
Totals	$2,700,000	$880,000	

Required:

a. Prepare an allocation schedule to compute goodwill.

b. Prepare a consolidated working paper.

Problem 3–17. On January 2, 19x4, P Company purchased 100 percent of the outstanding common stock of S Company for $542,000 payable in cash. On that date the assets and liabilities of S Company had fair market values as indicated below. Balance sheets of the companies on January 2, 19x4, are as follows:

Problem 3–18. Using the balance sheets that appear in Problem 3–17, assume that only 80 percent of the outstanding stock of S Company was acquired by P Company for $542,000 payable in cash. All other information in the problem is unchanged.

Required:

a. Prepare an allocation schedule to compute goodwill.

b. Prepare a consolidated working paper.

[Relates to Problem 3–17]	Book values		S Company fair market values
	P Company	S Company	
Cash	$ 100,000	$100,000	$100,000
Accounts receivable	200,000	150,000	150,000
Inventory	150,000	130,000	140,000
Land	50,000	80,000	120,000
Equipment (net of accumulated depreciation) .	300,000	200,000	180,000
Investment in S Company	542,000		
Long-term investments in marketable securities	100,000	125,000	140,000
Totals	$1,442,000	$785,000	
Accounts payable	175,000	115,000	115,000
Common stock—P Company	400,000		
Common stock—S Company		200,000	
Additional paid-in capital—P Company	200,000		
Retained earnings—P Company	667,000		
Retained earnings—S Company		470,000	
Totals	$1,442,000	$785,000	

Required:

a. Prepare an allocation schedule to compute goodwill.

b. Prepare a consolidated working paper.

Problem 3–19. On January 2, 19x5, P Company purchased 90 percent of the outstanding common stock of S Compnay for $323,500 payable in cash. On that date, the assets and liabilities of S Company had fair market values as indicated below. Balance sheets of the companies on January 2, 19x5, are as follows:

[Relates to Problem 3–19]	Book values		S Company fair market values
	P Company	S Company	
Cash	$ 100,000	$100,000	$100,000
Accounts receivable	200,000	150,000	150,000
Inventory	150,000	130,000	140,000
Land		80,000	120,000
Equipment (net of accumulated depreciation) .	300,000	200,000	180,000
Investment in S Company	323,500		
Long-term investments in marketable securities		125,000	140,000
Totals	$1,073,500	$785,000	
Accounts payable	$ 175,000	$115,000	115,000
Common stock—P Company	400,000		
Common stock—S Company		200,000	
Additional paid-in capital—S Company		100,000	
Retained earnings—P Company	498,500		
Retained earnings—S Company		370,000	
Totals	$1,073,500	$785,000	

Required:

a. Prepare an allocation schedule to compute (negative) goodwill.

b. Prepare a consolidated working paper.

Problem 3–20. On January 2, 19x6, P Company purchased 80 percent of the outstanding common stock of S Company and 70 percent of the outstanding common stock of T Company. On that date the book values of the assets and liabilities of S Company and T Company were approximately equal to their respective fair market values. Balance sheets of the companies are as follows:

Required:

Prepare a consolidated working paper.

Problem 3–21 (related to Appendix A, Chapter 24). Using the Mattel, Inc., pro forma balance sheet and related notes in Appendix A, Chapter 24, prepare the journal entry to —

a. Record the investment in Western, if Western is to continue operating as a 100 percent owned subsidiary. [*Hint:* See entry (10).]

b. Eliminate the investment account, if a consolidated balance sheet is to be prepared as of the date of acquisition.

[Relates to Problem 3–20]

	P Company	S Company	T Company
Cash	$ 300,000	$200,000	$100,000
Accounts receivable	200,000	100,000	80,000
Inventory	200,000	120,000	120,000
Land	100,000	50,000	
Equipment (net of accumu-			
lated depreciation)	600,000	350,000	675,000
Investment in S Company	600,000		
Investment in T Company	530,000		
Totals	$2,530,000	$820,000	$975,000
Accounts payable	$ 150,000	$120,000	$ 75,000
8 percent bonds payable (face amount $500,000)	520,000		
Common stock—P Company	500,000		
Common stock—S Company		300,000	
Common stock—T Company			200,000
Retained earnings—P Company	1,360,000		
Retained earnings—S Company		400,000	
Retained earnings—T Company			700,000
Totals	$2,530,000	$820,000	$975,000

4

Consolidated statements—subsequent to date of acquisition

OVERVIEW

There are three main methods used to account for investments in subsidiaries:

1. Under the cost method, *income is not recorded until dividends are declared by the subsidiary and amortization of excess is not recorded on the books of the parent company. This method is essentially equivalent to* cash basis *accounting and may be used to account for investments in subsidiaries that are to be consolidated with the parent company's financial statements. It may not be used to account for unconsolidated subsidiaries except under special circumstances.*

2. Under the incomplete equity method, *a parent company records on its books its share of a subsidiary's net income by debiting the Investment in Subsidiary account and crediting Investment Income. No entries are made for amortization of excess, and dividends received by a parent reduce the Investment in Subsidiary account. This method is considered to be a partial accrual method and may be used when consolidated financial statements are to be prepared. It is* not acceptable to use this method to account for unconsolidated subsidiaries.*

3. The complete equity method *represents a* full accrual method. This *method is similar to the incomplete equity method except that amortization of excess is recorded on the parent company's books. This method may be used to account for* both consolidated subsidiaries and unconsolidated subsidiaries.*

Although the three methods of accounting for investments in subsidiaries produce different results on the parent company's books, consolidated financial statements prepared under each method are identical because there is only one reality when presenting the financial statements of a consolidated entity. The identical result is achieved by altering the elimination entries on the consolidated working paper in a manner to produce the correct result.

As noted in Chapter 2, business combinations are an ongoing phenomenon in the continuum of business activity. Therefore, most purchase accounting business combinations will entail accounting procedures for subsidiaries already in existence, i.e., subsequent to the date of their incorporation or acquisition.

Basically, there are two methods of accounting for investments in other than temporary marketable securities. These methods are known as the equity method and the cost method. A discussion of each method follows.

EQUITY METHOD

The equity method of accounting, as will be seen later in this chapter, is required under certain conditions. Under this method the investment is recorded at its original purchase price (cost) and is subsequently adjusted to reflect the net effect of all income and capital transactions recorded on the subsidiary's books. The parent's share of a subsidiary's income or loss is recorded as income or loss on the parent's books, and the payment of dividends by the subsidiary is viewed as a transfer of cash to the parent corporation and thus a reduction of its investment in the subsidiary. If income and dividends were not treated in this manner, the managers of a parent corporation could manipulate its income by timing the declaration of the dividend to coincide with a particular goal. Even though the subsidiary technically declares the dividend, the parent actually controls this decision. Illustration 4–1 will be used to illustrate the equity method.

Illustration 4–1
P COMPANY AND S COMPANY
Trial Balances
January 1, 19x1

	P Company	S Company
Assets	$100,000	$20,000
Capital stock—common	$ 30,000	$ 5,000
Retained earnings	70,000	15,000
Totals	$100,000	$20,000

Additional information:
1. On January 1, 19x1, P Company purchases, for cash, 80 percent of the outstanding shares of S Company for $26,000.
2. During 19x1, S Company had sales of $50,000, costs and expenses of $30,000, leaving a net income of $20,000.
3. On October 31, 19x1, S Company paid a dividend of $12,000.
4. All of the assets of S Company were stated at fair market values on January 1, 19x1. The parent approach will be used to amortize goodwill over 40 years.*

*APB Opinion 17 provides for a maximum amortization period of 40 years. A shorter period of amortization is used when the estimated life is less than 40 years.

The following summary journal entries reflect all of the above using the equity method of accounting. Post-closing trial balances as of December 31, 19x1, are also presented.

S Company's Books

Assets	20,000	
Costs and Expenses	30,000	
Sales Revenue		50,000
Dividends Paid	12,000	
Assets		12,000

P Company's Books

1/1/x1	Investment in S Company	26,000	
	Assets		26,000
	Purchased 80 percent of S Company.		
10/1/x1	Assets	9,600	
	Investment in S Company		9,600
	To record the receipt of a dividend from S Company using the equity method (80 percent × $12,000).		
12/31/x1	Investment in S Company	16,000	
	Equity in Earnings of Subsidiary		16,000
	To record share of subsidiary income using the equity method (80 percent × $20,000).		
	Equity in Earnings of Subsidiary	250	
	Investment in S Company		250
	Goodwill on acquisition ($10,000 ÷ 40 = $250).		

Closing Entries—S Company Books

Sales Revenue	50,000	
Costs and Expenses		30,000
Income Summary		20,000
Income Summary	20,000	
Retained Earnings		20,000
Retained Earnings	12,000	
Dividends Paid		12,000

Closing Entries—P Company Books

Equity in Earnings of Subsidiary	15,750	
Retained Earnings (from Income Summary)		15,750

After posting the above entries (Illustration 4–1), the post-closing trial balances at December 31, 19x1, would appear as in Illustration 4–2.

Illustration 4–2
P COMPANY AND S COMPANY
Post-Closing Trial Balances
December 31, 19x1

Debits	P Company	S Company
Assets	$ 83,600	$28,000
Investment in S Company	32,150	
Totals	$115,750	$28,000

Credits

Capital stock—common	$ 30,000	$ 5,000
Retained earnings	85,750	23,000
Totals	$115,750	$28,000

To facilitate the discussion of the relationship between the investment account on the parent company's books and the net assets on the subsidiary's books, the following T-accounts are presented:

Accounts as of January 1, 19x1 (Date of Investment)

Parent's Books
Investment in S Company

19x1	
Jan. 1 26,000	

Subsidiary's Books

Common Stock

19x1
Jan. 1   5,000

Retained Earnings

19x1
Jan. 1 15,000

$20,000
80 percent of which is $16,000

As of December 31, 19x1

Investment in S Company

19x1		19x1	
Jan. 1	26,000	Oct. 1	9,600
Dec. 31	16,000	Dec. 31	250
Balance	32,150		

Common Stock

19x1
Jan. 1   5,000

Retained Earnings

19x1	19x1
	Jan. 1 15,000
Oct. 1 12,000	Dec. 31 20,000
	Balance 23,000

$28,000
80 percent of which is $22,400

The following is a reconciliation of the investment accounts (inclusive of goodwill) on the parent's books:

On date of investment:

Investment account—at cost	$26,000
80 percent of net assets acquired	16,000
Goodwill—at acquisition	$10,000

One year later:

Investment account—at equity	$32,150
80 percent of net assets of subsidiary	22,400
Goodwill net of amortization ($10,000 − $250)	$ 9,750

From the above it can be seen that under the complete equity method the investment account reflects the original cost of the investment and the parent company's share of all transactions recorded on the books of the subsidiary. Similar treatment will be accorded to subsidiary losses except that the income entry will be reversed.

When the incomplete equity method is used and the goodwill is not recorded on the books of the parent but instead is recorded on the consolidation working paper only (this method is illustrated in Appendix 4–B at the end of this chapter), the difference between the parent's investment account and 80 percent of the net assets of the subsidiary would always be $10,000, the amount of the difference on the date of acquisition.

COST METHOD

Under the cost method, income is recorded when the investee declares a dividend. However, an exception to this practice occurs when an investee pays dividends in excess of what it has earned from the date of the investor's acquisition of the investment. To demonstrate these concepts, the following is assumed:

1. Buymore Corporation purchases 80 percent of the outstanding shares of Expropriated Company, Inc., for $80,000 on January 2, 19x1.
2. Expropriated Company, Inc., earned $50,000 and $20,000 for the years 19x1 and 19x2, respectively. It also paid $40,000 in dividends during each year. Retained earnings prior to 19x1 amounted to $100,000.

Entries on Buymore Corporation's books are as follows:

19x1	Investment in Expropriated Company, Inc.	80,000	
	Cash		80,000
	Cash	32,000	
	Dividend Income		
	(80% of total dividend of $40,000)		32,000
19x2*	Cash	32,000	
	Dividend Income		24,000
	Investment in Expropriated Company, Inc.		8,000

*The computations for 19x2 are:

19x1 income	$50,000
19x2 income	20,000
Total income—cumulative	70,000
Less: 19x1 dividend (prior years)	40,000
Balance	$30,000
Dividend recognition limit—80 percent of balance	$24,000

Under the cost method whenever an investor's cumulative dividends exceed its share of cumulative earnings from the date of its investment, the excess dividends are considered a return of the investment. This problem does not arise under the equity method since all dividends are applied to reduce the investor's investment account.

UNCONSOLIDATED SUBSIDIARIES

Generally, the presentation of consolidated financial statements is mandatory and not elective. *Accounting Research Bulletin (ARB) 51* notes that:

> The purpose of consolidated statements is to present, primarily for the benefit of the shareholders and creditors of the parent company, the results of operations and the financial position of a parent company and its subsidiaries essentially as if the group were a single company with one or more branches or divisions. There is a presumption that consolidated statements are more meaningful than separate statements and that they are usually necessary for a fair presentation when one of the companies in the group directly or indirectly has a controlling financial interest in the other companies.[1]

However, not all subsidiaries are consolidated. *ARB 51* cites the following cases when a subsidiary should *not* be consolidated:

1. Where control is likely to be temporary.[2]
2. Where the subsidiary is in legal reorganization or in bankruptcy.[3]
3. Where a subsidiary is a bank or an insurance company and the parent and other subsidiaries are engaged in manufacturing operations.[4]

APB Opinion 18 sanctions the exclusion of foreign subsidiaries that are expropriated or where exchange restrictions prohibit cash remittances to the parent company.[5]

With the exception of subsidiaries that are expropriated by foreign powers, or that are subject to exchange restrictions or currency blockages, or that are in legal reorganization or in bankruptcy, any unconsolidated subsidiaries must be reported as under the equity method. It is appropriate to use the cost method in the case of the above exceptions. In any event, certain disclosures are required for all unconsolidated subsidiaries. These relate to the results of operations and to the composition of assets and liabilities of the unconsolidated subsidiary.

APB Opinion 18 reinforced and strengthened the requirements of consolidation accounting and the use of the equity method. It contains:

> The Board reaffirms the conclusion that investors should account for investments in common stock of unconsolidated domestic subsidiaries by the equity method in consolidated financial statements, and the Board now extends this conclusion to investments in common stock of all unconsolidated subsidiaries (foreign as well as domestic) in consolidated financial statements. The equity method is not, however, a valid substitute for consolida-

---

[1]AICPA, "Consolidated Financial Statements," *ARB Bulletin No. 51* (New York, 1959), par. 1. Copyright © (1959) by the American Institute of Certified Public Accountants, New York.

[2]Ibid., par. 2.

[3]Ibid.

[4]Ibid., par. 3.

[5]APB, "The Equity Method of Accounting for Investments in Common Stock," *APB Opinion No. 18* (New York: AICPA, 1971), par. 14. Copyright © (1971) by the American Institute of Certified Public Accountants, New York.

tion and should not be used to justify exclusion of a subsidiary when consolidation is otherwise appropriate. The Board also concludes that parent companies should account for investments in the common stock of subsidiaries by the equity method in parent-company financial statements prepared for issuance to stockholders as the financial statements of the primary reporting entity.[6]

Where the fiscal years of a parent corporation and that of a subsidiary differ, *ARB 51* permits consolidation without a need to conform the fiscal years as long as the time difference does not exceed three months. This can be seen from the following:

> A difference in fiscal periods of a parent and a subsidiary does not of itself justify the exclusion of the subsidiary from consolidation. It ordinarily is feasible for the subsidiary to prepare, for consolidation purposes, statements for a period which corresponds with or closely approaches the fiscal period of the parent. However, where the difference is not more than about three months, it usually is acceptable to use, for consolidation purposes, the subsidiary's statements for its fiscal period; when this is done, recognition should be given by disclosure or otherwise to the effect of intervening events which materially affect the financial position or results of operations.[7]

CONSOLIDATION PROCEDURES SUBSEQUENT TO DATE OF ACQUISITION

PARTIALLY OWNED SUBSIDIARY USING THE COMPLETE EQUITY METHOD

Heretofore we have only considered consolidation procedures as of the date of a parent's acquisition of a subsidiary's capital stock. These procedures were limited to the balance sheet only, since consolidated results of operations (income statement) were not yet affected. It is now appropriate to consider consolidation procedures for results of operations.

Two working paper formats are generally used in practice. One format, a traditional debit and credit format, requires *two columns* for each subsidiary that is to be consolidated and becomes lengthy as the number of subsidiaries to be consolidated increases. This type of working paper is illustrated in Appendix 4–D at the end of this chapter. The other format, a three-part working paper in statement format (one column each for parent and subsidiary) is less unwieldy since only *one column* is required for the parent company and one column for each subsidiary. For this reason, the three-part working paper will be the primary format used throughout this text. In either case, the end result (consolidated financial statements prepared from the working papers) would be identical.

There are three methods that are generally used in practice to account for investments in subsidiaries. They are:

1. The *complete equity* method where *all* entries affecting consolidated net income are recorded on the *books* of the parent company. (This method

[6]Ibid.
[7]*ARB 51*, par. 4.

is used exclusively in this chapter and the succeeding chapters dealing with consolidation procedures.)

2. The *incomplete equity* method where the parent company records *only* its share of a subsidiary's net income or losses on its *books* and all other entries affecting consolidated net income are recorded on the consolidated working papers only. (This method is illustrated in Appendix 4–B to this chapter and in appendixes to succeeding chapters.)

3. The *cost* method where the parent company maintains its investment at the price paid for it and all entries affecting consolidated net income are recorded only on the consolidated working papers. (This method is illustrated in Appendix 4–C to this chapter and in appendixes to succeeding chapters.)

Regardless of which method a parent company uses to account for its investments, the consolidated column(s) of the working papers will be identical. Because the trial balance amounts (per books) are different for each method, the adjusting and elimination entries for each method must of necessity differ so that the book amounts are in turn converted to "proper" consolidated amounts. This can be verified by comparing the illustrations in this and succeeding chapters with the illustrations in this and succeeding, related appendixes.

To illustrate the entries necessary to apply the complete equity method, the following assumptions are made:

1. The information used to prepare Illustration 3–18 is now extended to include the results of operations for the year ended December 31, 19x1.

2. The purchase price and the allocation of differences between market values and book values are the same as indicated in Illustration 3–17.

3. Branch, Inc., had a net income of $100,000 for the year ended December 31, 19x1, and it paid dividends of $40,000 during that year.

4. Branch, Inc., uses the first-in, first-out (FIFO) method to account for its inventories, and all inventories on hand on January 1, 19x1, were sold during 19x1. (All subsequent problems in connection with the preparation of consolidated statements, both in the text and in the problem material are to be solved using this assumption, unless indicated otherwise.)

5. Although the interest method is the correct approach for the amortization of the difference between the market value and book value of bonds payable, the straight-line method is used to simplify the illustration.

6. The remaining useful lives of the following assets on January 1, 19x1, were:
   a. Buildings, 40 years.
   b. Equipment, 8 years.
   c. Patent, 10 years.
   d. Goodwill, 40 years.

When the complete equity method is used to account for investments, the following entries are required on the investor's books.

Parent's Books—December 31, 19x1

(1)

Investment in Branch, Inc.	80,000	
Equity in Earnings of Subsidiary		80,000

To record 80 percent of $100,000 earned by Branch, Inc.

(2)

Cash	32,000	
Investment in Branch, Inc.		32,000

To record receipt of cash dividends from Branch, Inc. (80 percent × $40,000).

(3)

Equity in Earnings of Subsidiary	12,800	
Investment in Branch, Inc.		12,800

To write off excess of fair market price paid over the book value of inventories of Branch, Inc., which were sold by it during 19x1. (See Illustration 3–17 for calculation.)

(4)

Equity in Earnings of Subsidiary	200	
Investment in Branch, Inc.		200

To amortize excess paid over remaining useful lives as follows (see page 78):

Building	$16,000 ÷ 40 years =	$ 400
Equipment	(8,000) ÷ 8 years =	(1,000)
Patent	8,000 ÷ 10 years −	800
Total		$ 200

(5)

Equity in Earnings of Subsidiary	1,600	
Investment in Branch, Inc.		1,600

To amortize difference between book value and market value of Bonds Payable over remaining life of bonds on January 1, 19x1 ($8,000 ÷ 5 years = $1,600).

(6)

Equity in Earnings of Subsidiary	1,500	
Investment in Branch, Inc.		1,500

To amortize goodwill ($60,000 ÷ 40 years = $1,500).

It should be noted that:

1. *All entries* affecting a parent company's share of income from a subsidiary are channeled through the equity in earnings and investment accounts. The reasons for this will become obvious as the reader reviews the working papers in this chapter.

2. Entry (3) pertaining to undervalued inventories will not be repeated once the inventories are sold. The subsequent three entries, (4), (5), and (6), will be repeated until the respective useful lives expire or a particular asset is sold.

3. No entry is required on the parent's books for the excess of fair market over book value of the subsidiary's land. Since depreciation is generally not taken on land, the excess will remain unamortized until the land is sold by Branch, Inc. The treatment of this excess when the land is sold will be considered in Chapter 6.

Illustration 4–3
Investment in Branch, Inc.

19x1				19x1			
Jan. 1		Purchase	153,600	Dec. 31	(2)	Dividends	32,000
Dec. 31	(1)	Equity in earnings	80,000	31	(3)	Excess—inventories	12,800
			233,600	31	(4)	Amortization—building, equipment, patent	200
Bal.		185,500		31	(5)	Amortization—bonds payable	1,600
				31	(6)	Amortization—goodwill	1,500
							48,100

Equity in Earnings of Subsidiary

19x1				19x1			
Dec. 31	(3)	Excess inventories	12,800	Dec. 31	(1)	Equity in earnings	80,000
31	(4)	Amortization—building, equipment, patent	200	Balance			63,900
31	(5)	Amortization—bonds payable	1,600				
31	(6)	Amortization—goodwill	1,500				
			16,100				

The ledger account balances for the respective accounts on December 31, 19x1, are given in Illustration 4–3. The Investment in Branch, Inc., account balance can be viewed as an account containing the parent company's share of the subsidiary's net assets at book value on December 31, 19x1, plus/minus the unamortized balances assigned to overvalued and undervalued assets of the subsidiary. This can be seen in Illustration 4–4.

Illustration 4–4: Conceptual analysis
Investment in Branch, Inc.

80 percent of Branch, Inc., net assets on 12/31/X1 (80 percent × $121,000)	96,800	Equipment (7* × $1,000)	7,000
Land	8,000		
Building (39* × $400)	15,600		
Patent (9* × $800)	7,200		
Bonds payable (4* × $1,600)	6,400		
Goodwill (39* × $1,500)	58,500		
	192,500		7,000
Balance	185,500		

*Remaining life at year-end.

From Illustration 4–4 it can be seen that the complete equity method causes the parent company's investment account to reflect the *current* portion of a subsidiary's net assets at book value. It also causes the investment account to be amortized and be partially written-off so that 40 years later all that will remain in the account will be the parent's proportionate share of the subsidiary's net assets.

The consolidated working paper for the year ended December 31, 19x1, is shown in Illustration 4–5. The results of operations for 19x1 of both the parent company and the subsidiary are shown as assumed. The elimination entries for Illustration 4–5 are as follows:

(1)

Equity in Earnings—Subsidiary	63,900	
Dividends Paid—Branch, Inc.		32,000
Investment in Branch, Inc.		31,900

(2)

Cost of Sales (beginning inventory)	12,800	
Retained Earnings (1/1/x1)—Branch, Inc.	7,200	
Land	8,000	
Building	16,000	
Patents	8,000	
Goodwill	60,000	
Bonds Payable	8,000	
Common Stock—Branch, Inc.	32,000	
Additional Paid-In Capital	9,600	
Equipment		8,000
Investment in Branch, Inc.		153,600

(3)

Cost of Sales (depreciation and amortization)	200	
Accumulated Depreciation—Equipment	1,000	
Accumulated Depreciation—Building		400
Patents		800

(4)

Interest Expense	1,600	
Bonds Payable		1,600

(5)

Amortization of Goodwill	1,500	
Goodwill		1,500

In Illustration 4–5 the following is particularly noteworthy:

1. Although only 80 percent of Branch, Inc., is owned by the parent company, *100 percent* of sales, cost of sales, operating expenses, interest expense, and provision for income taxes are carried to the consolidated column. *ARB 51* indicated this to be the preferred treatment since the financial statements are considered to be those of a consolidated entity. This approach requires that the minority interest's share of the subsidiary's net income (20% × $100,000 = $20,000) be subtracted to arrive at consolidated net income (CNI). If not, CNI would have been $233,900 which is $20,000 higher than the correct net income as shown in the first column (taken from the parent company's books).

2. Although the $63,900 equity in earnings of the subsidiary appears on the parent's books, this amount must be eliminated on the consolidation working paper in order to prevent double counting of income because the components of the subsidiary's income are being carried forward to the consolidated column. Note that the amortization entries on the parent's books [entries (3), (4), (5), (6)] are reflected in the $63,900 and that this amount is in turn eliminated on the working paper. Con-

Illustration 4–5

Complete Equity Method
1st Year Subsequent to Acquisition
80% Subsidiary

CHROME SERIAL COMPANY, INC.
Consolidated Working Paper
For the Year Ended December 31, 19x1

	Chrome Serial Co., Inc.	Branch, Inc. (80%)	Eliminations Dr.	Eliminations Cr.	Minority Interest	Consolidated
Income Statement						
Sales	800,000	703,600	(3) 200			1,503,600
Cost of sales	350,000	300,000	(2) 12,800			663,000
Gross margin	450,000	403,600				840,600
Operating expenses	150,000	200,000	(5) 1,500			351,500
Operating income before taxes	300,000	203,600				489,100
Deduct: Interest expense		3,600	(4) 1,600			5,200
Add: Equity in earnings—subsidiary	63,900		(1) 63,900			
Income before income taxes	363,900	200,000				483,900
Provision for income taxes (50%)	150,000	100,000				250,000
						233,900
Minority interest net income					20,000	(20,000)
Net income—carried forward	213,900	100,000			20,000	213,900
Retained Earnings Statement						
Balance, 1/1/x1:						
Chrome Serial Co., Inc.	473,600					473,600
Branch, Inc.		9,000	(2) 7,200		1,800	
Net income—brought forward	213,900	100,000			20,000	213,900
Total	687,500	109,000			21,800	687,500
Less: Dividends paid						
Chrome Serial Co., Inc.	110,000					110,000
Branch, Inc.		40,000		(1) 32,000	8,000	
Balance, 12/31/x1—carried forward	577,500	69,000			13,800	577,500
Balance Sheet						
Cash in bank	98,500	40,000				138,500
Accounts receivable (net of estimated uncollectables)	100,000	45,000				145,000
Inventories	80,000	30,000				110,000
Land	70,000	10,000	(2) 8,000			88,000
Building (net of depreciation)	116,000	48,750	(2) 16,000	(3) 400		180,350
Equipment (net of depreciation)	250,000	26,250	(3) 1,000	(2) 8,000		269,250
Patents			(2) 8,000	(3) 800		7,200
Goodwill			(2) 60,000	(5) 1,500		58,500
				(2) 153,600		
Investment in Branch, Inc.	185,500			(1) 31,900		
Totals	900,000	200,000				996,800
Liabilities and Stockholders' Equity						
Accounts payable and other liabilities	122,500	27,400				149,900
8% bonds payable ($50,000)		51,600	(2) 8,000	(4) 1,600		45,200
Common stock:						
Chrome Serial Co., Inc.	200,000					200,000
Branch, Inc.		40,000	(2) 32,000		8,000	
Additional paid-in capital		12,000	(2) 9,600		2,400	
Retained earnings—brought forward	577,500	69,000			13,800	577,500
Minority interest					24,200	24,200
Totals	900,000	200,000	229,800	229,800		996,800

Illustration 4–5 *(continued)*

(1) To eliminate equity in earnings of subsidiary to prevent double counting of income; to eliminate parent's share of dividends paid and convert year-end balance of investment to beginning of the year balance.

(2) To eliminate balance of investment and to allocate excess in accordance with Illustration 3–16 except that inventory excess is charged to cost of sales since the inventory was sold in 19x1. [See journal entry (3) on parent's books as of December 31, 19x1.]

(3) To record amortization of excess for building, equipment, and patent. (See journal entry (4) on parent's books as of December 31, 19x1.)

(4) To record amortization of excess for bonds payable. [See journal entry (5) on parent's books as of December 31, 19x1.]

(5) To record amortization of Goodwill. [See journal entry (6) on parent's books as of December 31, 19x1.]

sequently, the amortization entries *must be repeated on the working paper* because along with the elimination of the $63,900 equity in earnings of subsidiary amount, they have been eliminated as well. Without the reinstatement of the elimination entries, CNI would *not* be $213,900. It should be borne in mind that CNI must *always* be equal to the parent's net income whenever the complete equity method is used. (Methods other than complete equity are discussed in appendixes B and C at the end of this chapter.)

3. Interest expense on the books of the subsidiary consists of the cash payment of $4,000 (8% × $50,000) minus the amortization of the bond premium in the amount of $400 ($2,000 ÷ 5 years). In consolidation, the $3,600 is increased by the amortization of $1,600 of the excess of book value over the market value of bonds payable. As already mentioned in the preceding chapter, the market rate of interest of the bonds payable is much higher than their stated rate of 8 percent (hence the discount of 80% × $10,000 or $8,000). Since the market rate of interest at the time of acquisition was higher than the adjusted stated rate of the bonds payable, the interest expense on a consolidated basis must exceed the interest expense on the subsidiary's books. (For a further discussion of this subject see Chapter 7.)

4. The provision for income taxes of the parent company is 50 percent of its income exclusive if its share of subsidiary earnings. Since the subsidiary accrued taxes on its own income, accrual by the parent on this income would have amounted to a double accrual. A discussion of the subject of consolidated tax returns versus separate corporate tax returns and of the impact of that decision on the consolidated provision for income taxes is contained in Appendix 4–A of this Chapter and Appendix 5–A of Chapter 5. In any event, the provision in Illustration 4–5 in the amount of $250,000 is not 50 percent of $483,900 (income before income taxes). In this context it should be borne in mind that the amortization of goodwill (per working paper of $1,500) is never deductible for tax purposes. The deductibility of the remaining items (amortization of building excess, equipment excess, etc.) involves tax complexities that are beyond the scope of this work.[8]

---

[8]An excellent text dealing with these matters is Boris I. Bittker and James S. Eustice, *Federal Income Taxation of Corporations and Shareholders*, latest ed. (Boston: Warren Gorham and Lamont).

5. The net income amounts in *all* columns (except the eliminations columns) are carried forward to the retained earnings statement. For easier identification, this is indicated by an arrow on the right-hand side of the working paper.

6. Entry (1) in the elimination columns converts the investment balance to the *beginning of the year* balance ($153,600). Therefore, the parent's 80 percent share of beginning retained earnings is eliminated. The minority interest's share of $1,800 is extended to the minority interest column. The same treatment is accorded dividends paid by the subsidiary. Thus, entry (1) eliminates 80 percent (the parent's share), and $8,000 (the minority interest's share) is extended as a *reduction* of minority interest. Just as their share of the income earned increases the minority's interest, so the receipt of dividends reduces their interest.

7. When the complete equity methods is used, consolidated retained earnings (beginning and ending) is always equal to the retained earnings (beginning and ending) on the parent company's books.

8. For the reason in 7 immediately above and the reason cited earlier in 1 above regarding CNI, if Chrome Serial Company, Inc., could not consolidate Branch, Inc., but was required to use the equity method—such as, if Branch, Inc., were a bank instead of a manufacturer—the financial statements of Chrome would be prepared from the first column (per its books). The results of operations ($213,900) and retained earnings would be the same as in consolidated statements, except the details (sales, cost of sales, etc.) would be different. This use of the equity method without consolidation is sometimes referred to as *one-line consolidation.*

9. The ending balances of retained earnings in all four columns are carried forward to the respective balance sheets (a treatment similar to the transfer of net income to retained earnings).

10. The following are *never* carried across to the consolidated column.
    a. Investment in Branch, Inc.
    b. Subsidiary capital stock.
    c. Subsidiary additional paid-in capital.
    d. Subsidiary retained earnings.

11. The minority interest can be verified independently by computing 20 percent of the subsidiary's net assets at the *end of the year.* The calculations are:

Capital stock	$ 40,000
APIC	12,000
Retained earnings	69,000
Total	$121,000
20% of above	$ 24,200

12. Elimination entry (2) in this example sets up the unamortized balances of allocated excess at the *beginning of the year.* A step can be saved by combining entries (3), (4), and (5) with entry (2). Thus, if the allocated excess at the *end* of the year were set up, i.e., $15,600 for building,

$7,200 for patent, etc., this results in a short cut. To promote a full understanding of these entries, it is recommended that the extra steps be performed in the initial stages of a student's study of this subject.

For 19x2, it is now assumed that Branch, Inc., earned $80,000 and paid no dividends. The investment account balance would be increased by $64,000 (80% of $80,000). Referring back to the journal entries on the parent's books as of December 31, 19x1 (see page 98), it should be noted that for 19x2 entry (2) is not required (no dividends were paid) and entry (3) is no longer required (the inventory was sold in 19x1). Entries (4), (5), and (6) would be repeated in 19x2. Therefore, the Investment in Branch, Inc., would have a balance of $246,200 on December 31, 19x2 (the beginning balance of $185,500 + $64,000 − $200 − $1,600 − $1,500). The Equity in Earnings of Subsidiary on December 31, 19x2, would be $60,700 ($64,000 − $200 − $1,600 − $1,500).

The working paper elimination entries for 19x2 would be:[9]

(1)		
Equity in Earnings—Subsidiary	60,700	
Investment in Branch, Inc.		60,700

(2)		
Retained Earnings (1/1/x2)—Branch, Inc. (80% × $69,000)	55,200	
Land	8,000	
Building	16,000	
Patents	7,200	
Goodwill	58,500	
8 Percent Bonds Payable	6,400	
Common Stock (80% × $40,000)	32,000	
Additional Paid-In Capital (80% × $12,000)	9,600	
Accumulated Depreciation—Equipment	1,000	
Equipment		8,000
Investment in Branch, Inc.		185,500
Accumulated Depreciation—Building		400

(3)		
Cost of Sales	200	
Accumulated Depreciation—Equipment	1,000	
Accumulated Depreciation—Building		400
Patents		800

(4)		
Interest Expense	1,600	
8 Percent Bonds Payable		1,600

(5)		
Operating Expenses	1,500	
Goodwill		1,500

The above entries should be compared with the comparable entries in Illustration 4–5. It can be seen that the setting up of the allocated excess in each category is the unamortized balance of the category at the *beginning* of the current year. Entries (3), (4), and (5) are repetitive.

---

[9]Explanations of these entries are similar to those found in Illustration 4–5.

MINORITY INTEREST

Normally, operating losses of a subsidiary are charged proportionately to majority (parent) and to minority interests. On rare occasions, the subsidiary's loss may be of such a magnitude as to completely eliminate the minority's share of the equity and then some. What disposition should be made of this *negative* minority interest balance? *ARB 51* clearly indicates that this negative amount should be charged against the parent's interest and that subsequent profits up to this negative amount should be credited to the parent's interest before the minority interest is restored to a positive position. The bulletin states:

> In the unusual case in which losses applicable to the minority interest in a subsidiary exceed the minority interest in the equity capital of the subsidiary, such excess and any further losses applicable to the minority interest should be charged against the majority interest, as there is no obligation of the minority interest to make good such losses. However, if future earnings do materialize, the majority interest should be credited to the extent of such losses previously absorbed.[10]

INTERCOMPANY TRANSACTIONS

When a parent and subsidiary have intercompany transactions (as is usual), additional elimination entries become necessary. Since a major objective of consolidated statements is to present the financial statements of a single economic unit (entity), transactions between members of the affiliated group must be eliminated or reversed. If consolidated statements are to be useful, the statements must be limited to transactions with parties other than members of the affiliated group, since transactions among affiliated members may lack objective economic substance.

Illustration 4–6 represents a working paper which includes typical intercompany transactions. Reference to this illustration will clarify the need for the additional elimination entries. The working paper elimination entries for Illustration 4–6 are as follows:

(1)

Equity in Earnings—Subsidiary	62,208	
Dividends Declared—Right Corporation		36,000
Investment in Right Corporation		26,208

(2)

Retained Earnings (1/1/x2)—Right Corporation	225,000	
Capital Stock—Right Corporation	180,000	
Investment in Right Corporation		405,000

(3)

Interest Income	4,800	
Interest Expense		4,800

(4)

Sales	80,000	
Cost of Sales		80,000

[10]Ibid., par. 15.

Illustration 4–6
BAKE CORPORATION
Consolidated Working Paper
For the Year Ended December 31, 19x2

Complete Equity Method
90 Percent Subsidiary

	Bake Corp.	Right Corp. (90%)	Eliminations Dr.	Eliminations Cr.	Minority Interest	Consol- idated
Income Statement						
Sales	800,000	300,000	(4) 80,000			1,020,000
Cost of sales	400,000	100,000		(4) 80,000		420,000
Gross margin	400,000	200,000				600,000
Expenses	180,000	80,000				260,000
Operating income before taxes	220,000	120,000				340,000
Equity in earnings— subsidiary	62,208		(1) 62,208			
Interest income	4,800		(3) 4,800			
Interest expense (deduction)		4,800		(3) 4,800		
Income before income taxes	287,008	115,200				
Provision for income taxes (40%)	89,920	46,080				136,000
						204,000
Minority interest net income					6,912	(6,912)
Net income—carried forward	197,088	69,120	147,008	84,800	6,912	197,088
Retained Earnings Statement						
Balance, 1/1/x2:						
Bake Corp.	400,000					400,000
Right Corp.		250,000	(2) 225,000		25,000	
Net income—brought forward	197,088	69,120	147,008	84,800	6,912	197,008
Totals	597,088	319,120			31,912	597,088
Less: Dividends declared:						
Bake Corp.	100,000					100,000
Right Corp.		40,000		(1) 36,000	4,000	
Balance 12/31/x2—carried forward	497,088	279,120	372,008	120,800	27,912	497,088
Balance Sheet						
Cash	111,000	50,000				161,000
Notes receivable	80,000			(6) 60,000		20,000
Accounts receivable (net)	100,000	80,000		(5) 40,000		140,000
Inventories	90,000	70,000				160,000
Investment in Right Corp.	431,208			(2) 405,000		
				(1) 26,208		
Other assets	375,880	429,120				805,000
Dividends receivable	9,000			(7) 9,000		
Totals	1,197,088	629,120				1,286,000
Notes payable	160,000	60,000	(6) 60,000			160,000
Accounts payable	90,000	50,000	(5) 40,000			100,000
Other liabilities—accruals	50,000	40,000	(7) 9,000			81,000
Capital stock:						
Bake Corp.	400,000					400,000
Right Corp.		200,000	(2) 180,000		20,000	
Retained earnings—brought forward	497,088	279,120	372,008	120,800	27,912	497,088
Minority interest					47,912	47,912
Totals	1,197,088	629,120	661,008	661,008		1,286,000

Illustration 4–6 *(continued)*

(1) To eliminate equity in earnings of subsidiary to prevent double counting of income; to eliminate parent's share of dividends paid and to convert year-end balance of investment to beginning of the year balance.

(2) To eliminate the balance of the investment.

(3) To eliminate intercompany interest transactions to prevent double counting.

(4) To eliminate intercompany sales.

(5) To eliminate intercompany receivables and payables on open account.

(6) To eliminate intercompany notes outstanding.

(7) To eliminate intercompany unpaid dividends.

(5)		
Accounts Payable	40,000	
Accounts Receivable		40,000
(6)		
Notes Payable	60,000	
Notes Receivable		60,000
(7)		
Other Liabilities (accruals)	9,000	
Dividends Receivable		9,000

The following observations should prove useful for understanding of Illustration 4–6:

1. Entries (1) and (2) are the usual elimination entries for an equity method working paper.

2. Although entry (3) has no effect on the net income of the consolidated entity, it nevertheless is necessary to eliminate the inference that the entity had interest income from, and paid interest expense to, outsiders. This entry eliminated intercompany interest income and expense.

3. The elimination of intercompany sales and purchases in entry (4) is necessary to prevent a double counting of these items.

4. Intercompany receivables and payables must be eliminated as shown in entries (5), (6), and (7).

5. Consolidated net income is the same as Bake's net income.

6. The minority interest of $47,912 is equal to 10 percent of Right's ending stockholders' equity ($200,000 + $279,120 = $479,120).

7. The adjustment columns were subtotaled after each statement. This variation is sometimes used by accountants.

Appendix 4–A: Income tax implications between parents and subsidiaries

Taxability of dividends

Section 243 of the Internal Revenue Code provides that under certain conditions, a parent corporation is entitled to a 100 percent deduction for dividends received from its subsidiaries. The problems used in this chapter, including the illustrative problems, were all prepared under the assumption that all earnings of subsidiaries will ultimately be remitted to the parent corporation and that the parent corporation will be entitled to this 100 percent dividends received deduction. A review of Illustration 4–5 will reveal that a 50 percent tax rate was assumed for both the parent and the subsidiary in each illustration. Notice that income taxes were *not* accrued for dividend income from the subsidiary on the parent's books. Similarly, income taxes were also *not* accrued for the parent's share of subsidiary income in Illustration 4–5, since the taxes on that income were accrued by the subsidiary and it will be liable for them on its own tax return.

In Illustration 4–6 it was assumed that the tax rate is 40 percent and that the parent company and the subsidiary will file separate corporate income tax returns. Accordingly, the interest income and interest expense would be taxable and deductible on the separately filed tax returns and the 40 percent tax accrual reflects the tax status of these items. A review of the consolidated column shows the tax provision at $136,000 which is 40 percent of $340,000 (consolidated operating income before taxes).

Undistributed earnings of subsidiaries

APB Opinion 23 contains the following:

> Including undistributed earnings of a subsidiary in the pretax accounting income of a parent company, either through consolidation or accounting for the investment by the equity method, may result in a timing difference . . . .[11]

> It should be presumed that all undistributed earnings of a subsidiary will be transferred to the parent company. Accordingly, the undistributed earnings of a subsidiary included in consolidated income should be accounted for as a timing difference, except to the extent that some or all of the undistributed earnings meet the criteria in paragraph 12 (indefinite reversal criteria—see below).[12]

This suggested treatment coincides with the approach used in this chapter. It was assumed that the undistributed earnings were timing differences and the appropriate tax rate (100 percent exclusion—no tax) was used to accrue the provision for income taxes on the timing difference. However, if a parent does *not* qualify for the 100 percent dividends received deduction, it should accrue income taxes on

---

[11]*APB,* "Accounting for Income Taxes—Special Areas," *APB Opinion No. 23* (New York: AICPA 1972), par. 9.
[12]Ibid.

the timing difference using the 85 percent exclusion (15 percent would be taxable) if the subsidiary were a domestic corporation or use foreign tax credits for foreign subsidiaries.

APB Opinion 23 also states:

The presumption that all undistributed earnings will be transferred to the parent company may be overcome, and no income taxes should be accrued by the parent company, if sufficient evidence shows that the subsidiary has invested or will invest the undistributed earnings indefinitely or that the earnings will be remitted in a tax-free liquidation. A parent company should have evidence of specific plans for reinvestment of undistributed earnings of a subsidiary which demonstrate that remttance of the earnings will be postponed indefinitely. Experience of the companies and definite future programs of operations and remittances are examples of the types of evidence required to substantiate the parent company's representation of indefinite postponement of remittances from a subsidiary. If circumstances change and it becomes apparent that some or all of the undistributed earnings of a subsidiary will be remitted in the foreseeable future but income taxes have not been recognized by the parent company, it should accrue as an expense of the current period income taxes attributable to that remittance; income tax expense for such undistributed earnings should not be accounted for as an extraordinary item. If it becomes apparent that some or all of the undistributed earnings of a subsidiary on which income taxes have been accrued will not be remitted in the foreseeable future, the parent company should adjust income tax expense of the current period; such adjustment of income tax expense should not be accounted for as an extraordinary item.[13]

Accordingly, if it appears that the undistributed earnings are invested indefinitely in the subsidiary, such as an investment in real estate used in the business or other long-term assets, and if it appears that the subsidiary is expanding by using its own retained earnings, no income taxes should be accrued on this timing difference. Any changes in circumstances should be treated as indicated in the preceding paragraph.

---

[13]Ibid., par. 12.

Appendix 4-B: Incomplete equity method

Aside from the *complete equity* method of consolidation which is used in the chapter, another prevalent method that is found in practice is the *incomplete equity* method. Users of this method record dividends received and their share of income as is done in the complete equity method [see entries (1) and (2) on the parent's books in the chapter]. However, none of the other entries for amortization, write-offs, etc.—e.g., entries (3), (4), (5), and (6)—are recorded on the books of the parent company. Since entries (3), (4), (5), and (6) must be recorded on the working papers under either method, the users of the incomplete method save bookkeeping effort by *not* recording entries (3) through (6) on the parent's books. However, the saving in labor is not without cost. When these entries are not recorded on the books, parent net income is not equal to CNI and a reconciliation of the two is highly recommended. In any event, CNI must be the same under either method. To demonstrate this method, the same data as used in Illustration 4–5 is now used except that only entries (1) and (2) are assumed to have been made on the parent company's books. Therefore, the balance in Investment in Branch, Inc., is $201,600 ($153,600 + $80,000 income − $32,000 dividends) on December 31, 19x1. The equity in earnings of subsidiary is $80,000, the amount from entry (1) (see page 98). The working paper elimination entries for Illustration 4–7 are:

(1)		
Equity in Earnings—Subsidiary	80,000	
Dividend Paid—Branch, Inc.		32,000
Investment in Branch, Inc.		48,000

(2)		
Cost of Sales (beginning inventory)	12,800	
Retained Earnings (1/1/x1)— Branch, Inc.	7,200	
Land	8,000	
Building	16,000	
Patents	8,000	
Goodwill	60,000	
Bonds Payable	8,000	
Common Stock—Branch, Inc.	32,000	
Additional Paid-In Capital	9,600	
Equipment		8,000
Investment in Branch, Inc.		153,600

(3)		
Cost of Sales (depreciation and amortization)	200	
Accumulated Depreciation— Equipment	1,000	
Accumulated Depreciation—Building		400
Patents		800

(4)		
Interest Expense	1,600	
Bonds Payable		1,600

(5)		
Amortization of Goodwill	1,500	
Goodwill		1,500

A review of Illustration 4–7 reveals that:

1. The second column (Branch, Inc.) is identical to the one in Illustration 4–5.
2. Entry (1) on the working paper is similar to entry (1) in Illustration 4–5, except that the amount of subsidiary earnings recognized by the parent company on its books is different.
3. Entries (2), (3), (4), and (5) on the working paper are identical to those entries in Illustration 4–5.
4. The minority interest column and the consoli-

Illustration 4–7
CHROME SERIAL COMPANY, INC.
Consolidated Working Paper
For the Year Ended December 31, 19x1

Incomplete Equity Method
1st Year Subsequent to Acquisition
80 Percent Subsidiary

	Chrome Serial Co., Inc.	Branch, Inc. (80%)	Eliminations Dr.	Eliminations Cr.	Minority Interest	Consol- idated
Income Statement						
Sales	800,000	703,600				1,503,600
			(3) 200			
Cost of sales	350,000	300,000	(2) 12,800			663,000
Gross margin	450,000	403,600				840,600
Operating expenses	150,000	200,000	(5) 1,500			351,500
Operating income before taxes	300,000	203,600				489,100
Deduct: Interest expense		3,600	(4) 1,600			5,200
Add: Equity in earnings—subsidiary	80,000		(1) 80,000			
Income before income taxes	380,000	200,000				483,900
Provision for income taxes (50%)	150,000	100,000				250,000
						233,900
Minority interest net income					20,000	(20,000)
Net income—carried forward	230,000	100,000			20,000	213,900
Retained Earnings Statement						
Balance, 1/1/x1:						
Chrome Serial Co., Inc.	473,600					473,600
Branch, Inc.		9,000	(2) 7,200		1,800	
Net income—brought forward	230,000	100,000			20,000	213,900
Total	703,600	109,000			21,800	687,500
Less: Dividends paid:						
Chrome Serial Co., Inc.	110,000					110,000
Branch, Inc.		40,000		(1) 32,000	8,000	
Balance, 12/31/x1—carried forward	593,600	69,000			13,800	577,500
Balance Sheet						
Cash in bank	98,500	40,000				138,500
Accounts receivable (net of estimated uncollectables)	100,000	45,000				145,000
Inventories	80,000	30,000				110,000
Land	70,000	10,000	(2) 8,000			88,000
Building (net of depreciation)	116,000	48,750	(2) 16,000	(3) 400		180,350
Equipment (net of depreciation)	250,000	26,250	(3) 1,000	(2) 8,000		269,250
Patents			(2) 8,000	(3) 800		7,200
Goodwill			(2) 60,000	(5) 1,500		58,500
				(2) 153,600		
Investment in Branch, Inc.	201,600			(1) 48,000		
Totals	916,100	200,000				996,800
Liabilities and Stockholders' Equity						
Accounts payable and other liabilities	122,500	27,400				149,900
8 percent bonds payable ($50,000)		51,600	(2) 8,000	(4) 1,600		45,200
Common stock:						
Chrome Serial Co., Inc.	200,000					200,000
Branch, Inc.		40,000	(2) 32,000		8,000	
Additional paid-in capital		12,000	(2) 9,600		2,400	
Retained earnings—brought forward	593,600	69,000			13,800	577,500
Minority interest					24,200	24,000
Totals	916,100	200,000	245,900	245,900		996,800

Illustration 4–7 (continued)

(1) To eliminate equity in earnings of subsidiary to prevent double counting of income; to eliminate parent's share of dividends paid and convert year-end balance of investment to beginning of the year balance.

(2) To eliminate balance of investment and to allocate excess in accordance with Illustration 3–16 except that inventory excess is charged to cost of sales since the inventory was sold in 19x1. [See journal entry (3) on parent's books as of December 31, 19x1.]

(3) To record amortization of excess for building, equipment, and patent. [See journal entry (4) on parent's books as of December 31, 19x1.]

(4) To record amortization of excess for bonds payable. [See journal entry (5) on parent's books as of December 31, 19x1.]

(5) To record amortization of goodwill. [See journal entry (6) on parent's books as of December 31, 19x1.]

---

dated column are identical to those respective columns in Illustration 4–5.

Whenever the incomplete equity method is used, it is highly desirable to reconcile parent net income with CNI and parent retained earnings with consolidated retained earnings. This can be accomplished as follows:

Parent net income	$230,000
Adjustments for:	
Inventory excess sold	(12,800)
Building amortization	(400)
Equipment amortization	1,000
Patent amortization	(800)
Goodwill amortization	(1,500)
Bonds payable amortization	(1,600)
CNI	$213,900
Parent—retained earnings, December 31, 19x1	$593,600
Less: Sum of above adjustments	(16,100)
Consolidated retained earnings	$577,500

For years after the first year, entries (2), (3), (4), and (5) on the working paper will *not be the same* for the two equity methods. The reason for this is that users of the complete equity method amortize and write off allocated amounts of excess on their books, and these amounts find their way into parent retained earnings when closing entries on the books are made, whereas users of the incomplete equity method do not make these entries. Therefore, the latter approach requires adjustments to parent retained earnings for accumulated amounts of amortization and write-offs, except for the current year's portion, in order to conform parent retained earnings (per books) to the amount shown in the preceding year's working papers. The amount of these adjustments will equal the amount shown in the reconciliation of retained earnings ($16,100). Using the same information for 19x2 as used in the chapter (subsidiary's net income of $80,000 and no dividends paid), the parent company records only its equity in the earnings of the subsidiary in the amount of $64,000 (80% × $80,000). The Investment in Branch, Inc., account on December 31, 19x2, now amounts

to $265,600 ($201,600 + $64,000). The *working paper* elimination entries for 19x2 would then be:

(1)

Equity in earnings—Subsidiary	64,000	
Investment in Branch, Inc.		64,000

(2)

Retained Earnings 1/1/x2—		
Parent	12,800	
Retained Earnings 1/1/x2—		
Branch, Inc. (80% × $69,000)	55,200	
Land	8,000	
Building	16,000	
Patents	8,000	
Goodwill	60,000	
8 Percent Bonds Payable	8,000	
Common Stock (80% × $40,000)	32,000	
Additional Paid-In Capital	9,600	
Equipment		8,000
Investment in Branch, Inc.		201,600

(3)

Retained Earnings (beginning)—		
Parent (prior years' amortization)	200	
Cost of Sales (current year's amortization)	200	
Accumulated Depreciation—		
Equipment ($1,000 × 2 years)	2,000	
Accumulated Depreciation—Building (2 × $400)		800
Patents (2 × $800)		1,600

(4)

Interest Expense (current year's portion)	1,600	
Retained Earnings (beginning)—		
Parent (prior years' portion)	1,600	
8 Percent Bonds Payable (2 × $1,600)		3,200

(5)

Operating Expenses (current year's portion)	1,500	
Retained Earnings (beginning)—		
Parent (prior years' portion)	1,500	
Goodwill (2 × $1,500)		3,000

The total adjustment to parent retained earnings on the working paper in year 19x2 would amount to $16,100 as noted earlier in the reconciliation and can be proven as follows:

From entry (2) above	$12,800
From entry (3) above	200
From entry (4) above	1,600
From entry (5) above	1,500
	$16,100

Appendix 4–C: Cost method—partially owned subsidiaries

A parent company can account for its investment in a subsidiary in different ways. *Unconsolidated* subsidiaries *must be* accounted for by the complete equity method unless they are in bankruptcy or have been expropriated, etc. Thus, viable subsidiaries (banks, insurance companies, etc.) of manufacturing or merchandising companies that are not consolidated must be handled in this manner. Consolidated subsidiaries, however, can be accounted for either by an equity method or the cost method, since the end result (consolidated financial statements) would be the same using either method.

It is now assumed that the Chrome Serial Company, Inc., as shown in Illustration 4–5, accounts for its investment in Branch, Inc., using the cost method. Accordingly, its investment account balance will be maintained at $153,600; the purchase price and dividends received from Branch, Inc., will be treated as income. The only entry made on the parent company's books would then be:

(1)

Cash	32,000	
Dividend Income		32,000

Illustration 4–8 contains the consolidated working paper for the cost method, and the elimination entries contained therein are:

(1)

Dividend Income	32,000	
Dividends Paid—Branch, Inc.		32,000

(2)

Cost of Sales (beginning inventory)	12,800	
Retained Earnings (1/1/x1)— Branch, Inc.	7,200	
Land	8,000	
Building	16,000	
Patents	8,000	
Goodwill	60,000	
Bonds Payable	8,000	
Common Stock—Branch, Inc. .	32,000	
Additional Paid-In Capital	9,600	
Equipment		8,000
Investment in Branch, Inc.		153,600

(3)

Cost of Sales (depreciation and amortization)	200	
Accumulated Depreciation— Equipment	1,000	
Accumulated Depreciation—Building .		400
Patents		800

(4)

Interest Expense	1,600	
Bonds Payable		1,600

(5)

Amortization of Goodwill	1,500	
Goodwill		1,500

The following should be noted:

1. Entry (1) eliminates the dividend income since it is not income from an entity viewpoint.
2. Entries (2), (3), (4), and (5) are the same as shown in Illustration 4–5 for the complete equity method and in Illustration 4–7 as shown for the incomplete equity method.
3. The *consolidated* financial statements (column) are the same for the cost method, the incomplete equity method, and the complete equity method.

Illustration 4–8

Cost Method
1st Year Subsequent to Acquisition
80 Percent Subsidiary

CHROME SERIAL COMPANY, INC.
Consolidated Working Paper
For the Year Ended December 31, 19x1

	Chrome Serial Co., Inc.	Branch, Inc. (80%)	Eliminations Dr.	Eliminations Cr.	Minority Interest	Consolidated
Income Statement						
Sales	800,000	703,600	(3) 200			1,503,600
Cost of sales	350,000	300,000	(2) 12,800			663,000
Gross margin	450,000	403,600				840,600
Operating expenses	150,000	200,000	(5) 1,500			351,500
Operating income before taxes	300,000	203,600				489,100
Deduct: Interest expense		3,600	(4) 1,600			5,200
Add: Dividend income	32,000		(1) 32,000			
Income before income taxes	332,000	200,000				483,900
Provision for income taxes (50%)	150,000	100,000				250,000
						233,900
Minority interest net income					20,000	(20,000)
Net income—carried forward	182,000	100,000			20,000	213,900
Retained Earnings Statement						
Balance, 1/1/x1						
Chrome Serial Co., Inc.	473,600					473,600
Branch, Inc.		9,000	(2) 7,200		1,800	
Net income—brought forward	182,000	100,000			20,000	213,900
Total	655,600	109,000			21,800	687,500
Less: Dividends paid:						
Chrome Serial Co., Inc.	110,000					110,000
Branch, Inc.		40,000		(1) 32,000	8,000	
Balance, 12/31/x1—carried forward	545,600	69,000			13,800	577,500
Balance Sheet						
Cash in bank	98,500	40,000				138,500
Accounts receivable (net of estimated uncollectibles)	100,000	45,000				145,000
Inventories	80,000	30,000				110,000
Land	70,000	10,000	(2) 8,000			88,000
Building (net of depreciation)	116,000	48,750	(2) 16,000	(3) 400		180,350
Equipment (net of depreciation)	250,000	26,250	(3) 1,000	(2) 8,000		269,250
Patents			(2) 8,000	(3) 800		7,200
Goodwill			(2) 60,000	(5) 1,500		58,500
Investment in Branch, Inc.	153,600			(2) 153,600		
Totals	868,100	200,000				996,800
Liabilities and Stockholders' Equity						
Accounts payable and other liabilities	122,500	27,400				149,900
8 percent bonds payable ($50,000)		51,600	(2) 8,000	(4) 1,600		45,200
Common Stock:						
Chrome Serial Co., Inc.	200,000					200,000
Branch, Inc.		40,000	(2) 32,000		8,000	
Additional paid-in capital		12,000	(2) 9,600		2,400	
Retained earnings—brought forward	545,600	69,000			13,800	577,500
Minority interest					24,200	24,200
Totals	868,100	200,000	197,900	197,900		996,800

Illustration 4–8 *(continued)*

(1) To eliminate dividend income and parent's share of dividends paid by subsidiary.

(2) To eliminate balance of investment and to allocate excess in accordance with Illustration 3–16 except that inventory excess is charged to cost of sales since the inventory was sold in 19x1. [See journal entry (3) on parent's books as of December 31, 19x1.]

(3) To record amortization of excess for building, equipment, and patent. [See journal entry (4) on parent's books as of December 31, 19x1.]

(4) To record amortization of excess for bonds payable [See journal entry (5) on parent's books as of December 31, 19x1.]

(5) To record amortization of goodwill. [See journal entry (6) on parent's books as of December 31, 19x1.]

Whenever the cost method is used, it is highly advisable that a reconciliation be made between parent net income and consolidated net income. The reconciliation can be made as follows:

Parent net income	$182,000
Add: 80 percent of subsidiary's retained	
income of $60,000 ($100,000 earned less	
dividends of $40,000 = $60,000)	48,000
Adjustments for write-offs and amortization:	
Inventory excess sold in 19x1	(12,800)
Building amortization	(400)
Equipment amortization	1,000
Patent amortization	(800)
8 percent bonds payable amortization	(1,600)
Goodwill amortization	(1,500)
CNI	$213,900

A reconciliation of parent retained earnings (per books) would be:

Parent retained earnings, December 31, 19x1 .	$545,600
Add: Subsidiary's not recorded by parent—as	
above	48,000
Less: Adjustments—as above	(16,100)
Consolidated retained earnings, December 31,	
19x1	$577,500

The elimination entries on the working paper for 19x2 assuming that Branch, Inc., earned $80,000 and paid no dividends during 19x2 would be:

(1)

Investment in Branch, Inc. . . .	48,000	
Retained Earnings		
(1/1/x2)—Parent		48,000

To record the parent's share of the increase in net assets of the subsidiary.

Branch, Inc.—		
retained		
earnings		
(1/1/x2)	$69,000	
Branch, Inc.—		
retained		
earnings (at		
date of		
acquisition) . .	9,000	
Increase in		
net assets	$60,000	
Parent's share—		
80 percent . .	$48,000	

(2)

Retained Earnings (1/1/x2)—		
Parent	12,800	
Retained Earnings (1/1/x2)—		
Branch, Inc. (80% × $69,000)	55,200	
Land	8,000	
Building	16,000	
Patents	8,000	
Goodwill	60,000	
8 Percent Bonds Payable	8,000	
Common Stock (80% × $40,000)	32,000	
Additional Paid In Capital		
(80% × $12,000)	9,600	
Equipment		8,000
Investment in Branch, Inc.		201,600

(3)

Retained Earnings (1/1/x2)—		
Parent (prior years'		
amortization)	200	
Cost of Sales (current year's		
amortization)	200	
Accumulated Depreciation—		
Equipment (2 × $1,000) . . .	2,000	
Accumulated		
Depreciation—Building		
(2 × $400)		800
Patents (2 × $800)		1,600

(4)

Interest Expense (current year's portion)	1,600	
Retained Earnings (1/1/x2)—		
Parent (prior years' portion) .	1,600	
8 Percent Bonds Payable (2 × $1,600)		3,200

(5)

Operating Expenses (current year's portion)	1,500	
Retained Earnings (1/1/x2)—		
Parent (prior years' portion) .	1,500	
Goodwill (2 × $1,500)		3,000

Although entry (1) above is in the same amount ($48,000) as that required in the reconciliation of parent net income to CNI, this will only be true for the first year subsequent to the acquisition. For later years, the *cumulative* amount is required. Therefore, the format in entry (1) is recommended. The retained earnings of the subsidiary at the *beginning* of a particular year should be compared with the retained earnings of the subsidiary on the date of acquisition and the difference should be computed. Then, the parent's share of that difference becomes the basis of entry (1). The remaining adjustments to parent retained earnings is the sum of the adjustments ($16,100) from entries (2), (3), (4), and (5). After these adjustments are recorded on the working paper for 19x2, the parent's beginning retained earnings in the first column of the working paper (the amount would be $545,600, shown as closing retained earnings for 19x1 in Illustration 4–8, first column) would coincide with the closing *consolidated* retained earnings of $577,500 for 19x1 (also shown in Illustration 4–8). Thus, the consolidated retained earnings statement for 19x2 will have as its beginning balance, $577,500 (also the 19x1 closing balance). These amounts can be reconciled as follows:

Retained earnings (1/1/x2)—per books		$545,600
Add: Entry (1)		48,000
		593,600
Deduct: Entry (2)	$12,800	
(3)	200	
(4)	1,600	
(5)	1,500	16,100
Retained earnings (1/1/x2)— consolidated		$577,500

Appendix 4–D: Trial balance working papers

Using the same information that was used to prepare Illustration 4–5, a trial balance approach to the preparation of consolidation working papers is now presented in Illustration 4–9. Accounts receivable, buildings, and equipment, instead of being shown at their net amounts are now shown at gross amounts with their respective contra asset accounts as given. The net amounts for these assets agree with those shown in Illustration 4–5.

The elimination entries for Illustration 4–9 are as follows:

(1)		
Equity in Earnings—Subsidiary	63,900	
Dividends Paid—Branch, Inc.		32,000
Investment in Branch, Inc.		31,900

(2)		
Cost of Sales (beginning inventory)	12,800	
Retained Earnings (1/1/x1)—Branch, Inc.	7,200	
Land	8,000	
Building	16,000	
Patents	8,000	
Goodwill	60,000	
Bonds Payable	8,000	
Common Stock—Branch, Inc.	32,000	
Additional Paid-In Capital	9,600	
Equipment		8,000
Investment in Branch, Inc.		153,600

(3)		
Cost of Sales (depreciation and amortization)	200	
Accumulated Depreciation—Equipment	1,000	
Accumulated Depreciation—Building		400
Patents		800

(4)		
Interest Expense	1,600	
Bonds Payable		1,600

(5)		
Amortization of Goodwill	1,500	
Goodwill		1,500

Although the format of the working papers is different, a review of the two illustrations reveals the following:

1. The elimination entries are identical except where contra asset accounts are involved. The net effect, however, is the same,
2. Although the financial statement approach (Illustration 4–5) is already in statement format, if statements are prepared from Illustration 4–9, they would coincide with those shown in Illustration 4–5.

Complete Equity Method
First Year Subsequent to Acquisition
80 Percent Subsidiary
Trial Balance Approach

Illustration 4–9
CHROME SERIAL COMPANY, INC.
Consolidated Working Paper
For the Year Ended December 31, 19x1

	Chrome Serial Co., Inc.	Branch, Inc. (80%)	Eliminations Dr.	Eliminations Cr.	Income Statement	Retained Earnings	Minority Interest	Balance Sheet
Debits								
Cash in bank	98,500	40,000						138,500
Accounts receivable	110,000	48,000						158,000
Inventories	80,000	30,000						110,000
Land	70,000	10,000	(2) 8,000					88,000
Buildings	150,000	62,500	(2) 16,000					228,500
Equipment	300,000	37,500		(2) 8,000				329,500
Patents			(2) 8,000	(3) 800				7,200
Goodwill			(2) 60,000	(5) 1,500				58,500
Investment in Branch, Inc.	185,500			(2) 153,600 (1) 31,900				
Cost of sales	350,000	300,000	(3) 200 (5) 12,800		(663,000)			
Operating expenses	150,000	200,000	(5) 1,500		(351,500)			
Interest expense		3,600	(4) 1,600		(5,200)			
Provision for income taxes	150,000	100,000			(250,000)			
Dividends paid—Chrome Serial Co., Inc.	110,000					(110,000)		
Dividends paid—Branch, Inc.		40,000		(1) 32,000			(8,000)	
	1,754,000	871,600						1,118,200
Credits								
Allowance for doubtful accounts	10,000	3,000						13,000
Accumulated depreciation—buildings	34,000	13,750		(3) 400				48,150
Accumulated depreciation—equipment	50,000	11,250	(3) 1,000					60,250
Accounts payable	122,500	27,400						149,900
Bond payable		50,000	(2) 8,000					43,600
Bond premium		1,600		(4) 1,600				1,600
Common stock—Chrome Serial Co., Inc.	200,000							200,000
Common stock—Branch, Inc.		40,000	(2) 32,000				8,000	
Additional paid-in capital		12,000	(2) 9,600				2,400	
Retained earnings—Chrome Serial Co., Inc.	473,600					473,600		
Retained earnings—Branch, Inc.		9,000	(2) 7,200				1,800	
Sales	800,000	703,600			1,503,600			
Equity in earnings—subsidiary	63,900		(1) 63,900					
	1,754,000	871,600	229,800	229,800				
Total net income					233,900		20,000	
Less: Minority interest net income					20,000			
Consolidated net income					213,900	213,900		
Consolidated retained earnings						577,500		577,500
Minority Interest							24,200	24,200
							24,200	1,118,200

QUESTIONS

1. When dividends are received from a subsidiary, how are they treated on a parent company's books when the complete equity method is used? Why should they be treated this way?

2. When the complete equity method is used, how is a parent's share of a subsidiary's income recorded by the parent company? Use a journal entry to demonstrate the procedure.

3. Is excess amortized when the complete equity method is used? If so, use an example to illustrate the procedure.

4. When the complete equity method is used, is there a relationship (congruity) between the parent's investment and the underlying net assets of the subsidiary? Explain.

5. Under the cost method, dividends received by a parent company from its subsidiary are credited to Dividend Income. Is there an exception to this procedure? Explain.

6. Is there a presumption that consolidated statements are more meaningful than unconsolidated statements? If so, is it mandatory to prepare consolidated statements in all cases? Explain.

7. Must the complete euity method be used in all cases where subsidiaries are not consolidated? If not, explain.

8. Is it possible to prepare consolidated financial statements even though the fiscal years of the parent company and its subsidiaries are different? Explain.

9. What can be said about a parent company's trial balances (per books) if it used either the complete equity method, the incomplete equity method, or the cost method to account for its investment in a subsidiary? What can be said about the consolidated financial statements prepared under each of the three methods? How is the result achieved?

10. What is meant by *one-line consolidation*?

11. Which accounts that appear in the parent company's trial balance are never carried across to the consolidated financial statements? Which accounts that appear in a subsidiary's trial balance are never carried across to consolidated financial statements?

12. What must be done with intercompany receivables and payables when consolidated financial statements are prepared? With intercompany sales and purchases? Why?

Questions for Appendix 4–A:

13. Is it possible that undistributed earnings of subsidiaries may give rise to a timing difference that requires income tax allocation? Explain.

14. If income tax allocation is required, what tax rates should be used?

15. Are there circumstances where undistributed earnings of subsidiaries do not require income tax allocation? Explain.

EXERCISES

Exercise 4–1.

1. On October 1, company X acquired for cash all of the outstanding common stock of company Y. Both companies have a December 31 year-end and have been in business for many years. Consolidated net income for the year ended December 31 should include net income of—

a. Company X for three months and company Y for three months.

b. Company X for 12 months and company Y for three months.

c. Company X for twelve months and company Y for twelve months.

d. Company X for twelve months; but no income from company Y until company Y distributes a dividend.

2. Polk Corporation purchased a controlling interest in Irwin Corporation for an amount which reflects the fact that Irwin's depreciable assets have a market value in excess of their book value. In the separate statements of Polk, this difference should be—

a. Charged against investment revenue over the remaining useful life of the assets.

b. Included in the carrying value of the investment until disposition of the stock.

c. Charged against investment revenue in the year of acquisition.

d. Charged to depreciation expense over the remaining useful life of the assets.

3. Under the equity method of accounting for investments, an investor recognizes its share of the earnings in the period in which the—

a. Investor sells the investment.

b. Investee declares a dividend.

c. Investee pays a dividend.

d. Earnings are reported by the investee in its financial statements.

4. If all other conditions for consolidation are met, how should subsidiaries acquired in a business combination be shown under each of the following methods?

	Purchase	Pooling of interests
a.	Consolidated	*Not* consolidated
b.	Consolidated	Consolidated
c.	*Not* consolidated	Consolidated
d.	*Not* consolidated	*Not* consolidated

5. What would be the effect on the financial statements if an unconsolidated subsidiary is accounted for by the equity method, but consolidated statements are being prepared with other subsidiaries?

a. All of the unconsolidated subsidiary's accounts will be included individually in the consolidated statements.

b. The consolidated retained earnings will not reflect the earnings of the unconsolidated subsidiary.

c. The consolidated retained earnings will be the same as if the subsidiary had been included in the consolidation.

d. Dividend revenue from the unconsolidated subsidiary will be reflected in consolidated net income.

6. Presenting consolidated financial statements this year when statements of individual companies were presented last year is—

a. A correction of an error.

b. An accounting change that should be reported prospectively.

c. An accounting change that should be reported by restating the financial statements of all prior periods presented.

d. *Not* an accounting change.   (AICPA adapted)

Exercise 4–2.

1. Aaron, Inc., owns 80 percent of the outstanding stock of Belle, Inc. Compare the consolidated net earnings of Aaron and Belle (X) and Aaron's net earnings if it does *not* consolidate with Belle (Y).

a. X greater than Y.

b. X equals Y.

c. X less than Y.

d. Cannot be determined.

2. When the equity method of accounting for an investment in a subsidiary is used, dividends from the subsidiary should be accounted for by the parent corporation as—

a. Revenue unless paid from retained earnings of the subsidiary earned before the date of acquisition.

b. Revenue so long as the dividends were declared from retained earnings.

c. A reduction of the carrying value of the investment account.

d. A deferred credit.

3. Investor, Inc., owns 40 percent of Alimand Corporation. During the calendar year 19x5, Alimand had net earnings of $100,000 and paid dividends of $10,000. Investor mistakenly recorded these transactions using the cost method rather than the equity method of accounting. What effect would this have on the investment account, net earnings, and retained earnings, respectively?

a. Understate, overstate, overstate.

b. Overstate, understate, understate.

c. Overstate, overstate, overstate.

d. Understate, understate, understate.

4. How should goodwill be written off?

a. As soon as possible to retained earnings.

b. By systematic charges to retained earnings over the period benefited, but not in excess of 40 years.

c. As soon as possible as a one-time charge to expense and reported as an extraordinary item.

d. By systematic charges to an operating expense over the period benefited, but not in excess of 40 years.

5. How is the portion of consolidated earnings to be assigned to minority interest in consolidated financial statements determined?

a. The net income of the parent is subtracted from the subsidiary's net income to determine the minority interest.

b. The subsidiary's net income is extended to the minority interest.

c. The amount of the subsidiary's earnings recognized for consolidation purposes is multiplied by the minority's percentage ownership.

d. The amount of consolidated earnings determined on the consolidated working papers is multiplied by the minority interest percentage at the balance sheet date. (AICPA adapted)

Exercise 4–3.

1. If Sweets Candy Company acquired an 80 percent interest in Honey Wrapper Company on December 31, 19x8, for $210,000 and the equity (or accrual) method of accounting for the investment was used, the amount of the debit to Investment in Stock of Honey Wrapper Company would have been—

a. $320,000.   *c.* $210,000.

b. $240,000.   *d.* $200,000.

2. If Sweets Candy Company acquired a 90 percent interest in Honey Wrapper Company on December 31, 19x8, for $270,000 and during 19x9 Honey Wrapper Company had net income of $22,000 and paid a cash dividend of $7,000, applying the cost method would give a debit balance in the Investment in Stock of Honey Wrapper Company account at the end of 19x9 of—

a. $285,000.

b. $283,500.

c. $276,300.

d. $270,000.

3. If Sweets Candy Company acquired a 90 percent interest in Honey Wrapper Company on December 31, 19x8, for $270,000 and during 19x9 Honey Wrapper Company had net income of $30,000 and paid a cash dividend of $15,000, applying the equity method would give a debit balance in the Investment in Stock of Honey Wrapper Company account at the end of 19x9 of—

a. $285,000.

b. $283,500.

c. $276,300.

d. $270,000.   (AICPA adapted)

Exercise 4–4.

1. On January 1, 19x7, the Pint Corporation paid $400,000 for 10,000 shares of Quart Company's common stock which represents a 10 percent investment in Quart. Pint received dividends of $1 per share from Quart in 19x7. Quart reported net income of $150,000 for the year ended December 31, 19x7. The market value of Quart's common stock on December 31, 19x7, was $42 per share. *Ignoring income taxes,* the amount reported in Pint's 19x7 income statement as a result of Pint's investment in Quart was—

a. $10,000.

b. $15,000.

c. $30,000.

d. $35,000.

2. On January 1, 19x5, the Swing Company purchased at book value 100,000 shares (20 percent) of the voting common stock of Harpo Instruments, Inc., for $1,200,000. Direct costs associated with the purchase were $50,000. On December 1, 19x5, the board of directors of Harpo declared a dividend of $2 per share payable to holders of record on December 28, 19x5. The net income of Harpo for the year ended December 31, 19x5, was $1,600,000.

What should be the balance in Swing's Investment in Harpo Instruments, Inc., account at December 31, 19x5?

a. $1,200,000.

b. $1,250,000.

c. $1,370,000.

d. $1,520,000.

3. In January 19x5, the Harold Corporation acquired 20 percent of the outstanding common stock of Otis Company for $400,000. This investment gave Harold the ability to exercise significant influence over Otis. The book value of these shares was $300,000. The excess of cost over book value was attributed to an identifiable intangible asset which was undervalued on Otis' balance sheet and which had a remaining useful life of 10 years.

For the year ended December 31, 19x5, Otis reported net income of $90,000 and paid cash dividends of $20,000 on its common stock. What is the carrying value of Harold's investment in Otis Company at December 31, 19x5?

a. $386,000.

b. $390,000.

c. $400,000.

d. $404,000.

4. A parent corporation which uses the equity method of accounting for its investment in a 40 percent owned subsidiary, which earned $20,000 and paid $5,000 in dividends, made the following entries:

Investment in Subsidiary	8,000	
Equity in Earnings of		
Subsidiary		8,000
Cash	2,000	
Dividend revenue		2,000

What effect will these entries have on the parent's statement of financial position?

a. Financial position will be fairly stated.

b. Investment in subsidiary overstated, retained earnings understated.

c. Investment in subsidiary understated, retained earnings understated.

d. Investment in subsidiary overstated, retained earnings overstated.

5. On January 1, 19x7, Wilson, Inc., issued 100,000 additional shares of $10 par value voting common stock in exchange for all of Thomson Company's voting common stock in a business combination appropriately accounted for by the pooling of interests method. Net income for the year ended December 31, 19x7, was $400,000 for Thomson and $1,300,000 for Wilson, exclusive of any consideration of Thomson. During 19x7, Wilson paid $900,000 in dividends to its stockholders and Thomson paid $250,000 in dividends to Wilson. What should be the consolidated net income for the year ended December 31, 19x7?

a. $1,150,000.

b. $1,450,000.

c. $1,550,000.

d. $1,700,000.   (AICPA adapted)

Exercise 4–5. Items 1 and 2 are based on the following information:

On January 1, 19x6, Tom Kat, Inc., purchased 25 percent of the outstanding shares of stock of Carmel for $115,000 cash. The investment will be accounted for by the equity method. On that date, Carmel's net assets (book and fair value) were $300,000. Tom Kat has determined that the excess of the cost of its investment in Carmel over its share of Carmel's net assets has an indeterminate life.

Carmel's net income for the year ended December 31, 19x6, was $50,000. During 19x6, Tom Kat received $5,000 cash dividends from Carmel. There were no other transactions between the two companies.

1. On January 1, 19x6, the investment in Carmel would be recorded on Tom Kat's books at—

a. $75,000.

b. $85,000.

c. $115,000.

d. $155,000.

2. Ignoring income taxes, Tom Kat's income statement for the year ended December 31, 19x6,

should include "equity in 1976 net income of Carmel" in the amount of

a. $7,500.

b. $11,500.

c. $12,500.

d. $13,500.

3. On December 1, 19x8, Drew Company issued shares of its voting common stock in exchange for all of the voting common stock of Art Company in a business combination appropriately accounted for by the pooling of interests method. Net income for each company is as follows:

	Drew	Art
12 months ended December 31, 19x8	$2,000,000	$1,200,000
1 month ended December 31, 19x8	220,000	115,000

During 19x8, Drew paid $900,000 in dividends to its stockholders. Art had paid $500,000 in dividends to its stockholders in September 19x8. Assuming that the net income of Drew given above does not include the equity in net income of Art, the consolidated net income for the year ended December 31, 19x8, should be—

a. $335,000.

b. $2,115,000.

c. $2,700,000.

d. $3,200,000.

4. On January 1, 19x7, the Robohn Company purchased for cash 40 percent of the 300,000 shares of voting common stock of the Lowell Company for $1,800,000 when 40 percent of the underlying equity in the net assets of Lowell was $1,400,000. Robohn amortizes goodwill over a 40-year period with a full year's amortization taken in the year of the purchase. The amortization is not deductible for income tax reporting. As a result of this transaction, Robohn has the ability to exercise significant influence over the operating and financial policies of Lowell. Lowell's net income for the year ended December 31, 19x7, was $600,000. During 19x7, Lowell paid $325,000 in dividends to its stockholders. The income reported by Robohn for its investment in Lowell should be—

a. $120,000.

b. $130,000.

c. $230,000.

d. $240,000.

5. Drab, Inc., owns 40 percent of the outstanding stock of Gloom Company. During 19x5, Drab received a $4,000 cash dividend from Gloom. What effect did this dividend have on Drab's 19x5 financial statements?

   a. Increased total assets.

   b. Decreased total assets.

   c. Increased income.

   d. Decreased investment account.

(AICPA adapted)

Exercise 4–6.

1. On December 1, 19x8, Chest Corporation purchased 200,000 shares representing 45 percent of the outstanding stock of Park Company for cash of $2,500,000. As a result of this purchase, Chest has the ability to exercise significant influence over the operating and financial policies of Park. Forty-five percent of the net income of Park amounted to $20,000 for the month of December and $350,000 for the year ended December 31, 19x8. The appropriate amount of goodwill amortization to be recorded by Chest in 19x8 as a result of its purchase of Park stock would be $10,000. On January 15, 19x9, cash dividends of 30 cents per share were paid to stockholders of record on December 31, 19x8. Chest's long-term investment in Park should be shown in Chest's December 31, 19x8, balance sheet at—

   a. $2,450,000.

   b. $2,460,000.

   c. $2,500,000.

   d. $2,510,000.

2. On January 1, 19x7, Barley Corporation, paid $600,000 for 60,000 shares of Oat Company's common stock which represents a 25 percent investment in Oat. Barley has the ability to exercise significant influence over Oat. Barley received a dividend of $1 per share from Oat in 19x7. Oat reported net income of $320,000 for the year ended December 31, 19x7. The balance in Barley's balance sheet account Investment in Oat Company at December 31, 19x7, should be—

   a. $600,000.

   b. $620,000.

   c. $680,000.

   d. $740,000.

3. On January 1, 19x8, Grade Company paid $300,000 for 20,000 shares of Medium Company's common stock which represents a 15 percent investment in Medium. Grade does not have the ability to exercise significant influence over Medium. Medium declared and paid a dividend of $1 a share to its stockholders during 19x8. Medium reported net income of $260,000 for the year ended December 31, 19x8. The balance in Grade's balance sheet account Investment in Medium Company at December 31, 19x8, should be—

   a. $280,000.

   b. $300,000.

   c. $319,000.

   d. $339,000.

Items 4 and 5 are based on the following information:

4. On January 1, 19x8, Avow, Inc., purchased 30 percent of the outstanding common stock of Depot Corporation for $129,000 cash. Avow is accounting for this investment on the equity method. On the date of acquisition, the fair value of Depot's net assets was $310,000. Avow has determined that the excess of the cost of the investment over its share of Depot's net assets has an indeterminate life. Depot's net income for the year ended December 31, 19x8, was $90,000. During 19x8, Depot declared and paid cash dividends of $10,000. There were no other transactions between the two companies. On January 1, 19x8, the investment in Depot should have been recorded as—

   a. $93,000.

   b. $120,000.

   c. $129,000.

   d. $165,000.

5. Ignoring income taxes, Avow's statement of income for the year ended December 31, 19x8, should include "equity in net income of Depot Corporation" in the amount of—

   a. $17,000.

   b. $26,100.

   c. $27,000.

   d. $27,900.   (AICPA adapted)

Exercise 4–7. On January 1, 19x1, P Company purchased 80 percent of the outstanding shares of S Company at a cost of $800,000. On that date, S Company had $500,000 of capital stock and $500,000 of retained earnings.

For 19x1, S Company reported income of $200,000 and paid dividends of $80,000. All the assets and liabilities of S Company are at fair market value.

Required:

   a. Prepare entries by P Company to record the purchase of the investment (at cash), the receipt of dividends, and the equity in subsidiary earnings for 19x1 (P Company uses the equity method).

b. Compute the balance of the Investment in S Company account on December 31, 19x1.

c. Compute minority interest net income for 19x1.

d. Compute the amount to be shown as minority interest on a consolidated statement as of December 31, 19x1.

Exercise 4–8. Using the information provided in Exercise 4–7, assume that the purchase price was $900,000 instead of $800,000 and all other information is the same.

Required:

Complete (*a*), (*b*), (*c*), and (*d*) as specified in Exercise 4–7 using the complete equity method.

Exercise 4–9. The following information was extracted from the books of S Company:

Year	Net income	Dividends paid
19x1	$100,000	$40,000
19x2	60,000	40,000
19x3	10,000	40,000
19x4	100,000	40,000

On January 1, 19x2, P Company purchased, at book value, 80 percent of S Company's outstanding stock. The price paid for the investment on January 1, 19x2, amounted to $400,000.

Required:

a. Prepare all of the required journal entries on P Company's books for 19x2, 19x3, and 19x4 under the *cost method.*

b. Compute the balance in the Investment in S Company account on December 31, 19x4, under the cost method.

c. Redo (*a*) above for the equity method.

d. Redo (*b*) above for the equity method.

Exercise 4–10. On January 1, 19x3, P Company purchased 80 percent of the outstanding shares of S Company at a cost of $800,000. On that date, S Company had $300,000 of capital stock and $600,000 of retained earnings.

For 19x3, P Company had income of $300,000 from its own operations (excluding its share of income from S Company) and paid dividends of $150,000. For 19x3, S Company reported a net income of $100,000 and paid dividends of $40,000. All the assets and liabilities of S Company have book val-

ues approximately equal to their respective market values.

P Company uses the complete equity method to account for its investment in S company.

Required:

a. Compute the amount that P Company should record as Equity in Earnings of S Company for 19x3.

b. Compute consolidated net income for 19x3.

c. Compute minority interest net income for 19x3.

d. Compute the total minority interest at December 31, 19x3.

e. Compute the balance in the investment account at December 31, 19x3.

Exercise 4–11. On January 1, 19x4, P Company purchased 80 percent of the outstanding shares of S Company at a cost of $700,000. On that date, S Company had $200,000 of capital stock and $500,000 of retained earnings.

For 19x4, P Company had income of $400,000 from its own operations (excluding its share of income from S Company) and paid dividends of $200,000. For 19x4, S Company reported a *loss of $50,000* and paid dividends of $40,000. All of the assets and liabilities of S Company have book values approximately equal to their respective market values.

P Company uses the complete equity method to account for its investment in S Company.

Required:

a. Prepare the journal entries necessary to record the equity in earnings of S Company on the books of P Company for 19x4.

b. Compute consolidated net income for 19x4.

c. Compute the balance in the Investment in S Company account at December 31, 19x4.

Exercise 4–12. On January 1, 19x5, P Company purchased 80 percent of the outstanding common stock of S Company. On that date, S Company had common stock of $200,000 and retained earnings of $300,000. For 19x5, P Company earned $200,000 from its own operations and reported a net income of $270,000, which includes its share of equity in earnings of S Company. For 19x5, S Company reported a net income of $90,000 and paid dividends of $40,000. All of the assets and liabilities of S Company have book values approximately equal to their respective market values. The excess, if any, is being amortized over a 40-year period.

P Company uses the complete equity method to account for its investment in S Company.

Required:

a. Compute the price paid for the investment in S Company.

b. Compute the balance in the Investment in S Company account at December 31, 19x5.

Exercise 4–13. On January 1, 19x6, Todd Corporation made the following investments:

Acquired for cash, 80 percent of the outstanding common stock of Meadow Corporation at $70 per share. The stockholders' equity of Meadow on January 1, 19x6, consisted of the following:

Common stock, par value, $50 . . . . $50,000
Retained earnings 20,000

Acquired for cash, 70 percent of the outstanding common stock of Van Corporation at $40 per share. The stockholders' equity of Van on January 1, 19x6, consisted of the following:

Common stock, par value, $20 . . . . $60,000
Capital in excess of par value 20,000
Retained earnings 40,000

After these investments were made, Todd was able to exercise significant influence over the operations of both companies.

An analysis of the retained earnings of each company for 19x6 is as follows:

	Todd	Meadow	Van
Balance, January 1, 19x6	$240,000	$20,000	$40,000
Net income (loss)	104,600	36,000	(12,000)
Cash dividends paid . .	(40,000)	(16,000)	(9,000)
Balance, December 31, 19x6	$304,600	$40,000	$19,000

Required:

a. What entries should have been made on the books of Todd during 19x6 to record the following?
   Investments in subsidiaries.
   Parent's share of subsidiary income or loss.
   Subsidiary dividends received.

b. Using the "parent company theory," compute the amount of minority interest in each subsidiary's stockholders' equity at December 31, 19x6.

c. What amount should be reported as consolidated retained earnings of Todd Corporation and subsidiaries as of December 31, 19x6?

(AICPA adapted)

Exercise 4–14 for Appendix 4–A.

1. With respect to the difference between taxable income and pretax accounting income, the tax effect of the undistributed earnings of a subsidiary included in consolidated income should normally be—
   a. Accounted for as a timing difference.
   b. Accounted for as a permanent difference.
   c. Ignored because it must be based on estimates and assumptions.
   d. Ignored because it cannot be presumed that all undistributed earnings of a subsidiary will be transferred to the parent company.

2. Simpson Company, a subsidiary of Rusk Company, did not distribute its 19x2 earnings in 19x2. Rusk should recognize income taxes on its share of the earnings in its 19x2 financial statements only if—
   a. Simpson is a domestic corporation.
   b. The earnings will be remitted in a tax-free transaction within the foreseeable future.
   c. The earnings will be remitted in a taxable transaction on or before March 15, 19x3.
   d. Remittance of the earnings in a taxable transaction will *not* be postponed indefinitely.

3. If it becomes apparent that the undistributed earnings of a subsidiary on which income taxes have been accrued will *not* be remitted in the foreseeable future, the parent company should—
   a. Increase income tax expense and increase deferred income taxes.
   b. Decrease income tax expense and decrease deferred income taxes.
   c. Increase extraordinary income and decrease deferred income taxes.
   d. Make *no* adjustment.

4. Smith Corporation owns only 25 percent of the voting stock of Jones Corporation but exercises significant influence over its operating and financial policies. The tax effect of differences between taxable income and pretax accounting income attributable to undistributed earnings of Jones Corporation should be—

a. Accounted for as a timing difference.

b. Accounted for as a permanent difference.

c. Ignored because it must be based on estimates and assumptions.

d. Ignored because Smith holds less than 51 percent of the voting stock of Jones.

5. Accounting for the tax effect of a difference between taxable income and pretax accounting income with respect to undistributed earnings of a subsidiary is similar to a situation involving—

a. Profits on assets within the consolidated group which are eliminated in consolidated financial statements.

b. Profits on intercompany transactions which are taxed when reported in separate tax returns.

c. Rents and royalties which are taxed when collected and deferred in financial statements until earned.

d. Profits on installment sales which are recognized in financial statements at the date of sale and reported in tax returns when collected.

6. When undistributed earnings of a subsidiary company have increased the pretax accounting income of a parent company because the latter consolidated the subsidiary or used the equity method to account for its investment—

a. Income tax allocation is necessary because there is an invariable presumption that undistributed earnings will ultimately be transferred to the parent.

b. Maximum tax rates should be applied as a matter of conservatism if income tax allocation is applied.

c. Income taxes need *not* be accrued where evidence shows the subsidiary will *not* remit undistributed earnings to the parent for an indefinite period.

d. Generally accepted accounting principles have been violated.   (AICPA adapted)

PROBLEMS

Problem 4–15. On January 1, 19x4, P Company acquired 80 percent of the outstanding capital stock of S Company for $280,000. On that date, the capital stock of S Company was $100,000 and its retained earnings were $100,000.

On the date of acquisition, the assets of S Company had the following values:

	Book value	Fair market value
Inventories	$80,000	$100,000
Plant and equipment	60,000	140,000

All other assets and liabilities had book values approximately equal to their respective fair market values. The plant and equipment had a remaining useful life of 10 years from January 1, 19x4, and S Company uses the FIFO inventory cost flow assumption.

The retained earnings of P Company on the date of acquisition was $600,000. For 19x4, P Company earned $200,000 exclusive of its share of the earnings of S Company. During 19x4, P Company paid dividends of $60,000. S Company earned $100,000 in 19x4 (per books) and paid dividends in that year of $40,000.

P Company uses the complete equity method to account for its investment in S Company.

Required:

a. Prepare a schedule of allocation of excess.

b. Compute consolidated net income for 19x4.

c. Compute consolidated retained earnings at December 31, 19x4.

d. Compute the balance in the investment account on December 31, 19x4.

e. Compute minority interest net income for 19x4.

f. Compute the total minority interest at December 31, 19x4.

Problem 4–16. Using the information provided in Problem 4–15, assume the following for 19x7:

	P Company	S Company
Retained earnings, January 1, 19x7	$900,000	$300,000
Separate incomes	250,000	150,000
Dividend payments	100,000	60,000

There were no other changes since the date of acquisition.

Required:

a. Compute consolidated net income for 19x7.

b. Compute consolidated retained earnings at December 31, 19x7.

c. Compute the balance in the investment account at December 31, 19x7.

d. Compute the total minority interest at December 31, 19x7.

Problem 4–17. On January 1, 19x5, P Company acquired 70 percent of the outstanding capital stock of S Company for $195,000. On that date, the capital stock of S Company was $200,000 and its retained earnings were $100,000.

On the date of acquisition, the assets of S Company had the following values:

	Book value	Fair market value
Inventories	$ 40,000	$60,000
Plant and equipment	120,000	50,000

All other assets and liabilities had book values approximately equal to their respective fair market values. The plant and equipment had a remaining useful life of 10 years from the date of acquisition, and S Company uses the FIFO inventory cost flow assumption.

The retained earnings of P Company on January 1, 19x5, was $500,000. For 19x5, P Company earned $300,000 exclusive of its share of the earnings of S Company. During 19x5, P Company paid dividends of $100,000. S Company earned $80,000 in 19x5 (per books) and paid dividends in that year of $30,000.

P Company uses the complete equity method to account for its investment in S Company.

Required:

a. Prepare a schedule of allocation of excess.

b. Compute consolidated net income for 19x5.

c. Compute consolidated retained earnings at December 31, 19x5.

d. Compute the balance in the investment account on December 31, 19x5.

e. Compute minority interest net income for 19x5.

f. Compute the total minority interest at December 31, 19x5.

Problem 4–18. Using the information provided in Problem 4–17, assume the following for 19x7:

	P Company	S Company
Retained earnings, January 1, 19x7	$800,000	$400,000
Separate incomes	200,000	100,000
Dividend payments	100,000	40,000

There were no other changes since the date of acquisition.

Required:

a. Compute consolidated net income for 19x7.

b. Compute consolidated retained earnings at December 31, 19x7.

c. Compute the balance in the investment account at December 31, 19x7.

d. Compute the total minority interest at December 31, 19x7.

Problem 4–19. On January 1, 19x1, P Company purchased 40,000 shares of S Company in the open market for $1,140,000. On that date, the assets and liabilities of S Company had book values that approximated their respective fair market values. Excess (goodwill), if any, is expected to last for 20 years and is to be amortized over that period.

P Company uses the complete equity method to account for its investment.

On December 31, 19x1, S Company owed P Company $10,000 on open account from purchases made last year.

Financial statements for the two corporations for the year ended December 31, 19x1, are as follows:

	P Company	S Company
Income Statement		
Sales	$2,000,000	$1,000,000
Cost of sales	800,000	600,000
Gross margin	1,200,000	400,000
Expenses	500,000	100,000
Operating income before taxes	700,000	300,000
Equity in earnings— subsidiary	139,000	
Income before income taxes .	839,000	300,000
Provision for income taxes . .	280,000	120,000
Minority interest net income		
Net income—carried forward	$ 559,000	$ 180,000

	P Company	S Company
Retained Earnings Statement		
Balance, January 1, 19x1:		
P Company	$3,000,000	
S Company		$ 800,000
Net income—brought		
forward	559,000	180,000
Totals	3,559,000	980,000
Less: Dividends declared:		
P Company	400,000	
S Company		60,000
Balance, December 31, 19x1—		
carried forward	$3,159,000	$ 920,000
Balance Sheet		
Cash	$ 300,000	$ 100,000
Accounts receivable	200,000	200,000
Inventories	400,000	300,000
Land	600,000	
Building (net of accumulated depreciation)	400,000	
Equipment (net of accumulated depreciation) .	1,228,000	1,000,000
Investment in S Company . .	1,231,000	
Totals	$4,359,000	$1,600,000
Accounts payable and accrued expenses	$ 302,000	$ 180,000
Bonds payable (face amount $100,000)		98,000
Common stock—P Company ($50 par)	500,000	
Common stock—S Company ($10 par)		500,000
Additional paid-in capital—P Company	300,000	
Retained earnings brought forward	3,159,000	920,000
Totals	$4,359,000	$1,600,000

Required:

a. Prepare a consolidated working paper.

b. Prepare consolidated financial statements.

Problem 4–20. On January 1, 19x1, P Company purchased 24,000 shares of S Company in the open market for $756,000. On that date, the following assets of S Company had book values that were different from their respective market values:

	Book value	Fair market value
Inventories	$ 40,000	$ 70,000
Land	150,000	200,000
Building (net)	200,000	300,000
Equipment (net)	450,000	375,000
Patent	–0–	40,000

All other assets and liabilities had book values approximately equal to their respective market values.

On January 1, 19x1, the building had a remaining useful life of 20 years. Equipment and the patent had remaining useful lives of 10 years each. FIFO inventory costing is used. Goodwill, if any, has an indeterminate life. P Company uses the complete equity method to account for this investment.

Financial statements for the companies for the year ended December 31, 19x1, are as follows:

	P Company	S Company
Income Statement		
Sales	$1,000,000	$ 500,000
Cost of sales	400,000	150,000
Gross margin	600,000	350,000
Expenses	200,000	100,000
Operating income before taxes	400,000	250,000
Equity in earnings— subsidiary	92,800	
Income before income taxes .	492,800	250,000
Provision for income taxes . .	160,000	100,000
Minority interest net income		
Net income—carried forward	$ 332,800	$ 150,000
Retained Earnings Statement		
Balance, January 1, 19x1:		
P Company	$ 600,000	
S Company		$ 400,000
Net income—brought forward	332,800	150,000
Totals	932,800	550,000
Less: Dividends declared:		
P Company	100,000	
S Company		50,000
Balance, December 31, 19x1— carried forward	$ 832,800	$ 500,000

	P Company	S Company
Balance Sheet		
Cash	$ 200,000	$ 100,000
Accounts receivable	150,000	50,000
Inventories	100,000	40,000
Land		150,000
Building		260,000
Equipment	700,000	490,000
Patent		—
Investment in S Company . .	808,800	
Totals	$1,958,800	$1,090,000
Accounts payable and accrued expenses	$ 124,000	$ 190,000
Accumulated depreciation— building		60,000
Accumulated depreciation— equipment	402,000	40,000
Common stock—P Company ($50 par)	200,000	
Common stock—S Company ($10 par)		300,000
Additional paid-in capital—P Company	400,000	
Retained earnings— brought forward	832,800	500,000
Totals	$1,958,800	$1,090,000

Required:

a. Prepare an allocation schedule of excess.

b. Prepare a consolidated working paper.

Problem 4–21. P Company acquired 80 percent of the outstanding common stock of S Company on January 1, 19x1. The price paid for the investment, book and market values of assets on the date of acquisition, and useful lives are provided in Problem 4–20.

P Company uses the complete equity method to account for its investment.

Financial statements for the companies for the year ended December 31, 19x2 (second year), are as follows:

	P Company	S Company
Income Statement		
Sales	$1,200,000	$700,000
Cost of sales	500,000	250,000
Gross margin	700,000	450,000
Expenses	200,000	120,000
Operating income before taxes	500,000	330,000
Equity in earnings— subsidiary	155,200	
Income before income taxes .	655,200	330,000
Provision for income taxes . .	200,000	132,000
Minority interest net income		
Net income—carried forward	$ 455,200	$198,000

	P Company	S Company
Retained Earnings Statement		
Balance, January 1, 19x2:		
P Company	$ 832,800	
S Company		$ 500,000
Net income—brought forward	455,200	198,000
Totals	1,288,000	698,000
Less: Dividends declared:		
P Company	150,000	
S Company		60,000
Balance, December 31, 19x2— carried forward	$1,138,000	$ 638,000
Balance Sheet		
Cash	$ 233,600	$ 48,000
Accounts receivable	240,000	70,000
Inventories	150,000	80,000
Land		150,000
Building		260,000
Equipment	800,000	633,000
Patent		—
Investment in S Company . .	916,000	
Totals	$2,339,600	$1,241,000
Accounts payable and accrued expenses	$ 150,600	$ 140,000
Accumulated depreciation— building		73,000
Accumulated depreciation— equipment	451,000	90,000
Common stock—P Company ($50 par)	200,000	
Common stock—S Company ($10 par)		300,000
Additional paid-in capital—P Company	400,000	
Retained earnings—P Company—brought forward	1,138,000	638,000
Totals	$2,339,600	$1,241,000

Required:

Prepare a consolidated working paper.

Problem 4–22. On January 1, 19x2, P Company acquired 80 percent of the outstanding common stock of S Company for $640,000. On that date, the retained earnings of S Company were $200,000 and there have been no changes in its capital stock and additional paid-in capital.

All of the assets and liabilities of S Company had book values approximately equal to their respective market values. Goodwill, if any, is to be amortized over a 20-year period.

On December 31, 19x4, P Company owes S Company $20,000 from sales made by S Company last year. This year, 19x4, there were no intercompany transactions.

The financial statements of the companies for the year ended December 31, 19x4, are as follows:

Income Statement

	P Company	S Company
Sales	$800,000	$200,000
Cost of sales	300,000	150,000
Gross margin	500,000	50,000
Expenses	200,000	100,000
Operating income (loss) before taxes	300,000	(50,000)
Equity in earnings— subsidiary	(28,000)	
Income (loss) before income taxes	272,000	(50,000)
Provision for income taxes . .	120,000	(20,000)
Minority interest net income		
Net income (loss)—carried forward	$152,000	$(30,000)

Retained Earnings Statement

	P Company	S Company
Balance, January 1, 19x4:		
P Company	$600,000	
S Company		$300,000
Net income (loss)—brought forward	152,000	(30,000)
Totals	752,000	270,000
Less: Dividends declared:		
P Company	80,000	
S Company		–
Balance, December 31, 19x4— carried forward	$672,000	$270,000

Balance Sheet

	P Company	S Company
Cash	$ 150,000	$ 50,000
Accounts receivable	80,000	30,000
Inventories	60,000	40,000
Equipment (net of accumulated depreciation) .	298,000	750,000
Investment in S Company . .	684,000	
Totals	$1,272,000	$870,000
Accounts payable and accrued expenses	$ 200,000	$100,000
Common stock—P Company ($50 par)	400,000	
Common stock—S Company ($10 par)		300,000
Additional paid-in capital—S Company		200,000
Retained earnings— brought forward	672,000	270,000
Totals	$1,272,000	$870,000

Required:

Prepare a consolidated working paper.

Problem 4–23 (for Appendix 4–B). On January 1, 19x1, P Company purchased 40,000 shares of S Company in the open market for $1,140,000. On that date, the assets and liabilities of S Company had book values that approximated their respective fair market values. Excess (goodwill), if any, is expected to last for 20 years and is to be amortized over that period.

P Company uses the incomplete equity method to account for its investment.

Financial statements for the two corporations for the year ended December 31, 19x1, are as follows:

Income Statement

	P Company	S Company
Sales	$2,000,000	$1,000,000
Cost of sales	800,000	600,000
Gross margin	1,200,000	400,000
Expenses	500,000	100,000
Operating income before taxes	700,000	300,000
Equity in earnings— subsidiary	144,000	
Income before income taxes .	844,000	300,000
Provision for income taxes . .	280,000	120,000
Minority interest net income		
Net income—carried forward	$ 564,000	$ 180,000

Retained Earnings Statement

	P Company	S Company
Balance, January 1, 19x1:		
P Company	$3,000,000	
S Company		$ 800,000
Net income—brought forward	564,000	180,000
Totals	3,564,000	980,000
Less: Dividends declared:		
P Company	400,000	
S Company		60,000
Balance, December 31, 19x1— carried forward	$3,164,000	$ 920,000

	P Company	S Company
Balance Sheet		
Cash	$ 300,000	$ 100,000
Accounts receivable	200,000	200,000
Inventories	400,000	300,000
Land	600,000	—
Building (net of accumulated depreciation)	400,000	—
Equipment (net of accumulated depreciation) .	1,228,000	1,000,000
Investment in S Company . .	1,236,000	
Totals	$4,364,000	$1,600,000
Accounts payable and accrued expenses	$ 400,000	$ 180,000
Common stock—P Company ($50 par)	500,000	
Common stock—S Company ($10 par)		500,000
Additional paid-in capital—P Company	300,000	
Retained earnings—brought forward	3,164,000	920,000
Totals	$4,364,000	$1,600,000

Required:

a. Prepare a consolidated working paper.

b. Prepare consolidated financial statements.

Problem 4–24 (Appendix 4–B). On January 1, 19x1, P Company purchased 24,000 shares of S Company in the open market for $756,000. On that date, the following assets of S Company had book values that were different from their respective market values:

	Book value	Fair market value
Inventories	$ 40,000	$ 70,000
Land	150,000	200,000
Building (net)	200,000	300,000
Equipment (net)	450,000	375,000
Patent	–0–	40,000

All other assets and liabilities had book values approximately equal to their respective market values.

On January 1, 19x1, the building had a remaining useful life of 20 years. Equipment and the patent had remaining useful lives of 10 years each. FIFO inventory costing is used. Goodwill, if any, has an indeterminate life. P Company uses the incomplete equity method to account for this investment.

Financial statements for the companies for the year ended December 31, 19x1, are as follows:

	P Company	S Company
Income Statement		
Sales	$1,000,000	$ 500,000
Cost of sales	400,000	150,000
Gross margin	600,000	350,000
Expenses	200,000	100,000
Operating income before taxes	400,000	250,000
Equity in earnings— subsidiary	120,000	
Income before income taxes .	520,000	250,000
Provision for income taxes . .	160,000	100,000
Minority interest net income		
Net income—carried forward	$ 360,000	$ 150,000
Retained Earnings Statement		
Balance, January 1, 19x1:		
P Company	$ 600,000	
S Company		$ 400,000
Net income—brought forward	360,000	150,000
Totals	$ 960,000	$ 550,000
Less: Dividends declared:		
P Company	100,000	
S Company		50,000
Balance, December 31, 19x1— carried forward	$ 860,000	$ 500,000
Balance Sheet		
Cash	$ 200,000	$ 100,000
Accounts receivable	150,000	50,000
Inventories	100,000	40,000
Land		150,000
Building		260,000
Equipment	700,000	490,000
Patent		—
Investment in S Company . .	836,000	
Totals	$1,986,000	$1,090,000
Accounts payable and accrued expenses	$ 124,000	$ 190,000
Accumulated depreciation— building		60,000
Accumulated depreciation— equipment	402,000	40,000
Common stock—P Company ($50 par)	200,000	
Common stock—S Company ($10 par)		300,000
Additional paid-in capital—P Company	400,000	
Retained earnings—brought forward	860,000	500,000
Totals	$1,986,000	$1,090,000

Required:

a. Prepare an allocation schedule of excess.

b. Prepare a consolidated working paper.

Problem 4–25 (Appendix 4–B). P Company acquired 80 percent of the outstanding common stock of S Company on January 1, 19x1. The price paid for the investment, book and market values of assets on the date of acquisition, and useful lives are provided in Problem 4–24.

P Company uses the incomplete equity method to account for its investment.

Financial statements for the companies for the year ended December 31, 19x2 (second year), are as follows:

Income Statement	P Company	S Company
Sales	$1,200,000	$ 700,000
Cost of sales	500,000	250,000
Gross margin	700,000	450,000
Expenses	200,000	120,000
Operating income before taxes	500,000	330,000
Equity in earnings— subsidiary	158,400	
Income before income taxes	658,400	330,000
Provision for income taxes	200,000	132,000
Minority interest net income		
Net income—carried forward	$ 458,400	$198,000

Retained Earnings Statement	P Company	S Company
Balance, January 1, 19x2:		
P Company	$ 860,000	
S Company		$ 500,000
Net income—brought forward	458,400	198,000
Totals	1,318,400	698,000
Less: Dividends declared:		
P Company	150,000	
S Company		60,000
Balance, December 31, 19x2— carried forward	$1,168,400	$ 638,000

Balance Sheet	P Company	S Company
Cash	$ 233,600	$ 48,000
Accounts receivable	240,000	70,000
Inventories	150,000	80,000
Land		150,000
Building		260,000
Equipment	800,000	633,000
Patent		—
Investment in S Company	946,400	
Totals	$2,370,000	$1,241,000
Accounts payable and accrued expenses	$ 150,600	$ 140,000
Accumulated depreciation— building		73,000
Accumulated depreciation— equipment	451,000	90,000
Common stock—P Company ($50 par)	200,000	
Common stock—S Company ($10 par)		300,000
Additional paid-in capital—P Company	400,000	
Retained earnings—brought forward	1,168,400	638,000
Totals	$2,370,000	$1,241,000

Required:

Prepare a consolidated working paper.

Problem 4–26 (Appendix 4–C). On January 1, 19x1, P Company purchased 40,000 shares (80 percent) of the outstanding common stock of S Company in the open market for $740,000. On that date, the retained earnings of S Company were $300,000. There have been no changes in capital stock since then. On January 1, 19x1, the assets and liabilities of S Company had book values that approximated their respective fair market values. Excess, if any, is to be amortized over 20 years.

P Company uses the cost method to account for its investment.

Financial statements for the two companies for the year ended December 31, 19x4, are as follows:

	P Company	S Company
Income Statement		
Sales	$2,000,000	$1,000,000
Cost of sales	800,000	600,000
Gross margin	1,200,000	400,000
Expenses	500,000	100,000
Operating income before		
taxes	700,000	300,000
Dividend income—subsidiary	48,000	
Income before income taxes .	748,000	300,000
Provision for income taxes . .	280,000	120,000
Minority interest net income		
Net income—carried forward	$ 468,000	$ 180,000

	P Company	S Company
Retained Earnings Statement		
Balance, January 1, 19x4:		
P Company	$2,000,000	
S Company		$ 800,000
Net income—brought		
forward	468,000	180,000
Totals	2,468,000	980,000
Less: Dividends declared:		
P Company	400,000	
S Company		60,000
Balance, December 31, 19x4—		
carried forward	$2,068,000	$ 920,000

	P Company	S Company
Balance Sheet		
Cash	$ 300,000	$ 100,000
Accounts receivable	200,000	200,000
Inventories	300,000	300,000
Land	500,000	
Equipment (net of		
accumulated depreciation) .	928,000	1,000,000
Investment in S Company . .	740,000	
Totals	$2,968,000	$1,600,000
Accounts payable and		
accrued expenses	$ 302,000	$ 180,000
Bonds payable (face amount		
$100,000)	98,000	
Common stock—P Company		
($50 par)	500,000	
Common stock—S Company		
($10 par)		500,000
Retained earnings—		
brought forward	2,068,000	920,000
Totals	$2,968,000	$1,600,000

Required:

a. Prepare a consolidated working paper.

b. Prepare consolidated financial statements.

Problem 4–27 (Appendix 4–C). On January 1, 19x1, P Company purchased 80 percent of the outstanding shares of S Company in the open market for $468,000. On that date, the following assets of S Company had book values that were different from their respective market values:

	Book value	Fair market value
Inventories	$ 40,000	$ 60,000
Land	100,000	140,000
Equipment (net)	600,000	550,000

On January 1, 19x1, S Company had retained earnings of $100,000 and there were no changes in capital stock or additional paid-in capital from that date.

The inventories were sold in 19x1, the land is still unsold and the equipment had a 20-year remaining life from January 1, 19x1. Goodwill, if any, had an indefinite life at that time and is still the case at present.

P Company uses the cost method to account for its investment.

Financial statements for the companies for the year ended December 31, 19x4, are as follows:

	P Company	S Company
Income Statement		
Sales	$1,200,000	$ 700,000
Cost of sales	500,000	250,000
Gross margin	700,000	450,000
Expenses	200,000	120,000
Operating income before		
taxes	500,000	330,000
Dividend income—subsidiary	48,000	
Income before income taxes .	548,000	330,000
Provision for income taxes . .	200,000	132,000
Minority interest net income		
Net income—carried forward	$ 348,000	$ 198,000

	P Company	S Company
Retained Earnings Statement		
Balance, January 1, 19x4:		
P Company	$ 800,000	
S Company		$ 500,000
Net income—brought		
forward	348,000	198,000
Totals	1,148,000	698,000
Less: Dividends declared:		
P Company	200,000	
S Company		60,000
Balance, December 31, 19x4—		
carried forward	$ 948,000	$ 638,000

Balance Sheet	P Company	S Company
Cash	$ 200,000	$ 50,000
Accounts receivable	120,000	70,000
Inventories	100,000	80,000
Land	100,000	100,000
Equipment	460,000	870,000
Investment in S Company . .	468,000	
Totals	$1,448,000	$1,170,000
Accounts payable and accrued expenses	$ 170,000	$ 32,000
Accumulated depreciation— equipment	30,000	100,000
Common stock—P Company ($50 par)	300,000	
Common stock—S Company ($10 par)		300,000
Additional paid-in capital—S Company		100,000
Retained earnings—carried forward	948,000	638,000
Totals	$1,448,000	$1,170,000

Required:

a. Prepare an allocation schedule of excess as of January 1, 19x1.

b. Prepare a consolidated working paper for 19x4.

Problem 4–28 (Appendix 4–D). On January 1, 19x1, P Company purchased 40,000 shares of S Company in the open market for $1,140,000. On that date, the assets and liabilities of S Company had book values that approximated their respective fair market values. Excess (goodwill), if any, is expected to last for 20 years and is to be amortized over that period.

P Company uses the complete equity method to account for its investment.

On December 31, 19x1, S Company owes P Company $10,000 on open account from purchases made last year.

Trial balances for the two corporations for the year ended December 31, 19x1, are as follows:

Debits	P Company	S Company
Cash	$ 300,000	$ 100,000
Accounts receivable	200,000	200,000
Inventories	400,000	300,000
Land	600,000	—
Building (net of accumulated depreciation)	400,000	—
Equipment (net of accumulated depreciation) .	1,228,000	1,000,000
Investment in S Company . .	1,231,000	
Cost of sales	800,000	600,000
Expenses	500,000	100,000
Provision for income taxes . .	280,000	120,000
Dividends paid	400,000	60,000
Bond discount	2,000	
Totals	$6,341,000	$2,480,000

Credits	P Company	S Company
Accounts payable and accrued expenses	$ 302,000	$ 180,000
Bonds payable	100,000	—
Common stock ($50 par; $10 par)	500,000	500,000
Additional paid-in capital . . .	300,000	—
Retained earnings	3,000,000	800,000
Sales	2,000,000	1,000,000
Equity in earnings— subsidiary	139,000	
Totals	$6,341,000	$2,480,000

Required:

a. Prepare a consolidated working paper using the trial balance approach.

b. Prepare consolidated financial statements.

Problem 4–29 (Appendix 4–D). On January 1, 19x1, P Company purchased 24,000 shares of S Company in the open market for $756,000. On that date the following assets of S Company had book values that were different from thier respective market values:

	Book value	Fair market value
Inventories	$ 40,000	$ 70,000
Land	150,000	200,000
Building (net)	200,000	300,000
Equipment (net)	450,000	375,000
Patent	—0—	40,000

All other assets and liabilities had book values approximately equal to their respective market values.

On January 1, 19x1, the building had a remaining

useful life of 20 years. Equipment and the patent had remaining useful lives of 10 years each. FIFO inventory costing is used. Goodwill, if any, has an indeterminate life. P Company uses the complete equity method to account for this investment.

Trial Balances for the companies for the year ended December 31, 19x1, are as follows:

Debits	P Company	S Company
Cash	$ 200,000	$ 100,000
Accounts receivable	150,000	50,000
Inventories	100,000	40,000
Land		150,000
Building		260,000
Equipment	700,000	490,000
Patents		—
Investment in S Company	808,800	
Cost of sales	400,000	150,000
Expenses	200,000	100,000
Provision for income taxes	160,000	100,000
Dividends paid	100,000	50,000
Totals	$2,818,800	$1,490,000

Credits	P Company	S Company
Accounts payable and accrued expenses	$ 124,000	$ 190,000
Accumulated depreciation— building		60,000
Accumulated depreciation equipment	402,000	40,000
Common stock ($50 par; $10 par)	200,000	300,000
Additional paid-in capital	400,000	
Retained earnings	600,000	400,000
Sales	1,000,000	500,000
Equity in earnings— subsidiary	92,800	
Totals	$2,818,800	$1,490,000

Required:

a. Prepare an allocation schedule of excess.

b. Prepare a consolidated working paper using the trial balance approach.

c. Prepare consolidated financial statements.

5

Consolidated statements— intercompany profits on inventories

OVERVIEW

Sales among members of an affiliated group of companies are made at prices in excess of cost. If any inventory from intercompany shipments is still held by an affiliate at the end of an accounting period, profits on the intercompany sale pertaining to that inventory must be eliminated when preparing a consolidated working paper. This unrealized profit is restored in a subsequent accounting period when the inventory is sold to outsiders.

When a sale is made by a parent company to a subsidiary—a downstream sale—any unrealized profit is charged entirely to the parent company. When a sale is made by a subsidiary to its parent company—an upstream sale—any unrealized profit is allocated between the parent company and the minority interest.

The elimination of intercompany profit in inventories is usually accomplished by eliminating 100 percent of the inventory profit. This is true for both upstream and downstream sales. Occasionally, another method, known as fractional elimination is used.

Most larger business organizations, especially diversified companies, use autonomous divisions as profit centers for purposes of motivation, return on investment measurement, and control. Rewards and penalties are usually a function of the division's performance in relation to invested capital and to a target income.

Billing above cost

As noted in Chapter 1, billings in excess of cost are necessary if a branch manager's performance is to be properly evaluated. The same procedures apply to divisons and subsidiaries. A parent company may sell to its subsidiaries at its normal selling price which is usually an amount in excess of its cost. In practice, subsidiaries also sell to a parent company at a price other than at cost. Because of these practices, problems arise in connection with income recognition of the consolidated entity.

UNCONFIRMED (UNREALIZED) PROFITS—SALES BY PARENT COMPANY (DOWNSTREAM)
First year

The procedures for eliminating unconfirmed profit in ending inventories which arise from a parent-subsidiary relationship are somewhat different from those in a home office–branch relationship.[1] In Chapter 1, unconfirmed profits were credited throughout the year to an Allowance for Overvaluation of Branch Inventory account, and at the year's end, an adjustment was made to this account for profits realized through sales to third parties. This account will not be used for consolidated statement purposes. A home office–branch relationship is always that within a single legal entity where 100 percent ownership is present, whereas in a parent-subsidiary relationship separate legal entities do exist and less than 100 percent ownership does occur. Accordingly, sales between a parent and its subsidiaries are credited to the respective seller's revenue accounts at the full selling price and purchases are debited by the purchaser at the same amount. If all of the inventory from an intercompany transaction is sold, income recognition problems do not exist since *all* of the intercompany profit is confirmed by a sale to third parties.

If, alternatively, some inventory from an intercompany transaction remains unsold at year's end, income recognition problems do exist and a postponement of this unconfirmed profit is necessary in order to prepare the consolidated statements in conformity with generally accepted accounting principles (GAAP). To illustrate the generally accepted approach when 100 percent of unconfirmed profits are eliminated, Illustration 5–1 is based on the following assumptions:

1. Mace Corporation acquired 90 percent of More Corporation on January 1, 19x1, in a transaction using purchase accounting. The price paid ($450,000) by Mace Corporation was equal to the book value of More Corporation, and the latter's book values approximated the respective fair market values of individuals assets and liabilities.
2. The Mace Corporation uses the complete equity method to account for its investment in More Corporation.
3. During 19x1, Mace Corporation sold to More Corporation merchandise (this is referred to as a "downstream" sale) and made the following entry on its books:

Accounts Receivable—More Corporation	100,000	
Sales		100,000

---

[1]*Unconfirmed* and *unrealized* are used interchangeably by accountants.

Mace Corporation normally sells its merchandise at 25 percent above cost (20 percent of selling price).

4. More Corporation made the following entry on its books:

Purchases	100,000	
Accounts Payable—Mace Corporation		100,000

More Corporation sold 60 percent of the above merchandise and has 40 percent of this inventory on hand on December 31, 19x1.

5. Income tax considerations are to be ignored (these will be discussed in Appendix 5–A at the end of this chapter).

6. More Corporation still owes Mace Corporation $30,000 for the intercompany purchases.

Paragraph .08 of *ARB 51* contains the following:

> In the preparation of consolidated statements, intercompany balances and transactions should be eliminated. This includes intercompany open account balances, security holdings, sales and purchases, interest, dividends, etc. As consolidated statements are based on the assumption that they represent the financial position and operating results of a single business enterprise, such statements should not include gain or loss on transactions among the companies in the group. Accordingly, any intercompany profit or loss on assets remaining within the group should be eliminated; the concept usually applied for this purpose is gross profit or loss.

Paragraph .14 of *ARB 51* states:

> The amount of intercompany profit or loss to be eliminated in accordance with paragraph .08 is not affected by the existence of a minority interest. The complete elimination of the intercompany profit or loss is consistent with the underlying assumption that consolidated statements represent the financial position and operating results of a single business enterprise. The elimination of the intercompany profit or loss may be allocated proportionately between the majority and minority interests.

Despite the recommendation that 100 percent of intercompany profits on assets still within the group be eliminated when minority interests exist, another method called fractional (partial) elimination is occasionally encountered in practice. This method is discussed in Appendix 5–B at the end of this chapter. The method used throughout the consolidation portion of this text is the 100 percent elimination approach recommended by *ARB 51*.

If the parent company uses the complete equity method to account for its investment, the following entries, based on the data previously assumed, would be recorded on the *books* of the parent company at the end of the year:

Parent Company Books—19x1

(1)

Investment in More Corporation	81,000	
Equity in Earnings of Subsidiary		81,000
To record 90 percent of the income ($90,000) earned by More Corporation for 19x1.		

(2)

Equity in Earnings of Subsidiary	8,000	
Investment in More Corporation		8,000

To remove 100 percent of the unconfirmed profit in More
Corporation's closing inventory purchased from Mace
Corporation. ($100,000 shipped less $60,000 sold equals $40,000
on hand at 20 percent profit based on the parent's selling price
which is the subsidiary's cost.)

In addition, the parent company would have made the following entry for
dividends received in 19x1:

(3)

Cash	36,000	
Investment in More Corporation		36,000

After giving effect to these entries, the parent's investment account would
appear as follows:

Investment in More Corporation

19x1				19x1			
Jan.	1	cost	450,000	Dec. 31	(2)		8,000
Dec. 31	(1)		81,000	Div.	(3)		36,000
Balance	487,000						

Initially, it may seem surprising that the unconfirmed profit of $8,000 on
a downstream sale (a profit that appears as income on the parent's books)
should be removed by entry (2). One may ask: Why whould the removal of
this profit affect the parent's Investment in More Corporation's account?
From Illustration 5–1 it can be seen that the net assets of More Corporation
on December 31, 19x1, are:

Capital stock	$300,000
Retained earnings	250,000
Total	$550,000
Parent's share—90%	$495,000
Less: Unconfirmed profit in	
subsidiary inventories	8,000
Parent's share of net assets	
in accordance with GAAP	$487,000

Since there was no excess in the purchase price paid ($450,000) by the
parent company for the investment in the subsidiary, the investment account should, in accordance with GAAP, be $487,000.

The working paper elimination entries for Illustration 5–1 are:

(1)

Equity in Earnings—Subsidiary	73,000	
Dividends Declared—More Corporation		36,000
Investment in More Corporation		37,000

(2)

Retained Earnings (1/1/x1)—More Corporation	180,000	
Capital Stock—More Corporation	270,000	
Investment in More Corporation		450,000

Illustration 5–1
MACE CORPORATION
Consolidated Working Paper
For the Year Ended December 31, 19x1

Complete Equity Method
End of First Year
90 Percent Subsidiary

	Mace Corp.	More Corp. (90%)	Eliminations		Minority Interest	Consol-idated
			Dr.	Cr.		
Income Statement						
Sales	900,000	400,000	(3) 100,000			1,200,000
Cost of sales	720,000	150,000	(4) 8,000	(3) 100,000		778,000
Gross margin	180,000	250,000				422,000
Expenses	100,000	100,000				200,000
Operating income before taxes	80,000	150,000				222,000
Equity in earnings—subsidiary	73,000		(1) 73,000			
Income before taxes	153,000	150,000				
Provision for income taxes (40%)	32,000	60,000				92,000
						130,000
Minority interest net income					9,000	(9,000)
Net income—carried forward	121,000	90,000			9,000	121,000
Retained Earnings Statement						
Balance, 1/1/x1:						
Mace Corp.	500,000					500,000
More Corp.		200,000	(2) 180,000		20,000	
Net income—brought forward	121,000	90,000			9,000	121,000
Totals	621,000	290,000			29,000	621,000
Less: Dividends declared						
Mace Corp.	20,000					20,000
More Corp.		40,000		(1) 36,000	4,000	
Balance, 12/31/x1—carried forward	601,000	250,000			25,000	601,000
Balance Sheet						
Cash	100,000	80,000				180,000
Accounts receivable (net)	80,000	50,000		(5) 30,000		100,000
Inventories	150,000	70,000		(4) 8,000		212,000
				(2) 450,000		
Investment in More Corp.	487,000			(1) 37,000		
Other assets	484,000	410,000				894,000
Totals	1,301,000	610,000				1,386,000
Accounts payable	90,000	40,000	(5) 30,000			100,000
Other liabilities	110,000	20,000				130,000
Capital stock:						
Mace Corp.	500,000					500,000
More Corp.		300,000	(2) 270,000		30,000	
Retained earnings—brought forward	601,000	250,000			25,000	601,000
Minority interest					55,000	55,000
Totals	1,301,000	610,000	661,000	661,000		1,386,000

(1) To eliminate equity in earnings of subsidiary and intercompany dividends.
(2) To eliminate balance of investment in subsidiary and subsidiary's stockholders equity (reciprocal accounts).
(3) Elimination of intercompany sales.
(4) Elimination of intercompany profit in closing inventory (40,000 × 20% = $8,000).
(5) Elimination of intercompany receivable and payable.

Illustration 5–1 *(continued)*

Computations and Proofs

Income apportionment:

	Total	Parent	Minority
Income—More Corp.	$ 90,000	$ 81,000	$ 9,000
Income—Mace Corp. ($121,000 − 73,000.)	48,000	48,000	
Unrealized profit in inventory	(8,000)	(8,000)	
Totals	$130,000	$121,000	$ 9,000

Reconciliation—minority interest:

More Corp.—capital stock	$300,000
—retained earnings (end of year)	250,000
Total equity	$550,000
Minority interest @ 10%	$ 55,000

	(3)		
Sales		100,000	
Cost of Sales			100,000
	(4)		
Cost of Sales (ending inventory)		8,000	
Inventories			8,000
	(5)		
Accounts Payable		30,000	
Accounts Receivable			30,000

The debit to Equity in Earnings of Subsidiary account can also be verified by reviewing Illustration 5–1 and noting the following:

1. Entry (1) eliminates $73,000 of income ($81,000 less the $8,000 of unconfirmed profit), the intercompany dividend of $36,000, and the net effect of other transactions of the subsidiary that affect the parent's share (90 percent) of these transactions—$37,000. The result of this elimination entry is to convert the 19x1 ending balance of the investment account ($487,000) to the beginning balance of $450,000 as of January 1, 19x1. This process permits the details (sales, cost of sales, etc.) of the subsidiary's operation for the year to be combined with those of the parent company.

2. Parent net income—per its books—of $121,000 agrees with CNI of $121,000. This result is always true whenever the complete equity method is used.

Additional observations from Illustration 5–1 that are noteworthy follow:

1. Entry (4) increases cost of sales and thereby decreases profit by the amount of the unconfirmed profit in the subsidiary's closing inventory. The entry also reduces the inventory in the balance sheet back to cost for the combined entity. Although this entry (removal of unconfirmed profit) was recorded on the books of the parent company through the

investment and equity in earnings accounts, entry (4) must be made on the working paper in order to remove the profit again because entries (1) and (2) on the working paper *eliminate* the accounts which reflected the profit removal on the parent's books.

2. Parent retained earnings and consolidated retained earnings are identical. This is always true for the complete equity method.

3. All intercompany sales ($100,000) are removed in the year the sales were made, despite the fact that $60,000 was sold to third parties and only $40,000 of these sales is still on hand in the subsidiary's inventory. Sales between related parties are not considered as sales (purchases) from the entity viewpoint.

4. Minority interest net income (see apportionment on working paper) and minority interest (see reconciliation on working paper) are unaffected by downstream sales.

Second year

In the second year, it is now assumed that the inventory on hand on December 31, 19x1 has been sold to third parties. If not, entry (4) from Illustration 5–1 would be repeated. When the inventory is sold to third parties, this completes the transaction and any unconfirmed profits carried over from 19x1 are now considered to be earned in accordance with GAAP. Accordingly, the $8,000 of unconfirmed profit from 19x1 that was removed in entry (2) on the parent's books must now be restored as earned income in 19x2, and this is accomplished by reversing that entry as follows:

Parent's Books—19x2

(1)

Investment in More Corporation	8,000	
Equity in Earnings of Subsidiary		8,000
To restore 100 percent of unconfirmed inventory profit on December 31, 19x1, because this inventory has been sold to third parties by More Corporation.		

In addition, if it is assumed that More Corporation earned $96,000 for 19x2 and paid dividends of $40,000 during the year, Mace Corporation would also make the following entries for 19x2:

(2)

Investment in More Corporation	86,400	
Equity in Earnings of Subsidiary		86,400
To record parent's share of subsidiary's earnings for 19x2 (90% × $96,000).		

(3)

Cash	36,000	
Investment in More Corporation		36,000
To record receipt of dividends from More Corporation (90% × $40,000).		

If there are no unconfirmed profits at the end of 19x2 and there were no intercompany transactions for 19x2, the partial consolidated working paper for 19x2 would appear as shown in Illustration 5–2. All information other than that previously given is assumed.

The working paper eliminations entries are:

(1)		
Equity in Earnings—Subsidiary	94,400	
Dividends Declared—More Corporation		36,000
Investment in More Corporation		58,400

(2)		
Investment in More Corporation	8,000	
Cost of Sales (beginning inventory)		8,000

(3)		
Retained Earnings (1/1/x2)—More Corporation	225,000	
Capital Stock—More Corporation	270,000	
Investment in More Corporation		495,000

Pertinent observations from this illustration are:

1. The equity in earnings from subsidiary ($94,400) consists of entries (1) and (2) on the parent's books for 19x2. The investment balance of $545,400 consists of last year's closing balance of $487,000 and the effect of entries (1), (2), and (3).

2. Elimination entry (1) is similar to entry (1) in Illustration 5–1. However, *before* the balance in the investment can be eliminated, it is necessary to restore the previously unconfirmed profit of $8,000 on the *working paper*. It should be remembered that when the complete equity method is used, it is necessary to repeat adjustment entries on the working paper even though these entries were previously recorded on the parent's books. *After* entry (2) has been recorded on the working paper, it is possible to proceed with the elimination of the investment balance as was done in entry (3).

3. Parent net income is the same as CNI, and parent retained earnings is the same as consolidated retained earnings. (This is always true when the complete equity method is used.)

4. The provision for income taxes in the consolidated column is not 40 percent of consolidated operating income. (The treatment required to correct this is covered in Appendix 5–A.)

5. The income apportionment schedule and reconciliation of minority interest are useful for purposes of achieving a better understanding of consolidation procedures.

UNCONFIRMED PROFITS—SALES BY SUBSIDIARIES (UPSTREAM)

First year

We turn now to sales by subsidiaries of a common parent. As noted earlier, *ARB 51* states:

> The amount of intercompany profit or loss to be eliminated is not affected by the existence of a minority interest. . . . The elimination of the intercompany profit or loss may be allocated proportionately between the majority and minority interests.

Accordingly, Illustration 5–1 will now be reworked incorporating the principles recommended by *ARB 51* with one modification. It is now assumed that More Corporation made the sale to the parent company at the same rate of gross profit (20 percent on selling price and 25 percent on cost).

Illustration 5–2
MACE CORPORATION
Partial Consolidated Working Paper
For the Year Ended December 31, 19x2

Complete Equity Method
End of Second Year
90 Percent Subsidiary

	Mace Corp.	More Corp. (90%)	Eliminations Dr.	Eliminations Cr.	Minority Interest	Consol- idated
Income Statement						
Sales	1,000,000	450,000				1,450,000
Cost of sales	750,000	180,000		(2) 8,000		922,000
Gross margin	250,000	270,000				528,000
Expenses	120,000	110,000				230,000
Operating income before taxes	130,000	160,000				298,000
Equity in earnings—subsidiary	94,400		(1) 94,400			
Income before taxes	224,400	160,000				
Provision for income taxes (40%)	52,000	64,000				116,000
						182,000
Minority interest net income					9,600	(9,600)
Net income—carried forward	172,400	96,000			9,600	172,400
Retained Earnings Statement						
Balance, 1/1/x2:						
Mace Corp.	601,000					601,000
More Corp.		250,000	(3) 225,000		25,000	
Net Income—brought forward	172,400	96,000			9,600	172,400
Totals	773,400	346,000			34,600	773,400
Less: Dividends declared						
Mace Corp.	40,000					40,000
More Corp.		40,000		(1) 36,000	4,000	
Balance, 12/31/x2—carried forward	773,400	306,000			30,600	733,400
Balance Sheet						
				(1) 58,400		
Investment in More Corp.	545,400		(2) 8,000	(3) 495,000		
Capital stock—More Corp.		300,000	(3) 270,000		30,000	
Retained earnings—brought forward	733,400	306,000			30,600	733,400
Minority interest					60,000	60,600

(1) To eliminate equity in earnings from subsidiary and intercompany dividends.
(2) Restoration of confirmed inventory profit.
(3) Elimination of balance of investment.

Computations and Proofs

Income apportionment:

	Total	Parent	Minority
Income—More Corp.	$ 96,000	$ 86,400	$ 9,600
Income—Mace Corp. ($172,400 − $94,400)	78,000	78,000	
Confirmed inventory profit	8,000	8,000	
Totals	$182,000	$172,000	$ 9,600

Reconciliation—minority interest:

More Corp.—capital stock	$300,000
—retained earnings (end of year)	306,000
Total equity	$606,000
Minority interest @ 10%	$ 60,600

Although *ARB 51* states that the elimination of intercompany profit *may* be allocated proportionately between the parent company and the minority interests, it is generally accepted that apportionment is the norm. Accordingly, this approach will be used throughout this book. If apportionment were not used, Illustration 5–1 and Illustration 5–3 would be identical. However, a comparison of the two illustrations show that apportionment produces a different result when the subsidiary sells merchandise to the parent company instead of vice versa. Therefore, for purposes of eliminating intercompany profit, it is important to determine who makes the sale. It should be noted that sales, receivables, and payables are the same for a parent making sales to a subsidiary as for a subsidiary making sales (for the same amount of dollars) to its parent company.

For 19x1, the parent company's entries on its books are:

Parent Company's Books—19x1

(1)

Investment in More Corporation	81,000	
Equity in Earnings of Subsidiary		81,000

To record parent's share of income earned by subsidiary (90% × $90,000) for 19x1.

(2)

Equity in Earnings of Subsidiary	7,200	
Investment in More Corporation		7,200

To remove *parent's share* of unconfirmed inventory profit on *upstream* sale (90% × $8,000).

(3)

Cash	36,000	
Investment in More Corporation		36,000

To record dividends received.

The working paper elimination entries for Illustration 5–3 are:

(1)

Equity in Earnings—Subsidiary	73,800	
Dividends Declared—More Corporation		36,000
Investment in More Corporation		37,800

(2)

Retained Earnings (1/1/x1)—More Corporation	180,000	
Capital Stock—More Corporation	270,000	
Investment in More Corporation		450,000

(3)

Sales	100,000	
Cost of Sales		100,000

(4)

Cost of Sales (ending inventory)	8,000	
Inventories		8,000

(5)

Accounts Payable	30,000	
Accounts Receivable		30,000

Illustration 5-3
MACE CORPORATION
Consolidated Working Paper
For the Year Ended December 31, 19x1

Complete Equity Method
End of First Year
90 Percent Subsidiary

	Mace Corp.	More Corp. (90%)	Eliminations Dr.	Eliminations Cr.	Minority Interest	Consolidated
Income Statement						
Sales	900,000	400,000	(3) 100,000			1,200,000
Cost of sales	720,000	150,000	(4) 8,000	(3) 100,000		778,000
Gross margin	180,000	250,000				422,000
Expenses	100,000	100,000				200,000
Operating income before taxes	80,000	150,000				222,000
Equity in earnings—subsidiary	73,800		(1) 73,800			
Income before taxes	153,800	150,000				
Provision for income taxes	32,000	60,000				92,000
						130,000
Minority interest net income					8,200	(8,200)
Net income—carried forward	121,800	90,000			8,200	121,800
Retained Earnings Statement						
Balance, 1/1/x1:						
Mace Corp.	500,000					500,000
More Corp.		200,000	(2) 180,000		20,000	
Net income—brought forward	121,800	90,000			8,200	121,800
Totals	621,800	290,000			28,200	621,800
Less: Dividends declared:						
Mace Corp.	20,000					20,000
More Corp.		40,000		(1) 36,000	4,000	
Balance, 12/31/x1—carried forward	601,800	250,000			24,200	601,800
Balance Sheet						
Cash	100,000	80,000				180,000
Accounts receivable (net)	80,000	50,000		(5) 30,000		100,000
Inventories	150,000	70,000		(4) 8,000		212,000
				(2) 450,000		
Investment in More Corp.	487,800			(1) 37,800		
Other Assets	484,000	410,000				894,000
Totals	1,301,800	610,000				1,386,000
Accounts payable	90,000	40,000	(5) 30,000			100,000
Other liabilities	110,000	20,000				130,000
Capital stock:						
Mace Corp.	500,000					500,000
More Corp.		300,000	(2) 270,000		30,000	
Retained earnings—brought forward	601,800	250,000			24,200	601,800
Minority interest					54,200	54,200
Totals	1,301,800	610,000	661,800	661,800		1,386,000

(1) Elimination of equity in earnings of subsidiary and intercompany dividend.
(2) Elimination of investment.
(3) Elimination of intercompany sales.
(4) Elimination of intercompany profit in closing inventory ($40,000 × 20% = $8,000).
(5) Elimination of intercompany receivable and payable.

Illustration 5–3 *(continued)*

Computations and Proofs

Income apportionment:

	Total	Parent	Minority
Income—More Corp.	$ 90,000	$ 81,000	$ 9,000
Less: Unrealized profit in inventory	(8,000)	(7,200)	(800)
Income—Mace Corp. ($121,800 − $73,800)	48,000	48,000	
Totals	$130,000	$121,800	$ 8,200

Reconciliation—minority interest:

More Corp.—capital stock	$300,000
—retained earnings (end of year)	250,000
Total equity	$550,000
Less: Unrealized profit in ending inventory	8,000
Balance	$542,000
Minority interest @ 10%	$ 54,200

Some salient observations of Illustration 5–3 are:

1. Although there is a 10 percent minority interest in the More Corporation, *100 percent of the inventory profit ($8,000) is eliminated,* and the $8,000 is then apportioned (90 percent or $7,200 against the parent and 10 percent or $800 against the minority interest).
2. The decision of whether or not to apportion is best reached by ascertaining who made the sale. The decision rule is as follows:
    a. If the subsidiary made the sale, apportionment is in order since the subsidiary has a minority ownership interest.
    b. If the parent made the sale, then *do not* apportion, since the parent has no minority interest.
3. Consolidated net income is the same as parent net income. Consolidated retained earnings is the same as parent retained earnings.
4. Minority interest net income must be reduced by 10 percent (its share) of the unconfirmed inventory profit. (See income apportionment computations.)
5. The balance of minority interest on December 31, 19x1, is $800 (10 percent × $8,000 unconfirmed profit) lower than 10 percent of $550,000 (net assets of More Corporation on December 31, 19x1). This can be seen in the reconciliation of minority interest schedule.

Second year

Using the same data as presented in Illustration 5–2 except that the subsidiary is assumed to have made the sale of merchandise, Illustration 5–4 provides the solution to the confirmed-profit problem for the year 19x2. The major differences between Illustration 5–2 (where the parent company made the sale) and Illustration 5–4 is in the apportionment of net income between majority and minority interests.

The following entries would be recorded on the parent's books for 19x2:

Illustration 5–4
MACE CORPORATION
Partial Consolidated Working Paper
For the Year Ended December 31, 19x2

Complete Equity Method
End of Second Year
90 Percent Subsidiary

	Mace Corp.	More Corp. (90%)	Eliminations Dr.	Eliminations Cr.	Minority Interest	Consol- idated
Income Statement						
Sales	1,000,000	450,000				1,450,000
Cost of sales	750,000	180,000		(2) 8,000		922,000
Gross margin	250,000	270,000				528,000
Expenses	120,000	110,000				230,000
Operating income before taxes	130,000	160,000				298,000
Equity in earnings—subsidiary	93,600		(1) 93,600			
Income before taxes	223,600	160,000				
Provision for income taxes	52,000	64,000				116,000
						182,000
Minority interest net income					10,400	(10,400)
Net income	171,600	96,000			10,400	171,600
Retained Earnings Statement						
Balance, 1/1/x2:						
Mace Corp.	601,800					601,800
More Corp.		250,000	(2) 800		24,200	
Net income—forward	171,600	96,000	(3) 225,000		10,400	171,600
Totals	773,400	346,000			34,600	773,400
Less: Dividends declared:						
Mace Corp.	40,000					40,000
More Corp.		40,000		(1) 36,000	4,000	
Balance, 12/31/x2:	733,400	306,000			30,600	733,400
Balance Sheet						
Investment in More Corp.	545,400		(2) 7,200	(3) 495,000 (1) 57,600		
Capital stock—More Corp.		300,000	(3) 270,000		30,000	
Retained earnings—forward	733,400	306,000			30,600	733,400
Minority interest					60,600	60,600

(1) Elimination of equity in earnings of subsidiary and intercompany dividends.
(2) Restoration of confirmed inventory profit.
(3) Elimination of Investment.

Illustration 5–4 (continued)

Computations and Proofs

Income apportionment:

	Total	Parent	Minority
Income—More Corp.	$ 96,000	$ 86,400	$ 9,600
Confirmed inventory profit	8,000	7,200	800
Income—Mace Corp. ($171,600 − $93,600)	78,000	78,000	
Totals	$182,000	$171,600	$ 10,400

Reconciliation—minority interest:

More Corp.—capital stock	$300,000
—retained earnings (end of year)	306,000
Total equity	$606,000
Minority interest @ 10%	$ 60,600

Parent Company's Books—19x2

(1)

Investment in More Corporation	7,200	
Equity in Earnings of Subsidiary		7,200

To restore 19x1 unconfirmed inventory profit for inventory sold by More Corporation in 19x2.

(2)

Investment in More Corporation	86,400	
Equity in Earnings of Subsidiary		86,400

To record parent's share of subsidiary's earnings for 19x2 (90% × $96,000).

(3)

Cash	36,000	
Investment in More Corporation		36,000

To record receipt of dividends received.

The working paper elimination entries for Illustration 5–4 are:

(1)

Equity in Earnings—Subsidiary	93,600	
Dividends Declared—More Corporation		36,000
Investment in More Corporation		57,600

(2)

Retained Earnings (1/1/x2)—More Corporation	800	
Investment in More Corporation	7,200	
Cost of Sales (beginning inventory)		8,000

(3)

Retained Earnings (1/1/x2)—More Corporation	225,000	
Capital Stock—More Corporation	270,000	
Investment in More Corporation		495,000

From Illustration 5–4, the following observations are particularly noteworthy:

1. The restoration of the $8,000 of unconfirmed profit from 19x1 should be done—entry (2)—*prior* to the elimination of the investment balance. If

not, the investment balance of $495,000 will have to be calculated taking into account the allocated portion of $7,200 (90% × $8,000). The reduction of cost of sales increases the profit. For the complete equity method, the parent's share ($7,200) is an adjustment to the investment balance. The minority interest's portion ($800) is an adjustment to the beginning retained earnings of the subsidiary. After entry (3) is made, the minority interest retained earnings becomes $24,200 ($250,000 − $225,000 = $25,000 − $800 = $24,200).

2. Minority interest net income of $10,400 can be calculated as 10% × $96,000 = $9,600 + $800 or $10,400. Thus, the minority interest's share of the restored inventory profit is proven.

3. The reconciliation of minority interest ($60,600) no longer requires an adjustment for inventory profit. Since the profit from the previous year (19x1) has now been cleared in 19x2, it is no longer a reconciling item. Reconciling items are those amounts that are uncleared at the *end* of any given year and awaiting clearance in subsequent years.

4. A comparison of Illustration 5–2 with 5–4 reveals that the parent retained earnings, consolidated retained earnings, minority interest, and the investment balance respectively all have *identical balances as of December 31, 19x2,* in both illustrations. From this comparison it can be noted that the differing treatments between downstream and upstream sales are matters of timing only. When the reconciling items have cleared (sales to third parties are completed), book balances and working paper balances coincide and no differences result between upstream and downstream sales. In essence, the deferral of income recognition is the required method used in order to comply with GAAP.

INVENTORIES— UNCONFIRMED PROFITS— COMPREHENSIVE ILLUSTRATION

Heretofore, each illustration dealt with only one aspect of unconfirmed inventory profits. A comprehensive illustration will now be presented. The following information is applicable to Illustration 5–5:

1. P Company acquired its investment in S Company at book value on January 2, 19x1. The book values of the assets and liabilities of S Company approximate their respective fair market values.

2. The acquisition required the use of purchase accounting, and P Company is using the complete equity method to account for its investment.

3. Income tax timing considerations are to be ignored.

4. The companies had intercompany transactions as follows:

	P Company	S Company
Sales	$50,000	$40,000
Unsold inventories:		
January 1, 19x2	20,000	10,000
December 31, 19x2	30,000	20,000
Receivables, December 31, 19x2	25,000	15,000

5. Intercompany sales are made at the same rate of gross margin as to third parties. The 19x1 margin was the same as that for 19x2. Thus, P Company sells to S Company at a profit of 60 percent of selling price and S Company sells to P Company at a profit of 70 percent of selling price.

Based on the above information and the information presented in Illustration 5–5, the parent company would make the following entries on its books for 19x2:

Parent Company's Books—19x2

(1)

Investment in S Company	108,000	
Equity in Earnings of Subsidiary		108,000

To record parent's share of subsidiary income (90% × $120,000).

(2)

Cash	54,000	
Investment in S Company		54,000

To record receipt of dividends.

(3)

Investment in S Company	18,600	
Equity in Earnings of Subsidiary		18,600

To restore profits in opening inventories:

Downstream (100% of 60% gross profit × $10,000 inventory)	$ 6,000	
Upstream (90%* of 70% gross profit × $20,000 inventory)	12,600	
Total	$18,600	

(4)

Equity in Earnings of Subsidiary	30,900	
Investment in S Company		30,900

To remove unconfirmed profit in closing inventories:

Downstream (100% of 60% gross profit × $20,000 inventory)	$12,000	
Upstream (90%* × 70% gross profit × $30,000 inventory)	18,900	
Total	$30,900	

*Due to 10 percent minority interest.

The working paper elimination entries for Illustration 5–5 are:

(1)

Equity in Earnings—Subsidiary	95,700	
Dividends Declared—S Company		54,000
Investment in S Company		41,700

(2)

Retained Earnings (1/1/x2)—S Company	1,400	
Investment in S Company	18,600	
Cost of Sales (beginning inventory)		20,000

(3)

Retained Earnings (1/1/x2)—S Company	360,000	
Capital Stock—S Company	270,000	
Investment in S Company		630,000

	(4)	
Sales	90,000	
Cost of Sales		90,000

	(5)	
Accounts Payable	40,000	
Accounts Receivable		40,000

	(6)	
Cost of Sales (ending inventory)	33,000	
Inventories		33,000

A close examination of Illustration 5–5 will reveal the following:

1. The elimination of intercompany receivables and payables of $25,000 and $15,000 can be combined into a single entry. It is also immaterial who the debtor is if there is only one receivable. These concepts can be demonstrated by the following analysis of book amounts and the resulting eliminations:

	P Company	S Company	Consolidated
Receivable from S Company	$ 25,000		
Receivable from P Company		$15,000	
Receivables from others	75,000	65,000	$140,000
Totals—per books	$100,000	$80,000	
Payable to S Company	$ 15,000		
Payable to P Company		$25,000	
Payables to others	65,000	35,000	100,000
Totals—per books	$ 80,000	$60,000	

It is clear that $40,000 ($25,000 + $15,000) must be eliminated from both the receivables and payables for purposes of consolidation. For elimination purposes, receivables and payables from parent to subsidiary and vice versa are *added—not netted.*

2. The elimination entry for unconfirmed profit in *closing inventories is not apportioned in* the entry [see entry (6)] to minority interest, but, rather, it is apportioned in the income that is allocated to the minority interest ($11,300).

3. The restoration (confirmation) of the profit in the *beginning inventories requires an apportionment* for minority interest ($1,400) which results in an adjustment of the minority interest's share in retained earnings [see entry (2) on working paper]. In addition, a net apportionment of the $1,400 is also required in the income allocated to the minority interest ($11,300). (See income allocation schedule.)

4. The reconciliation of the minority interest requires an adjustment for unconfirmed profit in the closing inventory *only.* No adjustment for the profit in the beginning inventory is necessary since the closing retained earnings already reflect the reversal of the intercompany profit in the beginning inventory.

Illustration 5–5
P COMPANY
Consolidated Working Paper
For the Year Ended December 31, 19x2

Complete Equity Method
End of Second Year
90 Percent Subsidiary

	P Co.	S Co. (90%)	Eliminations Dr.	Eliminations Cr.	Minority Interest	Consolidated
Income Statement						
Sales	800,000	500,000	(4) 90,000	(2) 20,000		1,210,000
Cost of sales	320,000	150,000	(6) 33,000	(4) 90,000		393,000
Gross margin	480,000	350,000				817,000
Expenses	280,000	150,000				430,000
Operating income before taxes	200,000	200,000				387,000
Equity in earnings—subsidiary	95,700		(1) 95,700			
Income before taxes	295,700	200,000				
Provision for income taxes	80,000	80,000				160,000
						227,000
Minority interest net income					11,300	(11,300)
Net income—carried forward	215,700	120,000			11,300	215,700
Retained Earnings Statement						
Balance, 1/1/x2:						
P Co.	581,400					581,400
			(2) 1,400			
S Co.		400,000	(3) 360,000		38,600	
Net income—brought forward	215,700	120,000			11,300	215,700
Totals	797,100	520,000			49,900	797,100
Less: Dividends declared—S Co.		60,000		(1) 54,000	6,000	
Balance, 12/31/x2—carried forward	797,100	460,000			43,900	797,100
Balance Sheet						
Cash	60,000	40,000				100,000
Accounts receivable (net)	100,000	80,000		(5) 40,000		140,000
Inventories	70,000	30,000		(6) 33,000		67,000
				(3) 630,000		
Investment in S Co.	653,100		(2) 18,600	(1) 41,700		
Other assets	444,000	700,000				1,144,000
Totals	1,327,100	850,000				1,451,000
Accounts payable	80,000	60,000	(5) 40,000			100,000
Other liabilities	50,000	30,000				80,000
Capital stock:						
P Co.	400,000					400,000
S Co.		300,000	(3) 270,000		30,000	
Retained earnings—brought forward	797,100	460,000			43,900	797,100
Minority interest					73,900	73,900
Totals	1,327,100	850,000	908,700	908,700		1,451,000

(1) Elimination of equity in earnings of subsidiary and intercorporate dividends.
(2) Confirmation of profit in beginning inventory.
(3) Elimination of investment.
(4) Elimination of intercompany sales.
(5) Elimination of intercompany receivables and payables.
(6) Intercompany profit in closing inventory.

Illustration 5–5 *(continued)*

Computations and Proofs

Elimination entries:

A. Profit in closing inventories:

P Co. inventory sold by S Co.	$30,000	
S Co. margin	70%	
Unconfirmed profit		$ 21,000
S Co. inventory sold by P Co.	$20,000	
P Co. margin	60%	
Unconfirmed profit		12,000
Total		$ 33,000

B. Profit in beginning inventories:

	Total	Parent	Minority Interest
P Co. inventory—sale by S Co. ($20,000 × 70%)	$ 14,000	$ 12,600	$ 1,400
S Co. inventory—sale by P Co. ($10,000 × 60%)	6,000	6,000	
Totals	$ 20,000	$ 18,600	$ 1,400

Income apportionment:

	Total	Parent	Minority
Income—S Co.	$120,000	$108,000	$ 12,000
Add: Confirmed profit (70% × $20,000)	14,000	12,600	1,400
Less: Unconfirmed profit (70% × $30,000)	(21,000)	(18,900)	(2,100)
Total—S Co.	$113,000	$101,700	$ 11,300
Income—P Co. ($215,700 − $95,700)	120,000	120,000	
Add: Confirmed profit (60% × $10,000)	6,000	6,000	
Less: Unconfirmed profit (60% × $20,000)	(12,000)	(12,000)	
Totals	$227,000	$215,700	$ 11,300

Reconciliation—minority interest:

S Co.—capital stock	$300,000
—retained earnings (end of year)	460,000
Total equity	$760,000
Less: Unconfirmed profit in closing inventory of P Co. (70% × $30,000)	21,000
Total	$739,000
Minority interest @ 10%	$ 73,900

Note: Adjustment for opening inventory confirmation is *not* required.

SALES BETWEEN SUBSIDIARIES OF ONE AFFILIATED GROUP— LATERAL SALES

No additional complications are created when the intercompany sale is a *lateral* one. The entire intercompany profit on unsold inventory will be eliminated and income apportionment between majority (parent) and minority interests will be handled in the same manner as illustrated in the case of upstream sales.

REDUCTIONS OF INVENTORIES—LOWER OF COST OR MARKET WRITE-DOWNS

Occasionally, unsold inventories which result from intercompany sales must be written down in order to comply with GAAP. When this occurs, the elimination of intercompany profit must be modified by the amount of the write-down. For example, if a parent company shipped to a subsidiary $100,000 of merchandise that had a cost price of $80,000 to the parent, and

50 percent of the inventory (i.e., $50,000) was unsold at the end of the year, the normal elimination entry for unconfirmed profit would be $10,000 (50 percent of the $20,000 gross profit). However, if the subsidiary already wrote the inventory down to $43,000 (a write-down of $7,000), the elimination entry would be for only $3,000. If the write-down carries the inventory to $40,000 or less, no additional elimination entry for unconfirmed profit would be required.

GROSS PROFIT VERSUS NET PROFIT

In discussions on the proper amount of profit to be eliminated, some theoreticians have advocated the elimination of *net* profits on intercompany sales rather than *gross* profits. This theory is difficult to sustain for the following reasons:

1. Selling and administrative expenses are not inventoriable and, therefore, are not subject to capitalization. Using net profit would, in effect, capitalize these expenses during the time that these inventories remain unsold. It is true that either profit deferral will ultimately be reversed, but this does not justify the deferral of the wrong amount in the interim.
2. The calculation of net profit on a specific item requires the use of arbitrary allocations of joint period costs which presents another argument against the use of this concept.

DISCLOSURE OF CONSOLIDATION POLICIES

APB Opinion 22 generally requires that the basis of consolidation be disclosed in the notes, or a section immediately preceding the notes, to the financial statements.[2] A typical note, taken from a recent General Motors Corporation Annual Report, follows:

Note 1: Significant Accounting Policies.

Principles of Consolidation

The consolidated financial statements include the accounts of the Corporation and all domestic and foreign subsidiaries which are more than 50 percent owned and engaged principally in manufacturing or wholesale marketing of General Motors products. General Motors' share of earnings or losses of nonconsolidated subsidiaries and of associates in which at least 20 percent of the voting securities is owned is generally included in consolidated income under the equity method of accounting. Intercompany items and transactions between companies included in the consolidation are eliminated and unrealized intercompany profits on sales to nonconsolidated subsidiaries and to associates are deferred.

---

[2]*APB*, "Disclosure of Accounting Policies," *APB Opinion No.* 22 (New York: AICPA, 1972), par. 13.

Appendix 5–A: Income tax considerations for consolidated financial statements

Members of an affiliated group (hereinafter defined) can elect to file either a consolidated income tax return for the group as a whole or they can file separate tax returns with each member paying taxes on its own income. The separate corporation's income tax provisions, and the combined provision as it appears in the consolidated column of the working paper, will be affected by the choice of income tax return(s) filed.

Separate income tax returns

When separate income tax returns are filed, each corporation will pay its own income taxes and, therefore, its tax provision will be based on *its* own taxable income. The calculation is relatively simple since there is *no* allowance for the elimination of unconfirmed intercompany profits. In this case, any unconfirmed intercompany profits will be taxed to the corporation making the sale. Since these unconfirmed profits will be eliminated in the consolidated financial statements, the consolidated entity is, in effect, prepaying the income taxes on the unconfirmed profits and a deferred income tax debit should be set up for such prepayment. There may be perfectly valid reasons for not filing consolidated tax returns as is the case when less than 80 percent of a subsidiary is owned and consequently the requisites for a consolidated income tax return have not been met. Notwithstanding the method of tax filing, consolidated financial statements must still be prepared. Consolidated income tax returns will usually produce lower income taxes and they will be considered later in this appendix.

Referring back to Illustration 5–1, we see that entry (4) eliminated $8,000 of unconfirmed inventory profit. If for some reasons, individual rather than consolidated tax returns are prepared, the working paper entry necessary to record the prepayment of $3,200 (40 percent × $8,000) in income taxes is as follows:

Deferred Income Tax	3,200	
Provision for Income Taxes . .		3,200

The deferred income tax would appear as a deferred charge in the consolidated column of the balance sheet section. The bottom portion of the income statement section would then appear as in Illustration 5–6.

A comparison of Illustration 5–1 with Illustration 5–6 reveals that the consolidated provision for income taxes of the latter ($88,800) is 40 percent of the consolidated income before income taxes ($222,000) whereas the provision in Illustration 5–1 is not. Obviously, the approach in Illustration 5–6 which uses elimination entries net of their tax effect is the correct one. However, in order to introduce concepts in a gradual manner, Illustrations 5–1 through 5–5 were presented without considering the net-of-tax concept.

In Illustration 5–2, the consolidated provision for income taxes ($116,000) is also *not* 40 percent of operating income before income taxes ($298,000). However, in that Illustration, the $8,000 of inventory profit is confirmed (reversed) and, accordingly, the deferred income tax expense shown in Illustration 5–6 should also be reversed. The consolidated provision for income taxes will then be $3,200 higher ($116,000 + $3,200 = $119,200) which will bring it

Illustration 5–6
Partial Consolidated Working Paper
For the Year Ended December 31, 19x1

	Make Corp.	More Corp.	Eliminations Dr.	Eliminations Cr.	Minority Interest	Consol- idated
Operating income before income taxes						222,000
Income before income taxes	153,000	150,000				
Provision for income taxes	32,000	60,000		(4) 3,200*		88,800
						133,200
Minority interest net income					9,000	(9,000)
Net income	121,000	90,000			9,000	124,200

*This represents an expansion of the entry (4) found in Illustration 5–1.

up to 40 percent of the consolidated operating income before income taxes ($298,000).

To summarize, whenever *separate* income tax returns are filed and intercompany unconfirmed profits exist, the deferral of profit from the intercompany sale of inventories will require that a prepaid income taxes provision be set up. When profit reversal (confirmation) occurs, the reversal of the related deferred income tax provision is also required. Stated differently, if the income tax rate is 40 percent, a deferral and confirmation of profit should net out at 60 percent of the profit adjustment.

The treatment is similar when the subsidiary is the seller. Referring to Illustration 5–3, we can now make the following additional working paper entry for the prepaid income taxes:

Deferred Income Tax	3,200	
Provision for Income Taxes . .		3,200

After giving effect to the above entry, the income apportionment schedule and the income statement portion of the working paper would appear as in Illustration 5–7. From this illustration, it is apparent that:

1. The provision for income taxes in the consolidated column is equal to 40 percent of the operating income before income taxes, whereas in Illustration 5–3 this was not the case.
2. The apportionments of income to the majority and minority interests are consistent, i.e., they are net of income taxes.
3. The reconciliation of minority interest requires an adjustment for unconfirmed profit at year's end—net of income taxes.

4. Parent net income does *not* equal consolidated net income. The difference is the parent's share of the deferred taxes (90 percent × $3,200 = $2,880).

Consolidated income tax returns

Section 1501 of the Internal Revenue Code (IRC) provides:

> An affiliated group of corporations shall, subject to the provisions of this chapter, have the privilege of making a consolidated return with respect to the income tax imposed by Chapter 1 for the taxable year in lieu of separate returns. The making of a consolidated return shall be upon the condition that all corporations which at any time during the taxable year have been members of the affiliated group consent to all the consolidated return regulations prescribed. . . .

Section 1504 (a) (IRC) provides:

> As used in this chapter, the term *affiliated group* means one or more chains of includible corporations connected through stock ownership with a common parent corporation which is an includible corporation if—
>
> 1. Stock possessing at least 80 percent of the voting power of all classes of stock and at least 80 percent of each class of the nonvoting stock of each of the includible corporations (except the common parent corporation) is owned directly by one or more of the other includible corporations; and
> 2. The common parent corporation owns directly stock possessing at least 80 percent of

the voting power of all classes of stock and at least 80 percent of each class of the nonvoting stock of at least one of the other includible corporations.

From the foregoing it is obvious that the conditions for filing a consolidated income tax return are different from those that govern the preparation of consolidated financial statements in accordance with GAAP. Income taxes may be substantially reduced by the filing of consolidated income tax returns. *Some* of the important reasons for this are:

1. Intercompany unrealized profits can be eliminated as they are in consolidated financial statements.
2. Losses of one subsidiary will offset income from other subsidiaries.
3. Credits against the consolidated income tax may be larger than are separate credits against the taxes of the individual corporation. An example of this is the case of a subsidiary with a taxable loss and an investment credit. The subsidiary would not be eligible to claim the credit (a carryback or carryforward might be possible), but a parent company that files a consolidated tax return would utilize the credit if sufficient consolidated taxable income were available to qualify for it.

When a consolidated income tax return is filed and unconfirmed intercompany profits are eliminated on the tax return, there occurs *no* prepayment of income taxes. Therefore, the Deferred Income Tax account is not used for this purpose. Since the accrued liabilities for income taxes payable shown on the books of the separate members of a group may not be equal to the consolidated income taxes liability, an adjustment on the parent's books may be required. In our example, this adjustment for $3,200 is a debit to Income Taxes Payable and a credit to the Provision for Income Taxes. Using the information from Illustration 5–6 as an example, the filing of a consolidated income tax return will require a tax payment of $88,800 instead of the $92,000 ($32,000 + $60,000) as indicated by the illustration. The income statement and income apportionment schedules, in this instance, will be identical for the separate and the consolidated income tax returns. Similarly, when the subsidiary makes the sale, and a consolidated income tax return is filed, the income statement portion of the working paper and the income apportionment schedule will also be identical with that in Illustration 5–7. The only difference in the treatments is the debit to *Income Taxes Payable (on the parent's books)* instead of the *working paper adjustments* as indicated in the illustrations. Needless to say, confirmation of profits in subsequent years requires a reversal of the book adjustment. This will be illustrated in the next chapter in Appendix 6–A.

Illustration 5–7
MACE CORPORATION
Partial Consolidated Working Paper
For the Year Ended December 31, 19x1

Complete Equity Method
End of First Year
90 Percent Subsidiary

	Mace Corp.	More Corp. (90%)	Eliminations Dr.	Eliminations Cr.	Minority Interest	Consolidated
Income Statement						
Sales	900,000	400,000	(2) 100,000			1,200,000
Cost of sales	720,000	150,000	(3) 8,000	(2) 100,000		778,000
Gross margin	180,000	250,000				422,000
Expenses	100,000	100,000				200,000
Operating income before taxes	80,000	150,000				222,000
Equity in earnings—subsidiary	73,800		(1) 73,800			
Income before taxes	153,800	150,000				
Provision for taxes	32,000	60,000		(3) 3,200		88,800
						133,200
Minority interest net income					8,520	(8,520)
Net income	121,800	90,000			8,520	124,680
Selected Balance Sheet Items						
Inventories	150,000	70,000		(3) 8,000		212,000
Deferred income tax			(3) 3,200			3,200

Computations and Proofs

Income apportionment:

	Total	Parent	Minority
Income—More Corp.	$ 90,000	$ 81,000	$ 9,000
Less: Unconfirmed profit in inventory	(8,000)	(7,200)	(800)
Add: Tax effect on profit (40%)	3,200	2,880	320
Income—Mace Corp. ($121,800 − $73,800)	48,000	48,000	
Totals	$133,200	$124,680	$ 8,520

Reconciliation—minority interest:

More Corp.—capital stock	$300,000
—retained earnings (end of year)	250,000
Total equity	$550,000
Less: Unconfirmed profit in ending inventory—net of tax ($8,000 × 60%)	4,800
Balance	$545,200
Minority interest @ 10%	$ 54,520

Partial working paper calculation:
Net income	$ 8,520
Retained earnings—beginning	20,000
Dividends	(4,000)
Capital stock	30,000
Total minority interest	$ 54,520

Appendix 5–B: Partial (fractional) elimination of intercompany profits—inventories

Although a 100 percent (total) elimination of intercompany profits for partially owned subsidiaries is the general practice, some accountants advocate the use of a partial (fractional) elimination for partially owned subsidiaries who sell, at a profit, to the parent or other members of a group. Essentially, partial elimination is a method whereby only the parent's share of an unconfirmed profit is eliminated while the minority interest's share of that profit is treated as confirmed in the year of the intercompany sale. The *only difference* between the two methods *is the period* in which the minority's share of unconfirmed profits is *recognized*. The *amount* recognized (after the parent's share is confirmed) *is the same under both methods.*

Theoretical justification for the method

Where the focal point of interest is the business entity as a whole, the entity method implies that total elimination should be used. Under this view, minority interests are part of the total stockholders' equity. However, as discussed in Chapter 3, the tendency is not to show minority interests as part of stockholders' equity but rather to present them between liabilities and stockholders' equity. While few, if any, practitioners or theoreticians consider minority interests as liabilities, many of the former consider a minority interest as being closer to "outsiders" rather than "insiders" (stockholders). It is under this view that a sale made by a partially owned subsidiary is sometimes viewed as being composed of two parts—a sale by insiders to the extent of the par-

ent's share, and a sale by outsiders and, therefore, immediately confirmed to the extent of the minority's share.

To illustrate the entries (ignoring income taxes) that are required for partial elimination, Illustrations 5–3 and 5–4 will be reworked as Illustrations 5–8 and 5–9.

The working paper elimination entries for Illustration 5–8 are:

(1)		
Equity in Earnings—Subsidiary	73,800	
Dividends Declared—More Corporation		36,000
Investment in More Corporation		37,800
(2)		
Retained Earnings (1/1/x1)— More Corporation	180,000	
Capital Stock—More Corporation	270,000	
Investment in More Corporation		450,000
(3)		
Sales	100,000	
Cost of Sales		100,000
(4)		
Cost of Sales (ending inventory)	7,200	
Inventories		7,200
(5)		
Accounts Payable	30,000	
Accounts Receivable		30,000

Illustration 5–8
MACE CORPORATION
Consolidated Working Paper
For the Year Ended December 31, 19x1

Complete Equity Method
End of First Year
90 Percent Subsidiary

	Mace Corp.	More Corp. (90%)	Eliminations		Minority Interest	Consolidated
			Dr.	Cr.		
Income Statement						
Sales	900,000	400,000	(3) 100,000			1,200,000
Cost of sales	720,000	150,000	(4) 7,200	(3) 100,000		777,200
Gross margin	180,000	250,000				422,800
Expenses	100,000	100,000				200,000
Operating income before taxes	80,000	150,000				222,800
Equity in earnings—subsidiary	73,800		(1) 73,800			
Income before taxes	153,800	150,000				
Provision for income taxes	32,000	60,000				92,000
						130,800
Minority interest net income					9,000	(9,000)
Net income—carried forward	121,800	90,000			9,000	121,800
Retained Earnings Statement						
Balance, 1/1/x1:						
Mace Corp.	500,000					500,000
More Corp.		200,000	(2) 180,000		20,000	
Net income—brought forward	121,800	90,000			9,000	121,800
Totals	621,800	290,000			29,000	621,800
Less: Dividends declared:						
Mace Corp.	20,000					20,000
More Corp.		40,000		(1) 36,000	4,000	
Balance, 12/31/x1—carried forward	601,800	250,000			25,000	601,800
Balance Sheet						
Cash	100,000	80,000				180,000
Accounts receivable (net)	80,000	50,000		(5) 30,000		100,000
Inventories	150,000	70,000		(4) 7,200		212,800
				(2) 450,000		
Investment in More Corp.	487,800			(1) 37,800		
Other assets	484,000	410,000				894,000
Totals	1,301,800	610,000				1,386,800
Accounts payable	90,000	40,000	(5) 30,000			100,000
Other liabilities	110,000	20,000				130,000
Capital stock:						
Mace Corp.	500,000					500,000
More Corp.		300,000	(2) 270,000		30,000	
Retained earnings—brought forward	601,800	250,000			25,000	601,800
Minority interest					55,000	55,000
Totals	1,301,800	610,000	661,000	661,000		1,386,800

(1) Elimination of equity in earnings of subsidiary and intercompany dividends.
(2) Elimination of investment.
(3) Elimination of intercompany sales.
(4) Elimination of intercompany profit in closing inventory ($40,000 × 20% = $8,000 × 90% = $7,200).
(5) Elimination of intercompany receivable and payable.

Illustration 5–9
MACE CORPORATION
Partial Consolidated Working Paper
For the Year Ended December 31, 19x2

Complete Equity Method
End of Second Year
90 Percent Subsidiary

	Mace Corp.	More Corp. (90%)	Eliminations		Minority Interest	Consol- idated
			Dr.	Cr.		
Income Statement						
Sales	1,000,000	450,000				1,450,000
Cost of sales	750,000	180,000		(2) 7,200		922,800
Gross margin	250,000	270,000				527,200
Expenses	120,000	110,000				230,000
Operating income before taxes	130,000	160,000				297,200
Equity in earnings—subsidiary	93,600		(1) 93,600			
Income before taxes	223,600	160,000				
Provision for income taxes	52,000	64,000				116,000
						181,200
Minority interest net income					9,600	(9,600)
Net income—carried forward	171,600	96,000			9,600	171,600
Retained Earnings Statement						
Balance, 1/1/x2:						
Mace Corp.	601,800					601,800
More Corp.		250,000	(3) 225,000		25,000	
Net income—brought forward	171,600	96,000			9,600	171,600
Totals	773,400	346,000			34,600	773,400
Less: Dividends declared:						
Mace Corp.	40,000					40,000
More Corp.		40,000		(1) 36,000	4,000	
Balance, 12/31/x2—carried forward	733,400	306,000			30,600	733,400
Balance Sheet						
				(3) 495,000		
Investment in More Corp.	545,400		(2) 7,200	(1) 57,600		
Capital stock—More Corp.		300,000	(3) 270,000		30,000	
Retained earnings—brought forward	733,400	306,000			30,600	733,400
Minority interest					60,600	60,600

(1) Elimination of equity in earnings of subsidiary and intercompany dividends.
(2) Restoration of confirmed inventory profit.
(3) Elimination of investment.

For Illustration 5–9, the elimination entries are:

(1)		
Equity in Earnings—Subsidiary	93,600	
Dividends Declared—More Corporation		36,000
Investment in More Corporation		57,600

(2)		
Investment in More Corporation	7,200	
Cost of Sales (beginning inventory)		7,200

(3)		
Retained Earnings (1/1/x2)—		
More Corporation	225,000	
Capital Stock—More		
Corporation	270,000	
Investment in More		
Corporation		495,000

After comparing Illustrations 5–8 and 5–9 with Illustrations 5–3 and 5–4, respectively, the following can be noted:

1. Consolidated net income (the parent's share) is the *same* under both methods for *each year.*

2. Minority interest net income is $800 higher in 19x1 for partial elimination, but is $800 lower for 19x2. Therefore, the two years combined are the same under either method.

3. For partial elimination, the proof of minority interest does *not* involve the use of any unconfirmed profit—it is merely 10 percent of the subsidiary's total equity *at year's end* for both years. For 19x1, it is 10 percent of $550,000 or $55,000; and for 19x2, it is 10 percent of $606,000 or $60,600.

4. Income apportionment schedules are not required. Minority interest net income for either year is merely 10 percent of the subsidiary's net income, i.e., for 19x1 it is 10 percent of $90,000 or $9,000.

5. Consolidated inventories at December 31, 19x1, are $800 higher under partial elimination. This can be explained theoretically from the viewpoint that the parent corporation purchased 10 percent of its inventories from the minority which are regarded as outsiders and, therefore, this cost is properly includable in its inventories.

6. *All differences* are *cleared* at the *end of 19x2*, and the financial statements, under either method, will be identical from 19x3 forward if no new differences arise.

7. The amounts of the minority interests are the same under either method, since the differences eventually clear. For valuation purposes, the minority interests must look to market values and the separate financial statements of the subsidiary. Consolidated statements, and the treatment of unconfirmed profits, are rarely of any significance to minority interest.

Appendix 5–C: Incomplete equity method—intercompany profit on inventories

The essential difference between the complete equity and incomplete equity methods as it relates to the treatment of intercompany profits is that in the former case the intercompany profit removal (and later restoration) are recorded on the parent's books whereas in the latter case they are not. On the working papers, however, the entries for both methods are comparable (although slightly different), and they reflect identical end results in the consolidated financial statements. It should be borne in mind that at the time of this writing *the Uniform CPA Examination unofficial solutions make use of the incomplete equity method,* and do *not* use fractional elimination.

To facilitate the comparison between the two methods, Illustrations 5–3, 5–4, and 5–5 will be reworked employing the incomplete equity method. The only items that are assumed to be recorded on the parent's books in each of these reworked illustrations (Illustrations 5–10, 5–11, and 5–12) are the parent's share of subsidiary income and the receipt of dividends. Accordingly, parent net income (first column of the working paper) does not coincide with consolidated net income (last column of the working paper) to the extent of the intercompany profit adjustments. (If excess existed in these illustrations, this would cause differences in addition to the intercompany profit difference.) Similarly, parent retained earnings does not equal consolidated retained earnings. However, the working paper contains appended reconciliations and proofs which reconcile these differences.

The working paper elimination entries for Illustration 5–10 are:

(1)		
Equity in Earnings—Subsidiary	81,000	
Dividends Declared—More Corporation		36,000
Investment in More Corporation		45,000

(2)		
Retained Earnings (1/1/x1)— More Corporation	180,000	
Capital Stock—More Corporation	270,000	
Investment in More Corporation		450,000

(3)		
Sales	100,000	
Cost of Sales		100,000

(4)		
Cost of Sales (ending inventory)	8,000	
Inventories		8,000

(5)		
Accounts Payable	30,000	
Accounts Receivable		30,000

A comparison of Illustration 5–3 with Illustration 5–10 will reveal that:

1. The consolidated columns of each illustration are identical, as they should be. The method used to account for an investment does not affect the consolidated financial statements. The

Illustration 5–10
MACE CORPORATION
Consolidated Working Paper
For the Year Ended December 31, 19x1

Incomplete Equity Method
End of First Year
90 Percent Subsidiary

	Mace Corp.	More Corp. (90%)	Eliminations		Minority Interest	Consolidated
			Dr.	Cr.		
Income Statement						
Sales	900,000	400,000	(3) 100,000			1,200,000
Cost of sales	720,000	150,000	(4) 8,000	(3) 100,000		778,000
Gross margin	180,000	250,000				422,000
Expenses	100,000	100,000				200,000
Operating income before taxes	80,000	150,000				222,000
Equity in earnings—subsidiary	81,000		(1) 81,000			
Income before taxes	161,000	150,000				
Provision for taxes	32,000	60,000				92,000
						130,000
Minority interest net income					8,200	(8,200)
Net income—carried forward	129,000	90,000			8,200	121,800
Retained Earnings Statement						
Balance, 1/1/x1:						
Mace Corp.	500,000					500,000
More Corp.		200,000	(2) 180,000		20,000	
Net income—brought forward	129,000	90,000			8,200	121,800
Totals	629,000	290,000			28,200	621,800
Less: Dividends declared:						
Mace Corp.	20,000					20,000
More Corp.		40,000		(1) 36,000	4,000	
Balance, 12/31/x1—carried forward	609,000	250,000			24,200	601,800
Balance Sheet						
Cash	100,000	80,000				180,000
Accounts receivable (net)	80,000	50,000		(5) 30,000		100,000
Inventories	150,000	70,000		(4) 8,000		212,000
				(1) 45,000		
Investment in More Corp.	495,000			(2) 450,000		
Other assets	484,000	410,000				894,000
Totals	1,309,000	610,000				1,386,000
Accounts payable	90,000	40,000	(5) 30,000			100,000
Other liabilities	110,000	20,000				130,000
Capital stock:						
Mace Corp.	500,000					500,000
More Corp.		300,000	(2) 270,000		30,000	
Retained earnings—brought forward	609,000	250,000			24,200	601,800
Minority interest					54,200	54,200
Totals	1,309,000	610,000	669,000	669,000		1,386,000

(1) Elimination of equity in earnings of subsidiary and intercompany dividends.
(2) Elimination of investment.
(3) Elimination of intercompany sales.
(4) Elimination of intercompany profit in closing inventory ($40,000 × 20% = $8,000).
(5) Elimination of intercompany receivable and payable.

Illustration 5–10 *(continued)*

Computations and Proofs

Income apportionment:

	Total	Parent	Minority
Income More Corp.	$ 90,000	$ 81,000	$ 9,000
Less: Unconfirmed profit in inventory	(8,000)	(7,200)	(800)
Income—Mace Corp. ($129,000 − $81,000)	48,000	48,000	
Totals	$130,000	$121,800	$ 8,200

Reconciliation—minority interest:

More Corp.—capital stock	$300,000
—retained earnings (end of year)	250,000
Total equity	$550,000
Less: Unconfirmed profit in ending inventory	8,000
Balance	$542,000
Minority interest @ 10%	$ 54,200

Reconciliation—retained earnings:

Balance per books, 12/31/x1	$609,000
Less: Unconfirmed profit in ending inventory—Parent's share (90% × $8,000)	7,200
Balance per worksheet, 12/31/x1	$601,800

---

elimination entries, however, are somewhat different.

2. Except for the amount of elimination entry (1), the remaining elimination entries are the same for both illustrations.

3. Parent net income for 19x1 and parent retained earnings at December 31, 19x1, in Illustration 5–10 differ from their respective consolidated amounts by $7,200, the parent's share of unconfirmed inventory profits. This is explained in the reconciliations appended to the working paper.

For Illustration 5–11, the elimination entries are:

(1)		
Equity in Earnings—Subsidiary	86,400	
Dividends Declared—More		
Corporation		36,000
Investment in More		
Corporation		50,400

(2)		
Retained Earnings (1/1/x2)—		
Mace Corporation	7,200	
Retained Earnings (1/1/x2)—		
More Corporation	800	
Cost of Sales (beginning		
inventory)		8,000

(3)		
Retained Earnings (1/1/x2)—		
More Corporation	225,000	
Capital Stock—More		
Corporation	270,000	
Investment in More		
Corporation		495,000

A comparison of Illustration 5–4 with Illustration 5–11 will reveal similar analyses as indicated for the two previous comparisons. There is *one additional* observation that should be made, however. In Illustration 5–4, entry (2) requires that the parent's share of intercompany profit restoration ($7,200) be debited to the investment, whereas in Illustration 5–11 the debit is to parent retained earnings at the beginning of 19x2. The reason for this is that in Illustration 5–4, the $7,200 was recorded on the *books* of the parent company and is thereby reflected in the investment account. In Illustration 5–11 this was not the case, and, therefore, the parent book retained earnings account is overstated on December 31, 19x1. Entry (2) on the working paper in this illustration corrects for the overstatement on January 1, 19x2, and it can be seen that the adjusted consolidated retained earnings is $601,800 in both illustra-

Illustration 5-11

Incomplete Equity Method
End of Second Year
90 Percent Subsidiary

MACE CORPORATION
Partial Consolidated Working Paper
For the Year Ended December 31, 19x2

	Mace Corp.	More Corp. (90%)	Eliminations Dr.	Eliminations Cr.	Minority Interest	Consolidated
Income Statement						
Sales	1,000,000	450,000				1,450,000
Cost of sales	750,000	180,000		(2) 8,000		922,000
Gross margin	250,000	270,000				528,000
Expenses	120,000	110,000				230,000
Operating income before taxes	130,000	160,000				298,000
Equity in earnings—subsidiary	86,400		(1) 86,400			
Income before taxes	216,400	160,000				
Provision for taxes	52,000	64,000				116,000
						182,000
Minority interest net income					10,400	(10,400)
Net income—carried forward	164,400	96,000			10,400	171,600
Retained Earnings Statement						
Balance, 1/1/x2:						
Mace Corp.	609,000		(2) 7,200			601,800
			(2) 800			
More Corp.		250,000	(3) 225,000		24,200	
Net income—brought forward	164,400	96,000			10,400	171,600
Totals	773,400	346,000			34,600	773,400
Less: Dividends declared:						
Mace Corp.	40,000					40,000
More Corp.		40,000		(1) 36,000	4,000	
Balance, 12/31/x2—carried forward	733,400	306,000			30,600	733,400
Balance Sheet						
				(1) 50,400		
Investment in More Corp.	545,400			(3) 495,000		
Capital stock—More Corp.		300,000	(3) 270,000		30,000	
Retained earnings—brought forward	733,400	306,000			30,600	733,400
Minority interest					60,600	60,600

(1) Elimination of equity in earnings of subsidiary and intercompany dividends.
(2) Restoration of confirmed inventory profit.
(3) Elimination of investment.

Computations and Proofs

Income appointment:

	Total	Parent	Minority
Income More Corp.	$ 96,000	$ 86,400	$ 9,600
Confirmed inventory profit	8,000	7,200	800
Income—Mace Corp. ($164,400 − $86,400)	78,000	78,000	
	$182,000	$171,600	$ 10,400

Reconciliation—minority interest:

More Corp.—capital stock	$300,000
—retained earnings (end of year)	306,000
Total equity	$606,000
Minority interest @ 10%	$ 60,600

Illustration 5–12
P COMPANY
Consolidated Working Paper
For the Year Ended December 31, 19x2

Incomplete Equity Method
End of Second Year
90 Percent Subsidiary

	P Co.	S Co. (90%)	Eliminations Dr.	Eliminations Cr.	Minority Interest	Consol- idated
Income Statement						
Sales	800,000	500,000	(3) 90,000	(5) 20,000		1,210,000
Cost of sales	320,000	150,000	(4) 33,000	(3) 90,000		393,000
Gross margin	480,000	350,000				817,000
Expenses	280,000	150,000				430,000
Operating income before taxes	200,000	200,000				387,000
Equity in earnings—subsidiary	108,000		(1) 108,000			
Income before taxes	308,000	200,000				
Provision for taxes	80,000	80,000				160,000
						227,000
Minority interest net income					11,300	(11,300)
Net income—carried forward	228,000	120,000			11,300	215,700
Retained Earnings Statement						
Balance, 1/1/x2:						
P Co.	600,000		(5) 18,600			581,400
			(5) 1,400			
S Co.		400,000	(2) 360,000		38,600	
Net income—brought forward	228,000	120,000			11,300	215,700
Totals	828,000	520,000			49,900	797,100
Less: Dividends declared—S Co.		60,000		(1) 54,000	6,000	
Balance, 12/31/x2—carried forward	828,000	460,000			43,900	797,100
Balance Sheet						
Cash	60,000	40,000				100,000
Accounts receivable (net)	100,000	80,000		(6) 40,000		140,000
Inventories	70,000	30,000		(4) 33,000		67,000
				(1) 54,000		
Investment in S Co.	684,000			(2) 630,000		
Other assets	444,000	700,000				1,144,000
Totals	1,358,000	850,000				1,451,000
Accounts payable	80,000	60,000	(6) 40,000			100,000
Other liabilities	50,000	30,000				80,000
Capital stock:						
P Co.	400,000					400,000
S Co.		300,000	(2) 270,000		30,000	
Retained earnings—brought forward	828,000	460,000			43,900	797,100
Minority interest					73,900	73,900
Totals	1,358,000	850,000	921,000	921,000		1,451,000

(1) Elimination of equity in earnings of subsidiary and intercompany dividends.
(2) Elimination of investment.
(3) Elimination of intercompany sales.
(4) Intercompany profit in closing inventory.
(5) Confirmation of profit in beginning inventory.
(6) Elimination of intercompany receivables and payables.

Illustration 5–12 *(continued)*

Computations and Proofs

Elimination entries:

A. Profit in closing inventories:

P Co. inventory sold by S Co.	$ 30,000	
S Co. margin	70%	
Unconfirmed profit		$ 21,000
S Co. inventory sold by P Co.	$ 20,000	
P Co. margin	60%	
Unconfirmed profit		12,000
Total		$ 33,000

B. Profit in beginning inventories:

	Total	Parent	Minority Interest
P Co. inventory—sale by S Co. ($20,000 × 70%)	$ 14,000	$ 12,600	$ 1,400
S Co. inventory—sale by P Co. ($10,000 × 60%)	6,000	6,000	
Totals	$ 20,000	$ 18,600	$ 1,400

Income apportionment:

	Total	Parent	Minority
Income—S Co.	$120,000	$108,000	$ 12,000
Add: Confirmed profit (70% × $20,000)	14,000	12,600	1,400
Less: Unconfirmed profit (70% × $30,000)	(21,000)	(18,900)	(2,100)
Total—S Co.	$113,000	$101,700	$ 11,300
Income—P Co. ($228,000 − $108,000)	120,000	120,000	
Add: Confirmed profit (60% × $10,000)	6,000	6,000	
Less: Unconfirmed profit (60% × $20,000)	(12,000)	(12,000)	
Totals	$227,000	$215,700	$ 11,300

Reconciliation—minority interest:

S Co.—capital stock	$300,000
—retained earnings (end of year)	460,000
Total equity	$760,000
Less: Unconfirmed profit in closing inventory of P Co. (70% × $30,000)	21,000
Total	$739,000
Minority interest @ 10%	$ 73,900

Reconciliation of retained earnings:

Balance per books, 12/31/x2	$828,000
Less: Unconfirmed profit in S Co. inventory at 12/31/x2 (60% × $20,000)	(12,000)
Less: Unconfirmed profit in P Co. inventory at 12/31/x2—Parent's share only (70% × $30,000) × 90%	(18,900)
Balance per working paper, 12/31/x2	$797,100

Note: Adjustment for opening inventory confirmation is not required.

tions after entry (2) is made. Similar comparisons between Illustrations 5–5 and 5–12 can also be made.

The working paper elimination entries for Illustration 5–12 are as follows:

(1)		
Equity in Earnings—Subsidiary	108,000	
Dividends Declared—S Company		54,000
Investment in S Company		54,000

(2)		
Retained Earnings (1/1/x2)—S Company	1,400	
Investment in S Company	18,600	
Cost of Sales		20,000

(3)		
Retained Earnings 1/1/x2—S Company	360,000	
Capital Stock—S Company	270,000	
Investment in S Company		630,000

(4)		
Sales	90,000	
Cost of Sales		90,000

(5)		
Accounts Payable	40,000	
Accounts Receivable		40,000

(6)		
Cost of Sales	33,000	
Inventories		33,000

Appendix 5–D: Cost method—intercompany profit on inventories

As previously discussed, the accounting for an investment by the cost method will not result in *consolidated* financial statements that are different from those prepared from books that reflect either the complete equity method or the incomplete equity method. Although the book balances of the investment and related accounts are different for each of the methods, the elimination entries on the working papers adjust for these differences to produce an identical consolidated column for each of the three methods. To demonstrate the procedures that are employed when the cost method is used, Illustrations 5–3 and 5–4 will now be reworked where it is assumed that the only entry on the parent's books is to record the receipt of intercompany dividends as a credit to Dividend Income. For this method, the original cost of the investment ($450,000) remains unchanged from year to year.

The working paper elimination entries for Illustration 5–13 are:

(1)		
Dividend Income—Subsidiary .	36,000	
Dividends Declared—More Corporation		36,000

(2)		
Retained Earnings (1/1/x1)— More Corporation	180,000	
Capital Stock—More Corporation	270,000	
Investment in More Corporation		450,000

(3)		
Sales	100,000	
Cost of Sales		100,000

(4)		
Cost of Sales (ending inventory)	8,000	
Inventories		8,000

(5)		
Accounts Payable	30,000	
Accounts Receivable		30,000

The following observations from Illustration 5–13 are noteworthy:

1. Since no equity in subsidiary earnings were recorded on the parent's books, as is the case in an equity method, entry (1) merely eliminates the intercompany dividends, the receipt of which was recorded on the parent's books.
2. Entries (2), (3), (4), and (5) are the same as in Illustration 5–3.
3. In Illustration 5–3 it was not necessary to reconcile retained earnings since the book retained earnings and consolidated retained earnings are the same. This is not the case for Illustration 5–13. In order to reconcile the retained earnings in this illustration, it is necessary to include the parent's share of the increase in subsidiary net assets. In addition, the unconfirmed profit in ending inventories must be allocated (90 percent) and subtracted to arrive at the consolidated balance of $601,800.

Illustration 5–13
MACE CORPORATION
Consolidated Working Paper
For the Year Ended December 31, 19x1

Cost Method
End of First Year
90 Percent Subsidiary

	Mace Corp.	More Corp. (90%)	Eliminations Dr.	Eliminations Cr.	Minority Interest	Consol-idated
Income Statement						
Sales	900,000	400,000	(3) 100,000			1,200,000
Cost of sales	720,000	150,000	(4) 8,000	(3) 100,000		778,000
Gross margin	180,000	250,000				422,000
Expenses	100,000	100,000				200,000
Operating income before taxes	80,000	150,000				222,000
Dividend income—subsidiary	36,000		(1) 36,000			
Income before taxes	116,000	150,000				
Provision for income taxes	32,000	60,000				92,000
						130,000
Minority interest net income					8,200	(8,200)
Net income—carried forward	84,000	90,000			8,200	121,800
Retained Earnings Statement						
Balance, 1/1/x1:						
Mace Corp.	500,000					500,000
More Corp.		200,000	(2) 180,000		20,000	
Net income—brought forward	84,000	90,000			8,200	121,800
Totals	584,000	290,000			28,200	621,800
Less: Dividends declared:						
Mace Corp.	20,000					20,000
More Corp.		40,000		(1) 36,000	4,000	
Balance, 12/31/x1—carried forward	564,000	250,000			24,200	601,800
Balance Sheet						
Cash	100,000	80,000				180,000
Accounts receivable—net	80,000	50,000		(5) 30,000		100,000
Inventories	150,000	70,000		(4) 8,000		212,000
Investment in More Corp. (cost)	450,000			(2) 450,000		
Other assets	484,000	410,000				894,000
Totals	1,264,000	610,000				1,386,000
Accounts payable	90,000	40,000	(5) 30,000			100,000
Other liabilities	110,000	20,000				130,000
Capital stock:						
Mace Corp.	500,000					500,000
More Corp.		300,000	(2) 270,000		30,000	
Retained earnings—brought forward	564,000	250,000			24,200	601,800
Minority interest					54,200	54,200
Totals	1,264,000	610,000	624,000	624,000		1,386,000

(1) Elimination of intercompany dividends.
(2) Elimination of investment.
(3) Elimination of intercompany sales.
(4) Elimination of intercompany profit in closing inventory ($40,000 × 20% = $8,000).
(5) Elimination of intercompany receivable and payable.

Illustration 5–13 *(continued)*

Computations and Proofs

Income apportionment:

	Total	Parent	Minority
Income—More Corp.	$ 90,000	$ 81,000	$ 9,000
Less: Unconfirmed profit in inventory	(8,000)	(7,200)	(800)
Income—Mace Corp. ($84,000 − $36,000)	48,000	48,000	
Totals	$130,000	$121,800	$ 8,200

Reconciliation—minority interest:

More Corp.—capital stock	$300,000
—retained earnings (end of year)	250,000
Total equity	550,000
Less: Unconfirmed profit in ending inventory	8,000
Balance	$542,000
Minority interest @ 10%	$ 54,200

Reconciliation—retained earnings:

Balance per books, 12/31/x1		$564,000
Add: Increase in parent's share of subsidiary's net assets:		
Subsidiary net assets:		
12/31/x1	$550,000	
Date of acquisition	500,000	
Increase	$ 50,000	
Parent's share—90% of above		45,000
Less: Parent's share of unconfirmed profit in ending inventory—upstream sale (90% × $8,000)		(7,200)
Consolidated balance, 12/31/x1		$601,800

The working paper eliminations entries for Illustration 5–14 are as follows:

(1)

Dividend Income—Subsidiary	36,000	
Dividends Declared—More Corporation		36,000

(2)

Investment in More Corporation	45,000	
Retained Earnings (1/1/x2)—Mace Corporation		45,000

(3)

Retained Earnings (1/1/x2)—Mace Corporation	7,200	
Retained Earnings (1/1/x2)—More Corporation	800	
Cost of Sales (beginning inventory)		8,000

(4)

Retained Earnings (1/1/x2)—More Corporation	225,000	
Capital Stock—More Corporation	270,000	
Investment in More Corporation		495,000

From Illustration 5–14 the following should be noted:

1. Entry (1) is similar to its counterpart in Illustration 5–13.
2. Entry (2) *must* be made *prior* to the elimination of the investment amount. The calculation supporting this entry is:

Subsidiary net assets, January 1, 19x2	$550,000
Subsidiary net assets on date of acquisition	500,000
Increase	$ 50,000
Parent's share at 90 percent	$ 45,000

Illustration 5–14
MACE CORPORATION
Partial Consolidated Working Paper
For the Year Ended December 31, 19x2

Cost Method
End of Second Year
90 Percent Subsidiary

	Mace Corp.	More Corp. (90%)	Eliminations Dr.	Eliminations Cr.	Minority Interest	Consol-idated
Income Statement						
Sales	1,000,000	450,000				1,450,000
Cost of sales	750,000	180,000		(3) 8,000		922,000
Gross margin	250,000	270,000				528,000
Expenses	120,000	110,000				230,000
Operating income before taxes	130,000	160,000				298,000
Dividend income—subsidiary	36,000		(1) 36,000			
Income before taxes	166,000	160,000				
Provision for income taxes	52,000	64,000				116,000
						182,000
Minority interest net income					10,400	(10,400)
Net income—carried forward	114,000	96,000			10,400	171,600
Retained Earnings Statement						
Balance, 1/1/x2:						
Mace Corp.	564,000		(3) 7,200	(2) 45,000		601,800
			(3) 800			
More Corp.		250,000	(4) 225,000		24,200	
Net income—brought forward	114,000	96,000			10,400	171,600
Totals	678,000	346,000			34,600	773,400
Less: Dividends declared:						
Mace Corp.	40,000					40,000
More Corp.		40,000		(1) 36,000	4,000	
Balance, 12/31/x2—carried forward	638,000	306,000			30,600	733,400
Balance Sheet						
Investment in More Corp. (cost)	450,000		(2) 450,000	(4) 495,000		
Capital stock—More Corp.		300,000	(4) 270,000		30,000	
Retained earnings—brought forward	638,000	306,000			30,600	733,400
Minority interest					60,600	60,600

(1) Elimination of intercompany dividends.
(2) To record parent's share of increase in subsidiary's net assets.
(3) Restoration of confirmed inventory profit.
(4) Elimination of investment.

It is essential to remember that when a working paper is prepared that *includes* an income statement, *beginning-of-the-year* net assets are used for purposes of computing the increase (decrease) in net assets. Alternatively, if a *balance sheet only* working paper is being prepared, one must use *end-of-the-year* net assets to compute the increase (decrease) in net assets, since that is

all that is available on that type of working paper.

3. After entry (2) is made to reflect the increase in net assets, entries (3) and (4) are comparable to entries (2) and (3) in Illustration 5–4 except for the debit of $7,200 in entry (3) in Illustration 5–14. In this illustration the debit is to parent retained earnings (beginning) since the intercom-

Illustration 5–14 *(continued)*

Computations and Proofs

Income apportionment:

	Total	Parent	Minority
Income—More Corp.	$ 96,000	$ 86,400	$ 9,600
Confirmed inventory profit	8,000	7,200	800
Income—Mace Corp. ($114,000 − $36,000)	78,000	78,000	
Totals	$182,000	$171,600	$ 10,400

Reconciliation—minority interest:

More Corp.—capital stock	$300,000
—retained earnings (end of year)	306,000
Total equity	$606,000
Minority interest @ 10%	$ 60,600

Reconciliation—retained earnings:

Balance per books, 12/31/x2		$638,000
Add: Increase in parent's share of subsidiary's net assets:		
Subsidiary net assets:		
12/31/x2	$606,000	
Date of acquisition	500,000	
Increase	$106,000	
Parent's share—90% of above		95,400
Consolidated balance, 12/31/x2		$733,400

pany profit removal was never recorded on the parent's books and book retained earnings (beginning) is consequently overstated. In Illustration 5–4 the $7,200 debit is to the investment account balance since the profit removal was recorded on the books and reinstated in 19x2 on the books.

4. The reconciliation of retained earnings requires that the parent's share of the increase in net assets of the subsidiary be considered. Since the intercompany profit in the beginning inventory is *already* reflected in the parent retained earnings, it is no longer used as a reconciling item as was necessary in the preceding year illustration.

QUESTIONS

1. Define:

a. Downstream sales.

b. Upstream sales.

2. Is the treatment of unconfirmed inventory profits in home office–branch relationships treated differently from those of parent-subsidiary relationships? Explain.

3. Two methods of intercompany profit elimination are used in practice. What are they? Which one is recommended by *ARB 51?* When "total" elimina-

tion is used, is it still necessary to allocate upstream sales? Explain.

4. When the complete equity method is used, intercompany profits on sales made by the parent company (downstream) are removed by debiting the Equity in Earnings of Subsidiary account and crediting the investment account. Why? Construct an example to illustrate your explanation.

5. When a parent owes money to a subsidiary and this same subsidiary owes money to the parent company, are the amounts added or netted for purposes of an eliminating entry? Explain.

6. When profit in an ending inventory is eliminated in year 1 on the working paper, it is then restored in year 2 (using a FIFO cost flow). Explain why it is necessary to do this.

7. In calculating the amount of profit to be eliminated on the consolidated working paper, is it gross profit or net profit that should be used? Why?

8. In addition to eliminating unrealized profit on the working paper, it is also necessary to eliminate the intercompany sale and purchase. Why? Does this elimination entry have any effect on the consolidated net income?

9. If unrealized profit exists at the end of 19x1, would the failure to eliminate this profit in 19x1 have any effect on the years 19x1 and 19x2 taken together (both years combined)? Explain.

10. When using the complete equity method, unrealized profits are eliminated on the books of the parent company. Is it necessary to remove the profits again when preparing a consolidated working paper? Why? Are the same accounts used? Explain.

Questions for Appendix 5–A:

11. If the conditions for consolidation are met, consolidated financial statements are mandatory. Is the same true for filing tax returns? Explain.

12. When separate tax returns are filed and intercompany profits are unrealized, income taxes are, in effect, paid in advance. Explain.

13. Are the requirements for filing a consolidated tax return different from those requiring consolidated financial statements? Explain.

14. When consolidated tax returns are filed, is it necessary to set up a "deferred tax" amount? Explain.

Questions for Appendix 5–B:

15. When partial (fractional) elimination is used, is there a difference between this method and "total" elimination *after* the unconfirmed profit is confirmed (in year 2)? Explain.

16. What is the theoretical justification for the use of partial elimination?

17. Is it necessary to allocate upstream unconfirmed inventory profits as in "total" elimination? Explain.

Questions for Appendix 5–C:

18. Is there a difference in treatment between the incomplete equity method and the complete equity method? If so, explain the difference.

19. What is true about consolidated financial statements prepared from working papers where the books reflect either the complete equity method or the incomplete equity method? Explain.

Question for Appendix 5–D:

20. What is true about the consolidated financial statements prepared from working papers where the books reflect either the cost method or the complete equity method? Explain.

EXERCISES

Exercise 5–1.

1. The Mon Corporation acquired a 30 percent interest in the Soon Company on January 1, 19x4, for $600,000. At that time, Soon had 2,000,000 shares of its $1 par value common stock issued and outstanding. During 19x4, Soon paid cash dividends of $20,000 and thereafter declared and issued a 5 percent common stock dividend when the market value was $2 per share. Soon's net income for 19x4 was $120,000. What should be the balance in Mon's Investment in Soon Company account at the end of 19x4?

a. $570,000.
b. $600,000.
c. $630,000.
d. $636,000.

2. Eltro Company acquired a 70 percent interest in the Samson Company in 19x2. For the years ended December 31, 19x3, and 19x4, Samson reported net income of $80,000 and $90,000, respectively. During 19x3, Samson sold merchandise to Eltro for $10,000 at a profit of $2,000. The merchandise was later resold by Eltro to outsiders for $15,000 during 19x4.

For consolidation purposes what is the minority interest's share of Samson's net income for 19x3 and 19x4, respectively?

a. $23,400 and $27,600.

b. $24,000 and $27,000.

c. $24,600 and $26,400.

d. $26,000 and $25,000. (AICPA adapted)

Exercise 5–2. On January 1, 19x1, P Company purchased 80 percent of the outstanding shares of S Company at a cost of $800,000. On that date, S Company had $500,000 of capital stock and $500,000 of retained earnings.

For 19x1, S Company reported income of $200,000 and paid dividends of $80,000. All the assets and liabilities of S Company are at fair market value.

During 19x1, P Company sold merchandise to S Company for $80,000 (billed price) which had a cost of $60,000. On December 31, 19x1, 20 percent of this merchandise was unsold and was included in the inventory of S Company.

For the year 19x1, P Company reported income from its *own* operations in the amount of $300,000. P Company uses the complete equity method to account for its investment in S Company.

Required:

a. Prepare the journal entries on the books of P Company to record its share of the equity in the earnings of S Company and the deferral of earnings due to unsold inventories.

b. Compute the amount to be shown as consolidated net income.

c. Compute the balance of the Investment in S Company account on December 31, 19x1.

d. Compute minority interest net income for 19x1.

e. Compute the amount to be shown as minority interest on a consolidated statement as of December 31, 19x1.

Exercise 5–3. Using the information provided in Exercise 5–2, assume that the intercompany sale of $80,000 was made by S Company (upstream sale) instead of by P Company. All other information is unchanged.

Required:

Complete (a), (b), (c), (d), and (e) from Exercise 5–2.

Exercise 5–4. On December 31, 19x2, P Company purchased 80 percent of the outstanding shares of S Company at a cost of $800,000. On that date, S Company had $300,000 of capital stock and $500,000 of retained earnings.

For 19x3, P Company had income of $400,000 from its own operations (excluding its share of income from S Company) and paid dividends of $100,000. For 19x3, S Company reported a net income of $200,000 and paid dividends of $40,000. All of the assets and liabilities of S Company have book values approximately equal to their respective market values.

During 19x3, P Company sold merchandise to S Company at 125 percent of its cost which is also the selling price used for 19x2 sales. The January 1, 19x3, inventory of S Company included $9,600 (at billed prices) of merchandise purchased from P Company on December 31, 19x2, while its December 31, 19x3, inventory included $18,000 of merchandise purchased from P Company at billed prices. S Company uses FIFO inventory costing.

P Company uses the complete equity method to account for its investment in S Company.

Required:

a. Compute the amount that P Company should record as equity in earnings of S Company for 19x3.

b. Compute consolidated net income for 19x3.

c. Compute minority interest net income for 19x3.

d. Compute the total minority interest at December 31, 19x3.

e. Compute the balance in the investment account at December 31, 19x3. (Optional.)

Exercise 5–5. On December 31, 19x3, P Company purchased 80 percent of the outstanding shares of S Company at a cost of $600,000. On that date, S Company had $200,000 of capital stock and $500,000 of retained earnings.

For 19x4, P Company had income of $400,000 from its own operations (excluding its share of income from S Company) and paid dividends of $200,000. For 19x4, S Company reported income of $60,000 and paid dividends of $40,000. All of the assets and liabilities of S Company have book values approximately equal to their respective market values.

The beginning inventory of P Company includes $12,000 of merchandise purchased from S Company on December 31, 19x3, at 120 percent of cost. The ending inventory of P Company includes $15,000 of merchandise purchased from S Company at the same prices. P Company uses FIFO inventory costing.

P Company uses the complete equity method to account for its investment in S Company.

Required:

a. Prepare the journal entries necessary to record the equity in earnings of S Company on the books of P Company for 19x4.

b. Compute consolidated net income for 19x4.

c. Compute minority interest net income for 19x4.

d. Compute the total minority interest at December 31, 19x4.

e. Compute the balance in the investment account at December 31, 19x4. (Optional.)

Exercise 5–6. On December 31, 19x2, P Company purchased 80 percent of the outstanding shares of S Company at a cost of $600,000. On that date, S Company had $300,000 of capital stock and $400,000 of retained earnings.

For 19x3, P Company had income of $200,000 from its own operations (excluding its share of income from S Company) and paid dividends of $50,000. For 19x3, S Company reported a net income of $180,000 and paid dividends of $70,000. All of the assets and liabilities of S Company have book values approximately equal to their respective market values.

The beginning inventory of S Company includes $21,000 of merchandise purchased from P Company on December 31, 19x3, who shipped this merchandise at 40 percent above its cost. The ending inventory of P Company includes $16,000 of merchandise purchased from S Company who shipped this merchandise at 33 1/3 percent above its cost. Both companies use FIFO inventory costing.

P Company uses the complete equity method to account for its investment in S Company.

Required:

a. Compute the amount that P Company should record as equity in earnings of S Company for 19x3.

b. Compute consolidated net income for 19x3.

c. Compute minority interest net income for 19x3.

d. Compute the total minority interest at December 31, 19x3.

e. Compute the balance in the investment account at December 31, 19x3. (Optional.)

Exercise 5–7. On December 31, 19x3, P Company purchased 80 percent of the outstanding shares of S Company at a cost of $700,000. On that date, S Company had $200,000 of capital stock and $500,000 of retained earnings.

For 19x4, P Company had income of $400,000 from its own operations (excluding its share of income from S Company) and paid dividends of $200,000. For 19x4, S Company reported a loss of $50,000 and paid dividends of $40,000. All of the asset and liabilities of S Company have book values approximately equal to their respective market values.

The beginning inventory of P Company includes $8,000 of merchandise purchased from S Company on December 31, 19x3, at 25 percent above its cost. The ending inventory of S Company includes $9,000 of merchandise purchased from P Company at 20 percent above its cost.

P Company uses the complete equity method to account for its investment in S Company.

Required:

a. Prepare the journal entries necessary to record the equity in earnings of S Company on the books of P Company for 19x4.

b. Compute consolidated net income for 19x4.

c. Compute minority interest net income for 19x4.

d. Compute the total minority interest at December 31, 19x4.

e. Compute the balance in the investment account at December 31, 19x4. (Optional.)

Exercise 5–8. On January 1, 19x5, P Company purchased 80 percent of the outstanding shares of S Company at a price that included $10,000 of excess attributable entirely to land that was undervalued.

For 19x5, P Company reported income of $159,120 computed under the complete equity method. Minority interest net income was $15,280. The minority interest reported on the consolidated balance sheet at December 31, 19x5, amounted to $79,280.

On December 31, 19x5, P Company had inventories which included $18,000 of merchandise purchased from S Company at 125 percent of its cost. On the same date, S Company had inventories which included $12,000 of merchandise purchased from P Company at 120 percent of its cost.

Neither company paid any dividends in 19x5.

Required:

a. Compute the amount of income the parent reported as equity in earnings of S Company.

b. Compute the amount of net assets on the books of S Company at December 31, 19x5.

c. Compute the price paid by P Company for its investment in S Company.

d. Compute the balance of the Investment in S Company account at December 31, 19x5.

PROBLEMS

Problem 5–9. On January 1, 19x2, P Company acquired 75 percent of the outstanding shares of S Company at book value.

During 19x4, P Company purchased merchandise from S Company in the amount of $200,000 at billed prices. S Company shipped this merchandise at 33 1/3 percent above its cost, and this price was also used for shipments made in 19x3 to P Company. The inventories of P Company included merchandise at billed prices from S Company as follows:

January 1, 19x4 . . . . $20,000
December 31, 19x4   30,000

Income statements for the two companies for the year 19x4 are as follows:

Income Statement	P Company	S Company
Sales	$1,000,000	$500,000
Cost of sales	400,000	250,000
Gross margin	600,000	250,000
Expenses	200,000	100,000
Operating income before taxes	400,000	150,000
Equity in earnings— subsidiary	65,625	
Income before income taxes .	465,625	150,000
Provision for income taxes . .	160,000	60,000
Minority interest net income		
Net income	$ 305,625	$ 90,000

Required:

Prepare a consolidated income statement.

Problem 5–10. On January 1, 19x3, P Company acquired 80 percent of the outstanding shares of S Company at book value.

During 19x5, P Company purchased merchandise from S Company who also purchased merchandise from P Company. Data regarding intercompany sales, inventories and profit percentages are as follows:

	P Company	S Company
Intercompany sales	$300,000	$200,000
Intercompany inventories:		
January 1, 19x5	50,000	30,000
December 31, 19x5	40,000	20,000
Gross profit percentages on intercompany sales—as a percentage of selling price. (see gross margin percentages on income statements below)	60%	50%

Income statements for the two companies for the year 19x5 are as follows:

Income Statement	P Company	S Company
Sales	$1,500,000	$800,000
Cost of sales	600,000	400,000
Gross margin	900,000	400,000
Expenses	300,000	200,000
Operating income before taxes	600,000	200,000
Equity in earnings— subsidiary	106,000	
Income before income taxes .	706,000	200,000
Provision for income taxes . .	240,000	80,000
Minority interest net income		
Net income	$ 466,000	$120,000

Required:

Prepare a consolidated income statement.

Problem 5–11. On January 1, 19x1, P Company purchased 40,000 shares of S Company in the open market for $740,000. On that date, the net assets of S Company amounted to $800,000 and had book values that approximated their respective fair market values. Excess (goodwill), if any, is expected to last for 20 years and is to be amortized over that period.

P Company uses the complete equity method to account for its investment.

On December 31, 19x4, S Company owed P Company $70,000 on open account from purchases made during 19x4.

The amount of the sales to S Company during 19x4 is $500,000. P Company shipped this merchandise to S Company at its normal shipping price and had a cost of $200,000. The entire closing inventory of S Company was purchased from P Company. The opening inventory of S Company included $100,000 of inventory acquired from P Company at the same rate of profit.

Financial statements for the two corporations for the year ended December 31, 19x4, are as follows:

Income Statement	P Company	S Company
Sales	$2,000,000	$1,000,000
Cost of sales	800,000	600,000
Gross margin	1,200,000	400,000
Expenses	500,000	200,000
Operating income before taxes	700,000	200,000
Equity in earnings—subsidiary	31,000	
Income before income taxes	731,000	200,000
Provision for income taxes	280,000	80,000
Minority interest net income		
Net income—carried forward	$ 451,000	$ 120,000

Retained Earnings Statement		
Balance, January 1, 19x4:		
P Company	$3,108,000	
S Company		$ 860,000
Net income—brought forward	451,000	120,000
Totals	3,559,000	980,000
Less: Dividends declared:		
P Company	400,000	
S Company		60,000
Balance, December 31, 19x4—carried forward	$3,159,000	$ 920,000

Balance Sheet	P Company	S Company
Cash	$ 300,000	$ 200,000
Accounts receivable	260,000	200,000
Inventories	400,000	200,000
Land	600,000	—
Building (net of accumulated depreciation)	400,000	—
Equipment (net of accumulated depreciation)	1,303,000	1,000,000
Investment in S Company	1,096,000	
Totals	$4,359,000	$1,600,000
Accounts payable and accrued expenses	$ 302,000	$ 180,000
Bonds payable (face amount $100,000)		98,000
Common stock—P Company ($50 par)	500,000	
Common stock—S Company ($10 par)		500,000
Additional paid-in capital—P Company	300,000	
Retained earnings—brought forward	3,159,000	920,000
Totals	$4,359,000	$1,600,000

Required:

Prepare a consolidated working paper.

Problem 5–12. On January 1, 19x4, P Company purchased 24,000 shares of S Company in the open market for $502,000. On that date the following assets of S Company had book values that were different from their respective market values:

	Book value	Fair market value
Equipment (net)	$450,000	$400,000
Patent	–0–	140,000

All other assets and liabilities had book values approximately equal to their respective market values, and the net assets amounted to $500,000.

On January 1, 19x4, the equipment and the patent had remaining useful lives of 10 years each. Goodwill, if any, has a 10-year estimated life. P Company uses the complete equity method to account for this investment.

During 19x7, S Company sold $200,000 of merchandise to P Company at 33⅓ percent above its cost. The inventories of P Company contain merchandise purchased from S Company as follows:

	Billed price
January 1, 19x7	$12,000
December 31, 19x7	60,000

On December 31, 19x7, P Company owed S Company $50,000 on open account.

Financial statements for the companies for the year ended December 31, 19x7, are as follows:

Income Statement	P Company	S Company
Sales	$1,000,000	$ 600,000
Cost of sales	400,000	400,000
Gross margin	600,000	200,000
Expenses	200,000	160,000
Operating income before taxes	400,000	40,000
Equity in earnings— subsidiary	(600)	
Income before income taxes .	399,400	40,000
Provision for income taxes . .	160,000	16,000
Minority interest net income		
Net income—carried forward	$ 239,400	$ 24,000

Retained Earnings Statement		
Balance, January 1, 19x7:		
P Company	$ 693,400	
S Company		$ 526,000
Net income—brought forward	239,400	24,000
Totals	932,800	550,000
Less: Dividends declared:		
P Company	100,000	
S Company		50,000
Balance, December 31, 19x7— carried forward	$ 832,800	$ 500,000

Balance Sheet		
Cash	$ 200,000	$ 100,000
Accounts receivable	150,000	50,000
Inventories	110,000	40,000
Land		150,000
Building		260,000
Equipment	809,600	690,000
Patent		—
Investment in S Company . .	689,200	
Totals	$1,958,800	$1,290,000
Accounts payable and accrued expenses	$ 124,000	$ 190,000
Accumulated depreciation— building		60,000
Accumulated depreciation— equipment	402,000	240,000
Common stock—P Company ($50 par)	200,000	
Common stock—S Company ($10 par)		300,000
Additional paid-in capital—P Company	400,000	
Retained earnings—brought forward	832,800	500,000
Totals	$1,958,800	$1,290,000

Required:

a. Prepare an allocation schedule of excess.

b. Prepare a consolidated working paper.

Problem 5–13. On January 1, 19x2, P Company acquired 80 percent of the outstanding common stock of S Company for $600,000. On that date, the retained earnings of S Company were $200,000 and there have been no changes in its capital stock and additional paid-in capital.

All of the assets and liabilities of S Company had book values approximately equal to their respective market values. Goodwill, if any, is to be amortized over a 20-year period.

On December 31, 19x4, P Company owed S Company $20,000 from sales made by S Company. P Company uses the complete equity method.

During 19x4, there were intercompany sales. Information relating to sales, inventories and profit percentages are as follows:

	P Company	S Company
Intercompany sales	$100,000	$80,000
Intercompany inventories:		
January 1, 19x4	60,000	40,000
December 31, 19x4	6,000	8,000
Profit percentage on cost . . .	100%	33 1/3%

The financial statements of the companies for the year ended December 31, 19x4, are as follows:

Income Statement	P Company	S Company
Sales	$ 800,000	$200,000
Cost of sales	400,000	150,000
Gross margin	400,000	50,000
Expenses	100,000	100,000
Operating income (loss) before taxes	300,000	(50,000)
Equity in earnings— subsidiary	800	
Income (loss) before income taxes	300,800	(50,000)
Provision for income taxes . .	120,000	(20,000)
Minority interest net income		
Net income (loss)—carried forward	$ 180,800	$(30,000)

	P Company	S Company
Retained Earnings Statement		
Balance, January 1, 19x4:		
P Company	$ 571,200	
S Company		$300,000
Net income (loss)—brought		
forward	180,800	(30,000)
Totals	752,000	270,000
Less: Dividends declared:		
P Company	80,000	
S Company		—
Balance, December 31, 19x7—		
carried forward	$ 672,000	$270,000

Balance Sheet		
Cash	$ 150,000	$ 50,000
Accounts receivable	90,000	30,000
Inventories	60,000	40,000
Equipment (net of		
accumulated depreciation) .	327,200	750,000
Investment in S Company . .	644,800	
Totals	$1,272,000	$870,000
Accounts payable and		
accrued expenses	$ 200,000	$100,000
Common stock—P Company		
($50 par)	400,000	
Common stock—S Company		
($10 par)		300,000
Additional paid-in capital—S		
Company		200,000
Retained earnings—brought		
forward	672,000	270,000
Totals	$1,272,000	$870,000

Required:

Prepare a consolidated working paper.

Problem 5–14. On June 30, 19x6, Paul Corporation acquired for cash of $19 per share all of the outstanding voting common stock of Sand Corporation. Both companies continued to operate as separate entities and both companies have calendar years.

1. On June 30, 19x6, after closing the nominal accounts, Sand's condensed balance sheet was as follows:

Assets	
Cash	$ 700,000
Accounts receivable (net)	600,000
Inventories	1,400,000
Property, plant, and equipment (net) . .	3,300,000
Other assets	500,000
Total assets	$6,500,000

Liabilities and Stockholders' Equity	
Accounts payable and other current . . .	
liabilities	$ 700,000
Long-term debt	2,600,000
Other liabilities	200,000
Common stock, par value $1	
per share	1,000,000
Additional paid-in capital	400,000
Retained earnings	1,600,000
Total liabilities and	
stockholders' equity	$6,500,000

2. On June 30, 19x6, Sand's assets and liabilities that had fair values that were different than the book values were as follows:

	Fair value
Property, plant, and equipment (net) . .	$16,400,000
Other assets	200,000
Long-term debt	2,200,000

The differences between fair values and book values resulted in a charge or credit to depreciation or amortization for the consolidated statements for the six-month period ending December 31, 19x6, as follows:

Property, plant, and equipment	
(net)	$500,000 charge
Other assets	10,000 credit
Long-term debt	5,000 charge
	$495,000 charge

3. The amount paid by Paul in excess of the fair value of the net assets of Sand is attributable to expected future earnings of Sand and will be amortized over the maximum allowable period.

4. On June 30, 19x6, there were no intercompany receivables or payables.

5. During the six-month period ending December 31, 19x6, Sand acquired merchandise from Paul at an invoice price of $500,000. The cost of the merchandise to Paul was $300,000. At December 31, 19x6, one half of the merchandise was not sold and Sand had not yet paid for any of the merchandise.

6. The 19x6 net income (loss) for both companies was as follows:

	Paul	Sand
January 1 to June 30	$ 250,000	$ (750,000)
July 1 to December 31 . . .	1,600,000	1,250,000

The $1,600,000 net income of Paul includes the equity in the net income of Sand.

7. On December 31, 19x6, after closing the nominal

accounts, the condensed balance sheets for both companies were as follows:

	Paul	Sand
Assets		
Cash	$ 3,500,000	$ 600,000
Accounts receivable (net) .	1,400,000	1,500,000
Inventories	1,000,000	2,500,000
Property, plant, and		
equipment (net)	2,000,000	3,100,000
Investment in subsidiary,		
at equity	20,250,000	—
Other assets	100,000	500,000
Total assets	$28,250,000	$8,200,000
Liabilities and Stockholders' Equity		
Accounts payable and		
other current liabilities .	$ 1,500,000	$1,100,000
Long-term debt	4,000,000	2,600,000
Other liabilities	750,000	250,000
Common stock, par value		
$1 per share	10,000,000	1,000,000
Additional paid-in capital .	5,000,000	400,000
Retained earnings	7,000,000	2,850,000
Total liabilities and stockholders'		
equity	$28,250,000	$8,200,000

Required:

Prepare a condensed *consolidated* balance sheet of Paul Corporation and its wholly owned subsidiary, Sand Corporation, as of December 31, 19x6. Show supporting computations in good form. *Ignore Income tax and deferred tax considerations in your answer.* (AICPA adapted)

Problem 5–15 (for Appendix 5–A). Using the information provided in Problem 5–9, prepare a consolidated income statement using a 40 percent income tax rate and assume that separate income tax returns are to be filed.

Problem 5–16 (for Appendix 5–A). Using the information provided in Problem 5–10, prepare a consolidated income statement using a 40 percent income tax rate and assume that separate income tax returns are to be filed. Show your supporting computations and income allocation schedule.

Problem 5–17 (for Appendix 5–A). Using the information provided in Problem 5–11, prepare a consolidated working paper using a 40 percent income tax rate and assume that separate income tax returns are to be filed. (*Hint:* Open a caption for Deferred Tax Debit Account for deferred taxes relating to the closing inventory and adjust the parent company's beginning retained earnings account for the deferred taxes relating to the beginning inventory.)

Problem 5–18 (for Appendix 5–B). Using the information provided in Problem 5–9, prepare a consolidated income statement using fractional (partial) elimination instead of total elimination.

Problem 5–19 (for Appendix 5–B). Using the information provided in Problem 5–10, prepare a consolidated income statement using the fractional (partial) elimination method.

Problem 5–20 (for Appendix 5–B). Using the information provided in Problem 5–12, prepare a consolidated working paper using the fractional (partial) elimination method.

Problem 5–21 (for Appendix 5–B). Using the information provided in Problem 5–13, prepare a consolidated working paper using the fractional (partial) elimination method.

Problem 5–22 (for Appendix 5–C). On January 1, 19x1, P Company purchased 40,000 shares of S Company in the open market for $740,000. On that date, the net assets of S Company amounted to $800,000 and had book values that approximated their respective fair market values. Excess (goodwill), if any, is expected to last for 20 years and is to be amortized over that period.

P Company uses the incomplete equity method to account for its investment.

On December 31, 19x4, S Company owed P Company $70,000 on open account for purchases made during 19x4.

The amount of the sales to S Company during 19x4 is $500,000. P Company shipped this merchandise to S Company at 250 percent of its cost. The entire closing inventory of S Company was purchased from P Company. The opening inventory of S Company included $100,000 of inventory acquired from P Company at the same rate of profit.

Financial statements for the two corporations for the year ended December 31, 19x4, are as follows:

	P Company	S Company
Income Statement		
Sales	$2,000,000	$1,000,000
Cost of sales	800,000	600,000
Gross margin	1,200,000	400,000
Expenses	500,000	200,000
Operating income before taxes	700,000	200,000
Equity in earnings— subsidiary	96,000	
Income before income taxes .	796,000	200,000
Provision for income taxes . .	280,000	80,000
Minority interest net income		
Net income—carried forward	$ 516,000	$ 120,000
Retained Earnings Statement		
Balance, January 1, 19x4:		
P Company	$3,183,000	
S Company		$ 860,000
Net income—brought forward	516,000	120,000
Totals	3,699,000	980,000
Less: Dividends declared:		
P Company	400,000	
S Company		60,000
Balance, December 31, 19x4— carried forward	$3,299,000	$ 920,000
Balance Sheet		
Cash	$ 300,000	$ 200,000
Accounts receivable	260,000	200,000
Inventories	400,000	200,000
Land	600,000	—
Building (net of accumulated depreciation)	400,000	—
Equipment (net of accumulated depreciation) .	1,303,000	1,000,000
Investment of S. Company . .	1,236,000	
Totals	$4,499,000	$1,600,000
Accounts payable and accrued expenses	$ 302,000	$ 180,000
Bonds payable (face amount $100,000)	98,000	
Common stock—P Company ($50 par)	500,000	
Common stock—S Company ($10 par)		500,000
Additional paid-in capital—P Company	300,000	
Retained earnings—brought forward	3,299,000	920,000
Totals	$4,499,000	$1,600,000

Required:

Prepare a consolidated working paper.

Problem 5–23 (for Appendix 5–C). On January 1, 19x4, P Company purchased 24,000 shares of S Company in the open market for $502,000. On that date the following assets of S Company had book values that were different from their respective market values:

	Book value	Fair market value
Equipment (net)	$450,000	$400,000
Patent	–0–	140,000

All other assets and liabilities had book values approximately equal to their respective market values and the net assets amounted to $500,000.

On January 1, 19x4, the equipment and the patent had remaining useful lives of 10 years each. Goodwill, if any, has a 10-year estimated life. P Company uses the incomplete equity method to account for this investment.

During 19x7, S Company sold $200,000 of merchandise to P Company at 33 1/3 percent above its cost. The inventories of P Company contain merchandise purchased from S Company as follows:

	Billed price
January 1, 19x7	$12,000
December 31, 19x7	60,000

On December 31, 19x7, P Company owed S Company $50,000 on open account.

Financial statements for the companies for the year ended December 31, 19x7, are as follows:

	P Company	S Company
Income Statement		
Sales	$1,000,000	$ 600,000
Cost of sales	400,000	400,000
Gross margin	600,000	200,000
Expenses	200,000	160,000
Operating income before taxes	400,000	40,000
Equity in earnings— subsidiary	19,200	
Income before income taxes .	419,200	40,000
Provision for income taxes . .	160,000	16,000
Minority interest net income		
Net income—carried forward	$ 259,200	$ 24,000

Retained Earnings Statement	P Company	S Company
Balance, January 1, 19x7:		
P Company	$ 726,400	
S Company		$ 526,000
Net income—brought forward	259,200	24,000
Totals	985,600	550,000
Less: Dividends declared:		
P Company	100,000	
S Company		50,000
Balance, December 31, 19x7—carried forward	$ 885,600	$ 500,000

Balance Sheet		
Cash	$ 200,000	$ 100,000
Accounts receivable	150,000	50,000
Inventories	110,000	40,000
Land		150,000
Building		260,000
Equipment	809,600	690,000
Patent		—
Investment in S Company	742,000	
Totals	$2,011,600	$1,290,000
Accounts payable and accrued expenses	$ 124,000	$ 190,000
Accumulated depreciation—building		60,000
Accumulated depreciation—equipment	402,000	240,000
Common stock—P Company ($50 par)	200,000	
Common stock—S Company ($10 par)		300,000
Additional paid-in capital—P Company	400,000	
Retained earnings—brought forward	885,600	500,000
Totals	$2,011,600	$1,290,000

Required:

a. Prepare an allocation schedule of excess.

b. Prepare a consolidated working paper.

Problem 5–24 (for Appendix 5–C). On January 1, 19x2, P Company acquired 80 percent of the outstanding common stock of S Company for $600,000. On that date, the retained earnings of S Company were $200,000 and there have been no changes in its capital stock and additional paid-in capital.

All of the assets and liabilities of S Company had book values approximately equal to their respective market values. Goodwill, if any, is to be amortized over a 20-year period.

On December 31, 19x4, P Company owed S Company $20,000 from sales made by S Company. P Company uses the incomplete equity method.

During 19x4, there were intercompany sales. In-formation relating to sales, inventories and profit percentages are as follows:

	P Company	S Company
Intercompany sales	$100,000	$80,000
Intercompany inventories:		
January 1, 19x4	60,000	40,000
December 31, 19x4	6,000	8,000
Profit percentage on cost	100%	33⅓%

The financial statements of the companies for the year ended December 31, 19x4, are as follows:

Income Statement	P Company	S Company
Sales	$ 800,000	$200,000
Cost of sales	400,000	150,000
Gross margin	400,000	50,000
Expenses	100,000	100,000
Operating income (loss) before taxes	300,000	(50,000)
Equity in earnings—subsidiary	(24,000)	
Income (loss) before income taxes	276,000	(50,000)
Provision for income taxes	120,000	(20,000)
Minority interest net income		
Net income (loss)—carried forward	$ 156,000	$(30,000)

Retained Earnings Statement		
Balance, January 1, 19x4:		
P Company	$ 607,200	
S Company		$300,000
Net income (loss)—brought forward	156,000	(30,000)
Totals	763,200	270,000
Less: Dividends declared:		
P Company	80,000	
S Company		—
Balance, December 31, 19x4—carried forward	$ 683,200	$270,000

Balance Sheet		
Cash	$ 150,000	$ 50,000
Accounts receivable	90,000	30,000
Inventories	60,000	40,000
Equipment (net of accumulated depreciation)	327,200	750,000
Investment in S Company	656,000	
Totals	$1,283,200	$870,000
Accounts payable and accrued expenses	$ 200,000	$100,000
Common stock—P Company ($50 par)	400,000	
Common stock—S Company ($10 par)		300,000
Additional paid-in capital—S Company		200,000
Retained earnings—brought forward	683,200	270,000
Totals	$1,283,200	$870,000

Required:

Prepare a consolidated working paper.

Problem 5–25 (for Appendix 5–D). On January 1, 19x1, P Company purchased 40,000 shares of S Company in the open market for $740,000. On that date, the net assets of S Company amounted to $800,000 and had book values that approximated their respective fair market values. Excess (goodwill), if any, is expected to last for 20 years and is to amortized over that period.

P Company uses the cost method to account for its investment.

On December 31, 19x4, S Company owed P Company $70,000 on open account for purchases made during 19x4.

The amount of the sales to S Company during 19x4 is $500,000. P Company shipped this merchandise to S Company at 250 percent of its cost. The entire closing inventory of S Company was purchased from P Company. The opening inventory of S Company included $100,000 of inventory acquired from P Company at the same rate of profit.

Financial statements for the two corporations for the year ended December 31, 19x4, are as follows:

	P Company	S Company
Income Statement		
Sales	$2,000,000	$1,000,000
Cost of sales	800,000	600,000
Gross margin	1,200,000	400,000
Expenses	500,000	200,000
Operating income before taxes	700,000	200,000
Dividend income—subsidiary	48,000	
Income before income taxes	748,000	200,000
Provision for income taxes	280,000	80,000
Minority interest net income		
Net income—carried forward	$ 468,000	$ 120,000

	P Company	S Company
Retained Earnings Statement		
Balance, January 1, 19x4:		
P Company	$2,735,000	
S Company		$ 860,000
Net income—brought forward	468,000	120,000
Totals	$3,203,000	$ 980,000
Less: Dividends declared:		
P Company	400,000	
S Company		60,000
Balance, December 31, 19x4— carried forward	$2,803,000	$ 920,000

	P Company	S Company
Balance Sheet		
Cash	$ 300,000	$ 200,000
Accounts receivable	260,000	200,000
Inventories	400,000	200,000
Land	600,000	—
Building (net of accumulated depreciation)	400,000	
Equipment (net of accumulated depreciation)	1,303,000	1,000,000
Investment in S Company	740,000	
Totals	$4,003,000	$1,600,000
Accounts payable and accrued expenses	$ 302,000	$ 180,000
Bonds payable (face amount $100,000)	98,000	
Common stock—P Company ($50 par)	500,000	
Common stock—S Company ($10 par)		500,000
Additional paid-in capital—P Company	300,000	
Retained earnings—brought forward	2,803,000	920,000
Totals	$4,003,000	$1,600,000

Required:

Prepare a consolidated working paper.

Problem 5–26 (for Appendix 5–D). On January 1, 19x4, P Company purchased 24,000 shares of S Company in the open market for $502,000. On that date, the following assets of S Company had book values that were different from their respective market values:

	Book value	Fair market value
Equipment (net)	$450,000	$400,000
Patent	–0–	140,000

All other assets and liabilities had book values approximately equal to their respective market values and the net assets amounted to $500,000.

On January 1, 19x4, the equipment and the patent had remaining useful lives of 10 years each. Goodwill, if any, has a 10-year estimated life. P Company uses the cost method to account for this investment.

During 19x7, S Company sold $200,000 of merchandise to P Company at 33 1/3 percent above its cost. The inventories of P Company contain merchandise purchased from S Company as follows:

	Billed price
January 1, 19x7	$12,000
December 31, 19x7	60,000

On December 31, 19x7, P Company owed S Company $50,000 on open account.

Financial statements for the companies for the year ended December 31, 19x7, are as follows:

Income Statement	P Company	S Company
Sales	$1,000,000	$ 600,000
Cost of sales	400,000	400,000
Gross margin	600,000	200,000
Expenses	200,000	160,000
Operating income before taxes	400,000	40,000
Dividend income—subsidiary	40,000	
Income before income taxes .	440,000	40,000
Provision for income taxes . .	160,000	16,000
Minority interest net income		
Net income—carried forward	$ 280,000	$ 24,000

Retained Earnings Statement		
Balance, January 1, 19x7:		
P Company	$ 465,600	
S Company		$ 526,000
Net income—brought forward	280,000	24,000
Totals	745,600	550,000
Less: Dividends declared:		
P Company	100,000	
S Company		50,000
Balance, December 31, 19x7—carried forward	$ 645,600	$ 500,000

Balance Sheet	P Company	S Company
Cash	$ 200,000	$ 100,000
Accounts receivable	150,000	50,000
Inventories	110,000	40,000
Land		150,000
Building		260,000
Equipment	809,600	690,000
Patent		—
Investment in S Company . .	502,000	
Totals	$1,771,600	$1,290,000
Accounts payable and accrued expenses	$ 124,000	$ 190,000
Accumulated depreciation—building		60,000
Accumulated depreciation—equipment	402,000	240,000
Common stock—P Company ($50 par)	200,000	
Common stock—S Company ($10 par)		300,000
Additional paid-in capital—P Company	400,000	
Retained earnings—brought forward	645,600	500,000
Totals	$1,771,600	$1,290,000

Required:

a. Prepare an allocation schedule of excess.

b. Prepare a consolidated working paper.

Problem 5–27 (for Appendix 5–D). On January 1, 19x2, P Company acquired 80 percent of the outstanding common stock of S Company for $600,000. On that date, the retained earnings of S Company were $200,000 and there have been no changes in its capital stock and additional paid-in capital.

All of the assets and liabilities of S Company had book values approximately equal to their respective market values. Goodwill, if any, is to be amortized over a 20-year period.

On December 31, 19x4, P Company owed S Company $20,000 from sales made by S Company. P Company uses the cost method.

During 19x4, there were intercompany sales. Information relating to sales, inventories, and profit percentages are as follows:

	P Company	S Company
Intercompany sales	$100,000	$80,000
Intercompany inventories:		
January 1, 19x4	60,000	40,000
December 31, 19x4	6,000	8,000
Profit percentage on cost . . .	100%	33 1/3%

The financial statements of the companies for the year ended December 31, 19x4, are as follows:

	P Company	S Company
Income Statement:		
Sales	$ 800,000	$200,000
Cost of sales	400,000	150,000
Gross margin	400,000	50,000
Expenses	100,000	100,000
Operating income (loss) before taxes	300,000	(50,000)
Dividend income—subsidiary	—	
Income (loss) before income taxes	300,000	(50,000)
Provision for income taxes . .	120,000	(20,000)
Minority interest net income		
Net income (loss)—carried forward	$ 180,000	$(30,000)

	P Company	S Company
Retained Earnings Statement		
Balance, January 1, 19x4:		
P Company	$ 527,200	
S Company		$300,000
Net income (loss)—brought forward	180,000	(30,000)
Totals	$ 707,200	$270,000
Less: Dividends declared:		
P Company	80,000	
S Company		—
Balance, December 31, 19x4— carried forward	$ 627,200	$270,000

	P Company	S Company
Balance Sheet		
Cash	$ 150,000	$ 50,000
Accounts receivable	90,000	30,000
Inventories	60,000	40,000
Equipment (net of accumulated depreciation) .	327,200	750,000
Investment in S Company . .	600,000	
Totals	$1,227,200	$870,000
Accounts payable and accrued expenses	$ 200,000	$100,000
Common stock—P Company ($50 par)	400,000	
Common stock—S Company ($10 par)		300,000
Additional paid-in capital—S Company		200,000
Retained earnings—brought forward	627,200	270,000
Totals	$1,227,200	$870,000

Required:

Prepare a consolidated working paper.

6

Consolidated statements— intercompany profit on plant asset transfers and other related matters

OVERVIEW

Just as in Chapter 5 where it was shown that the profit on an intercompany sale of inventory must be removed until the inventory is resold to third parties, the profit or loss on an intercompany sale of plant assets must similarly be removed until the profit or loss is confirmed. The confirmation process, however, is somewhat more complex than for inventories. For inventories, the unrealized profit is usually confirmed in the very next accounting period that follows the profit's deferral. For plant assets such as buildings, machinery, and equipment, the confirmation of a gain or loss on an intercompany sale occurs on a piecemeal basis over the remaining productive life of the property. For land, the confirmation of a gain or loss on an intercompany sale must await its resale to third parties.

The concept of downstream sales and upstream sales applies to plant assets as well as to inventories. Thus, for downstream sales, the entire gain or loss is attributable to the parent company. For upstream sales the gain or loss is allocated to majority and minority interests.

Basically, there are two main areas in the consolidation of financial statements that affect the accounting for plant assets. As discussed earlier in Chapters 3 and 4, under the purchase method of accounting, the price paid by a parent company for its investment in a subsidiary usually differs from the amount at which the underlying net asset values are reflected on the books of the subsidiary. The allocation of excess[1] was illustrated in

---

[1]The difference between the price paid and the parent's share of the *book value* of the net assets of the subsidiary.

these chapters, and it was mentioned therein that upon a subsequent sale of a subsidiary's plant asset, this excess must be taken into account in order to properly reflect the consolidated gain or loss on such sale by the subsidiary. The other main area that affects consolidated statements is the intercompany sale of plant assets, usually at an amount that differs from book value. Both of these areas will be considered in this chapter.

SALES OF PLANT ASSETS BY SUBSIDIARIES SUBSEQUENT TO THE DATE OF ACQUISITION

To illustrate the procedures to be used when a subsidiary sells a plant asset at a gain or loss, the following assumptions are made:

1. On January 1, 19x1, P Company purchased its investment at the book value of S company's net assets except for a difference (excess) attributable to the Land account. P Company purchased 80 percent of S Company.
2. On the date of acquisition, the Land account on the books of S Company had a balance of $10,000 and its fair market value was $20,000. Thus P Company paid $8,000 [80 percent × ($20,000 − $10,000)] in excess as attributable to land and represents the entire excess arising from this acquisition.
3. On December 31, 19x5, the subsidiary sold the land to third parties for $40,000.
4. All the other information in Illustration 6–1 is stated as assumed.

Based on the information provided, the parent company would make the following entries on its *books* for 19x5:

Parent's Books—19x5
(1)

Investment in S Company	86,400	
Equity in Earnings of Subsidiary		86,400

To record parent's share of subsidiary's earnings (80 percent × $108,000).

(2)

Equity in Earnings of Subsidiary	8,000	
Investment in S Company		8,000

To remove excess attributable to land sold by S Company in 19x5 which also serves to adjust the equity in subsidiary earnings to complete equity accounting.

The Illustration 6–1 elimination entries are:

(1)

Equity in Earnings—Subsidiary	78,400	
Investment in S Company		78,400

(2)

Gain on Sale of Land	8,000	
Investment in S Company		8,000

(3)

Retained Earnings (1/1/x5)—S Company	240,000	
Capital Stock—S Company	160,000	
Investment in S Company		400,000

Illustration 6–1
P COMPANY
Consolidated Working Paper
For the Year Ended December 31, 19x5

Complete Equity Method
80 Percent Subsidiary

	P Co.	S Co. (80%)	Eliminations Dr.	Eliminations Cr.	Minority Interest	Consol- idated
Income Statement						
Sales	900,000	400,000				1,300,000
Cost of sales	360,000	160,000				520,000
Gross margin	540,000	240,000				780,000
Operating expenses	240,000	90,000				330,000
Operating income before taxes	300,000	150,000				450,000
Equity in earnings—subsidiary	78,400		(1) 78,400			
Gain on sale of land		30,000	(2) 8,000			22,000
Income before income taxes	378,400	180,000				472,000
Provision for income taxes (40%)	120,000	72,000				192,000
						280,000
Minority interest net income					21,600	(21,600)
Net income—carried forward	258,400	108,000			21,600	258,400
Retained Earnings Statement						
Balance, 1/1/x5:						
P Co.	400,000					400,000
S Co.		300,000	(3) 240,000		60,000	
Net income—brought forward	258,400	108,000			21,600	258,400
Total—balance, 12/31/x5—carried forward	658,400	408,000			81,600	658,400
Selected Balance Sheet Items						
				(3) 400,000		
				(2) 8,000		
Investment in S Co.	486,400			(1) 78,400		
Land	–0–	–0–				
Capital stock:						
P Co.	500,000					500,000
S Co.		200,000	(3) 160,000		40,000	
Retained earnings—brought forward	658,400	408,000			81,600	658,400
Minority interest					121,600	121,600

(1) To eliminate equity in earnings of subsidiary.
(2) To transfer excess attributable to land and to adjust the gain on land sold by subsidiary.
(3) To eliminate the balance of the investment.

Reconciliations

Minority interest:

Capital stock—S Co.	$200,000
Retained earnings—end of year	408,000
Total—net assets	$608,000
20% of above—minority interest	$121,600

Noteworthy observations from Illustration 6–1 are:

1. Parent net income is the same as consolidated net income. Retained earnings per books also agrees with consolidated retained earnings.
2. The investment account at the beginning of the year was $408,000, which was $8,000 in excess of the net assets of S Company's book value or 80 percent ($200,000 + $300,000) = $400,000. After entry (2) is posted (on the parent's books), the investment account represents 80 percent of S Company's book value. If the net assets figure of S Company at December 31, 19x5 ($608,000), is multiplied by 80 percent, the result ($486,400) agrees with the balance in the investment account at December 31, 19x5.
3. Although 20 percent of the full gain on sale of land before taxes ($30,000) or $6,000 is included in the minority interest's total share of net income of $21,600, the parent's share of the gain before taxes is computed at only $16,000 ($30,000 − $6,000 − $8,000).

Let us now assume that instead of land an asset subject to depreciation is sold by a subsidiary to third parties. Moreover, if the parent's investment account included excess from the time of acquisition of the subsidiary attributable to that depreciable asset being sold, the treatment illustrated in the sale of land above would be modified so that the exclusion from the share of the parent's profit on the sale would be based on the amount of unamortized (undepreciated) "excess" still remaining in the investment account on the date of sale.

INTERCOMPANY SALES OF PLANT ASSETS

Intercompany sales of property, plant, and equipment may require elimination entries that are similar to those required when intercompany sales of inventory occur. However, the process of profit confirmation becomes somewhat more complex. Instead of confirmation of profit in one year, as is the usual case with inventories costed on a FIFO basis, confirmation of profit on the sale of plant assets is accomplished through the depreciation process and, therefore, lasts for the remaining useful life of the acquired asset. For example, if a depreciable asset with a remaining useful life of 10 years is sold to a member of the affiliated group at a $50,000 profit, $5,000 per annum of that profit will be confirmed each year over 10 years assuming the straight-line depreciation method is used. An analogy to the sale of inventories can be made if it is assumed that an intercompany sale of inventory occurs at the end of 19x1 and that only 10 percent of that inventory is sold to third parties each year of the following 10 years.

PLANT ASSET SALE BY PARENT COMPANY—DOWNSTREAM SALE

Just as in the case of intercompany inventory sales where it was necessary to ascertain who made the sale, it is necessary to determine whether a plant asset sale is an upstream or downstream sale. Downstream sales of plant assets require profit removals that are attributable 100 percent to the parent company. The following information is assumed for purposes of demonstrating the treatment of downstream plant asset sales:

1. Date of sale—December 31, 19x1.
2. Selling price—$60,000.
3. Cost of office equipment—$80,000.
4. Accumulated depreciation—$40,000.
5. Remaining life of equipment—5 years.
6. Depreciation method—straight line.
7. Salvage value—none.
8. Income taxes—ignored.

For the year ended December 31, 19x1, Major Corporation would make the following entries on its books:

Parent's Books—19x1

(1)

Cash	60,000	
Accumulated Depreciation	40,000	
Equipment		80,000
Gain on Sale of Equipment		20,000

    To record the sale of equipment to Minor Corporation on December 31, 19x1.

(2)

Investment in Minor Corporation	24,000	
Equity in Earnings of Subsidiary		24,000

    To record the parent's share of subsidiary's income (80 percent × $30,000).

(3)

Equity in Earnings of Subsidiary	20,000	
Investment in Minor Corporation		20,000

    To remove 100 percent of the unconfirmed profit on sale of equipment to Minor Corporation in 19x1 and to adjust equity in earnings of subsidiary to the complete equity method.

The entry to record the purchase of the equipment on Minor's books is:

Subsidiary's Books—December 31, 19x1

(4)

Equipment	60,000	
Cash		60,000

    To record purchase of equipment from parent company.

The working paper elimination entries on Illustration 6–2 are:

(1)

Equity in Earnings—Subsidiary	4,000	
Investment in Minor Corporation		4,000

(2)

Retained Earnings (1/1/x1)—Minor Corporation	240,000	
Capital Stock—Minor Corporation	160,000	
Investment in Minor Corporation		400,000

(3)

Gain on Sale of Equipment	20,000	
Property, Plant, and Equipment	20,000	
Accumulated Depreciation		40,000

Illustration 6–2

Complete Equity Method
End of First Year
80 Percent Subsidiary

MAJOR CORPORATION
Partial Consolidated Working Paper
For the Year Ended December 31, 19x1

	Major Corp.	Minor Corp. (80%)	Eliminations Dr.	Eliminations Cr.	Minority Interest	Consol- idated
Income Statement						
Sales	800,000	300,000				1,100,000
Operating income before taxes	80,000	50,000				130,000
Equity in earnings—subsidiary	4,000		(1) 4,000			
Gain on sale of equipment	20,000		(3) 20,000			
Income before taxes	104,000	50,000				130,000
Provision for taxes (40%)	40,000	20,000				60,000
						70,000
Minority interest net income					6,000	(6,000)
Net income—carried forward	64,000	30,000			6,000	64,000
Retained Earnings Statement						
Balance, 1/1/x1:						
Major Corp.	400,000					400,000
Minor Corp.		300,000	(2) 240,000		60,000	
Net income—brought forward	64,000	30,000			6,000	64,000
Balance, 12/31/x1—carried forward	464,000	330,000			66,000	464,000
Balance Sheet						
Investment in Minor Corp.	404,000			(2) 400,000		
				(1) 4,000		
Property, plant, and equipment	200,000	100,000	(3) 20,000			320,000
Accumulated depreciation	(80,000)	(20,000)		(3) 40,000		(140,000)
Other assets	430,000	490,000				920,000
Totals	954,000	570,000				1,100,000
Liabilities	90,000	40,000				130,000
Capital Stock:						
Major Corp.	400,000					400,000
Minor Corp.		200,000	(2) 160,000		40,000	
Retained earnings—brought forward	464,000	330,000			66,000	464,000
Minority interest					106,000	106,000
Totals	954,000	570,000	444,000	444,000		1,100,000

(1) To eliminate equity in earnings of subsidiary.
(2) Elimination of investment.
(3) Elimination of gain on sale of equipment and restoration of original book values.

Computations and Proofs

Income apportionment:

	Total	Parent	Minority
Income—Minor Corp.	$30,000	$24,000	$ 6,000
Income—Major Corp. ($64,000 − $4,000)	60,000	60,000	
Less: Unconfirmed gain on sale of equipment	(20,000)	(20,000)	
Totals	$70,000	$64,000	$ 6,000

Reconciliation—minority interest:

Minor Corp.—capital stock	$200,000
—retained earnings (end of year)	330,000
Total equity	$530,000
20%—minority interest	$106,000

Illustration 6–2 contains the working paper that would be used to prepare consolidated statements for Major Corporation. Pertinent observations are:

1. The gain on the sale of the equipment is removed [see working paper entry (3)] and the book values that were removed when the gain was recorded are restored. Elimination entry (3) in the working paper reverses the *net effect* of *book* entries (1) and (4) above.

2. Since the sale was made on the last day of the year, depreciation on the equipment was taken by the parent for the full year and none was taken by the subsidiary; hence there is no profit confirmation in 19x1. Had the sale been made during 19x1, the appropriate depreciation expense would have been recorded by the subsidiary on its new cost of $60,000 instead of on the parent's former historical book value of $40,000. The additional depreciation taken on this $20,000 differential would have constituted confirmed profit in the year of the sale. (The profit-confirmation procedure is shown in Illustration 6–3.)

3. The income apportionment and the reconciliation of the minority interest schedules are compatible with entry (3) and should be studied carefully.

For 19x2, Major would make the following entry on its books:

Parent's Books—19x2
(5)

Investment in Minor Corporation	42,400	
Equity in Earnings of Subsidiary		42,400

To record the parent's share of equity in earnings of Minor Corporation as follows:

80% of $48,000 net income	$38,400
Add: piecemeal confirmation of gain on sale of	
equipment ($20,000 ÷ 5 years = $4,000)	4,000
	$42,400

The working paper for 19x2 is shown in Illustration 6–3.
The working paper elimination entries on Illustration 6–3 are:

(1)

Equity in Earnings—Subsidiary	42,400	
Investment in Minor Corporation		42,400

(2)

Investment in Minor Corporation	20,000	
Property, Plant, and Equipment	20,000	
Accumulated Depreciation		40,000

(3)

Accumulated Depreciation	4,000	
Depreciation Expense		4,000

(4)

Retained Earnings (1/1/x2)—Minor Corporation	264,000	
Capital Stock—Minor Corporation	160,000	
Investment in Minor Corporation		424,000

Illustration 6–3
MAJOR CORPORATION
Consolidated Working Paper
For the Year Ended December 31, 19x2

Complete Equity Method
End of Second Year
80 Percent Subsidiary

	Major Corp.	Minor Corp. (80 %)	Eliminations Dr.	Eliminations Cr.	Minority Interest	Consol- idated
Income Statement						
Sales	1,000,000	400,000				1,400,000
Cost of sales	600,000	200,000				800,000
Gross margin	400,000	200,000				600,000
Expenses	250,000	120,000		(3) 4,000		366,000
Operating income before taxes	150,000	80,000				234,000
Equity in earnings—subsidiary	42,400		(1) 42,400			
Income before taxes	192,400	80,000				
Provision for taxes	60,000	32,000				92,000
						142,000
Minority interest net income					9,600	(9,600)
Net income—carried forward	132,400	48,000			9,600	132,400
Retained Earnings Statement						
Balance, 1/1/x2:						
Major Corp.	464,000					464,000
Minor Corp.		330,000	(4) 264,000		66,000	
Net income—brought forward	132,400	48,000			9,600	132,400
Balance, 12/31/x2—carried forward	596,400	378,000			75,600	596,400
Balance Sheet						
Cash	80,000	130,000				210,000
Accounts receivable (net)	120,000	60,000				180,000
Inventories	100,000	40,000				140,000
Investment in Minor Corp.	446,400		(2) 20,000	(4) 424,000		
				(1) 42,400		
Property, plant, and equipment	200,000	200,000	(2) 20,000			420,000
Accumulated depreciation	(100,000)	(40,000)	(3) 4,000	(2) 40,000		(176,000)
Other assets	270,000	238,000				508,000
Totals	1,116,400	628,000				1,282,000
Liabilities	120,000	50,000				170,000
Capital stock:						
Major Corp.	400,000					400,000
Minor Corp.		200,000	(4) 160,000		40,000	
Retained earnings—brought forward	596,400	378,000			75,600	596,400
Minority interest					115,600	115,600
Totals	1,116,400	628,000	510,400	510,400		1,282,000

(1) Elimination of equity in earnings of subsidiary.
(2) Elimination of gain on sale of equipment and restoration of book values.
(3) Confirmation of the current year's gain on sale ($20,000 ÷ 5 years = $4,000).
(4) Elimination of investment.

Illustration 6–3 *(continued)*

Computations and Proofs

Income apportionment:

	Total	Parent	Minority
Income—Minor Corp.	$ 48,000	$ 38,400	$ 9,600
Income—Major Corp. ($132,400 − $42,400)	90,000	90,000	
Confirmed profit on sale of equipment (1 year @ $4,000)	4,000	4,000	
Totals	$142,000	$132,400	$ 9,600

Reconciliation—minority interest:

Minor Corp.—capital stock	$200,000
—retained earnings (end of the year)	378,000
Total equity	$578,000
20%—minority interest	$115,600

A study of this illustration reveals that:

1. Entry (2) restores the Property, Plant, and Equipment account and the related Accumulated Depreciation account to their book values prior to the sale. This portion of entry (2) will be repeated for the remaining life of the property or until its prior sale to third parties. The remaining $20,000 of debit that is required to balance the entry is an adjustment to the investment account since the $20,000 was removed therefrom on the *parent's books* in 19x1. If not handled in this manner, elimination entry (4) would not be in balance to the extent of $20,000, since the investment account balance on the parent's books must agree with the amount of net assets of the subsidiary.

2. Entry (3) reduces the consolidated depreciation expense and the related accumulated depreciation since the subsidiary depreciated an unconfirmed profit ($20,000 ÷ 5 years = $4,000). The process of depreciating the $20,000 profit is sometimes referred to as "piecemeal recognition" (confirmation). In essence, this depreciation can be viewed as consuming 20 percent (over five years) of the transferred property each year for the production of income earned from third parties. Stated differently, it can be viewed as if one fifth of the equipment is sold to third parties each year over the next five years and, therefore, one-fifth of the profit is earned each year.

3. The credit in entry (3) went to Expenses, since the equipment involved was office equipment. If the equipment had been used for manufacturing, the credit would be to cost of sales (cost of goods manufactured).

For the years 19x3 through 19x6, entries (2) and (3) could be combined, and if they were, the entry would be as follows:

	19x3		19x4		19x5		19x6	
Investment in Minor Corporation	16,000		12,000		8,000		4,000	
Property, Plant, and Equipment	20,000		20,000		20,000		20,000	
Accumulated Depreciation	8,000		12,000		16,000		20,000	
Accumulated Depreciation		40,000		40,000		40,000		40,000
Depreciation Expense		4,000		4,000		4,000		4,000

INTERCOMPANY SALE OF MANUFACTURING EQUIPMENT

If the equipment involved in an intercompany sale is equipment used in manufacturing, some accounting theorists would attempt to ascertain how much of the related excess depreciation is still in the closing inventories and then consider this portion as unconfirmed until the inventories are sold to third parties. As a practical matter, unless this excess depreciation is material, this refinement is usually ignored and the entire excess depreciation is treated as confirmed profit in the year in which it is recorded.

SALE OF EQUIPMENT PRIOR TO EXPIRATION OF USEFUL LIFE

Occasionally, the equipment involved in an intercompany sale is sold to a third party prior to the expiration of its useful life. When this happens, any remaining unconfirmed profit on the transfer automatically becomes confirmed. To demonstrate the entries necessary to complete the confirmation process, it will now be assumed that the office equipment sold by Major Corporation to its subsidiary in Illustration 6–2 is now sold by the subsidiary on December 31, 19x3, for $42,000 to a third party. The subsidiary would make the following entry on its books:

Cash	42,000	
Accumulated Depreciation	24,000	
Equipment		60,000
Gain on Sale of Equipment		6,000

From a consolidated standpoint, the sale by the subsidiary produces not only a gain of $6,000 but also a gain of $12,000 which represents the remaining amount of unconfirmed profit arising from the sale of the equipment by the parent company to the subsidiary on December 31, 19x1. Had the subsidiary sold the equipment at a loss, the procedure would be the same except that the loss on the sale would be netted against the balance of the parent's remaining gain of $12,000 in order to arrive at the net consolidated gain (or loss) on the transactions. Illustration 6–4 demonstrates the procedures that are necessary to record this transaction in accordance with GAAP.

The following entry would be recorded on the books of the parent company:

Parent's Books—19x3

Investment in Minor Corporation	73,600	
Equity in Earnings of Subsidiary		73,600

To record parent's share of earnings:

80% × $72,000 =	$57,600
Confirmation of equipment profit for 19x3	4,000
Confirmation of the balance of intercompany equipment profit on 12/31/x3	12,000
	$73,600

The working paper elimination entries for Illustration 6–4 are:

(1)

Equity in Earnings—Subsidiary	73,600	
Investment in Minor Corporation		73,600

(2)

Investment in Minor Corporation	12,000	
Gain on Sale of Equipment		12,000

Complete Equity Method
End of Third Year
80 Percent Subsidiary

Illustration 6–4
MAJOR CORPORATION
Consolidated Working Paper
For the Year Ended December 31, 19x3

	Major Corp.	Minor Corp. (80%)	Eliminations Dr.	Eliminations Cr.	Minority Interest	Consolidated
Income Statement						
Sales	1,100,000	500,000				1,600,000
Cost of sales	650,000	250,000				900,000
Gross margin	450,000	250,000				700,000
Expenses	250,000	136,000		(3) 4,000		382,000
Operating income before taxes	200,000	114,000				318,000
Equity in earnings—subsidiary	73,600		(1) 73,600			
Gain on sale of equipment		6,000		(2) 12,000		18,000
Income before taxes	273,600	120,000				336,000
Provision for taxes	80,000	48,000				128,000
						208,000
Minority interest net income					14,400	(14,400)
Net income—carried forward	193,600	72,000			14,400	193,600
Retained Earnings Statement						
Balance, 1/1/x3:						
Major Corp.	596,000					596,400
Minor Corp.		378,000	(4) 302,400		75,600	
Net income—brought forward	193,600	72,000			14,400	193,600
Balance, 12/31/x3—carried forward	790,000	450,000			90,000	790,000
Balance Sheet						
Cash	100,000	150,000				250,000
Accounts receivable (net)	90,000	80,000				170,000
Inventories	110,000	50,000	(3) 4,000	(4) 462,400		160,000
Investment in Minor Corp.	520,000		(2) 12,000	(1) 73,600		
Property, plant, and equipment	200,000	140,000				340,000
Accumulated depreciation	(120,000)	(56,000)				(176,000)
Other assets	420,000	346,000				766,000
Total assets	1,320,000	710,000				1,510,000
Liabilities	130,000	60,000				190,000
Capital stock:						
Major Corp.	400,000					400,000
Minor Corp.		200,000	(4) 160,000		40,000	
Retained earnings—brought forward	790,000	450,000			90,000	790,000
Minority interest					130,000	130,000
Totals	1,320,000	710,000	552,000	552,000		1,510,000

(1) Elimination of equity in earnings of subsidiary.
(2) Confirmation of balance of profit on resale of equipment as of 12/31/x3.
(3) Confirmation of profit for the year 19x3.
(4) Elimination of investment balance.

Computations and Proofs

Income apportionment:

	Total	*Parent*	*Minority*
Income—Minor Corp.	$ 72,000	$ 57,600	$ 14,400
Income—Major Corp. ($177,600 − $57,600)	120,000	120,000	
Confirmed profit on sale of equipment (1 year @ $4,000)	4,000	4,000	
Balance of unconfirmed profit of equipment on resale by subsidiary	12,000	12,000	
Totals	$208,000	$193,600	$ 14,400

Illustration 6–4 *(continued)*

Reconciliation—minority interest:

Minor Corp.—capital stock	$200,000
—retained earnings (end of year)	450,000
Total equity	$650,000
20%—minority interest	$130,000

(3)		
Investment in Minor Corporation	4,000	
Depreciation Expense		4,000

(4)		
Retained Earnings (1/1/x3)—Minor Corporation	302,400	
Capital Stock—Minor Corporation	160,000	
Investment in Minor Corporation		462,400

From Illustration 6–4 and the assumed information, it should be noted that:

1. The *consolidated* gain on sale of the equipment can be computed using the original book value of the equipment. This will prove that the gain is in accordance with GAAP.

    Computations are:

Original cost		$80,000
Accumulated depreciation on date of		
sale to subsidiary		40,000
Book value, December 31, 19x1:		40,000
Depreciation, 19x2	$8,000	
Depreciation, 19x3	8,000	16,000
Book value, December 31, 19x3		24,000
Selling price on resale by subsidiary		42,000
Total gain		$18,000

2. The $6,000 portion of the gain on sale of the equipment (on the subsidiary's books) is, in effect, apportioned 80 percent to the parent and 20 percent to the minority interest through the apportionment of the $72,000 of subsidiary net income.
3. Since income tax effects have been ignored (they will be considered in the Appendix at the end of this chapter), the consolidated provision for taxes does not equal 40 percent (the assumed rate in this chapter) of the operating income before taxes.

SALE BY PARENT OF NONDEPRECIABLE ASSETS

If a parent company were to sell land to a subsidiary at a profit, no confirmation of the resulting unconfirmed profit would be possible because land is not depreciable (except for the extractive industries where depletion is required). Therefore, entry (3) in Illustration 6–3 would not apply as long as the subsidiary owned the land. Entry (2) (Illustration 6–3) would be repeated until such time as the land is sold to a third party.

PLANT ASSETS—SALE BY SUBSIDIARIES— UPSTREAM SALE

The basic difference between sales of plant assets by subsidiaries to other members of a group and sales by the parent to a subsidiary relates to the apportionment of income. When a subsidiary makes the sale, the unrealized (unconfirmed) gain (or loss) and subsequent confirmation through depreciation must be apportioned between the majority and the minority interests. To demonstrate the technique that is applicable, the data from Illustration 6–2 will be amended so that Minor Corporation rather than Major Corporation will be the seller of the equipment. The result can be viewed in Illustration 6–5. The illustration is based on the assumption that the following entry would have been made on the parent's books:

Parent's Books—19x1

Investment in Minor Corporation		17,600
Equity in Earnings of Subsidiary			17,600
To record parent's share of subsidiary earnings:		
80% × $42,000 = ...	$33,600	
Less: Parent's share of upstream profit on sale		
of equipment (80% × $20,000)	16,000	
Total	$17,600	

The elimination entries on the working paper shown on Illustration 6–5 are:

(1)

Equity in Earnings—Subsidiary	17,600	
Investment in Minor Corporation		17,600

(2)

Gain on Sale of Equipment	20,000	
Property, Plant, and Equipment	20,000	
Accumulated Depreciation		40,000

(3)

Retained Earnings (1/1/x1)—Minor Corporation	240,000	
Capital Stock—Minor Corporation	160,000	
Investment in Minor Corporation		400,000

The following noteworthy observations stem from Illustration 6–5:

1. Although this sale was an upstream sale, 100 percent of the unconfirmed profit ($20,000) is eliminated [see entry (2) on the working paper]. However, in the income apportionment schedule appended to the working paper, the $20,000 is allocated 80 percent to the parent and 20 percent to the minority interest.
2. The reconciliation of the minority interest as of December 31, 19x1, requires the removal of its share of this unconfirmed profit. The net assets of the subsidiary as of December 31, 19x1, amount to $542,000 and 20 percent of this amount is $108,400. By reducing the latter amount by the $4,000 of minority-interest unconfirmed profit, it is possible to reconcile to the $104,400 figure shown in the consolidated balance as minority interest.

For 19x2, the following working paper entries would be required:

Illustration 6–5
MAJOR CORPORATION
Partial Consolidated Working Paper
For the Year Ended December 31, 19x1

	Major Corp.	Minor Corp. (80%)	Eliminations Dr.	Eliminations Cr.	Minority Interest	Consolidated
Income Statement						
Sales	800,000	300,000				1,100,000
Operating income before taxes	80,000	50,000				130,000
Equity in earnings—subsidiary	17,600		(1) 17,600			
Gain on sale of equipment		20,000	(2) 20,000			
Income before taxes	97,600	70,000				130,000
Provision for taxes (40%)	32,000	28,000				60,000
						70,000
Minority interest net income					4,400	(4,400)
Net income—carried forward	65,600	42,000			4,400	65,600
Retained Earnings Statement						
Balance, 1/1/x1:						
Major Corp.	400,000					400,000
Minor Corp.		300,000	(3) 240,000		60,000	
Net income—brought forward	65,600	42,000			4,400	65,600
Balance, 12/31/x1—carried forward	465,600	342,000			64,400	465,600
Balance Sheet						
				(3) 400,000		
Investment in Minor Corp.	417,600			(1) 17,600		
Property, plant, and equipment	200,000	100,000	(2) 20,000			320,000
Accumulated depreciation	(80,000)	(20,000)		(2) 40,000		(140,000)
Other assets	420,400	490,000				910,400
Totals	958,000	570,000				1,090,400
Liabilities	92,400	28,000				120,400
Capital stock:						
Major Corp.	400,000					400,000
Minor Corp.		200,000	(3) 160,000		40,000	
Retained earnings—brought forward	465,600	342,000			64,400	465,600
Minority interest					104,400	104,400
Totals	958,000	570,000	457,600	457,600		1,090,400

(1) Elimination of equity in earnings of subsidiary.
(2) Elimination of gain on sale of equipment and restoration of original book values.
(3) Elimination of investment balance.

Computations and Proofs

Income apportionment:

	Total	Parent	Minority
Income—Minor Corp.	$42,000	$33,600	$ 8,400
Less: Unconfirmed gain on sale of equipment	(20,000)	(16,000)	(4,000)
Income—Major Corp. ($65,600 − $17,600)	48,000	48,000	
Totals	$70,000	$65,600	$ 4,400

Reconciliation—minority interest:

Minor Corp.—capital stock	$200,000
—retained earnings (end of year)	342,000
Total equity	542,000
Less: Unconfirmed gain on sale of equipment	20,000
Total	$522,000
20%—minority interest	$104,400

(2)		
Investment in Minor Corporation	16,000	
Retained Earnings (1/1/x2)—Minor Corporation	4,000	
Property, Plant, and Equipment	20,000	
Accumulated Depreciation		40,000

(3)		
Accumulated Depreciation	4,000	
Depreciation Expense		4,000

These entries should be compared with the same-numbered entries in Illustration 6–3. From this comparison it can be seen that the only difference between them is the apportionment of unconfirmed gain of $20,000. In Illustration 6–3, the full amount was debited to the investment account since, in that case, the sale was *downstream*. For *upstream* sales, only the parent's share ($16,000) is debited to the investment account and the minority interest's share ($4,000) is debited to the subsidiary's retained earnings at the beginning of the year. The latter debit reduced the minority interest's share of the beginning net assets *per books* (20 percent × $542,000 or $108,400) to the proper amount of $104,400 as explained in Illustration 6–5. For 19x2, 19x3, 19x4, 19x5, and 19x6, the parent company will record on *its books* its share ($3,200) of piecemeal confirmation of the profit, instead of the full $4,000 as demonstrated for downstream sales. The $3,200 can be computed either as $16,000 ÷ 5 years or 80 percent of $4,000 (the total confirmation per year on downstream sales).

The elimination entries for the years 19x3, 19x4, 19x5, and 19x6 can be condensed as follows:

	19x3		19x4		19x5		19x6	
Investment—Minor Corporation	12,800		9,600		6,400		3,200	
Retained Earnings (1/1)—Minor	3,200		2,400		1,600		800	
Property, Plant, and Equipment	20,000		20,000		20,000		20,000	
Accumulated Depreciation		32,000		28,000		24,000		20,000
Depreciation Expense		4,000		4,000		4,000		4,000

The separate entries which form the basis of the above condensed entries for 19x3 and 19x4 are as follows:

(2)				
	19x3		19x4	
Investment in Minor Corporation	16,000		16,000	
Retained Earnings (1/1)—Minor	4,000		4,000	
Property, Plant, and Equipment	20,000		20,000	
Accumulated Depreciation		40,000		40,000

(3)				
Accumulated Depreciation	8,000		12,000	
Depreciation Expense		4,000		4,000
Investment—Minor Corporation		3,200		6,400
Retained Earnings (1/1)—Minor		800		1,600

SALES OF ASSETS AT OTHER THAN END OF A YEAR—UPSTREAM SALE

If an intercompany sale occurs at a time other than the end of a year, it becomes necessary to combine the previously illustrated separate concepts in the year of the sale. Thus, in the year of the sale the removal of the intercompany profit must be combined with the piecemeal confirmation for the portion of the year subsequent to the sale. For example, if the sale were made on April 1, 19x2, at a gain, the gain would be removed and three fourths of a year's confirmation of profit would be restored in the year of the sale (19x2). Conversely, if the sale produced a loss, the loss would be removed and three fourths of a year's loss would be confirmed in 19x2.

To demonstrate the techniques to be employed when a sale of this type occurs, information similar to that used in Illustration 6–5 will be used except that it is now assumed that the sale was made on January 1, 19x1, instead of December 31, 19x1. Illustration 6–6 is the result and is based upon the assumption that the following entry was made on the parent's books:

Parent's Books—19x1

Investment in Minor Corporation		20,800
Equity in Earnings of Subsidiary		20,800
80% × $42,000 =	$33,600	
Less: Parent's share of unconfirmed profit on		
sale of equipment (80% × $20,000)	(16,000)	
Plus: one year's confirmation of above ($16,000		
÷ 5 years)	3,200	
	$20,800	

The Illustration 6–6 working paper elimination entries are:

(1)

Equity in Earnings—Subsidiary	20,800	
Investment in Minor Corporation		20,800

(2)

Gain on Sale of Equipment	20,000	
Property, Plant, and Equipment	20,000	
Accumulated Depreciation		40,000

(3)

Accumulated Depreciation	4,000	
Depreciation Expense		4,000

(4)

Retained Earnings (1/1/x1)—Minor Corporation	240,000	
Capital Stock—Minor Corporation	160,000	
Investment in Minor Corporation		400,000

The procedures used to prepare Illustration 6–6 are similar to those used previously except for the reconciliation of the minority interest. In previously prepared illustrations, the subsidiary's net assets were adjusted for the gross amounts of uncleared items (unsold intercompany inventory, unconfirmed profit on sales of plant assets, etc.) and the result was then multiplied by the minority interest's share to arrive at the reconciling result. In Illustration 6–6, however, each element of the net assets and reconciling items was

Illustration 6–6
MAJOR CORPORATION
Condensed Consolidated Working Paper
For the Year Ended December 31, 19x1

Complete Equity Method
End of First Year
80 Percent Subsidiary

	Major Corp.	Minor Corp. (80%)	Eliminations Dr.	Eliminations Cr.	Minority Interest	Consolidated
Income Statement						
Sales	800,000	300,000				1,100,000
Cost of sales and operating expenses	720,000	250,000		(3) 4,000		966,000
Operating income before taxes	80,000	50,000				134,000
Equity in earnings—subsidiary	20,800		(1) 20,800			
Gain on sale of equipment		20,000	(2) 20,000			
Income before taxes	100,800	70,000				
Provision for taxes	32,000	28,000				60,000
						74,000
Minority interest net income					5,200	(5,200)
Net income—carried forward	68,800	42,000			5,200	68,800
Retained Earnings Statement						
Balance, 1/1/x1:						
Major Corp.	400,000					400,000
Minor Corp.		300,000	(4) 240,000		60,000	
Net income—brought forward	68,800	42,000			5,200	68,800
Balance, 12/31/x1—carried forward	468,800	342,000			65,200	468,800
Balance Sheet						
				(4) 400,000		
Investment in Minor Corp.	420,800			(1) 20,800		
Property, plant, and equipment	200,000	100,000	(2) 20,000			320,000
Accumulated depreciation	(80,000)	(20,000)	(3) 4,000	(2) 40,000		(136,000)
Other assets	420,400	490,000				910,400
Total	961,200	570,000				1,094,400
Liabilities	92,400	28,000				120,400
Capital stock:						
Major Corp.	400,000					400,000
Minor Corp.		200,000	(4) 160,000		40,000	
Retained earnings—brought forward	468,800	342,000			65,200	468,800
Minority interest					105,200	105,200
Totals	961,200	570,000	464,800	464,800		1,094,400

(1) Elimination of equity in earnings of subsidiary.
(2) Elimination of gain on sale of equipment and restoration of book values.
(3) To record confirmation of current year's profit on sale of equipment.
(4) Elimination of investment.

Illustration 6–6 *(continued)*

Computations and Proofs

Income apportionment:

	Total	Parent	Minority
Income—Minor Corp.	$42,000	$33,600	$ 8,400
Less: Gain on sale of equipment	(20,000)	(16,000)	(4,000)
Add: One year's confirmation on sale of equipment	4,000	3,200	800
Income—Major Corp. ($68,800 − $20,800)	48,000	48,000	
Totals	$74,000	$68,800	$ 5,200

Reconciliation—minority interest:

Capital stock—Minor Corp. (20% × $200,000)		$ 40,000
Retained earnings—12/31/x1 (20% × $342,000)		68,400
Less: Unconfirmed profit on sale of equipment, 1/1/x1	$20,000	
Less: Confirmed in 19x1	(4,000)	
Balance unconfirmed as of 12/31/x1	$16,000	
20% of above		(3,200)
Minority interest, 12/31/x1		$105,200

multiplied by the minority interest's percentage and then totaled. Of course, either procedure produces the same result, but it is worthwhile to understand both methods.

The *working paper* elimination entries relating to the intercompany sale of equipment for 19x2 and 19x3 can be condensed into the following:

	19x2		19x3	
Investment in Minor Corporation	12,800		9,600	
Retained Earnings(1/1)—Minor	3,200		2,400	
Property, Plant, and Equipment	20,000		20,000	
Accumulated Depreciation		32,000		28,000
Depreciation Expense		4,000		4,000

For 19x2, the adjustment to retained earnings amounts to $3,200 which is the balance of unconfirmed profit as of the *beginning* of the current year. This amount should agree with the amount used for the reconciliation of minority interest at the *end* of the preceding year (see Illustration 6–6). The advantage of the reconciliation in Illustration 6–6 is apparent if it is to be used for the following year's working paper entry. Of course, the adjustment of $12,800 for 19x2 is the parent's share of the same $16,000 of unconfirmed profit used in the reconciliation at the *beginning* of the year.

BALANCE SHEET ONLY WORKING PAPERS

On CPA examinations and in selected other instances it may be necessary to prepare a working paper for the balance sheet only. The elimination entries are somewhat different from those presented thus far, and the balance sheet from Illustration 6–6 will be used to demonstrate the required procedures for this type of working paper.

The Illustration 6–7 working paper elimination entries are:

Illustration 6–7
MAJOR CORPORATION
Balance Sheet Consolidated Working Paper
December 31, 19x1

Complete Equity Method
End of First Year
80 Percent Subsidiary

	Major Corp.	Minor Corp. (80%)	Eliminations Dr.	Eliminations Cr.	Minority Interest	Consolidated
Assets						
Investment in Minor Corp.	420,800		(1) 12,800	(2) 433,600		
Property, plant, and equipment	200,000	100,000	(1) 20,000			320,000
Accumulated depreciation	(80,000)	(20,000)		(1) 36,000		(136,000)
Other assets	420,400	490,000				910,400
Totals	961,200	570,000				1,094,400
Liabilities and Stockholders' Equity						
Liabilities	92,400	28,000				120,400
Capital stock:						
Major Corp.	400,000					400,000
Minor Corp.		200,000	(2) 160,000		40,000	
Retained earnings:						
Major Corp.	468,800					468,800
			(2) 273,600		65,200	
Minor Corp.		342,000	(1) 3,200			
Minority interest					105,200	105,200
Totals	961,200	570,000	469,600	469,600		1,094,400

(1) To restore equipment and related accounts to original book values as of 12/31/x1.
(2) To eliminate investment balances.

(1)

Investment in Minor Corporation	12,800	
Property, Plant, and Equipment	20,000	
Retained Earnings—Minor Corporation	3,200	
Accumulated Depreciation		36,000

(2)

Capital Stock—Minor Corporation	160,000	
Retained Earnings—Minor Corporation	273,600	
Investment in Minor Corporation		433,600

A comparison of the elimination entries in Illustration 6–7 with the elimination entries in Illustration 6–6 for 19x2 reveals that they are the same on a net effect basis. The reason for this is that on Illustration 6–7 (a "closed" working paper) the entries *are as of December 31, 19x1,* and for the next year's working paper that includes an *income statement* ("open" working paper), the elimination entry is *as of January 1, 19x2,* which is the same point in time from an accounting viewpoint, although they are different years. It should be obvious that the balance sheets in Illustration 6–6 and 6–7 are identical, despite the differences in elimination entries.

Appendix: Consolidated statements—provision for income taxes on consolidated income tax returns involving intercompany profits on asset transfers

In Appendix A of Chapter 5, the treatment of deferred income taxes and the income tax provision were considered for those cases where a parent company and its subsidiary file separate income tax returns. In this Appendix the treatment of the income tax provision will be considered for those cases when consolidated income tax returns are filed. The requirements for filing a consolidated income tax return were already considered in Appendix A of Chapter 5.

In practice, the income tax provision is treated in a variety of ways when consolidated income tax returns are filed by a parent company. In some cases, subsidiary managements are instructed to accrue income taxes as if separate income tax returns are to be filed and then remit such amount to the parent. Only in rare cases will this amount coincide with the actual liability arising from the subsidiary's portion of the total taxable income. Book income will usually contain one or more of the following modifications needed to arrive at taxable income and the actual tax liability:

1. Intercompany profit transactions.
2. Amortization of goodwill.
3. Tax credits such as, investment tax credits, foreign tax credits, work incentive credits, etc.

4. Net operating loss carry forwards.
(Note: The above list is not all-inclusive.)

Some parent companies attribute tax reductions and modifications to the parent company only; others use percentage prorations to allocate the tax modifications between majority and minority interests. The treatment in this appendix is to prorate tax modifications arising from intercompany profits on asset transfers between majority and minority interests. In effect, unconfirmed profit adjustments are made on a net-of-tax basis.

To demonstrate the procedures involved in the net-of-tax approach, the following is now assumed:

1. P Company purchased 90 percent of the outstanding shares of S Company on January 1, 19x1, for $625,000. The retained earnings of S Company on that date were $350,000. All identifiable assets on the books of S Company are approximately equal to their respective fair market values. Any excess is attributable to goodwill and is to be amortized over the longest permissible period since the excess has an indeterminate life.
2. During 19x1, the following intercompany transactions occurred:

	Billed price	Cost	On hand—12/31/x1
Upstream . . .	$20,000	$ 6,000	$20,000 (100%)
Downstream .	40,000	16,000	10,000 (25%)

3. On December 31, 19x1, P Company sold equipment with a remaining useful life of five years to S Company and made the following entry on its books to record the sale:

Cash	60,000	
Accumulated Depreciation .	40,000	
Equipment		80,000
Gain on Sale of		
Equipment		20,000

4. Income taxes are 40 percent of taxable income. Income taxes are to be taken into account for intercompany transactions, and a consolidated income tax return is to be filed.

5. The subsidiary remitted $60,000 to the parent company for its share of income taxes. The parent company paid estimated income taxes of $120,000 ($60,000 for its own income and the $60,000 received from the subsidiary).

The following entries were made on the books of the parent company (see Illustration 6–8 for information):

Parent's Books—December 31, 19x1

(1)

Cash	36,000	
Investment in S Company		36,000

To record the receipt of dividends (90% × $40,000).

(2)

Investment in S Company	41,400	
Equity in Earnings of Subsidiary . .		41,400

To record parent's share of income as follows:

90% × $90,000 =	$81,000
Less: Unconfirmed inventory profit— downstream sale: 100% ($10,000 − $4,000)	(6,000)
Upstream sale 90% ($20,000 − $6,000)	(12,600)
Unconfirmed gain on sale of equipment— Downstream (100% × $20,000) .	(20,000)
Amortization of goodwill* ($40,000 ÷ 40 years)	(1,000)
Total	$41,400

(3)

Provision for Income Taxes	72,560	
Income Taxes Payable		72,560

To accrue income taxes:

P Company operating income	$200,000
Less: Unconfirmed inventory profits ($6,000 + $12,500) . . .	(18,600)
Taxable income	$181,400
Tax @ 40%	$ 72,560

*The calculation of goodwill is $625,000 − 90% (net assets of $650,000) or $40,000.

The calculation of the income tax provision can also be computed as follows:

P Company income before taxes	$261,400
Less: Parent's share of subsidiary income (90% × $90,000)	(81,000)
Add: Amortization of goodwill—not deductible for tax purposes	1,000
Taxable Income	$181,400
Tax @ 40%	$ 72,560

The Illustration 6–8 working paper elimination entries are:

Complete Equity Method
End of First Year
90 Percent Subsidiary

	P Co.	S Co. (90%)	Eliminations Dr.	Eliminations Cr.	Minority Interest	Consol-idated
Income Statement						
Sales	700,000	300,000	(4) 60,000			940,000
Cost of sales	280,000	90,000	(5) 20,000	(4) 60,000		330,000
Gross margin	420,000	210,000				610,000
Expenses	220,000	60,000	(3) 1,000			281,000
Operating income before taxes	200,000	150,000				329,000
Equity in earnings—subsidiary	41,400		(1) 41,400			
Gain on sale of equipment	20,000		(6) 20,000			
Income before income taxes	261,400	150,000				
Provision for income taxes (40%)	72,560	60,000		(7) 560		132,000
						197,000
Minority interest net income					8,160	(8,160)
Net income—carried forward	188,840	90,000			8,160	188,840
Retained Earnings Statement						
Balance, 1/1/x1:						
P Co.	389,400					389,400
S Co.		350,000	(2) 315,000		35,000	
Net income—brought forward	188,840	90,000			8,160	188,840
Totals	578,240	440,000			43,160	578,240
Less: Dividends declared—S Co.		40,000		(1) 36,000	4,000	
Balance, 12/31/x1—carried forward	578,240	400,000			39,160	578,240
Balance Sheet						
Cash	100,000	80,000				180,000
Accounts receivable (net)	60,000	30,000				90,000
Inventories	80,000	40,000		(5) 20,000		100,000
				(2) 625,000		
Investment in S Co.	630,400			(1) 5,400		
Property, plant, and equipment	200,000	200,000	(6) 20,000			420,000
Less: Accumulated depreciation	(80,000)	(20,000)		(6) 40,000		(140,000)
Other assets	142,860	400,000				542,860
Goodwill			(2) 40,000	(3) 1,000		39,000
Totals	1,133,260	730,000				1,231,860
Accounts payable	62,400	20,000				82,400
Income taxes payable	12,560	—	(7) 560			12,000
Other liabilities	80,060	10,000				90,060
Capital stock:						
P Co.	400,000					400,000
S Co.		300,000	(2) 270,000		30,000	
Retained earnings—brought forward	578,240	400,000			39,160	578,240
Minority interest					69,160	69,160
Totals	1,133,260	730,000	787,960	787,960		1,231,860

(1) Elimination of equity in earnings of subsidiary.
(2) Elimination of investment balance.
(3) One year's amortization of goodwill.
(4) Elimination of intercompany sales.
(5) Elimination of unconfirmed profit in ending inventory.
(6) Elimination of unconfirmed gain on intercompany sale of equipment and restoration of book values.
(7) Adjustment of income taxes on minority interest's share of unconfirmed inventory profit at 12/31/x1.

Illustration 6–8 (*continued*)

Computations and Proofs

Income apportionment—net of tax:

	Total	Parent	Minority
Income—S Co.	$ 90,000	$ 81,000	$ 9,000
Less: Unconfirmed inventory profit, 12/31/x1—upstream sale	(14,000)	(12,600)	(1,400)
Income—P Co. ($188,840 − $41,400)	147,440	147,440	
Less: Unconfirmed inventory profit, 12/31/x1—downstream	(6,000)	(6,000)	
Less: Unconfirmed profit on sale of equipment	(20,000)	(20,000)	
Less: Amortization of goodwill	(1,000)	(1,000)	
Totals	196,440	188,840	7,600
Add: Tax adjustment for minority interest ($1,400 × 40%)	560		560
	$197,000	$188,840	$ 8,160

Reconciliation—minority interest:

S Co. capital stock (10% × $300,000)		$30,000
S Co. retained earnings, 12/31/x1 (10% × $400,000)		40,000
Less: Unconfirmed inventory profit, 12/31/x1	$ 1,400	
Tax—40%	(560)	
Net of tax		(840)
Minority interest, 12/31/x1		$69,160

(1)		
Equity in Earnings—Subsidiary	41,400	
Dividends Declared—S Company	36,000	
Investment in S Company		5,400

(2)		
Retained Earnings (1/1/x1)—S Company	315,000	
Capital Stock—S Company	270,000	
Goodwill	40,000	
Investment in S Company		625,000

(3)		
Amortization of Goodwill	1,000	
Goodwill		1,000

(4)		
Sales	60,000	
Cost of Sales		60,000

(5)		
Cost of Sales (ending inventory)	20,000	
Inventories		20,000

(6)		
Gain on Sale of Equipment	20,000	
Property, Plant, and Equipment	20,000	
Accumulated Depreciation		40,000

(7)		
Income Taxes Payable	560	
Provision for Income Taxes		560

From Illustration 6–8 it should be noted that:

1. Entries (1) to (6) are similar to the respective entries used in previous illustrations.

2. Entry (7) was not previously discussed. A review of the appended income apportionment schedule (in Illustration 6–8) indicates that a $560 adjustment to minority interest net income is necessary if the net-of-tax concept is to be used. This same amount must be used to adjust the income tax provision and the liability for income taxes since they were adjusted only for the parent's share of intercompany profits [see book entry (3) above]. After the posting of working paper entry (7), the income tax provision in the consolidated column is $132,000 or 40 percent of consolidated operating income increased by the nondeductible goodwill amortization ($329,000 + $1,000 = $330,000 × 40 percent = $132,000).

3. Income taxes payable in the consolidated column are $12,000. Since the total liability for the year equals $132,000 and estimated taxes of

$120,000 have been paid, the unpaid balance is, in fact, $12,000.

4. The reconciliation of minority interest as at December 31, 19x1, requires an inventory adjustment, but in this case it must be made on a *net-of-tax basis* in the amount of $840 rather than $1,400 as was done in Chapter 5. This reconciliation, appended to Illustration 6–8, should be studied carefully.

5. Just as in previous illustrations that employed the complete equity method, the net-of-tax approach also results in the parent's net income and the parent's retained earnings agreeing with the respective consolidated amounts.

The example will now be continued for 19x2 with the following assumptions:

1. All unsold inventories on January 1, 19x2, were sold during 19x2.
2. Intercompany sales (both downstream and upstream) for the year amounted to $90,000.
3. Intercompany profit in unsold inventories on December 31, 19x2, are:

| Downstream | $12,000 profit |
| Upstream | 21,000 profit |

4. Intercompany receivables and payables on December 31, 19x2, amount to $40,000.
5. Estimated income tax payments were $120,000.

The parent company made the following entries on its books for 19x2:

Parent's Books—December 31, 19x2

(4)

| Cash | 54,000 | |
| Investment in S Company | | 54,000 |

To record dividends received (90% × $60,000).

(5)

| Investment in S Company | 98,700 | |
| Equity in Earnings of Subsidiary | | 98,700 |

To record parent's share of income as follows:

90% × $120,000 =	$108,000
Add: Confirmation of inventory profits (1/1/x2):	
Downstream (100% × $6,000)	6,000
Upstream (90% × $14,000)	12,600
Confirmation of gain on sale of equipment ($20,000 ÷ 5 years)	4,000
Deduct: Unconfirmed inventory profits (12/31/x2):	
Downstream (100% × $12,000)	(12,000)
Upstream (90% × $21,000)	(18,900)
Amortization of goodwill	(1,000)
Total	$ 98,700

(6)

| Provision for Income Taxes | 76,680 | |
| Income Taxes Payable | | 76,680 |

To accrue income taxes as follows:

P Company operating income	$200,000
Add: Beginning inventory profits ($6,000 + $12,600)	18,600
Confirmed gain on equipment sale	4,000
Deduct: Ending inventory profits ($12,000 + $18,900)	(30,900)
Taxable income	$191,700
Tax @ 40%	$ 76,680

Alternatively, the income tax provision can be computed as follows:

P Company income before taxes	$298,700
Less: Parent's share of subsidiary income (90% × $120,000)	(108,000)
Add: Amortization of goodwill not deductible on tax return	1,000
Taxable income	$191,700
Tax @ 40%	$ 76,680

Illustration 6–9

Complete Equity Method
End of Second Year
90 Percent Subsidiary

P COMPANY
Consolidated Working Paper
For the Year Ended December 31, 19x2

	P Co.	S Co. (90%)	Eliminations Dr.	Eliminations Cr.	Minority Interest	Consolidated
Income Statement						
Sales	800,000	500,000	(7) 90,000	(2) 20,000		1,210,000
Cost of sales	320,000	150,000	(8) 33,000	(7) 90,000		393,000
Gross margin	480,000	350,000				817,000
Expenses	280,000	150,000	(6) 1,000	(4) 4,000		427,000
Operating income before taxes	200,000	200,000				390,000
Equity in earnings—subsidiary	98,700		(1) 98,700			
Income before taxes	298,700	200,000				
Provision for taxes (40%)	76,680	80,000		(10) 280		156,400
						233,600
Minority interest net income					11,580	(11,580)
Net income—carried forward	222,020	120,000			11,580	222,020
Retained Earnings Statement						
Balance, 1/1/x2:						
P Co.	578,240					578,200
			(2) 1,400	(10) 560		
S Co.		400,000	(5) 360,000		39,160	
Net income—brought forward	222,020	120,000			11,580	222,020
Totals	800,260	520,000			50,740	800,260
Less: Dividends declared—S Co.		60,000		(1) 54,000	6,000	
Balance, 12/31/x2—carried forward	800,260	460,000			44,740	800,260
Balance Sheet						
Cash	60,000	40,000				100,000
Accounts receivable (net)	100,000	80,000		(9) 40,000		140,000
Inventories	70,000	30,000		(8) 33,000		67,000
			(3) 20,000	(5) 669,000		
Investment in S Co.	675,100		(2) 18,600	(1) 44,700		
Property, plant, and equipment	200,000	200,000	(3) 20,000			420,000
Less: Accumulated depreciation	(100,000)	(40,000)	(4) 4,000	(3) 40,000		(176,000)
Other assets	352,900	540,000				892,900
Goodwill			(5) 39,000	(6) 1,000		38,000
Total assets	1,358,000	850,000				1,481,900
Accounts payable	80,000	60,000	(9) 40,000			100,000
Income taxes payable	17,240	20,000	(10) 840			36,400
Other liabilities	60,500	10,000				70,500
Capital stock:						
P Co.	400,000					400,000
S Co.		300,000	(5) 270,000		30,000	
Retained earnings—brought forward	800,260	460,000			44,740	800,260
Minority interest					74,740	74,740
Totals	1,358,000	850,000	996,540	996,540		1,481,900

(1) Elimination of equity in earnings of subsidiary.
(2) Confirmation of intercompany profit in beginning inventories.
(3) Elimination of intercompany gain on sale of equipment and restoration of book values.
(4) Confirmation of one year's profit on intercompany sale of equipment.
(5) Elimination of the balance of investment.
(6) Amortization of current year's goodwill amount.
(7) Elimination of intercompany sales.
(8) Elimination of unconfirmed profits in closing inventories.
(9) Elimination of intercompany payables and receivable.
(10) Income tax adjustments on minority interest's share of profit in beginning and ending inventories.

Illustration 6–9 *(continued)*

Computations and Proofs

Adjustment—income tax provision:

Schedule A

	Total	Parent	Minority
Confirmed Profit			
Beginning inventory:			
Sale by P Co.	$ 6,000	$ 6,000	
Sale by S Co.	14,000	12,600	$ 1,400
Office machine depreciation sale by P Co.	4,000	4,000	
Unconfirmed Profit			
Ending inventory:			
Sale by P Co.	(12,000)	(12,000)	
Sale by S Co.	(21,000)	(18,900)	(2,100)
Net—Unconfirmed	$ (9,000)	$ (8,300)	$ (700)
Tax @ 40%	$ (9,000)	$ (3,320)	$ (280)

Income apportionment:

Schedule B

	Total	Parent	Minority
Income—S Co.	$120,000	$108,000	$12,000
Add: Confirmed inventory profit—beginning	14,000	12,600	1,400
Deduct: Unconfirmed inventory profit end	(21,000)	(18,900)	(2,100)
Income—P Co. ($222,020 − $98,700)	123,320	123,320	
Add: Confirmed inventory profit—beginning	6,000	6,000	
Deduct: Unconfirmed inventory profit—end	(12,000)	(12,000)	
Add: Confirmed equipment profit	4,000	4,000	
Deduct: Goodwill amortization	(1,000)	(1,000)	
Add: Tax reduction adjustment—Minority (Schedule A)	280		280
	$233,600	$222,020	$11,580

Reconciliation of minority interest:

S Co.—capital stock (10% × $300,000)		$30,000
S Co.—retained earnings, 12/31/x2 (10% × $460,000)		46,000
Less: Unconfirmed inventory profit, 12/31/x2 (10% × $21,000)	$ 2,100	
Tax @ 40%	(840)	
Net of tax		(1,260)
Minority interest, 12/31/x2		$74,740

The Illustration 6–9 working paper elimination entries are:

(1)

Equity in Earnings—Subsidiary	98,700	
Dividends Declared—S Company		54,000
Investment in S Company		44,700

(2)

Retained Earnings (1/1/x2)—S Company	1,400	
Investment in S Company ...	18,600	
Cost of Sales (beginning inventory)		20,000

(3)

Investment in S Company ...	20,000	
Property, Plant, and Equipment	20,000	
Accumulated Depreciation		40,000

(4)

Accumulated Depreciation ...	4,000	
Depreciation Expense ...		4,000

(5)

Retained Earnings (1/1/x2)—S Company	360,000	
Capital Stock—S Company ..	270,000	
Goodwill	39,000	
Investment in S Company		669,000

	(6)		
Amortization of Goodwill . . .	1,000	
Goodwill		1,000

	(7)		
Sales	90,000	
Cost of Sales		90,000

	(8)		
Cost of Sales (ending		
inventory)	33,000	
Inventories		33,000

	(9)		
Accounts Payable	40,000	
Accounts Receivable		40,000

	(10)		
Income Taxes Payable	840	
Provison for Income Taxes		280
Retained Earnings,		
(1/1/x2)—S Company . . .		560

The following observations from Illustration 6–9 should be carefully reviewed:

1. Elimination entries (1) to (9) are similar to entries previously discussed.
2. The tax reduction adjustment of $280 (see income apportionment schedule) is really a *reversal* of the 19x1 adjustment of $560 plus a new adjustment for 19x2 of $840 ($2,100 × 40% tax) for a net adjustment of $280. Accordingly, entry (10) represents the net effect of these two amounts.
3. After entry (10) is made on the working paper, the income tax provision is $156,400 which is 40% × $391,000 (operating income of $390,000 plus the nondeductible goodwill amortization of $1,000).
4. The income tax liability of $36,400 is the total tax liability of $156,400 reduced by the estimated income tax payments of $120,000.
5. The $560 adjustment in entry (10) is necessary to adjust the minority interest's share of beginning retained earnings to agree with last year's closing amount. This can be verified by comparing the closing amount of $39,160 in Illustration 6–8 with the beginning amount of $39,160 in Illustration 6–9. Without the $560 adjustment, they would not agree.
6. The reconciliation of the minority interest requires an adjustment for the closing inventory (on a net-of-tax basis) only. The beginning inventory is now a "cleared item" and does not enter into the reconciliation.

QUESTIONS

1. When a parent company computes excess as of the date of acquisition, it is usual for a portion of this excess to be allocated to specific plant assets owned by the subsidiary. If the subsidiary later sells a plant asset to which excess has been allocated, what treatment is accorded to the excess thus allocated?

2. When an intercompany sale of depreciable plant assets takes place, how is the gain or loss on the sale treated in the year of the sale? In subsequent years?

3. Is it necessary to ascertain if an intercompany sale of plant assets is either downstream or upstream? Why?

4. What is meant by piecemeal confirmation (recognition)?

5. Occasionally, a plant asset acquired in an intercompany sale is disposed of prior to the expiration of its estimated useful life. From a consolidated viewpoint, what accounting treatment is necessary to record this event?

6. Is the treatment of the confirmation of an intercompany gain or loss the same for land as for depreciable plant assets? If not, how do they differ?

7. The *date* of an intercompany *sale of inventory* does not affect the accounting entries for profit deferral and confirmation. The relevant information is the amount of *unsold* inventory on the last day of the accounting period. Is the same true for an intercompany sale of depreciable plant assets? Explain your answer by considering the following dates of sale:

a. Beginning of the year.
b. An interim date.
c. End of the year.

8. Are the elimination entries different for a working paper used to prepare only a balance sheet and a three-part working paper when an intercompany sale of plant assets is involved? Explain.

Questions for Appendix:

9. Are there different treatments in use regarding the allocation of the provision for income taxes when consolidated income tax returns are filed? Explain.

10. What is meant by the net-of-tax approach?

EXERCISES

Exercise 6–1.

1. On January 1, 19x8, Harry Corporation sold equipment costing $2,000,000 with accumulated depreciation of $500,000 to Anna Corporation, its wholly owned subsidiary, for $1,800,000. Harry was depreciating the equipment on the straight-line method over 20 years with *no* salvage value, which Anna continued. In consolidation at December 31, 19x8, the cost and accumulated depreciation, respectively, should be

a. $1,500,000 and $100,000.
b. $1,800,000 and $100,000.
c. $2,000,000 and $100,000.
d. $2,000,000 and $600,000.

Items 2 and 3 are based on the following information:

Corporation A purchased the net assets of corporation B for $80,000. On the date of A's purchase, corporation B had no long-term investments in marketable securities and $10,000 (book and fair value) of liabilities. The fair values of corporation B's assets, when acquired, were:

Current assets	$ 40,000
Noncurrent assets	60,000
Total	$100,000

2. How should the $10,000 difference between the fair value of the net assets acquired ($90,000) and the cost ($80,000) be accounted for by corporation A?

a. The $10,000 difference should be credited to retained earnings.

b. The noncurrent assets should be recorded at $50,000.

c. The current assets should be recorded at $36,000, and the noncurrent assets should be recorded at $54,000.

d. A deferred credit of $10,000 should be set up and then amortized to income over a period not to exceed 40 years.

3. Assume that corporation A paid $110,000 for corporation B's net assets, and that all other information given above remains the same. What is the minimum annual difference between financial accounting income and tax income because of this purchase?

a. Zero.
b. $500.
c. $2,000.
d. *Cannot* be determined from the information given. (AICPA adapted)

Exercise 6–2. On January 1, 19x1, P Company purchased 80 percent of the outstanding shares of S Company at a cost of $800,000. On that date, S Company had $500,000 of capital stock and $500,000 of retained earnings.

For 19x1, S Company reported income of $200,000 and paid dividends of $80,000. All of the assets and liabilities of S Company are at fair market value.

On December 31, 19x1, P Company sold equipment to S Company for $80,000 which had a cost of $60,000. The equipment is expected to have a useful life of 10 years from this date. P Company uses the complete equity method to account for its investment in S Company.

For the year 19x1, P Company reported income from its *own* operations in the amount of $300,000, which included the gain of $20,000 on equipment sold to S Company.

Required:

a. Prepare the journal entries on the books of P Company to record the equity in earnings of S Company, including the deferral of earnings due to the sale of equipment.

b. Compute the amount to be shown as consolidated net income.

c. Compute the balance of the Investment in S Company account on December 31, 19x1.

d. Compute minority interest net income for 19x1.

e. Compute the amount to be shown as minority interest on a consolidated statement as of December 31, 19x1.

f. For 19x2, the separate incomes of P Company and S Company were $350,000 and $250,000, respectively. Prepare the journal entry (entries) to record the equity in earnings of S Company to be recorded on the books of P Company. Compute consolidated net income for 19x2.

Exercise 6–3. Using the information provided in Exercise 6–2, assume that the intercompany sale of equipment was made by S Company (upstream sale) instead of by P Company. All other information is unchanged.

Required:

Complete *(a)*, *(b)*, *(c)*, *(d)*, *(e)*, and *(f)* from Exercise 6–2.

Exercise 6–4. On January 1, 19x3, P Company purchased 80 percent of the outstanding shares of S Company at a cost of $800,000. On that date, S Company had $300,000 of capital stock and $500,000 of retained earnings.

For 19x3, P Company had income of $400,000 from its own operations (excluding its share of income from S Company) and paid dividends of $100,000. For 19x3, S Company reported a net income of $200,000 and paid dividends of $40,000. All of the assets and liabilities of S Company have book values approximately equal to their respective market values.

On April 1, 19x3, P Company sold equipment with a book value of $40,000 to S Company for $80,000. The gain on the sale is included in the income of P Company indicated above. The equipment is expected to have a useful life of five years from the date of the sale.

P Company uses the complete equity method to account for its investment in S Company.

Required:

a. Compute the amount that P Company should record as equity in earnings of S Company for 19x3.

b. Compute consolidated net income for 19x3.

c. Compute minority interest net income for 19x3.

d. Compute the total minority interest at December 31, 19x3.

e. Compute the balance in the investment account at December 31, 19x3.

f. For 19x4, the separate incomes of P Company and S Company were $450,000 and $300,000, respectively. Prepare the journal entry (entries) to record the equity in earnings of S Company to be recorded on the books of P Company. Compute consolidated net income for 19x4.

Exercise 6–5. Using the information provided in

Exercise 6–4, assume that the intercompany sale of equipment was made by S Company (upstream sale) instead of by P Company. All other information is unchanged.

Required:

Complete *(a)*, *(b)*, *(c)*, *(d)*, *(e)*, and *(f)* from Exercise 6–4.

Exercise 6–6. On January 1, 19x4, P Company purchased 80 percent of the outstanding shares of S Company at a cost of $600,000. On that date, S Company had $200,000 of capital stock and $500,000 of retained earnings.

For 19x4, P Company had income of $400,000 from its own operations (excluding its share of income from S Company) and paid dividends of $200,000.

For 19x4, S Company reported income of $60,000 and paid dividends of $40,000. All of the assets and liabilities of S Company have book values approximately equal to their respective market values.

On January 2, 19x4, P Company sold equipment to S Company for $100,000. The book value of the equipment on that date was $150,000. The loss of $50,000 is reflected in the income of P Company indicated above. The equipment is expected to have a useful life of five years from the date of the sale.

P Company uses the complete equity method to account for its investment in S Company.

Required:

a. Prepare the journal entries necessary to record the equity in earnings of S Company on the books of P Company for 19x4.

b. Compute consolidated net income for 19x4.

c. Compute the balance in the investment in S Company at December 31, 19x4.

d. Compute minority interest net income for 19x4.

e. Compute the total minority interest at December 31, 19x4.

f. For 19x4, the separate incomes of P Company and S Company were $350,000 and $100,000, respectively. Prepare the journal entry (entries) to record the equity in earnings of S Company to be recorded on the books of P Company. Compute consolidated net income for 19x4.

Exercise 6–7. Using the information provided in Exercise 6–6 assume that the intercompany sale of equipment was made by S Company (upstream sale) instead of by P Company. All other information is unchanged.

Required:

Complete (a), (b), (c), (d), (e), and (f) from Exercise 6–6.

Exercise 6–8. On January 1, 19x4, P Company purchased 80 percent of the outstanding shares of S Company at a cost of $700,000. On that date, S Company had $200,000 of capital stock and $500,000 of retained earnings.

For 19x4, P Company had income of $400,000 from its own operations (excluding its share of income from S Company) and paid dividends of $200,000.

For 19x4, S Company reported a loss of $50,000 and paid dividends of $40,000. All of the asset and liabilities of S Company have book values approximately equal to their respective market values.

On July 1, 19x4, P Company sold equipment to S Company at a profit of $30,000. The equipment is expected to last 10 years from the date of the sale. On January 1, 19x4, S Company sold equipment to P Company at a loss of $20,000. The equipment is expected to have a useful life of five years from the date of the sale. Both the gain and the loss are reflected in the respective incomes indicated above.

P Company uses the complete equity method to account for its investment in S Company.

Required:

a. Prepare the journal entries necessary to record the equity in earnings of S Company on the books of P Company for 19x4.

b. Compute consolidated net income for 19x4.

c. Compute the balance in the investment in S Company at December 31, 19x4.

d. Compute minority interest net income for 19x4.

e. Compute the total minority interest at December 31, 19x4.

Exercise 6–9. On January 1, 19x2, P Company purchased 80 percent of the outstanding shares of S Company at a cost of $600,000. On that date, S Company had $300,000 of capital stock and $400,000 of retained earnings.

For 19x3, P Company had income of $200,000 from its own operations (excluding its share of income from S Company) and paid dividends of $50,000. For 19x3, S Company reported a net income of $180,000 and paid dividends of $70,000. All of the assets and liabilities of S Company have book values approximately equal to their respective market values.

The beginning inventory of S Company includes $21,000 of merchandise purchased from P Company who shipped this merchandise at 40 percent above its cost. The ending inventory of P Company includes $16,000 of merchandise purchased from S Company who shipped this merchandise at 33 1/3 percent above its cost. Both companies use Fifo inventory costing.

On July 1, 19x3, S Company sold equipment to P Company at a gain of $60,000. This gain is reflected in the net income of S Company as indicated above. This equipment is expected to have a useful life of 10 years from the date of the sale.

P Company uses the complete equity method to account for its investment in S Company.

Required:

a. Compute the amount that P Company should record as equity in earnings of S Company for 19x3.

b. Compute consolidated net income for 19x3.

c. Compute minority interest net income for 19x3.

d. Compute the total minority interest at December 31, 19x3.

Exercise 6–10. On January 1, 19x5, P Company purchased 80 percent of the outstanding shares of S Company at a price that included $10,000 of excess attributable entirely to land that was undervalued.

For 19x5, P Company reported income of $155,920 computed under the complete equity method. Minority interest net income was $18,480. The minority interest reported on the consolidated balance sheet at December 31, 19x5, amounted to $94,480.

On December 31, 19x5, P Company had inventories which included $18,000 of merchandise purchased from S Company at 125 percent of its cost. On the same date S Company had inventories which included $12,000 of merchandise purchased from P Company at 120 percent of its cost.

On January 1, 19x5, S Company sold equipment to P Company at a gain of $30,000. This equipment is expected to have a useful life of five years from the date of the sale.

Neither company paid any dividends in 19x5.

Required:

a. Compute the amount of income the parent reported as equity in earnings of S Company.

b. Compute the amount of net assets on the books of S Company at December 31, 19x5.

c. Compute the price paid by P Company for its investment in S Company.

d. Compute the balance of the investment in S Company at December 31, 19x5.

PROBLEMS

Problem 6–11. On January 1, 19x2, P Company acquired 75 percent of the outstanding shares of S Company at book value.

For the year 19x4, P Company purchased merchandise from S Company in the amount of $200,000 at billed prices. S Company shipped this merchandise at 33 $\frac{1}{3}$ percent above its cost, and this price was also used for shipments made in 19x3 to P Company. The inventories of P Company included merchandise at billed prices from S Company as follows:

January 1, 19x4	$20,000
December 31, 19x4	30,000

On January 1, 19x4, P Company sold equipment to S Company at a gain of $40,000. This equipment is estimated to have a useful life of eight years.

Income statements for the two companies for the year 19x4 are as follows:

Income Statement	P Company	S Company
Sales	$1,000,000	$500,000
Cost of sales	400,000	250,000
Gross margin	600,000	250,000
Expenses	200,000	100,000
Operating income before taxes	400,000	150,000
Gain on sale of equipment . .	40,000	
Equity in earnings— subsidiary	30,625	
Income before income taxes .	470,625	150,000
Provision for income taxes . .	176,000	60,000
Minority interest net income		
Net income	$ 294,625	$ 90,000

Required:

Prepared a consolidated income statement.

Problem 6–12. On January 1, 19x3, P Company acquired 80 percent of the outstanding shares of S Company at book value.

For the year 19x5, P Company purchased merchandise from S Company who also purchased merchandise from P Company. Data regarding inter-

company sales, inventories, and profit percentages are as follows:

	P Company	S Company
Intercompany sales	$300,000	$200,000
Intercompany inventories:		
January 1, 19x5	30,000	40,000
December 31, 19x5	20,000	50,000
Gross profit percentages on intercompany sales—as a percentage of selling price. (See gross margin percentages on income statements below.)	60%	50%

On July 1, 19x3, S Company sold equipment to P Company at a gain of $30,000. This equipment is estimated to have a useful life of five years from the date of the sale.

Income statements for the two companies for the year 19x5 are as follows:

Income Statement	P Company	S Company
Sales	$1,500,000	$800,000
Cost of sales	600,000	400,000
Gross margin	900,000	400,000
Expenses	300,000	200,000
Operating income before taxes	600,000	200,000
Gain on sale of equipment . .		30,000
Equity in earnings— subsidiary	86,800	
Income before income taxes .	686,800	230,000
Provision for income taxes . .	240,000	92,000
Minority interest net income		
Net income	$ 446,800	$138,000

Required:

Prepare a consolidated income statement.

Problem 6–13 (complete equity method). On January 1, 19x1, P Company purchased 40,000 shares of S Company in the open market for $640,000. On that date, the net assets of S Company amounted to $800,000 and had book values that approximated their respective fair market values.

P Company uses the complete equity method to account for its investment.

On January 1, 19x4, P Company sold equipment to S Company at a gain of $50,000. P Company made the following entry on its *books*:

Cash	150,000	
Accumulated Depreciation—		
Equipment	100,000	
Equipment		200,000
Gain on Sale of		
Equipment		50,000

The equipment is estimated to have a remaining useful life of five years from the date of the sale.

Financial statements for the two corporations for the year ended December 31, 19x4, are as follows:

	P Company	S Company
Income Statement		
Sales	$2,000,000	$1,000,000
Cost of sales	800,000	600,000
Gross margin	1,200,000	400,000
Expenses	500,000	200,000
Operating income before		
taxes	700,000	200,000
Gain on sale of equipment	50,000	
Equity in earnings—		
subsidiary	56,000	
Income before income taxes	806,000	200,000
Provision for income taxes	300,000	80,000
Minority interest net income		
Net income—carried forward	$ 506,000	$ 120,000
Retained Earnings Statement		
Balance, January 1, 19x4:		
P Company	$3,053,000	
S Company		$ 860,000
Net income—brought		
forward	506,000	120,000
Totals	3,559,000	980,000
Less: Dividends declared:		
P Company	400,000	
S Company		60,000
Balance, December 31, 19x4—		
carried forward	$3,159,000	$ 920,000

	P Company	S Company
Balance Sheet		
Cash	$ 300,000	$ 200,000
Accounts receivable	260,000	200,000
Inventories	400,000	200,000
Land	600,000	—
Building	400,000	—
Equipment	1,303,000	1,000,000
Investment in S Company	1,096,000	
Totals	$4,359,000	$1,600,000
Accounts payable and		
accrued expenses	$ 302,000	$ 20,000
Accumulated depreciation—		
building	40,000	—
Accumulated depreciation—		
equipment	58,000	160,000
Common stock—P Company		
($50 par)	500,000	
Common stock—S Company		
($10 par)		500,000
Additional paid-in capital—P		
Company	300,000	
Retained earnings—brought		
forward	3,159,000	920,000
Totals	$4,359,000	$1,600,000

Required:

Prepare a consolidated working paper.

Problem 6–14 (complete equity method). On January 1, 19x2, P Company acquired 80 percent of the outstanding common stock of S Company for $560,000. On that date, the retained earnings of S Company were $200,000 and there have been no changes in its capital stock and additional paid-in capital.

All of the assets and liabilities of S Company had book values approximately equal to their respective market values.

P Company uses the complete equity method to account for this investment.

On August 1, 19x4, S Company sold equipment to P Company at a loss of $36,000. S Company made the following entry on its *books*:

Cash	30,000	
Accumulated Depreciation	20,000	
Loss on Sale of Equipment	36,000	
Equipment		86,000

The equipment is estimated to have a remaining useful life of three years from the date of the sale.

The financial statements of the companies for the year ended December 31, 19x4 are as follows:

	P Company	S Company
Income Statement		
Sales	$ 800,000	$200,000
Cost of sales	400,000	150,000
Gross margin	400,000	50,000
Expenses	100,000	64,000
Operating income (loss) before taxes	300,000	(14,000)
Loss on sale of equipment . .		(36,000)
Equity in earnings— subsidiary	800	
Income (loss) before income taxes	300,800	(50,000)
Provision for income taxes . .	120,000	(20,000)
Minority interest net income		
Net income (loss)—carried forward	$ 180,800	$(30,000)
Retained Earnings Statement		
Balance, January 1, 19x5:		
P Company	$ 571,200	
S Company		$300,000
Net income—brought forward	180,800	(30,000)
Totals	752,000	270,000
Less: Dividends declared:		
P Company	80,000	
S Company		—
Balance, December 31, 19x7— carried forward	$ 672,000	$270,000
Balance Sheet		
Cash	$ 154,000	$ 50,000
Accounts receivable	90,000	30,000
Inventories	60,000	40,000
Equipment	327,200	750,000
Investment in S Company . .	640,800	
Totals	$1,272,000	$870,000
Accounts payable and accrued expenses	$ 160,000	$ 40,000
Accumulated depreciation— equipment	40,000	60,000
Common stock—P Company ($50 par)	400,000	
Common stock—S Company ($10 par)		300,000
Additional paid-in capital—S Company		200,000
Retained earnings—brought forward	672,000	270,000
Totals	$1,272,000	$870,000

Required:

Prepare a consolidated working paper.

Problem 6–15 (complete equity method). On January 1, 19x4, P Company purchased 24,000 shares of S Company in the open market for $502,000. On that date the following assets of S Company had book values that were different from their respective market values:

	Book value	Fair market value
Equipment (net)	$450,000	$400,000
Patent	–0–	140,000

All other assets and liabilities had book values approximately equal to their respective market values and the net assets amounted to $500,000.

On January 1, 19x4, the equipment and the patent had remaining useful lives of 10 years each. Goodwill, if any, has a 10-year estimated life. P Company uses the complete equity method to account for this investment.

During 19x7, S Company sold $200,000 of merchandise to P Company at 33 1/3 percent above its cost. The inventories of P Company contain merchandise purchased from S Company as follows:

	Billed price
January 1, 19x7	$12,000
December 31, 19x7	60,000

On December 31, 19x7, P Company owed S Company $50,000 on open account.

On July 1, 19x6, S Company sold equipment to P Company at a gain of $30,000. On that date, S Company made the following entry on its *books*:

Cash	90,000	
Accumulated Depreciation	20,000	
Equipment		80,000
Gain on Sale of Equipment .		30,000

This equipment is estimated to have a remaining useful life of five years. This equipment had a book value on January 1, 19x4 (date of acquisition), equal to its fair market value on that date. Accordingly, no excess was allocated to this equipment.

Financial statements for the companies for the year ended December 31, 19x7, are as follows:

	P Company	S Company
Income Statement		
Sales	$1,000,000	$ 600,000
Cost of sales	400,000	400,000
Gross margin	600,000	200,000
Expenses	200,000	160,000
Operating income before taxes	400,000	40,000
Equity in earnings— subsidiary	4,200	
Income before income taxes .	404,200	40,000
Provision for income taxes . .	160,000	16,000
Minority interest net income		
Net income—carried forward	$ 244,200	$ 24,000

Retained Earnings Statement		
Balance, January 1, 19x7:		
P Company	$ 688,600	
S Company		$ 526,000
Net income—brought forward	244,200	24,000
Totals	932,800	550,000
Less: Dividends declared:		
P Company	100,000	
S Company		50,000
Balance, December 31, 19x7— brought forward	$ 832,800	$ 500,000

Balance Sheet		
Cash	$ 200,000	$ 100,000
Accounts receivable	150,000	50,000
Inventories	110,000	40,000
Land		150,000
Building		260,000
Equipment	826,400	690,000
Patent		—
Investment in S Company . .	672,400	
Totals	$1,958,800	$1,290,000
Accounts payable and accrued expenses	$ 124,000	$ 190,000
Accumulated depreciation— building		60,000
Accumulated depreciation— equipment	402,000	240,000
Common stock—P Company ($50 par)	200,000	
Common stock—S Company ($10 par)		300,000
Additional paid-in capital—P Company	400,000	
Retained earnings—brought forward	832,800	500,000
Totals	$1,958,800	$1,290,000

Required:

a. Prepare an allocation schedule of excess.

b. Prepare a consolidated working paper.

Problem 6–16 (complete equity method). On January 1, 19x1, P Company purchased 40,000 shares of S Company in the open market for $640,000. On that date, the net assets of S Company amounted to $800,000 and had book values that approximated their respective fair market values.

P Company uses the complete equity method to account for its investment.

On December 31, 19x2, S Company sold equipment to P Company at a loss of $40,000. S Company made the following entry on its *books* to record the sale:

Cash	50,000	
Accumulated Depreciation . . .	10,000	
Loss on Sale of Equipment . . .	40,000	
Equipment		100,000

This equipment is estimated to have a remaining useful life of eight years from the date of the sale.

On July 1, 19x4, P Company sold equipment to S Company at a gain of $60,000. P Company made the following entry on its *books* to record the sale:

Cash	120,000	
Accumulated Depreciation . . .	80,000	
Equipment		140,000
Gain on Sale of Equipment		60,000

This equipment is estimated to have a remaining useful life of six years from the date of sale.

Financial statements for the two corporations for the year ended December 31, 19x4, are as follows:

	P Company	S Company
Income Statement		
Sales	$2,000,000	$1,000,000
Cost of sales	800,000	600,000
Gross margin	1,200,000	400,000
Expenses	500,000	200,000
Operating income before taxes	700,000	200,000
Gain on sale of equipment . .	60,000	
Equity in earnings— subsidiary	37,000	
Income before income taxes .	797,000	200,000
Provision for income taxes . .	304,000	80,000
Minority interest net income		
Net income—carried forward	$ 493,000	$ 120,000

	P Company	S Company
Retained Earnings Statement		
Balance, January 1, 19x4:		
P Company	$2,066,000	
S Company		$ 860,000
Net income—brought forward	493,000	120,000
Totals	2,559,000	980,000
Less: Dividends declared:		
P Company	400,000	
S Company		60,000
Balance, December 31, 19x4—carried forward	$2,159,000	$ 920,000

Balance Sheet

	P Company	S Company
Cash	$ 300,000	$ 200,000
Accounts receivable	260,000	200,000
Inventories	400,000	200,000
Equipment	1,294,000	1,000,000
Investment in S Company ..	1,105,000	
Totals	$3,359,000	$1,600,000
Accounts payable and accrued expenses	$ 302,000	$ 80,000
Accumulated depreciation—equipment	98,000	100,000
Common stock—P Company ($50 par)	500,000	
Common stock—S Company ($10 par)		500,000
Additional paid-in capital—P Company	300,000	
Retained earnings—brought forward	2,159,000	920,000
Totals	$3,359,000	$1,600,000

Required:

Prepare a consolidated working paper.

Problem 6–17 (complete equity method). On January 1, 19x4, P Company purchased 24,000 shares of S Company in the open market for $424,000. On that date the following asset of S Company had a book value that was different from its market value:

	Book value	Fair market value
Land	$50,000	$80,000

All other assets and liabilities had book values approximately equal to their respective market values and the net assets amounted to $500,000.

P Company uses the complete equity method to account for this investment.

On January 1, 19x5, P Company sold land to S Company at a gain of $40,000. The cost of the land to P Company was $60,000; thus, the selling price to S Company was $100,000. On July 1, 19x7, all of the land owned by S Company was sold for $200,000.

Financial statements for the companies for the year ended December 31, 19x7, are as follows:

	P Company	S Company
Income Statement		
Sales	$1,000,000	$600,000
Cost of sales	400,000	400,000
Gross margin	600,000	200,000
Expenses	200,000	160,000
Operating income before taxes	400,000	40,000
Gain on sale of land		50,000
Equity in earnings—subsidiary	59,200	
Income before income taxes .	459,200	90,000
Provision for income taxes ..	160,000	36,000
Minority interest net income		
Net income—carried forward	$ 299,200	$ 54,000

	P Company	S Company
Retained Earnings Statement		
Balance, January 1, 19x7:		
P Company	$ 633,600	
S Company		$526,000
Net income—brought forward	299,200	54,000
Totals	932,800	580,000
Less: Dividends declared:		
P Company	100,000	
S Company		80,000
Balance, December 31, 19x7—brought forward	$ 832,800	$500,000

	P Company	S Company
Balance Sheet		
Cash	$ 200,000	$250,000
Accounts receivable	150,000	50,000
Inventories	110,000	40,000
Other assets	858,800	650,000
Investment in S Company ..	640,000	
Totals	$1,958,800	$990,000
Accounts payable and accrued expenses	$ 124,000	$190,000
Bonds payable (face amount $400,000)	402,000	
Common stock—P Company ($50 par)	200,000	
Common stock—S Company ($10 par)		300,000
Additional paid-in capital—P Company	400,000	
Retained earnings—brought forward	832,800	500,000
Totals	$1,958,800	$990,000

Required:

Prepare a consolidated working paper.

Problem 6–18 (incomplete equity method). On January 1, 19x1, P Company purchased 40,000 shares of S Company in the open market for $640,000. On that date, the net assets of S Company amounted to $800,000 and had book values that approximated their respective fair market values.

P Company uses the incomplete equity method to account for its investment.

On January 1, 19x4, P Company sold equipment to S Company at a gain of $50,000. P Company made the following entry on its *books*:

Cash	150,000	
Accumulated Depreciation—		
Equipment	100,000	
Equipment		200,000
Gain on Sale of		
Equipment		50,000

The equipment is estimated to have a remaining useful life of five years from the date of the sale.

Financial statements for the two corporations for the year ended December 31, 19x4, are as follows:

	P Company	S Company
Income Statement		
Sales	$2,000,000	$1,000,000
Cost of sales	800,000	600,000
Gross margin	1,200,000	400,000
Expenses	500,000	200,000
Operating income before		
taxes	700,000	200,000
Gain on sale of equipment	50,000	
Equity in earnings—		
subsidiary	96,000	
Income before income taxes	846,000	200,000
Provision for income taxes	300,000	80,000
Minority interest net income		
Net income—carried forward	$ 546,000	$ 120,000
Retained Earnings Statement		
Balance, January 1, 19x4:		
P Company	$3,053,000	
S Company		$ 860,000
Net income—brought		
forward	546,000	120,000
Totals	3,599,000	980,000
Less: Dividends declared:		
P Company	400,000	
S Company		60,000
Balance, December 31, 19x4—		
carried forward	$3,199,000	$ 920,000

	P Company	S Company
Balance Sheet		
Cash	$ 300,000	$ 200,000
Accounts receivable	260,000	200,000
Inventories	400,000	200,000
Land	600,000	—
Building	400,000	—
Equipment	1,303,000	1,000,000
Investment in S Company	1,136,000	
Totals	$4,399,000	$1,600,000
Accounts payable and		
accrued expenses	$ 302,000	$ 20,000
Accumulated depreciation—		
building	40,000	—
Accumulated depreciation—		
equipment	58,000	160,000
Common stock—P Company		
($50 par)	500,000	
Common stock—S Company		
($10 par)		500,000
Additional paid-in capital—P		
Company	300,000	
Retained earnings—brought		
forward	3,199,000	920,000
Totals	$4,399,000	$1,600,000

Required:

Prepare a consolidated working paper.

Problem 6–19 (incomplete equity method). On January 1, 19x2, P Company acquired 80 percent of the outstanding common stock of S Company for $560,000. On that date, the retained earnings of S Company were $200,000 and there have been no changes in its capital stock and additional paid-in capital.

All of the assets and liabilities of S Company had book values approximately equal to their respective market values.

P Company uses the incomplete equity method.

On August 1, 19x4, S Company sold equipment to P Company at a loss of $36,000. S Company made the following entry on its *books*:

Cash	30,000	
Accumulated Depreciation	20,000	
Loss on Sale of Equipment	36,000	
Equipment		86,000

The equipment is estimated to have a remaining useful life of three years from the date of the sale.

The financial statements of the companies for the year ended December 31, 19x4, are as follows:

	P Company	S Company
Income Statement		
Sales	$ 800,000	$200,000
Cost of sales	400,000	150,000
Gross margin	400,000	50,000
Expenses	100,000	64,000
Operating income (loss) before taxes	300,000	(14,000)
Loss on sale of equipment . .		(36,000)
Equity in earnings— subsidiary	(24,000)	
Income (loss) before income taxes	276,000	(50,000)
Provision for income taxes . .	120,000	(20,000)
Minority interest net income		
Net income (loss)—carried forward	$ 156,000	$(30,000)
Retained Earnings Statement		
Balance, January 1, 19x4:		
P Company	$ 571,200	
S Company		$300,000
Net income (loss) brought forward	156,000	(30,000)
Totals	727,200	270,000
Less: Dividends declared:		
P Company	80,000	
S Company		—
Balance, December 31, 19x4— carried forward	$ 647,200	$270,000
Balance Sheet		
Cash	$ 154,000	$ 50,000
Account receivable	90,000	30,000
Inventories	60,000	40,000
Equipment	327,200	750,000
Investment in S Company . .	616,000	
Totals	$1,247,200	$870,000
Accounts payable and accrued expenses	$ 160,000	$ 40,000
Accumulated depreciation— equipment	40,000	60,000
Common stock—P Company ($50 par)	400,000	
Common stock—S Company ($10 par)		300,000
Additional paid-in capital—S Company		200,000
Retained earnings—brought forward	647,200	270,000
Totals	$1,247,200	$870,000

Required:

Prepare a consolidated working paper.

Problem 6–20 (incomplete equity method). On January 1, 19x4, P Company purchased 24,000 shares of S Company in the open market for $502,000. On that date the following assets of S Company had book values that were different from their respective market values:

	Book value	Fair market value
Equipment (net)	$450,000	$400,000
Patent	–0–	140,000

All other assets and liabilities had book values approximately equal to their respective market values and the net assets amounted to $500,000.

On January 1, 19x4, the equipment and the patent had remaining useful lives of 10 years each. Goodwill, if any, has a 10-year estimated life. P Company uses the incomplete equity method to account for this investment.

During 19x7, S Company sold $200,000 of merchandise to P Company at 33 ⅓ percent above its cost. The inventories of P Company contain merchandise purchased from S Company as follows:

	Billed price
January 1, 19x7	$12,000
December 31, 19x7	60,000

On December 31, 19x7, P Company owed S Company $50,000 on open account.

On July 1, 19x6, S Company sold equipment to P Company at a gain of $30,000. On that date, S Company made the following entry on its *books*:

Cash	90,000	
Accumulated Depreciation	20,000	
Equipment		80,000
Gain on Sale of Equipment .		30,000

This equipment is estimated to have a remaining useful life of five years. This equipment had a book value on January 1, 19x4 (date of acquisition), equal to its fair market value on that date. Accordingly, no excess was allocated to this equipment.

Financial statements for the companies for the year ended December 31, 19x7, are as follows:

	P Company	S Company
Income Statement		
Sales	$1,000,000	$ 600,000
Cost of sales	400,000	400,000
Gross margin	600,000	200,000
Expenses	200,000	160,000
Operating income before taxes	400,000	40,000
Equity in earnings— subsidiary	19,200	
Income before income taxes .	419,200	40,000
Provision for income taxes . .	160,000	16,000
Minority interest net income		
Net income—carried forward	$ 259,200	$ 24,000
Retained Earnings Statement		
Balance, January 1, 19x7:		
P Company	$ 743,200	
S Company		$ 526,000
Net income—brought forward	259,200	24,000
Totals	1,002,400	550,000
Less: Dividends declared:		
P Company	100,000	
S Company		50,000
Balance, December 31, 19x7— carried forward	$ 902,400	$ 500,000
Balance Sheet		
Cash	$ 200,000	$ 100,000
Accounts receivable	150,000	50,000
Inventories	110,000	40,000
Land		150,000
Building		260,000
Equipment	826,400	690,000
Patent		—
Investment in S Company . .	742,000	
Totals	$2,028,400	$1,290,000
Accounts payable and accrued expenses	$ 124,000	$ 190,000
Accumulated depreciation— building		60,000
Accumulated depreciation— equipment	402,000	240,000
Common stock—P Company ($50 par)	200,000	
Common stock—S Company ($10 par)		300,000
Additional paid-in capital—P Company	400,000	
Retained earnings—brought forward	902,400	500,000
Totals	$2,028,400	$1,290,000

Required:

a. Prepare an allocation schedule of excess.

b. Prepare a consolidated working paper.

Problem 6–21 (cost method). On January 1, 19x1, P Company purchased 40,000 shares of S Company in the open market for $640,000. On that date, the net assets of S Company amounted to $800,000 and had book values that approximated their respective fair market values.

P Company uses the cost method to account for its investment.

On January 1, 19x4, P Company sold equipment to S Company at a gain of $50,000. P Company made the following entry on its *books*:

Cash	150,000	
Accumulated Depreciation— Equipment	100,000	
Equipment		200,000
Gain on Sale of Equipment		50,000

The equipment is estimated to have a remaining useful life of five years from the date of the sale.

Financial statements for the two corporations for the year ended December 31, 19x4, are as follows:

	P Company	S Company
Income Statement		
Sales	$2,000,000	$1,000,000
Cost of sales	800,000	600,000
Gross margin	1,200,000	400,000
Expenses	500,000	200,000
Operating income before taxes	700,000	200,000
Gain on sale of equipment . .	50,000	
Dividend income	48,000	
Income before income taxes .	798,000	200,000
Provision for income taxes . .	300,000	80,000
Minority interest net income		
Net income—carried forward	$ 498,000	$ 120,000
Retained Earnings Statement		
Balance, January 1, 19x4:		
P Company	$2,605,000	
S Company		$ 860,000
Net income—brought forward	498,000	120,000
Totals	3,103,000	980,000
Less: Dividends declared:		
P Company	400,000	
S Company		60,000
Balance, December 31, 19x4— carried forward	$2,703,000	$ 920,000

Balance Sheet

	P Company	S Company
Cash	$ 300,000	$ 200,000
Accounts receivable	260,000	200,000
Inventories	400,000	200,000
Land	600,000	—
Building	400,000	—
Equipment	1,303,000	1,000,000
Investment in S Company . .	640,000	
Totals	$3,903,000	$1,600,000
Accounts payable and accrued expenses	$ 302,000	$ 20,000
Accumulated depreciation— building	40,000	—
Accumulated depreciation— equipment	58,000	160,000
Common stock—P Company ($50 par)	500,000	
Common stock—S Company ($10 par)		500,000
Additional paid-in capital—P Company	300,000	
Retained earnings—brought forward	2,703,000	920,000
Totals	$3,903,000	$1,600,000

Required:

Prepare a consolidated working paper.

Problem 6–22 (cost method). On January 1, 19x2, P Company acquired 80 percent of the outstanding common stock of S Company for $560,000. On that date, the retained earnings of S Company were $200,000 and there have been no changes in its capital stock and additional paid-in capital.

All of the assets and liabilities of S Company had book values approximately equal to their respective market values.

P Company uses the cost method.

On August 1, 19x4, S Company sold equipment to P Company at a loss of $36,000. S Company made the following entry on its *books*:

Cash	30,000	
Accumulated Depreciation	20,000	
Loss on Sale of Equipment	36,000	
Equipment		86,000

The equipment is estimated to have a remaining useful life of three years from the date of the sale.

The financial statements of the companies for the year ended December 31, 19x4, are as follows:

Income Statement

	P Company	S Company
Sales	$ 800,000	$200,000
Cost of sales	400,000	150,000
Gross margin	400,000	50,000
Expenses	100,000	64,000
Operating income (loss) before taxes	300,000	(14,000)
Loss on sale of equipment . .		(36,000)
Dividend income	—	
Income (loss) before income taxes	300,000	(50,000)
Provision for income taxes . .	120,000	(20,000)
Minority interest net income		
Net income (loss)—carried forward	$ 180,000	$(30,000)

Retained Earnings Statement

	P Company	S Company
Balance, January 1, 19x4:		
P Company	$ 491,200	
S Company		$300,000
Net income (loss)—brought forward	180,000	(30,000)
Totals	671,200	270,000
Less: Dividends declared:		
P Company	80,000	
S Company		—
Balance, December 31, 19x4— carried forward	$ 591,200	$270,000

Balance Sheet

	P Company	S Company
Cash	$ 154,000	$ 50,000
Accounts receivable	90,000	30,000
Inventories	60,000	40,000
Equipment	327,200	750,000
Investment in S Company . .	560,000	
Totals	$1,191,200	$870,000
Accounts payable and accrued expenses	$ 160,000	$ 40,000
Accumulated depreciation— equipment	40,000	60,000
Common stock—P Company ($50 par)	400,000	
Common stock—S Company ($10 par)		300,000
Additional paid-in capital—S Company		200,000
Retained earnings—brought forward	591,200	270,000
Totals	$1,191,200	$870,000

Required:

Prepare a consolidated working paper.

Problem 6–23 (cost method). On January 1, 19x4, P Company purchased 24,000 shares of S Company in the open market for $502,000. On that date the following assets of S Company had book values that were different from their respective market values:

	Book value	Fair market value
Equipment (net)	$450,000	$400,000
Patent	–0–	140,000

All other assets and liabilities had book values approximately equal to their respective market values, and the net assets amounted to $500,000.

On January 1, 19x4, the equipment and the patent had remaining useful lives of 10 years each. Goodwill, if any, has a 10-year estimated life. P Company uses the cost method to account for this investment.

During 19x7, S Company sold $200,000 of merchandise to P Company at 33 1/3 percent above its cost. The inventories of P Company contain merchandise purchased from S Company as follows:

	Billed price
January 1, 19x7	$12,000
December 31, 19x7	60,000

On December 31, 19x7, P Company owed S Company $50,000 on open account.

On July 1, 19x6, S Company sold equipment to P Company at a gain of $30,000. On that date, S Company made the following entry on its *books*:

Cash	90,000	
Accumulated Depreciation	20,000	
Equipment		80,000
Gain on Sale of Equipment .		30,000

This equipment is estimated to have a remaining useful life of five years. This equipment had a book value on January 1, 19x4 (date of acquisition), equal to its fair market value on that date. Accordingly, no excess was allocated to this equipment.

Financial statements for the companies for the year ended December 31, 19x7, are as follows:

	P Company	S Company
Income Statement		
Sales	$1,000,000	$ 600,000
Cost of sales	400,000	400,000
Gross margin	600,000	200,000
Expenses	200,000	160,000
Operating income before taxes	400,000	40,000
Dividend income	40,000	
Income before income taxes .	440,000	40,000
Provision for income taxes . .	160,000	16,000
Minority interest net income		
Net income—carried forward	$ 280,000	$ 24,000
Retained Earnings Statement		
Balance, January 1, 19x7:		
P Company	$ 482,400	
S Company		$ 526,000
Net income—brought forward	280,000	24,000
Totals	762,400	550,000
Less: Dividends declared:		
P Company	100,000	
S Company		50,000
Balance, December 31, 19x7— carried forward	$ 662,400	$ 500,000
Balance Sheet		
Cash	$ 200,000	$ 100,000
Accounts receivable	150,000	50,000
Inventories	110,000	40,000
Land		150,000
Building		260,000
Equipment	826,400	690,000
Patent		—
Investment in S Company . .	502,000	
Totals	$1,788,400	$1,290,000
Accounts payable and accrued expenses	$ 124,000	$ 190,000
Accumulated depreciation— building		60,000
Accumulated depreciation— equipment	402,000	240,000
Common stock—P Company ($50 par)	200,000	
Common stock—S Company ($10 par)		300,000
Additional paid-in capital—P Company	400,000	
Retained earnings—brought forward	662,400	500,000
Totals	$1,788,400	$1,290,000

Required:

a. Prepare an allocation schedule of excess.

b. Prepare a consolidated working paper.

Problem 6–24 (for appendix, complete equity). Using the information provided in Problem 6–13, prepare a consolidated working paper using a 40 percent income tax rate and assume that consolidated income tax returns are to be filed. Show your supporting computations and income allocation schedule.

(Note: Assume that income taxes payable are included in accrued expenses.)

Problem 6–25 (for appendix, complete equity). Using the information provided in Problem 6–14, prepare a consolidated working paper using a 40 percent income tax rate and assume that consolidated income tax returns are to be filed. Show your supporting computations and income allocation schedule.

(Note: Assume that income taxes payable are included in Accrued Expenses.)

Problem 6–26 (for appendix, complete equity). Using the information provided in Problem 6–15, prepare a consolidated working paper using a 40 percent income tax rate and assume that consolidated income tax returns are to be filed. Show your supporting computations and income allocation schedule.

(Note: Assume that income taxes payable are included in accrued expenses.)

Problem 6–27 (for appendix, incomplete equity). Using the information provided in Problem 6–20, prepare a consolidated working paper using a 40 percent income tax rate and assume that consolidated income tax returns are to be filed. Show your supporting computations and income allocation schedule.

(Note: Assume that income taxes payable are included in accrued expenses.)

Problem 6–28 (for appendix, cost method). Using the information provided in Problem 6–23, prepare a consolidated working paper using a 40 percent income tax rate and assume that consolidated income tax returns are to be filed. Show your supporting computations and income allocation schedule.

(Note: Assume that income taxes payable are included in accrued expenses.)

7

Consolidated statements— transactions in intercompany bonds and preferred stock

OVERVIEW

An investment by one member of a consolidated group of companies in the bonds of another member of that group is, in substance, the same thing as the purchase by a member of its own bonds. Although the bonds cannot physically be retired, since two separate entities are involved in the transaction, from a consolidated viewpoint, the transaction is treated as a constructive retirement of the bonds payable to the extent of the investment in the bonds. Thus, the consolidated financial statements will reflect a gain or loss (if there is one) on the constructive retirement of bonds in the year of the purchase. This is true despite the fact that the books of the individual members involved in the transaction continue to reflect the investment in bonds and bonds payable accounts respectively.

If a parent company purchases the preferred stock of a subsidiary, the parent company must calculate the excess, if any, as is done for purchases of common stock. However, in this case the parent company must now calculate how much of the net assets of the subsidiary can be attributed to the preferred stock interests as well as the common stock interests. This will enable the parent company to calculate the excess separately for its purchase of the preferred and common stocks. Additionally, each year's income must be allocated between the preferred stock and common stock interests.

Occasionally a business entity may find it advantageous to invest its excess cash in its own outstanding bonds. When a parent company purchases its own bonds, or a subsidiary purchases its own bonds, no consolidation problems are created thereby; the individual company treats the purchase as either treasury bonds or as retirement of bonds. In either case, a gain or loss is recorded on the purchaser-issuer's books and is treated as an *early extinguishment of debt,* and if it is material, it is recorded as an extraordinary item on its income statement.[1] Treasury bonds are carried at par value (face value) and shown as a deduction from bonds issued in order to arrive at bonds outstanding. The net effect on a company's financial statements is the same whether the acquired bonds are treated as treasury bonds or as retired bonds.

OVERVIEW OF ACCOUNTING FOR THE RETIREMENT OF TREASURY BONDS

It is essential to have a firm grasp on the accounting treatment of bonds repurchased for retirement purposes before one can understand the consolidation complexities encountered when intercompany bonds are purchased. Therefore, a demonstration problem dealing with bonds repurchased for retirement will now be discussed. The facts in Illustration 7–1 are assumed.

Illustration 7–1
P COMPANY
Partial Trial Balance
June 30, 19x1

	Debit	Credit
Unamortized bond discount	$ 5,000	
8% bonds payable, due December 31, 19x3		$1,000,000
Interest expense	41,000	

It is further assumed that interest is payable June 30 and December 31 and that on July 1, 19x1, P Company purchased $400,000 (40 percent) face value of bonds for $399,500 and the bonds are to be retired. The entry to record the purchase and retirement would be:

Bonds Payable	400,000	
Loss on Retirement of Bonds	1,500	
Unamortized Bond Discount (4/10 of $5,000)		2,000
Cash		399,500

The loss can also be calculated as follows:

Bonds payable outstanding, June 30, 19x1.	$1,000,000
Less: Unamortized bond discount	5,000
Total carrying amount	$ 995,000
Carrying amount repurchased—40 % of above	$ 398,000
Price paid	399,500
Loss on retirement	$ 1,500

From the above it can be seen that:

---

[1] *FASB Statement of Financial Accounting Standards No. 4,* "Reporting Gains and Losses from Extinguishment of Debt" (Stamford, Conn., 1975), par. 8.

1. Since 40 percent of the outstanding bonds were reacquired, 40 percent of the unamortized discount must be written off in order to properly compute the gain or loss on retirement.

2. The price paid for the bonds exceeds their carrying amount, and consequently this results in a loss. When the reverse is the case, i.e., when the price paid is less than the carrying amount of repurchased bonds, a gain results.

3. Interest expense of $41,000 represents the cash payment on June 30 of $40,000 (8% × $1,000,000 × ½ year) plus $1,000 of bond discount amortization ($6,000 ÷ 3 years = $2,000 × ½ year = $1,000). On January 1, 19x1, the unamortized bond discount was $6,000. Straight-line amortization[2] of $1,000 reduced this amount to $5,000 as of July 1, 19x1.

Interest expense for the year 19x1, assuming that no other changes occur for the remainder of the year would be:

Cash payment, January 1, 19x1, to June 30, 19x1	$40,000
Bond discount amortization—first 6 months	1,000
Cash payment—second half of the year ($600,000 × 8% × ½ year)	24,000
Bond discount amortization—second half of the year ($5,000 − $2,000 = $3,000 ÷ 30 months = $100 per month × 6 months or $600)	600
Interest expense for 19x1	$65,600

PURCHASE OF INTERCOMPANY BONDS

Although the *net effect* on consolidated statements of an intercompany bond purchase *is the same* as when a company purchases its own bonds, elimination entry complexities are introduced when an intercompany purchase of bonds occurs. It is physically impossible to retire the bonds when an intercompany purchase occurs, since the investment (purchase) appears on one set of books and the bonds payable appear on another set of books. Yet, the purchased bonds must be treated on the consolidated financial statements as if the bonds were liabilities only to those holders who are *not* part of the consolidated group of companies.

TREATMENT OF GAIN OR LOSS ON CONSOLIDATED STATEMENTS

As stated earlier, no allocation problem exists when a company purchases its own bonds, but when an intercompany purchase of bonds occurs, allocation problems do arise. Generally, four theories have been advanced regarding the allocation of a gain or loss on the purchase of intercompany bonds. They can be summarized as follows:

1. Attribute the entire gain or loss to the purchaser of the bonds.
2. Attribute the entire gain or loss to the parent company in all cases.
3. Attribute a portion of the gain or loss to both the issuer of the bonds and the purchaser of the bonds. The latter's portion is equal to the difference between face value and the price paid. The issuer's portion is equal to purchased percentage multiplied by the unamortized bond dis-

[2]Straight-line amortization is used exclusively in this chapter. The "interest" method should be used in practice.

count (premium) on the date of purchase. (The net of these two amounts is, of course, the gain or loss.)

4. Attribute the entire gain or loss to the issuer.

The first approach is difficult to justify on a theoretical basis. Since any decision to purchase intercompany bonds usually emanates from the majority interest (the parent company), a subsidiary that purchases parent company bonds is merely following instructions by the parent and is, therefore, not an independent decision maker. Furthermore, it is difficult to justify a gain or loss on the *retirement* of bonds purchased as a proper item on the *purchaser's* books. Retirement gains and losses should logically appear on the issuer's books if there is any unamortized discount (premium) remaining on the books of the issuer.

The second method has found some acceptance because of the fact that a consolidated entity is primarily dominated by the parent company and that gains and losses on bond purchases should consequently belong to the decision-making parent company.

The third method has substantial theoretical support. Since the individual books of account of the parent company and its subsidiary each reflect the *carrying amounts* of the investment in bonds and the liability for bonds payable respectively, each of the company's books will also reflect the necessary piecemeal removal (discussed later in this chapter) of the gain or loss through the amortization of their respective discounts and/or premiums. The allocation of the gain or loss between parent and subsidiary is the one that is compatible with the treatment on each company's books of account. This method will be used in this chapter.

The fourth method also has substantial theoretical support since the consolidated statements are prepared using the assumption that the bonds are retired from an *entity* viewpoint. Since gains and losses on early retirement of bonds can only be reflected on the books of an issuer, any gain or loss on the purchase of intercompany bonds should be attributable to the issuer of the bonds. It is interesting to note that the unofficial solutions to CPA examination problems utilize this approach, and while this does not necessarily make this approach preferable, CPA candidates should be familiar with this method which will be demonstrated in Appendix 7–A at the end of this chapter.

SUBSIDIARY PURCHASES PARENT'S BONDS

The least complicated type of intercompany bond transaction that involves a gain or loss is one where a subsidiary purchases, at par, bonds issued by its parent company. For this type of transaction, accountants are generally in agreement that the entire gain or loss on the purchase should be attributed to the parent company without any allocation to minority interests. To demonstrate the procedures necessary to eliminate an intercompany transaction in bonds, the following is assumed:

1. P Company has $1,000,000 of 8 percent bonds outstanding on December 31, 19x5. Interest is payable June 30 and December 31. The bonds were sold on January 2, 19x1, at 98, and they mature in 20 years on December

31, 19z0. The discount has been amortized on a straight-line basis since the result is not materially different from the interest method.
2. S Company purchased $300,000 of P Company bonds on December 31, 19x5, at par (face value).
3. All of the remaining data in the working paper are assumed. (P Company purchased its investment at book value and "excess" is nil.)

To facilitate the preparation of the necessary journal entries on the books of the parent company, we recommend that the gain or loss on the purchase of intercompany bonds be computed independently to verify the amount arrived at in the journalizing process. Using the information above, the independent calculation would be:

Bonds payable	$1,000,000
Less: Unamortized bond discount ($20,000 − $5,000)	15,000
Carrying amount	$ 985,000
Price paid for purchased bonds (30%)	$ 300,000
Carrying amount eliminated (30% × $985,000)	295,500
Loss on purchase	$ (4,500)

The parent company would make the following entry on its books for 19x5.

Parent's Books—19x5

Investment in S Company	103,500	
Equity in Earnings of Subsidiary		103,500
To record parent's share of income as follows:		
90% × $120,000 =	$108,000	
Less: 100% of loss on purchase of		
intercompany bonds	4,500	
Total	$103,500	

The entire loss is attributable to the parent company since it arises from the unamortized bond discount (30% × $15,000 = $4,500) on the parent's books. It should be noted that the original issue bond discount amounted to $20,000. With an original life of 20 years, the discount was amortized for five years at $1,000 per annum leaving an unamortized balance of $15,000.

Illustration 7–2 presents a consolidation working paper giving effect to these transactions.

The Illustration 7–2 elimination entries are:

(1)

Equity in Earnings—Subsidiary	103,500	
Investment in S Company		103,500

(2)

Retained Earnings (1/1/x5)—S Company	900,000	
Capital Stock—S Company	360,000	
Investment in S Company		1,260,000

	(3)		
Bonds Payable		300,000	
Loss on Purchase of Intercompany Bonds		4,500	
Unamortized Bond Discount			4,500
Investment in P Company Bonds			300,000

From this illustration it can be seen that:

1. Since only 70 percent of the bonds are held by outsiders, only $10,500 ($15,000 × 70%) of the bond discount is carried to the consolidated column.

2. Since the bonds purchased by S Company were purchased on the last day of the year (19x5), all of the interest was paid to outsiders and, therefore, no adjustment to interest expense is required. This will not be true in subsequent years.

3. In this example the loss on the purchase of intercompany bonds is equal to the portion of bond discount eliminated. This will only occur when the intercompany bonds are purchased at *par*. In some subsequent examples, bonds will not be assumed to be purchased at par.

4. Although the loss on the purchase of intercompany bonds will never appear on the *books* of either company in the year of the purchase, it, nevertheless, does appear on the *consolidated* financial statements issued by P Company.

For 19x6, the parent company would make the following entry on its books (see Illustration 7–3 for income data):

Parent's Books—19x6

Investment in S Company	175,260	
Equity in Earnings of Subsidiary		175,260
To record parent's share of income as follows:		
90% × $194,400 =	$174,960	
Add: Piecemeal removal of loss on purchase		
of intercompany bonds ($4,500 ÷ 15 years		
= $300)	300	
Total	$175,260	

An analogy can be made between the treatments accorded plant assets and bonds since they both involve piecemeal treatments. However, the process of recognition is exactly opposite. For plant assets the process is:

1. A gain or loss on an intercompany sale of an asset *is recorded on the books* of the seller *and is removed on the working paper.*

2. The gain or loss is recognized in years subsequent to the sale through piecemeal recognition—excess depreciation if a gain was recorded and lower depreciation if a loss was recorded. The depreciation process is in effect equated to the gradual "sales" of the equipment to outsiders.

For bonds the process is:

1. A gain or loss on an intercompany purchase of bonds *is not recorded on the books* and *is recorded on the working paper.*

2. On the books of the issuer of the bonds, the discount or premium attri-

Illustration 7–2
P COMPANY
Condensed Consolidated Working Paper
For the Year Ended December 31, 19x5

Complete Equity Method
End of Fifth Year—Year of Bond Purchase
90 Percent Subsidiary

	P Co.	S Co. (90%)	Eliminations Dr.	Eliminations Cr.	Minority Interest	Consolidated
Income Statement						
Sales	1,000,000	600,000				1,600,000
Cost of sales and expenses	700,000	400,000				1,100,000
Operating income before taxes	300,000	200,000				500,000
Equity in earnings—subsidiary	103,500		(1) 103,500			
Loss on purchase of intercompany bonds			(3) 4,500			(4,500)
Income before income taxes	403,500	200,000				495,500
Provision for income taxes (40%)	120,000	80,000				200,000
						295,500
Minority interest net income					12,000	(12,000)
Net income—carried forward	283,500	120,000			12,000	283,500
Retained Earnings Statement						
Balance, 1/1/x5:						
P Co.	2,000,000					2,000,000
S Co.		1,000,000	(1) 900,000		100,000	
Net income—brought forward	283,500	120,000			12,000	283,500
Balance, 12/31/x5—carried forward	2,283,500	1,120,000			112,000	2,283,500
Balance Sheet						
				(2) 1,260,000		
Investment in S Co.	1,363,500			(1) 103,500		
Investment in P Co. bonds		300,000		(3) 300,000		
Unamortized bond discount	15,000			(3) 4,500		10,500
Other assets	2,721,500	1,400,000				4,121,500
Totals	4,100,000	1,700,000				4,132,000
8% bonds payable	1,000,000		(3) 300,000			700,000
Liabilities—other	316,500	180,000				496,500
Capital stock:						
P Co.	500,000					500,000
S Co.		400,000	(2) 360,000		40,000	
Retained earnings—brought forward	2,283,500	1,120,000			112,000	2,283,500
Minority interest					152,000	152,000
Totals	4,100,000	1,700,000	1,668,000	1,668,000		4,132,000

(1) Elimination of equity in earnings of subsidiary.
(2) Elimination of balance of investment.
(3) Elimination of intercompany purchase of bonds and to record the loss in the year of purchase.

Note: Minority interest net income is 10 percent of S Company income, and the minority interest at 12/31/x5 is 10 percent of S Company net assets on that date. There are no reconciling items.

butable to the intercompany bonds continues to be amortized to interest expense as if the intercompany bonds have not been purchased by another member of the group. Thus, the issuer's books reflected interest expense that is not correct from a consolidated entity viewpoint. On the working paper an adjustment of interest expense is necessary to remove the amortization attributable to the intercompany bonds.

If an issuer has on its books an unamortized discount at the time of the purchase of intercompany bonds, the portion of the discount attributable to the purchased bonds will become part of the *consolidated* gain or loss on this transaction. The continued amortization on the books of this discount in subsequent years overstates interest expense and understates income on the issuer's books from a consolidated viewpoint. Therefore, on the working papers of subsequent years, and in picking up earnings from the subsidiary under the complete equity method, income must be increased by the amount of the amortization in that particular year. Thus, for consolidation purposes (working papers only) the loss is recorded in full in the year of the purchase and is removed in a piecemeal fashion in years subsequent to the purchase. When the bonds mature, the cumulative total of the individual piecemeal removals will equal the amount of the loss recorded in the year of the bond purchase.

If an issuer of bonds has an unamortized premium, at the time of the intercompany purchase, the result would be a gain which becomes part of the consolidated gain or loss on this transaction. Since amortization of a bond premium increases income, piecemeal removal requires that income be reduced.

A purchaser's discount or premium has similar effects except that discount amortization *increases* income and premium amortization *reduces* income.

The Illustration 7–3 elimination entries are:

	(1)		
Equity in Earnings—Subsidiary		175,260	
Investment in S Company			175,260
	(2)		
Bonds Payable		300,000	
Investment in S Company		4,200	
Investment in P Company Bonds			300,000
Unamortized Bond Discount			4,200
	(3)		
Interest Income		24,000	
Investment in S Company		300	
Interest Expense			24,300
	(4)		
Retained Earnings (1/1/x6)—S Company		1,008,000	
Capital Stock—S Company		360,000	
Investment in S Company			1,368,000

Illustration 7–3 which presents the elimination entries in 19x6, the subsequent year, reveals the following:

Illustration 7-3
P COMPANY
Condensed Consolidated Working Paper
For the Year Ended December 31, 19x6

Complete Equity Method
First Year After Bond Purchase
90 Percent Subsidiary

	P Co.	S Co. (90%)	Eliminations Dr.	Eliminations Cr.	Minority Interest	Consol- idated
Income Statement						
Sales	1,200,000	800,000				2,000,000
Cost of sales and operating expenses	800,000	500,000				1,300,000
Operating income before taxes	400,000	300,000				700,000
Equity in earnings—subsidiary	175,260		(1) 175,260			
Interest income		24,000	(2) 24,000			
Interest expense	(81,000)			(3) 24,300		(56,700)
Income before income taxes	494,260	324,000				643,300
Provision for income taxes (40%)	127,600	129,600				257,200
						386,100
Minority interest net income					19,440	(19,440)
Net income—carried forward	366,660	194,400			19,440	366,660
Retained Earnings Statement						
Balance, 1/1/x6:						
P Co.	2,283,500					2,283,500
S Co.		1,120,000	(4) 1,008,000		112,000	
Net income—brought forward	366,660	194,400			19,440	366,660
Balance, 12/31/x6—carried forward	2,650,160	1,314,400			131,440	2,650,160
Balance Sheet						
			(3) 300	(4) 1,368,000		
Investment in S Co.	1,538,760		(2) 4,200	(1) 175,260		
Investment in P Co. bonds		300,000		(2) 300,000		
Unamortized bond discount	14,000			(2) 4,200		9,800
Other assets	2,847,240	1,500,000				4,347,240
Totals	4,400,000	1,800,000				4,357,040
8% bonds payable	1,000,000		(2) 300,000			700,000
Liabilities—other	249,840	85,600				335,440
Capital stock:						
P Co.	500,000					500,000
S Co.		400,000	(4) 360,000		40,000	
Retained earnings—brought forward	2,650,160	1,314,400			131,440	2,650,160
Minority interest					171,440	171,440
Totals	4,400,000	1,800,000	1,871,760	1,871,760		4,357,040

(1) Elimination of equity in earnings of subsidiary.
(2) To eliminate intercompany bonds and proportionate share of unamortized bond discount and unrecognized portion of loss.
(3) To eliminate intercompany interest on bonds and the piecemeal recognition of loss.
(4) Elimination of the balance of the investment.
Note: Minority interest net income is 10 percent of S Company income, and the minority interest at 12/31/x6 is 10 percent of S Company net assets on that date. There are no reconciling items.

1. Although S Company received $24,000 of interest from P Company, it is completely eliminated. From a consolidated viewpoint, the interest is viewed as an intraentity transfer of cash.
2. Although interest expense on the books of P Company amounts to $81,000, only 70 percent of this amount ($56,700) is applicable to outsiders and appears in the consolidated column.
3. The difference between the elimination of interest income and interest expense is $300, and this amount is 30 percent (insider's percentage) of the bond discount amortization of $1,000 per annum. This difference of $300 will be repeated each year for the remaining life of the bonds and must be part of an adjustment to the parent's investment in the subsidiary. The remainder of the adjustment to the parent's investment (30% × $14,000 = $4,200) represents the insider's portion of unamortized bond discount. Together, the $4,500 adjustment converts the parent's investment back to what it would have been if the loss on purchase of intercompany bonds did not occur.

Working paper elimination entries for the following three years would be as in Illustration 7–4.

Illustration 7–4
P COMPANY AND SUBSIDIARY
Elimination Entries—Bonds
For the Years Ended December 31

	19x7	19x8	19x9
(2)			
Debits:			
Bonds Payable	300,000	300,000	300,000
Investment in S Company	3,900	3,600	3,300
Credits:			
Investment in Bonds	300,000	300,000	300,000
Unamortized Bond Discount	3,900	3,600	3,300
(3)			
Debits:			
Interest Income	24,000	24,000	24,000
Investment in S Company	300	300	300
Credit:			
Interest Expense	24,300	24,300	24,300

Although the loss of $4,500 appears on the working paper *only* in the year of the intercompany purchase of bonds and thereby on the consolidated financial statements, the loss finds its way onto the books of the parent company through the amortization of bond discount in $300 installments each year. In effect, the recognition on the books of $300 each year and the removal of the $300 as part of elimination entry (3) causes the books of the parent company to agree with the working paper at the end of 15 years (the maturity date of the bonds).

We now turn to an intercompany bond purchase at 85% percent of par. It is now assumed that S Company purchased the bonds on January 1, 19x6, instead of on December 31, 19x5, and all other assumptions remain the same. The gain or loss on purchase of intercompany bonds can be computed as follows:

Bonds payable	$1,000,000
Less: Unamortized bond discount	15,000
Carrying value	$ 985,000
Price paid for purchased bonds (30% × $1,000,000 = $300,000 × 85%)	$ 255,000
Carrying value eliminated (30% × $985,000)	295,500
Gain on purchase	$ 40,500

As indicated earlier, the approach that will be used in this chapter is the one that has the greatest amount of theoretical support, i.e., the proration of the gain or loss in accordance with the difference between the carrying amounts and the face values on the respective sets of books. Thus, the $40,500 gain can be allocated as follows:

Face amount of bonds purchased	$300,000	
Price paid	255,000	
Gain allocated to purchaser		$45,000
Face amount of bonds constructively retired	300,000	
Carrying value of bonds constructively retired	295,500	
Loss allocated to issuer		(4,500)
Consolidated gain		$40,500

After the above analysis is prepared, the parent company should prepare an income apportionment schedule similar to the one appended to Illustration 7–5. That schedule then becomes the basis for recording the following entry on the parent's books:

Parent's Books—19x6

Investment in S Company	210,180	
Equity in Earnings of Subsidiary		210,180
As per income apportionment schedule ($401,580 − $191,400)		

The Illustration 7–5 elimination entries are:

(1)

Equity in Earnings—Subsidiary	210,180	
Investment in S Company		210,180

(2)

Bonds Payable	300,000	
Gain on Purchase of Intercompany Bonds		37,800
Investment in P Company Bonds		258,000
Unamortized Bond Discount		4,200

(3)

Interest Income	27,000	
Interest Expense		24,300
Gain on Purchase of Intercompany Bonds		2,700

(4)

Retained Earnings (1/1/x6)—S Company	1,008,000	
Capital Stock—S Company	360,000	
Investment in S Company		1,368,000

For the year ended December 31, 19x6 (Illustration 7–5), the following should be noted:

1. The investment in bonds on S Company's books increased to $258,000 from $225,000 (the price paid for the bonds), because on its books S Company amortized the discount on bonds ($45,000 ÷ 15 years) as follows:

Investment in P Company Bonds	3,000	
Interest Income		3,000

2. Interest income of S Company consists of $24,000 received in cash ($300,000 × 8 percent) plus the $3,000 of amortization for a total of $27,000.

3. Elimination entry (2) eliminates 30 percent of the bonds payable and 30 percent of the unamortized discount. It also removes the entire balance in the Investment in P Company Bonds account. The balancing amount ($37,800) represents the unrecorded gain of $40,500 minus the $2,700 of amortization recorded on the respective sets of books as follows:

Amortization of purchaser's discount on S Company books	$3,000
Amortization of issuer's discount on P Company books ($1,000 × intercompany % of 30%)	(300)
Net amortization—insiders	$2,700

4. Entry (3) eliminates all interest income and 30 percent of interest expense. The difference of $2,700 is due entirely to net amortizations as explained in the preceding paragraph.

5. When the combined amounts of entries (2) and (3) are extended to the consolidated column as a gain on purchase of intercompany bonds, the amount equals the $40,500 computed independently on page 244. The independent proof is useful for the allocation shown earlier and acts as a proof for entries (2) and (3) in the year of purchase of intercompany bonds.

6. Since the bonds were purchased at the beginning of the year, parent income and minority interest net income both have gains (losses) to be recorded and piecemeal removals in the same year. For subsequent years, only piecemeal removals will be required.

7. The reconciliation of the minority interest requires a reconciling item for its share of the gain that will be recorded on the subsidiary's books in subsequent years. Another way of computing this amount is to multiply the annual amortization by the remaining life of the bonds—10 percent ($3,000 x 14 years) = $4,200.

Illustration 7–5
P COMPANY
Condensed Consolidated Working Paper
For the Year Ended December 31, 19x6

Complete Equity Method
Year of Bond Purchase
90 Percent Subsidiary

	P Co.	S Co. (90%)	Eliminations Dr.	Eliminations Cr.	Minority Interest	Consol- idated
Income Statement						
Sales	1,200,000	800,000				2,000,000
Cost of sales and operating expenses	800,000	500,000				1,300,000
Operating income before taxes	400,000	300,000				700,000
Equity in earnings—subsidiary	210,180		(1) 210,180			
Interest income		27,000	(3) 27,000			
Interest expense	(81,000)			(3) 24,300		(56,700)
				(3) 2,700		
Gain on purchase of intercompany bonds				(2) 37,800		40,500
Income before income taxes	529,180	327,000				683,800
Provision for income taxes (40%)	127,600	130,800				258,400
						425,400
Minority interest net income					23,820	(23,820)
Net income—carried forward	401,580	196,200			23,820	401,580
Retained Earnings Statement						
Balance, 1/1/x6:						
P Co.	2,288,000					2,288,000
S Co.		1,120,000	(4) 1,008,000		112,000	
Net income—brought forward	401,580	196,200			23,820	401,580
Balance, 12/31/x6	2,689,580	1,316,200			135,820	2,689,580
Balance Sheet						
Investment in S Co.	1,578,180			(4) 1,368,000		
				(1) 210,180		
Investment in P Co. bonds		258,000		(2) 258,000		
Unamortized bond discount	14,000			(2) 4,200		9,800
Other assets	2,847,240	1,545,000				4,392,240
Totals	4,439,420	1,803,000				4,402,040
8% bonds payable	1,000,000		(2) 300,000			700,000
Other liabilities	249,840	86,800				336,640
Capital stock:						
P Co.	500,000					500,000
S Co.		400,000	(4) 360,000		40,000	
Retained earnings—brought forward	2,689,580	1,316,200			135,820	2,689,580
Minority interest					175,820	175,820
Totals	4,439,420	1,803,000	1,905,180	1,905,180		4,402,040

(1) Elimination of equity in earnings of subsidiary.
(2) Elimination of intercompany bonds and to record a portion of the gain on purchase of intercompany bonds.
(3) Elimination of intercompany bond interest and to record the balance of the gain.
(4) Elimination of the balance of investment.

Illustration 7–5 (continued)

Computations and Proofs

Income apportionment:

	Total	Parent	Minority
S Co. income	$196,200	$176,580	$ 19,620
Intercompany purchase of bonds:			
Loss allocated to parent	(4,500)	(4,500)	
Gain allocated to subsidiary	45,000	40,500	4,500
Piecemeal recognition of parent's loss ($4,500 ÷ 15 years)	300	300	
Piecemeal recognition of subsidiary's share of gain ($45,000 ÷ 15 years)	(3,000)	(2,700)	(300)
P Co. income ($401,580 − $210,180)	191,400	191,400	
Totals	$425,400	$401,580	$ 23,820

Reconciliation—minority interest:

S Co.—capital stock		$ 400,000
—retained earnings 12/31/x6		1,316,200
Net assets, 12/31/x6		$1,716,200
10% of above		$ 171,620
Add: Gain on intercompany purchase of bonds	$ 45,000	
Less: piecemeal recording for 19x6	(3,000)	
Unrecorded balance	$ 42,000	
10% of above		4,200
Minority interest, 12/31/x6		$ 175,820

For 19x7, the consolidated working paper would appear as is shown in Illustration 7–6. The Illustration 7–6 elimination entries are:

(1)

Equity in Earnings—Subsidiary	174,180	
Investment in S Company		174,180

(2)

Bonds Payable	300,000	
Retained Earnings (1/1/x7)—S Company		3,900
Investment in P Company Bonds		261,000
Unamortized Bond Discount		3,900
Investment in S Company		31,200

(3)

Interest Income	27,000	
Interest Expense		24,300
Retained Earnings (1/1/x7)—S Company		300
Investment in S Company		2,400

(4)

Retained Earnings (1/1/x7)—S Company	1,184,580	
Capital Stock—S Company	360,000	
Investment in S Company		1,544,580

The following observations are noteworthy:

1. Equity in earnings of subsidiary in the amount of $174,180 can be obtained from the income apportionment schedule appended to the work-

Illustration 7–6
P COMPANY
Condensed Consolidated Working Paper
For the Year Ended December 31, 19x7

Complete Equity Method
First Year After Bond Purchase
90 Percent Subsidiary

	P Co.	S Co. (90%)	Eliminations Dr.	Eliminations Cr.	Minority Interest	Consol- idated
Income Statement						
Sales	1,000,000	700,000				1,700,000
Cost of sales and operating expenses	600,000	400,000				1,000,000
Operating income before taxes	400,000	300,000				700,000
Equity in earnings—subsidiary	174,180		(1) 174,180			
Interest income		27,000	(3) 27,000			
Interest expense	(81,000)			(3) 24,300		(56,700)
Income before income taxes	493,180	327,000				643,300
Provision for income taxes (40%)	127,600	130,800				258,400
						384,900
Minority interest net income					19,320	(19,320)
Net income—carried forward	365,580	196,200			19,320	365,580
Retained Earnings Statement						
Balance, 1/1/x7:						
P Co.	2,689,580					2,689,580
				(3) 300		
S Co.		1,316,200	(4) 1,184,580	(2) 3,900	135,820	
Net income—brought forward	365,580	196,200			19,320	365,580
Balance, 12/31/x7—carried forward	3,055,160	1,512,400			155,140	3,055,160
Balance Sheet						
				(4) 1,544,580		
				(3) 2,400		
				(2) 31,200		
Investment in S Co.	1,752,360			(1) 174,180		
Investment in P Co. bonds		261,000		(2) 261,000		
Unamortized bond discount	13,000			(2) 3,900		9,100
Other assets	3,089,800	1,739,000				4,828,800
Totals	4,855,160	2,000,000				4,837,900
8% bonds payable	1,000,000		(2) 300,000			700,000
Liabilities—other	300,000	87,600				387,600
Capital stock:						
P Co.	500,000					500,000
S Co.		400,000	(4) 360,000		40,000	
Retained earnings—brought forward	3,055,160	1,512,400			155,140	3,055,160
Minority interest					195,140	195,140
Totals	4,855,160	2,000,000	2,045,760	2,045,760		4,837,900

(1) Elimination of equity in earnings of subsidiary.
(2) Elimination of intercompany bonds.
(3) Elimination of intercompany bond interest.
(4) Elimination of the balance of investment.

Illustration 7–6 *(continued)*

Computations and Proofs

Income apportionment:

	Total	Parent	Minority
S Co. income	$196,200	$176,580	$ 19,620
Piecemeal recognition of parent's share of loss on bonds ($4,500 ÷ 15 years)	300	300	
Piecemeal recognition of subsidiary's share of gain ($45,000 ÷ 15 years)	(3,000)	(2,700)	(300)
P Co. income ($365,580 − $174,180)	191,400	191,400	
Totals	$384,900	$365,580	$ 19,320

Reconciliation—minority interest:

S Co.—capital stock		$ 400,000
—retained earnings, 12/31/x7		1,512,400
Net assets, 12/31/x7		$1,912,400
10% of above		$ 191,240
Add: Subsidiary gain on intercompany purchase of bonds	$ 45,000	
Less: Piecemeal book recording for 2 years (19x6 and 19x7)	(6,000)	
Unrecorded balance	$ 39,000	
10% of above		3,900
Minority interest, 12/31/x7		$ 195,140

ing paper. Included in these earnings are 100% × $300 (the parent's share of the parent's amortization) and 90% x ($3,000) (the parent's share of the amortization on the books of the subsidiary). The $300 and ($2,700) are the piecemeal removals of the respective gain and loss. These plus the parent's 90 percent share of the S Company's income add up to $174,180.

2. In entry (2) the Investment in S Company is credited for $31,200. This amount is the remaining balance of the parent's *net gain* on purchase of bonds remaining to be amortized in subsequent years and can be computed as follows:

Gain—(90% × $3,000) = $2,700 × 13 years =	$35,100
Loss—(100% × $300) = $300 × 13 years =	(3,900)
Total	$31,200

The $3,900 credit to subsidiary retaining earnings for the minority's share can similarly be computed as follows:

Gain − (10% × $3,000) = $300 × 13 years = $3,900

3. Entry (3) eliminates 100 percent of intercompany interest income, 30 percent of interest expense and $2,400 of parent piecemeal removal ($2,700 − $300), and $300 of minority interest piecemeal removal in accordance with the income apportionment schedule appended to the working paper.

4. After posting elimination entries (2), (3), and (4) to the subsidiary's *beginning* retained earnings, the resulting minority interest balance of $135,820 agrees with the *closing* amount in the preceding working paper, Illustration 7–5.

5. The reconciliation of minority interest requires a reconciling item of $3,900. This $3,900 can be computed either as it was done in the reconciliation appended to the working paper, or as it was done immediately above in the explanation of elimination entry (2). (See item 2 in this series of noteworthy observations.)

For the next two years, 19x8 and 19x9, the working paper elimination entries would be:

	(2)			
		19x8		19x9
Bonds Payable	300,000		300,000	
Investment in Bonds		264,000		267,000
Unamortized Bond Discount		3,600		3,300
Investment in S Company		28,800		26,400
Retained Earnings (1/1)—S Company .		3,600		3,300

	(3)			
		19x8		19x9
Interest Income	27,000		27,000	
Interest Expense		24,300		24,300
Investment in S Company		2,400		2,400
Retained Earnings (1/1)—S Company .		300		300

From the foregoing it can be seen that over the years the books of the two companies will reflect the recording of the total $40,500 gain in a piecemeal fashion—$3,000 of income on S Company's books and $300 of expense on P. Company's books for a net amount of $2,700 of income. At the end of 15 years the full $40,500 ($2,700 × 15) will have been recognized on the books of the two companies.

PARENT PURCHASES SUBSIDIARY'S BONDS

When a parent company invests its cash in bonds of its *wholly owned* subsidiary, any gain or loss on the purchase of the bonds may be attributed partially to the subsidiary, but since the subsidiary is wholly owned, that portion of the gain or loss is, in effect, attributed entirely to the parent company in the consolidated statements. Since the net result of this type of transaction is identical with that shown in Illustrations 7–2 and 7–3 in this chapter, it will not be illustrated again. However, when a subsidiary has a minority interest, the results of this type of transaction are similar to the results shown in Illustrations 7–5 and 7–6, except for the allocation of income. If, for example, the information used in these two illustrations was assumed for the years 19x6 and 19x7 except that the subsidiary was the issuer and the parent company was the purchaser of the bonds, the apportionment of income would appear as shown in Illustrations 7–7 and 7–8. The calculations of the consolidated gain of $40,500, the respective elements of the gain [$45,000 and ($4,500)] interest income and interest expense would all be the same except for the attribution of the gain and the sets of books on which the interest income and expense appear. The consolidated statements of income would reflect the same gain on purchase of intercompany bonds, interest expense, and interest income. CNI and minority interest net income would be different as shown in Illustrations 7–5 and 7–7 and in Illustrations 7–6 and 7–8. The total net income (CNI and minority interest net income), however, is the same. Working paper elimination entries relating to a parent's purchase of subsidiary bonds are similar to those in Illustrations 7–5 and 7–6 except for the difference in the amounts of net income apportioned to the respective interests.

Illustration 7–7
P COMPANY
Schedule of Income Apportionment
For the Year Ended December 31, 19x6

		Total	Parent	10 Percent minority
S Company income ($300,000 − $81,000) × 60% . . .		$131,400	$118,260	$13,140
Intercompany purchase of bonds:				
Gain allocated to parent		45,000	45,000	
Loss allocated to subsidiary		(4,500)	(4,050)	(450)
Piecemeal recognition of parent's gain		(3,000)	(3,000)	
Piecemeal recognition of subsidiary's loss		300	270	30
P Company income:				
Operating income	$400,000			
Interest income	27,000			
Income before taxes	427,000			
Income taxes (40%)	170,800			
Net income—P Company alone		256,200	256,200	
Allocated net income		$425,400	$412,680	$12,720

Illustration 7–8
P COMPANY
Schedule of Income Apportionment
For the Year Ended December 31, 19x7

	Total	Parent	10 Percent Minority
S Company income (see Illustration 7–7)	$131,400	$118,260	$13,140
Piecemeal recognition of intercompany bond transaction:			
Parent's share of gain ($45,000 ÷ 15 years)	(3,000)	(3,000)	
Subsidiary's share of loss ($4,500 ÷ 15 years) . . .	300	270	30
P Company income (see Illustration 7–7)	256,200	256,200	
Allocated net income	$384,900	$371,730	$13,170

PURCHASE BETWEEN INTEREST DATES

When bonds are purchased between interest dates, they are purchased "plus accrued interest." In addition, amortization of discount or premium will now occur from the date of purchase through the maturity date. Since no special *consolidation* problems are created when bonds are purchased between interest dates, a review of these matters can be obtained by referring to an intermediate accounting text.

PREFERRED STOCK

INVESTMENTS IN PREFERRED STOCK

Occasionally, a parent company acquires preferred stock issued by its subsidiary. When this occurs, two additional consolidation aspects are introduced. First, the subsidiary's retained earnings on the date of acquisition must be apportioned between preferred stock interests and common stock interests in order to ascertain if any "excess of cost over equity in net assets acquired" exists for either interest. Second, the subsidiary's net income for each year must be apportioned between preferred stock interests and common stock interests. These calculations will be affected by whether or not the preferred stock is *(a)* cumulative, *(b)* participating, or *(c)* preferred as to assets in liquidation. Additional considerations that may affect these calculations are dividend arrearages and call premiums. Familiarity with these terms is assumed here.[3]

ALLOCATION OF RETAINED EARNINGS

The computations of excess in Illustration 7–9 are based on the following assumptions:

1. Saul Corporation has 10,000 shares of 8 percent, $10 par value, cumulative, fully participating preferred stock outstanding. The corporation also has 100,000 shares of $20 par value, common stock outstanding. Both stock issues were sold at par value.
2. There are no dividends in arrears and the preferred stock is callable at par.
3. On January 2, 19x1, Peter Corporation purchased 60 percent of the outstanding preferred stock for $420,000 and 90 percent of the outstanding common stock for $12,600,000. On this date the retained earnings of Saul Corporation amounts to $10,500,000.
4. Identifiable net assets of the Saul Corporation at book values approximate their respective fair values. (Excess, if any, is attributable only to goodwill.)
5. The preferred stock of Saul Corporation is preferred as to assets in liquidation.

The fully participating calculations in Schedule A, Illustration 7–9, are based on the above data without modification. If we assume, however, that the preferred stock is nonparticipating, that dividends are in arrears for two years, and that the preferred stock is callable at 104, the calculations would be as in Schedule B of Illustration 7–9. From Illustration 7–9 it can be seen that different preferred stock characteristics can produce different results. Preferred stock can also be partially participating, and the principles that were applied in Illustration 7–9 could also be applied to such stock.

INCOME APPORTIONMENT

The apportionment of a subsidiary's net income between preferred stock interests and common stock interests depends on whether or not the pre-

---

[3]A review of these topics can be obtained from an intermediate accounting text.

Illustration 7-9
PETER CORPORATION
Calculation of Excess on Investment
January 1, 19x1

	Capital stock	Retained earnings	Total net assets	Percent owned	Percent of net assets	Price paid	Excess
			Schedule A				
Fully participating:							
Preferred stock	$ 100,000	$ 500,000*	$ 600,000	60	$ 360,000	$ 420,000	$ 60,000
Common stock	2,000,000	10,000,000†	12,000,000	90	10,800,000	12,600,000	1,800,000
Totals	$2,100,000	$10,500,000	$12,600,000	—	$11,160,000	$13,020,000	$1,860,000

$* \dfrac{\$100,000}{\$2,100,000} \times \$10,500,000 = \$500,000$

$\dagger \dfrac{\$2,000,000}{\$2,100,000} \times \$10,500,000 = \$10,000,000$

	Capital stock	Retained earnings	Total net assets	Percent owned	Percent of net assets	Price paid	Excess
			Schedule B				
Nonparticipating, dividends in arrears for two years and callable at 104:							
Preferred stock	$ 100,000	$ 20,000*	$ 120,000	60	$ 72,000	$ 420,000	$ 348,000
Common stock	2,000,000	10,480,000†	12,480,000	90	11,232,000	12,600,000	1,368,000
Totals	$2,100,000	$10,500,000	$12,600,000	—	$11,304,000	$13,020,000	$1,716,000

*Dividends in arrears:

2 years @ $8,000 (8% × $100,000)	$16,000	
Call premium 4% × $100,000	4,000	
	$20,000	

†Balance.

ferred stock is participating. If the preferred stock is nonparticipating, the net income of a subsidiary is allocated by allowing the current year's dividend to the preferred stock interests and attributing any balance of net income to the common stock interests. If the preferred dividend is not declared but the preferred stock is cumulative, the dividend is nevertheless allocated to the preferred stock interests. If the preferred stock is not cumulative and the dividend is not declared, no portion of the subsidiary's net income need be allocated to preferred stock interests.

Alternately, if a subsidiary's preferred stock is fully participating, the apportionment of its net income is based on the sharing ratio of the respective preferred and common stocks outstanding. To demonstrate such an apportionment, the five assumptions used to prepare Illustration 7-9 are now used to prepare Illustration 7-10. In addition, it is also assumed that Saul Corporation paid the current preferred dividend (8% × $100,000 = $8,000) and no dividends on common were paid in 19x1.

The Illustration 7-10 elimination entries are:

	(1)		
Equity in Subsidiary Earnings—Preferred		22,500	
Dividends Declared—Saul Corporation			4,800
Investment in Saul—Preferred			17,700

Illustration 7–10

PETER CORPORATION
Partial Consolidated Working Paper
For the Year Ended December 31, 19x1

Complete Equity Method
First Year Fully Participating Preferred Stock
90 Percent Owned Subsidiary

	Peter Corp.	Saul Corp. (90%)	Eliminations Dr.	Eliminations Cr.	Minority Interest	Consolidated
Income Statement						
Sales	2,400,000	1,640,000				4,040,000
			(6) 45,000			
Cost of sales, expenses, and income taxes	1,000,000	800,000	(3) 1,500			1,846,500
Operating income	1,400,000	840,000				2,193,500
Equity in subsidiary earnings—preferred	22,500		(1) 22,500			
Equity in subsidiary earnings—common	675,000		(4) 675,000			
Minority interest net income—preferred					16,000	(16,000)
Minority interest net income—common					80,000	(80,000)
Net income—carried forward	2,097,500	840,000			96,000	2,097,500
Retained Earnings Statement						
Balance, 1/1/x1—Peter Corp.	3,000,000					3,000,000
			(5) 9,000,000			
—Saul Corp.		10,500,000	(2) 300,000		1,200,000	
Net income—brought forward	2,097,500	840,000			96,000	2,097,500
Total	5,097,500	11,340,000			1,296,000	5,097,500
Less: Dividends—Saul Corp.		8,000		(1) 4,800	3,200	
Balance, 12/31/x1—carried forward	5,097,500	11,332,000			1,292,800	5,097,500
Balance Sheet						
				(2) 420,000		
Investment in Saul—preferred	437,700			(1) 17,700		
				(5) 12,600,000		
Investment in Saul—common	13,275,000			(4) 675,000		
Excess of cost—preferred			(2) 60,000	(3) 1,500		58,500
Excess of cost—common			(5) 1,800,000	(6) 45,000		1,755,000
Preferred stock—Saul Corp.		100,000	(2) 60,000		40,000	
Common stock—Saul Corp.		2,000,000	(5) 1,800,000		200,000	
Retained earnings—brought forward	5,097,500	11,332,000			1,292,800	5,097,500
					1,532,800	1,532,800

(1) Elimination of preferred stock equity in earnings.
(2) Elimination of preferred investment balance.
(3) Amortization of excess—40-year life.
(4) Elimination of common stock equity in earnings.
(5) Elimination of common investment balance.
(6) Amortization of excess—40-year life.

Illustration 7–10 *(continued)*

Computations and Proofs

Income apportionment:

	Total	Parent	Minority
Subsidiary income:			
Preferred stock income*	$ 40,000	$ 24,000	$ 16,000
Common stock income†	800,000	720,000	80,000
Amortization of excess:			
Preferred	(1,500)	(1,500)	
Common	(45,000)	(45,000)	
Parent income—exclusive of subsidiary income	1,400,000	1,400,000	
Totals	$2,193,500	$2,097,500	$ 96,000

$* \dfrac{\$100,000}{\$2,100,000} \times \$840,000 = \$40,000 \times 60\% = \$24,000$

$†\$840,000 - \$40,000 = \$800,000 \times 90\% = \$720,000$

Minority interest:

Total net assets on 1/1/x1 (per Illustration 7–9, Schedule A)	$12,600,000
Less: Allocated to Peter Corp.	11,160,000
Allocated to minority interest	1,440,000
Add: Preferred income	16,000
Common income	80,000
Deduct: Preferred dividend	(3,200)
Minority interest, 12/31/x1	$ 1,532,800

(2)

Retained Earnings (1/1/x1)—Saul Corporation	300,000	
Excess of Cost—Preferred	60,000	
Preferred Stock—Saul Corporation	60,000	
Investment in Saul—Preferred		420,000

(3)

Amortization of Excess of Cost (expenses)	1,500	
Excess of Cost—Preferred		1,500

(4)

Equity in Subsidiary Earnings—Common	675,000	
Investment in Saul—Common		675,000

(5)

Retained Earnings (1/1/x1)—Saul Corporation	9,000,000	
Excess of Cost—Common	1,800,000	
Common Stock—Saul Corporation	1,800,000	
Investment in Saul—Common		12,600,000

(6)

Amortization of Excess of Cost (expenses)	45,000	
Excess of Cost—Common		45,000

A careful review of Illustration 7–10 reveals that Saul Corporation's net income results in the apportionment as is given in Illustration 7–11.

Illustration 7–11
PETER CORPORATION
Income Apportionment of
Saul Subsidiary
For the Year Ended December 31, 19x1

Type of stock	Stock par value	Frac- tion	Income appor- tionment	Parent's owner- ship %	Income allocation	
					Parent	Minority
Preferred	$ 100,000	$1/21$	$ 40,000	60%	$ 24,000	$16,000
Common	2,000,000	$20/21$	800,000	90	$720,000	$80,000
	$2,100,000		$840,000			

The balances in the parent's investment accounts include the original costs of the respective investments adjusted for the following entries that appear on the parent's books of account.

Parent's Books—19x1
(1)

Investment in Saul Corporation—Preferred	22,500	
Equity in Saul Corporation Earnings—Preferred		22,500

To record income from Saul Corporation subsidiary—per apportionment schedule ($24,000 − $1,500 goodwill amortization).

(2)

Cash	4,800	
Investment in Saul Corporation—Preferred		4,800

To record dividend received on preferred stock (60% × $8,000).

(3)

Investment in Saul Corporation—Common	675,000	
Equity in Saul Corporation Earnings—Common		675,000

To record income from Saul Corporation subsidiary—per apportionment schedule ($720,000 − $45,000 of goodwill amortization).

If the preferred stock were nonparticipating and the current year's dividends on preferred stock were paid, the entries on Peter's books would be:

Parent's Books—19x1
(1)

Investment in Saul Corporation—Preferred	3,300	
Equity in Saul Corporation Earnings—Preferred		3,300

To record share of income—(60% × $8,000		
dividend) = ...	$4,800	
Less: Amortization of excess	1,500	
	$3,300	

(2)

Cash	4,800	
Investment in Saul Corporation—Preferred		4,800

To record receipt of dividend.

(3)

Investment in Saul Corporation—Common   703,800
    Equity in Saul Corporation Earnings—Common   703,800
(90% [$840,000 − $8,000]) = $748,800 − $45,000
amortization of excess.

The working paper elimination entries for the year ended December 31, 19x1, would then be modified to:

(1)

Equity in Earnings—Preferred   3,300
    Investment in Saul—Preferred   3,300

(2)

Same as in Illustration 7–10.

(3)

Same as in Illustration 7–10.

(4)

Equity in Earnings —Common   703,800
    Investment in Saul—Common   703,800

(5)

Same as in Illustration 7–10.

(6)

Same as in Illustration 7–10.

Appendix 7–A: Gain or loss on purchase of intercompany bonds attributable to issuer— complete equity method

As indicated earlier in the chapter, the unofficial solutions to CPA examination questions indicate a preference for attributing gains and losses on the purchase of intercompany bonds to the issuer of the bonds rather than allocating the gains or losses between purchaser and issuer. To illustrate this method and to contrast it with the approach used in the chapter, Illustration 7–5 is now reworked as Illustration 7–12 wherein the gain on purchase of intercompany bonds is attributed to the issuer of the bonds.

The Illustration 7–12 elimination entries are:

(1)		
Equity in Earnings— Subsidiary	214,380	
Investment in S Company		214,380

(2)		
Bonds Payable	300,000	
Gain on Purchase of Intercompany Bonds .		37,800
Investment in P Company Bonds		258,000
Unamortized Bond Discount		4,200

(3)		
Interest Income	27,000	
Interest Expense		24,300
Gain on Purchase of Intercompany Bonds .		2,700

(4)		
Retained Earnings (1/1/x6) —S Company	1,008,000	
Capital Stock—S Company	360,000	
Investment in S Company		1,368,000

A comparison of Illustrations 7–5 and 7–12 reveals that the only differences between them are:

1. The apportionment of minority interest net income differs by $4,200 which causes a difference in consolidated net income in the same amount.
2. Consolidated retained earnings and minority interest differ in the two illustrations by the same $4,200.

For 19x7 and 19x8, working paper elimination entries (2) and (3) would be:

258

Illustration 7–12
P COMPANY
Condensed Consolidated Working Paper
For the Year Ended December 31, 19x6

Complete Equity Method
Year of Bond Purchase
90 Percent Subsidiary

	P Co.	S Co. (90%)	Eliminations Dr.	Eliminations Cr.	Minority Interest	Consol- idated
Income Statement						
Sales	1,200,000	800,000				2,000,000
Cost of sales and operating expenses	800,000	500,000				1,300,000
Operating income before taxes	400,000	300,000				700,000
Equity in earnings—subsidiary	214,380		(1) 214,380			
Interest income		27,000	(3) 27,000			
Interest expense	(81,000)			(3) 24,300		(56,700)
				(3) 2,700		
Gain on purchase of intercompany bonds				(2) 37,800		40,500
Income before income taxes	533,380	327,000				683,800
Provision for income taxes (40%)	127,600	130,800				258,400
						425,400
Minority interest net income					19,620	(19,620)
Net income—carried forward	405,780	196,200			19,620	405,780
Retained Earnings Statement						
Balance, 1/1/x6:						
P Co.	2,288,000					2,288,000
S Co.		1,120,000	(4) 1,008,000		112,000	
Net income—brought forward	405,780	196,200			19,620	405,780
Balance, 12/31/x6—carried forward	2,693,780	1,316,200			131,620	2,693,780
Balance Sheet						
Investment in S Co.	1,582,380			(4) 1,368,000		
				(1) 214,380		
Investment in P Co. bonds		258,000		(2) 258,000		
Unamortized bond discount	14,000			(2) 4,200		9,800
Other assets	2,847,240	1,545,000				4,392,240
Totals	4,443,620	1,803,000				4,402,040
8% bonds payable	1,000,000		(2) 300,000			700,000
Other liabilities	249,840	86,800				336,640
Capital stock:						
P Co.	500,000					500,000
S Co.		400,000	(4) 360,000		40,000	
Retained earnings—brought forward	2,693,780	1,316,200			131,620	2,693,780
Minority interest					171,620	171,620
Totals	4,443,620	1,803,000	1,909,380	1,909,380		4,402,040

(1) Elimination of equity in earnings of subsidiary.
(2) Elimination of intercompany bonds and to record a portion of the gain on purchase of intercompany bonds.
(3) Elimination of intercompany bond interest and to record the balance of the gain.
(4) Elimination of the balance of investment.

Illustration 7–12 *(continued)*

Computations and Proofs

Income apportionment:

	Total	Parent	Minority
S Co. income	$196,200	$176,580	$ 19,620
Intercompany purchase of bonds:			
Gain attributed to parent co.	40,500	40,500	
Piecemeal removal of gain for 19x6 ($40,500 ÷ 15 years)	(2,700)	(2,700)	
P Co. income ($405,780 − $214,380)	191,400	191,400	
Totals	$425,400	$405,780	$ 19,620

Reconciliation of minority interest:

S Co.—capital stock	$ 400,000
—retained earnings, 12/31/x6	1,316,200
Net assets, 12/31/x6	$1,716,200
10% of above	$ 171,620

Note: There are no reconciling items for minority interest.

	(2)			
	19x7		*19x8*	
8% Bonds Payable	300,000		300,000	
Investment in P Company Bonds . . .		261,000		264,000
Unamortized Bond Discount		3,900		3,600
Investment in S Company		35,100		32,400
	(3)			
Interest Income	27,000		27,000	
Interest Expense		24,300		24,300
Investment in S Company		2,700		2,700

Since the entire gain of $40,500 was attributed to the parent company (issuer of the bonds), the minority interest is unaffected by the piecemeal adjustments in subsequent years and the entire $2,700 adjustment flows through the parent's investment in S Company. In the chapter illustrations, the $2,700 was apportioned as $2,400 to the parent company and $300 to the minority interest.

It should be remembered that although the treatments of the two methods differ throughout the life of the bonds, the net effect of these treatments will ultimately coincide by the time the bonds mature. This result is achieved because, during the life of the bonds, the separate books of the parent company and the subsidiary are the same under either method and only the consolidation working papers reflect the differing treatments. When the bonds mature, book balances are the same regardless of which method was used on the working papers.

Appendix 7–B: Intercompany bond transactions—cost method

The basic difference between the cost method and the complete equity method is in the recording of the increase in net assets of the subsidiary from the date of acquisition. The entries relating to the bond transactions are the same for either method. Thus, the entries that affect the intercompany bond accounts and interest expense/income accounts on the working papers illustrated in this chapter would be the same for either method. Therefore, the illustrations in the chapter will not be reworked to demonstrate the cost method working papers. Instead, a different example will be used to demonstrate the cost method, and it is now assumed that the subsidiary is the issuer of the bonds and:

1. P Company purchased 90 percent of S Company's stock on January 1, 19x0, at book value when S Company's retained earnings were $500,000.
2. P Company purchased $600,000 face value of S Company's bonds for $540,000 on January 2, 19x6. The bonds mature in five years and interest is paid on January 1 and July 1 each year.
3. The bonds of S Company bear interest at 6 percent per annum and were sold at 90 on January 2, 19x1. (Five years prior to the purchase of these bonds by P Company.)
4. P Company uses the cost method to account for its investment in S Company. (No income is recorded by the parent company on its books until it is received as dividends.)
5. Income taxes are 40 percent.

Since Illustration 7–13 is a cost-method working paper, it is necessary to calculate the parent company's share of the increase in S Company's net assets from the date of acquisition to the beginning of the current year. This can be accomplished as follows:

S Company retained earnings, January 1, 19x6	$2,500,000
S Company retained earnings on date of acquisition, January 1, 19x0	500,000
Increase	$2,000,000
Parent's share, 90%	$1,800,000

This calculation becomes the basis of entry (1) in Illustration 7–13. Entry (1), in effect, converts the investment in S Company to the incomplete equity method as of the *beginning* of the current year (19x6).

The Illustration 7–13 elimination entries are:

(1)		
Investment in S Company	1,800,000	
Retained Earnings (1/1/x6)—P Company		1,800,000

(2)		
Retained Earnings (1/1/x6)— S Company	2,250,000	
Capital Stock—S Company	1,350,000	
Investment in S Company		3,600,000

(3)		
Bonds Payable	600,000	
Gain on Purchase of Intercompany Bonds		24,000
Investment in S Company Bonds		552,000
Unamortized Bond Discount		24,000

Illustration 7–13
P COMPANY
Condensed Consolidated Working Paper
For the Year Ended December 31, 19x6

90 Percent Subsidiary
Cost Method
First Year of Bond Purchase

	P Co.	S Co. (90%)	Eliminations Dr.	Eliminations Cr.	Minority Interest	Consolidated
Income Statement						
Sales	4,000,000	4,900,000				8,900,000
Cost of sales	2,000,000	1,900,000				3,900,000
Gross margin	2,000,000	3,000,000				5,000,000
Expenses	1,000,000	1,400,000				2,400,000
Operating income before interest	1,000,000	1,600,000				2,600,000
Interest income	48,000		(4) 48,000			
Interest expense		70,000		(4) 42,000		28,000
				(4) 6,000		
Gain on purchase in intercompany bonds				(3) 24,000		30,000
Income before income taxes	1,048,000	1,530,000				2,602,000
Provision for income taxes	419,200	612,000				1,031,200
						1,570,800
Minority interest net income					89,400	(89,400)
Net income—carried forward	628,800	918,000			89,400	1,481,400
Retained Earnings Statement						
Balance, 1/1/x6:						
P Co.	4,000,000			(1) 1,800,000		5,800,000
S Co.		2,500,000	(2) 2,250,000		250,000	
Net income—brought forward	628,800	918,000			89,400	1,481,400
Balance, 12/31/x6—carried forward	4,628,800	3,418,000			339,400	7,281,400
Balance Sheet						
Accrued interest receivable	18,000			(5) 18,000		
Investment in S Co.	1,800,000		(1) 1,800,000	(2) 3,600,000		
Investment in S Co. bonds	552,000			(3) 552,000		
Unamortized bond discount		40,000		(3) 24,000		16,000
Other assets	3,758,800	6,408,000				10,166,800
Totals	6,128,800	6,448,000				10,182,800
Accrued interest payable		30,000	(5) 18,000			12,000
6% bonds payable		1,000,000	(3) 600,000			400,000
Other liabilities	500,000	500,000				1,000,000
Capital stock:						
P Co.	1,000,000					1,000,000
S Co.		1,500,000	(2) 1,350,000		150,000	
Retained earnings—brought forward	4,628,800	3,418,000			339,400	7,281,400
Minority interest					489,400	489,400
Totals	6,128,800	6,448,000	6,066,000	6,066,000		10,182,800

(1) To record parent's share of increase in net assets from date of acquisition.
(2) Elimination of investment account balance.
(3) Elimination of intercompany bonds and related accounts and to record part of the gain on purchase.
(4) Elimination of intercompany interest and to record the balance of the gain.
(5) Elimination of intercompany receivables and payables.

Illustration 7–13 *(continued)*

Computations and Proofs

Schedules

Computation of gain on purchase of intercompany bonds:

Bonds payable—issued and outstanding	$1,000,000
Less: Unamortized discount on 1/2/x0	50,000
Carrying value	$ 950,000
Carrying value of % purchased—60% of above	$ 570,000
Price paid	540,000
Gain on purchase	$ 30,000

Income apportionment:

	Total	Parent	Minority Interest
Net income—per books:			
Parent	$ 628,800	$ 628,800	
Subsidiary	918,000	826,200	$ 91,800
Add: Gain on purchase of intercompany bonds:			
Discount on purchase	60,000	60,000	
Unamortized discount of issuer (60% × $50,000)	(30,000)	(27,000)	(3,000)
Deduct: Piecemeal recognition of gain:			
Purchaser	(12,000)	(12,000)	
Issuer (60% × $10,000)	6,000	5,400	600
Allocated net income	$1,570,800	$1,481,400	$ 89,400

Reconciliation-minority interest:

S Co.—capital stock	$1,500,000
S Co.—retained earnings 12/31/x6	3,418,000
Net assets, 12/31/x6	$4,918,000
10% of above	$ 491,800
Deduct: Share of intercompany bond loss (10% × $30,000)	(3,000)
Add: Piecemeal recognition of loss ($3,000 ÷ 5 years)	600
Minority interest, 12/31/x6	$ 489,400

Reconciliation parent retained earnings:

Retained earnings per books—12/31/x6		$4,628,800
Add: Increase in net assets:		
S Co. retained earnings:		
12/31/x6	$3,418,000	
1/1/x0	500,000	
Increase in net assets	$2,918,000	
90% of above		2,626,200
Add: Intercompany bond transaction:		
Balance of unrecognized gian attributable to parent ($60,000 − $12,000)	$ 48,000	
Balance of unrecognized loss attributable to subsidiary 90% ($30,000 − $6,000)	(21,600)	
Net amount		26,400
Consolidated retained earnings		$7,281,400

	(4)	
Interest Income	48,000	
Interest Expense		42,000
Gain on Purchase of		
Intercompany Bonds .		6,000

	(5)	
Accrued Interest Payable . .	18,000	
Accrued Interest		
Receivable		18,000

The following observations from Illustration 7–13 are pertinent:

1. Since the bonds were purchased at the *beginning of the year 19x6,* the working paper contains the gain on the purchase of intercompany bonds *and* the piecemeal recognition of the gain in the *same* year.

2. Although the unamortized bond discount was $50,000 on the date of the purchase, the balance at year's end is $40,000 ($10,000 of amortization per annum on a straight-line basis). Interest expense of $70,000 consists of the $10,000 of amortization plus the $60,000 (6% × $1,000,000) cash payment for interest.

3. Since interest is payable on January 1, $30,000 (one-half year) was accrued as payable by S Company and 60 percent of this was accrued as a receivable by P Company. For consolidation purposes intercompany receivables and payables are eliminated, and this was done in entry (5).

4. P Company must amortize its investment in bonds so that it amounts to $600,000 at maturity. Accordingly, the discount of $60,000 ($600,000 − $540,000) is amortized at $12,000 per annum. This increased the carrying value of the investment to $552,000 and interest income was correspondingly increased from $36,000 (cash portion) to $48,000. This amount is eliminated by entry (4) since it is an intercompany transaction.

5. Since 60 percent of the outstanding bonds payable are now owned by P Company, 60 percent of the unamortized bond discount ($40,000) must be eliminated. This is reflected in entry (3).

6. The computation of the minority interest net income should be studied carefully. Although the net gain on the purchase of intercompany bonds is $30,000 from a consolidated viewpoint, it consists of two elements, namely, (1) a $60,000 gain attributable to P Company (its purchase discount), and (2) a $30,000 loss attributable to S Company (60 percent of its unamortized issuance discount). Since the net gain of $30,000 consists of these two elements, the piecemeal removal of this gain (one-fifth each year for five years) will similarly consist of two elements. It should be noted that each portion of the removal

Illustration 7–14
P·COMPANY
Working Paper Elimination Entries
For the Years Ended December 31

	19x7	19x8	19x9	19y0
		(2)		
Retained Earnings (1/1)—S Company	1,800	1,200	600	—
Bonds Payable	600,000	600,000	600,000	600,000
Unamortized Bond Discount . .	18,000	12,000	6,000	—
Investment in S Company Bonds	564,000	576,000	588,000	600,000
Retained Earnings (1/1)—P Company	19,800	13,200	6,600	—
		(3)		
Retained Earnings (1/1)—S Company	600	600	600	600
Interest Income	48,000	48,000	48,000	48,000
Interest Expense	42,000	42,000	42,000	42,000
Retained Earnings (1/1/)—P Company	6,600	6,600	6,600	6,600

is equal to one-fifth of the net gain elements and the piecemeal removal is added or deducted in the opposite direction from the gain elements. Thus, the P Company gain of $60,000 causes a $12,000 piecemeal reduction of income and the S Company loss of $30,000 causes a $6,000 piecemeal addition to income. Of course, at the end of five years the process will cease and the books of the individual companies will then be in agreement with the consolidation working paper.

For subsequent years the working paper elimination entries are similar to those illustrated in this chapter except for the adjustments that affect the investment account. Under the cost method, the original cost of the investment in S Company must be maintained intact, and, therefore, no adjustments to this account are permitted as in the complete equity method. Accordingly, the required adjustments are reflected through the retained earnings accounts. Thus, entries (3) and (4) for subsequent years would be as shown in Illustration 7–14. When the bonds are redeemed on January 2, 19y1, the accounts on the respective sets of books (parent and subsidiary) will then be in agreement with the working papers for intercompany bond purchases and no longer require adjustments or reconciliations.

QUESTIONS

1. How is the purchase of intercompany bonds treated from a consolidated viewpoint?

2. Is there more than one method to treat the consolidated gain or loss on the purchase of intercompany bonds? Explain. Discuss the various theories.

3. In the year of the purchase, how is the consolidated gain or loss on the purchase of intercompany bonds treated on the parent's *books* when the complete equity method is used?

4. In the year of the purchase, how is the consolidated gain or loss on the purchase of intercompany bonds treated on the consolidated working paper? Compare your answer to 3 above. Are the treatments different? Why?

5. How is the consolidated gain or loss treated in years subsequent to the purchase of intercompany bonds (until maturity)?

6. Is the treatment of "piecemeal removal" different from that accorded to gains and losses on the sales of intercompany plant assets? Why are they different?

7. Is it possible to compute the consolidated gain or loss independently from arriving at it through journal entires? Construct an example to show how this is done.

8. Is it necessary to allocate a subsidiary's retained earnings when an investor company purchases a majority of both preferred and common stock? Explain.

9. What steps are necessary to calculate excess when an investor company purchases a majority of both common and preferred stock of an investee?

10. Is the equity in earnings of a subsidiary calculated differently when a subsidiary has both common and preferred stock compared to a subsidiary that has common stock only? Explain.

Questions for Appendix 7–A:

11. In the chapter, a consolidated gain or loss on the intercompany purchase of bonds was allocated in accordance with the discounts and/or premiums on the purchaser's and issuer's books. How is the consolidated gain or loss treated in the appendix? Does this method have theoretical support? Explain.

12. Do the treatments in the chapter and the appendix produce different results in the year of the intercompany purchase? In the years subsequent to the purchase (until maturity)? Why?

13. What is true about the treatments followed in the chapter and the appendix after the bonds mature and are paid? Why is this so?

EXERCISES

Exercise 7–1. Given the following:

[Relates to Exercise 7–1]

	Parent's books		Subsidiary's purchase of bonds	
	Bonds payable	Premium or (discount)	Face value	Price paid
Case A	$500,000	$40,000	$150,000	$155,000
Case B	500,000	20,000	100,000	98,000
Case C	500,000	(30,000)	200,000	210,000
Case D	500,000	(50,000)	250,000	235,000
Case E	500,000	—	175,000	165,000
Case F	500,000	25,000	90,000	90,000

Required:

For each of the above cases compute:

a. The consolidated gain or loss that would appear on a consolidated income statement.

b. The amounts of gain or loss that would be attributed to the parent company and to the minority interest if, in each case, the parent company owned 80 percent of the outstanding shares of the subsidiary.

Exercise 7–2. On January 1, 19x3, P Company had the following on its books:

	Debit	Credit
Bond discount	$30,000	
10% bonds payable, due January 1, 19x8		$400,000
Accrued interest payable		20,000

Interest is payable on January 1 and July 1.

On July 1, 19x3, S Company purchased 40 percent (face value, $160,000) of P Company's bonds for $151,000.

Required:

a. Prepare all of the entries pertaining to bonds payable for P Company. Your entries should include entries for the payment and accrual of interest and any amortization that is required.

b. Prepare all of the entries pertaining to S Company's investment in the bonds of P Company. S Company is a wholly owned subsidiary. (Include the entry for the purchase of the bonds.)

Exercise 7–3. Selected accounts from the books of the companies are as follows:

[Relates to Exercise 7–3]

At December 31, 19x3

	P Company		S Company	
	Dr.	Cr.	Dr.	Cr.
Interest income				–0–
Interest expense	$53,000			
Interest receivable			$ 12,500	
Investment in P Company bonds			250,000	
Discount on bonds payable	15,000			
Interest payable		$ 25,000		
10% bonds payable		500,000		

Additional information:

1. The bonds mature on January 1, 19x9.
2. The subsidiary purchased the P Company bonds at face value on December 31, 19x3. (Ignore accrued interest.)
3. P Company owns 80 percent of the outstanding shares of S Company.
4. Interest is payable on January 1 and July 1.

Required:

a. What was the balance in the Discount on Bonds Payable account at the beginning of the year?

b. Compute the consolidated gain or loss on the purchase of the bonds.

c. Prepare the working paper elimination entry (entries).

d. What effect will the above gain or loss have on the parent's income for 19x3?

Exercise 7–4. Selected accounts from the books of the companies are as follows:

Additional information:

1. The bonds mature on January 1, 19x9.
2. P Company purchased the bonds on December 31, 19x2. (Ignore accrued interest.)
3. P Company owns 80 percent of the outstanding shares of S Company.
4. Interest is payable on January 1 and July 1.

Required:

a. What was the balance in the Premium on Bonds Payable account at the beginning of the year?

b. Compute the consolidated gain or loss on the purchase of the bonds.

c. Prepare the working paper elimination entry (entries).

d. What effect will the above gain (loss) have on the parent's income for 19x2? On the minority interest net income for 19x2?

Exercise 7–5. Selected accounts from the books of the companies are as follows:

[Relates to Exercise 7–4]

At December 31, 19x2

	P Company Dr.	Cr.	S Company Dr.	Cr.
Interest income		–0–		
Interest expense			$34,000	
Interest receivable	$ 7,200			
Investment in S Company bonds	$148,000			
Premium on bonds payable				$ 12,000
Interest payable				18,000
9% bonds payable				400,000

[Relates to Exercise 7–5]

At December 31, 19x1

	P Company Dr.	Cr.	S Company Dr.	Cr.
Interest income		$8,200		
Interest expense			$51,000	
Interest receivable	$ 7,200			
Investment in S Company bonds	168,000			
Discount on bonds payable			18,000	
Interest payable				$ 24,000
8% bonds payable				600,000

Additional information:

1. The bonds mature on January 1, 19x8.
2. P Company purchased the bonds on July 1, 19x1, for $167,000. The face amount of the bonds (par) was $180,000.
3. P Company owns 80 percent of the outstanding shares of S Company.
4. Interest is payable on January 1 and July 1.

Required:

a. What was the balance in the Discount on Bonds Payable account on July 1, 19x1?

b. Compute the consolidated gain or loss on the purchase of the bonds.

c. Prepare the working paper elimination entry (entries).

d. What effect will the above gain (loss) have on the parent's income for 19x1? On the minority interest net income for 19x1? (Include in your answer any piecemeal removal required.)

Exercise 7–6. Selected accounts from the books of the companies are as follows:

b. What was the price paid for the bonds by S Company?

c. Compute the consolidated gain or loss on the purchase of the bonds.

d. Prepare the working paper elimination entries.

e. What effect will the above gain (loss) have on the parent's income for 19x1? On the minority interest net income for 19x1? (Include in your answer any piecemeal removal required.)

Exercise 7–7. On January 1, 19x1, P Company purchased 80 percent of the outstanding shares of S Company at a cost of $800,000. On that date, S Company had $500,000 of capital stock and $500,000 of retained earnings.

For 19x4, S Company reported income of $200,000 and paid dividends of $80,000. All of the assets and liabilities of S Company are at fair market value. For the year 19x4, P Company reported income from its *own* operations in the amount of $300,000. P Company uses the complete equity method to account for its investment in S Company.

[Relates to Exercise 7–6]

At December 31, 19x1

	P Company		S Company	
	Dr.	Cr.	Dr.	Cr.
Interest income				$24,500
Interest expense	$100,000			
Interest receivable			$ 24,000	
Investment in P Company bonds			396,000	
Discount on bonds payable	16,000			
Interest payable		$ 48,000		
12% bonds payable		800,000		

Additional information:

1. The bonds mature on January 1, 19x6.
2. S Company purchased the bonds on July 1, 19x1. The face value of the bonds purchased was $400,000.
3. P Company owns 80 percent of the outstanding shares of S Company.
4. Interest is payable on January 1 and July 1.

Required:

a. What was the balance in the Discount on Bonds Payable account on July 1, 19x1?

Required:

Using the information provided in Exercise 7–3 together with the above information you are asked to:

a. Prepare the journal entries on the books of P Company to record its share of the equity in earnings of S Company.

b. Compute the amount to be shown as consolidated net income.

c. Compute minority interest net income for 19x4.

Exercise 7–8. On January 1, 19x2, P Company

purchased 80 percent of the outstanding shares of S Company at a cost of $800,000. On that date, S Company had $500,000 of capital stock and $500,000 of retained earnings.

For 19x3, P Company had income of $400,000 from its own operations (excluding its share of income from S Company) and paid dividends of $100,000. For 19x3, S Company reported a net income of $200,000 and paid dividends of $40,000. All of the assets and liabilities of S Company have book values approximately equal to their respective market values.

P Company uses the complete equity method to account for its investment in S Company.

Required:

Using the information provided in Exercise 7–4 together with the above information you are asked to:

a. Compute the amount that P Company should record as equity in earnings of S Company for 19x3.

b. Compute consolidated net income for 19x3.

c. Compute minority interest net income for 19x3.

Exercise 7–9. On January 1, 19x1, P Company purchased 80 percent of the outstanding shares of S Company at a cost of $600,000. On that date, S Company had $200,000 of capital stock and $500,000 of retained earnings.

For 19x4, P Company had income of $400,000 from its own operations (excluding its share of income from S Company) and paid dividends of $200,000. For 19x4, S Company reported income of $60,000 and paid dividends of $40,000. All of the assets and liabilities of S Company have book values approximately equal to their respective market values.

P Company uses the complete equity method to account for its investment in S Company.

Required:

Using the information provided in Exercise 7–5 together with the above information you are asked to:

a. Prepare the journal entries necessary to record the equity in earnings of S Company on the books of P Company for 19x4.

b. Compute consolidated net income for 19x4.

c. Compute minority interest net income for 19x4.

Exercise 7–10. On January 1, 19x1, P Company purchased 80 percent of the outstanding shares of S Company at a cost of $600,000. On that date, S Company had $200,000 of capital stock and $500,000 of retained earnings.

For 19x1, P Company had income of $400,000 from its own operations (excluding its share of income from S Company) and paid dividends of $200,000. For 19x1, S Company reported a loss of $50,000 and paid dividends of $40,000. All of the asset and liabilities of S Company have book values approximately equal to their respective market values.

P Company uses the complete equity method to account for its investment in S Company.

Required:

Using the information provided in Exercise 7–6 together with the above information you are asked to:

a. Prepare the journal entries necessary to record the equity in earnings of S Company on the books of P Company for 19x1.

b. Compute consolidated net income for 19x1.

c. Compute the balance in the Investment in S Company at December 31, 19x1.

d. Compute minority interest net income for 19x1.

e. Compute the total minority interest at December 31, 19x1.

Exercise 7–11. On January 1, 19x5, P Company purchased 80 percent of the outstanding shares of S Company at a price that included $10,000 of excess attributable entirely to land that was undervalued.

For 19x5, P Company reported income of $174,000 computed under the complete equity method. Minority interest net income was $18,500. The minority interest reported on the consolidated balance sheet at December 31, 19x5, amounted to $78,500.

On July 1, 19x5, S Company purchased bonds issued by P Company. The purchase of the bonds produced a constructive gain on purchase of $15,000. The bonds mature on July 1, 19x8. P Company had no unamortized bond discount or premium (P Company originally sold these bonds at par).

Neither company paid any dividends in 19x5.

Required:

a. Compute the amount of income the parent reported as equity in earnings of S Company.

b. Compute the amount of net assets on the books of S Company at December 31, 19x5.

c. Compute the price paid by P Company for its investment in S Company.

d. Compute the balance of the investment in S Company at December 31, 19x5.

Exercise 7–12 (preferred stock). Par Corporation purchased the following stock of Sharp Corporation on December 31, 19x8:

	Price paid
80% of common	$360,000
60% of preferred	200,000

The net assets of Sharp Corporation on December 31, 19x8, were:

10% preferred stock ($50 par), cumulative, nonparticipating, callable at $55	$150,000
Common stock ($10 par)	300,000
Retained earnings	150,000
Total	$600,000

Note: Preferred dividends have not been paid, or declared, for 19x7 and 19x8.

Required:

Calculate excess for investment in:

a. Preferred stock.

b. Common stock.

Exercise 7–13 (preferred stock). Press Corporation purchased the following stock of Sleep Products Corporation on January 1, 19x3:

	Price paid
30% of preferred	$ 150,400
80% of common	1,665,600

The net assets of Sleep Products Corporation on January 1, 19x3, consisted of:

12% preferred stock ($100 par)	$ 400,000
Common stock ($10 par)	1,000,000
Premium on preferred stock	100,000
Premium on common stock	300,000
Retained earnings	700,000
Total	$2,500,000

The preferred stock is cumulative, nonparticipating, and is callable at 105. Dividends are in arrears for 19x2, and no dividends have been declared for

19x3. Sleep Products Corporation reported a net income of $98,000 for 19x3.

Required:

a. Calculate excess for the parent's purchases of preferred and common stocks (excess has an indeterminate life).

b. Calculate the amount of income (using the complete equity method) Press Corporation should report from its investment in:

1. Preferred stock.

2. Common stock.

c. Calculate minority interest net income. (*Hint:* Seventy percent of preferred income is part of minority interest net income.)

d. Calculate the amount of minority interest to be shown on the December 31, 19x3, consolidated balance sheet.

Exercise 7–14 (preferred stock). Using the information provided in Exercise 7–13, assume that Press Corporation purchased the stock on July 1, 19x3, instead of on January 1, 19x3. All other information is unchanged. (*Hint:* Although preferred dividends do not legally accrue until declared, for accounting purposes they should be treated as if they accrue.)

Required:

Complete (*a*), (*b*), (*c*), and (*d*) of Exercise 7–13.

Exercise 7–15 (preferred stock). Prest Corporation purchased the following stock of Walk Products Corporation on January 1, 19x4:

	Price paid
60% of preferred	$ 880,000
75% of common	1,430,000

The net assets of Walk Products Corporation on January 1, 19x4, consisted of:

10% preferred stock ($100 par)	$ 500,000
Common stock ($50 par)	1,000,000
Additional paid-in capital	200,000
Retained earnings	1,000,000
Total	$2,700,000

The preferred stock is cumulative, fully participating, and is callable at 110. Dividends are in arrears for 19x3, and no dividends have been declared for 19x4. Walk Products Corporation reported a net income of $210,000 for 19x4.

Required:

a. Calculate excess for the parent's purchases of preferred and common stocks (excess has a 20-year life).

b. Calculate the amount of income (using the complete equity method) Prest Corporation should report from its investment in:

1. Preferred stock.
2. Common stock.

PROBLEMS

Problem 7–16 (complete equity method). On January 1, 19x2, P Company acquired 75 percent of the outstanding shares of S Company at book value.

On July 1, 19x2, P Company purchased 40 percent of the outstanding bonds of S Company for $152,500. On that date, S Company had $400,000 of 10 percent bonds payable outstanding. The bond discount on that date amounted to $20,000. The bonds mature on July 1, 19x7. Interest is payable January 1 and July 1.

P Company uses the complete equity method to account for its investment.

Income statements for the two companies for the year 19x2 are as follows:

Income Statement	P Company	S Company
Sales	$1,000,000	$500,000
Cost of sales	400,000	250,000
Gross margin	600,000	250,000
Expenses	200,000	100,000
Operating income before taxes	400,000	150,000
Deduct: Interest expense		(44,000)
Add: Interest income	8,750	
Equity in earnings—subsidiary	49,050	
Income before income taxes	457,800	106,000
Provision for income taxes	163,500	42,400
Minority interest net income		
Net income	$ 294,300	$ 63,600

Required:

Prepare a consolidated income statement.

Problem 7–17 (complete equity method). On January 1, 19x1, P Company purchased 40,000 shares of S Company in the open market for $640,000. On that date, the net assets of S Company amounted to $800,000 and had book values that approximated their respective fair market values.

On April 1, 19x1, P Company purchased 30 percent of the outstanding bonds of S Company for $170,000. Interest is payable April 1 and October 1.

P Company uses the complete equity method.

Financial statements for the two corporation for the year ended December 31, 19x1, are as follows:

Income Statement	P Company	S Company
Sales	$2,000,000	$1,000,000
Cost of sales, expenses, and income taxes	1,580,000	880,000
Subtotal	420,000	120,000
Interest income	12,300	
Interest expense		(58,000)
Equity in earnings—subsidiary	47,900	
Net income—carried forward	$ 480,200	$ 62,000

Retained Earnings Statement	P Company	S Company
Balance, January 1, 19x1:		
P Company	$2,000,000	
S Company		$ 300,000
Add: Net income—brought forward	480,200	62,000
Balance, December 31, 19x1—carried forward	$2,480,200	$ 362,000

Balance Sheet	P Company	S Company
Interest receivable	$ 3,600	
Investment in S Company bonds	171,500	
Investment in S Company stock	687,900	
Other assets	2,417,200	$1,631,500
Bond discount		42,500
Totals	$3,280,200	$1,674,000
Interest payable		$ 12,000
Bonds payable, 8%—due April 1, 19x6		600,000
Other liabilities	$ 300,000	200,000
Capital stock—P Company ($50 par)	500,000	
Capital stock—S Company ($10 par)		500,000
Retained earnings—brought forward	2,480,200	362,000
Totals	$3,280,200	$1,674,000

Required:

a. Compute the balance in the Bond Discount account at April 1, 19x1.

b. Compute the consolidated gain or loss on the purchase of intercompany bonds.

c. Prepare a consolidated working paper.

Problem 7–18 (complete equity method). On January 1, 19x2, P Company acquired 80 percent of the outstanding common stock of S Company for $600,000 and there have been no changes in its capital stock. The book values of the net assets of S Company approximated their respective fair market values.

On October 1, 19x2, S Company purchased 60 percent of the outstanding bonds of P Company. Interest is payable on April 1 and October 1.

P Company uses the complete equity method.

The financial statements of the companies for the year ended December 31, 19x2, are as follows:

	P Company	S Company
Income Statement		
Sales	$1,000,000	$500,000
Cost of sales, expenses, and		
income taxes	790,000	440,000
Subtotal	210,000	60,000
Interest income		5,500
Interest expense	(46,000)	
Equity in earnings—		
subsidiary	30,300	
Net income—carried forward	$ 194,300	$ 65,500
Retained Earnings Statement		
Balance, January 1, 19x2:		
P Company	$ 800,000	
S Company		$250,000
Add: Net income—brought		
forward	194,300	65,500
Balance, December 31, 19x2—		
carried forward	$ 994,300	$315,500

	P Company	S Company
Balance Sheet		
Interest receivable		$ 6,000
Investment in P Company		
bonds		248,500
Investment in S Company		
stock	$ 630,300	
Other assets	1,448,500	661,000
Bond discount	25,500	
Totals	$2,104,300	$915,500
Interest payable	$ 10,000	
Bonds payable, 10%—due		
April 1, 19x7	400,000	
Other liabilities	200,000	$100,000
Capital stock—P Company		
($50 par)	500,000	
Capital stock—S Company		
($10 par)		500,000
Retained earnings—brought		
forward	994,300	315,500
Totals	$2,104,300	$915,500

Required:

a. Compute the balance in the Bond Discount account at October 1, 19x2.

b. Compute the price paid by S Company for its investment in P Company bonds.

c. Compute the consolidated gain or loss on the purchase of intercompany bonds.

d. Prepare a consolidated working paper.

Problem 7–19 (complete equity method). On January 1, 19x4, P Company purchased 24,000 shares of S Company in the open market for $500,000. On that date the following asset of S Company had a book value that was different from its respective market value:

	Book value	Fair market value
Patent	–0–	$140,000

All other assets and liabilities had book values approximately equal to their respective market values.

On January 1, 19x4, the patent had a remaining useful life of 10 years. Goodwill, if any, has a 40-year estimated life. P Company uses the complete equity method to account for this investment.

During 19x4, S Company sold $200,000 of merchandise to P Company at 33 ⅓ percent above its cost. The closing inventory of P Company contains merchandise purchased from S Company at a billed price of $60,000.

On July 1, 19x4, P Company bonds were purchased by S Company for $92,000. The face value of the bonds amounts to $100,000. Interest is payable on January 1 and July 1.

On December 31, 19x4, P Company owed S Company $50,000 on open acount.

Financial statements for the companies for the year ended December 31, 19x4, are as follows:

	P Company	S Company
Income Statement		
Sales	$2,000,000	$1,000,000
Cost of sales	800,000	600,000
Gross margin	1,200,000	400,000
Expenses	500,000	200,000
Operating income before taxes	700,000	200,000
Add: Interest income		5,800
Equity in earnings—subsidiary	79,969	
Deduct: Interest expense	(39,000)	
Gain (loss) on purchase of intercompany bonds		
Income before income taxes	740,969	205,800
Provision for income taxes	264,400	82,320
Minority interest net income		
Net income—carried forward	$ 476,569	$ 123,480

	P Company	S Company
Retained Earnings Statement		
Balance, January 1,19x4:		
P Company	$ 209,900	
S Company		$ 60,000
Net income—brought forward	476,569	123,480
Totals	686,469	183,480
Less: Dividends declared:		
P Company	200,000	
S Company		40,000
Balance, December 31, 19x4—carried forward	$ 486,469	$ 143,480

	P Company	S Company
Balance Sheet		
Cash	$ 300,000	$ 200,000
Accounts receivable	260,000	100,000
Accrued interest receivable		5,000
Inventories	400,000	100,000
Equipment (net of accumulated depreciation)	303,000	200,000
Investment in P Company bonds		92,800
Investment in S Company stock	547,969	
Totals	$1,810,969	$ 697,800
Accounts payable and accrued expenses payable	$ 300,000	$ 254,320
Interest payable	20,000	
10% bonds payable—due July 1, 19x9	400,000	
Bond premium	4,500	
Common stock—P Company ($50 par)	500,000	
Common stock—S Company ($10 par)		300,000
Additional paid-in capital—P Company	100,000	
Retained earnings—brought forward	486,469	143,480
Totals	$1,810,969	$ 697,800

Required:

a. Compute the balance in the Bond Premium account at July 1, 19x4.

b. Compute the consolidated gain or loss on the purchase of intercompany bonds.

c. Prepare a consolidated working paper.

Problem 7–20 (complete equity method). Continuing Problem 7–17, financial statements for the next year, 19x2, are as follows:

	P Company	S Company
Income Statement		
Sales	$2,500,000	$1,500,000
Cost of sales, expenses, and income taxes	1,800,000	1,200,000
Subtotal	700,000	300,000
Interest income	16,400	
Interest expense		(58,000)
Equity in earnings—subsidiary	194,000	
Net income—carried forward	$ 910,400	$ 242,000

	P Company	S Company
Retained Earnings Statement		
Balance, January 1,19x2:		
P Company	$2,480,200	
S Company		$ 362,000
Add: Net income—brought forward	910,400	242,000
Balance, December 31, 19x2— carried forward	$3,390,600	$ 604,000
Balance Sheet		
Interest receivable	$ 3,600	
Investment in S Company bonds	173,500	
Investment in S Company stock	881,900	
Other assets	3,181,600	$1,933,500
Bond discount		32,500
Totals	$4,240,600	$1,966,000
Interest payable		$ 12,000
Bonds payable, 8%—due April 1, 19x6		600,000
Other liabilities	$ 350,000	250,000
Capital stock—P Company ($50 par)	500,000	
Capital stock—S Company ($10)		500,000
Retained earnings—brought forward	3,390,600	604,000
Totals	$4,240,600	$1,966,000

Required:

Prepare a consolidated working paper.

Problem 7–21 (incomplete equity method). On January 1, 19x1, P Company purchased 40,000 shares of S Company in the open market for $640,000. On that date, the net assets of S Company amounted to $800,000 and had book values that approximated their respective fair market values.

On April 1, 19x1, P Company purchased 30 percent of the outstanding bonds of S Company for $170,000. Interest is payable April 1 and October 1.

P Company uses the incomplete equity method.

Financial statements for the two corporations for the year ended December 31, 19x1, are as follows:

	P Company	S Company
Income Statement		
Sales	$2,000,000	$1,000,000
Cost of sales, expenses, and income taxes	1,580,000	880,000
Subtotal	420,000	120,000
Interest income	12,300	
Interest expense		(58,000)
Equity in earnings— subsidiary	49,600	
Net income—carried forward	$ 481,900	$ 62,000
Retained Earnings Statement		
Balance, January 19x1:		
P Company	$2,000,000	
S Company		$ 300,000
Add: Net income—brought forward	481,900	62,000
Balance, December 31, 19x1— carried forward	$2,481,900	$ 362,000
Balance Sheet		
Interest receivable	$ 3,600	
Investment in S Company bonds	171,500	
Investment in S Company stock	689,600	
Other assets	2,417,200	$1,631,500
Bond discount		42,500
Totals	$3,281,900	$1,674,000
Interest payable		$ 12,000
Bonds payable, 8%—due April 1, 19x6		600,000
Other liabilities	$ 300,000	200,000
Capital stock—P Company ($50 par)	500,000	
Capital stock—S Company ($10 par)		500,000
Retained earnings—brought forward	2,481,900	362,000
Totals	$3,281,900	$1,674,000

Required:

a. Compute the balance in the Bond Discount account at April 1, 19x1.

b. Compute the consolidated gain or loss on the purchase of intercompany bonds.

c. Prepare a consolidated working paper.

Problem 7–22 (incomplete equity method). On January 1, 19x2, P Company acquired 80 percent of the outstanding common stock of S Company for $600,000, and there have been no changes in its capital stock. The book values of the net assets of S Company approximated their respective fair market values.

On October 1, 19x2, S Company purchased 60 percent of the outstanding bonds of P Company. Interest is payable on April 1 and October 1.

P Company uses the incomplete equity method.

The financial statements of the companies for the year ended December 31, 19x2, are as follows:

	P Company	S Company
Income Statement		
Sales	$1,000,000	$500,000
Cost of sales, expenses, and income taxes	790,000	440,000
Subtotal	210,000	60,000
Interest income		5,500
Interest expense	(46,000)	
Equity in earnings—subsidiary	52,400	
Net income—carried forward	$ 216,400	$ 65,500
Retained Earnings Statement		
Balance, January 1, 19x2:		
P Company	$ 800,000	
S Company		$250,000
Add: Net income—brought forward	216,400	65,500
Balance, December 31, 19x2—carried forward	$1,016,400	$315,500
Balance Sheet		
Interest receivable		$ 6,000
Investment in P Company bonds		248,500
Investment in S Company stock	$ 652,400	
Other assets	1,448,500	661,000
Bond discount	25,500	
Totals	$2,126,400	$915,500
Interest payable	$ 10,000	
Bonds payable, 10%—due April 1, 19x7	400,000	
Other liabilities	200,000	$100,000
Capital stock—P Company ($50 par)	500,000	
Capital stock—S Company ($10 par)		500,000
Retained earings—brought forward	1,016,400	315,500
Totals	$2,126,400	$915,500

Required:

a. Compute the balance in the Bond Discount account at October 1, 19x2.

b. Compute the price paid by S Company for its investment in P Company bonds.

c. Compute the consolidated gain or loss on the purchase of intercompany bonds.

d. Prepare a consolidated working paper.

Problem 7–23. On October 1, 19x1, the Arba Company acquired a 90 percent interest in the common stock of Braginetz Company on the open market for $750,000; the book value was $712,500 at that date. Since the excess could not be attributed to the undervaluation of any specific assets, Arba reported $37,500 of consolidated goodwill on its consolidated balance sheet at September 30, 19x2. During fiscal 19x3, it was decided that the Braginetz goodwill should be amortized in equal amounts over 10 years beginning with fiscal 19x2.

On October 1, 19x2, Arba purchased new equipment for $14,500 from Braginetz. The equipment cost Braginetz $9,000 and had an estimated life of 10 years as of October 1, 19x2. Arba uses the sum-of-the-years'-digits depreciation method for both financial and income tax reporting.

During fiscal 19x4, Arba had merchandise sales to Braginetz of $100,000; the merchandise was priced at 25 percent above Arba's cost. Braginetz still owes Arba $17,500 on open account and has 20 percent of this merchandise in inventory at September 30, 19x4.

On August 1, 19x4, Braginetz borrowed $30,000 from Arba by issuing twelve, $2,500, 9 percent, 90-day notes. Arba discounted four of the notes at its bank on August 31 at 6 percent.

Required:

a. What are criteria which could influence Arba in its decision to include or exclude Braginetz as a subsidiary in consolidated financial statements? Explain.

b. For each of the following items give the elimination entry (including explanation) that should be made on the working papers for the preparation of the indicated consolidated statement(s) at September 30, 19x4.

1. For the consolidated goodwill—to prepare all consolidated statements.
2. For the equipment:
   (a) To prepare only a consolidated balance sheet.
   (b) To prepare all consolidated statements.
3. For the intercompany merchandise transactions—to prepare all consolidated statements.
4. For the note transactions—to prepare only a consolidated balance sheet. (AICPA adapted)

Problem 7–24 (preferred stock). Using the information provided in Exercise 7–13, you are asked to:

a. Prepare the journal entries for—

1. The purchase of the preferred stock.

2. The purchase of the common stock.

3. Recording the equity in earnings from preferred stock of subsidiary (complete equity basis).

4. Recording the equity in earnings from common stock of subsidiary (complete equity basis).

b. Prepare the elimination entries for a consolidated working paper for the—

1. Investment in preferred stock.

2. Investment in common stock.

Problem 7–25 (preferred stock). Using the information provided in Exercise 7–15, you are asked to:

a. Prepare the journal entries for—

1. The purchase of the preferred stock.

2. The purchase of the common stock.

3. Recording the equity in earnings from preferred stock of subsidiary (complete equity basis).

4. Recording the equity in earnings from common stock of subsidiary (complete equity basis).

b. Prepare the elimination entries for a consolidated working paper for the—

1. Investment in preferred stock.

2. Investment in common stock.

Problem 7–26. Brighton Corporation acquired 80 percent of the 1,250 shares of $100 par value common stock outstanding of Solvo Corporation on July 1, 19x9, for $158,600. Brighton uses the incomplete equity method of accounting for its investment in Solvo.

The December 31, 19x9, trial balances for both companies appear below:

BRIGHTON CORPORATION AND SUBSIDIARY
Trial Balances
December 31, 19x9

	Brighton Corporation	Solvo Corporation
Cash	$ 200,000	$ 20,000
Accounts receivable	205,000	55,000
Notes receivable	180,000	11,000
Notes receivable discounted	(4,000)	
Accrued interest receivable .	1,600	400
Dividends receivable	6,400	
Inventories	300,000	75,000
Plant and equipment	794,000	280,600
Allowance for depreciation .	(260,000)	(30,000)
Investment in Solvo Corporation stock	167,400	
Investment in Solvo Corporation bonds	40,000	
Advance to Solvo Corporation	35,000	
Totals	$1,665,400	$412,000
Accounts payable	$ 220,400	$ 54,800
Notes payable	142,000	24,200
Dividends payable		8,000
Accrued interest payable . .	22,100	3,900
Other accrued liabilities . .	7,900	3,100
Advance from Brighton Corporation		35,000
Bonds payable	600,000	85,000
Capital stock	360,000	125,000
Capital in excess of par value	49,000	12,000
Retained earnings	264,000	61,000
Totals	$1,665,400	$412,000

The following information is also available:

1. Solvo Corporation reported net income and dividends for 19x9 as follows:

Net income for six months ending:

June 30	$10,000
December 31	20,000

Dividends declared:

March 31	4,000
June 30	4,000
September 30	1,000
December 31	8,000

2. Data pertaining to 19x9 intercompany sales and ending inventories were as follows:

	Brighton Corporation	Solvo Corporation
Intercompany sales:		
January 1 to June 30	$40,000	$ 95,000
July 1 to December 31	60,000	105,000
Markup on cost	20%	25%
Intercompany payable at year-end	$13,000	$ 5,500
Year-end inventory of intercompany purchases at Fifo cost	25,000	18,000

3. Sales of equipment by Brighton Corporation to Solvo Corporation during 19x9 were as follows:

[Relates to Problem 7–26]

Date		Book value on Brighton's records	Price paid by Solvo	Depreciation method	Estimated life
February 1	. . . .	$11,000	$13,500	Double-declining balance	10 years
October 1	. . . .	14,000	12,000	Straight line	5 years

For depreciation purposes Solvo Corporation estimates salvage at 10 percent of the equipment's cost.

4. Brighton Corporation acquired $40,000 of the 6 percent Solvo Corporation bonds at par value on July 1, 19x9. Interest is paid each July 1 and January 1 by Solvo Corporation.

5. On December 1, 19x9, Brighton Corporation discounted $4,000 of noninterest-bearing notes payable of Solvo Corporation.

Required:

Complete a worksheet for the preparation of a consolidated balance sheet for Brighton Corporation and its subsidiary, Solvo, Inc., as of December 31, 19x9. Formal statements and journal entries are not required. You may assume that both companies made all of the adjusting entries required for separate financial statements unless an obvious discrepancy exists. Income taxes should not be considered in your solution. (AICPA adapted)

Problem 7–27. On April 1, 19x4, Jared, Inc., purchased 100 percent of the common stock of Munson Manufacturing Company for $5,850,000 and 20 percent of its preferred stock for $150,000. At the date of purchase the book and fair values of Munson's assets and liabilities were as follows:

	Book value	Fair value
Cash	$ 200,000	$ 200,000
Notes receivable	85,000	85,000
Accounts receivable (net) . . .	980,000	980,000
Inventories	828,000	700,000
Land	1,560,000	2,100,000
Machinery and equipment . .	7,850,000	10,600,000
Accumulated depreciation . .	(3,250,000)	(4,000,000)
Other assets	140,000	50,000
Totals	$8,393,000	$10,715,000
Notes payable	$ 115,000	$ 115,000
Accounts payable	400,000	400,000
Subordinated debentures— 7%	5,000,000	5,000,000
Preferred stock; noncumulative, nonparticipating, par value $5 per share; authorized, issued and outstanding 150,000 shares	750,000	—
Common stock; par value $10 per share; authorized, issued, and outstanding 100,000 shares	1,000,000	—
Additional paid-in capital (common stock)	122,000	—
Retained earnings	1,006,000	—
Totals	$8,393,000	

Additional information:

By the year-end, December 31, 19x4, the following transactions had occurred:

1. The balance of Munson's net accounts receivable at April 1, 19x4, had been collected.
2. The inventory on hand at April 1, 19x4, had been charged to cost of sales. Munson used a perpetual inventory system in accounting for inventories.
3. Prior to 19x4, Jared had purchased at face value $1,500,000 of Munson's 7 percent subordinated debentures. These debentures mature on October 31, 19y0 (six years hence), with interest payable annually on October 31.
4. As of April 1, 19x4, the machinery and equipment had an estimated remaining life of six years. Munson uses the straight-line method of depreciation. Munson's depreciation expense calculation for the nine months ended December 31, 19x4, was based upon the old depreciation rates.
5. The other assets consist entirely of long-term investments made by Munson and do not include any investment in Jared.
6. During the last nine months of 19x4, the following intercompany transactions occurred between Jared and Munson.

    Intercompany sales:

	Jared to Munson	Munson to Jared
Net sales	$158,000	$230,000
Included in purchaser's inventory at December 31, 19x4	36,000	12,000
Balance unpaid at December 31, 19x4	16,800	22,000

Jared sells merchandise to Munson at cost. Munson sells merchandise to Jared at regular selling price including a normal gross profit margin of 35 percent. There were no intercompany sales between the two companies prior to April 1, 19x4.

    Accrued interest on intercompany debt is recorded by both companies in their respective accounts receivable and accounts payable accounts.

7. The account Investment in Munson Manufacturing Company includes Jared's investment in Munson's debentures and its investment in the common and preferred stock of Munson.
8. Jared's policy is to amortize intangible assets over a 20-year period.

Required:

Complete the worksheet to prepare the consolidated trial balance for Jared, Inc., and its subsidiary, Munson Manufacturing Company, at December 31, 19x4. Show computations in good form where appropriate to support worksheet entries.

Jared's revenue and expense figures are for the 12-month period while Munson's are for the last 9 months of 19x4. You may assume that both companies made all the adjusting entries required for separate financial statements unless stated to the contrary. Round all computations to the nearest dollar. *Ignore income taxes.*

Problem 7–28. Parent, Inc., purchased for $151,000 cash 100 percent of the common stock and 20 percent of the 5 percent noncumulative, nonparticipating preferred stock of Subsidiary Manufacturing Corporation on June 30, 19x1. At that date, Subsidiary's stockholders' equity was as follows: 5,000 shares of $10 par value preferred stock, $50,000; 100,000 shares of $1 par value common stock, $100,000; and retained earnings, $41,000. The fair values of the assets, liabilities, and preferred stock did not differ materially from their book values. Subsidiary has made no adjustments to its books to reflect the purchase by Parent. At December 31, 19x1, Parent and Subsidiary prepared consolidated financial statements.

Transactions between Parent and Subsidiary during the year ended December 31, 19x2, follow:

1. On January 3, 19x2, Parent sold land with an $11,000 book value to Subsidiary for $15,000. Subsidiary made a $3,000 down payment and signed an 8 percent mortgage-note payable in 12 equal quarterly payments of $1,135, including interest, beginning March 31, 19x2.
2. Subsidiary produced equipment for Parent under two separate contracts. The first contract, which was for office equipment, was begun and completed during the year at a cost to Subsidiary of $17,500. Parent paid $22,000 cash for the equipment on April 17, 19x2. The second contract was begun on February 15, 19x2, but will not be completed until May 19x3. Subsidiary has incurred $45,000 costs as of December 31, 19x2, and anticipates an additional $30,000 cost to complete the $95,000 contract. Subsidiary accounts for all contracts under the percentage-of-completion method of accounting. Parent has made no account on its books for this uncompleted contract as of December 31, 19x2.

[Relates to Problem 7–27]

JARED, INC., AND SUBSIDIARY
Worksheet to Prepare Consolidated Trial Balance
For the Year Ended December 31, 19x4

	Jared, Inc. Dr., (Cr.)	Munson Mfg. Co. Dr. (Cr.)	Adjustments and Eliminations		Consolidated Balances	
			Debit	Credit	Debit	Credit
Cash	822,000	530,000				
Notes receivable	—	85,000				
Accounts receivable (net)	2,758,000	1,368,400				
Inventories	3,204,000	1,182,000				
Land	4,000,000	1,560,000				
Machinery and equipment	15,875,000	7,850,000				
Accumulated depreciation— machinery and equipment	(6,301,000)	(3,838,750)				
Buildings	1,286,000	—				
Accumulated depreciation— buildings	(372,000)	—				
Investment in Munson Manufacturing Company	7,500,000	—				
Other assets	263,000	140,000				
Notes payable	—	(115,000)				
Accounts payable	(1,364,000)	(204,000)				
Long-term debt	(10,000,000)	—				
Subordinated debentures—7%	—	(5,000,000)				
Preferred stock	—	(750,000)				
Common stock	(2,400,000)	(1,000,000)				
Additional paid-in capital	(240,000)	(122,000)				
Retained earnings	(12,683,500)	—				
Retained earnings	—	(1,006,000)				
Sales	(18,200,000)	(5,760,000)				
Cost of sales	10,600,000	3,160,000				
Selling, general, and administrative expenses	3,448,500	1,063,900				
Depreciation expense—machinery and equipment	976,000	588,750				
Depreciation expense—buildings	127,000	—				
Interest revenue	(105,000)	(1,700)				
Interest expense	806,000	269,400				
	–0–	–0–				

(AICPA adapted)

3. On December 1, 19x2, Subsidiary declared a 5 percent cash dividend on its preferred stock, payable on January 15, 19x3, to stockholders to record as of December 14, 19x2.

4. Parent sells merchandise to Subsidiary at an average mark up of 12 percent of costs. During the year, Parent charged Subsidiary $238,000 for merchandise purchased, of which Subsidiary paid $211,000. Subsidiary has $11,200 of this merchandise on hand at December 31, 19x2.

Parent depreciates all its equipment over a 10-

year estimated economic life with no salvage value. Parent takes a half-year's depreciation in the year of purchase.

Both companies have made all of the adjusting entries required for separate financial statements unless an obvious discrepancy exists.

Required:

Complete the worksheet for the preparation of a consolidated balance sheet and income statement for Parent, Inc., and its subsidiary, Subsidiary Man-

[Relates to Problem 7–28]

PARENT, INC., AND SUBSIDIARY
Worksheet to Prepare Consolidated Balance
Sheet and Income Statement
For the Year Ended December 31, 19x2

	Parent, Inc. Dr. (Cr.)	Subsidiary Corp. Dr. (Cr.)	Adjustments and Eliminations		Consolidated Balances	
			Debit	Credit	Debit	Credit
Cash	43,000	31,211				
Accounts receivable	119,000	53,000				
Costs and estimated earnings in excess of billings and uncompleted contracts	—	87,100				
Dividends receivable	500	—				
Mortgage receivable	8,311	—				
Unsecured notes receivable	18,000	—				
Inventories	217,000	117,500				
Land	34,000	42,000				
Plant and equipment (net)	717,000	408,000				
Investment in Subsidiary Corporation	151,000	—				
Accounts payable	(203,000)	(97,000)				
Dividends payable	—	(2,500)				
Mortgages payable	(592,000)	(397,311)				
Preferred stock	—	(50,000)				
Common stock	(250,000)	(100,000)				
Retained earnings	(139,311)	(47,000)				
Sales	(1,800,000)	—				
Earned revenues on contracts	—	(1,289,000)				
Cost of sales	1,155,000	—				
Cost of earned revenues on contracts	—	852,000				
Selling, general, and administrative expenses	497,000	360,000				
Interest revenue	(20,000)	—				
Interest expense	49,000	32,000				
Dividend revenue	(500)	—				
Gain on sale of land	(4,000)	—				

(AICPA adapted)

ufacturing Corporation, for the year ended December 31, 19x2. Formal statements, journal entries, and worksheet totals are not required. Round all computations to the nearest dollar. *Ignore income tax considerations.*

Problem 7–29 (for Appendix 7–A). Using the information provided in Problem 7–16, rework the problem attributing the gain or loss on the purchase of intercompany bonds entirely to the issuer. (*Hint:* Change Equity in Earnings—Subsidiary to $47,362.)

Problem 7–30 (for Appendix 7–A). Using the information provided in Problem 7–17, rework the problem attributing the gain or loss on the purchase of intercompany bonds entirely to the issuer. (*Hint:* Change Equity in Earnings—Subsidiary to $46,200

and change the Investment in S Company to $686,200.)

Problem 7–31 (for Appendix 7–A). Using the information provided in Problem 7–18, rework the problem attributing the gain or loss on the purchase of intercompany bonds entirely to the issuer. (*Hint:* Change Equity in Earnings—Subsidiary to $28,600 and change Investment in S Company to $628,600.)

Problem 7–32 (cost method). On June 30, 19x2, Linskey, Inc., purchased 100 percent of the outstanding common stock of Cresswell Corporation for $3,605,000 cash and Linskey's common stock valued at $4,100,000. At the date of purchase the book and fair values of Cresswell's assets and liabilities were as follows:

	Book value	Fair value
Cash	$ 160,000	$ 160,000
Accounts receivable, net	910,000	910,000
Inventory	860,000	1,025,186
Furniture, fixtures, and machinery	3,000,000	2,550,000
Building	9,000,000	7,250,000
Accumulated depreciation . . .	(5,450,000)	—
Intangible assets, net	150,000	220,000
Total	$8,630,000	
Accounts payable	$ 580,000	580,000
Note payable	500,000	500,000
5% mortgage note payable . . .	4,000,000	3,710,186
Common stock	2,900,000	—
Retained earnings	650,000	—
Total	$8,630,000	

By the year-end, December 31, 19x2, the net balance of Cresswell's accounts receivable at June 30, 19x2, had been collected; the inventory on hand at June 30, 19x2, had been charged to cost of goods sold; the accounts payable at June 30, 19x2, had been paid; and the $500,000 note had been paid.

As of June 30, 19x2, Cresswell's furniture, fixtures, and machinery and building had an estimated remaining life of 8 and 10 years, respectively. All intangible assets had an estimated remaining life of 20 years. All depreciation and amortization is to be computed using the straight-line method.

As of June 30, 19x2, the 5 percent mortgage note payable had eight equal annual payments remaining with the next payment due June 30, 19x3. The fair value of the note was based on a 7 percent rate.

Prior to June 30, 19x2, there were no intercompany transactions between Linskey and Cresswell; however, during the last six months of 19x2 the following intercompany transactions occurred:

1. Linskey sold $400,000 of merchandise to Cresswell. The cost of the merchandise to Linskey was $360,000. Of this merchandise, $75,000 remained on hand at December 31, 19x2.
2. On December 29, 19x2, Cresswell purchased, in the market, $300,000 of Linskey's 7 ½ percent bonds payable for $312,500, including $22,500 interest receivable. Linskey had issued $1,000,000 of these 20-year 7 ½ percent bonds payable eight years ago (January 1, 19w5) for $960,000.
3. Many of the management functions of the two companies have been consolidated since the merger. Linskey charges Cresswell a $30,000 per month management fee.

4. At December 31, 19x2, Cresswell owes Linskey two months' management fees and $18,000 for merchandise purchases.

Required:

Complete the worksheet for the preparation of a consolidated balance sheet and income statement for Linskey, Inc., and its subsidiary, Cresswell Corporation, for the year ended December 31, 19x2. Provide computations in good form where appropriate to support entries.

Linskey's profit and loss figures are for the 12-month period while Cresswell's are for the last six months. You may assume that both companies made all the adjusting entries required for separate financial statements unless an obvious discrepancy exists. *Income taxes should not be considered in your solution.* Round all computations to the nearest dollar.

Problem 7–33 (cost method). On January 1, 19x1, P Company purchased 40,000 shares of S Company in the open market for $640,000. On that date, the net assets of S Company amounted to $800,000 and had book values that approximated their respective fair market values.

On April 1, 19x1, P Company purchased 30 percent of the outstanding bonds of S Company for $170,000. Interest is payable April 1 and October 1. P Company uses the cost method to account for its investment.

Financial statements for the two corporations for the year ended December 31, 19x1, are as follows:

	P Company	S Company
Income Statement		
Sales	$2,000,000	$1,000,000
Cost of sales, expenses, and income taxes	1,580,000	880,000
Subtotal	420,000	120,000
Interest income	12,300	
Interest expense		(58,000)
Net income—carried forward	$ 432,300	$ 62,000
Retained Earnings Statement		
Balance, January 1, 19x1:		
P Company	$2,000,000	
S Company		$ 300,000
Add: Net income—brought forward	432,300	62,000
Balance, December 31, 19x1— carried forward	$2,432,300	$ 362,000

[Relates to Problem 7–32]

LINSKEY, INC., AND SUBSIDIARY
Worksheet for Consolidated Statements
For the Year Ended December 31, 19x2

	Debit	(Credit)	Consolidating Entries		Consol-idated Balances Debit (Credit)
	Linskey, Inc.	Cresswell Corpora-tion	Debit	Credit	
Cash	507,000	200,750			
Accounts receivable, net	1,890,000	817,125			
Inventory	2,031,000	1,009,500			
Furniture, fixtures, and machinery	4,200,000	3,000,000			
Buildings	17,000,000	9,000,000			
Accumulated depreciation	(8,000,000)	(6,050,000)			
Intangible assets, net	—	146,250			
Investment in subsidiary	7,705,000	—			
Investment in Linskey 7½% bonds payable, net	—	290,000			
Interest receivable	—	22,500			
Discount on 7½% bonds	24,000	—			
Accounts payable	(1,843,000)	(575,875)			
Interest payable	(200,500)	(100,000)			
Morgage notes payable	(6,786,500)	(4,000,000)			
7½% bonds payable	(1,000,000)	—			
8¼% bonds payable	(3,900,000)	—			
Common stock	(8,772,500)	(2,900,000)			
Retained earnings	(2,167,500)	(650,000)			
Sales	(26,000,000)	(6,000,000)			
Cost of goods sold	18,000,000	3,950,000			
Selling, general, and administrative expenses	3,130,000	956,000			
Management service income	(180,000)	—			
Management service expense	—	180,000			
Interest expense	662,000	100,000			
Depreciation expense	3,701,000	600,000			
Amortization expense	—	3,750			
	–0–	–0–			

(AICPA adapted)

	P Company	S Company
Balance Sheet		
Interest receivable	$ 3,600	
Investment in S Company bonds	171,500	
Investment in S Company stock	640,000	
Other assets	2,417,200	$1,631,500
Bond discount		42,500
Totals	$3,232,300	$1,674,000
Interest payable		$ 12,000
Bonds payable, 8%—due April 1, 19x6		600,000
Other liabilities	$ 300,000	200,000
Capital stock—P Company ($50 par)	500,000	
Capital stock—S Company ($10 par)		500,000
Retained earnings—brought forward	2,432,300	362,000
Totals	$3,232,300	$1,674,000

Required:

a. Compute the balance in the Bond Discount account at April 1, 19x1.

b. Compute the consolidated gain or loss on the purchase of intercompany bonds.

c. Prepare a consolidated working paper.

Problem 7–34 *(cost method).* On January 1, 19x2 P Company acquired 80 percent of the outstanding common stock of S Company for $600,000, and there have been no changes in its capital stock. The book values of the net assets of S Company approximated their respective fair market values.

On October 1, 19x2, S Company purchased 60 percent of the outstanding bonds of P Company. Interest is payable on April 1 and October 1.

P Company uses the cost method to account for its investment in S Company.

The financial statements of the companies for the year ended December 31, 19x2, are as follows:

	P Company	S Company
Income Statement		
Sales	$1,000,000	$500,000
Cost of sales, expenses, and income taxes	790,000	440,000
Subtotal	210,000	60,000
Interest income		5,500
Interest expense	(46,000)	
Net income—carried forward	$ 164,000	$ 65,500

	P Company	S Company
Retained Earnings Statement		
Balance, January 1, 19x2:		
P Company	$ 800,000	
S Company		$250,000
Add: Net income—brought forward	164,000	65,500
Balance, December 31, 19x2— carried forward	$ 964,000	$315,500
Balance Sheet		
Interest receivable		$ 6,000
Investment in P Company bonds		248,500
Investment in S Company stock	$ 600,000	
Other assets	1,448,500	661,000
Bond discount	25,500	
Totals	$2,074,000	$915,500
Interest payable	$ 10,000	
Bonds payable, 10%—due April 1, 19x7	400,000	
Other liabilities	200,000	$100,000
Capital stock—P Company ($50 par)	500,000	
Capital stock—S Company ($10 par)		500,000
Retained earings—brought forward	964,000	315,500
Totals	$2,074,000	$915,500

Required:

a. Compute the balance in the Bond Discount account at October 1, 19x2.

b. Compute the price paid by S Company for its investment in P Company bonds.

c. Compute the consolidated gain or loss on the purchase of intercompany bonds.

d. Prepare a consolidated working paper.

8

Consolidated statements—increases in parent's percentages of ownership by purchases of stock

OVERVIEW

It is not unusual for an investor (or parent company) to acquire shares of an investee in a piecemeal fashion. When this occurs, excess must be calculated separately for each purchase if consolidated statements are prepared or if the equity method must be used.

Occasionally, a parent company may acquire additional shares from its subsidiary rather than in the open market. In this case the calculation of excess becomes somewhat more complex.

Since most purchases of shares by an investor (parent company) take place at interim dates rather than at the end of a fiscal period, this necessitates the calculation of preacquisition earnings from the beginning of the fiscal period to the date of purchase.

When a business combination occurs at an interim date and pooling accounting (as discussed in Chapter 2) is to be used, a consolidated working paper for the year of the combination must be prepared as if the combination took place at the beginning of the year.

In preceding chapters the focus has been on the preparation of consolidated financial statements rather than on the manner in which the shares of a subsidiary were acquired by a parent company. This chapter deals with the problems associated with a parent company's acquisition of shares in a subsidiary. The next chapter will deal with the disposal of shares in parent-subsidiary relationships.

A parent company can purchase shares of an investee either directly from the investee or from existing stockholders. Both the percentage of the ownership interest and the manner of calculating excess are significantly affected by the method of acquisition. When shares of stock are purchased in the marketplace, the change in ownership has a full impact. For example, if a parent company owns 6,000 shares out of 10,000 total shares outstanding, or 60 percent and it purchases 2,000 shares in the marketplace, its ownership percentage increases to 80 percent. However, if instead, the parent company purchases the 2,000 shares from its subsidiary, its percentage of ownership increases to only 66 $\frac{2}{3}$ percent because the total number of shares outstanding is increased. This can be computed as follows:

	Before	After
Parent shares:	$\frac{6,000}{10,000} = 60\%$	$\frac{8,000}{12,000} = 66\frac{2}{3}\%$
Total shares:		

When shares of stock are purchased from a subsidiary, the calculation of excess, as will now be demonstrated in detail involves a different kind of calculation from that used in previous chapters where it was assumed that the shares were purchased in the open market.

PIECEMEAL ACQUISITIONS

ARB 51 contains, in part:

> When one company purchases two or more blocks of stock of another company at various dates and eventually obtains control of the other company, the date of acquisition (for the purpose of preparing consolidated statements) depends on the circumstances. If two or more purchases are made over a period of time, the earned surplus of the subsidiary at acquisition should generally be determined on a step-by-step basis; however, if small purchases are made over a period of time and then a purchase is made which results in control, the date of the latest purchase, as a matter of convenience, may be considered as the date of acquisition.[1]

To demonstrate the step-by-step principle mandated by *ARB 51*, it is assumed that P Company made the following open-market purchases of S Company's·common stock:

Date	Number of shares	Percent of total	Price paid
January 2, 19x1	2,000	20	$300,000
January 2, 19x3	2,000	20	320,000
January 2, 19x5	4,000	40	900,000

---

[1]*AICPA,* "Consolidated Financial Statements," *ARB Bulletin No. 51* (New York, 1959), par. 10. © American Institute of Certified Public Accountants.

It is also assumed that S Company had no changes in its $100 Par Value Common Stock account, had additional paid-in capital of $20,000, and that its retained earnings were:

Date	Amount
January 2, 19x1	$300,000
January 2, 19x3	500,000
January 2, 19x5	800,000

The step-by-step calculation of excess would be:

Date	Common stock	Additional paid-in capital	Retained earnings	Total net assets	Percent purchased	Percent of net assets	Price paid	Excess
January 2, 19x1 .	$1,000,000	$20,000	$300,000	$1,320,000	20	$ 264,000	$ 300,000	$ 36,000
January 2, 19x3 .	1,000,000	20,000	500,000	1,520,000	20	304,000	320,000	16,000
January 2, 19x5 .	1,000,000	20,000	800,000	1,820,000	40	728,000	900,000	172,000
Totals					80	$1,296,000	$1,520,000	$224,000

The calculation of excess on the date control is achieved (January 2, 19x5), would be:

Total price paid	$1,520,000
Less: 80% of net assets (80% × $1,820,000)	1,456,000
Excess of cost	$ 64,000

The difference between the two methods ($224,000 − $64,000) is $160,000, and this amount consists of:

20% ($1,820,000 − $1,320,000)	$100,000
20% ($1,820,000 − $1,520,000)	60,000
Total	$160,000

In essence, the calculation of excess on the date control is achieved fails to take into account the increase in the net assets of S Company in relation to the price paid for the shares on a specific earlier date. The price paid for shares of stock usually bears some relationship to the net assets acquired and, therefore, the step-by-step calculation of excess is the proper one because it relates the price paid on a specific date to the proportion of net assets acquired on that date. The net result of the difference in this example is an understatement of $160,000 of the excess and retained earnings, respectively. In this example, the first purchase was for 20 percent of the investee's outstanding shares, and *APB Opinion 18* requires that excess be calculated on this and subsequent purchases in the application of the equity method.[2]

---

[2]APB, "The Equity Method of Accounting for Investments in Common Stock," *APB Opinion No. 18* (New York: AICPA, 1971), par. 19b.

CONVERSION FROM COST METHOD TO EQUITY METHOD

If an investor owns less than 20 percent of an investee and is unable to exercise significant influence over its operating and financial policies, the investor should account for its investment using the cost method.[3] However, if the investor increases its percentage of ownership to 20 percent or more and is able to exercise substantial influence over the affairs of the investee, conversion to the equity method is required including the *retroactive* application of the equity method to the earlier purchases on a step-by-step basis.[4] The retroactive application for the earlier years is treated as a change in the reporting entity[5] and a restatement of the prior period comparative results is required, if the effects are material.[6]

Illustration 8–1
SUN COMPANY
Selected Data

	19x4	19x5	19x6
Retained earnings, January 1	$150,000	$200,000	$260,000
Net income for the year ended December 31	80,000	100,000	120,000
Dividends paid for the year ended December 31	30,000	40,000	50,000

It is now assumed that Prop Corporation made the following purchases of Sun Company's common stock:

Date	Number of shares	Percent of total	Price paid
January 2, 19x4	1,000	10	$ 30,000
January 2, 19x6	3,000	30	148,000
January 2, 19x7	5,000	50	300,000

In addition, the following is also assumed:

1. There were no changes in Sun Company's Common Stock account from the original issuance of 10,000 shares at a par value of $10 per share. The shares were issued at par value, and there is no capital in excess of par value.
2. All of the assets and liabilities of the investee are stated at fair market values.
3. The excess, if any, is to be amortized over 40 years.
4. The retained earnings, net income, and dividends of Sun Company are as shown in Illustration 8–1.
5. Income tax effects are to be ignored.

The calculation of excess appears in Illustration 8–2. The journal entries below on the books of Prop Corporation for 19x4 and 19x5 reflect the use of the cost method, and for 19x6, the equity method was used together with a retroactive application of the equity method for 19x4 and 19x5. The entries for dividends and income are summary entries for the respective years.

[3]Ibid., par. 17.
[4]Ibid., par 19m.
[5]*AICPA Codification of Statement on Auditing Standards,* (New York, 1978), par. AU 420.07.
[6]APB, "Accounting Changes," *APB Opinion No. 20* AICPA (New York: AICPA, 1971), par. 34.

Illustration 8–2
PROP CORPORATION
Calculation of Excess of Cost

Date	Common stock	Retained earnings	Total net assets	Percent purchased	Net assets purchased	Price paid	Excess
January 2, 19x4	$100,000	$150,000	$250,000	10	$ 25,000	$ 30,000	$ 5,000
January 2, 19x6	100,000	260,000	360,000	30	108,000	148,000	40,000
January 2, 19x7	100,000	330,000	430,000	50	215,000	300,000	85,000

Parent's Books

(1)

1/2/x4	Investment in Sun Company	30,000	
	Cash		30,000
	Purchased 1,000 shares.		

(2)

12/31/x4	Cash	3,000	
	Dividend Income		3,000

(3)

12/31/x5	Cash	4,000	
	Dividend Income		4,000

(4)

1/2/x6	Investment in Sun Company	148,000	
	Cash		148,000
	Purchased 3,000 shares.		

(5)

Investment in Sun Company	4,875	
Retained Earnings—Adjustment for Equity in Earnings of Investee for 19x4		4,875

To convert the investment to the equity method from the cost method as follows:

19x4 income	$ 80,000
Less: Dividends paid	30,000
Undistributed income	$ 50,000
10% of above	$ 5,000
Less: Amortization of excess: $5,000 ÷ 40 years (see Illustration 8–2) =	125
Net adjustment	$ 4,875

(6)

Investment in Sun Company	5,875	
Retained Earnings—Adjustment for Equity in Earnings of Investee for 19x5		5,875

To convert the investment to the equity method from the cost method as follows:

19x5 income	$100,000
Less: Dividends paid	40,000
Undistributed income	$ 60,000
10% of above	$ 6,000
Less: Amortization of excess: $5,000 ÷ 40 years =	125
Net adjustment	$ 5,875

(7)

12/31/x6	Investment in Sun Company	48,000	
	Equity in Earnings of Investee		48,000
	40% × $120,000 (19x6 earnings).		

(8)

Equity in Earnings of Investee	1,125	
Investment in Sun Company		1,125
To record amortization of excess for 19x6 as		
follows (see Illustration 8–2):		

$5,000 ÷ 40 years =	$ 125
$40,000 ÷ 40 years =	1,000
	$1,125

(9)

Cash	20,000	
Investment in Sun Company		20,000
To record dividends received in 19x6 (40% ×		
$50,000 = $20,000).		

(10)

1/2/x7	Investment in Sun Company	300,000	
	Cash		300,000
	Purchased 5,000 shares.		

Subsequent accounting and consolidation procedures will be handled in accordance with the principles discussed in preceding chapters.

PURCHASE OF SHARES FROM A SUBSIDIARY

Occasionally, a parent company purchases shares of stock from its subsidiary in order to increase its share of ownership. If, for instance, a parent company owns 70 percent of the outstanding shares of its subsidiary and it wishes to increase its ownership to 80 percent in order to derive a favorable tax treatment (see appendix in Chapter 2 and Appendix 5–A in Chapter 5), it may purchase the necessary shares directly from the subsidiary provided the stock is not subject to preemptive rights (the right of stockholders to subscribe to new issuances of stock on a prorata basis). As indicated earlier, the percentage purchased and the calculation of excess is different from that when shares are purchased in the open market.

To illustrate the difference in treatment, it is now assumed that:

1. Prop Corporation on January 2, 19x2, purchased in the open market 7,000 shares of Set Company stock for $300,000. On that date Set Company's net assets consisted of:

$10 par value common stock	$100,000
Additional paid-in capital	50,000
Retained earnings	250,000
	$400,000

2. On January 2, 19x3, Prop Corporation purchased 5,000 shares of common stock directly from Set Company for $400,000.

3. All of the net assets on the books of Set Company were stated at fair market values on January 2, 19x2, and January 2, 19x3.

4. During 19x2, Set Company earned $160,000 and paid dividends of $60,000. This resulted in a net increase in retained earnings of $100,000 for 19x2.

The calculation of excess can be computed as follows:

First purchase, January 2, 19x2:
Price paid $300,000
Less: 70% of Set Company's net assets of $400,000 280,000
Excess of cost . . . . $ 20,000

Second purchase, January 2, 19x3:

	Ownership percentages	
	Before	*After*
Shares owned =	$\frac{7,000}{10,000}$ = 70%	$\frac{12,000}{15,000}$ = 80%
Total shares		

	Net assets	
	Before	*After*
$400,000 plus $100,000 net increase in retained earnings for 19x2	$500,000	
$500,000 plus $400,000 cash payment . . .		$900,000

	Calculation of excess
After second purchase:	
80% × $900,000	$720,000
Before second purchase:	
70% × $500,000	350,000
Difference	370,000
Price paid	400,000
Excess of cost	$ 30,000

This can be verified by computing the $50 book value per share before the purchase ($500,000 ÷ 10,000 shares outstanding) and comparing this to the price paid per share of $80 ($400,000 ÷ 5,000 shares). The difference of $30 per share paid in excess of book value multiplied by the 5,000 shares purchased produces a total excess of $150,000. Of this amount, 80 percent reverts back to the parent company and 20 percent or $30,000 inures to the benefit of the minority interest. The portion applicable to the minority interest represents the excess paid by the parent company.

PURCHASES OF STOCK AT INTERIM DATES— PURCHASE ACCOUNTING

Most investments in stock are usually made on days other than the first or last day of a particular year. Previously, all illustrations were assumed to be made at the beginning of a year. Interim purchases will now be considered.

As is the case when a depreciable asset is purchased on an interim date and the depreciation expense is apportioned within the fiscal year, income from a subsidiary purchased on an interim date must also be apportioned. *ARB 51* contains

> When a subsidiary is purchased during the year, there are alternative ways of dealing with the results of its operations in the consolidated income statement. One method, which usually is preferable, especially where there are several dates of acquisition of blocks of shares, is to include the subsidiary in the consolidation as though it had been acquired at the beginning of the year, and to deduct at the bottom of the consolidated income statement the preacquisition earnings applicable to each block of stock. This method presents results which are more indicative of the current status of the group, and facilitates future comparison with subsequent years.[7]

Since the preferable treatment, as indicated above, is to deduct the preacquisition income on the bottom of the income statement, this method will be used henceforth. To illustrate this method, it is assumed that Gurd Corporation purchased 80 percent of the outstanding shares of Drum Corporation for $460,000 on April 1, 19x3. It is also assumed that:

1. Drum Corporation's income is earned uniformly throughout the year. (If this were not the case, an income statement would be required for the first three months in addition to the annual statement and the income apportionment would be based on such income statements.)
2. Gurd Corporation uses the complete equity method to account for its investment in Drum Corporation.
3. The retained earnings of Drum Corporation were $220,000 on January 1, 19x3. There were no changes in the Capital Stock account during 19x3.
4. The recorded net assets of Drum Corporation approximated their fair market values on April 1, 19x3.
5. Goodwill is to be amortized over 40 years.
6. Dividends are paid ratably, on the last day of each quarter.
7. For the year ended December 31, 19x3, Gurd Corporation had the following summary entries recorded on its books:

Parent's Books

(1)

Cash	24,000	
Investment in Drum Corporation		24,000
For dividends received 3 × (80% × $10,000 per quarter).		

(2)

Investment in Drum Corporation	35,250	
Equity in Earnings of Subsidiary		35,250

To record income earned by subsidiary (80% × $60,000

$\times \frac{9}{12}$) = $36,000 minus $750 of goodwill amortization

($40,000 ÷ 40 years) × $\frac{9}{12}$.

The elimination entries for Illustration 8–3 are:

---

[7]*ARB 51,* par. 11.

	(1)		
Equity in Earnings—Subsidiary		35,250	
Dividends Declared—Drum Corporation			32,000
Investment in Drum Corporation			3,250

	(2)		
Preacquisition Income		12,000	
Retained Earnings (1/1/x3)—Drum Corporation		176,000	
Goodwill		40,000	
Capital Stock—Drum Corporation		240,000	
Investment in Drum Corporation			468,000

	(3)		
Amortization of Goodwill (expenses)		750	
Goodwill			750

Illustration 8–3 contains the appropriate consolidated working paper. The following should be noted:

1. Goodwill of $40,000 is arrived at as follows:

Price paid for investment		$460,000
Less: *80% of net assets on April 1, 19x3:*		
Capital stock	$300,000	
Retained earnings, January 1, 19x3	220,000	
Add: Income, January 1, 19x3 to March 31, 19x3 (3/12 × $60,000)	15,000	
Less: Dividends paid March 31, 19x3 (1/4 × $40,000)	(10,000)	
Net assets, April 1, 19x3	$525,000	
80% of above		420,000
Goodwill		$ 40,000

2. Preacquisition income ($12,000) is deducted in the consolidated income statement to arrive at net income, since sales, cost of sales, expenses, etc., are carried to the consolidated statement for the *full* year even though the income from the subsidiary is earned for only nine months.

3. Although Gurd Corporation received only dividends for three quarters of the year, the full year's dividends (80% × $40,000) are eliminated. Since it is necessary for $8,000 of dividends (20% × $40,000) to be allocated to the minority interest, the dividend paid to the prior owners of the parent's shares are eliminated together with the dividends received by the parents.

4. The amortization of goodwill as shown in entry (3) is for nine months and is computed as $750 ($40,000 ÷ 40 years = $1,000 × 9/12 = $750).

PREFERRED STOCK PURCHASES ON INTERIM DATES

The principles governing interim purchases of common stocks apply also to interim purchases of preferred stocks with one modification pertaining to preacquisition income. The procedure for calculating excess on an interim date is the same for all classes of stock, and by incorporating the principles discussed in this chapter and in the preceding chapter, the calculation of excess on preferred stock purchases presents no new problems. The treatment of preacquisition income, however, is different for preferred stock

Illustration 8–3
GURD CORPORATION
Consolidated Working Paper
December 31, 19x3

Complete Equity Method
First year
80 Percent Subsidiary

	Gurd Corp.	Drum Corp. (80%)	Eliminations Dr.	Eliminations Cr.	Minority Interest	Consol-idated
Income Statement						
Sales	900,000	400,000				1,300,000
Cost of sales	300,000	150,000				450,000
Gross margin	600,000	250,000				850,000
Expenses	200,000	150,000	(3) 750			350,750
Operating income before taxes	400,000	100,000				499,250
Equity in earnings—subsidiary	35,250		(1) 35,250			
Income before taxes	435,250	100,000				
Provision for income taxes	160,000	40,000				200,000
						299,250
Minority interest net income					12,000	(12,000)
Preacquisition income			(2) 12,000			(12,000)
Net income—carried forward	275,250	60,000			12,000	275,250
Retained Earnings Statement						
Balance, 1/1/x3:						
Gurd Corp.	500,000					500,000
Drum Corp.		220,000	(2) 176,000		44,000	
Net income—brought forward	275,250	60,000			12,000	275,250
Totals	775,250	280,000			56,000	775,250
Less: Dividends declared:						
Gurd Corp.	100,000					100,000
Drum Corp.		40,000		(1) 32,000	8,000	
Balance, 12/31/x3—carried forward	675,250	240,000			48,000	675,250
Balance Sheet						
Other assets	888,000	600,000				1,488,000
				(2) 468,000		
Investment in Drum Corp.	471,250			(1) 3,250		
Goodwill			(2) 40,000	(3) 750		39,250
Totals	1,359,250	600,000				1,527,250
Liabilities	184,000	60,000				244,000
Capital stock:						
Gurd Corp.	500,000					500,000
Drum Corp.		300,000	(2) 240,000		60,000	
Retained earnings—brought forward	675,250	240,000			48,000	675,250
Minority interest					108,000	108,000
Totals	1,359,250	600,000	504,000	504,000		1,527,250

(1) Elimination of equity in earnings of subsidiary.
(2) Elimination of balance of investment and to record preacquisition income.
(3) Amortization of goodwill ($40,000 ÷ 40 years = $1000 × $\frac{9}{12}$ = $750.

Illustration 8–3 (*continued*)

Computations and Proofs

Income apportionment:

	Total	Parent	Minority
Income—Drum Corp.	$ 60,000	$ 48,000	$ 12,000
Less: Preacquisition income	(12,000)	(12,000)	
Income—Gurd Corp. ($275,250 − $35,250)	240,000	240,000	
Amortization—goodwill	(750)	(750)	
	$287,250	$275,250	$ 12,000

Reconciliation—minority interest:

Capital stock	$300,000
Retained earnings—end of year	240,000
Total equity	$540,000
Minority interest—20%	$108,000

from that of common stock. For common stock, income is prorated if it is earned uniformly or the actual income for interim periods is used when income is not earned uniformly. For preferred stocks, however, preacquisition income relates to dividend declaration rather than to earnings. For cumulative preferred stock it is customary to assume that dividends accrue ratably during the year—even though this is not the case, legally. In the case of noncumulative preferred stock, however, recognition of preacquisition dividend income depends on actual dividend declaration. Thus, if a preferred stock is noncumulative, preacquisition income is limited to actual dividends *declared.*

POOLING ACCOUNTING

In Chapter 2 on business combinations, the attributes of pooling accounting were discussed and statutory mergers accounted for as poolings were illustrated. We turn now to pooling accounting for parent-subsidiary relationships.

It should be remembered that the end-products, i.e., the financial statements, are the same for a merger and a parent-subsidiary relationship. In the latter case there are two independent sets of books, but after preparing the consolidated working papers, the consolidated financial statements which result are identical to those prepared when a statutory merger has taken place. Therefore, although there are different amounts that an investment can be recorded at for pooling accounting, the end-product (the financial statements) will always be the same regardless of the amount recorded for the investment. The two most widely used methods are: (1) to record the investment at the book value of the net assets, and (2) to record the investment at the legal capital (par value). The simplest one to use is the book value method and this is the one that will be used exclusively in this book.

Illustration 8–4
JAMES COMPANY AND POOL COMPANY
Post-Closing Trial Balances
January 1,19x2

	James Company	Pool Company
Assets	$900,000	$700,000
Liabilities	$100,000	$200,000
Common stock—$100 par value	500,000	200,000
Additional paid-in capital	—	150,000
Retained earnings	300,000	150,000
Totals	$900,000	$700,000

If the James Company were to acquire 90 percent of the Pool Company on January 1, 19x2, by exchanging 3,000 of its $100 par value common stock for 1,800 shares (90 percent) of Pool Company, the entry to record the acquisition, assuming that all requisites for a pooling have been met, would be:

Parent's Books

Investment in Pool Company	450,000	
Common Stock		300,000
Retained Earnings—From Pool Company		135,000
Additional Paid-In Capital		15,000

To record the acquisition of 90 percent of Pool Company's outstanding shares, to record the investment at 90 percent of the net assets ($700,000 − $200,000), and to carry forward 90 percent of Pool Company's retained earnings.

If, immediately after the business combination, a consolidated working paper were to be prepared, it would appear as in Illustration 8–5. The trial balances in Illustration 8–4 combined with the journal entry above comprise the basis for the first two columns of the working paper.

The elimination entry for Illustration 8–5 is:

(1)		
Capital Stock—Pool Company	180,000	
Additional Paid-In Capital—Pool Company	135,000	
Retained Earnings—Pool Company	135,000	
Investment in Pool Company		450,000

A study of Illustration 8–5 reveals that the elimination entry has been simplified so that 90 percent of each element of stockholders' equity is eliminated and the minority interest calculation is proven since it represents exactly 10 percent of each element. Recording the investment at any amount other than $450,000 complicates the elimination entry even though the final result would be the same. It should be recalled that pooling accounting leaves the acquiree's book values intact and, therefore, no goodwill can ever arise in such a business combination.

Except for acquisitions on interim dates, a consolidated working paper, subsequent to the date of acquisition, is no different for pooling accounting that it would be for purchase accounting. Under either method, the investment can be carried at equity or cost and the elimination procedures would be the same for pooling as for purchase accounting. The difference between the pooling and purchase methods is significant *on the date of acquisition*

Illustration 8–5
JAMES COMPANY
Consolidated Working Paper
January 1, 19x2

Date of Acquisition—Pooling
90 Percent Subsidiary

	James Co.	Pool Co. (90%)	Eliminations Dr.	Eliminations Cr.	Minority Interest	Consol- idated
Balance Sheet						
Assets	900,000	700,000				1,600,000
Investment in Pool Co.	450,000			(1) 450,000		
Totals	1,350,000	700,000				
Liabilities	100,000	200,000				300,000
Capital stock:						
James Co.	800,000					800,000
Pool Co.		200,000	(1) 180,000		20,000	
Additional paid-in capital:						
James Co.	15,000					15,000
Pool Co.		150,000	(1) 135,000		15,000	
Retained earnings:						
James Co.	435,000					435,000
Pool Co.		150,000	(1) 135,000		15,000	
Minority interest					50,000	50,000
	1,350,000	700,000	450,000	450,000		1,600,000

only. Once the business combination is recorded, consolidation procedures are the same for either method except for acquisitions made on interim dates.

ACQUISITION ON AN INTERIM DATE

For purchase accounting only, subsidiary income earned subsequent to the date of acquisition is included in consolidated net income. This is not true for pooling accounting. For pooling accounting, subsidiary income for the entire year is included in consolidated net income regardless of the date of the combination. Even if the combination takes place on the last day of a year (December 31), the entire year's income is included. The reason for this is that a pooling is considered a change of entity[8] and restatement is required.[9] Not only is restatement required for the year of the acquisition, but all comparative statements presented (5-year or 10-year comparatives) must also be restated as if the combination had taken place prior to the earliest statement presented. Therefore, when a pooling takes place on an interim date such as April 1, 19x3, the simplest treatment is to work on the assump-

[8]*APB 20,* par. 12.
[9]*APB 20,* par. 34.

tion as if the combination took place at the beginning of the period, i.e., January 1, 19x3. Consequently, we would use the book value on this date to record the investment, rather than use the April 1, 19x3, book value. Under this procedure the treatment of income for the year 19x3 will be the same as if purchase accounting was used as of January 1, 19x3.

However, if a dividend was declared prior to the date of a pooling, the dividend must be considered in the calculation of the amount at which to record the investment. To demonstrate the nature of this problem, it is now assumed that:

1. Gurd Corporation issued 5,400 shares of its $50 par value common stock to acquire 90 percent of Drum Corporation's outstanding stock on July 1, 19x3, and all conditions for a pooling have been met.
2. Trial balance data as of December 31, 19x3, appear in Illustration 8–6. Dividends were paid equally for the year on the last day of each quarter.

The entry on Gurd's books to record the acquisition on July 1, 19x3, would be:

Parent's Books

7/1/x3	Investment in Drum Corporation	441,000	
	Common Stock		270,000
	Retained Earnings—Pooled Subsidiary		171,000

To record the issuance of 5,400 shares of common stock to acquire 27,000 shares of Drum Corporation common stock and to record the transaction at book value as of January 1, 19x3, as follows:

Drum Corporation—common stock	$300,000
Drum Corporation—retained earnings as of 1/1/x3	200,000
Net assets at book value	500,000
Less: Dividends declared prior to acquisition (2 × $5,000 per quarter)	(10,000)
Basis for recording pooling	$490,000
90% of above	$441,000

Using the complete equity method to account for its investment, the parent company would make the following additional entries for 19x3:

Parent's Books

9/30/x3	Cash	4,500	
	Investment in Drum Corporation		4,500
	To record dividends received (90% × $5,000).		

12/31/x3	Cash	4,500	
	Investment in Drum Corporation		4,500
	To record dividends received.		

Investment in Drum Corporation	54,000	
Equity in Earnings of Subsidiary		54,000

To record 90% × $60,000 of net income earned for a full year by the pooled subsidiary.

The elimination entries for Illustration 8–6 are:

(1)		
Equity in Earnings—Subsidiary	54,000	
Dividends Declared—Drum Corporation		9,000
Investment in Drum Corporation		45,000

(2)		
Retained Earnings (1/1/x3)—Drum Corporation	180,000	
Capital Stock—Drum Corporation	270,000	
Dividends Declared—Drum Corporation		9,000
Investment in Drum Corporation		441,000

The following observations pertaining to Illustration 8–6 should be noted:

1. Although the journal entry on July 1, 19x3, segregates the pooling retained earnings of the subsidiary on the parent's books for management's use, on the working papers the $171,000 was combined with the parent's retained earnings of $329,000 to arrive at the combined amount of $500,000. It is not customary to segregate the source of retained earnings on financial statements for external use.

2. In elimination entry (1), $9,000 of dividends were eliminated. This approach causes the investment balance to revert back to the amount at which the investment was initially recorded ($441,000). An alternate approach which results in identical consolidated statements is to credit dividends for the full 90 percent of $20,000 or $18,000. If this approach were used, the working paper elimination entries would be:

(1)		
Equity in Earnings of Subsidiary	54,000	
Dividends		18,000
Investment in Drum Corporation		36,000

(2)		
Retained Earnings(1/1/x3)—Drum	180,000	
Common Stock—Drum	270,000	
Investment in Drum Corporation		450,000

Thus it can be seen that the net effect of the above elimination entries are identical to the ones used in Illustration 8–6 and either approach is acceptable.

3. The full year's income is included in the consolidated income statement despite the fact that the business combination was consummated on July 1, 19x3.

4. The common stock of the parent company includes the $270,000 from its book entry on July 1, 19x3.

INTERCOMPANY TRANSACTIONS

Intercompany profits in inventories, plant assets, and intercompany purchases of bonds present no new problems in pooling accounting. Since pooling accounting affects only the amount at which the business combination is recorded on the date of acquisition, the only difference between

Illustration 8–6
GURD CORPORATION
Consolidated Working Paper
December 31, 19x3

Complete Equity Method
First Year—Pooling
90 Percent Subsidiary

	Gurd Corp.	Drum Corp. (90%)	Eliminations		Minority Interest	Consol-idated
			Dr.	Cr.		
Income Statement						
Sales	900,000	400,000				1,300,000
Cost of sales	300,000	150,000				450,000
Gross margin	600,000	250,000				850,000
Expenses	200,000	150,000				350,000
Operating income before taxes	400,000	100,000				500,000
Equity in earnings—subsidiary	54,000		(1) 54,000			
Income before taxes	454,000	100,000				
Provision for income taxes	160,000	40,000				200,000
						300,000
Minority interest net income					6,000	(6,000)
Net income—carried forward	294,000	60,000			6,000	294,000
Retained Earnings Statement						
Balance, 1/1/x3:						
Gurd Corp.	500,000					500,000
Drum Corp.		200,000	(2) 180,000		20,000	
Net income—brought forward	294,000	60,000			6,000	294,000
Totals	794,000	260,000			26,000	794,000
Less: Dividends declared:						
Gurd Corp.	100,000					100,000
				(2) 9,000		
Drum Corp.		20,000		(1) 9,000	2,000	
Balance, 12/31/x3—carried forward	694,000	240,000			24,000	694,000
Balance Sheet						
Other assets	862,000	600,000				1,462,000
				(2) 441,000		
Investment in Drum Corp.	486,000			(1) 45,000		
Totals	1,348,000	600,000				1,462,000
Liabilities	84,000	60,000				144,000
Capital stock:						
Gurd Corp.—$50 P.V.	570,000					570,000
Drum Corp.—$10 P.V.		300,000	(2) 270,000		30,000	
Retained earnings—brought forward	694,000	240,000			24,000	694,000
Minority interest					54,000	54,000
Totals	1,348,000	600,000	504,000	504,000		1,462,000

(1) Elimination of equity in earnings of subsidiary, dividends received and to restore investment back to balance on date of business combination.

(2) Elimination of investment balance and dividends paid prior to date of business combination.

Note: Minority interest net income is 10 percent of subsidiary net income and minority interest is 10 percent of the subsidiary's net assets on 12/31/73. There are no reconciling items.

purchase accounting and pooling accounting is in the carrying amounts of specific assets and liabilities and their subsequent amortization. Under pooling accounting excess cannot exist, and, therefore, no amortization is possible. However, transactions *subsequent* to the date of the business combination are treated identically, regardless of how a business combination is recorded. Therefore, the principles enunciated in Chapters 5, 6, and 7 apply equally to purchase and pooling accounting.

Appendix:
Preacquisition income—
cost method

When the investment is accounted for by the cost method, consolidation working papers that involve preacquisition income for purchase accounting are slightly different from those using the complete equity method. To demonstrate the differences, Illustration 8–3 will be reworked using the cost method and the result is Illustration 8–7.

The elimination entries for Illustration 8–7 are:

(1)

Dividend Income	24,000	
Dividends Declared—		
Drum Corporation		24,000

(2)

Purchased Income	12,000	
Retained Earnings (1/1/x3)—		
Drum Corporation	176,000	
Goodwill	40,000	
Capital Stock—Drum		
Corporation	240,000	
Dividends Declared—		
Drum Corporation		8,000
Investment in Drum		
Corporation		460,000

(3)

Amortization of Goodwill		
(Expenses)	750	
Goodwill		750

The major differences between these two illustrations are:

1. Instead of $35,250 of income from the subsidiary, the parent company's books reflect only dividend income of $24,000.
2. The investment in Drum Corporation would be carried at $460,000, the price paid for the investment.

The consolidated columns of the two illustrations are, of course, identical. (See illustration 8–7.)

Illustration 8–7
GURD CORPORATION
Consolidated Working Paper
December 31, 19x3

Cost Method
First Year
80 Percent Subsidiary

	Gurd Corp.	Drum Corp. (80%)	Eliminations Dr.	Eliminations Cr.	Minority Interest	Consol-idated
Income Statement						
Sales	900,000	400,000				1,300,000
Cost of sales	300,000	150,000				450,000
Gross margin	600,000	250,000				850,000
Expenses	200,000	150,000	(3) 750			350,750
Operating income before taxes	400,000	100,000				499,250
Dividend income	24,000		(1) 24,000			
Income before taxes	424,000	100,000				
Provision for income taxes	160,000	40,000				200,000
						299,250
Minority interest net income					12,000	(12,000)
Preacqusition income			(2) 12,000			(12,000)
Net income—carried forward	264,000	60,000			12,000	275,250
Retained Earnings Statement						
Balance, 1/1/x3:						
Gurd Corp.	500,000					500,000
Drum Corp.		220,000	(2) 176,000		44,000	
Net income—brought forward	264,000	60,000			12,000	275,250
Totals	764,000	280,000			56,000	775,250
Less: Dividends declared:						
Gurd Corp.	100,000					100,000
				(2) 8,000		
Drum Corp.		40,000		(1) 24,000	8,000	
Balance, 12/31/x3—carried forward	664,000	240,000			48,000	675,250
Balance Sheet						
Other assets	888,000	600,000				1,488,000
Investment in Drum Corp.	460,000			(2) 460,000		
Goodwill			(2) 40,000	(3) 750		39,250
Totals	1,348,000	600,000				1,527,250
Liabilities	184,000	60,000				244,000
Capital stock:						
Gurd Corp.	500,000					500,000
Drum Corp.		300,000	(2) 240,000		60,000	
Retained earnings—brought forward	664,000	240,000			48,000	675,250
Minority interest					108,000	108,000
Totals	1,348,000	600,000	492,750	492,750		1,527,250

(1) Elimination of intercompany dividend.
(2) Elimination of balance of investment and to record preqcquisition income.
(3) Amortization of goodwill.

Illustration 8–7 (*continued*)

Computations and Proofs

See Illustration 8–3 for income apportionment and reconciliation of minority interest.

Reconciliation—retained earnings:

Retained earnings—per books, 12/31/x3		$664,000
Add: Increase in net assets:		
S Co. retained earnings, 12/31/x3	$240,000	
Date of acquisition ($220,000 + $15,000 income minus $10,000 of dividends)	225,000	
Net increase	$ 15,000	
80% of above		12,000
Less: Amortization of goodwill ($40,000 ÷ 40 years = $1,000 × 9/12)		(750)
Consolidated retained earnings . . . . : . .		$675,250

QUESTIONS

1. An investor (parent company) can purchase shares either in the open market or from the investee (subsidiary) directly. From the point of view of accounting, does the source of such purchase make a difference? Explain.

2. What is the appropriate treatment for calculating excess when an investor acquires its shares on a piecemeal basis instead of all in one purchase? Explain and discuss your answer.

3. When an investor owns less than 20 percent of an investee's outstanding shares and then purchases additional shares to increase its percentage to 20 percent or more, what is the appropriate treatment with regard to the shares acquired prior to the date on which 20 percent or more ownership is achieved? Does this treatment constitute a change in accordance with *APB Opinion 20?* If so, what type of change and what treatment is appropriate in the circumstances?

4. How is excess calculated when a parent company purchases additional shares from its subsidiary? Is this the same way excess is calculated when shares are purchased in the open market?

5. What procedure is used with regard to income earned by a subsidiary when a parent company ac-

quires its investment during an interim period? How is this income treated on a consolidated working paper for the year in which the interim purchase is made? Does this procedure also apply for piecemeal acquisitions made at interim dates?

6. Does the procedure above in 5 also apply to interim preferred stock purchases? Is there a difference between the application for common stock purchases and preferred stock purchases? Explain.

7. When a parent company acquires its shares on an interim date, is there a difference between a pooling working paper and a purchase working paper? Why is this so?

8. When a dividend is declared by an investee prior to the date of a pooling, how is this dividend treated for purposes of calculating the amount at which to record the investment by the parent company?

9. Is there a difference in the treatment of intercompany transactions between pooling working papers and purchase working paper? Why?

10. Is there a difference in calculating excess for purchase working papers as opposed to pooling working papers? Explain.

EXERCISES

Exercise 8–1. P Company made the following purchases of S Company's common stock in the open market:

Date	Number of shares	Percent of total	Price paid
January 2, 19x3	4,000	20	$120,000
July 2, 19x3	2,000	10	60,000

On January 2, 19x3, S Company had 20,000 shares outstanding. The stock has a par value of $10 per share and the retained earnings on that date were $300,000. For 19x3, S Company earned $80,000 (earned evenly) and paid dividends of $1 per share on December 1, 19x3. Excess, if any, cannot be assigned to any specific assets of S Company, and it has an indefinite useful life.

Required:

   a. Calculate excess on a step-by-step basis.

   b. Calculate the amount that P Company should report as equity in earnings of investee for 19x3.

   c. Calculate the balance that P Company should have in its investment account at December 31, 19x3.

Exercise 8–2. P Company made the following purchases of S Company's common stock in the open market:

Date	Number of shares	Percent of total	Price paid
January 2, 19x3	2,000	10	$ 60,000
January 2, 19x5	4,000	20	148,000

On January 2, 19x3, S Company had 20,000 shares outstanding. The stock had a par value of $10 per share, and the retained earnings on that date were $300,000. For 19x3, S Company earned $80,000 (earned evenly) and paid dividends of $1 per share on December 1, 19x3. Excess, if any, cannot be assigned to any specific assets of S Company, and it has an indefinite useful life.

For 19x4 and 19x5, S Company earned $100,000 and $140,000, respectively. Dividends for both years were $1 per share paid in December of each year.

Required:

   a. Calculate excess on a step-by-step basis.

   b. Calculate the amount that P Company should have reported as investment income for:

   1. 19x3.
   2. 19x4.
   3. 19x5.

   c. Calculate the amount of the retroactive adjustment for 19x5 that should be treated as a prior period adjustment.

   d. Calculate the balance in the investment account at December 31, 19x5.

Exercise 8–3. On January 2, 19x4, P Company owned 50 percent of the outstanding common stock of S Company. These shares were purchased at book value.

On that date, S Company had 20,000 shares of common stock outstanding with a par value of $10 per share. Retained earnings on that date amounted to $200,000.

P Company purchased 5,000 additional shares of common stock directly from S Company on January 2, 19x4, paying $50 per share for the shares. For 19x4, S Company reported a net income of $80,000 and paid dividends of 30,000.

Required:

   a. Prepare the journal entry to be made by S Company to record the sale of the 5,000 shares to P Company.

   b. What percentage of stock does P Company own after its purchase of the 5,000 additional shares?

   c. Compute the excess on the purchase of the 5,000 shares.

   d. Compute the amount of investment income that P Company should record for 19x4. (Use the complete equity method and 40-year amortization of excess.)

   e. Compute the balance in the investment account at December 31, 19x4.

Exercise 8–4. P Company made the following purchases of the common stock of S Company in the open market:

Date	Number of shares	Percent purchased	Price paid
January 2, 19x1 . .	10,000	25	$ 75,000
May 1, 19x1	8,000	20	68,000
October 1, 19x1 . .	12,000	30	117,000

All purchases were made at book value.

S Company earned $120,000 evenly for 19x1 and paid no dividends.

Required:

a. Compute the net assets of S company at January 2, 19x1.

b. Compute the amount of preacquisition income P Company should report in its consolidated income statement for 19x1.

c. Compute the amount of minority interest net income.

d. Compute the amount of equity in earnings of subsidiary that P Company would record.

e. Reconcile your answers for (b), (c), and (d) above with the net income of S Company for 19x1.

Exercise 8–5 (preferred stock). Press Corporation purchased the following stock of Sleep Products Corporation on July 1, 19x3:

	Price paid
30% of preferred	$ 147,600
80% of common	1,665,600

The net assets of Sleep Products Corporation on January 1, 19x3, consisted of:

12% preferred stock ($100 par)	$ 400,000
Common stock ($10 par)	1,000,000
Premium on preferred stock	100,000
Premium on common stock	300,000
Retained earnings	700,000
Total	$2,500,000

The preferred stock is cumulative, nonparticipating, and is callable at 105. Dividends are in arrears for 19x2, and no dividends have been declared for 19x3. Sleep Products Corporation reported a net income of $98,000 for 19x3. (*Hint:* Accrue preferred dividends.)

Required:

a. Calculate excess for the parent's purchases of preferred and common stocks. (Excess has an indeterminate life.)

b. Calculate the amount of income (using the complete equity method) Press Corporation should report from its investment in:

1. Preferred stock.
2. Common stock.

c. Calculate the amount of preacquisition income for both common and preferred.

d. Calculate minority interest net income. (*Hint:*

Seventy percent of preferred income is part of minority interest net income.)

e. Calculate the amount of minority interest to be shown on the December 31, 19x3, consolidated balance sheet.

f. Prepare the elimination entries for a consolidated working paper for 19x3. (*Hint:* Update the investment accounts for the amounts calculated in (b) above.)

Exercise 8–6. On September 1, 19x7, the Horn Company purchased 200,000 shares representing 45 percent of the outstanding stock of Mat Company for cash. As a result of the purchase, Horn has the ability to exercise significant influence over the operating and financial policies of Mat. Goodwill of $500,000 was appropriately recognized by Horn at the date of the purchase.

On December 1, 19x8, Horn purchased 300,000 shares representing 30 percent of the outstanding stock of Simon Company for cash of $2,500,000. The stockholders' equity section of Simon's balance sheet at the date of the acquisition was as follows:

Common stock, par value $2 a share	$2,000,000
Additional paid-in capital	1,000,000
Retained earnings	4,000,000
	$7,000,000

Furthermore, at the date of acquisition, the fair value of Simon's property, plant, and equipment (net) was $3,800,000 whereas the book value was $3,500,000. For all of the other assets and liabilities of Simon, the fair value and book value was equal. As a result of the transaction, Horn has the ability to exercise significant influence over the operating and financial policies of Simon.

Assume that Horn amortizes goodwill over the maximum period allowed and takes a full year's amortization in the year of purchase.

Required:

Prepare a schedule computing the amount of goodwill and accumulated amortization at December 31, 19x8, and the goodwill amortization for the year ended December 31, 19x8. Show supporting computations in good form. (AICPA adapted)

Exercise 8–7. For the past five years Herbert has maintained an investment (properly accounted for and reported upon) in Broome amounting to a 10 percent interest in the voting common stock of Broome. The purchase price was $700,000, and the underlying net equity in Broome at the date of purchase was $620,000. On January 2 of the current year, Herbert purchased an additional 15 percent of the voting common stock of Broome for $1,200,000; the underlying net equity of the additional investment at January 2 was $1,000,000. Broome has been profitable and has paid dividends annually since Herbert's initial acquisition.

Required:

Discuss how this increase in ownership affects the accounting for and reporting upon the investment in Broome. Include in your discussion adjustments, if any, to the amount shown prior to the increase in investment to bring the amount into conformity with generally accepted accounting principles. Also include how current and subsequent periods would be reported upon.   (AICPA adapted)

Exercise 8–8. 1. On January 1, 19x2, Investor Corporation purchased for $20,000 a 15 percent common stock interest in Investee Corporation whose total common stock equity had a fair and a book value of $100,000. The investment is accounted for by the cost method. If Investee's net income during 19x2 is $30,000 and Investor receives dividends of $5,000 from Investee, for 19x2, Investor Corporation should report income from this investment of—
   a. $5,000.
   b. $4,875.
   c. $4,500.
   d. $4,375.
   e. None of the above or not determinable from the above facts.

2. Assume the same facts as in item 1 above except that Investor Corporation pays $50,000 for a 40 percent common stock interest in Investee Corporation, accounts for the investment by the equity method, and received $13,333 in dividends from Investee during 19x2. For 19x2, Investor Corporation should report as income from this investment the single amount of—
   a. $13,333.
   b. $13,083.
   c. $12,000.
   d. $11,750.
   e. None of the above or not determinable from the above facts.

3. Assume that Operating Corporation purchases a 10 percent common stock interest in Service Corporation for $10,000 on January 1, 19x2, and an additional 20 percent interest for $22,000 on January 1,

19x3. The balance sheets of Service Corporation, which pays no dividends, follow:

	December 31, 19x3	December 31, 19x2	January 1, 19x2
Cash	$130,000	$110,000	$100,000
Total assets	$130,000	$110,000	$100,000
Common stock . . .	$100,000	$100,000	$100,000
Retained earnings .	30,000	10,000	–0–
Total owners' equity	$130,000	$110,000	$100,000

During 19x2, Operating Corporation carries this investment under the cost method and on January 1, 19x3, adopts the equity method. For 19x3, Operating Corporation should report as income from this 30 percent investment the single amount of—
   a. $9,000.
   b. $7,000.
   c. $6,000.
   d. $5,950.
   e. None of the above or not determinable from the above facts.

4. The investment described in item 3 above should be reported as a long-term investment in Operating Corporation's balance sheet at December 31, 19x3, as a single amount of—
   a. $41,000.
   b. $39,000.
   c. $38,000.
   d. $37,900.
   e. None of the above or not determinable from the above facts.   (AICPA adapted)

Exercise 8–9. P Company owns 15,000 shares of the common stock of S Company. On January 2, 19x5, the net assets of S Company were $500,000, and, on this date, P Company was contemplating the purchase of another 5,000 shares of S Company's stock directly from the latter. Prior to the sale, S Company had 20,000 shares issued and outstanding. The following prices per share were contemplated as the price to pay:

Case A	$20 per share
Case B	$25 per share
Case C	$40 per share

The net assets of S Company have book values approximately equal to their respective market values.

Required:

a. What percentage of S Company does P Company presently own?

b. What percentage of S Company will P Company own after the purchase?

c. For each case, calculate the excess that P Company will assign to goodwill.

Exercise 8–10. On January 1, 19x6, Peters, Inc., issued 200,000 additional shares of its voting common stock in exchange for 100,000 shares of Clarkin Company's outstanding voting common stock in a business combination appropriately accounted for by the pooling of interests method. The market value of Peters's voting common stock was $40 per share on the date of the business combination. The balance sheets of Peters and Clarkin immediately before the business combination contained the following information:

Peters, Inc.

Common stock, par value $5 per share; authorized 1,000,000 shares; issued and outstanding 600,000 shares	$ 3,000,000
Additional paid-in capital	6,000,000
Retained earnings	11,000,000
Total stockholders' equity	$20,000,000

Clarkin Company

Common stock, par value $10 per share; authorized 250,000 shares; issued and outstanding 100,000 shares	$1,000,000
Additional paid-in capital	2,000,000
Retained earnings	4,000,000
Total stockholders' equity	$7,000,000

Additional information:

1. Net income for the year ended December 31, 19x6, was $1,150,000 for Peters and $350,000 for Clarkin.
2. During 19x6, Peters paid $900,000 in dividends to its stockholders and Clarkin paid $210,000 in dividends to Peters.

Required:

Prepare the *consolidated* stockholders' equity section of the balance sheet of Peters, Inc., and its subsidiary, Clarkin Company at December 31, 19x6. Provide a supporting schedule for retained earnings. *Ignore income tax and deferred tax considerations.*

(AICPA adapted)

PROBLEMS

Problem 8–11. Pasta Corporation made the following purchases of Shasta's common stock (total outstanding shares are 20,000) in the open market:

Date	Number purchased	Price paid
January 1, 19x5	4,000	$160,000
April 1, 19x5	4,000	159,000
October 1, 19x5	6,000	213,500

Shasta's stockholders' equity at the beginning of the year consisted of:

Common stock ($20 PV)	$400,000
Retained earnings	200,000
Total	$600,000

Shasta's income for the year was $60,000, and it was earned uniformly. Dividends of $1 per share were paid on December 1, 19x5.

All assets and liabilities of Shasta are at fair market value. Excess, if any, has an indeterminate life.

Required:

a. Compute the amount of goodwill for each purchase.

b. Compute the equity in earnings of subsidiary for 19x5. Pasta uses the complete equity method to account for its investment.

c. Compute the amount of preacquisition income.

d. Compute the amount of minority interest net income.

e. Compute the balance in the investment account on December 31, 19x5, after all entries that are required are posted.

Problem 8–12. P Company purchased the following shares of the common stock of S Company in the open market:

Date	Number purchased	Percent of total	Price paid
January 2, 19x6	40,000	50	$500,000
July 1, 19x6	20,000	25	265,000

On January 2, 19x6, S Company had 80,000 shares of common stock issued and outstanding. The par value of these shares is $10 per share. The retained earnings on this date was $200,000.

Income for 19x6 earned by S Company was as follows:

January 1 to June 30	. . . .	$ 60,000
July 1 to December 31	. . . .	120,000
Total for 19x6	. . . .	$180,000

Dividends were paid on the last day of the year at the rate of $1 per share.

All identifiable assets and liabilities of S Company have book values equal to their respective market values.

Required:

a. Prepare the entries to record the purchase of the shares by P Company, the entry (entries) to record the parent's equity in the earnings of S Company and the receipt of dividends.

b. Compute the balance in the investment account at December 31, 19x6.

c. Compute preacquisition income.

d. Compute minority interest net income.

e. Prepare the elimination entries that would appear on a consolidated working paper for 19x6.

f. Reconcile your income allocation from *(a)*, *(c)*, and *(d)* above to the total income for 19x6.

Problem 8–13. P Company made the following purchases of S Company's common stock:

b. What percentage of ownership did P Company have on January 2, 19x3? on April 1, 19x3?

c. Compute excess on the second purchase (5,000 shares).

d. Compute the amount that P Company should report as preacquisition income on a consolidated income statement for 19x3.

e. Compute the amount that P Company should record as equity in earnings of S Company for 19x3. (Use the complete equity method and use 40-year amortization for each excess.)

f. Compute minority interest net income.

g. Compute the balance in the investment account at December 31, 19x3.

h. Prepare the elimination entries that would be required for a consolidated working paper for 19x3.

Problem 8–14 (complete equity method). On April 1, 19x1, P Company purchased 80 percent of the shares of S Company in the open market for $590,000. On that date, the assets and liabilities of S Company had book values that approximated their respective fair market values. Excess (goodwill), if any, is expected to last for 20 years and is to be amortized over that period.

The income of S Company was earned uniformly during the year. P Company uses the complete equity method.

Dividends are paid on June 30 and December 31.

[Relates to Problem 8–13]

Date	Number of shares	Source of shares	Price paid
January 2, 19x3	10,000	Open market	$270,000
April 1, 19x3	5,000	From S Company	180,000

On January 2, 19x3, S Company had 20,000 shares of common stock outstanding. The stock has a par value of $10 per share. The only change in the number of shares in 19x3 is from the sale of the 5,000 shares to P Company.

The balance of retained earnings on January 2, 19x3, amounted to $300,000. For 19x3, S Company earned $80,000 which was earned evenly throughout the year. No dividends were paid in 19x3.

Required:

a. Compute excess on the first purchase of 10,000 shares.

Financial statements for the companies for the year ended December 31, 19x1, are as follows:

	P Company	S Company
Income Statement		
Sales	$1,000,000	$500,000
Cost of sales	400,000	150,000
Gross margin	600,000	350,000
Expenses	200,000	100,000
Operating income before taxes	400,000	250,000
Equity in earnings— subsidiary	90,000	
Income before income taxes .	490,000	250,000
Provision for income taxes . .	160,000	100,000
Minority interest net income		
Net income—carried forward	$ 330,000	$150,000

	P Company	S Company
Retained Earnings Statement		
Balance, January 1, 19x1:		
P Company	$ 602,800	
S Company		$400,000
Net income—brought forward	330,000	150,000
Totals	932,800	550,000
Less: Dividends declared:		
P Company	100,000	
S Company		50,000
Balance, December 31, 19x1— carried forward	$ 832,800	$500,000

	P Company	S Company
Balance Sheet		
Cash	$ 200,000	$100,000
Accounts receivable	150,000	50,000
Inventories	100,000	40,000
Land		150,000
Building—(net of accumulated depreciation) .		200,000
Equipment—(net of accumulated depreciation) .	868,800	450,000
Investment in S Company . .	640,000	
Totals	$1,958,800	$990,000
Accounts payable and accrued expenses	$124,000	$190,000
Bonds payable (face amount $400,000)	402,000	
Common stock—P Company ($50 par)	200,000	
Common stock—S Company ($10 par)		300,000
Additional paid-in capital—P Company	400,000	
Retained earnings—brought forward	832,800	500,000
Totals	$1,958,800	$990,000

Required:

Prepare a consolidated working paper.

Problem 8–15. The December 31, 19x8, balance sheets of the Major Corporation and its two subsidiaries appear below:

MAJOR CORPORATION AND SUBSIDIARIES
Trial Balances
December 31, 19x8

	Major Corporation	Minor Corporation	Mode Corporation
Cash	$ 100,000	$ 75,000	$ 95,000
Accounts receivable	158,200	210,000	105,000
Inventories	290,000	90,000	115,000
Advance to Minor Corporation . . .	17,000		
Dividends receivable	24,000		
Property, plant, and equipment	777,600	325,000	470,000
Allowance for depreciation . . .	(180,000)	(55,000)	(160,000)
Investment in Minor Corporation:			
6% bonds	23,800		
Common stock . .	308,600		
Investment in Mode Corporation:			
Preferred stock .	7,000		
Common stock . .	196,000		
Totals	$1,722,200	$645,000	$625,000
Accounts payable . .	$ 170,000	$ 96,000	$ 86,000
Notes payable	45,000	14,000	44,000
Bonds payable . . .	285,000	150,000	125,000
Discount on bonds payable	(8,000)	(12,000)	
Dividends payable .	22,000	30,000	
Preferred stock, $20 par	400,000		
Mode Corporation			50,000
Common stock, $10 par	600,000		
Minor Corporation . . .		250,000	
Mode Corporation			200,000
Retained earnings .	208,200		
Minor Corporation . . .		117,000	
Mode Corporation			120,000
Totals	$1,722,200	$645,000	$625,000

Additional information:

1. The investment in Minor Corporation stock by the Major Corporation is composed of the following items:

Date	Description	Amount
April 1, 19x7	Cost of 5,000 shares of Minor Corporation stock	$ 71,400
December 31, 19x7	20% of the dividends declared in December 19x7 by the Minor Corporation . . .	(9,000)
December 31, 19x7	20% of the 19x7 net income of the Minor Corporation . . .	12,000
July 1, 19x8	Cost of 15,000 shares of Minor Corporation stock	226,200
December 31, 19x8	80% of the dividends declared in December 19x8 by Minor Corporation . . .	(24,000)
December 31, 19x8	80% of the 19x8 net income of the Minor Corporation . . .	32,000
December 31, 19x8	Total	$308,600

2. Major Corporation acquired 250 shares of fully participating preferred stock for $7,000 and 14,000 shares of common stock for $196,000 of the Mode Corporation on January 2, 19x8. Mode Corporation had a net income of $20,000 in 19x8 and did not declare any dividends.

3. Mode Corporation's inventory includes $22,400 of merchandise acquired from Minor Corporation for which no payment had been made. Minor Corporation marked up the merchandise 40 percent on cost.

4. Major Corporation acquired in the open market 25 $1,000 face value 6 percent bonds of Minor Corporation for $21,400 on January 5, 19x5. The Minor Corporation bonds mature December 31, 19y0 (six years hence). Interest is paid each June 30 and December 31.

5. The three corporations are all in the same industry, and their operations are homogeneous. Major Corporation exercises control over the boards of directors of both Minor Corporation and Mode Corporation and has installed new principal officers in both.

Required:

Prepare a worksheet for the preparation of a consolidated balance sheet as of December 31, 19x8, for Major Corporation and its subsidiaries. Consolidated retained earnings should be allocated to Major Corporation, and minority interests should be shown separately. The consolidation is to be accounted for as a purchase. Formal financial statements and journal entries are not required. Supporting computations should be in good form.   (AICPA adapted)

Problem 8–16. Williard, Inc., acquired 10 percent of the 100,000 shares of $2.50 par value common stock outstanding of Thorne Corporation on December 31, 19x9, for $38,000. An additional 70,000 shares were acquired for $331,600 on June 30, 19y1 (at which time there was no material difference between the fair and book values of Thorne's assets and liabilities). Williard uses the equity method of accounting for its investment in Thorne.

Enclosed are the balance sheets for both companies for the year ended December 31, 19y1. The following information is also available:

1. An analysis of investment in Thorne Corporation:

Date	Description	Amount
December 31, 19x9	Investment	$ 38,000
June 30, 19y1	Investment	331,600
December 31, 19y1	80% of net increase in retained earnings of Thorne Corporation during 19y1	36,000
		$405,600

2. Analysis of the companies' Retained Earnings accounts:

	Williard, Inc.	Thorne Corporation
Balance, December 31, 19x9 .	$540,000	$101,000
Net income for 19y0	55,000	40,000
Cash dividends in 19y0		(5,000)
Balance, December 31, 19y0 .	595,000	136,000
Net income:		
January 1–June 30, 19y1 . .	31,000	23,000
June 30–December 31, 19y1	40,800	33,000
Dividends declared,		
December 15, 19y1	(20,000)	(11,000)
80% of net increase in retained earnings of Thorne Corporation during 19y1	36,000	
Balance, December 31, 19y1 .	$682,800	$181,000

3. Thorne's other equity accounts have not changed since 19x5.

4. Data on 19y1 intercompany sales and ending inventories were as follows:

	Williard, Inc.	Thorne Corporation
Intercompany sales:		
January 1–June 30	$39,000	$24,000
June 30–December 31	41,600	41,000
Gross profit on sales	30%	25%
Intercompany payable at year-end	$12,000	$ 7,000
Year-end inventory of intercompany purchases at FIFO cost	26,000	22,000

WILLIARD, INC. AND SUBSIDIARY
Worksheet to Prepare Consolidated Balance Sheet
December 31, 19y1

	Williard, Inc.	Thorne Corporation	Adjustments and Eliminations		Consolidated Balance Sheet	
			Debit	Credit	Debit	Credit
Debits						
Cash	130,000	60,000				
Accounts receivable	160,000	75,000				
Notes receivable	15,000	12,200				
Interest receivable	2,100	1,600				
Dividends receivable	8,800					
Marketable securities	31,220	9,700				
Inventories	180,000	96,000				
Plant and equipment	781,500	510,000				
Investment in Thorne Corporation stock	405,600					
Investment in Thorne Corporation bonds	30,580					
Advance to Thorne Corporation	32,000					
Unamortized bond discount		7,500				
	1,776,800	772,000				
Credits						
Allowance for depreciation	87,000	85,000				
Accounts payable	34,500	16,000				
Notes payable	5,500	3,800				
Dividends payable	20,000	11,000				
Interest payable	18,000	13,000				
Other accrued liabilities	15,000	1,200				
Advance from Williard, Inc.		32,000				
Bonds payable	400,000	150,000				
Capital stock	500,000	250,000				
Capital in excess of par value	14,000	29,000				
Retained earnings	682,800	181,000				
	1,776,800	772,000				

(AICPA adapted)

5. Williard, Inc., acquired $30,000 of the Thorne Corporation 6 percent bonds on August 31, 19y1, for $30,599 plus accrued interest. Thorne Corporation issued the 20-year bonds on January 1, 19x2, at 90 and has been paying the interest on each January 1 and July 1 due date.

6. On September 1, 19y1, Williard, Inc., sold equipment with a cost of $40,000 and accumulated depreciation of $9,300 to Thorne Corporation for $20,200. Thorne Corporation recorded the equipment as having a cost of $29,500 with accumulated depreciation of $9,300. At that date the equipment had an estimated salvage value of $500 and an estimated life of 10 years.

7. Included in Williard, Inc.'s notes receivable are $2,000 in noninterest bearing notes of Thorne Corporation.

Required:

Complete the worksheet for the preparation of a consolidated balance sheet for Williard, Inc., and its subsidiary, Thorne Corporation, as of December 31, 19x1. Formal statements and journal entries are not required. You may assume that both companies made all of the adjusting entries required for separate financial statements unless an obvious discrepancy exists. Income taxes should not be considered in your solution. Any amortization required by *APB Opinion 17*, "Intangible Assets," is to be computed by the straight-line method over a 40-year period.

Problem 8–17. Sterling, Inc., a domestic corporation having a fiscal year ending June 30, has purchased common stock in several other domestic corporations. As of June 30, 19y2, the balance in Sterling's investments account was $870,600, the total cost of stock purchased less the cost of stock sold. Sterling wishes to restate the investments account to reflect the provisions of *APB Opinion 18*, "The Equity Method of Accounting for Investments in Common Stock."

Data concerning the investment follow:

[Relates to Problem 8–17]

		Turner, Inc.	Grotex, Inc.	Scott, Inc.
Shares of common stock outstanding		3,000	32,000	100,000
Shares purchased by Sterling	(a)	300	8,000	30,000
	(b)	810		
Date of purchase	(a)	7/1/x9	6/30/y0	6/30/y1
	(b)	7/1/y1		
Cost of shares purchased .	(a)	$ 49,400	$ 46,000	$ 670,000
	(b)	142,000		
Balance sheet at date indicated:				
Assets		*July 1, 19y1*	*June 30, 19y0*	*June 30, 19y1*
Current assets		$ 362,000	$ 39,600	$ 994,500
Fixed assets (net of depreciation		1,638,000	716,400	3,300,000
Patent (net of amortization)				148,500
		$2,000,000	$756,000	$4,443,000

Liabilities and Capital	Turner, Inc.	Grotex, Inc.	Scott, Inc.
Liabilities	$1,500,000	$572,000	$2,494,500
Common stock	260,000	80,000	1,400,000
Retained earnings	240,000	104,000	548,500
	$2,000,000	$756,000	$4,443,000
Changes in common stock since July 1, 19x9 . . .	None	None	None
Average remaining life of fixed assets at date of balance sheet (above) .	12 years	9 years	22 years
Analysis of retained earnings:			
Balance, July 1, 19x9 . . .	$ 234,000		
Net income, July 1, 19x9 to June 30, 19y0	53,400		
Dividend paid—April 1, 19y0	(51,000)		
Balance, June, 30, 19y0 .	236,400	$104,000	
Net income (loss), July 1, 19y0 to June 30, 19y1	55,600	(2,000)	
Dividend paid—April 1, 19y1	(52,000)		
Balance, June 30, 19y1 . .	240,000	102,000	$ 548,500
Net income, July 1, 19y1 to June 30, 19y2	25,000	18,000	330,000
Dividends paid:			
December 28, 19y1 . .			(150,000)
June 1, 19y2		(5,600)	
Balance, June 30, 19y2 . . .	$ 265,000	$114,400	$ 728,500

Sterling's first purchase of Turner's stock was made because of the high rate of return expected on the investment. All later purchases of stock have been made to gain substantial influence over the operations of the various companies.

In December 19y1, changing market conditions caused Sterling to reevaluate its relation to Grotex. On December 31, 19y1, Sterling sold 6,400 shares of Grotex for $54,400.

For Turner and Grotex, the fair values of the net assets did not differ materially from the book values as shown in the above balance sheets. For Scott, fair values exceeded book values only with respect to the patent which had a fair value of $300,000 and a remaining life of 15 years as of June 30, 19y1.

At June 30, 19y2, Sterling's inventory included $48,600 of items purchased from Scott during May and June at a 20 percent markup over Scott's cost.

Required:

Prepare a working paper to restate Sterling's investments account as of June 30, 19y2, and its investment income by year for the three years then ended. Transactions should be listed in chronological order and supporting computations should be in good form. *Ignore income taxes.* Amortization of goodwill, if any, is to be over a 40-year period. Use the following columnar headings for your working paper:

Date	Description	Investments			Investment Income, Year Ended June 30			Other Accounts	
		Turner Dr. (Cr.)	Grotex Dr. (Cr.)	Scott Dr. (Cr.)	19y0 Cr. (Dr.)	19y1 Cr. (Dr.)	19y2 Cr. (Dr.)	Amount Dr. (Cr.)	Name

(ACIPA adapted)

Problem 8-18. The North Salem Company has supplied you with information regarding two investments which were made during 19x5 as follows:

1. On January 1, 19x5, North Salem purchased for cash 40 percent of the 500,000 shares of voting common stock of the Yorktown Company for $2,400,000 representing 40 percent of the net worth of Yorktown. Yorktown's net income for the year ended December 31, 19x5, was $750,000. Yorktown paid dividends of 50 cents per share in 19x5. The market value of Yorktown's common stock was $14 per share on December 31, 19x5. North Salem exercised significant influence over the operating and financial policies of Yorktown.

2. On July 1, 19x5, North Salem purchased for cash 15,000 shares representing 5 percent of the voting common stock of the Mahopac Company for $450,000. Mahopac's net income for the six months ended December 31, 19x5, was $350,000 and for the year ended December 31, 19x5, was $600,000. Mahopac paid dividends of 30 cents per share each quarter during 19x5 to stockholders of record on the last day of each quarter. The market value of Mahopac's common stock was $32 per share on January 1, 19x5, and $34 per share on December 31, 19x5.

Required:

a. As a result of these two investments, what should be the balance in the investments account for North Salem at December 31, 19x5? Show supporting computations in good form. *Ignore income taxes and deferred tax considerations in your answer.*

b. As a result of these two investments, what should be the income reported by North Salem for the year ended December 31, 19x5? Show supporting computations in good form. *Ignore income taxes and deferred tax considerations in your answer.*

(AICPA adapted)

Problem 8-19. You have been assigned to the audit of Wright, Inc., a manufacturing company. You have been asked to summarize the transactions for the year ended December 31, 19x3, affecting stockholders' equity and other related accounts, particularly investments and long-term liabilities. The stockholders' equity section of Wright's December 31, 19x2, balance sheet follows:

Stockholders' Equity

Common stock, par value $10; shares authorized 500,000; shares issued 90,000 .	$ 900,000
Capital in excess of par value	11,250
Retained earnings	424,689
Less cost of 1,210 shares of common stock in treasury	(36,300)
Total stockholders' equity	$1,299,639

You have extracted the following information from the accounting records and audit working papers.

1. On March 31, 19x3, Wright paid $146,960 cash for all of the stock of Buller Company. A summary of Buller's adjusted trial balance including operations for the three months ended March 31, 19x3, follows. Fair market value (FMV) is shown parenthetically when different from book value.

Receivables	$28,901
Land (FMV, $96,000)	78,000
Other assets	12,876
Liabilities	(35,777)
Common stock	(22,180)
Paid-in capital	(26,320)
Retained earnings	(25,299)
Revenues	(97,249)
Expenses	87,048
	-0-

The excess cost over the sum of the fair values of the net assets acquired as shown on the above adjusted trial balance was deemed attributable to the future earnings potential of Buller. This excess cost should be amortized over the maximum period recommended by generally accepted accounting principles.

Earnings of Buller from January 1 to March 31, 19x3, were $10,201; earnings from April 1 to December 31, 19x3, were $14,434.

Buller is to retain its separate corporate identity and operate as a subsidiary. There were no intercompany accounts requiring elimination or adjustment at December 31, 19x3. Wright desires to maintain its accounting records to produce information for the preparation of its statements (unconsolidated) for issuance to stockholders as the financial statements of the primary reporting entity.

2. On August 31, 19x3, Wright exchanged 12,400 previously authorized but unissued shares of its common stock for all of the stock of Clark Corporation. A summary of Clark's balance sheet at August 31, 19x3, follows:

Assets	
Assets	$318,000
Total assets	$318,000

Liabilities and Stockholders' Equity	
Liabilities	$ 39,366
Common stock ($1 par)	104,000
Paid-in capital	80,243
Retained earnings	94,391
Total liabilities and stockholders' equity	$318,000

The combination was appropriately accounted for as a pooling of interests. Clark's retained earnings included $17,426 of earnings from January 1 to August 31, 19x3. Clark's earnings from September 1 to December 31, 19x3, were $8,111.

Clark is to retain its separate corporate identity and operate as a subsidiary. In accordance with generally accepted accounting principles, the investment in Clark on Wright's books is to be recorded at the book value of the net assets acquired as shown on the above balance sheet; stockholders' equity accounts are to be charged and credited in the same manner as if the companies were combined (or consolidated). Wright will continue to account for its investment in Clark by the equity method. There were no intercompany accounts requiring elimination or adjustment at December 31, 19x3.

Other data:

The market price at which Wright's common stock traded on a midwest exchange at various dates follows.

January 2	$19	July 5	$32
January 15	20	August 1	32
January 26	21	August 31	33
March 30	22	September 4	34
April 2	22	October 1	33
May 1	28	November 1	36
June 1	31	December 3	38
June 30	32	December 31	42

Required:

Complete the worksheet to summarize the above transaction of Wright.

Problem 8–20. The December 31, 19x9, balance sheets of Encanto Corporation and its subsidiary, Norris Corporation, are presented as follows:

Assets	Encanto Corporation	Norris Corporation
Cash	$ 167,250	$101,000
Accounts receivable	178,450	72,000
Notes receivable	87,500	28,000
Dividends receivable	36,000	
Inventories	122,000	68,000
Property, plant, and equipment	487,000	252,000
Accumulated depreciation .	(117,000)	(64,000)
Investment in Norris Corporation	240,800	
	$1,202,000	$457,000

Liabilities and Stockholders' Equity		
Accounts payable	$ 222,000	$ 76,000
Notes payable	79,000	89,000
Dividend payable		40,000
Common stock, $10 par value:		
Encanto Corporation . . .	400,000	
Norris Corporation		100,000
Retained earnings:		
Encanto Corporation . . .	501,000	
Norris Corporation		152,000
	$1,202,000	$457,000

Additional information:

1. Encanto initially acquired 60 percent of the outstanding common stock of Norris in 19x7. This purchase resulted in no difference between cost and net assets acquired. As of December 31, 19x9, the percentage owned is 90 percent. An analysis of the account Investment in Norris Corporation is as follows:

Date	Description	Amount
December 31, 19x7	Acquired 6,000 shares	$ 70,800
December 31, 19x8	60% of 19x8 net income of $78,000	46,800
September 1, 19x9	Acquired 3,000 shares	92,000
December 31, 19x9	Subsidiary income for 19x9	67,200*
December 31, 19x9	90% of dividends declared	(36,000)
		$240,800

*Subsidiary income for 19x9:	
60% of $96,000	$57,600
30% of $96,000 × 33⅓%	9,600
	$67,200

Assume that Norris's net income is earned ratably during the year. Amortization of the excess

[Relates to Problem 8–19]

WRIGHT, INC.
Transactions Affecting Stockholders'
Equity and Other Related Accounts
Year Ended December 31, 19x3

No.	Description	Common Stock Dr. (Cr.)	Common Stock Subscribed Dr. (Cr.)	Capital in Excess of Par Value Dr. (Cr.)	Treasury Stock Dr. (Cr.)	Cash Dr. (Cr.)	Subscriptions Receivable Dr. (Cr.)	Investments Dr. (Cr.)	Equity in Earnings of Unconsolidated Subsidiaries Dr. (Cr.)	Other Accounts	
										Account	Amount Dr. (Cr.)
	Opening balances	(900,000)	—	(11,250)	36,300	—	—	—	—	Retained earnings	(424,689)

(AICPA adapted)

of cost over the net assets acquired is to be recorded over 60 months.

2. On December 15, 19x9, Norris declared a cash dividend of $4 per share of common stock, payable to shareholders on January 7, 19y0.
3. During 19x9, Encanto sold merchandise to Norris. Encanto's cost for this merchandise was $68,000, and the sale was made at 125% of cost. Norris's inventory at December 31, 19x9, included merchandise purchased from Encanto at a cost to Norris of $35,000.
4. In December 19x8, Norris sold merchandise to Encanto for $67,000, which was at a markup of 35% over Norris's cost. On January 1, 19x9, $54,000 of this merchandise remained in Encanto's inventory. This merchandise was subsequently sold by Encanto at a profit of $11,000 during 19x9.
5. On October 1, 19x9, Encanto sold for $42,000, excess equipment to Norris. Data relating to this equipment is as follows:

Book value on Encanto's records . . .	$36,000
Method of depreciation	Straight line
Estimated remaining life on October 1, 19x9	10 years

6. Near the end of 19x9, Norris reduced the balance of its intercompany account payable to Encanto to zero by transferring $8,000 to Encanto. This payment was still in transit on December 31, 19x9.

Required:

Complete the consolidated balance sheet worksheet on Encanto Corporation and its subsidiary, Norris Corporation, as of December 31, 19x9.

(AICPA adapted)

Problem 8–21 *(complete equity method).* On July 1, 19x1, P Company acquired 90 percent of the outstanding shares of S Company by exchanging 4,000 shares of its $50 par value stock for 90 percent of the outstanding shares of S Company. All conditions for a pooling were met.

The dividends paid by S Company were paid quarterly on the last day of each quarter.

The parent company uses the complete equity method to account for its investment.

Trial balances for the two corporations for the year ended December 31, 19x1, are as follows:

	P Company	S Company
Debits		
Cash	$ 300,000	$ 100,000
Accounts receivable	200,000	200,000
Inventories	400,000	300,000
Land	600,000	—
Building (net of accumulated depreciation)	400,000	—
Equipment (net of accumulated depreciation) .	1,181,000	1,000,000
Investment in S Company . .	1,278,000	
Cost of sales	800,000	600,000
Expenses	500,000	100,000
Provision for income taxes . .	280,000	120,000
Dividends paid	400,000	60,000
Bond discount	2,000	
Totals	$6,341,000	$2,480,000
Credits		
Accounts payable and accrued expenses	$ 279,000	$ 180,000
Bonds payable	100,000	—
Common stock ($50 par; $10 par)	500,000	500,000
Additional paid-in capital . . .	300,000	—
Retained earnings	3,000,000	800,000
Sales	2,000,000	1,000,000
Equity in earnings— subsidiary	162,000	
Totals	$6,341,000	$2,480,000

Required:

a. Prepare the journal entry that the parent company used to record its investment in S Company.

b. Prepare the journal entries that the parent company used to record its share of income from S Company and for the receipt of dividends.

c. Prepare a consolidated working paper. (Use the three-part financial statement approach.)

Problem 8–22 *(for appendix).* On April 1, 19x1, P Company purchased 80 percent of the shares of S Company in the open market for $590,000. On that date, the assets and liabilities of S Company had book values that approximated their respective fair market values. Excess (goodwill), if any, is expected to last for 20 years and is to be amortized over that period.

The income of S Company was earned uniformly during the year. P Company uses the cost method to account for its investment. Dividends are paid June 30 and December 31.

Financial statements for the companies for the year ended December 31, 19x1, are as follows:

	P Company	S Company
Income Statement		
Sales	$1,000,000	$500,000
Cost of sales . . . . , ...	400,000	150,000
Gross margin	600,000	350,000
Expenses	200,000	100,000
Operating income before taxes	400,000	250,000
Dividend income—subsidiary	40,000	
Income before income taxes .	440,000	250,000
Provision for income taxes . .	160,000	100,000
Minority interest net income		
Net income—carried forward	$ 280,000	$150,000

	P Company	S Company
Retained Earnings Statement		
Balance, January 1, 19x1:		
P Company	$ 602,800	
S Company		$400,000
Net income—brought forward	280,000	150,000
Totals	882,800	550,000
Less: Dividends declared:		
P Company	100,000	
S Company		50,000
Balance, December 31, 19x1— carried forward	$ 782,800	$500,000

	P Company	S Company
Balance Sheet		
Cash	$ 200,000	$100,000
Accounts receivable	150,000	50,000
Inventories	100,000	40,000
Land		150,000
Building—(net of accumulated depreciation) .		200,000
Equipment—(net of accumulated depreciation) .	868,800	450,000
Investment in S Company . .	590,000	
Totals	$1,908,800	$990,000
Accounts payable and accrued expenses	$ 124,000	$190,000
Bonds payable (face amount $400,000)	402,000	
Common stock—P Company ($50 par)	200,000	
Common stock—S Company ($10 par)		300,000
Additional paid-in capital—P Company	400,000	
Retained earnings—brought forward	782,800	500,000
Totals	$1,908,800	$990,000

Required:

Prepare a consolidated working paper.

Problem 8–23 (cost method). The following trial balances were prepared after completion of the examination of the December 31, 19x4, financial statements of Adam Corporation and its subsidiaries, Seth Corporation and Cain Corporation. The subsidiary investments are accounted for by the cost method.

The audit working papers provide the following additional information:

1. The Seth Corporation was formed by the Adam Corporation on January 1, 19x4. To secure additional capital, 25 percent of the capital stock was sold at par value in the securities market. Adam purchased the remaining capital stock at par value for cash.

2. On July 1, 19x4, Adam acquired from stockholders 4,000 shares of Cain Corporation capital stock for $175,000. A condensed trial balance for Cain Corporation at July 1, 19x4, follows:

	Debit	Credit
Current assets	$165,000	
Fixed assets (net)	60,000	
Current liabilities		$ 45,000
Capital stock, par value $20 . .		100,000
Retained earnings		36,000
Sales		200,000
Cost of sales	140,000	
Operating expenses	16,000	
Totals	$381,000	$381,000

[Relates to Problem 8–23]

ADAM CORPORATION AND SUBSIDIARIES
Consolidated Statements Working Paper
For the Year Ended December 31, 19x4

	Trial Balances, December 31, 19x4		
	Adam Corp.	Seth Corp.	Cain Corp.
Debits			
Cash	82,000	11,000	27,000
Accounts receivable	104,000	41,000	143,000
Inventories	241,000	70,000	78,000
Investment in Seth Corporation	150,000		
Investment in Cain Corporation	175,000		
Investments—other	185,000		
Fixed assets	375,000	58,000	99,000
Accumulated depreciation	(96,000)	(7,000)	(21,000)
Cost of sales	820,000	300,000	350,000
Operating expenses	60,000	35,000	40,000
Totals	2,096,000	508,000	716,000
Credits			
Accounts payable	46,000	33,000	24,000
Sales	960,000	275,000	570,000
Gain on sales of assets	9,000		
Dividend income	18,000		
Capital stock, $20 par value			
Adam	500,000		
Seth		200,000	
Cain			100,000
Retained earnings:			
Adam	563,000		
Cain			12,000
Appropriation for contingency			10,000
Totals	2,096,000	508,000	716,000

3. The following intercompany sales of certain products were made in 19x4:

[Relates to Problem 8–23]

	Sales	Gross profit on sales	Included in purchaser's inventory at December 31, 19x4 at lower of cost or market
Adam Corporation to Cain Corporation	$ 40,000	20%	$15,000
Seth Corporation to Cain Corporation	30,000	10	10,000
Cain Corporation to Adam Corporation	60,000	30	20,000
Total	$130,000		$45,000

In valuing the Adam Corporation inventory at the lower of cost or market, the portion of the inventory purchased from the Cain Corporation was written down by $1,900.

4. On January 2, 19x4, Adam Corporation sold a punch press to Seth Corporation. The machine

was purchased on January 1, 19x2, and was being depreciated by the straight-line method over a 10-year life. Seth Corporation computed depreciation by the same method based on the remaining useful life. Details of the sale are as follows:

Cost of punch press	$25,000
Accumulated depreciation	5,000
Net book value	20,000
Sales price	24,000
Gain on sale	$ 4,000

5. Cash dividends were paid on the following dates in 19x4:

	Adam	Cain
June 30	$22,000	$ 6,000
December 31	26,000	14,000
Total	$48,000	$20,000

6. Adam Corporation billed $6,000 to each subsidiary at year-end for executive services in 19x4. The billing was treated as an operating expense and reduction of operating expenses. The invoices were paid in January 19x5.

7. At year-end Cain Corporation appropriated $10,-000 for a contingent loss in connection with a lawsuit that had been pending since 19x2.

Required:

Prepare a working paper for consolidated statements for Adam Corporation and its subsidiaries for the year ended December 31, 19x4. The sales, costs, and expenses of the subsidiaries are to be included in the consolidation as though the subsidiaries had been acquired at the beginning of the year. You plan to deduct the current year's preacquisition earnings of Cain Corporation at the bottom of the consolidated income statement. (AICPA adapted)

9

Consolidated statements—decreases in parent's (investor's) share of ownership and other related matters

OVERVIEW

An investor's (parent's) percentage of ownership can be decreased in two ways. The investor may sell some of its shares in the investee. In this case the investor's gain or loss on the sale is measured by the difference between the proceeds from the sale and the carrying value of the shares sold determined by the equity method. An exception to this method of measurement, applies to investors who own less than 20 percent of an investee. In this case, the gain or loss is the difference between the cost of the shares sold and the proceeds received.

The other method by which an investor can reduce ownership in an investee is to have the investee sell shares to outsiders. If the shares are sold at book value, there is no impact on the investor's carrying value of its investment. If, however, the shares are sold at an amount other than book value, there is an impact on the investor's (20 percent or more ownership) carrying value and the investment account must be adjusted for the difference between the selling price and the book value per share.

An investee's purchase of its own shares (treasury stock) will either increase or decrease the investor's percentage of ownership depending on who the seller of the shares is, i.e., outsiders or the investor. Here too, the price paid for its shares by the investee will have an impact on the investor's investment account, if the price is other than book value.

Since a stock dividend issued by an investee has no effect on its net assets, the dividend does not affect the carrying value of an investor's investment account.

In the preceding chapter, various aspects of the accounting for increases in ownership percentages were discussed. The reverse—decreases in ownership—will now be considered. Decreases in ownership can occur for a variety of reasons, such as, the need to raise cash, for tax reasons, a desire to discontinue parent company status, compliance with antitrust regulations, and other reasons.

While the basic principles associated with disinvestment are similar to those governing increases in ownership percentages, there are some differences which will be the focus of this chapter.

Disinvestment can occur in either of two ways. Either the parent company sells shares of its subsidiary which it owns to third parties or the subsidiary sells stock (treasury or unissued) to third parties. Treasury stock transactions can result in either increased investment or disinvestment, and this topic will be considered separately. Our discussion at this point will be limited to a consideration of the effect of sales of stock to third parties by either the parent company or by the subsidiary.

SALE OF SHARES BY SUBSIDIARY TO THIRD PARTIES

At book value

A sale of stock to third parties by a subsidiary at book value does not require any adjustment to a parent's investment account balance. This is so because the parent's excess, if any, in relation to its investment in the net assets of the subsidiary at book value remains unchanged. To demonstrate this it is assumed that:

1. Farley Corporation purchased 9,000 shares (90 percent) of Sorley Corporation's outstanding common stock for $550,000 on January 1, 19x2.
2. On January 1, 19x2, Sorley Corporation's $10 par value common stock and paid-in capital accounts amounted to $100,000 and its retained earnings were $400,000. The carrying amounts of all assets and liabilities approximated their respective fair market values.
3. On January 2, 19x2, Sorley Corporation sold 2,000 shares of unissued stock to third parties for $50 per share, or $100,000.

The entry to record the sale on Sorley Corporation's books of its $10 par value stock would be:

Cash	100,000	
Common Stock		20,000
Additional Paid-In Capital		80,000

As a result of the sale of stock by the subsidiary, the parent's percentage of ownership decreases to 75 percent from 90 percent. This can be calculated as follows:

	Before	After
Parent's shares:		
Total shares:	$\frac{9,000}{10,000} = 90\%$	$\frac{9,000}{12,000} = 75\%$

Goodwill can be calculated on January 1, 19x2, as follows:

Price paid by parent company	$550,000
90% of subsidiary's net assets of $500,000	450,000
Excess (goodwill)	$100,000

The $100,000 of goodwill must be maintained (except for periodic amortization) since the parent company retained its investment intact. Therefore, a similar calculation must be made after the sale by the subsidiary using the *new* net assets of the subsidiary and the reduced percentage of ownership by the parent. Thus, if a different amount of goodwill results from such a computation, an adjustment to the parent's investment account will be required. On January 1, 19x2, the new computation is as follows:

Price paid by parent company	$550,000
75% of subsidiary's net assets of $600,000 ($500,000 + $100,000 from proceeds of sale)	450,000
Excess (goodwill)	$100,000

Since the amount of computed excess after the sale by the subsidiary is unaltered, no adjustment to the parent's investment is required. This occurs *only* when the sale by the subsidiary is made at its *book value* per share. Sales at amounts other than book value do require adjustments and these will now be considered.

At a price in excess of book value

If, in the above example, the sale of the shares by the subsidiary would be at $80 per share rather than at $50 per share, or for a total price of $160,000, and with all other conditions remaining the same, the entry on the subsidiary's books would be:

Subsidiary's Books

Cash	160,000	
Common Stock		20,000
Additional Paid-In Capital		140,000

The computation of excess following the sale of stock by the subsidiary on January 2, 19x2, would be:

Price paid by parent company	$550,000
75% of subsidiary's net assets of $660,000 ($500,000 + $160,000)	495,000
Difference	$ 55,000

If the excess on the parent's books is to be maintained at the original $100,000, an adjustment on the parent's books in the amount of $45,000 will now be required. The reason for this is that changes in the amount of goodwill should result only from purchases or sale by the parent rather than from sales by others. From a consolidated entity viewpoint, the transaction causing this adjustment arises from a *capital transaction*—a sale of *capital stock* by the subsidiary that is part of the consolidated entity—and, therefore, the adjustment must be to the stockholders' equity section of the parent company and *not* to income. The entry to record the adjustment on the *parent's books* would be:

Parent's Books—January 2, 19x2

Investment in Sorley Corporation	45,000	
Additional Paid-In Capital		45,000

To record the adjustment necessary to restore excess to
$100,000 on account of sale of stock by Sorley Corporation.

After posting the above entry, the balance in the investment account is
$595,000 which is $100,000 greater that the $495,000 computed as the par-
ent's share (75 percent) of the subsidiary's net assets.

The adjustment of $45,000 can be proven in the following manner:

Selling price per share	$80
Book value per share	50
Difference	$30
Number of shares sold	2,000
Proceeds of sale in excess of book value (2,000 × $30)	$60,000
Parent's percentage—new	75%
Adjustment required—(75% × $60,000)	$45,000

Since the selling price was greater than book value, the adjustment resulted
in an increase in the investment account and an increase in paid-in capital.

At a price below book value

Sales of stock by a subsidiary at a price below book value per share will
result in adjustments similar to those discussed above but in the opposite
direction. For example, if the 2,000 shares in the above example were sold at
$40 per share for a total of $80,000, the required adjustment could be calculated as:

Price paid by parent company	$550,000
75% of subsidiary's net assets of $580,000 ($500,000 + $80,000)	435,000
Difference	$115,000

Since the parent's excess must be $100,000 as originally computed, a
downward adjustment of $15,000 is now required. The proof of this calcu-
lation is:

Book value per share	$50
Selling price per share	40
Difference	$10
Number of shares sold	2,000
Proceeds of sale below book value (2,000 × $10)	$20,000
Parent's percentage—new	75%
Adjustment required (75% × $20,000)	$15,000

Since the selling price was less than book value, the investment account
must be decreased and paid-in capital (and if not available, retained earnings)
must be charged as follows:

Additional Paid-In Capital . . . . ·.   15,000
    Investment in Sorley Corporation   15,000
    To adjust the investment account by an amount necessary to
    reduce excess to the required $100,000 because of the sale of
    stock by Sorley Corporation.

SALES BY INVESTORS OF INVESTEE'S STOCK—EQUITY METHOD

A reduction in an investor's percentage of ownership in an investee can be accomplished either by a sale of shares by the investee as discussed earlier, or by a sale by the investor of investee shares owned by it. In either case, similar results can be achieved. Thus, for example, the investor's ownership percentage can be reduced from 90 percent to 75 percent, as shown in the preceding illustration, or by the investor's sale of 1,500 shares of the 9,000 shares it owned. However, in the latter case, the transaction gives rise to a gain or loss on its income statement because the transaction represents the sale of investments.[1] The gain or loss is measured by the difference between the proceeds received from the sale of the shares and the carrying value of the shares sold. By *carrying value* is meant the book balance assigned to the shares sold using the complete equity method.

In Chapter 8, an example was given where an investor increased its investment percentage of ownership from 10 percent to 40 percent. In that example it was shown that the 10 percent investment was accounted for on a cost basis and when the additional 30 percent was acquired, not only did the investor convert to the complete equity method but the investor also made a *retroactive* application of the equity method for the 10 percent shares originally accounted for on the cost basis. When a change results in a decline in ownership percentage, i.e., when a 40 percent ownership interest accounted for under the complete equity method is reduced by sale to only a 10 percent interest, the procedure is *not* reversed. Instead, the *equity method is discontinued,* and the cost method is applied *prospectively* to the remaining 10 percent investment and no *retroactive adjustment* is involved.[2] The use of the cost method requires that dividends received in any subsequent period which are in excess of the investor's share of income earned by the investee, be recorded as a reduction of the investor's investment account.[3]

SALES BY AN INVESTOR OF PART OF ITS INVESTMENT IN A SUBSIDIARY OR AFFILIATE

Since the accounting for gains or losses on the sale of investments is the same for any percentage of ownership between 20–100 percent, the accounting for a sale by a parent company will obviously apply to an investor owning between 20 percent and 50 percent of an investee. To demonstrate the procedures involved when an investor sells part of its investment, it is now assumed that:

1. Anthony Corporation purchased 16,000 shares (or 80 percent) of Beta

---

[1]*APB*, "The Equity Method of Accounting for Investments in Common Stock," *APB Opinion No. 18* (New York: AICPA, 1971), par. 19f.

[2]Ibid., par. 19l.

[3]Ibid.

Corporation's outstanding common stock for $440,000 on January 1, 19x2. On this date, Beta's retained earnings were $200,000. Beta's net assets on its books approximate their respective fair market values. Excess, if any, is entirely attributable to goodwill with an indeterminate life. (*Hint:* Forty-year amortization should be used.)

2. For 19x2, Beta had a net income of $150,000 and paid dividends of $50,000. The 19x3 operating results and dividends appear in Illustration 9–1. Income is earned uniformly throughout the year, and dividends are paid quarterly on the last day of the quarter.

3. On October 1, 19x3, Anthony sold 2,000 shares of Beta's stock to third parties for $75,500.

4. There were no intercompany transactions other than the payment of dividends in either 19x2 or 19x3.

For 19x2, the parent company would make the following entries on its books:

Parent's Books—19x2

Cash	40,000	
Investment in Beta Corporation		40,000
To record dividends received (80% × $50,000).		
Investment in Beta Corporation	119,000	
Equity in Earnings of Subsidiary		119,000
To record share of income as follows:		

80% × $150,000 =	$120,000	
Less: Amortization of goodwill* ($40,000 ÷		
40 years)	1,000	
	$119,000	

*Goodwill is calculated as:

Price paid	$440,000
Less: 80% of Beta's stock ($300,000)	(240,000)
80% of Beta's retained earnings on the date of acquisition ($200,000)	(160,000)
Goodwill	$ 40,000

For 19x3, the parent company would make the following entries on its books:

Parent's Books

3/31/x3	Cash	12,000	
	Investment in Beta Corporation		12,000
	To record dividend received (80% × $15,000).		
6/30/x3	Same entry.		
9/30/x3	Same entry.		
10/1/x3	Investment in Beta Corporation	95,250	
	Equity in Earnings of Subsidiary		95,250
	To record share of income for nine months as follows:		

80% × $120,000 =	$96,000	
Less: Goodwill amortization		
($1,000 × 9/12)	750	
	$95,250	

Parent's Books

Cash		75,500	
Investment in Beta Corporation			72,281
Gain on sale of investments			3,219

To record the sale of 2,000 shares of Beta common
stock as follows:

Price paid—16,000 shares		$440,000	
Income 19x2		119,000	
Income 19x3		95,250	
Less: Dividends 19x2	$40,000		
Dividends 19x3	36,000	(76,000)	
Investment balance, 10/1/x3 . .		$578,250	
Carrying amount of shares sold (2,000/16,000 = ⅛ of above) .		$ 72,281*	

12/31/x3 Cash		10,500	
Investment in Beta Corporation			10,500

To record receipt of dividend (70% × $15,000).

Investment in Beta Corporation		27,781	
Equity in Earnings of Subsidiary			27,781

To record equity in earnings for the fourth quarter of
19x3 as follows:

70% × $40,000 =		$28,000
Amortization of goodwill ($40,000 − ⅛ sold on 10/1/x3 = $35,000 ÷ 40 years = $875 per annum × ¼ year) .		(219)
Total		$27,781

*Rounded to nearest dollar.

Illustration 9–1 presents a condensed consolidated working paper which reflects the above sale.

The elimination entries for Illustration 9–1 are:

(1)		
Equity in Earnings—Subsidiary	123,031	
Dividends Declared—Beta Corporation		46,500
Investment in Beta Corporation		76,531

(2)		
Investment in Beta Corporation	7,500	
Retained Earnings (1/1/x3)—Beta Corporation		7,500

(3)		
Amortization of Goodwill (Expenses)	969	
Retained Earnings (1/1/x3)—Beta Corporation	210,000	
Capital Stock—Beta Corporation	210,000	
Goodwill	33,250	
Investment in Beta Corporation		454,219

From the working paper it can be noted that:

1. The intercompany dividends that are eliminated as part of entry (1) are the actual dividends received by the parent company ($12,000 + $12,000 + $12,000 + $10,500 = $46,500).

Illustration 9–1
ANTHONY CORPORATION
Condensed Consolidated Working Paper
For the Year Ended December 31, 19x3

Complete Equity Method
Sale of Investment by Parent Co.
70 Percent Subsidiary

	Anthony Corp.	Beta Corp. (70%)	Eliminations Dr.	Eliminations Cr.	Minority Interest	Consol-idated
Income Statement						
Sales	1,000,000	310,000				1,310,000
Cost of sales, expenses, and income taxes	600,000	150,000	(3) 969			750,969
Operating income	400,000	160,000				559,031
Equity in earnings—subsidiary	123,031		(1) 123,031			
Gain on sale of investments	3,219					3,219
						562,250
Minority interest net income					36,000	(36,000)
Net income—carried forward	526,250	160,000			36,000	526,250
Retained Earnings Statement						
Balance, 1/1/x3:						
Anthony Corp.	500,000					500,000
Beta Corp.		300,000	(3) 210,000	(2) 7,500	97,500	
Net income—brought forward	526,250	160,000			36,000	526,250
Totals	1,026,250	460,000			133,500	1,026,250
Less: Dividends declared:						
Beta Corp.		60,000		(1) 46,500	13,500	
Balance, 12/31/x3—carried forward	1,026,250	400,000			120,000	1,026,250
Balance Sheet						
Miscellaneous assets	1,103,000	750,000				1,853,000
				(3) 454,219		
Investment in Beta Corp.	523,250		(2) 7,500	(1) 76,531		
Goodwill			(3) 33,250			33,250
Totals	1,626,250	750,000				1,886,250
Liabilities	100,000	50,000				150,000
Capital stock:						
Anthony Corp.	500,000					500,000
Beta Corp.		300,000	(3) 210,000		90,000	
Retained earnings—brought forward	1,026,250	400,000			120,000	1,026,250
Minority interest					210,000	210,000
Totals	1,626,250	750,000	584,750	584,750		1,886,250

(1) Elimination of equity in earnings of subsidiary and dividends paid to parent company.

(2) To restore 19x3 investment increase in net assets on shares sold during the year—10 percent ($40,000 quarterly income − $15,000 quarterly dividend × 3 quarters). This amount was removed from investment to calculate gain on sale of investments and becomes part of minority interest.

(3) To remove balance of investment, record unamortized goodwill and amortization for 19x3.

Illustration 9–1 (*continued*)

Computations and Proofs

Income apportionment:

	Total	Parent	Minority
Beta's income:			
1/1/x3–10/1/x3—80%	120,000	96,000	24,000
10/1/x3–12/31/x3—70%	40,000	28,000	12,000
Amortization of goodwill:			
1/1/x3–10/1/x3—($40,000 ÷ 40 years = $1,000 × $^9/_{12}$)	(750)	(750)	
10/1/x3–12/31/x3 (33,469 ÷ 38$^1/_4$ years = $875 × $^3/_{12}$)	(219)	(219)	
Anthony's income:			
($526,250 − $123,031)	403,219	403,219	
Totals	562,250	526,250	36,000

Reconciliation minority interest:

The minority interest of $210,000 is 30 percent of the net assets on 12/31/x3 ($700,000).

2. Entry (2) represents the increase in net assets on Beta's books for the first nine months of 19x3 that is applicable to the 10 percent (2,000 shares) sold by Anthony. Since this increase in net assets was recorded on Anthony's books in 19x3 and then removed from the investment because of the sale, the $7,500 is now shifted to the minority interest.[4] This is necessary if the minority interest of 30 percent is to reconcile to $210,000. Another way of viewing this adjustment of $7,500 is:

Retained earnings January 1, 19x3—Beta	$300,000
Add: Income, January 1, 19x3, to September 30, 10x3	120,000
Deduct: Dividends, January 1, 19x3 to September 30, 19x3	(45,000)
Retained earnings, October 1, 19x3—Beta	$375,000

Minority interest's share of retained earnings:	
20% of retained earnings, January 1, 19x3 (see above)—$300,000	$60,000
10% of retained earnings, October 1, 19x3 (see above)—$375,000	37,500
Required balance of retained earnings in minority interest column (see Illustration 9–1)	$97,500
Less: 30% of retained earnings on January 1, 19x3 ($300,000)	90,000
Adjustment required	$ 7,500*

*This adjustment would also be required for interim sales when a subsidiary sells shares to third parties since, in substance, a sale of this type is equivalent to a sale by an investor of its shares in the investee. The calculation would be identical.

In essence, the $7,500 did not flow to the minority interest through

---

[4]Income for the period January 1, 19x3 to September 30, 19x3	$120,000
Dividends for the period January 1, 19x3 to September 30, 19x3	45,000
Increase in net assets	$ 75,000
10% of the above	$ 7,500

the income statement and, therefore, it must be shifted through the retained earnings statement. A proof of the above would be:

Beta's net assets (capital stock and retained earnings), January 1, 19x3 . . .	$600,000
Beta's net assets, October 1, 19x3	675,000

Computation of minority interest, December 31, 19x3:	
20% of net assets at January 1, 19x3	$120,000
Add: Net income	36,000
Less: Dividends	(13,500)
Add: 10% of net assets, October 1, 19x3	67,500
Minority interest (30% total), December 31, 19x3	$210,000

3. Entry (3) accomplishes the following:
    a. Eliminates 70 percent of Beta's capital stock.
    b. Eliminates 70 percent of Beta's beginning retained earnings.
    c. Records the total amortization of goodwill for the year ($750 + $219 or $969).
    d. Records the unamortized balance of goodwill on the remaining shares ($40,000 − $\frac{1}{8}$ sold = $35,000 − $875 each for 19x2 and 19x3 or $33,250). ($35,000 ÷ 40 years = $875 per year.)
    e. Eliminates the balance of the investment.

The adjustment to minority interest as indicated above is not required for *interim purchases* of subsidiary shares by the parent, and the procedures indicated above should be contrasted with those shown in Chapter 8. For interim purchases of stock, it is merely necessary to adjust for preacquisition income with no adjustments beyond that. In essence, the minority interest on the last day of the accounting period governs the treatment for the entire accounting period. For interim sales, however, a split in minority interest and minority interest net income is required for the change in percentage of ownership.

TREASURY STOCK TRANSACTIONS— SUBSIDIARY'S PURCHASE OF SHARES FROM THIRD PARTIES

Another method of increasing a parent's percentage of ownership is to have the subsidiary purchase its own shares from the minority interest. When a subsidiary does this, and regardless of whether it retires the shares or keeps them as treasury stock, the parent's percentage of ownership is thereby increased. Thus, if P Company owns 9,000 shares out of 12,000 issued by S Company and S Company purchases 2,000 shares from the minority shareholders, the percentages of ownership are:

	Before	*After*
Parent's shares:	$\frac{9,000}{12,000}$ = 75%	$\frac{9,000}{10,000}$ = 90%
Total shares:		

Earlier in this chapter it was seen that the above change in percentage ownership is the exact reverse of the case where the subsidiary sold shares to third parties. The discussion that followed is equally applicable here, i.e., if the purchase of the shares is made at S Company's book value, no adjustment to the investment on the parent's books is required. To demonstrate this, the following is assumed:

1. S Company has 12,000 shares outstanding, and its net assets are $600,000 ($50 book value per share).
2. P Company purchases 9,000 shares for $550,000. Later that day, S. Company purchases 2,000 shares @ $50 per share for a total of $100,000

The calculations of excess before and after the purchase of the treasury shares are:

	Before	After
Price paid by P Company	$550,000	$550,000
75% of net assets of $600,000	450,000	
90% of net assets of $500,000 ($600,000 − $100,000)		450,000
Excess	$100,000	$100,000

Thus it can be seen that no adjustment is required for a purchase of treasury shares at book value. However, purchases of treasury shares do require adjustments when the prices differ from book value. The discussions in the earlier part of this chapter dealing with sales at other than book value are also applicable to treasury stock transactions but with one adjustment. When shares are sold by a subsidiary at a price in excess of book value, the parent's investment account is *increased.* However, if a subsidiary purchases treasury shares in excess of book value, the parent's investment account is *decreased.* The dollar amounts of the calculations are exactly the same as discussed earlier in the chapter and, therefore, need not be repeated here. Of course, sales and purchases below book also parallel that discussion except that the effect is in the opposite direction of increasing and decreasing the investment account on the parent's books.

STOCK DIVIDENDS

A stock dividend merely affects the composition of stockholders' equity while leaving the total unchanged. Therefore, a parent's investment account is unaffected by the issuance of a stock dividend and the reciprocity of the parent's investment and the subsidiary's net assets is unaffected. Thus, the aggregate of working paper elimination entries are the same whether a stock dividend is issued or not. The only difference between the two is in the amounts of the component retained earnings, capital stock and additional paid-in capital.

A simple illustration will indicate the working paper elimination entries that are required to reflect a stock dividend. It is assumed that:

1. P Company purchases 80 percent of S Company's outstanding shares on January 1, 19x1, at book value. All assets and liabilities are at their respective fair market values on this date and consequently no goodwill arises.
2. On January 1, 19x1, S Company's common stock consists of 10,000 shares of $50 par value, or $500,000, and its retained earnings amount to $500,000. On January 2, 19x1, S Company declares a 10 percent stock dividend on which date its stock is selling at $100 per share.

Based on the above, the parent company would make the following entries:

Parent's Books

1/1/x1	Investment in S Company	800,000	
	Cash		800,000

To record the purchase of 8,000 shares of S Company.

1/2/x1   Memo entry to record the receipt of 800 shares of S Company as a 10 percent stock dividend.

Subsidiary's Books

1/2/x1	Stock Dividend Declared	100,000	
	Common Stock		50,000
	Additional Paid-In Capital from Stock Dividend . . .		50,000

To record the issuance of a 10 percent stock dividend of 1,000 shares at a fair market value of $100 per share.

If a consolidation working paper is prepared as of January 1, 19x1, the elimination entry would be:

1/1/x1	Retained Earnings (80% × $500,000)	400,000	
	Common Stock (80% × $500,000)	400,000	
	Investment in S Company		800,000

Alternatively, if a consolidation working paper is prepared as of January 2, 19x1, the elimination entry would be:

(1)

1/2/x1	Common Stock	40,000	
	Additional Paid-In Capital	40,000	
	Stock Dividends Declared		80,000

(2)

	Common Stock	400,000	
	Retained Earnings	400,000	
	Investment in S Company		800,000

The latter entries serve to reverse the parent's share of the stock dividend, and thereby causes the parent's share of S Company's stockholders' equity to revert back to the beginning-of-the-year balances. For subsequent years, working paper elimination entries would be as discussed in preceding chapters with no further modifications.

Appendix: Decreases in parent's ownership percentage—cost method

Sales of shares by a subsidiary to third parties

The *calculations* and *journal entries* pertaining to *sales* of shares by a subsidiary to third parties apply equally to investments accounted for by the cost method as to those accounted for by the complete equity method. In fact, the entries illustrated in the chapter are identical for the same transactions where the cost method is used. The only difference between the two methods is that for the complete equity method the entries are recorded on the *parent's books*—as shown in the chapter—while for the cost method *the same entries* are recorded on the consolidation *working papers.* The reason for this is that for the cost method the investment account is carried at original cost on the books and all needed adjustments are, therefore, posted on the working papers only. It should be remembered that once an adjustment to APIC is made on the parent's books under the complete equity method it is not necessary to repeat it. Alternatively, for the cost method it is necessary to repeat the entry, year after year, since the entry is posted to the *working paper only* and each year's trial balance is taken from the books.

Treasury stock transactions of a subsidiary

What was noted above as applicable to sales of stock by a subsidiary also applies to purchases of treasury stock. Since the purchase of treasury stock can be viewed as a negative sale, treasury stock transactions are the exact oppposite of the sale of additional shares. Consequently, the discussion of treasury share transactions in the chapter coupled with this discussion should enable the reader to fully understand the appropriate accounting in this case.

Sale of a subsidiary's shares by a parent company

Although the end result—consolidated financial statements—is the same for investments accounted for by the cost method as they are under the complete equity method, the accounting treatment and the consolidated working papers are different for the two methods. In order to demonstrate the differences and the same end product, the information that was used to prepare Illustration 9–1 will now be used to prepare Illustration 9–2. The only change between the two will be that the parent company is now assumed to use the cost method to account for its investment instead of the complete equity method. Using the cost method, the parent company would record $40,000 of dividend income on its books for 19x2 and for 19x3 the amount would be $46,500. One other entry would be recorded on the books of the parent company pertaining to its investment in Beta Corporation. This entry is the gain on the sale of 2,000 shares of Beta's stock.

The elimination entries for Illustration 9–2 are:

	(1)	
Dividend Income	46,500	
Dividends Declared—Beta Corporation		46,500
	(2)	
Investment in Beta Corporation	80,000	
Retained Earnings (1/1/x3) —Anthony Corporation . .		80,000

(3)		
Gain on Sale of Investments . .	9,875	
Investment in Beta		
Corporation		9,875

(4)		
Amortization of Goodwill		
(expenses)	94	
Gain on Sale of Investments . .	7,406	
Retained Earnings (1/1/x3)		
—Beta Corporation		7,500

(5)		
Retained Earnings (1/1/x3)—		
Anthony Corporation	125	
Retained Earnings (1/1/x3)—		
Beta Corporation	210,000	
Goodwill	35,000	
Capital Stock—Beta		
Corporation	210,000	
Investment in Beta		
Corporation		455,125

(6)		
Amortization of Goodwill		
(expenses)	875	
Retained Earnings (1/1/x3)—		
Anthony Corporation	875	
Goodwill		1,750

From the consolidated working paper for 19x3 (Illustration 9–2), the following can be noted:

1. The difference between the parent's book retained earnings on January 1, 19x3, ($421,000) and its working paper retained earnings on that date ($500,000) is $79,000. This amount can be computed as follows:

Increase in Beta's net assets from date of	
acquisition ($300,000 − $200,000)	$100,000
80% of above—parent's share	$80,000
Less: Amortization of goodwill ($40,00 ÷	
40 years = $1,000 × 1 year)	(1,000)
Difference	$ 79,000

2. Dividend income is eliminated in entry (1), and

the parent's share of the increase in the net assets of Beta Corporation is recorded in entry (2).

3. The book gain on the sale of Bet's stock can be computed as follows:

Selling price of stock	$75,500
Cost of shares sold (original cost of	
$440,000 × 2,000/16,000)	55,000
Gain on sale—cost method	$20,500

4. The above gain must be converted to the equity method.
   This is accomplished by:
   a. Adjusting the gain for income recorded on prior years' working papers pertaining to the shares sold. The computation appears in explanation (3) on the working paper. See entry (3).
   b. Adjusting the gain in entry (4) for the 19x3 increase in net assets pertaining to the shares sold and by recording the current year's amortization of goodwill for these shares.
   After recording the above adjustments, the gain is converted to $3,219 which amount agrees with that shown in Illustration 9–1. The credit of $7,500 in entry (4) is explained in Illustration 9–1.

5. In entry (5), only the remaining portion of goodwill is recorded ($40,000 × 14,000/16,000 = $35,000). The portion sold ($5,000) entered into the calculation of the gain on sale ($20,500).

6. Amortization of goodwill is now $875 per annum ($35,000 ÷ 40 years). Since the cost method is used, amortization must be recorded for the current year as well as for prior years since none of the amortization is recorded on the parent's books.

A comparison of Illustration 9–1 with Illustration 9–2 reveals that the minority interest columns as well as the consolidated statement columns of both illustrations are identical.

QUESTIONS

1. What is the effect on a parent's investment account when its subsidiary sells common stock to third parties at book value? Does the parent's percentage of ownership change as a result of such a sale? How do you reconcile your answers? (Use an example to prove your answer.)

2. What is the effect on a parent's investment account when its subsidiary sells common stock to third parties at a price per share which is in excess of its book value? Are any other accounts affected by the sale? What reason(s) can you offer to justify your answers?

Illustration 9–2
ANTHONY CORPORATION
Condensed Consolidated Working Paper
For the Year Ended December 31, 19x3

Cost Method
Sale of Investment by Parent Co.
70 Percent Subsidiary

	Anthony Corp.	Beta Corp. (70%)	Eliminations Dr.	Eliminations Cr.	Minority Interest	Consolidated
Income Statement						
Sales	1,000,000	310,000				1,310,000
			(6) 875			
Cost of sales, expenses, and income taxes	600,000	150,000	(4) 94			750,969
Operating income	400,000	160,000	(1) 46,500			559,031
Dividend income	46,500		(3) 9,875			
Gain on sale of investments	20,500		(4) 7,406			3,219
						562,250
Minority interest net income					36,000	(36,000)
Net income—carried forward	467,000	160,000			36,000	526,250
Retained Earnings Statement						
Balance, 1/1/x3:						
			(6) 875			
Anthony Corp.	421,000		(5) 125	(2) 80,000		500,000
Beta Corp.		300,000	(5) 210,000	(4) 7,500	97,500	
Net income—brought forward	467,000	160,000			36,000	526,250
Totals	888,000	460,000			133,500	1,026,250
Less: Dividends declared:						
Beta Corp.		60,000		(1) 46,500	13,500	
Balance, 12/31/x3—carried forward	888,000	400,000			120,000	1,026,250
Balance Sheet						
Miscellaneous assets	1,103,000	750,000				1,853,000
			(2) 80,000	(5) 455,125		
Investment in Beta Corp.	385,000			(3) 9,875		
Goodwill			(5) 35,000	(6) 1,750		33,250
Totals	1,488,000	750,000				1,886,250
Liabilities	100,000	50,000				150,000
Capital stock:						
Anthony Corp.	500,000					500,000
Beta Corp.		300,000	(5) 210,000		90,000	
Retained earnings—brought forward	888,000	400,000			120,000	1,026,250
Minority interest					210,000	210,000
Totals	1,488,000	750,000				1,886,250

(1) Elimination of intercompany dividends.

(2) To record parent's share of increase in net assets from date of acquisition 80% × ($300,000 − $200,000).

(3) To reduce gain on sale by income recorded on prior years' working papers (¹/₈ of entry (2) = $10,000 less amortization of ¹/₈ × $1,000) for shares sold by parent company.

(4) To record increase in net assets on shares sold for period 1/1/x3—9/30/x3 and amortization for the period 10% ($120,000 income minus $45,000 dividends = $75,000) minus ¹/₈ × $750.

(5) To eliminate balance of investment.

(6) To record amortization at $875 per annum on remaining shares ($35,000 ÷ 40 years = $875).

Illustration 9–2 (*continued*)

Computations and Proofs

Income apportionment:
  (See Illustration 9–1.)

Reconciliation minority interest:
  (See Illustration 9–1.)

Reconciliation of Retained Earnings:

Balance per books, 12/31/x3		$888,000
Add: Increase in Beta's retained earnings:		
Balance, 12/31/x3	$400,000	
Balance, date of acquisition	200,000	
Increase	$200,000	
70% of above	$140,000	
Less: Amortization of goodwill ($875 × 2 years)	(1,750)	138,250
Balance per workpaper		$1,026,250

3. What happens to the congruity between a parent's investment account and the parent's share of the net assets of the subsidiary when the latter sells common stock to third parties at a price per share which is less than book value? What treatment on the parent's books becomes necessary when this occurs?

4. Is the treatment consistent for piecemeal acquisitions when a purchase of shares increases the investor's percentage from below 20 percent to a greater amount, on the one hand, and that of a sale of shares that decreases the percentage of ownership from 20 percent or more to an amount less than 20 percent on the other hand? Explain.

5. How is the gain or loss on the sale of shares computed when an investor of 20 percent or more sells shares of an investee's stock? Are the procedures the same for a 20 percent to 50 percent investor as for a parent company?

6. When shares are sold by a 20 percent or greater investor on an interim date, are there additional calculations to be made as opposed to a sale at the beginning of a year? If so, what calculations are required to calculate the gain or loss on the sale?

7. When treasury shares are purchased from third parties, what is the effect on the parent's percentage of ownership? Does the price paid have an effect on the parent's investment account in *all* cases? Discuss.

8. Does a stock dividend issued by a subsidiary have an effect on the parent's investment account? Does the dividend have an effect on the consolidated working paper elimination entries? Explain.

Questions for appendix—cost method:

9. Are the calculations for a gain or loss on the sale of shares by a parent company the same for the cost method as for the complete equity method? Are the amounts per *books* the same? Are the amounts per consolidated working paper (consolidated column) the same? How do you explain your answers?

10. In the context of changes in percentages of ownership how should treasury stock purchases by a subsidiary be viewed?

EXERCISES

Exercise 9–1. On January 2, 19x2, P Company purchased, in the open market, 12,000 shares of the common stock of S Company for $480,000. On that date, S Company had 15,000 shares outstanding and its net assets were $600,000 composed of the common stock at $10 par value and the balance in retained earnings.

Immediately after the purchase by P Company, S Company sold an additional 3,000 shares of stock to outsiders.

Required:

a. Prepare the entry to record the sale of the shares @ $40 per share (on S Company's books).

b. What percentage of stock does P Company own after its purchase but *before* the sale by S Company? *After* the sale by S Company?

c. Prepare any necessary entry on the books of P Company if the price received by S Company is:

1. $40 per share.
2. $30 per share.
3. $60 per share.

(Note: P Company has $50,000 of additional paid-in capital on its books at January 1, 19x2.)

Exercise 9–2. On January 2, 19x3, P Company purchased for cash, in the open market, 18,000 shares of the common stock of S Company for $300,000. On that date, S Company had 20,000 shares outstanding and its net assets consisted of:

Common stock ($10 par)	$200,000
Retained earnings	100,000
Total	$300,000

On July 1, 19x3, S Company sold 4,000 shares of stock to outsiders at $20 per share.

For the year 19x3, S Company earned $80,000 uniformly and paid no dividends.

Required:

a. Prepare the entry to record the sale of the shares by S Company.

b. What percentage of ownership did P Company have on January 2, 19x3? On July 1, 19x3, *after* the sale by S Company?

c. Prepare the required entry on the books of P Company as a result of the sale of the shares by S Company.

d. What amount should P Company record as equity in earnings of S Company? (All of the liabilities and assets of S Company have book values equal to their respective fair market values.)

Exercise 9–3. Using the information from Exercise 9–2, rework the exercise if the selling price per share were $12 instead of $20. Assume that P Company has $40,000 of additional paid-in capital on its books. All other conditions remain unchanged.

Exercise 9–4. P Company purchased, in the open market, 9,000 shares of the common stock of S Company for $400,000. On January 2, 19x4, the date of the purchase by P Company, the net assets of S Company consisted of:

Common stock ($10 par)	$100,000
Retained earnings	300,000
Total	$400,000

Shortly after the purchase by P Company, on the same day, S Company sold 5,000 additional share of stock. *P Company purchased 4,500* shares and 500 shares were purchased by outsiders.

Required:

a. Prepare the entry to record the sale of the shares by S Company, if the shares were sold for—

1. $40 per share.
2. $30 per share.
3. $60 per share.

b. What is the parent's percentage of ownership before the sale? After the sale?

c. For each case in (a) above, compute any adjustment required to the investment account on the books of P Company.

d. What conclusion can you reach about the effect of the price at which shares are sold when an investor purchases a pro rata portion of the shares sold by an investee?

Exercise 9–5. Using the information in Exercise 9–4, assume that P Company only purchased 3,000 shares of stock instead of 4,500 shares. All other conditions remain unchanged.

Required:

Complete (a), (b), and (c) of Exercise 9–4.

Exercise 9–6. On January 2, 19x3, P Company purchased 80 percent of the outstanding common stock of S Company for $720,000. On that date, the net assets of S Company consisted of:

Common stock ($50 par)	$500,000
Retained earnings	300,000
Total	$800,000

S Company had the following incomes earned uniformly and paid the following dividends:

Year	Net income	Dividends (paid quarterly)
19x3	$120,000	$40,000
19x4	150,000	50,000

On July 1, 19x4, P Company sold 1,000 of the 8,000 shares it owned for $110,000.

P Company uses the complete equity method to account for its investment in S Company.

Required:

a. Prepare the journal entries to record the equity in earnings of S Company for:

1. 19x3.

2. 19x4.

(*Hint:* Income must be prorated for 19x4.) Excess is to be amortized over a 40-year period.

b. Compute the balance of the investment account at July 1, 19x4.

c. Prepare the journal entry to record the sale of the 1,000 shares of stock by P Company.

d. Compute the balance in the investment account at December 31, 19x4.

Exercise 9–7. On January 2, 19x2, P Company purchased 20,000 shares of common stock directly from S Company for $2,000,000. On that date, S Company had net assets consisting of:

Common stock ($10 par)	$ 50,000
Retained earnings	250,000
Total	$300,000

All of the assets and liabilities of S Company had book values approximately equal to their respective market values.

Required:

a. What percentage of ownership does P Company have after its purchase of the shares?

b. Compute the amount of excess that P Company paid for its investment.

c. Prepare the elimination entry that would be required for a consolidated working paper prepared on January 2, 19x2.

Exercise 9–8. Pasta Corporation made the following purchases of Shasta's common stock (total outstanding shares are 40,000) in the open market:

Date	Number purchased	Price paid
January 1, 19x5	8,000	$168,000
April 1, 19x5	12,000	219,000
July 1, 19x5	12,000	248,000

Shasta's stockholders' equity at the beginning of the year consisted of:

Common stock ($10 PV)	$400,000
Retained earnings	200,000
Total	$600,000

Shasta's income for the year was $120,000, and it was earned uniformly. Dividends of $1 per share were paid on Decmeber 1, of the current year.

Pasta sold 2,000 shares of its investment in Shasta for $47,275 on October 1, 19x5. All assets and liabilities of Shasta are at fair market value.

Required:

a. The amount of goodwill for each purchase.

b. Compute the equity in earnings of the subsidiary for 19x5. Pasta uses the complete equity method to account for its investment.

c. Compute the gain or loss on sale of the 2,000 shares (use FIFO).

Exercise 9–9. On January 2, 19x5, P Company purchased, in the open market, 6,000 shares of the outstanding common stock of S Company for $500,000. The net assets of S Company on that date consisted of:

Common stock ($30 par)	$300,000
Retained earnings	400,000
Total	$700,000

The day after the purchase of the shares by P Company, the subsidiary purchased 2,000 shares of its own stock in the open market.

Required:

a. Calculate the excess on the purchase by P Company.

b. What percentage of ownership did P Company have after its purchase but *before* the purchase by S Company? *After* the purchase by S Company?

c. Compute the adjustment to the investment account required on the books of P Company if the 2,000 shares are purchased at:

1. $70 per share.

2. $50 per share.

3. $90 per share. (Assume that P Company has additional paid-in capital of $50,000 on its books.)

(*Hint:* Reduce the net assets of S Company by the amount paid for the shares.)

Exercise 9–10. On January 2, 19x3, P Company purchased, in the open market, 8,000 shares of the outstanding common stock of S Company for $460,000. The net assets of S Company on that date consisted of:

Common stock ($40 par)	$400,000
Retained earnings	100,000
Total	$500,000

On the following day, S Company purchased 2,000 shares of its own stock directly from P Company.

Required:

a. Calculate excess on the purchase by P Company.

b. What percentage of ownership does P Company have on January 2, 19x3? On January 3, 19x3?

c. For each case, compute the required adjustment, if any, to the investment account of P Company as a result of the purchase by S Company *and* the gain or loss on the sale by P Company. (Two calculations are required for each case.)

	Selling price per share
Case I	$50.00
Case II	40.00
Case III	57.50
Case IV	70.00

Exercise 9–11. On January 2, 19x5, P Company purchased 80 percent of the outstanding common stock of S Company for $600,000. The net assets of S Company on that date consisted of:

Common stock ($20 par)	$200,000
Retained earnings	400,000
Total	$600,000

On the following day, S Company declared a 10 percent stock dividend and made the following entry on its books:

Retained Earnings	75,000	
Common Stock		20,000
Additional Paid-In Capital . .		55,000
To record the issuance of 1,000 shares as a 10 percent stock dividend at the fair market value of $75 per share.		

Required:

a. Prepare the consolidated working paper elimination entry, if a working paper were prepared on January 2, 19x5, *before* the stock dividend was issued.

b. Prepare the consolidated working paper elimination entry as of January 3, 19x5, *after* the stock was issued.

Exercise 9–12 (for appendix). Using the information provided in Exercise 9–6, assume that the Parent Company uses the cost method to account for its investment in S Company and all other information remains unchanged.

Required:

a. Compute the gain or loss on the shares sold that would be recorded on the *books* of P Company.

b. Prepare the entry that would be required on a consolidated working paper to convert the amount computed in *(a)* above to the proper amount on a consolidated financial statement.

PROBLEMS

Problem 9–13. On January 2, 19x1, P Company purchased, for cash in the open market, 36,000 shares of the common stock of S Company for $900,000. On that date, S Company had net assets consisting of:

Common stock ($10 par)	$400,000
Retained earnings	500,000
Total	$900,000

On July 1, 19x1, S Company sold an additional 8,000 shares of stock to outsiders at $30 per share.

For the year 19x1, S Company earned $200,000 uniformly and paid a dividend of $2 per share on December 1, 19x1.

The assets and liabilities of S Company had book values equal to their respective market values on January 2, 19x1. Excess, if any, has an indeterminate life.

P Company uses the complete equity method to account for its investment in S Company.

Required:

a. What percentage of ownership did P Company have on January 2, 19x1? On July 1, 19x1?

b. Prepare the required entry on the books of P Company as a result of the sale of the shares by S Company.

c. What amount should P Company record as equity in earnings of S Company?

d. Compute minority interest net income for 19x1.

e. Compute the balance in the investment account at December 31, 19x1.

f. Compute the amount that would appear as minority interest in a consolidated balance sheet at December 31, 19x1.

g. Prepare the consolidated working paper elimination entries for 19x1. (*Hint:* See footnote on page 330.)

Problem 9–14. Past Corporation made the following purchases of Soasta's common stock (total outstanding shares are 20,000) in the open market:

Date	Number purchased	Price paid
January 1, 19x5	4,000	$180,000
April 1, 19x5	4,000	123,000
October 1, 19x5	6,000	243,500

Soasta's stockholders' equity at the beginning of the year consisted of:

Common stock ($20 PV)	$400,000
Retained earnings	200,000
Total	$600,000

Soasta's income for the year was $60,000, and it was earned uniformly. Dividends of $1 per share were paid on December 1, 19x5.

Past Corporation sold 2,000 shares of its investment in Soasta for $85,000 on June 30, 19x5. All assets and liabilities of Soasta are at fair market value.

Required:

a. The amount of goodwill for each purchase.

b. Compute the equity in earnings of subsidiary for 19x5. Past uses the complete equity method to account for its investment.

c. Compute the gain or loss on sale of the 2,000 shares (use FIFO).

d. The balance in the investment account on December 31, 19x5, after all entries that are required are posted.

e. Compute the amount of minority interest net income.

f. Compute the amount that would be shown as minority interest on a consolidated balance sheet at December 31, 19x5.

g. Prepare the consolidated working paper elimination entries for 19x5.

Problem 9–15. On January 2, 19x4, P Company purchased, in the open market, 9,000 shares of the outstanding common stock of S Company for $660,000. The net assets of S Company on that date consisted of:

Common stock ($20 par)	$240,000
Retained earnings	560,000
Total	$800,000

On July 1, 19x5, S Company purchased 2,000 shares of its stock in the open market for $140,000.

Income, earned uniformly, and dividends paid by S Company are as follows:

Year	Income	Dividends (paid annually in December)
19x4	$100,000	$2.50 per share
19x5	120,000	3.00 per share*

*Paid on only 10,000 shares.

All of the assets and liabilities of S Company had book values approximately equal to their respective fair market values.

P Company uses the complete equity method to account for its investment in S Company.

Required:

a. What percentage of ownership did P Company have on January 2, 19x4? On July 1, 19x5?

b. Prepare the required entry on the books of P Company as a result of the purchase of the shares by S Company.

c. Compute the amount P Company should record as Equity in earnings of S Company for:

1. 19x4.

2. 19x5.

d. Compute minority interest net income for 19x5.

e. Compute the balance in the investment account on:

1. July 1, 19x5.

2. December 31, 19x5.

f. Compute the amount that would appear as minority interest in a consolidated balance sheet at December 31, 19x5.

Problem 9–16. Using the information provided in Problem 9–15, rework the problem but assume now that the 2,000 shares were purchased directly from P Company instead of in the open market.

Required:

The same requirements as in Problem 9–15.

Problem 9–17 (complete equity method). On January 1, 19x2, P Company acquired 80 percent of the outstanding common stock of S Company for $640,000. On that date, the retained earnings of S Company were $200,000 and there have been no changes in its capital stock and additional paid-in capital.

All of the assets and liabilities of S Company had book values approximately equal to their respective market values. Goodwill, if any, is to be amortized over a 40-year period.

This year, 19x4, there were no intercompany transactions except for the dividends which were paid in December.

P Company uses the complete equity method to account for its investment in S Company.

On July 1, 19x4, P Company sold 3,000 shares (10 percent of the outstanding shares of S Company) of its investment in S Company to outsiders for $130,000. Income for 19x4 was earned uniformly.

The financial statements of the companies for the year ended December 31, 19x4, are as follows:

Income Statement	P Company	S Company
Sales	$1,200,000	$ 700,000
Cost of sales	500,000	250,000
Gross margin	700,000	450,000
Expenses	200,000	120,000
Operating income before taxes	500,000	330,000
Gain on sale of investments	11,975	
Equity in earnings— subsidiary	142,875	
Income before income taxes	654,850	330,000
Provision for income taxes	204,790	132,000
Minority interest net income		
Net income—carried forward	$ 450,060	$ 198,000

Retained Earnings Statement	P Company	S Company
Balance, January 1, 19x2:		
P Company	$ 837,940	
S Company		$ 500,000
Net income—brought forward	450,060	198,000
Totals	1,288,000	698,000
Less: Dividends declared:		
P Company	150,000	
S Company		60,000
Balance, December 31, 19x2— carried forward	$1,138,000	$ 638,000

	P Company	S Company
Balance Sheet		
Cash	$ 298,750	$ 48,000
Accounts receivable	240,000	70,000
Inventories	150,000	80,000
Land		150,000
Building—(net of accumulated depreciation)		190,000
Equipment—(net of accumulated depreciation)	800,000	540,000
Investment in S Company	850,850	
Totals	$2,339,600	$1,078,000
Accounts payable and accrued expenses	$ 200,000	$ 140,000
Bonds payable (face amount $400,000)	401,600	
Common stock—P Company ($50 par)	200,000	
Common stock—S Company ($10 par)		300,000
Additional paid-in capital—P Company	400,000	
Retained earnings—P Company—brought forward	1,138,000	
Retained earnings—S Company—brought forward		638,000
Totals	$2,339,600	$1,078,000

Required:

a. Prepare a schedule to verify the gain on sale of investments.

b. Prepare an income allocation schedule for the parent company and the minority interest.

c. Prepare a consolidated working paper. (*Hint:* An adjustment to minority interest is required. See page 330.)

Problem 9–18 (complete equity method). On January 1, 19x1, P Company purchased 40,000 shares of S Company in the open market for $1,140,000. On that date, the assets and liabilities of S Company had book values that approximated their respective fair market values. Excess (goodwill), if any, is expected to last for 20 years and is to be amortized over that period.

P Company uses the complete equity method to account for its investment.

After the preparation of the financial statements presented below but before the close of business on December 31, 19x1, S Company sold 12,500 additional shares of common stock to outsiders for $500,000.

Financial statements for the two corporations,

before giving effect to the sale, for the year ended December 31, 19x1, are as follows:

	P Company	S Company
Income Statement		
Sales	$2,000,000	$1,000,000
Cost of sales	800,000	600,000
Gross margin	1,200,000	400,000
Expenses	500,000	100,000
Operating income before taxes	700,000	300,000
Equity in earnings—subsidiary	139,000	
Income before income taxes .	839,000	300,000
Provision for income taxes . .	280,000	120,000
Minority interest net income		
Net income—carried forward	$ 559,000	$ 180,000
Retained Earnings Statement		
Balance, January 1, 19x1:		
P Company	$3,000,000	
S Company		$ 800,000
Net income—brought forward	559,000	180,000
Totals	3,559,000	980,000
Less: Dividends declared:		
P Company	400,000	
S Company		60,000
Balance, December 31, 19x1—carried forward	$3,159,000	$ 920,000
Balance Sheet		
Cash	$ 300,000	$ 100,000
Accounts receivable	200,000	200,000
Inventories	400,000	300,000
Land	600,000	
Building—(net of accumulated depreciation) .	400,000	
Equipment—(net of accumulated depreciation) .	1,228,000	1,000,000
Investment in S Company . .	1,231,000	
Totals	$4,359,000	$1,600,000
Accounts payable and accrued expenses	$ 302,000	$ 180,000
Bonds payable (face amount $100,000)	98,000	
Common stock—P Company ($50 par)	500,000	
Common stock—S Company ($10 par)		500,000
Additional paid-in capital—P Company	300,000	
Retained earnings—P Company—brought forward	3,159,000	
Retained earnings—S Company—brought forward		920,000
Totals	$4,359,000	$1,600,000

Required:

a. Prepare the journal entry to record the sale of the 12,500 shares by S Company.

b. What is the percentage of parent ownership after the sale?

c. Prepare the journal entry required to adjust the investment account on the books of P Company as a result of the sale of the 12,500 shares by S Company.

d. Adjust the financial statements of P Company and S Company above to give effect to the journal entries in *(a)* and *(c)*.

e. Prepare a consolidated working paper.

(*Hint:* An adjustment to minority interest is required as in the case where a parent sells part of its investment in a subsidiary. See page 330.)

Problem 9–19 (for appendix). On January 1, 19x2, P Company acquired 80 percent of the outstanding common stock of S Company for $640,000. On that date, the retained earnings of S Company were $200,000 and there have been no changes in its capital stock and additional paid-in capital.

All of the assets and liabilities of S Company had book values approximately equal to their respective market values. Goodwill, if any, is to be amortized over a 40-year period.

This year, 19x4, there were no intercompany transactions except for the dividends which were paid in December.

P Company uses the cost method to account for its investment in S Company.

On July 1, 19x4, P Company sold 3,000 shares (10 percent of the outstanding shares of S Company) of its investment in S Company to outsiders for $130,000. Income for 19x4 was earned uniformly.

The financial statements of the companies for the year ended December 31, 19x4, are as follows:

	P Company	S Company
Income Statement		
Sales	$1,200,000	$ 700,000
Cost of sales	500,000	250,000
Gross margin	700,000	450,000
Expenses	200,000	120,000
Operating income before taxes	500,000	330,000
Gain on sale of investments .	50,000	
Dividend income—subsidiary	42,000	
Income before income taxes .	592,000	330,000
Provision for income taxes . .	204,790	132,000
Minority interest net income		
Net income—carried forward	$ 387,210	$ 198,000

	P Company	S Company
Retained Earnings Statement		
Balance, January 1, 19x2:		
P Company	$ 609,940	
S Company		$ 500,000
Net income—brought		
forward	387,210	198,000
Totals . , ...	997,150	698,000
Less: Dividends declared:		
P Company	150,000	
S Company		60,000
Balance, December 31, 19x2—		
carried forward	$ 847,150	$ 638,000
Balance Sheet		
Cash	$ 298,750	$ 48,000
Accounts receivable	240,000	70,000
Inventories	150,000	80,000
Land		150,000
Building (net of accumulated depreciation)		190,000
Equipment (net of accumulated depreciation) .	800,000	540,000
Investment in S Company—at cost	560,000	
Totals	$2,048,750	$1,078,000
Accounts payable and accrued expenses	$ 200,000	$ 140,000
Bonds payable (face amount $400,000)	401,600	
Common stock—P Company ($50 par)	200,000	
Common stock—S Company ($10 par)		300,000
Additional paid-in capital—P Company	400,000	
Retained earnings—P Company—brought forward	847,150	
Retained earnings—S Company—brought forward		638,000
Totals	$2,048,750	$1,078,000

Required:

a. Prepare a schedule to compute the gain on sale of investments under the *equity* method.

b. Prepare an income allocation schedule for the parent company and the minority interest.

c. Prepare a consolidated working paper. (*Hint:* an adjustment to minority interest is required. See page 330.)

Problem 9–20 (incomplete equity method). Presented below are condensed statements of income (unconsolidated) for the year ended December 31, 19x5, of Royal Company and its subsidiary, Butler Company:

Condensed Statements of Income

	Royal Company	Butler Company
Sales	$4,000,000	$1,700,000
Cost of sales	(2,982,000)	(1,015,000)
Operating expenses	(400,000)	(377,200)
Dividend income	75,000	—
Subsidiary income	232,000	—
Interest expense	—	(7,800)
Net income	$ 925,000	$ 300,000

The statements of retained earnings for the year ended December 31, 19x5, and the balance sheets as of December 31, 19x5, of the companies are presented on the enclosed worksheet.

Additional information:

1. On January 3, 19x3, Royal acquired from John Roth, the sole stockholder of Butler Company, for $440,000 cash, both a patent valued at $40,000 and 80 percent of the outstanding stock of Butler. The net book value of Butler's stock on the date of acquisition was $500,000, and the book values of the individual assets and liabilities were equal to their fair market values. Royal charged the entire $440,000 to the account Investment in Stock of Butler Company. The patent, for which no amortization has been charged, had a remaining legal life of four years as of January 3, 19x3.

2. On July 1, 19x5, Royal reduced its investment in Butler to 75 percent of Butler's outstanding common stock, by selling shares for $70,000 to an unaffiliated company at a profit of $16,000. Royal recorded the proceeds as a credit to its investment account.

3. For the six months ended June 30, 19x5, Butler had net income of $140,000. Royal recorded 80 percent of this amount on its books of account prior to the time of sale.

4. During 19x4, Butler sold merchandise to Royal for $130,000, which was at a markup of 30 percent over Butler's cost. On January 1, 19x5, $52,000 of this merchandise remained in Royal's inventory. This merchandise was subsequently sold by Royal in February 19x5 at a profit of $8,000.

5. In November 19x5, Royal sold merchandise to Butler for the first time. Royal's cost for this merchandise was $80,000, and the sale was made at 120 percent of cost. Butler's inventory at December 31, 19x5, contained merchandise that

[Relates to Problem 9-20]

ROYAL COMPANY AND SUBSIDIARY
Worksheet to Prepare Consolidated
Statement of Retained Earnings and Balance Sheet
As of December 31, 19x5

	Royal Company Dr. (Cr.)	Butler Company Dr. (Cr.)	Consolidating totals Dr. (Cr.)	Adjustments and Eliminations		Minority Interest Dr. (Cr.)	Consolidated Dr. (Cr.)
				Debit	Cr.		
Statement of Retained Earnings							
Balance, January 1, 19x5							
Royal Company	(2,100,000)	—	(2,100,000)				
Butler Company	—	(640,000)	(640,000)				
Net income	(925,000)	(300,000)	(1,225,000)				
Dividends	170,000	100,000	270,000				
Balance, December 31, 19x5	(2,855,000)	(840,000)	(3,695,000)				
Balance Sheet							
Assets							
Cash	486,000	249,600	735,600				
Accounts receivable	235,000	185,000	420,000				
Inventories	475,000	355,000	830,000				
Machinery and equipment	2,231,000	530,000	2,761,000				
Investment in stock of Butler Company	954,000	—	954,000				
Investment in bonds of Butler Company	58,000	—	58,000				
	(4,439,000)	(1,319,600)	(5,758,600)				
Liabilities and Owners' Equity							
Accounts payable	(384,000)	(62,000)	(446,000)				
Bonds payable	—	(120,000)	(120,000)				
Unamortized discounts on bonds payable	—	2,400	2,400				
Common stock:							
Royal Company	(1,200,000)	—	(1,200,000)				
Butler Company	—	(250,000)	(250,000)				
Contributed capital	—	(50,000)	(50,000)				
Retained earnings (brought forward)	(2,855,000)	(840,000)	(3,695,000)				
Minority interest							
	(4,439,000)	(1,319,600)	(5,758,600)				

(AICPA adapted)

was purchased from Royal at a cost to Butler of $24,000.

6. On December 31, 19x5, there was a $45,000 payment in transit from Butler Company to Royal Company. Accounts receivable and accounts payable include intercompany receivables and payables.

7. In December 19x5, Butler declared and paid cash dividends of $100,000 to its stockholders.

8. On December 31, 19x5, Royal purchased for $58,000, 50 percent of the outstanding bonds issued by Butler. The bonds mature on December 31, 19x9, and were originally issued at a discount. On December 31, 19x5, the balance in Butler's account, Unamortized Discount on Bonds Payable was $2,400. It is the intention of the management of Royal to hold these bonds until their maturity.

Required:

Complete the worksheet to prepare a consolidated statement of retained earnings and a consolidated balance sheet of Royal Company and its subsidiary as of December 31, 19x5.

Formal statements and journal entries are not required. Ignore income taxes.

(*Hint:* For the current year, Royal recorded its share of subsidiary income *and* also recorded its receipt of intercompany dividends as dividend income.)

Problem 9–21 (cost method). On January 1, 19x6, Prent Company purchased a controlling interest in Alec Company. The general ledger trial balances for Prent Company and Alec Company at December 31, 19x6 are as follows:

PRENT COMPANY AND SUBSIDIARY
General Ledger Trial Balances
December 31, 19x6

	Prent Company	Alec Company
Debits		
Cash	$ 37,900	$ 29,050
Marketable securities	33,000	18,000
Trade accounts receivable . . .	210,000	88,000
Intercompany receivables	24,000	
Inventories	275,000	135,000
Machinery and equipment . . .	518,000	279,000
Investment in Alex Company at cost	96,000	
Patents	35,000	
Cost of sales	510,000	374,000
Depreciation expense	65,600	11,200
Administrative and selling expenses	130,000	110,500
Total debits	$1,934,500	$1,044,750

	Prent Company	Alec Company
Credits		
Dividends payable	$ 7,500	
Trade accounts payable	103,900	$ 96,050
Accrued expenses	91,600	78,000
Intercompany payables	8,000	
Allowance for bad debts	6,800	2,300
Accumulated depreciation . . .	298,200	196,700
Capital stock, par value $10 . . .	150,000	
Capital stock, par value $5 . . .		22,000
Paid-in capital in excess of par value	36,000	
Paid-in capital in excess of par value		14,000
Retained earnings	370,500	
Retained earnings		102,000
Sales and services	850,000	530,000
Dividend income	4,800	
Other income	7,200	3,700
Total credits	$1,934,500	$1,044,750

The following information is also available:

1. Prent Company purchased 1,600 shares of Alec Company's outstanding stock on January 1, 19x5, for $50,000 and on January 1, 19x6, purchased an additional 1,400 shares for $46,000.

2. An analysis of the stockholders' equity accounts at December 31, 19x5, and 19x4 follows:

[Relates to Problem 9–21]

	Prent Company December 31		Alec Company December 31	
	19x5	19x4	19x5	19x4
Capital stock, par $10	$150,000	$150,000		
Capital stock, par $5			$ 20,000	$ 20,000
Paid-in capital in excess of par value	36,000	36,000	10,000	10,000
Retained earnings	378,000	285,000	112,000	82,000
Totals	$564,000	$471,000	$142,000	$112,000

3. Alec Company's marketable securities consist of 1,500 shares of Prent Company stock purchased on June 15, 19x6, in the open market for $18,000. The securities were purchased as a temporary investment and were sold on January 15, 19x7, for $25,000.

4. On December 10, 19x6, Prent Company declared a cash dividend of 50 cents per share payable January 10, 19x7, to stockholders of record on December 20, 19x6. Alec Company paid a cash dividend of $1 per share on June 30, 19x6, and distributed a 10 percent stock dividend on September 30, 19x6. The stock was selling for $15 per share ex-dividend on September 30, 19x6. Alec Company paid no dividends in 19x5.

5. Alec Company sold machinery with a book value of $4,000, and a remaining life of five years to Prent Company for $4,800 on December 31, 19x6. The gain on the sale was credited to the Other Income account.

6. Alec Company includes all intercompany receivable and payable accounts in its Trade Accounts Receivable and Trade Accounts Payable accounts.

7. During 19x6, the following intercompany sales were made:

	Net Sales	Included in Purchaser's Inventory at 12/31/x6
Prent Company to Alec Company	$ 78,000	$24,300
Alec Company to Prent Company	104,000	18,000
Totals	$182,000	$42,300

Prent Company sells merchandise to Alec Company at cost. Alec Company sells merchandise to Prent Company at regular selling price to make a normal profit margin of 30 percent. The market value of all inventory was in excess of cost at December 31, 19x6. There were no intercompany sales in prior years.

Required:

Prepare a consolidated worksheet for Prent Company and its subsidiary, Alec Company, for the year ended December 31, 19x6. The worksheet should show adjustments and eliminations, minority interest, consolidated income statement, and consolidated balance sheet and should include the names of

other accounts affected by adjustments or reclassifications. Formal journal entries are not necessary. Schedules or supporting computations should be in good form. Disregard tax considerations.

(AICPA adapted)

Problem 9–22 (cost method). After completing the audit of company P and its subsidiaries for the year ended December 31, 19x2, you have prepared the following trial balances:

	Company P	Company X	Company Y
Debits			
Cash	$ 33,000	$ 41,500	$ 175,200
Accounts receivable	85,000	97,500	105,000
Inventories	137,500	163,000	150,000
Investment in company X . . .	350,000		
Investment in company Y . . .	650,000		
Bonds of company Y		147,000	
Plant and equipment . . .	700,000	525,000	834,000
Unamortized bond discount			800
Cost of sales	2,500,000	1,200,000	1,400,000
Operating expenses	405,000	280,000	290,500
Interest expense .	16,200	2,500	9,500
	$4,876,700	$2,456,500	$2,965,000
Credits			
Accounts payable .	$ 202,000	$ 150,500	$ 90,000
Dividends payable	12,000	5,000	
Bonds payable . .	400,000		200,000
Accumulated depreciation . .	402,000	325,000	240,000
Sales	2,950,000	1,550,000	1,750,000
Interest income on bonds		6,000	
Dividend income .	30,500		
Capital stock, par $50	600,000		
Capital stock, par $50		250,000	
Capital stock, par $50			500,000
Capital in excess of par			70,000
Retained earnings, company P . . .	280,200		
Retained earnings, company X . . .		170,000	
Retained earnings, company Y . . .			115,000
	$4,876,700	$2,456,500	$2,965,000

Your working papers contain the following information:

1. Company P acquired 4,000 shares of company X common stock for $310,000 on January 1, 19x1, and an additional 500 shares for $40,000 on January 1, 19x2.
2. Company P acquired all of company Y's 8,000 outstanding shares on January 1, 19x1, for $650,000. On January 1, 19x2, company Y issued 2,000 additional shares to the public at $85 per share. Company P has no investments other than the stock of companies X and Y.
3. On January 1, 19w5, company Y issued $200,000 of 10-year, 4 percent first-mortgage bonds at 98. On January 1, 19x2, company X purchased $150,000 (face value) of these bonds in the open market at 98. Interest is paid on the bonds on June 30 and December 31.
4. Condensed balance sheets for company X and company Y at the start of business on January 1, 19x1 and January 1, 19x2 are presented below:

the straight-line method based on a 10-year life. Company P credited the gain on the sale to Retained Earnings.

7. Company P consistently sells to its subsidiaries at a price which realizes a gross profit of 25 percent on sales. Companies X and Y sell to each other and to company P at cost. Prior to 19x2, intercompany sales were negligible, but during 19x2 the following intercompany sales were made:

	Total sales	Included in purchaser's inventory at 12/31/x2
Company P to company X . .	$172,000	$20,000
Company P to company Y . .	160,000	40,000
Company X to company Y . .	25,000	5,000
Company X to company P . .	28,000	8,000
	$385,000	$73,000

[Relates to Problem 9–22]

	Company X		Company Y	
	1/1/x2	1/1/x1	1/1/x2	1/1/x1
Current assets	$225,000	$195,000	$205,000	$280,400
Plant and equipment	350,000	305,000	623,800	613,000
Unamortized bond discount			1,200	1,600
Totals	$575,000	$500,000	$830,000	$895,000
Current liabilities	$125,000	$100,000	$105,000	$ 95,000
Bonds payable			200,000	200,000
Capital stock—par $50	250,000	250,000	400,000	400,000
Retained earnings	200,000	150,000	125,000	200,000
Totals	$575,000	$500,000	$830,000	$895,000

5. Total dividends paid during 19x2 were as follows:

Company P	$24,000
Company X	25,000
Company Y	10,000

In addition to the dividend payments, company P and company X had each declared dividends of $1 per share payable in January 19x3.

6. On June 30, 19x2, company P sold equipment with a book value of $8,000 to company X for $10,000. Company X depreciates equipment by

8. At December 31, 19x2:

Company P owed company X	$24,000
Company X owed company Y	16,000
Company Y owed company P	12,000
	$52,000

Required:

Prepare consolidated working papers for company P and subsidiaries for the year ended December 31, 19x2. (*Note:* Ignore income tax considerations.)

(AICPA adapted)

10

Consolidated statements—complex affiliation structures

OVERVIEW

Affiliation structures come in a variety of patterns. They can be tiered lineally, such as, a father-son-grandson structure; they can be lateral where one of the subsidiaries of a common parent owns shares in the other; or they can be mutually owned where a subsidiary owns shares of the parent company.

It may also be necessary to prepare consolidated financial statements when a parent company has indirect holdings of less than 50 percent in the grandson company if the son company owns more than 50 percent of the grandson, since control is present at each level of the tier.

Two methods are principally used in consolidation when mutual stockholdings exist. One method, known as the treasury stock approach, *treats a subsidiary's investment in its parent company as treasury stock in the consolidated balance sheet. The other method sometimes referred to as the* conventional *or* traditional *approach, treats the subsidiary's investment in its parent company as a constructive retirement of the parent's outstanding stock. This method requires the use of algebraic equations to arrive at consolidated net income.*

In our consideration of consolidation procedures we have so far considered only parent-subsidiary structures of an affiliated group without mutual holdings. These may be referred to as simple structures. We turn now to a consideration of other possible structures that can be called complex structures.

We can classify complex structures into:

1. Lineal relationships such as a father-son-grandson relationship which can be diagramed as shown in Illustration 10–1.

Illustration 10–1

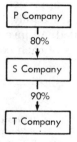

2. Lateral relationships which can be diagramed as shown in Illustration 10–2.

Illustration 10–2

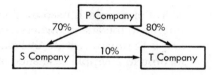

3. Mutual relationships where the subsidiary(s) own stock of the parent and can be diagramed as shown in Illustration 10–3.

Illustration 10–3

4. Other mutual relationships an example of which can be diagramed as is shown in Illustration 10–4.

Illustration 10–4

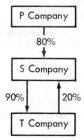

It is also possible to have additional combinations such as mutual relationships coupled with lateral relationships. Each grouping above requires a different type of calculation for consolidation purposes and, therefore, will be dealt with individually.

LINEAL STRUCTURES

The simplest structure of the four types is the lineal type. In Illustration 10–1 it can be said that, in effect, P Company owns 80 percent of S Company and also owns 72 percent (80% × 90%) of T Company. In practice, two different approaches, each producing the same result, are used to calculate a parent's equity in the earnings of subsidiaries. Both techniques will be illustrated. All investments were purchased at book value, and the separate earnings of each company for 19x4 is as follows:

	Separate earnings
P Company	$100,000
S Company (80% owned)	50,000
T Company (90% owned)	40,000
Total	$190,000

In the approach used in Illustration 10–5, income is allocated in an order *inverse* to the line of ownership. Thus, T Company's income is allocated first and S Company's next. Alternately, a direct approach for calculating parent income in a simple case such as this would be:

P Company (100% × $100,000)	$100,000
S Company (80% × $50,000)	40,000
T Company (72% × $40,000)	28,800
Total	$168,800

Illustration 10–5
P COMPANY AND SUBSIDIARIES
Allocation of Income
For the Year 19x4

	P Company	*S Company*	*T Company*
Separate income—per books	$100,000	$50,000	$40,000
Allocation—T Company (90%)		36,000	(36,000)
Subtotals	$100,000	$86,000	$ 4,000
Allocation—S Company (80%)	68,800	(68,800)	
Allocated income	$168,800	$17,200	$ 4,000

Parent income	$168,800
Minority interest income	21,200
Total	$190,000

However, when the allocation of income becomes more involved, the approach used in Illustration 10–5 is a very useful one, especially when intercompany profits are to be eliminated and/or lateral relationships are present. Continuing this example, it is now assumed that the following occurred in 19x4:

1. P Company sold to S Company merchandise at a profit of $10,000. Half of this merchandise is unsold on December 31, 19x4.
2. S Company sold to T Company merchandise in 19x3. On December 31, 19x3, there remained $10,000 of unconfirmed profit on this merchandise. This merchandise was completely sold by P Company in 19x4.
3. T Company sold to S Company equipment on January 1, 19x4. The equipment had a book value of $30,000 and was sold for $50,000. The equipment has a remaining life of five years, and straight-line depreciation was used in 19x4.
4. On January 1, 19x4, T Company purchased $200,000 of P Company bonds payable at par (face value). This represents 20 percent of P Company bonds outstanding. The unamortized bond premium on P Company's books on January 1, 19x4, (the date of the intercompany purchase) amounted to $100,000, and the bonds mature in 10 years from that date.

Illustration 10–6 contains the income allocation schedule used to calculate parent net income and minority interest net income. The advantage of this type of format in place of the direct calculation is readily apparent.

Illustration 10–6
P COMPANY AND SUBSIDIARIES
Income Apportionment Schedule
For the Year Ended December 31, 19x4

	P Company	S Company	T Company
Separate income—per books	$100,000	$50,000	$40,000
Deduct: Unconfirmed profit on downstream merchandise sale ($\frac{1}{2}$ × $10,000)—ending inventory	(5,000)		
Add: Confirmed profit on downstream merchandise sale—beginning inventory		10,000	
Deduct: Gain on sale of equipment			(20,000)
Add: Piecemeal recognition of gain ($20,000 ÷ 5)			4,000
Add: Gain on purchase of intercompany bonds (20% × $100,000 premium)	20,000		
Deduct: Piecemeal removal of gain ($20,000 ÷ 10 years)	(2,000)		
Adjusted incomes	$113,000	$60,000	$24,000
Allocation—T Company (90%)		21,600	(21,600)
Allocation—S Company (80% × $81,600)	65,280	(65,280)	
Allocated income	$178,280	$16,320	$ 2,400
Minority interest net income		$18,720	

After performing the computations shown in Illustration 10–6, the parent company would make the following entries on its books (intercompany dividend payments are assumed):

Parent's Books—19x4

(1)

| Investment in S Company | 65,280 | |
| Equity in Earnings of S Company | | 65,280 |

To record income per schedule (see Illustration 10–6).

(2)

| Cash | 24,000 | |
| Investment in S Company | | 24,000 |

To record receipt of dividends (80% × $30,000 = $24,000).

(3)

| Investment in S Company | 13,000 | |
| Equity in Earnings of S Company | | 13,000 |

To record equity in earnings for:

Gain on purchase of intercompany bonds	$20,000
Less: Piecemeal removal of above	(2,000)
Less: Unconfirmed profit on downstream merchandise inventory sale	(5,000)
Total	$13,000

Additionally, S Company would make the following entries on its books:

S Company Books—19x4

(1)

| Investment in T Company | 21,600 | |
| Equity in Earnings of T Company | | 21,600 |

To record income per schedule (see Illustration 10–6).

(2)

| Investment in T Company | 10,000 | |
| Equity in Earnings of T Company | | 10,000 |

To record confirmed profit in beginning inventory.

(3)

| Cash | 9,000 | |
| Investment in T Company | | 9,000 |

To record receipt of dividends (90% × $10,000 = $9,000).

It is now also assumed that:

1. On the date of the acquisition of T Company, all of T's assets and liabilities at book value approximated their respective market values and that S Company purchased its 90 percent investment at book value (there is no excess).

2. The same conditions prevail for the net assets of S Company, and there was no excess when P Company purchased its 80 percent investment.

Consolidation working papers can be found in Illustration 10–7.

The elimination entries for Illustration 10–7 are:

(1)

Equity in Earnings—S Company	78,280	
Dividends Declared—S Company		24,000
Investment in S Company		54,280

(2)

Retained Earnings (1/1/x4)—S Company	240,000	
Capital Stock—S Company	240,000	
Investment in S Company		480,000

(3)

Equity in Earnings of T Company	31,600	
Dividends Declared—T Company		9,000
Investment in T Company		22,600

(4)

Investment in T Company	10,000	
Cost of Sales (beginning inventory)		10,000

(5)

Retained Earnings (1/1/x4)—T Company	180,000	
Capital Stock—T Company	90,000	
Investment in T Company		270,000

(6)

Cost of Sales (ending inventory)	5,000	
Inventories		5,000

(7)

Sales	100,000	
Cost of Sales		100,000

(8)

Gain on Sale of Equipment	20,000	
Equipment		20,000

(9)

Accumulated Depreciation—Equipment	4,000	
Expenses (depreciation)		4,000

(10)

Interest Income	16,000	
Bonds Payable	200,000	
Unamortized Bond Premium	18,000	
Interest Expense (expenses)		14,000
Gain on Purchase of Intercompany Bonds		20,000
Investment in P Company Bonds		200,000

From the illustration it can be seen that:

1. Consolidated net income is the same as P Company income per illustration 10–6.
2. Minority interest net income is also in agreement with the calculation shown in Illustration 10–6.
3. Minority interest contains two components—20 percent of the net assets of S Company and 10 percent of the net assets of T Company (exclusive of unconfirmed profits).

We will now change the example so that instead of a lineal relationship, which prevailed in the preceding example, we now assume a lateral relationship between companies P, S, and T, with ownership percentages as shown

Illustration 10–7

P COMPANY
Consolidated Working Paper
For the Year Ended December 31, 19x4

Complete Equity Method

	P Co.	S Co. (80%)	T Co. (90%)	Eliminations Dr.	Eliminations Cr.	Minority Interest	Consolidated
Income Statement							
Sales	2,000,000	1,000,000	800,000	(7) 100,000			3,700,000
Cost of sales	1,200,000	700,000	480,000	(6) 5,000	(7) 100,000 (4) 10,000		2,275,000
Gross margin	800,000	300,000	320,000				1,425,000
Expenses and income taxes	700,000	250,000	316,000		(10) 14,000		1,248,000
Income before investment and other income	100,000	50,000	4,000		(9) 4,000		177,000
Equity in earnings of S Co.	78,280			(1) 78,280			
Equity in earnings of T Co.		31,600		(3) 31,600			
Interest income			16,000	(10) 16,000			
Gain on sale of equipment			20,000	(8) 20,000			
Gain on purchase in intercompany bonds					(10) 20,000		20,000
Minority interest net income						18,720	(18,720)
Net income	178,280	81,600	40,000			18,720	178,280
Retained Earnings Statement							
Balance, 1/1/x4:							
P Co.	500,000						500,000
S Co.		300,000		(2) 240,000		60,000	
T Co.			200,000	(5) 180,000		20,000	
Net income—brought forward	178,280	81,600	40,000			18,720	178,280
Totals	678,280	381,600	240,000			98,720	678,280
Less: Dividends declared:							
P Co.	80,000						80,000
S Co.		30,000			(1) 24,000	6,000	
T Co.			10,000		(3) 9,000	1,000	
Balance, 12/31/x4—carried forward	598,280	351,600	230,000			91,720	598,280

Balance Sheet

Balance Sheet	P Co.	S Co.	T Co.	Eliminations Dr	Eliminations Cr	Minority interest	Consolidated
Cash	300,000	40,000	30,000				370,000
Inventories	80,000	50,000	40,000		(6) 5,000		165,000
Investment in S Co.	534,280				(2) 480,000 / (1) 54,280		
Investment in T Co.		282,600		(4) 10,000	(5) 270,000 / (3) 22,600		
Investment in P Co. bonds					(10) 200,000		
Equipment	200,000	150,000	100,000		(8) 20,000		430,000
Accumulated depreciation	(80,000)	(30,000)	(40,000)	(9) 4,000			(146,000)
Other assets	1,204,000	239,000	70,000				1,513,000
Totals	2,238,280	731,600	400,000				2,332,000
Accounts payable	50,000	30,000	40,000				120,000
Bonds payable, 8%	1,000,000			(10) 200,000			800,000
Unamortized bond premium	90,000			(10) 18,000			72,000
Other liabilities	100,000	50,000	30,000				180,000
Capital stock: P Co.	400,000						400,000
S Co.		300,000		(2) 240,000		60,000	
T Co.			100,000	(5) 90,000		10,000	
Retained earnings—brought forward	598,280	351,600	230,000			91,720	598,280
Minority interest						161,720	161,720
Totals	2,238,280	731,600	400,000	1,232,880	1,232,880	161,720	2,332,000

(1) Elimination of equity in earnings of S Company.
(2) Elimination of balance of investment in S Company.
(3) Elimination of equity in earnings of T Company.
(4) Restoration of confirmed profit in beginning inventory.
(5) Elimination of balance of investment in T Company.
(6) Elimination of unconfirmed profit in ending inventory.
(7) Elimination of intercompany sales (assumed).
(8) Elimination of unconfirmed gain on intercompany sale of equipment.
(9) Elimination of portion of depreciation taken on intercompany sale of equipment.
(10) Elimination of intercompany bonds and related unamortized bond premium (20% × $90,000 = $18,000), interest income ($16,000), and interest expense (*see calculation below) and to record gain on purchase of intercompany bonds.

*Calculation of interest expense elimination:

Cash portion of interest expense (8% × $1,000,000)	$80,000
Amortization of bond premium ($100,000 ÷ 10 years)	(10,000)
Interest expense (net)	$70,000
Intercompany portion—20% of above	$14,000

Reconciliations

Minority interest:

Net assets of S Co., 12/31/x4—20% ($300,000 + $351,600)	$130,320
Net assets of T Co., 12/31/x4—10% ($100,000 + $230,000)	33,000
Less: Unconfirmed profit on upstream sale of equipment—10% ($20,000 − $4,000)	(1,600)
Minority interest, 12/31/x4	$161,720

in Illustration 10–2. The separate incomes and the intercompany transactions remain the same as used in Illustration 10–6. The income apportionment schedule is as follows:

Illustration 10–8
P COMPANY AND SUBSIDIARIES
Income Apportionment Schedule
For the Year Ended December 31, 19x4

	P Company	S Company	T Company
Adjusted incomes—per Illustration 10–6	$113,000	$60,000	$24,000
Allocation—T Company:			
10% to S Company		2,400	(2,400)
80% to P Company	19,200		(19,200)
Allocation—S Company:			
(70% × $62,400)	43,680	(43,680)	
Allocated income	$175,880	$18,720	$ 2,400
Minority interest net income		$21,120	

When this type of apportionment schedule is used, it is necessary to allocate income in a direction that is inverse to the arrows in the affiliation diagram. Thus, in Illustration 10–2 it can be seen that T Company is the terminal point in the ownership sequence and, therefore, is the first one to be allocated. Through this approach, 10 percent of T Company income is allocated to S Company of which 70 percent is, in turn, allocated to P Company. Thus, in effect, 7 percent (10% × 70%) of T Company's income is allocated to P Company. This can be proven as follows:

P Company adjusted income	$113,000
Direct holdings:	
Add: 70% of S Company adjusted income ($60,000)	42,000
80% of T Company adjusted income ($24,000)	19,200
Indirect holdings:	
7% of T Company adjusted income ($24,000)	1,680
Consolidated net income (per Illustration 10–8)	$175,880

Except for the differences in consolidated net income and minority interest net income, the consolidated working paper and the entries on the respective sets of books are similar to those previously illustrated.

MUTUAL HOLDINGS

From Illustration 10–3 it can be seen that S Company owns 10 percent of the parent company's outstanding common stock. In cases such as these, two approaches are generally used to account for *reciprocal holdings*. One method, known as the *treasury stock* approach is to treat the subsidiary's ownership of the parent company's shares as treasury stock in the consolidated financial statements. The other method, sometimes referred to as the *conventional* or *traditional* approach, involves the use of simultaneous linear equations. Since this latter approach is used less frequently in practice the authors elected to discuss it in the appendix at the end of this chapter.[1]

TREASURY STOCK APPROACH—EQUITY METHOD

The equity method will be used to illustrate the treasury stock approach in accounting for mutual holdings. The following is now assumed:

1. Phillips Corporation purchased 90 percent of Sousa Corporation's outstanding common stock at book value on January 1, 19x1, which approximated fair market value (i.e., there is no excess).
2. Sousa Corporation purchased 10 percent of Phillips's outstanding common stock for $30,000 and carries this investment at cost.
3. The trial balances on December 31, 19x1, of the respective corporations have been recast as shown in Illustration 10–9. Phillips Corporation uses the equity method to account for its investment in Sousa Corporation. In computing its share of subsidiary earnings, it excludes the dividends which the subsidiary recieves from it. The percentage (90 percent) of ownership is applied to subsidiary earnings *exclusive* of such dividends.
4. There were no intercompany transactions between the companies in 19x1 other than the payment of dividends.

The elimination entries for Illustration 10–9 are:

(1)

Equity in Earnings—Subsidiary	90,000	
Dividends Declared—Sousa Corporation		45,000
Investment in Sousa Corporation		45,000

(2)

Retained Earnings (1/1/x1)—Sousa Corporation	540,000	
Capital Stock—Sousa Corporation	360,000	
Investment in Sousa Corporation		900,000

(3)

Treasury Stock	230,000	
Investment in Phillips Corporation		230,000

A review of Illustration 10–9 reveals the following:

1. Phillips Corporation recorded $90,000 as its share of subsidiary earnings (90% × $100,000 operating income). The parent company *does not* record as earnings its share of the dividend income of the subsidiary (90% × $10,000) which represent dividends it paid to the subsidiary (income taxes ignored).
2. Entries (1) and (2) are the usual entries as shown in earlier chapters.
3. Entry (3) transfers the subsidiary's investment in the parent to treasury stock.
4. Entry (4) eliminates 100 percent (rather than 90 percent) of the dividends paid to the subsidiary by the parent company. If this were not done,

[1]Accountants International Study Group, *Consolidated Financial Statements*, 1973, par. 67.

some dividend income would be extended to the consolidated column and this is not acceptable. This is so because from a consolidated viewpoint only dividends received from outsiders constitute dividend income and dividends received from insiders, or members of the consolidated group, must be completely eliminated in the consolidated income state-

Illustration 10–9
PHILLIPS CORPORATION
Consolidated Working Paper
For the Year Ended December 31, 19x1

Equity Method
First Year Treasury Stock Method
90 Percent Subsidiary

	Phillips Corp.	Sousa Corp. (90%)	Eliminations		Minority Interest	Consol- idated
			Dr.	Cr.		
Income Statement						
Sales	1,000,000	400,000				1,400,000
Cost of sales, expenses, income taxes	800,000	300,000				1,100,000
Operating income	200,000	100,000				300,000
Equity in earnings—subsidiary	90,000		(1) 90,000			
Dividend income		10,000	(4) 10,000			
Minority interest net income					11,000	(11,000)
Net income—carried forward	290,000	110,000			11,000	289,000
Retained Earnings Statement						
Balance, 1/1/x1:						
Phillips Corp.	1,000,000					1,000,000
Sousa Corp.		600,000	(2) 540,000		60,000	
Net income—brought forward	290,000	110,000			11,000	289,000
Totals	1,290,000	710,000			71,000	1,289,000
Less: Dividends declared:						
Phillips Corp.	100,000			(4) 10,000		90,000
Sousa Corp.		50,000		(1) 45,000	5,000	
Balance, 12/31/x1—carried forward	1,190,000	660,000			66,000	1,199,000
Balance Sheet						
Miscellaneous assets	1,045,000	920,000				1,965,000
Investment in Sousa Corp.	945,000			(2) 900,000		
Investment in Phillips Corp.		230,000		(1) 45,000		
				(3) 230,000		
Totals	1,990,000	1,150,000				1,965,000
Liabilities	200,000	90,000				290,000
Capital stock:						
Phillips Corp.	600,000					600,000
Sousa Corp.		400,000	(2) 360,000		40,000	
Retained earnings—brought forward	1,190,000	660,000			66,000	1,199,000
Treasury stock			(3) 230,000			(230,000)
Minority interest					106,000	106,000
Totals	1,990,000	1,150,000	1,230,000	1,230,000		1,965,000

(1) Elimination of equity in earnings and intercompany dividend paid to the parent company.
(2) Elimination of the balance of investment.
(3) To set up treasury stock.
(4) Elimination of dividends paid to the subsidiary by the parent company.

Illustration 10–9 (continued)

Computations and Proofs

Minority interest net income—10% ($110,000) . . . . $ 11,000

Minority interest, 12/31/x1—10% ($400,000 + $660,000) . . . . $ 106,000

Reconciliation—consolidated net income:
Net income—per parent's books . . . . $ 290,000
Less: Portion of parent's dividend paid and earned by minority interest of Sousa (10% × $10,000) . . . 1,000
Consolidated net income . . . . $ 289,000

Reconciliation—consolidated retained earnings:
Retained earnings, 12/31/x1—per books $1,190,000
Add: Parent's share of its dividend paid to Sousa—in effect paid to itself (90% × $10,000) 9,000
Retained earnings—working paper $1,199,000

ment. It should be noted, however, that although the intercompany dividend is entirely eliminated, the minority interest net income is based on the subsidiary's net income which includes the intercompany dividend (10% × $110,000 or $11,000). Thus, in effect, the minority interest is credited with 10 percent of the intercompany dividend.

5. Consolidated net income is $1,000 less than parent net income. This difference arises from the fact that the minority interest is credited with 10 percent of the intercompany dividend.

6. Consolidated retained earnings are different from the parent's retained earnings. This difference is explained in the computations and proofs included in Illustration 10–9.

Illustration 10–10 is a continuation of Illustration 10–9 and covers the following year. The operating data are assumed. The procedures used to prepare Illustration 10–9 were continued in the preparation of Illustration 10–10.

The elimination entries for Illustration 10–10 are:

(1)

Equity in Earnings—Subsidiary 153,000
    Dividends Declared—Sousa Corporation 63,000
    Investment in Sousa Corporation 90,000

(2)

Investment in Sousa Corporation 9,000
    Retained Earnings (1/1/x1)—Phillips Corporation 9,000

(3)

Retained Earnings (1/1/x1)—Sousa Corporation. 594,000
Capital Stock—Sousa Corporation 360,000
    Investment in Sousa Corporation 954,000

(4)

Dividend Income 15,000
    Dividends Declared—Phillips Corporation 15,000

(5)

Treasury Stock 230,000
    Investment in Phillips Corporation 230,000

Chapter 10

Illustration 10–10
PHILLIPS CORPORATION
Consolidated Working Paper
For the Year Ended December 31, 19x2

Equity Method
90 Percent Subsidiary
Second Year—Treasury Stock Method

	Phillips Corp.	Sousa Corp. (90%)	Eliminations Dr.	Eliminations Cr.	Minority Interest	Consol-idated
Income Statement						
Sales	1,200,000	500,000				1,700,000
Cost of sales, expenses, income taxes	870,000	330,000				1,200,000
Operating income	330,000	170,000				500,000
Equity in earnings—subsidiary	153,000		(1) 153,000			
Dividend income		15,000	(4) 15,000			
Minority interest net income					18,500	(18,500)
Net income—carried forward	483,000	185,000			18,500	481,500
Retained Earnings Statement						
Balance, 1/1/x1:						
Phillips Corp.	1,190,000			(2) 9,000		1,199,000
Sousa Corp.		660,000	(3) 594,000		66,000	
Net income—brought forward	483,000	185,000			18,500	481,500
Totals	1,673,000	845,000			84,500	1,680,500
Less: Dividends declared:						
Phillips Corp.	150,000			(4) 15,000		135,000
Sousa Corp.		70,000		(1) 63,000	7,000	
Balance, 12/31/x1—carried forward	1,523,000	775,000			77,500	1,545,500
Balance Sheet						
Miscellaneous assets	1,365,000	1,270,000				2,635,000
Investment in Sousa Corp.	1,035,000		(2) 9,000	(3) 954,000 (1) 90,000		
Investment in Phillips Corp.		230,000		(5) 230,000		
Totals	2,400,000	1,500,000				2,635,000
Liabilities	277,000	325,000				602,000
Capital stock:						
Phillips Corp.	600,000					600,000
Sousa Corp.		400,000	(3) 360,000		40,000	
Retained earnings—brought forward	1,523,000	775,000			77,500	1,545,500
Treasury stock			(5) 230,000			(230,000)
Minority interest					117,500	117,500
Totals	2,400,000	1,500,000	1,361,000	1,361,000		2,635,000

(1) Elimination of equity in subsidiary earnings and intercompany dividends paid to parent company.

(2) Adjustment to investment account and parent's retained earnings for the *cumulative* amount of dividends paid by the parent company to the subsidiary in prior years multiplied by the parent's percentage of ownership (90%). This represents dividends paid by the parent company—in effect—paid to itself.

(3) Elimination of the balance of the investment.

(4) Elimination of dividends paid to the subsidiary by the parent company.

(5) To set up treasury stock.

Illustration 10–10 (*continued*)

Computations and Proofs

Minority interest net income—10% ($185,000) . . . . $ 18,500

Minority interest, 12/31/x2—10% ($400,000 + $775,000) . . . . $ 117,500

Reconciliation—Consolidated net income:
Net income—per parent's books . . . . $ 483,000
Less: Portion of parent's dividend paid and earned by minority interest of Sousa (10% × $15,000) . . .   1,500
Consolidated net income   . . . . $ 481,500

Reconciliation—consolidated retained earnings:
Retained earnings, 12/31/x2—per books $1,523,000
Add: Parent's share of its dividend paid to Sousa—in effect paid to itself—19x2 (90% × $15,000)   13,500
Add: Cumulative amount from prior years (see Illustration 10–9 reconciliation)   9,000
Retained earnings—working paper $1,545,500

The only additional entry required in any year after the first is entry (2). This entry is for the *cumulative* amount necessary to reconcile consolidated retained earnings with parent retained earnings at the *close of the preceding year.* Thus, in this illustration the balance is obtained from the 19x1 working paper (Illustration 10–9). For 19x3, the amount would be $22,500 ($13,500 + $9,000) (see computations and proofs on Illustration 10–10). Other than entry (2), the remaining entries are similar to those in Illustration 10–9.

The consolidation accounting for an affiliation structure such as shown in Illustration 10–4 cannot be performed by use of the treasury stock method. Instead, the algebraic method illustrated in the appendix must be used.

INDIRECT HOLDINGS OF LESS THAN 50 PERCENT— CONSOLIDATED STATEMENTS

In practice it is common to find affiliation structures such as shown in Illustration 10–11.

Illustration 10–11

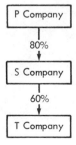

From the above structure it can be seen that P Company indirectly owns 48 percent (80% × 60%) of T Company which is less than a majority interest. Nevertheless, P effectively controls T Company through its ownership of

S Company, and it is entirely proper (and required) to consolidate T Company with P Company assuming there are no reasons not to consolidate (such as currency blockage, etc.). Except for the differences in percentages owned, the consolidation procedures for this type of structure are handled in the same manner as was previously shown in Illustrations 10–6 and 10–7.

Appendix: Reciprocal holdings—algebraic solution

In Illustrations 10–9 and 10–10 the investment in Phillips Corporation held by the subsidiary was treated in consolidation as treasury stock of Phillips Corporation. However, another approach sometimes encountered in practice is to treat a subsidiary's investment in a parent company's stock as constructively retired from a consolidated viewpoint. This method can be justified by comparing it to the treatment accorded to the purchase of intercompany bonds. In Chapter 7, which deals with this subject, it can be seen that intercompany bonds are eliminated (constructively retired) on consolidation working papers. When this method is applied to an investment in a parent company's stock, the calculations required for apportioning income can either be solved algebraically (simultaneous linear equations) or, in simple situations, by successive trial and error attempts until the solution is arrived at.

Investment in subsidiary carried at equity and investment in parent carried at cost

Illustrations 10–9 and 10–10 are now reworked and presented as Illustrations 10–12 and 10–13 using the constructive retirement approach. When this approach is used, an investment carried at cost must be treated as if the *equity method* is applied. Therefore, excess must be determined. For purposes of calculating excess on the purchase of Sousa's investment in Phillips, it is assumed that Phillips identifiable net assets are at approximate fair market values and the excess, if any, is attributable to goodwill with an indefinite life. The calculation of excess would be:

Price paid	$230,000
Less: 10% of Phillips's net assets ($1,600,000)	
on January 1, 19x1	160,000
Goodwill	$ 70,000
Amortization per annum = $70,000 ÷ 40	
years	$ 1,750

For 19x1 (Illustration 10–12), the calculation of income for apportionment purposes is:

Let P_E = Allocable parent net income using equity
Let S_E = Allocable subsidiary net income using equity
Let P_S = Parent's separate operating income
Let S_S = Subsidiary's separate operating income

$$P_S = \$200,000$$
$$S_S = \$100,000$$
$$P_E = \$200,000 + .9\,S_E$$
$$S_E = \$100,000 - \$1,750 \text{ amortization} + .1\,P_E$$

Solving by substitution:
$$P_E = \$200,000 + .9(\$98,250 + .1P_E)$$
$$P_E = \$200,000 + \$88,425 + .09P_E$$
$$.91\,P_E = \$288,425$$
$$P_E = \frac{\$288,425}{.91}$$
$$P_E = \$316,950$$

Substituting in S_E:
$$S_E = \$100,000 - \$1,750 + .1(\$316,950)$$
$$S_E = \$98,250 + \$31,695$$
$$S_E = \$129,945$$

It should be obvious that the algebraic solution contains double counting since consolidated net income plus the minority interest's net income must equal $298,250 ($200,000 + $100,000 − $1,750). Therefore, the computed amounts must be allocated as follows:

Parent net income—90% × $316,950 = ...	$285,256
Minority interest net income—10% × $129,945	12,994
Total net income	$298,250

Illustration 10–12
PHILLIPS CORPORATION
Consolidated Working Paper
For the Year Ended December 31, 19x1

Equity Method—Parent Only
90 Percent Subsidiary
First Year—Algebraic Method

	Phillips Corp.	Sousa Corp. (90%)	Eliminations Dr.	Eliminations Cr.	Minority Interest	Consol-idated
Income Statement						
Sales	1,000,000	400,000				1,400,000
Cost of sales, expenses, income taxes	800,000	300,000	(3) 1,750			1,101,750
Operating income	200,000	100,000				298,250
Equity in earnings—subsidiary	85,256		(4) 85,256			
Dividend income		10,000	(1) 10,000			
Minority interest net income					12,994	(12,994)
Net income—carried forward	285,256	110,000			12,994	285,256
Retained Earnings Statement						
Balance, 1/1/x1:						
Phillips Corp.	1,000,000	/	(2) 100,000			900,000
Sousa Corp.		600,000	(5) 540,000		60,000	
Net income—brought forward	285,256	110,000			12,994	285,256
Totals	1,285,256	710,000			72,994	1,185,256
Less: Dividends declared:						
Phillips Corp.	100,000			(1) 10,000		90,000
Sousa Corp.		50,000		(4) 45,000	5,000	
Balance, 12/31/x1—carried forward	1,185,256	660,000			67,994	1,095,256
Balance Sheet						
Miscellaneous assets	1,045,000	920,000				1,965,000
Investment in Sousa Corp.	940,256			(5) 900,000		
				(4) 40,256		
Investment in Phillips Corp.		230,000		(2) 230,000		
Goodwill			(2) 70,000	(3) 1,750		68,250
Totals	1,985,256	1,150,000				2,033,250
Liabilities	200,000	90,000				290,000
Capital stock:						
Phillips Corp.	600,000		(2) 60,000			540,000
Sousa Corp.		400,000	(5) 360,000		40,000	
Retained earnings—brought forward	1,185,256	660,000			67,994	1,095,256
Minority interest					107,994	··107,994
Totals	1,985,256	1,150,000	1,227,006	1,227,006		2,033,250

(1) To eliminate dividends paid by the parent company to the subsidiary.
(2) To eliminate subsidiary's investment in parent company and to set up goodwill of $70,000.
(3) To record current year's amortization of goodwill ($70,000 ÷ 40 years).
(4) To eliminate equity in earnings of subsidiary and dividends paid to parent company.
(5) To eliminate balance of investment and parent's share of Sousa's net assets at 1/1/x1.

Illustration 10–12 (continued)

Computations and Proofs

Minority interest:

Sousa Corp.—12/31/x1:

Capital stock	$ 400,000
Retained earnings	660,000
Net assets—per books	1,060,000
Add: 10% of Phillips net income per algebraic solution to simultaneous linear equations (10% × $316,950)	31,695
Less: Dividends received by Sousa—cost method	(10,000)
Amortization of excess ($70,000 ÷ 40 years)	(1,750)
Net assets—complete equity method	$1,079,945
10% of above	$ 107,994

Consolidated retained earnings:

Parent retained earnings 12/31/x1—per books	$1,185,256
Less: Retained earnings constructively retired 10% of parent retained earnings on the date of purchase by Sousa (10% × $1,000,000)	(100,000)
Add: Dividends paid to Sousa by Phillips	10,000
Balance, 12/31/x1	$1,095,256

The elimination entries for Illustration 10–12 are:

(1)

Dividend Income	10,000	
Dividends Declared—		
Phillips Corporation		10,000

(2)

Retained Earnings (1/1/x1)—		
Phillips Corporation	100,000	
Goodwill	70,000	
Capital Stock—Phillips		
Corporation	60,000	
Investment in Phillips		
Corporation		230,000

(3)

Amortization of Goodwill		
(expenses)	1,750	
Goodwill		1,750

(4)

Equity in Earnings—Subsidiary	85,256	
Dividends Declared—		
Sousa Corporation		45,000
Investment in Sousa		
Corporation		40,256

(5)

Retained Earnings (1/1/x1)—		
Sousa Corporation	540,000	
Capital Stock—Sousa		
Corporation	360,000	
Investment in Sousa		
Corporation		900,000

In comparing Illustration 10–12 with Illustration 10–9 it can be seen that the consolidated columns are different, as they should be because Illustration 10–9 uses the treasury stock approach whereas Illustration 10–12 uses the constructive retirement approach. Further, a review of Illustration 10–12 reveals that:

1. Consolidated net income is the same as parent net income. This is true because the parent company uses the equity method to account for its investment.

2. Minority interest net income ($12,994) is the algebraically computed amount and not 10 percent of Sousa Corporation's income of $110,000. This is so because the subsidiary uses the cost method to account for its investment in the parent.

3. Parent retained earnings is not the same as consolidated retained earnings. Since the subsidiary's investment in the parent company is viewed, in this case, as a constructive retirement of the parent's stock, 10 percent of the parent's retained earnings on the date of acquisition (January 1, 19x1) and 10 percent of its dividend payments are eliminated on the working paper *only*. These become reconciling items in the appended computations and proofs.

4. The reconciliation of the minority interest entails complexities not previously encountered

Illustration 10–13
PHILLIPS CORPORATION
Consolidated Working Paper
For the Year Ended December 31, 19x2

Equity Method—Parent only
90 Percent Subsidiary
2nd Year—Algebraic Method

	Phillips Corp.	Sousa Corp. (90%)	Eliminations Dr.	Eliminations Cr.	Minority Interest	Consolidated
Income Statement						
Sales	1,200,000	500,000				1,700,000
Cost of sales, expenses, income taxes	870,000	330,000	(3) 1,750			1,201,750
Operating income	330,000	170,000				498,250
Equity in earnings—subsidiary	146,134		(5) 146,134			
Dividend income		15,000	(1) 15,000			
Minority interest net income					22,116	(22,116)
Net income—carried forward	476,134	185,000			22,116	476,134
Retained Earnings Statement						
Balance, 1/1/x2:						
Phillips Corp.	1,185,256		(2) 100,000	(4) 10,000		1,095,256
			(3) 1,750			
Sousa Corp.		660,000	(6) 590,256		67,994	
Net income—brought forward	476,134	185,000			22,116	476,134
Totals	1,661,390	845,000			90,110	1,571,390
Less: Dividends declared:						
Phillips Corp.	150,000			(1) 15,000		135,000
Sousa Corp.		70,000		(5) 63,000	7,000	
Balance, 12/31/x2—carried forward	1,511,390	775,000			83,110	1,436,390
Balance Sheet						
Miscellaneous assets	1,365,000	1,270,000				2,635,000
				(6) 950,256		
Investment in Sousa Corp.	1,023,390		(4) 10,000	(5) 83,134		
Investment in Phillips Corp.		230,000		(2) 230,000		
Goodwill			(2) 70,000	(3) 3,500		66,500
Totals	2,388,390	1,500,000				2,701,500
Liabilities	277,000	325,000				602,000
Capital stock:						
Phillips Corp.	600,000		(2) 60,000			540,000
Sousa Corp.		400,000	(6) 360,000		40,000	
Retained earnings—brought forward	1,511,390	775,000			83,110	1,436,390
Minority interest					123,110	123,110
Totals	2,388,390	1,500,000	1,354,890	1,354,890		2,701,500

(1) To eliminate current year's dividends paid by parent company to subsidiary.

(2) To eliminate subsidiary's investment in parent company and to set up goodwill of $70,000.

(3) To record current and prior years' amortization of goodwill.

(4) To adjust parent's retained earnings for prior years' dividends paid by parent company to subsidiary and to maintain reciprocity of parent's investment in subsidiary with intercompany dividends received by subsidiary.

(5) To eliminate equity in earnings of subsidiary and dividends paid by subsidiary to parent company.

(6) To eliminate the balance of the parent's investment account. (90% of capital stock and the balance to retained earnings.)

Illustration 10–13 (*continued*)

Computations and Proofs

Minority interest:

Sousa Corp.—12/31/x2:

Capital stock	$ 400,000
Retained earnings	775,000
Net assets—per books	1,175,000
Add: 10% of Phillips net income per algebraic solution to simultaneous linear equations (10% × $529,038)	52,904
Add: Algebraically determined amounts per prior working papers (see Illustration 10–12)	31,695
Less: Dividends Received by Sousa:	
This year	(15,000)
Prior years	(10,000)
Accumulated amortization of excess (2 × $1750)	(3,500)
Net assets—complete equity method	$1,231,099
10% of above	$ 123,110

Consolidated retained earnings:

Parent retained earnings 12/31/x2—per books	$1,511,390
Less: Retained earnings constructively retired as of 1/1/x1 (see Illustration 10–12)	(100,000)
Add: Dividends paid to Sousa by Phillips:	
This year	15,000
Prior years	10,000
Balance, 12/31/x2	$1,436,390

and should be reviewed carefully. (See computations and proofs in Illustration 10–12.)

5. Elimination entries (4) and (5) are the normal entries used in the earlier chapters. Entry (2) eliminates 10 percent of the parent's beginning retained earnings and capital stock (net assets) and sets up the goodwill as previously computed. Entry (3) records one year's amortization of goodwill, and entry (1) eliminates the intercompany dividends paid by the parent company.

For 19x2, the algebraic solutions using the separate incomes shown in Illustration 10–13 are as follows:

Let P_E = Allocable parent net income using equity
Let S_E = Allocable subsidiary net income using equity

$$P_E = \$330,000 + .9S_E$$
$$S_E = \$170,000 - \$1,750 \text{ amortization} + .1P_E$$

By substitution:

$$P_E = \$330,000 + .9(\$168,250 + .1P_E)$$
$$P_E = \$330,000 + \$151,425 + .09P_E$$
$$.91P_E = \$481,425$$
$$P_E = \frac{\$481,425}{.91}$$
$$P_E = \$529,038$$

Substituting in S_E:

$$S_E = \$170,000 - \$1,750 + .1(\$529,038)$$
$$S_E = \$168,250 + \$52,904$$
$$S_E = \$221,154$$

Allocated income can now be computed as:

Parent net income—90% × $529,038 = ...	$476,134
Minority interest net income—10% × $221,154 = ...	22,116*
Total net income	$498,250

*Rounded to produce total net income of $498,250.

The elimination entries for Illustration 10–13 are:

(1)

Dividend Income	15,000	
Dividends Declared—		
Phillips Corporation		15,000

(2)

Goodwill	70,000	
Retained Earnings (1/1/x2)—		
Phillips Corporation	100,000	
Capital Stock—Phillips		
Corporation	60,000	
Investment in Phillips		
Corporation		230,000

	(3)		
Amortization of Goodwill . . .	1,750	
Retained Earnings (1/1/x2)—		
Sousa Corporation	1,750	
Goodwill		3,500

	(4)		
Investment in Sousa		
Corporation	10,000	
Retained Earnings (1/1/x2)		
—Phillips Corporation . .		10,000

	(5)		
Equity in Earnings—Subsidiary	146,134	
Dividends Declared—		
Sousa Corporation		63,000
Investment in Sousa		
Corporation		83,134

	(6)		
Retained Earnings (1/1/x2)—		
Sousa Corporation.	590,256	
Capital Stock—Sousa		
Corporation	360,000	
Investment in Sousa Corp.		950,256

From Illustration 10–13 it can be seen that it contains similar entries to those in Illustration 10–12. However, there are differences between the two illustrations that are worth noting. These are:

1. Entry (4) in Illustration 10–13 must be made prior to eliminating the parent's investment in the subsidiary. This entry is for the cumulative amount of dividends paid by the parent to the subsidiary as of the beginning of the year. Since these dividends are not counted as income but they increase the retained earnings of the subsidiary, the parent's investment in the subsidiary is increased in order to maintain the reciprocity between the investment and the subsidiary's net assets.

2. The reconciliation of the minority interest now requires cumulative amounts for (a) equity net income, (b) dividends received, and (c) amortization of goodwill.

3. The beginning balance ($67,994) of retained earnings in the minority interest column agrees with the ending balance in Illustration 10–12.

4. The reconciliation of consolidated retained earnings requires a reconciling item for 10 percent of the parent's retained earnings on January 1, 19x1 (the date of the subsidiary's investment in the parent) and a reconciling item for the cumulative dividends paid to the subsidiary.

Investment in subsidiary carried at equity and investment in parent carried at equity

Although *APB Opinion 18* specifies that, except in certain cases, investments of less than 20 percent are to be carried at cost, this requirement is not applicable to our present discussion. This is so because, in our example, the 10 percent investment by the subsidiary in the parent stock is *eliminated* in the consolidated working papers, and consequently, it does not matter whether the investment is carried at cost or equity.

The algebraic solution for Illustration 10–14 is the same as that used for Illustration 10–12. The parent records its share of subsidiary income as $85,256 ($285,256 − $200,000), and the subsidiary records its share of parent income as $29,945 ($129,945 − $100,000). (Each amount of allocated income reduced by the respective separate income equals the share of income to be recorded.)

The elimination entries for Illustration 10–14 are:

	(1)		
Equity in Earnings—Subsidiary	85,256	
Dividends Declared—		
Sousa Corporation		45,000
Investment in Sousa		
Corporation		40,256

	(2)		
Retained Earnings (1/1/x1)—		
Sousa Corporation	540,000	
Capital Stock—Sousa		
Corporation	360,000	
Investment in Sousa		
Corporation		900,000

	(3)		
Equity in Earnings—Parent . .	29,945	
Dividends Declared—		
Phillips Corporation		10,000
Investment in Phillips		
Corporation		19,945

	(4)		
Retained Earnings (1/1/x1)—		
Phillips Corporation	100,000	
Goodwill	70,000	
Capital Stock—Phillips		
Corporation	60,000	
Investment in Phillips		
Corporation		230,000

	(5)		
Amortization of Goodwill		
(expenses)	1,750	
Goodwill		1,750

Illustration 10–14
PHILLIPS CORPORATION
Consolidated Working Paper
For the Year Ended December 31, 19x1

Complete Equity Method—Parent and Subsidiary
90 Percent Subsidiary First Year

	Phillips Corp.	Sousa Corp. (90%)	Eliminations Dr.	Eliminations Cr.	Minority Interest	Consolidated
Income Statement						
Sales	1,000,000	400,000				1,400,000
Cost of sales, expenses, income taxes	800,000	300,000	(5) 1,750			1,101,750
Operating income	200,000	100,000				298,250
Equity in earnings—subsidiary	85,256		(1) 85,256			
Equity in earnings—parent		29,945	(3) 29,945			
Minority interest net income					12,994	(12,994)
Net income—carried forward	285,256	129,945			12,994	285,256
Retained Earnings Statement						
Balance, 1/1/x1:						
Phillips Corp.	1,000,000		(4) 100,000			900,000
Sousa Corp.		600,000	(2) 540,000		60,000	
Net income—brought forward	285,256	129,945			12,994	285,256
Totals	1,285,256	729,945			72,994	1,185,256
Less: Dividends declared:						
Phillips Corp.	100,000			(3) 10,000		90,000
Sousa Corp.		50,000		(1) 45,000	5,000	
Balance, 12/31/x1—carried forward	1,185,256	679,945			67,994	1,095,256
Balance Sheet						
Miscellaneous assets	1,045,000	920,000				1,965,000
Investment in Sousa Corp.	940,256			(2) 900,000 (1) 40,256 (4) 230,000		
Investment in Phillips Corp.		249,945		(3) 19,945		
Goodwill			(4) 70,000	(5) 1,750		68,250
Totals	1,985,256	1,169,945				2,033,250
Liabilities	200,000	90,000				290,000
Capital stock:						
Phillips Corp.	600,000		(4) 60,000			540,000
Sousa Corp.		400,000	(2) 360,000		40,000	
Retained earnings—brought forward	1,185,256	679,945			67,994	1,095,256
Minority interest					107,994	107,994
Totals	1,985,256	1,169,945	1,246,951	1,246,951		2,033,250

(1) To eliminate equity in earnings of subsidiary and dividends paid by subsidiary.
(2) To eliminate balance of investment.
(3) To eiminate equity in earnings of parent and dividends paid by parent.
(4) To eliminate balance of investment and to set up original amount paid for goodwill.
(5) To record amortization of goodwill for the current year.

Computations and Proofs

Minority interest:

10% of Sousa's net assets at 12/31/x1:

Capital stock	$ 400,000
Retained earnings	679,945
Total net assets	$1,079,945
10% of above	$ 107,994

Consolidated retained earnings:

Same as in Illustration 10–12 reconciliation.

Illustration 10–15
PHILLIPS CORPORATION
Consolidated Working Paper
For the Year Ended December 31, 19x2

Complete Equity Method—Parent and Subsidiary
90 Percent Subsidiary
Second year

	Phillips Corp.	Sousa Corp. (90%)	Eliminations Dr.	Eliminations Cr.	Minority Interest	Consolidated
Income Statement						
Sales	1,200,000	500,000				1,700,000
Cost of sales, expenses, income taxes	870,000	330,000	(6) 1,750			1,201,750
Operating income	330,000	170,000				498,250
Equity in earnings—subsidiary	146,134		(1) 146,134			
Equity in earnings—parent		51,154	(4) 51,154			
Minority interest net income					22,116	(22,116)
Net income—carried forward	476,134	221,154			22,116	476,134
Retained Earnings Statement						
Balance, 1/1/x2:						
Phillips Corp.	1,185,256		(5) 100,000 (6) 1,750	(2) 10,000		1,095,256
Sousa Corp.		679,945	(3) 590,256 (5) 19,945		67,994	
Net income—brought forward	476,134	221,154			22,116	476,134
Totals	1,661,390	901,099			90,110	1,571,390
Less: Dividends declared:						
Phillips Corp.	150,000			(4) 15,000		135,000
Sousa Corp.		70,000		(1) 63,000	7,000	
Balance, 12/31/x2—carried forward	1,511,390	831,099			83,110	1,436,390
Balance Sheet						
Miscellaneous assets	1,365,000	1,270,000				2,635,000
Investment in Sousa Corp.	1,023,390		(2) 10,000	(3) 950,256 (1) 83,134 (5) 249,945		
Investment in Phillips Corp.		286,099		(4) 36,154		
Goodwill			(5) 70,000	(6) 3,500		66,500
Totals	2,388,390	1,556,099				2,701,500
Liabilities	277,000	325,000				602,000
Capital stock:						
Phillips Corp.	600,000		(5) 60,000			540,000
Sousa Corp.		400,000	(3) 360,000		40,000	
Retained earnings—brought forward	1,511,390	831,099			83,110	1,436,390
Minority interest					123,110	123,110
Totals	2,388,390	1,556,099	1,410,989	1,410,989		2,701,500

(1) To eliminate equity in earnings of subsidiary and dividends paid by subsidiary.

(2) To restore reciprocity of investment account with net assets of subsidiary for cumulative amount of prior years' dividends paid to subsidiary.

(3) To eliminate balance of investment (90 percent of capital stock and remainder to retained earnings).

(4) To eliminate equity in earnings of parent and dividends paid by parent.

(5) To eliminate balance of investment, set up original goodwill of $70,000, eliminate 10 percent of capital stock and remainder to:
    a). Parent retained earnings ($100,000 per 1/1/x1 amount).
    b). Subsidiary retained earnings.

(6) To amortize goodwill for current year and for prior years.

Computations and Proofs

(Same as in Illustration 10–13.)

A comparison of Illustrations 10–12 and 10–14 reveals that the consolidated columns are identical, as they should be. The method of accounting for investments should not affect the end product (financial statements). The elimination entries used in Illustration 10–14 are similar to the entries used in previous chapters and require no further elaboration. However, they should be reviewed in order to enhance understanding.

For 19x2, the working paper would appear as in Illustration 10–15. The elimination entries for Illustration 10–15 are:

(1)

Equity in Earnings—Subsidiary	146,134	
Dividends Declared—		
Sousa Corporation		63,000
Investment in Sousa		
Corporation		83,134

(2)

Investment in Sousa		
Corporation	10,000	
Retained Earnings (1/1/x2)		
—Phillips Corporation . .		10,000

(3)

Retained Earnings (1/1/x2)—		
Sousa Corporation	590,256	
Capital Stock—Sousa		
Corporation	360,000	
Investment in Sousa		
Corporation		950,256

(4)

Equity in Earnings—Parent . .	51,154	
Dividends Declared—		
Phillips Corporation		15,000
Investment in Phillips		
Corporation		36,154

(5)

Retained Earnings (1/1/x2)—		
Phillips Corporation	100,000	
Retained Earnings (1/1/x2)—		
Sousa Corporation	19,945	
Goodwill	70,000	
Capital Stock—Phillips		
Corporation	60,000	
Investment in Phillips		
Corporation		249,945

(6)

Amortization of Goodwill		
(expenses)	1,750	
Retained Earnings (1/1/x2)—		
Sousa Corporation	1,750	
Goodwill		3,500

As expected, the working paper consolidated column agrees with that in Illustration 10–13. A comparison of the elimination entries and the explanations appended to the working papers will aid in achieving a fuller understanding of the procedures that are required in each case.

Indirect holdings and mutual relationships

Illustration 10–11 exemplifies a situation where even though the parent does not own directly more than 50 percent of a subsidiary consolidation is still mandatory because effective control is nevertheless present.

If Illustration 10–11 is changed so that, in addition, T Company owns 20 percent of S Company, we are now faced with a mutual holding relationship that must be solved algebraically because the treasury stock method is inappropriate here. The treasury stock approach can only be used when the mutual relationship is with the parent company directly. If it is assumed that the separate income of P Company is $200,000 while S Company has $100,000 of separate income and T Company has $80,000 of separate income, the algebraic solution would be:

Let P_E = Parent's net income using equity
Let S_E = Allocable net income using equity
Let T_E = Allocable net income using equity

$$P_E = \$200,000 + .8S_E$$
$$S_E = \$100,000 + .6T_E$$
$$T_E = \$\ 80,000 + .2S_E$$

By substitution:
$$T_E = \$80,000 + .2(\$100,000 + .6T_E)$$
$$T_E = \$80,000 + \$20,000 + .12T_E$$
$$.88T_E = \$100,000$$
$$T_E = \frac{\$100,000}{.88}$$
$$T_E = \$113,636$$

Substituting in S_E:
$$S_E = \$100,000 + .6(\$113,636)$$
$$S_E = \$100,000 + \$68,182$$
$$S_E = \$168,182$$

Substituting in P_E:
$$P_E = \$200,000 + .8(\$168,182)$$
$$P_E = \$200,000 + \$134,546$$
$$P_E = \$334,546$$

Allocated income would be:

P Company—100% × $334,546 =	$334,546
Minority interest income in S Company	−0−*
Minority interest income in T Company (40%	
× T Company $113,636) =	45,454
Total income	$380,000

*The minority interest of S Company is equal to [100% − (80% owned by P Company + 20% owned by T Company) = 0].

The entries to record equitites in income on the respective books would be as follows:

P Company Books

Investment in S Company	134,546	
Equity in Earnings of Subsidiary		134,546
To record share of income ($334,546 − $200,000 separate income).		

S Company Books

Investment in T Company	68,182	
Equity in Earnings of Subsidiary		68,182
To record share of income ($168,182 − $100,000 separate income).		

T Company Books

Investment in S Company	33,636	
Equity in Earnings of S Company		33,636
To record share of income ($113,636 − $80,000 separate income).*		

*This could also be calculated as:

S Company income allocated to P Company	$134,546
Balance of S Company income to T Company	33,636
Total S Company income	$168,182

Working paper procedures would be handled in the same manner as Illustrations 10–14 and 10–15 if the equity method were used to account for all investments. If one or more of the investments were accounted for by the cost method, Illustrations 10–12 and 10–13 show the necessary working paper procedures.

QUESTIONS

1. Complex affiliation structures can be varied. Explain what is meant by:

   a. Lineal relationships.
   b. Lateral relationships.
   c. Mutual relationships.

2. When income is allocated in a lineal or lateral relationship, what order should the allocation assume? Use an affiliation diagram to illustrate your answer.

3. What is meant by indirect holdings? When would it be necessary to consolidate an indirect holding of less than 50%?

4. There are two approaches used to account for reciprocal holdings. What are they? Which one is most often encountered in practice?

5. How is the treasury stock approach treated on consolidated financial statements? What theoretical justification can you offer for this treatment?

6. A Company owns 70 percent of B company, and B Company owns 60 percent of C Company. Are consolidated statements required that include C Company? Explain.

7. P Company owns 80 percent of S Company, and S Company owns 80 percent of T Company. What is P Company's indirect ownership percentage of T Company? Can this percentage be used to allocate T Company's income between majority and minority interests? Use an example to illustrate your answer.

Questions for appendix:

8. What theoretical justification is there for the use of the algebraic solution?

9. What steps are necessary to apportion income when the algebraic method is used? You may describe the steps; it is not necessary to use algebraic equations in your answer.

10. What is true about consolidated net income under the treasury stock method and consolidated net income under the algebraic method? Why is this so?

EXERCISES

Exercise 10–1. P Company has two affiliates, and all investments were purchased at book value. P Company owns 90 percent of S Company who, in turn, owns 70 percent of T Company. During 19x1, P Company sold land to S Company at a gain of $30,000. The land is still owned by S Company. Separate incomes for 19x1 are:

P Company	$300,000
S Company	100,000
T Company	150,000

Required:

a. Construct an affiliation diagram.
b. Compute:
1. Consolidated net income.
2. Minority interest net income.

Exercise 10–2. P Company has two affiliates, and all investments were purchased at book value. P Company owns 80 percent of Q Company and 90 percent of R Company. R Company owns 10 percent of Q Company. During 19x2, P Company sold land to R Company at a gain of $20,000 and Q Company sold merchandise to P Company at a profit of $10,000. Both items are still owned by the purchasers as of the end of 19x2. Separate incomes for 19x2 are:

P Company	$200,000
Q Company	150,000
R Company	90,000

Required:

a. Construct an affiliation diagram.
b. Compute:
1. Consolidated net income.
2. Minority interest net income.

Exercise 10–3. P Company has three affiliates, and all investments were purchased at book value. P Company owns 70 percent of A Company and 80 percent of B Company. A Company owns 80 percent of D Company and 10 percent of B Company. B company owns 10 percent of D Company.

During 19x3, P Company sold merchandise to B Company at a profit of $20,000. Half of this merchandise is unsold at the end of 19x3. On December 31, 19x3, D Company sold equipment to B Company at a gain of $25,000.

Separate incomes (losses) for 19x3 are:

P Company	$400,000
A Company	(100,000)
B Company	80,000
D Company	120,000

Required:

a. Construct an affiliation diagram.
b. Compute:
1. Consolidated net income.
2. Minority interest net income.

Exercise 10–4. P Company has four affiliates, and all investments were purchased at book value. P Company owns 70 percent of E Company and 90 percent of G Company. E Company owns 60 percent of F Company. G Company owns 20 percent of E Company and 70 percent of H Company. F Company also owns 20 percent of H Company.

During 19x4, E Company sold inventory to F Company at a profit of $30,000. Half of this inventory is unsold at the end of 19x4. On December 31, 19x4, G Company purchased $200,000 (face value) of the outstanding bonds payable of P Company for $190,000. P Company originally sold these bonds at par.

Separate incomes (losses) for 19x4 are:

P Company	$400,000
E Company	(100,000)
F Company	200,000
G Company	(50,000)
H Company	150,000

Required:

a. Construct an affiliation diagram.
b. Compute:
1. Consolidated net income.
2. Minority interest net income.

Exercise 10–5. P Company has three affiliates, and all investments were purchased at book value. P Company owns 80 percent of K Company who, in turn owns 70 percent of M Company and 60 percent of N Company.

During 19x5, the following intercompany transactions are to be considered:

1. The *beginning* inventory of N Company contains $20,000 of unconfirmed profit from sales made in 19x4 by K Company.
2. The *ending* inventory of M Company contains $10,000 of unconfirmed profit from sales made in 19x5 by K Company.
3. On July 1, 19x5 K Company sold equipment to P Company at a gain of $40,000. The equipment was estimated to have a useful life of five years from the date of the sale.
4. On January 1, 19x5, P Company purchased $200,000 (face value) of the bonds payable issued by N Company and paid $190,000 for the bonds.

The bonds mature five years from the date of the purchase. On the date of the purchase, N Company had an unamortized bond discount on its books in the amount of $20,000 and the bonds payable balance was $500,000.

The 19x5 separate incomes (per books) of the companies are:

P Company	$400,000
K Company	20,000
M Company	150,000
N Company	80,000

Required:

a. Prepare an affiliation diagram.

b. Compute:

1. Consolidated net income.

2. Minority interest net income.

Exercise 10–6. Using the information provided in Exercise 10–5, you are to prepare all entries that would appear on the books of P Company and K Company that affect equity in earnings of subsidiaries when the complete equity method is used.

Exercise 10–7 (for appendix). Akron, Inc., owns 80 percent of the capital stock of Benson Co. and 70 percent of the capital stock of Cashin, Inc. Benson Co. owns 15 percent of the capital sotck of Cashin, Inc. Cashin, Inc., in turn, owns 25 percent of the capital stock of Akron, Inc. These ownership inter-relationships are illustrated in the following diagram:

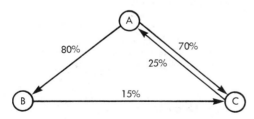

Net income before adjusting for interests in inter-company net income for each corporation follows:

Akron, Inc.	$190,000
Benson Co.	$170,000
Cashin, Inc.	$230,000

The following notations relate to items 1 through 4. Ignore all income tax considerations.

A_e = Akron's consolidated net income; i.e., its net income plus its share of the consolidated net incomes of Benson and Cashin.

B_e = Benson's consolidated net income; i.e., its net income plus its share of the consoli-dated net income of Cashin.

C_e = Cashin's consolidated net income; i.e., its net income plus its share of the consoli-dated income of Akron.

1. The equation, in a set of simultaneous equa-tions, which computes A_e is—

a. $A_e = .75(190,000 + .8B_e + .7C_e)$.

b. $A_e = 190,000 + .8B_e + .7C_e$.

c. $A_e = .75(190,000) + .8(170,000) + .7(230,000)$.

d. $A_e = .75(190,000) + .8B_e + .7C_e$.

2. The equation, in a set of simultaneous equa-tions, which computes B_e is—

a. $B_e = 170,000 + .15C_e - .75A_e$.

b. $B_e = 170,000 + .15C_e$.

c. $B_e = .2(170,000) + .15(230,000)$.

d. $B_e = .2(170,000) + .15C_e$.

3. Cashin's minority interest in consolidated net income is—

a. $.15 (230,000)$.

b. $230,000 + .25A_e$.

c. $.15 (230,000) + .25A_e$.

d. $.15C_e$.

4. Benson's minority interest in consolidated net income is—

a. $34,316.

b. $25,500.

c. $45,755.

d. $30,675.   (AICPA adapted)

Exercise 10–8 (for appendix). P Company pur-chased 80 percent of S Company at book value. S Company purchased 10 percent of P Company at book value.

The separate incomes for 19x2 are:

P Company	$100,000
S Company	80,000

Required:

Compute:

a. Consolidated net income.

b. Minority interest net income.

Exercise 10–9 (for appendix). P Company has two affiliates, and all investments were purchased at book value. P Company owns 80 percent of A Com-pany and 70 percent of B Company. In addition, A Company owns 20 percent of P Company.

The separate incomes for 19x3 are:

P Company	$200,000
A Company	80,000
B Company	50,000

Required:

a. Construct an affiliation diagram.

b. Compute:

1. Consolidated net income.

2. Minority interest net income.

Exercise 10–10 (for appendix). P Company has two affiliates, and all investments were purchased at book value. P Company owns 90 percent of C Company who, in turn, owns 60 percent of D Company. D Company owns 10 percent of C Company. The separate incomes for 19x4 are:

P Company $300,000
C Company 200,000
D Company 100,000

Required:

a. Construct an affiliation diagram.

b. Compute:

1. Consolidated net income.

2. Minority interest net income.

Exercise 10–11 (for appendix). P Company has two affiliates, and all investments were purchased at book value. P Company owns 80 percent of E Company who, in turn, owns 70 percent of F Company. F Company owns 10 percent of P Company. The separate incomes for 19x5 were:

P Company $300,000
E Company 200,000
F Company 100,000

Required:

a. Construct an affiliation diagram.

b. Compute:

1. Consolidated net income.

2. Minority interest net income.

(*Hint:* The problem can be solved by performing one substitution in an equation and then a second substitution in the same equation.)

Exercise 10–12 (for appendix). Using the information provided in Exercise 10–9, rework the exercise assuming that P Company purchased A Company at an amount which included $40,000 for goodwill. Goodwill of $20,000 was also paid when B Company was purchased. Amortization of goodwill is to be provided over a 20-year useful life.

Exercise 10–13 (for appendix). Using the information provided in Exercise 10–10, rework the exercise if P Company purchased C Company at an amount which included $60,000 for goodwill and C Company purchased D Company at an amount which included $40,000 for goodwill. Assume goodwill amortization over a 40-year period.

PROBLEMS

Problem 10–14. P Company and its affiliates acquired all of their investments at book value. The investments consist of:

	Percentage owned
P Company:	
R Company	80
S Company	70
T Company	90
R Company:	
V Company	60
S Company	10
S Company:	
W Company	70
T Company	10
T Company:	
W Company	20

During 19x7, S Company sold inventory to R Company at a profit of $40,000. Half of this inventory is unsold at the end of 19x7. On January 1, 19x7, W Company sold equipment to S Company at a gain of $30,000. The equipment had a remaining useful life of five years from the date of sale.

Separate incomes (losses) for 19x7 are:

P Company $400,000
R Company 200,000
S Company . . . . (30,000)
T Company 80,000
V Company . . . . (60,000)
W Company 20,000

Required:

a. Construct an affiliation diagram.

b. Compute:

1. Consolidated net income.

2. Minority interest net income.

Problem 10–15. Selected accounts from the trial balances of P Company and its affiliates at December 31, 19x4, are as follows:

	P Company dr. (cr.)	S Company dr. (cr.)	T Company dr. (cr.)
Retained earnings, January 1, 19x4	$(600,000)	$(200,000)	$(300,000)
Common stock ($10 par) . . .	(400,000)	(300,000)	(200,000)
Dividends declared . . .	100,000	80,000	50,000

All investments were made at book value. Ownership percentages are:

P Company owns 80 percent of S Company and 70 percent of T Company. S Company owns 10 percent of T Company.

The separate incomes for 19x4 are:

P Company $300,000
S Company 200,000
T Company 150,000

There were no intercompany transactions in 19x4. All companies use the complete equity method.

Required:

a. Prepare all entries to record equity in earnings of subsidiary by P Company and its affiliates.

b. Prepare all entries to record the *receipt* of dividends paid by the companies.

c. Compute the balances in the investment accounts at December 31, 19x4.

d. Prepare *all* possible working paper elimination entries.

e. Compute:
1. Consolidated net income.
2. Minority interest net income.

f. Prepare a consolidated statement of retained earnings for the year ended December 31, 19x4.

Problem 10–16 (complete equity method). On January 1, 19x2, P Company purchased 80 percent of the outstanding shares of S Company for $600,000 and 70 percent of the outstanding shares of T Company for $420,000. The following day, S Company purchased 20 percent of the outstanding shares of T Company for $120,000.

All of the assets and liabilities of S Company and T Company have book values that approximate their respective fair market values. Excess, if any, has an indeterminate life.

During 19x2, T Company sold merchandise with a cost of $30,000 to S Company for $50,000. Half of this merchandise is unsold at December 31, 19x2. In addition, P Company sold merchandise with a cost of $40,000 to T Company for $80,000. One fourth of this merchandise is still unsold at December 31, 19x2.

S Company owes T Company $10,000 on open account.

Both P Company and S Company use the complete equity method to account for investments.

Financial statements for the companies for the year ended December 31, 19x2, are as follows:

[Relates to Problem 10–16]

	P Company	S Company	T Company
Income Statement			
Sales	$1,200,000	$700,000	$500,000
Cost of sales	500,000	250,000	200,000
Gross margin	700,000	450,000	300,000
Expenses	200,000	120,000	100,000
Operating income before taxes . .	500,000	330,000	200,000
Equity in earnings—S Company . .	174,600		
Equity in earnings—T Company . .	65,250	21,500	
Income before income taxes	739,850	351,500	200,000
Provision for income taxes	200,000	132,000	80,000
Minority interest net income			
Net income—carried forward . . .	$ 539,850	$219,500	$120,000

	P Company	S Company	T Company
Retained Earnings Statement			
Balance, January 1, 19x2:			
P Company	$ 860,000		
S Company		$500,000	
T Company			$400,000
Net income—brought forward ...	539,850	219,500	120,000
Totals	1,399,850	719,500	520,000
Less: Dividends declared:			
P Company	150,000		
S Company		60,000	
T Company			40,000
Balance, December 31, 19x2—			
carried forward	$1,249,850	$659,500	$480,000
Balance Sheet			
Cash	$ 300,000	$100,000	$100,000
Accounts receivable	200,000	80,000	50,000
Inventories	150,000	70,000	30,000
Land	300,000		
Equipment (net of accumulated			
depreciation)	264,000	556,000	450,000
Investment in S Company	726,600		
Investment in T Company	457,250		
Investment in T Company		133,500	
Totals	$2,397,850	$939,500	$630,000
Accounts payable and accrued			
expenses	$ 250,000	$ 80,000	$ 50,000
Bonds payable (face amount			
$400,000)	398,000		
Common stock—P Company ($50			
par)	500,000		
Common stock—S Company ($10			
par)		200,000	
Common stock—T Company ($10			
par)			100,000
Retained earnings—brought			
forward	1,249,850	659,500	480,000
Totals	$2,397,850	$939,500	$630,000

Required:

a. Prepare an income apportionment schedule and verify the amounts recorded as equity in earnings from subsidiaries.

b. Prepare a consolidated working paper.

Problem 10–17 (for appendix). P Company has two affiliates, V Company and W Company. Ownership percentages and prices paid for goodwill are as follows:

	Percentage acquired	Goodwill
P Company:		
V Company	80	$20,000
W Company	60	40,000
V Company:		
W Company	20	10,000
W Company:		
V Company	10	–0–

There were no intercompany transactions during 19x5.

Goodwill is to be amortized over a 10-year period.

The separate incomes for 19x5 are: P Company, $100,000; V Company, $40,000; and W Company, $60,000.

Required:

a. Prepare an affiliation diagram.

b. Compute:

1. Consolidated net income.

2. Minority interest net income.

Problem 10–18 (for appendix). On January 1, 19x1, P Company purchased 80 percent of the outstanding shares of S Company for $600,000. The excess is due entirely to the undervaluation of land. The following day, S Company purchased 10 percent of the outstanding shares of P Company at book value.

P Company uses the equity method to account for its investment. S Company uses the cost method to account for its investment.

	P Company	S Company
Income Statement		
Sales	$1,000,000	$500,000
Cost of sales, expenses, and		
income taxes	782,000	360,000
Subtotal	218,000	140,000
Equity in earnings—		
subsidiary	112,000	
Dividend income		10,000
Minority interest net income		
Net income—carried forward	$ 330,000	$150,000

	P Company	S Company
Retained Earnings Statement		
Balance, January 1, 19x1:		
P Company	$ 600,000	
S Company		$400,000
Net income—brought		
forward	330,000	150,000
Totals	930,000	550,000
Less: Dividends declared:		
P Company	100,000	
S Company		50,000
Balance, December 31, 19x1—		
carried forward	$ 830,000	$500,000

	P Company	S Company
Balance Sheet		
Cash	$ 200,000	$100,000
Accounts receivable	150,000	50,000
Inventories	100,000	40,000
Land		250,000
Equipment (net of		
accumulated depreciation) . .	228,000	450,000
Investment in P Company . .		100,000
Investment in S Company . .	672,000	
Totals	$1,350,000	$990,000
Accounts payable and		
accrued expenses	$ 120,000	$190,000
Common stock—P Company		
($50 par)	400,000	
Common stock—S Company		
($10 par)		300,000
Retained earnings—brought		
forward	830,000	500,000
Totals	$1,350,000	$990,000

Required:

Prepare a consolidated working paper using the treasury stock approach.

Problem 10–19 (for appendix). On January 1, 19x1, P Company purchased 80 percent of the outstanding shares of S Company for $600,000. The excess is due entirely to the undervaluation of land. The following day, S Company purchased 10 percent of the outstanding shares of P Company at book value.

P Company uses the equity method to account for its investment. S Company uses the cost method to account for its investment.

	P Company	S Company
Income Statement		
Sales	$1,000,000	$500,000
Cost of sales, expenses, and		
income taxes	782,000	360,000
Subtotal	218,000	140,000
Equity in earnings—		
subsidiary	104,826	
Dividend income		10,000
Minority interest net income		
Net income—carried forward	$ 322,826	$150,000

	P Company	S Company
Retained Earnings Statement		
Balance, January 1, 19x1:		
P Company	$ 600,000	
S Company		$400,000
Net income—brought forward	322,826	150,000
Totals	922,826	$550,000
Less: Dividends declared:		
P Company	100,000	
S Company		50,000
Balance, December 31, 19x1— carried forward	$ 822,826	$500,000
Balance Sheet		
Cash	$ 200,000	$100,000
Accounts receivable	150,000	50,000
Inventories	100,000	40,000
Land		250,000
Equipment (net of accumulated depreciation)	228,000	450,000
Investment in P Company		100,000
Investment in S Company	664,826	
Totals	$1,342,826	$990,000
Accounts payable and accrued expenses	$ 120,000	$190,000
Common stock—P Company ($50 par)	400,000	
Common stock—S Company ($10 par)		300,000
Retained earnings—brought forward	822,826	500,000
Totals	$1,342,826	$990,000

	P Company	S Company
Income Statement		
Sales	$1,000,000	$ 500,000
Cost of sales, expenses, and income taxes	782,000	360,000
Subtotal	218,000	140,000
Equity in earnings—P Company		35,870
Equity in earnings—S Company	104,826	
Minority interest net income		
Net income—carried forward	$ 322,826	$ 175,870
Retained Earnings Statement		
Balance, January 1, 19x1:		
P Company	$ 600,000	
S Company		$ 400,000
Net income—brought forward	322,826	175,870
Totals	$ 922,826	$ 575,870
Less: Dividends declared:		
P Company	100,000	
S Company		50,000
Balance, December 31, 19x1— carried forward	$ 822,826	$ 525,870
Balance Sheet		
Cash	$ 200,000	$ 100,000
Accounts receivable	150,000	50,000
Inventories	100,000	40,000
Land		250,000
Equipment (net of accumulated depreciation)	228,000	450,000
Investment in P Company		125,870
Investment in S Company	664,826	
Totals	$1,342,826	$1,015,870
Accounts payable and accrued expenses	$ 120,000	$ 190,000
Common stock—P Company ($50 par)	400,000	
Common stock—S Company ($10 par)		300,000
Retained earnings—brought forward	822,826	525,870
Totals	$1,342,826	$1,015,870

Required:

a. Solve a set of simultaneous equations to determine consolidated net income and minority interest net income on a complete equity basis.

b. Prepare a consolidated working paper using the constructive retirement approach.

Problem 10–20 (for appendix). On January 1, 19x1, P Company purchased 80 percent of the outstanding shares of S Company for $600,000. The excess is due entirely to the undervaluation of land. The following day, S Company purchased 10 percent of the outstanding shares of P Company at book value.

Both P Company and S Company use the equity method to account for their investments.

Required:

a. Solve a set of simultaneous equations to determine consolidated net income and minority interest net income on a complete equity basis. Compare your solution with the amounts shown in the income statements.

b. Prepare a consolidated working paper using the constructive retirement approach.

11

Consolidated statements— consolidation theories and other topics

OVERVIEW

Thus far, our treatment of consolidations consisted of the method generally used in practice, known as the parent *theory. Another method, known as the* entity *theory, is occasionally encountered in practice. Under the entity theory, the minority interest is viewed as an equity interest which must merely be differentiated from the majority interest (the parent's share). Accordingly, under this theory, assets and liabilities of the subsidiary are revalued for the minority interest as is done for the parent company when the parent theory is employed. Moreover, unlike the treatment under the parent theory, the minority interest is not considered to be a liability but is rather shown on the balance sheet as a part of stockholders' equity.*

Although consolidated statements are required in accordance with GAAP, they do have limitations. They are not useful for minority stockholders, creditors of subsidiaries, and possibly creditors of the parent company. They also do not reveal financial statement ratios of the individual companies.

A consolidated statement of changes in financial position usually contains items not found in statements of single companies. These items, among others, include minority interest net income, dividends received in excess of the equity in earnings of subsidiaries or vice versa, and amortization of excess.

As noted in Chapter 3, this text emphasizes consolidation principles that comprise the method known as the *parent* approach. In fact, a strict interpretation of this method and the procedures usually encountered in practice differ somewhat. The differences involve principally the treatment of the minority's interest's share of net income as well as the location of the minority interest on the balance sheet. The strictest interpretation of the parent approach is to show the minority interest's share of income as an expense rather than a deduction from income. However, practice differs. U. I. International (Illustration 11–1) shows the minority interest's share of income as an expense under the caption "Costs and Expenses" and Alcan Aluminum Ltd. (Illustration 11–2) shows the minority interest's share in net income as an "other deduction."

Either of these income statements is consistent with the procedures used in this book, that is, the parent approach. The parent approach has been described as follows:

> The "parent company" concept views consolidated statements as an extension of parent company statements, in which the investment account of the parent is replaced by the individual assets and liabilities underlying the parent's investment, and subsidiaries are viewed as almost the equivalent of

Illustration 11–1
I U INTERNATIONAL CORPORATION
Consolidated Statements of Earnings
In thousands except per share data
For the Years Ended December 31, 1979, and 1978

	1979	1978*
Revenues and other income	$2,662,013	$2,459,539
Costs and expenses:		
Cost of products sold, other operating costs and expenses, excluding depreciation and amortization	2,061,716	1,898,027
Selling, general, and administrative expenses, excluding depreciation and amortization	287,727	278,248
Depreciation and amortization	91,127	83,988
Interest and debt expense	61,532	62,650
Foreign currency adjustments	5,428	(14,637)
Income taxes	56,925	55,819
Minority interest	29,438	29,838
	2,593,893	2,393,933
Earnings from continuing operations	68,120	65,606
Loss from discontinued ocean shipping operations	(1,100)	(53,546)
Net earnings	$ 67,020	$ 12,060
Earnings per share:		
Primary:		
Continuing operations	$1.91	$1.91
Discontinued ocean shipping operations	(0.03)	(1.61)
	$1.88	$0.30
Assuming full dilution:†		
Continuing operations	$1.79	$1.80
Discontinued ocean shipping operations	(0.03)	(1.48)
	$1.76	—

*Restated to segregate discontinued ocean shipping operations.
†Not reported for 1978 due to antidilutive effect of convertible securities.

Illustration 11–2
ALCAN ALUMINUM LTD.
Consolidated Statement of Income
For the Years Ended December 31, 1979, and 1978

	Year Ending December 31 ($000)	
	1979	1978
Revenues:		
Sales	$4,194,961	$3,552,350
Operating revenues	186,261	158,854
Other income	60,164	26,497
	4,441,386	3,737,701
Costs and expenses:		
Cost of sales and operating expenses	3,231,490	2,716,163
Depreciation	148,873	137,593
Selling, research, and administrative expenses	307,846	268,412
Interest on debt not maturing within one year	84,683	71,384
Other interest	28,945	16,277
Other expenses	14,382	16,585
	3,816,219	3,226,414
Income before income taxes and other items	625,167	511,287
Income taxes:		
Current	154,613	107,096
Deferred	56,431	83,161
	211,044	190,257
Income before other items	414,123	321,030
Equity income	21,299	5,122
Minority interests	(29,464)	(29,168)
Income before extraordinary gain	405,958	296,984
Gain on sale of investment	21,509	—
Net income	$ 427,467	$ 296,984
Income per common share:		
Before extraordinary gain	$10.04	$7.34
Extraordinary gain	0.53	—
Dividends per common share	$10.57	$7.34
	2.10	1.55

branches. When subsidiary ownership is not complete, the consolidation process segregates the minority interest in the partially owned subsidiary. The minority interest is considered to be an outside group and a liability as far as the parent shareholder group is concerned.[1]

THE ENTITY METHOD

There is another method, referred to as the *entity* approach. This method has been described as follows:

> In contrast to the parent company concept, the "entity" concept view consolidated statements as those of an economic entity with two classes of proprietary interest—the major or dominant interest and the minority interest.

---

[1]Accountants International Study Group, *Consolidated Financial Statements: Current Recommended Practices in Canada, the United Kingdom, and the United States* (Plainstow, England: The Curwen Press Ltd., 1973), par. 24.

It holds that in consolidation these interests should be treated consistently. The consolidated statements are not viewed as an extension of parent company statements; rather, they are viewed as an expression of the financial position and operating results of a distinct "consolidated entity" consisting of a number of related companies whose relationship arises from common control (based on powers conferred by share ownership). When related companies are viewed as parts of such an entity, the minority interest, instead of representing an accountability to an outside group by the parent, represents a part of capital.[2]

Discussion

In 1944, the American Accounting Association published Professor Maurice Moonitz's monograph entitled *The Entity Theory of Consolidated Statements.* The entity theory focuses on the entity as the unit of interest and, accordingly, consolidated financial statements that are prepared in accordance with this theory emphasize the entity as a whole rather than the parent's interest. Thus, if a subsidiary's net assets were purchased at an amount different from their book value, and the transaction was accounted for as a *purchase,* under the entity theory the *full* amount of the difference between book value and market value would be reflected in the consolidated statements. Accordingly, the minority interest's share of these differences would be reflected in the consolidated financial statements and the minority interest would thus be shown at its implied fair market value rather than at book value as is the practice under the parent approach. The same procedure applies to the calculation of unidentifiable intangibles (goodwill). A variation of the method known as the *push-down theory* appears at the end of this chapter—see appendix at end of this Chapter.

When the parent approach is used, only the parent's share of the net assets is reflected in the consolidated statements at neither book value nor market value, but at a hybrid amount involving a combination of both.

For example, if a parent company purchased 80 percent of a subsidiary and if that subsidiary's inventories were carried on its books at $100,000 on the purchase date, and if the fair market value was $300,000, these inventories would be reflected on the consolidated statements at $260,000, i.e., the $100,000 book value plus 80 percent of $200,000 (the excess of fair market value over book value). By contrast, the inventory valuation under the *entity* theory would be the fair market value of $300,000 with a concommitant increase in minority interest of $40,000 (20% × $200,000 of excess). Even though the entity approach is considered by some as theoretically preferable, it is rarely encountered in practice. One reason for this may be that the $40,000 increment is not the result of an arm's-length transaction, but for the inventory as such it is derived from the parent's willingness to pay more than book value for the business. The parent's payment for excess is considered as part of an arm's-length negotiated transaction and, therefore, is compatible with GAAP, but so is the entity method.

---

[2]Ibid., par. 25.

The parent approach can be theoretically justified when the payment for excess is deemed to be made for economies of scale or other advantages that accrue to the benefit of the parent company only. For example, if the acquired subsidiary has efficient marketing channels similar to those needed by the parent company, the parent company may be able to reduce overall marketing costs by using the subsidiary's marketing channels. In this case, the parent company is the major beneficiary of the acquisition of superior or more economical marketing channels and the excess paid by the parent company for this feature does not necessarily benefit the minority interest directly. The entity approach would have little theoretical justification in such cases. The entity approach can best be justified theoretically when the payment of excess is attributable to overvalued or undervalued assets.

Entity method—date of acquisition

In order to contrast the two approaches, Illustration 3–15 will now be reworked using the entity method. Based on the purchase price of $153,600 for an 80 percent interest in Branch, Inc., it can be inferred that the total market value of Branch, Inc., is $192,000 ($153,600 ÷ 80%). Using the book and market values shown in Illustration 3–3, the allocation of the purchase price would now be as shown in Illustration 11–3.

Illustration 11–3
BRANCH, INC.
Allocation of Purchase Price
January 1, 19x1

	Total	(80%) Parent	(20%) Minority
Market value of Branch, Inc.	$192,000	$153,600	$38,400
Less: (differences between market values and book values):			
Undervalued inventories	(16,000)	(12,800)	(3,200)
Undervalued land	(10,000)	(8,000)	(2,000)
Undervalued building	(20,000)	(16,000)	(4,000)
Overvalued equipment	10,000	8,000	2,000
Undervalued patent	(10,000)	(8,000)	(2,000)
Overvalued bonds payable	(10,000)	(8,000)	(2,000)
Balances of excess	$136,000	$108,800	$27,200
Less: Net assets at book value	61,000	48,800	12,200
Goodwill	$ 75,000	$ 60,000	$15,000

A proof of the calculation of goodwill is:

Total market value—as calculated	$192,000
Less: Net assets at market value (see Illustration 3–3)	117,000
Goodwill	$ 75,000

The working paper shown in Illustration 3–16 is recast using the entity approach, as shown as Illustration 11–4.

The elimination entry for Illustration 11–4 is:

(1)

Retained Earnings—Branch, Inc.	7,200
Common Stock—Branch, Inc.	32,000
Additional Paid-In Capital—Branch, Inc.	9,600
Inventories	16,000
Land	10,000
Building	20,000
Patents	10,000
Goodwill	75,000
Bonds Payable	10,000

Equipment	10,000
Investment in Branch, Inc.	153,600
Minority Interest Excess	26,200

Illustration 11–4
CHROME SERIAL COMPANY, INC.
Consolidated Working Paper
January 1, 19x1

80 Percent Subsidiary
Date of Acquisition
Entity Method

	Chrome Serial Co., Inc.	Branch, Inc. (80%)	Eliminations Dr.	Eliminations Cr.	Minority Interest	Consolidated
Assets						
Cash in bank	80,000	13,000				93,000
Accounts receivable (net of estimated uncollectibles)	50,000	26,000				76,000
Inventories	60,000	14,000	(1) 16,000			90,000
Land	70,000	10,000	(1) 10,000			90,000
Building (net of depreciation)	120,000	50,000	(1) 20,000			190,000
Equipment (net of depreciation)	200,000	30,000		(1) 10,000		220,000
Patents			(1) 10,000			10,000
Goodwill			(1) 75,000			75,000
Investment in Branch, Inc.	153,600			(1) 153,600		
Total assets	733,600	143,000				844,000
Liabilities and Stockholders' Equity						
Accounts payable and other liabilities	60,000	30,000				90,000
8% bonds payable ($50,000)		52,000	(1) 10,000			42,000
Common stock:						
Chrome Serial Co., Inc.	200,000					200,000
Branch, Inc.		40,000	(1) 32,000		8,000	
Additional paid-in capital		12,000	(1) 9,600		2,400	
Retained earnings:						
Chrome Serial Co., Inc.	473,600					473,600
Branch, Inc.		9,000	(1) 7,200		1,800	
Minority interest excess				(1) 26,200	26,200	
Total minority interest					38,400	38,400
Total liabilities and stockholders' equity	773,600	143,000	189,800	189,800		844,000

From Illustration 11–4 the following can be noted:

1. The assets and liabilities of Branch, Inc. are adjusted to their *full* market values and not to their partial values as was done previously.
2. Goodwill of $75,000 is recorded instead of the 60,000 shown in Chapter 3.
3. Minority interest is shown at the *implied market value* of $38,400 instead of $12,200 which is 20 percent of the *book value* of $61,000. The calculation of minority interest excess is the difference between the two amounts ($38,400 − $12,200 = $26,200).

Entity method— subsequent to date of acquisition

Consolidated working papers that are prepared subsequent to the date of an acquisition under the entity method require similar elimination entries to those prepared under the parent method. However, the amortization of excess (inventory, plant assets, goodwill, etc.) now involves the minority interest which was not involved under the parent approach. Since under the entity approach implied excess is allocated to the minority interest, the minority interest's share of net income in years subsequent to the date of acquisition must be changed by the respective amortizations attributable to it. It should be noted that *no new problems are created by the use of the entity method with regard to intercompany profits* and, therefore, this topic will not be illustrated in this chapter.

To demonstrate the procedures required to amortize the excess attributable to the minority interest, the example used for Illustration 11–4 will now be extended to one year after the date of acquisition; this is shown now as Illustration 11–5. All operating data for 19x1 coincide with the assumptions in Illustration 4–5. After reviewing Illustration 11–5 it would be useful to compare the two illustrations and note the differences in results.

The elimination entries for Illustration 11–5 are:

(1)		
Equity in Earnings—Subsidiary	63,900	
Dividends Paid—Branch, Inc.		32,000
Investment in Branch, Inc.		31,900

(2)		
Retained Earnings (1/1/x1)—Branch, Inc.	7,200	
Cost of Sales	16,000	
Land	10,000	
Building	20,000	
Patents	10,000	
Goodwill	75,000	
Bonds Payable	10,000	
Common Stock—Branch, Inc.	32,000	
Additional Paid-In Capital—Branch, Inc.	9,600	
Equipment		10,000
Investment in Branch, Inc.		153,600
Minority Interest Excess		26,200

(3)		
Cost of Sales (depreciation and amortization)	250	
Accumulated Depreciation—Equipment	1,250	
Accumulated Depreciation—Building		500
Patents		1,000

(4)		
Interest Expense	2,000	
Bonds Payable		2,000
(5)		
Amortization of Goodwill (expenses)	1,875	
Goodwill		1,875

From Illustration 11–5 it can be seen that:

1. Elimination entry (1) is the usual entry when the complete equity method is used.
2. Entry (2) is also the usual entry except that the *full* values are used (as computed in Illustration 11–3) instead of only the parent's portion.
3. The calculation of the minority interest's net income (see computations and proofs) must now be adjusted for its share of amortization instead of merely using $20,000 (20% × $100,000). It can also be calculated by taking 25 percent (20% ÷ 80%) of the parent's equity in subsidiary earnings—25% × $63,900 = $15,975.
4. The reconciliation of the minority interest must now include its share of *unamortized excess* instead of merely its share of the net assets at the end of the year. (For years after the first year, the reconciliation will require an adjustment for the cumulative amortization if the original excess is added in as in this illustration. Alternatively, the unamortized excess could be used if the original excess is *not* added in as part of the reconciliation.)

A comparison of Illustration 11–5 with Illustration 4–5 reveals that:

1. Consolidated net income is the same even though the components of the income statement are different. Minority interest net income adjusts for these differences.
2. The consolidated retained earnings statements are the same.
3. The components of the balance sheet are different wherever excess is involved. Illustration 11–5 reflects the full market value (parent's and minority interest's) less amortization while Illustration 4–5 reflects only the parent's share.

LIMITATIONS OF CONSOLIDATED STATEMENTS

While consolidated financial statements are mandatory in accordance with GAAP, some useful information is lost in the consolidation process; that is, a trade-off occurs in giving up the individual company data in favor of consolidated data. Moreover, there are instances where separate statements are meaningful, and in these, separate statements are appended to the consolidated statements. This is especially so where the consolidated statements include the investment in one or more unconsolidated subsidiaries. In such cases the separate statements of unconsolidated subsidiaries are often included as part of the annual report.

Illustration 11–5

CHROME SERIAL COMPANY, INC.
Consolidated Working Paper
For the Year Ended December 31, 19x1

	Chrome Serial Co., Inc.	Branch, Inc. (80%)	Eliminations Dr.	Eliminations Cr.	Minority Interest	Consolidated
Income Statements						
Sales	800,000	703,600				1,503,600
			(3) 250			
Cost of sales	350,000	300,000	(2) 16,000			666,250
Gross margin	450,000	403,600				837,350
Operating expenses	150,000	200,000	(5) 1,875			351,875
Operating income before taxes	300,000	203,600				485,475
Deduct: Interest expense		3,600	(4) 2,000			5,600
Add: Equity in earnings—subsidiary	63,900		(1) 63,900			
Income before income taxes	363,900	200,000				479,875
Provision for income taxes (50%)	150,000	100,000				250,000
						229,875
Minority interest net income					15,975	(15,975)
Net income—carried forward	213,900	100,000			15,975	213,900
Retained Earnings Statement						
Balance, 1/1/x1:						
Chrome Serial Co., Inc.	473,600					473,600
Branch, Inc.		9,000	(2) 7,200		1,800	
Net income—brought forward	213,900	100,000			15,975	213,900
Total	687,500	109,000			17,775	687,500
Less: Dividends paid:						
Chrome Serial Co., Inc.	110,000					110,000
Branch, Inc.		40,000		(1) 32,000	8,000	
Balance, 12/31/x1—carried forward	577,500	69,000			9,775	577,500
Balance Sheet						
Cash in bank	98,500	40,000				138,500
Accounts receivable (net of estimated uncollectables)	100,000	45,000				145,000
Inventories	80,000	30,000				110,000
Land	70,000	10,000	(2) 10,000			90,000
Building (net of depreciation)	116,000	48,750	(2) 20,000	(3) 500		184,250
Equipment (net of depreciation)	250,000	26,250	(3) 1,250	(2) 10,000		267,500
Patents			(2) 10,000	(3) 1,000		9,000
Goodwill			(2) 75,000	(5) 1,875		73,125
				(2) 153,600		
Investment in Branch, Inc.	185,500			(1) 31,900		
Totals	900,000	200,000				1,017,375
Liabilities and Stockholders' Equity						
Accounts payable and other liabilities	122,500	27,400				149,900
8% bonds payable ($50,000)		51,600	(2) 10,000	(4) 2,000		43,600
Common stock:						
Chrome Serial Co., Inc.	200,000					200,000
Branch, Inc.		40,000	(2) 32,000		8,000	
Additional paid-in capital		12,000	(2) 9,600		2,400	
Retained earnings—brought forward	577,500	69,000			9,775	577,500
Minority interest excess				(2) 26,200	26,200	
Minority interest					46,375	46,375
Totals	900,000	200,000	259,075	259,075		1,017,375

Illustration 11–5 (continued)

(1) To eliminate equity in earnings of subsidiary to prevent double counting of income; to eliminate parent's share of dividends paid and convert year-end balance of investment to beginning-of-the-year balance.

(2) To eliminate balance of investment and to allocate excess. (Note: Inventory excess is charged to cost of sales since it is assumed that the inventory has been sold.)

(3) To record amortization of excess for building, equipment, and patent.

(4) To record amortization of excess for bonds payable.

(5) To record amortization of goodwill.

Computations and Proofs

Income apportionment:

	Total	Parent	Minority Interest
Parent income from operations ($213,900 − $63,900)	$150,000	$150,000	—
Subsidiary income	100,000	80,000	$ 20,000
Amortization of excess:			
Inventory—sold in 19x1	(16,000)	(12,800)	(3,200)
Building ($20,000 ÷ 40 years)	(500)	(400)	(100)
Equipment ($10,000 ÷ 8 years)	1,250	1,000	250
Patent ($10,000 ÷ 10 years)	(1,000)	(800)	(200)
Bonds payable ($10,000 ÷ 5 years)	(2,000)	(1,600)	(400)
Goodwill ($75,000 ÷ 40 years)	(1,875)	(1,500)	(375)
Totals	$229,875	$213,900	$ 15,975

Minority interest:

Net assets of Branch, 12/31/x1:	
Capital stock	$ 40,000
Additional paid-in capital	12,000
Retained earnings	69,000
Total	$121,000
20% of above	$ 24,200
Add: Minority interest excess	26,200
Less: Amortization and write-offs as above:	
Inventory	(3,200)
Building	(100)
Equipment	250
Patent	(200)
Bonds	(400)
Goodwill	(375)
Minority interest, 12/31/x1	$ 46,375

Minority interest stockholders

Consolidated statements rarely present specific information that is useful to minority interest stockholders. Since in consolidation the details of a specific subsidiary's financial statements are combined with those of the parent company and other subsidiaries, minority interest stockholders must obtain the subsidiary's separate financial statements if they are to obtain meaningful data regarding their investment. Such separate statements are usually provided to minority interest stockholders.

Creditors of subsidiary companies

Potential creditors of subsidiary companies are usually unable to assess the credit-worthiness of a subsidiary company from consolidated statements. Unless the parent company guarantees a subsidiary's debts, a credit grantor will usually require the subsidiary's separate financial statements in addition to those of the consolidated entity. Consolidated financial statements do not provide credit grantors of a subsidiary with information about the legal status of the contemplated debt nor with data on the debt-paying ability of a subsidiary. It is conceivable that a subsidiary's insolvency (excess of liabilities over assets) could be masked in the consolidated financial statements. In practice, there have been cases where a subsidiary has gone into bankruptcy and the parent company paid the subsidiary's debts although it was not legally obligated to do so. This is mostly done in order to uphold the credit standing of other members of the consolidated group.

Creditors of the parent company

Problems similar to those discussed above exist for the creditors of a parent company. Consolidated financial statements contain liabilities in excess of those of the parent company alone. Similarly, the details of consolidated assets are different from those of the parent company. Accordingly, potential creditors of a parent company are usually unable to assess the legal status of contemplated debts from the consolidated statements alone and, therefore, will obtain parent company statements as well. Annual report filings with the SEC (Form 10-K) contain both consolidated as well as parent company unconsolidated financial statements.

Financial statement ratios

Financial analysts, investors, creditors, and others analyze financial statements by using various measures of liquidity, operating performance, and rate of return on investment. The analysis of aggregate consolidated data can present problems of interpretation. For example, consolidated financial statements, when analyzed by means of ratios, will provide *average* ratios of the combined entity while masking the relationships for individual members of the group. While segment reporting, as required by *SFAS 14*, provides some data regarding the parts of the aggregate entity, that is often not adequate for an in-depth analysis of particular segments of a consolidated entity. Furthermore, the legal separation between subsidiaries does not necessarily provide the optimum basis for segment analysis. If, for example, an integrated entity has manufacturing and retail operations, each retail location could be a separate subsidiary owned by another subsidiary in a tiered holding company structure. The combined retail operation might provide a more meaningful basis for analysis than would each individual retail subsidiary.

Consolidated retained earnings

Consolidated retained earnings shown on consolidated financial statements rarely represent the amount legally available for dividends. Subsidiaries that were acquired under the purchase method of accounting have their retained earnings eliminated in consolidation. In many cases, the amount of retained earnings available for dividends is not a significant item in analysis, but if it is relevant, this factor cannot usually be obtained from an examination of consolidated financial statements only.

CONSOLIDATED STATEMENT OF CHANGES IN FINANCIAL POSITION

A consolidated statement of changes in financial position is similar to such a statement of an individual company. Since this topic is usually covered in intermediate accounting courses, a familiarity with the subject is assumed and the focus here will be only on the differences between a consolidated statement and a statement for a single company. The major differences between the two statements are the treatments of the minority interest's share of net income and dividends paid to minority interest stockholders. The treatment of these items are found in Illustrations 11–6, 11–7, and 11–8. The declaration and payment of dividends by a subsidiary to minority stockholders can either be combined with the parent company's dividend payments and shown as an application (use) of working capital or the minority interest dividends can be deducted from the minority interest's share of net income.

Illustration 11–6
INTERLAKE, INC.
Statement of Changes in Financial Position
For the Years Ended December 30, 1979, and December 31, 1978

	1979 (52 weeks)	1978 (53 weeks)
Financial resources were provided by:		
Net income	$ 39,735	$ 10,488
Depreciation, depletion, and amortization	25,015	23,012
Equity in earnings of affiliates and joint ventures less dividends received	(923)	1,490
(Decrease) increase in noncurrent portion of shutdown/ disposal provision	(1,960)	13,739
Future income taxes	3,941	3,478
Other long-term liabilities	1,680	355
→Minority interest in net income of subsidiary, less dividend paid	715	758
Working capital provided from operations	68,203	53,320
Long-term borrowings	2,864	54,350
Disposals of property, plant, and equipment	2,133	5,503
Decrease (increase) in construction funds held by trustees	8,016	(9,164)
Other	4,029	1,122
	85,245	105,131
Financial resources were used for:		
Capital expenditures	69,556	65,974
Reduction of long-term debt	3,640	3,414
Cash dividends	13,127	13,077
	86,323	82,465
(Decrease) increase in working capital	$ (1,078)	$ 22,666
(Decrease) increase in working capital comprises:		
Cash and short-term investments	$ (9,897)	$ 6,509
Receivables	33,587	40,402
Inventories	21,694	12,367
Other current assets	(2,689)	4,132
Accounts payable and accrued liabilities	(27,325)	(36,514)
Income taxes payable	8,421	(128)
Debt due within one year	(24,869)	(4,102)
	(1,078)	22,666
Working capital at beginning of year	163,348	140,682
Working capital at end of year	$162,270	$163,348

In Illustration 11–6 (see arrow) the dividends paid to minority stockholders were netted against their share of net income. The resulting net amount is added back as a "charge to income not requiring the outlay of working capital in the current period." This is done because this charge to income does not decrease working capital but rather increases a noncurrent account, i.e., the amount of the minority interest. This add-back is similar to the treatment accorded to depreciation and amortization expense in the statement of changes in financial position.

The treatment accorded to the equity in earnings of unconsolidated associated companies (see, for example, the arrow in Illustration 11–7), is noteworthy. The equity in earnings of unconsolidated affiliates is deducted in arriving at funds (i.e. working capital) provided by operations, because this income, net of any dividends received, increases a noncurrent (nonworking

Illustration 11–7
THE NEW YORK TIMES COMPANY
Consolidated Statements of Changes in Financial Position
For the Years Ended December 31, 1979, and 1978
($000)

	1979	1978
Source of funds:		
From operations:		
Net income	$36,408	$15,550
Charges (credits) to income not requiring (providing) funds:		
Depreciation	11,909	9,957
Amortization	3,952	3,429
Deferred income taxes, net	3,715	1,870
→ Equity in earnings of associated companies, net	(9,781)	(8,226)
Other	1,358	630
Total from operations	47,561	23,210
Property, plant, and equipment:		
Reclassification (see contra below)	—	1,584
Disposals	655	1,196
Decrease (increase) in investments:		
Dividends received from associated companies	7,162	3,176
Other	178	(856)
Increase in other liabilities	1,809	2,150
Increase in noncurrent portion of notes payable	13,678	289
Employee stock purchase and stock option plans, etc.	5,633	5,840
Total source of funds	$76,676	$36,589
Application of funds:		
Additions to property, plant, and equipment	$19,787	$29,765
Cash dividends	10,226	9,199
Miscellaneous assets:		
Reclassification (see contra above)	—	1,584
Increase	3,972	5,001
Increase in cost in excess of net assets acquired	14,074	—
Reduction in noncurrent portion of notes payable	2,190	2,112
Purchase of company stock	2,531	3,321
Net noncurrent assets of businesses acquired	4,374	1,188
Other	329	1,722
Increase (decrease) in working capital	19,193	(17,303)
Total application of funds	$76,676	$36,589

See notes to consolidated financial statements.

capital) account, i.e., the investment in unconsolidated (associated) company. Illustration 11–8 (see arrow) includes an example of an add-back for dividends in excess of equity in earnings of unconsolidated affiliates. This is a treatment opposite to that in Illustration 11–7 and is required since the receipt of the dividend increases working capital notwithstanding the fact that the dividend is not considered income under the equity method of accounting.

Whenever consolidated financial statements include a goodwill account which is subject to amortization, the resulting amortization expense does not represent a use of funds and, consequently, is added back to net income in arriving at "funds provided by operations." This treatment is similar to that accorded to the amortization of any other intangible which is a noncurrent asset.

Illustration 11–8
MOORE, MCCORMACK RESOURCES, INC.
Consolidated Statement of Changes in Financial Position
For the Year Ended December 31, 1979

Funds provided from operations:

Net income	$ 40,513,000
Charges not affecting working capital:	
Depreciation, amortization, and depletion	24,768,000
Increase in deferred income taxes	8,948,000
Increase in estimated liability for claims, etc.	835,000
→ Dividends received in excess of equity in earnings of affiliates	541,000
Total from operations	75,605,000
Other sources:	
Long-term debt and construction borrowings	87,244,000
Sale of interest in joint venture, net of gain	8,285,000
Decrease in restricted funds, net	1,272,000
Increase (decrease) in net unterminated voyage revenue	6,111,000
Total funds provided	$178,517,000

Funds used for:

Purchase of net assets of Florida Mining & Materials Corp., net of working capital acquired of $20,788,000	$ 67,312,000
Additions to capital assets, net	64,389,000
Reduction of long-term debt and obligations under capital leases	31,481,000
Note received on sale of interest in joint venture	9,668,000
Dividends	6,219,000
Increase in Capital Construction Fund	4,081,000
Other, net	434,000
Total funds used	183,584,000
Net increase (decrease) in working capital	$ (5,067,000)

Analysis of changes in working capital:

Cash and short-term investments	$ (5,803,000)
Receivables	24,612,000
Inventories	(2,134,000)
Other current assets	1,247,000
Accounts payable and accrued liabilities	(12,029,000)
Long-term debt due within one year	(7,218,000)
Obligations under capital leases due within one year	(103,000)
Income taxes payable	(3,639,000)
Net increase (decrease) in working capital	$ (5,067,000)

The Notes to Consolidated Financial Statements are an integral part of these statements.

Appendix: Push-down theory

Although not widely used in practice, the push-down theory received some degree of attention in 1973 when the SEC recommended its selective use. Shortly thereafter, the recommendation was tabled for further study, and the use of this method is not usually found in practice. However the Accounting Standards Executive Committee (AcSEC) of the AICPA is presently considering the use of this method.

Essentially, this theory is analogous to the entity theory except that instead of reflecting complete market values on the consolidation working papers (see Illustrations 11–4 and 11–5), the individual assets and liabilities including goodwill are adjusted to market values on the *books* of the subsidiary. When this is done, the elimination of the parent's investment on the working paper requires no allocation or assignment to excess, since the net assets of the subsidiary (after the adjustment) are equal to the price paid by the parent for the investment. The minority interest is similarly valued at the fair market value of the net assets of the subsidiary. For years subsequent to the business combination, the amortization of assets (including goodwill) is based on the adjusted values and thus the subsidiary's net income requires no further adjustments (except for unrealized intercompany profits)—see Illustration 11–5. The end product, however, would be the same, i.e., consolidated financial statements prepared under the entity method are identical to those prepared under the push-down method. However, major differences between the two approaches occur when:

1. Unconsolidated individual financial statements of the subsidiary are issued. Under the entity theory they would be based on the original historical carrying amounts, whereas under the push down theory they would be based on the fair market values on the date of the business combination.
2. The subsidiary sells assets. The *book* gain or loss on the sale of an asset would be different if the historical and market values are different.

One major consideration in the application of the push-down theory is to determine the degree of ownership needed for its implementation. In theory, such percentage of ownership can vary from 20 percent to 100 percent. Some advocates of the theory would use the 20 percent standard of ownership as enunciated by *APB 18*. Others maintain that control should be the standard rather than mere application of the equity method where control is not present. Still others maintain that a small minority interest (no more than 10 percent as allowed for pooling accounting) would be allowed for its use, while at the other extreme others maintain that 100 percent ownership should be required. Of course, in the latter case (100 percent), the concept is moot, since there is no minority interest and, therefore, individual financial statements of the subsidiary would rarely be issued. In any event, while the push-down method is occasionally encountered in practice, it does not enjoy wide support at this time. However, this may change after the AcSEC completes its review of the method.

QUESTIONS

1. How are consolidated statements viewed under the parent approach?

2. How is the minority interest viewed when the parent approach is used? Give examples from practical usage.

3. How are consolidated statements viewed under the entity approach?

4. How is the minority interest viewed when the entity approach is used? Is this treatment frequently used in practice?

5. When an investor purchases a majority of the net assets of an investee at other than book value, how is the difference between the price paid and book value treated under the *parent* approach? Under the *entity* approach?

6. When can the parent approach be theoretically justified?

7. When can the entity approach be theoretically justified?

8. How is excess allocated to the minority interest on consolidated working papers when the entity method is used? Is this treatment different from the manner in which excess is allocated when the parent approach is used? Explain.

9. What treatment is necessary for the excess allocated to the minority interest in periods subsequent to the date of acquisition?

10. Are there limitations to consolidated statements? Discuss the possible limitations that might affect:

    a. Minority interest stockholders.

    b. Creditors of subsidiaries.

    c. Creditors of the parent company.

11. What happens to the individual financial statement ratios of subsidiaries and of the parent company when consolidated financial statements are prepared? Discuss.

12. What items are likely to be found on a consolidated statement of changes in financial position that would not usually be found on such statements of individual companies? Discuss the nature of each of the items you mention.

Questions for Appendix (push-down theory):

13. What is meant by push-down theory?

14. Is there any difference in the end product—consolidated financial statements—between statements prepared under the entity method and those prepared under the push-down theory? Explain. Between the parent method and push-down theory? Explain.

15. Is there a difference of opinion regarding the percentage of ownership necessary before the push-down theory is appropriately used? Discuss.

EXERCISES

Exercise 11–1. For each of the following independent cases, prepare the consolidated *working paper* elimination entry for P Company and its subsidiary S Company using the entity approach. Assume that purchase accounting is to be used and that all of the assets and liabilities of S Company have fair market values approximately equal to their respec-

tive book values. (*Hint:* Calculate excess prior to preparing entry.)

Exercise 11–2. On January 1, 19x2, P Company purchased an 80 percent interest in S Company for $528,000. On that date, the assets and liabilities of S Company had book values and fair values as shown

[Relates to Exercise 11–1]

| | | Percent of stock acquired | S Company balances | | |
| | | | Capital stock | Additional paid-in capital | Retained earnings (deficit) |
Case	Price paid				
A	$1,300,000	80	$500,000	$200,000	$600,000
B	640,000	80	500,000	300,000	(200,000)

below. S Company's balance sheet on January 1, 19x2, was as follows:

	Book values	Market values
Assets		
Cash	$ 50,000	$ 50,000
Accounts receivable	30,000	30,000
Inventory	20,000	40,000
Long-term investments in marketable securities	40,000	60,000
Plant and equipment (net of accumulated depreciation)	240,000	280,000
Land	120,000	200,000
Total assets	$500,000	$660,000
Liabilities and Stockholders' Equity		
Liabilities	$100,000	$100,000
Common stock	100,000	
Retained earnings	300,000	
Total liabilities and stockholders' equity	$500,000	

Required:

Prepare the working paper elimination entry for P Company as of January 1, 19x2, using:

a. Parent theory.

b. Entity theory.

Exercise 11-3. Using the data provided in Exercise 11-2 assume the P Company purchased the investment (80 percent) for $352,000. All other information is unchanged.

Required:

Prepare the working paper elimination entry (entries) for P Company on January 1, 19x3, using the entity theory.

Exercise 11-4. On January 1, 19x3, P Company purchased an 80 percent interest in S Company. On that date, the book values and fair market values of S Company's assets and liabilities were the same. An entity approach *consolidated* balance sheet prepared on that date appeared as follows:

P COMPANY AND SUBSIDIARY
Consolidated Balance Sheet
January 1, 19x3

Assets

Current assets	$200,000
Plant assets (net of accumulated depreciation)	500,000
Goodwill from consolidation	250,000
Total assets	$950,000

Liabilities and Stockholders' Equity

Current liabilities	$150,000
Common stock	200,000
Retained earnings	500,000
Minority interest	100,000
Total liabilities and stockholders' equity	$950,000

Required:

Calculate the following:

a. Common stock of P Company.

b. Retained earnings of P Company.

c. The identifiable net assets of S Company at fair market value.

d. The price paid by P Company for its 80 percent investment in S Company.

Exercise 11-5. On January 1, 19x3, P Company purchased 80 percent of the outstanding shares of S Company at a cost of $800,000. On that date, S Company had $300,000 of capital stock and $600,000 of retained earnings.

For 19x3, P Company had income of $300,000 from its own operations (excluding its share of income from S Company) and paid dividends of $150,000. For 19x3, S Company reported a net income of $100,000 and paid dividends of $40,000. All of the assets and liabilities of S Company have book values approximately equal to their respective market values.

P Company uses the complete equity method to account for its investment in S Company.

Required:

Using the entity concept:

a. Compute the amount that P Company should record as equity in earnings of S Company for 19x3.

b. Compute the parent's share of consolidated net income for 19x3.

c. Compute the minority interest's share of consolidated net income for 19x3.

d. Compute the total minority interest at December 31, 19x3.

e. Prepare the consolidated working paper elimination entries for a 19x3 working paper.

Exercise 11-6. On January 1, 19x2, P Company purchased 80 percent of the outstanding shares of S Company at a cost of $800,000. On that date, S Company had $300,000 of capital stock and $500,000 of retained earnings.

For 19x3, P Company had income of $400,000 from its own operations (excluding its share of income from S Company) and paid dividends of $100,000. For 19x3, S Company reported a net income of $200,000 and paid dividends of $40,000. All of the assets and liabilities of S Company have book values approximately equal to their respective market values.

During 19x3, P Company sold merchandise to S Company at 125 percent of its cost which is also the selling price used for 19x2 sales. The January 1, 19x3, inventory of S Company included $9,600 (at billed prices) of merchandise purchased from P Company; and its December 31, 19x3, inventory included $18,000 of merchandise purchased from P Company at billed prices. S Company uses FIFO inventory costing.

P Company uses the complete equity method to account for its investment in S Company.

Required:

Using the entity approach—

a. Compute the amount that P Company should record as equity in earnings of S Company for 19x3.

b. Compute the parent's share of consolidated net income for 19x3.

c. Compute the minority interest's share of consolidated net income for 19x3.

Exercise 11–7. On January 1, 19x3, P Company purchased 80 percent of the outstanding shares of S Company at a cost of $600,000. On that date, S Company had $200,000 of capital stock and $500,000 of retained earnings.

For 19x4, P Company had income of $400,000 from its own operations (excluding its share of income from S Company) and paid dividends of $200,000.

For 19x4, S Company reported income of $60,000 and paid dividends of $40,000. All of the assets and liabilities of S Company have book values approximately equal to their respective market values.

The beginning inventory of P Company includes $12,000 of merchandise purchased from S Company at 120 percent of cost. The ending inventory of P Company includes $15,000 of merchandise purchased from S Company at the same prices. P Company uses FIFO inventory costing.

P Company uses the complete equity method to account for its investment in S Company.

Required:

Using the entity approach:

a. Compute the amount that P Company should record as equity in earnings of S Company.

b. Compute the parent's share of consolidated net income for 19x4.

c. Compute the minority interest's share of consolidated net income for 19x4.

Exercise 11–8. On January 2, 19x2, P Company purchased 80 percent of the outstanding common stock of S Company for $950,000 payable in cash. On that date, the assets and liabilities of S Company had fair market values as indicated below. Balance sheets of the companies on January 2, 19x2, are as follows:

[Relates to Exercise 11–8]

	Book values		S Company fair market values
	P Company	S Company	
Cash	$ 300,000	$ 50,000	$ 50,000
Account receivable	200,000	100,000	100,000
Inventory	150,000	60,000	90,000
Land		70,000	120,000
Equipment (net of accumulated depreciation)	600,000	470,000	600,000
Investment in S Company	950,000		
Totals	$2,200,000	$750,000	$960,000
Accounts payable	$ 100,000	$ 50,000	$ 50,000
Common stock—P Company	600,000		
Common stock—S Company		200,000	
Additional paid-in capital		100,000	
Retained earnings—P Company	1,500,000		
Retained earnings—S Company		400,000	
Totals	$2,200,000	$750,000	

Required:

Using the entity approach—

a. Prepare an allocation schedule to compute goodwill.

b. Prepare a consolidated balance sheet.

PROBLEMS

Problem 11–9. On January 1, 19x4, P Company acquired 80 percent of the outstanding capital stock of S Company for $280,000. On that date, the capital stock of S Company was $100,000 and its retained earnings were $100,000.

On the date of acquisition, the assets of S Company had the following values:

	Book value	Fair market value
Inventories	$80,000	$100,000
Plant and equipment	60,000	140,000

All other assets and liabilities had book values approximately equal to their respective fair market values. The plant and equipment had a remaining useful life of 10 years from January 1, 19x4, and S Company uses the FIFO inventory cost flow assumption.

The retained earnings of P Company on the date of acquisition were $600,000. For 19x4, P Company earned $200,000 exclusive of its share of the earnings of S Company. During 19x4, P Company paid dividends of $60,000. S Company earned $100,000 in 19x4 (per books) and paid dividends in that year of $40,000.

P Company uses the complete equity method to account for its investment in S Company.

Required (use the entity approach):

a. Prepare a schedule of allocation of excess.

b. Compute the parent's share of consolidated net income for 19x4.

c. Compute consolidated retained earnings at December 31, 19x4.

d. Compute the balance in the investment account on December 31, 19x4.

e. Compute the minority interest's share of consolidated net income for 19x4.

f. Compute the total minority interest at December 31, 19x4.

g. Prepare the elimination entries for a consolidated working paper at December 31, 19x4.

Problem 11–10 (complete equity method). On January 1, 19x1, P Company purchased 40,000 shares of S Company in the open market for $1,140,000. On that date, the assets and liabilities of S Company had book values that approximated their respective fair market values. Excess (goodwill), if any, is expected to last for 20 years and is to be amortized over that period.

P Company uses the complete equity method to account for its investment.

On December 31, 19x1, S Company owed P Company $10,000 on open account from purchases made last year.

Financial statements for the two corporations for the year ended December 31, 19x1, are as follows:

	P Company	S Company
Income Statement		
Sales	$2,000,000	$1,000,000
Cost of sales	800,000	600,000
Gross margin	1,200,000	400,000
Expenses	500,000	100,000
Operating income before taxes	700,000	300,000
Equity in earnings— subsidiary	139,000	
Income before income taxes .	839,000	300,000
Provision for income taxes . .	280,000	120,000
Minority interest net income		
Net income—carried forward	$ 559,000	$ 180,000

	P Company	S Company
Retained Earnings Statement		
Balance, January 1, 19x1:		
P Company	$3,000,000	
S Company		$ 800,000
Net income—brought forward	559,000	180,000
Totals	3,559,000	980,000
Less: Dividends declared:		
P Company	400,000	
S Company		60,000
Balance, December 31, 19x1— carried forward	$3,159,000	$ 920,000

Balance Sheet		
Cash	$ 300,000	$ 100,000
Accounts receivable	200,000	200,000
Inventories	400,000	300,000
Land	600,000	
Building (net of accumulated depreciation)	400,000	
Equipment (net of accumulated depreciation) .	1,228,000	1,000,000
Investment in S Company . .	1,231,000	
Totals	$4,359,000	$1,600,000
Accounts payable and accrued expenses	$ 302,000	$ 180,000
Bonds payable (face amount $100,000)	98,000	
Common stock—P Company ($50 par)	500,000	
Common stock—S Company ($10 par)		500,000
Additional paid-in capital—P Company	300,000	
Retained earnings—P Company—brought forward . . . . :	3,159,000	
Retained earnings—S Company—brought forward		920,000
Totals	$4,359,000	$1,600,000

Required:

a. Prepare a consolidated working paper (use the entity approach).

b. Prepare consolidated financial statements.

Problem 11–11 (complete equity method). On January 1, 19x1, P Company purchased 24,000 shares of S Company in the open market for $756,000. On that date, the following assets of S Company had book values that were different from their respective market values:

	Book value	Fair market value
Inventories	$ 40,000	$ 70,000
Land	150,000	200,000
Building (net)	200,000	300,000
Equipment (net)	450,000	375,000
Patent	–0–	40,000

All other assets and liabilities had book values approximately equal to their respective market values.

On January 1, 19x1, the building had a remaining useful life of 20 years. Equipment and the patent had remaining useful lives of 10 years each. FIFO inventory costing is used. Goodwill, if any, has an indeterminate life. P Company uses the complete equity method to account for this investment.

Financial statements for the companies for the year ended December 31, 19x1, are as follows:

	P Company	S Company
Income Statement		
Sales	$1,000,000	$500,000
Cost of sales	400,000	150,000
Gross margin	600,000	350,000
Expenses	200,000	100,000
Operating income before taxes	400,000	250,000
Equity in earnings— subsidiary	92,800	
Income before income taxes .	492,800	250,000
Provision for income taxes . .	160,000	100,000
Minority interest net income		
Net income—carried forward	$ 332,800	$150,000

	P Company	S Company
Retained Earnings Statement		
Balance, January 1, 19x1:		
P Company	$ 600,000	
S Company		$400,000
Net income—brought forward	332,800	150,000
Totals	932,800	550,000
Less: Dividends declared:		
P Company	100,000	
S Company		50,000
Balance, December 31, 19x1— carried forward	$ 832,800	$500,000

Balance Sheet	P Company	S Company
Cash	$ 200,000	$100,000
Accounts receivable	150,000	50,000
Inventories	100,000	40,000
Land		150,000
Building (net of accumulated depreciation)		200,000
Equipment (net of accumulated depreciation) .	700,000	450,000
Patent		—
Investment in S Company . .	808,800	
Totals	$1,958,800	$990,000
Accounts payable and accrued expenses	$ 124,000	$190,000
Bonds payable (face amount, $400,000)	402,000	
Common stock—P Company ($50 par)	200,000	
Common stock—S Company ($10 par)		300,000
Additional paid-in capital—P Company	400,000	
Retained earnings—P Company—brought forward	832,800	
Retained earnings—S Company—brought forward		500,000
Totals	$1,958,800	$990,000

Income Statement	P Company	S Company
Sales	$1,200,000	$ 700,000
Cost of sales	500,000	250,000
Gross margin	700,000	450,000
Expenses	200,000	120,000
Operating income before taxes	500,000	330,000
Equity in earnings— subsidiary	155,200	
Income before income taxes .	655,200	330,000
Provision for income taxes . .	200,000	132,000
Minority interest net income		
Net income—carried forward	$ 455,200	$ 198,000

Retained Earnings Statement	P Company	S Company
Balance, January 1, 19x2:		
P Company	$ 832,800	
S Company		$ 500,000
Net income—brought forward	455,200	198,000
Totals	1,288,000	698,000
Less: Dividends declared:		
P Company	150,000	
S Company		60,000
Balance, December 31, 19x2— carried forward	$1,138,000	$ 638,000

Balance Sheet	P Company	S Company
Cash	$ 233,600	$ 48,000
Accounts receivable	240,000	70,000
Inventories	150,000	80,000
Land		150,000
Building (net of accumulated depreciation)		190,000
Equipment (net of accumulated depreciation) .	800,000	540,000
Patent		—
Investment in S Company . .	916,000	
Totals	$2,339,600	$1,078,000
Accounts payable and accrued expenses	$ 200,000	$ 140,000
Bonds payable (face amount $400,000)	401,600	
Common stock—P Company ($50 par)	200,000	
Common stock—S Company ($10 par)		300,000
Additional paid-in capital—P Company	400,000	
Retained earnings—P Company—brought forward	1,138,000	
Retained earnings—S Company—brought forward		638,000
Totals	$2,339,600	$1,078,000

Required:

a. Prepare an allocation schedule of excess (use the entity approach).

b. Prepare a consolidated working paper.

Problem 11–12 (*complete equity method*). P Company acquired 80 percent of the outstanding common stock of S Company on January 1, 19x1. The price paid for the investment, book, and market values of assets on the date of acquisition, and useful lives are provided in Problem 11–11.

P Company uses the complete equity method to account for its investment.

Financial statements for the companies for the year ended December 31, 19x2 (second year), are as follows:

Required:

Prepare a consolidated working paper (use the entity approach).

Problem 11–13 (*complete equity method*). On January 1, 19x2, P Company acquired 80 percent of the outstanding common stock of S Company for $640,000. On that date, the retained earnings of S Company were $200,000, and there have been no changes in its capital stock and additional paid-in capital.

All of the assets and liabilities of S Company had book values approximately equal to their respective market values. Goodwill, if any, is to be amortized over a 20-year period.

On December 31, 19x4, P Company owed S Company $20,000 from sales made by S Company last year. This year, 19x4, there were no intercompany transactions.

The financial statements of the companies for the year ended December 31, 19x4, are as follows:

Income Statement	P Company	S Company
Sales	$ 800,000	$200,000
Cost of sales	300,000	150,000
Gross margin	500,000	50,600
Expenses	200,000	100,000
Operating income (loss) before taxes	300,000	(50,000)
Equity in earnings—subsidiary	(28,000)	
Income (loss) before income taxes	272,000	(50,000)
Provision for income taxes	120,000	(20,000)
Minority interest net income		
Net income (loss)—carried forward	$ 152,000	$(30,000)

Retained Earnings Statement	P Company	S Company
Balance, January 1, 19x4:		
P Company	$ 600,000	
S Company		$300,000
Net income—brought forward	152,000	(30,000)
Totals	752,000	270,000
Less: Dividends declared:		
P Company	80,000	
S Company		—
Balance, December 31, 19x4—carried forward	$ 672,000	$270,000

	P Company	S Company
Balance Sheet		
Cash	$ 150,000	$ 50,000
Accounts receivable	80,000	30,000
Inventories	60,000	40,000
Equipment (net of accumulated depreciation)	298,000	750,000
Investment in S Company	684,000	
Totals	$1,272,000	$870,000
Accounts payable and accrued expenses	$ 200,000	$100,000
Common stock—P Company ($50 par)	400,000	
Common stock—S Company ($10 par)		300,000
Additional paid-in capital—S Company		200,000
Retained earnings—P Company—brought forward	672,000	
Retained earnings—S Company—brought forward		270,000
Totals	$1,272,000	$870,000

Required:

Prepare a consolidated working paper (use the entity approach).

Problem 11–14 (*complete equity method*). On January 1, 19x4, P Company purchased 24,000 shares of S Company in the open market for $502,000. On that date, the following assets of S Company had book values that were different from their respective market values:

	Book value	Fair market value
Equipment (net)	$450,000	$400,000
Patent	–0–	140,000

All other assets and liabilities had book values approximately equal to their respective market values, and the net assets amounted to $500,000.

On January 1, 19x4, the equipment and the patent

had remaining useful lives of 10 years each. Good-will, if any, has a 10-year estimated life. P Company uses the complete equtiy method to account for this investment.

During 19x7, S Company sold $200,000 of merchandise to P Company at 33⅓ percent above its cost. The inventories of P Company contain merchandise purchased from S Company as follows:

	Billed price
January 1, 19x7	$12,000
December 31, 19x7	60,000

On December 31, 19x7, P Company owed S Company $50,000 on open account.

Financial statements for the companies for the year ended December 31, 19x7, are as follows:

Income Statement	P Company	S Company
Sales	$1,000,000	$ 600,000
Cost of sales	400,000	400,000
Gross margin	600,000	200,000
Expenses	200,000	160,000
Operating income before taxes	400,000	40,000
Equity in earnings—subsidiary	(600)	
Income before income taxes .	399,400	40,000
Provision for income taxes . .	160,000	16,000
Minority interest net income		
Net income—carried forward	$ 239,400	$ 24,000

Retained Earnings Statement		
Balance, January 1, 19x7:		
P Company	$ 693,400	
S Company		$ 526,000
Net income—brought forward	239,400	24,000
Totals	932,800	550,000
Less: Dividends declared:		
P Company	100,000	
S Company		50,000
Balance, December 31, 19x7—carried forward	$ 832,800	$ 500,000

Balance Sheet	P Company	S Company
Cash	$ 200,000	$ 100,000
Accounts receivable	150,000	50,000
Inventories	110,000	40,000
Land		150,000
Building		260,000
Equipment	809,600	690,000
Patent		—
Investment in S Company . .	689,200	
Totals	$1,958,800	$1,290,000
Accounts payable and accrued expenses	$ 124,000	$ 190,000
Accumulated depreciation—building		60,000
Accumulated depreciation—equipment	402,000	240,000
Common stock—P Company ($50 par)	200,000	
Common stock—S Company ($10 par)		300,000
Additional paid-in capital—P Company	400,000	
Retained earnings—P Company—brought forward	832,800	
Retained earnings—S Company—brought forward		500,000
Totals	$1,958,800	$1,290,000

Required:

a. Prepare an allocation schedule of excess (use the entity approach).

b. Prepare a consolidated working paper.

Problem 11–15 (incomplete equity method). On January 1, 19x4, P Company purchased 24,000 shares of S Company in the open market for $502,000. On that date, the following assets of S Company had book values that were different from their respective market values:

	Book value	Fair market value
Equipment (net)	$450,000	$400,000
Patent	–0–	140,000

All other assets and liabilities had book values approximately equal to their respective market values, and the net assets amounted to $500,000.

On January 1, 19x4, the equipment and the patent

had remaining useful lives of 10 years each. Goodwill, if any, has a 10-year estimated life. P Company uses the incomplete equity method to account for this investment.

During 19x7, S Company sold $200,000 of merchandise to P Company at $33\frac{1}{3}$ percent above its cost. The inventories of P Company contain merchandise purchased from S Company as follows:

	Billed price
January 1, 19x7	$12,000
December 31, 19x7	60,000

On December 31, 19x7, P Co. owed S Co. $50,000 on open account.

Financial statements for the companies for the year ended December 31, 19x7, are as follows:

	P Company	S Company
Income Statement		
Sales	$1,000,000	$ 600,000
Cost of sales	400,000	400,000
Gross margin	600,000	200,000
Expenses	200,000	160,000
Operating income before		
taxes	400,000	40,000
Equity in earnings—		
subsidiary	19,200	
Income before income taxes .	419,200	40,000
Provision for income taxes . .	160,000	16,000
Minority interest net income		
Net income—carried forward	$ 259,200	$ 24,000

Retained Earnings		
Statement		
Balance, January 1, 19x7:		
P Company	$ 726,400	
S Company		$ 526,000
Net income—brought		
forward	259,200	24,000
Totals	985,600	550,000
Less: Dividends declared:		
P Company	100,000	
S Company		50,000
Balance, December 31, 19x7—		
carried forward	$ 885,600	$ 500,000

	P Company	S Company
Balance Sheet		
Cash	$ 200,000	$ 100,000
Accounts receivable	150,000	50,000
Inventories	110,000	40,000
Land		150,000
Building		260,000
Equipment	809,600	690,000
Patent		—
Investment in S Company . .	742,000	
Totals	$2,011,600	$1,290,000
Accounts payable and		
accrued expenses	$ 124,000	$ 190,000
Accumulated depreciation—		
building		60,000
Accumulated depreciation—		
equipment	402,000	240,000
Common stock—P Company		
($50 par)	200,000	
Common stock—S Company		
($10 par)		300,000
Additional paid-in capital—P		
Company	400,000	
Retained earnings—P		
Company—brought		
forward	885,600	
Retained earnings—S		
Company—brought		
forward		500,000
Totals	$2,011,600	$1,290,000

Required:

a. Prepare an allocation schedule of excess (use the entity approach).

b. Prepare a consolidated working paper.

Problem 11–16 (cost method). On January 1, 19x4, P Company purchased 24,000 shares of S Company in the open market for $502,000. On that date, the following assets of S Company had book values that were different from their respective market values:

	Book Value	Fair market value
Equipment (net)	$450,000	$400,000
Patent	–0–	140,000

All other assets and liabilities had book values approximately equal to their respective market values, and the net assets amounted to $500,000.

On January 1, 19x4, the equipment and the patent

had remaining useful lives of 10 years each. Good-will, if any, has a 10-year estimated life. P Company uses the cost method to account for this investment.

During 19x7, S Company sold $200,000 of merchandise to P Company at 33⅓ percent above its cost. The inventories of P Company contain merchandise purchased from S Company as follows:

	Billed price
January 1, 19x7	$12,000
December 31, 19x7	60,000

On December 31, 19x7, P Company owed S Company $50,000 on open account.

Financial statements for the companies for the year ended December 31, 19x7, are as follows:

	P Company	S Company
Income Statement		
Sales	$1,000,000	$ 600,000
Cost of sales	400,000	400,000
Gross margin	600,000	200,000
Expenses	200,000	160,000
Operating income before		
taxes	400,000	40,000
Dividend income	40,000	
Income before income taxes .	440,000	40,000
Provision for income taxes . .	160,000	16,000
Minority interest net income		
Net income—carried forward	$ 280,000	$ 24,000

Retained Earnings Statement		
Balance, January 1, 19x7:		
P Company	$ 465,600	
S Company		$ 526,000
Net income—brought		
forward	280,000	24,000
Totals	745,600	550,000
Less: Dividends declared:		
P Company	100,000	
S Company		50,000
Balance, December 31, 19x7 .	$ 645,600	$ 500,000

	P Company	S Company
Balance Sheet		
Cash	$ 200,000	$ 100,000
Accounts receivable	150,000	50,000
Inventories	110,000	40,000
Land		150,000
Building		260,000
Equipment	809,600	690,000
Patent		—
Investment in S Company . .	502,000	
Totals	$1,771,600	$1,290,000
Accounts payable and		
accrued expenses	$ 124,000	$ 190,000
Accumulated depreciation—		
building		60,000
Accumulated depreciation—		
equipment	402,000	240,000
Common stock—P Company		
($50 par)	200,000	
Common stock—S Company		
($10 par)		300,000
Additional paid-in capital—P		
Company	400,000	
Retained earnings—P		
Company—brought		
forward	645,600	
Retained earnings—S		
Company—brought		
forward		500,000
Totals	$1,771,600	$1,290,000

Required:

a. Prepare an allocation schedule of excess (use the entity approach).

b. Prepare a consolidated working paper.

Problem 11–17. The consolidated financial statements for P Company and its 80% owned subsidiary are as follows:

P COMPANY
Consolidated Income Statement
For the Year Ended December 31, 19x3

Sales		$2,000,000
Cost of sales		800,000
Gross margin		1,200,000
Expenses		500,000
Operating income before taxes . .		700,000
Equity in earnings of		
unconsolidated subsidiary . . .		144,000
Combined income before income		
taxes		844,000
Provision for income taxes	$260,000	
Minority interest net income . . .	20,000	280,000
Net income		$ 564,000

P COMPANY
Consolidated Balance Sheets
December 31, 19x3, and 19x2

	19x3	19x2
Assets		
Cash	$ 300,000	$ 250,000
Accounts receivable	200,000	225,000
Inventories	400,000	350,000
Land	600,000	600,000
Building (net of accumulated depreciation)	400,000	425,000
Equipment (net of accumulated depreciation)	1,228,000	1,128,000
Investment in unconsolidated subsidiary (at equity)	1,236,000	1,144,000
Total assets	$4,364,000	$4,122,000
Equities		
Liabilities:		
Accounts payable and accrued expenses	$ 400,000	$ 534,000
Minority interest	100,000	88,000
Stockholders' equity:		
Common stock	500,000	500,000
Additional paid-in capital . . .	300,000	300,000
Retained earnings	3,064,000	2,700,000
Total stockholders' equity	3,864,000	3,500,000
Total equities	$4,364,000	$4,122,000

Additional information:

1. P Company has a subsidiary engaged in financial activities and, therefore, its operations were not consolidated in the above statements. However, one-line consolidation (complete equity basis) was used to account for this investment.

2. Depreciation and amortization of goodwill amounted to:
   a. Depreciation of building, $25,000.
   b. Depreciation of equipment, $100,000.
   c. Amortization of goodwill, $16,000.
      (This amount reduced the equity in earnings of unconsolidated subsidiary from $160,000 to the $144,000 shown in the income statement.)

3. Dividend payments consisted of:
   a. Payments by P Company, $200,000.
   b. Payments by S Company, $40,000 ($32,000 to P Company and $8,000 to minority interest; S Company was consolidated).
   c. Payments by the unconsolidated subsidiary—P Company received $52,000.

4. Equipment purchased in 19x3, $200,000.

Required:

Prepare a consolidated statement of changes in financial position using the working capital concept.

Problem 11–18. The consolidated financial statements for P Company and its 90 percent owned subsidiary are as follows:

P COMPANY
Consolidated Income Statement
For the Year Ended December 31, 19x4

Sales		$1,000,000
Cost of sales		400,000
Gross margin		600,000
Expenses		200,000
Operating income before taxes . .		400,000
Equity in earnings of unconsolidated subsidiary . . .		92,800
Combined income before income taxes		492,800
Provision for income taxes	$160,000	
Minority interest net income . . .	25,000	185,000
Net income		$ 307,800

P COMPANY
Consolidated Balance Sheets
December 31, 19x4, and 19x3

	19x4	19x3
Assets		
Cash	$ 110,000	$ 300,000
Accounts receivable	150,000	100,000
Inventories	100,000	125,000
Equipment (net of accumulated depreciation)	700,000	253,000
Investment in unconsolidated subsidiary (at equity)	808,000	755,200
Goodwill	90,000	100,000
Total assets	$1,958,000	$1,633,200
Equities		
Liabilities:		
Accounts payable and accrued expenses	$ 200,000	$ 750,000
Bonds payable (face amount $400,000)	402,000	—
Total liabilities	602,000	750,000
Minority interest	80,000	65,000
Stockholders' equity:		
Common stock ($10 par value)	500,000	300,000
Additional paid-in capital . . .	100,000	50,000
Retained earnings	676,000	468,200
Total stockholders' equity	1,276,000	818,200
Total equities	$1,958,000	$1,633,200

Additional information:

1. P Company has a subsidiary that is engaged in insurance activities and, accordingly, its operations were not consolidated in the above statements. However, one-line consolidation (complete equity basis) was used to account for this investment.

2. Depreciation and amortization of goodwill amounted to:

    a. Depreciation, $45,000.

    b. Goodwill, $10,000 (included in expenses).

3. Dividend payments consisted of:

    a. Payments by P Company, $100,000

    b. Payments by S Company, $100,000 ($90,000 to P Company and $10,000 to minority interest).

    c. Payments by the unconsolidated subsidiary—P Company received $40,000.

4. Equipment was purchased in 19x4 for $492,000.

5. The bonds payable were sold on June 30, 19x4, for $402,200. Interest is payable June 30 and December 31.

6. The only change in common stock was the sale of 20,000 additional shares.

Required:

Prepare a consolidated statement of changes in financial position using the working capital concept.

12

Accounting for foreign operations

OVERVIEW

The significant expansion of foreign trade in recent decades and the concurrent growth of multinational companies has resulted in increasing attention being paid to international accounting practices and problems. The accounting for transactions and operations that cross international boundaries is subject to complexities that extend beyond those to which accounting is normally subject. These subdivide, generally speaking, into three broad areas:

1. *Problems related to differences in accounting principles and practices which are peculiar to the foreign country in which the operations are conducted.*
2. *Problems related to transactions which give rise to receivables and payables which are denominated in foreign currencies but which must be measured in the currency of the reporting entity.*
3. *Problems which arise from the translation of foreign assets, liabilities, equities, and results of operations from the local currency into the currency of the base (home) country or, in our focus, the U.S. dollar.*

A discussion of the nature of these problem areas and of the related accounting issues is the subject of this chapter.

Foreign accounting practices

The preparation of consolidated financial statements which include foreign subsidiaries or affiliates accounted for on the equity basis often requires that the financial statements of these foreign entities be adjusted in order that they be conformed to the accounting principles acceptable in the home country (e.g., the U.S.A.). Moreover, investors and credit grantors who must make decisions on the basis of foreign financial statements must have a thorough understanding of the accounting standards which governed the preparation of those statements.

Accounting practices can vary significantly among countries. There are a variety of reasons for this including a lack of agreement on objectives of financial statements, the requirements of national company laws, the influence of tax laws and differences in the strength, and the development patterns of local professional bodies. Moreover, it must be understood that accounting is a social science whose objectives are socially determined and expressed. Thus, for example, in many countries accounting is used as a means of implementing specific social and economic objectives and is not viewed solely as a discipline for the communication of economic data.

Peculiarities of foreign accounting practices. Accounting practices in the United States and those in other countries can differ significantly. The following examples, are indicative of the nature and the extent of such differences. Thus, in some countries—

1. Inventory reserves and other secret reserves may be sanctioned.
2. Excessive depreciation may be recorded.
3. Because of substantial price-level changes, restatements of property accounts may be effected based on coefficients established by, and frequently revised by, the local government.
4. "Legal reserves" amounting to a fixed percentage of net income may be established.
5. Tax allocation may not be practiced.
6. Stock dividends may be recorded only on the basis of the par value of the stock issued.
7. Pooling of interests accounting may not be sanctioned.
8. Consolidation of parent and subsidiary financial statements may not be required.
9. The recognition of pension liabilities can vary widely.
10. General provisions (reserves) and subsequent reversals of such reserves may be used to shift income between periods.
11. Certain assets may be omitted from the financial statements.
12. No significance may be attached to consistency of application of accounting policies, and no disclosure of changes therein may be required.

Efforts to develop worldwide accounting standards

In recent years serious attempts have begun to bring more conformity into international accounting practices. The most ambitious program for the establishment of international accounting standards was the establishment in 1973 of the International Accounting Standards Committee (IASC) by the professional institutes of nine countries. Its objective is to formulate and publish in the public interest, basic standards to be observed in the presentation of audited accounts and financial statements and to promote their worldwide acceptance and observance. Since its foundation, IASC has grown in membership to over 50 accounting bodies from over 40 nations.

In its efforts to publish basic worldwide accounting standards, the IASC has issued a number of standards covering important areas such as disclosure of accounting policies, valuation and presentation of inventories, consolidated financial statements, depreciation, information to be disclosed in financial statements, accounting for changing prices, statement of changes in financial position, unusual and prior period items, changes in accounting policies, research and development costs, contingencies, foreign statement translation, construction contracts, income taxes, and others.

While these international standards do not override local standards, member bodies of IASC work within their respective countries to assure that local standards conform to IASC pronouncements or that there is disclosure of the extent of nonconformance. In the United States, the AICPA is working to encourage business support of IASC efforts and has submitted to the FASB a list of differences between U.S. and IASC standards (most of which are minor) for its consideration and any action it may deem appropriate.

A particularly encouraging development is the adoption of ISAC standards by a number of countries with small accounting bodies and few codified standards.

The procedures followed by ISAC include circulation of exposure drafts for comment before a standard is issued. This assures comment by all interested parties and ensures a wider degree of acceptance of the standard-setting process.

In spite of these important developments, generally accepted worldwide accounting standards seem to be a long way off; and consequently, all those concerned with foreign financial statements, be they preparers wishing to consolidate them with a domestic parent or decision makers, such as investors or credit grantors, must become thoroughly familiar with the accounting standards as well as the actual practices of the countries in which the financial statements have been prepared. In this connection it is best to consult one or more of the published sources of information on foreign accounting practices.[1]

TRANSACTIONS IN FOREIGN CURRENCIES

There are numerous ways, in our world of expanding trade and economic relationships, in which an enterprise in the home country (i.e., the United States) can be involved in transactions involving the currencies of other countries.

---

[1]See, for example, *Professional Accounting in 30 Countries* (New York: AICPA, 1975); *Accouting Principles and Reporting Practices: A Survey in 46 Countries* (Price Waterhouse International, 1975); and *International Accounting Standards and Guidelines* (DeCoite Haskins & Sells, 1981).

Import and export transactions

The simplest of these transactions involve the importation of foreign goods to the United States or the export of domestic goods to a foreign buyer. If settlement is to be made in U.S. dollars, foreign currency transactions do not arise. However, if settlement is to be made in the foreign currency, then foreign currency issues arise. In the first instance the U.S. importer must purchase foreign currency to pay the foreign supplier, and in the latter case the U.S. exporter must convert into U.S. dollars the foreign currency received for the goods exported.

Conducting foreign operations

Should the U.S. enterprise wish to engage in more extensive operations abroad (e.g., manufacturing, buying, financing), it will usually do so through a business entity stationed in the foreign country or countries in which it operates. This can be done through a branch or through a fully or partially owned subsidiary or affiliated company

This involves a higher degree of complexity of operations and accounting because the U.S. enterprise will now own foreign assets and incur foreign liabilities which, before they can be incorporated in the financial statements of the U.S. parent company, must be *translated* into U.S. dollars.

Measured versus denominated

It is useful to have a clear understanding of these two widely used terms. Assets and liabilities are *denominated* in one currency if their amount is fixed in terms of that currency. However, they may be *measured* (for financial reporting purposes) in another currency.

When a transaction is to be settled by the receipt or payment of a fixed amount of a specified currency, the receivable or payable is said to be *denominated* in that currency. Regardless of the currency in which a transaction is denominated, the party to the transaction *measures* and records the transaction in the currency of the country in which the party is located (i.e., its functional currency). For example, a U.S. importer purchases goods on credit from a British exporter who is to be paid in pounds sterling. The transaction is deonominated in £ but measured and recorded by the U.S. importer in dollars. However, the British exporter's transaction is both denominated and measured in pounds sterling.

As a further example of the difference between measurement and denomination, consider the case of the Swiss subsidiary of a U.S. parent which purchases goods from an Italian exporter who is to be paid in lira. The subsidiary will *measure* and record the liability in Swiss francs even though it is denominated in lira. From the viewpoint of the U.S. parent, the subsidiary's liability is denominated in foreign currency because it is not payable in dollars. When the parent translates this liability into dollars, it is said to *measure* it in dollars.

Conversion versus translation

It is important to understand the distinction between the conversion and the translation of foreign currencies. In the case of our import example above, the U.S. importer *converts* U.S. dollars on the day of payment into the necessary amount of foreign currency. There is no question what the rate of exchange is; it is the rate paid to obtain the required amount of foreign exchange. It represents an actual exchange of foreign currency into dollars or vice versa.

On the other hand, the assets, liabilities, and operating items of a foreign branch or subsidiary are *translated* into U.S. dollars from time to time in order to incorporate them into the financial statements of the U.S. home office or owner. No actual exchange of currencies is involved, and we deal here only with translation into a single currency. The question of the rates at which these are translated is, as we shall see, at the heart of the problem of accounting for foreign operations.

Currency exchange rates

Before we begin our discussion of the accounting for foreign exchange we must understand the terminology used.

From the perspective of a home, or base, country foreign currencies are commodities which fluctuate in price based on a multitude of factors which influence supply and demand. An exchange rate is the ratio between a unit of one currency and the amount of another currency into which that unit can be converted at a given point in time. A rate determined only by supply and demand in the marketplace is known as the *free* rate of exchange. When the government of a country wants to influence the rate of exchange for purposes of economic policy or other reasons, *multiple* exchange rates may prevail. Thus, the importation of certain desirable goods may be subject to a *preferential* rate of exchange while the rate which will apply to transactions which are to be discouraged (e.g., importation of luxury goods) is known as the *penalty* rate of exchange. A *dividend* rate of exchange may prevail for payment of dividends to nonresident shareholders. Official interference with free market rates of exchange may give rise to *black-market* rates of exchange at which the currency is bought and sold by unauthorized dealers in foreign exchange in contravention of governmental regulations. Governmental regulations may result in bank accounts of nonresidents to become restricted to use only within the country. Such accounts are known as *blocked accounts* and can be contrasted to freely *convertible currency* which can be used without restriction for all kinds of transactions.

In the quotation of currency exchange rates, if the exchange is to occur immediately, the rate is known as the *spot rate*. If, for whatever reasons, delivery of the exchanged currency is desired at a future date (say in 30, 90, or 180 days), a future or *forward rate of exchange* will apply.

ACCOUNTING FOR FOREIGN CURRENCY TRANSACTIONS

Foreign currency *transactions* encompass a wide variety of activities such as:

The purchase or sale on credit of goods or services whose prices are stated in a foreign currency.

The borrowing or lending of funds expressed in terms of foreign currencies and repayable or receivable in such currencies. For any other reasons, the acquisition of assets or the incurrence of liabilities *denominated* in terms of foreign currencies.

Unlike the accounting for foreign currency statement translation, which is now undergoing major change and which is discussed later in this chapter, the accounting for foreign currency transactions is more settled and less controversial. In our discussion of the accounting for foreign currency transactions we are including some changes incorporated in the June 1981 FASB Revised Exposure Draft entitled "Foreign Currency Translation."

As an example of a foreign currency transaction, let us assume that U.S. Importers Inc., purchased from Swisswatch SFr100,000 worth of watches when the exchange rate was SFr = 50 cents. U.S. Importers recorded the transaction as follows:

```
Inventory . . . . . . . . . . . . . . . . . . . . . . . . . . . . . . . . . . .    50,000
    Accounts Payable (SFr100,000) . . . . . . . . . . . . . . . . . . .                50,000
    (SFr100 × $0.50 = $50,000.)
```

Terms of payment were two months and by the time payment was effected the Swiss franc strengthened to 55 cents. Thus, at the time that payment to Swisswatch was made, U.S. Importers recorded the payment as follows:

```
Accounts payable . . . . . . . . . . . . . . . . . . . . . . . . . . . . .    50,000
Exchange Loss . . . . . . . . . . . . . . . . . . . . . . . . . . . . . .     5,000
    Cash . . . . . . . . . . . . . . . . . . . . . . . . . . . . . . . . . .            55,000
```

This treatment is in accordance with the FASB's conclusion, reaffirmed in SFAS 52 (see discussion later in chapter), that the purchase of an asset is a transaction separate and distinct from the subsequent payment for it. This view, also known as the *two-transaction perspective,* maintains that the dollar cost of an imported asset (or similarly the revenue of an export sale) is determined by the exchange rate which prevails at the time of purchase (or sale). An exchange gain or loss can occur only if payment is delayed and an exposure to foreign exchange fluctuations is assumed by such delay. The payment is viewed as a separate transaction, and any related exchange gain or loss does not affect the original transaction but must be recorded separately, as was done in the Journal entry above.

This view is to be contrasted with the *one-transaction perspective* which considers the purchase and payment as a single transaction. Thus, under this view the initial recorded dollar amount of the purchase is viewed as an estimate which is subject to final adjustment when payment is made in the foreign currency. The FASB has rejected this view.

Unsettled transactions in foreign currency

Assume that in our above example the purchase by U.S. Importers took place on June 1, 19x1, and that its fiscal year-end is on June 30, 19x1, at which date the exchange rate was SFr = 48 cents. If a foreign currency transaction is unsettled by year-end, an exchange gain or loss must be recognized to reflect a difference in the exchange rate between the transaction date (or last valuation date) and the year-end. In this instance the payable must be reduced to reflect the decline in the Swiss franc (SFr100,000 ×

$0.48 = \$48,000; \$50,000 - \$48,000 = 12,000$). The following entry will be made at year-end (June 30, 19x1):

Accounts Payable	2,000	
Exchange Gain		2,000

As we know from the preceding example, actual payment to Swisswatch was made on August 1, 19x1 (two months after purchase). Since the SFr had strengthened by that date to 55 cents and the accounts payable had been written down to $48,000 by year-end, the entry at date of payment is as follows:

Accounts Payable	48,000	
Exchange Loss	7,000	
Cash		55,000
Remittance of SFr100,000 at an exchange rate of 55 cents to the SFr.		

We can recapitulate the theoretical argument in support of recording an exchange gain at year-end and an exchange loss at time of payment as follows: At the time of purchase, the buying transaction was completed and that fixes the cost of the asset acquired. The decision to delay payment requires that the account payable be valued at year-end, i.e., a determination of how many dollars it would take to liquidate the SFr100,000 liability. Since the SFr has weakened between the time of purchase and year-end, a gain was recorded on that date, i.e., the decision to delay payment resulted in a gain. Between the year-end and the time of payment, the SFr strengthened against the dollar and that resulted in an exchange loss. The year-end exchange gain resulted from a currency *translation* of an unsettled transaction. The exchange loss at time of payment was the result of actual *conversion* of dollars in SFr, and thus it became final.

Forward exchange contracts

Let us now continue with our example of the purchase on June 1, 19x1, by U.S. Importers of SFr100,000 worth of watches. In our discussion so far we assume that U.S. Importers were willing to assume the risks of exchange rate changes between the date of purchase and the date of payment two months later. U.S. Importers have, however, another option and that is to hedge this risk and fix their liability to Swisswatch at the time of purchase by buying on June 1, 19x1, a contract that will entitle them to receive SFr 100,000 on August 1, 19x1, when this amount is due to be paid. Such a contract is known as a forward exchange contract.

A forward exchange contract is thus an agreement to exchange on a specified future date currencies of different countries at a specified rate. That rate is referred to as the *forward rate* of exchange, and it usually differs from the present or spot rate because of expectations of future exchange rate changes and because of the time value of money. This difference is known as the premium or discount on the forward contract.

The purpose of a foreign exchange contract is either to speculate in anticipation of a gain or to hedge (protect against possible losses from fluctuations in the exchange rate by buying foreign currency futures) one of the following:

Foreign currency commitment.

Foreign currency net asset position (the excess of assets over liabilities measured or denominated in a foreign currency and translated at the current rate).

Foreign currency net liability position (the excess of liabilities over assets measured or denominated in a foreign currency and translated at the current rate).

Accounting for forward exchange contracts

Gains or losses on forward exchange contracts should normally be included in the determination of the net income of the period in which the exchange rate changes which caused them occurred. There are several exceptions to this, and they will be taken up later in this section.

As we know from our discussion of the U.S. Importers illustration, the spot rate for SFr on the date of purchase was SFr = 50 cents. On that date U.S. Importers bought SFr100,000 for delivery on August 1, 19x1, at the forward exchange rate of SFr = 51 cents. We also know that the spot rate on June 30, 19x1, was SFr = 48 cents and on August 1, 19x1, it was SFr = 55 cents. Because this forward contract qualifies as a hedge on an *existing* foreign currency *transaction*, the gain or loss on the contract is recognized currently rather than being deferred. The following entries will be made:

(1)

19x1	Inventory	50,000	
June 1	Accounts Payable		50,000
	Purchase of watches for SFr100,000 when SFr = 50 cents.		

(2)

Foreign Currency Due from Broker	50,000	
Deferred Forward Exchange Premium	1,000	
Liability to Currency Broker		51,000
Purchase of SFr100,000 for delivery in 60 days at ISFr = 51 cents.		

(3)

June 30	Accounts Payable	2,000	
(fiscal	Exchange Gain		2,000
year-end)	To accrue exchange gain on unperformed transaction when SFr = 48 cents ($50,000 − $48,000).		

(4)

Forward Exchange Expense	500	
Deferred Forward Exchange Premium		500
To record the expired portion (30 days/60 days) of the forward exchange premium.		

(5)

Exchange Loss	2,000	
Foreign Currency Due from Broker		2,000

To record loss on forward exchange contract, the
SFr having declined to 48 cents ($48,000) from 50
cents ($50,000) when contract was entered into.

(6)

Aug. 1	Liability to Currency Broker	51,000	
	Position in Swiss Francs (100,000 × 0.55)	55,000	
	Cash		51,000
	Foreign Currency Due from Broker		48,000
	Exchange Gain		7,000

To record settlement of forward exchange contract
when SFr = 55 cents.

(7)

Accounts Payable	48,000	
Exchange Loss	7,000	
Position in Swiss Francs		55,000

Remittance of SFr100,000 at an exchange rate of SFr
= 55 cents.

(8)

Forward Exchange Expense	500	
Deferred Forward Exchange Premium		500

To record the balance of the unexpired forward
exchange premium.

It should be noted that due to the executory nature of the forward currency contract, journal entry (2) is sometimes recorded in memorandum form only. In that case the recognition of exchange gains and losses would be made by use of an allowance account and the following entry would be made instead of journal entry (5) above:

Exchange Loss	2,000	
Allowance for Exchange Gains or Losses		2,000

A comparison of the above journal entries which reflect the hedged foreign currency position with the earlier entries reflecting the same transaction in unhedged form will reveal that in the hedged transaction no net gain or loss on foreign exchange was incurred (i.e., the exchange gains and losses cancel each other out), which is, of course, the objective of the hedge. The cost of this protection is reflected as forward exchange expense, which is the premium paid for the contract.

Accounting for a hedge on a foreign currency net asset or liability position

Assume that U.S. Importers sell watches to a Mexican firm on February 1, 19x2, for 100,000 pesos payable on May 1, 19x2. Assuming no other outstanding peso position, U.S. Importers now have an exposed net peso (asset) position. If U.S. Importers do not want to assume this peso risk, they can hedge by selling 100,000 pesos for delivery in 90 days. This is merely a variation of the type of forward contract illustrated in the preceding case, and the accounting for it will be similar.

In practice, it may be difficult at times to relate specific hedging transactions with specific exposed positions. However, in order to determine that particular forward contract may be computed as a hedge, as opposed to a speculative foreign exchange contract, it is necessary to be able to relate such forward contract, at least on an aggregate basis, to an exposed foreign currency position resulting form either foreign currency transactions and/or investments in foreign operations.

Accounting for a hedge of an identifiable foreign currency commitment

One of the exceptions to the requirement that gains and losses on forward exchange contracts be recognized currently is as follows:

> A gain or loss should be deferred on forward exchange contracts intended to be a hedge of an identifiable foreign currency commitment when the following conditions are met:
>
> a. The foreign currency transaction is designated as, and is effective as, a hedge of a foreign currency commitment. (The required accounting shall commence as of the designation date.)
> b. The foreign currency commitment is firm.

To illustrate this, let us assume that on January 1, 19x1 U.S. Importers entered into an uncancelable commitment with Japan Watch to buy and accept delivery of 10,000,000 yen worth of watches at a date 10 months later. Concerned that the dollar may decline against the yen and not wishing to expose itself to currency fluctuations, U.S. Importers enter into a forward contract to obtain 10,000,000 yen on November 1, 19x1. While the purchase transaction will not be recorded until the watches are shipped, U.S. Importers could incur gains or losses on the forward contract due to large rate changes between the commitment date and the transaction date. Since the dollar basis for a foreign currency transaction should be established at the transaction date rather than the commitment date, such gains or losses prior to the transaction date should be deferred and included in the final computation of the purchase transaction.

Assume that due to a strengthening of the yen against the dollar, the forward contract entered into by U.S. Importers shows a profit of $1,000 by June 30, 19x1 (the fiscal year-end). This would be recorded as follows:

Foreign Currency Due from Broker	1,000	
Deferred Exchange Gain		1,000

On November 1, 19x1, when the purchase is recorded and the U.S. $ = 200 yen, the entry will be as follows:

Inventory	49,000	
Deferred Exchange Gain	1,000	
Accounts Payable (10,000,000 yen)		50,000

The portion of gains or losses on the forward exchange contract that may be deferred is limited to that arising from a specific commitment. A gain or loss in excess of the aforementioned may be deferred to the extent that the forward contract is intended to provide a hedge on an *aftertax* basis.

Transaction gains and losses to be excluded from determination of net income

As will be seen from the discussion later in this chapter, the *Statement of Financial Accounting Standards 52* established the concept of a separate component of stockholders' equity in which translation adjustments are accumulated.

The gains and losses on foreign currency *transactions* that are not to be included in determining net income but are to be reported separately and included with translation adjustments in the separate component of equity are:

a. Gains and losses attributable to a foreign currency transaction that is designated as, and is effective as, an economic hedge of a net investment in a foreign entity (the required accounting shall commence as of the designation date).

b. Gains or losses attributable to intercompany foreign currency transactions that are of a long-term investment nature (i.e. settlement is not anticipated or planned in the foreseeable future) when the entities to the transaction are consolidated, combined, or accounted for by the equity method in the reporting enterprise's financial statements.

Accounting for gains and losses on speculative forward exchange contracts

Let us assume that U.S. Importers, without having any identifiable foreign currency commitments outstanding, decides to speculate on the value of a foreign currency by entering into a forward contract. Such a speculative contract is valued at the current forward rate for its remaining life and any gains or losses thereon are recognized currently in the income statement.

TRANSLATION OF FOREIGN CURRENCY FINANCIAL STATEMENTS

An important area in the accounting for foreign operations is the translation of account balances which are expressed in a foreign currency into the currency of the reporting (or home-base) company. This translation is necessary when we wish to record a domestic entity's equity in the earnings of its foreign investee or subsidiary or when we want to combine or consolidate the financial statements of a foreign branch or subsidiary with those of the domestic entity.

Evolution of the accounting for foreign exchange translation

Early pronouncements on the accounting for foreign operations were concerned mostly with foreign currency translations and not with foreign currency transactions. The principal differences among the various methods of translation which were advanced concerned which assets, liabilities, and operating items were to be translated at the current exchange rate (i.e., generally the rate of exchange prevailing at the end of a period) as opposed to the historical rate (i.e., the rate which prevailed when a given transaction occurred in the past).

Chapter 12 of *ARB 43* as modified by paragraph 18 of *APB Opinion 6* was the basic authoritative pronouncement on the subject before the FASB undertook to reconsider it. Chapter 12 of *ARB 43* called for the use of the *current-noncurrent* method of translation, i.e., the translation of current assets and liabilities at current rates and the translation of noncurrent assets and liabilities at historical rates. A research report described the current-noncurrent distinction, however, as one that "seems to reflect the use of an established balance sheet classification for a purpose to which it is not relevant."[2] The pronouncement contained some exceptions to the current-noncurrent rule, and in 1965 paragraph 18 of *APB Opinion 6* sanctioned further changes such as the translation of all payables and receivables at the current rate. This, in effect, was a move to permit another method of translation known as the *monetary-nonmonetary method*. Under this method, monetary assets and liabilities are translated at the current rate while nonmonetary assets and liabilities are translated at applicable historical rates. Assets and liabilities are regarded as monetary if they are expressed in terms of a fixed number of foreign currency units, e.g., cash, receivables, liabilities expressed in the foreign currency; all other assets and liabilities are regarded as nonmonetary.

Two other methods of foreign currency translation were also advanced during protracted discussions which preceded and continued during the FASB's consideration of the subject.[3]

The *current rate method* provides for the translation of all assets and liabilities at the current rate.

Under the *temporal method*, cash, receivables, payables, as well as assets and liabilities carried at present or future prices, are translated at current rates while assets and liabilities carried at past prices (historical costs) are translated at applicable historical rates.

The following table summarizes the salient features of the four translation methods discussed above:

	Monetary-nonmonetary method	Current-noncurrent method	Current rate method	Temporal method
Cash, current receivables, current payables	Current	Current	Current	Current
Inventories, current prepaids, current unearned revenue	Historical	Current	Current	Historical*
Noncurrent receivable, long-term liabilities	Current	Historical	Current	Current
Fixed assets, deferred charges, noncurrent unearned revenue . .	Historical	Historical	Current	Historical

*With some exceptions.

In 1975 the FASB adopted *SFAS 8 "Accounting for the Translation of Foreign Currency Transactions and Foreign Currency Financial Statements"* which basically follows the temporal method. The Appendix to this chapter

[2]S. R. Hepworth, *Reporting Foreign Operations* (Ann Arbor, Mich.: University of Michigan, 1956).

[3]In fact, nine distinct methods of foreign currency translations are illustrated in the FASB's *Financial Statement Model on Accounting for Foreign Currency Translation* (Stamford, Conn.: FASB, 1974).

presents this method because its application will remain optional until 1983 and because it applies in certain situations under *SFAS 52* (the statement which replaced *SFAS 8*).

Since its issuance *SFAS 8* has been one of the most controversial of all the standards promulgated by the FASB. In response to repeated criticism of this standard, the Board decided in 1979 to reconsider this statement. In August 1980, the Board issued an Exposure Draft of a proposed statement of financial accounting standards that would replace *SFAS 8*. This was followed in June 1981 by a revised exposure draft that was designed to meet some remaining objections. In December 1981, the Board issued *SFAS 52* which replaces *SFAS 8* and which is effective for fiscal years beginning on or after December 15, 1982, with earlier application encouraged.

STATEMENT OF FINANCIAL ACCOUNTING STANDARDS 52

Basic objectives

Statement of Financial Accounting Standards 52 "Foreign Currency Translation" represents a clear shift away from the philosophy of *SFAS 8* (see Appendix). *SFAS 8* was based on the parent company perspective, which is consistent with the temporal method, and which required all transactions to be measured as if the transactions occurred in U.S. dollars. The shift is to a "local" perspective, i.e., that of the foreign entity itself and the economic relationships expressed within its operations as a separate business unit whose factual financial statements are those prepared in the currency of its own environment.

Thus, SFAS 52 has as its major objective to (1) provide information that is generally compatible with the expected economic effects of a change in exchange rates on an enterprise's cash flows and equity and (2) to reflect in consolidated statements the financial results and relationships as measured in the primary currency of the economic environment in which the entity operates which is referred to as its *functional currency*.[4] The proposed draft places reliance on management's judgment in determining what the functional currency of a foreign subsidiary is.

A major feature of the functional currency approach is the current rate translation method. A foreign entity's assets, liabilities, and operations exist basically in the economic environment of its functional currency. Its costs are incurred in its functional currency, and its revenues are produced in its functional currency. Use of a current exchange rate retains those historical costs and other measurements but restates them in terms of the reporting currency, thereby preserving the relationships established in the entity's economic environment. Accordingly, use of the current exchange rate reflects in the consolidated financial statements the inherent relationships appearing in the functional currency financial statements.

---

[4]For an entity with operations that are relatively self-contained and integrated within a country, the functional currency will generally be the currency of that country. However, for example, if the foreign operations are a direct component or extension of a parent company's operations, then the parent's currency would be the functional currency. In this case the translation principles of *SFAS 8* would generally hold, including the requirement for current inclusion in income of all gains and losses. Under *SFAS 52* all deferred income taxes are to be translated at current exchange rates.

The functional currency approach entails:

a.   Identifying the functional currency of the entity's economic environment.

b.   Measuring all elements of the financial statements in the functional currency.

c.   Using the current exchange rate for translation from the functional currency to the reporting currency, if they are different.

d.   Distinguishing the economic impact of changes in exchange rates on a net investment from the impact of such changes on individual assets and liabilities that are receivable or payable in currencies other than the functional currency.

In adopting the functional currency approach the Board had the following overall objectives of foreign currency translation in mind:

a.   To provide information that is generally compatible with the expected economic effects of a rate change on an enterprise's cash flows and equity.

b.   To present the consolidated financial statements of an enterprise in conformity with U.S. generally accepted accounting principles.

c.   To reflect in consolidated financial statements the financial results and relationships of the individual consolidated entities as measured in their functional currencies.

Another major change in the Board's approach is to report the adjustment resulting from translation of foreign financial statements not as a gain or loss in the income of the period but as a separate accumulation as part of equity which, in accordance with FASB *Concepts Statement No. 3*, can be viewed as part of "comprehensive income." This must be clearly distinguished from gains or losses on foreign currency *transactions* which, subject to exceptions mentioned earlier, must be currently included in *income.* These include gains and losses on settled as well as *unsettled* transactions, such as may occur when, for example, a U.S. company takes out a 20-year debt denominated in Swiss francs.

A change in the exchange rate between the U.S. dollar and the other currency produces a change in the U.S. dollar equivalent of the net investment, although there is no change in the net assets of the other entity measured in its functional currency. A strengthening of the foreign currency against the dollar enhances the U.S. dollar equivalent; a weakening reduces the U.S. dollar equivalent. Accordingly, the translation adjustment reflects an economic effect of exchange rate changes. However, that change in the U.S. dollar equivalent of the net investment is an unrealized enhancement or reduction, having no effect on the functional currency net cash flows generated by the foreign entity which may be currently reinvested or distributed to the parent. It is for this reason that the translation adjustment is reported separately from the determination of net income.

Based on the objectives and the considerations outlined above, the following are the major provisions of *SFAS 52*:

Major provisions

1. The translation process requires that the functional currency of the entity be identified first. Ordinarily it will be the currency of the country in which the entity is located or the U.S. dollar. All financial statement elements of the foreign entity must then be measured in terms of the functional currency in conformity with U.S. generally accepted accounting principles.

2. Translation from the functional currency into the reporting currency, if they are different, is to be at the *current* exchange rate[5] except that revenues and expenses are to be translated at the *average* exchange rates prevailing during the period.[6] The functional currency translation approach generally considers the effect of exchange rate changes to be on the net investment in a foreign entity rather than on its individual assets and liabilities which was the focus of *SFAS 8.*

3. Translation adjustments are not to be included in net income but are to be disclosed and accumulated as a separate component of stockholders' equity until such time that the net investment in the foreign entity is sold or completely or substantially liquidated. To the extent that the sale or liquidation represents realization, the relevant amounts should be removed from the separate equity component and included as a gain or loss in the determination of the net income of the period during which the sale or liquidation occurs.

4. The statement of changes in financial position is to be translated by applying the current exchange rate as of the balance sheet date, except that those changes which result from revenues, expenses, gains and losses are to be translated at the rates at which these items are translated in the income statement.

5. Exchange gains and losses attributable to intercompany foreign currency transactions and balances that are of a trading nature are to be included in income, while those that are of a long-term financing or capital nature, for which settlement is not contemplated in the foreseeable future, are to be reported in the separate component of shareholder's equity where adjustments arising from the translation of foreign currency financial statements are accumulated.

Using the current rate method to translate the nonmonetary assets of foreign subsidiaries located in highly inflationary economies can produce

---

[5]Usually the year-end rate which can be used for purposes of dividend remittances.

[6]A foreign entity's revenues, expenses, gains, and losses should be translated in a manner that produces amounts approximately as if the underlying elements had been translated on the dates they were recognized (sometimes referred to as the weighted average exchange rate). This also applies to accounting allocations (e.g., depreciation, cost of sales, and amortization of deferred revenues and expenses) and requires translation at the current exchange rates applicable to the dates those allocations are included in revenues and expenses (i.e., not the rates on the dates the related items originated). In most cases the average exchange rate prevailing during the year would be used.

distorted results. The Board concluded that if a foreign entity's functional currency has been affected by cumulative inflation of 100 percent or more over a three-year period, it is to be considered not stable enough to serve as a functional currency and consequently, the financial statements of the entity shall be remeasured into the reporting (i.e. parent) currency. This remeasurement process, in effect, results in translation by the temporal method (see the Appendix).

Illustration 12–1 presents an example of the translation procedure which reflects the foregoing provisions.

**Illustration 12–1:
Illustration of the
translation of the
financial statements of a
foreign subsidiary**

Forco is a wholly owned foreign subsidiary of Dollarco and has been since its incorporation in 19v8. On July 1, 19x6, the dollar was devalued in relation to the foreign currency (FC) from FC 1 = U.S. $1.20 to FC 1 = $1.40. This was the only significant change in the exchange rate since 19x0. A summary trial balance of Forco in FC at December 31, 19x6, is given below:

Cash	FC 100,000
Accounts receivable	300,000
Inventories, at cost	500,000
Prepaid expenses	25,000
Property, plant, and equipment (net)	1,000,000
Long-term note receivable	75,000
	FC 2,000,000
Accounts payable	FC 500,000
Current portion of long-term debt	100,000
Long-term debt	900,000
Capital stock	300,000
Retained earnings, January 1, 19x6	50,000
Sales	5,000,000
Cost of sales	(4,000,000)
Depreciation	(300,000)
Other expense	(550,000)
	FC 2,000,000

Additional information:

1. Fixed assets were purchased prior to July 1, 19x6.
2. The long-term note receivable was executed on January 31, 19x6.
3. FC 100,000 of the inventory on hand at year-end was purchased prior to July 1, 19x6.
4. Prepaid expenses represent unexpired insurance premiums which were paid on March 31, 19x6.
5. Long-term debt was incurred prior to July 1, 19x6.
6. All of the common stock was issued on the date of incorporation.
7. All accounts receivable and payable and long-term debt amounts are denominated in the local currency.
8. Sales, purchases and all operating expenses are assumed to have occurred evenly throughout the year so that the application of the average exchange rate produced results as if each individual month's revenues and expenses were translated using the rate in effect during each month. It is appropriate to convert the cost of goods sold by use of the average rate.

9. The balance at the beginning of the year of the "equity adjustment from translation of foreign currency statements" is assumed to be $45,000 (debit). Income tax consequences, if any, relating to this account are to be ignored* in this illustration.

*Generally interperiod tax allocation is required in accordance with *APB N 11*, "Accounting for Income Taxes," if taxable exchange gains or tax-deductible exchange losses resulting from an entity's foreign currency transactions are included in net income in a different period for financial statement purposes than for tax purposes. Translation adjustments shall be accounted for in the same way as timing differences under the provisions of *APB Opinions 11, 23,* and *24. APB Opinion 23,* "Accounting for Income Taxes—Special Areas," provides that deferred taxes shall not be provided for unremitted earnings of a subsidiary in certain instances; in those instances, deferred taxes shall not be provided on translation adjustments.

FORCO COMPANY
Translation Working Paper
Year Ended December 31, 19x6

	FC	Exchange rate	Translation code or explanation	U.S. dollars
Balance Sheet				
Cash	100,000	1.4	C	140,000
Accounts receivable	300,000	1.4	C	420,000
Inventories, at cost	500,000	1.4	C	700,000
Prepaid expenses	25,000	1.4	C	35,000
Property, plant, and equipment (net)	1,000,000	1.4	C	1,400,000
Long-term note receivable	75,000	1.4	C	105,000
Total assets	2,000,000			2,800,000
Accounts payable	500,000	1.4	C	700,000
Current portion of long-term debt	100,000	1.4	C	140,000
Long-term debt	900,000	1.4	C	1,260,000
Total liabilities	1,500,000			2,100,000
Capital stock	300,000	1.2	H	360,000
Retained earnings:				
Balance, 1/1/x6	50,000		E	60,000
Current year net income	150,000		F	195,000
Balance, 12/31/x6	200,000			255,000
Equity adjustment from translation of foreign currency statements:				
Balance, 1/1/x6			E	(45,000)
Current year translation adjustment			G	130,000
Balance, 12/31/x6				85,000
Total stockholders' equity	500,000			700,000
Total liabilities and equity	2,000,000			2,800,000
Income Statement				
Sales	5,000,000	1.3	A	6,500,000
Cost of sales	(4,000,000)	1.3	A	(5,200,000)
Depreciation	(300,000)	1.3	A	(390,000)
Other expenses	(550,000)	1.3	A	(715,000)
Net income	150,000			195,000

Translation code or explanation:
C = current rate.
H = historical rate.
A = average rate.
E = balance in U.S. dollars at the beginning of the period.
F = per income statement.
G = amount needed to balance the financial statements.

In the solution on page 426 the translation is done in balance sheet and income statement (versus the trial balance)[7] format so as to highlight the FASB's proposed treatment of classifying translation adjustments as a separate component of stockholders' equity.

A review of the translation working paper of the FORCO Company reveals the following noteworthy elements:

1. All items in the simplified income statement are converted at the average rate of exchange prevailing during the year.

2. All assets and liabilities are translated at the current rate of exchange. The capital stock account is translated at the historical rate. If all of a foreign entity's assets and liabilities are measured in its functional currency and are translated at the current exchange rate, the net accounting effect of a change in the exchange rate is the effect on the net assets of the entity. That accounting result is compatible with the broad concept of economic hedging on which the net investment view is based. No gains or losses arise from hedged assets and liabilities, and the dollar equivalent of the unhedged net investment increases or decreases when the functional currency strengthens or weakens.

3. It will be noted that after the translated net income for 19x6 of $195,000 is added to the retained earnings section of the balance sheet, a translation adjustment of $130,000 must be inserted in order to balance the balance sheet. When this current year translation adjustment (credit) of $130,000 is added to the $45,000 opening debit balance of the Equity Adjustment from Translation of Foreign Currency Statements account, the resulting ending balance for this account is a credit of $85,000. This will be the opening balance of this equity account as of January 1, 19x7.

4. In this particular example the Equity Adjustment from Translation of Foreign Currency Statements account was affected only by the translation adjustment that was required in order to balance the translated balance sheet. In different circumstances this account could also be debited or credited for:

   a. Gains and losses attributable to a foreign currency transaction that is designated as, and is effective as, an economic hedge of a net investment in a foreign entity.

---

[7]In the trial balance format where, instead of a "cost of goods sold" figure, the opening inventory, purchases as well as ending inventory are given, the translated dollar amount of the opening inventory will represent a forced figure computed as in the following example:

	FC	Exchange rate	U.S. dollars
Opening inventory	400,000	*	570,000
Add: Purchases	4,100,000	(A) 1.3	5,330,000
	4,500,000		5,900,000
Less: Ending inventory	500,000	(C) 1.4	700,000
Equals Cost of goods sold	4,000,000	(A) 1.3	5,200,000

*U.S. amount needed to allow cost of goods sold figure to be translated at current rate.
A = Average rate.
C = Current rate.

  b. Gains or losses attributable to intercompany foreign currency transactions and balances that are of a long-term financing or capital nature when the entities to the transaction are consolidated, combined, or accounted for by the equity method in the reporting entity's financial statements.

Accounting for investment by parent company

When the investment in the foreign subsidiary is accounted for by the parent company on the equity method the parent will have to pick up *its*[8] share of the translation adjustment. Thus, in the case and our Illustration 12–1 Dollarco will, for the year 19x6, make the following entries (figures in U.S. dollars):

```
Investment in Forco  ........................    195,000
     Equity in Earnings of Subsidiary ...............            195,000
   To pick up earnings of Forco.

Investment in Forco  ........................    130,000
     Translation Adjustment ....................            130,000
   To pick up the current year translation adjustment.
```

Accounting when an investment in subsidiary is sold or liquidated

Continuing with the example in Illustration 12–1, should Dollarco sell its investment in Forco on January 1, 19x7, then, *in addition* to recording a gain or loss on the difference between the proceeds of the sale and the carrying (book) value of the investment, Dollarco will close out the Equity Adjustment from Translation of Foreign Currency Statements account with a credit balance of $85,000 into income as part of this completed and realized sales transaction.

Disclosure requirements

SFAS 52 requires disclosure of the aggregate transaction gain or loss included in net income for the period as well as presentation of an analysis of the changes during the period in the separate component of equity for cumulative translation adjustments.

Exposure to foreign exchange losses

Any enterprise which conducts business abroad either through a foreign based branch or subsidiary or through direct dealings with foreign suppliers or customers is exposed to the risk of foreign exchange loss. Before that risk can be managed, it must be measured.

  The exposure to exchange *translation* losses is not necessarily the same as the *economic* exposure to exchange losses, although the FASB's current rate translation approach aims at narrowing this gap. The latter depends on many complex factors including economic conditions, relative rates of inflation, regulation, and other factors. Translation exposure, on the other hand, depends on what has to be translated at current exchange rates which now

---

[8]Thus, if a parent owns only 80 percent of a subsidiary, it will pick up 80 percent of the translation adjustment.

encompasses all assets and liabilities. Thus the exposure position can be defined as the net balance of all accounts translated at *current* exchange rates. Accounts translated at historical rates are not exposed to translation adjustments because the same old conversion rate is used each year.

The net exposure position may be calculated as follows:

Items contributing to exposure:

a. Current assets (exclusive of prepaid expenses).
b. Investments denominated in fixed amounts of local currency.
c. Long-term receivables (net of allowances).

Items reducing exposure:

d. Inventories (sale of which is not subject to price controls).
e. U.S. dollar assets included in *(a)*, *(b)*, and *(c)* above and not already included in *(d)*.
f. Local currency liabilities (including reserves).

The algebraic sum of the above items equals the net exposure to risk of loss (or exposure to gain) through exchange fluctuations. Based on given assumption as to the future behavior of exchange rates, an exposed position can be managed by carefully controlling the company's position in the listed items and by such additional measures as the use of forward exchange contracts.

Appendix: The temporal method of translation

(The methodology of *SFAS 8*)

Applicability

Under *SFAS 52*, when the functional currency of a foreign subsidiary is that of the parent company or when a foreign entity's functional currency has been affected by cumulative inflation of 100 percent or more over a three year period, translation will follow the principles of the temporal method (as sanctioned by *SFAS 8*) The only change to that method made by *SFAS 52* is to require the translation of deferred taxes at the current rate of exchange.

The conceptual basis of *SFAS 8*

In *SFAS 8*, the FASB did not adopt any translation method by name (see discussion of alternative methods in the chapter) but, in effect chose a method very similar to the temporal method. The basic aim was that translation should change the unit of measure without changing the accounting principles employed.

Thus, the translation method adopted results in translated statements in which the measurement basis of assets and liabilities in terms of U.S. generally accepted accounting principles, (GAAP) remains the same after translation as before. In contrast, the current and the current-noncurrent methods do *not* retain the same measurement basis before and after translation. For example, inventory that is measured at *historical* cost would be translated at the *current* rate under both the current and the current-noncurrent methods.

The monetary-nonmonetary method seems to coincide with the temporal method, but it is purely coincidence that most monetary assets and liabilities are measured at current or future prices whereas nonmonetary assets and liabilities are measured at past prices.

The following illustrates the differences between the various translation methods, under the assumption that the acquisition of a fixed asset is financed by issuance of long-term debt:

Fixed asset cost . . . . FC 1,000
Long-term debt . . . . FC 1,000
At acquisition date . . . . FC 1 = $4
At balance sheet date . . . . FC 1 = $5

(Ignore depreciation and assume that no principal payment is required and that interest is paid to date.)

	Current noncurrent method	Current rate method	Temporal method
Fixed asset	$4,000	$5,000*	$4,000
Long-term debt . . .	$4,000†	$5,000	$5,000

*Result departs from historical based accounting.

†No recognition is given to loss from holding long-term debt payable in a foreign currency when that currency increased in value compared to the dollar.

Note that in the above illustration, the current-noncurrent method translates long-term debt at *past exchange rates* despite the fact that, in accordance with GAAP, long-term debt is stated at its *future price*. The current rate method ignores the fact that fixed assets are stated at *past prices* (historical cost) and translates them at the *current exchange rate*. Only the temporal method translates assets and liabilities without changing their measurement bases according to U.S. GAAP.

BASIC PROVISIONS OF *SFAS 8*

Foreign financial statements, prepared in conformity with U.S. GAAP, should be translated into U.S. dollars in such a manner so as to preserve the same measurement basis of assets, liabilities, revenues, and expenses after translation. This is accomplished as follows:

1. Cash, amounts receivable and payable, both short and long term, should be translated at the *current* exchange rate.
2. Other assets and liabilities should be translated *according to their measurement basis under U.S. GAAP.*
   a. Accounts carried at past prices should be translated at *historical* rates.
      Examples: Inventory carried at cost; marketable equity securities carried at cost; property, plant, and equipment; intangibles; deferred taxes; and prepaid assets.
   b. Accounts carried at current or future prices (future settlement) should be translated at the *current* exchange rate.
      Examples: Inventory carried at market (under the lower of cost or market rule), marketable equity securities carried at current market price.
   c. The foreign statements of an investee that are accounted for by the equity method first shall be translated into dollars in conformity with the requirements of the *Statement*; then the equity method shall be applied.

Revenues and expenses should be translated in a manner that produces approximately the same dollar amounts as the use of the transaction method, that is, at the exchange rate in effect on the applicable transaction dates. (As a practical matter, average rates may be employed to achieve this result.) An exception to the above rule is that revenue and expenses that relate to balance sheet items translated at historical rates (such as depreciation) should be translated at historical rates.

The following table summarizes the appropriate use of the translation rates (*SFAS 8*, par. 38):

	Translation rates	
	Current	Historical
Assets		
Cash on hand and demand and time deposits	X	
Marketable equity securities:		
Carried at cost		X
Carried at current market price	X	
Accounts and notes receivable and related unearned discount	X	
Allowance for doubtful accounts and notes receivable	X	
Inventories:		
Carried at cost		X
Carried at current replacement price or current selling price .	X	
Carried at net realizable value . .	X	
Carried at contract price (produced under fixed price contracts)	X	
Prepaid insurance, advertising, and rent		X
Refundable deposits	X	
Advances to unconsolidated subsidiaries	X	
Property, plant, and equipment . .		X
Accumulated depreciation of property, plant, and equipment .		X
Cash surrender value of life insurance	X	
Patents, trademarks, licenses, and formulas		X
Goodwill		X
Other tangible assets		X
Liabilities		
Accounts and notes payable and overdrafts	X	
Accrued expenses payable	X	
Accrued losses on firm purchase commitments	X	
Refundable deposits	X	
Deferred income		X
Bonds payable or other long-term debt	X	
Unamortized premium or discount on bonds or notes payable	X	
Convertible bonds payable	X	
Accrued pension obligations	X	
Obligations under warranties . . .	X	

The following are translation procedures applying to specific situations:

1. *Holding of debt securities:* A bond that will be held to maturity must be translated at the current rate. A bond not held to maturity is translated at the historical rate if carried at cost and at the current rate if carried at market value.

2. *Deferred taxes:* In general, deferred taxes are translated at the same rate as the item which gives rise to them. Thus, deferred taxes which relate to items translated at historical rates (e.g., fixed assets) are translated at historical rates. However, *SFAS 52* requires the translation of deferred taxes at the current rate.

3. *Translation after a business combination:* Pooling—translation shall be as if the foreign operation were always a subsidiary and historical rates will be used where appropriate. Purchase—assets and liabilities are first adjusted to fair values, and the *rates in effect on the date of the acquisition* are then used.

4. *Investments accounted for by the equity method:* Foreign statements of an investee are first translated into dollars; then the equity method is applied.

5. *Minority interests:* The minority interest of a consolidated statement shall be based on the subsidiary's statements after translation.

6. *Preferred stock:* Normally, if preferred stock is a permanent investment, it is translated at historical rates. However, if it is carried at its liquidation or redemption price *and* liquidation or redemption is *required or imminent,* the current rate is to be used.

7. *Applying the rule of cost or market, whichever is lower:* Translated historical cost must be compared with translated market. Application of the rule in dollars may require write-downs even though none would be required in the foreign currency. A write-down in dollars becomes the new cost in dollars until the inventory is sold or written down further.

Illustration of the application of translation standards to inventories:

Facts:

Unit of inventory purchased during the year at :		FC 1,000
Exchange rate at purchase date		FC1 = $2.00

At balance sheet date:

	Foreign	U.S.

Assumption A: No change in market value or exchange rate

Inventory at cost	FC 1,000	$2,000
Inventory at market	FC 1,000	$2,000
Inventory at the lower cost or market	FC 1,000	$2,000

Assumption B: Change in exchange rate FC 1 = $2.50; no change in market value

Inventory at cost	FC 1,000	$2,000
Inventory at market	FC 1,000	$2,000
Inventory at the lower of cost or market	FC 1,000	$2,000

Assumption C: Change in exchange rate FC 1 = $1.75; no change in market value

Inventory at cost	FC 1,000	$2,000
Inventory at market	FC 1,000	$1,750
Inventory at the lower of cost or market	FC 1,000	$1,750

Assumption D: Change in market value to FC 800; no change in exchange rate

Inventory at cost	FC 1,000	$2,000
Inventory at market	FC 800	$1,600
Inventory at the lower of cost or market	FC 800	$1,600

Assumption E: Change in market value to FC 800; Exchange rate changes to FC 1 = $3

Inventory at cost	FC 1,000	$2,000
Inventory at market	FC 800	$2,400
Inventory at the lower of cost or market	FC 800	$2,000

Exchange gains and losses:

1. Exchange gains and losses which result from a rate change between the dollar and the foreign currency occur in connection with *foreign transactions* as well as *translation of foreign statements.* Presently all exchange gains and losses enter into the determination of income for the period in which they are measured. This rule applies equally to interim statements. (See, for example, Appendix A, Chapter 24.)

2. Interperiod tax allocation is required where exchange gains and losses enter into taxable income in a period different from that of accounting income. For example, U.S. Company purchases factory supplies on credit for FC1,000 when the exchange rate is FC1 = $1. The purchase is unpaid at balance sheet date when FC1 = $1.50. Therefore, an exchange loss of $500 is recognized for financial statement purposes, but is not currently deductible for tax purposes since the loss is not fixed or certain.

Assuming that U.S. Company is otherwise profitable and a 50 percent tax rate, the following entry would be made:

Loss on Translation	500	
Deferred Income Taxes	250	
Accounts Payable		500
Provision for Income Taxes (deferred portion)		250

3. Using historical rates for certain revenue and expense items, such as depreciation, may create an unusual relationship between translated pretax foreign income and foreign income taxes; this is *not* a timing difference, and interperiod tax allocation is not required. To the extent that exchange gains and losses arise from translation of foreign subsidiary and foreign investee statements, the requirements of *APB Opinions 23* and *24* shall apply.

4. In accordance with *APB Opinion 30 all* gains or losses from translations of foreign currencies, including those relating to major devaluations and revaluations, are to be treated as ordinary rather than extraordinary items. Such treatment does not, however, imply that such gains and losses cannot be separately disclosed in the income statement as "one-line" items above "income before extraordinary items."

Disclosure requirements:

1. Aggregate exchange gain or loss included in determining net income for the period.
2. Effects of rate changes on reported results of operations, other than the effects included in the disclosure required above, if practicable, should be described and quantified. If quantified, the methods and the underlying assumptions used to determine the estimated effects should be explained.

Illustration of the translation of the financial statements of a foreign subsidiary

Using the data for FORCO Company given in Illustration 12–1 in the Chapter (Except for point 9 of the additional information given) we are to translate the accounts of FORCO into U.S. dollars in accordance with *SFAS 8* standards Illustration 12A–1 presents the translation process:

Illustration 12A–1
FORCO COMPANY
Translation Working Paper
Year Ended December 31, 19x6

	F.C.	Exchange rate	U.S. dollars
Cash	100,000	1.40 (A)	140,000
Accounts receivable	300,000	1.40 (A)	420,000
Inventories, at cost	500,000	100,000 @ 1.20 (B) 400,000 @ 1.40 (A)	→ 680,000
Prepaid expenses	25,000	1.20 (B)	30,000
Property, plant, and equipment (net)	1,000,000	1.20 (B)	1,200,000
Long-term note receivable	75,000	1.40 (A)	105,000
	2,000,000		2,575,000
Accounts payable	500,000	1.40 (A)	700,000
Current portion of long-term debt	100,000	1.40 (A)	140,000
Long-term debt	900,000	1.40 (A)	1,260,000
Capital stock	300,000	1.20 (C)	360,000
Retained earnings, 1/1/x6	50,000	(E)	60,000
Sales	5,000,000	1.30 (D)	6,500,000
Cost of sales	(4,000,000)	(F)	(5,120,000)
Depreciation	(300,000)	1.20 (D)	(360,000)
Other expenses	(550,000)	1.30 (D)	(715,000)
Translation loss*			(250,000)
	2,000,000		2,575,000

*To balance.

Illustration 12A–1 (*continued*)

Key to translation rates:
  (A) Current rate at balance sheet date.
  (B) Rate in effect when acquired (historical rate).
  (C) Rate in effect at date of incorporation.
  (D) Revenue and expenses are translated at average rates in effect during the period except when they relate to a balance sheet item translated at a historical rate, then the revenue or expense is translated at the historical rate.
  (E) Balance in U.S. dollars at the beginning of the period.
  (F) Cost of sales are translated as follows:

	FC		Exchange rate	U.S. dollars
Opening inventory	500,000		1.20	600,000
Purchase	4,000,000		1.30	5,200,000
Available for sale	4,500,000			5,800,000
		100,000	1.20)	
Closing inventories	500,000	400,000	1.40)	680,000
	4,000,000			5,120,000

Translation of a branch

The accounts of a branch are translated by following the same principles followed in the translation of the accounts of a subsidiary with the only exception that the reciprocal accounts (i.e., branch control account and home office control account) are stated at dollar amounts at which they are carried on the home office books and are not translated by use of translation exchange rates.

Illustration of booking of translation gains and losses and related tax effects

On April 1, 19x6, Dollarco borrowed FC 450,000 from a foreign concern when FC 4.50 = $1. Repayment is due in 10 equal annual installments each April 1 plus interest at 10 percent per annum. At December 31, 19x6, FC 5.00 = $1.

The following journal entries will be made at De-cember 31, 19x6, by Dollarco to adjust the loan payable at that date and to reflect the deferred tax related to the translation gain (at an assumed tax rate of 50 percent):

(A)

Loan Payable	10,000	
Accrued Interest	750	
Gain on Translation		10,750

A translation gain is recorded for a loan payable denominated in a foreign currency when the dollar has increased in value compared to the foreign currency. Computed as follows:

	Conversion		
	April 1, 19x6 (FC 4.50 = $1)	December 31, 19x6 (FC 5.00 = $1)	Translation Gain Loss
Loan payable FC 450,000	$100,000	$90,000	$10,000
Interest on FC 450,000 @ 10% for 9 months = FC 33,750	7,500	6,750	750
			$10,750

(B)

| Deferred Income Tax Provision | 5,375 | |
| Deferred Income Tax Liability | | 5,375 |

Gain on translation is a timing difference requiring interperiod tax allocation since the gain is not taxable until realized.

QUESTIONS

1. Accounting practices can vary significantly among countries.

a. Give some reasons for these variations.

b. Give some examples indicative of the nature and extent of such differences.

2. Discuss some of the ways in which an enterprise in the home country can be involved in transactions involving the currencies of other countries.

3. Differentiate between conversion and translation of foreign curriencies.

4. Explain the difference amont the following exchange rates:

a. Free rate.

b. Multiple rates.

c. Preferential rate.

d. Penalty rate.

e. Dividend rate.

f. Black market rate.

g. Spot rate.

h. Forward exchange rate.

5. Foreign currency transactions encompass a wide variety of activities. Give some examples of such activities.

6. Distinguish between the *two-transaction perspective* and the *one-transaction perspective* stating which perspective the FASB supports.

7. Explain what is meant by a forward exchange contract and indicate its purpose.

8. What are the conditions that must be met in order to defer a gain or loss on a forward exchange contract intended to be a hedge of an identifiable foreign currency committment?

9. What are the salient features of the four methods used for translating foreign currency financial statements? Give your answer in a summary format.

10. Which method of translation was adopted by the FASB and what is its conceptual basis?

11. What are the basic objectives of the FASB's new approach to foreign currency translation?

12. What is the "functional currency" of an enterprise?

13. How are revenues, expenses, gains, and losses to be translated?

14. How is the statement of changes in financial position to be translated?

15. How are translation adjustments to be accounted for?

16. Differentiate between exposure to exchange *translation* losses and *economic* exposure to exchange losses.

17. How may the net exposure position be calculated?

Questions for Appendix— The Temporal Method: SFAS 8.

18. List and discuss some of the translation procedures which should be applied in specific situations such as, the holding of debt securities, deferred taxes, business combinations, minority interests, preferred stock, and so forth.

19. What is the proper accounting treatment of all gains and losses from translation of foreign currencies?

20. What are the disclosure requirements under *SFAS 8?*

EXERCISES

Exercise 12–1. On February 20, 19x7, merchandise was purchased by NCR Corporation for 50,000 Florins, payable in Florins. At this date, the exchange rate was 40 cents. On March 31, 19x7, the exchange rate was 39 cents.
On April 20, 19x7, the account was paid, at which date the exchange rate was 41 cents.

Required:

Entries for the above, assuming that an interim statement was issued as of March 31, 19x7.

Exercise 12-2. On August 1, 19x7, Lorin Corporation entered into a forward exchange contract with Kell Corporation in order to hedge against *general* foreign currency commitments totaling 600,000 FCU. The forward contract calls for the parties to exchange currencies on December 1 at a forward rate of 3.00 FCU to $1. (Lorin Corporation will receive 600,000 FCU on December 1 and will pay $200,000 to Kell Corporation.) Spot rates were 3.10 FCU to $1 on August 1, 2.90 FCU to $1 on September 30, and 3.20 FCU to $1 on December 1.

Required:

Entries for Lorin Corporation on August 1, September 30 (interim statement), and December 1.

Exercise 12–3. On January 1, 19x7, Alpha Corporation contracts with Beta Corporation (both are U.S. corporations) to sell for $200,000 some equipment that will be manufactured by a German supplier and delivered in 18 months. At this date, the spot rate for the German mark is 40 cents, and the cost of the equipment to Alpha Corporation is 400,000 marks or $160,000 (400,000 marks × 40 cents). Thus, the selling price of $200,000 to Beta Corporation provides a gross margin of $40,000 to Alpha Corporation (based upon current exchange rates).

In order to ensure that this gross margin will be realized, Alpha Corporation enters into a forward exchange contract with an exchange broker to receive 400,000 German marks in 18 months at the current forward rate of 41 cents.

The following spot rates prevail in the future: December 31, 19x7 — 45 cents, and June 30, 19x8 — 51 cents.

Required:

Entries for Alpha Corporation on January 1, 19x7, December 31, 19x7, and June 30, 19x8, assuming that the forward contract entered into by Alpha Corporation met the requisites as a hedge against an identifiable commitment.

Exercise 12–4. On May 1, 19x7, Howe Corporation entered into a forward exchange contract for speculation. The contract called for Howe Corporation to deliver to Bell Corporation 400,000 FCU on August 1, 19x7, at a forward rate of 5.00 FCU to $1, and therefore to receive $80,000. Spot rates were 4.80 FCU to $1 on May 1, 19x7, and 5.20 FCU to $1 on

August 1, 19x7. On June 30, 19x7, the rate for an August 1, 19x7, forward contract was 4.90 FCU to $1.

Required:

Entries for Howe Corporation on May 1, 19x7, June 30, 19x7 (interim statement date), and August 1, 19x7.

Exercise 12–5. Part A. The FASB discusses certain terminology essential to both the translation of foreign currency transactions and foreign currency financial statements. Included in the discussion is a definition of and distinction between the terms *measure* and *denominate*.

Required:

Define the terms *measure* and *denominate* as discussed by the FASB and give a brief example that demonstrates the distinction between accounts measured in a particular currency and accounts denominated in a particular currency.

Part B. There are several methods of translating foreign currency transactions or accounts reflected in foreign currency financial statements. Among these methods are: current-noncurrent, monetary-nonmonetary, current rate, and the temporal method.

Required:

Define the temporal method of translating foreign currency financial statements. Specifically include in your answer the treatment of the following four accounts:

a. Long-term accounts receivable.

b. Deferred income.

c. Inventory valued at cost.

d. Long-term debt.   (AICPA adapted)

PROBLEMS

Problem 12–6. American International Corporation (AMICO) purchased goods from Japanco of Japan on August 1, 19x1, for 20,000 yen to be paid October 31, 19x1, in yens.

Required:

a. Assume that on August 1, 1 yen = 15 cents, and on October 31, 1 yen = 17 cents, and that AMICO's fiscal year-end is December 31. Give all journal entries necessary to record the purchase and the payments on AMICO's books.

b. Answer (a) above if AMICO fiscal year-end is September 30 at which date 1 yen = (1) 16 cents; and (2) 13 cents.

c. Assume same facts as in (a), except that on August 1, 19x1, AMICO enters into a forward exchange contract to receive 20,000 yen from a foreign currency broker on October 31, at a rate of 1 yen = 16 cents. Give all necessary journal entries to record the purchase, the payment, and the forward contract on AMICO's books.

d. Answer (c) above if AMICO's fiscal year-end is

September 30 at which date 1 yen = (1) 16 cents; and (2) 13 cents.

Problem 12–7. U.S. International manufactures TV sets which it sells in domestic as well as international markets. Late in 19x7, USI has been preparing for purchasing subassemblies from a foreign manufacturer to assemble the newly introduced pocket TV. Following are selected transactions for 19x8.

1. On January 15, USI sold TV sets to a Mexican importer for a total price of $15,000 to be paid in dollars on March 13. On January 15, $1 = 12 pesos, and on March 13, $1 = 11 pesos.
2. On February 7, USI purchased subassemblies from the foreign manufacturer for 10,000 FC to be paid in FC on April 6. On February 7, FCI = 20 cents, and on April 6, FCI = 19 cents.
3. On May 1, USI sold TV sets to a Swiss wholesaler for a total price of SFr 20,000. To hedge against SFr fluctuations, USI entered on May 1 into a contract with a foreign currency broker to deliver to him SFr 20,000 on June 15 (the date the SFr due from the Swiss wholesaler) at a rate of SFr 1 = 40 cents. On May 1, SFr 1 = 39 cents, and on June 15, SFr 1 = 37 cents.
4. Because the demand for the foreign subassemblies for pocket TV sets was rising rapidly, USI entered on July 1 into a noncancelable purchase committment of 5,000 subassemblies to be shipped August 1. The total price for the shipment was FC 5 million to be paid in FC on August 15. On July 1, USI entered into a forward exchange contract to receive from the foreign currency broker FC 5 million on August 15, at a rate of FCI = 21 cents.

     On July 1,   FCI = 20 cents.
     On August 1,   FCI = 22 cents.
     On August 15,   FCI = 23 cents.

5. On December 1, USI sold pocket TV sets to a German importer for a total price of DM 10,000 to be paid in DM on February 1, 19x9. At the same date (December 1, 19x8), USI entered into a forward exchange contract with a foreign currency broker to deliver to him DM 10,000 on February 1, 19x9, at a rate of DMI = 40 cents. On December 1, 19x8, DMI = 41 cents; on December 31, 19x8, DMI = 39 cents; but on February 1, 19x9, DMI = 42 cents.

Required:

Prepare all necessary journal entries for the above transactions on USI's books, assuming its fiscal year-end is December 31.

Problem 12–8. USCO (A U.S. corporation) had the following transactions during 19x7:

1. On January 5, USCO sold goods to BRCO (a British company) for $36,000 (£20,000).
2. On February 5, purchased merchandise from FRCO (a French corporation) for $10,000 (equivalent FF 50,000).
3. On March 5, USCO received payment from BRCO when the exchange rate was £ = $1.83.
4. On April 5, USCO paid FRCO when the exchange rate was FF = 22 cents.
5. On May 5, USCO sold goods to GRCO (a German company) for DM 40,000 when the exchange rate was DM = 25 cents (i.e., for $10,000). On the same date, USCO sold DM 40,000 at 25 cents for delivery on June 5.
6. On June 5, USCO received payment from GRCO, when the exchange rate was 24 cents; thereupon the deutsche marks were delivered in settlement of the future contract.

Required:

Record the above transactions on USCO books under two alternatives:

     a. If the billing is in domestic currency (dollars).
     b. If the billing is in foreign currency.

Problem 12–9. Referring to Problem 12–8 assume that USCO contracts on July 5 with an American customer to sell him for $100,000 equipment that will be manufactured by FRCO and delivered in one year. On July 5, the exchange rate was FF = 20 cents and the cost of the equipment to USCO is FF400,000.

Since the transaction cannot be completed before one year, USCO, in order to ensure that the gross margin will be realized, enters into a forward exchange contract to receive FF400,000 in one year at the present forward rate of 21 cents.

USCO closes its books on December 31.

Required:

Assuming that the exchange rate on December 31, 19x7, was 22 cents and on July 5, 19x8, was 25 cents, record the above transactions on the USCO books.

Problem 12–10. Assume that USCO of Problem 12–8 has neither identifiable foreign currency committments nor an exposed net asset or liability position but wants to speculate in fluctuations in the value of the Swiss franc. Thus on December 1, 19x7, USCO purchases SFr40,000 for delivery in two months. On December 1, the spot rate for the Swiss franc was 40 cents and the two-month future rate was 38 cents.

Required:

Record the entries in USCO's books if the forward exchange rate on December 31 for one-month delivery is 36 cents, and on February 1, 19x8, when the spot rate was 39 cents.

Problem 12–11. The trial balance of Swisco Corporation, a Swiss corporation at December 31, 19x8, is shown below (in Swiss francs).

	Debit	Credit
Cash	50,000	
Accounts receivable	100,000	
Property, plant, and equipment, net	800,000	
Depreciation expense	100,000	
Other expenses (including taxes)	200,000	
Inventory, January 1, 19x8	150,000	
Sales		2,000,000
Allowance for doubtful accounts		10,000
Accounts payable		80,000
Notes payable		20,000
Capital stock		100,000
Retained earnings, January 1, 19x8		190,000
Purchases	1,000,000	
	2,400,000	2,400,000

Additional information:

1. Swisco uses the periodical inventory system as well as the Fifo method for measuring inventory and cost of good sold. On December 31, 19x8, inventory on hand was SFr120,000. It is carried at cost.

2. The capital stock was issued six years ago when the company was established, at which time the exchange rate was SFr1 = 30 cents. Plant and equipment was purchased five years ago when the exchange rate was SFr1 = 35 cents; the note payable was made out to a local bank at the same time.

3. Revenue and expense items were realized or incurred uniformly throughout 19x8. However, inventory on hand on December 31, 19x8, was purchased throughout the second half of 19x8.

4. The retained earnings balance in the December 31, 19x7, balance sheets (in dollars) of Swisco Corporation was $61,000, and the inventory balance was $47,000.

5. The spot rates for SFr in 19x8 were as follows:

January 1, 19x8	32 cents
Average for 19x8	37
Average for second half of 19x8	36
December 31, 19x8	38

6. Management determined that the functional currency of Swisco is the Swiss franc.

Required:

a. Prepare a trial balance in dollars for Swisco Corporation at December 31, 19x8.

b. Prepare the income statement for the year ending December 31, 19x8, and the balance sheet at that date (in dollars) for Swisco Corporation.

c. Assuming that Unisco Corporation, a U.S. firm, purchased a 75 percent ownership interest in Swisco Corporation at book value on January 1, 19x8, prepare the entry that Unisco would make at December 31, 19x8, to record its equity in Swisco's 19x8 earnings (Unisco uses the complete equity method, to account for its investments in Swisco).

Problem 12–12. The American Eagle Corporation (AEC) is a U.S. corporation which acquired its wholly owned subsidiary, the British International Corporation (BIC), on January 1, 19x1 in a transaction accounted for as a purchase.

On December 31, 19x2, BIC's trial balance in £ was as follows:

BIC
Trial Balance
December 31, 19x2
(in pounds sterling)

	Debit	Credit
Cash	50,000	
Accounts receivable	40,000	
Allowance for doubtful accounts		2,000
Inventories, December 31, 19x2 (at cost)	200,000	
Prepaid expenses	5,000	
Plant and equipment	420,000	
Accumulated depreciation, plant, and equipment		153,000
Accounts payable		25,000
Income tax payable		80,000
Notes payable, short term		40,000
Bonds payable		120,000
Due from AEC	60,000	
Capital stock		100,000
Retained earnings, January 1, 19x2		160,000
Sales		750,000
Cost of goods sold	415,000	
Depreciation expense	45,000	
Selling and administrative expenses	125,000	
Provision for income taxes	82,000	
Gain on sale of plant and equipment		12,000
Totals	1,442,000	1,442,000

The following additional information is available.

1. Certain plant and equipment acquired on January 1, 19x1, was sold on December 31, 19x2, for £30,000 and accumulated depreciation of £12,000.

2. Capital stock and bonds were issued on January 1, 19x0.

3. BIC uses the LIFO inventory valuation method. The December 31, 19x1, ending inventory was £60,000, and 19x2 purchases of inventory took place uniformly throughout the year. The December 31, 19x1, balance of £60,000 also existed on January 1, 19x1.

4. Other than the net income for 19x1, no entries were made in the Retained Earnings account of BIC since its acquisition. The Retained Earnings account at December 31, 19x1, in dollars was $207,000.

5. The Equity Adjustment from Translation had a credit balance of $100,000 at January 1, 19x2.

6. The following exchange rates prevailed on the following dates:

	Dollars per £1
January 1, 19x1	$2.10
Average for 19x1	2.20
December 31, 19x1	2.30
Average for 19x2	2.40
December 31, 19x2	2.50

7. Management determined that the functional currency of BIC is the pound sterling.

8. Revenue and expense items were realized or incurred uniformly throughout 19x2.

Required:

Prepare a working paper to convert the December 31, 19x2, trial balance of BIC from £ to U.S. dollars. Supporting schedules should be in good form.

(AICPA adapted)

Problem 12–13. On January 1, 19x8, American Shoes, Inc. (ASI), a U.S. corporation acquired Swiss Shoes, International (SSI), a Geneva-based Shoe Company. The 100 percent acquisition was accounted for as a pooling. On December 31, 19x9, SSI, which started operations on January 1, 19x5, had the following trial balance in Swiss francs:

	Debit	Credit
Cash	3,000	
Accounts receivable	40,000	
Allowance for doubtful accounts		4,000
Marketable securities	25,000	
Inventories	110,000	
Due from ASI	25,000	
Prepaid expense (advertising)	2,000	
Land (acquired January 1, 19x5)	70,000	
Buildings	100,000	
Accumulated depreciation—buildings		21,500
Equipment	220,000	
Accumulated depreciation—equipment		65,700
Cost of goods sold	210,000	
Selling and adminstrative expenses	50,000	
Depreciation expense—buildings	5,000	
Depreciation expense—equipment	18,900	
Advertising expense	5,000	
Warranty expense	20,000	
Loss on sale of equipment	8,000	
Accounts payable		60,000
Taxes payable		55,000
Obligations under warranties		12,000
Deferred income tax	500	
6% convertible debentures (issued January 1, 19x9		150,000
Common stock (issued January 1, 19x5)		100,000
Retained earnings, January 1, 19x9		31,800
Sales		490,000
Unrealized gain on marketable securities		2,000
Income tax expense	75,500	
Uncollectible accounts expense	4,100	
Totals	992,000	992,000

Additional information:

1. Inventory is valued on the FIFO basis.

2. The prepaid expense represents a two-year advertising campaign started on July 1, 19x8.

3. The marketable securities were acquired on June 30, 19x9, at a cost of SFr23,000. The parent company carries its own marketable securities at cost and does not recognize any gain in the value of marketable securities above original cost.

4. Buildings are depreciated on a straight-line basis using an estimated useful life of 20 years and no salvage value. The company uses the same depreciation method for tax purposes except that the useful life is estimated at 16 years.

5. Equipment is depreciated on a straight-line ba-

sis using an estimated useful life of 10 years and a salvage value of 10 percent of original cost.

6. The dollar balance of retained earnings on January 1, 19x9, was $15,700.

7. The Equity Adjustment from Translation Account had a credit balance of $10,000 on January 1, 19x9.

8. The income tax rate is 50 percent.

9. The following exchange rates prevailed on the dates shown below:

	Dollars per SFrI
January 1, 19x5	$0.35
December 31, 19x7	0.42
July 1, 19x8	0.45
December 31, 19x8	0.48
June 30, 19x9	0.49
March 31, 19x9	0.50
Average for 19x9	0.51
December 31, 19x9	0.52

Required:

a. Prepare a working paper to convert the December 31, 19x9, trial balance of SSI from SFr to U.S. dollars.

b. Prepare the income statement for 19x9 and the balance sheet as at December 31, 19x9, for SSI as translated into dollars using the trial balance above.

Problem 12–14. BRITCO is a foreign subsidiary (in London) of U.S. CORP. (a U.S. corporation) and has been since its incorporation in 19x1. The following are the financial statements of BRITCO for 19x8:

BRITCO
Income Statement
For Year Ending December 31, 19x8
(in millions of pounds sterling)

Sales		£ 5,000
Inventory, January 1, 19x8	£ 700	
Purchases	3,800	
	4,500	
Less: Inventory, December 31, 19x8	500	
Cost of Sales		40,000
Gross profit		1,000
Depreciation	300	
Selling, general, and administrative expenses	450	750
Pretax income		250
Income tax @ 40%		100
Net income		£ 150

BRITCO
Balance Sheet
December 31, 19x8
(in millions of £)

Assets

Current assets:		
Cash		£ 100
Accounts receivable		300
Inventories, at cost		500
Prepaid expenses		25
Total current assets		925
Long-term note receivable		75
Property, plant, and equipment		2,200
Less: Accumulated depreciation		1,200
Property, plant, and equipment, net		1,000
Total assets		£2,000

Liabilities and equity

Current liabilities:		
Accounts payable		£ 500
Notes payable		80
Accrued liabilities		20
Total current liabilities		600
Long-term debt		900
Stock holders' equity:		
Capital stock		300
Retained earnings		200
Total equity		500
Total liabilities and equity		£2,000

Additional information:

1. On January 1, 19x1, date of incorporation of BRITCO, the exchange rate was £ = $2.

2. On January 1, 19x8, the exchange rate was £1 = $2.20.

3. The average exchange rate for 19x8 was £1 = $2.35.

4. Property, plant, and equipment were purchased on January 1, 19x5, when the exchange rate was $2.30.

5. Long-term note receivable was executed on January 1, 19x8.

6. £100 of inventory on hand at year-end was purchased during the first half of 19x8 when the exchange rate was approximately £1 = $2.20.

7. Prepaid expenses represent unexpired insurance premiums which were paid on April 1, 19x8, when the exchange rate was $2.20.

8. Long-term debt was incurred on January 1, 19x8.

9. All of the capital stock was issued on date of incorporation.

10. All accounts receivable and payable and long-

term debt amounts are denominated in pounds sterling.

11. Sales, purchases, expenses (including taxes), and depreciation were evenly distributed during the year.

12. Exchange rate on December 31, 19x8, was £1 = $2.50.

13. Balance of retained earnings on January 1, 19x8, was $110.

14. Management determined that the functional currency of BRITCO is the pound sterling.

Required:

Translate the financial statements of BRITCO into U.S. dollars.

Problem 12–15. On January 1, 19x2, P Company purchased at book value 100 percent of the outstanding shares of English Company for £1,000,000 when the exchange rate was $2. per pound sterling. In the same date, P Company borrowed £1,000,000 from a bank in England. This borrowing is to be repaid three years hence and requires an interest payment of 18 percent per annum each year end.

This loan qualifies as a hedge of a net investment in a foreign entity.

For the years subsequent to the purchase, the following is provided:

On January 1, 19x5, P Company sold its investment in English Company for $2,500,000 and repaid the loan, the exchange rate on that date being $2.30.

Required:

Prepare all of the necessary entries on the books of P Company to account for its investment in the English Company using the complete equity method. For each year you should record:

a. The purchase of the investment and the proceeds of the loan (19x2 only).

b. The equity in earnings of English Company, the receipt of dividends, and the translation adjustment for the year.

c. The payment of interest on the loan (December 31).

d. The adjustment of the loan for the preparation of the annual report of P Company.

e. The sale of the Investment in English Company and the repayment of the loan (19x5 only).

[Relates to Problem 12–15]

Year	Net income of English company	Dividends received, December 31	Exchange rate, December 31	Exchange rate, Average	Equity Translation adjustment for year
19x2	£200,000	£ 0	$2.20	$2.10	$40,000 Cr.
19x3	250,000	100,000	1.80	2.00	60,000 Cr.
19x4	300,000	150,000	2.30	2.25	20,000 Dr.

Exercises and problems related to appendix—The temporal method (SFAS 8)

Exercise 12–16.

1. When translating foreign currency financial statements, which of the following items would be translated using current exchange rates?

a. Inventories carried at cost.

b. Prepaid insurance.

c. Goodwill.

d. Marketable equity securities carried at current market price.

2. When translating foreign currency financial statements, which of the following items would be translated using historical exchange rates?

a. Notes payable.

b. Long-term debt.

c. Deferred income.

d. Accrued expenses payable.

3. At what translation rates should the following

balance sheet accounts in foreign statements be translated into U.S. dollars?

		Equipment	Accumulated depreciation of equipment
a.	. . . .	Current	Current
b.	. . . .	Current	Average for year
c.	. . . .	Historical	Current
d.	. . . .	Historical	Historical

(AICPA adapted)

Exercise 12–17.

1. How should exchange gains and losses resulting from translating foreign currency financial statements into U.S. dollars be accounted for?

a. Included as an ordinary item in net earnings for the period in which the rate changes.

b. Included as an extraordinary item in net earnings for the period in which the rate changes.

c. Included in the statement of financial position as a deferred item.

d. Included as an ordinary item in net earnings for gains, but deferred for losses.

2. A material loss arising from the devaluation of the currency of a country in which a corporation was conducting foreign operations through a branch would be reflected in the company's year-end financial statements as—

a. An asset to be subsequently offset against gains from foreign currency revaluations.

b. A factor in determining earnings before extraordinary items in the year during which the loss occurred.

c. An extraordinary item on the earnings statement of the year during which the loss occurred.

d. A prior period adjustment unless the operations of the foreign branch had begun during the year in which the loss occurred.

3. When preparing combined or consolidated financial statements for a domestic and a foreign company, the account balances expressed in the foreign currency must be translated into the domestic currency. The objective of the translation process is to obtain currency valuations that—

a. Are conservative.

b. Reflect current monetary equivalents.

c. Are expressed in domestic units of measure and are in conformity with domestic generally accepted accounting principles.

d. Reflect the translated account at its unexpired historical cost.

4. A company is translating account balances from another currency into dollars for its December 31, 19x5, statement of financial position and its calendar year 19x5 earnings statement and statement of changes in financial position. The average exchange rate for the year 19x5 should be used to translate—

a. Cash at December 31, 19x5.

b. Land purchased in 19x3.

c. Retained earnings at January 1, 19x5.

d. Sales for 19x5.

5. A foreign exchange gain that is a consequence of translation should be—

a. Included in net income in the period it occurs.

b. Deferred and amortized over a period *not* to exceed 40 years.

c. Deferred until a subsequent year when a loss occurs and offset against that loss.

d. Included as a separate item in the equity section of the balance sheet.   (AICPA adapted)

Exercise 12–18.

1. The France Company owns a foreign subsidiary with 2,400,000 local currency units (LCU) of property, plant, and equipment before accumulated depreciation at December 31, 19x8. Of this amount, 1,500,000 LCU were acquired in 19x6 when the rate of exchange was 1.5 LCU to $1, and 900,000 LCU were acquired in 19x7 when the rate of exchange was 1.6 LCU to $1. The rate of exchange in effect at December 31, 19x8, was 1.9 LCU to $1. The weighted average of exchange rates which were in effect during 19x8 was 1.8 LCU to $1. Assuming that the property, plant, and equipment are depreciated using the straight-line method over a 10-year period with no salvage value, how much depreciation expense relating to the foreign subsidiary's property, plant, and equipment should be charged in France's income statement for 19x8?

a. $126,316.

b. $133,333.

c. $150,000.

d. $156,250.

2. On January 1, 19x8, the Ben Company formed a foreign subsidiary. On February 15, 19x8, Ben's subsidiary purchased 100,000 local currency units (LCU) of inventory. 25,000 LCU of the original inventory purchased on February 15, 19x8, made up the entire inventory on December 31, 19x8. The exchange rates were 2.2 LCU to $1 from January 1, 19x8, to June 30, 19x8, and 2 LCU to $1 from July 1, 19x8, to December 31, 1978. The December 31, 19x8, inventory balance for Ben's foreign subsidiary should be translated into U.S. dollars of —

a. $10,500.

b. $11,364.

c. $11,905.

d. $12,500.

3. Seed Company has receivable from a foreign customer which is payable in the local currency of the foreign customer. On December 31, 19x6, this receivable was appropriately included in the accounts receivable section of Seed's balance sheet at $450,000. When the receivable was collected on January 4, 19x7, Seed converted the local currency of the foreign customer into $440,000. Seed also owns a foreign subsidiary in which exchange gains of $45,000 resulted as a consequence of translation in 19x7. What amount, if any, should be included as an exchange gain or loss in Seed's 19x7 consolidated income statement?

a. $0.

b. $10,000 exchange loss.

c. $35,000 exchange gain.

d. $45,000 exchange gain.   (AICPA adapted)

Exercise 12–19. The following is the translated balance of the Foreign Subsidiary at the end of year 1 when 1 FC = $4.

	Foreign	U.S.
Cash	FC 1,000	$ 4,000
Land	2,000	8,000
	FC 3,000	$12,000
Capital stock	FC 1,000	$ 4,000
Retained earnings	2,000	8,000
	FC 3,000	$12,000

Required:

Assuming no activity during the years convert the balance sheets of the Foreign Subsidiary at—

a. End of year 2 when 1 FC = $5.

b. End of year 3 when 1 FC = $4.50.

In each case give the journal entry on the parent's books to reflect the gain or loss on translation in the Investment in Subsidiary account.

Exercise 12–20.

1. Fore Company had a $30,000 exchange loss resulting from the translation of the accounts of its wholly owned foreign subsidiary for the year ended December 31, 19x8. Fore also had a receivable from a foreign customer which was payable in the local currency of the foreign customer. On December 31, 19x7, this receivable for 500,000 local currency units (LCU) was appropriately included in the accounts receivable section of Fore's balance sheet at $245,000. When the receivable was collected on February 5, 19x8, the exchange rate was 2 LCU to $1. What amount should be included as an exchange gain or loss in the 19x8 consolidated income statement of Fore Company and its wholly owned foreign subsidiary as a result of the above?

a. $5,000 exchange gain.

b. $20,000 exchange loss.

c. $25,000 exchange loss.

d. $30,000 exchange loss.

2. The Clark Company owns a foreign subsidiary which had net income for the year ended December 31, 19x5, of 4,800,000 local currency units (LCU) which was appropriately translated into $800,000. On October 15, 19x5, when the rate of exchange was 5.7 LCU to $1, the foreign subsidiary paid a dividend to Clark of 2,400,000 LCU. The dividend represented the net income of the foreign subsidiary for the six months ended June 30, 19x5, during which time the weighted average of exchange rates was 5.8 LCU to $1. The rate of exchange in effect at December 31, 19x5, was 5.9 LCU to $1. What rate of exchange should be used to translate the dividend for the December 31, 19x5, financial statements?

a. 5.7 LCU to $1.

b. 5.8 LCU to $1.

c. 5.9 LCU to $1.

d. 6.0 LCU to $1.

3. The Dease Company owns a foreign subsidiary with 3,600,000 local currency units (LCU) of property, plant, and equipment before accumulated depreciation at December 31, 19x5. Of this amount, 2,400,000 LCU were acquired in 19x3 when the rate of exchange was 1.6 LCU to $1, and 1,200,000 LCU were acquired in 19x4 when the rate of exchange was 1.8 LCU to $1. The rate of exchange in effect at December 31, 19x5, was 2 LCU to $1. The weighted average of exchange rates which were in effect during 19x5 was 1.92 LCU to $1. Assuming that the property, plant, and equipment are depreciated using the straight-line method over a 10-year period with *no* salvage value, how much depreciation expense relating to the foreign subsidiary's property, plant, and equipment should be charged in Dease's income statement for 19x5?

a. $180,000.

b. $187,500.

c. $200,000.

d. $216,667.

4. The Marvin Company has a receivable from a foreign customer which is payable in the local currency of the foreign customer. The amount receivable for 900,000 local currency units (LCU), has been translated into $315,000 on Marvin's December 31, 19x5, balance sheet. On January 15, 19x6, the receivable was collected in full when the exchange rate was 3 LCU to $1. What journal entry should Marvin make to record the collection of this receivable?

a. Cash 300,000
    Accounts Receivable   300,000

b. Cash 300,000
    Exchange loss 15,000
    Accounts Receivable   315,000

c. Cash 300,000
    Deferred Exchange loss 15,000
    Accounts Receivable   315,000

d. Cash 315,000
    Accounts Receivable   315,000

                            (AICPA adapted)

Exercise 12–21.

1. Certain balance sheet accounts in a foreign subsidiary of the Brogan Company at December 31, 19x7, have been translated into U.S. dollars as follows:

	Translated at	
	Current rates	Historical rates
Marketable equity securities carried at cost	$100,000	$110,000
Marketable equity securities carried at current market price	120,000	125,000
Inventories carried at cost	130,000	132,000
Inventories carried at net realizable value	80,000	$184,000
	$430,000	$451,000

What amount should be shown in Brogan's balance sheet at December 31, 19x7, as a result of the above information?

a. $430,000.
b. $436,000.
c. $442,000.
d. $451,000.

2. When translating an amount for fixed assets shown on the statement of financial position of a foreign subsidiary, the appropriate rate of translation is the—

a. Current exchange rate.
b. Average exchange rate for the current year.
c. Historical exchange rate.

d. Average exchange rate over the life of each fixed asset.

3. A wholly owned foreign subsidiary of Union Corporation has certain expense accounts for the year ended December 31, 19x9, stated in local currency units (LCU) as follows:

	LCU
Amortization of patent (related patent was acquired January 1, 19x7)	40,000
Provision for doubtful accounts	60,000
Rent	100,000

The exchange rates at various dates are as follows:

	Dollar equivalent of 1 LCU
December 31, 19x9	$.20
Average for the year ended December 31, 19x9	.22
January 1, 19x7	.25

What total dollar amount should be included in Union's income statement to reflect the above expenses for the year ended December 31, 19x9?

a. $40,000.
b. $42,000.
c. $44,000.
d. $45,200.

4. The Jem Company used the monetary-nonmonetary approach when translating foreign currency amounts at December 31, 19x5. At that time, Jem had foreign subsidiaries with 1,500,000 local currency units (LCU) in long-term receivables and 2,400,000 LCU in long-term debt. The rate of exchange in effect when the specific transactions occurred involving those foreign currency amounts was 2 LCU to $1. The rate of exchange in effect at December 31, 19x5, was 1.5 LCU to $1. The translation of the above foreign currency amounts into U.S. dollars would result in long-term receivables and long-term debt, respectively, of—

a. $750,000 and $1,200,000.
b. $750,000 and $1,600,000.
c. $1,000,000 and $1,200,000.
d. $1,000,000 and $1,600,000.   (AICPA adapted)

Exercise 12–22.

On November 28, 19x6, merchandise was purchased by a Dutch branch for 50,000 Florins when the rate was 40 cents. The merchandise was on hand at December 31, 19x6, when the market was 52,000 FL and the rate was 38 cents.

Required:

Valuation of inventory on the subsidiary's statements at December 31, 19x6, and translated dollar amount at that date under the lower-of-cost-or-market rule.

Exercise 12–23. Assume that the inventory is stated at the lower of cost or market, and that the component makeup of the inventory at December 31, 19x6, is as follows:

Item	Purchase date	Cost	Market	Lower of cost or market
AA . . .	11/x6	FC 90,000	FC 80,000	FC 80,000
AB . . .	12/x6	140,000	140,000	140,000
AC . . .	5/x6	55,000	50,000	50,000
AD . . .	2/x6	50,000	55,000	50,000
AE . . .	7/x6	130,000	150,000	130,000
AF . . .	9/x6	50,000	60,000	50,000
				FC 500,000

Required:

Translate the inventory into U.S. dollars using the standards established by *SFAS 8.*

Current rate at balance sheet date 1 $ = FC 1.40.
Rate at date of acquisition (historical rate) 1 $ = FC 1.20.

Exercise 12–24. A British subsidiary of an American corporation has the following components of inventory of December 31, 19x8 (in millions of £):

[Relates to Exercise 12–24]

Item	Purchase date	Cost	Market	Lower of cost or market	Exchange rate at purchase date
A	11/x8	90	80	80	$2.50
B	12/x8	140	140	140	2.50
C	5/x8	55	50	50	2.20
D	2/x8	50	55	50	2.20
E	9/x8	180	210	180	2.50
				£ 500	

Exchange rate at December 31, 19x8, was $2.50.

Required:

Translate the inventory into U.S. dollars using *SFAS 8* standards.

Problem 12–25. The trial balance of Swisco Corporation, a Swiss corporation at December 31, 19x8, is shown below (in Swiss francs).

	Debit	Credit
Cash	50,000	
Accounts receivable	100,000	
Property, plant, and equipment, net	800,000	
Depreciation expense	100,000	
Other expenses (including taxes) .	200,000	
Inventory, January 1, 19x8	150,000	
Sales		2,000,000
Allowance for doubtful accounts .		10,000
Accounts payable		80,000
Notes payable		20,000
Capital stock		100,000
Retained earnings, January 1, 19x8		190,000
Purchases	1,000,000	
	2,400,000	2,400,000

Additional information:

1. Swisco uses the periodical inventory system as well as the FIFO method for measuring inventory and cost of good sold. On December 31, inventory on hand was SFr120,000. It is carried at cost.

2. The capital stock was issued six years ago when the company was established, at which time the exchange rate was SFr1 = 30 cents. Plant and equipment was purchased five years ago when the exchange rate was SFr1 = 35 cents the note payable was made out to a local bank at the same time.

3. Revenue and expense items were realized or incurred uniformly throughout 19x8. However, inventory on hand on December 31, 19x8, was purchased throughout the second half of 19x8.

4. The retained earnings balance in the December 31, 19x7, balance sheets (in dollars) of Swisco Corporation was $61,000, and the inventory balance was $47,000.

5. The spot rates for SFr in 19x8 were as follows:

January 1, 19x8	32 cents
Average for 19x8	37
Average for second half of 19x8	36
December 31, 19x8	38

Required:

a. Prepare a trial balance in dollars for Swisco Corporation at December 31, 19x8.

b. Prepare the income statement for the year ending December 31, 19x8, and the balance sheet at that date (in dollars) for Swisco Corporation.

c. Assuming that Unisco Corporation, a U.S. firm, purchased a 75 percent ownership interest in Swisco Corporation at book value on January 1, 19x8, prepare the entry that Unisco would make at December 31, 19x8, to record its equity in Swisco's 19x8 earnings (Unisco uses the complete equity method to account for its investments in Swisco).

Problem 12–26. The American Eagle Corporation (AEC) is a U.S. corporation with international operations mainly in Europe. On January 1, 19x1, AEC acquired British International Corporation (BIC), a London-based corporation with international operations also in Europe. The 100 percent acquisition was accounted for as a purchase. On December 31, 19x0 BIC had the following balance sheet in pounds sterling (£).

BRITISH INTERNATIONAL CORPORATION
Balance Sheet
December 31, 19x0
(in pounds sterling)

Assets

Current assets:

Cash	£ 6,000
Accounts receivable	10,000
Inventories	60,000
Total current assets	76,000
Plant and equipment	400,000
Accumulated depreciation	(80,000)
Total assets	£396,000

Liabilities and Equity

Accounts payable	£ 40,000
Bonds payable	120,000
Capital stock	100,000
Retained earnings	136,000
Total liabilities and equity	£396,000

On December 31, 19x2, BIC's trial balance in £ was as follows:

BIC
Trial Balance
December 31, 19x2
(in pounds sterling)

	Debit	Credit
Cash	50,000	
Accounts receivable	40,000	
Allowance for doubtful accounts .		2,000
Inventories, December 31, 19x2 (at cost)	200,000	
Prepaid expenses	5,000	
Plant and equipment	420,000	
Accumulated depreciation, plant and equipment		153,000
Accounts payable		25,000
Income tax payable		80,000
Notes payable, short term		40,000
Bonds payable		120,000
Due from AEC	60,000	
Capital stock		100,000
Retained earnings, January 1, 19x2		160,000
Sales—domestic		350,000
Sales—foreign		400,000
Cost of goods sold	415,000	
Depreciation expense	45,000	
Selling and administrative expenses	125,000	
Provision for income taxes	82,000	
Gain on sale of plant and equipment		12,000
Totals	1,442,000	1,442,000

The following additional information is available.

1. Certain plant and equipment acquired on January 1, 19x1, was sold on December 31, 19x2, for £30,000 and accumulated depreciation of £12,000.

2. Depreciation of plant and equipment is computed on a straight-line basis and an estimated useful life of 10 years for both old and new plant and equipment. On December 31, 19x1, new equipment was purchased at a cost of £50,000.

3. All of BIC's foreign sales are made to its parent, AEC, and billed in U.S. dollars. The reciprocal accounts on AEC's books show total 19x2 purchases as $942,000 and balance due to BIC on December 31, 19x2, as $141,000.

4. The prepaid expenses were incurred on December 31, 19x1.

5. Capital stock and bonds were issued on January 1, 19x0.

6. BIC uses the LIFO inventory valuation method. The December 31, 19x1, ending inventory was £60,000, and 19x2 purchases of inventory took place uniformly throughout the year. The De-

cember 31, 19x1, balance of £60,000 also existed on January 1, 19x1.

7. Other than the net income for 19x1, no entries were made in the Retained Earnings account of BIC since its acquisition. The Retained Earnings account at December 31, 19x1, in dollars was $337,000.

8. The following exchange rates prevailed on the following dated:

	Dollars per £1
January 1, 19x1	$2.10
Average for 19x1	2.20
December 31, 19x1	2.30
Average for 19x2	2.40
December 31, 19x2	2.50

Required:

Prepare a working paper to convert the December 31, 19x2, trial balance of BIC from £ to U.S. dollars. Supporting schedules should be in good form.

(AICPA adapted)

Problem 12–27. On January 1, 19x8, American Shoes, Inc. (ASI), a U.S. corporation acquired Swiss Shoes, January 1, International (SSI), a Geneva-based Shoe Company. The 100 percent acquisition was accounted for as a pooling. On December 31, 19x9, SSI, which started operations on January 1, 19x5, had the following trial balance in Swiss francs:

	Debit	Credit
Cash	3,000	
Accounts receivable	40,000	
Allowance for doubtful accounts		4,000
Marketable securities	25,000	
Inventories (raw materials and finished goods)	110,000	
Due from ASI	25,000	
Prepaid expense (advertising)	2,000	
Land (acquired January 1, 19x5)	70,000	
Buildings	100,000	
Accumulated depreciation—buildings		21,500
Equipment	220,000	
Accumulated depreciation—equipment		65,700
Cost of goods sold	210,000	
Selling and administrative expenses	50,000	
Depreciation expense—buildings	5,000	
Depreciation expense—equipment	18,900	
Advertising expense	5,000	
Warranty expense	20,000	
Loss on sale of equipment	8,000	
Loss due to decline in value of ending inventory	18,000	
Accounts payable		60,000
Taxes payable		55,000
Obligations under warranties		12,000
Deferred income tax	500	
6% convertible debentures (issued January 1, 19x9)		150,000
Common stock (issued January 1, 19x5)		31,800
Sales		490,000
Unrealized gain on marketable securities		2,000
Allowance for decline in inventory valuation		18,000
Income tax expense	75,500	
Uncollectible accounts expense	4,100	
Totals	1,010,000	1,010,000

Additional information:

1. Inventory is valued on the FIFO basis. Only finished goods which had a cost of SFr50,000 was costed at the lower-of-cost-or-market (market value was SFr32,000). The January 1, 19x9, inventory was acquired evenly throughout 19x8. Purchases during 19x9 were made evenly throughout the year.

2. The amount due from ASI represents an advance from SSI made on October 1, 19x9. The amount will be collected in SFr.

3. The prepaid expense represents a two-year advertising campaign started on July 1, 19x8.

4. The marketable securities were acquired on

June 30, 19x9, at a cost of SFr23,000. The parent company carries its own marketable securities at cost and does not recognize any gain in the value of marketable securities above original cost.

5. The balance in the buildings account resulted from the following transactions:

Acquired January 1, 19x5 . . . .   SFr80,000
Acquired July 1, 19x8 . . . .   SFr20,000

Buildings are depreciated on a straight-line basis using an estimated useful life of 20 years and no salvage value. The company uses the same depreciation method for tax purposes except that the useful life is estimated at 16 years.

6. The balance in the equipment account resulted from the following transactions:

Acquired January 1, 19x5	SFr150,000
Acquired December 31, 19x8	SFr 50,000
Acquired March 31, 19x9	SFr 40,000
	240,000
Sold July 1, (from equipment acquired January 1, 19x5)	20,000
Ending balance December 31, 19x9 . . .	220,000

Equipment is depreciated on a straight-line basis using an estimated useful life of 10 years and a salvage value of 10 percent of original cost.

7. The dollar balance of retained earnings on January 1, 19x9, was $15,700.

8. The January 1, 19x9, credit balance of SFr8,875 in the deferred tax account has a translated dollar value of $3,460 and is based on the net change method. The following timing differences have occurred in 19x9:

a. The unrealized gain on marketable securities is not recognized for tax purposes. However, the unrealized gain is included in book income.

b. Taxable income in 19x9 includes SFr10,000 gross profit on past installment sales which was recognized as income for book purposes in the year of sale.

c. The depreciation expense on buildings for tax purposes is greater than the expense for book purposes. See 5 above.

d. SSI instituted on January 1, 19x9, a product warranty program. Related expenses are recognized for tax purposes only when paid.

e. The income tax rate is 50 percent.

9. The following exchange rates prevailed on the dates as follows:

	Dollars per SFrl
January 1, 19x5	$0.35
December 31, 19x7	0.42
July 1, 19x8	0.45
December 31, 19x8	0.48
June 30, 19x9	0.49
March 31, 19x9	0.50
Average for 19x9	0.51
December 31, 19x9	0.52

Required:

a. Prepare a working paper to convert the December 31, 19x9, trial balance of SSI from SFr to U.S. dollars. Supporting schedules and necessary adjustments should be in good form.

b. Prepare the income statement for 19x9 and the balance sheet as at December 31, 19x9, for SSI as translated into dollars using the trial balance above.

Problem 12–28. BRITCO is a foreign subsidiary (in London) of U.S. CORP (a U.S. corporation) and has been since its incorporation in 19x1. The following are the financial statements of BRITCO for 19x8:

BRITCO
Income Statement
For Year Ending December 31, 19x8
(in millions of pounds sterling)

Sales		£5,000
Inventory, January 1,19x8	£ 700	
Purchases	3,800	
	4,500	
Less: Inventory, December 31, 19x8 . .	500	
Cost of sales		4,000
Gross profit		1,000
Depreciation	300	
Selling, general, and administrative expenses	450	750
Pretax income		250
Income tax @ 40%		100
Net income		£ 150

BRITCO
Balance Sheet
At December 31, 19x8
(in millions of £)

Assets

Current assets:

Cash	£ 100
Accounts receivable	300
Inventories, at cost	500
Prepaid expenses	25
Total current assets	925
Long-term note receivable	75
Property, plant, and equipment	2,200
Less: Accumulated depreciation	1,200
Property, plant, and equipment, net	1,000
Total assets	£2,000

Liabilities and Equity

Current liabilities:

Accounts payable	£ 500
Notes payable	80
Accrued liabilities	20
Total current liabilities	600
Long-term debt	900

Stockholders' equity:

Capital stock	300
Retained earnings	200
Total stockholders' equity	500
Total liabilities and equity	£2,000

Additional information:

1. On January 1, 19x1, date of incorporation of BRITCO, the exchange rate was £1 = $2.
2. On January 1, 19x8, the exchange rate was £1 = $2.20.
3. On July 1, 19x8, the exchange rate was £1 = $2.50.
4. Property, plant, and equipment were purchased on January 1, 19x5, when the exchange rate was $2.30.
5. Long-term note receivable was executed on January 1, 19x8.
6. £100 of inventory on hand at year-end was purchased during the first half of 19x8 when the exchange rate was approximately £1 = $2.20.
7. Prepaid expenses represent unexpired insurance premiums which were paid on April 1, 19x8, when the exchange rate was $2.20.
8. Long-term debt was incurred on January 1, 19x8.
9. All of the capital stock was issued on date of incorporation.
10. All accounts receivable and payable and long-term debt amounts are denominated in pounds sterling.
11. Sales, purchases, expenses (including taxes), and depreciation were evenly distributed during the year.
12. Exchange rate on December 31, 19x8, was £1 = $2.50 which was also the average for the second half of the year. The average for the first half of the year was £1 = $2.20.
13. Balance of retained earnings on January 1, 19x8, was $110.

Required:

Translate the financial statements of BRITCO into U.S. dollars in accordance with the provisions of *SFAS 8.*

Problem 12–29. On January 1, 19x5, the Franklin Company formed a foreign subsidiary which issued all of its currently outstanding common stock on that date. Selected captions from the balance sheets, all of which are shown in local currency units (LCU), are as follows:

	December 31	
	19x6	*19x5*
Accounts receivable (net of allowance for uncollectible accounts of 2,200 LCU at December 31, 19x6, and 2,000 LCU at December 31, 19x5)	40,000 LCU	35,000 LCU
Inventories, at cost	80,000	75,000
Property, plant, and equipment (net of allowance for accumulated depreciation of 31,000 LCU at December 31, 19x6, and 14,000 LCU at December 31, 19x5)	163,000	150,000
Long-term debt	100,000	120,000
Common stock, authorized 10,000 shares, par value 10 LCU per share, issued and outstanding 5,000 shares at December 31, 19x6, and December 31, 19x5	50,000	50,000

Additional information:

1. Exchange rates are as follows:

January 1, 19x5–July 31, 19x5	2 LCU to $1
August 1, 19x5–October 31, 19x5	1.8 LCU to $1
November 1, 19x5–June 30, 19x6	1.7 LCU to $1
July 1, 19x6–December 31, 19x6	1.5 LCU to $1
Average monthly rate for 19x5	1.9 LCU to $1
Average monthly rate for 19x6	1.6 LCU to $1

2. An analysis of the accounts receivable balance is as follows:

	19x6	19x5
Accounts receivable:		
Balance at beginning of year	37,000 LCU	— LCU
Sales (36,000 LCU per month in 19x6 and 31,000 LCU per month in 19x5) . . .	432,000	372,000
Collections	423,600	334,000
Write-offs (May 19x6 and December 19x5)	3,200	1,000
Balance at end of year	42,200 LCU	37,000 LCU
Allowance for uncollectible accounts:		
Balance at beginning of year	2,000 LCU	— LCU
Provision for uncollectible accounts	3,400	3,000
Write-offs (May 19x6 and December 19x5)	3,200	1,000
Balance at end of year	2,200 LCU	2,000 LCU

3. An analysis of inventories, for which the first-in, first-out (FIFO) inventory method is used, is as follows:

	19x6	19x5
Inventory at beginning of year	75,000 LCU	— LCU
Purchases (June 19x6 and June 19x5)	335,000	375,000
Goods available for sale	410,000	375,000
Inventory at end of year	80,000	75,000
Cost of goods sold . . .	330,000 LCU	300,000 LCU

4. On January 1, 19x5, Franklin's foreign subsidiary purchased land for 24,000 LCU and plant and equipment for 140,000 LCU On July 4, 19x6, additional equipment was purchased for 30,000 LCU. Plant and equipment is being depreciated on a straight-line basis over a 10-year period with no salvage value. A full year's depreciation is taken in the year of purchase.

5. On January 15, 19x5, 7 percent bonds with a face value of 120,000 LCU were sold. These bonds mature on January 15, 19y1, and interest is paid semiannually on July 15 and January 15. The first payment was made on January 15, 19x6.

Required:

Prepare a schedule translating the selected captions above into U.S. dollars at December 31, 19x6, and December 31, 19x5, respectively. Show supporting computations in good form.   (AICPA adapted)

13

Segment reporting by diversified enterprises

OVERVIEW

In recent decades, a growing number of companies have diversified their operations into a variety of related and unrelated industry areas. This increase in the diversity of overall operations has made it increasingly difficult for financial analysts and other users of financial statements to analyse and interpret them.

The reasons for these difficulties are not hard to find. Different industry segments can have greatly differing growth potentials, capital requirements, and profitability characteristics. Consider, for example, a company composed of a bakery, a recreational vehicle division, and an electronic instrument division. The bakery division operates in a stable industry, has modest capital requirements, and its profitability is limited because of fiercely competitive conditions. The recreational vehicle division is highly cyclical depending, as it does, on the availability of discretionary income by its buying public. It is also capital intensive, and because of large fixed costs its profitability is subject to wide fluctuations. The electronic instrument division operates in a high demand, high growth, technology area of great promise. Capital requirements are modest, and high demand ensures significant profitability. The resulting return on investment is impressive. However, its relatively small size will prevent it from making a significant contribution to overall company profitability for some years to come.

Imagine now the task of the analyst who wants to evaluate this company's growth potential and future profitability on the basis of financial statements which combine all three divisions. Stagnation in one division may mask the growth of another; the profits of one may obscure the losses of another. The only meaningful solution to this problem is disaggregation of total enterprise financial data or segment reporting, and over the years the demand for this type of disclosure has grown and that demand is now being increasingly met.

This chapter examines the accounting standards and the reporting requirements which have evolved and which govern the reporting of segmental data.

The evolving interest in segmental reporting

Original interest in diversified reporting was sparked by hearings of the Subcommittee on Antitrust and Monopoly of the Senate Committee on the Judiciary held in the mid 1960s concerned with economic concentration in American industry. This was followed by increasing attention being accorded to the subject by the SEC and the accounting profession.

Interest in the subject of reporting by diversified companies has sparked research efforts into the types of disclosures which are necessary and feasible and the problems related thereto.[1] The most extensive research effort was that undertaken by Professor R. K. Mautz.[2] In 1974, the FASB published an extensive Discussion Memorandum on the subject. Subsequently, in 1976, the FASB issued *Statement of Financial Accounting Standards 14*, "Financial Reporting for Segments of a Business Enterprise."

SEC reporting requirements

The SEC took an early lead in requiring line of business information.

In 1969, the SEC amended its registration forms S-1 and S-7 under the 1933 Act, and Form 10 under the 1934 Act. The effect of the amendment was to include a requirement for comprehensive lines of business information to be disclosed by registrants who, with their subsidiaries, are engaged in more than one line of business.

In 1970, the Commission revised its annual report form (Form 10-K) to include a requirement of annual reporting of line of business information identical with the requirements referred to above.

In 1974, these reporting requirements were extended to annual reports to security holders of companies filing with the SEC.

Following the promulgation of *SFAS 14*, the SEC has substantially conformed its reporting requirements to those contained in the *FASB Standard*. However, as has been its policy and practice, the SEC extended the requirements beyond those of the FASB whenever and wherever it determined that the required disclosure did not go far enough to meet the needs of investors and others.

Thus, an additional narrative description is called for in Form S-K covering the registrant's business by reportable segments including information on competition, dependence on a few customers, principal products and services, backlog, sources and availability of raw materials, patents, research and development costs, number of employees, and the seasonality of the business.

Generally, *SFAS 14* requires reporting on only two years while in the 1980 revision of Form 10-K the SEC requires information for a three-year period. Other areas where the SEC requires additional disclosures will be identified later in this chapter.

---

[1] See Morton Backer and Walter B. McFarland, *External Reporting for Segments of a Business* (New York: National Association of Accountants, 1968). Also see Robert T. Sprouse, "Diversified Views about Diversified Companies," *Journal of Accounting Research* 7, no. 1 (Spring 1969): 137–59; and A. Rappaport and E. H. Lerner, A *Framework for Financial Reporting by Diversified Companies* (New York: National Association of Accountants, 1969).

[2] R. K. Mautz, *Financial Reporting by Diversified Companies* (New York: Financial Executives Research Foundation, 1968).

FASB *SFAS 14,* "FINANCIAL REPORTING FOR SEGMENTS OF A BUSINESS ENTERPRISE"

SFAS 14 (hereafter also referred to as "the *Statement*"), which was issued in 1976, represents the culmination of a project which had been under consideration by the FASB for over three years. It is the authoritative pronouncement on the subject, and most of the discussion in this chapter will be based on it. *SFAS 21* amended *SFAS 14* to exclude nonpublic enterprises from its requirements.[3] *SFAS 19* exempts interim information from the disclosure requirements of *SFAS 14*. Segment information *may* be included in interim reports on an elective basis, and if so included must be consistent with segment reporting requirements.

OBJECTIVES OF SEGMENT DISCLOSURE

In the view of the FASB, financial information about business segments will "assist financial statement users in analyzing and understanding the enterprise's financial statements by permitting better assessment of the enterprise's past performance and future prospects."

APPLICABLE ACCOUNTING STANDARDS

In general, segment information should be based on the totals of consolidated financial statements, and thus the principles governing consolidations are those to be used for segmental reporting. For example, a subsidiary acquired under the purchase method would be included in segment disclosures at amount shown in consolidation and not at the amounts appearing on the subsidiary's books. Segmental accounting standards apply as well to companies whose segments are divisions rather than subsidiaries.

Transactions between segments are not to be eliminated for purposes of segment disclosures with the exception of intersegment loans, advances, and related interest which should generally be excluded from segment assets and revenues.

UNCONSOLIDATED INVESTMENTS

Segmental disclosures are not required for unconsolidated subsidiaries or other investees accounted for by the equity method except that, in addition to information now required by *APB Opinion 18*, the industry and geographic area (i.e., foreign and domestic) in which such entities operate should also be disclosed. Segmental disclosures are, however, required when complete (rather than mere capsule) financial statements of investees accounted under the equity method are presented.

AREAS COVERED BY SEGMENTAL DISCLOSURES

Under the provisions of *SFAS 14* an enterprise may have to disclose data for one or more of the following areas:

---

[3]*SFAS 21* defines a nonpublic enterprise as "an enterprise other than one (a) whose debt or equity securities trade in a public market or a foreign or domestic stock exchange or in the over the counter market. . . or (b) that is required to file financial statements with the SEC.

Operations in different industries.

Domestic and foreign operations.

Export sales.

Major customers.

Whether or not an enterprise must report on one or more of these areas is determined by the application of specific tests for each area as discussed below.

OPERATIONS IN DIFFERENT INDUSTRIES

The first step in determining whether an enterprise must report its operations in different industries is to identify the industry segments in which it operates. Basically, a reportable segment is a significant component of an enterprise which provides related products and services primarily to unaffiliated customers.

Selecting the method of identifying separate industry segments is the most basic, yet one of the most difficult problems in segmental reporting. The *Statement* is relatively flexible in its prescriptions for the segmentation of a company's business. It recognizes that no single set of characteristics is universally applicable and concludes that "the determination of an enterprise's industry segments must depend to a considerable extent on the judgment of the management of the enterprise."

While the Standard Industrial Classification (SIC) system may provide guidance in grouping an enterprise's products and services by industry lines, they are not in themselves suitable in determining industry segments for purposes of the *Statement*. A good place to start with the segmentation process is a company's existing profit centers, i.e., the smallest unit of activity for which revenues and expenses information is accumulated for internal planning and control purposes. But judgment may indicate that in some cases profit centers must be disaggregated into smaller groups of related products and services while in other cases it is advisable to combine related units of activity into one industry segment.

Other factors which should be considered in determining whether products and services are related or unrelated include:

The nature of the products: Do they have similar purposes or end uses?

The nature of the production process: Are there shared or interchangeable raw materials or production facilities and equipment?

Markets and marketing methods: Are there similar customers or marketing organizations?

The ultimate determination of separate industry segments should be supportable on the basis that the information set forth achieves the objective of providing information on those separate and distinct lines of business which are subject to different risks, rates of profitability, and prospects for the future.

The *Statement* contains specific materiality standards for determining "reportable" industry segments once the segments of a diversified company have been identified.

Revenue test

An industry segment is reportable if its revenue is 10 percent or more of the combined revenue of all industry segments. Revenue is defined to include intersegment sales and transfers. Interest, inclusive of interest on interseg ment trade receivables, is included in the revenue test if the assets on which the interest is earned are included in that segment's identifiable assets. How ever, interest on intersegment loans and advances is not to be included in revenue for this purpose except for interest of a segment the operations of which are primarily of a financial nature.

Example of identification of reportable segments by the revenue test. Assume that Diverso Company has segments with sales as follows (in mil lions of dollars):

	Segments					Total	Elimi- nation	Consolidated
	A	B	C	D	E			
Sales to unaffiliated outsiders	30	30	30	200	40	330		330
Intersegment sales	10	20		80		110	(110)	—
Total sales	40	50	30	280	40	440	(110)	330

The bench mark for the 10 percent test of revenues is $44 (10 percent of total sales of $440). Consequently, segments B and D meet the sales test because their sales exceed the bench mark sales amount and are conse quently reportable.

Operating profit test

For purposes of this test, *operating profit* is defined as an industry segment's revenue minus all operating expenses. Operating profit includes expenses that relate to intersegment sales or transfers and expenses allocated among segments on a reasonable basis. Excluded from the computation of operat ing profit are revenues earned at the corporate level, general corporate ex penses, interest expense (except for financial segments), domestic and for eign income taxes, income or loss from equity investees, gain or loss on discontinued operations, extraordinary items, minority interest, and the cu mulative effect of an accounting change. Intersegment interest expenses and revenues of an industry segment that is primarily financial in nature are included in determining that segment's operating profit or loss.

An industry segment is reportable if the absolute amount of its operating profit or loss is 10 percent or more of the *greater,* in absolute amount, of (1) the combined operating profits of all industry segments that *did not* in cur an operating loss or (2) the combined operating loss of all industry seg ments that *did* incur an operating loss.

Example of identification of reportable segments by the operating profit test.
Assume that Diverso Company has segments with operating profits and losses as follows (in millions of dollars):

	Segments					Corporate administration	Consolidated
	A	B	C	D	E		
Operating profit (loss) . . .	(8)	(40)	8	75	5		40
Equity investment income .					10	10	20
Corporate expenses						(20)	(20)
Interest						(10)	(10)
Totals	(8)	(40)	8	75	15	(20)	30

To determine the bench mark for the profit test we first add up the profits of all segments which did report a profit and the losses of all segments which reported a loss as follows (in millions of dollars):

Segment	Profits	Losses
A		8
B		40
C	8	
D	75	
E	5	—
Totals	88	48

Thus, the bench mark for determining reportable segments under the operating profits test is 10 percent of $88 or $8.8 million. Accordingly, segments B (with a $40 million loss) and D (with a $75 million profit) are reportable. All other segments have operating profits or losses lower than $8.8 million and are not reportable under this test.

Asset test

An industry segment is reportable if its identifiable assets are 10 percent or more of the combined identifiable assets of all industry segments. Identifiable assets include tangible and intangible assets (inclusive of goodwill) used exclusively by an industry segment and an allocated portion of assets used jointly by two or more industry segments. They exclude assets maintained for general corporate purposes and intersegment loans, advances, or investments, except for those of a financial segment which are included. Asset valuation allowances, such as allowance for doubtful accounts, accumulated depreciation, and marketable securities valuation allowances, should be taken into account in computing the amount of an industry segment's identifiable assets.

Example of identification of reportable segments by the asset test. Assume that Diverso Company has segments with identifiable assets as follows (in millions of dollars):

		Segments				Corporate	Total	Elimi-nations	Consoli-dated
	A	B	C	D	E				
Identifiable assets	30	40	60	330	40		500		500
Investments (intersegment)					50	50	100		100
Corporate						30	30		30
Loans (intersegment)		20		20		10	50	(50)	—
Totals	30	60	60	350	90	90	680	(50)	630

The bench mark for the 10 percent of identifiable assets test is $50 (10 percent of total identifiable assets of $500). Intersegment investments and loans can be included only in the identifiable assets of a financial segment (none of the segments are assumed here to be financial). General corporate assets are also excluded from identifiable assets. The assets of segments C and D meet the 10 percent test and are consequently reportable.

Evaluation of reportable segments

Industry segments meeting any *one* of the above three tests are considered as reportable segments. The *Statement* specifies, however, additional rules and criteria that are to be used for a final determination of which segments are reportable. Thus, where a segment meets only one of the tests but is not expected to meet the test in the future, it should not be considered a reportable segment. On the other hand, a segment that does not meet any of the tests may nevertheless be considered reportable if it has been reportable in prior years and is expected to meet one or more of the tests in future years.

There is the additional requirement that the combined reportable segments must represent a substantial portion of the total operations of the enterprise. Thus, if the combined revenues from sales to unaffiliated customers of all reportable segments is less than 75 percent of the combined revenue from sales to unaffiliated customers of all industry segments, additional segments must be identified as reportable segments so as to bring the total up to 75 percent. Conversely, if the number of reportable segments exceeds 10, it may be appropriate to combine the most closely related industry segments into broader reportable segments with a view of reducing their number.

Foreign operations which are not disaggregated along industry lines because of impracticality should nevertheless be included in segment revenues, profits, and assets as a separate segment provided such a segment meets one of the size tests discussed above.

Application of the tests to the Diverso Company examples. As was brought out in the preceding illustrations, the various segments of Diverso Company met the tests as follows:

Type of test	Segments meeting test
Revenues	B and D
Operating profits	B and D
Assets	C and D

Consequently, segments B, C, and D are reportable. The additional 75 percent test which was discussed above can be applied as follows:

	($ millions)
Total unaffiliated revenues (sales) of all segments	$330
75 percent of above	$248
Unaffiliated revenues (sales) of all reportable segments (B = 30 + C = 30 + D = 200)	$260

Since $260 > than $248, the test is met and the reporting of the three segments is appropriate.

Dominant segments

Where an enterprise has only one reportable segment and that segment comprises more than 90 percent of the related combined revenues *and* combined profits *and* combined assets of all industry segments, then only a description of that dominant industry segment is required. However, as will be discussed below, disclosures of foreign operations, export sales, and major customers would still be required if the separate tests for these disclosures are met.

Operation in different industries—criteria for disclosure

Once the reportable segments of a company have been identified, all other industry segments are combined into a reporting category by a name such as "other industry segments." The *Statement* specifies the disclosures which must be made for each year for which financial statements are presented. The following information, which may be presented in the body of the financial statements, in footnotes or in a separate schedule, must be provided for *each* reportable segment *and* for the aggregate of "other industry segments."

Revenue:

Revenue from unaffiliated customers.

Revenue from affiliated customers.

A reconciliation of revenue from all reportable segments with the total revenue reported in the income statement.

The basis of accounting for intersegment sales and transfers, and the effect of any changes in basis on the operating profit and loss of the segment.

Profitability:

Operating profit or loss.

The nature and amount of unusual or infrequently occurring items.

A reconciliation of operating profit and loss for all reportable segments and other industry segments with the *pretax* income from continuing operations as shown in the consolidated income statement. Corporate expenses are to be separately disclosed.

The effect on operating profit or loss of reportable segments of any changes in allocating operating expenses among segments.

The effect on operating profit of each reportable segment of a change in accounting principles.

In the determination of segment operating profit and loss the following items are to excluded:

1. General corporate revenues (e.g., gain on sales of securities).
2. General corporate expenses.
3. Interest (except for financial segments).
4. Income taxes (domestic and foreign).
5. Equity in income or loss of unconsolidated subsidiaries or investees.
6. Gain or loss from discontinued operations.
7. Minority interest.
8. Extraordinary items.
9. Cumulative effect of a change in accounting principles.

Assets:

Amount of identifiable assets.

A reconciliation of identifiable assets for all reportable segments and other industry segments with total consolidated assets. The identifiable assets should exclude: (1) assets maintained for general corporate purposes, (2) intersegment loans and advances (except for financial segments), and (3) investments in unconsolidated subsidiaries and other investments carried at equity.

Appendix 24–A of Chapter 24 presents an illustration of financial statement disclosures as required by *SFAS 14*.

FOREIGN OPERATIONS

The *Statement* requires that multinational companies disclose separately domestic and significant foreign operations. Foreign operations include those located outside a "home country" (e.g., the United States) and which produce revenue either by unaffiliated customer sales or by intercompany sales. They do not include the operation of unconsolidated subsidiaries and investees.

Operations in individual foreign countries may be grouped by geographical area. Such groupings can be determined on the basis of such factors as proximity, economic affinity, or similarity in business environment.

A significant foreign operation is defined as meeting *either* of the following two tests:

1. Revenue from sales to unaffiliated customers is 10 percent or more of consolidated revenue.
2. Identifiable assets are 10 percent or more of consolidated assets.

Illustration of application of sales for determining significant foreign operations. Worldwide Company has far-flung operations summarized in the following tabulations:

Revenues
($000)

	Domestic	Western Europe	South America	Australia	Combined	Elimi- nations	Consolidated
Sales to unaffiliated customers	$47,000	$5,000	$6,000	$2,000	$60,000		$60,000
Interarea sales	11,000	3,000	—	2,000	16,000	$(16,000)	—
Total revenue	$58,000	$8,000	$6,000	$4,000	$76,000	$(16,000)	$60,000

The revenue test bench mark is 10 percent of consolidated revenues of $60,000, or $6,000. Domestic operations and South American operations have sales to unaffiliated customers equal to or in excess of $6,000 and are separately reportable.

Assets
($000)

	Domestic	Western Europe	South America	Australia	Combined	Elimi- nations	Consolidated
Identifiable assets	$70,000	$12,000	$14,000	$4,000	$100,000		$100,000
Investments affiliates	10,000	10,000			20,000		20,000
General corporate assets	6,000				6,000		6,000
Interarea advances	6,000	2,000		2,000	10,000	$(10,000)	—
Total assets	$92,000	$24,000	$14,000	$6,000	$136,000	$(10,000)	$126,000

The asset test bench mark is 10 percent of consolidated assets of $126,000, or $12,600. Domestic operations as well as the South American operations have identifiable assets of at least equal to or in excess of $12,600 and are separately reportable under this test.

Worldwide Company will consequently report domestic operations and South American operations separately while the operations in Western Europe and Australia will be combined and disclosed as operations in "other foreign areas."

Disclosure requirements   If foreign operations' revenue from sales to unaffiliated customers and foreign operations identifiable assets are less than 10 percent of related consolidated amounts, they need not be reported separately.

For all separately reportable areas as well as for the combined areas, revenue, profitability information, and identifiable assets must be disclosed.

In addition, the geographic areas into which foreign operations have been disaggregated should be identified. An enterprise may operate in one major industry on a worldwide basis and may therefore have to report operations in different geographic areas but not in different industries.

Export sales

The boundary between foreign operations and export sales is not always clear and obvious. Generally, foreign operations include those located outside the "home country" (e.g., United States) and which produce revenue from either sales to unaffiliated customers or to members of a group of companies. Export sales represent generally revenue generated abroad from services provided by domestic offices.

If sales by a company's domestic operations to unaffiliated foreign customers are at least 10 percent of consolidated revenues, such export sales should be disclosed in total and, where appropriate, by geographic area.

Major customers

If 10 percent or more of revenue is derived from sales to any single customer, that fact should be disclosed. *SFAS 30* which modifies the *Statement* now requires companies to disclose the amount of revenue derived from sales to an individual domestic or foreign government entity only when those revenues are 10 percent or more of total revenue. The *aggregation* of revenues from all domestic or foreign government entities for purposes of this test is no longer required. Disclosure of sales to major customers should identify the industry segments making such sales, but the names of individual customers need not be disclosed.

The SEC's position on segmental reporting

Following the promulgation of *SFAS 14* which satisfied most of the reporting objectives which the Commission had previously identified in this area, the SEC conformed its disclosure rules substantially to those of the *Statement.* Some of the few exceptions which remain are as follows:

> In SEC filings, data must be reported for a three-year historical period whereas the *Statement* requires segmental data only for those years for which a complete set of financial statements is presented.

> The SEC requires identification of a major *customer* or customers if the loss of such a customer or customers would have a materially adverse effect on the enterprise.

Problem areas of segmental reporting

The SEC's expanded disclosure requirements relating to the prices at which transfers are made from one segment to another (deleted in the 1980 form 10-K revision) were based on concern stemming from the lack of firm rules or standards which would govern the establishment of realistic and meaningful transfer prices. It is obvious that a lack of realism or objectivity in such pricing practices can affect and possibly distort individual segment results to a considerable degree. Nevertheless, recognizing the lack of transfer pricing standards, the *SFAS 14* concluded that revenue from intersegment sales or transfers shall be accounted for on whatever basis is used by the enterprise to price intersegment sales or transfers. No single basis was prescribed.

Another major problem area is presented by the need to allocate joint costs among segments. Bases of allocating joint expenses are largely arbitrary and subject to differences of opinions as to their validity and precision. Some specific types of joint expenses which present particularly difficult problems are general and administrative expenses of central headquarters, research and development costs, certain selling costs, advertising, interest, and federal and state income taxes. As was seen earlier in this chapter, the Board has, for purposes of segmental disclosure, specifically excluded a whole list of expenses from the allocation process. The *Cost Accounting Standards Board* has in recent years begun to tackle the problem of forging uniform and consistent recommendations to govern the allocation of joint costs.[4] While these recommendations address the problems of allocating joint costs to segments of an enterprise involved in defense contracts, they should have general usefulness and applicability as well. In this area, as in the area of transfer pricing, much work remains to be done before meaningful and objective standards of measurement will be devised.

QUESTIONS

1. What is an industry segment?

2. What is a reportable industry segment?

3. What are the objectives of segment disclosure in view of the FASB?

4. Under what conditions is an industry segment considered to be a reportable segment?

5. Briefly describe the major types of information disclosures required by FASB *SFAS 14.*

6. Briefly describe the revenue test for determining whether a specific industry segment is a reportable segment.

7. Briefly describe the operating profit test for determining a reportable segment.

8. Briefly describe the asset test to be used in determining whether an industry segment is a reportable segment.

9. What items are excluded from operating profits for the purpose of determining whether a segment meets the operating profit test for reporting it as a separate segment?

10. What determines whether an industry segment is a dominant segment?

11. Define a significant foreign operation.

12. What disclosures are required for foreign operations?

13. What are the disclosure requirements for export sales?

14. Describe the SEC's position on segmental reporting.

15. What are some remaining problem areas in segmental reporting?

---

[4] See, for example, *Cost Accounting Standard 403*, "Allocation of Home Office Expenses to Segments" (as of now the CASB is no longer in operation).

EXERCISES

Exercise 13–1. A diversified company has five segments. The following information is available:

Segment	Operating profit (loss) 19x6	19x7
A	$3,000	$ 200
B	(1,000)	500
C	2,000	(400)
D	300	(420)
E	100	50
	$4,400	$ (70)

[Relates to Exercise 13–3]

Segment	Sales to unaffiliated customers	Sales to affiliated customers	Profit or (loss)	Identifiable assets
Coal	$ 800	$ 50	$200	$1,000
Iron ore	600	—	120	500
Steel	150	100	(100)	300
Auto parts	1,100	150	350	1,200
Paint	150	—	(20)	200
Totals	$2,800	$300	$550	$3,200

Required:

Indicate which segments are reportable for each year.

Exercise 13–2. The following is selected information for the segments of Texas Electric Company for the year ended December 31, 19x8:

Segment	Revenues	Operating profit (loss)	Identifiable assets
N	$15,000	$ 3,500	$ 5,000
O	43,000*	10,200	34,000
P	6,000	1,000	5,600
Q	21,000*	1,300	51,000
R	2,500	(200)	6,000
	$87,500	$15,800	$101,600

*Only 95 percent of the revenues of segment O and 90 percent of segments Q's revenues are from sales to unaffiliated customers.

Required:

a. Determine which, if any, of these segments would qualify as reportable segments.

b. Determine whether a substantial portion or Texas Company's total operations is represented by reportable segments.

Exercise 13–3. Diversified Mid-America Corporation has five industry segments. Measures of sales, operating profit and loss, and identifiable assets for each segment are as follows:

For each of the following, select the letter which best represents the correct answer:

1. Each of the above segments would qualify as reportable segment under the 10 percent revenue test if—

a. Its sales to unaffiliated customers = $280.

b. Its sales to unaffiliated customers = $310.

c. Its sales to affiliated and unaffiliated customers = $230.

d. Its sales to affiliated and unaffiliated customers = $310.

2. Each of the above segments would qualify as a reportable segment under the 10 percent operating profit test it—

a. Its operating profit = $55.

b. Its operating profit or loss = $55.

c. Its operating profit = $67 or its operating loss = $1.

d. Its operating profit or loss = $67.

3. The following segments would qualify as reportable segments under one or more of the revenue, operating profit, or assets tests:

a. Coal, iron ore, steel, auto parts, and paint.

b. Coal, iron ore, and paint.

c. Iron ore, steel, auto parts, and paint.

d. Coal, iron ore, steel, and auto parts.

4. The test value for determining if the 75 percent revenue test for *reevaluation* of reportable segments is met would be computed as follows:

a. $2,800 × 75 percent.

b. $3,100 × 75 percent.

c. $2,650 × 75 percent.

d. $2,950 × 75 percent.

Exercise 13–4. Waverly Corporation has four industry segments. The operating data for each segment during 19x8 are as follows:

[Relates to Exercise 13–4]

	Industry segment			
	K	L	M	N
Sales to unaffiliated customers	$ 6,000	$ 42,000	$20,100	$ 4,000
Cost of goods sold	3,500	15,000	7,000	1,200
Administrative expenses	1,700	3,500	1,700	500
Selling expenses	1,100	6,000	1,000	400
Total identifiable expenses	6,300	24,500	9,700	2,100
Operating income (loss)	$ (300)	$ 17,500	$10,400	$ 1,900
Intersegment sales (purchases)	—	$ (2,000)	$ 2,000	—
Identifiable assets	$12,000	$120,500	$15,000	$13,000

Additional data:

General Corporate expenses, $2,000, Interest expense, $1,500, and income taxes, $5,600. The general corporate office has assets of $12,000.

Required:

a. Determine which of the industry segments of Waverly Corporation should be reported separately in a segment report.

b. Using the information mentioned above, prepare a schedule for disclosure of Waverly's industry segments.

Exercise 13–5. Many accountants and financial analysts contend that companies should report financial data for segments of the enterprise.

Required:

a. What does financial reporting for segments of a business enterprise involve?

b. Identify the reasons for requiring financial data to be reported by segments.

c. Identify the possible disadvantages of requiring financial data to be reported by segments.

d. Identify the accounting difficulties inherent in segment reporting.   (AICPA adapted)

Exercise 13–6. Part A. In order to properly understand current generally accepted accounting principles with respect to accounting for and reporting upon segments of a business enterprise, as stated by the FASB in its *SFAS 14*, it is necessary to be familiar with certain unique terminology.

Required:

With respect to segments of a business enterprise, explain the following terms:

a. Industry segment.

b. Revenue.

c. Operating profit and loss.

d. Identifiable assets.

Part B. A central issue in reporting on industry segments of a business enterprise is the determination of which segments are reportable.

Required:

a. What are the tests to determine whether or not an industry segment is reportable?

b. What is the test to determine if enough industry segments have been separately reported upon and what is the guideline on the maximum number of industry segments to be shown?   (AICPA adapted)

Exercise 13–7.

1. The Jonas Company is a diversified company that discloses supplemental financial information as to industry segments of its business. The following information is available for 19x9:

	Sales	Traceable costs	Allocable costs
Product A	$400,000	$225,000	
Product B	300,000	240,000	
Product C	200,000	135,000	
Totals	$900,000	$600,000	$150,000

Allocable costs are allocated based on the ratio of a segment's income before allocable costs to total income before allocable costs. This should be considered an appropriate method of allocation. What is the operating profit for product B for 19x9?

  a. $0.

  b. $10,000.

  c. $30,000.

  d. $50,000.

2. The profitability information that should be reported for each reportable segment of a business enterprise consists of—

  a. An operating profit or loss figure consisting of segment revenues less traceable costs and allocated common costs.

  b. An operating profit or loss figure consisting of segment revenues less traceable costs but *not* allocated common costs.

  c. An operating profit or loss figure consisting of segment revenues less allocated common costs but *not* traceable costs.

  d. Segment revenues only.

3. Chip Company operates in four different industries, each of which is appropriately regarded as a reportable segment. Total sales for 19x8 for all the segments combined were $1,000,000. Sales for segment 2 were $400,000, and traceable costs were $150,000. Total common costs for all the segments combined were $500,000. Chip allocates common costs based on the ratio of a segment's sales to total sales, an appropriate method of allocation. The operating profit presented for Segment No. 2 for 19x8 should be—

  a. $50,000.

  b. $125,000.

  c. $200,000.

  d. $250,000.   (CPA adapted)

Exercise 13–8.

  1. Erick Company is a diversified company that discloses supplemental financial information as to industry segments of its business. The following information is available for 19x6:

	Sales	Traceable costs	Common costs
Product A	$300,000	$240,000	
Product B	200,000	100,000	
Product C	100,000	60,000	
Totals	$600,000	$400,000	$100,000

Common costs are allocated based on the ratio of a segment's income before common costs to total income before common costs. This should be considered an appropriate method of allocation. What should be the common costs allocated to product A for 19x6?

  a. Zero, because allocation of common costs is never allowed for segment reporting.

  b. $30,000.

  c. $50,000.

  d. $60,000.

2. Which of the following is *not* a consideration in segment reporting for diversified enterprises?

  a. Allocation of joint costs.

  b. Transfer pricing.

  c. Defining the segments.

  d. Consolidation policy.

3. Mill Company operates in three different industries, each of which is appropriately regarded as a reportable segment. Segment 1 contributed 60 percent of Mill Company's total sales. Sales for segment 1 were $900,000, and traceable costs were $400,000. Total common costs for Mill were $600,000. Mill allocates common costs based on the ratio of a segment's sales to total sales, an appropriate method of allocation. What should be the operating profit presented for segment 1 for 19x7?

  a. $140,000.

  b. $360,000.

  c. $500,000.

  d. $540,000.   (AICPA adapted)

PROBLEMS

Problem 13–9. Super Corporation is a diversified company that discloses supplemental financial information as to industry segments of its business. Summary information for its segments is as follows:

	Segment		
	A	B	C
Information for segments:			
Sales to unaffiliated customers	$12,200	$ 800	$300
Sales to affiliated customers	200	500	200
Operating profit	700	(50)	30
Identifiable assets	11,500	1,360	420
Depreciation and depletion .	1,200	140	110
Capital expenditures	1,600	80	230

Other information:		
Total operating profit		$680
Less: General expenses	$ 20	
Interest expense	35	
Minority interest income	15	
Income taxes	300	370
Net income		$310

Required:

a. Which of the Super Corporation segments are reportable segments? (Support your answer computationally.)

b. Is the A segment a dominant segment?

Problem 13–10. United Corporation has operations in the United States and in some foreign countries. Information relevant to United Corporation for the year ended December 31, 19x8, is as follows:

Required:

a. Which, if any, of United's foreign geographic areas require separate disclosure under the following tests:

(1) Revenue test.

(2) Asset test.

b. Prepare a schedule for disclosure of United's domestic and foreign operation from the above information. (Assume that reconciliations to related consolidated statements amounts have already been made in the segment reporting disclosure.)

[Relates to Problem 13–10]

	Domestic	Mexico	North Africa	Brazil	Consolidated
Sales to unaffiliated customers	$140,000	$15,000	$28,000	$25,000	$208,000
Interarea transfers	30,000	10,000		5,000	
Total revenue	$170,000	$25,000	$28,000	$30,000	$208,000
Operating profit	$ 20,000	$ 5,000	$ 7,000	$ 6,000	$ 38,000
Identifiable assets	160,000	25,000	28,000	22,000	235,000
Total assets	195,000	27,000	29,000	22,000	273,000

Problem 13–11. Navar Company operates in four industry segments. The information available concerning calendar year 19x7 for Navar is as follows:

operating expenses were $1,500, general Corporate expenses were $1,100, and interest expense was $300. Erick's total assets were $16,000 of which $12,000

[Relates to Problem 13–11]

	Industry segment			
	W	X	Y	Z
Sales to unaffiliated customers	$26,000	$ 5,000	$4,000	$ 6,000
Intersegment sales	13,000	3,000	—	—
Operating profit (loss)	12,000	(4,000)	1,000	(1,500)
Identifiable assets	55,000	9,000	3,000	8,000
Capital expenditures	7,000	500	1,500	500
Depreciation, depletion, and amortization	3,000	700	800	600

Additional information:

1. *From the income statement:*

Consolidated sales	$41,000
Earnings from investment	1,500
General corporate expenses	2,900
Interest expense	1,400
Income taxes	2,000

2. *From the balance sheet:*

Investment	14,000
General corporate assets	9,000

Required:

Prepare a schedule to show segment information and all reconciliations needed to be included in the financial statements of Navar Company.

Problem 13–12. Erick Company's home country is the United States, but it also has operations in Western Europe and Canada.

During 19x7, Erick had sales of $9,000 of which $2,500 were to the Canadian affiliate and $3,000 to the U.S. government. Erick's cost of sales was $6,300,

were identifiable with U.S. operations and the balance were general corporate assets.

The Western Europe geographic area's sales during 19x7 were $3,200, its cost of sales amounted to $1,800, and other operating expenses were $600. Its identifiable assets were $7,500.

Sales of the Canadian area during 19x7 were $4,000. Its cost of goods sold amounted to $2,600, all of which were obtained from Erick at its cost plus its regular markup. Total identifiable assets of the Canadian area were $10,500, of which $500 was ending inventory. Other operating expenses were $400.

Required:

Prepare a schedule for disclosure of Erick's domestic and foreign operation using the information given above.

Problem 13–13. Carson Steel Company has operations in four industry segments, E, F, G, and H. Summary information for these segments for 19x9 is as follows:

[Relates to Problem 13–13]

	E	F	G	H
Sales	$12,300	$95,000	$9,000	$8,500
Cost of sales	4,000	30,500	3,200	3,600
General and administrative expenses	1,200	13,000	2,900	3,000
Selling expenses	1,000	2,500	2,900	2,100
Total costs and expenses	$ 6,200	$46,000	$8,000	$8,700
Operating profit (loss)	$ 6,100	$49,000	$1,000	$ (200)
Identifiable assets	$10,000	$50,000	$6,000	$5,500

Additional information:

1. On December 31, 19x9, General Corporate assets were $25,000.
2. The sales of segment E included $1,200 made to segment G during the year. Segment G has zero ending inventory on December 31, 19x9.
3. General corporate expenses were $2,500 and income taxes were $15,000.

Required:

a. Prepare schedules to show which, if any, of Carson's segments are reportable.

b. Prepare a financial report by segments reconciled to consolidated data for the year ended December 31, 19x9.

Problem 13–14. The Century Company, a diversified manufacturing company, had four separate operating divisions engaged in the manufacture of products in each of the following areas: food products, health aids, textiles, and office equipment.

Financial data for the two years ended December 31, 19x5, and 19x4 are presented below:

The company's textiles division had six manufacturing plants which produced a variety of textile products. In April 19x5, the company sold one of these plants and realized a gain of $130,000. After the sale, the operations at the plant that was sold were transferred to the remaining five textile plants which the company continued to operate.

In August 19x5, the main warehouse of the food products division, located on the banks of the Bayer River, was flooded when the river overflowed. The resulting damage of $420,000 is not included in the financial data given above. Historical records indicate that the Bayer River normally overflows every four to five years causing flood damage to adjacent property.

For the two years ended December 31, 19x5, and 19x4, the company had interest revenue earned on investments of $70,000 and $40,000, respectively.

For the two years ended December 31, 19x5, and 19x4, the company's net income was $960,000 and $670,000, respectively.

The provision for income tax expense for each of

[Relates to Problem 13–14]

	Net sales		Cost of sales		Operating expenses	
	19x5	*19x4*	*19x5*	*19x4*	*19x5*	*19x4*
Food products	$3,500,000	$3,000,000	$2,400,000	$1,800,000	$ 550,000	$ 275,000
Health aids	2,000,000	1,270,000	1,100,000	700,000	300,000	125,000
Textiles	1,580,000	1,400,000	500,000	900,000	200,000	150,000
Office equipment	920,000	1,330,000	800,000	1,000,000	650,000	750,000
Totals	$8,000,000	$7,000,000	$4,800,000	$4,400,000	$1,700,000	$1,300,000

On January 1, 19x5, Century adopted a plan to sell the assets and product line of the office equipment division and expected to realize a gain on this disposal. On September 1, 19x5, the division's assets and product line were sold for $2,100,000 cash resulting in a gain of $640,000 (exclusive of operations during the phase-out period).

the two years should be computed at a rate of 50 percent.

Required:

Prepare in proper form a comparative statement of income of the Century Company for the two years ended December 31, 19x5, and December 31, 19x4. Footnotes are *not* required.   (AICPA adapted)

14

Interim financial reporting

OVERVIEW

Investors, creditors, and other decision makers need information about enterprise performance on a continuous and timely basis. Quarterly reports fill these needs in the periods between two annual reports.

This chapter discusses the important issues raised in interim reporting, i.e., whether the preparation of interim financial statements should use the same accounting principles and practices as are used in the preparation of annual financial statements. It contrasts the discrete period approach, which measures interim period earnings by viewing it as an independent period on its own, with the integral period approach which views each interim period as an integral part of the annual reporting period. Following a discussion of these issues we present, discuss, and illustrate in detail the current generally accepted accounting standards (GAAP) in this area.

THE NEED FOR INTERIM REPORTS

The demand for financial statements covering periods shorter than one year arises primarily from the need of decision makers to receive frequent and timely updated information about the financial position and results of operations of enterprises in which they have an interest.

The need of participants in active securities markets for timely updated information on financial and operating developments in traded companies is long-standing and indeed, the New York Stock Exchange has for a long time now required its listed companies to publish interim financial reports. Similarly, lenders to enterprises, whether by means of bond purchases or by direct loans, are always interested in monitoring closely the progress of borrowers so that problem areas can be identified as early as possible.

Close monitoring of results is one major reason for the interest in interim reports. Another important objective is to use such reports as a basis for projecting annual results.

PROBLEM AREAS

While the need for interim reports is unmistakeable, so are the problems associated with financial reporting for short periods.

As anyone familiar with accounting knows, financial statements covering an entire year include many estimates and judgments, particularly of future revenues, costs, and expenses, and that only time and future events can tell whether such estimates and judgments are reasonably accurate and valid. The problem with estimates and judgments is greatly compounded the more we shorten the time period covered by the accounting.

Thus, for example, a full understanding of a highly seasonal business characterized by peaks and valleys of revenue can be achieved only on the basis of at least one complete annual cycle. In practice, few companies experience equal amounts of revenue and expense in equal time intervals, and thus the problems of interim reporting tend to be pervasive. These are problems of associating revenues with and allocating costs and expenses to specific short periods of time such as one quarter. Such questions as how to treat fixed costs incurred in one interim period but expected to benefit another period or what to do with expenses which relate to a full year's activity but which occur randomly during the year must be constantly faced by those preparing interim reports.

TWO DIVERGENT VIEWS

Accountants hold two divergent views on how to regard an interim period.

One view regards each interim period as a basic and distinct accounting period. Under this view, known as the *discrete period approach*, interim net income is determined by employing the same processes and principles as are used in the determination of annual results. Under this method, for example, any outlay such as for advertising or repairs and maintenance would be expensed in the interim period in which it occurs if such expense would usually be expensed in an annual period as well, and no deferral to future interim periods would occur. Similarly, under this method a low tax accrual for an interim period would be made even if the benefit from the investment tax credit which gave rise to this low effective tax rate is not expected to recur in other interim periods and thus a higher effective tax rate is expected to prevail for the entire year.

The other view holds that an interim period is an integral part of the annual period and, consequently, does not stand as a distinct and separate accounting period. Under this view, known as the *integral period approach*, accruals, deferrals, estimates, and allocations depend on overall estimates of the relationship between estimated annual revenues and expenses. Under this method, expenses such as advertising or benefits such as the investment tax credit mentioned above will be deferred so that a proper allocation between interim periods within one year can be achieved.

APB OPINION 28

APB Opinion 28, "Interim Financial Reporting," issued in 1973, is based primarily on the conclusion that an interim period be viewed as an integral part of the annual reporting period, even though, as we shall see, it allows some departures from this approach in the interest of relating the interim statement more closely to its annual counterpart. *APB Opinion 28* also stresses its concern for consistency by emphasizing that financial statements for each interim period should be based on the same accounting principles and practices as are used in the preparation of annual financial statements.

STANDARDS FOR INTERIM REPORTING OF REVENUES, COSTS, AND EXPENSES

Revenues from products sold or services rendered should be recognized as earned during an interim period on the same basis as followed for the full year. Moreover, businesses having significant seasonal variations in revenue should disclose the seasonal nature of their activities. This is usually accomplished by issuing data for the latest 12 months in addition to the interim data.

Costs and expenses may be classified as (1) those associated with revenues, that is, those allocated to or directly associated with the products sold or services rendered; or (2) all other costs and expenses that are not allocated as in (1) but which are charged as incurred against income in the interim periods or allocated on the basis of time expired, benefits received, or other activities associated with the interim periods.

Direct or allocated product costs encompass all inventoriable costs such as direct material, labor, and manufacturing overhead. The accounting for these costs for interim periods should be on the same basis as used for the full year. However, *APB Opinion 28* provided the following exceptions with respect to the determination of costs of goods sold for interim financial statements.

1. Enterprises which use the gross profit method at interim dates to estimate cost of goods sold should disclose this practice in the interim financial statements. Moreover, any material adjustments reconciling estimated interim inventories with annual physical inventories should also be disclosed.

2. Enterprises using the LIFO method of inventory may dip into LIFO layers *temporarily* during an interim period. Since LIFO is an annual con-

cept, if the enterprise expects to replenish this inventory reduction before year-end, it should provide in the interim cost of goods for such replacement of inventory.

3. Inventory losses resulting from market declines should generally not be deferred beyond the interim period in which they occur. Recovery of such losses in subsequent interim periods should be recognized as gains in such period, but only to the extent of losses previously recognized. In those instances when inventory losses in interim periods are viewed as *temporary,* such losses need not be recognized since no loss is expected for the fiscal year as a whole.

Illustration of the application of the lower of cost or market rule to interim reporting

The Empire Company accounts for its single merchandise item on the FIFO basis by applying the lower of cost or market measure. On January 1, 19x5, the company had an inventory of 12,000 units in stock with a cost of $48,000 (or $4 per unit). For simplicity of illustration we assume that no purchases were made during 19x5. Quarterly unit sales as well as end-of-quarter market quotations for the merchandise items were as follows:

Quarter	Sales for quarter (units)	End of quarter market quote per unit
First	3,000	$5
Second	2,000	3
Third	2,600	6
Fourth	1,000	2

On the assumption that Empire did not consider the market decline at the end of the second quarter as temporary, the costs of goods sold for the four quarters would be computed as follows:

Quarter	Computation		Cost of goods sold For quarter	Cost of goods sold Year to date
First	3,000 units at $4		$12,000	$12,000
Second	2,000 units at $4	$8,000		
	Write-down of remaining 7,000 units to market (7,000 × $1)	7,000	15,000	27,000
Third	2,600 units at $3 (cost at end of 2nd quarter)	7,800		
	Less: Write-up to original cost of 4,400 remaining units (4,400 × $1)	4,400	3,400	30,400
Fourth	1,000 units at $4	4,000		
	Add: Write-down to market of remaining 3,400 units × $2	6,800	10,800	41,200*

*The cost of goods sold for 19x5 can be reconciled as follows:
Cost of 8,600 units sold at $4	$34,400
Write-down of 1975 ending inventory to market 3,400 units at $2	6,800
	$41,200

4. Enterprises using standard cost accounting for the determination of inventory and cost of goods sold should follow for interim periods the same procedures as would apply to the entire fiscal year. Thus, planned or normal variances at the end of interim periods which are expected to be absorbed by the end of the fiscal year should be deferred at the interim date. However, unplanned or not normal variances should be reflected in income in the interim period in which they occur.

With regard to the reporting of costs and expenses which are not allocated to products sold or services rendered the following standards are enumerated in paragraph 15 of *APB Opinion 28:*

a. Cost and expenses other than product costs should be charged to income in interim periods as incurred, or be allocated among interim periods based on an estimate of time expired, benefit received or activity associated with the periods. Procedures adopted for assigning specific cost and expense items to an interim period should be consistent with the bases followed by the company in reporting results of operations at annual reporting dates. However, when a specific cost or expense item charged to expense for annual reporting purposes benefits more than one interim period, the cost or expense item may be allocated to those interim periods.

b. Some costs and expenses incurred in an interim period, however, cannot be readily identified with the activities or benefits of other interim periods and should be charged to the interim period in which incurred. Disclosure should be made as to the nature and amount of such costs unless items of a comparable nature are included in both the current interim period and in the corresponding interim period of the preceding year.

c. Arbitrary assignment of the amount of such costs to an interim period should not be made.

d. Gains and losses that arise in any interim period similar to those that would not be deferred at year end should not be deferred to later interim periods within the same fiscal year.

Examples of items to which the above standards apply are major repairs, quantity discounts, property taxes, and advertising costs.

The *Opinion* encourages enterprises to avoid year-end adjustments as much as possible by making quarterly estimates of those items, such as inventory shortages, bad debt losses, and contract adjustments that usually result in year-end adjustments. Thus, a portion of such items will be properly assigned to each interim period.

INCOME TAXES IN INTERIM STATEMENTS

The estimate of the required income tax provision is one of the more important factors in the determination of interim operating results. The accouting for income taxes in interim financial statements is generally based on the application of the relevant principles established in *APB Opinions 11, 23, 24,* and *28* as well as in *FASB Interpretation No. 18.*

The basic position taken by *APB Opinion 28* is that the amount of tax charged to an interim period should be related to the expected annual income tax provision. To this end, the effective tax rate for the entire current fiscal period must be estimated at the end of each interim period and applied to interim income. The interim tax expense (or benefit) should consequently be the difference between (1) the year-to-date tax expense or benefit and (2) the cumulative amounts of tax reported in previous interim period.

In determining the estimated effective annual tax rate, the effect of permanent tax differences such as investment tax credits, capital gains, percentage depletion, and other nontaxable income or nondeductible expense must be estimated. For example, if investment tax credits were allowed to affect net income on a quarter-by-quarter basis, when property happened to be acquired, these credits could cause very serious distortions of income, particularly that reported for short interim periods. By annualizing the effective tax rate, this type of erratic effect in interim reporting is avoided.

The tax effect of operating loss carry-forwards should not be recognized unless such losses can be offset against the income of subsequent interim periods and such ability to offset is assured beyond any reasonable doubt.

The computation of the estimated effective tax rate should *not* include the tax effect of *nonordinary* items of income or loss, which are shown net of their tax effect, such as extraordinary items, discontinued operations, and the cumulative effect of changes in accounting principles. The effects of changes in tax legislation should be reflected only in interim periods which follow the effective date of the legislation.

The following examples illustrate the determination of the effective tax rate for the year as well as the computation of quarterly tax provisions:

Illustration of the computation of interim statement tax provision

At the end of its first quarter, the Apex Company had $100,000 in pretax income and no nonordinary items of income or loss. In computing the tax provision for the quarter, the first step is to determine the estimated effective tax rate for the entire year. This is usually done for both federal and state income taxes on a combined basis.

Apex estimates that it will have no timing tax differences and that its taxable income will be as follows:

Estimated income before income taxes	$400,000
Add: Nondeductible goodwill amortization	6,000
Taxable income	$406,000
Combined federal and state income tax rate, 62%.	
Estimated tax (62% of $406,000)	$251,720
Less: Investment tax credit	20,000
Estimated tax payable	$231,720
Effective tax rate $231,720/$400,000	57.93%

The tax provision for the first quarter will be computed as follows:

$100,000 (pretax income) × 57.93% (estimated effective tax rate) = $57,930

For its second quarter, Apex had a pretax income of $110,000. Because of expected dividend exclusions and capital gain rates, which have the effect of lowering the tax rates the effective combined tax rate for the full year is now expected to be 52 percent. The tax provision for the second quarter will be computed as follows:

Cumulative pretax income (year to date) ($100,000 + $110,000) =	$210,000
Tax at estimated combined rate of 52%	$109,200
Less: Income tax accrued for first quarter	57,930
Income tax to be provided for the second quarter	$ 51,270

As can be seen, the effect of any change in the estimated full year tax rate is included in the tax provision of the second (the latest) quarter and no retroactive revision is undertaken. This process will be repeated for the third and fourth quarters as well.

Let us now consider the case where losses occur in certain quarters. The following illustrates the computation of the interim period tax provision under such circumstances.

Illustration of interim tax provision when losses occur

Assume now that in one of the subsequent years Apex incurred a loss in the first quarter, that carryback to prior years was not available, and that the tax benefit which may arise from such loss is *not* assured beyond a reasonable doubt. The following tabulation illustrates the computation of the quarterly tax provisions:

	Pretax income (loss)			Tax expense (benefit)		
Quarter	Current	Year to date	Estimated tax rate for year	Year to date	Previously reported to date	Current quarter
First	$(60,000)	$(60,000)	60%	—	—	—
Second	40,000	(20,000)	60	—	—	—
Third	80,000	60,000	60	$36,000	—	$36,000
Fourth	100,000	160,000	50	80,000	$36,000	44,000

As can be seen from the above, no tax benefits (credits) were recorded in the first two quarters since their realization was not assured beyond a reasonable doubt. A regular tax provision at the estimated yearly effective rate was made on the year to date pretax income of $60,000 occurring in the third quarter. In the fourth quarter, the provision was made on the basis of a revised effective tax rate for the year.

Given the same facts as in the tabulation above, but assuming that the realization of tax benefits from the first quarter loss *was assured*, the following is the computation of interim tax provisions:

| Quarter | Pretax income (loss) | | Estimated tax rate for year | Tax expense (benefit) | | |
	Current	Year to date		Year to date	Previously reported to date	Current quarter
First	$(60,000)	$(60,000)	60%	$(36,000)	—	$(36,000)
Second	40,000	(20,000)	60	(12,000)	$(36,000)	24,000
Third	80,000	60,000	60	36,000	(12,000)	48,000
Fourth	100,000	160,000	50	80,000	36,000	44,000

It should be noted that due to assurance beyond any reasonable doubt that the tax benefit from the first quarter loss can be realized in the future, tax provision of the first quarter reflects that benefit in the form of a credit of $36,000 (the debit is to an asset "future tax benefits" or similar title). The second quarter's tax provision already reflects the proper accrual for year-to-date results. It will be noted that the total tax provision for the year in the above tabulations is identical to that in the preceding table.

FASB Interpretation No. 18 provides many other examples of complex interim tax computations.

Reporting of accounting changes and extraordinary and other nonoperating items

While *APB Opinion 28* generally encourages relating items, such as income taxes, to the annual period, it does not encourage smoothing the effects of unusual or infrequently occurring events and transactions that arise in an interim period. Thus, extraordinary and unusual items and gains or losses from disposals of segments of a business must be reported in full as they occur so that their impact is immediately known. Because these items are always shown net of taxes, the tax effects must be shown as adjustments of these items to the extent that they are realized.

APB Opinion 28 recommends that when an enterprise is to make a change in accounting policy, the change should be adopted during the first period of the fiscal year. For a cumulative-effect change in an accounting principle that is made, pursuant to *APB Opinion 20*, in the first reporting period of the year, the cumulative effect of the change up to the end of the previous fiscal year is included in determining net income of that interim period.[1]

With respect to changes in accounting principles which are made after the first interim period of a given year, *SFAS 3* provided that no cumulative effect of the change shall be included in net income of the period of change. Instead, the interim periods preceding the period of the change should be restated by applying the newly adopted accounting standard. The cumulative effect of the change in retained earnings at the beginning of that fiscal year shall be included in the restated net income of the first interim period of

---

[1] In accordance with *APB Opinion 20*, a cumulative-effect change in an accounting principle does not include changes that require restatements of prior period financial statements such as changes from LIFO inventory or a change in accounting for long-term construction contracts.

the fiscal year in which the change is made (and in any period reported on that includes the first interim period).

The effect of a change in accounting *estimates* (e.g., useful life of property) should be accounted for in the period in which the change of estimate was made, and no restatement of previously reported interim data should be undertaken.

Disclosure of summarized interim financial data

APB Opinion 28 recognizes that in order to be timely, interim reporting may provide considerably less detailed information than is found in annual reports. Thus, the *Opinion* requires disclosure of the following information at a minimum, including the disclosure of any significant change in financial position in the event condensed balance sheets are not provided:

1. Sales or gross revenues, provision for income taxes, extraordinary items, cumulative effect of accounting principles, and net income.
2. Primary and fully diluted earnings per share data for each period presented.
3. Seasonal revenue, costs, or expenses.
4. Significant changes in estimates or provisions for income taxes.
5. Disposal of a segment of a business, extraordinary, unusual, or infrequently occurring items.
6. Contingent items.
7. Changes in accounting principles or estimates.
8. Sigificant changes in financial position.

The above data should be provided for the current quarter, the current year-to-date or the last 12 months-to-date plus comparable data for the preceding year.

When a company does not issue a fourth quarter report, the annual financial statements should disclose the effects of the following for the fourth quarter: disposals of a segment, extraordinary items, unusual or infrequently occurring items, changes in accounting principles, as well as the aggregate effect of year-end adjustments which are material to the fourth quarter results.

SEC disclosure requirements

As part of its integrated disclosure program (see also discussion in Chapter 24), the SEC has established standard requirements for both interim financial statements and management's discussion and analysis of interim period results.

The new provisions require, for Form 10-Q filings, the inclusion of balance sheets as of the end of the most recent interim period and the end of the preceding fiscal year. Interim period discussions should focus on the same information discussed for annual periods in order to provide an update of the annual discussion. Only material changes in financial condition and results of operations occurring during the periods covered by the interim financial statements need be discussed. This discussion of material changes must cover:

The period from the end of the preceding fiscal year to the date of the most recent interim balance sheet provided.

The most recent interim year-to-date period and fiscal quarter for which income statements are provided and the corresponding periods of the preceding fiscal year.

The same items required to be addressed in annual discussions of results of operations must, with the exception of the impact of inflation, also be addressed in discussions of interim periods.

Appendix 24–A in Chapter 24 presents an example of unaudited interim financial information presented in an SEC filing. In this filing a management discussion and analysis was not yet required. It would be similar to that presented in Appendix 24–B, Chapter 24.

While significant improvements in interim financial reporting have occurred in recent years, the controversy (see earlier discussion in this chapter) surrounding the proper relationship of the interim period to the fiscal year of which it is a part, as well as other aspects of reporting, continues.

As a first step in the process of reconsideration of this topic, the FASB on May 25, 1978, issued a Discussion Memorandum entitled "Interim Financial Accounting and Reporting." At the present time this topic does not enjoy a high degree of priority.

QUESTIONS

1. Accountants hold two divergent views on how to regard an interim period. Discuss.

2. Discuss the standards for interim reporting of revenues, costs, and expenses as provided by *APB Opinion 28*, "Interim Financial Reporting."

3. What are the exceptions provided by *APB Opinion 28* with respect to the determination of costs of goods sold for interim financial statements?

4. Explain how income tax provisions in interim financial statements can be computed according to *APB Opinion 28*.

5. Explain the treatment of accounting changes and extraordinary and other nonoperating items in interim financial statements.

6. How should the changes in accouting principles which are made after the first interim period be disclosed in the interim statement?

EXERCISES

Exercise 14–1.

1. In considering interim financial reporting, how did the Accounting Principles Board conclude that such reporting should be viewed?

a. As a "special" type of reporting that need *not* follow generally accepted accounting principles.

b. As useful only if activity is evenly spread throughout the year so that estimates are unnecessary.

c. As reporting for a basic accounting period.

d. As reporting for an integral part of an annual period.

2. Which of the following is an inherent difficulty in the determination of the results of operations on an interim baisis?

a. Cost of sales reflects only the amount of product expense allocable to revenue recognized as of the interim date.

b. Depreciation on an interim basis is a partial estimate of the actual annual amount.

c. Costs expensed in one interim period may benefit other periods.

d. Revenues from long-term construction contracts accounted for by the percentage of completion method are based on annual completion and interim estimates may be incorrect.

3. Minimum disclosure requirements for companies issuing interim financial information would include which of the following?

a. An interim statement of financial position and statement of changes in financial position data.

b. Primary and fully diluted earnings per share data for each period presented.

c. Sales and cost of goods sold for the current quarter and the current year-to-date.

d. The contribution margin by product line for the current quarter and the current year-to-date.

4. Which of the following reporting practices is permissible for interim financial reporting?

a. Use of the gross profit method for interim inventory pricing.

b. Use of the direct-costing method for determining manufacturing inventories.

c. Deferral of unplanned variances under a standard cost system until year-end.

d. Deferral of inventory market declines until year-end.   (AICPA adapted)

Exercise 14–2. The following account titles are found on the books of XYZ Corporation:

1. Inventory.
2. Prepaid Expenses.
3. Advertising.
4. Research and Development Costs.
5. Accounts Payable.

Required:

Discuss the method that is used for evaluating each of the above accounts for presentation in interim financial statements and indicate the deviation, if any, from normal accounting procedures that is required for such presentation.

Exercise 14–3. Tempo Company sells a single product. On June 1, 19x7, the company had an inventory of 1,000 units priced at FIFO cost of $4,500. The company's product transactions for the year ended May 31, 19x8, were as follows:

[Relates to Exercise 14–3]

Quarter	Units purchased	Cost per unit purchased	Units sold	End of quarter current cost per unit
First	2,000	$4.00	2,500	$4.50
Second	4,000	4.50	4,000	5.00
Third	5,000	5.00	3,500	4.50*
Fourth	3,000	4.50	4,000	5.50

*Decline not considered to be temporary.

Required:

Compute for Tempo Company the cost of goods sold for each of the four quarters of the year ended May 31, 19x8.

Exercise 14–4. FOX Company anticipates that its ordinary income for the fiscal year will be $200,000. The anticipated tax credits are $20,000, and the income tax rate is 50 percent. No permanent differences are anticipated for the year.

Required:

a. Compute the estimated annual effective tax rate for FOX Company.

b. Compute the tax provision for each quarter, assuming quarterly income to be as follows:

$50,000 in the first quarter.
$60,000 in the second quarter.
$50,000 in the third quarter.
$70,000 in the fourth quarter.

Assume also that no changes in the tax rate or in the tax credits occurred during the year and that the projection for ordinary income did not change in the first three quarters of the fiscal year.

Exercise 14–5. The expected ordinary income of BBC Company for the full fiscal year is $300,000. BBC's income is taxable at a 40 percent rate, and its anticipated tax credits for the coming year amount to $30,000. The quarterly income (loss) figures for BBC are as follows:

$100,000 in the first quarter.
$(40,000) in the second quarter.
$120,000 in the third quarter.
$110,000 in the fourth quarter.

During the third quarter of the year, the projection for ordinary income changed from $300,000 to $280,000.

Required:

Compute the quarterly income tax provision for BBC Company assuming that no changes in the tax rate or in the tax credits occurred during the year.

Exercise 14–6. Interim financial reporting has become an important topic in accounting. There has been considerable discussion as to the proper method of reflecting results of operations at interim dates. Accordingly, the Accounting Principles Board issued an *Opinion* clarifying some aspects of interim financial reporting.

Required:

a. Discuss generally how revenue should be recognized at interim dates and specifically how revenue should be recognized for industries subject to large seasonal fluctuations in revenue and for long-term contracts using the percentage-of-completion method at annual reporting dates.

b. Discuss generally how product and period costs should be recognized at interim dates. Also discuss how inventory and cost of goods sold may be afforded special accounting treatment at interim dates.

c. Discuss how the provision for income taxes is computed and reflected in interim financial statements. (CPA adapted)

Exercise 14–7.

1. A company that uses the last-in, first-out (LIFO) method of inventory pricing finds at an interim reporting date that there has been a partial liquidation of the base period inventory level. The decline is considered temporary, and the partial liquidation will be replaced prior to year-end. The amount shown as inventory at the interim reporting date should—

a. Not give effect to the LIFO liquidation, and cost of sales for the interim reporting period should in-

clude the expected cost of replacement of the liquidated LIFO base.

b. Be shown at the actual level, and cost of sales for the interim reporting period should reflect the decrease in LIFO base period inventory level.

c. Not give effect to the LIFO liquidation, and cost of sales for the interim reporting period should reflect the decrease in the LIFO base period inventory level.

d. Be shown at the actual level, and the decrease in inventory level should *not* be reflected in the cost of sales for the interim reporting period.

2. Which of the following is *not* an acceptable treatment of factory overhead variances at an interim reporting date?

a. Apportion the total only between work in process and finished goods inventories on hand at the end of the interim reporting period.

b. Apportion the total only between that part of the current period's production remaining in inventories at the end of the period and that part sold during the period.

c. Carry forward the total to be offset by opposite balances in later periods.

d. Charge or credit the total to the cost of goods sold during the period.

3. Bailey Company, a calendar-year corporation, has the following income before income tax provision and estimated effective annual income tax rates for the first three quarters of 19x9:

Quarter	Income before income tax provision	Estimated effective annual tax rate at end of quarter
First	$60,000	40%
Second	70,000	40
Third	40,000	45

Bailey's income tax provision in its interim income statement for the third quarter should be—

a. $18,000.
b. $24,500.
c. $25,500.
d. $76,500.

PROBLEMS

Problem 14–8. The results of operations by quarter for Brett Corporation for 19x7 are as follows:

Quarter	Ordinary income (or loss)	Extraordinary items (loss)
First	$20,000	
Second	40,000	$(65,000)
Third	(60,000)	
Fourth	70,000	

The tax rate applicable for Brett Corporation is 50 percent.

Required:

a. Show how the tax expense (benefit) for each quarter would be disclosed on the interim financial statements for Brett Corporation (assuming that the tax benefits of all net operating losses are assured beyond reasonable doubt).

b. How would the solution to (a) change if it is assumed that at the time of incurring a net operating loss, it does not appear that such losses can be carried forward.

Problem 14–9. Following are some of Jay Company's annual budgeted income statement items for 19x8:

Sales	$200,000
Cost of sales	140,000
Operating expenses	30,000
Income tax expense	11,000
Net income	19,000

The budgeted sales by quarter were $50,000, $25,000, $75,000, and $50,000. The cost of sales is estimated to be 70 percent of sales. Operating expenses usually do not benefit more than one interim period. The tax expense is based on a rate of 30 percent on the first $10,000 of income and 40 percent on all income over $10,000. Some transactions which took place in 19x8 are as follows:

1. Actual sales by quarters were $40,000, $35,000, $80,000, and $40,000.
2. The cost of goods sold percentage to sales for the year was as budgeted, except that at year-end, the inventory was written down by $1,000 to record it at the lower of cost or market.
3. Operating expenses by quarter were $6,000, $5,000, $12,000, and $7,000.

Required:

Prepare a four-column presentation (a column for each quarter) showing the amount of sales, cost of goods sold, operating expenses, income tax expense, and net income that should be reported on Jay Company's 19x8 interim financial statements.

Problem 14–10. ABC Company forecast pretax income of $400,000 for the year ending July 31, 19x8. No timing difference between pretax accounting income and taxable income was anticipated. However, the forecast permanent differences between accounting and taxable income for 19x8 were as follows:

Dividend exclusion	$80,000
Goodwill amortization	10,000

The anticipated investment tax credits for ABC for 19x8 were $30,000. The company's combined federal and state income tax rate is 50 percent.

ABC's quarterly pretax accounting income for the year ended July 31, 19x8, were as follows:

First quarter	$100,000
Second quarter	90,000
Third quarter	110,000
Fourth quarter	115,000

In the second quarter, ABC altered its permanent difference estimate for 19x8 for dividend exclusion to $90,000, and its investment tax credits to $40,000.

As of July 31, 19x8, the actual amounts for permanent differences and investment credit were as follows:

Dividend exclusion	$85,000
Goodwill amortization	10,000
Investment tax credit	50,000

Required:

Compute the effective combined federal and state income tax rates which ABC should use for its quarterly interim financial statements for the year ended July 31, 19x8.

Problem 14–11. On January 1, 19x4, Polar Corporation paid $84,000 for a piece of equipment with no salvage value and a useful life of six years. Polar depreciated the equipment on the sum-of-the-years'-digits (SYD) method until the third quarter of 19x8, at which time it changed to the straight-line (SL) method of depreciation. Polar's income before tax (45 percent rate), depreciation on the equipment, cumulative effect of the accounting change, and extraordinary items is $100,000 in each year and $25,000 in each quarter. The only extraordinary item is a gain in the fourth quarter of 19x8 of $20,000 (net of related income tax).

Required:

a. Prepare SYD and SL depreciation schedules (and income tax expense) showing the income effect of the depreciation change.

b. Determine the cumulative effect (net of income taxes) of the change in accounting principle from the SYD to the SL depreciation or retained earnings at January 1, 19x8.

c. Prepare partial comparative statements of annual income for 19x8 and 19x7, including pro forma disclosures of income before extraordinary items and net income.

d. Prepare partial comparative statements of interim income for the third quarter of 19x8; include also year-to-date amounts for both 19x8 and 19x7.

e. Prepare a schedule showing the effect of the change in accounting principle on the income of the first and second quarters of 19x8. Begin with net income as originally reported and calculate income as restated.

Problem 14–12. The Anderson Manufacturing Company, a California corporation listed on the Pacific Coast Stock Exchange, budgeted activities for 19x5 as follows:

	Amount	Units
Net sales	$6,000,000	1,000,000
Cost of goods sold	3,600,000	1,000,000
Gross margin	2,400,000	
Selling, general, and administrative expenses	1,400,000	
Operating earnings	1,000,000	
Nonoperating revenues and expenses	–0–	
Earnings before income taxes	1,000,000	
Estimated income taxes (current and deferred)	550,000	
Net earnings	$ 450,000	
Earnings per share of common stock	$4.50	

Anderson has operated profitably for many years and has experienced a seasonal pattern of sales volume and production similar to the following ones forecasted for 19x5. Sales volume is expected to fol-

low a quarterly pattern of 10, 20, 35, and 35 percent, respectively, because of the seasonality of the industry. Also, due to production and storage capacity limitations it is expected that production will follow a pattern of 20, 25, 30, and 25 percent per quarter, respectively.

At the conclusion of the first quarter of 19x5, the controller of Anderson has prepared and issued the following interim report for public release:

	Amount	Units
Net sales	$ 600,000	100,000
Cost of goods sold	360,000	100,000
Gross margin	240,000	
Selling, general, and administrative expenses	275,000	
Operating loss	(35,000)	
Loss from warehouse fire	(175,000)	
Loss before income taxes	(210,000)	
Estimated income taxes	–0–	
Net loss	$(210,000)	
Loss per share of common stock	$(2.10)	

The following additional information is available for the first quarter just completed, but was not included in the public information released:

1. The company uses a standard cost system in which standards are set at currently attainable levels on an annual basis. At the end of the first quarter there was underapplied fixed factory overhead (volume variance) of $50,000 that was treated as an asset at the end of the quarter. Production during the quarter was 200,000 units, of which 100,000 were sold.

2. The selling, general, and administrative expenses were budgeted on a basis of $900,000 fixed expenses for the year plus 50 cents variable expenses per unit of sales.

3. Assume that the warehouse fire loss met the conditions of an extraordinary loss. The warehouse had an undepreciated cost of $320,000; $145,000 was recovered from insurance on the warehouse. No other gains or losses are anticipated this year from similiar events or transactions, nor has Anderson had any similar losses in preceding years; thus, the full loss will be deductible as an ordinary loss for income tax purposes.

4. The effective income tax rate, for federal and state taxes combined, is expected to average 55

percent of earnings before income taxes 19x5. There are no permanent differences between pretax accounting earnings and taxable income.

5. Earnings per share were computed on the basis of 100,000 shares of capital stock outstanding. Anderson has only one class of stock issued, no long-term debt outstanding, and no stock option plan.

Required:

a. Without reference to the specific situation described above, what are the standards of disclosure for interim financial data (published interim financial reports) for publicly traded companies? Explain.

b. Identify the weaknesses in form and content of Anderson's interim report without reference to the additional information.

c. For each of the five items of additional information, indicate the preferable treatment for each item for interim-reporting purposes and explain why that treatment is preferable.   (AICPA adapted)

Problem 14–13. The controller of Predictive Corporation wants to issue to stockholders quarterly income statements that will be predictive of expected annual income. He proposes to allocate all fixed costs for the year among quarters in proportion to the number of units expected to be sold in each quarter, stating that the annual income can then be predicted through the use of the following equation:

$$\text{Expected annual income} = \text{Quarterly income} \times \frac{100 \text{ percent}}{\text{Percent of unit sales applicable to quarter.}}$$

Predictive Corporation's budget calls for the following activity during 19x5 (in thousands except per unit data):

	Units	Average sales price per unit	Total
Sales revenue:			
First quarter	500	$2.00	$1,000
Second quarter	100	1.50	150
Third quarter	200	2.00	400
Fourth quarter	200	2.00	400
Total for year	1,000		$1,950
Cost to be incurred:			
Variable:			
Manufacturing		$0.70	$ 700
Selling and administrative . . .		0.25	250
		$0.95	$ 950
Fixed:			
Manufacturing			$ 380
Selling and administrative . . .			220
			600
Income before taxes			$ 400

Required (ignore income taxes):

Assuming that Predictive's actual activities do not vary from budgeted expectations, will the controller's plan achieve his objectives? If not, how can it be modified to do so? Explain and give illustrative computations.   (AICPA adapted)

15

Earnings per share

OVERVIEW

The earnings per share (EPS) statistic is the most widely used and quoted measure of corporate performance. The net income number expresses in one figure the net results of operations achieved by an enterprise in a given period of time. While accountants and others recognize or should recognize the limited significance that can be attached to any one figure taken out of the context of the financial statements taken as a whole, such a figure is nevertheless useful in computing such widely used measures of management performance as return on equity and return on total assets.

The owners of the enterprise, its equity shareholders, must however relate the earnings per individual share to the price at which they can buy or sell the common stock and to the dividend which is paid on each share. Thus, the earnings per share figure forms the basis of such important investment measures as the price earnings ratio and dividend yield and is, consequently, a most widely used measure.

This chapter reviews the standards and the proceedures which govern the computation of earnings per share under a variety of circumstances ranging from the simple to the more complex, including those which involve business combinations.

EVOLUTION OF THE EARNINGS PER SHARE COMPUTATION

For many years accountants were not closely associated with either the computation or the presentation of earnings per share. In an early prouncement on the subject (*ARB 49*—issued in 1958), the main concern was with averaging the number of shares in cases where there was significant change during the year.

In the mid-1960s, when a wave of mergers brought with it the widespread use of convertible securities as financing devides, the attention of analysts and of accountants turned to the denominator of the EPS computation, that is, the number of shares of common stock by which the earnings should be divided. It became obvious that the prior practice of considering only the common shares actually outstanding, without a consideration of the future potential dilution which is inherent in convertible securities, had often led to an overstatement of EPS.

The managements of merger-minded companies had discovered that it was possible to buy the earnings of a company by compensating its owners with low-yield convertible securities which in effect represented a deferred equity interest. Since the acquired earnings were immediately included in the combined income of the merged enterprise while the dilutive effect of the issuance of convertible securities was ignored, an illusory increase in EPS was thus achieved. Such growth in EPS increased the value of the securities, thus enabling the merger-minded company to carry this value enhancing process even further by using its attractive securities to effect business combinations at increasingly advantageous terms for its existing stockholders.

The distortion to which EPS figures which ignored the dilutive effect of convertible securities and other instruments and provisions were subject became more and more apparent and led to calls for reform.

The Accounting Principles Board first tackled the subject in Part II of *APB Opinion 9,* and in 1969 refined its thinking on the subject in *APB Opinion 15,* which remains the authoritative guide on the computation and presentation of EPS.

MAJOR PROVISIONS OF *APB OPINION 15*

APB Opinion 15 looks to the substance of a securities issue rather than merely to its legalistic form. It requires that EPS be presented on the face of the income statement. It contains the following provisions to guide in the computation of both primary and fully diluted EPS.

Simple capital structure

If a corporation has a simple capital structure which consists only of common stock and nonconvertible senior securites and does not include potentially dilutive securities, then most of the provisions of the *Opinion* do not apply. In that case a single presentation of EPS is called for and is computed as follows:

$$\frac{\text{Net income less claims of senior equity securities}}{\begin{array}{c}\text{Weighted average number of common shares outstanding during the}\\\text{period after adjustments for stock splits and dividends (including those}\\\text{effected after balance sheet date but before completion of financial}\\\text{statements)}\end{array}}$$

In the above computation, dividends of cumulative senior equity securities, whether earned or not, should be deducted from net income or added to net loss.

Computation of weighted average of common shares outstanding

The theoretically correct weighted average number of shares is the sum of shares outstanding each day divided by the number of days in the period. Less precise averaging methods, such as on a monthly or quarterly basis, where there is little change in the number of shares outstanding, is also permissible.

In the computation:

1. Reacquired shares should be excluded from date of acquisition.
2. Shares sold or issued in a purchase of assets should be included from date of issuance.
3. Previously reported EPS data should be adjusted retroactively for changes in outstanding shares resulting from stock splits or stock dividends.

Example of computation of weighted average number of shares outstanding

19x1	Transactions in common stock	Number of shares
January 1	Outstanding	1,200
February 2	Stock options exercised	200
April 15	Issued as 5% stock dividend	70
August 16	Issued in pooling of interests	400
September 2	Sale for cash	300
October 18	Repurchase of treasury shares	(100)
		2,070

Computation of weighted average number of shares

		Shares outstanding		Product:
		Number	Days	Share—days
Date of change:				
January 1		1,200		
Retroactive adjustment:				
For stock dividend (5%)		60		
Issued in pooling		400		
January 1—adjusted		1,660	32	53,120
February 2—stock option	200			
+ 5% stock dividend	10	210		
		1,870	212	396,440
September 2—sale for cash		300		
		2,170	46	99,820
October 18—repurchase		(100)		
		2,070	75	155,250
			365	704,630

19x1 weighted average number of shares $\dfrac{704,630}{365}$ = 1,930 shares

As can be seen in the illustrations above, shares issued in a pooling of interests are included in the computation of EPS as of the beginning of all periods presented. This is so because under the pooling of interests concept the merged companies are assumed to have been combined since their respective inceptions. In the case of purchases the EPS reflect new shares issued only from date of acquisition.

Stock dividends are also adjusted retroactively, thus applying to the computation of the entire year. Issuances of stock (as a result of stock options or sale) as well as repurchases of stock all involve changes in entity resources and thus enter the computation only from the date of the transaction.

The term *earnings per common share* should be used without qualifying language only when the company has in fact a simple capital structure and no agreements exist for contingent issuances of common stock. A company can also make such presentation of earnings per share if the total dilution from dilutive securities or other provisions does not exceed 3 percent. (i.e., if the adjusted net income divided into total shares which include dilutive securities results in an EPS number not lower than 97 percent of that arrived at without considering such dilutive securities).

COMPLEX CAPITAL STRUCTURE

A company is deemed to have a complex capital structure if it has outstanding potentially dilutive securities such as convertible securities, options, warrants, or other stock issue agreements.

By dilution is meant a reduction in EPS (or increase in net loss per share) resulting from the assumption that convertible securities have been converted into common stock, or that options and warrants have been exercised, or that shares have been issued in compliance with certain contracts.

A company having a complex capital structure has to give a dual presentation of EPS if the aggregate dilutive effect of convertible and other securities is more than 3 percent. Such dual presentation is to be effected with equal prominence on the income statement and show (1) primary EPS and (2) fully diluted EPS.

Primary EPS.

Primary EPS is the amount of earnings attributable to each share of common stock outstanding plus dilutive common stock equivalents.

Definition of common stock equivalents (CSE). The concept of CSE is basic to the approach adopted in the *APB Opinion 15*. It denotes a security which derives the major portion of its value from its common stock characteristics or conversion privileges. Thus, a CSE is a security which, because of its terms or the circumstances under which it was issued, is deemed to be in substance equivalent to common stock. The following are examples of CSE:

1. *Convertible debt and convertible preferred stocks* are CSE only if at the time of issuance they have a cash yield (based on market price) of less than $66^2/_3$ percent of the then current bank prime[1] interest rate.

---

[1] The FASB is expected to substitute in 1982 the average Aa corporate bond yield in this CSE test.

If a convertible security is issued which is a CSE and that same security was previously issued when it was not a CSE at time of issuance, the earlier issued shares or debt should be considered a CSE *from the date of issuance of the later shares or debt.* Prior periods EPS should not be restated. Similarly, any subsequent issuance of shares or debt with the same terms as previously issued shares or debt classified as a CSE should be classified as a CSE at its time of issuance even though the later issue of shares or debt would not be a CSE under the yield test at the later date of issue. This requirement can be overcome by a change in a term or condition having economic significance which is expected to affect prices in the securities market.

2. *Stock options and warrants (including stock purchase contracts)* are always to be considered as CSE.

3. *Participating securities and two-class common stocks* are CSE if their praticipation features enable their holders to share in the earnings potential of the issuing corporation, on substantially the same basis as common stock, even though the securities may not give the holder the right to exchange his shares for common stock.

4. *Contingent shares*—if shares are to be issued in the future upon the mere passage of time, they should be considered as outstanding for purposes of computing EPS. If additional shares of stock are issuable for little or no consideration upon the satisfaction of certain conditions, they should be considered as outstanding when the conditions are met.

5. *Securities of subsidiaries* may be considered common stock equivalents and conversion or exercise assumed for computing consolidated or parent company EPS when—

    a. *As to the subsidiary:*
       (1) Certain of the subsidiary's securities are CSE in relation to its own common stock.
       (2) Other of the subsidiary's convertible securities, although not CSE in relation to its own common stock, would enter into the computation of its fully diluted earnings per share.

    b. *As to the parent:*
       (1) The subsidiary's securities are convertible into the parent company's common stock.
       (2) The subsidiary issues options and warrants to purchase the parent company's common stock.

Computation of primary EPS.   If CSE with a dilutive effect are present, then primary EPS should be based on the weighted average number of shares of common stock and CSE. The computation is also based on the assumption that convertible securities which are CSE were converted at the beginning of the period (or at time of issuance, if later), and that requires adding back to net income any deductions for interest or dividends, net of tax effect, related to such securities, a procedure known as the "if converted" method. It can be summarized as follows:

Numerator	**Denominator**
Net income for the period.	Average of shares outstanding.
(Less preferred dividends applicable to preferred stock considered as CSE).	Add—number of common shares into which convertible preferred shares and convertible bonds (which are deemed to be CSE) are convertible adjusted for proportion of time outstanding.
Add back tax adjusted interest on convertible bonds considered as CSE.	

This method recognizes that if a security issue is considered the equivalent of common stock for a period, any related effects on income must also be removed.

OPTIONS AND WARRANTS

Options and warrants are instruments which entitle the holder to buy a given amount (or fraction) of common shares at a given price for a specified period of time (usually shorter in the case of options than in the case of warrants). The computation of the dilutive effects of options and warrants, which are always considered as CSE, must, in turn, recognize the benefits accruing from the cash, or "boot" which the converter of these instruments into common must pay to the issuing company. This has given rise to the *treasury stock* method.

The treasury stock method recognizes the use of proceeds that would be obtained upon exercise of options and warrants in computing EPS. It assumes that any proceeds would be used to purchase common stock at current market prices. For options and warrants, the treasury stock method of computing the dilution to be reflected in EPS should be used (except for two exceptions to be explained). Under the treasury stock method:

1. EPS data are computed as if the options and warrants were exercised at the beginning of the period (or at time of issuance, if later) and as if the funds obtained thereby were used to purchase common stock at the average market price during the period.
2. But the assumption of exercise is not reflected in EPS data until the market price of the common stock obtainable has been in excess of the exercise price for substantially all of three consecutive months ending with the last month of the period to which EPS relate.[2]

---

[2]The following formula will yield the number of incremental shares which will result from applying the treasury stock method to options or warrants (Y):

$$Y = \frac{M - E}{M} (N)$$

where M is the market price per share, E is the exercise price of option or warrant per common share and N is the total number of shares obtainable on exercise.

Example of treasury stock method

Assumptions:
   1,000,000 common shares outstanding (no change during year)
   $80 average market price for the common stock for the year
   100,000 warrants outstanding exercisable at $48

Computation:
  Shares
     100,000 shares issuable on exercise of warrants (proceeds $4,800,000)
    (60,000) shares acquirable with $4,800,000 proceeds (at $80 per share)
     40,000 CSE
  1,000,000 common shares
  1,040,000 shares used for computing primary EPS

First exception to treasury stock method. Warrants or debt indentures may permit or require certain uses of funds with exercise of warrants. Examples:

1. Debt is permitted or required to be tendered towards exercise price.
2. Proceeds of exercise are required to retire debt.
3. Convertible securities require cash payments upon conversion.

In these cases, an "if converted" method, which assumes conversion on exercise at the beginning of the period should be applied as if retirement or conversion of the securities had occurred and as if the excess proceeds, if any, had been applied to the purchase of common stock under the treasury stock method.

Second exception to treasury stock method. If the number of shares of common stock obtainable upon exercise of outstanding options and warrants in the aggregate exceeds 20 percent of the number of common shares outstanding at the end of the period for which the computation is being made, the treasury stock method should be modified. In this circumstances all the options and warrants should be assumed to have been exercised and the aggregate proceeds therefrom to have been applied in two steps:

1. As if the funds obtained were first applied to the repurchase of outstanding common shares at the average market price during the period (treasury stock method) but not to exceed 20 percent of the outstanding shares; and then
2. As if the balance of the funds were applied first to reduce any short-term or long-term borrowings and any remaining funds were invested in U.S. government securities or commercial paper, with appropriate recognition of any income tax effect.
3. The results of steps 1 and 2 of the computation (whether dilutive or antidilutive) should be aggregated, and if the net effect is dilutive, it should enter into the EPS computation.

Example of second exception of treasury stock method

	Case 1	Case 2
Assumptions:		
Net income for year	$ 4,000,000	$ 3,000,000
Common shares outstanding (no change during year)	3,000,000	3,000,000
Options and warrants outstanding to purchase equivalent		
shares.	1,000,000	1,000,000
20% limitation on assumed repurchase	600,000	600,000
Exercise price per share	$15	$15
Average market value per common share to be used	$20	$14*
Interest rate on borrowings	6%	6%
Computations:		
Application of assumed proceeds ($15 × 1,000,000 shares)		
toward repurchase of outstanding common shares at		
applicable market value (600,000 × $20) and (600,000 ×		
$14)	$12,000,000	$ 8,400,000
Reduction of debt	3,000,000	6,600,000
	$15,000,000	$15,000,000
Adjustment of net income:		
Actual net income	$ 4,000,000	$ 3,000,000
Interest reduction on debt (6%) less 50% tax effect	90,000	198,000
Adjusted net income (A)	$ 4,090,000	$ 3,198,000
Adjustment of shares outstanding:		
Actual number outstanding	3,000,000	3,000,000
Net additional shares issuable (1,00,000 − 600,000)	400,000	400,000
Adjusted shares outstanding (B)	3,400,000	3,400,000
Primary EPS:		
Before adjustment	$1.33	$1.00
After adjustment (A ÷ B)	$1.20	$0.94

*The three consecutive months test has previously been met.

Provisions concerning antidilution. Antidilution is an increase in EPS resulting from the assumption that convertible securities have been converted or that options and warrants have been exercised or other shares have been issued upon the fulfillment of certain conditions. For example, although stock options and warrants (and their equivalents) and stock purchase contracts should always be considered CSE, they should not enter into EPS calculations until the average market price of the common stock exceeds the exercise price of the option or warrant for preferably three consecutive months before the reporting period.

Computations of primary EPS should not give effect to CSE or other contingent issuance for any period in which their inclusion would have the effect of increasing the EPS amount or decreasing the loss per share amount otherwise computed.

Fully diluted EPS

Definition of fully diluted EPS. Fully diluted EPS is designed to show the maximum potential dilution of current EPS on a prospective basis. Fully diluted EPS is the amount of current EPS reflecting the maximum dilution that would have resulted from conversions of all convertible securities whether they are CSEs or not, as long as they are dilutive. Also to reflect dilution resulting from exercises and other contingent issuances that individually would have decreased EPS and in the aggregate would have had a dilutive effect. All such issuances are assumed to have taken place at the beginning of the period (or at the time the event or contingency arose, if later).

When required.   Fully diluted EPS data are required for each period presented if shares of common stock (1) were issued during the period on conversions, exercise, etc., or (2) were contingently issuable at the close of any period presented and if primary EPS for such period would have been affected (dilutively or incrementally) had such actual issuances taken place at the beginning of the period or would have been reduced had such contingent issuances taken place at the beginning of the period.

Computation of fully diluted EPS.   The computation should be based on the assumption that all such issued and issuable shares were outstanding from the beginning of the period (or from the time the contingency arose, if after the beginning of the period). Interest charges applicable to convertible securities and nondiscretionary adjustments that would have been made to items based on net income or income before taxes—such as profit-sharing expense, certain royalties, and investment credit—or preferred dividends applicable to the convertible securities should be taken into account in determining the balance of income applicable to common stock.

Use ending market price for treasury stock method.   The treasury stock method (along with the two exceptions) should be used to compute fully diluted EPS if dilution results from outstanding options and warrants; however, in order to reflect maximum potential dilution, the market price at the close of the period reported upon should be used to determine the number of shares which would be assumed to be repurchased (under the treasury stock method) if such market price is higher than the average price used in computing primary EPS.

Example of computation of fully diluted EPS.   Assume that there are 1,000,000 shares of class A preferred stock and 1,500,000 shares of class B preferred stock outstanding, both issues convertible into common on a share-for-share basis. Two million shares of common are outstanding. Class A preferred is a CSE with a $1.80 dividend; class B is a nonCSE preferred with a $1 dividend. Net income before either preferred dividend was $7,300,000.

Computation

	Shares	Net income	EPS
Net income		$ 7,300,000	
Shares outstanding	2,000,000		
$1.80 preferred dividend		(1,800,000)	
$1.00 preferred dividend		(1,500,000)	
	2,000,000	4,000,000	$2.00
Assume conversion of CSE class A preferred	1,000,000	1,800,000	
	3,000,000	5,800,000	
Primary EPS			1.93
Assume conversion of nonCSE class B preferred	1,500,000	1,500,000*	
	4,500,000	$ 7,300,000	
Fully diluted EPS (beginning with primary EPS			1.62

*Add back $1 preferred dividend.

Since the intention in presenting fully diluted EPS is to show the *maximum* dilution possible, an alternative computation is possible in this case which would yield a lower figure of fully diluted EPS. This computation has as a starting point the outstanding common shares and income after preferred dividends rather than the primary EPS.

Computation

	Shares	Net income	EPS
Shares outstanding and income after dividends	2,000,000	$4,000,000	
Assume conversion of nonCSE class B preferred	1,500,000	1,500,000	
	3,500,000	$5,500,000	
Fully diluted EPS—beginning with outstanding shares and income after preferred dividends			$1.57

The reason why the alternative computation yields a lower fully diluted EPS is that while the $1.80 preferred issue is dilutive for purposes of computing primary EPS, it is antidilutive for purposes of computing the fully diluted EPS.

Provisions regarding antidilution. As with primary EPS, no antidilution should be recognized. Consequently, computations should exclude those securities whose conversion, exercise, or other contingent issuance would have the effect of increasing the EPS amount or decreasing the loss per share amount for each period. Therefore, fully diluted EPS should be $1.57 rather than the $1.62 shown in the preceding computation.

Illustration of the computation of primary and fully diluted EPS

The Complex Corporation had the following changes in its capital structure during 19x6:

	Number of shares
Common stock:	
Balance on January 1	500,000
April 1—issued in conversion of preferred stock	200,000
July 1—sold for cash	100,000
Balance on December 31	800,000
Preferred stock:	
$10 par 8 percent, each convertible into two common shares, issued in 19x3 at $12 per share when the bank prime rate was 7½ percent (Dividend requirement on outstanding shares is $80,000)	
Outstanding January 1	175,000
Converted on April 1, 19x6 (into 200,000 common)	100,000
Outstanding on December 31	75,000
Subordinated debentures:	
$800,000 of 4 percent debentures issued at par in 19x4 when the bank prime rate was 9 percent. The debentures are convertible into 12,000 shares of common and are all outstanding.	
Warrants:	
100,000 warrants issued in 19x4, each to purchase one common share at $80 per share until December 31, 19x9. So far none have been exercised.	

Additional information:

Market prices of common for 19x6 were as follows:

	Average for quarter	End of quarter
First quarter	$78	$79
Second quarter	80	85
Third quarter	90	89
Fourth quarter	88	86

Preferred dividends paid in 19x6:	
First quarter	$35,000
Second quarter	15,000
Third quarter	15,000
Fourth quarter	15,000
Income before extraordinary item in 19x6	$1,200,000
Extraordinary item—condemnation gain (net of tax effect)	300,000
Income tax rate	50%

The following are the steps in the computation of primary and fully diluted EPS of the Complex Corporation for 19x6:

Primary earnings per share

Step No. 1: Computation of weighted average number of common shares outstanding in 19x6.

	Shares outstanding	No. of months	Product
January 1	500,000	3	1,500,000
April 1	700,000	3	2,100,000
July 1	800,000	6	4,800,000
		12	8,400,000

$$\text{Weighted average: } \frac{8,400,000}{12} = 700,000 \text{ shares}$$

Step No. 2: Identification of common stock equivalents (CSE).

Security	(A) Cash yield at issuance	(B) Two/thirds of prime* interest rate at date of issuance	Classification and elaboration
8% convertible preferred	$\frac{\$0.80}{\$12} = 6.67\%$	$^2/_3$ of $7^1/_2\% = 5\%$	Not a CSE because (A) exceeds (B)
4% subordinated debentures	4% (issued at par)	$^2/_3$ of $9\% = 6\%$	A CSE because (B) exceeds (A)
Warrants	—	—	Warrants are always considered as CSE

*Expected to be replaced in 1982 with the average Aa corporate bond yield.

Step No. 3: Computation of primary EPS.

	Shares	Earnings
Income before extraordinary item		$1,200,000
Dividend requirements of outstanding preferred stock (as given) . . .		80,000
		$1,120,000
Weighted average of common shares outstanding	700,000	
Assumed conversion of 4% subordinated debentures	12,000	

Add back to income interest:

4% of $800,000 = ...	$32,000		
Less tax effect at 50%	16,000		16,000

Effect of assumed conversion of warrants:

First quarter: Assumed exercise of warrants should not be reflected until market price of common has been in excess of exercise price for
Second quarter: substantially all of 3 consecutive months (a one time test).

Third quarter: In this quarter above condition was fulfilled.

Total shares issuable on conversion	100,000
$\dfrac{\text{Proceeds}}{\text{Average price for quarter}} = \dfrac{\$8,000,000}{\$90} =$	88,889
Incremental shares for quarter	11,111

Fourth quarter:

Total shares available for conversion	100,000
$\dfrac{\text{Proceeds}}{\text{Average price for quarter}} = \dfrac{\$8,000,000}{88} =$	90,090
Incremental shares for quarter	9,091
Total incremental shares for all quarters	20,202

20,202 divided by 4	5,050	
Totals	717,050	$1,136,000

Primary EPS—before extraordinary item	$\dfrac{\$1,136,000}{717,050} =$	$1.58
Extraordinary item	$\dfrac{\$300,000}{717,050} =$	0.42
Net income per share	$\dfrac{\$1,436,000}{717,050} =$	$2.00

Step 4: Computation of fully diluted EPS.

	Shares	Earnings
Income before extraordinary item		$1,200,000
Weighted average of common shares (as above)	700,000	

Add: Assumed conversion of 4% debentures*

Assumed conversion of 8% convertible Preferred (175,000 × 2)	350,000		
Less: Converted preferred already included in 700,000 weighted average (200,000 × ³⁄₄ year‡) . .	150,000	200,000	—§

Warrants: Assumed conversion

Total shares available for conversion	100,000	
$\dfrac{\text{Proceeds}}{\text{Year-end market price}} = \dfrac{100,000 \times \$80†}{\$86} =$	93,023	
Incremental shares (three year)		6,977
		906,977
		$1,200,000

*These debentures are excluded from this computation because they are antidilutive (i.e., they result in an EPS increment of $1.33). Interest requirement is $32,000 (4% of 800,000) less 50% tax = $16,000. $16,000 ÷ 12,000 (shares) = $1.33. Thus the inclusion of the debentures in the computation would *increase* EPS.

†Note that a computation using individual quarters would have resulted in *fewer* incremental shares.

‡Issued in conversion April 1,19x6.

§If we include the convertible preferred as a CSE dividend requirements need not be deducted.

Fully diluted EPS:

Income before extraordinary item:	$\dfrac{\$1,200,000}{906,977} =$	$1.32
Extraordinary item:	$\dfrac{\$300,000}{906,977} =$	0.33
Net income:	$\dfrac{\$1,500,000}{906,977} =$	$1.65

We will now consider some more complex aspects of earnings per share computations.

MORE COMPLEX ASPECTS OF THE COMPUTATION OF EARNINGS PER SHARE

First, we will consider an example of the classification of contingently issuable shares in the computation of EPS:

Illustration of classification of contingently issuable shares

Rand Consolidated, acquired several companies over the past few years. The company's consolidated net income for 19x6 amounted to $18,450,000. Based on weighted average common shares and common equivalent shares of 4,350,000, the *primary EPS* for the year was $4.24.

Excerpts from specific purchase agreements thought to affect EPS follow. There are no other potentially dilutive securities other than those mentioned in this case.

1. *Collins, Inc.*, was purchased for an initial issuance of 700,000 shares in July of 19x5. For the three years prior to the purchase, Collins reported annual net income of $1,075,000, $1,150,000, and $1,025,000. Under terms of the purchase agreement, an additional 200,000 shares would be issued as a part of the transaction contingent upon the company attaining an earnings level of $1,250,000 in any of the year's 19x6, 19x7, and 19x8 (or a total of 600,000 shares contingently issuable under the agreement). The earnings level of $1,250,000 must be attained in each of these years individually, not for all years on a cumulative or average basis. Collins's earnings amounted to $990,000 in 19x5 and $1,150,000 in 19x6.
2. *Sunburn Unlimited*, a manufacturer of suntan lotions, was purchased in January of 19x3. In the three years prior to the purchase (19x0 through 19x2), earnings had averaged $2,000,000. As a part of the transaction, the prior owners were offered, on a contingent basis, an additional 500,000 shares of common stock deliverable in 19x8, if they could maintain this average earnings over the five years 19x3 through 19x7. A reduced number of shares would be issued (based on a graduated scale in the agreement), if lower earnings levels were maintained. However, the specified $2,000,000 average has thus far been maintained.
3. *Seacoast Apartments, Inc.*, Florida's largest builder of high rise apartment complexes, was purchased in September, 19x6. The purchase agreement called for the immediate issuance of 275,000 shares of common stock and additional blocks of 50,000 shares in each of the years 19x7, 19x8, and 19x9.

We are to present the calculation of fully diluted earnings per share. (For purposes of this calculation, we assume the 4,350,000 weighted average common *and common equivalent shares* is correct for primary EPS calculations and can be properly used, after giving effect to adjustments for other potentially dilutive securities, for fully diluted earnings per share calculations.

Solution:

Determinations of classification of securities as common stock equivalents should be made at the time of issuance. The contingently issuable shares of Rand Consolidated would be classified as follows:

1. 600,000 shares contingently issuable through purchase of Collins, Inc. Since the specified earnings level was not attained in 19x6, 200,000 of these shares will not have to be issued under the agreement. The remaining 400,000 shares are not common stock equivalents since the required earnings level is not currently being attained.
2. 500,000 shares contingently issuable through purchase of Sunburn Unlimited. These shares would be included in calculation of primary earnings per share since maintenance of a level of earnings currently being attained is the condition to the issuance.
3. 150,000 shares issuable through purchase of Seacoast Apartments, Inc. These shares are common stock equivalents since their issuance is contingent only on the mere passage of time.

Calculation of number of shares to be used in computation of fully diluted earnings per share:

Weighted average common and common equivalent shares used for primary EPS (this amount includes the 500,000 and 150,000 shares contingently issuable under the above described Sunburn Unlimited and Seacoast Apartments, Inc. purchase agreements).	4,350,000
Additional shares issuable under the Collins, Inc., purchase agreement. . .	400,000
Weighted average number of shares used for fully diluted EPS.	4,750,000
Calculation of adjusted net income for purpose of fully diluted earnings per share calculation.	
Net income	$18,450,000
Adjustment to give effect to increase in earnings specified by Collins, Inc. purchase agreement ($1,250,000 − $1,150,000 = $100,000)	100,000
	$18,550,000
Calculation of fully diluted earnings per share ($18,550,000 ÷ 4,750,000) . .	$3.91

Next we will consider an example of the effects of issuance of options on the computation of EPS.

Illustration of option agreements in the computation of EPS

Apex Manufacturing Company, a fabricator of precision bearings, has run into production problems over the past four years. This resulted in a steady decline in profits. In an attempt to alleviate this problem, the company hired a vice president for production, a new plant foreman, and a production control specialist. As an incentive, the company entered into stock purchase agreements with these individuals in June of 19x1. Details of the agreements are as follows:

Individual	Number of shares	Purchase price
Production VP	30,000	$1.75
Plant foreman	15,000	2.75
Production control specialist	20,000	2.10

The options can be exercised at any time, once the company's earnings exceed $100,000 per year. Through production planning and quality control, these individuals reduced the company's cost of production, resulting in net income of $160,000 for the year ended June 30, 19x2. None of the options had been exercised prior to June 30, 19x2.

The market price of the company's common stock ranged from a high of $2.21 to a low of $2.12. Asssuming a weighted-average common stock outstanding of 400,000 shares and an average market price of $2.15 per share for the full year, we are to compute the primary EPS for 19x2.

Solution:

Average weighted shares of common stock outstanding		400,000
Incremental shares resulting from stock purchase agreements:		
Production VP:		
Assumed proceeds 30,000 shares at $1.75 or $52,500.		
Shares issuable	30,000	
Shares purchased on market, $52,500 ÷ 2.15	24,418	
Net incremental shares		5,582
Plant foreman—15,000 shares at $2.75.		
Assumption of exercise not made since there is antidilution due to purchase price in excess of market. The rule regarding "reasonable groupings" does not mean that dilutive and antidilutive securities can be combined for computational purposes.		
Production control specialist:		
Assumed proceeds 20,000 shares at $2.10 or $42,000.		
Shares issuable	20,000	
Shares purchased on market, $42,000 ÷ $2.15	19,535	
Net incremental shares		465
Total common shares and common equivalent shares		406,047
Earnings		$160,000
Primary EPS		$0.39

(Please note that the 39 cents EPS obtained above represents dilution of less than 3 percent from the 40 cents ($160,000 ÷ 400,000 shares) that would result if the options were ignored. Therefore, the options may be ignored; immaterial dilution *may be* but does not have to be shown.)

Computations involving changing conversion rates or exercise prices

When the terms of convertible securities change in the future, such as is the case when conversion rates of debentures or exercise prices of warrants change over time, recognition must be accorded to these factors in EPS computations. In the case of *fully diluted* EPS, *APB Opinion 15* requires that only the most attractive rate or price during the 10 years following the latest fiscal period be used. Concerning the computation of primary EPS, the *Opinion* provides (par. 57):

> For primary earnings per share computations, the conversion rate or exercise price in effect for the period presented is used. If the holder does not have the right to convert or exercise the security until after that period, the earliest effective conversion rate or exercise price during the five years following the close of the period is used.

Examples of EPS computations in a period during which a business combination occurs

The conceptual difference between a business combination accounted for under the pooling of interests method and that accounted for under the purchase method calls for different treatments in the computation of EPS.

Thus, in the case of a purchase, the EPS computation should reflect new shares only from the date of acquisition as income of the acquired entity is included only from this date.

In the case of a pooling of interests, on the other hand, the computation should be based on the total weighted average of outstanding shares of the combining companies, adjusted to equivalent shares of the surviving company for all periods presented. This is so because under the pooling of interests concept the results of operations are combined for all periods presented.

Example of computation

Pooling of interests

Assumptions: On July 1, 19x2, company A and B merged to form company C. The transaction was accounted for as a *pooling of interests.*

	Company A	Company B
Net income January 1 to June 30, 19x2	$100,000	$150,000
Outstanding shares of common stock at June 30, 19x2	20,000	8,000
Shares sold to public April 1, 19x2	10,000	

		Company C
Net income July 1 to December 31, 19x2		$325,000
Common shares issued for acquisition of:		
Company A		200,000
Company B		400,000
Computation:		
Net income ($100,000 + $150,000 + $325,000)		$575,000
Average shares outstanding during year, using equivalent shares for pooled companies:		
Company A:		
100,000 × 3 months	300,000	
200,000 × 3 months	600,000	
Company B:		
400,000 × 6	2,400,000	
Company C:		
600,000 × 6	3,600,000	
	6,900,000	
Weighted average (6,900,000 ÷ 12)	575,000	
Net income per weighted average number of shares of common stock outstanding during the year (equivalent shares used for pooled companies)		$1.00

Purchase

Assumptions: Company X has outstanding on January 1, 19x3, 90,000 shares of common stock. On October 1, 19x3, company X issued 30,000 shares of its own common stock for another company. This transaction was accounted for as purchase. Net income for 19x3 for company X was $250,000 to October 1, and the net income of the combined entities for the last three months of the fiscal year ending December 31, 19x3, was $42,500. The acquired company had net income of $40,000 during the first nine months of the year. There were no other capital transactions during the year.

Computation:

9 months × 90,000 shares outstanding	810,000
3 months × 120,000 shares outstanding	360,000
	1,170,000

$$\text{Average shares } \frac{1,170,000}{12} = 97,500$$

Net income per weighted average number of shares of common stock outstanding during the year $\dfrac{\$292,500}{97,500} = \$3.00$

EPS computations of investor companies with affiliates

An investor corporation must, in computing its EPS, recognize the dilution inherent in the capital structure of an investee corporation whose results of operations it picks up on the equity method. Similar considerations also apply in the case of EPS computations for consolidated financial statements.

The first step in this recognition process is to compute the primary and fully diluted EPS of the investee corporation. The second step is to exclude from the Investor Company income the net income derived from picking up the equity in earnings of the Investee Company. That income is replaced in the numerator by the shares of common shares of the Investee which are owned times the above computed primary EPS of the Investee. Assuming the Investor Company owns 1,500 shares of the Investee, the computation will be as follows:

$$\frac{\text{Investor's primary earnings } less \text{ equity in earnings of Investee} + 1,500 \left(\begin{array}{l} \text{Investee's} \\ \text{primary} \\ \text{EPS} \end{array} \right)}{\text{Investor's common shares plus dilutive common stock equivalents}}$$

In a consistent fashion the Investor Company's fully diluted EPS will be computed as follows:

$$\frac{\text{Investor's fully diluted earnings } less \text{ equity in earnings of Investee} + 1,500 \left(\begin{array}{l} \text{Investee's fully} \\ \text{diluted EPS} \end{array} \right)}{\left(\begin{array}{l} \text{Investor's common} \\ \text{shares plus dilutive} \\ \text{common stock} \\ \text{equivalents} \end{array} \right) + \left(\begin{array}{l} \text{Additional Investor Company's} \\ \text{common which would result} \\ \text{from conversion of} \\ \text{dilutive senior securities} \end{array} \right)}$$

Illustration of EPS computation involving an affiliate

The following data from the EPS computations of Investor Company are available for the fiscal year ended December 31, 19x8:

Primary earnings (numerator)	$100,000
Fully diluted earnings (numerator)	112,500
Equity in earnings of affiliate included in both above figures	20,000
Number of share in primary EPS computation (denominator)	50,000 shares
Number of share in fully diluted EPS computation (denominator)	75,000 shares

Additional information:

Affiliated Company's—primary EPS	. . . . . .	$1.20
	fully diluted EPS	1.00

Investor Company is holding 8,000 out of Investee Company's 16,000 common shares outstanding.

Computation of Investor Company's—

1. *Primary EPS:*
$$\frac{(\$100,000 - \$20,000) + (8,000 \times \$1.20)}{50,000} = 1.79$$

2. *Fully diluted EPS:*
$$\frac{(\$112,500 - \$20,000) + (8,000 \times \$1)}{75,000} = 1.34$$

Restatement of prior period EPS

Whenever comparative EPS figures are presented for a number of years, these must be restated to reflect changes in the number of common shares outstanding due to stock dividends, stock splits (and reverse stock splits), issuance of shares in an acquisition accounted under the pooling of interests method, and prior period adjustments of net income. On the other hand, issues of stock for cash or in an acquisition or the repurchase of stock do not require adjustment because the earnings generated are deemed to be affected by the new resources acquired or relinquished in exchange for the shares.

Illustration of prior period EPS restatement

The following are the reported EPS of the Taylor Company for the respective fiscal years shown:

	19x9	19x8	19x7	19x6	19x5	19x4
EPS	$5	$5	$9	$6	$3	$4

The following changes in capitalization took place at the beginning of each of the years shown:

19x5	100% stock dividend paid
19x6	500,000 shares of common stock issued for cash
19x7	200,000 share of common issued on conversion of bonds
19x8	3-for-1 stock split
19x9	50% stock dividend paid

The table adjusting the reported EPS figures for the above changes follows. Note that since the change of the 50 percent stock dividend, for example, occurred in 19x9, it has already been allowed for in that year's EPS computation. All prior years, however, must be adjusted for that dividend by multiplying reported EPS figures by a factor of 100/150.

	Year	Reported EPS	Adjustments			Adjusted EPS
50% stock dividend accounted for:	19x9	$5.00	None			$5.00
	19x8	5.00			(100/150)	3.33
3-for-1 stock split accounted for:	19x7	9.00		$(^1/_3)$	(100/150)	2.00
	19x6	6.00		$(^1/_3)$	(100/150)	1.33
	19x5	3.00		$(^1/_3)$	(100/150)	0.67
100% stock dividend accounted for:	19x4	4.00	$(^1/_2)$	$(^1/_3)$	(100/150)	0.44

Requirements for additional disclosures in conjunction with the presentation of EPS data

Complex capital structures require additional disclosures either on the balance sheet or in notes. Financial statements should include a description sufficient to explain the pertinent rights and privileges of the various securities outstanding.

With regard to EPS data, disclosure is required for—

1. The bases upon which both primary and fully diluted EPS are calculated, identifying the securities entering into computations.
2. All assumptions and any resulting adjustments used in computations.
3. The number of shares issued upon conversion, exercise, etc., during at least the most recent year.

Supplementary EPS data should be disclosed (preferably in a note) if—

1. Conversions during the period would have affected primary EPS (either dilutive *or* incremental effect) if they had taken place at the beginning of the period, or
2. Similar conversions occur after the close of the period but before completion of the financial report.

This supplementary information should show what primary EPS would have been if such conversions had taken place at the *beginning* of the period or date of issuance of security if within the period.

It should be understood that the designation of securities as CSE is done solely for the purpose of determining primary EPS. No changes from present practices in the accounting for such securities or in their presentation within the financial statements are required.

Note E in Appendix A of Chapter 24 represents an example of disclosure in published financial statements of the computation of income (loss) per common and common equivalent share.

Alleged weaknesses of *APB Opinion 15*

As is the case with almost every accounting pronouncement which has a real effect on parties at interest, *APB Opinion 15* has been criticized by members of the APB, by other accountants, by analysts, and others. The major objections center around the following points:

1. That some provisions of the *Opinion* are arbitrary and subjectively determined. This applies to such provisions as to the prime bank rate–cash yield test, the treasury stock method assumptions, the 20 percent limitation on the use of the treasury stock method, and the timing in the determination of when a security actually becomes a common stock equivalent.

2. That there are basic inconsistencies in the *Opinion*. Thus, it is alleged that it is inconsistent to treat certain securities as the equivalent of common stock for purposes of computing EPS while not considering them as part of the stockholder's equity in the balance sheet. As a consequence, the reader may experience difficulty in relating reported EPS with the debt-leverage position pertaining to the same earnings. The other inconsistency often cited is the lack of direct relationship between the bank prime rate, which is a short-term rate, and the interest rate placed on convertible securities which is mostly a *long-term* interest rate.

3. That the determination of EPS often involves a degree of circularity of effect. Thus, reported EPS influence the market price of a security which in turn can influence the classification of a security's status, which in turn influences the EPS computation, which in turn influences the security's market price. As a consequence, under these rules the projection of future EPS requires not only the projection of earning levels but also the projection of future market prices.

While there is considerable validity to many of the above criticisms of *APB Opinion 15,* it must be recognized that accounting, being a social science, cannot benefit, from rules and bench marks which approach scientifically determined precision. These rules are, rather, the result of a compromise of many varied interests and views. It is not quite fair to say that the *Opinion* focuses on a single EPS figure to the exclusion of other factors which properly enter the full analysis of results of operations. What is true is that the public and the marketplace do attach considerable significance to the EPS number and that the organized accounting profession had the obligation to step in and to promulgate rules that would make the computation and presentation of EPS as free of distortion and possible misinterpretation as possible.

QUESTIONS

1. Under what circumstances can the term *earnings per common share* be used without qualifying language?

2. What is the difference between a simple capital structure and a complex capital structure?

3. What type of EPS presentation is required when a company has a complex capital structure?

4. Define common stock equivalents and give examples thereof.

5. How is the primary EPS figure computed when dilutive CSE exist and the "if converted" method is used?

6. *(a)* What are options and warrants? How do they affect the computation of EPS? *(b)* Describe the treasury stock method used in the computation of EPS.

7. Discuss the two major exceptions to the treasury stock method.

8. How does the computation of fully diluted EPS differ from the computaton of primary EPS?

9. Describe the computations of EPS involving changing conversion rates or exercise prices.

10. How are primary EPS and fully diluted EPS computed for investor companies with affiliates?

11. What are the basic additional disclosure requirements in conjunction with the presentation of EPS data?

12. Discuss some of the alleged weaknesses of *APB Opinion 15.*

EXERCISES

Exercise 15–1. Public enterprises are required to present earnings per share data on the face of the income statement.

Required:

Compare and contrast primary earnings per share with fully diluted earnings per share for each of the following:

a. The effect of common stock equivalents on the number of shares used in the computation of earnings per share data.

b. The effect of convertible securities that are *not* common stock equivalents on the number of shares used in the computation of earnings per share data.

c. The effect of antidilutive securities.

(CPA adapted)

Exercise 15–2. The earnings per share data required of a company depend on the nature of its capital structure. A corporation may have a simple capital structure and only compute "earnings per common share" or may have a complex capital structure and have to compute "primary earnings per share" and "fully diluted earnings per share."

Required:

a. Define the term *common stock equivalent* and describe what securities could be considered common stock equivalents in the computation of earnings per share.

b. Define the term *complex capital structure* and discuss the disclosures (both financial and explanatory) necessary for earnings per share when a corporation has a complex capital structure.

(CPA adapted)

Exercise 15–3. You have been assigned to check the X Company's calculation of earnings per share for the current year. You have been supplied with the following calculations:

Net income	$2,079,524
Common shares issued and outstanding:	
Beginning of year	1,106,417
End of year	906,557
Average	1,006,487

Earnings per share:
$$\frac{\$2,079,524}{1,006,487} = \qquad \$2.07 \text{ per share}$$

You have developed the following additional information:

1. There are no other equity securities in addition to the common shares.
2. There are no options or warrants outstanding to purchase common shares.
3. There are no convertible debt securities.
4. Activity in common shares during the year was as follows:

Outstanding, January 1	1,106,417
Treasury shares acquired October 1 . . .	(300,000)
	806,417
Shares reissued, December 1	100,140
Outstanding, December 31	906,557

Required:

Based upon the foregoing information, do you agree with the company's computation of earnings per share for the year? If not, show a corrected computation of EPS.

Exercise 15–4. Items 1 and 2 are based on the following information:

Information concerning the capital structure of the Petrock Corporation is as follows:

	December 31,	
	19x5	19x6
Common stock	90,000 shares	90,000 shares
Covertible preferred stock	10,000 shares	10,000 shares
8% convertible bonds . .	$1,000,000	$1,000,000

During 19x6, Petrock paid dividends of $1 per share on its common stock and $2.40 per share on its preferred stock. The preferred stock is convertible into 20,000 shares of common stock; but is *not* considered a common stock equivalent. The 8 percent convertible bonds are convertible into 30,000 shares of common stock and are considered common stock equivalents. The net income for the year ended December 31, 19x6, was $285,000. Assume that the income tax rate was 50 percent.

1. What should be the primary earnings per share for the year ended December 31, 19x6, rounded to the nearest penny?

    a. $2.38.

    b. $2.51.

    c. $2.84.

    d. $3.13.

2. What should be the fully diluted earnings per share for the year ended December 31, 19x6, rounded to the nearest penny?

    a. $2.15.

    b. $2.32.

    c. $2.61.

    d. $2.74.

3. The Madden Company had 600,000 shares of common stock issued and outstanding at December 31, 19x7. During 19x8, no additional common stock was issued. On January 1, 19x8, Madden issued 400,000 shares of nonconvertible preferred stock. During 19x8, Madden declared and paid $200,000 cash dividends on the common stock and $110,000 on the noncovertible preferred stock. Net income for the year ended December 31, 19x8, was $750,000. What should be Madden's 19x8 earnings per common share, rounded to the nearest penny?

    a. $0.73.

    b. $0.92.

    c. $1.07.

    d. $1.25.   (AICPA adapted)

Exercise 15–5.

1. The 19x3 net income of Mack Company was $100,000, and 100,000 shares of its common stock were outstanding during the entire year. In addition, there were outstanding options to purchase 10,000 shares of common stock at $10 per share. These options were granted in 19x1, and none had been exercised by December 31, 19x3. Market prices of Mack's common stock during 19x3 were:

January 1	$20 per share
December 31	40
Average price	25

The amount which should be shown as Mack's fully diluted earnings per share for 19x3 is (rounded to the nearest cent).

    a. $\dfrac{\$100,000}{110,000 \text{ shares}} = 91$ cents.

    b. $\dfrac{\$100,000}{105,000 \text{ shares}} = 95$ cents.

    c. $\dfrac{\$100,000}{106,000 \text{ shares}} = 94$ cents.

    d. $\dfrac{\$100,000}{107,500 \text{ shares}} = 93$ cents.

2. What is the inherent justification underlying the concept of common stock equivalents in an earnings per share computation?

    a. Form over substance.

    b. Substance over form.

    c. Form and substance considered equally.

    d. Substance over form or form over substance depending on the circumstances.

3. At December 31, 19x4, the Back Company had 350,000 shares of common stock outstanding. On September 1, 19x5, an additional 150,000 shares of common stock were issued. In addition, Back had $10,000,000 of 8 percent convertible bonds outstanding at December 31, 19x4, which are convertible into 200,000 shares of common stock. The bonds were *not* considered common stock equivalents at the time of their issuance, and *no* bonds were converted into common stock in 19x5. The net income for the year ended December 31, 19x5, was $3,000,000. Assuming the income tax rate was 50 percent, what should be the fully diluted earnings per share for the year ended December 31, 19x5?

    a. $4.33.

    b. $5.00.

    c. $5.67.

    d. $7.50.   (AICPA adapted)

Exercise 15–6.

1. A company has net income of $900,000 for computation of primary earnings per share (EPS) and net income of $960,000 for computation of fully diluted EPS. Its capital structure consists only of common stock and $2,000,000 of bonds convertible into common stock, all outstanding all year. The bonds were issued at face value and are *not* common stock equivalents. Assuming an effective income tax rate of 40 percent what is the stated interest rate on these bonds?

a. 3 percent.
b. 5 percent.
c. 7.5 percent.
d. *Cannot* be determined from the information given.

2. The Tam Company's net income for the year ended December 31, 19x6, was $10,000. During 19x6, Tam declared and paid $1,000 cash dividends on preferred stock and $1,750 cash dividends on common stock.

At December 31, 19x6, 12,000 shares of common stock were issued and outstanding, 10,000 of which had been issued and outstanding throughout the year and 2,000 of which were issued on July 1, 19x6. There were *no* other common stock transactions during the year, and there is *no* potential dilution of earnings per share. What should be the 19x6 earnings per common share of Tam, rounded to the nearest penny?

a. 75 cents.
b. 82 cents.
c. 90 cents.
d. $1.

3. In a primary earnings per share computation, the treasury stock method is used for options and warrants to reflect assumed reacquisition of common stock at the average market price during the period. If the exercise price of the options or warrants exceeds the average market price, the computation would—

a. Fairly present primary earnings per share on a prospective basis.
b. Fairly present the maximum potential dilution of primary earnings per share on a prospective basis.
c. Reflect the excess of the number of shares assumed issued over the number of shares assumed reacquired as the potential dilution of earnings per share.
d. Be antidilutive. (AICPA adapted)

Exercise 15–7.

1. At December 31, 19x5, the Hillery Company had 2,000,000 shares of common stock outstanding. On January 1, 19x6, Hillery issued 1,000,000 shares of convertible preferred stock which were considered common stock equivalents at the time of their issuance. During 19x6, Hillery declared and paid $2,000,000 cash dividends on the common stock and $1,000,000 cash dividends on the preferred stock. Net income for the year ended December 31, 19x6, was $9,000,000. Assuming an income tax rate of 50 percent, what should be earnings per share for the year ended December 31, 19x6?

a. $3.
b. $4.
c. $4.25.
d. $4.50.

2. The nature of primary earnings per share involving adjustment for stock options can be described as—

a. Historical because earnings are historical.
b. Historical because it indicates the firm's valuation.
c. Pro forma because it indicates potential changes in number of shares.
d. Pro forma because it indicates potential changes in earnings.

3. At December 31, 19x6, the Front Company had 400,000 shares of common stock outstanding. On October 1, 19x7, an additional 100,000 shares of common stock were issued. In addition, Front had $10,000,000 of 8 percent convertible bonds outstanding at December 31, 19x6, which are convertible into 225,000 shares of common stock. The bonds were considered common stock equivalents at the time of their issuance and *no* bonds were converted into common stock in 19x7. The net income for the year ended December 31, 19x7, was $3,500,000. Assuming the income tax rate was 50 percent, the primary earnings per share for the year ended December 31, 19x7, should be—

a. $6.
b. $6.62.
c. $7.
d. $8.24. (AICPA adapted)

Exercise 15–8.

1. Faucet Company has 2,500,000 shares of common stock outstanding on December 31, 19x7. An additional 500,000 shares of common stock were issued on April 1, 19x8, and 250,000 more on July 1, 19x8. On October 1, 19x8, Faucet issued 5,000, $1,000 face value, 7 percent convertible bonds. Each bond is convertible into 40 shares of common stock. The bonds were *not* considered common stock equivalents at the time of their issuance, and *no* bonds were converted into common stock in 19x8. What is the number of shares to be used in computing primary earnings per share and fully diluted earnings per share, respectively, for the year ended December 31, 19x8?

a. 2,875,000 and 2,975,000.

b. 2,875,000 and 3,075,000.

c. 3,000,000 and 3,050,000.

d. 3,000,000 and 3,200,000.

2. Weaver Company had 100,000 shares of common stock issued and outstanding at December 31, 19x8. On July 1, 19x9, Weaver issued a 10 percent stock dividend, Unexercised stock options to purchase 20,000 shares of common sotck (adjusted for the 19x9 stock dividend) at $20 per share were outstanding at the beginning and end of 19x9. The average market price of Weaver's common stock (which was not affected by the stock dividend) was $25 per share during 19x9. Net income for the year ended December 31, 19x9, was $550,000. What should be Weaver's 19x9 primary earnings per common share, rounded to the nearest penny?

a. $4.82.

b. $5.

c. $5.05.

d. $5.24.

3. During 19x2, Hoffman Company had a net income of $50,000 (no extraordinary items) and 50,000 shares of common stock and 10,000 shares of preferred stock outstanding. Hoffman declared and paid dividends of 50 cents per share to common and $6 per share to preferred. Although the preferred stock is convertible into common stock on a share-for-share basis, it is not classified as a common stock equivalent. For 19x2, Hoffman Company should report fully diluted earnings (loss) per share of—

a. 83 ⅓ cents.

b. $1.

c. (20 cents).

d. 50 cents.   (AICPA adapted)

Exercise 15–9. The Splitting Company, in its annual reports for the years ending December 31, reported per share earnings as shown below:

19x0	$3.00
19x1	2.00
19x2	1.50
19x3	3.00
19x4	1.80
19x5	2.50
19x6	2.50

The following changes in capitalization took place in December of each of the years shown:

19x1	50% stock dividend paid
19x2	400,000 shares of common stock issued for cash
19x3	2-for-1 stock split
19x5	300,000 shares issued on conversion of an outstanding debenture issue
19x6	80% stock dividend paid

The head of the research department has asked you to make the necessary adjustments to the reported figures so that a better comparison of changes in earnings on the common stock can be made.

(CFA adapted)

PROBLEMS

Problem 15–10. Earnings per share (EPS) is the most featured single financial statistic about modern corporations. Daily published quotations of stock prices have recently been expanded to include a "times earnings" figure for many securities which is based on EPS. Often the focus of analysts' discussions will be on the EPS of the corporations receiving their attention.

Required:

a. Explain how dividends or dividend requirements on any class of preferred stock that may be outstanding affect the computation of EPS.

b. One of the technical procedures applicable in EPS computations is the treasury stock method.

(1) Briefly describe the circumstances under which it might be appropriate to apply the treasury stock method.

(2) There is a limit to the extent to which the treasury stock method is applicable. Indicate what this limit is and give a succinct indication of the procedures that should be followed beyond the treasury stock limits.

c. Under some circumstances, convertible debentures would be considered "common stock equivalents" while under other circumstances they would not.

(1) When is it proper to treat convertible debentures as common stock equivalents? What is the effect on computation of EPS in such cases?

(2) In case convertible debentures are not considered as common stock equivalents, explain how they are handled for purposes of EPS computations.

(AICPA adapted)

Problem 15–11. Foster, Inc., showed the following for 19x6:

Income before extraordinary item	$600,000
Extraordinary item—casualty loss (net after	
taxes)	100,000
Net income for period	$500,000

At January 1, 19x6, there were 190,000 shares of common stock outstanding. On October 1, 19x6, an additional 40,000 shares were sold for cash.

In 19x4, 6 percent bonds were issued at par, $1,000,000. These are convertible into 20,000 shares of common stock. None have been converted. At date of issue, the bank prime rate was 8 percent.

In 19x2, 25,000 shares of $3 cumulative preferred stock were issued at $90 per share. Each preferred share is convertible into two shares of common stock. None have been converted. At date of issue, the bank prime rate was 9 percent.

In 19x3, 40,000 options were granted to purchase common stock (one option for each share) at $48 per share. None have been exercised. During 19x6, the average market price per share of common stock was $50 and on December 31, 19x6, the market price was $60. Assume an income tax rate of 40 percent.

Required:

a. Calculate primary earnings per share.

b. Calculate fully diluted earnings per share.

Problem 15–12. The controller of Lafayette Corporation has requested assistance in determining income, primary earnings per share, and fully diluted earnings per share for presentation in the company's income statement for the year ended September 30, 19x2. The company's net income is $540,000 for fiscal year 19x1–x2, and there are no extraordinary items.

Your working papers disclose the following opening balances and transactions in the company's capital stock accounts during the year:

1. Common stock (at October 1, 19x1, stated value $10, authorized 300,000 shares; effective December 1, 19x1, stated value $5, authorized 600,000 shares):

   Balance, October 1, 19x1—issued and outstanding 60,000 shares.

   December 1, 19x1—60,000 shares issued in a 2-for-1 stock split.

   December 1, 19x1—280,000 shares (stated value $5) issued at $39 per share.

2. Treasury stock—common:

   March 1, 19x2—purchased 40,000 shares at $38 per share.

   April 1, 19x2—sold 40,000 shares at $40 per share.

3. Stock purchase warrants, series A (initially, each warrant was exchangeable with $60 for one common share; effective December 1, 19x1, each warrant became exchangeable for two common shares at $30 per share):

   October 1, 19x1—25,000 warrants issued at $6 each.

4. Stock purchase warrants, series B (each warrant is exchangeable with $40 for one common share):

   April 1, 19x2—20,000 warrants issued at $10 each.

5. First-mortgage bonds, $5\frac{1}{2}$ percent, due 19y6 (nonconvertible; priced to yield 5 percent when issued):

   Balance October 1, 19x1—authorized, issued and outstanding—the face value of $1,400,000.

6. Convertible debentures, 7 percent, due 19y9 (initially each $1,000 bond was convertible at any time until maturity into $12\frac{1}{2}$ common shares; effective December 1, 19x1, the conversion rate became 25 shares for each bond):

   October 1, 19x1—authorized and issued at their face value (no premium or discount) of $2,400,000.

The following table shows market prices for the company's securities and the assumed bank prime interest rate during 19x1–x2:

[Relates to Problem 15–12]

	Price (or rate) at			Average for year ended September 30, 19x2
	October 1, 19x1	April 1, 19x2	September 30, 19x2	
Common stock	66	40	36¼	37½*
First-mortgage bonds	88½	87	86	87
Convertible debentures	100	120	119	115
Series A warrants	6	22	19½	15
Series B warrants	—	10	9	9½
Bank prime interest rate	8%	7¾%	7½%	7¾%

*Adjusted for stock split.

Required:

Prepare a schedule computing (1) the primary earnings per share and (2) the fully diluted earnings per share which should be presented in the company's income statement for the year ended September 30, 19x2. A supporting schedule computing the numbers of shares to be used in these computations should also be prepared. (Because of the relative stability of the market price for its common shares, the annual average market price may be used where appropriate in your calculations. Assume an income tax rate of 48 percent.   (AICPA adapted)

Problem 15–13. The following are extracts from two agreements regarding the issue of $5,000,000 and $2,000,000 in convertible debentures, respectively:

Agreement I:
1. Issue price—par.
2. Interest rate—5 percent.
3. Conversion provisions—can be converted into common shares at the rate of two common shares for each $100 of debentures, at any time prior to maturity.
4. Maturity date—July 1, 19y1.
5. Date of issue—July 1, 19x1.
6. Amount of issue—$5,000,000.

Agreement II:
1. Issue price—par.
2. Interest rate—6 percent.
3. Conversion provisions—can be converted into common shares at the rate of two common shares for each $100 of debentures, at any time prior to maturity.
4. Maturity date—September 1, 19x6.

5. Date of issue—September 1, 19x1.
6. Amount of issue—$2,000,000.

In addition you are aware of the following facts:
1. The prime interest rate of July 1, 19x1, and September 1, 19x1, was 8 percent.
2. The market price of the stock at July 1, 19x1, and September 1, 19x1, was $45.
3. The capital structure of the company is as follows:

    Capital stock:
       Common—300,000 shares @ $10 = $3,000,000
    Preferred:
       Series A, 5 percent
          100,000 @ $20 = $2,000,000
       Series B, 7 percent
          500,000 @ $10 = $5,000,000
    Both classes of preferred shares are nonparticipating, that is, are not entitled to more than the dividends stated. The dividends are cumulative for both classes of preferred shares.
4. Earnings for 19x1 are $6,000,000.

Required:

a. What are the implications of these two debenture issues on the reporting of earnings per share?

b. Calculate the earnings per share as of December 31, 19x1 (assume 50 percent tax rate).

Problem 15–14. The following schedule sets forth the short-term debt, long-term debt, and stockholders' equity of Darren Company as of December 31, 19x4. The president of Darren has requested that you assist the controller in preparing figures for earnings per share computations.

Short-term debt:

Notes payable—banks	$ 4,000,000
Current portion of long-term debt	10,000,000
Total short-term debt	$ 14,000,000

Long-term debt:

4% convertible debentures due April 15, 19y6	$ 30,000,000
Other long-term debt less current portions	20,000,000
Total long-term debt	50,000,000

Stockholders' equity:

$4 cumulative, convertible preferred stock; par value $20 per share; authorized 2,000,000 shares; issued and outstanding 1,200,000 shares; liquidation preference $30 per share aggregating $36,000,000	24,000,000
Common stock; par value $1 per share; authorized 20,000,000 shares; issued 7,500,000 shares including 600,000 shares held in treasury	7,500,000
Additional paid-in capital	4,200,000
Retained earnings	76,500,000
Total	112,200,000
Less cost of 600,000 shares of common stock held in treasury (acquired prior to 19x4)	900,000
Total stockholders' equity	111,300,000
Total long-term debt and stockholders' equity	$161,300,000

Explanation of short-term debt, long-term debt, and stockholders' equity including transactions during the year ended December 31, 19x4:

1. The "Other long-term debt" and the related amounts due within one year are amounts due on unsecured promissory notes which require payments each year to maturity. The interest rates on these borrowings range from 6 percent to 7 percent. At the time that these monies were borrowed, the bank prime interest rate was 7 percent.

2. The 4 percent convertible debentures were issued at their face value of $30,000,000 in 19x6 when the bank prime interest rate was 5 percent. The debentures are due in 19x6 and until then are convertible into the common stock of Darren at the rate of 25 shares for each $1,000 debenture.

3. The $4 cumulative, convertible preferred stock was issued in 19x3. The stock had a market value of $75 at the time of issuance when the bank prime interest rate was 9 percent. On July 1, 19x4, and on October 1, 19x4, holders of the pre-

ferred stock converted 80,000 and 20,000 preferred shares, respectively, into common stock. Each share of preferred stock is convertible into 1.2 shares of common stock.

4. On April 1, 19x4, Darren acquired the assets and business of Brett Industries by the issuance of 800,000 shares of Darren common stock in a transaction appropriately accounted for as a purchase.

5. On October 1, 19x3, the company granted options to its officers and selected employees to purchase 100,000 shares of Darren's common stock at a price of $33 per share. The options are *not* exercisable until 19x6.

Additional information:

1. The average and ending market prices during 19x4 of Darren common stock were as follows:

	Average market price	Ending market price
First quarter	$31	$29
Second quarter	33	32
Third quarter	35	33
Fourth quarter	37	34
Average for the year	34	—
December 31, 19x4	—	34

2. Dividends on the preferred stock have been paid through December 31, 19x4. Dividends paid on the common stock were 50 cents per share for each quarter.

3. The net income of Darren Company for the year ended December 31, 19x4, was $8,600,000. There were no extraordinary items. The provision for income taxes was computed at a rate of 48 percent.

Required:

a. Prepare a schedule which shows the adjusted number of shares for 19x4 to compute:

(1) Primary earnings per share.

(2) Fully diluted earnings per share.

b. Prepare a schedule which shows the adjusted net income for 19x4 to compute:

(1) Primary earnings per share.

(2) Fully diluted earnings per share.

Do not compute earnings per share.

(AICPA adapted)

Problem 15–15. On July 1, 19x8, the board of directors of Movie Company decided to acquire the Camera and Projector Corporations. Following is some additional information on this purchase transaction:

[Relates to Problem 15–15]

	Movie Company	Camera Company	Projector Company
Net income from 1/1 to 6/30/x8	$300,000	$200,000	$100,000
Common shares outstanding on 7/1/x8 .	100,000	50,000	200,000
Shares issued after 1/1/x8:			
Shares issued on 4/1/x8		30,000	
Shares issued on 5/1/x8			100,000
Shares issued on 7/1/x8 for acquisition of:			
Camera (3 for 1)	150,000		
Projector (1 for 2)	100,000		
Net income from 7/1 to 12/31/x8	$750,000		

Required:

Calculate EPS for Movie Company for the year ending December 31, 19x8.

Problem 15–16. On October 1, 19x5, the management of the Morning Corporation decided to merge the Afternoon and Evening Corporations. Following is some additional information: (the merger was accounted for as a pooling)

[Relates to Problem 15–16]

	Afternoon Corporation	Evening Corporation	Morning Corporation
Net income from 1/1 to 9/30/x5	$200,000	$300,000	–0–
Common shares outstanding on 10/1/x5	100,000	80,000	300,000
Shares issued on 7/1/x5	50,000		
Shares issued on 9/1/x5		20,000	
Net income from 10/1 to 12/31/x5			$500,000
Number of shares issued for acquisition of:			
Afternoon Corporation (2 for 1)			200,000
Evening Corporation (5 for 1)			400,000

Required:

Compute earnings per share for the Consolidated Company on December 31, 19x5.

Problem 15–17. Ex Company owns 1,800 shares of Zee Company's outstanding common stock. The following data pertains to these companies' financial operation and status during 19x8:

	Ex Company	Zee Company
1. Net income, excluding subsidiary's earnings	$40,000	$ 10,000
2. Common shares outstanding all year	12,000	2,000
3. 6% convertible bonds, issued at par ($1,000)—convertible into five shares of common per bond, prime interest rate at issuance was 10%		$400,000
4. 7% convertible preferred stock, issued at par ($100)—convertible into five shares of common per share of preferred. Bank prime rate at date of issue was 12%—shares outstanding	1,600	
5. Average price of common stock during 19x8	$ 100	$ 300
6. Warrants outstanding to purchase Zee Company's common stock at $50 per share		1,200
7. Tax rate	50%	50%

Required:

Calculate consolidated primary EPS for Ex Company and its subsidiary.

Problem 15–18. The following information is available for Parent Company for 19x8:

Parent Company's income including equity in earnings of its Subsidiary Company of $20,000 to be used in computing:

Primary EPS	$100,000
Fully diluted EPS	112,500

Number of Parent Company shares used in computing:

Primary EPS	50,000 shares
Fully diluted EPS	75,000 shares

Parent hold 800 shares out of 1,000 shares Subsidiary Company has outstanding:

Subsidiary's primary EPS	$1.20
Subsidiary's fully diluted EPS	1.00

Required:

a. Calculate primary EPS for Parent and its Subsidiary Company.

b. Calculate fully diluted EPS for Parent and its Subsidiary Company.

Problem 15–19. The Expanding Company has the following capital structure:

7% *subordinated convertible debentures* (issued at par.) Prime rate at time of issuance, 6½%.

Convertible into common stock at $25 per share:

Outstanding, 1/1/x3	$4,000,000
Converted into common stock, 6/30/x3 .	1,000,000
Outstanding, 12/31/x3	$3,000,000
Interest expense for year on above	$ 245,000

4% *convertible preferred stock* (issued at par in a prior year):
Prime rate at date of issuance, 6½%.

Par value	Shares outstanding	Aggregate
$100	$20,000	$2,000,000

Convertible into common stock at $40 per share (i.e., 2½ shares).

Warrants to purchase common stock at $30 per share:

	Shares
Outstanding, 1/1/x3 and 12/31/x3	50,000
Common stock:	
Shares outstanding, 1/1/x3	1,000,000
Issued 6/30/x3 on conversion of debentures	40,000
Shares outstanding, 12/31/x3	1,040,000

Shares contingently issuable in connection with prior year acquisition:

Based on earnings:

If the aggregate net earnings of the acquired company for the three years 19x3–x5 are, *in total,* at least equal to certain amounts, a total number of additional shares will then be issued, as shown:

$1,500,000	10,000 shares
2,250,000	20,000
3,000,000	40,000

19x3 earnings of the acquired company were $520,000.

Based on market value of stock:

Market value of 50,000 shares of common stock was guaranteed to be $75 per share by the end of 19x6. Additional shares to be issued in settlement.

Additional data:

Market price of common stock:		
Closing price, 12/31/x3	$	60
Average price for 19x3		40
Net income for year 19x3		3,000,000
Dividend on preferred stock . .		40,000

Required:

Compute primary and fully diluted EPS.

16

Partnerships—formation and operation

OVERVIEW

Legally, partnerships have many attributes in common with individual proprietorships. However, from an accounting viewpoint, some partnerships, such as large accounting firms, have many of the attributes of corporations, such as continued existence after changes in ownership occur, and, therefore, are treated as entities separate from the individual partners.

The division of profits and losses of partnerships is handled in a manner similar to that of proprietorships, i.e., income is creditied to the individual capital accounts. However, the treatment becomes somewhat more complex because of the differences (1) in capital contributions; (2) in abilities and talents of individual partners; and (3) in time spent on partnership duties by the individual partners. These differences can be compensated for by allowing (1) interest on capital balances; (2) different profit and loss ratios; and (3) salary allowances.

Whenever disagreements arise among the partners, they are usually resolved in accordance with the Uniform Partnership Act. While a partnership agreement may be in oral form, it is usually best for the partners to have a written agreement to minimize later disagreements.

There are distinct differences between the taxation of partnerships and of corporations. While a corporation is subject to income taxes on its taxable income, a partnership is not subject to an income tax. Instead, the individual partners are personally subject to these taxes on their distributive share of the partnership's income.

DEFINITIONS AND FEATURES OF PARTNERSHIPS

The Uniform Partnership Act (UPA), reproduced at the end of this chapter as Appendix 16–B, has been adopted by all but a few states and defines a partnership as "an association of two or more persons to carry on as co-owners a business for profit."[1] The co-ownership of property—joint tenancy, tenancy in common, etc.—does not, by itself, establish a partnership.[2]

Mutual agency

Every partner is an agent of the partnership, and any partner can legally bind the other partners by an action that is part of the usual conduct of partnership business, unless the partner has no authority to act and the person with whom the partner is dealing knows this.[3]

Unlimited liability

While stockholders of corporations have limited their investment liabilities to the extent of their investments, partners generally do not avail themselves of this feature. Except for a special class of partners, referred to as "limited" partners, general partners are subject to personal liabilities for partnership debts that are not satisfied by partnership assets. In order to eliminate this feature, also present in proprietorships, the owners of many small businesses choose to operate them as corporations instead of as partnerships. However, the corporate form of business has certain disadvantages (double taxation, franchise taxes, record keeping for minutes and resolutions, etc.) that are not present in partnerships and in those cases where business risks can be adequately covered by insurance, the partnership form of business is used extensively.

Assignment of partner's interest

An assignment of a partner's interest does not automatically dissolve a partnership.[4] Since a partner's relationship to the other partners is a personal one, an assignment does not automatically admit the assignee into partnership. The assignee can become a partner only by acceptance and agreement by the remaining partners. If the assignee is not admitted as a partner, the assignee has no right to participate in managing the partnership; the assignee's rights are limited to participating in profits and losses of the partnership and the right to receive the assignor's proceeds upon the dissolution of the partnership.[5]

Limited life

Generally, corporations continue in existence indefinitely. Partnerships, however, either have a limited life for a fixed term or are dissolved as a result of one or more specified actions. A partnership is usually dissolved when one of the following occurs:

---

[1]Uniform Partnership Act, sec. 6 (1).
[2]Ibid., sec. 7 (2).
[3]Ibid., sec. 9 (1).
[4]Ibid., sec. 27 (1).
[5]Ibid.

1. A defined period of time has elapsed or a specified undertaking has been completed.
2. A partner requests that the partnership be dissolved.
3. A partner dies.
4. A partner or the partnership becomes bankrupt.
5. A court issues a decree ordering a dissolution when a partner is of unsound mind, incapable of performing partnership duties, guilty of acts prejudicial to the continued existence of the partnership, or when the partnership can only operate at a loss.[6]

Taxation

Whereas corporations are taxable entities and are subject to income and other taxes, partnerships are not subject to income taxes. Instead, the individual partners pay taxes personally on their distributive shares of the income earned by the partnership. Appendix 16–A at the end of this chapter contains selected aspects of partnership taxation and also considers a partner's tax basis which may differ from the amounts shown on partnership books as capital accounts.

ENTITY VERSUS PROPRIETORSHIP THEORIES

The proprietorship theory views the assets of a business as belonging to the proprietor, the liabilities of a business are viewed as debts of the proprietor, and the income of the business is viewed as an increase in the proprietor's net worth (capital). In practice, however, proprietorship assets and liabilities are treated as having a separate existence from the personal assets and liabilities of the proprietor. Thus, in practice, proprietorships are treated as separate entities, even though, in theory, they are not.

Although there are many similarities between partnerships and proprietorships (unlimited liability, dissolution upon death, etc.), partnerships are generally viewed as entities separate and apart from the individual partners. Assets are viewed as belonging to the partnership and *not* to the partners, individually. This view is consistent with the UPA, in that the Act provides that: "All property originally brought into the partnership stock or subsequently acquired by purchase or otherwise, on account of the partnership, is partnership property."[7] Stated differently, a partner whose share of the partnership is 30 percent does not have a claim to 30 percent of the cash, or of any specific asset, of the partnership; rather, the partner has a claim of 30 percent of the net assets (assets minus liabilities) of the partnership. Income earned by the partnership is usually viewed as income to the "entity" with each partner entitled to a distributive share of the income. This view is especially true for the so-called Big Eight accounting firms and many other large law and accounting firms that use the partnership form of organization. The legal life of firms in this category transcends the death or admission of a partner, and it is usually found that partnership agreements for these large firms provide for the continued existence of the partnership

[6]Ibid., secs. 31 and 32.
[7]Ibid., sec. 8 (1).

beyond the death of a partner. It is, thus, not necessary to have an automatic dissolution upon the death or other condition specified in the UPA, if an agreement among the partners provides otherwise.

On the other hand, small partnerships are usually viewed as a combination of two or more proprietorships, and the "proprietorship" theory would be the pertinent one for firms of this size. The death of one partner would usually cause a dissolution—especially if there are only two partners.

INITIAL CONTRIBUTIONS TO CAPITAL

If there are no implicit intangibles contributed by the individuals forming a new partnership and only cash is contributed to the partnership, the entries to record the cash contributions are rather simple. If, for example, Good and York form a partnership with a capital of $100,000 and the cash contributions are 40 percent and 60 percent, respectively, the entries would be:

Cash	40,000	
Good—Capital		40,000
Cash	60,000	
York—Capital		60,000

In many cases a partner's contribution to the partnership may consist of property and/or intangible assets in addition to cash or in place of cash. When this occurs, valuation problems can arise. Theoretically, independent appraisals of the property should be obtained since to record property at other than its fair market value can affect the interests of individual partners. For example, if R and S form a partnership and R contributes a parcel of land to the partnership that he acquired some years ago at a cost of $50,000, but which is presently worth $100,000, then recording the land at $50,000 would result in a $25,000 disadvantage to R and a $25,000 windfall to S, assuming they share profits and losses equally. This can be demonstrated if it is assumed that R contributes the land, S contributes $50,000 in cash, the land is sold on the following day, and the partnership is dissolved. In that case the entries would be:

Cash	50,000	
S—Capital		50,000
Land	50,000	
R—Capital		50,000
Cash	100,000	
Land		50,000
Gain on Sale of Land		50,000
Gain on Sale of Land	50,000	
S—Capital		25,000
R—Capital		25,000
S—Capital	75,000	
R—Capital	75,000	
Cash		150,000

If instead of recording the land at $50,000, the fair market value of $100,000 was used, there would be no gain on the sale and R would have been credited with the full $100,000 fair market value of his capital contribution. Despite the theoretical soundness of the independent appraisal procedure, partners often bypass this procedure and agree to use instead arbitrary valuations for property contributions. The following example illustrates the accounting for the formation of a partnership:

1. Tung and Waterhose formed a partnership to sell garden supplies.
2. Tung contributed $50,000 in cash to the partnership.
3. Waterhose contributed land and a building having an agreed to fair market value of $80,000 and fixtures having a fair market value of $10,000. The building was encumbered by a mortgage of $40,000 which the partnership will assume. The land was appraised at $20,000.

Entries to record the above are as follows:

Cash	50,000	
Tung—Capital		50,000
To record initial capital contribution.		
Building	60,000	
Land	20,000	
Fixtures	10,000	
Mortgage Payable—Land and Building		40,000
Waterhose—Capital		50,000
To record initial capital contribution.		

WRITTEN PARTNERSHIP AGREEMENTS

While it is perfectly acceptable to have an oral partnership agreement, it is preferable to commit such an agreement to writing. Lapses of memory and future misunderstandings are usually avoided when agreements are written. A written agreement is called the *articles of partnership* and usually provides for:

1. The date of the agreement.
2. The name of the partnership and the names of the individual partners.
3. The nature of the business.
4. The term of partnership.
5. Capital contributions and agreed to valuations of property contributions.
6. Sharing of profits and losses.
7. Salaries and drawings.
8. Interest on capital balances and/or loan balances.
9. The duties of the partners.
10. Record-keeping procedures.
11. Termination—retirement, liquidation.
12. Use of the partnership name upon death of a partner.
13. Expulsion of a partner for cause.
14. Arbitration of disputes among the partners.

The above list is not all-inclusive.

DIVISION OF OPERATING RESULTS

The results of operations can be apportioned in any manner that the partners desire. If the articles of partnership are silent on this matter, profits and losses are *shared equally* regardless of differences in capital account balances, services rendered, time spent on partnership duties, and differing abilities of individual partners. Therefore, if a profit and loss sharing ratio which is other than equal is desired, it must be specified.

SALARIES TO PARTNERS

When the services rendered to the partnership by the individual partners are not equal—i.e., because of differing abilities of partners or differences in time spent on partnership duties—it is virtually impossible to provide for such differences through the use of profit and loss sharing ratios. Since profits and losses may fluctuate from year to year, a fair profit-sharing ratio in one year may produce an unfair division in another year. Accordingly, the best way to provide for these differences is to allow salaries to each partner which are commensurate with the services the partner renders to the partnership.

It should be rememberd that providing for partners' salaries is still an income-sharing device and, therefore, is *usually* not considered an expense of the partnership in the same sense as are salaries paid to employees. In any event, such salaries reduce the balance that is available in the Income Summary account at year's end and for profit and loss sharing purposes. To demonstrate the use of partners' salaries for profit and loss division purposes, it is assumed that Anders and Mitchell are partners and:

1. Anders is to be allowed a salary of $40,000 and Mitchell is to be allowed a salary of $20,000.
2. Their profit and loss sharing ratio is 50:50.
3. The balance in the Income Summary account is $80,000 before the allowance for salaries.

The entries to close the Income Summary account would be:

(1)

Income Summary	60,000	
Anders—Capital		40,000
Mitchell—Capital		20,000

To credit partners' capital for salary allowances.

(2)

Income Summary	20,000	
Anders—Capital		10,000
Mitchell—Capital		10,000

To distribute balance of income in the income and loss sharing ratio.

Instead of two separate entries, one combining entry could also have been made.

If the partners had drawn their salaries during the year, the two above entries would still be the same, but the following additional entry would be required:

(3)

Anders—Capital	40,000	
Mitchell—Capital	20,000	
Anders—Salary		40,000
Mitchell—Salary		20,000

To close salaries drawn during the year to the respective
capital accounts.

If there were any other drawings by the partners during the year, they
would be closed out as in entry (3).

A partnership agreement should provide not only for salaries and the
sharing of profits, it should provide also for the treatment of salaries when
losses are incurred. In the absence of agreement to the contrary, salaries
are automatically allowed even when losses are incurred. For example, if the
Income Summary account of Anders and Mitchell shows a debit balance of
$20,000 after allowance for salaries and the articles of partnership are silent
concerning the treatment of losses, the entries for salaries and losses can be
combined as follows:

(4)

| Mitchell—Capital . . . . | 20,000 | |
| Income Summary . . . . | | 20,000 |

To close Income Summary as follows:

	Mitchell	Anders	Total
Salaries credited	$ 20,000	$40,000	$ 60,000
Division of loss	(40,000)	(40,000)	(80,000)
Balance per			
Income Summary	$(20,000)	–0–	$(20,000)

If the articles of partnership provide that salaries are allowed to the extent
of earnings only, no salaries are allowed when a loss occurs and salaries are
allowed on a pro rata basis if earnings are lower than the total of salaries
that can be earned by partners. Thus, for example, if a partnership agreement provides that salaries are allowed only to the extent earned, and the
agreement also provides for salaries of $24,000 and $36,000 to A and B, respectively, a profit of $30,000 would be divided as follows:

Partner	Salary allowance	Percent of total	Allocated salary allowance
A	$24,000	40	$12,000
B	36,000	60	18,000
Total	$60,000	100	$30,000

Alternatively, the allocation may be made as follows:

$$\frac{\text{Net income}}{\text{Salary allowance}} = \frac{\$30,000}{\$60,000} = 50\%$$

Salary allowance to A = 50% × $24,000 =	$12,000
Salary allowance to B = 50% × 36,000 =	18,000
Total allocated salary allowance . . .	$30,000

INTEREST ON CAPITAL AND LOAN ACCOUNTS

Loans to a partnership by an individual partner are properly shown as liabilities of the partnership. In addition, Section 18 (c) of the UPA provides that interest shall accrue on advances or loans made by partners beyond that of their capital accounts. To avoid any misunderstanding regarding the rate of interest to be paid, the articles of partnership should provide the necessary provisions on interest to be paid on loans and advances.

In order to recognize the possibility of different capital contributions and balances, a partnership agreement may provide that interest at a specified percentage shall be allowed on either: (1) average capital, (2) beginning capital, (3) ending capital, or (4) capital in excess of a specified amount. If the partnership agreement is silent on this subject, interest is allowed on loan advances but *not* on capital balances. If Anders and Mitchell agree that interest is to be allowed on average capital balances at 6 percent per annum, and their respective capital accounts are shown in Illustration 16–1, the division of income would be as follows assuming that the Income Summary account had a credit balance of $60,000 before the allowance for interest on average capitals (the calculation of average capitals and interest allowances appear in Illustration 16–2:

Illustration 16–1
ANDERS AND MITCHELL
Capital Accounts
As at December 31, 19x1
Anders—Capital

		Debit	Credit	Balance
19x1				
Jan. 1	Beginning balance			40,000
Mar. 1	Additional contribution		20,000	60,000
Aug. 1	Additional contribution		20,000	80,000
Oct. 1	Withdrawal	20,000		60,000

Mitchell—Capital

		Debit	Credit	Balance
19x1				
Jan. 1	Beginning balance			60,000
Mar. 1	Additional contribution		50,000	110,000
Aug. 1	Additional contribution		40,000	150,000
Nov. 1	Withdrawal	50,000		100,000

Illustration 16–2
ANDERS AND MITCHELL
Calculation of Average Capital and
Allowance of Interest Thereon
For the Year Ended December 31, 19x1

Anders—Capital

	Capital balance	Months unchanged	Product
19x1			
Jan. 1	$40,000	2	$ 80,000
Mar. 1	60,000	5	300,000
Aug. 1	80,000	2	160,000
Oct. 1	60,000	3	180,000
Totals		12	$720,000

Average capital = $720,000 ÷ 12 = $60,000
Interest allowed = 60,000 × 6% = 3,600

Illustration 16–2 (continued)

Mitchell—Capital

	Capital balance	*Months unchanged*	*Product*
19x1			
Jan. 1	$ 60,000	2	$ 120,000
Mar. 1	110,000	5	550,000
Aug. 1	150,000	3	450,000
Nov. 1	100,000	2	200,000
	Totals	12	$1,320,000

Average capital = $1,320,000 ÷ 12 = $110,000
Interest allowed =   110,000 × 6% =   6,600

(5)*

Income Summary	10,200	
Anders—Capital		3,600
Mitchell—Capital		6,600

To allow interest at 6% on average capital balances

(6)*

Income Summary	49,800	
Anders—Capital		24,900
Mitchell—Capital		24,900

To distribute balance of income after allowance for interest on
average capital.

*Entries (5) and (6) are usually combined into one compound entry.

DIVISION OF INCOME IN CAPITAL RATIO

The division of income on the basis of the capital ratios occurs infrequently in practice since this method of profit and loss sharing may ignore the value of services rendered to the partnership by the individual partners. Also, under this method, a partner can increase or decrease his share of income and losses by increasing or decreasing his capital balance. To avoid such possible distortions, the relative capital balances may be specified in the articles of partnership, and this, in effect, becomes a specified method of profit and loss sharing ratio.

To illustrate this approach, it is assumed that Anders and Mitchell have capital balances as shown in Illustration 16–2 and that the articles of partnership do not specify required capital balances. If the Income Summary account shows a credit balance of $80,000, the entry to record the division of profit is:

(7)

Income Summary	80,000	
Anders—Capital		28,232
Mitchell—Capital		51,768

To record the division of income in the capital ratio of
720:1,320, respectively.
(720/2,040 = 35.29%)
(1,320/2,040 = 64.71%)

It should be noted that it is not necessary to compute the average capital balance in order to use this method. The relationship of the "Product" column in our earlier computation will serve to produce the same result as would the relationship of average capital ($60,000:$110,000).

This method of profit and loss sharing is best used where capital is the most important income-producing factor and any services that the partners perform for the partnership are relatively negligible.

BONUS TO PARTNERS In some partnerships a wide disparity may exist between the services rendered to the partnership by individual partners. For instance, one partner may assume the complete responsibility for the daily operations of the partnership and the other partner(s) may be inactive or semiretired. In such cases, it may be desirable to allow a basic salary to the operating partner and then allow him a bonus based on profits in order to motivate him to maximize the profits of the partnership. When bonuses are to be allowed, the articles of partnership must be explicit in specifying the method of computation. The computation of the bonus can be based on (1) income before an allowance for salaries and/or interest on capital balances, (2) income after salaries and interest and/or *before* the bonus, and (3) income after salaries and interest and/or *after* the bonus. The first and second methods are relatively simple to compute and, therefore, only the third method will be illustrated. If the Income Summary account was a credit balance of $190,200 and Anders is to be allowed a 20 percent bonus after deducting salaries of $60,000 to both partners (previously illustrated) and after deducting interest of $10,200 on balances of average capital (previously illustrated), the calculation of the bonus *after* deducting the bonus is as follows:

Let x = income after salaries, interest, and bonus.

$$\text{Bonus} = .2x$$
$$x + .2x + \$60{,}000 + \$10{,}200 = \$190{,}200$$
$$1.2x = \$190{,}200 - \$60{,}000 - \$10{,}200$$
$$1.2x = \$120{,}000$$
$$x = \$100{,}000$$
$$\text{Bonus} = .2\,(\$100{,}000) = \$20{,}000$$

Assuming the condensed trial balance of Anders and Mitchell to be as in Illustration 16–3 and assuming the division of profits and losses to be as indicated immediately above, the closing entries would be as follows (using the schedule of income apportionment in Illustration 16–4):

Illustration 16–3
ANDERS AND MITCHELL
Condensed Trial Balance
December 31, 19x1

	Debit	Credit
Cash in bank	$100,200	
Accounts receivable	40,000	
Merchandise inventory	45,000	
Fixtures and equipment	132,000	
Accumulated depreciation		$ 15,000
Accounts payable		12,000
Anders—capital		60,000
Anders—drawings	40,000	
Mitchell—capital		100,000
Mitchell—drawings	20,000	
Revenues		800,000
Cost of goods sold	400,000	
Expenses	209,800	
Totals	$987,000	$987,000

Illustration 16–4
ANDERS AND MITCHELL
Schedule of Income Apportionment
For the Year Ended December 31, 19x1

	Anders	Mitchell	Total
Salaries	$ 40,000	$20,000	$ 60,000
Interest on capital balances	3,600	6,600	10,200
Bonus	20,000	–0–	20,000
Balance	50,000	50,000	100,000
Totals	$113,600	$76,600	$190,200

(8)

Revenues	800,000	
Cost of Goods Sold		400,000
Expenses		209,800
Income Summary		190,200

To close revenue and expense accounts.

(9)

Income Summary	190,200	
Anders—Capital		113,600
Mitchell—Capital		76,600

To apportion and close Income Summary account as per schedule annexed hereto.

(10)

Anders—Capital	40,000	
Mitchell—Capital	20,000	
Anders—Drawings		40,000
Mitchell—Drawings		20,000

To close drawings accounts.

FINANCIAL STATEMENTS   The financial statements of a partnership are only slightly different from those of an individual proprietorship. The income statements are the same; the only difference is in the capital section of the balance sheet. Therefore, only the balance sheet and supporting statements will be demonstrated. Illustrations 16–5 and 16–6 illustrate the balance sheet and the statement of partners' capital balances. The latter statement includes a supporting schedule of income apportionment. However, since the apportionment schedule was presented in Illustration 16–4 as part of the closing entries, it will not be repeated despite its usual *inclusion as part of the financial statements* to be prepared for either internal or external users.

Illustration 16–5
ANDERS AND MITCHELL
Balance Sheet
December 31, 19x1

Assets

Current assets:		
Cash in bank	$100,200	
Accounts receivable	40,000	
Merchandise inventory	45,000	
Total current assets		$185,200
Plant assets:		
Fixtures and equipment	132,000	
Less: Accumulated depreciation	15,000	
Total plant assets		117,000
Total assets		$302,200

Liabilities and Capital

Current liabilities:		
Accounts payable		$ 12,000
Capital:		
Anders—capital (per statement)	133,600	
Mitchell—capital (per statement)	156,600	
Total capital		290,200
Total liabilities and capital		$302,200

Illustration 16–6
ANDERS AND MITCHELL
Statement of Partners' Capital
For the Year Ended December 31, 19x1

	Anders	Mitchell	Total
Balances, January 1, 19x1	$ 40,000	$ 60,000	$100,000
Additional contributions	40,000	90,000	130,000
Net income—per apportionment schedule	113,600	76,600	190,200
Totals	193,600	226,600	420,200
Less: Drawings	40,000*	20,000*	60,000*
Withdrawals of capital	20,000*	50,000*	70,000*
Balances, December 31, 19x1	$133,600	$156,600	$290,200

*Deductions.

Appendix 16–A: Selected principles of partnership taxation and basis of partnership interests

Taxation of partnership income

Partnerships, per se, are not subject to federal income taxes. Rather, partnerships file an informational tax return which contains (1) an income statement, (2) beginning and ending balance sheets for the tax year, and (3) distributive shares of taxable income to the partners. On their personal income tax returns, the individual partners record their distributive shares of taxable income and personally pay the taxes due on this income. The various categories of the partnership's taxable income, e.g., ordinary, capital gain, etc.—are carried over to the partners' individual tax returns. It is for this reason that partnership net income on its income statement contains no provision for income taxes. This differs, for example, from corporate income statements where such a provision is made.

Tax basis of partnership property

An individual who contributes property to a partnership generally recognizes no gain or loss at that time. Accordingly, the tax basis of the property to the partnership is the same as the tax basis to the individual partner. Therefore, a partnership, while often recording contributed property at its fair market value for accounting purposes, must use different amounts in order to arrive at taxable income.

The need for separate book and tax records is especially evident in the case of inventory and depreciable property. Thus, depreciation for accounting purposes is computed using fair market values, but depreciation for tax purposes can be significantly different. This will require the keeping of separate sets of records, book and tax, for depreciation, plant assets, inventories, and any other assets where book-tax differences occur.

Such differences can be material already at the time when the partnership is formed. For instance, if D and E form a new partnership and D contributes inventory having a tax basis of $20,000 and a fair market value of $100,000, the partnership will recognize $30,000 of income for accounting purposes if the inventory is sold for $130,000, while the partners will pay taxes on a gain of $110,000 ($130,000 − $20,000). If this increased tax liability is not provided for in the partnership agreement, E would be placed in the position of paying taxes on income that he never in fact realized. In fact, E would probably pay *more* in taxes than the economic income allocated to him.[8] This difference between fair market value and tax basis should be provided for by the partners in the partnership agreement whenever property with differing book and tax bases is contributed to a partnership.

---

[8]Reg. § 1.704-1(c) requires that each partner be taxed on the taxable gain—in this case, $55,000 each—even though, for accounting purposes, E's capital account would be credited for $15,000—one half the accounting gain—if the profit and loss ratio were equal.

Basis of partner's interest

In accordance with partnership tax law, whenever a partner contributes property to a partnership, the basis of the partner's interest is equal to cash contributed plus the tax basis of property contributed less the portion of any personal indebtedness assumed by the other partners. The other partners' bases are equal to cash contributed plus the tax bases of property contributed plus the portions of indebtedness assumed from other partners. This can be illustrated by considering the following example wherein D and E are equal partners.

Illustration 16–7
D AND E
Analysis of Capital Contributions
As at January 2, 19x1

	Tax basis	Fair market value
D:		
Cash	$30,000	$ 30,000
Fixtures	30,000	50,000
Inventory	20,000	20,000
Totals	$80,000	$100,000
E:		
Cash	$20,000	$ 20,000
Land	20,000	40,000
Building	30,000	80,000
Totals	70,000	140,000
Less: Mortgage assumed by partnership	40,000	40,000
Totals	$30,000	$100,000

The entry for accounting purposes to record the formation of the partnership is:

Cash	50,000	
Inventory	20,000	
Land	40,000	
Building	80,000	
Fixtures	50,000	
Mortgage Payable		40,000
D—Capital		100,000
E—Capital		100,000

To record the contribution of cash and property upon the formation of the partnership.

However, for tax purposes, the partners' bases of their partnership interests are computed as follows (see Illustration 16–7):

	D	E
Cash	$ 30,000	$20,000
Inventory	20,000	
Land		20,000
Building		30,000
Fixtures	30,000	
Liabilities (50% × $40,000)	20,000	(20,000)
Totals	$100,000	$50,000

If, immediately after the partnership was formed on January 2, 19x1, but before any business was transacted, T was admitted into partnership with a 20 percent interest by investing $50,000, the accounting entry to record the admission would be:

Cash	50,000	
T-Capital		50,000

The tax basis of each partner would be:

	T	D	E
Tax basis—as above . . .		$100,000	$50,000
Cash investment	$50,000		
Liabilities assumed by T (20% of $40,000)	8,000	(4,000)	(4,000)
New basis	$58,000	$ 96,000	$46,000

If in Illustration 16–7, E had contributed the same assets but the land and building were subject to a mortgage of $115,000 instead of $40,000, and E's percentage in the partnership was 20 percent (rather than 50 percent), his tax basis would be zero and he would be required to report a taxable capital gain of $22,000 upon the formation of the partnership[9] calculated as follows:

	D	E
Tax basis of cash and property contributed	$ 80,000	$70,000
Mortgage assumed by D (80% × $115,000)	92,000	(92,000)
Totals	172,000	(22,000)
Taxable gain added		22,000
Tax basis	$172,000	–0–

---

[9] Relief from a personal liability is treated as being equivalent to the receipt of cash.

Appendix 16–B: Uniform Partnership Act

Part and Section Analysis

PART I. PRELIMINARY PROVISIONS

Sec.
1. Name of Act.
2. Definition of Terms.
3. Interpretation of Knowledge and Notice.
4. Rules of Construction.
5. Rules for Cases Not Provided for in This Act.

PART II. NATURE OF PARTNERSHIP

6. Partnership Defined.
7. Rules for Determining the Existence of a Partnership.
8. Partnership Property.

PART III. RELATIONS OF PARTNERS TO PERSONS DEALING WITH THE PARTNERSHIP

9. Partner Agent of Partnership as to Partnership Business.
10. Conveyance of Real Property of the Partnership.
11. Partnership Bound by Admission of Partner.
12. Partnership Charged with Knowledge of or Notice to Partner.
13. Partnership Bound by Partner's Wrongful Act.
14. Partnership Bound by Partner's Breach of Trust.
15. Nature of Partner's Liability.
16. Partner by Estoppel.
17. Liability of Incoming Partner.

PART IV. RELATIONS OF PARTNERS TO ONE ANOTHER

18. Rules Determining Rights and Duties of Partners.
19. Partnership Books.
20. Duty of Partners to Render Information.
21. Partner Accountable as a Fiduciary.
22. Right to an Account.
23. Continuation of Partnership Beyond Fixed Term.

PART V. PROPERTY RIGHTS OF A PARTNER

24. Extent of Property Rights of a Partner.
25. Nature of a Partner's Right in Specific Partnership Property.
26. Nature of Partner's Interest in the Partnership.
27. Assignment of Partner's Interest.
28. Partner's Interest Subject to Charging Order.

PART VI. DISSOLUTION AND WINDING UP

Sec.
29. Dissolution Defined.
30. Partnership not Terminated by Dissolution.
31. Causes of Dissolution.
32. Dissolution by Decree of Court.
33. General Effect of Dissolution on Authority of Partner.
34. Right of Partner to Contribution from Co-partners after Dissolution.
35. Power of Partner to Bind Partnership to Third Persons after Dissolution.
36. Effect of Dissolution on Partner's Existing Liability.
37. Right to Wind Up.
38. Rights of Partners to Application of Partnership Property.
39. Rights Where Partnership Is Dissolved for Fraud or Misrepresentation.
40. Rules for Distribution.
41. Liability of Persons Continuing the Business in Certain Cases.
42. Rights of Retiring or Estate of Deceased Partner When the Business Is Continued.
43. Accrual of Actions.

PART VII. MISCELLANEOUS PROVISIONS
44.   When Act Takes Effect.
45.   Legislation Repealed.

PART I

PRELIMINARY PROVISIONS

§ 1.   Name of act

This act may be cited as Uniform Partnership Act.

§ 2.   Definition of terms

In this act, "Court" includes every court and judge having jurisdiction in the case.

"Business" includes every trade, occupation, or profession.

"Person" includes individuals, partnerships, corporations, and other associations.

"Bankrupt" includes bankrupt under the Federal Bankruptcy Act or insolvent under any state insolvent act.

"Conveyance" includes every assignment, lease, mortgage, or encumbrance.

"Real property" includes land and any interest or estate in land.

§ 3.   Interpretation of knowledge and notice

(1) A person has "knowledge" of a fact within the meaning of this act not only when he has actual knowledge thereof, but also when he has knowledge of such other facts as in the circumstances shows bad faith.

(2) A person has "notice" of a fact within the meaning of this act when the person who claims the benefit of the notice:

(a) States the fact to such person, or

(b) Delivers through the mail, or by other means of communication, a written statement of the fact to such person or to a proper person at his place of business or residence.

§ 4.   Rules of construction

(1) The rule that statutes in derogation of the common law are to be strictly construed shall have no application to this act.

(2) The law of estoppel shall apply under this act.

(3) The law of agency shall apply under this act.

(4) This act shall be so interpreted and construed as to effect its general purpose to make uniform the law of those states which enact it.

(5) This act shall not be construed so as to impair the obligations of any contract existing when the act goes into effect, nor to affect any action or proceedings begun or right accrued before this act takes effect.

§ 5.   Rules for cases not provided for in this act

In any case not provided for in this act the rules of law and equity, including the law merchant, shall govern.

PART II

NATURE OF PARTNERSHIP

§ 6.   Partnership defined

(1) A partnership is an association of two or more persons to carry on as co-owners a business for profit.

(2) But any association formed under any other statute of this state, or any statute adopted by authority, other than the authority of this state, is not a partnership under this act, unless such association would have been a partnership in this state prior to the adoption of this act; but this act shall apply to limited partnerships except in so far as the statutes relating to such partnerships are inconsistent herewith.

§ 7.   Rules for determining the existence of a partnership

In determining whether a partnership exists, these rules shall apply:

(1) Except as provided by section 16 persons who are not partners as to each other are not partners as to third persons.

(2) Joint tenancy, tenancy in common, tenancy by the entireties, joint property, common property, or part ownership does not of itself establish a partnership, whether such co-owners do or do not share any profits made by the use of the property.

(3) The sharing of gross returns does not of itself establish a partnership, whether or not the persons sharing them have a joint or common right or interest in any property from which the returns are derived.

(4) The receipt by a person of a share of the profits of a business is prima facie evidence that he is a

partner in the business, but no such inference shall be drawn if such profits were received in payment:

(a) As a debt by installments or otherwise,

(b) As wages of an employee or rent to a landlord,

(c) As an annuity to a widow or representative of a deceased partner,

(d) As interest on a loan, though the amount of payment vary with the profits of the business,

(e) As the consideration for the sale of a good-will of a business or other property by installments or otherwise.

§ 8. Partnership property

(1) All property originally brought into the partnership stock or subsequently acquired by purchase or otherwise, on account of the partnership, is partnership property.

(2) Unless the contrary intention appears, property acquired with partnership funds is partnership property.

(3) Any estate in real property may be acquired in the partnership name. Title so acquired can be conveyed only in the partnership name.

(4) A conveyance to a partnership in the partnership name, though without words of inheritance, passes the entire estate of the grantor unless a contrary intent appears.

PART III

RELATIONS OF PARTNERS TO PERSONS DEALING WITH THE PARTNERSHIP

§ 9. Partner agent of partnership as to partnership business

(1) Every partner is an agent of the partnership for the purpose of its business, and the act of every partner, including the execution in the partnership name of any instrument, for apparently carrying on in the usual way the business of the partnership of which he is a member binds the partnership, unless the partner so acting has in fact no authority to act for the partnership in the particular matter, and the person with whom he is dealing has knowledge of the fact that he has no such authority.

(2) An act of a partner which is not apparently for the carrying on of the business of the partnership in the usual way does not bind the partnership unless authorized by the other partners.

(3) Unless authorized by the other partners or un-

less they have abandoned the business, one or more but less than all the partners have no authority to:

(a) Assign the partnership property in trust for creditors or on the assignee's promise to pay the debts of the partnership,

(b) Dispose of the good-will of the business,

(c) Do any other act which would make it impossible to carry on the ordinary business of a partnership,

(d) Confess a judgment,

(e) Submit a partnership claim or liability to arbitration or reference.

(4) No act of a partner in contravention of a restriction on authority shall bind the partnership to persons having knowledge of the restriction.

§ 10. Conveyance of real property of the partnership

(1) Where title to real property is in the partnership name, any partner may convey title to such property by a conveyance executed in the partnership name; but the partnership may recover such property unless the partner's act binds the partnership under the provisions of paragraph (1) of section 9, or unless such property has been conveyed by the grantee or a person claiming through such grantee to a holder for value without knowledge that the partner, in making the conveyance, has exceeded his authority.

(2) Where title to real property is in the name of the partnership, a conveyance executed by a partner, in his own name, passes the equitable interest of the partnership, provided the act is one within the authority of the partner under the provisions of paragraph (1) of section 9.

(3) Where title to real property is in the name of one or more but not all the partners, and the record does not disclose the right of the partnership, the partners in whose name the title stands may convey title to such property, but the partnership may recover such property if the partners' act does not bind the partnership under the provisions of paragraph (1) of section 9, unless the purchaser or his assignee, is a holder for value, without knowledge.

(4) Where the title to real property is in the name of one or more or all the partners, or in a third person in trust for the partnership, a conveyance executed by a partner in the partnership name, or in his own name, passes the equitable interest of the partnership, provided the act is one within the au-

thority of the partner under the provisions of paragraph (1) of section 9.

(5) Where the title to real property is in the names of all the partners a conveyance executed by all the partners passes all their rights in such property.

§ 11. Partnership bound by admission of partner

An admission or representation made by any partner concerning partnership affairs within the scope of his authority as conferred by this act is evidence against the partnership.

§ 12. Partnership charged with knowledge of or notice to partner

Notice to any partner of any matter relating to partnership affairs, and the knowledge of the partner acting in the particular matter, acquired while a partner or then present to his mind, and the knowledge of any other partner who reasonably could and should have communicated it to the acting partner, operate as notice to or knowledge of the partnership, except in the case of a fraud on the partnership committed by or with the consent of that partner.

§ 13. Partnership bound by partner's wrongful act

Where, by any wrongful act or omission of any partner acting in the ordinary course of the business of the partnership or with the authority of his copartners, loss or injury is caused to any person, not being a partner in the partnership, or any penalty is incurred, the partnership is liable therefor to the same extent as the partner so acting or omitting to act.

§ 14. Partnership bound by partner's breach of trust

The partnership is bound to make good the loss:

(a) Where one partner acting within the scope of his apparent authority receives money or property of a third person and misapplies it; and

(b) Where the partnership in the course of its business receives money or property of a third person and the money or property so received is misapplied by any partner while it is in the custody of the partnership. .

§ 15. Nature of partner's liability

All partners are liable

(a) Jointly and severally for everything chargeable to the partnership under sections 13 and 14.

(b) Jointly for all other debts and obligations of the partnership; but any partner may enter into a separate obligation to perform a partnership contract.

§ 16. Partner by estoppel

(1) When a person, by words spoken or written or by conduct, represents himself, or consents to another representing him to any one, as a partner in an existing partnership or with one or more persons not actual partners, he is liable to any such person to whom such representation has been made, who has, on the faith of such representation, given credit to the actual or apparent partnership, and if he has made such representation or consented to its being made in a public manner he is liable to such person, whether the representation has or has not been made or communicated to such person so giving credit by or with the knowledge of the apparent partner making the representation or consenting to its being made.

(a) When a partnership liability results, he is liable as though he were an actual member of the partnership.

(b) When no partnership liability results, he is liable jointly with the other person, if any, so consenting to the contract or representation as to incur liability, otherwise separately.

(2) When a person has been thus represented to be a partner in an existing partnership, or with one or more persons not actual partners, he is an agent of the persons consenting to such representation to bind them to the same extent and in the same manner as though he were a partner in fact, with respect to persons who rely upon the representation. Where all the members of the existing partnership consent to the representation, a partnership act or obligation results; but in all other cases it is the joint act or obligation of the person acting and the persons consenting to the representation.

§ 17. Liability of incoming partner

A person admitted as a partner into an existing partnership is liable for all the obligations of the partnership arising before his admission as though he had been a partner when such obligations were incurred, except that this liability shall be satisfied only out of partnership property.

PART IV

RELATIONS OF PARTNERS TO ONE ANOTHER

§ 18. Rules determining rights and duties of partners

The rights and duties of the partners in relation to the partnership shall be determined, subject to any agreement between them, by the following rules:

(a) Each partner shall be repaid his contributions, whether by way of capital or advances to the partnership property and share equally in the profits and surplus remaining after all liabilities, including those to partners, are satisfied; and must contribute towards the losses, whether of capital or otherwise, sustained by the partnership according to his share in the profits.

(b) The partnership must indemnify every partner in respect of payments made and personal liabilities reasonably incurred by him in the ordinary and proper conduct of its business, or for the preservation of its business or property.

(c) A partner, who in aid of the partnership makes any payment or advance beyond the amount of capital which he agreed to contribute, shall be paid interest from the date of the payment or advance.

(d) A partner shall receive interest on the capital contributed by him only from the date when repayment should be made.

(e) All partners have equal rights in the management and conduct of the partnership business.

(f) No partner is entitled to remuneration for acting in the partnership business, except that a surviving partner is entitled to reasonable compensation for his services in winding up the partnership affairs.

(g) No person can become a member of a partnership without the consent of all the partners.

(h) Any difference arising as to ordinary matters connected with the partnership business may be decided by a majority of the partners; but no act in contravention of any agreement between the partners may be done rightfully without the consent of all the partners.

§ 19. Partnership books

The partnership books shall be kept, subject to any agreement between the partners, at the principal place of business of the partnership, and every partner shall at all times have access to and may inspect and copy any of them.

§ 20. Duty of partners to render information

Partners shall render on demand true and full information of all things affecting the partnership to any partner or the legal representative of any deceased partner or partner under legal disability.

§ 21. Partner accountable as a fiduciary

(1) Every partner must account to the partnership for any benefit, and hold as trustee for it any profits derived by him without the consent of the other partners from any transaction connected with the formation, conduct, or liquidation of the partnership or from any use by him of its property.

(2) This section applies also to the representatives of a deceased partner engaged in the liquidation of the affairs of the partnership as the personal representatives of the last surviving partner.

§ 22. Right to an account

Any partner shall have the right to a formal account as to partnership affairs:

(a) If he is wrongfully excluded from the partnership business or possession of its property by his co-partners,

(b) If the right exists under the terms of any agreement,

(c) As provided by section 21,

(d) Whenever other circumstances render it just and reasonable.

§ 23. Continuation of partnership beyond fixed term

(1) When a partnership for a fixed term or particular undertaking is continued after the termination of such term or particular undertaking without any express agreement, the rights and duties of the partners remain the same as they were at such termination, so far as is consistent with a partnership at will.

(2) A continuation of the business by the partners or such of them as habitually acted therin during the

term, without any settlement or liquidation of the partnership affairs, is prima facie evidence of a continuation of the partnership.

PART V

PROPERTY RIGHTS OF A PARTNER

§ 24. Extent of property rights of a partner

The property rights of a partner are (1) his rights in specfic partnership property, (2) his interest in the partnership, and (3) his right to participate in the management.

§ 25. Nature of a partner's right in specific partnership property

(1) A partner is co-owner with his partners of specific partnership property holding as a tenant in partnership.

(2) The incidents of this tenancy are such that:

(a) A partner, subject to the provisions of this act and to any agreement between the partners, has an equal right with his partners to posses specific partnership property for partnership purposes; but he has no right to possess such property for any other purpose without the consent of his partners.

(b) A partner's right in specific partnership property is not assignable except in connection with the assignment of rights of all the partners in the same property.

(c) A partner's right in specific partnership property is not subject to attachment or execution, except on a claim against the partnership. When partnership property is attached for a partnership debt the partners, or any of them, or the representatives of a deceased partner, cannot claim any right under the homestead or exemption laws.

(d) On the death of a partner his right in specific partnership property vests in the surviving partner or partners, except where the deceased was the last surviving partner, when his right in such property vests in his legal representative. Such surviving partner or partners, or the legal representative of the last surviving partner, has no right to possess the partnership property for any but a partnership purpose.

(e) A partner's right in specific partnership property is not subject to dower, curtesy, or allowances to widows, heirs, or next of kin.

§ 26. Nature of partner's interest in the partnership

A partner's interest in the partnership is his share of the profits and surplus, and the same is personal property.

§ 27. Assignment of partner's interest

(1) A conveyance by a partner of his interest in the partnership does not of itself dissolve the partnership, nor, as against the other partners in the absence of agreement, entitle the assignee, during the continuance of the partnership, to interfere in the management or administration of the partnership business or affairs, or to require any information or account of partnership transactions, or to inspect the partnership books; but it merely entitles the assignee to receive in accordance with his contract the profits to which the assigning partner would otherwise be entitled.

(2) In case of a dissolution of the partnership, the assignee is entitled to receive his assignor's interest and may require an account from the date only of the last account agreed to by all the partners.

§ 28. Partner's interest subject to charging order

(1) On due application to a competent court by any judgment creditor of a partner, the court which entered the judgment, order, or decree, or any other court, may charge the interest of the debtor partner with payment of the unsatisfied amount of such judgment debt with interest thereon; and may then or later appoint a receiver of his share of the profits, and of any other money due or to fall due to him in respect of the partnership, and make all other orders, directions, accounts and inquiries which the debtor partner might have made, or which the circumstances of the case may require.

(2) The interest charged may be redeemed at any time before foreclosure, or in case of a sale being directed by the court may be purchased without thereby causing a dissolution:

(a) With separate property, by any one or more of the partners, or

(b) With partnership property, by any one or more of the partners with the consent of all the partners whose interests are not so charged or sold.

(3) Nothing in this act shall be held to deprive a partner of his right, if any, under the exemption laws, as regards his interest in the partnership.

PART VI

DISSOLUTION AND WINDING UP

§ 29. Dissolution defined

The dissolution of a partnership is the change in the relation of the partners caused by any partner ceasing to be associated in the carrying on as distinguished from the winding up of the business.

§ 30. Partnership not terminated by dissolution

On dissolution the partnership is not terminated, but continues until the winding up of partnership affairs is completed.

§ 31. Causes of dissolution

Dissolution is caused:

(1) Without violation of the agreement between the partners,

(a) By the termination of the definite term or particular undertaking specified in the agreement,

(b) By the express will of any partner when no definite term or particular undertaking is specified,

(c) By the express will of all the partners who have not assigned their interests or suffered them to be charged for their separate debts, either before or after the termination of any specified term or particular undertaking,

(d) By the expulsion of any partner from the business bona fide in accordance with such a power conferred by the agreement between the partners;

(2) In contravention of the agreement between the partners, where the circumstances do not permit a dissolution under any other provision of this section, by the express will of any partner at any time;

(3) By any event which makes it unlawful for the business of the partnership to be carried on or for the members to carry it on in partnership;

(4) By the death of any partner;

(5) By the bankruptcy of any partner or the partnership;

(6) By decree of court under section 32.

§ 32. Dissolution by decree of court

(1) On application by or for a partner the court shall decree a dissolution whenever:

(a) A partner has been declared a lunatic in any judicial proceeding or is shown to be of unsound mind,

(b) A partner becomes in any other way incapable of performing his part of the partnership contract,

(c) A partner has been guilty of such conduct as tends to affect prejudicially the carrying on of the business,

(d) A partner wilfully or persistently commits a breach of the partnership agreement, or otherwise so conducts himself in matters relating to the partnership business that it is not reasonably practicable to carry on the business in partnership with him,

(e) The business of the partnership can only be carried on at a loss,

(f) Other circumstances render a dissolution equitable.

(2) On the application of the purchaser of a partner's interest under sections 28 or 29:

(a) After the termination of the specified term or particular undertaking,

(b) At any time if the partnership was a partnership at will when the interest was assigned or when the charging order was issued.

§ 33. General effect of dissolution on authority of partner

Except so far as may be necessary to wind up partnership affairs or to complete transactions begun but not then finished, dissolution terminates all authority of any partner to act for the partnership,

(1) With respect to the partners,

(a) When the dissolution is not by the act, bankruptcy or death of a partner; or

(b) When the dissolution is by such act, bankruptcy or death of a partner, cases were section 34 so requires.

(2) With respect to persons not partners, as declared in section 35.

§ 34. Right of partner to contribution from co-partners after dissolution

Where the dissolution is caused by the act, death or bankruptcy of a partner, each partner is liable to his co-partners for his share of any liability created by any partner acting for the partnership as if the partnership had not been dissolved unless

(a) The dissolution being an act of any partner, the partner acting for the partnership had knowledge of the dissolution, or

(b) The dissolution being by the death or bankruptcy of a partner, the partner acting for the partnership had knowledge or notice of the death or bankruptcy.

§ 35. Power of partner to bind partnership to third persons after dissolution

(1) After dissolution a partner can bind the partnership except as provided in Paragraph (3).

(a) By any act appropriate for winding up partnership affairs or completing transactions unfinished at dissolution;

(b) By any transaction which would bind the partnership if dissolution had not taken place, provided the other party to the transaction

(I) Had extended credit to the partnership prior to dissolution and had no knowledge or notice of the dissolution; or

(II) Though he had not so extended credit, had nevertheless known of the partnership prior to dissolution, and, having no knowledge or notice of dissolution, the fact of dissolution had not been advertised in a newspaper of general circulation in the place (or in each place if more than one) at which the partnership business was regularly carried on.

(2) The liability of a parnter under Paragraph (1b) shall be satisfied out of partnership assets alone when such partner had been prior to dissolution

(a) Unknown as a partner to the person with whom the contract is made; and

(b) So far unknown and inactive in partnership affairs that the business reputation of the partnership could not be said to have been in any degree due to his connection with it.

(3) The partnership is in no case bound by any act of a partner after dissolution

(a) Where the partnership is dissolved because it is unlawful to carry on the business, unless the act is appropriate for winding up partnership affairs; or

(b) Where the partner has become bankrupt; or

(c) Where the partner has no authority to wind up partnership affairs; except by a transaction with one who

(I) Had extended credit to the partnership prior to dissolution and had no knowledge or notice of his want of authority; or

(II) Had not extended credit to the partnership prior to disolution, and, having no knowledge or notice of his want of authority, the fact of his want of authority has not been advertised in the manner provided for advertising the fact of dissolution in Paragraph (1bII).

(4) Nothing in this section shall affect the liability under Section 16 of any person who after dissolution represents himself or consents to another representing him as a partner in a partnership engaged in carrying on business.

§ 36. Effect of dissolution on partner's existing liability

(1) The dissolution of the partnership does not of itself discharge the existing liability of any partner.

(2) A partner is discharged from any existing liability upon dissolution of the partnership by an agreement to that effect between himself, the partnership creditor and the person or partnership continuing the business; and such agreement may be inferred from the course of dealing between the creditor having knowledge of the dissolution and the person or partnership continuing the business.

(3) Where a person agrees to assume the existing obligations of a dissolved partnership, the partners whose obligations have been assumed shall be discharged from any liability to any creditor of the partnership who, knowing of the agreement, consents to a material alteration in the nature or time of payment of such obligations.

(4) The individual property of a deceased partner shall be liable for all obligations of the partnership incurred while he was a partner but subject to the prior payment of his separate debts.

§ 37. Right to wind up

Unless otherwise agreed the partners who have not wrongfully dissolved the partnership or the legal representative of the last surviving partner, not bankrupt, has the right to wind up the partnership affairs; provided, however, that any partner, his legal representative or his assignee, upon cause shown, may obtain winding up by the court.

§ 38. Rights of partners to application of partnership property

(1) When dissolution is caused in any way, except in contravention of the partnership agreement, each partner, as against his co-partners and all persons claiming through them in respect of their interests in the partnership, unless otherwise agreed, may have the partnership property applied to discharge its liabilities, and the surplus applied to pay in cash the net amount owing to the respective partners. But if dissolution is caused by expulsion of a partner, bona fide under the partnership agreement and if the expelled partner is discharged from all partnership liabilities, either by payment or agreement under section 36(2), he shall receive in cash only the net amount due him from the partnership.

(2) When dissolution is caused in contravention of

the partnership agreement the rights of the partners shall be as follows:

(a) Each partner who has not caused dissolution wrongfully shall have,

I. All the rights specified in paragraph (1) of this section, and

II. The right, as against each partner who has caused the dissolution wrongfully, to damages for breach of the agreement.

(b) The partners who have not caused the dissolution wrongfully, if they all desire to continue the business in the same name, either by themselves or jointly with others, may do so, during the agreed term for the partnership and for that purpose may possess the partnership property, provided they secure the payment by bond approved by the court, or pay to any partner who has caused the dissolution wrongfully, the value of his interest in the partnership at the dissolution, less any damages recoverable under clause (2a II) of this section, and in like manner indemnify him against all present or future partnership liabilities.

(c) A partner who has caused the dissolution wrongfully shall have:

I. If the business is not continued under the provisions of paragraph (2b) all the rights of a partner under paragraph (1), subject to cause (2a II), of this section,

II. If the business is continued under paragraph (2b) of this section the right as against his co-partners and all claiming through them in respect of their interests in the partnership, to have the value of his interest in the partnership, less any damages caused to his co-partners by the dissolution, ascertained and paid to him in cash, or the payment secured by bond approved by the court, and to be released from all existing liabilities of the partnership; but in ascertaining the value of the partner's interest the value of the good-will of the business shall not be considered.

§ 39. Rights where partnership is dissolved for fraud or misrepresentation

Where a partnership contract is rescinded on the ground of the fraud or misrepresentation of one of the parties thereto, the party entitled to rescind is, without prejudice to any other right, entitled,

(a) To a lien on, or a right of retention of, the surplus of the partnership property after satisfying the partnership liabilities to third persons for any sum of money paid by him for the purchase of an interest in the partnership and for any capital or advances contributed by him; and

(b) To stand, after all liabilities to third persons have been satisfied, in the place of the creditors of the partnership for any payments made by him in respect of the partnership liabilities; and

(c) To be indemnified by the person guilty of the fraud or making the representation against all debts and liabilities of the partnership.

§ 40. Rules for distribution

In settling accounts between the partners after dissolution, the following rules shall be observed, subject to any agreement to the contrary:

(a) The assets of the partnership are:

I. The partnership property,

II. The contributions of the partners necessary for the payment of all the liabilities specified in clause (b) of this paragraph.

(b) The liabilities of the partnership shall rank in order of payment, as follows:

I. Those owing to creditors other than partners,

II. Those owing to partners other than for capital and profits,

III. Those owing to partners in respect of capital,

IV. Those owing to partners in respect of profits.

(c) The assets shall be applied in order of their declaration in clause (a) of this paragraph to the satisfaction of the liabilities.

(d) The partners shall contribute, as provided by section 18 (a) the amount necessary to satisfy the liabilities; but if any, but not all, of the partners are insolvent, or, not being subject to process, refuse to contribute, the other partners shall contribute their share of the liabilities, and, in the relative proportions in which they share the profits, the additional amount necessary to pay the liabilities.

(e) An assignee for the benefit of creditors or any person appointed by the court shall have the right to enforce the contributions specified in clause (d) of this paragraph.

(f) Any partner or his legal representative shall have the right to enforce the contributions specified in clause (d) of this paragraph, to the extent of the amount which he has paid in excess of his share of the liability.

(g) The individual property of a deceased partner shall be liable for the contributions specified in clause (d) of this paragraph.

(h) When partnership property and the individual properties of the partners are in possession of a court for distribution, partnership creditors shall have priority on partnership property and separate creditors on individual property, saving the rights of lien or secured creditors as heretofore.

(i) Where a partner has become bankrupt or his estate is insolvent the claims against his separate property shall rank in the following order:

I.   Those owing to separate creditors,

II.   Those owing to partnership creditors,

III. Those owing to partners by way of contribution.

§ 41.   Liability of persons continuing the business in certain cases

(1) When any new partner is admitted into an existing partnership, or when any partner retires and assigns (or the representative of the deceased partner assigns) his rights in partnership property to two or more of the partners, or to one or more of the partners and one or more third persons, if the business is continued without liquidation of the partnership affairs, creditors of the first or dissolved partnership are also creditors of the partnership so continuing the business.

(2) When all but one partner retire and assign (or the representative of a deceased partner assigns) their rights in partnership property to the remaining partner, who continues the business without liquidation of partnership affairs, either alone or with others, creditors of the dissolved partnership are also creditors of the person or partnership so continuing the business.

(3) When any partner retires or dies and the business of the dissolved partnership is continued as set forth in paragraphs (1) and (2) of this section, with the consent of the retired partners or the representative of the deceased partner, but without any assignment of his right in partnership property, rights of creditors of the dissolved partnership and of the creditors of the person or partnership continuing the business shall be as if such assignment had been made.

(4) When all the partners or their representatives assign their rights in partnership property to one or more third persons who promise to pay the debts and who continue the business of the dissolved partnership, creditors of the dissolved partnership are also creditors of the person or partnership continuing the business.

(5) When any partner wrongfully causes a dissolution and the remaining partners continue the business under the provisions of section 38(2b), either alone or with others, and without liquidation of the partnership affairs, creditors of the dissolved partnership are also creditors of the person or partnership continuing the business.

(6) When a partner is expelled and the remaining partners continue the business either alone or with others, without liquidation of the partnership affairs, creditors of the dissolved partnership are also creditors of the person or partnership continuing the business.

(7) The liability of a third person becoming a partner in the partnership continuing the business, under this section, to the creditors of the dissolved partnership shall be satisfied out of partnership property only.

(8) When the business of a partnership after dissolution is continued under any conditions set forth in this section the creditors of the dissolved partnership, as against the separate creditors of the retiring or deceased partner or the representative of the deceased partner, have a prior right to any claim of the retired partner or the representative of the deceased partner against the person or partnership continuing the business, on account of the retired or deceased partner's interest in the dissolved partnership or on account of any consideration promised for such interest or for his right in partnership property.

(9) Nothing in this section shall be held to modify any right of creditors to set aside any assignment on the ground of fraud.

(10) The use by the person or partnership continuing the business of the partnership name, or the name of a deceased partner as part thereof, shall not of itself make the individual property of the deceased partner liable for any debts contracted by such person or partnership.

§ 42.   Rights of retiring or estate of deceased partner when the business is continued

When any partner retires or dies, and the business is continued under any of the conditions set forth in section 41 (1, 2, 3, 5, 6), or section 38 (2b) without any settlement of accounts as between him or his estate and the person or partnership continuing the business, unless otherwise agreed, he or his legal representative as against such persons or partnership may have the value of his interest at the date of dissolution ascertained, and shall receive as an ordinary creditor an amount equal to the value of his interest in the dissolved partnership with interest, or, at his option or at the option of his legal representative, in lieu of interest, the profits attributable to the use of his right in the property of the dissolved partnership; provided that the creditors of the dissolved partnership as against the separate creditors, or the representative of the retired or deceased partner, shall have priority on any claim arising under this section, as provided by section 41 (8) of this act.

§ 43. Accrual of actions

The right to an account of his interest shall accrue to any partner, or his legal representative, as against the winding up partners or the surviving partners or the person or partnership continuing the business, at the date of dissolution, in the absence of any agreement to the contrary.

PART VII

MISCELLANEOUS PROVISIONS

§ 44. When act takes effect

This act shall take effect on the . . . . day of . . . . one thousand nine hundred and . . . .

§ 45. Legislation repealed

All acts or parts of acts inconsistent with this act are hereby repealed.

QUESTIONS

1. According to the Uniform Partnership Act (UPA), what is a partnership?

2. What is meant by a *mutual agency?*

3. Does the assignment of a partner's interest automatically dissolve a partnership? Explain.

4. When is a partnership usually forced to dissolve? Are there exceptions to your examples? Explain.

5. Are partnerships treated differently from corporations with regard to income taxes? Explain.

6. Contrast the proprietorship theory with the entity theory as they relate to partnerships.

7. Does an individual partner have a claim against specific partnership assets? Explain.

8. When a partner contributes property to a partnership, at what value should the property be recorded at? Why?

9. What items should be provided for in a written partnership agreement?

10. In what way can a partnership agreement best provide for differences in—

a. Individual partner's abilities?

b. Time spent on partnership duties?

c. Capital contributions?

11. Are partnership salary allowances always allowed even when partnership profits are less than salary allowances? Explain.

12. When interest is allowed on capital accounts, should end-of-the-year balances be used or should average balances be used? Why?

13. Are financial statements of partnerships different from those of—

a. Individual proprietorships?

b. Corporations?

For each of the above explain the nature of the differences and the similarities.

Questions for Appendix 16–B:

14. Are partnerships subject to income tax? How are the individual partners taxed on partnership income?

15. Is there a possibility of a difference between the tax basis of partnership property and the amount recorded on the books of the partnership for accounting purposes? If so, how will this effect the individual partners? In what way?

16. Does the assumption of liabilities by a partnership affect a partner's tax basis of his partnership interest? In what way? Use an example to illustrate your answer.

EXERCISES

Exercise 16–1.

1. On March 1, 19x7, Smith and Dale formed a partnership with each contributing the following assets:

	Smith	Dale
Cash	$30,000	$ 70,000
Machinery and equipment	25,000	75,000
Building	—	225,000
Furniture and fixtures	10,000	—

The building is subject to a mortgage loan of $80,000, which is to be assumed by the partnership. The partnership agreement provides that Smith and Dale share profits and losses 30 percent and 70 percent, respectively. On March 1, 19x7, the balance in Dales's capital account should be—

  a. $290,000.

  b. $305,000.

  c. $314,000.

  d. $370,000.

2. Arthur Plack a partner in the Brite Partnership, has a 30 percent participation in partnership profits and losses. Plack's capital account had a net decrease of $60,000 during the calendar year 19x4. During 19x4, Plack withdrew $130,000 (charged against his capital account) and contributed property valued at $25,000 to the partnership. What was the net income of the Brite Partnership for 19x4?

  a. $150,000.

  b. $233,333.

  c. $350,000.

  d. $550,000.   (AICPA adapted)

Exercise 16–2.
Aldo and Mitchell are partners with beginning capital account balances (credit) of $40,000 and $20,000, respectively. During 19x2, the following additional contributions and withdrawals of capital appeared in the capital accounts:

	Aldo		Mitchell	
	Dr.	Cr.	Dr.	Cr.
19x4				
January 31	$5,000			
February 28		$ 8,000		$10,000
March 31			$6,000	
May 31			2,000	
August 31		10,000		
October 31				12,000
November 28 . . .		7,000		4,000

Required:

Compute the average capital balances for Aldo and Mitchell for 19x4.

Exercise 16–3.
Baylor and Smith are partners operating a chain of retail stores. The partnership agreement provides for:

	Baylor	Smith
Salaries	$22,000	$36,000
Interest on average capital balances . . .	10%	10%
Bonus	20% of net income *before* salaries and bonus, but *after* interest on capital	None
Remainder	40%	60%

The Income Summary account for 19x3 shows a credit balance of $180,000 before any allocations. Average capital balances for Baylor and Smith are $100,000 and $160,000, respectively.

Required:

  a. Prepare a schedule of income apportionment.

  b. Prepare the journal entry to close the Income Summary account.

Exercise 16–4.
Rework Exercise 16–3 if the partnership agreement provides that the bonus is to be calculated *after* the allowance for interest, salaries, *and* the bonus.

Exercise 16–5.
Rework Exercise 16–3 if the Income Summary account has a *debit* balance of $10,000 before any allocations and the partnership agreement is silent with regard to the earning of salaries.

Exercise 16–6.
Caldor and Burstyn are partners operating an automobile repair shop. For 19x4, the Income Summary account has a credit balance of $20,000. Caldor and Burstyn withdrew their salary allowances of $18,000 and $12,000, respectively, and profits and losses are shared 3:7.

Required:

Prepare an income apportionment schedule and closing entries for drawings and income summary if—

  a. The partnership agreement is silent with regard to the earnings of salaries.

  b. The partnership agreement specifies that salaries are allowed only to the extent earned.

Exercise 16-7. Darwin and Sanders are joining their separate businesses to form a partnership. Property and cash is to be contributed for a total capital of $300,000. The property to be contributed and liabilities to be assumed are:

	Darwin		Sanders	
	Book value	Fair market value	Book value	Fair market value
Accounts receivable . .	$20,000	$20,000		
Inventories . . .	30,000	40,000	$20,000	$25,000
Equipment . . .	60,000	45,000	40,000	50,000
Accounts payable	15,000	15,000	10,000	10,000

The partners' capital accounts are to be equal after all contributions and assumptions of liabilities.

Required:

a. Calculate the amount of cash that each partner must contribute.

b. Prepare the journal entry (entries) necessary to record the formation of the partnership.

Exercise 16-8.

1. Geller and Harden formed a partnership on January 2, 19x4, and agreed to share profits 90 percent, 10 percent, respectively. Geller contributed capital of $25,000. Harden contributed *no* capital but has a specialized expertise and manages the firm full time. There were *no* withdrawals during the year. The partnership agreement provides for the following:

1. Capital accounts are to be credited annually with interest at 5 percent of beginning capital.
2. Harden is to be paid a salary of $1,000 a month.
3. Harden is to receive a bonus of 20 percent of income calculated before deducting his salary and interest on both capital accounts.
4. Bonus, interest, and Harden's salary are to be considered partnership expenses.

The partnership 19x4 income statement follows:

Revenues	$96,450
Expenses (including salary, interest, and bonus)	49,700
Net income	$46,750

What is Harden's 19x4 bonus?
a. $11,688.
b. $12,000.

c. $15,000.
d. $15,738.

2. Partners C and K share profits and losses equally after each has been credited in all circumstances with annual salary allowance of $15,000 and $12,000, respectively. Under this arrangement, C will benefit by $3,000 more than K in which of the following circumstances?

a. Only if the partnership has earnings of $27,000 or more for the year.

b. Only if the partnership does not incur a loss for the year.

c. In all earnings or loss situations.

d. Only if the partnership has earnings of at least $3,000 for the year. (AICPA adapted)

Exercise 16-9. Elton and How are partners in a merchandising business. During 19x5, they withdrew their salary allowances of $20,000 and $30,000, respectively. Profits and losses are shared in the ratio of 3:2. The Income Summary account has a credit balance of $60,000 before any income allocation. Their capital accounts reflect the following:

	Elton	How
Beginning balance	$60,000	$40,000
Additional investments	10,000	20,000
Withdrawals other than for salary allowances	(20,000)	(10,000)
Ending balance	$50,000	$50,000

Required:

Prepare a statement of partner's capital for the year 19x5 after closing the Income Summary and withdrawals accounts.

Exercise 16-10 (for Appendix 16-A).

1. During 19x3, Norman contributed property held more than six months to the MaryAnn Partnership for a 40 percent interest. The total capital after his contribution was $50,000. His tax basis in the property was $8,000, and it had a fair market value of $10,000 at the time of the contribution to the partnership. What gain or loss should Norman report on the contribution of his property to the partnership?

a. No gain or loss.

b. $2,000 long-term capital gain.

c. $12,000 long-term capital gain.

d. $12,000 long-term capital gain of which $10,000 is deferred.

e. None of the above. (AICPA adapted)

Exercise 16-11 (for Appendix 16-A). Davis and Polk are forming a partnership. An analysis of their contributions to capital is as follows:

DAVIS AND POLK
Analysis of Capital Contributions
As at January 2, 19x8

	Tax basis	Fair market value
Davis:		
Cash	$ 60,000	$ 60,000
Fixtures	40,000	30,000
Inventory	20,000	50,000
Totals	$120,000	$140,000
Polk:		
Cash	$ 10,000	$ 10,000
Land	20,000	50,000
Building	50,000	100,000
Totals	80,000	160,000
Less: Mortgage assumed by partnership	20,000	20,000
Totals	$ 60,000	$140,000

Required:

a. Prepare the journal entry (entries) to record the formation of the partnership and the contributions by the partners.

b. Compute the tax basis of each partner's interest in the partnership.

Exercise 16–12 (for Appendix 16–A). Using the information provided in Exercise 16–11, compute the tax basis of each partner:

a. If the mortgage on the building were $90,000 and the profit and loss ratio were 90 percent for Davis and 10 percent for Polk. Would there be any tax consequences to Polk? What are they?

b. If, independently of (a), Wilkie were admitted into partnership with a 20 percent interest in profits and losses for $70,000 in cash.

PROBLEMS

Problem 16–13. Farragut and Geneen are partners with capital accounts that had the following transactions during 19x6:

	Farragut		Geneen	
	Dr.	Cr.	Dr.	Cr.
Balance, January 1, 19x4		$60,000		$80,000
February 28 . .	$10,000			
March 31				20,000
April 30		10,000		
June 30			$15,000	
August 31				10,000
September 30 .		15,000		
October 31 . . .	12,500		5,000	

The Income Summary account has a credit balance of $150,000.

Required:

Prepare an income apportionment schedule for each of the following independent profit-sharing agreements:

a. Interest on average capital at 8 percent, salaries of $20,000 and $40,000 to Farragut and Geneen, respectively, a bonus to Farragut of 20 percent of net income after interest and salaries but before the bonus, and the balance equally.

b. In the average capital ratio.

c. Interest at 10 percent on the amount by which the ending capital balance exceeds the beginning balance.

d. Salaries of $20,000 and $40,000 to Farragut and Geneen, respectively, a bonus to Farragut of 20 percent of net income after salaries *and* the bonus, and the balance equally.

Problem 16–14. The partnership of Gary, Jerome, and Paul was formed on January 1, 19x6. The original investments were as follows:

Gary	$ 80,000
Jerome	120,000
Paul	180,000

According to the partnership agreement, net income or loss will be divided among the respective partners as follows:

1. Salaries of $12,000 for Gary, $10,000 for Jerome, and $8,000 for Paul.
2. Interest of 8 percent on the average capital balances during the year of Gary, Jerome, and Paul.
3. Remainder divided equally.

Additional information:

1. Net income of the partnership for the year ended December 31, 19x6, was $70,000.
2. Gary invested an additional $20,000 in the partnership on July 1, 19x6.
3. Paul withdrew $30,000 from the partnership on October 1, 19x6.

4. Gary, Jerome, and Paul made regular drawings against their shares of net income during 19x6 of $10,000 each.

Required:

a. Prepare a schedule showing the division of net income among the three partners. Show supporting computations in good form.

b. Prepare a schedule showing each partner's capital balance at December 31, 19x6. Show supporting computations in good form.   (AICPA adapted)

Problem 16–15. A, B, and C, attorneys, agreed to consolidate their individual practices as of January 1, 19x3. The partnership agreement included the following features:

1. Each partner's capital contribution was the net amount of the assets and liabilities taken over by the partnership, which were as follows:

	A	B	C
Cash	$ 5,000	$ 5,000	$ 5,000
Accounts receivable . .	14,000	6,000	16,000
Furniture and library .	4,300	2,500	6,200
	23,300	13,500	27,200
Allowance for			
depreciation	2,400	1,500	4,700
Accounts payable . . .	300	1,400	700
	2,700	2,900	5,400
Capital contributions .	$20,600	$10,600	$21,800

Each partner guaranteed the collectibility of his receivables.

2. C had leased office space and was bound by the lease until June 30, 19x3. The monthly rental was $600. The partners agreed to occupy C's office space until the expiration of the lease and to pay the rent. The partners concurred that the rent was too high for the space and that a fair rental value would be $450 per month. The excess rent was to be charged to C at year-end. On July 1 the partners moved to new quarters with a monthly rental of $500.

3. No salaries were to be paid to the partners. The individual partners were to receive 20 percent of the gross fees billed to their respective clients during the first year of the partnership. After deducting operating expenses, the balance of the fees billed was to be credited to the partners'

capital accounts in the following ratios: A, 40 percent; B, 35 percent; and C, 25 percent.

On April 1, 19x3, D was admitted to the partnership; he was to receive 20 percent of the fees from new business obtained after April 1 after deducting expenses applicable to that new business. Expenses were to be apportioned to the new business in the same ratio that total expenses, other than bad debt losses, bore to total gross fees.

The following information pertains to the partnership's activities in 19x3:

1. Fees were billed as follows:

A's clients	$22,000
B's clients	12,000
C's clients	11,000
New business:	
Prior to April 1	3,000
After April 1	12,000
Total	$60,000

2. Total expenses, excluding depreciation and bad debt expenses, were $19,350 including the total amount paid for rent. Depreciation was to be computed at the rate of 10 percent. Depreciable assets purchased during 19x3, on which one-half year's depreciation was to be taken, totaled $5,000.

3. Cash charges to the partners' accounts during the year were:

A	$ 5,200
B	4,400
C	5,800
D	2,500
	$17,900

4. Of A's and B's receivables, $1,200 and $450, respectively, proved to be uncollectible. A new client billed in March for $1,600 had been adjudged bankrupt and a settlement of 50 cents on the dollar was made.

Required (disregard income taxes):

Prepare a statement of the partners' capital accounts for the year ended December 31, 19x3. Supporting computations should be in good form.

(AICPA adapted)

17

Partnerships—changes in ownership

OVERVIEW

Changes in partnership interests occur for a variety of reasons. These can be summarized as:

1. *A change in a partner's percentage of participation in either profits or capital without a change in the identities of the partners.*
2. *Admission of a new partner.*
3. *Retirement of a partner.*
4. *Death of a partner.*

In most cases, when a change in ownership occurs, the market values and book values of individual partnership assets and liabilities are different. These differences are accounted for either by recording them on the partnership books by adjusting the assets and liabilities—in many cases goodwill is recorded in the process—or by adjusting the partners' capital accounts for these differences. The net effect of the latter approach is usually the same as if the differences were recorded and then immediately written off to bring the accounts back to their original book values.

A partner can be admitted either by purchasing an interest in the partnership from an existing partner(s), or by investing in the partnership itself. In the former case the net assets of the partnership are usually unchanged, while in the latter case the net assets are usually increased.

The death or retirement of a partner requires procedures similar to those used for the admission of a partner except that the process is reversed.

CHANGES IN THE PROFIT AND LOSS RATIOS

A change in the profit and loss ratios and/or capital ratios of partners occurs frequently in large partnerships, and occasionally in smaller ones as well. It is not unusual for the older members of a partnership to reduce their partnership responsibilities with a concomitant decrease in either their profit and loss ratios, their capital ratios, or both. Conversely, younger partners may accept increased responsibilities with a concurrent increase in their participation ratios. Such changes will occur with frequency in the case of large CPA and law firms. When changes in participation ratios occur, several problems are encountered in the valuation of partners' interests among which are the following:

1. There may be a difference between the book value of the tangible assets and the current fair market value of these assets.
2. The partnership might have intangibles, such as goodwill, that are not reflected on the books of the partnership, but which must be considered in arriving at the fair value of the respective partnership interests.
3. The partnership might keep its books on a cash basis, and as a result of this, there may be unrecorded assets such as receivables for work in progress, and unrecorded liabilities such as payables for unpaid purchases. These, too, must be reflected for purposes of determining the fair value of the respective partnership interests.

It is obvious that if a realignment of partnership interests is to be fair and equitable, the above items, if material, must be taken into account to reflect fair valuations of all the partners' interests. To use a simplified example for purposes of illustrating the problem indicated above, let us consider the A-B Partnership where A's share of profits and losses is 10 percent and where B's share of profits and losses is 90 percent. If the partnership owns a piece of land which it had acquired 10 years ago for $50,000 and the fair market value of which is currently $350,000, there is an unrealized and unrecorded potential profit of $300,000 that has accrued to the partners in their profit-sharing ratio of 10 percent and 90 percent respectively. If a realignment of interests is to take place between A and B resulting in a new profit-sharing ratio of 25 percent for A and 75 percent for B, nonrecognition of the increase in the value of the land would result in a $45,000 (15% × $300,000) advantage to A to the detriment of B. Therefore, it is necessary to reflect this differential whenever a realignment of partnership interests occurs.

There are two general approaches to this:

1. Write up or down all assets and liabilities to reflect their fair market values, and book any unrecorded assets or liabilities. The resulting net gain or loss should be reflected in the partners' capital accounts in accordance with their old profit and loss ratios.
2. Calculate the effects of all differences between book values and fair market values as well as the unrecorded assets and liabilities, and adjust only the respective partners' capital accounts for the *net* effects of these adjustments utilizing the old profit and loss ratio. Under this method no write-ups or write-downs of assets and/or liabilities are reflected on the books of the partnership.

The argument advanced by some accountants to justify the first approach is that a realignment of partnership interests, is, in effect, a two-step transaction under which the old partnership is dissolved and a new one is formed. Under this theory, it is acceptable to write-up and write-down assets and liabilities to reflect fair market values. This argument is not a very convincing one, although there is some merit to it. The second approach accomplishes the same result in the partners' capital accounts but it avoids a possible violation of generally accepted accounting principles (GAAP) by retaining the individual assets and liabilities at original book values.

To illustrate the application of the principles discussed above, it is assumed that the only difference between the book and fair value of assets concerns the earlier mentioned land which has a fair market value of $350,000 and a book value of $50,000. The change in the profit and loss ratios are also as cited earlier. The second approach can be implemented with the following journal entry:

```
A—Capital .................................................   45,000
    B—Capital .............................................              45,000
    To credit B with 15% (90% − 75%) of $300,000 ($350,000 −
    $50,000) for his share of the increase in the fair market value of
    the land account and to charge A's capital accordingly.
```

If the first approach were to be used, the required entry would be as follows:

```
Land  ...................................................   300,000
    A—Capital ............................................              30,000
    B—Capital ............................................             270,000
    To record the increase in the Land account and to credit the
    respective partners' capital in the ratio of 10 percent and 90
    percent.
```

If, at a later date, it becomes necessary, for whatever reason, to reverse the write-up of the Land account, the entry necessary to reduce that account back to its original historical cost would be as follows:

```
A—Capital  .............................................   75,000
B—Capital  .............................................  225,000
    Land ................................................             300,000
    To reverse the write-up of Land back to historical cost in the
    new profit-sharing ratio of 25 percent and 75 percent for A
    and B, respectively.
```

It should be noted that if the above write-up entry were combined with the write-down entry which preceded it, the net effect on the partners' capital accounts is identical to that achieved by the simple entry which implemented the second approach and thus proving that the net effect of both methods on the *capital accounts* is the same.

ADMISSION OF A PARTNER—PURCHASE FROM EXISTING PARTNERS

The admission of a new partner into a partnership can be accomplished in a number of ways. One option is for the incoming partner to purchase an interest from one or more of the existing partners. When this occurs, the partnership assets remain unchanged and no cash or other assets are flowing from the new partner to the partnership. Rather, any cash or assets that are exchanged as consideration for admission into the partnership form part of the transactions that are affected by the partners outside the firm. Accordingly, in such cases, the entries to record the admission of a partner will reflect a debit to the capital accounts of the partners selling some or all of their interests, and a credit to the capital account of the partner buying in. The amounts of the capital transferred will be governed not by the amount of cash and other consideration that is transferred, but rather, by the fair value of the share in the firm that is being sold. Illustration 17–1 contains the trial balance of the ABD Partnership on December 31, 19x1. The partners, A, B, and D, share profits and losses in the ratio of 2:3:5. On this date, X is admitted into the partnership with a 50 percent interest in the profits and losses of the partnership.

Illustration 17–1
ABD PARTNERSHIP
Trial Balance
December 31, 19x1

	Debit	Credit
Cash in bank	$15,000	
Other assets	65,000	
Liabilities		$10,000
A—capital		20,000
B—capital		20,000
D—capital		30,000
Totals	$80,000	$80,000

The old partners (A, B, and D) are to retain their original capital and profit-sharing relationships to each other and are to transfer sufficient amounts (50 percent) of their own capital accounts to X in order to accomplish his admission as planned. If X agreed to pay a total of $50,000 to A, B, and D in this transaction, the entry necessary to record this transaction will appear as follows:

A—Capital	10,000	
B—Capital	10,000	
D—Capital	15,000	
X—Capital		35,000

To record the admission of X into the ABD partnership with a 50 percent interest in profits and losses.

The foregoing entry makes it clear that the transaction involves no cash being transferred into or out of the partnership. Moreover, the $50,000 of consideration passes outside of the partnership framework and, in this example, has no effect on the capital accounts. The amounts of capital transferred are equal to the incoming partner's new ratio multiplied by the balance in the capital accounts of the existing partners.

As to the question of how the $50,000 of cash is to be divided among the individual partners, the advice of accountants and others may have to be sought. One fair and equitable arrangement would be as shown in Illustration 17–2.

Illustration 17–2:
Division of cash between
partners A, B, and D
December 31, 19x1

	Total	A	B	D
Amount of capital transferred	$35,000	$10,000	$10,000	$15,000
Excess of $15,000 divided in the profit and loss sharing ratio	15,000	3,000	4,500	7,500
Totals of cash division	$50,000	$13,000	$14,500	$22,500

From Illustration 17–2 it can be seen that one fair and equitable method for dividing the cash among the existing partners is (1) to allow credit for the amounts of capital transferred by the existing partners since they have given up the right to receive this amount of capital upon liquidation; and (2) to apportion any excess (or deficiency) in their respective profit and loss sharing ratio because the excess (or deficiency) represents the implied difference between book and fair market values at the time of the transaction. It should be noted, however, that the partnership books are unaffected by the size of the consideration that passes outside of the partnership entity. This lack of accounting impact is analogous to the situation where a stockholder of a publicly-traded corporation sells stock to another individual. In that case, the price paid for the shares of stock has, of course, no effect on the accounting records of the corporation, but is merely reflected in its stockholders' transfer ledger.

However, a case can be made for adjusting the net assets of the partnership using the price paid by the purchaser as the implicit value of the firm. In fact, this practice has appeared on recent CPA examinations. Thus, if partner X purchases a 50 percent interest in the ABD Partnership for $50,000, as in the preceding example, and it is decided that the implicit goodwill should be recognized, the calculation would be:

Implicit value of the firm ($50,000 ÷ 50%)	$100,000
Less: Existing capital accounts	70,000
Implied goodwill	$ 30,000

The entries to record the admission of X into the partnership would then be:

Goodwill	30,000	
A—Capital		6,000
B—Capital		9,000
C—Capital		15,000

To record the implicit goodwill of the firm based upon the admission of X into the partnership and to credit the existing partners for their shares of the goodwill in their profit and loss ratios.

A—Capital	13,000	
B—Capital	14,500	
C—Capital	22,500	
X—Capital		50,000

To record the admission of X into the partnership by payment of $50,000 to the existing partners.

It is interesting to note that the debits to the existing partners' accounts are exactly equal to the division of cash as shown in Illustration 17–2. Thus, when it is decided to record the implicit goodwill in this manner, it is unnecessary to prepare a cash division schedule, since the division of cash coincides with the partners' charges to their capital accounts.

ADMISSION OF A PARTNER—INVESTMENT INTO THE PARTNERSHIP

Instead of *purchasing* a partnership interest outside of the partnership entity, an incoming partner may be admitted on the basis of a direct investment in the partnership. Under this option the assets agreed upon as consideration for admission will flow into the firm and consequently enlarge its total assets. Occasionally, the investment will be at book value, but more often it will reflect the underlying fair value of the interest acquired.

Based on the data in Illustration 17–1, it is now assumed that Z is to be admitted into the partnership with a 20 percent interest in the profits and losses and with an investment to be made at book value. Computing the investment amount is a relatively simple procedure. The total existing capital (in this case, $70,000) is divided by the percentage that the remaining partners will have after the admission of the new partner. The result is the total capital of the new firm. Subtracting the amount of present capital from the new capital yields the investment required from the incoming partner. The computations are:

1. $70,000 ÷ 80% = $87,500.
2. $87,500 − $70,000 = $17,500.
3. Proof: 20% × $87,500 = $17,500.

The entry to record the admission of Z would be:

Cash 17,500
    Z—Capital 17,500
To record the admission of Z into the partnership for a 20 percent interest in profits and losses and the investment computed at book value.

ADMISSION OF A PARTNER—INVESTMENT AT OTHER THAN BOOK VALUE—PROFIT AND LOSS RATIO AND CAPITAL RATIO COINCIDE

In most instances, the investment by an incoming partner will be at an amount other than book value. The reasons for this are varied: (1) the assets on the books of the partnership may be carried at amounts that differ from their fair market values; (2) there may be unrecorded intangibles, such as goodwill; (3) the incoming partner may be very anxious to join the partnership, or, conversely, the existing partners may be very anxious for the incoming partner to be admitted into the partnership which factors will affect the price asked for a given partnership share. It was previously pointed out that revaluing the assets and liabilities of the partnership upon the admission of a partner is generally not in accordance with GAAP. Therefore, there are two approaches for handling these differences. One method is to revalue the assets and liabilities in accordance with the values agreed upon by the new and existing partners. If goodwill is recorded as part of the process of recording the revaluation, this approach is sometimes referred to as the "goodwill" approach.

Another approach is to record the difference between the investment by the incoming partner and his share of the book value of the partnership as a "bonus." Under this method, the bonus can either be attributable to the existing partners when the investment is greater than the incoming partner's proportionate share of book value, or the bonus can be attributable to the incoming partner if the investment is less than the proportionate share of the pre-admission book value.

Whenever an incoming partner makes the investment at other than book value, then, in the absence of an agreed-upon procedure, there are three ways of recording the total capitalization of the new firm.

Using the data from Illustration 17–1 above, it is now assumed that W invests $45,000 for a 30 percent share of the capital and a 30 percent share of the profits and losses of the ABD Partnership. The existing partners' profit and loss ratio remains the same as it was in relation to each other. Stated differently, A's percentage is now 14 percent (20% × 70%), B's percentage is 21 percent (30% × 70%) and D's percentage is 35 percent (50% × 70%). Using these assumptions, it is now theoretically possible to compute three different capitalizations of the firm:

Computation 1:

$$\$70,000 + \$45,000 = \underline{\$115,000}$$

The capital accounts of the existing partners are added to the cash contributed by the incoming partner to form the capitalization of the new firm.

Computation 2:

$$\$70,000 \div 70\% = \underline{\$100,000}$$

The existing partners' total capital is divided by their share of the partnership after the incoming partner is admitted in order to "gross up" the amount of the capital of the new firm.

Computation 3:

$$\$45,000 \div 30\% = \underline{\$150,000}$$

The incoming partner's cash contribution is divided by his incoming profit and loss percentage to arrive at the new firm's total capital.

An analysis of the three amounts computed above reveals that the first computation (the bonus method) increases the total capitalization by the amount of cash invested. Therefore, any differences pertaining to goodwill or other assets whose market values are different from their book values are not recorded on the books of the partnership but are, instead, adjusted to the partners' capital accounts. This treatment is considered by many accountants to be the most conservative treatment and is in accordance with GAAP. The other two amounts, $100,000 and $150,000, require further analysis. The amount computed using the existing partners' capital accounts ($100,000) is less than the amount computed under the bonus method. If the capitalization of the firm were to be set at $100,000, it is clear that assets equal to $15,000 ($115,000 − $100,000) would have to be written off. In most cases the lowest value of the three—in this case $100,000—is rejected as a possible capitalization unless the assets of the firm are overvalued and write-downs of assets are appropriate. For our purposes, the lowest of the three methods of computation will be rejected in future discussions. Turning now to the amount computed in the third instance ($150,000), if this amount is to be the total capitalization of the firm, it is clear that $35,000 ($150,000 − $115,000) of assets will have to be written up. When the "goodwill" method is used, it is customary to record the $35,000 as goodwill. Since the incoming partner's calculation produced the higher figure, the goodwill is attributable to the existing partners. The reverse could also occur. When the existing partners' calcuation produces the higher amount, the goodwill would then be attributable to the incoming partner. This latter case will be further demonstrated after the completion of this illustration. The recording of the two alternative methods of computation discussed above are as follows:

Bonus Method

Cash	45,000	
W—Capital		34,500
A—Capital		2,100
B—Capital		3,150
D—Capital		5,250

The amount credited to W's capital account is 30% × $115,000 = $34,500. The credits to the remaining partners' capital accounts are computed by allocating this differential bonus of $10,500 in proportion to the profit and loss ratios of each of the remaining partners.

Goodwill Method

Cash	45,000	
W—Capital		45,000
Goodwill	35,000	
A—Capital		7,000
B—Capital		10,500
D—Capital		17,500

Under the goodwill method the incoming partner's capital account is credited for the full amount of his investment. In this example, the goodwill was attributable to the existing partners and consequently the existing partners' capital accounts are credited proportionately for their share of the goodwill implicit in the transaction.

If, at a later date, the goodwill is to be written off, the entry to record the write-off would appear as follows:

W—Capital	10,500	
A—Capital	4,900	
B—Capital	7,350	
D—Capital	12,250	
Goodwill		35,000

Under the goodwill method, the write-up of goodwill and its subsequent write-off produces a net effect which is equal to that of the bonus method. This will always be true provided there is *no realignment* of partnership interests after the admission of the incoming partner. This can be verified

Illustration 17–3
Comparison of Bonus and Goodwill
Methods for Admission of a Partner
December 31, 19x1
Bonus Method

	Total	A	B	D	W
Capital balances prior to admission	$ 70,000	$20,000	$20,000	$30,000	$ –0–
Journal entry on admission	45,000	2,100	3,150	5,250	34,500
Balances after admission	$115,000	$22,100	$23,150	$35,250	$34,500

Goodwill Method

	Total	A	B	D	W
Capital balances prior to admission	$ 70,000	$20,000	$20,000	$30,000	$ –0–
Journal entries on admission	80,000	7,000	10,500	17,500	45,000
Balances after admission	150,000	27,000	30,500	47,500	45,000
Less: Subsequent entry to write off goodwill .	35,000	4,900	7,350	12,250	10,500
Balances after goodwill write-off	$115,000	$22,100	$23,150	$35,250	$34,500

by reviewing Illustration 17–3. If there is a realignment of partnership interests, either on the date of the admission of the new partner, or at a subsequent point in time, this will no longer be true. If the partnership books are to be kept free of goodwill and of revaluations of other assets, the admission of a partner coupled with a realignment of profit and loss ratios can be handled in a manner similar to the "realignment" discussed earlier in this chapter. The differentials between book values and fair market values can be reflected using the original profit and loss ratios, and then the differential can immediately be written off using the profit and loss ratios prevailing subsequent to the realignment.

In order to illustrate the case where an incoming partner will be credited with goodwill, it is now assumed that T is to be admitted into the ABD Partnership (see Illustration 17–1) by investing $15,000 for a 20 percent share in the profits and losses of the firm. A, B, and D will continue to maintain their relative pre-admission ratios. The three possible computations of total partnership capital are:

1. $70,000 + $15,000 = $85,000.
2. $70,000 ÷ 80% = $87,500.
3. $15,000 ÷ 20% = $75,000.

The third computation ($75,000) results in a capitalization which is less than the "bonus" computation ($85,000) and will, therefore, not be considered here. The implicit goodwill of $2,500 ($87,500 − $85,000) is simply the difference between the other two computations. The entries to record the admission of T would be:

Bonus Method

Cash	15,000	
A—Capital	400	
B—Capital	600	
D—Capital	1,000	
T—Capital		17,000

To record the admission of T into partnership with a 20 percent interest in profits and losses.

Goodwill Method

Cash	15,000	
Goodwill	2,500	
T—Capital		17,500

To record the admission of T into partnership with a 20 percent interest in profits and losses.

It should be noted that in both cases T is credited with 20 percent of the respective total capitalizations—"bonus" equals 20 percent of $85,000 and "goodwill" equals 20 percent of $87,500. If the goodwill were subsequently written off, the net result would be the same as the "bonus" method provided a subsequent realignment of ratios did not occur.

ADMISSION OF A PARTNER—PROFIT AND LOSS RATIOS AND CAPITAL RATIOS ARE DIFFERENT

Frequently, a partner may be admitted into partership with a profit and loss ratio that differs from the capital ratio. With one modification, the admission principles discussed previously apply to cases where the ratios are different. Previously, only one ratio was given and, therefore, a choice of ratios was not required. When two ratios are given, i.e., a profit and loss ratio of 20 percent and a capital ratio of 30 percent, only the capital ratio is used for the purpose of calculating the implied goodwill or to calculate the bonus. Thus, referring to the preceding discussion, if W is admitted with a 20 percent interest in profits and losses and a 30 percent interest in the capital of the partnership, the calculations would be identical to those on page 552 since the 20 percent ratio would be ignored and only the 30 percent ratio would be used. The journal entries that follow would also be the same.

RETIREMENT OF A PARTNER

As is the case with the admission of a partner, the retirement of a partner also occurs rarely at book value. When the valuation of a retiring partner's capital differs from the balance in his capital account, three accounting approaches are in general usage:

1. Record only the difference between the payments to the retired partner and the balance in his capital account. (Record only the differential.)
2. Compute the difference as in (1) above, but divide this amount by the retiring partner's percentage and enter the resulting difference (implied differential) in the partnership books of account.
3. Do not record the difference, but instead, adjust the remaining partners' capital accounts by the difference (differential) computed in (1) above.

Again using the basic data in Illustration 17–1, it is now assumed that D is retiring from the partnership and A and B agree to pay D $40,000, which D accepts, as a retirement payment in full. The entries to record the retirement under each of the above three approaches are as follows:

Record Differential only

D—Capital	30,000	
Goodwill (or other assets)	10,000	
Liability to retired partner		40,000

To record the retirement of D from the partnership.

Record the Implicit Differential

D—Capital	30,000	
Goodwill (or other assets)	20,000	
Liability to Retired Partner		40,000
A—Capital		4,000
B—Capital		6,000

To record the retirement of D and to book the implicit excess ($40,000 − $30,000) ÷ 50% = $20,000 and credit the remaining partners for their share in it in the ratio of 2:3.

Record No Differential

D—Capital	30,000	
A—Capital	4,000	
B—Capital	6,000	
Liability to Retired Partner		40,000

To record the retirement of D and to allocate the excess payment to A and B in the ratio of 2:3.

The first of the above three approaches is the one most nearly in compliance with GAAP since under it assets or goodwill are recorded in accordance with the price paid for them. The second approach is less conservative, since under it, goodwill (or other assets) attributable to the remaining partners (to whom no payment is made) are recorded. The third method is overly conservative since the payment for goodwill (or other assets) is, in effect, immediately written off against the remaining partners' capital accounts.

Although most often, particularly in successful partnerships, retirements of partners require payments in excess of a partner's capital balance, in some cases retirements may occur where the payments are less than a partner's capital balance. In such cases an attempt should be made to allocate the differential to specific assets. If we assume a payment of $15,000 to D for his partnership interest, the resulting entry will be as follows:

D—Capital	30,000	
Liability to Retired Partner		15,000
Specific Assets (to be identified)		15,000

If the causes of the differential are not ascertainable or assignable to specific assets, then the "bonus" method should be used as follows:

D—Capital	30,000	
Liability to Retired Partner		15,000
A—Capital		6,000
B—Capital		9,000

To record the retirement of D and the allocation of the differential to A and B in the ratio of 2:3.

DEATH OF A PARTNER

The Uniform Partnership Act (UPA) specifies that a partnership is dissolved by the death of a partner (sec. 31). However, a partnership agreement may countermand this provision and permit the partnership to continue. In any event, the partnership books should be closed as of the date of death in order to permit the partnership to render an accounting to the estate of the deceased partner. A partnership agreement usually specifies the basis to be used to arrive at the value of the deceased partner's interest. The deceased partner's estate is entitled to participate in the profits and losses of the partnership up to the date of death, and, in addition, is entitled to compensation for the value of the deceased partner's interest in the partnership as of that date. The entries to record payments to a deceased partner's estate are not different from those illustrated above with regard to the retirement of a partner, except that the liability account would be called, Liability to the Estate of D.

INCORPORATION OF A PARTNERSHIP

For a variety of reasons, including legal and/or tax, the partners of a partnership may choose to incorporate. Two approaches of opening the corporate books are in general use. One is to retain the books of the partnership and to record all assets and liabilities at fair market value concomitant with the closing of the partners' capital accounts and the opening of a Common Stock account. The other approach is to close out the partnership books completely and to open a new set of books for the corporation using fair market values as the basis for recording all assets and liabilities with the balancing amount credited to Common Stock. Occasionally, additional cash or other assets may be invested in the corporation. As an example, Illustration 17–4 contains a partnership trial balance together with the fair market values of those assets that differ from their book values. In addition, it is assumed that the profit and loss ratios of D, E, and F are 2:3:5, respectively. Each partner wishes to contribute or withdraw a sufficient amount of cash so that the stockholders' equity shall amount to $200,000 after revaluation and the partner's relative stockholdings in the new corporation shall be in proportion to their former profit and loss ratio.

Illustration 17–4
DEF PARTNERSHIP
Trial Balance
December 31, 19x1

	Debit	Credit	Market value
Cash	$ 30,000		
Accounts receivable	20,000		
Merchandise inventory	25,000		$40,000
Prepaid expenses	3,000		
Property, plant, and equipment	100,000		
Accumulated depreciation		$ 30,000	80,000
Accounts payable		20,000	
D—loan payable		30,000	
D—capital		15,000	
E—capital		28,000	
F—capital		55,000	
Totals	$178,000	$178,000	

The following entries which give effect to the incorporation assume that the partnership books will be continued.

Merchandise Inventory	15,000	
Accumulated Depreciation	30,000	
Property, Plant, and Equipment		20,000
Revaluation Account		25,000

To revalue partnership assets and close Accumulated
Depreciation upon incorporation of the DEF Partnership.

Revaluation Account	25,000	
D—Capital		5,000
E—Capital		7,500
F—Capital		12,500

To close Revaluation Account and credit the partners'
accounts in the ratio of 2:3:5.

D—Loan Payable	30,000	
D—Capital		20,000
Cash		10,000

To bring D—Capital up to 20% × $200,000.

Cash	57,000	
E—Capital		24,500
F—Capital		32,500

To bring the capital accounts up to a total of $200,000 in the
desired proportions.

D—Capital	40,000	
E—Capital	60,000	
F—Capital	100,000	
Common Stock		200,000

To close capital accounts and record the issuance of
corporate common stock to the partners.

If the corporation were to open a new set of books, the net results would
be the same and would appear as follows:

Cash	77,000	
Accounts Receivable	20,000	
Merchandise Inventory	40,000	
Prepaid Expenses	3,000	
Property, Plant, and Equipment	80,000	
Accounts Payable		20,000
Common Stock		200,000

To record the incorporation of the DEF Partnership.

In this case the partnership's books would be completely closed out.

QUESTIONS

1. Very often, a partner's participation in profits and losses and/or capital may change. When the change arises for reasons other than the admission, death, or retirement of a partner, explain why the change may occur, and indicate the problems that are usually encountered when the change is to be recorded on the partnership's books.

2. What equitable treatments may be used to overcome the problems you noted in the previous question? Illustrate them by the use of an example.

3. A partner may be admitted into a partnership in either of two ways. What are they? What is the usual effect on the net assets of the firm for each method?

4. When a partner is admitted into partnership by investing in the partnership, two approaches exist to record the admission. What are they called? Explain each method.

5. Explain how goodwill may be calculated when the goodwill method is used to record the admission

of a partner and the profit and loss ratio coincides with the capital ratio.

6. When the bonus method is used to record the admission of a partner, it can be compared to the goodwill method under a certain set of conditions and assumptions. Explain these conditions and assumptions.

7. Is there any authoritative support for adjusting the book values of the net assets of a partnership to market values when an incoming partner purchases a partnership interest from an existing partner? Explain.

8. Is it possible for a partner to be admitted into partnership with a profit and loss ratio different from the capital ratio? If so, how is the goodwill or bonus calculated for these cases?

9. When a partner retires, rarely will the payments to a partner equal the balance in the partner's capital account. When the payments to the retiring partner exceed the balance in the partner's capital account, there are three generally accepted approaches to account for the excess payment. What are they? Illustrate each one with an example.

10. When the payments to a retiring partner are less than the balance in the partner's capital account, there are two generally accepted approaches to account for the difference. What are they? Illustrate each one with an example.

11. When a partner dies, is the partnership automatically dissolved? If one wishes to overcome the provisions of Section 31 of the UPA, how can this be accomplished? In either case, what should be done with regard to the partnership's books as of the date of a partner's death? Why?

12. Is it necessary to close the partnership's books upon incorporation? If not, how are the differences between the book values and market values of the individual assets and liabilities treated? What is true about the opening balances of the corporation's books when the partnership's books are closed or continued?

EXERCISES

Exercise 17–1. Arlen and Babcox are partners with a profit and loss ratio of 80:20, respectively. Their credit balance capital accounts on January 1, 19x3, are $60,000 for Arlen and $40,000 for Babcox. For each of the following cases, prepare journal entries to admit Coren:

a. Coren invests an amount of cash for a 20 percent interest in profits, losses, and capital.

b. Coren invests $40,000 for a one-fourth interest in the capital of the firm and goodwill is not to be recorded.

c. Coren invests $30,000 for a one-fourth interest in the capital of the firm and goodwill is not to be recorded.

d. Coren invests $40,000 for a 20 percent interest in the capital of the firm and goodwill is to be recorded.

e. Coren invests $20,000 for a 20 percent interest in the capital of the firm and goodwill is to be recorded.

Exercise 17–2. Baton and Carey are partners and share profits and losses in the ratio of 6:4. On January 1, 19x4, their credit balance capital accounts are $80,000 for Baton and $20,000 for Carey. Devon is to be admitted for a 20 percent interest in the capital of partnership which is to be purchased directly from the partners for $30,000. Each partner's capital account is to be charged pro rata for amounts in their capital ratio which will provide Devon with the 20 percent interest.

Required:

a. Prepare the entry on the partnership's books to record the admission of Devon into partnership.

b. Prepare a schedule to show how the $30,000 of cash should be divided by Baton and Carey.

Exercise 17–3. Corwin and David, who share profits and losses in the ratio of 6:4, are partners in a partnership with credit capital balances of $30,000 and $70,000, respectively. Edwards is to be admitted into the partnership with a cash contribution of $30,000 for a 20 percent interest in the capital of the firm.

Required:

a. Prepare the journal entries to record the admission of Edwards using three possible solutions.

b. For each solution, give a brief description when that method would be most appropriate.

Exercise 17–4. Darrell and Evers, who share profits and losses in ratio of 3:7, are partners in a partnership with credit capital balances of $40,000 and $60,000, respectively. Flint is to be admitted into the partnership for a 20 percent interest in the capital of the firm.

Required:

a. Calculate the cash payment by Flint if, after the cash payment is recorded, the capital balances of Darrell and Evers are $52,000 and $88,000 and goodwill *was* recorded.

b. Calculate the cash payment by Flint if, after the cash payment is recorded, the capital balances of Darrell and Evers are $38,800 and $57,200 and goodwill *was not* recorded.

Exercise 17–5.

1. Pat, Helma, and Diane are partners with capital balances of $50,000, $30,000, and $20,000, respectively. The partners share profits and losses equally. For an investment of $50,000 cash, Mary Ann is to be admitted as a partner with a one-fourth interest in capital and profits. Based on this information, the amount of Mary Ann's investment can best be justified by which of the following?

a. Mary Ann will receive a bonus from the other partners upon her admission to the partnership.

b. Assets of the partnership were overvalued immediately prior to Mary Ann's investment.

c. The book value of the partnership's net assets was less than their fair value immediately prior to Mary Ann's investment.

d. Mary Ann is apparently bringing goodwill into the partnership, and her capital account will be credited for the appropriate amount.

2. The capital accounts for the partnership of Lance and Dey at October 31, 19x5, are as follows:

Lance, capital	$ 80,000
Dey, capital	40,000
	$120,000

The partners share profits and losses in the ratio of 6:4, respectively.

The partnership is in desperate need of cash, and the partners agree to admit Carey as a partner with a one-third interest in the capital and profits and losses upon his investment of $30,000. Immediately after Carey's admission, what should be the capital balances of Lance, Dey, and Carey, respectively, assuming goodwill is *not* to be recognized?

a. $50,000; $50,000; $50,000.

b. $60,000; 60,000; $60,000.

c. $66,667; $33,333; $50,000.

d. $68,000; $32,000; $50,000.   (AICPA adapted)

Exercise 17–6.

1. Frank and Moore are partners who share profits and losses equally in a highly successful partnership. The capital accounts of Frank and Moore have tripled in five years and at present stand at $90,000 and $60,000, respectively. Swoop desires to join the firm and offered to invest $50,000 for a one-third interest in the capital and profits and losses of the firm. Frank and Moore declined this offer but extended a counter offer to Swoop of $70,000 for a one-fourth interest in the capital and profits and losses of the firm. If Swoop accepted this offer and goodwill is recorded, what should be the balances in the capital accounts of Frank and Moore after Swoop's admission?

a. Frank, $90,000; Moore, $60,000.

b. Frank, $97,500; Moore, $67,500.

c. Frank, $100,000; Moore, $70,000.

d. Frank $120,000; Moore, $90,000.

2. Partners Allen, Baker, and Coe share profits and losses 50:30:20, respectively. The balance sheet at April 30, 19x5, follows:

Assets	
Cash	$ 40,000
Other assets	360,000
Total assets	$400,000

Liabilities and Capital	
Accounts payable	$100,000
Allen, capital	74,000
Baker, capital	130,000
Coe, capital	96,000
Total liabilities and capital	$400,000

The assets and liabilities are recorded and presented at their respective fair values.

Jones is to be admitted as a new partner with a 20 percent capital interest and a 20 percent share of profits and losses in exchange for a cash contribution. **No** goodwill or bonus is to be recorded. How much cash should Jones contribute?

a. $60,000.

b. $72,000.

c. $75,000.

d. $80,000.   (AICPA adapted)

Exercise 17–7.

1. Elton and Don are partners who share profits and losses in the ratio of 7:3, respectively. On November 5, 19x8, their respective capital accounts were as follows:

Elton	$ 70,000
Don	60,000
	$130,000

On that date they agreed to admit Kravitz as a partner with a one-third interest in the capital and profits and losses upon his investment of $50,000. The new partnership will begin with a total capital of $180,000. Immediately after Kravitz's admission what are the capital balances of Elton, Don, and Kravitz, respectively?

a. $60,000; $60,000; $60,000.
b. $63,000; $57,000; $60,000.
c. $63,333; $56,667; $60,000.
d. $70,000; $60,000; $50,000.

2. William desires to purchase a one-fourth capital and profit and loss interest in the partnership of Eli, George, and Dick. The three partners agree to sell William one-fourth of their respective capital and profit and loss interest in exchange for a total payment of $40,000. The capital accounts and the respective percentage interests in profits and losses immediately before the sale to William follow:

	Capital accounts	Percentage interest in profits and losses
Eli	$ 80,000	60
George	40,000	30
Dick	20,000	10
Totals	$140,000	100

All other assets and liabilities are fairly valued and implied goodwill is to be recorded prior to the acquisition by William. Immediately after William's acquisition, what should be the capital balances of Eli, George, and Dick, respectively?

a. $60,000; $30,000; $15,000.
b. $69,000; $34,500; $16,500.
c. $77,000; $38,500; $19,500.
d. $92,000; $46,000; $22,000.   (AICPA adapted)

Exercise 17–8. Presented below is the condensed balance sheet of the partnership of Kane, Clark, and Lane who share profits and losses in the ratio of 6:3:1, respectively:

Cash	$ 85,000
Other assets	415,000
	$500,000
Liabilities	$ 80,000
Kane, capital	252,000
Clark, capital	126,000
Lane, capital	42,000
	$500,000

1. The assets and liabilities on the above balance sheet are fairly valued, and the partnership wishes to admit Bayer with a 25 percent interest in the capital and profits/losses *without* recording goodwill or bonus. How much should Bayer contribute in cash or other assets?

a. $70,000.
b. $105,000.
c. $125,000.
d. $140,000.

2. Assume that the partners agree instead to sell Bayer 20 percent of their respective capital and profit and loss interests for a total payment of $90,000. The payment by Bayer is to be made directly to the individual partners. The partners agree that implied goodwill is to be recorded prior to the acquisition by Bayer. What are the capital balances of Kane, Clark, and Lane, respectively, after the acquisition by Bayer?

a. $198,000; $99,000; $33,000.
b. $201,600; $100,800; $33,600.
c. $216,000; $108,000; $36,000.
d. $255,600; $127,800; $42,600.

3. The capital accounts of the partnership of Newton, Sharman, and Jackson on June 1, 19x7, are presented below with their respective profit and loss ratios:

Newton	$139,200	$\frac{1}{2}$
Sharman	208,800	$\frac{1}{3}$
Jackson	96,000	$\frac{1}{6}$
	$444,000	

On June 1, 19x7, Sidney was admitted to the partnership when he purchased, for $132,000, a proportionate interest from Newton and Sharman in the net assets and profits of the partnership. As a result of this transaction, Sidney acquired a one-fifth interest in the net assets and profits of the firm. Assuming that implied goodwill is *not* to be recorded, what is the combined gain realized by Newton and Sharman upon the sale of a portion of their interests in the partnership to Sidney?

a. $0.

b. $43,200.

c. $62,400.

d. $82,000.   (AICPA adapted)

Exercise 17–9. On January 1, 19x3, Garvey and Harold agree to adjust their profit and loss ratio from 70:30 to 60:40. A balance sheet on that date, together with the related fair market values, is as follows:

GARVEY AND HAROLD
Balance Sheet
January 1, 19x3

	Book value	Market value
Current assets	$100,000	$100,000
Land	50,000	150,000
Equipment (net of accumulated depreciation)	100,000	90,000
Total	$250,000	
Liabilities	$ 50,000	
Garvey—capital	120,000	
Harold—capital	80,000	
Total	$250,000	

Required:

Prepare the journal entries to record the change in ratios, if:

a. The assets are to be revalued.

b. The assets are not to be revalued.

Exercise 17–10. Horatio, Imobile, and Johnson are partners with a profit and loss ratio of 2:5:3 and credit capital balances of $40,000, $80,000, and $60,000, respectively. Keller is to be admitted into the partnership, for a 20 percent interest by purchasing a prorata amount of capital from each partner. Keller will give the partners $48,000 to accomplish his purchase of the 20 percent interest.

The partners decided that goodwill should be recorded on the books of the partnership based upon the price paid by Keller.

Required:

Prepare the entries that would be necessary to record the admission of Keller and to record the goodwill as indicated.

Exercise 17–11. Innes, Jackson, and Kabob are partners with a profit and loss ratio of 3:3:4 and credit capital balances of $60,000, $40,000, and $40,000, respectively. Lomar is to be admitted into the partnership by investing $60,000 for a 20 percent interest in the capital and a 30 percent interest in the profits and losses of the firm.

Required:

Prepare the journal entries to record the admission of Lomar, if:

a. Goodwill is to be recorded.

b. Goodwill is not to be recorded.

Exercise 17–12. James, Kelly, and Lumet are partners with a profit and loss ratio of 5:3:2 and credit capital balances of $50,000, $40,000, and $30,000, respectively. James is to retire, and he is to be paid $80,000 in full settlement of his partnership interest.

Required:

Prepare journal entries to record the retirement of James (set up a liability to the retiring partner) using *three* different methods.

Exercise 17–13. Rework Exercise 17–12 if, instead of $80,000, James is to be paid $40,000 for his entire partnership interest.

Required:

Prepare journal entries to record the retirement of James (set up a liability to the retiring partner) using *two* different methods.

Exercise 17–14.

1. The balance sheet for the partnership of Lang, Monte, and Newton at April 30, 19x5, follows. The partners share profits and losses in the ratio of 2:2:6, respectively.

Assets, at cost	$100,000
Lang, loan	$ 9,000
Lang, capital	15,000
Monte, capital	31,000
Newton, capital	45,000
Total	$100,000

Lang is retiring from the partnership. By mutual agreement, the assets are to be adjusted to their fair value of $130,000 at April 30, 19x5. Monte and Newton agree that the partnership will pay Lang $37,000 cash for his partnership interest, exclusive of his loan which is to be paid in full. **No** goodwill is to be recorded. What is the balance of Newton's capital account after Lang's retirement?

a. $51,000.

b. $53,400.

c. $59,000.

d. $63,000.

2. James Dixon, a partner in an accounting firm, decided to withdraw from the partnership. Dixon's share of the partnership profits and losses was 20 percent. Upon withdrawing from the partnership he was paid $74,000 in final settlement for his interest. The total of the partners' capital accounts *before* recognition of partnership goodwill prior to Dixon's withdrawal was $210,000. After his withdrawal the remaining partners' capital accounts, excluding their share of goodwill, totaled $160,000. The total agreed upon goodwill of the firm was—

a. $120,000.

b. $140,000.

c. $160,000.

d. $250,000.

3. On June 30, 19x8, the balance sheet for the partnership of Williams, Brown, and Lowe together with their respective profit and loss ratios was as follows:

Assets, at cost	$300,000
Williams, loan	$ 15,000
Williams, capital (20%)	70,000
Brown, capital (20%)	65,000
Lowe, capital (60%)	150,000
Total	$300,000

Williams has decided to retire from the partnership and by mutual agreement the assets are to be adjusted to their fair value of $360,000 at June 30, 19x8. It was agreed that the partnership would pay Williams $102,000 cash for his partnership interest exclusive of his loan which is to be repaid in full. *No* goodwill is to be recorded in this transaction. After Williams' retirement what are the capital account balances of Brown and Lowe, respectively?

a. $65,000 and $150,000.

b. $72,000 and $171,000.

c. $73,000 and $174,000.

d. $77,000 and $186,000.   (AICPA adapted)

PROBLEMS

Problem 17–15. Kapok, Lind, and Mitchell are partners with a profit and loss ratio of 4:3:3 and credit capital balances of $80,000, $60,000, and $60,000. Nolan is to be admitted into the partnership with an investment of $60,000 for a 20 percent interest in the capital, profits and losses of the firm.

Required:

a. Prepare journal entries to record the admission of Nolan, if:

1. Goodwill is to be recorded.

2. Goodwill is not to be recorded.

b. Prepare journal entries to record the admission of Nolan if, instead of investing into the partnership, he purchases his interest from the partners at the same $60,000, and:

1. Implicit goodwill is to be recorded.

2. Goodwill is not to be recorded.

c. Compare your answers in (a) and (b). Write a brief explanation explaining any differences you note between the solutions in (a) and (b).

Problem 17–16. Leonard and Mack are partners with a profit and loss ratio of 75:25 and credit capital balances of $100,000 and $50,000, respectively. Nixon is to be admitted into the partnership by purchasing a 20 percent interest in the capital, profits, and losses for $60,000.

Required:

a. Prepare a schedule of partners' capital balances after the admission of Nixon, if:

1. Goodwill is not to be recorded.

2. Goodwill is to be recorded.

3. Goodwill is to be recorded and then written off.

b. Prepare a schedule of partners' capital balances after the admission of Nixon, and goodwill is to be recorded and then written off but the new profit and loss ratio is 4:4:2 for Leonard, Mack, and Nixon instead of 6:2:2 as in (a) (3) above.

c. Briefly comment on your solutions after comparing (a) (1) with (a) (3), and (b) with (a) (3).

Problem 17–17. Monard, Nelson, and Opel are partners with a profit and loss ratio of 5:3:2. They decided to incorporate as at January 1, 19x5. On that date, the partnership's trial balance was as follows:

MONARD, NELSON, AND OPEL
Trial Balance
January 1, 19x5

	Book values	Market values
Debits		
Cash in bank	$ 40,000	$40,000
Accounts receivable (net of estimated uncollectibles)	26,000	26,000
Inventories	34,000	60,000
Land	20,000	60,000
Building	50,000	70,000
Equipment	80,000	60,000
Totals	$250,000	
Credits		
Accounts payable	$ 30,000	$30,000
Accumulated depreciation—building	20,000	
Accumulated depreciation—equipment	30,000	
Loan payable—Nelson	40,000	
Monard—capital	60,000	
Nelson—capital	20,000	
Opel—capital	50,000	
Totals	$250,000	

Capital stock is to be issued in the ratio of 4:3:3 for Monard, Nelson, and Opel. The partners are either to receive cash or pay into the partnership amounts of cash sufficient to bring their capital accounts into the ratio of 4:3:3 after any required revaluation of assets.

Required:

a. Prepare the journal entries to record the incorporation if the partnership books are to be continued.

b. Prepare the journal entry (entries) to record the incorporation if the corporation is to start a new set of books.

Problem 17–18. You have been engaged to prepare financial statements for the partnership of Alexander, Randolph, and Ware as of June 30, 19x2. You have obtained the following information from the partnership agreement as amended and from the accounting records.

1. The partnership was formed originally by Alexander and Barnes on July 1, 19x1. At that date:

   a. Barnes contributed $400,000 cash.

   b. Alexander contributed land, building, and equipment with fair market values of $110,000, $520,000, and $185,000, respec-

tively. The land and building were subject to a mortgage securing an 8 percent per annum note (interest rate of similar notes at July 1, 19x1). The note is due in quarterly payments of $5,000 plus interest on January 1, April 1, July 1, and October 1 of each year. Alexander made the July 1, 19x1, principal and interest payment personally. The partnership then assumed the obligation for the remaining $300,000 balance.

   c. The agreement further provided that Alexander had contributed a certain intangible benefit to the partnership due to his many years of business activity in the area to be serviced by the new partnership. The assigned value of this intangible asset plus the net tangible assets he contributed gave Alexander a 60 percent initial capital interest in the partnership.

   d. Alexander was designated the only active partner at an annual salary of $24,000 plus an annual bonus of 4 percent of net income after deducting his salary but before deducting interest on partners' capital investments (see below). Both the salary and the bonus are operating expenses of the partnership.

   e. Each partner is to receive a 6 percent return on his average capital investment, such interest to be an expense of the partnership.

   f. All remaining profits or losses are to be shared equally.

2. On October 1, 19x1, Barnes sold his partnership interest and rights as of July 1, 19x1, to Ware for $370,000. Alexander agreed to accept Ware as a partner if he would contribute sufficient cash to meet the October 1, 19x1, principal and interest payment on the mortgage note. Ware made the payment from personal funds.

3. On January 1, 19x2, Alexander and Ware admitted a new partner, Randolph. Randolph invested $150,000 cash for a 10 percent capital interest based on the initial investments at July 1, 19x1, of Alexander and Barnes. At January 1, 19x2, the book value of the partnership's assets and liabilities approximated their fair market values. Randolph contributed no intangible benefit to the partnership.

   Similar to the other partners, Randolph is to receive a 6 percent return on his average capital investment. His investment also entitled him to 20 percent of the partnership's profits or losses as defined above. However, for the year ended June 30, 19x2, Randolph would receive one half of his pro rata share of the profits or losses.

4. The accounting records show that on February 1, 19x2, Other Miscellaneous Expenses had been charged $3,600 in payment of hospital expenses incurred by Alexander's eight-year-old daughter.

5. All salary payments to Alexander have been charged to his personal account. On June 1, 19x2, Ware made a $33,000 withdrawal. These are the only transactions recorded in the partners' personal accounts.

6. Presented below is a trial balance which summarizes the partnership's general ledger balances at June 30, 19x2. The general ledger has not been closed.

	Dr. (cr.)
Current assets	$ 307,100
Fixed assets, net	1,285,800
Current liabilities	(157,000)
8% mortgage note payable	(290,000)
Alexander, capital	(515,000)
Randolph, capital	(150,000)
Ware, capital	(400,000)
Alexander, personal	24,000
Randolph, personal	—
Ware, personal	33,000
Sales	(872,600)
Cost of sales	695,000
Administrative expenses	16,900
Other miscellaneous expenses	11,100
Interest expense	11,700

Required:

Prepare a working paper to adjust the net income (loss) and partners' capital accounts for the year ended June 30, 19x2, and to close the net income (loss) to the partner's capital accounts at June 30, 19x2. Supporting schedules should be in good form. Amortization of goodwill, if any, is to be over a 10-year period. *Ignore all tax considerations.* Use the following column headings and begin with balances per books as shown:

Problem 17–19. The partnership agreement of Jones, McDill, Gilrey, Carter, and Adams contained a buy and sell agreement, among numerous other provisions, which would become operative in case of the death of any partner. Some provisions contained in the buy and sell agreement were as follows:

ARTICLE V. Buy and Sell Agreement

1. *Purposes of the buy and sell agreement.*
   a. The partners mutually desire that the business shall be continued by the survivors without interruption or liquidation upon the death of one of the partners.
   b. The partners also mutually desire that the deceased partner's estate shall receive the full value of the deceased partner's interest in the partnership and that the estate shall share in the earnings of the partnership until the deceased partner's interest shall be fully purchased by the surviving partners.
2. *Purchase and sale of deceased partner's interest.*
   a. Upon the death of the partner first to die, the partnership shall continue to operate without dissolution.
   b. Upon the decedent's death, the survivors shall purchase and the executor or administrator of the deceased partner's estate shall sell to the surviving partners the deceased partner's interest in the partnership for the price and upon the terms and conditions hereinafter set forth.
   c. The deceased partner's estate shall retain the deceased partner's interest until the amount specified in the next paragraph shall be paid in full by the surviving partners.
   d. The parties agree that the purchase price for the partnership interest shall be an amount equal to the deceased partner's capital account at the date of death. Said amount shall

[Relates to Problem 17–18]

Description	Net Income (loss)		Partners' Capital						Other Accounts		
			Alexander		Randolph		Ware		Amount		
	Cr.	(Dr.)	Cr.	(Dr.)	Cr.	(Dr.)	Cr.	(Dr.)	Dr.	(Cr.)	Name
Book balances at June 30, 19x2	$137,900		$515,000		$150,000		$400,000				

(AICPA adapted)

be paid to the legal representative of decedent as follows:

(i) The first installment of 30 percent of said capital account shall be paid within 60 days from the date of death of the partner or within 30 days from the date on which the personal representative of decedent becomes qualified by law, whichever date is later, and

(ii) The balance shall be due in four equal installments which shall be due and payable annually on the anniversary date of said death.

3. *Deceased partner's estate's share of the earnings.*

a. The partners mutually desire that the deceased partner's estate shall be guaranteed a share in the earnings of the partnership over the period said estate retains an interest in the partnership. Said estate shall not be deemed to have an interest in the partnership after the final installment for the deceased partner's capital account is paid even though a portion of the guaranteed payments specified below may be unpaid and may be due and owing.

b. The deceased partner's estate's guaranteed share of the earnings of the partnership shall be determined from two items and shall be paid at different times as follows:

(i) First, interest shall be paid on the unpaid balance of the deceased partner's capital account at the same date the installment on the purchase price is paid. The amount to be paid shall be an amount equal to accrued interest at the rate of 6 percent per annum on the un-

the partnership earnings shall be an amount equal to 25 percent of the deceased partner's share of the aggregate gross receipts of the partnership for the full 36 months preceding the month of the partner's death. Said amount shall be payable in 48 equal monthly installments without interest, and the first payment shall be made within 60 days following the death of the partner or within 30 days from the date on which the personal representative of deceased becomes qualified, whichever date is later; provided, however, that the payments so made under this provision during any 12-month period shall not exceed the highest annual salary on a calendar-year basis received by the partner for the three calendar years immediately preceding the date of his death. In the event that said payment would exceed said salary, then an amount per month shall be paid which does not so exceed said highest monthly salary, and the term over which payments shall be paid to the beneficiary shall be lengthened out beyond the said 48 months in order to complete said payment.

Jones and Adams were both killed simultaneously in an automobile accident on January 10, 19x6. The surviving partners notified the executors of both estates that the first payment due under the buy and sell agreement would be paid on March 10, 19x6, and that subsequent payments would be paid on the tenth day of each month as due.

The following information was determined from the partnership's records:

[Relates to Problem 17–19]

Partner	P & L sharing ratio	Capital account on January 10, 19x6	Annual salaries to partners by years		
			19x3	19x4	19x5
Jones	30	$25,140	$16,500	$17,000	$17,400
McDill	25	21,970	15,000	15,750	16,500
Gilrey	20	4,780	12,000	13,000	14,000
Carter	15	5,860	9,600	10,800	12,000
Adams	10	2,540	8,400	9,600	10,800

paid balance of the purchase price for the deceased partner's capital account.

(ii) Second, the parties agree that the balance of the guaranteed payment from

The partnership's gross receipts for the three prior years were:

19x3	$296,470
19x4	325,310
19x5	363,220

Required:

Prepare a schedule of the amounts to be paid to the Jones Estate and to the Adams Estate in March 19x6, December 19x6, and January 19x7. The schedule should identify the amounts attributable to earnings and to interest in the guaranteed payments and to capital. Supporting computation should be in good form.   (AICPA adapted)

18

Partnerships— liquidation and dissolution

OVERVIEW

When a partnership is in the process of liquidation and dissolution, creditors other than partners have a prior claim to partnership assets over partners' claims.

If the partnership liquidation is accomplished in one transaction, the accounting for the liquidation is simpler than the accounting for a liquidation which occurs over an extended period of time. For a one-transaction liquidation, the creditors are paid and any remaining assets are distributed to the partners. For an extended liquidation, however, liquidation is usually accomplished in instalments. This involves the calculation of instalment payments to partners while creditors' claims or potential creditors' claims may still be unpaid. The calculation of these instalment payments requires a calculation to arrive at what is called the safe payment.

In the process of a partnership liquidation it often becomes necessary to examine each partner's personal assets and liabilities in conjunction with his or her capital account. A partner may have a deficiency in his personal assets, his partnership capital account, or both. This process is known as marshaling of assets.

When a partner dies, the partnership may continue in business rather than liquidate. This chapter is concerned with the accounting that occurs when either because of the death of a partner or for other reasons, a partnership decides to liquidate its assets and to dissolve.

RIGHTS OF PARTNERS IN LIQUIDATION

The liabilities of a partnership rank in order of payment as follows:

1. Those owing to creditors other than partners.
2. Those owing to partners other than for capital and profits.
3. Those owing to partners in respect of capital.
4. Those owing to partners in respect of profits.[1]

From the above ranking it is clear that partnership liabilities to creditors (other than partners) must be paid (actual payment may be delayed provided sufficient funds are reserved) prior to any payments to partners. The Uniform Partnership Act (UPA) classifies partners' loans and advances ahead of capital. This distinction is usually not an important one when a partnership is in the process of liquidation because a partner's loan account is subject to a *right of offset* if the partner has a debit balance (or a potential debit balance) in his capital account. The right to transfer balances *from a partner's loan account* to cover a capital deficiency has been judicially established. This eliminates the need for partners who have capital account credit balances to pursue personal remedies against the partner with a capital account debit balance. When a partner has a capital account credit balance, however, the partner's loan account does rank before capital, and is shown as a liability, but this is usually a moot distinction, since the loan and capital balances are usually paid at or nearly the same time.

LIQUIDATION IN ONE TRANSACTION

PARTNERS' CAPITAL AND LOAN ACCOUNTS SUFFICIENT TO ABSORB LOSSES

The simplest form of liquidation is one where all of the partnership's assets are sold in one transaction as a package—such as to another business entity—and the gain or loss on liquidation is recognized in full. When this occurs, the partnership's only asset is cash, and after paying creditors, the remaining cash is distributed to the partners. Illustration 18–1 presents a condensed trial balance for Skins, Wick, and Pelts; and Illustration 18–2 presents the statement of partnership liquidation for the firm after the noncash assets were sold for $70,000. It should be noted in Illustration 18–2 that the loss on liquidation must *first* be allocated to the partners before the amount each partner is to receive in liquidation can be ascertained. Further, gains and losses on liquidation are allocated in the partners' profit and loss sharing ratio (2:3:5) and *not* in their capital ratios. Illustration 18–2 demonstrates the case where a partner's loan account was used to offset a debit capital account balance as discussed earlier.

---

[1]Uniform Partnership Act, sec. 40 (b).

PARTNERS' CAPITAL AND LOAN ACCOUNTS INSUFFICIENT TO ABSORB LOSSES

When a liquidation loss is of such magnitude that a partner's capital and loan balances are insufficient to absorb the loss, the first priority is to request the partner with the debt balance to contribute to the partnership an amount sufficient to eliminate such debit balance. If this is not possible, the partner with the debit balance may be personally insolvent, then the debit balance must be charged against the partners with credit balances using the *remaining* profit and loss sharing ratio. The partners that are thus charged then have a personal claim against the partner with the debit balance. Collection, however, may be a difficult matter.

Illustration 18–1
SKINS, WICK, AND PELTS
Post-Closing Trial Balance
December 31, 19x6

	Debit	Credit
Cash in bank	$ 20,000	
Noncash assets	170,000	
Liabilities to creditors		$ 40,000
Loan payable—Skins		30,000
Skins—capital		10,000
Wick—capital		30,000
Pelts—capital		80,000
Totals	$190,000	$190,000

Note: The profit and loss sharing ratio for the partners is 2:3:5, respectively.

Illustration 18–2
SKINS, WICK, AND PELTS
Statement of Partnership Liquidation
December 31, 19x6

	Cash	Noncash assets		Liabilities	Loan Skins	(20%) Capital— Skins	(30%) Capital— Wick	(50%) Capital— Pelts
Balances, December 31, 19x6	$20,000	$170,000	=	$40,000	$30,000	$10,000	$30,000	$80,000
Sale of assets and realization loss	70,000	170,000*				20,000*	30,000*	50,000*
Totals	90,000	–0–	=	40,000	30,000	(10,000)	–0–	30,000
Offset of loan—Skins					10,000*	10,000		
Totals	90,000	–0–	=	40,000	20,000	–0–	–0–	30,000
Payments—creditors	40,000*			40,000*				
Totals	50,000	–0–	=	–0–	20,000	–0–	–0–	30,000
Payments—partners	50,000*				20,000*			30,000*
Balances	–0–	–0–	=	–0–	–0–	–0–	–0–	–0–

Note: All partners are solvent; All partners have credit balances.
*Deduction
( ) Negative balance.

Referring again to Illustration 18–1, it is assumed in preparing Illustration 18–3 that the noncash assets were sold for $49,000 and that Wick, being personally solvent, is willing and able to contribute an amount sufficient to cover the debit balance in his capital account.

Illustration 18–4 presents a statement of partnership liquidation using the same assumptions as in Illustration 18–3 except that Wick has a debit capital

Illustration 18–3
SKINS, WICKS, AND PELTS
Statement of Partnership Liquidation
December 31, 19x6

	Cash	Noncash assets		Liabilities	Loan— Skins	Capital— Skins (20%)	Capital— Wick (30%)	Capital— Pelts (50%)
Balances, December 31 19x6 .	$20,000	$170,000	=	$40,000	$30,000	$10,000	$30,000	$80,000
Sale of assets and realization loss	49,000	170,000				24,200*	36,300*	60,500*
Totals	69,000	–0–	=	40,000	30,000	(14,200)	(6,300)	19,500
Offset of loan—Skins					14,200*	14,200		
Cash receipt—Wick	6,300						6,300	
Totals	75,300	–0–	=	40,000	15,800	–0–	–0–	19,500
Payments—creditors	40,000*			40,000*				
Totals	35,300	–0–	=	–0–	15,800	–0–	–0–	19,500
Payments—partners	35,300*				15,800*			19,500*
Balances	–0–	–0–	=	–0–	–0–	–0–	–0–	–0–

Note: All partners are solvent; one partner has a debit balance.
*Deduction.
( ) Negative balance.

balance after the assets are liquidated, is insolvent, and is unable to repay the partnership for the debit balance. Of course, Skins and Pelts will have personal claims of $1,800 and $4,500, respectively, against Wick. It is noteworthy that the allocation of Wick's debit balance preceded the offset of Skins's loan account. If not done this way, the loan offset would have required one offset for $14,200 followed by another offset for $1,800.

Illustration 18–4
SKINS, WICK, AND PELTS
Statement of Partnership Liquidation
December 31, 19x6

	Cash	Noncash assets		Liabilities	Loan— Skins	(20%) Capital— Skins	(30%) Capital— Wick	(50%) Capital— Pelts
Balances, December 31, 19x6 .	$20,000	$170,000	=	$40,000	$30,000	$10,000	$30,000	$80,000
Sale of assets and realization loss	49,000	170,000*				24,200*	36,300*	60,500*
Totals	69,000	–0–	=	40,000	30,000	(14,200)	(6,300)	19,500
Allocation of Wick Debit balance in the ratio of 2:5 .						1,800*	6,300	4,500*
Offset of loan—Skins					16,000*	16,000		
Totals	69,000	–0–	=	40,000	14,000	–0–	–0–	15,000
Payment—creditors	40,000*			40,000*				
Totals	29,000	–0–	=	–0–	14,000	–0–	–0–	15,000
Payments—partners	29,000*				14,000*			15,000*
Balances	–0–	–0–	=	–0–	–0–		–0–	–0–

Note: One partner is insolvent, and has a debit balance.
*Deduction.
( ) Negative balance.

MARSHALING OF ASSETS

Marshaling of assets is defined as:

> The arrangement of assets or claims so as to secure the proper application of the assets to the various claims; especially when there are two

classes of assets, and some creditors can enforce their claims against both, and others against only one, and the creditors of the former class are compelled to exhaust the assets against which they alone have a claim before having recourse to other assets, thus providing for the settlement of as many claims as possible.[2]

There are a number of ways in which a partnership can be insolvent. It can become insolvent by virture of operating losses or due to losses incurred in the sale of its assets. In either case its labilities will exceed its assets. The complexities of liquidation and dissolution are increased if one or more partners are personally insolvent. If all partners are solvent and have sufficient personal assets to satisfy their debit capital account balances, the problem of partnerhip insolvency is no different from that presented in Illustration 18–3. However, if the partnership is insolvent, and one or more partners are insolvent as well, then the *marshaling of assets* is required. The UPA sets forth the following rules:

> Where a partner has become bankrupt or his estate is insolvent the claims against his separate property shall rank in the following order:
>
> 1. Those owing to separate creditors,
> 2. Those owing to partnership creditors,
> 3. Those owing to partners by way of contribution.[3]

Combining the above rankings together with the ranking of partnership liabilities cited earlier in this chapter, it is obvious that the marshaling of assets can be an important process in the liquidation of insolvent partnerships.

To demonstrate the principles involved, the trial balance in Illustration 18–1 will be used in conjunction with the following additional information:

1. The noncash assets are sold for $3,000, and liquidation expenses amount to $3,000.
2. The partners' separable (personal) assets and liabilities are:

	Assets	Liabilities
Skins	$ 30,000	$20,000
Wick	40,000	60,000
Pelts	100,000	30,000

3. After receiving a notification from the unpaid creditors of the partnership of an impending lawsuit to enforce collection, Pelts advances $20,000 to pay the partnership creditors.

Illustration 18–5 contains the statement of partnership liquidation using the principles of marshaling of assets. If, however, the personal assets and liabilities of the partners were as presented in Illustration 18–6, the maximum collection that the partnership creditors could enforce would be $15,000 ($10,000 from Wick and $5,000 from Pelts). This is so because the

---

[2]*Black's Law Dictionary* (St. Paul, Minn.: West Publishing, 1968).
[3]Uniform Partnership Act, sec. 40 (h).

Illustration 18–5
SKINS, WICK, AND PELTS
Statement of Partnership Liquidation
December 31, 19x6

	Cash	Noncash assets		Liabilities	Loan— Skins	Capital— Skins (20%)	Capital— Wick (30%)	Capital— Pelts (50%)
Balances, December 31, 19x6 .	$20,000	$170,000	=	$40,000	$30,000	$10,000	$30,000	$80,000
Sale of assets and payment of liquidation expenses plus loss	–0–	170,000				34,000*	51,000*	85,000*
Totals	20,000	–0–	=	40,000	30,000	(24,000)	(21,000)	(5,000)
Payment of creditors	20,000*			20,000*				
Transfer of loan—Skins					24,000*	24,000		
Totals	–0–	–0–	=	20,000	6,000	–0–	(21,000)	(5,000)
Cash advance—Pelts	20,000							20,000
Payment of creditors	20,000*			20,000*				
Totals	–0–	–0–	=	–0–	6,000	–0–	(21,000)	15,000
Allocation of Wick debit balance—personally insolvent—ratio 2:5					6,000*		21,000	15,000*
Balances	–0–	–0–	=	–0–	–0–	–0–	–0–	–0–

Note: Partnership is insolvent, and a partner is insolvent.
*Deduction.
( ) Negative balance.

personal creditors of Wick and Pelts must be paid prior to any partnership claims against their personal assets. Since Skins is personally insolvent, partnership creditors will be unable to enforce any collection from his assets. Skins's personal creditors would normally have a claim against the credit balance in his loan account, but, Wick and Pelts have no personal assets left after satisfying partnership creditors to the extent possible and, therefore, the claim against Skins's credit balance becomes unenforceable.

Illustration 18–6
SKINS, WICK, AND PELTS
Analysis of Personal Assets and Liabilities
December 31, 19x6

	Assets	Liabilities
Skins	$30,000	$60,000
Wick	40,000	30,000
Pelts	50,000	45,000

Illustration 18–7
BRAND, RUSS, NAVEN, AND RICE
Post-Closing Trial Balance
December 31, 19x5

	Debit	Credit
Cash	$ 10,000	
Noncash assets	200,000	
Liabilities		$100,000
Brand—capital		80,000
Russ—capital		20,000
Naven—capital	20,000	
Rice—capital		30,000
Totals	$230,000	$230,000

Note: Income and losses are shared equally.

Illustration 18–8
BRAND, RUSS, NAVEN, AND RICE
Statement of Partnership Liquidation
December 31, 19x5

	Cash	Noncash Assets		Liabilities	(25%) Capital— Brand	(25%) Capital— Russ	(25%) Capital— Naven	(25%) Capital— Rice
Balances, December 31, 19x5	$10,000	$200,000	=	$100,000	$80,000	$20,000	$(20,000)	$30,000
Sale of assets and liquidation loss	40,000	200,000*			40,000*	40,000*	40,000*	40,000*
Totals	50,000	–0–	=	100,000	40,000	(20,000)	(60,000)	(10,000)
Payment of creditors	50,000*			50,000*				
Totals	–0–	–0–	=	50,000	40,000	(20,000)	(60,000)	(10,000)
Contribution by Naven	50,000						50,000	
Payment of creditors	50,000*			50,000*				
Totals	–0–	–0–	=	–0–	40,000	(20,000)	(10,000)	(10,000)
Contribution by Russ	10,000					10,000		
Allocation of Naven and Russ debit balances 1:1					10,000*	10,000	10,000	10,000*
Totals	$10,000	–0–	=	–0–	30,000	–0–	–0–	(20,000)
Contribution by Rice	20,000							20,000
Payment to Brand	30,000*				30,000*			
Balances	–0–	–0–	=	–0–	–0–	–0–	–0–	–0–

Note: Partnership is insolvent; one partner is insolvent and another becomes insolvent.
*Deduction.
( ) Negative balance.

A more extensive example will now be considered. Based on the trial balance in Illustration 18–7 (on the preceding page) and the following additional information, we can prepare the statement of partnership liquidation as shown in Illustration 18–8.

Additional information:

1. The noncash assets were sold for $40,000.
2. The personal assets and liabilities of the partners are:

	Assets	Liabilities
Brand	$20,000	$60,000
Russ	40,000	30,000
Naven	80,000	30,000
Rice	50,000	20,000

3. Naven is notified of an impending lawsuit to effect collection of $50,000 by partnership creditors. Accordingly, Naven contributed $50,000 to the partnership.
4. Brand's personal creditors notify the partners of Brand's $40,000 unpaid liabilities and commence collection proceedings from the remaining partners.

A review of Illustrations 18–7 and 18–8 together with the additional information provided reveals the following:

1. The personal creditors of Russ, Naven, and Rice must be paid, or sufficient assets reserved for them, before any personal assets can be used to satisfy partnership creditors.

2. Although Naven has a debit capital balance of $60,000 after the sale of the partnership assets, only $50,000 of personal assets are available to satisfy partnership creditors. This leaves a $10,000 debit capital balance that is uncollectible.

3. Since Russ' personal assets in excess of personal liabilities is only $10,000, it only partially satisfies Russ' debit capital balance and the remaining $10,000 debit balance is uncollectible.

4. The two $10,000 debit balances are allocated in the remaining ratio of 1:1 to Brand and Rice.

5. After allocating the Russ and Naven debit capital balances, Rice has a $20,000 debit capital balance which is satisfied by personal assets.

6. Brand has a $30,000 credit capital balance after all allocations and the sale of partnership assets. Although Brand's personal creditors have unsatisfied claims of $40,000, they will receive only the $30,000 available from partnership assets. Brand's personal creditors have no claim against Rice even though Rice is personally solvent.

The rules enunciated above are in accord with the UPA. Common law and bankruptcy laws provide for a somewhat different rule for the marshaling of assets. However, since only a few states have not adopted the UPA, the common law rule will not be illustrated here.

LIQUIDATION IN INSTALLMENTS

In many cases partnership assets are all sold as a package in which case the statement of partnership liquidation previously illustrated is the appropriate one. In other cases, however, partnership assets may be liquidated piecemeal over extended periods of time. When this occurs, the partners are usually not prepared to wait until the liquidation is complete before receiving any cash proceeds from the partnership. Consequently, the partners will usually ask the firm's accountant to compute the amount of cash that can be safely distributed to partners while partnership liabilities are still outstanding. The calculation of such a *safe payment* is usually prepared on a *working paper* and requires basically the following steps:

1. *Assume* that all remaining noncash assets are worthless and distribute this hypothetical loss to the partners' capital balances in the profit and loss sharing ratio.

2. Retain a sufficient amount of cash which equals partnership liabilities to others than partners.

3. If liquidation expenses are expected, retain an amount of cash sufficient to cover these and allocate the resulting hypothetical charges to the partners' capital balances in the profit and loss sharing ratio.

4. If a partner has a debit balance after steps (1), (2), and (3), allocate the debit balance to the remaining partners in their remaining profit and loss sharing ratio. Since this computational debit balance is *hypothetical* the partner with such a debit balance cannot be expected to contribute money to the partnership.

5. Any cash in excess of the amounts reserved for steps (2) and (3) above can then be distributed to those partners with credit capital balances up to the amounts of such balances.

To illustrate the steps involved in calculating the safe payment, the date in Illustration 18–9 was used along with the information which follows and the results are summarized in Illustration 18–10, while Illustrations 18–11, 18–12, and 18–13 present the monthly computations of the safe payments.

1. The profit and loss sharing ratio is 2:2:2:4 for Good, Buddy, Fitz, and Colin, respectively.

2. The assets were sold in installments as follows:

Month	Cash realized	Book value of assets sold
January	$60,000	$100,000
February	40,000	100,000
March	60,000	50,000

Illustration 18–9
GOOD, BUDDY, FITZ, AND COLIN
Post-Closing Trial Balance
December 31, 19x4

	Debit	Credit
Cash	$ 50,000	
Noncash assets	250,000	
Liabilities		$ 30,000
Good—capital		60,000
Buddy—capital		40,000
Fitz—capital		50,000
Colin—capital		120,000
Totals	$300,000	$300,000

3. Legal and accounting fees will be paid when the liquidation of the partnership is complete. Therefore, $4,000 of cash will be retained by the partnership throughout the liquidation process to provide for unpaid (estimated) professional fees, other liquidation expenses, and any other liabilities of the partnership that may subsequently be discovered. At the end of March 19x5, it is ascertained that the actual fees and liquidation expenses amounted to $2,000.

4. *Required:* Calculate safe payments to partners on December 31, January 31, and February 28 and prepare a statement of partnership liquidation assuming the partners pay creditors on February 28, 19x5.

A careful review of these illustrations will reveal the following that is particularly noteworthy:

1. In Illustration 18–11, the allocation of Buddy's hypothetical debit balance creates a hypothetical debit balance for Fitz which is then allocated to Good and Colin. In situations of this sort, the Buddy allocation could have been limited to Good and Colin for $3,333 and $6,667 and thereby avoiding the Fitz reallocation.

Illustration 18–10
GOOD, BUDDY, FITZ, AND COLIN
Statement of Partnership Liquidation
For the Period From December 31, 19x4, to March 31, 19x5

	Cash	Noncash assets		Liabilities	20% Capital— Good	20% Capital— Buddy	20% Capital— Fitz	40% Capital— Colin
Balances, December 31, 19x4	$50,000	$250,000	=	$30,000	$60,000	$40,000	$50,000	$120,000
Payment to partners . . . (A)	20,000*				6,667*			13,333*
Totals, December 31, 19x4	30,000	250,000	=	30,000	53,333	40,000	50,000	106,667
Sale of assets, January 19x5 . . . . (D)	60,000	100,000*			8,000*	8,000*	8,000*	16,000*
Totals	90,000	150,000	=	30,000	45,333	32,000	42,000	90,667
Payment to partners . . . (B)	56,000*				14,533*	1,200*	11,200*	29,067*
Balances, January 31, 19x5 . .	34,000	150,000	=	30,000	30,800	30,800	30,800	61,600
Sale of assets, February 19x5 . . . . (D)	40,000	100,000*			12,000*	12,000*	12,000*	24,000*
Totals	74,000	50,000	=	30,000	18,800	18,800	18,800	37,600
Payment to partners . . . (C)	40,000*				8,000*	8,000*	8,000*	16,000*
Totals	34,000	50,000	=	30,000	10,800	10,800	10,800	21,600
Payment to creditors	30,000*			30,000*				
Balances, February 28, 19x5 .	4,000	50,000	=	–0–	10,800	10,800	10,800	21,600
Sale of assets, March 19x5 . .	60,000	50,000*			2,000	2,000	2,000	4,000
Payment of liquidation expenses	2,000*				400*	400*	400*	800*
Totals	62,000	–0–	=	–0–	12,400	12,400	12,400	24,800
Final payment to partners . .	62,000*				12,400*	12,400*	12,400*	24,800*
Balances	–0–	–0–	=	–0–	–0–	–0–	–0–	–0–

*Deduction.
(A) See Illustration 18–11.
(B) See Illustration 18–12.
(C) See Illustration 18–13.
(D) Realization losses on the sale (or write-down of assets) can arise from: (1) inventory sales at amounts less than book values; (2) inability to collect receivables on the books; and (3) write-offs of intangibles, especially goodwill; and similar items.

Illustration 18–11
GOOD, BUDDY, FITZ, AND COLIN
Calculation of Safe Payment
December 31, 19x4

	Cash	Noncash assets		Liabilities	20% Capital— Good	20% Capital— Buddy	20% Capital— Fitz	40% Capital— Colin
Balances, December 31, 19x4	$50,000	$250,000	=	$30,000	$60,000	$40,000	$50,000	$120,000
Assumed realization loss . .		250,000*			50,000*	50,000*	50,000*	100,000*
Totals	50,000	–0–	=	30,000	10,000	(10,000)	–0–	20,000
Allocate Buddy debit balance 2:2:4					2,500*	10,000	2,500*	5,000*(a)
Allocate Fitz debit balance 2:4					833*		2,500	1,667*(a)
Totals	50,000	–0–	=	30,000	6,667	–0–	–0–	13,333
Retained for liabilities . . .	30,000*			30,000*				
Safe payment to partners .	$20,000	–0–	=	–0–	$ 6,667	–0–	–0–	$ 13,333

*Deduction.
( ) Negative balance.
(a) These could have been combined by allocating Buddy's $10,000 debit directly to Good and Colin in the ratio of 2:4.

Illustration 18–12
GOOD, BUDDY, FITZ, AND COLIN
Calculation of Safe Payment
January 31, 19x5

	Cash	Noncash assets		Liabilities	20% Capital— Good	20% Capital— Buddy	20% Capital— Fitz	40% Capital— Colin
Balances after January sale of assets	$90,000	$150,000	=	$30,000	$45,333	$32,000	$42,000	$90,667
Assumed realization loss . . .		150,000*			30,000*	30,000*	30,000*	60,000*
Liquidation expense retainage	4,000*				800*	800*	800*	1,600*
Totals	86,000	–0–	=	30,000	14,533	1,200	11,200	29,067
Retained for liabilities	30,000*			30,000*				
Safe payment to partners . .	$56,000	–0–	=	–0–	$14,533	$ 1,200	$11,200	$29,067

*Deduction.

Illustration 18–13
GOOD, BUDDY, FITZ, AND COLIN
Calculation of Safe Payment
February 28, 19x5

Cash available after sale of assets in February 19x5		$74,000
Less: Retained for:		
Liquidation expenses	$ 4,000	
Liabilities	30,000	34,000
Safe Payment to partners in profit and loss sharing ratio		$40,000

2. After the safe payment on January 31, 19x5, the partners' capital account balances (see Illustration 18–10) are in the profit and loss sharing ratio. Once this point is reached, it is *no longer* necessary to *allocate an assumed loss* to partners since all future payments to them will be in the profit and loss sharing ratio. All that remains to be done in order to calculate the safe payment is to withhold sufficient cash for the payment of unpaid liabilities and estimated liquidation expenses.

An error in the calculation of a safe payment can have serious repercussions. If a partner is overpaid in one instalment and subsequently becomes personally bankrupt or insolvent, recovery of the overpayment may be impossible resulting in a loss to the remaining partners.

ADVANCE CASH DISTRIBUTION PLANS

Instead of preparing a safe payment calculation every time cash is to be distributed to partners—especially when the liquidation process is protracted—it is possible to prepare a cash distribution plan in advance. The steps necessary to prepare the plan are:

1. Compute the liquidation loss which will eliminate each partner's capital balance.
2. Rank the partners according to the size of the computed loss using the smallest loss first.
3. Prepare a statement of partnership liquidation starting with the first ranked partner's loss and then adding incrementally an additional layer

to reach the next partner's loss and continue until this is done for all partners.

4. Prepare a statement of advance cash distribution using the statement of partnership liquidation in an order inverse to that in 3 above.

Based on Illustration 18–9, Illustration 18–16 shows an advance cash distribution plan.

Illustration 18–14
GOOD, BUDDY, FITZ, AND COLIN
Computation of Liquidation Loss which Will Eliminate
Partners' Capital Balances
December 31, 19x4

Partner	Capital balance		Profit-sharing ratio		Loss to eliminate	Vulnerability to loss ranking (1 most vulnerable)
Good	$ 60,000	÷	0.2	=	$300,000	3
Buddy	40,000	÷	0.2	=	200,000	1
Fitz	50,000	÷	0.2	=	250,000	2
Colin	120,000	÷	0.4	=	300,000	3

The amount of loss which would eliminate a partner's capital balance is computed by dividing the partner's capital balance by his profit-sharing ratio as shown in Illustration 18–14. These amounts are then used to prepare the advance cash statement of partnership liquidation as shown in Illustration 18–15. On the first level ($200,000) of this illustration, the amount used is as computed in Illustration 18–14. However, as we go down Illustration 18–15, the amount computed for each succeeding level is reduced by the amount used in the preceding level and is then multiplied by the total percentage of partners that have capital balances left. The amount at each level can also be calculated by taking the partner's capital balance and dividing it by his

Illustration 18–15
GOOD, BUDDY, FITZ, AND COLIN
Advance Statement of Partnership Liquidation
December 31, 19x4

	Loss necessary to eliminate partner's capital balance	(20%) Capital— Good	(20%) Capital— Buddy	(20%) Capital— Fitz	(40%) Capital— Colin
Capital balances, December 31, 19x4		$60,000	$40,000	$50,000	$120,000
Buddy loss	$200,000	40,000*	40,000*	40,000*	80,000*
Totals		20,000	–0–	10,000	40,000
Fitz loss 80% ($250,000 − $200,000)	40,000	10,000*		10,000*	20,000*
Totals		10,000	–0–	–0–	20,000
Good and Colin losses 60% ($300,000 − $250,000)	30,000	10,000*			20,000*
Totals		–0–	–0–	–0–	–0–

*Deduction.

profit-sharing ratio in relation to those partners which still have capital balances. For instance, on the second level the amount of $40,000 can be obtained by using Fitz's balance of $10,000 and dividing it by 25 percent (the remaining ratio is 2:2:4). On the third level ($30,000), the balance of either Good or Colin can be used. Using Good's balance of $10,000 and dividing it by one-third (the ratio is now 2:4) will produce the amount of $30,000. Illustration 18–16 contains a detailed statement of advance cash distribution.

Illustration 18–16
GOOD, BUDDY, FITZ, AND COLIN
Statement of Cash Distribution
December 31, 19x4

Amount	Liabilities	Good	Buddy	Fitz	Colin
First $30,000	$30,000				
Next $30,000		$1/3$	—	—	$2/3$
Next $40,000		$1/4$	—	$1/4$	$1/2$
Next $200,000		$1/5$	$1/5$	$1/5$	$2/5$
Any excess		$1/5$	$1/5$	$1/5$	$2/5$

LOAN BALANCES

In the event of a liquidation, if a partner has a loan balance and instalment payments are desired, such a balance can, for practical purposes, be combined with the partner's capital account since the loan account is subject to the right of offset as discussed earlier in this chapter. In liquidation, the distinction between a partner's loan account and his capital account is a moot point.

QUESTIONS

1. Section 40 (b) of the UPA provides for a ranking of claims against partnership assets. What is the order of the ranking?

2. What is meant by the *right of offset?*

3. What is *marshaling of assets?*

4. When a partner becomes bankrupt, what is the ranking of claims against the partner's separate property?

5. What general approach is used to calculate the *safe payment* for installment liquidations?

6. How are potential liquidation expenses treated when calculating the safe payment?

7. If an error is made in calculating the safe payment, what are some of the possible consequences?

8. Is it possible to avoid the practice of calculating a safe payment each time a payment is to be made to partners? How can this be accomplished?

9. What are the necessary steps to prepare an advance cash distribution plan?

10. Legally, is there a difference in priority between a partner's loan balance and his capital balance? What is the difference? Does this difference retain its importance when a partnership is being liquidated? Why?

EXERCISES

Exercise 18–1. The following balance sheet is for the AdGenDa partnership. The partners, Ad, Gen, and Da, share profits and losses in the ratio of 5:3:2, respectively.

Cash	$ 30,000
Other assets	270,000
	$300,000

Liabilities	$ 70,000
Ad, capital	140,000
Gen, capital	80,000
Da, capital	10,000
	$300,000

1. The assets and liabilities are fairly valued on the above balance sheet, and the partnership wishes to admit Melvin as a new partner with a one-fifth interest *without* recording goodwill or bonus. How much should Melvin contribute in cash or other assets?

a. $36,800.
b. $46,000.
c. $57,500.
d. $60,000.

2. Assume that the original partners have agreed to liquidate the partnership by selling the other assets. What should each of the respective partners receive if the other assets are sold for $200,000?

a. Ad, $102,500; Gen, $57,500; Da, $0.
b. Ad, $103,000; Gen, $57,000; Da, $0.
c. Ad, $105,000; Gen, $59,000; Da, $4,000.
d. Ad, $140,000; Gen, $80,000; Da, $10,000.

(AICPA adapted)

Exercise 18–2.

1. Q, R, S, and T are partners sharing profits and losses equally. The partnership is insolvent and is to be liquidated; the status of the partnership and each partner is as follows:

proceed legally because the partnership assets are less than the partnership liabilities.

c. Will have to share R's interest in the partnership on a pro rata basis with R's personal creditors.

d. Have first claim to the partnership assets before any partner's personal creditors have rights to the partnership assets.

2. The following condensed balance sheet is presented for the partnership of Fisher, Taylor, and Simon who share profits and losses in the ratio of 6:2:2, respectively:

Cash	$ 40,000
Other assets	140,000
	$180,000

Liabilities	$ 70,000
Fisher, capital	50,000
Taylor, capital	50,000
Simon, capital	10,000
	$180,000

The assets and liabilities are fairly valued on the above balance sheet, and it was agreed to by all the partners that the partnership would be liquidated after selling the other assets. What would each of the partners receive at this time if the other assets are sold for $80,000?

	Fisher	Taylor	Simon
a.	$12,500	$37,500	–0–
b.	13,000	37,000	–0–
c.	14,000	38,000	$ 2,000
d.	50,000	50,000	10,000

(AICPA adapted)

[Relates to Exercise 18–2]

	Partnership capital balance	Personal assets (exclusive of partnership interest)	Personal liabilities (exclusive of partnership interest)
Q	$ 15,000	$100,000	$40,000
R	10,000	30,000	60,000
S	(20,000)	80,000	5,000
T	(30,000)	1,000	28,000
Total	$(25,000)		

Assuming the Uniform Partnership Act applies, the partnership creditors—

a. Must first seek recovery against S because he is solvent personally and he has a negative capital balance.

b. Will *not* be paid in full regardless of how they

Exercise 18–3. The following balance sheet is presented for the partnership of Davis, Wright, and Dover who share profits and losses in the ratio of 5:3:2, respectively:

Cash	$ 60,000
Other assets	540,000
	$600,000

Liabilities	$140,000
Davis, capital	280,000
Wright, capital	160,000
Dover, capital	20,000
	$600,000

1. Assume that the assets and liabilities are fairly valued on the balance sheet and the partnership decided to admit Hank as a new partner with a one-fifth interest. **No** goodwill or bonus is to be recorded. How much should Hank contribute in cash or other assets?

    a. $120,000.
    b. $115,000.
    c. $92,000.
    d. $73,000.

2. Assume that instead of admitting a new partner, the partners decided to liquidate the partnership. If the other assets are sold for $400,000, how should the available cash be distributed to each partner?

    a. Davis, $280,000; Wright, $160,000; Dover, $20,000.

    b. Davis, $210,000; Wright, $118,000; Dover, $8,000.

    c. Davis, $206,000; Wright, $114,000; Dover, $0.

    d. Davis, $205,000; Wright, $115,000; Dover, $0.

                      (AICPA adapted)

Exercise 18–4. Alston, Boyer, and Cane are partners with a profit and loss ratio of 5:4:1. The partnership was liquidated, and prior to the liquidation process, the partnership balance sheet was as follows:

ALSTON, BOYER, AND CANE
Balance Sheet
January 1, 19x3

Assets

Cash	$ 20,000
Other assets	180,000
Total assets	$200,000

Equities

Alston—capital	$ 80,000
Boyer—capital	80,000
Cane—capital	40,000
Total equities	$200,000

After the partnership was liquidated and the cash was distributed, Boyer received $32,000 in cash in full settlement of his interest.

Required

    a. Compute the amount of the realization loss on the sale of the other assets.

    b. Prepare a statement of partnership liquidation.

Exercise 18–5. The following information is provided in connection with the liquidation of a partnership:

[Relates to Exercise 18–5]

Partner	Profit and loss ratio	Partnership capital balance— cr. (dr.)	Personal assets	Personal liabilities
Brill	30%	$80,000	$100,000	$20,000
Cravath	10	40,000	60,000	50,000
Duluth	20	(60,000)	80,000	50,000
Edwards	40	(90,000)	40,000	60,000
Capital deficiency		$(30,000)		

Required:

    a. For each partner, indicate the maximum amount that partnership creditors can enforce their claims against the partner's personal assets. (Use UPA rules)

    b. Assume that Brill advances the $30,000 to pay the partnership creditors. Prepare a statement of partnership liquidation. (*Hint:* Duluth must deposit $30,000 of personal assets.)

    c. Rework *(b)* if Duluth advances the $30,000 instead of Brill.

d. Reconcile the net cash positions of Brill and Cravath in *(b)* and *(c)*. What conclusion can you reach about which partner makes up the capital deficiency? (You may wish to try another combination such as a $10,000 payment by Cravath and a $20,000 payment by Brill and then compare the net cash positions.)

Exercise 18–6. Calvert, Doyle, and Eagle are partners with a profit and loss ratio of 5:2:3. Due to operating unprofitably, the partners decided to liquidate the partnership. On January 1, 19x6, the trial balance of the partnership was as follows:

CALVERT, DOYLE, AND EAGLE
Trial Balance
January 1, 19x6

	Debit	Credit
Cash	$ 80,000	
Other assets	200,000	
Liabilities		$ 50,000
Calvert—loan payable		10,000
Calvert—capital		60,000
Doyle—capital		60,000
Eagle—capital		100,000
Totals	$280,000	$280,000

Required:

a. Compute the safe payment if the $80,000 is to be distributed prior to the liquidation of the other assets.

b. Independent of your solution to part *(a)* it is now decided to liquidate the other assets first and distribute all of the cash at the same time. The other assets are sold for $50,000. Prepare a statement of partnership liquidation (none of the partners have personal assets in excess of personal liabilities).

Exercise 18–7. Denton, English, and Frumer are partners with a profit and loss ratio of 5:2:3. The partners decided to liquidate the partnership effective January 1, 19x4. On that date, the partnership's trial balance was as follows:

DENTON, ENGLISH, AND FRUMER
Trial Balance
January 1, 19x4

	Debit	Credit
Cash	$120,000	
Other assets	300,000	
Liabilities		$180,000
English—loan payable		60,000
Denton—capital		200,000
English—capital	80,000	
Frumer—capital		60,000
Totals	$500,000	$500,000

Required:

Prepare a statement of partnership liquidation if the other assets were sold for $250,000 and liquidation expenses amounted to $10,000.

Exercise 18–8. The following balance sheet is for the partnership of Able, Boyer, and Cain:

Cash	$ 20,000
Other assets	180,000
Total	$200,000
Liabilities	$ 50,000
Able, capital (40%)	37,000
Boyer, capital (40%)	65,000
Cain, capital (20%)	48,000
Total	$200,000

Figures shown parenthetically reflect agreed profit and loss sharing percentages.

1. If the assets are fairly valued on the above balance sheet and the partnership wishes to admit Day as a new one-sixth partner without recording goodwill or bonus, Day should contribute cash or other assets of —

    a. $40,000.

    b. $36,000.

    c. $33,333.

    d. $30,000.

2. If assets on the initial balance sheet are fairly valued, Able and Boyer consent and Day pays Cain $51,000 for his interest; the revised capital balances of the partners would be—

    a. Able, $38,500; Boyer, $66,500; Day, $51,000.

    b. Able, $38,500; Boyer, $66,500; Day, $48,000.

    c. Able, $37,000; Boyer, $65,000; Day, $51,000.

    d. Able, $37,000; Boyer, $65,000; Day, $48,000.

3. If the firm, as shown on the original balance sheet, is dissolved and liquidated by selling assets in installments, the first sale of noncash assets having a book value of $90,000 realizes $50,000 and all cash available after settlement with creditors is distributed; the respective partners would receive (to the nearest dollar)—

    a. Able, $8,000; Boyer, $8,000; Cain, $4,000.

    b. Able, $6,667; Boyer, $6,667; Cain, $6,666.

    c. Able, $0; Boyer, $13,333; Cain, $6,667.

    d. Able, $0; Boyer, $3,000; Cain, $17,000.

4. If the facts are as in item 3 above except that $3,000 cash is to be withheld, the respective partners would then receive (to the nearest dollar)—

    a. Able, $6,800; Boyer, $6,800; Cain, $3,400.

    b. Able, $5,667; Boyer, $5,667; Cain, $5,666.

c. Able, $0; Boyer, $11,333; Cain, $5,667.

d. Able, $0; Boyer, $1,000; Cain, $16,000.

5. If each partner properly received some cash in the distribution after the second sale, the cash to be distributed amounts to $12,000 from the third sale and unsold assets with an $8,000 book value remain; ignoring items 3 and 4, the respective partners would receive—

a. Able, $4,800; Boyer, $4,800; Cain, $2,400.

b. Able, $4,000; Boyer, $4,000; Cain, $4,000.

c. Able, $^{37}/_{150}$ of $12,000; Boyer, $^{65}/_{150}$ of $12,000; Cain $^{48}/_{150}$ of $12,000.

d. Able, $0; Boyer, $8,000; Cain, $4,000.

(AICPA adapted)

Exercise 18–9. The partnership of Jenson, Smith, and Hart share profits and losses in the ratio of 5:3:2, respectively. The partners voted to disolve the partnership when its assets, liabilities, and capital were as follows:

Assets

Cash	$ 40,000
Other assets	210,000
Total assets	$250,000

Liabilities and Capital

Liabilities	$ 60,000
Jenson, capital	48,000
Smith, capital	72,000
Hart, capital	70,000
Total liabilities and capital	$250,000

The partnership will be liquidated over a prolonged period of time. As cash is available it will be distributed to the partners. The first sale of noncash assets having a book value of $120,000 realized $90,000. How much cash should be distributed to each partner after this sale?

a. Jenson, $0; Smith, $28,800; Hart, $41,200.

b. Jenson, $0; Smith, $30,000; Hart, $40,000.

c. Jenson, $35,000; Smith, $21,000; Hart, $14,000.

d. Jenson, $45,000; Smith, $27,000; Hart, $18,000.

(AICPA adapted)

Exercise 18–10. Using the information provided in Exercise 18–9, how much cash should be distributed to each partner if it was decided to withhold $20,000 in the event the remaining other assets are worthless and liquidation expenses (legal, accounting, etc.) amount to $20,000?

Exercise 18–11. Using the information provided in Exercise 18–9 and assuming that no assets have been sold, prepare an advance cash distribution plan as cash becomes available.

PROBLEMS

Problem 18–12. Edwin, Field, and Garrison are partners with a profit and loss ratio of 2:2:6. The partners are retiring and plan to liquidate the partnership. On January 1, 19x2, the trial balance of the partnership is as follows:

EDWIN, FIELD, AND GARRISON
Trial Balance
January 1, 19x2

	Debit	Credit
Cash	$ 20,000	
Other assets	350,000	
Liabilities		$ 80,000
Edwin—loan		30,000
Edwin—capital	10,000	
Field—capital		50,000
Garrison—capital		220,000
Totals	$380,000	$380,000

Sales of assets, amounts realized, and cash withheld for liquidation expenses are:

Month ending	Assets sold	Amount realized	Cash to be withheld
January 31	$200,000	$160,000	$10,000
February 28	100,000	50,000	5,000
March 31	50,000	30,000	–0–

Required:

Prepare a statement of partnership liquidation showing, in separate schedules, the safe payments to partners at January 31, February 28, and the final payment on March 31.

Problem 18–13. Using the information provided

in Problem 18–12 and ignoring the monthly sales of assets, etc., you are asked to:

a. Prepare an advance cash distribution plan as the cash becomes available.

b. *(1)* Compute the amounts to be paid for liabilities and to each partner if $220,000 of cash is available for distribution (the $20,000 in the trial balance is part of the $220,000).

(2) Which partners would get the next $60,000 that is available?

(3) How would any future cash that becomes available be divided?

Problem 18–14. X, Y, and Z are partners sharing profits in the ratio of 4, 3, and 2, respectively. The partnership and two of the partners are currently unable to pay their creditors. The firm balance sheet and personal status of the partners are as follows:

X, Y, AND Z PARTNERSHIP
Balance Sheet

Assets

Cash	$ 500
Other assets	60,500
Total assets	$61,000

Liabilities

Accounts and bills payable	$37,000
Capital: X	10,000
Y	6,000
Z	8,000
Total liabilities	$61,000

Personal status of partners
(excluding partnership interests)

Partner	Cash and cash value of personal assets	Liabilities
X	$31,000	$20,000
Y	9,450	11,900
Z	4,000	5,000

Required:

a. Prepare a worksheet showing distribution to partnership and personal creditors in the event of dissolution under the provisions of the Uniform Partnership Act, assuming that the "other assets" are sold for $33,500.

b. Prepare a computation showing the minimum amount which must be realized from the sale of the partnership assets other than cash, so that the personal creditors of Y would receive full settlement of their claims.   (AICPA adapted)

Problem 18–15. The law firm of Shroyer, Curry, and Jones has decided to dissolve partnership as of June 30, 19x8, and has called you in to render an accounting. The only records maintained are the checkbook and a daily record of cash received. The firm has been in existence for four years with equal capital investments, and profits are divided equally. The prior year's tax return indicates that the following expenditures had been capitalized for tax purposes prior to January 1, 19x8:

	Assets	Allowance January 1, 19x8
Office furniture and fixtures	$1,500	$ 450
Books	900	180
Automobile—Shroyer	2,000	600
Automobile—Curry	1,000	200
Automobile—Jones	3,000	600
	$8,400	$2,030

Cash receipts to June 30, 19x8, amount to $60,000. A summary of cash disbursements follows:

Rent	$ 1,400
Wages and salaries	2,102
Entertainment	4,000
Automobile and miscellaneous	1,000
Withdrawals—Shroyer	9,000
Withdrawals—Curry	10,000
Withdrawals—Jones	12,000
	$39,502

The capital accounts of the partners as of January 1, 19x8, were equal. Depreciation has been charged against partnership profits. Automobiles are depreciated over a five-year period, and office furniture and fixtures and books over a 10-year period. The bank balance at June 30, 19x8, is $29,998. The three partners have agreed to distribute the office furniture and fixtures in kind, and they feel that the distribution will be equal. The automobiles, which are purchased from partnership funds, will be retained by the partners to whom they have been assigned. The books will be distributed to Shroyer.

Required:

A schedule of changes in partners' capital accounts from January 1, 19x8, to June 30, 19x8, and the final cash distribution to each partner.

(AICPA adapted)

Problem 18–16. Part A. The partnership of Adams, Baker, and Crane have called upon you to assist them in winding up the affairs of their partnership.

You are able to gather the following information:

1. The trial balance of the partnership at June 30, 19x2, is as follows:

	Debit	Credit
Cash	$ 6,000	
Accounts receivable	22,000	
Inventory	14,000	
Plant and equipment (net) .	99,000	
Adams, loan	12,000	
Crane, loan	7,500	
Accounts payable		$ 17,000
Adams, capital		67,000
Baker, capital		45,000
Crane, capital		31,500
Totals	$160,500	$160,500

2. The partners share profits and losses as follows: Adams, 50 percent; Baker, 30 percent, and Crane, 20 percent.

3. The partners are considering an offer of $100,000 for the accounts receivable, inventory, and plant and equipment as of June 30. The $100,000 would be paid to the partners in installments, the number and amounts of which are to be negotiated.

Required:

Prepare a cash distribution schedule as of June 30, 19x2, showing how the $100,000 would be distributed as it becomes available.

Part B. Assume the same facts as in Part A except that the partners have decided to liquidate their partnership instead of accepting the offer of $100,000. Cash is distributed to the partners at the end of each month.

A summary of the liquidation transactions follows:

July	$16,500	Collected on accounts receivable, balance is uncollectible.
	10,000	Received for the entire inventory.
	1,000	Liquidation expenses paid.
	8,000	Cash retained in the business at end of the month.
Aug.	1,500	Liquidation expenses paid.
		As part payment of his capital, Crane accepted a piece of special equipment that he developed which had a book value of $4,000. The partners agreed that a value of $10,000 should be placed on the machine for liquidation purposes.
	2,500	Cash retained in the business at end of the month.
Sept.	75,000	Received on sale of remaining plant and equipment.
	1,000	Liquidation expenses paid.
		No cash retained in the business.

Required:

Prepare a schedule of cash payment as of September 30, 19x2, showing how the cash was actually distributed.   (AICPA adapted)

19

Accounting for estates and trusts

OVERVIEW

The planning for and the administration of estates and trusts involves accounting skills as well as knowledge of tax and other specialized areas of law.

Fiduciaries whose function it is to administer estates and trusts are concerned primarily with preservation of assets, the discharging of liabilities, and the equitable distribution of principal and income to those entitled to them in accordance with applicable law and the intent of legal instruments such as wills or trusts. Thus the focus is not on compliance with generally accepted accounting principles but rather on specialized bookkeeping practices and accounting statements which aim at carrying out the intent of the law as well as the intent of those who leave estates or create trusts.

The net assets owned by an individual at the time of death are referred to as that person's estate. An individual may also at any time transfer property by will or lifetime gift, to be held in trust for someone else. Individuals or corporations which are entrusted with the custody, the management, and the disposition of estate or trust assets are known as fiduciaries. In this chapter we shall first examine briefly the legal aspects of estates and follow this by a consideration of the accounting responsibilities of the fiduciary. The chapter will conclude with an examination of the legal and accounting aspects of trusts.

ESTATE PLANNING

The legal and particularly the tax implications inherent in the administration and disposition of an estate are best understood and planned for before a person's death. For this reason this chapter starts with a brief consideration of estate planning.

Estate planning is an informed series of steps which aim at maximizing the net resources which will be left for the beneficiaries of a person's estate. The planning and execution of these steps often require the skills of a number of professionals such as accountants, attorneys, and insurance specialists.

The Economic Recovery Tax Act of 1981 (the "1981 Act"), following up on the significant changes in the federal taxation of gifts, estates, and trusts, initiated by the Tax Reform Act of 1976, increased unified credits of estate and gift taxes, reduced top bracket rates of estate taxation, and provided for an unlimited marital deduction. The 1981 Act also increased the annual gift tax exclusion to $10,000.

Under the unified tax on estates and gifts, a single progressive schedule is applied to cumulative gifts and bequests made by an individual. The 1981 Act, when fully implemented in 1987, will virtually eliminate estate taxes on estates under $600,000 not left to spouses.

LEGAL ASPECTS OF ESTATE ADMINISTRATION

The administration, the distribution of, and the accountability for the estates of decreased persons (decedents) or missing persons is generally governed by state laws (probate codes). Since these laws vary from state to state, the National Conference of Commissioners on Uniform State Laws has drafted a Uniform Probate Code which has been approved by the American Bar Association. While the Uniform Probate Code has thus far been adopted by only a few states, we shall nevertheless base our discussion of the legal and accounting issues governing the administration of an estate on the provisions of that Code as the most representative provisions of law on this subject.

A person who leaves a valid *will* is considered to have died *testate,* and the will of the testator largely governs the disposition of the decedent's real and personal property. The person who does not leave a valid will in whole or in part, is considered to have died *intestate,* with respect to the involved portion, and the distribution of property in this case is governed by the provisions of the Code.

The administration of an estate is normally under the jurisdiction of a court which may be referred to as a probate, surrogate's, orphan's, or county court. The process by which the validity of a will is established is known as *probating the will.* Once a will has been admitted to probate, the court will proceed to appoint a personal representative of the deceased whose function is to administer the estate. A personal representative named in the will is called an *executor* or *executrix.* If the deceased dies intestate, the court will appoint a personal representative who is then called an *administrator* or *administratrix.* If the individual named in the will is able and willing to serve, *letters testamentary* will be issued as evidence of formal authority for the exercise by him of the fiduciary function. A court appointed representative is issued *letters of administration* as evidence of that individual's authority to act as a fiduciary.

While nobody is forced to accept the role of a fiduciary, once that role is accepted, the representative must observe highest standards of fairness and equity in the administration and disposition of the estate. Such a representative is entitled to reasonable compensation for services rendered.

Inventory of assets

One of the first steps the representative takes will be to take possession and control of the decedent's property. In the interest of asset conservation, the representative may continue to operate a business owned by the deceased for not longer than four months.

Within three months of appointment, the personal representative must submit to the probate court an inventory of property owned by the decedent on the date of death and a listing of any liens which exist against the property. Since the assets comprising the inventory must be valued at fair value as of the date of death, the services of an appraiser may be necessary. If, after the filing of the inventory with the probate court, additional assets of the decedent are discovered, supplementary inventory reports must be filed with the court.

Claims against the estate

Once appointed, the representative must give public notice in a newspaper of general circulation, once a week for three weeks, requesting that those who have claims against the estate present them within four months, or be forever barred from asserting such claims.

Preceding all claims against the estate are certain allowances and exemptions specified by the Code. These are as follows:

Homestead allowance: A surviving spouse or surviving minor and dependent children of a decedent are entitled to a homestead allowance of $5,000 in the aggregate. This allowance is additional to any other share of the estate which passes to the spouse or children by the will.

Family allowance: During the administration of the estate, the surviving spouse and children who were supported by the decedent are entitled to a reasonable cash allowance not to exceed $6,000 or $500 per month for 12 months. The family allowance has priority over all claims against the estate except for the homestead allowance.

Exempt property: The surviving spouse or children of the deceased are entitled to automobiles, household furniture and furnishing, appliances, and other personal effects up to a value of $3,500.

Unless the total claims against the estate exceed the assets available, the personal representative must pay claims in the following order:

1. The expenses of administering the estate.
2. The funeral expenses as well as the hospital and medical expenses of the decedent's last illness.
3. Debts and taxes which have preference under federal or state laws.
4. All remaining claims.

The settlement of an estate

Once an inventory of the deceased's property has been taken and the claims against the estate have been established and paid, the personal representative has the duty to distribute the remaining assets of the estate to persons entitled to it.

Intestate distribution. When a person has died intestate, i.e., without leaving a valid will, his or her estate will be distributed in accordance with the applicable state law, generally only to a spouse or a blood relative. *Real property* is distributed to heirs under the laws of descent of the state where the property is located. *Personal property* is distributed to *next of kin* under the laws of distribution of the state in which the decedent is domiciled.

Testate distribution. If a person dies testate, the distribution of the decedant's property is mostly governed by the terms of the will. In such a situation, the gift of real property is called a *devise* and the recipient is referred to as a *devisee.* Testamentary gifts of personal property are called *bequests* or *legacies,* and the recipient is called the *legatee.*

THE CLASSIFICATIONS OF LEGACIES

While a devise is ordinarily a gift of a specific piece of real property, a legacy may be one of a number of types as follows:

A *specific* legacy is a gift of personal property specifically identified in the will, such as a specific piece of jewelry or a painting.

A *demonstrative* legacy is a bequest payable out of a source specified in the will, such as a bank account or the proceeds from a specific insurance policy. The will may specify that if the source proves inadequate to meet the amount specified, the shortfall shall constitute a general legacy.

A *general* legacy is a gift of an indicated amount of money or quantity of something without designation as to source.

A *residual* legacy is the distribution of the property remaining after all debts have been satisfied and all other legacies distributed or otherwise provided for.

ACCOUNTING ASPECTS OF ESTATE ADMINISTRATION

A major purpose of estate accounting is to facilitate the reporting by the fiduciary (the personal representative) to the court. Two aspects of that reporting are accountability, and where a trust is created, the distinction between principal and income.

Accountability stresses the fiduciary's responsibility for the assets of the deceased and for their proper administration and disposition. Thus the accounting reflects the assets for whose responsibility the fiduciary is charged and distributions and payments to creditors and beneficiaries with which the fiduciary is created.

The distinction between principal and income

Basic to the accounting for an estate is the distinction between principal (also known as *corpus*) and income. This distinction is important because wills frequently provide that the income of the estate, or a portion of it, accrue for the benefit of one party, known as the *income beneficiary*, for a stipulated period of time after which the principal is to be distributed to another party known as the *remainderman*. For example, under a will, the income of certain assets may be distributed to the spouse for life (i.e., the life tenant), and upon death of the spouse the principal is distributed to the children of the deceased (i.e., the remaindermen).

A will or a trust instrument can specify how income and principal should be defined and allocated. In the absence of such instructions state laws apply. This discussion of the distinction between income and principal will be based on the Revised Uniform Principal and Income Act which has been adopted, in some cases with modifications, by many states. The following definitions and descriptions convey an overall idea of the intent of the Act.

> *Income* is defined as the return in money or property derived from the use of principal including rent, interest, cash dividends including certain corporate distributions, receipts from business and farming operations as specified and any other revenue earned or received during the administration of a decedent's estate.
>
> *Principal* is defined as the property set aside by the owner, or the person legally entitled to do so, so that it is held in trust for eventual delivery to a remainderman. Principal includes proceeds of insurance on property forming part of the principal, stock dividends and liquidating corporate distributions, and allowances for depreciation. Principal also includes any rents or other types of revenues which already accrued at the date of death of the testator. Premium or discount on investments in bonds included in principal is not amortized and all proceeds from the sale or redemption of bonds are considered principal.[1]

The credits to and charges against income and principal are, in the absence of contrary provisions in the will, governed by the following general provisions of the Revised Uniform Principal and Income Act:

All expenses incurred in connection with the settlement of an estate including funeral expenses, debts, estate taxes and interest and penalties in respect of those taxes, and family allowances are to be charged against principal. Court costs and accountants', attorneys', and personal representative fees as well as trustees' fees are to be apportioned between principal and income.

Principal is charged with costs incurred in preparing principal property for sale or rent, the cost of investing and reinvesting principal assets, major repairs to principal assets, and income taxes on receipts or gains allocable to principal.

Income is charged with ordinary expenses incurred in the management and preservation of estate or trust property, including regularly recurring taxes assessed against the principal, water charges, insurance premiums, interest, and ordinary repairs (as opposed to capital improvements).

---

[1]Section 3, 7A, U.L.A., 1978 edition.

DEPRECIATION AND DEPLETION

The question of whether depreciation is or is not chargeable against income depends on the expressed intention of the testator with respect to the preservation of the principal of the estate as indicated in a will or trust instrument. In the absence of such indication of intent, state law generally controls.

Where repairs or other maintenance outlays materially enhance or improve the value of estate or trust properties, they are properly chargeable to principal. Expenditures which are required for the preservation of the normal operating efficiency of depreciable assets are normally regarded as income charges.

The wishes of the testator or, in the absence of a clear statement of intent, state law will generally determine how depletion charges for wasting assets, such as mineral deposits, etc., are treated. If the preservation of principal was the clear intent of the testor, income will be charged for depletion.

ACCOUNTING AND REPORTING FOR ESTATES

The major focus of estate accounting is on the accountability by the fiduciary for estate assets and for their proper administration and distribution. Thus, the fundamental accounting equation as regards fiduciaries is modified in these situations to:

$$\text{Assets} = \text{Accountability}$$

The accounting for an estate which involves a trust must reflect the distinction between principal and income. Thus, the accounts which the fiduciary will use are primarily designed to maintain the distinction between capital (corpus) and income and should be sufficiently detailed so as to facilitate a full and meaningful report to the court.

Accounts relating to principal

The accounting for an estate begins when the fiduciary files with the court an inventory of the decedent's property. At that time each asset account is debited with the assets's fair market value at date of death with the credit going to an *Estate Principal* account. This is the basic equity (or corpus) of the estate and includes interest earned and dividends declared prior to the date of death. When assets not originally inventoried are subsequently discovered, the increase in accountability is booked by a credit to an *Assets Subsequently Discovered* account.

When assets are disposed of, any gains or losses sustaned in relation to amounts originally inventoried are posted to a *Gain (Loss) on Realization* account. The accountability of the fiduciary is satisfied by payments of *funeral, medical, and administration expenses,* by payments of *debts of the decedent* and by distributions of *legacies.* It should be noted that debts are recorded in the accounts only as they are paid unless they represent liens on specific estate property, in which case they are recorded as part of the property inventory. The Debts of Decedent Paid account represents a reduction of the executor's accountability for estate assets.

The number of detailed accounts used depends on the size and complexity of the estate. The major objective is for the accounting system to be sufficiently detailed so as to facilitate a proper reporting to the court.

Accounts relating to income

Income collections are credited to an *Estate Income* account (or to a number of subsidiary accounts which detail the nature of the income received). Expenses allocable against the interests of income beneficiaries are charged to various categories of *expense (income)* accounts. Final accountability is achieved by distributions to income beneficiaries which are charged to *Distributions to Income Beneficiaries* accounts.

Reporting

The form of reporting by a fiduciary to the court is governed by applicable state statutes. Generally these reports include (1) a *charge and discharge statement (as to principal)* and (2) a *charge and discharge statement (as to income)*. These statements account for the fiduciary's activities over a period of time and are combined in his overall accounting to the court.

ACCOUNTING FOR AN ESTATE—AN ILLUSTRATION

The following simplified illustration of the accounting for an estate is designed to illustrate major accounting concepts:

Walter Cox died testate on May 31, 19x1. His will, admitted to probate on July 10, 19x1, provided that his son, Andrew Cox, be appointed executor. The will also provided that general legacies of $3,000 each, in cash, be paid to William and Mark, grandsons of the decedent; $12,000 and the decedent's personal automobile to go to Andrew; all personal effects to the widow, Alice; and the remainder of the estate property, after payments of debts and proper charges and distribution of legacies, to be distributed to the widow, Alice.

On July 20, Andrew Cox filed the following inventory with the probate court:

Cash in bank	$25,000
Personal effects	1,000
Automobile	4,000
Life insurance policy payable to the estate	30,000
U.S. Savings Bonds, Series E (redemption value on May 31, 19x1)	6,000
Edna Corporation, common stock 1,000 shares (market value)	5,000
Toto Corporation 5% bonds due 19x8, par $10,000	9,600
Dividend declared (on May 15) on Edna common stock	400
Accrued interest (Toto Corporation bonds)	250
Total inventory of assets	$81,250

The following transaction and events occurred as follows:

Date

July 28 Public notice was given that creditors of the estate should make a presentment of their claims.

Aug. 15 Paid funeral expenses, $1,500.

16 Collected dividend on Edna stock, $400.

20 Undeposited cash of $1,000 discovered among the decedent's personal belongings.

31 Received payment on insurance policy.

Sept 1 Interest earned, subsequent to date of death on cash in bank, was credited, $200.

15 Paid debts of the decedent, $2,900.

30 Collected interest on Toto Corporation bonds.

Oct. 1 Paid cash legacies provided for in the will.

3 Delivered automobile to Andrew Cox and personal effects to widow.

8 Collected cash dividend $300 on Edna Corporation stocks.

12 Paid attorney's fees, $1,000, and other administration expenses of $2,500 of which $200 relate to income.

15 Sold Edna Corporation stock for $4,900.

Dec. 15 Interest accrued on Toto Corporation bonds, $250.

15 Distributed remaining assets to residuary beneficiaries.

On the basis of the above information the following will be prepared:

1. Journal entries of the fiduciary.

2. Charge and discharge statement of Andrew Cox as to principal and income for period May 31 to December 15, 19x1.

3. Closing entries reflecting the distribution of remaining assets to residuary beneficiaries and closing the fiduciary books.

(1) Journal Entries

Date	Details	Debit	Credit
July 20	Cash—Principal	25,000	
	Personal Effects	1,000	
	Automobile	4,000	
	Life Insurance Policy—Payable to Estate	30,000	
	U.S. Savings Bonds	6,000	
	Edna Corporation Common Stock	5,000	
	Toto Corporation 5% Bonds Due 19x8	9,600	
	Dividends Receivable	400	
	Interest Receivable	250	
	Estate Principal		81,250
	Inventory of estate of Walter Cox.		
28	Public notice was given that creditors of the estate of the decedent should make a presentment of their claims.		
Aug. 15	Funeral and Administration Expenses	1,500	
	Cash—Principal		1,500
	Funeral expenses paid.		
16	Cash—Principal	400	
	Dividend Receivable		400
	Collected dividends on Edna common stock.		
20	Cash—Principal	1,000	
	Assets Subsequently Discovered		1,000
	Undeposited cash discovered today.		
31	Cash—Principal	30,000	
	Life Insurance Policy		30,000
	Received payment on life insurance.		

Date	Details	Debit	Credit
Sept. 1	Cash—Income	200	
	Estate Income		200
	Interest credited on cash in bank.		
15	Debts of Decedent Paid	2,900	
	Cash—Principal		2,900
	Paid debts of decedent.		
30	Cash—Principal	250	
	Interest Receivable		250
	Collected accrued interest accrued before death on Toto Corporation bonds.		
Oct. 1	Legacy—Andrew Cox	12,000	
	Legacy—William Cox	3,000	
	Legacy—Mark Cox	3,000	
	Cash—Principal		18,000
	Paid legacies provided for in the will.		
3	Legacy—Andrew Cox	4,000	
	Legacy—Alice Cox	1,000	
	Automobile		4,000
	Personal Effects		1,000
	Delivered automobile and personal effects as per will.		
8	Cash—Income	300	
	Estate Income		300
	Cash dividend on Edna Corporation common stock.		
12	Funeral and Administration Expenses	3,300	
	Expenses—Income	200	
	Cash—Principal		3,300
	Cash—Income		200
	Paid attorney's fees ($1,000) and administration expenses ($2,500).		
15	Cash—Principal	4,900	
	Loss on Realization	100	
	Edna Corporation common stock		5,000
	Sold Edna Corporation stock.		
Dec.15	Interest Receivable	250	
	Estate Income		250
	Interest accrued on Toto Corporation bonds.		

(2) Charge and Discharge Statements

ESTATE OF WALTER COX, DECEASED
Andrew Cox, Executor
Charge and Discharge Statement
May 31 to December 15, 19x1

I charge myself with:

Assets per original inventory		$81,250
Assets subsequently discovered		1,000
Total		82,250

I credit myself with:

Loss on realization of assets	$ 100	
Funeral and administration expenses	4,800	
Debts of decedent paid	2,900	
Legacies paid or distributed:		
Andrew Cox (cash, $12,000; automobile, $4,000)	16,000	
William Cox (cash)	3,000	
Mark Cox (cash)	3,000	
Alice Cox (personal effects)	1,000	30,800
Balance as to principal		$51,450

Which consists of:

Cash*	$35,850
U.S. Savings Bonds	6,000
Toto Corporation bonds	9,600
	$51,450

*Cash—principal balance is computed as follows:

Debit	Cash—Principal		Credit
7/20 Inventory	25,000		
8/16	400	8/15	1,500
8/20	1,000	9/15	2,900
8/31	30,000	10/1	18,000
9/30	250	10/2	3,300
10/15	4,900	12/15 Balance	35,850
	61,550		61,550

As to Income

I charge myself with:

Income collected or accrued		$ 750

I credit myself with:

Expenses chargeable to income		200
Balance as to income		$ 550

Which consists of:

Cash	$ 300
Interest Receivable (Toto Corporation bonds)	250
	$ 550

(3) Closing Entries Reflecting the Distribution of Estate Assets

Dec 15	Legacy—Alice Cox	51,450	
	Cash—Principal		35,850
	U.S. Savings Bonds		6,000
	Toto Corporation Bonds		9,600
	Distribution of residual assets to residuary beneficiary.		
15	Estate Principal	81,250	
	Assets Subsequently Discovered	1,000	
	Loss on Realization		100
	Debts of Decedent Paid		2,900
	Legacy—Andrew Cox		16,000
	Legacy—William Cox		3,000
	Legacy—Mark Cox		3,000
	Legacy—Alice Cox		52,450
	Funeral and Administrative Expenses		4,800
	To close open accounts as to Estate Principal.		
15	Distribution to Alice Cox	550	
	Cash—Income		300
	Interest Receivable		250
	Distribution of remaining cash and interest receivable.		
15	Estate Income	750	
	Expenses—Income		200
	Distribution to Income Beneficiary—Alice Cox		550
	To close open accounts as to Estate Income.		

It should be noted that in the case of more complex estates the charge and discharge statements will be supported by detailed schedules providing information regarding many of the totals aggregated in these statements. Referring to our simplified illustration above, the following items could be supported by schedules:

> Schedule of: Assets per original inventory.
>   Assets subsequently discovered.
>   Expenses.
>   Debts.
>   Legacies paid or distributed.
>   Loss on realization of assets.

LEGAL AND ACCOUNTING ASPECTS OF TRUSTS

An *inter vivos* trust may be created by a living *grantor* by a transfer of property to a *trustee* who holds it for the benefit of a person called the *beneficiary* or *cestuique trust*. When a trust is created by a will it is called a *testamentary trust*. As was noted earlier in this chapter, the income from a trust is ordinarily distributed periodically to an *income beneficiary* while the principal ultimately goes to a beneficiary known as a *remainderman*. The income beneficiary and remainderman may, of course, be the same person. As is the case in estate accounting the distinction between income and principal is also very important in trust accounting.

Whereas estate administration is generally a short-run process which aims at the expeditious distribution of estate assets, trust administration consists of the prudent management of funds over longer periods of time. Most intervivos trusts are not court supervised. Testamentary trustees as well as some other kinds of fiduciaries (such as guardians) must make periodic reports to a court. Although the laws of individual states may vary, the *Uniform Trustees Accouting Act* requires an accounting system similar to that used for estates and a reporting system very much like the charge and discharge statement illustrated earlier in this chapter.

Among other important provisions of the Uniform Trustees Accounting Act are the requirements that trustees file within 30 days after the end of each yearly period, an accounting with the court concerning events of the previous period, that the accounting period be specified and that the names and addresses of living beneficiaries be given. A statement of unpaid claims and reasons for nonpayment within the reporting period must also be given.

At the termination of the trust, a final accounting should be rendered covering the period since the last intermediate accounting. A plan for the distribution of trust assets still on hand must also be presented.

Since the accounting procedures for a trust are very similar to those of an estate, it suffices that we illustrate here the opening entries on a trustee's books. If we assume that, following the previous illustration, on December 15, 19x1, the balance of the Estate Principal account of $51,450 and of the Estate Income account of $550 were to be transferred to the First National Bank as trustee for the benefit of Nancy Cox, the decedent's grandaughter, the following opening entries would be appropriate.

NANCY COX TRUST
First National Bank—Trustee
General Journal

19x1
Dec. 15   Cash—Principal 35,850
       Cash—Income 300
       U.S. Savings Bonds 6,000
       Toto Corporation Bonds 9,600
       Interest Receivable 250
          Trust Principal 51,450
          Trust Income 550

       To record receipt by trustee of principal and income assets from Andrew Cox, executor of the estate of Walter Cox, pursuant to decree of court.

In a testamentary trust the trustee will generally record assets at the amounts which were used to value the estate even though a period of time may have elapsed since the date of valuation for estate purposes.

In order to demonstrate adherence to the terms of the trust instrument, the trustee must, in addition to required court reports, also provide private reports to income beneficiaries and remaindermen. The periodic reports are essentially similar to the charge and discharge statements illustrated earlier in this chapter.

QUESTIONS

1. Differentiate between a person who died testate and a person who died intestate.

2. Describe the meaning of the following terms: probating the will, executor, administrator, letters testamentary, and letters of administration.

3. Certain allowances and exemptions specified by the Code have to be satisfied before all claims against the estate. What are they?

4. What is the sequence of payment for the various claims against the estate?

5. Briefly explain the meaning of a devise, a devisee, legacies, and legatee in the testate distribution of an estate.

6. What are the various types of legacies that may exist in a will?

7. Define and describe the following with respect to a decedent's estate:

a. Income.

b. Principal.

8. Why is the distinction between principal and income in the administration of an estate important?

9. Compare the following:

a. Testamentary trust and invervivos trust.

b. An income beneficiary and remainderman.

EXERCISES

Exercise 19–1. The following items are related to a testamentary trust. Indicate as to each of them whether they would be charged to principal or to income.

1. Legal fees for the management of the trust assets.
2. Depreciation on office building.
3. Interest on mortgage note payable.
4. Loss realized on sale of trust investment.
5. Major repairs to property before the sale of the property.

Exercise 19–2. It is stated in the will of Robert Alex that the balance of his estate is to be transferred to a testamentary trust. On June 12, 19x8, the following trial balance was prepared from the accounts of the estate:

	Debit	Credit
Cash—principal	$90,100	
Cash—income	9,800	
Marketable securities	22,000	
Estate balance		$120,200
Assets subsequently discovered . . .		15,300
Gains on disposal of assets		2,200
Funeral and administration		
expenses	4,100	
Debts of decedent paid	12,500	
Interest revenue		2,000
Expenses chargable to income . . .	1,200	

Required:

a. Prepare the journal entry to close the accounts of the estate.

b. Prepare the journal entry to open the accounting books for the trust.

Exercise 19–3. The following activities related to the Estate of Kim Myers who died on March 28, 19x7.

a. Inventory of estate assets was filed with the court as follows:

Cash	$30,000
Capital stock of Block Company	20,500
Real estate	55,000
Personal effects	23,200

b. Funeral and administrative expenses paid, $3,200.

c. Dividends collected, $950 on Block Company's stock.

d. $10,000 of 10 percent bonds of ABC, Inc., were discovered.

e. Half of the capital stock of Block Company was sold for $12,000 cash.

f. Rent collected from the real estate was $1,200.

g. The personal effects were given to Robert, the son of Kim, as stipulated in the will.

h. The executor's fee of $2,300 was approved by the court and paid on August 1, 19x7. Of this amount, $300 is to be charged against income of the estate.

Required:

As the approved executor, prepare the journal entries to record the above activities.

Exercise 19–4. Prepare a charge and discharge statement for the estate detailed in Exercise 19–3.

Exercise 19–5. The will of Kim Myers in Exercise 19–3 stipulated that all remaining assets should be used to establish a trust at New York bank.

Required:

a. Prepare journal entries to transfer estate principal and income assets to the trust.

b. Prepare journal entries to close the executor's books of account.

PROBLEMS

Problem 19–6. Arthur Dodd died on May 30, 19x7. On November 30, 19x7, the accountant for the executor of the estate in the will, Perry Donald, prepared the following trial balance:

PERRY DONALD
Executor of the Will of Arthur Dodd
Trial Balance
November 30, 19x7

	Debit	Credit
Cash—principal	$ 20,000	
Cash—income	700	
Investments in bonds	110,000	
Household effects	17,800	
Gains on disposal of principal		
assets		$ 2,000
Assets discovered		20,400
Liabilities paid	22,400	
Administrative expense	8,100	
Estate principal balance		155,900
Interest revenue		7,400
Expenses chargeable to income . .	530	
Distributions to income		
beneficiaries	6,170	
Totals	$185,700	$185,700

The estate principal balance of $155,900 represents the inventory of assets as of May 30, 19x7.

Required:

Prepare a charge and discharge statement of the estate of Arthur Dodd.

Problem 19–7. Alex Dunn died on April 5, 19x8. Tom Dacey was named executor of the estate in the will which consisted of the following:

Cash	$20,000
Gantry Company debentures, includes accrued	
interest of $900	80,900
Personal effects	15,300
Automobile	4,000
Investment in common stocks	60,000

The will instructed the executor to transfer the personal effects and automobile to his son David, to pay estate taxes, liabilities, and administrative expenses of the estate, and to transfer the remaining assets to a trust for the benefit of his son. Income from the estate and the trust is to be paid to the son.

Transactions of the executor during the period of April 5–December 12, 19x8, were:

1. Paid administrative expenses for the estate, $4,500.
2. Sold 50 percent of investment in common stock for $32,100.
3. Discovered a saving account of $5,900 in the name of Alex Dunn.
4. Received interest income, $5,400.
5. Received dividends, $1,200.
6. Transferred personal effects and automobile to the son, David.
7. Paid debts of decedent, $9,100.
8. Distributed the income of the estate to David.
9. Paid estate taxes, $25,000.

Required:

a. Prepare journal entries on the books of the executor to record the transactions including opening entry and to close the accounting records for the estate on December 12, 19x8.

b. Prepare a charge and discharge statement prior to the transfer of estate assets to the Alex Dunn trust.

c. Prepare journal entry to establish the accounting records for the trust.

Problem 19–8. Scott Clason was appointed executor of the estate of Leland Robinson who died in an accident on March 20, 19x7. During the executorial period, April 15 through October 10, 19x7, the following transactions were made:

a. An inventory of estate assets was filed with the court as follows:

Cash	$ 5,000
Common stock, Jenson Company 2,000	
shares (par $7) @ $14	28,000
7% bonds of Delta Corporation	2,500
Accrued interest on bonds of Delta	
Corporation	20
Dividends receivable, Jenson Company . . .	700
Automobile	4,200
Personal and household effects	2,000
Life insurance, payable to the estate	12,000

b. Administration expenses of $926 were paid by the executor.
c. The life insurance policy proceeds were collected.
d. ABC Company bonds of $7,000 were discovered; the related accrued interest was $100.
e. After publishing a notice for the presentation of claims against the estate, debts of the decedent of $1,620 were validated and paid.
f. The common stock of Jenson Company was sold for $25,400 cash.
g. The dividend on Jenson stock was collected.

h. The accrued interest on ABC Company bonds of $100 and that on Delta bonds of $20 were collected.

i. Executorial fees of $1,900 were paid to Clason.

j. A cash legacy of $8,000 was paid to Mary Robinson, the widow, as stated in the will.

k. The automobile was sold for $4,190 cash.

l. All the remaining assets in the estate were distributed to Albert and Sam, sons of the decedent, equally.

Required:

a. Prepare the journal entries for the above transactions on the books of the executor.

b. Prepare a charge and discharge statement of Clason for the period April 15 to October 10, 19x7.

c. Prepare the closing entries on October 10, 19x7, to close the executor's books.

Problem 19–9. Alex Fess was named executor of the estate of Charles Howard, who died on January 10, 19x8. The transactions completed by Fess are listed below:

1. Inventory of estate assets was filed with the court as follows:

Cash, City bank . . . . $ 5,200
200 shares of WV common stock 10,000
6% bonds of Texas, Inc., including $700
    accrued interest 22,300
Office building 51,100
Household effects 15,000
Land 23,200

2. A diamond ring belonging to decedent was discovered and sold for $8,700 cash.

3. The office building was sold for $45,500 cash.

4. One hundred shares of WV common stock were sold for $4,300 cash.

5. One half of the land was sold for $15,000.

6. Interest receivable on Texas, Inc., bonds of $300 was collected.

7. Funeral and administrative expenses of $4,100 were paid.

8. Debts of the decedent of $15,000 were validated and paid.

9. Dividends declared and collected on WV common stock, $400.

10. Legacies and income were distributed according to the terms of the will as follows:

   To son, William: cash, $10,000; Texas, Inc., bonds.

   To son, Donald: cash, $25,000; land, $11,600; household effects, and the residue of the estate, if any.

   To widow, Lucy: cash, $14,700; 100 shares of WV common stock; and income of estate.

Required:

a. Prepare the executor's journal entries for the estate transactions.

b. Prepare a charge and discharge statement for the estate of Charles Howard.

c. Prepare the entries on April 28, 19x8, necessary to close the executor's books.

Problem 19–10. Fred Stone, one of three trustees appointed under the terms of a testamentary trust established by the will of Jac Allen, a bachelor, engaged you to prepare a consolidated balance sheet of the various interests in properties controlled and managed by the trustees as of September 30, 19x9. These properties consist of estate assets, undistributed income, and a 90 percent stock interest in the Bass Corporation purchased when the corporation was formed. Bass Corporation in turn owns 80 percent of the stock of the Crane Investments, Inc. All assets were valued for federal estate tax purposes as of the date of Allen's death.

Allen died on June 30, 19x3, leaving his entire estate in trust for the benefit of his sister to pass upon her death to her children. Under the terms of the will, the three appointed trustees are authorized to (1) act as directors of the two corporations and may, at their discretion, combine or dissolve them; (2) pay a minimum of $4,000 monthly as the sister's maintenance allowance from interest and dividend income remaining after payment of expenses of the trust; and (3) buy or sell trust investments, reinvest estate assets, and/or undistributed income. Gains or losses from the sale of trust assets are to be allocated to corpus.

The September 30, 19x9, trial balances for the Allen Estate, Bass Corporation, and Crane Investments, Inc., are as follows:

[Relates to Problem 19–10]

ALLEN ESTATE, BASS CORPORATION, AND CRANE INVESTMENTS, INC.
Trial Balances
September 30, 19x9

Debits	Allen Estate	Bass Corporation	Crane Investments, Inc.
Cash in bank	$ 45,000	$ 195,000	$ 45,000
Due from Crane Investments, Inc.		4,500	
Investments at cost:			
Corporate bonds	300,000	500,000	
Marketable securities:			
Purchased prior to June 30, 19x3		794,000	
Purchased after June 30, 19x3		2,000,000	439,000
Stock of Bass Corporation—90% interest at			
cost	2,250,000		
Stock of Crane Investments, Inc.—80% interest			
at cost		156,000	
Accrued interest receivable		21,000	
Trustee's expenses, taxes, etc. paid	218,000		
Distributions to sister	296,000		
	$3,109,000	$3,670,500	$484,000

Credits	Allen Estate	Bass Corporation	Crane Investments, Inc.
Sundry liabilities		$ 373,500	$ 38,250
Due to Bass Corporation			4,500
Income from dividends	$ 460,000		
Interest income	72,000		
Gain on sale of bonds	2,000		
Equity of Jac Allen:			
Estate Corpus	2,575,000		
Estate income			
Capital stock:			
Bass Corporation:			
Allen Estate		2,250,000	
Minority interest		250,000	
Crane Investments, Inc.:			
Bass Corporation:			160,000
Minority interest			40,000
Retained earnings:			
Bass Corporation:			
Allen Estate		717,300	
Minority interest		79,700	
Crane Investments, Inc.:			
Bass Corporation			193,000
Minority interest			48,250
	$3,109,000	$3,670,500	$484,000

Stone requested that you use, in lieu of cost for balance sheet valuation purposes, the fair market value of the securities *at the date of Allen's death* in order that the accountability of the trustees for subsequent events may be properly disclosed.

The following information was available:

1. Investments in bonds are reported at cost and represent their present market value. Interest of $9,000 had accrued on the bonds held by the Al-

len Estate but was not recorded on September 30, 19x9.

2. Marketable securities held by Bass Corporation costing $794,000 and having a market value of $800,000 on Allen's death were still on hand at September 30, 19x9. The market value of marketable securities purchased after Allen's death and held by Bass Corporation on September 30, 19x9, was $2,200,000.

3. The market value of the securities held by Crane

Investments, Inc., on June 30, 19x3, as determined for federal estate tax purposes, was $250,000. These securities cost $240,000 on January 2, 19x3, and were sold in 19x5 for $295,000. The securities on hand at September 30, 19x9, were purchased on May 10, 19x9, at a cost of $439,000 and had a market value of $441,000 on September 30, 19x9.

4. The investment in Bass Corporation is reported on the trial balance at cost. The value of the investment reported for federal estate tax purposes was $2,700,000 which the trustees believe to be fair and represents the original cost plus appreciation of securities to June 30, 19x3.

5. Bass Corporation's investment in Crane Investments, Inc., is reported on the trial balance at cost. On June 30, 19x3, total owners' equity of Crane Investments, Inc., consisted of $200,000 in capital stock at par value and $20,000 in retained earnings. No dividends have been paid to Crane Investments, Inc.

Required:

Prepare a worksheet for the preparation of a consolidated balance sheet. Supporting computations should be in good form. Worksheet adjusting and eliminating entries should be numbered. Formal adjusting and eliminating entries and financial statements are not required.   (AICPA adapted)

Problem 19–11. Clarence Morning died January 1, 19x3, and left his property in trust for his daughter, Cindy. Income from the trust was to be paid to her as she requested it, and at her death the trust principal was to go to his nephew, Mike Morning. Any income, including accrued interest, not withdrawn by Cindy at the time of her death would be paid to her estate. Clarence appointed Charles Wayne as trustee at a fixed fee of $6,000 per year. All expenses of settling Clarence's estate were paid and accounted for by the executor before the trustee took over.

Cindy died on September 30, 19x6, and left her property in trust to her cousin, Natalie Wagner. Mr. Wayne was also appointed executor and trustee of the estate, and he agreed not to make any additional charges for these services. All income subsequent to September 30, 19x6, was to be paid to Natalie. The estate of Cindy Morning consisted solely of her unexpended income from the Clarence Morning Trust, which was invested on October 1, 19x6, to yield 10 percent.

Pending preparation of legal papers and the official transfer of the property to Mike on December 31, 19x7, he received payments from the trustee totaling $40,000. The property received by Charles Wayne, trustee, under the will of Clarence Morning, as of January 1, 19x3, was:

10,000 shares of Flex Corporation, valued at $100 each.

$200,000 of Flex Corporation 9 percent bonds, paying interest semiannually on June 30 and December 31. Their market value and face value were identical at the date of death.

On February 1, 19x3, 19x4, and 19x5, the trustee received $40,000 of annual dividends from the Flex stock. Dividends increased to $60,000 on February 1, 19x6, and 19x7.

Payments made by the trustee were as follows:

Expenses averaged $100 per month.
Trustee's fee was $500 per month.
To the beneficiaries:

Cindy Morning:		
19x3	$30,000	
19x4	35,000	
19x5	30,000	
19x6	25,000	$120,000
Mike Morning:		
19x6	$10,000	
19x7	20,000	30,000
Natalie Wagner—19x6 and 19x7—		
all income received during the respective periods.		

Required:

a. Prepare a statement of income for the Clarence Morning Trust during the period Cindy Morning was the life tenant, showing the undistributed income that became the principal of the Cindy Morning Trust.

b. Prepare a schedule showing the computation of the total assets released to Mike Morning on December 31, 19x7.

c. Prepare a schedule showing the amount of income received by Natalie Wagner in 19x6 and 19x7.
                                            (AICPA adapted)

20

Corporate reorganizations and liquidations

OVERVIEW

Under ordinary circumstances, financial statements of business enterprises, prepared in accordance with generally accepted accounting standards, rest on the going-concern assumption. Thus, in the absence of evidence to the contrary, the going-concern concept views the economic entity as continuing in operation indefinitely.

This chapter is concerned with the accounting for enterprises doing business in corporate form which are in financial difficulty and for which the going-concern assumption may no longer be valid.

ENTERPRISES IN FINANCIAL DIFFICULTY

Business failure is a common phenomenon in a free enterprise economy and may be due to a variety of reasons such as incompetent management, poor operating control, inadequate financing, fraud, or other unexpected adverse developments. Among the inevitable symptoms of business failure is a shortage of funds or a lack of liquidity which results in the enterprise's inability to meet its current obligations as they become due.

Liquidity refers mainly to a firm's ability to meet its short-term obligations while solvency relates to the longer run financial viability of an enterprise. Both states are interrelated, and both are matters of degree. An auditor who examines the financial statements of an enterprise which has a history of losses has resulting financial difficulties, and may even be in default of loan agreement covenants must at some point evaluate the enterprise's ability to survive financially. If there is evidence that the ability of the enterprise to continue as a going concern can no longer be safely assumed, the auditor may have to qualify his opinion or in some cases disclaim an opinion.

INSOLVENCY

A business enterprise can be insolvent in the conventional sense when it is unable to pay off its liabilities as they become due. It is insolvent in the legal sense when, as defined in Section 101 of the Bankruptcy Reform Act of 1978, its "financial condition is such that the sum of such entity's debts is greater than all of such entity's property at fair valuation." Thus, in a legal sense an enterprise remains solvent as long as the fair value of its assets exceeds its liabilities, even though it cannot meet its current obligation because of an insufficiency of liquid resources.

ENTERPRISES IN FINANCIAL DIFFICULTY—AVAILABLE OPTIONS

At some stage of financial difficulty an enterprise may voluntarily reach some kind of agreement or arrangement with its creditors or else it may seek the protection of a court while attempting to work its way out of a financial stringency. Alternatively, creditors who lack patience or who have lost confidence in the debtor firm may seek to force a judicial reorganization or liquidation of the firm. Thus, the resolution of financial difficulties or of insolvency can take either a nonjudicial or a judicial route as shown in the following diagram:

Options available to a firm in financial difficulty

Debtor in Control	
Nonjudicial route	*Judicial route*
Maturity date extension	Reorganization
Composition agreement	(Debtor in possession)

Others in Control	
Nonjudicial route	*Judicial route*
Creditor committee	Reorganization
Voluntary assignment	(Trustee in possession)
	Liquidation

Following is a brief discussion of the above alternatives.

The nonjudicial route

Maturity date extension.   When a debtor finds itself in what it considers to be only a temporary financial difficulty, it may request agreement with its creditors to extend the maturity date of liabilities, i.e., additional time to work out the financial problems. This approach is generally possible when the creditors are few and when they perceive it to be to their advantage to give the debtor additional time. There are almost no accounting implications to this course of action.

The composition agreement.   An alternative to a maturity extension is for the debtor to offer creditors a certain percentage of their claims in full settlement. Such an agreement, called a composition agreement, can generally occur only when the creditors are few and if there is no substantial dissent from such an arrangement. Here, too, creditors must consider it in their interest to accept less than the full amount due them, and they must be willing to consent to higher proportional payments to dissenters, if any. For a composition agreement to be fully binding, the debtor enterprise must disclose its assets in full and must accord no preferential treatment to any creditor before the agreement is reached.

If, as is often the case under such agreements, the debtor is left with some assets to continue its business, then the ensuing accounting will, in accordance with *SFAS 4*, recognize the gain on discharge of debt net of related income tax effect as an extraordinary item in the income statement.

The creditor committee.   When, in the opinion of the creditors, the debtor cannot be relied upon to turn its business around, they may consent to a contractual arrangment under which a committee of creditors is formed to control and manage the business enterprise. Under such an arrangement the debtor loses control, at least temporarily, and a representative appointed by the creditor committee manages the business and attempts to restore it to financial health. If this course of action is successful, the creditors are ultimately paid off and the debtor regains control of its firm. Alternatively, a formal reorganization or liquidation may ensue. In the latter case there are accounting implications which will be described more fully later in this chapter.

The voluntary assignment.   Under some state insolvency laws it is possible for the debtor to execute a voluntary assignment of all property to a trust for the benefit of its creditors. The trustee or assignee, acting on behalf of the creditors, proceeds then to liquidate the debtor's property and to distribute the proceeds to creditors as a pro rata basis. Should the liquidation process result in an excess of proceeds over creditor claims, such excess is returned to the debtor.

As may often be the case, creditors who dissent from such an assignment may force the debtor into a more formal (judicial) bankruptcy process of liquidation.

The judicial route

Any business corporation can initiate bankruptcy proceedings by filing a petition with the court and asserting that it is unable to pay its debts as they become due. This is the *voluntary bankruptcy* process. If a company is reluctant to take such a voluntary step, proceedings can be initiated by creditors who may file a petition for involuntary bankruptcy. In such a petition the creditors must allege that the corporate debtor has committed one of the specific acts of bankruptcy specified in the law.

BANKRUPTCY REFORM ACT OF 1978

The original Federal Bankruptcy Act was enacted by Congress in 1898 and was subsequently revised by the Chandler Act in 1938. In November 1978 Congress enacted Title II of the United States Code thus providing a thorough revision of the federal bankruptcy laws which take effect on October 1, 1979. The Bankruptcy Reform Act of 1978 created a new bankruptcy court (to become operative in 1984) which will be presided by bankruptcy judges who will be appointed for 14-year terms.

The 1978 Act represents a significant simplication and modernization of the law. The major objectives of the bankruptcy act are to ensure a fair distribution of a debtor's assets among all creditors in settlement of their claims and to avoid the favoring of some creditors to the detriment of others. It also aims to provide a fresh start for a debtor by releasing it from all previous debts after the surrender of its assets and to enable the rehabilitation and reorganization of business corporations.

When an enterprise experiences financial difficulty, it may file a *voluntary petition* with the bankruptcy court seeking relief and protection. Should the firm's plight become known to its unsecured creditors, they may seek to force the firm into bankruptcy by filing an *involuntary petition* with the court. For creditors to be able to do this, there must exist three or more creditors having an aggregate unsecured debt of $5,000 or more. Alternately, if the total number of unsecured creditors is less than 12 (exclusive of insiders and employees), any single creditor with an unsecured claim of $5,000 or more may file a petition with the court.

Judicial action is commenced with the filing of the voluntary or involuntary petition. The individual or group filing such a petition must also indicate whether it is seeking relief under Chapter II of the new act which deals with reorganization or under Chapter VII which deals with liquidation. The court may start the judicial process under the chapter petitioned for and may later transfer it to the other chapter in response to a petition by the creditors or, in limited circumstances, by the debtor. There are other chapters and procedures under which bankruptcy proceedings can proceed, but we shall limit our consideration here to the accounting aspects of *reorganizations* (under Chapter XI of the new act) and *liquidations* (under Chapter VII of the new act).

REORGANIZATIONS

The 1978 Act made significant changes in the area of business reorganizations in order to improve the process of restructuring of a business's finances so that it may be able to continue to operate and to serve all segments of society. The act accomplishes this by a consolidation of four former chapters into a new Chapter XI which allows for a great deal of operational flexibility. Public creditors are protected under the act by providing for adequate disclosure to interested parties. Section 1125 of the act defines adequate information as: "information of a kind, and in sufficient detail, as far as reasonably practicable in light of the nature and history of the debtor and the condition of the debtor's books and records, that would enable a hypothetical reasonable investor typical of holders of claims or interests of the relevant class to make an informed judgment about the plan."

With regard to the management of the business which is to be reorganized under Chapter XI, the act adopts a flexible approach by leaving the debtor in possession of its property and business unless a request is made for the appointment of a trustee (Section 1104). If such a request is made by a party at interest for cause shown, including fraud, dishonesty, incompetence or gross mismanagement, or if the appointment of a trustee is in the interests of creditors, equity security holders and others, the court will order the appointment of a trustee or of an examiner, in lieu of a trustee, to examine the acts of management.

The following duties for a trustee are specified by the law:

1. To be accountable for all properties received from the debtor.
2. To file a "schedule of assets and liabilities," a "list of creditors" and a "statement of the debtor's financial affairs" if not already done by the debtor.
3. To investigate the debtor and file a statement of investigation with the court, the creditor's committee, the stockholder's committee or any other parties at interest as ordered by the court.
4. To furnish information and financial reports about the debtor's estate with the court, the creditors, tax authorities, and other parties at interest.
5. To examine proofs of claim of creditors.
6. To file all necessary tax returns.
7. To prepare a reorganization plan.

After the court approves and confirms a reorganization plan the trustee will "file such reports as are necessary as the court orders" and on termination of the trusteeship he or she will submit a final accounting and report of the administration of the estate with the court. If the debtor continues to operate the business *(debtor in possession)*, he or she will perform the same functions as the trustee except for those of an investigative nature.

As soon as practicable after the court grants the petition for a reorganization it will appoint a creditor's committee selected from unsecured creditors which have the largest claims against the debtor. The committee has consultative and investigative powers and generally aids the debtor or the trustee in the formulation of a reorganization plan.

A reorganization plan, which must be submitted by the debtor within 120 days of the approval of the petition for reorganization, or which is otherwise filed by a creditor committee, the trustee, or any party at interest, must specify the treatment that is to be accorded to each class of creditors and stockholders as well as provide proof that such plan can in actuality be carried out.

Following presentation of a plan of reorganization the creditors must vote to accept or reject it. Generally, to be accepted, at least two thirds in amount and more than one half in number of each class of creditors must vote in favor of the plan. The court may continue a plan it considers fair even though some classes of creditors have voted against it.

Confirmation of a plan of reorganization by the court will generally have the following effects:

1. The property covered by the plan will be free and clear of all claims except as provided for under the plan.
2. Unless otherwise provided, the debtor is discharged from any debt arising prior to date of confirmation and it terminates the rights and interests of old stockholders.
3. The plan is binding on the debtor, or any creditor or stockholder of the debtor and on any entity which issues securities under the plan.

ACCOUNTING FOR A REORGANIZATION

While the legal forms which a corporate reorganization can take will vary, the accounting treatments will be similar. Most students will be familiar with the accounting for *quasi-reorganizations* which are usually covered in intermediate accounting texts. The basic difference between a quasi reorganization and a court-approved reorganization with which we are concerned here is that the former derives its authority from a vote by stockholders while the latter depends on the sanction of the bankruptcy court.

In most cases, corporate reorganizations, as is the case with arrangements, involve the liquidation and the writing down of assets, reductions in the par or stated values of capital stock needed to absorb deficits, extensions of due dates and changes in terms of debts, exchanges of securities for debts, and the acceptance by creditors of less than the full amount for debts due to them.

Corporate reorganizations can be carried out by the corporate management under the supervision of creditor committees and others appointed by the court or they can be implemented by a court appointed trustee who takes charge. The accounting for these forms or reorganizations does not vary significantly, and thus, in the illustration which follows, we shall examine the journal entries that record a management implemented reorganization.

The Lowcash Company has experienced substantial financial difficulties and has filed a voluntary petition for a reorganization under Chapter 11 of the 1978 Act. The following is a balance sheet as at March 31, 19x1.

LOWCASH COMPANY
Balance Sheet
As of March 31, 19x1

Assets		Liabilities and equity	
Cash	$ 2,000	Notes payable, 7% due	
Accounts receivable	23,000	February 28, 19x2	$ 35,000
Merchandise	50,000	Accounts payable	72,000
Ace Company common stock		Salaries and wages payable	10,000
(at cost)	5,800	Taxes payable	2,000
Land	22,000	Bank loan	10,000
Buildings	92,000	Morgage payable	100,000
Machinery and equipment	80,000	Stockholders' equity:	
Goodwill	30,000	Capital stock	140,000
		Retained earnings	(64,200)
		Total liabilities and	
Total assets	$304,800	equity	$304,800

The following plan for reorganization was confirmed by the court:

1. Management will speed up the collection of accounts receivable and will liquidate inventories to raise the cash needed to implement the initial phase of the reorganization plan. The Ace Company common stock will be sold for $6,600.

2. The mortgage on the land and buildings which is payable with interest at 8 percent in 27 remaining annual installments will remain in effect and unchanged on all its terms.

3. The bank loan will be paid off now in the amount of $6,000 with the balance of $4,000 rescheduled to become due on March 31, 19x5, at 9 percent interest.

4. Salaries and wages payable as well as taxes payable will be paid in full.

5. The capital stock will be changed from $100 par to $1 par value with the resulting paid-in capital available for the absorption of the deficit and other losses and expenses of the reorganization.

6. The holder of the 7 percent notes payable due February 28, 19x2, will accept a new 9 percent note payable due February 28, 19x8, in the amount of $20,000 as well as 1,000 shares of new common stock having a fair market value of $15 per share.

7. The accounts payable creditors have accepted a settlement of 70 cents on the dollar with 10 cents on the dollar to be paid immediately and the balance in four equal annual installments.

8. Reorganization expenses (inclusive of auditor fees) of $8,000 will be paid currently.

The following journal entries give effect to the confirmed arrangements in the initial phase of the reorganization:

(1a)

Cash	6,600	
Ace Company Common		5,800
Gain on Sale of Stock		800
Sale of Ace Company common stock.		

(1b)

No entries are given for the assumed accelerated collection of receivables and the sale of inventories.

(2)

No entry.

(3)

Bank Loan (old)	10,000	
Bank Loan, (due March 31, 19x5)		4,000
Cash		6,000

To pay part of the bank loan and reschedule the balance.

(4)

Salaries and Wages Payable	10,000	
Taxes Payable	2,000	
Cash		12,000

To record the payment of salaries, wages, and taxes.

(5)

Capital Stock, $100 Par	140,000	
Capital Stock, $1 Par		1,400
Paid-In Capital in Excess of Par		138,600

To record issuance of 1,400 shares of $1 par capital stock in
exchange for 1,400 shares of $100 par capital stock in
accordance with the reorganization plan.

(6)

7% Notes Payable, (due February 28 ,19x2)	35,000	
9% Notes Payable, (due February 28, 19x8)		20,000
Capital Stock $1 par		1,000
Paid-In Capital in Excess of Par		14,000

To record exchange of the 7% notes payable due February
28, 19x2, for $20,000 of notes payable due February 28, 19x8,
with interest of 9 percent plus 1,000 shares of $1 par having
fair market value of $15 per share.

(7)

Accounts Payable (old)	72,000	
Cash		7,200
Accounts Payable (new)		43,100
Gain from Discharge of Indebtedness in Reorganization . .		21,600

To record settlement of accounts payable at 70 cents on the
dollar with 10 cents on the dollar payable now and the
balance in four equal annual installments.

(8)

Reorganization Expenses	8,000	
Cash		8,000

To record the payment of reorganization expenses.

The accelerated collection of receivables and the sale of inventories is
likely to result in some losses. However, proceeding on the assumption that
no such losses will be incurred the following entry will transfer all presently
known gains and losses to the deficit account.

Gain on Sale of Stock	800	
Gain from Discharge of Indebtedness in Reorganization	21,600	
Reorganization Expenses		8,000
Retained Earnings (deficit)		14,400

To close out income and expense accounts to deficit.

At the conclusion of the reorganization the remaining balance of the deficit of $49,800 ($64,200 − $14,400) would be eliminated against the paid-in capital by the following entry:

Paid-In Capital	49,800	
Retained Earnings (deficit)		49,800

    To eliminate the deficit remaining at the conclusion of the
reorganization by charge to the Paid-In Capital account.

The above entry will now allow Lowcash Company to begin with a "clean slate" after the reorganization and to resume operations as a going concern. For a reasonable number of years after the reorganization, the retained earnings should be dated so as to disclose to readers of subsequent financial statements the fact that the Retained Earnings account reflects only the earnings subsequent to the reorganization.

If, as already discussed above, a trustee is appointed to effect a court-approved reorganization, he or she will open accounts based on the book values of the reorganizing entity and these book values will form the initial basis for accountability.

Should a reorganization plan prove unworkable or inadequate within a reasonable period of time the creditors may petition to transfer the proceeding to a Chapter 7 liquidation under the act.

LIQUIDATIONS

When the financial position of the debtor is such that it cannot resolve its financial difficulties by any of the means discussed so far, it will have to resort to a liquidation under Chapter 7 of the 1978 Act. This process may be started by the debtor filing a voluntary petition or by creditors filing an involuntary petition. All businesses (or individuals) may file for a Chapter 7 liquidation with the exception of railroads, insurance companies, and a variety of banking institutions.

TRUSTEE IN BANKRUPTCY

Promptly following the filing of a petition for voluntary or involuntary liquidation, the court is required to appoint an interim trustee. Such an interim trustee may later be replaced by a different trustee at the request and vote of a specified number of unsecured creditors.

The duties of the trustee are similar to those in a reorganization except that in a liquidation the focus is on a realization of assets and a liquidation of liabilities rather than on preservation and continuation of a business. In addition, the trustee must assume control over the assets of the debtor, convert assets into cash, and liquidate the business as expeditiously as is compatible with the best interests of affected parties. In the course of liquidation the trustee may continue business activities if that is in the interest of an orderly liquidation. Also depending on circumstances and the conduct of the debtor, the trustee can oppose the discharge of the debtor. In most actions the trustee will consult with a creditor's committee if one is elected by the unsecured creditors.

DISTRIBUTION OF THE ESTATE IN BANKRUPTCY

Following disposition of assets to satisfy liens or security interests and the conversion of all remaining noncash assets into cash, that cash is distributed as follows:

1. Liabilities having priority in the following order:
   a. Costs of administering and preserving the bankrupt's estate.
   b. Unsecured claims allowed after an involuntary petition is filed but prior to appointment of the trustee.
   c. Unsecured claims of wage earners up to $2,000 per individual and earned 90 days preceding the petition.
   d. Unsecured claims for contributions to employee benefit plans up to $2,000 per employee arising from services performed 180 days prior to the filing of the petition.
   e. Unsecured claims of up to $900 cash, arising before the filing of the petition from deposit of money in connection with the purchase, lease, or rental of property or purchase of services that were not provided.
   f. Unsecured claims of governmental units for income taxes, property taxes, excise, and other taxes which have become due for specified periods preceding the filing of the petition in bankruptcy.
2. Unsecured claims which have been allowed and that have been filed on a timely basis.
3. Unsecured claims which have been allowed and that have been filed late.
4. Claims which have been allowed for fines, penalties, and a variety of other damages preceding the petition or the appointment of the trustee.
5. Interest on above at legal rate from the time the petition was filed to the date of payment of claim.
6. Any balance of assets to be distributed to the debtor.

When there is insufficient cash to pay the entire claim to any group the cash available will be distributed on a pro rata basis to that group. Each class of claims above has priority over the next class.

In the case of corporations, which are our focus here, all assets are available for the payment of liabilities because unlike the situation with individuals, there are no exempt assets. Similarly, a corporation, unlike an individual, cannot receive a discharge from the bankruptcy court. A corporation can simply cease to exist by giving up its charter, and thus it will not have the post-bankruptcy obligations that individuals can, under certain conditions, retain.

ACCOUNTING AND REPORTING FOR A LIQUIDATION

The basic focus of accounting for a bankrupt in liquidation is that of a "quitting concert" rather than a "going concern" which is the usual assumption in accounting. The statement which has been devised for that purpose is the *statement of affairs* which is hypothetical or pro forma in nature and which represents the best estimate as to the outcome of the liquidation of a debtor's business over an assumed period of time. The degree of realization of assets can, of course, vary depending on the time allowed for liquidation. Generally, the shorter the time allowed the lower the probable proceeds to be realized from sales.

While the statement of affairs is most useful in assessing the probable effects of a liquidation, it is obvious that this statement is also the appropriate tool to be used by those who want to decide on possible courses of action open to any entity which finds itself in financial difficulty.

The statement of affairs presents the pro forma position of the debtor at *any given point in time.* The trustee in bankruptcy must also report periodically to those interested in learning the progress of the liquidation process, and for this purpose a statement of realization and liquidation has been devised.

THE STATEMENT OF AFFAIRS

As was noted above the focus of this statement is on what assets will bring in liquidation and how much and in what order the proceeds can be expected to be paid to creditors.

The construction of a statement of affairs requires a number of preparatory steps:

1. A balance sheet as of the most recent date possible should be prepared.
2. Estimates and appraisals of amounts which are likely to be realized on various assets should be obtained.
3. A listing of the pledge of assets for specific obligations should be made.
4. Obligations not presently reflected on the balance sheet but which are expected to emerge in the course of liquidation should be identified.

Statement of affairs format

The basic form of classification on the statement of affairs is the availability of assets to unsecured creditors. The link to the original balance sheet is preserved by having book values in columns to the left of the captions. Asset classifications which are related to the liability classifications on the opposite side of the statement are ordinarily shown in the following order:

1. *Assets pledged with fully secured creditors,* i.e., those which by law must be paid in full before anything may be paid to unsecured creditors.
2. *Fully secured liabilities.*
3. *Partly secured liabilities.*
4. *Unsecured liabilities.*
5. *Stockholder's equity.*

Illustration of the statement of affairs

Based on the balance sheet of the Lowcash Company as at March 31, 19x1 (see page 612), and on the additional data presented below, a statement of affairs should be prepared as of March 31, 19x1.

1. Assuming a given interval of time for liquidation, the land is appraised at $25,000, and the building is estimated to have a current market value

of $85,000. Both land and buildings were pledged for the mortgage payable and accrued interest.

2. The machinery and equipment are valueless, except as salvage of $12,000.

3. The Ace Company common stock has current market value of $6,600. The bank loan is secured by these common shares.

4. Receivables are estimated to be collectible according to the following schedule:

$18,000	. . . .	100%
4,000	. . . .	50%
1,000	. . . .	Uncollectible

5. Merchandise has a current salable value of $40,000.

6. The unrecorded accrued interest on mortgage payable is $2,000.

7. The audit fee for the year ended December 31, 19x0, was $3,000, but a bill has not been submitted. In addition, liquidation expenses are estimated at about $8,000.

8. The salaries and wages payable do not exceed the limitations imposed by the National Bankruptcy Act.

The statement of affairs follows:

Book value		Net realizable value	Estimated amount available	Loss or (gain) on realization
	Assets			
	Assets pledged with fully secured creditors:			
$ 22,000	Land	$ 25,000		$ (3,000)
92,000	Buildings	85,000		7,000
		110,000		
	Less: Fully secured creditors (contra A)	102,000	$ 8,000	
	Assets pledged with partially secured creditors:			
5,800	Ace Co. common stock (contra B) .	6,600		(800)
	Free assets:			
2,000	Cash	$ 2,000		
23,000	Accounts receivable	20,000		3,000
50,000	Merchandise	40,000		10,000
80,000	Machinery and equipment	12,000		68,000
30,000	Goodwill			30,000
	Total estimated amount available	74,000		
	Less: Liabilities with priority (contra C)	20,000		
	Estimated amount available for unsecured creditors		54,000	
	Estimated deficiency to unsecured creditors (to balance)		51,400(3)	
$304,800	Totals	$128,600(1)	$113,400	$114,200(1)

		Amount secured	Amount Unsecured
	Liabilities and Equity		
	Liabilities with priority		
$ 10,000	Salaries and wages payable	$ 10,000	
2,000	Taxes payable	2,000	
	Estimated liquidation expenses . . .	8,000	
	Total (contra C)	$ 20,000	
	Fully secured creditors:		
100,000	Mortage payable	100,000	
	Accrued interest	2,000	
	Total (contra A)	$102,000	
	Partially secured creditors:		
10,000	Bank loan	$ 10,000	
	Less Security: Ace Co. common		
	stock (contra B)	6,600	$ 3,400
	Unsecured creditors:		
35,000	Notes payable 7% due 2/28/x2		35,000
72,000	Accounts payable		72,000
	Unbilled auditor's fees		3,000
	Stockholders' equity:		
140,000	Capital stock		
(64,200)	Retained earnings		
$304,800	Totals		$113,400(1)

Notes:
(1) Total of contra A, contra B, and contra C.
(2) Net loss on realization.
(3) Estimated deficiency to unsecured creditors.

While it is possible to reconcile the amount of the estimated deficiency to unsecured creditors quite readily to the data already provided in the statement of affairs, some accountants prefer to present such a reconciliation in a more formal statement titled the "Statement of Estimated Deficiency to Unsecured Creditors" which is presented below:

LOWCASH COMPANY
Statement of Estimated Deficiency to Unsecured Creditors
March 31, 19x1

Estimated losses on realization:		
On building		$ 7,000
On accounts receivable		3,000
On merchandise		10,000
On machinery and equipment		68,000
On goodwill		30,000
		118,000
Less: Estimated gains on realization:		
On land	$ 3,000	
On Ace Company stock	800	3,800
Net loss or realization		114,200
Add: Unrecorded expenses:		
Accrued interest on mortgage payable	2,000	
Unbilled auditors' fees	3,000	5,000
Add: Estimated liquidation expenses		8,000
		127,200

Less: Stockholders' equity:

Capital stock	140,000	
Retained earnings	(64,200)	75,800
Estimated deficiency to unsecured creditors		$ 51,400

STATEMENT OF REALIZATION AND LIQUIDATION

Following the appointment of a trustee and the preparation of a statement of affairs as of a given point in time, the court, as well as other interested parties, expect to receive progress reports on the liquidation process.

The statement that has evolved for this purpose has been called the *Realization and Liquidation account.* As the title implies it is in T account form and is a rather cumbersome and archaic statement and one that has certainly not been devised with clarity as an objective. Here we shall illustrate a much more simplified and understandable version of such a *statement.*

Illustrative example

Assume that Jean Smith, the trustee in bankruptcy of Lowcash Company, took custody of and title to the assets of the company at March 31, 19x1, as per the statement of affairs of that date. The following journal entry would be prepared to reflect this fact:

LOWCASH COMPANY IN BANKRUPTCY
Jean Smith, Trustee
General Journal
March 31, 19x1

Cash	2,000	
Accounts Receivable	20,000	
Merchandise	40,000	
Ace Company Common Stock	6,600	
Land	25,000	
Buildings	85,000	
Machinery and Equipment	12,000	
Estate Deficit	43,400	
7% Notes Payable (due February 28, 19x2)		35,000
Accounts Payable		72,000
Salaries and Wages Payable		10,000
Taxes Payable		2,000
Bank Loan		10,000
Accrued Auditors' Fees		3,000
Mortgage Payable (including accrued interest)		102,000

To record current fair values of assets and liabilities of Lowcash Company in bankruptcy.

Note that the estate deficit in the journal entry above differs from the estimated deficiency to unsecured creditors shown on the statement of affairs because it does not include a provision for estimated liquidation expenses of $8,000. These expenses will affect the deficit balance as they are incurred as will be shown on the statement of realization and liquidation below.

As the trustee undertakes the realization of assets and the payment of liabilities, she would prepare periodically a statement of realization and liquidation, and an accompanying statement of cash receipts and disbursements for the period in question showing total realization proceeds, and the dates, check numbers, payees, and amounts paid for liabilities and estate administration expenses. Supporting schedules would summarize assets not yet realized and liabilities not yet liquidated.

Assume that during the six month period ending September 30, 19x1, the trustee sold the investment in Ace Company common stock for $6,500, realized $21,000 for the accounts receivable, sold the merchandise for $38,000, paid off $6,500 of the bank loan and all liabilities with priorities (salaries and wages payable, taxes payable), as well as $1,860 for estate administration expenses. The statement of realization and liquidation for the six months ended September 30, 19x1, would then be prepared as shown below:

LOWCASH COMPANY IN BANKRUPTCY
Jean Smith, Trustee
Statement of Realization and Liquidation
For the Six Months Ended September 30, 19x1

Estate deficit, March 31, 19x1 . . . . . $43,400*

	Estimated current fair value March 31, 19x1	Realization proceeds	Loss or (gain)	
Assets realized				
Accounts receivable	$20,000	$21,000	$(1,000)	
Merchandise	40,000	38,000	2,000	
Ace Company common stock . . .	6,600	6,500	100	
Totals	$66,600	$65,500		1,100

Liabilities with priority liquidated at carrying amounts:		
Salaries and wages payable	$10,000	
Taxes payable	2,000	
Totals	$12,000	

Partially secured creditors liquided in part:		
Bank loan	$ 6,500	

Estate administration expenses paid . . .   1,860

Estate deficit, September 30, 19x1 . . . . $46,360

*Estate deficit per statement of affairs, $51,400 less $8,000 in estimated liquidation costs not provided for.

The cash receipts and disbursement schedule for the six months ended September 30, 19x1, which is simple and will not be illustrated here, will show a cash balance of $47,140.

As the liquidation process proceeds, the trustee will issue additional periodic reports showing all cash receipts and disbursements and their effect on the estate deficit. After all liabilities with priority, fully and partly secured creditors have been paid off the number of cents on the dollar which will be distributed on a pro rata basis to unsecured creditors, which includes the unpaid portion of partly secured liabilities, will be determined as follows:

Cash available for unsecured creditors
_____
Total claims of unsecured creditors

In the event that the cash remaining exceeds the total claims of unsecured creditors the balance is paid to equity holders.

QUESTIONS

1. Briefly describe what is meant by insolvency.

2. The resolution of financial difficulties or of insolvency can take either a nonjudicial or a jucicial route. Outline the various options available to a firm in financial difficulty under each of these routes.

3. Briefly discuss the alternatives available under the nonjudicial route to a firm in financial difficulty.

4. Who may file (a) a voluntary petition with the bankruptcy court? (b) an involuntary petition with the bankruptcy court?

5. What major duties are specified by law for a trustee in a business reorganization?

6. What are the general effects of a confirmation, by the court, of a plan of reorganization?

7. What is the basic difference between a quasi reorganization and a court-approved reorganization?

8. What is the sequence that has to be followed when distributing the cash received in a business liquidation in satisfaction of all claims and liabilities?

9. What does a statement of affairs represent and what is its purpose?

10. What is the purpose of the preparation of a realization and liquidation account?

EXERCISES

Exercise 20–1. Among the provisions of Hogan Company's arrangement confirmed by the bankruptcy court on September 30, 19x7, under the provision of Chapter 11 of the Bankruptcy Act were the following:

1. Amend articles of incorporation to provide for 200,000 shares of $1 par authorized capital stock, 2,000 shares to be exchanged on a share-for-share basis for 2,000 shares of $30 par capital stock currently outstanding.
2. Issue 2,000 shares of $1 par capital stock with a current fair value of $15 a share and $20,000 cash to unsecured trade creditors, in full settlement of their claims totaling $60,000.

Required:

Prepare journal entries for the above provisions of Hogan Company's arrangement at September 30, 19x7.

Exercise 20–2. Compute the amount that will probably be paid to each class of creditors, using the following information taken from the statement of affairs of Carol Company:

Assets pledged with fully secured creditors (current fair value, $37,500)	$45,000
Assets pledged with partially secured creditors (current fair value, $26,000)	37,000
Free assets (current fair value, $20,000)	35,000
Liability with priority	3,500
Fully secured creditors	15,000
Partially secured creditors	30,000
Unsecured creditors	56,000

Exercise 20–3. The following information for Duke Book Company was obtained by an accountant retained by the company's major creditors:

1. Furniture and fixtures: carrying amount, $50,000; current fair value, $40,500; pledged on a note payable of $32,000 on which unpaid interest of $700 has accrued.
2. Book manuscripts owned: carrying amount, $10,000; current fair value, $5,200; pledged on a note payable of $7,000; interest is paid up to date specified on the note.
3. Books in process of production: accumulated cost (direct materials, direct labor, and factory overhead), $30,000; net realizable value upon completion, $50,000; additional out-of-pocket costs of $9,200 will be required to complete the books in process.

Required:

Prepare the headings for the asset side of a statement of affairs and illustrate how each of the three items described above should be shown in the statement.

Exercise 20–4. Jason Jones, appointed receiver of Brown's Bootery, has prepared a statement of affairs. Assets against which there are no claims or liens are expected to produce $65,000, which must be allocated to unsecured claimants in all classes totaling $100,000.

The following claims are outstanding:

1. Fee for Jason Jones, receiver, $1,400.
2. Judy Bart, who holds a note for $1,100 on which

$70 of interest has accrued. The note is not secured.

3. Linda Gamble, who holds a note for $3,300, secured by $4,500 of receivables, estimated to be 60 percent collectible.

4. Scott Landger, who holds a $1,600 note on which $30 of interest has accrued. Property with a book value of $1,000 and a market value of $1,700 is pledged to guarantee payment of principal and interest.

5. Unpaid property tax of $4,000.

Required:

From the information given above:

a. Determine the amount allocable to each class in order of priority.

b. Determine the amount each of the claimants may expect to realize.

Exercise 20–5. During the examination of the financial statements of Hogan Corporation, you note that as of September 30, 19x9:

1. Current liabilities exceed current assets.
2. Total assets substantially exceed total liabilities.
3. Cash position is poor and current payables are past due.
4. Trade and secured creditors are pressing for payment, and several lawsuits have been commenced against Hogan.

Further investigation reveals the following:

1. In August 31, 19x9, Hogan made $1,000 payment to Delta on a $21,000 mortgage indebtedness over one year in arrears. The fair market value of the mortgage property is $40,000.

2. On September 20, 19x9, a trade creditor, Zuber, obtained a judgment against Hogan which under applicable law constitutes a lien on Hogan's real property.

3. On September 22, 19x9, Hogan paid a substantial amount to Miller, a supplier, on an account over one year old.

4. On September 27, 19x9, Hogan executed and delivered a financing statement to Helms, a vendor, from whom Hogan had purchased some new machinery six months earlier. Helms duly filed and perfected the financing statement.

Required:

a. As of September 30, 19x9, did any of the above transactions legally constitute an act of bankruptcy? Explain.

b. As of September 30, 19x9, could the creditors of Hogan file an involuntary petition in bankruptcy against Hogan if a sufficient number of them having a sufficient amount of claims decide to do so? Explain.

c. Independent of your answers to (*a*) and (*b*) above, assume the same facts set out above except that Hogan files a voluntary petition in bankruptcy and a trustee has been appointed.

(*1*) What are the rights, if any, of the trustee against each of the creditors involved in the four transactions stated in the problem? Explain.

(*2*) What are the general requirements for creditors to be entitled to vote on and participate in a bankruptcy proceeding? Explain for each of the four creditors involved whether he meets these requirements? Why?

(AICPA adapted)

PROBLEMS

Problem 20–6. On October 31, 19x8, M. Martin, a toy manufacturer, prepared the following enumeration of resources and creditor claims:

Resources:

Petty cash, $300, including expense vouchers for $120.

Cash, $2,620.

Accounts receivable, $3,670 of which $3,370 are believed to be collectible.

Toy materials and supplies, $12,100; estimated market value, $8,600.

Toys in process, $8,100; estimated market value, $3,000.

Building, $19,900; estimated market value, $8,000.

Display equipment, $11,500; estimated market value, $8,100.

Claims:

Accounts payable:

A & Z Supply Company	$ 3,000
Brown Company	6,000
Irwin, Inc.	16,000

Notes payable:

City Bank, $22,000. The display equipment is pledged as collateral.

Indiana Finance Company, $15,500. Unsecured notes receivable, $11,000, and warehouse receipts for finished goods are pledged as collateral. The finished goods (manufactured toys) have a book value of $7,500 and an estimated current value of $7,000. The notes receivable are estimated to be fully collectible.

Accrued wages, $1,700.

Required:

a. Prepare a statement of affairs as of October 31, 19x8.

b. Prepare a schedule of payment to creditors on this date indicating whether the amount of the settlement is a full or a partial liquidation.

Problem 20-7. On November 30, 19x6, a receiver was appointed for Brown, Inc., and on this date, the following was its balance sheet:

Assets

Petty cash		$ 150
Cash in bank		2,500
Accounts receivable . . .	$30,000	
Notes receivable	22,000	$52,000
Less: Allowance for bad debts		350	51,650
Accrued interest, notes receivable		500
Merchandise		29,000
Prepaid insurance		340
Prepaid advertising		160
Building	81,000	
Less: Accumulated depreciation	21,000	60,000
Furniture and fixtures . .	7,300	
Less: Accumulated depreciation	1,600	5,700
Organization costs		1,800
Goodwill		5,000
		$156,800

Liabilities and Equity

Accrued wages	$ 2,900		
Accrued property tax . . .	1,800		
Accounts payable	79,000		
Notes payable	15,600		
Accrued interest payable .	200		$ 99,500
Contributed capital:			
Common stock, par value	72,000		
Paid-in capital in excess of par	3,000	$75,000	
Retained earnings:			
Deficit		(17,700)	57,300
			$156,800

It is estimated that the conversion of assets will realize cash in the following amounts:

Notes receivable (with accrued interest)	$20,200
Accounts receivable	22,000
Merchandise	21,300
Building	24,000
Fixtures and furniture	2,100

Notes payable of $11,000 are secured by merchandise, the book value of which is $22,000. Notes payable of $4,600 are secured by the furniture and fixtures. Interest expense is allocable ratably to all outstanding notes payable.

Required:

a. Prepare a statement of affairs as of November 31, 19x6.

b. Prepare a supporting deficiency account as of this date.

Problem 20-8. Jones Manufacturing Corporation had a very unstable financial condition caused by a deficiency of quick assets. On June 25, 19x8, the following information was available:

Cash	$ 300
Accounts receivable	5,100
Raw material	12,200
Work in process	39,000
Finished goods	6,800
Machinery	38,000
Accounts payable	29,400
Capital stock	65,000
Retained earnings	7,200

In order to continue operations it became necessary to obtain sufficient cash to pay for payroll and other expenses. The principal creditors decided to advance $7,000 to Jones Corporation to enable it to meet its current obligations, and they also decided to continue operations until the present work in process stock is completed and sold. A trustee was appointed by the creditors to conduct these operations.

During the trusteeship period, from June 26 to November 30, 19x8, the following transactions were completed:

Cash disbursements:

For labor	$15,000
For other expenses	4,250
Purchasing of raw material on account	5,300
Sales on account	75,000
Expenses incurred on account	12,500
Loss on collection of old accounts	290

At the end of the trusteeship period, the unliquidated account balances were accounts receivable (new), $4,210; raw materials, $2,500; finished goods, $32,000; machinery, $38,000; and accounts payable (new), $400.

Required:

Prepare a statement of realization and liquidation with supporting schedules. Ignore the effects of depreciation on operating profit determination.

Problem 20–9. Rainbow Company is having considerable difficulty paying its liabilities as they become due. At November 20, 19x6, the following information for Rainbow Company is available:

	Carrying amount
Cash	$ 5,000
Accounts receivable (current fair value is equal to carrying amount)	40,000
Inventories (net realizable value, $20,000; pledged on $23,000 of notes payable)	41,000
Equipment (current fair value $70,500; pledged on mortgage note payable)	140,000
Accumulated depreciation	30,000
Supplies (current fair value, $2,000)	3,000
Wages payable	6,400
Income taxes payable	2,500
Accounts payable	65,000
Notes payable	43,000
Morgage note payable, including interest of $500	60,500
Capital stock, $10 par	110,000
Deficit	88,400

Required:

a. Prepare a statement of affairs at November 20, 19x6.

b. Prepare a working paper showing the estimated percentage of claim each group of creditors should expect to receive if Rainbow Company petitions for bankruptcy.

Problem 20–10. Duke Corporation was in financial difficulty. Its stockholders and creditors had asked for the liquidation of the corporation. The current fair values of Duke Corporation's assets and liabilities on January 1, 19x7, were as follows:

Assets

Cash	$ 800
Accounts receivable	20,000
Inventories	18,000
Marketable securities	1,000
Land	25,000
Building	35,000
Equipment	15,000

Liabilities

Wages payable	$ 2,000
Income taxes payable	1,000
Estimated liquidation costs payable	3,800
Morgage note payable	45,000
Accrued mortgage interest payable	400
Notes payable—bank	34,600
Accounts payable	35,000

Duke Corporation filed a voluntary petition for bankruptcy under the bankruptcy Act on January 2, 19x7. The bankruptcy court appointed a trustee to implement the liquidation of the company. The following transactions were completed by the trustee in January 19x7:

Jan. 5 Sold the land and the building for $63,000 cash and paid $45,500 to the mortgagee. The payment included interest of $100 which accrued in January.

9 Made the following cash payments:

Wages payable	$ 2,000
Income tax payable	1,000
Completion of inventories	500
Liquidation costs	800

31 Cash receipts for the period from January 7 to January 31 were as follows:

Collections on accounts receivable	$18,000
Sale of inventories	17,800
Sale of marketable securities	1,100

31 Additional cash payments were:

Liquidation costs	$ 1,300
Notes payable to bank (secured portion)	11,000
Dividend to unsecured creditors (60 cents on the dollar)	34,160

Required:

a. Prepare the journal entries for the transactions listed above in the accounting records of the trustee.

b. Prepare a statement of realization and liquidation for the month of January 19x7.

c. Prepare a trial balance for the trustee at January 31, 19x7.

Problem 20–11. A receiver was appointed on December 31, 19x6, to take charge of the Ruptbank Corporation. On that day, the following information was available:

RUPTBANK CORPORATION
Balance Sheet
December 31, 19x6

Assets

Cash	$ 12,000
Accounts receivable (net)	13,000
Inventories	20,000
Land	5,000
Building (net)	20,000
Equipment (net)	30,000
Total	$100,000

Liabilities and Equity

Accrued wages	$ 6,000
Bank note payable	20,000
Accounts payable	32,000
Interest payable—note	1,200
Interest payable—bonds	800
Bonds payable	20,000
Common stock	50,000
Retained earnings (deficit)	(30,000)
Total	$100,000

a. Realization estimates are as follows:
  1. Accounts receivable, $9,000.
  2. Land, $12,000.
  3. Building, $18,000.
  4. Equipment, $10,000.
  5. Inventories, $14,000.
b. The accounts receivable were pledged as security for the bank note payable.
c. Liquidation expenses are $5,000.
d. The land and building are pledged as collateral to the bondholders.

21

Accounting for nonbusiness organizations: State and local governments— general fund

OVERVIEW

At present the principles and standards relating to accounting for nonbusiness organizations differ from those relating to accounting for business organizations. One school of thought believes that the objectives and, consequently, the reporting for nonbusiness organizations should be different from those of business organizations because of the many restrictions imposed on nonbusiness organizations to which business organizations are not subject. The other school of thought believes that the similarities between the objectives of business and nonbusiness organizations far outweigh their differences and that it is possible to design one framework of principles and reporting standards that could be used by both types of organizations. The resolution of these differences between the two schools of thought is still in an early stage.

State and local governments presently use accounting methods known as fund accounting. The fundamental equation for fund accounting theory is Assets = Restrictions on assets. Budgeting plays an extremely important role in fund accounting, and may be unique in that role since budgeting is required and forms the basis of entries that are journalized in the government's journals. State and local governments make use of several different funds which are subject to separate accountability. Transactions which are not recorded in a specialized fund are recorded in the General Fund which is used for most day-to-day operations.

The objectives of this and the following chapter are twofold. The first is to impart to the reader an understanding of current thinking in the field of accounting for nonbusiness organizations, particularly in the light of the many changes which occurred recently and the likelihood of further changes occurring in this area in the near future. At the present time the form and the type of changes that are desirable is subject to controversy. The second objective is to impart to the reader a good understanding of the principles and the standards which are applicable to this field of study. A more comprehensive treatment of this subject can be found in specialized texts devoted entirely to this subject.[1]

CONCEPTUAL MATTERS

The basic issues which presently concern the accounting for nonbusiness organizations can be stated as follows:

1. Should the accounting for nonbusiness organizations be different from that of the accounting for business entities?
2. If such difference is warranted, should there also be a further differentiation between accounting for state and local governments as distinct from other nonbusiness organizations such as hospitals, colleges, and membership organizations?

Prior to the 1920s business and nonbusiness accounting were essentially the same. It was during the 1920s that municipalities began using fund accounting, and over the years mutations occurred to the point where five types of fund accouting are in use today.[2]

State and local governments generally use a version of fund accounting that is different from others, and yet, is in many respects similar to them. The American Institute of CPAs issued an audit guide on this topic.[3] In addition, they issued four audit guides covering other types of nonbusiness organizations. They are:

1. *Audits of Colleges and Universities* (1973).
2. *Hospital Audit Guide* (1972).
3. *Audits of Voluntary Health and Welfare Organizations* (1974).
4. *Accounting Principles and Reporting Practices for Certain Nonprofit Organizations* (1979).

Both business and nonbusiness entities are similar in many respects. For example:

> The operating environments of nonbusiness organizations and business enterprises are similar in many ways. Both nonbusiness organizations and business enterprises produce and distribute goods or services and use scarce resources in doing so. They sometimes provide essentially the same

---

[1] For example, see Leon E. Hay, *Accounting for Governmental and Nonprofit Entities*, 6th ed. (Homewood, Ill.: Richard D. Irwin, 1980).

[2] Robert N. Anthony, "Making Sense of Nonbusiness Accounting, " *Harvard Business Review* (May–June 1980), p. 84.

[3] Committee on Governmental Accounting and Auditing, *Audits of State and Local Government Units*, 2d ed. (New York, AICPA, 1980).

goods or services. For example, both municipal transportation systems significantly subsidized by general tax revenues and private bus lines may carry passengers within a large city, and both private nonprofit organizations supported by significant philanthropy and investor-owned enterprises may operate theatrical, dance, and musical organizations. Both nonbusiness organizations and business enterprises obtain resources from external sources and are accountable to those who provide resources or their representatives. Both are integral parts of the national economy and interrelate directly or indirectly with other organizations. Both own or control supplies of resources, some of which are used in current operations and some of which are held for use in future periods. Both incur obligations. Some nonbusiness organizations, as well as business enterprises, incur and pay taxes, and both are subject to governmental laws and regulations. Both must be financially viable: to achieve their operating objectives, they must, *in the long run*, receive at least as many resources as they need to provide goods and services at levels satisfactory to resource providers and other constituents. Both generally obtain resources from the same pool of resource providers, and the resources available for use by all organizations are limited.[4]

Both nonbusiness organizations and business enterprises obtain resources in exchange transactions in markets. Both obtain labor, materials, and facilities or their use by paying for them or agreeing to pay for them in the future. Both may borrow funds through bank loans, mortgages, or other direct loans or through issuing debt securities to creditors who commonly may evaluate and compare the risks and returns of securities of both nonbusiness organizations and business enterprises.[5]

There are, however, differences between these types of entities, and these can be summarized as follows:

1. Business organizations are organized for profit while nonbusiness organizations are not.
2. Business organizations obtain revenues from the sale of goods and services. While nonbusiness organizations may get some revenues from the sale of goods and services, they generally obtain revenues from taxes, donations, dues, and assessments.
3. Nonbusiness organizations may have restrictions imposed on them by donors or governments, and, accordingly, their revenues may be expendable only in accordance with such imposed restrictions.
4. In many nonbusiness organizations such as governments, budgetary accounting may be a significant control mechanism and is almost universally used whereas in business entities budgetary accounting is usually optional. The degree of control may be radically different even when both types of organizations use budgetary accounting. Exceeding a budgetary allowance in a governmental unit usually requires compelling reasons and possible reductions elsewhere, while business entities may not be subject to similar control aspects.

---

[4]FASB, *Statement of Financial Accounting Concepts No. 4,* "Objectives of Financial Reporting by Nonbusiness Organizations" (Stamford, Conn., 1980), p. 8. Copyright © (1980) by Financial Accounting Standards Board, High Ridge Park, Stamford, Connecticut, 06905, U.S.A. Reprinted with permission. Copies of the complete document are available from the FASB.

[5]Ibid., p. 9.

DICHOTOMY OF NONBUSINESS ACCOUNTING

Currently there are two main schools of thought regarding the accounting for nonbusiness organizations. One school of thought believes that there is little difference between business and nonbusiness accounting and, therefore, its advocates believe that nonbusiness accounting could, with minor exceptions, make use of the principles applicable to business accounting. Robert N. Anthony, author of an FASB *Research Report* entitled "Financial Accounting in Nonbusiness Organizations: An Exploratory Study of Conceptual Issues," states, in his analysis of the Exposure Draft (ED)[6]:

> I think the ED leads clearly to the conclusion that nonbusiness accounting is going to be essentially like business accounting. Nonbusiness organizations will prepare operating statements, balance sheets and funds flow statements. The primary focus will be on the operating statement, and its preparation will be governed by the same principles that now apply in business accounting. Furthermore, these principles will apply to all nonbusiness organizations, including state and local governments.[7]

Professor Anthony also notes that there are certain differences between fund accounting and commercial accounting. As an example, he states:

> A nonbusiness organization, however, has one type of resource inflow that has no counterpart in business. This is contributed capital. Many organizations receive funds for endowment, and the essential nature of such funds is that the principal must be maintained intact, leaving only the earnings on this principal available for operating purposes.[8]

Paragraph 45 of the Exposure Draft contains the following:

> Financial reporting should provide information about the service efforts of a nonbusiness organization. . . .[9]

Additionally, footnote 23 contains:

> Accrual accounting is concerned with the timing of recognizing transactions, events, and circumstances that have financial effects on an organization. . . .
>
> For example, whether certain inflows of financial resources, such as taxes, grants, and contributions, should be recognized in the period when a claim arises, when they are received, when they are appropriated for use, when they are used, or when other events occur, is beyond the scope of this Statement.[10]

The other school of thought believes that fund accounting, as it is presently practiced, will remain in vogue, and rightly so. In a recent article, the advantages of fund accounting were extolled both from the legal point of

---

[6]FASB Exposure Draft, *Objectives of Financial Reporting by Nonbusiness Organizations* (Stamford, Conn., 1980).

[7]Robert N. Anthony, "Nonbusiness Financial Reporting: Is there Enough Guidance?" *Journal of Accountancy* (August 1980), p. 49.

[8]Robert N. Anthony, "Making Sense of Nonbusiness Accounting," *Harvard Business Review* (May–June 1980), p. 88.

[9]FASB, *SFAC 4*, p. 25.

[10]Ibid.

view and from a management control evaluation viewpoint. The authors of the article maintain that, for many reasons, fund accounting should be maintained. Some of these are:

1. Funds have legal restrictions or discretionary restrictions and, accordingly, they must be segregated between "restricted" and "unrestricted" funds.
2. The use of budgetary accounting acts as a control mechanism in measuring the progress of desired financial results.
3. The use of encumbrances permits ready access to unencumbered (amounts available for future spending) balances even though purchases for future delivery have not yet been vouchered.
4. The segregation of funds provides information regarding the legal limits on their use, their purpose, and the discretionary restrictions imposed by the board of directors. Transfers between funds are also highlighted.[11]

Fund accounting, as presently practiced and as discussed in this article will be the focus of the remainder of this chapter as well as the next one.

FUND ACCOUNTING—STATE AND LOCAL GOVERNMENTS

Various organizations contribute to the development of standards used in governmental accounting. The federal government is generally not included in this standard-setting activity because the General Accounting Office (GAO) by law has jurisdiction over accounting standards for the federal government. Federal government accounting is beyond the scope of this text. State and local governments, however, are subject to standards set by state governments and the National Council of Governmental Accounting (NCGA) as organized by the Municipal Finance Officers Association (MFOA). In 1968, the NCGA issued *Government Accounting, Auditing and Financial Reporting* (GAAFR), and this publication was considered to be the authoritative pronouncement on the subject until 1974 when the AICPA issued its Industry Audit Guide. At that time the MFOA convened a new committee of NCGA to restudy and restate GAAFR and that culminated in the issuance of an Exposure Draft in 1978 and NCGA *Statement No. 1*[12] in March 1979. The latter pronouncement now is considered the authoritative source of reporting in accordance with generally accepted accounting principles (GAAP) for state and local governments. In some cases a conflict may arise between GAAP and compliance with legal provisions. When this occurs, the books can be maintained to comply with the legal requirements and the reporting can include adjustments that are necessary to comply with GAAP. The first principle in the NCGA *Statement* states that:

A governmental accounting system must make it possible both: (a) to present fairly and with full disclosure the financial position and results of finan-

---

[11]Regina E. Herzlinger and H. David Sherman, "Advantages of Fund Accounting in 'Nonprofits,'" *Harvard Business Review* (May–June 1980), pp. 94–105.

[12]National Council on Government Accounting, *Governmental Accounting and Financial Reporting Principles, Statement 1* (Chicago: Municipal Finance Officers Association, 1979).

cial operations of the funds and account groups of the governmental unit in conformity with generally accepted accounting principles; and (b) to determine and demonstrate compliance with finance-related legal and contractual provisions.[13]

DEFINITION AND TYPES OF FUNDS

A *fund* has a specific meaning in nonbusiness accounting. The second principle in the NCGA *Statement* contains:

> A fund is defined as a fiscal and accounting entity with a self-balancing set of accounts recording cash and other financial resources, together with all related liabilities and residual equities, or balances, and changes therein which are segregated for the purpose of carrying on specific activities or attaining certain objectives in accordance with special regulations, restrictions, or limitations.[14]

While there are no limits on the number of funds that a state or local government may use, it is best to use only those funds that are needed. Thus, a state or local government would use separate funds to account for, (1) the construction of capital projects; (2) the payment of interest and principal on bonded indebtedness; (3) services rendered to the community on a user-charge basis, such as an electric or water utility; (4) activities where the state or local government acts as a trustee or agent for other individuals or governments; and (5) its ongoing activities not accounted for elsewhere.

The *Statement* lists eight types of funds that should be used by state and local governments. These funds are categorized as:

A. *Governmental Funds*

    (1) *The General Fund*—to account for all financial resources except those required to be accounted for in another fund.

    (2) *Special Revenue Funds*—to account for the proceeds of specific revenue sources (other than special assessments, expendable trusts, or for major capital projects) that are legally restricted to expenditure for specified purposes.

    (3) *Capital Projects Funds*—to account for financial resources to be used for the acquisition or construction of major capital facilities (other than those financed by proprietary funds, Special Assessment Funds, and Trust Funds).

    (4) *Debt Service Funds*—to account for the accumulation of resources for, and the payment of, general long-term debt principal and interest.

    (5) *Special Assessment Funds*—to account for the financing of public improvements or services deemed to benefit the properties against which special assessments are levied.

B. *Proprietary Funds*

    (6) *Enterprise Funds*—to account for operations *(a)* that are financed and operated in a manner similar to private business enterprises—where the intent of the governing body is that the costs

[13]Ibid., p. 4.
[14]Ibid., pp. 5–6.

(expenses, including depreciation) of providing goods or services
to the general public on a continuing basis be financed or recovered primarily through user charges; or *(b)* where the governing
body has decided that periodic determination of revenues earned,
expenses incurred, and/or net income is appropriate for capital
maintenance, public policy, management control, accountability,
or other purposes.

(7) *Internal Service Funds*—to account for the financing of goods or
services provided by one department or agency to other departments or agencies of the governmental unit, or to other governmental units, on a cost-reimbursement basis.

C. *Fiduciary Funds*

(8) *Trust and Agency Funds*—to account for assets held by a governmental unit in a trustee capacity or as an agent for individuals,
private organizations, other governmental units and/or other
funds. These include *(a)* Expendable Trust Funds, *(b)* Nonexpendable Trust Funds, *(c)* Pension Trust Funds, and *(d)* Agency
Funds.[15]

NUMBER OF FUNDS

The number of funds is covered by the fourth principle which contains:

> Governmental units should establish and maintain those funds required by
> law and sound financial administration. Only the minimum number of
> funds consistent with legal and operating requirements should be estab
> lished, however, since unnecessary funds result in inflexibility, undue com
> plexity, and inefficient financial administration.[16]

ACCOUNTING FOR FIXED ASSETS AND LONG-TERM LIABILITIES

The fifth principle covers fixed assets other than those accounted for in
proprietary or trust funds and liabilities not accounted for elsewhere. The
principle is as follows:

a. Fixed assets related to specific proprietary funds or Trust Funds should
be accounted for through those funds. All other fixed assets of a governmental unit should be accounted for through the General Fixed Assets
Account Group.

b. Long-term liabilities of proprietary funds, Special Assessment Funds,
and Trust Funds should be accounted for through those funds. All other
unmatured general long-term liabilities of the governmental unit should
be accounted for through the General Long-Term Debt Account Group.[17]

The cost of fixed assets which are accounted for by a proprietary fund,
such as a water or electric utility, is recovered through user charges. Therefore, these fixed assets are accounted for separately. General fixed assets,
however, are not accounted for in a fund. The reason for this is that they
are not resources that can be used to meet obligations nor are their costs

[15]Ibid., p. 7.
[16]Ibid., p. 8.
[17]Ibid.

recovered through user charges. Since the objectives of state and local governments are to render services, rather than to earn profits, it is not necessary to provide depreciation on these fixed assets. Instead, they are recorded in a self-balancing group of accounts rather than in fund.

Except for the liabilities of proprietary, trust, and special assessment funds where the liabilities of these funds are liquidated from resources provided by these funds, unmatured general long-term debt is not accounted for in a fund. The reasoning for this is similar to that noted above for general fixed assets. This unmatured debt will not require the use of any current operating funds, and when they do mature, general revenues rather than specific revenues will be needed to satisfy the debt.

Thus, the unmatured general long-term debt is accounted for in a self-balancing group of accounts rather than in a fund.

VALUATION OF FIXED ASSETS

The sixth principle covers the valuation of fixed assets as follows:

> Fixed assets should be accounted for at cost or, if the cost is not practicably determinable, at estimated cost. Donated fixed assets should be recorded at their estimated fair value at the time received.[18]

DEPRECIATION OF FIXED ASSETS

Depreciation of fixed assets is covered by the seventh principle as follows:

   a. Depreciation of general fixed assets should not be recorded in the accounts of governmental funds. Depreciation of general fixed assets may be recorded in cost accounting systems or calculated for cost finding analyses; and accumulated depreciation may be recorded in the General Fixed Assets Account Group.

   b. Depreciation of fixed assets accounted for in a proprietary fund should be recorded in the accounts of that fund. Depreciation is also recognized in those Trust Funds where expenses, net income, and/or capital maintenance are measured.[19]

In commercial accounting an attempt is made to match revenues with the cost of generating them. Accordingly, if a piece of equipment is used in a manufacturing process, the portion of the equipment consumed in the revenue-generating process is matched against the revenue earned through the use of a depreciation charge. Whenever a state or local government uses equipment in this manner, such as in providing electricity, depreciation of fixed assets is appropriate. However, the bulk of a state or local government's equipment is not used for such purposes. For example, fixed assets used to provide police protection do not generate revenue on a user-charge basis and, therefore, depreciation expense is not required to match revenues and costs.

The seventh principle above notwithstanding, many accountants believe that depreciation should be reflected in the above example. They contend that the *total cost* of providing services should be reported even though the

[18]Ibid., p. 9.
[19]Ibid., p. 10.

matching principle does not apply. Thus far, the practice is not employed except in the case of proprietary funds and trust funds where capital maintenance is measured.

BASIS OF ACCOUNTING—ACCRUAL BASIS IN GOVERNMENTAL ACCOUNTING

The eighth principle deals with the appropriate use of the accrual basis and the modified accrual basis of accounting. The accrual basis in nonbusiness accounting is the same as in business accounting. Modified accrual accounting, however, requires elucidation. Generally, with regard to revenues, the cash basis is used *except* when *both* of the following are present:

1. The revenues are *available* for financing governmental operations.
2. The revenues can be measured objectively.

If both conditions are present, then accrual accounting is used. An example of a case where accrual would be used is when real estate property taxes are levied and the tax invoices are sent to property owners. The revenues are objectively measurable since they are based on assessed property values, and when the taxes are levied they become available for use by the government. Since collection is virtually assured, estimated uncollectibles can be provided for as in business accounting. Examples of revenues that are not usually susceptible of accrual are self-assessed taxes such as income taxes and sales taxes. These are accounted for on the cash basis when they are received.

Alternatively, expenditures are on the accrual basis if they can be objectively measured, except for interest on general long-term debt and the long-term portion of unfunded pension liability which is recognized as an expenditure when it is due. The *Statement* contains the following:

The modified accrual or accrual basis of accounting, as appropriate, should be utilized in measuring financial position and operating results.

a. *Governmental fund* revenues and expenditures should be recognized on the modified accrual basis. Revenues should be recognized in the accounting period in which they become available and measurable. Expenditures should be recognized in the accounting period in which the fund liability is incurred, if measurable, except for unmatured interest on general long-term debt and on special assessment indebtedness secured by interest-bearing special assessment levies, which should be recognized when due.

b. *Proprietary fund* revenues and expenses should be recognized on the accrual basis. Revenues should be recognized in the accounting period in which they are earned and become measurable; expenses should be recognized in the period incurred, if measurable.

c. *Fiduciary fund* revenues and expenses or expenditures (as appropriate) should be recognized on the basis consistent with the fund's accounting measurement objective. Nonexpendable Trust and Pension Trust Funds should be accounted for on the accrual basis; Expendable Trust Funds should be accounted for on the modified accrual basis. Agency Fund assets and liabilities should be accounted for on the modified accrual basis.

    d.   *Transfers* should be recognized in the accounting period in which the interfund receivable and payable arise.[20]

The term *expenditure* has a slightly different meaning in fund accounting from that used in commercial accounting. In fund accounting, an expenditure is recorded for any good or service received regardless of whether or not the utility of that good or service has expired. Thus, rent paid for the use of premises is an expenditure that may be an expired cost while the purchase of a long-lived piece of equipment is also an expenditure even though it represents an unexpired cost in commercial accounting. The distinction between expired and unexpired costs is not relevant in fund accounting except for proprietary funds and trust funds that measure capital maintenance.

Alternatively, expenses in fund accounting have the same meaning as in commercial accounting. An example to refine the distinction might be the purchase of supplies that are to be carried as inventory. The purchase of the supplies would be considered an expenditure while the use of the supplies would be considered an expense. Recording the purchase of supplies as an expenditure and not as an inventory item of supplies is a departure from accrual accounting. Usually, the amounts involved are not material and can be ignored as is often the case in commercial accounting. However, where the amounts involved are significant, NCGA *Statement 1* provides that the inventory should be reported in the balance sheet.[21]

Interfund transfers are peculiar to fund accounting. Transfers to and from specific funds, such as from the General Fund to the Debt Service Fund for the payment of interest are classified as *operating transfers* (in and out). Other transfers, classified as *residual equity transfers,* are transfers such as from the Capital Projects Fund to the General Fund when the capital project construction is completed and any balance in the Capital Projects Fund is transferred in order to close the fund.

BUDGETING, ACCOUNT CLASSIFICATION, TERMINOLOGY, AND FINANCIAL REPORTING
Budgeting, budgetary control, and budgetary reporting
	The 9th, 10th, 11th, and 12th principles are reproduced as follows:
	
	9. *a.* An annual budget(s) should be adopted by every governmental unit.
	    b. The accounting system should provide the basis for appropriate budgetary control.
	    c. Budgetary comparisons should be included in the appropriate financial statements and schedules for governmental funds for which an annual budget has been adopted.

Transfer, revenue, expenditure, and expense account classifications	10. *a.* Interfund transfers and proceeds of general long-term debt issues should be classified separately from fund revenues and expenditures or expenses. *b.* Governmental fund revenues should be classified by fund and source. Expenditures should be classified by fund, function (or pro-

---

[20]Ibid., pp. 10–11.
[21]Ibid., p. 12.

gram), organization unit, activity, character, and principal classes
of objects.

    c. Proprietary fund revenues and expenses should be classified in essentially the same manner as those of similar business organizations, functions, or activities.

Common terminology and classification

11. A common terminology and classification should be used consistently throughout the budget, the accounts, and the financial reports of each fund.

Interim and annual financial reports

12. *a.* Appropriate interim financial statements and reports of financial position, operating results, and other pertinent information should be prepared to facilitate management control of financial operations, legislative oversight, and, where necessary or desired, for external reporting purposes.

    b. A comprehensive annual financial report covering all funds and account groups of the governmental unit—including appropriate combined, combining, and individual fund statements; notes to the financial statements; schedules; narrative explanations; and statistical tables—should be prepared and published.

    c. General purpose financial statements may be issued separately from the comprehensive annual financial report. Such statements should include the basic financial statements and notes to the financial statements that are essential to fair presentation of financial position and operating results (and changes in financial position of proprietary funds and similar Trust Funds).[22]

BUDGETING, CONTROL, AND REPORTING

BUDGETING

In business accounting, budgeting is primarily used for purposes of planning and control. However, the use of budgeting is optional in the business sector, while for governmental accounting, the ninth principle, cited earlier, prescribes the use of budgets for every governmental unit. Effective planning and control for governmental units are best achieved through the use of budgets.

Budgets are submitted by the heads of governmental units to their legislatures for adoption by the legislative bodies. Approval may either be for segment totals or for line items. The latter approach provides the greatest degree of control.

Of course, when the budget is approved, the revenues and appropriations are estimated since a budget is for a subsequent fiscal period. Nevertheless, in fund accounting, these estimated amounts are journalized. It is through journalization that control is achieved, since the actual amounts incurred as the fiscal year progresses are then available for comparison with the esti-

---

[22]Ibid., pp. 12–18.

mated amounts already journalized. A typical entry to record the budget would be:

Estimated Revenues	2,500,000	
Appropriations		2,400,000
Fund Balance		100,000

It is customary for governmental units to project a small surplus, as in the example above, in case the estimated revenues fall short or unforeseen expenditures arise. The fund balance is considered to be a residual equity account. By comparing the debits (estimated revenues) with the credits (actual revenues) in the ledger, it is readily apparent whether a shortfall or surplus will prevail. Similar comparisons can be made for appropriations and expenditures. An additional safeguard regarding the expenditure control mechanism is the use of encumbrances.

ENCUMBRANCES AND EXPENDITURES

The use of encumbrances acts as a brake on overspending when unfilled purchase orders are outstanding. Since encumbrances are journalized prior to the receipt of the goods or services, the encumbrances together with the expenditures are compared to the appropriation to prevent overspending. For example, if a department's appropriation for the year were $500,000 and expenditures, thus far, totaled $470,000, the unencumbered balance would be $30,000. If a purchase order were then issued for $30,000, the required journal entry would be:

Encumbrances	30,000	
Reserve for Encumbrances		30,000
To record the issuance of a purchase order.		

If further expenditures were contemplated, the encumbrance above plus the prior expenditures would total $500,000 and would equal the appropriation for the year, thereby acting to prevent further expenditures.

When the goods are received, the following entries would then be made:

Reserve for Encumbrances	30,000	
Encumbrances		30,000
To reverse encumbrance upon receipt of goods ordered.		

Expenditures	30,000	
Vouchers Payable		30,000
To voucher expenditures for merchandise received.		

If the invoice were for only $29,000, the reversal of the encumbrance would still be for $30,000 (assuming that the $29,000 were not a partial shipment) and the entry to record the expenditure would be for $29,000. An extended discussion of this aspect can be found in the comprehensive illustration in the next section of this chapter.

Encumbrances that are outstanding at the end of the year can be handled in two different ways depending upon the lapsing or nonlapsing of the encumbrance. This facet of encumbrances is illustrated in the comprehensive illustration that follows this section.

In the discussion that follows, the 12 principles will be illustrated and elaborated upon as appropriate. The remainder of this chapter will be devoted to a comprehensive illustration of the operation of the General Fund. The chapter which follows will cover the remaining funds used by state and local governments.

As noted earlier, the General Fund is used to account for all activities that are not reflected in another fund. As such, this fund usually contains most of the accounting for the day-to-day activities of a state or local government. Principal revenues of this fund consist of real estate taxes, self-assessed taxes, fines, license fees, and penalties. Expenditures generally consist of those costs necessary to provide services, such as fire and police protection and sanitation. Expenditures are classified by each function (service) performed. In addition, expenditures are also classified by object, such as wages, supplies, and others as a subset of each functional classification.

In accordance with the principles discussed earlier (see principle nine), a budgetary system is used and is reflected in the journalizing of General Fund entries. Since expenditures are limited by law and are reflected in the budget, encumbrances are generally used in General Fund accounting. When a purchase order is issued, the amount of the order is journalized as an encumbrance until the good or service is received, at which time the encumbrance is reversed and the purchase is journalized. Through this procedure, outstanding purchase orders reduce the unencumbered amount available for future spending and thereby prohibits excess expenditures which might be made if outstanding purchase orders were not reflected in the accounts of the General Fund.

To demonstrate the types of entries that would be used in a General Fund, the following is assumed:

General Fund

The City of Watertown is beginning its first year of operations. The city's first fiscal budget has been approved, and the following data are available:

1. Estimated revenues for the year are $600,000. Estimated appropriations are $590,000.
2. Property taxes of $400,000 are levied. It is estimated that 3 percent ($12,000) will not be collected.
3. Other revenues of $10,000 meet the criteria for accrual. Estimated uncollectible revenues amount to $400.
4. An order was placed for supplies for the police department in the amount of $3,000. When the supplies were received, the invoice amounted to $3,050 which included freight charges.
5. Payroll costs of $40,000 were vouchered.
6. Cash collections amounted to $350,000 for property taxes levied and $5,000 of previously accrued revenues for a total of $355,000.
7. Uncollected property taxes are now delinquent.

8. Self-assessed taxes, license fees, and fines were collected amounting to $205,000.
9. The supplies ordered in 4 above, was paid.
10. Miscellaneous supplies were ordered from various vendors. The total of the orders amounts to $30,000.
11. Invoices were received for the items ordered in 10 above amounting to $20,000. There were no differences between the respective purchase orders and the invoices.
12. Taxes were collected in advance in the amount of $800.
13. Delinquent taxes of $8,000 are uncollectible and are to be written off.
14. Delinquent taxes of $12,000 and $800 of interest and penalties were collected. The interest has not yet been accrued.
15. Interest and penalties on delinquent taxes amount to $4,000. This is in addition to the amount in 14 above. Uncollectible interest is estimated at $300.
16. Other expenditures during the year amount to $420,000. For purposes of this discussion, these expenditures are paid without vouchering them.
17. The Internal Service Fund furnished the fire department with $2,000 of operating supplies.
18. Interest and principal was paid to the Debt Service Fund amounting to $99,000.
19. Entries to close the estimated and actual revenues are made.
20. All other closing entries are made.

The entries to record the above follows:

(1)

Estimated Revenues	600,000	
Appropriations		590,000
Fund Balance		10,000

Entry (1) is the budgetary entry. This budget anticipates a $10,000 surplus.

(2)

Taxes Receivable—Current	400,000	
Estimated Uncollectible Taxes—Current		12,000
Revenues		388,000

Under the modified accrual method property taxes are usually "available" and "measurable." Accordingly, they meet the test for accrual.

(3)

Accounts Receivable	10,000	
Estimated Uncollectible Accounts Receivable		400
Revenues		9,600

These receivables meet the test for accrual and, therefore, they are accrued.

(4a)

Encumbrances	3,000	
Reserve for Encumbrances		3,000

(4b)

| Reserve for Encumbrances | 3,000 | |
| Encumbrances | | 3,000 |

(4c)

| Expenditures (Police Supplies) | 3,050 | |
| Vouchers Payable | | 3,050 |

The purchase order was issued for $3,000. Because of possible weight uncertainties and freight charges, the actual invoice was for $3,050. In entry (4a) the encumbrance is recorded for the amount of the purchase order. When the invoice is received, entry (4b) reverses the encumbrance in the original amount and entry (4c) records the actual expenditure. In this example, the supplies are not treated as inventory because they are assumed to be immaterial. In an appropriation account for the police department, the above transaction would be handled as follows:

	Encumbrances			Expenditures		Unencumbered balance
	Dr.	Cr.	Bal.	Item	Cumulative	
Appropriation . . .						$100,000
Salaries				$10,000	$10,000	90,000
Supplies ordered .	$3,000		$3,000			87,000
Supplies received .		$3,000	–0–	3,050	13,050	86,950

It should be noted how the encumbrance reduces the amount available for future expenditures even though the supplies were not received until a later date. The $50 difference reduces the unencumbered balance when the supplies are received.

(5)

| Expenditures (payroll) | 40,000 | |
| Vouchers Payable | | 40,000 |

An encumbrance is not required for expenditures such as payroll. Since there is no time lag (or a minor one) between the vouchering and incurrence of the expenditure, the encumbrance is usually omitted.

(6)

Cash	355,000	
Taxes Receivable—Current		350,000
Accounts Receivable		5,000

(7)

Taxes Receivable—Delinquent	50,000	
Taxes Receivable—Current		50,000
Estimated Uncollectible Taxes—Current	12,000	
Estimated Uncollectible Taxes—Delinquent		12,000

Not only are the current taxes receivable reclassified as delinquent, but the reclassification is also applied to the estimated uncollectibles as well.

(8)

| Cash | 205,000 | |
| Revenues | | 205,000 |

Revenues that do not meet the criteria for accrual are recorded when collected under the modified accrual method. Revenues that fall into this category are self-assessment taxes such as income taxes and sales taxes as well as fines and penalties.

(9)

Vouchers Payable	3,050	
Cash		3,050

(10)

Encumbrances	30,000	
Reserve for Encumbrances		30,000

(11)

Reserve for Encumbrances	20,000	
Encumbrances		20,000
Expenditures (police, fire supplies)	20,000	
Vouchers Payable		20,000

Sometimes partial shipments are received. When this occurs, only the portion received is reversed and vouchered. The remainder, in this case $10,000, still remains as an open encumbrance.

(12)

Cash	800	
Taxes Collected in Advance		800

Taxes collected in advance are not revenues in the year collected; instead, they are a balance sheet item (shown as a liability) as in business accounting.

(13)

Estimated Uncollectible Taxes—Delinquent	8,000	
Taxes Receivable—Delinquent		8,000

(14)

Cash	12,800	
Taxes Receivable—Delinquent		12,000
Revenues		800

(15)

Interest and Penalties Receivable	4,000	
Estimated Uncollectible Interest and Penalties		300
Revenues		3,700

In entry (14) the interest on delinquent taxes is recorded as revenue since the collection occurred prior to the year's end. In entry (15) an accrual is made for interest on delinquent taxes to be collected subsequent to the current year.

(16)

Expenditures (miscellaneous)	420,000	
Cash		420,000

The above entry is a summary entry summarizing many transactions occurring during the year.

(17)

Expenditures (fire department supplies)	2,000	
Due to Internal Service Fund		2,000

A contra entry on the books of the Internal Service Fund would be made as follows:

Due from General Fund	2,000	
Billings to Departments		2,000

In additional, one entry adjusting the supplies inventory could be made. The operation of an Internal Service Fund is covered in the next chapter.

(18)

Operating Transfers-Out	99,000	
Cash		99,000

Entries in the Debt Service Fund and in the General Long-Term Debt Account Group would also be made as a result of entry (18). These entries are covered in the next chapter.

(19)

Revenues	607,100	
Fund Balance		7,100
Estimated Revenues		600,000

It would be unusual for actual revenues to equal budgeted revenues. Accordingly, both revenue accounts are closed and the net difference between them treated as an adjustment of the Fund Balance. In this case the excess of $7,100 increases the anticipated surplus of $10,000

(20)

Appropriations	590,000	
Fund Balance	4,050	
Expenditures		485,050
Operating Transfers-Out		99,000
Encumbrances		10,000

Here, too, the actual expenditures (plus open encumbrances) did not equal the appropriations.

In entry (20) the open encumbrances were closed to the Fund Balance and the Reserve for Encumbrances was left open. This procedure is used when the open encumbrances are *nonlapsing*. The Reserve for Encumbrances is a balance sheet item and is shown as part of the Fund Equity. This can be seen in Illustration 21–1.

In the following year the following entry would be made:

Reserve for Encumbrances	10,000	
Reserve for Encumbrances—Prior Year		10,000
To reclassify prior year's reserve.		

When the goods are received, the following entry would be made:

Expenditures—Prior Year	10,000	
Vouchers Payable		10,000

At year's end, the following closing entry would be required:

Reserve for Encumbrances—Prior Year	10,000	
Expenditures—Prior Year		10,000
To close.		

If the expenditure were for a different amount from the open encumbr-

Illustration 21–1
CITY OF WATERTOWN
General Fund
Balance Sheet
December 31, 19x1

Assets

Cash		$51,550
Taxes receivable—delinquent	$30,000	
Less: Estimated uncollectible delinquent taxes	4,000	26,000
Interest and penalties receivable	4,000	
Less: Estimated uncollectible interest and penalties	300	3,700
Accounts receivable	5,000	
Less: Estimated uncollectible accounts	400	4,600
Total assets		$85,850

Liabilities and Fund Equity

Liabilities:		
Vouchers payable	$60,000	
Due to Internal Service Fund	2,000	
Taxes collected in advance	800	$62,800
Fund equity:		
Reserved for encumbrances	10,000	
Fund balance (unrestricted)	13,050	23,050
Total liabilities and fund equity		$85,850

ance, the difference would become an adjustment to the Fund Balance account when the closing entries are made.

The above procedure is the one that has been used throughout the tenure of GAAFR. With the advent of NCGA *Statement 1* (effective for fiscal years after June 30, 1980), an alternate procedure is recommended. Instead of the above treatment, the encumbrance is reversed at year-end as follows:

Reserve for Encumbrances	10,000	
Encumbrances		10,000
To reverse open encumbrance.		

In addition, a portion of the Fund Equity would be reserved for the open encumbrance as follows:

Fund Balance	10,000	
Fund Balance—Reserved for Encumbrances		10,000
To appropriate Fund Balances for open encumbrances.		

At the beginning of the following year, the above entries would be reversed. The essential difference between the two methods is that in the former case, the expenditure does not appear as an expenditure in the current year when the goods are received, while in the latter case the expenditure does appear as an expenditure in the current year. The balance sheet treatment is the same in both cases.

If the appropriation instead lapses, the encumbrance is reversed without any appropriation of the Fund Balance. If the goods are still needed, in the following year, they would then be reappropriated and encumbered the same as any new encumbrance.

INVENTORY OF SUPPLIES

Thus far, our treatment of supplies has been to treat them as expenditures since the amounts were considered immaterial. If the amounts were material, the following entry would be made.

Inventory of Supplies	2,000	
Expenditures		2,000
Fund Balance	2,000	
Reserve for Inventory of Supplies		2,000

The inventory and reserve would be adjusted each accounting period in accordance with the actual amount of supplies in inventory.

Illustration 21–2
CITY OF WATERTOWN
Statement of Revenues, Expenditures, and
Changes in Fund Balances—Budget and Actual—
General Fund
For the Fiscal Year Ended December 31, 19x1

	Budget	Actual	Variance favorable (unfavorable)
Revenues:			
Property taxes	$390,000	$388,000	$(2,000)
Licenses and permits	150,000	160,000	10,000
Intergovernmental revenues	10,000	12,000	2,000
Charges for services	15,000	10,000	(5,000)
Fines and forfeits	10,000	9,100	(900)
Miscellaneous revenues	25,000	28,000	3,000
Total revenues	$600,000	$607,100	$ 7,100
Expenditures:			
Current:			
General government	$160,000	$155,000	$ 5,000
Public safety	80,000	79,050	950
Highways and streets	40,000	32,000	8,000
Sanitation	35,000	36,000	(1,000)
Health	26,000	30,000	(4,000)
Welfare	30,000	29,000	1,000
Culture and recreation	80,000	85,000	(5,000)
Education	40,000	39,000	1,000
Total expenditures	491,000	485,050	5,950
Excess of revenues over (under) expenditures	$109,000	$122,050	$13,050
Other financing sources (uses):			
Operating transfers-out	$(99,000)	$(99,000)	—
Operating transfers-in	–0–	–0–	—
Excess of revenues over (under) expenditures and other uses	10,000	23,050	13,050
Less: Reserve for encumbrances—December 31, 19x1	–0–	10,000	(10,000)
Fund balances—January 1	–0–	–0–	–0–
Fund balances—December 31	$ 10,000	$ 13,050	$ 3,050

Note: The details of revenues and expenditures not apparent from the comprehensive Illustration are assumed for illustrative purposes.

FINANCIAL STATEMENTS   Although, in practice, combined statements are normally presented, for purposes of illustration separate statements for the General Fund are presented. A complete set of *combined* statements prepared in accordance with NCGA requirements appears at the end of Chapter 22 in the appendix.

A balance sheet for the General Fund at the end of 19x1 appears as Illustration 21–1, and a statement of revenues, expenditures and changes in fund balance appears as Illustration 21–2.

QUESTIONS

1. Fund accounting has a common body of principles, yet five different audit guides have been issued for different types of organizations that use fund accounting. What are the types of organizations that use fund accounting?

2. There are differences and similarities between business and nonbusiness organizations. What are some of each?

3. Two schools of thought exist regarding the future of fund accounting. What are they? Discuss each school of thought.

4. State and local governments are subject to standards set by various organizations. Which organizations set these standards?

5. What is a fund?

6. There are eight types of funds that state and local governments use. What are they? Give a brief description of their use.

7. Are all fixed assets and long-term liabilities generally accounted for in a fund? Explain. Are they sometimes accounted for in a fund? If so, when?

8. What is the valuation basis for fixed assets?

9. Are fixed assets generally depreciated? If not, why not? Are they sometimes depreciated? If so, when?

10. What is meant by the modified accrual basis?

11. There are two different types of interfund transfers. What are they? Use an example to illustrate each type.

12. What role does the use of budgets play in fund accounting?

13. What is meant by an encumbrance and how is it used?

14. Are there alternate treatments for open encumbrances at the end of a fiscal year? What are they?

15. If an open encumbrance is nonlapsing, where is it shown in the balance sheet? Why is it shown there?

16. When the inventory of supplies on hand is not material, how is it usually treated? When it is material, how should it be treated? Where is the reserve for inventory of supplies shown in the balance sheet?

17. What financial statements are customarily prepared at the end of a fiscal year for a General Fund?

EXERCISES

Exercise 21–1.

1. What is *not* a major concern of governmental units?

  a. Budgets.
  b. Funds.
  c. Legal requirements.
  d. Consolidated statements.

2. The initial transfer of cash from the general fund in order to establish an Internal Service Fund would require the General Fund to credit cash and debit—

  a. Accounts receivable—Internal Service Fund.
  b. Transfer to Internal Service Fund.
  c. Reserve for encumbrances.
  d. Appropriations.

3. Which of the following steps in the acquisition of goods and services occurs first?

a. Appropriation.

b. Encumbrance.

c. Budget.

d. Expenditure.

4. Which of the following terms refers to an actual cost rather than an estimate?

a. Expenditure.

b. Appropriation.

c. Budget.

d. Encumbrance.

5. When the budget of a governmental unit is adopted and the estimated revenues exceed the appropriations, the excess is—

a. Debited to reserve for encumbrances.

b. Credited to reserve for encumbrances.

c. Debited to fund balance.

d. Credited to fund balance.

6. Which of the following will increase the fund balance of a governmental unit at the end of the fiscal year?

a. Appropriations are less than expenditures and reserve for encumbrances.

b. Appropriations are less than expenditures and encumbrances.

c. Appropriations are more than estimated revenues.

d. Appropriations are more than expenditures and encumbrances.

7. If a credit was made to the fund balance in the process of recording a budget for a governmental unit, it can be assumed that—

a. Estimated expenses exceed actual revenues.

b. Actual expenses exceed estimated expenses.

c. Estimated revenues exceed appropriations.

d. Appropriations exceed estimated revenues.

8. Which of the following is a basic principle of governmental accounting?

a. In financial reporting legal provisions take precedence over generally accepted governmental accounting principles if there is a conflict.

b. The basis of accounting to be followed in recording transactions in the respective funds depends on the purpose for which the fund has been established. Funds must be matched with the appropriate budgetary accounts.

c. Depreciation can be ignored because no attempt is made to measure profit.

d. Every transaction must equally affect the General Fund and at least one other fund.

(AICPA adapted)

Exercise 21–2.

1. Of the items listed below, those most likely to have parallel accounting procedures, account titles, and financial statements are—

a. Special Revenue Funds and Special Assessment Funds.

b. Internal Service Funds and Debt Service Funds.

c. The General Fixed Assets Group of Accounts and the General Long-Term Debt Group of Accounts.

d. The General Fund and Special Revenue Funds.

2. Authority granted by a legislative body to make expenditures and to incur obligations during a fiscal year is the definition of an—

a. Appropriation.

b. Authorization.

c. Encumbrance.

d. Expenditure.

3. What type of account is used to earmark the fund balance to liquidate the contingent obligations of goods ordered but not yet received?

a. Appropriations.

b. Encumbrances.

c. Obligations.

d. Reserve for encumbrances.

4. Repairs that have been made for a governmental unit, and for which a bill has been received, should be recorded in the General Fund as an—

a. Appropriation.

b. Encumbrance.

c. Expenditure.

d. Expense.

5. The Reserve for Encumbrances—Past Year account represents amounts recorded by a governmental unit for—

a. Anticipated expenditures in the next year.

b. Expenditures for which purchase orders were made in the prior year but disbursement will be in the current year.

c. Excess expenditures in the prior year that will be offset against the current-year budgeted amounts.

d. Unanticipated expenditures of the prior year that become evident in the current year.

6. When a truck is received by a governmental unit, it should be recorded in the General Fund as a (an)—

a. Appropriation.
b. Encumbrance.
c. Expenditure.
d. Fixed asset.

7. How should wages that have been earned by the employees of a governmental unit, but *not* paid, be recorded in the General Fund?
a. Appropriation.
b. Encumbrance.
c. Expenditure.
d. Expense.

8. What financial statement is *not* recommended for the general fund?
a. Analysis of changes in fund balance.
b. Statement of cash receipts and disbursements.
c. Statement of expenditures and encumbrances compared with authorizations.
d. Statement of revenue—actual and estimated.

(AICPA adapted)

Exercise 21–3.

1. A city's General Fund budget for the forthcoming fiscal year shows estimated revenues in excess of appropriations. The initial effect of recording this will result in an increase in—
a. Taxes receivable.
b. Fund balance.
c. Reserve for encumbrances.
d. Encumbrances.

2. Under the modified accrual method of accounting used by a local governmental unit, which of the following would be a revenue susceptible to accrual?
a. Income taxes.
b. Business licenses.
c. Property taxes.
d. Sales taxes.

3. Which of the following accounts is a budgetary account in governmental accounting?
a. Reserve for inventory of supplies.
b. Fund balance.
c. Appropriations.
d. Estimated uncollectible property taxes.

4. What is the underlying reason a governmental unit uses separate funds to account for its transactions?
a. Governmental units are so large that it would be unduly cumbersome to account for all transactions as a single unit.
b. Because of the diverse nature of the services

offered and legal provisions regarding activities of a governmental unit, it is necessary to segregate activities by functional nature.
c. Generally accepted accounting principles require that not-for-profit entities report on a funds basis.
d. Many activities carried on by governmental units are short-lived and their inclusion in a general set of accounts could cause undue probability of error and omission.

5. Which of the following should be accrued as revenues by the General Fund of a local government?
a. Sales taxes held by the state which will be remitted to the local government.
b. Parking meter revenues.
c. Sales taxes collected by merchants.
d. Income taxes currently due.

6. Which account represents the equity of a nonenterprise fund?
a. Net assets.
b. Fund balance.
c. Reserves.
d. Unencumbered balance.

7. Which of the following expenditures is normally recorded on the accrual basis in the General Fund?
a. Interest.
b. Personal services.
c. Inventory items.
d. Prepaid expenses.

8. When reporting for governmental units, what type of costs should be presented in the financial statements?
a. Historical.
b. Historical adjusted for price-level changes.
c. Current appraisal.
d. Historical and current presented in two separate columns.

(AICPA adapted)

Exercise 21–4. The following related entries were recorded in sequence in the General Fund of a municipality:

1.	Encumbrances	12,000	
	Reserve for Encumbrances		12,000
2.	Reserve for Encumbrances .	12,000	
	Encumbrances		12,000
3.	Expenditures	12,350	
	Vouchers Payable		12,350

The following statements relate to the above entries.

1. The sequence of entries indicates that—

a. An adverse event was foreseen and a reserve of $12,000 was created; later the reserve was cancelled and a liability for the item was acknowledged.

b. An order was placed for goods or services estimated to cost $12,000; the actual cost was $12,350 for which a liability was acknowledged upon receipt.

c. Encumbrances were anticipated but later failed to materialize and were reversed. A liability of $12,350 was incurred.

d. The first entry was erroneous and was reversed; a liability of $12,350 was acknowledged.

2. Assuming appropriate governmental accounting principles were followed, the entries—

a. Occurred in the same fiscal period.

b. Did *not* occur in the same fiscal period.

c. Could have occurred in the same fiscal period, but it is impossible to be sure of this.

d. Reflect the equivalent of a "prior period adjustment" had the entity concerned been one operated for profit.

3. Immediately after entry number one was recorded, the municipality had a balanced general fund budget for all transactions. What would be the effect of recording entries two and three?

a. *Not* change the balanced condition of the budget.

b. Cause the municipality to show a surplus.

c. Cause the municipality to show a deficit.

d. *Not* affect the current budget but would affect the budget of the following fiscal period.

(AICPA adapted)

Exercise 21–5.

1. In preparing the General Fund budget of Brockton City for the forthcoming fiscal year the city council appropriated a sum greater than expected revenues. This action of the council will result in—

a. A cash overdraft during that fiscal year.

b. An increase in encumbrances by the end of that fiscal year.

c. A decrease in the fund balance.

d. A necessity for compensatory offsetting action in the Debt Service Fund.

2. The Town of Newbold's General Fund issued purchase orders to vendors and suppliers of $630,000. Which of the following entries should be made to record this transaction?

		Debit	Credit
a.	Encumbrances	630,000	
	Reserve for encumbrances		630,000
b.	Expenditures	630,000	
	Vouchers Payable		630,000
c.	Expenses	630,000	
	Accounts Payable		630,000
d.	Reserve for Encumbrances	630,000	
	Encumbrances		630,000

3. What would be the effect on the General Fund balance in the current fiscal year of recording a $15,000 purchase for a new fire truck out of General Fund resources, for which a $14,600 encumbrance had been recorded in the General Fund in the previous fiscal year?

a. Reduce the General Fund balance $15,000.

b. Reduce the General Fund balance $14,600.

c. Reduce the General Fund balance $400.

d. Have *no* effect on the General Fund balance.

4. Which of the following changes would *not* appear in an analysis of changes in fund balance statement of a General Fund?

a. The difference between actual revenues and actual expenditures during the period.

b. Increases or decreases of reserves established in a prior period or periods.

c. Direct debits or credits to fund balance to record corrections or prior period transactions.

d. The difference between appropriations and actual expenditures during the period.

5. A city's general-fund budget for the forthcoming fiscal year shows estimated revenues in excess of appropriations. The initial effect of recording this will result in an increase in

a. Taxes receivable.

b. Fund balance.

c. Reserve for encumbrances.

d. Encumbrances. (AICPA adapted)

Exercise 21–6. William Bates is executive vice president of Mavis Industries, Inc., a publicly held industrial corporation. Bates has just been elected to the city council of Gotham City. Prior to assuming office as a city councilman, he asks you as his CPA to explain the major differences that exist in accounting and financial reporting for a large city when compared to a large industrial corporation.

Required:

a. Describe the major differences that exist in the purpose of accounting and financial reporting and in the types of financial reports of a large city when compared to a large industrial corporation.

b. Why are inventories often ignored in accounting for local governmental units? Explain.

c. Under what circumstances should depreciation be recognized in accounting for local governmental units? Explain. (AICPA adapted)

PROBLEMS

Problem 21–7. The following transactions and information relates to the General Fund for the Town of Mountainview for 19x3:

1. The budget for the year was adopted. Estimated revenues are $900,000, and appropriations are $870,000.
2. The property tax levy was $700,000. It was estimated that 2 percent of the levy would prove to uncollectible.
3. Collections from property taxes amounted to $650,000. The balance of taxes receivable are now deliquent.
4. Salaries of $300,000 were approved for payment. (*Hint:* There is no need to encumber this.)
5. Purchase orders were issued for various items amounting to $400,000.
6. Invoices were received for $325,000. The purchase orders for these items amounted to $320,000.
7. Collections from miscellaneous taxes, licenses, and permits amounted to $210,000.
8. Payments were made for salaries approved for payment and for $275,000 of the invoices noted in 6 above. In addition, $40,000 was transferred to the Debt Service Fund for interest payments.
9. Supplies were received from an Internal Service Fund amounting to $35,000.
10. Utility invoices from the city's electric company amounted to $90,000.

Required:

a. Prepare the necessary journal entries to record the above.

b. Prepare the closing entries assuming that the unfilled purchase orders at December 31, 19x3, do not lapse and supplies are not inventoried.

Problem 21–8. The trial balance of the General Fund for the Town of Mountainview on January 1, 19x3, was:

TOWN OF MOUNTAINVIEW
General Fund Trial Balance
January 1, 19x3

Debits

Cash	$130,000
Taxes receivable—delinquent	40,000
Materials and supplies	5,000
Total	$175,000

Credits

Allowance for uncollectible taxes receivable—delinquent	$ 8,000
Vouchers payable	10,000
Fund balance:	
Reserved for encumbrances	8,000
Reserved for supplies	5,000
Unreserved	144,000
Total	$175,000

The following information is to be combined with the information provided in Problem 21–7:

1. Vouchers payable of $10,000 were paid.
2. The unfilled purchase order of $8,000 was received. The amount paid was $8,000.
3. Materials and supplies inventory is considered a material item. The value of the inventory at December 31, 19x3, amounted to $15,000.
4. Delinquent taxes receivable were collected in the amount of $36,000. The balance of $4,000 was written off. (*Hint:* Write off the unused $4,000 balance in the Uncollectible Taxes account to Fund Balance.)

Required:

a. Prepare the journal entries to record the additional information.

b. Using the information from Problem 21–7 combined with the additional information in this problem, prepare:

(1) A balance sheet at December 31, 19x3.
(2) A statement of revenues, expenditures, and changes in fund balance for 19x3.

Problem 21–9. The following summary of transactions was taken from the accounts of the Annaville School District General Fund *before* the books had been closed for the fiscal year ended June 30, 19x5:

	Post-closing balances, June 30, 19x4	Pre-closing balances, June 30, 19x5
Cash	$400,000	$ 700,000
Taxes receivable	150,000	170,000
Estimated uncollectible taxes	(40,000)	(70,000)
Estimated revenues	—	3,000,000
Expenditures	—	2,842,000
Expenditures—prior year . .	—	—
Encumbrances	—	91,000
	$510,000	$6,733,000
Vouchers payable	$ 80,000	$ 408,000
Due to other funds	210,000	142,000
Reserve for encumbrances .	60,000	91,000
Fund balance	160,000	182,000
Revenues from taxes	—	2,800,000
Miscellaneous revenues . . .	—	130,000
Appropriations	—	2,980,000
	$510,000	$6,733,000

1. The estimated taxes receivable for the year ended June 30, 19x5, were $2,870,000, and taxes collected during the year totaled $2,810,000.
2. An analysis of the transactions in the vouchers payable account for the year ended June 30, 19x5, follows:

	Dr. (cr.)
Current expenditures	$(2,700,000)
Expenditures for prior year	(58,000)
Vouchers for payment to other funds .	(210,000)
Cash payments during year	2,640,000
Net change	$ (328,000)

3. During the year the General Fund was billed $142,000 for services performed on its behalf by other city funds.
4. On May 2, 19x5, commitment documents were issued for the purchase of new textbooks at a cost of $91,000.

Required:

Based upon the data presented above, reconstruct the *original detailed journal entries* that were required to record all transactions for the fiscal year ended June 30, 19x5, including the recording of the current year's budget. Do *not* prepare closing entries at June 30, 19x5.   (AICPA adapted)

Problem 21–10.

CITY OF WATERFORD
General Fund Trial Balance
December 31, 19x9

	Debit	Credit
Cash	$ 207,500	
Taxes receivable—current . . .	148,500	
Allowance for uncollectible taxes—current		$ 6,000
Expenditures	760,000	
Revenues		802,500
Vouchers payable		7,500
Fund balance		300,000
Total	$1,116,000	$1,116,000

Your examination disclosed the following:

1. The budget for the year 19x9, not recorded on the books, estimated revenues and expenditures as follows: revenues, $815,000; expenditures, $775,000.
2. Outstanding purchase orders at December 31, 19x9, for operating expenses not recorded on the books totaled $2,500. These do not lapse.
3. Examination of the subledger containing the details of the Expenditures account revealed the following items included therein:

Current operating expenses	$472,000
Additions to structures and improvements	210,000
Equipment purchases	10,000
General obligation bonds paid	50,000
Interest paid on general obligation bonds .	18,000

Required:

a. Prepare the entries necessary to correct the books of the City of Waterford. (*Hint:* Items have been omitted and other items have been misclassified.)

b. Prepare closing entries.

c. Prepare:

(1) A balance sheet at December 31, 19x9.

(2) A statement of revenues, expenditures and changes in fund balance for 19x9.

(AICPA adapted)

Problem 21–11. The following information pertains to the operations of the General Fund of the X County. Functions of this county government include operating the county jail and caring for the county courts.

Funds to finance the operations are provided

from a levy of county tax against the various towns of the county, from the state distribution of unincorporated business taxes, from board of jail prisoners assessed against the towns and against the state and from interest on savings accounts.

The balances in the accounts of the fund on January 1, 19x0, were as follows:

Cash in savings accounts	$ 60,650
Cash in checking accounts	41,380
Cash on hand (undeposited prisoners' board receipts)	320
Inventory of jail supplies	3,070
Due from towns and state for board of prisoners	3,550
General Fund balance	108,970

The budget for the year 19x0 as adopted by the county commissioners provided for the following items of revenue and expenditure:

(1) Town and county taxes	$20,000
(2) Jail operating costs	55,500
(3) Court operating costs	7,500
(4) Unincorporated business tax	18,000
(5) Board of prisoners (revenue)	5,000
(6) Commissioners' salaries and expenses	8,000
(7) Interest on savings	1,000
(8) Miscellaneous expenses	1,000

General Fund balance was appropriated in sufficient amount to balance the budget. At December 31, 19x0, the jail supply inventory amounted to $5,120, cash of $380 was on hand, and $1,325 of prisoners' board bills were unpaid. The following items represent all of the transactions which occurred during the year, with all current bills vouchered and paid by December 31, 19x0:

Item (1) was transacted exactly as budgeted.	
Item (2) cash expenditures amounted to	$55,230
Item (3) amounted to	7,110
Item (4) amounted to	18,070
Item (5) billings amounted to	4,550
Item (6) amounted to	6,670
Item (7) amounted to	1,050
Item (8) amounted to	2,310

During the year, $25,000 was transferred from the savings accounts to the checking accounts.

Required:

From the above information, prepare a worksheet providing columns to show:

a. The transactions for the year. (Journal entries not required.)

b. Variances between budgeted and actual revenues and expenditures for the year.

c. Balance sheet of the General Fund, December 31, 19x0. (AICPA adapted)

Problem 21–12. You were engaged to examine the financial statements of the Mayfair School District for the year ended June 30, 19x7, and were furnished the General Fund trial balance which appears below:

MAYFAIR SCHOOL DISTRICT
General Fund Trial Balance
June 30, 19x7

	Debit	Credit
Cash	$ 47,250	
Taxes receivable—current year .	31,800	
Estimated losses—current year taxes		$ 1,800
Temporary investments	11,300	
Inventory of supplies	11,450	
Estimated revenues	1,007,000	
Appropriations		1,000,000
Vouchers payable		10,200
Due to Internal Service Fund . .		950
Operating expenditures:		
Administration	24,950	
Instruction	601,800	
Other	221,450	
Operating transfers-out— Principal and interest . . .	130,000	
Capital outlays (equipment) . . .	22,000	
Revenues from tax levy, licenses and fines		1,008,200
Reserve for inventory of supplies		11,450
Fund balance		76,400
Totals	$2,109,000	$2,109,000

Your examination disclosed the following information:

1. The recorded estimate of losses for the current year taxes receivable was considered to be sufficient.

2. Purchases of classroom and playground equipment costing $22,000 were paid from general funds.

3. Five years ago a 4 percent, 10-year, sinking fund bond issue in the amount of $1,000,000 for constructing school buildings was made and is outstanding. Interest on the issue is payable at maturity. Budgetary requirements of an annual contribution of $90,000 and interest of $40,000 were accounted for in separate sinking fund accounts.

4. Outstanding purchase orders for operating expenses not recorded in the accounts at year-end were as follows:

Administration	$1,000
Instruction	1,200
Other	600
Total	$2,800

5. The school district operated a central machine shop. Billings amounting to $950 were properly recorded in the accounts of the General Fund.

Required:

a. Prepare the formal adjusting and closing entries for the General Fund.

b. Prepare a balance sheet at June 30, 19x7.

(AICPA adapted)

Problem 21–13. The following data were taken from the accounts of the Town of Ridgedale after the books had been closed for the fiscal year ending June 30, 19x3:

[Relates to Problem 21–13]

		19x3 Changes		
	Balances June 30, 19x2	Debits	Credits	Balances June 30, 19x3
Cash	$180,000	$ 955,000	$ 880,000	$255,000
Taxes receivable	20,000	809,000	781,000	48,000
	$200,000			$303,000
Allowances for uncollectible taxes	$ 4,000	6,000	9,000	$ 7,000
Vouchers payable	44,000	880,000	889,000	53,000
Due to other funds	12,000	67,000	110,000	55,000
Reserve for encumbrances . . .	40,000	40,000	47,000	47,000
Fund balance	100,000	20,000	61,000	141,000
	$200,000	$2,777,000	$2,777,000	$303,000

The following additional data are available:

1. The budget for the year provided for estimated revenues of $1,000,000 and appropriations of $965,000.
2. Expenditures totaling $895,000, in addition to those chargeable against Reserve for Encumbrances, were made.
3. The actual expenditures chargeable against Reserve for Encumbrances were $37,000.

Required:

Prepare a worksheet to compare estimated revenues with actual revenues, and encumbrances and expenditures with appropriations and other authorizations. The worksheet should have the following column headings:

Column Number	Heading
1	Balance Sheet, June 30, 19x2
2 and 3	19x3 Transactions (Debit and Credit)
4	Estimated Revenues
5	Actual Revenues
6	Encumbrances and Expenditures
7	Appropriations and Other Authorizations
8	Balance Sheet, June 30, 19x3

(AICPA adapted)

Problem 21–14. The Crescent City Council has employed you to examine the General Fund. The following information is made available to you directly or as the result of your examination:

1. The account balances of the General Fund at the end of the fiscal year are as follows:

Debits	
Cash	$ 600,000
Taxes receivable—current	500,000
Expenditures	9,300,000
Total	$10,400,000

Credits	
Revenues received	$ 9,900,000
Deferred tax collections	500,000
Total	$10,400,000

2. At the beginning of the year the Council formally approved the budget for the fiscal year. The budget is presented with the cash receipts and disbursements information in 3 below.
3. Cash receipts and disbursements, together with budgeting information, is presented below.

	Estimated Revenues	Actual Receipts
Taxes:		
Current year	$ 9,700,000	$9,500,000
Collected in advance .	–0–	20,000
Licenses and permits . .	200,000	250,000
Fines and forfeits	70,000	78,000
Rentals from use of		
properties	30,000	32,000
Miscellaneous:		
Refunds and rebates		
of current service		
charges by other		
agencies:		
Utility Fund		
(Enterprise Fund)	–0–	6,000
Internal Service		
Fund	–0–	4,000
Unused (excess) cash		
from Debt		
Service Fund . . .	–0–	10,000
Totals	$10,000,000	$9,900,000

Accrued salaries	$60,000	
Invoices for materials and		
supplies received	19,000	$79,000
Orders placed by the city but		
not filled		30,000

7. Services billed by the Internal Service Fund, not recorded on the books of General Fund, amounted to $1,000.

8. The General Fund stores inventory amounted to $35,000 at end of period and is to be recorded. The city's charter provides that expenditures are based on purchases.

9. The city's charter specifies that purchase orders unfilled at the end of the year do not lapse.

Required:

Prepare a worksheet for the General Fund with columns for Balances per Books, Corrections and Adjustments, and Corrected Balances. Key the corrections and adjustments to the related transaction

[Relates to Problem 21–14]

	Planned expenditures	Actual disbursements
Departmental expenses*	$7,100,000	$6,894,000
Contribution to Retirement Pension Fund	150,000	140,000
Creation of petty cash fund	–0–	5,000
City's share of cost of special assessments	150,000	150,000
Establishment of Internal Service Fund	50,000	50,000
Equipment—general office	420,000	421,000
Land for building site	500,000	500,000
Sinking Fund contribution	1,000,000	1,000,000
Matured serial general obligation bonds	100,000	100,000
Interest on bonds:		
Sinking Fund bonds	20,000	20,000
Serial bonds	10,000	10,000
Temporary loan to Internal Service Fund	–0–	10,000
Totals	$9,500,000	$9,300,000
*Include the following:		
Billed by Utility Fund	$ 70,000	$ 80,000
Billed by Internal Service Fund	–0–	$ 39,000

4. City taxes receivable, per tax roll, amounted to $10,000,000.

5. All unpaid city taxes become delinquent at the end of the year in which levied.

6. Unrecorded amounts at the close of the fiscal year consisted of

numbers. Formal general journal entries are not required.   (AICPA adapted)

Problem 21–15. The Sleepy Haven Township's adjusted trial balance for the General Fund as at the close of its fiscal year ending June 30, 19x2, is shown as follows:

SLEEPY HAVEN TOWNSHIP
General Fund Trial Balance
June 30, 19x2

	Debit	Credit
Cash	$ 1,100	
Taxes receivable—current (note 1) .	8,200	
Allowance for uncollectible taxes—current		$ 150
Taxes receivable—delinquent	2,500	
Allowance for uncollectible taxes—deliquent		1,650
Miscellaneous accounts receivable .	4,000	
Allowance for uncollectible —accounts		400
Due from Internal Service Fund . .	5,000	
Expenditures (note 2)	75,500	
Encumbrances	3,700	
Revenues (note 3)		6,700
Due to Utility Fund (Enterprise Fund)		1,000
Vouchers payable		2,000
Reserve for encumbrances—prior year		4,400
Reserve for encumbrances		3,700
Appropriations		72,000
Fund balance		8,000
Totals	$100,000	$100,000

Note 1: The current tax roll and miscellaneous accounts receivable, recorded on the accrual basis as sources of revenue, amounted to $50,000 and $20,000, respectively. These items have been recorded on the books subject to a 2 percent provision for uncollectible accounts.

Note 2: Includes $4,250 paid during the fiscal year in settlement of all purchase orders outstanding at the beginning of the fiscal year.

Note 3: Represents the difference between the budgeted (estimated) revenue of $70,000 and the actual revenue realized during the fiscal year.

Required:

a. Prepare in columnar form an Analysis of Changes in Fund Balance for the year ending June 30, 19x2, with the following column headings: Estimated, Actual, and Excess or Deficiency of Actual Compared with Estimated.

b. Prepare a formal balance sheet at June 30, 19x2.   (AICPA adapted)

22

Accounting for state and local governments— special funds

OVERVIEW

In addition to the General Fund, state and local governments use a variety of other funds. Separate funds are used for special revenues, such as from gasoline taxes that must be used for road improvements, construction of buildings, the payment of interest and principal for general long-term indebtedness. In addition, the state or local government may sell goods and services, such as water and electricity, on a user-charge basis. The accounting for each fund has certain similarities to the accounting for a General Fund, yet each fund has certain unique characteristics. Although separate financial statements can be prepared for each fund, it is customary to prepare combined statements with separate columnar headings for each fund.

In addition to the use of separate funds, state and local governments also use groups of accounts. Examples of these are for general fixed assets and for general long-term liabilities. Each of these are self-balancing and have certain unique features.

The preceding chapter concerned itself with the state of the art in the accounting for nonbusiness organizations. Moreover, it also demonstrated the procedures used to account for transactions in the General Fund. This chapter discusses other types of funds used by state and local governments.

SPECIAL REVENUE FUNDS

The accounting for Special Revenue Funds is identical to that of a General Fund. While the General Fund is used to account for the day-to-day activities of a state or local government and, therefore, accounts for various types of revenues and expenditures, a Special Revenue Fund, as its name implies, is used to account for a special type of revenue that can be used only for a specific purpose. An example of this type of revenue would be that portion of gasoline taxes that must be used for road improvements. Since this portion of the gasoline tax cannot legally be used for the general operations of the government, it is accounted for separately. A Special Revenue Fund uses budgetary and encumbrance accounting as demonstrated previously, and therefore, the entries will not be repeated.

CAPITAL PROJECTS FUND

The NCGA recommends that the modified accrual method of accounting be used to account for Capital Projects Funds. To demonstrate the entries used for this fund, the following is assumed.

On December 31, 19x0, the town council of Watertown authorized a bond issue in the amount of $200,000 for the purpose of constructing a building to house the police station. In addition, the town is contributing $50,000 from its General Fund, the county is contributing $50,000 and the state is contributing $50,000. The project is estimated to cost $350,000. The following transactions occurred:

1. On January 2, 19x1, a firm commitment was received for the $150,000 due from the various segments of government.
2. Purchase orders for $50,000 were sent out for various supplies and building materials.
3. A construction contract was signed in the amount of $295,000.
4. The bonds were sold on January 2, 19x1, at 101 with a coupon rate of 9 percent.
5. Supplies and building materials were received. The invoice amount is $51,000.
6. The invoice in 5 above is paid.
7. The amounts committed in 1 above are received.
8. The project is completed, and the contractor is paid in full.
9. The remaining excess funds are transferred to the General Fund.

The entries to record the above are as follows:

(1)

Due from General Fund	50,000	
Due from Other Governmental Units	100,000	
Operating Transfers-In		50,000
Revenues		100,000

To record the $50,000 due from the General Fund and
$100,000 from other governmental units.

(2)

Encumbrances	50,000	
Reserve for Encumbrances		50,000

As in the General Fund, encumbrances are used in the Capital Projects Fund.

(3)

Encumbrances	295,000	
Reserve for Encumbrances		295,000

(4a)

Cash	202,000	
Proceeds of Bonds		200,000
Premium on Bonds		2,000

Bonds payable are not carried in the Capital Projects Fund. Instead, they are
carried in the General Long-Term Debt Account Group. Accordingly, in that
group the following additional entry would be made:

General Long-Term Debt Account Group

Amount to Be Provided for Payment of Serial Bonds	200,000	
Serial Bonds Payable		200,000

Capital Projects Fund

(4b)

Premium on Bonds	2,000	
Cash		2,000

Since the bonds were sold at a premium of $2,000, the premium is not
usually available for expenditures by the Capital Projects Fund. Instead, it is
usually transferred to the Debt Service Fund for the payment of interest and
principal. In the Debt Service Fund cash would be debited for $2,000 and
Operating Transfers-In (Capital Projects Fund) would be credited for $2,000.
If the bonds were sold at a discount, either of two courses of action would
be required. First, the General Fund could make a transfer in the amount of
the discount and the project would proceed as planned. Alternatively, the
proposed cost of the project could be reduced by the amount of the discount. Cash from the Debt Service Fund is not available for compensating
the Capital Projects Fund for discounts on the sale of bonds.

(5a)

Reserve for Encumbrances	50,000	
Encumbrances		50,000

(5b)

Expenditures	51,000	
Vouchers Payable		51,000

(6)

Vouchers Payable	51,000	
Cash		51,000

(7)

Cash	150,000	
Due from General Fund		50,000
Due from Other Governmental Units		100,000

(8a)

Reserve for Encumbrances	295,000	
Encumbrances		295,000

(8b)

Expenditures	295,000	
Contracts Payable		295,000

(8c)

Contracts Payable	295,000	
Cash		295,000

It should be noted that the police station is not carried as a fixed asset in this fund. Fixed assets are generally carried in the General Fixed Assets Account Group. Thus, when the project is completed, the following entry is made in the General Fixed Assets Account Group:

General Fixed Assets Account Group

Buildings	346,000	
Investment in Fixed Assets—Capital Projects Fund		346,000

In this particular example no amount was withheld from the contractor pending the satisfactory completion of the project. In many cases, however, a percentage, such as 10 percent, is withheld from payments due to the contractor until it is determined that the construction project is satisfactorily completed at which time the retained percentage is paid.

(9a)

Residual Equity Transfer-Out	4,000	
Cash		4,000

The excess cash of $4,000 is transferred to the General Fund. A corresponding entry would be made in the General Fund to record the receipt of the $4,000.

(9b)

Proceeds of Bonds	200,000	
Operating Transfer-In	50,000	
Revenues	100,000	
Expenditures		346,000
Residual Equity Transfers-Out		4,000
To close fund.		

A statement of revenues, expenditures, and changes in fund balance for 19x1 would appear as in Illustration 22–1.

Illustration 22–1
TOWN OF WATERTOWN
Capital Projects Fund—Police Station
Statement of Revenues, Expenditures, and Changes in Fund Balance
For the Year Ended December 31, 19x1

Revenues and other sources:		
Revenues:		
Intergovernmental revenues		$100,000
Other sources:		
Proceeds from sale of bonds	$200,000	
Operating transfers-in—General Fund	50,000	250,000
Total revenues and other sources		350,000
Expenditures:		
Capital outlays		346,000
Excess of revenues and other sources over expenditures		4,000
Fund balance—January 1, 19x1		—
Residual equity transfers-out		(4,000)
Fund balance—December 31, 19x1		–0–

Since the fund has been closed at the end of the year, the balance sheet accounts have all been reduced to zero balances. However, a typical balance sheet might appear as in Illustration 22–2.

Illustration 22–2
TOWN OF WATERTOWN
Capital Projects Fund—Police Station
Balance Sheet
December 31, 19x–

Assets

Cash		$xxx
Due from General Fund		xxx
Due from other governmental units		xxx
Total assets		$xxx

Liabilities and Fund Balance

Vouchers payable		$xxx
Contracts payable		xxx
Total liabilities		xxx
Fund balance:		
Reserved for encumbrances	$xxx	
Unreserved	xxx	xxx
Total liabilities and fund balance		$xxx

DEBT SERVICE FUND

It is now assumed that the bond issue authorized for the construction of the police station in Watertown requires interest payments on the last day of June and December until maturity. The bonds are serial bonds and mature at the end of each calendar year in the amount of $20,000 per annum. Thus, the first maturity of $20,000 is payable on December 31, 19x1. Amounts in excess of requirements by the Capital Projects Fund will be applied first to interest payments and then to principal. The entries to record the transactions in the Debt Service Fund for 19x1 are:

January 2, 19x1

Cash	2,000	
Operating Transfers-In—Capital Projects Fund		2,000
For bonds sold at a premium.		

June 30, 19x1

Cash	7,000	
Operating Transfers-In—General Fund		7,000
Expenditures	9,000	
Interest Payable		9,000
Interest Payable	9,000	
Cash		9,000

Only $7,000 was required from the General Fund for the first interest payment ($9\% \times \$200,000 \times {}^{6}/_{12}$) since $2,000 of premium from the sale of the bonds is available for this interest payment. It should be noted that the NCGA recommends that, in general, the modified accrual basis be used but makes an exception for interest and principal on general long-term indebtedness. Accordingly, no accrual entries for interest are made in this fund; instead, interest and principal is recorded only when it is due.

December 31, 19x1

Cash	29,000	
Operating Transfers-In—General Fund		29,000
Expenditures	29,000	
Bonds Payable		20,000
Interest Payable		9,000
Bonds Payable	20,000	
Interest Payable	9,000	
Cash		29,000

If the interest and principal were due on January 1 instead of December 31, as in this case, no accrual entries would be made on December 31, unless the funds were received in 19x1. Instead, the entries would have been deferred until January 1, 19x2.

The illustration of the Debt Service Fund has been kept simple for ease of illustration. Normally, the fund would have some cash in its accounts, some investments and possibly some receivables. Also, the fund might have some matured bonds payable and some interest payable. The format of the financial statements for this fund would be similar to that shown in Illustrations 22–3 and 22–4. Therefore, they are not shown here. For a more realistic view of what the financial statements should look like, the reader should refer to the combined financial statements presented in the appendix to this chapter (see Illustration 22–17 and Illustration 22–18).

SPECIAL ASSESSMENT FUNDS	Special Assessment Funds are established to provide local improvements to a certain group of taxpayers which benefit from them directly and benefit other taxpayers indirectly. Examples of this type of improvement might be sewers or street lighting for a particular group of property owners. While

the particular group might be the direct beneficiaries of the service, all tax-payers may benefit indirectly because of the decrease in seepage of sewage pollutants and a possible reduction in crime rates. When this occurs, the property owners directly benefited are assessed a significant portion of the cost of the improvement and the General Fund may contribute the balance of the cost for those taxpayers indirectly benefited by it.

Just as is the case with the Debt Service Fund, the General Fund, and the Special Revenue Fund, the modified accrual basis is used for this fund as well. However, if bonds are sold to finance a portion of these improvements, the bonds are *not* accounted for in the General Long-Term Debt Account Group, since the bonds will *not* be paid from General Fund revenues. These bonds will be paid from the special assessment on property owners and, therefore, are accounted for in this fund. Accordingly, bonds in this fund are treated in the same manner, i.e., interest is *not* accrued; it is rather recorded when due.

To illustrate the operation of this fund the following is assumed:

The town council of Watertown authorized the construction of a sewer project for a section of the town. Property in that section of town will be hooked up to the sewer system, and these property owners will be assessed for the cost of this hookup, payable over a 10-year period. The town will pay for the remaining cost of the sewer system. It is estimated that the cost of the entire project will amount to $1,000,000 of which $700,000 will be as-sessed against property owners and $300,000 will come from general reve-nues. The $700,000 assessment will be financed by a bond issue of $630,000 at an interest rate of 8 percent per annum. Unpaid balances of assessments will bear interest at 8 percent per annum. The following transactions oc-curred during the first year of operations:

1. The 8 percent bonds were sold at par.
2. A contract for the construction of the sewers and hookups was awarded in the amount of $1,000,000.
3. Assessments against property owners were levied.
4. The portion of the improvements to be paid from general revenues came due.
5. The first installments of the property assessment were collected except for 5 percent (5% × $70,000) which is now delinquent.
6. The General Fund paid its share of the improvements.
7. The first six months interest on bonds payable was paid.
8. Foreclosure proceedings were instituted on property with an original assessment of $2,000. Costs of holding the sale amounted to $150.
9. The $2,000 of unpaid assessment in 8 above was received together with $80 of interest and $150 of expenses of holding the sale.
10. A progress payment of $800,000 was vouchered and paid to the con-tractor.
11. Interest receivable of $50,520 was accrued on unpaid assessments.
12. The second installment of assessments came due.
13. Closing entries were prepared.

The entries to record the above would be:

Memorandum (Optional)
Sewer Improvements Authorized, $1,000,000

(1)

Cash	630,000	
Bonds Payable		630,000

Bonds payable is credited since the bonds are carried as
liabilities of this fund.

(2)

Encumbrances	1,000,000	
Reserve for Encumbrances		1,000,000

(3)

Assessments Receivable—Current	70,000	
Assessment Receivable—Deferred	630,000	
Revenues		700,000

Deferred assessment are classified as such.

(4)

Due from General Fund	300,000	
Operating Transfers-In—General Fund		300,000

(5)

Cash	66,500	
Assessments Receivable—Delinquent	3,500	
Assessments Receivable—Current		70,000

(6)

Cash	300,000	
Due from General Fund		300,000

(7)

Interest Expense	25,200	
Cash		25,200

Interest expense is debited instead of expenditures.

(8)

Cost of Holding Sale	150	
Cash		150

(9)

Cash	2,230	
Assessments Receivable—Delinquent		200
Assessments Receivable—Deferred		1,800
Cost of Holding Sale		150
Interest Revenue		80

Interest Revenue is credited instead of Revenues. Ten
percent of the $2,000 assessment is delinquent, and the
balance is deferred.

(10a)

Reserve for Encumbrances	800,000	
Encumbrances		800,000

(10b)

Expenditures	800,000	
Vouchers Payable		800,000

(10c)

| Vouchers Payable | 800,000 | |
| Cash | | 800,000 |

(11)

| Interest Receivable | 50,520 | |
| Interest Revenue | | 50,520 |

Interest receivable is accrued while interest payable is not in accordance with modified accrual accounting.

(12)

| Assessments Receivable—Current | 70,000 | |
| Assessments Receivable—Deferred | | 70,000 |

Revenues	700,000	
Operating Transfers-In—General Fund	300,000	
Interest Revenue	50,600	
Expenditures		800,000
Encumbrances		200,000
Interest Expense		25,200
Fund Balance		25,400

The closing entry above is optional. The advantage of making the entry is to place this fund on a par with other funds in order to facilitate the preparation of financial statements (a complete set of financial statements for all funds appears in the appendix at the end of this chapter). If the closing entry is made, the Encumbrances account ($200,000) should be reopened next period by a reversal entry. It should be remembered that an entry is also required in the General Fixed Assets Account Group for the above construction. A Construction in Progress account is used until the project is completed at which time it is transferred to the Sewers account.

Financial statements for this fund would appear as shown in Illustrations 22–3 and 22–4.

Illustration 22–3
CITY OF WATERTOWN
Sewer Special Assessment Fund
Statement of Revenues, Expenditures, and Changes in Fund Balance
For the Fiscal Year Ended December 31, 19x1

Revenues:		
Special assessments levied	$700,000	
Interest on assessments	50,600	
Total revenues		$750,600
Expenditures:		
Progress payment to contractor	800,000	
Interest on bonds payable	25,200	
Total expenditures		825,200
Excess of expenditures over revenues		74,600
Other financing sources: Operating transfers-in		300,000
Excess of revenues and other sources over expenditures		225,400
Less: Reserve for encumbrances, December 31, 19x1		200,000
Increase in fund balance for year		25,400
Fund balance, January 1, 19x1		–0–
Fund balance, December 31, 19x1		$ 25,400

Illustration 22–4
CITY OF WATERTOWN
Sewer Special Assessment Fund
Balance Sheet
December 31, 19x1

Assets

Cash		$173,380
Assessments receivable:		
Delinquent	$ 3,300	
Current	70,000	
Deferred	558,200	631,500
Interest receivable		50,520
Total assets		$855,400

Liabilities and Fund Equity

Liabilities:		
Bonds payable		$630,000
Fund equity:		
Reserved for encumbrances	200,000	
Fund balance	25,400	
Total fund equity		225,400
Total liabilities and fund equity		$855,400

In the following year (19x2), a reversal entry would be made as follows:

Encumbrances	200,000	
Fund Balance		200,000
To reestablish encumbrances closed in 19x1.		

INTERNAL SERVICE FUNDS

Internal Service Funds and Enterprise Funds are classified as proprietary funds by the NCGA. Accordingly, these funds use the same accounts and accounting procedures used by business organizations. Thus, these funds contain fixed assets; bonds payable to be paid from the revenues generated in these funds, and regular depreciation accounting is used to account for fixed assets.

To illustrate the operation of this fund it is assumed that the city of Watertown centralizes the purchasing and the administration of supplies. All entries for 19x1 are assumed.

(1)

Cash	225,000	
Contribution from General Fund		225,000

(2)

Land	30,000	
Building	100,000	
Machinery and Equipment	50,000	
Equipment—Delivery	20,000	
Cash		200,000

(3)

Inventory of Supplies	150,000	
Vouchers Payable		150,000

(4a)

Cost of Supplies Issued	80,000	
Inventory of Supplies		80,000

(4b)

Due from General Fund	160,000	
Billings to Departments		160,000

(5)

Administrative Expenses	5,000	
Purchasing Expenses	20,000	
Warehousing Expenses	10,000	
Delivery Expenses	8,000	
Vouchers Payable		43,000

(6)

Cash	150,000	
Due from General Fund		150,000

(7)

Vouchers Payable	140,000	
Cash		140,000

(8)

Purchasing Expenses	1,000	
Warehousing Expenses	8,000	
Delivery Expenses	4,000	
Accumulated Depreciation—Building		4,000
Accumulated Depreciation—Machinery and Equipment . .		5,000
Accumulated Depreciation—Delivery		4,000

The closing entries would be:

(9)

Billings to Departments	160,000	
Cost of Supplies Issued		80,000
Purchasing Expenses		21,000
Warehousing Expenses		18,000
Delivery Expenses		12,000
Administrative Expenses		5,000
Retained Earnings		24,000

The financial statements prepared for this type of fund are similar to those prepared for commercial establishments. Thus, a balance sheet, a statement of retained earnings, an operating (income) statement, and a statement of changes in financial position are all customarily prepared. The balance sheet is classified as in a commercial business balance sheet. The only difference from a commercial balance sheet would be in the stockholders' equity section. Instead of capital stock, the section would contain "Contributions from General Fund" followed by "Retained earnings." The remaining statements would appear as normally used for commercial establishments as in Illustration 22–5, 22–6, and 22–7.

Illustration 22–5
CITY OF WATERTOWN
Supplies Fund
Balance Sheet
December 31, 19x1

Assets

Current assets:			
Cash			$ 35,000
Due from General Fund			10,000
Inventory of supplies			70,000
Total current assets			115,000
Fixed assets:			
Land			$ 30,000
Building	$100,000		
Less: Accumulated depreciation	4,000		96,000
Machinery and equipment—warehouse	50,000		
Less: Accumulated depreciation	5,000		45,000
Equipment—delivery	20,000		
Less: Accumulated depreciation	4,000		16,000
Total fixed assets			187,000
Total assets			$302,000

Liabilities and Fund Equity

Current liabilities:		
Vouchers payable	53,000	
Total liabilities		53,000
Fund equity:		
Contributions from General Fund	225,000	
Retained earnings	24,000	
Total fund equity		249,000
Total liabilities and fund equity		$302,000

Illustration 22–6
CITY OF WATERTOWN
Supplies Fund
Statement of Revenues, Expenses, and Changes in Retained Earnings
For the Year Ended December 31, 19x1

Billings to departments		$160,000
Less: Cost of supplies issued		80,000
Gross margin		80,000
Less: Purchasing expenses	$21,000	
Warehousing expenses	18,000	
Delivery expenses	12,000	
Administrative expenses	5,000	
Total operating expenses		56,000
Excess of net billings to departments over costs for the year		24,000
Retained earnings, January 1, 19x1		–0–
Retained earnings, December 31, 19x1		$ 24,000

Illustration 22–7
CITY OF WATERTOWN
Supplies Fund
Statement of Changes in Financial Position
For the Year Ended December 31, 19x1

Resources provided:		
Operations:		
Excess of billings to departments over costs		$ 24,000
Add: Charges that do not require the use of working capital:		
Depreciation expenses		13,000
Total from operations		37,000
Capital additions:		
Contribution from General Fund		225,000
Total resources provided		262,000
Resources used:		
Purchase of land, buildings, and equipment	$200,000	
Total resources used		200,000
Net increase in working capital		$ 62,000
Net increase in working capital:		
Increases in working capital:		
Increase in cash	$ 35,000	
Increase in receivables from General Fund	10,000	
Increase in inventory of supplies	70,000	
Increases in working capital		$115,000
Decreases in working capital:		
Increases in vouchers payable		53,000
Net increase in working capital		$62,000

ENTERPRISE FUNDS

Enterprise Funds are also Proprietary Funds and also use commercial accounting procedures. Therefore, the entries shown for the Internal Service Fund apply to Enterprise Funds as well. Enterprise Funds are formed for the purpose of providing services to residents on a user-charge basis. Examples of the types of services that may be provided are electric and gas companies, water companies, garbage collection (where residents are charged specifically for the service), swimming pools, and golf courses and others.

Since the entries for this type of fund would be essentially the same as shown previously, they are not repeated except for the entry to record revenues. Instead of Billings to Departments as shown in the Internal Service Fund on page 666, the entry to record revenue would be:

Customer Accounts Receivable   xxxx
     Sales of Water (electricity, etc.)   xxxx

Financial statements for this type of fund are the same as those for an Internal Service Fund.

FIDUCIARY FUNDS

Governmental units frequently act as trustees or agents for employees, other governmental units, organizations, and invidivuals. Because of this, Fiduciary Funds are usually referred to as *Trust* and *Agency* Funds. Although there is a legal distinction between agency relationships and trust relationships, the distinction is not germane to our discussion of these funds.

AGENCY FUNDS

Agency Funds can technically be used for the accounting of taxes withheld from employees for the benefit of the federal government and state governments. This use of the fund is, however, not customary. In many instances collections of tax levies by different governmental units are centralized in one tax collection agency. When this occurs, each governmental unit sets up the *gross* amount receivable together with an amount for estimated uncollectible taxes. The Agency Fund, however, merely records the gross amount receivable for all units and *does not* record an amount for uncollectible taxes since it is not concerned with revenues; it is merely acting as a conduit.

To demonstrate the operation of this type of fund it is assumed that:

1. The county of Watertown levies its taxes for $100,000 of which $3,000 is estimated to be uncollectible.
2. The town of Waterburg levies a tax of $50,000 of which $2,000 is estimated to be uncollectible and the village of Vilglo levies a tax of $20,000 of which $1,000 is expected to be uncollectible.
3. The county acts as agent to collect all taxes for which it charges a collection fee of 1 percent to the town and the village.

The entries to record the above would be:

General Fund—County

Taxes Receivable—Current	100,000	
Estimated Uncollectible Taxes—Current		3,000
Revenues		97,000

The town and the village would record entries similar to the above in order to record their respective tax levies. In addition, the county would make the following entries in its agency fund:

Agency Fund

Taxes Receivable for Other Funds and Units	170,000	
Due to Other Funds and Units		170,000
Note: The gross amount of all levies is recorded.		

Cash	150,000	
Taxes Receivable for Other Funds and Units		150,000

To record collections for:

General Fund	$ 90,000
Town of Waterburg	45,000
Village of Vilglo	15,000
	$150,000

Due to Other Funds and Units	150,000	
Cash		149,400
Due to General Fund		600

To record remittances as follows:

General Fund	$ 90,000
Waterburg ($45,000—1% collection)	44,550
Vilglo ($15,000—1% collection)	14,850
Total	$149,400

The County General Fund entry would be:

General Fund—County

Cash	90,000	
Due from Agency Fund	600	
Taxes Receivable—Current		90,000
Revenues		600

The Town General Fund entry would be:

General Fund—Waterburg

Cash	44,550	
Expenditures (collection fee)	450	
Taxes Receivable—Current		45,000

TRUST FUNDS

Trust Funds can be classified as either *expendable* or *nonexpendable.* Expendable Trust Funds are those that are set up for a specific purpose, such as a bequest for the construction and the related acquisitions of a business periodicals room in the library. In this type of fund, the trust principal (corpus) is expended for a specific purpose. Because a fund of this type uses the same accounting procedures as were illustrated in the preceding chapter, they are not repeated here.

Nonexpendable Trust Funds, however, require the use of different accounting procedures. Nonexpendable Trust Funds may contain provisions where the income may be expendable for a particular purpose, such as for scholarships, with the corpus maintained intact. A fund of this type is known as an *Endowment Fund.* Alternatively, Nonexpendable Trust Funds that are not Endowment Funds, such as Student Loan Funds, usually require that the income and principal be kept intact for the purposes specified in the trust, namely, the making of student loans.

Nonexpendable Trust Funds are accounted for in the same manner as Proprietary Funds. Thus, accrual accounting is used and fixed assets, if any, are depreciated as is the case in commercial accounting. Likewise, interest on any long-term indebtedness is also accrued. The proper distinction between corpus and income is crucial if the corpus is to be maintained intact.

Accounting for Nonexpendable Trust Funds

To illustrate the accounting procedures for this type of fund it is assumed that:

1. John Doe died on January 2, 19x1, leaving a Trust Fund to the city of Watertown consisting of a portfolio of common stocks valued at $100,000 and an office building having a fair market value of $200,000 with $50,000 of this amount attributable to land. The trust specifies that the income of the fund is to be used to operate and maintain the business periodicals reading room at the main library. The corpus is to be maintained intact.
2. The building has a remaining useful life of 30 years. No amount is assignable to salvage value. Straight-line depreciation is to be used.

The necessary entries (income and expenditures are assumed) would be:

(1)

Investments	100,000	
Land	50,000	
Building	150,000	
Trust Fund Balance		300,000

(2)

Cash	40,000	
Dividend Revenue		10,000
Rental Revenue		30,000

(3)

Accrued Rentals Receivable	2,000	
Rental Revenue		2,000

(4)

Maintenance Expenses	11,000	
Cash		8,000
Accounts Payable		3,000

(5)

Depreciation Expense	5,000	
Accumulated Depreciation ($150,000 ÷ 30 years = $5,000)		5,000

(6)

Rental Revenue	32,000	
Dividend Revenue	10,000	
Maintenance Expenses		11,000
Depreciation Expenses		5,000
Retained Earnings		26,000
To close.		

(7)

Retained Earnings	26,000	
Due to Library Fund		26,000
To record earnings due to library fund.		

(8)

Due to Library Fund	26,000	
Cash		26,000

The financial statements for this fund would appear as in Illustrations 22–8, 22–9, and 22–10.

Illustration 22–8
CITY OF WATERTOWN
Doe Library Endowment Fund
Balance Sheet
December 31, 19x1

Assets

Current assets:		
Cash	$ 6,000	
Accrued rent receivable	2,000	
Total current assets		$ 8,000
Plant assets:		
Land	50,000	
Building (net of $5,000 accumulated depreciation)	145,000	
Total plant assets		195,000
Investments:		
Common stock (market value, $102,000)		100,000
Total assets		$303,000

Liabilities and Fund Equity

Current liabilities:		
Accounts payable		$ 3,000
Fund equity:		
Fund balance		300,000
Total liabilities and fund equity		$303,000

Illustration 22–9
CITY OF WATERTOWN
Doe Library Endowment Fund
Statement of Revenues, Expenses, and Changes in Fund Balances
For the Year Ended December 31, 19x1

Revenues earned for transfer to Library Operating Fund:		
Rental revenue		$ 32,000
Less: Operating costs and expenses:		
Maintenance	$11,000	
Depreciation of building	5,000	16,000
Net operating income		16,000
Add: Dividends on stock investments		10,000
Net income		26,000
Less: Revenues transferred to Library Fund		26,000
Retained income		–0–
Fund balance received from Doe estate—January 2, 19x1		300,000
Fund balance, December 31, 19x1		$300,000

Illustration 22-10
CITY OF WATERTOWN
Doe Library Endowment Fund
Statement of Changes in Financial Position
For the Year Ended December 31, 19x1

Resources provided:
From operations:

Net income	$26,000
Add: Charges not requiring the outlay of working capital:	
Depreciation expense	5,000
Total resources provided	31,000
Resources used:	
Distribution Library Fund	26,000
Increase in working capital	5,000

Schedule of Changes in Working Capital

	December 31, 19x1	January 1, 19x1	Increase decrease*
Cash	$6,000	–0–	$6,000
Rent receivable	2,000	–0–	2,000
Current assets	8,000	–0–	8,000
Accounts payable	3,000	–0–	3,000*
Increase in working capital	$5,000	–0–	$5,000

GENERAL FIXED ASSETS ACCOUNT GROUP

Fixed assets are usually accounted for in this group of accounts except for the assets in Enterprise, Internal Service, and Fiduciary Funds. This account group is not a fund; it contains no current assets or liabilities. Essentially, it is availed of for purposes of accounting control. Thus, fixed assets are recorded at acquisition cost or fair market value if donated. Depreciation (accumulated) is not usually recorded. However, the NCGA *Statement* provides:

> Depreciation of general fixed assets should not be recorded in the accounts of governmental funds. Depreciation of general fixed assets may be recorded in cost accounting systems or calculated for cost finding analyses; and accumulated depreciation may be recorded in the General Fixed Assets Account Group.[1]

Therefore, if accumulated depreciation is to be provided, the debit is *not* to Depreciation Expense, but rather to the equity portion of the account called, Investment in General Fixed Assets.

To illustrate the operation of this account group the following illustrative entries are assumed.

General Fund

Expenditures (equipment)	50,000	
Vouchers Payable		50,000

General Fixed Assets Account Group

Equipment	50,000	
Investment in General Fixed Assets—General Fund Revenues		50,000

---

[1]Governmental Accounting and Financial Reporting Principles, *Statement 1*, p. 10.

If the equipment were acquired with federal funds, donations, Trust Funds, etc., the source of the funds would be part of the credit portion of the entry and would replace the General Fund Revenues account. If, instead of purchasing equipment, fixed assets were constructed using the funds in the Capital Projects Fund, the entry would be:

General Fixed Assets Account Group

Construction Work in Progress	300,000	
Investment in General Fixed Assets—Capital Projects Fund—Federal Grant		300,000

If the project were completed in the following year, the entry would be:

General Fixed Assets Account Group

Buildings	500,000	
Construction Work in Progress		300,000
Investment in General Fixed Assets—Capital Projects Fund—Federal Grant		200,000

Illustration 22–11
CITY OF RUTLAND, VERMONT
Statement of General Fixed Assets—by Functions and Activities
Fiscal Year Ended June 30, 19x8

	Total	Land	Buildings	Improvements other than buildings	Machinery and Equipment
General government:					
Control					
Legislative	$ 1,067.00				$ 1,067.00
Executive	587.88				587.88
Total control	1,654.88				1,654.88
Staff agencies:					
Finance					
Assessors and constable	2,359.85				2,359.85
Clerk	35,641.85				35,641.85
Treasurer	7,065.70				7,065.70
Zoning	2,329.84				2,329.84
Law	2,159.50				2,159.50
Public buildings	787,484.97	$175,229.00	$ 599,313.40	$ 11,326.27	1,616.30
Total staff agencies	837,041.71	175,229.00	599,313.40	11,326.27	51,173.04
Total general government	838,696.59	175,229.00	599,313.40	11,326.27	52,827.92
Public safety:					
Police department	74,723.59				74,723.59
Fire department	907,801.44	61,500.00	505,985.19	1,212.27	339,103.98
Civilian defense	3,388.08				3,388.08
Total public safety	985,913.11	61,500.00	505,985.19	1,212.27	417,215.65
Public works	4,340,132.01	23,000.00	429,369.38	3,233,081.80	654,680.83
Sanitation and waste removal	3,352,114.51	—	2,935.16	3,137,152.43	212,026.92
Public welfare	1,045.00	—	—	—	1,045.00
Libraries	333,693.28	15,000.00	318,693.28	—	—
Schools	9,183,898.97	324,531.25	7,085,840.98	463,920.57	1,309,606.17
Recreation	1,449,571.04	97,300.00	953,312.65	310,652.07	88,306.32
Total fixed assets allocated to functions	20,485,064.51	$696,560.25	$9,895,450.04	$7,157,345.41	$2,735,708.81
Work in progress	836,487.62				
Total general fixed assets	$21,321,552.13				

The financial statements for this account group consist of a statement of general fixed assets which contains a functional listing of the assets (land, building, etc.) with dollar amounts for each and a contralisting showing the investment in general fixed assets by sources of the funds used to acquire the fixed assets. Needless to say, the totals of each listing should agree. The other statement for this account group is a statement of changes in general fixed assets. The statement usually has four columns. The first column contains a functional listing of fixed assets at the beginning of the accounting period, a column for additions, a column for retirements, and a column for balances at the end of the accounting period (by functional category).

A sample set of financial statements for the city of Rutland, Vermont for this account group would appear as in Illustrations 22–11, 22–12, and 22–13.

Illustration 22–12
CITY OF RUTLAND, VERMONT
Statement of Changes in General Fixed Assets—by Functions and Activities
Fiscal Year Ended June 30, 19x8

	General fixed assets July 1, 19x7	Additions	Deductions	General fixed assets June 30, 19x8
General government				
Control				
Legislature	$ 1,067.00			$ 1,067.00
Executive	587.88			587.88
Total control	1,654.88			1,654.88
Staff agencies				
Finance				
Assessors and constable	2,359.85			2,359.85
Clerk	34,440.35	$ 1,201.50		35,641.85
Treasurer	7,065.70			7,065.70
Zoning	1,464.12	865.72		2,329.84
Law	–0–	2,159.50		2,159.50
Public buildings	767,718.22	19,766.75		787,484.97
Total staff agencies	813,048.24	23,993.47		837,041.71
Total general government	814,703.12	23,993.47		838,696.59
Public safety				
Police department	74,102.07	15,091.02	$ 14,469.50	74,723.59
Fire department	893,507.06	14,294.38		907,801.44
Civilian defense	1,403.08	1,985.00		3,388.08
Total public safety	969,012.21	31,370.40	14,469.50	985,913.11
Public works	3,871,809.25	488,682.26	20,359.50	4,340,132.01
Sanitation and waste removal	3,344,114.51	8,000.00	–0–	3,352,114.51
Public welfare	1,045.00	—	—	1,045.00
Libraries	333,693.28	—	—	333,693.28
Recreation	1,269,047.49	180,523.55	—	1,449,571.04
Schools	6,263,994.56	2,919,904.41	—	9,183,898.97
Work in progress	3,164,896.54	985,992.06	3,314,400.98	836,487.62
Total general fixed assets	$20,032,315.96	$4,638,466.15	$3,349,229.98	$21,321,552.13

Illustration 22–13
CITY OF RUTLAND, VERMONT
Statement of General Fixed Assets—by Sources
Fiscal Year Ended June 30, 19x8

	Total	Land	Buildings	Improvements other than buildings	Machinery and equipment	Construction work in progress
General fixed assets, July 1, 19x7	$20,032,315.96	$695,160.25	$7,417,545.77	$6,660,516.65	$2,094,196.75	$3,164,896.54
Add:						
Expenditures—capital outlay:						
General fund	16,312.95	1,400.00	615.96	7,103.48	7,193.51	
School fund	85,754.48		19,299.00	3,910.90	62,544.58	
Revenue sharing	177,934.50		13,489.60	43,326.01	53,843.89	67,275.00
State and federal	488,740.65		332,729.71	147,281.36	8,729.58	
Antirecession	125,346.18		11,770.00	45,092.68	68,483.50	
Other	3,744,377.39		2,100,000.00	250,114.33	475,546.00	918,717.06
Total additions	4,638,466.15	1,400.00	2,477,904.27	496,828.76	676,341.06	985,992.06
Total	24,670,782.11	696,560.25	9,895,450.04	7,157,345.41	2,770,537.81	4,150,888.60
Deduct:						
Fixed assets written off	34,829.00				34,829.00	
Completed projects	3,314,400.98					3,314,400.98
Total deductions	3,349,229.98				34,829.00	3,314,400.98
General fixed assets, June 30, 19x8	$21,321,552.13	$696,560.25	$9,895,450.04	$7,157,345.41	$2,735,708.81	$ 836,487.62

GENERAL LONG-TERM DEBT ACCOUNT GROUP

It should be remembered that Enterprise Funds, Internal Service Funds, Special Assessment Funds, and Trust Funds generally account for their own long-term debt. This account group does contain liabilities, but since no assets appear in this group, it is not a fund. Nevertheless, debits and credits are required for this account group to be in balance.

When bonds to be accounted for in this group are issued, the proceeds of sale appear elsewhere, and the following entry is made in this account group:

Amount to Be Provided for Payment of Term (Serial) Bonds . . .   500,000
    Term (Serial) Bonds Payable   500,000
Note: Either *Term* or *Serial* is used depending on the maturities of the bonds.

If the Debt Service Fund were accumulating amounts in accordance with a sinking fund requirement, the following entry would be made:

General Long-Term Debt Account Group

Amount Available in Debt Service Fund for Payment of Term
    (Serial) Bonds   75,000
     Amount to be Provided for Payment of Term (Serial) Bonds .   75,000
    Note: This entry would be repeated for earnings on the accumulation and for subsequent accumulations.

When the bonds mature, the payment of principal would be made from the Debt Service Fund, and the following entry would be made if the bonds were term bonds:

General Long-Term Debt Account Group

Term Bonds Payable   500,000
    Amount Available in Debt Service Fund for Payment of
    Term Bonds   500,000

Illustration 22–14
CITY OF WATERTOWN
Statement of General Long-Term Debt
December 31, 19x1

Amount available and to be provided for the payment of general
    long-term debt:

Term bonds:		
Amount available in Debt Service Fund		$ 75,000
Amount to be provided		125,000
Subtotal		200,000
Serial bonds:		
Amount available in Debt Service Fund	$ 80,000	
Amount to be provided	220,000	300,000
Total available and to be provided		$500,000

General long-term debt:

9% term bonds payable December 31, 19x9	$200,000
8% serial bonds payable $50,000 annually	300,000
Total general long-term debt	$500,000

Illustration 22–15
CITY OF RICHMOND
City Debt
Statement of Changes in General Long-Term Debt
For the Fiscal Year Ended June 30, 19x8

Bonds and notes payable—July 1, 19x7			$262,823,565
Notes issued:			
United Virginia Bank, dated July 13, 19x7,			
4.51%, $155,917 maturing annually from			
June 30, 19x8, to June 30, 19y2			779,585
			263,603,150
Bonds retired:			
City of Richmond:			
2½%	$ 342,000		
2¾%	1,540,000		
3%	880,000		
3¼%	1,055,000		
3½%	715,000		
4¼%	2,000,000		
5%	6,650,000		
6¼%	3,150,000		
6½%	1,000,000		
6¾%	1,350,000	$18,682,000	
County of Chesterfield (assumed by			
annexation):			
3%	161,050		
3$\frac{1}{10}$%	64,876		
3$\frac{2}{10}$%	142,853		
3$\frac{4}{10}$%	47,724		
3½%	210,965		
3$\frac{6}{10}$%	58,900		
4$\frac{3}{10}$%	65,791		
4¾%	104,120	856,279	
Total bonds retired			19,538,279
Notes retired United Virginia Bank 4.51%			155,917
Total retirements			19,694,196
Bonds and notes payable—June 30, 19x8			$243,908,954

Illustration 22–16

	Governmental Funds					Fiduciary Funds		Proprietary Funds		Account Groups	
	General Fund	Special Revenue Fund	Capital Projects Fund	Debt Service Fund	Special Assessment Fund	Agency Fund	Trust Fund—Nonexpendable	Internal Service Fund	Enterprise Fund	General Fixed Assets Account Group	General Long-Term Debt Account Group
Budgetary accounts	Yes	Yes	No	Yes	No	—	—	—	—	—	—
Basis of accounting	Modified	Modified	Modified	Modified	Modified	Cash	Accrual	Accrual	Accrual	—	—
Uses encumbrance system	Yes	No	No	No	Yes	No	Yes	Yes	Yes	Yes	No
Fixed assets	No	No	Yes	No	No	—	—	No	Yes	—	—
Proceeds of bond sales	No	No	No	No	Yes	—	—	No	Yes	—	Yes
Liability for bonds	Yes	Yes	No	When due	Yes	—	—	No	Yes	—	No
Payment of bonds				Yes	Yes				Yes		
Required Financial Statements											
Balance sheet	Yes	Yes	Yes	Yes	Yes	Yes	Yes	Yes	Yes	Yes	Yes
Statement of revenue and expenditures	Yes	Yes	Yes	Yes	Yes	No	No	No	No	No	No
Analysis of changes in fund balance	Yes	Yes	Yes	Yes	Yes	Yes	No	No	No	No	No
Statement of cash receipts and disbursements	No	No	No	No	No	Yes	No	No	No	No	No
Statement of revenues and expenses	No	No	No	No	No	No	Yes	Yes	Yes	No	No
Analysis of changes in retained earnings	No	No	No	No	No	No	Yes	Yes	Yes	No	No
Statement of changes in financial position	No	No	No	No	No	No	Yes	Yes	Yes	No	No

If the bonds were serial bonds, the entry would be similar except that the amount would only be for the portion maturing in a particular year.

The financial statements required for this account group are similar to those required for the General Fixed Assets Account Group. A typical statement of general long-term debt contains a listing of amounts available for payment of bonds and amounts to be provided for payment of bonds and appears as Illustration 22–14. The total of these listings should agree with a listing of outstanding bonds payable described as to type of bond, maturity date and interest rate. The second statement is a statement of changes in long-term debt. This statement (not related to Illustration 22–14) is taken from the annual report of the City of Richmond, Virginia, and appears as Illustration 22–15.

A complete set of financial statements, as recommended by the NCGA is included in the appendix at the end of this chapter. These should be reviewed by the reader. A master checklist of financial statements and accounting requirements for each fund is presented as Illustration 22–16.

Appendix: Financial statements for a state or local government

Illustration 22–17
NAME OF GOVERNMENTAL UNIT
Combined Balance Sheet—All Fund Types and Account Groups*
December 31, 19x2

		Governmental Fund types			
	General	Special Revenue	Debt Service	Capital Projects	Special Assessment
Assets					
Cash	$258,500	$101,385	$ 43,834	$ 431,600	$232,185
Cash with fiscal agent	—	—	102,000	—	—
Investments, at cost or amortized cost . . .	65,000	37,200	160,990	—	—
Receivables (net of allowances for uncollectibles):					
Taxes	58,300	2,500	3,829	—	—
Accounts	8,300	3,300	—	100	—
Special assessments	—	—	—	—	646,035
Notes	—	—	—	—	—
Loans	—	—	—	—	—
Accrued interest	50	25	1,557	—	350
Due from other funds	2,000	—	—	—	—
Due from other governments	30,000	75,260	—	640,000	—
Advances to Internal Service Funds	65,000	—	—	—	—
Inventory of supplies, at cost	7,200	5,190	—	—	—
Prepaid expenses	—	—	—	—	—
Restricted assets:					
Cash	—	—	—	—	—
Investments, at cost or amortized cost . .	—	—	—	—	—
Land	—	—	—	—	—
Buildings	—	—	—	—	—
Accumulated depreciation	—	—	—	—	—
Improvements other than buildings	—	—	—	—	—
Accumulated depreciation	—	—	—	—	—
Machinery and equipment	—	—	—	—	—
Accumulated depreciation	—	—	—	—	—
Construction in progress	—	—	—	—	—
Amount available in Debt Service Funds . . .	—	—	—	—	—
Amount to be provided for retirement of general long-term debt	—	—	—	—	—
Total assets	$494,350	$224,860	$312,210	$1,071,700	$878,570

Proprietary Fund types		Fiduciary Fund type	Account groups		Totals (memorandum only)	
Enterprise	Internal Service	Trust and Agency	General fixed assets	General long-term debt	December 31, 19x2	December 31, 19x1
$ 257,036	$ 29,700	$ 216,701	—	—	$ 1,570,941	$ 1,258,909
—	—	—	—	—	102,000	—
—	—	1,239,260	—	—	1,502,450	1,974,354
—	—	580,000	—	—	644,629	255,400
29,130	—	—	—	—	40,830	32,600
—	—	—	—	—	646,035	462,035
2,350	—	—	—	—	2,350	1,250
—	—	35,000	—	—	35,000	40,000
650	—	2,666	—	—	5,298	3,340
2,000	12,000	11,189	—	—	27,189	17,499
—	—	—	—	—	745,260	101,400
—	—	—	—	—	65,000	75,000
23,030	40,000	—	—	—	75,420	70,900
1,200	—	—	—	—	1,200	900
113,559	—	—	—	—	113,559	272,968
176,800	—	—	—	—	176,800	143,800
211,100	20,000	—	$1,259,500	—	1,490,600	1,456,100
447,700	60,000	—	2,855,500	—	3,363,200	2,836,700
(90,718)	(4,500)	—	—	—	(95,218)	(83,500)
3,887,901	15,000	—	1,036,750	—	4,939,651	3,922,200
(348,944)	(3,000)	—	—	—	(351,944)	(283,750)
1,841,145	25,000	—	452,500	—	2,318,645	1,924,100
(201,138)	(9,400)	—	—	—	(210,538)	(141,900)
22,713	—	—	1,722,250	—	1,744,963	1,359,606
—	—	—	—	$ 210,210	210,210	284,813
—	—	—	—	1,889,790	1,889,790	1,075,187
$6,375,514	$184,800	$2,084,816	$7,326,500	$2,100,000	$21,053,320	$17,059,911

Illustration 22–17 *(continued)*

	Governmental Fund types				
Liabilities and Fund Equity	*General*	*Special Revenue*	*Debt Service*	*Capital Projects*	*Special Assessment*
Liabilities:					
Vouchers payable	$118,261	$ 33,850	—	$ 29,000	$ 20,600
Contracts payable	57,600	18,300	—	69,000	50,000
Judgments payable	—	2,000	—	22,600	11,200
Accrued liabilities	—	—	—	—	10,700
Payable from restricted assets:					
Construction contracts	—	—	—	—	—
Fiscal agent	—	—	—	—	—
Accrued interest	—	—	—	—	—
Revenue bonds	—	—	—	—	—
Deposits	—	—	—	—	—
Due to other taxing units	—	—	—	—	—
Due to other funds	24,189	2,000	—	1,000	—
Due to student groups	—	—	—	—	—
Deferred revenue	15,000	—	—	—	—
Advance from General Fund	—	—	—	—	—
Matured bonds payable	—	—	$100,000	—	—
Matured interest payable	—	—	2,000	—	—
General obligation bonds payable	—	—	—	—	—
Revenue bonds payable	—	—	—	—	—
Special assessment bonds payable	—	—	—	—	555,000
Total liabilities	215,050	56,150	102,000	121,600	647,500
Fund equity:					
Contributed capital	—	—	—	—	—
Investment in general fixed assets	—	—	—	—	—
Retained earnings:					
Reserved for revenue bond retirement .	—	—	—	—	—
Unreserved	—	—	—	—	—
Fund balances:					
Reserved for encumbrances	38,000	46,500	—	941,500	185,000
Reserved for inventory of supplies . . .	7,200	5,190	—	—	—
Reserved for advance to Internal Service Funds	65,000	—	—	—	—
Reserved for loans	—	—	—	—	—
Reserved for endowments	—	—	—	—	—
Reserved for employees' retirement system	—	—	—	—	—
Unreserved:					
Designated for debt service	—	—	210,210	—	46,070
Designated for subsequent years' expenditures	50,000	—	—	—	—
Undesignated	119,100	117,020	—	8,600	—
Total fund equity	279,300	168,710	210,210	950,100	231,070
Total liabilities and fund equity .	$494,350	$224,860	$312,210	$1,071,700	$878,570

*Source: NCGA, *Statement No. 1.*

Assets

	Proprietary Fund types		Fiduciary Fund type	Account groups		Totals (memorandum only)	
	Enterprise	Internal Service	Trust and Agency	General fixed assets	General long-term debt	December 31, 19x2	December 31, 19x1
	$ 131,071	$ 15,000	$ 3,350	—	—	$ 351,132	$ 223,412
	8,347	—	—	—	—	203,247	1,326,511
	—	—	—	—	—	35,800	32,400
	16,870	—	4,700	—	—	32,270	27,417
	17,760	—	—	—	—	17,760	—
	139	—	—	—	—	139	—
	32,305	—	—	—	—	32,305	67,150
	48,000	—	—	—	—	48,000	52,000
	63,000	—	—	—	—	63,000	55,000
	—	—	680,800	—	—	680,800	200,000
	—	—	—	—	—	27,189	17,499
	—	—	1,850	—	—	1,850	1,600
	—	—	—	—	—	15,000	3,000
	—	65,000	—	—	—	65,000	75,000
	—	—	—	—	—	100,000	—
	—	—	—	—	—	2,000	—
	700,000	—	—	—	$2,100,000	2,800,000	2,110,000
	1,798,000	—	—	—	—	1,798,000	1,846,000
	—	—	—	—	—	555,000	420,000
	2,815,492	80,000	690,700	—	2,100,000	6,828,492	6,456,989
	1,392,666	95,000	—	—	—	1,487,666	815,000
	—	—	—	$7,326,500	—	7,326,500	5,299,600
	129,155	—	—	—	—	129,155	96,975
	2,038,201	9,800	—	—	—	2,048,011	1,998,119
	—	—	—	—	—	1,211,000	410,050
	—	—	—	—	—	12,390	10,890
	—	—	—	—	—	65,000	75,000
	—	—	50,050	—	—	50,050	45,100
	—	—	134,000	—	—	134,000	94,000
	—	—	1,426,201	—	—	1,426,201	1,276,150
	—	—	—	—	—	256,280	325,888
	—	—	—	—	—	50,000	50,000
	—	—	(216,135)	—	—	28,585	106,150
	3,560,022	104,800	1,394,116	7,326,500	—	14,224,828	10,602,922
	$6,375,514	$184,800	$2,084,816	$7,326,500	$2,100,000	$21,053,320	$17,059,911

Illustration 22–18
NAME OF GOVERNMENTAL UNIT
Combined Statement of Revenues, Expenditures, and Changes in Fund Balances—
All Governmental Fund Types and Expendable Trust Funds
For the Fiscal Year Ended December 31, 19x2

	Governmental Fund types		
	General	Special Revenue	Debt Service
Revenues:			
Taxes	$ 881,300	$ 189,300	$ 79,177
Special assessments levied	—	—	—
Licenses and permits	103,000	—	—
Intergovernmental revenues	186,500	831,100	41,500
Charges for services	91,000	79,100	—
Fines and forfeits	33,200	—	—
Miscellaneous revenues	19,500	71,625	7,140
Total revenues	1,314,500	1,171,125	127,817
Expenditures:			
Current:			
General government	121,805	—	—
Public safety	258,395	480,000	—
Highways and streets	85,400	417,000	—
Sanitation	56,250	—	—
Health	44,500	—	—
Welfare	46,800	—	—
Culture and recreation	40,900	256,450	—
Education	509,150	—	—
Capital outlay	—	—	—
Debt service:			
Principal retirement	—	—	60,000
Interest and fiscal charges	—	—	40,420
Total expenditures	1,163,200	1,153,450	100,420
Excess of revenues over (under) expenditures	151,300	17,675	27,397
Other financing sources (uses):			
Proceeds of general obligation bonds	—	—	—
Operating transfers-in	—	—	—
Operating transfers-out	(74,500)	—	—
Total other financing sources (uses)	(74,500)	—	—
Excess of revenues and other sources over (under) expenditures and other uses . . .	76,800	17,675	27,397
Fund balances—January 1	202,500	151,035	182,813
Fund balances—December 31	$ 279,300	$ 168,710	$210,210

	Governmental Fund types (continued)		Fiduciary Fund type	Totals (memorandum only) Year ended	
	Capital Projects	Special Assess- ment	Expend- able Trust	Decem- ber 31, 19x2	Decem- ber 31, 19x2
	—	—	—	$1,149,777	$1,137,900
	—	$240,000	—	240,000	250,400
	—	—	—	103,000	96,500
	$1,250,000	—	—	2,309,100	1,258,800
	—	—	—	170,100	160,400
	—	—	—	33,200	26,300
	3,750	29,095	$ 200	131,310	111,500
	1,253,750	269,095	200	4,136,487	3,041,800
	—	—	—	121,805	134,200
	—	—	—	738,395	671,300
	—	—	—	502,400	408,700
	—	—	—	56,250	44,100
	—	—	—	44,500	36,600
	—	—	—	46,800	41,400
	—	—	—	297,350	286,400
	—	—	2,420	511,570	512,000
	1,625,500	313,100	—	1,938,600	803,000
	—	—	—	60,000	52,100
	—	28,000	—	68,420	50,000
	1,625,500	341,100	2,420	4,386,090	3,039,800
	(371,750)	(72,005)	(2,220)	(249,603)	2,000
	900,000	—	—	900,000	—
	64,500	10,000	2,530	77,030	89,120
	—	—	—	(74,500)	(87,000)
	964,500	10,000	2,530	902,530	2,120
	592,750	(62,005)	310	652,927	4,120
	357,350	293,075	26,555	1,213,328	1,209,208
	$ 950,100	$231,070	$26,865	$1,866,255	$1,213,328

Illustration 22–19
NAME OF GOVERNMENTAL UNIT
**Combined Statement of Revenues, Expenditures, and
Changes in Fund Balances—Budget and Actual—
General and Special Revenue Fund Types
For the Fiscal Year Ended December 31, 19x2**

	General Fund		
	Budget	*Actual*	*Variance—favorable (unfavorable)*
Revenues:			
Taxes	$ 882,500	$ 881,300	$ (1,200)
Licenses and permits	125,500	103,000	(22,500)
Intergovernmental revenues	200,000	186,500	(13,500)
Charges for services	90,000	91,000	1,000
Fines and forfeits	32,500	33,200	700
Miscellaneous revenues	19,500	19,500	—
Total revenues	1,350,000	1,314,500	(35,500)
Expenditures:			
Current:			
General government	129,000	121,805	7,195
Public safety	277,300	258,395	18,905
Highways and streets	84,500	85,400	(900)
Sanitation	50,000	56,250	(6,250)
Health	47,750	44,500	3,250
Welfare	51,000	46,800	4,200
Culture and recreation	44,500	40,900	3,600
Education	541,450	509,150	32,300
Total expenditures	1,225,500	1,163,200	62,300
Excess of revenues over (under) expenditures	124,500	151,300	26,800
Other financing sources (uses):			
Operating transfers-out	(74,500)	(74,500)	—
Excess of revenues over (under) expenditures and other uses	50,000	76,800	26,800
Fund balances—January 1	202,500	202,500	—
Fund balances—December 31	$ 252,500	$ 279,300	$ 26,800

Special Revenue Funds			Totals (memorandum only)		
Budget	Actual	Variance— favorable (unfavorable)	Budget	Actual	Variance— favorable (unfavorable)
$ 189,500	$ 189,300	$ (200)	$1,072,000	$1,070,600	$ (1,400)
—	—	—	125,500	103,000	(22,500)
837,600	831,100	(6,500)	1,037,600	1,017,600	(20,000)
78,000	79,100	1,100	168,000	170,100	2,100
—	—	—	32,500	33,200	700
81,475	71,625	(9,850)	100,975	91,125	(9,850)
1,186,575	1,171,125	(15,450)	2,536,575	2,485,625	(50,950)
—	—	—	129,000	121,805	7,195
494,500	480,000	14,500	771,800	738,395	33,405
436,000	417,000	19,000	520,500	502,400	18,100
—	—	—	50,000	56,250	(6,250)
—	—	—	47,750	44,500	3,250
—	—	—	51,000	46,800	4,200
272,000	256,450	15,550	316,500	297,350	19,150
—	—	—	541,450	509,150	32,300
1,202,500	1,153,450	49,050	2,248,000	2,316,650	111,350
(15,925)	17,675	33,600	108,575	168,975	60,400
—	—	—	(74,500)	(74,500)	—
(15,925)	17,675	33,600	34,075	94,475	60,400
151,035	151,035	—	353,535	353,535	—
$ 135,110	$ 168,710	$33,600	$ 387,610	$ 448,010	$ 60,400

Illustration 22–20
NAME OF GOVERNMENTAL UNIT
**Combined Statement of Revenues, Expenses, and Changes in
Retained Earnings/Fund Balances—All Proprietary Fund Types
and Similar Trust Funds
For the Fiscal Year Ended December 31, 19x2**

	Proprietary Fund types		Fiduciary Fund type		Totals (memorandum only)	
					Year ended	
	Enterprise	Internal Service	Nonexpendable Trust	Pension Trust	December 31, 19x2	December 31, 19x1
Operating revenues:						
Charges for services	$ 672,150	$88,000	—	—	$ 760,150	$ 686,563
Interest	—	—	$ 2,480	$ 28,460	30,940	26,118
Contributions	—	—	—	160,686	160,686	144,670
Gifts	—	—	45,000	—	45,000	—
Total operating revenues	672,150	88,000	47,480	189,146	996,776	857,351
Operating expenses:						
Personal services	247,450	32,500	—	—	279,950	250,418
Contractual services	75,330	400	—	—	75,730	68,214
Supplies	20,310	1,900	—	—	22,210	17,329
Materials	50,940	44,000	—	—	94,940	87,644
Heat, light, and power	26,050	1,500	—	—	27,550	22,975
Depreciation	144,100	4,450	—	—	148,550	133,210
Benefit payments	—	—	—	21,000	21,000	12,000
Refunds	—	—	—	25,745	25,745	13,243
Total operating expenses	564,180	84,750	—	46,745	695,675	605,033
Operating income	107,970	3,250	47,480	142,401	301,101	252,318
Nonoperating revenues (expenses):						
Operating grants	55,000	—	—	—	55,000	50,000
Interest revenue	3,830	—	—	—	3,830	3,200
Rent	5,000	—	—	—	5,000	5,000
Interest expense and fiscal charges . . .	(92,988)	—	—	—	(92,988)	(102,408)
Total nonoperating revenues (expenses)	(29,158)	—	—	—	(29,158)	(44,208)
Income before operating transfers .	78,812	3,250	47,480	142,401	271,943	208,110
Operating transfers-in (out)	—	—	(2,530)	—	(2,530)	(2,120)
Net income	78,812	3,250	44,950	142,401	269,413	205,990
Retained earnings/fund balances— January 1	2,088,544	6,550	139,100	1,040,800	3,274,994	3,069,004
Retained earnings/fund balances— December 31	$2,167,356	$ 9,800	$184,050	$1,183,201	$3,544,407	$3,274,994

Illustration 22–21
NAME OF GOVERNMENTAL UNIT
Combined Statement of Changes in
Financial Position—All Proprietary Fund Types and
Similar Trust Funds
For the Fiscal Year Ended December 31, 19x2

	Proprietary Fund types		Fiduciary Fund type		Totals (memorandum only)	
	Enterprise	Internal Service	Non-expendable Trust	Pension Trust	Dec. 31, 19x2	Dec. 31, 19x1
Sources of working capital:						
Operations:						
Net income	$ 78,812	$ 3,250	$44,950	$142,401	$ 269,413	$ 205,990
Items not requiring (providing) working capital:						
Depreciation	144,100	4,450	—	—	148,550	133,210
Working capital provided by operations	222,912	7,700	44,950	142,401	417,963	339,200
Cash from revenue bond construction account	127,883	—	—	—	127,883	743,800
Contributions	672,666	—	—	—	672,666	—
Total sources of working capital	1,023,461	7,700	44,950	142,401	1,218,512	1,083,000
Uses of working capital:						
Acquisition of property, plant, and equipment	324,453	7,000	—	—	331,453	842,812
Retirement of general obligation bonds	50,000	—	—	—	50,000	50,000
Retirement of revenue bonds payable	52,000	—	—	—	52,000	48,000
Repayment of advance from General Fund	—	10,000	—	—	10,000	10,000
Net decrease in other current liabilities payable from						
restricted assets	8,946	—	—	—	8,946	4,318
Net increase in other restricted assets	1,624	—	—	—	1,624	414
Total uses of working capital	437,023	17,000	—	—	454,023	955,544
Net increase (decrease) in working capital . . .	$ 586,438	$ (9,300)	$44,950	$142,401	$ 764,489	$ 127,456
Elements of net increase (decrease) in working capital:						
Cash	$ 119,276	$(20,300)	$ 4,310	$ 20,121	$ 123,407	$ 796,412
Investments	—	—	45,640	118,341	163,981	(84,286)
Receivables (net of allowances for uncollectibles) . . .	(5,570)	—	(5,000)	—	(10,570)	2,396
Due from other funds	(6,000)	(8,000)	—	2,189	(11,811)	(4,923)
Inventory of supplies	11,250	14,000	—	—	25,250	(3,414)
Prepaid expenses	460	—	—	—	460	520
Vouchers payable	(72,471)	5,000	—	—	(67,471)	(42,427)
Contracts payable	551,653	—	—	1,750	553,403	(525,400)
Accrued liabilities	(12,160)	—	—	—	(12,160)	(11,422)
Net increase (decrease) in working capital . . .	$ 586,438	$ (9,300)	$44,950	$142,401	$ 764,489	$ 127,456

Illustration 22–22

NAME OF GOVERNMENTAL UNIT
Combining Balance Sheet—
All Special Revenue Funds
December 31, 19x2

	Parks	State gasoline tax	Motor vehicle license	Parking meter	Juvenile rehabil- itation	Totals Dec. 31, 19x2	Dec. 31, 19x1
Assets							
Cash	$39,525	$22,460	$ 5,420	$16,260	$17,720	$101,385	$ 91,459
Investments, at cost	16,200	—	—	15,000	6,000	37,200	25,000
Receivables:							
Taxes receivable—delinquent (net of allowance for uncollectibles of $500)	2,500	—	—	—	—	2,500	—
Accounts receivable (net of allowance for uncollectibles of $800)	3,300	—	—	—	—	3,300	2,700
Accrued interest	25	—	—	—	—	25	—
Due from state government	—	47,250	28,010	—	—	75,260	62,400
Inventory of supplies, at cost	1,100	990	702	1,066	1,332	5,190	5,190
Total assets	$62,650	$70,700	$34,132	$32,326	$25,052	$224,860	$186,749
Liabilities and Fund Balances							
Liabilities:							
Vouchers payable	$10,000	$11,220	$ 4,260	$ 3,220	$ 5,150	$ 33,850	$ 23,414
Contracts payable	12,500	4,000	—	1,800	—	18,300	12,300
Judgments payable	2,000	—	—	—	—	2,000	—
Due to General Fund	2,000	—	—	—	—	2,000	—
Total liabilities	26,500	15,220	4,260	5,020	5,150	56,150	35,714
Fund balances:							
Reserved for encumbrances	14,000	16,500	10,000	500	5,500	46,500	12,550
Reserved for inventory of supplies	1,100	990	702	1,066	1,332	5,190	5,190
Unreserved	21,050	37,990	19,170	25,740	13,070	117,020	133,295
Total fund balances	36,150	55,480	29,872	27,306	19,902	168,710	151,035
Total liabilities and fund balances	$62,650	$70,700	$34,132	$32,326	$25,052	$224,860	$186,749

Illustration 22–23

NAME OF GOVERNMENTAL UNIT
Combining Statement of Revenues, Expenditures, and Changes in Fund Balances—
All Special Revenue Funds
For the Fiscal Year Ended December 31, 19x2

	Parks	State gasoline tax	Motor vehicle license	Parking meter	Juvenile rehabil- itation	Totals year ended Dec. 31, 19x2	Dec. 31, 19x1
Revenues:							
Taxes	$189,300	—	—	—	—	$ 189,300	$ 168,400
Intergovernmental revenues	—	$422,500	$201,000	—	$207,600	831,100	749,990
Charges for services	—	—	—	$79,100	—	79,100	71,420
Miscellaneous revenues	70,700	—	—	600	325	71,625	63,614
Total revenues	260,000	422,500	201,000	79,700	207,925	1,171,125	1,053,424
Expenditures:							
Public safety	—	—	199,400	80,900	199,700	480,000	414,040
Highways and streets	—	417,000	—	—	—	417,000	346,414
Culture and recreation	256,450	—	—	—	—	256,450	238,419
Total expenditures	256,450	417,000	199,400	80,900	199,700	1,153,450	998,873
Excess of revenues over (under) expenditures	3,550	5,500	1,600	(1,200)	8,225	17,675	54,551
Fund balances—January 1	32,600	49,980	28,272	28,506	11,677	151,035	96,484
Fund balances—December 31	$ 36,150	$ 55,480	$ 29,872	$27,306	$ 19,902	$ 168,710	$ 151,035

QUESTIONS

1. What is a Special Revenue Fund used for? Are the entries in this fund similar to those of another fund? Which one?

2. What type of accounting does the Capital Projects Fund use? Does this fund use encumbrances? Are bonds payable recorded in this fund? Why? What is the appropriate treatment of bond premium in this fund? Of bond discount?

3. What type of accounting does the Debt Service Fund use? Is interest expense accrued? Why? Do the bonds payable appear in this fund? When?

4. When are Special Assessment Funds used? Does the General Fund sometimes share in the cost of these improvements? When? Who bears the remainder of the cost? Why? Are bonds payable recorded in this fund? Why?

5. What is an Internal Service Fund used for? What type of accounting does this fund use? What is meant by a Proprietary Fund? Is this fund a Proprietary Fund? Does this fund record depreciation expense? Why? Does this fund have an account for retained earnings? Are there any differences between the financial statements of this fund and those used by business organizations? If so, what are the differences?

6. When is an Enterprise Fund used? What kind of accounting is used for this fund? What kind of financial statements are used for this fund?

7. What is an Agency Fund? When is it used? What kind of accounting is used for this fund?

8. What is the difference between an Expendable Trust Fund and a Nonexpendable Trust Fund? What type of accounting is used for each type of fund? Give an example of each type of fund.

9. What is an Endowment Fund? Give an example of its use.

10. Is the General Fixed Assets Account Group a fund? Why? Is depreciation expense recorded in this account? Why? Is it possible to record accumulated depreciation? If so, what account is debited?

11. Is the General Long-Term Debt Account Group a fund? Why? Is interest expense recorded in this account? If not, where is it recorded?

EXERCISES

Exercise 22–1.

1. The operations of a public library receiving the majority of its support from property taxes levied for that purpose should be accounted for in—
a. The General Fund.
b. A Special Revenue Fund.
c. An Enterprise Fund.
d. An Internal Service Fund.
e. None of the above.

2. The liability for general obligation bonds issued for the benfit of a municipal electric company and serviced by its earnings should be recorded in—
a. An Enterprise Fund.
b. The General Fund.
c. An Enterprise Fund and the General Long-Term Debt Account Group.
d. An Enterprise Fund and disclosed in a footnote in the statement of general long-term debt.
e. None of the above.

3. The liability for special assessment bonds which carry a secondary pledge of a municipality's general credit should be recorded in—
a. An Enterprise Fund.
b. A Special Revenue Fund and General Long-Term Debt Account Group.
c. A Special Assessment Fund and the General Long-Term Debt Account Group.
d. A Special Assessment Fund and disclosed in a footnote in the statement of general long-term debt.
e. None of the above.

4. The proceeds of a federal grant made to assist in financing the future construction of an adult training center should be recorded in —
a. The General Fund.
b. A Special Revenue Fund.
c. A Capital Projects Fund.
d. A Special Assessment Fund.
e. None of the above.

5. The receipts from a special tax levy to retire and pay interest on general obligation bonds issued to finance the construction of a new city hall should be recorded in a—
a. Debt Service Fund.
b. Capital Projects Fund.

c. Revolving Interest Fund.

d. Special Revenue Fund.

e. None of the above.

6. The operations of a municipal swimming pool receiving the majority of its support from charges to users should be accounted for in—

a. A Special Revenue Fund.

b. The General Fund.

c. An Internal Service Fund.

d. An Enterprise Fund.

e. None of the above.   (AICPA adapted)

Exercise 22–2.

1. The fixed assets of a central purchasing and stores department organized to serve all municipal departments should be recorded in—

a. An Enterprise Fund and the General Fixed Assets Account Group.

b. An Enterprise Fund.

c. The General Fixed Assets Account Group.

d. The General Fund.

e. None of the above.

2. The monthly remittance to an insurance company of the lump sum of hospital-surgical insurance premiums collected as payroll deductions from employees should be recorded in—

a. The General Fund.

b. An Agency Fund.

c. A Special Revenue Fund.

d. An Internal Service Fund.

e. None of the above.

3. Several years ago a city provided for the establishment of a sinking fund to retire an issue of general obligation bonds. This year the city made a $50,000 contribution to the sinking fund from general revenues and realized $15,000 in revenue from securities in the sinking fund. The bonds due this year were retired. These transactions require accounting recognition in—

a. The General Fund.

b. A Debt Service Fund and the General Long-Term Debt Account Group.

c. A Debt Service Fund, the General Fund, and the General Long-Term Debt Account Group.

d. A Capital Projects Fund, a Debt Service Fund, the General Fund, and the General Long-Term Debt Account Group.

e. None of the above.

4. A city realized large capital gains and losses on securities in its library endowment fund. In the absence of specific instructions from the donor or state statutory requirements, the general rule of law holds that these amounts should be charged or credited to—

a. General Fund income.

b. General Fund principal.

c. Trust Fund income.

d. Trust Fund principal.

e. None of the above.

5. The activities of a central motor pool which provides and services vehicles for the use of municipal employees on official business should be accounted for in—

a. An Agency Fund.

b. The General Fund.

c. An Internal Service Fund.

d. A Special Revenue Fund.

e. None of the above.

6. A transaction in which a municipal electric utility paid $150,000 out of its earnings for new equipment requires accounting recognition in—

a. An Enterprise Fund.

b. The General Fund.

c. The General Fund and the General Fixed Assets Account Group.

d. An Enterprise Fund and the General Fixed Assets Account Group.

e. None of the above.   (AICPA adapted)

Exercise 22–3.

1. In order to provide for the retirement of general obligation bonds, a city invests a portion of its general revenue receipts in marketable securities. This investment activity should be accounted for in—

a. A Trust Fund.

b. The Enterprise Fund.

c. A Special Assessment Fund.

d. A Special Revenue Fund.

e. None of the above.

2. The activities of a municipal employee retirement plan which is financed by equal employer and employee contributions should be accounted for in—

a. An Agency Fund.

b. An Internal Service Fund.

c. A Special Assessment Fund.

d. A Trust Fund.

e. None of the above.

3. A city collects property taxes for the benefit of the local sanitary, park, and school districts and periodically remits collections to these units. This activity should be accounted for in—

a. An Agency Fund.

b. The General Fund.

c. An Internal Service Fund.

d. A Special Assessment Fund.

e. None of the above.

4. A transaction in which a municipal electric utility issues bonds (to be repaid from its own operations) requires accounting recognition in—

a. The General Fund.

b. A Debt Service Fund.

c. Enterprise and Debt Service Funds.

d. An Enterprise Fund, a Debt Service Fund, and the General Long-Term Debt Account Group.

e. None of the above.

5. A transaction in which a municipality issued general obligation serial bonds to finance the construction of a fire station requires accounting recognition in the

a. General Fund.

b. Capital Projects and General Funds.

c. Capital Projects Fund and the General Long-Term Debt Account Group.

d. General Fund and the General Long-Term Debt Account Group.

e. None of the above.

6. Expenditures of $200,000 were made during the year on the fire station in 5 above. This transaction requires accounting recognition in the—

a. General Fund.

b. Capital Projects Fund and the General Fixed Assets Account Group.

c. Capital Projects Fund and the General Long-Term Debt Account Group.

d. General Fund and the General Fixed Assets Account Group.

e. None of the above. (AICPA adapted)

Exercise 22–4.

1. The city of Paden should use a Capital Projects Fund to account for—

a. Structures and improvements constructed with the proceeds of a special assessment.

b. Proceeds of a bond issue to be used to acquire land for city parks.

c. Construction in progress on the city-owned electric utility plant, financed by an issue of revenue bonds.

d. Assets to be used to retire bonds issued to finance an addition to the city hall.

2. Activities of a central print shop offering printing services at cost to various city departments should be accounted for in—

a. The General Fund.

b. An Internal Service Fund.

c. A Special Revenue Fund.

d. A Special Assessment Fund.

3. Sanders County collects property taxes for the benefit of the state government and the local school districts and periodically remits collections to these units. These activities should be accounted for in—

a. An Agency Fund.

b. The General Fund.

c. An Internal Service Fund.

d. A Special Assessment Fund.

4. In order to provide for the retirement of general obligation bonds, the city of Osborn invests a portion of its receipts from general property taxes in marketable securities. This investment activity should be accounted for in—

a. A Capital Projects fund.

b. A Debt Service Fund.

c. A Trust Fund.

d. The General Fund.

5. The transactions of a municipal police retirement system should be recorded in—

a. The General Fund.

b. A Special Revenue Fund.

c. A Trust Fund.

d. An Internal Service Fund.

6. The activities of a municipal golf course which receives three fourths of its total revenue from a special tax levy should be accounted for in—

a. An Enterprise Fund.

b. The General Fund.

c. A Special Assessment Fund.

d. A Special Revenue Fund.

7. Recreational facilities run by a governmental unit and financed on a user-charge basis would be accounted for in which fund?

a. General.

b. Trust.

c. Enterprise.

d. Capital Projects. (AICPA adapted)

Exercise 22–5.

1. The presence of the Electric Plant Acquisiton Adjustments account in a city's Electric Utility Fund indicates that, according to the predominant rule in utility regulation—

a. The fund's assets have been appraised and written up to current market value.

b. Interest on money borrowed to finance construction has been capitalized during the construction period.

c. The estimated useful lives of fixed assets have been revised and the chage recorded.

d. The city paid more for the utility's assets than their net book value in the hands of the owner who first devoted them to public use.

2. Rogers City should record depreciation as an expense in its—

a. Enterprise Fund and Internal Service Fund.

b. Internal Service Fund and General Fixed Assets Account Group.

c. General Fund and Enterprise Fund.

d. Enterprise Fund and Capital Projects Funds.

3. In municipal accounting the accrual basis is recommended for—

a. Only Agency, Debt Service, Enterprise, General, and Special Revenue Funds.

b. Only Capital Projects, Enterprise, Internal Service, Special Assessment, and Trust Funds.

c. Only Enterprise and Internal Service Funds.

d. None of the funds.

4. The balance sheet in the financial report of a municipality may be prepared—

a. On a consolidated basis after eliminating the effects of interfund transactions.

b. On a combined basis showing the assets and equities of each fund with a total column indicating the aggregate balance for each identical account in all of the funds.

c. On a combined basis showing the assets and equities of each fund, but without a total column indicating the aggregate balance for each identical account in all of the funds.

d. For each fund in a separate statement but never presenting all funds together in the same statement.

5. Which of the following types of revenue would generally be recorded directly in the General Fund of a governmental unit?

a. Receipts from a city-owned parking structure.

b. Property taxes.

c. Interest earned on investments held for retirement of employees.

d. Revenues from Internal Service Funds.

6. Which of the following funds should use the modified accrual basis of accounting?

a. Capital Projects.

b. Internal Service.

c. Special Revenue.

d. Trust.

7. Which of the following funds frequently does *not* have a fund balance?

a. General Fund.

b. Agency Fund.

c. Special Revenue Fund.

d. Capital Projects Fund.

8. Which governmental fund would account for fixed assets in a manner similar to a "for-profit" organization?

a. Enterprise.

b. Capital Projects.

c. General Fixed Assets Account Group.

d. General.

9. If a governmental unit established a data processing center to service all agencies within the unit, the data processing center should be accounted for as a (an)—

a. Capital Projects Fund.

b. Internal Service Fund.

c. Agency Fund.

d. Trust Fund.   (AICPA adapted)

Exercise 22–6.

1. An "actuarial deficiency" would appear in which fund?

a. Agency.

b. Trust.

c. General.

d. Debt Service.

2. "Excess of net billings to departments over costs" would appear in the financial statement of which fund?

a. Internal Service.

b. Enterprise.

c. Capital Projects.

d. Special Revenue.

3. Which type of fund can be either expendable or nonexpendable?

a. Debt Service.

b. Enterprise.

c. Trust.

d. Special Revenues.

4. A statement of changes in financial position is prepared for which fund?

a. Enterprise.   *c.* Special Assessment.

b. General.   *d.* Trust.

5. The General Fixed Assets Account Group for a municipality can *best* be described as—

a. A fiscal entity.

b. An accounting entity.

c. An integral part of the General Fund.

d. The only fund in which to properly account for fixed assets.

6. An account for expenditures does not appear in which fund?

a. Capital Projects.

b. Enterprise.

c. Special Assessment.

d. Special Revenue.

7. Part of the general obligation bond proceeds from a new issuance was used to pay for the cost of a new city hall as soon as construction was completed. The remainder of the proceeds was transferred to repay the debt. Entries are needed to record these transactions in the—

a. General Fund and General Long-Term Debt Account Group.

b. General Fund, General Long-Term Debt Account Group, and Debt Service Fund.

c. Trust Fund, Debt Service Fund, and General Fixed Assets Account Group.

d. General Long-Term Debt Account Group, Debt Service Fund, General Fixed Assets Account Group, and Capital Projects Fund.

8. Cash secured from property tax revenue was transferred for the eventual payment of principal and interest on general obligation bonds. The bonds had been issued when land had been acquired several years ago for a city park. Upon the transfer, an entry would not be made in which of the following?

a. Debt Service Fund.

b. General Fixed Assets Account Group.

c. General Long-Term Debt Account Group.

d. General Fund.   (AICPA adapted)

Exercise 22–7.

1. Entries similar to those for the General Fund may also appear on the books of the municipality's—

a. General Fixed Assets Account Group.

b. General Long-Term Debt Account Group.

c. Trust Fund.

d. Special Revenue Fund.

2. Premiums received on general obligation

bonds are generally transferred to what fund or group of accounts?

a. Debt Service.

b. General Long-Term Debt.

c. General.

d. Special Revenue.

3. Self-supporting activities that are provided on a user charge basis are accounted for in what fund?

a. Agency.

b. Enterprise.

c. Internal Service.

d. Special Revenue.

4. Which fund is *not* an expendable fund?

a. Capital Projects.

b. General.

c. Special Revenue.

d. Internal Service.

5. Encumbrances would *not* appear in which fund?

a. Capital Projects.

b. Special Revenue.

c. General.

d. Enterprise.

6. Interest expense on bonds payable should be recorded in a Debt Service Fund—

a. At the end of the fiscal period if the interest due date does *not* coincide with the end of the fiscal period.

b. When bonds are issued.

c. When legally payable.

d. When paid.

7. An expenditures account appears in—

a. The General Fixed Assets Account Group.

b. The General Long-Term Debt Account Group.

c. A Special Revenue Fund.

d. An Internal Service Fund.

8. The city of Rover has two Special Assessment Funds. In the preparation of the statement of financial position of these funds as of the end of the fiscal year, these funds may be reported on—

a. A combined basis which shows the total for both funds and has separate columns to present account balances for each fund.

b. A consolidated basis after eliminating the effects of interfund transactions.

c. A separate basis, but never together in the same statement.

d. A consolidated basis with the general fund after eliminating the effects of interfund transactions.

(AICPA adapted)

Exercise 22–8.

1. The accounting for Special Revenue Funds is most similar to which type of fund?
   a. Capital Projects.
   b. Enterprise.
   c. General.
   d. Special Assessment.

2. The General Fixed Assets Account Group would be used for the fixed assets of the—
   a. Special Assessment Fund.
   b. Enterprise Fund.
   c. Trust Fund.
   d. Internal Service Fund.

3. Which of the following requires the use of the encumbrance system?
   a. Special Assessment Fund.
   b. Debt Service Fund.
   c. General Fixed Assets Account Group.
   d. Enterprise Fund.

4. When should revenues from interest on assessments receivable be recorded in a special assessment fund?
   a. When legally due.
   b. When assessed.
   c. When collected in cash.
   d. When the amount is known.

5. "Investment in general fixed assets" accounts would appear in which fund or group of accounts?
   a. General Fixed Assets.
   b. Enterprise.
   c. Capital Projects.
   d. General.

6. Equipment in general governmental service that had been constructed 10 years before by a Capital Projects Fund was sold. The receipts were accounted for as unrestricted revenue. Entries are necessary in the—
   a. General Fund and Capital Projects Fund.
   b. General Fund and General Fixed Assets Account Group.
   c. General Fund, Capital Projects Fund, and Enterprise Fund.
   d. General Fund, Capital Projects Fund, and General Fixes Assets Account Group.

7. The town of Boyd Electric Utility Fund, which is an Enterprise Fund, had the following:

Prepaid insurance paid in December 19x6 . . .	$ 43,000
Depreciation for 19x6	129,000
Provision for doubtful accounts for 19x6	14,000

What amount should be reflected in the state-ment of revenues and expenses (income statement) of the town of Boyd Electric Utility Fund for the above items?
   a. $(43,000).
   b. $0.
   c. $129,000.
   d. $143,000.   (AICPA adapted)

Exercise 22–9.

1. Brockton City's water utility, which is an Enterprise Fund, submits a bill for $9,000 to the General Fund for water service supplied to city departments and agencies. Submission of this bill would result in—
   a. Creation of balances which will be eliminated on the city's combined balance sheet.
   b. Recognition of revenue by the Water Utility Fund and of an expenditure by the General Fund.
   c. Recognition of an encumbrance by both the Water Utility Fund and the General Fund.
   d. Creation of a balance which will be eliminated on the city's combined statement of changes in fund balances.

2. Brockton City's water utility, which is an Enterprise Fund, transferred land and a building to the general city administration for public use at no charge to the city. The land was carried on the water utility books at $4,000 and the building at a cost of $30,000 on which $23,000 depreciation had been recorded. In the year of the transfer what would be the effect of the transaction?
   a. Reduce retained earnings of the water utility by $11,000 and increase the fund balance of the General Fund by $11,000.
   b. Reduce retained earnings of the water utility by $11,000 and increase the total assets in the General Fixed Assets Account Group by $11,000.
   c. Reduce retained earnings of the water utility by $11,000 and increase the total assets in the General Fixed Assets Account Group by $34,000.
   d. Have no effect on a combined balance sheet for the city.

3. Brockton City has approved a special assessment project in accordance with applicable laws. Total assessments of $500,000, including 10 percent for the city's share of the cost, have been levied. The levy will be collected from property owners in 10 equal annual installments commencing with the current year. Recognition of the approval and levy will result in entries of—
   a. $500,000 in the Special Assessment Fund and $50,000 in the General Fund.

b. $450,000 in the Special Assessment Fund and $50,000 in the General Fund.

c. $50,000 in the Special Assessment Fund and $50,000 in the General Fund.

d. $50,000 in the Special Assessment Fund and *no* entry in the General Fund.

4. Brocktown City's Debt-Service Fund (for term bonds) recorded required additions and required earnings for the current fiscal year of $15,000 and $7,000, respectively. The actual revenues and interest earnings were $16,000 and $6,500, respectively. What are the necessary entries to record the year's actual additions and earnings in the Debt Service Fund and in the General Long-Term Debt Account Group, respectively?

a. $22,500 and $22,000.

b. $22,000 and $22,000.

c. $22,500 and $22,500.

d. $22,500 and no entry.

5. Brockton City serves as collecting agency for the local independent school district and for a local water district. For this purpose, Brockton has created a single Agency Fund and charges the other entities a fee of 1 percent of the gross amounts collected. (The service fee is treated as General Fund revenue.) During the latest fiscal year a gross amount of $268,000 was collected for the independent school district and $80,000 for the water district. As a consequence of the foregoing, Brockton's General Fund should—

a. Recognize receipts of $348,000.

b. Recognize receipts of $344,520.

c. Record revenue of $3,480.

d. Record encumbrances of $344,520.

6. When Brockton City realized $1,020,000 from the sale of a $1,000,000 bond issue, the entry in its capital-project fund was

Cash	1,020,000	
Proceeds of Bonds . . .		1,000,000
Premium on Bonds . .		20,000

Recording the transaction in this manner indicates that—

a. The $20,000 cannot be used for the designated purpose of the fund but must be transferred to another fund.

b. The full $1,020,000 can be used by the Capital Project Fund to accomplish its purpose.

c. The nominal rate of interest on the bonds is below the market rate for bonds of such term and risk.

d. A safety factor is being set aside to cover possible contract defaults on the construction.

7. What will be the balance sheet effect of recording $50,000 of depreciation in the accounts of a utility, an Enterprise Fund, owned by Brockton City?

a. Reduce total assets of the Utility Fund and the General Fixed Assets Account group by $50,000.

b. Reduce total assets of the Utility Fund by $50,000 but have no affect on the General Fixed Assets Account Group.

c. Reduce total assets of the General Fixed Assets Account Group by $50,000 but have no effect on assets of the Utility Fund.

d. Have no effect on total assets of either the Utility Fund or the General Fixed Assets Accounts Group.

(AICPA adapted)

PROBLEMS

Problems 22–10. The village of Ramaco had the following transactions during 19x1:

1. On January 2, 19x1, term bonds were sold at par for $2,000,000. The interest rate is 10 percent, and interest is payable January 1 and July 1. The proceeds are to be used for the construction of a new village hall.

2. On February 1, 19x1, a contract for $2,000,000 was awarded for the construction of the village hall.

3. On June 25, 19x1, a transfer of $100,000 was made from the General Fund to the Debt Service Fund for interest payments.

4. The village hall was completed on December 15, 19x1, and the contractor was paid, less a 10 percent retained percentage. Occupancy commenced December 10, 19x1.

5. A transfer from the General Fund to the Debt Service Fund was made for $150,000 to cover interest payments and a sinking fund contribution.

Required:

Prepare journal entries in all of the appropriate funds to record the above transactions.

Problem 22–11 (Capital Projects Fund). On January 2, 19x3, the town council of Ramago authorized a bond issued in the amount of $2,000,000 for the purpose of constructing a town hall. In addition, the town is contributing $300,000 from its General Fund and other governmental units are contributing $500,000. The project is estimated to cost $2,800,000. The following transactions occurred:

1. On January 4, 19x3, a firm commitment was received for the $800,000 due from the various segments of governments.
2. Purchase orders for $500,000 were sent out for various supplies and materials.
3. A construction contract was signed in the amount of $2,300,000.
4. The bonds were sold on January 2, 19x3, at 98. The General Fund is to transfer an additional $40,000 to this fund.
5. Supplies and building materials were received. The invoice amount is $499,000.
6. The invoice in 5 above is paid.
7. The amounts committed in 1 above are received.
8. The amount committed in 4 above is received.
9. The project is completed, and the contractor is paid in full.
10. The remaining excess funds are transferred to the Debt Service Fund.

Required:

a. Prepare all of the necessary journal entries for the Capital Projects Fund.

b. Prepare a statement of revenues, expenditures, and changes in fund balance.

Problem 22–12 (Debt Service Fund). The balance sheet for the Debt Service Fund for the town of Ramo at December 31, 19x1, is as follows:

TOWN OF RAMO
Debt Service Fund
Balance Sheet as of December 31, 19x1

Assets

Cash	$125,000
Investments	480,000
Interest receivable on investments	20,000
Total assets	$625,000

Liabilities and Fund Equity

Interest payable	$ 3,000
Fund balance	622,000
Total liabilities and fund equity	$625,000

Additional information:

1. The town issued $3,000,000 in bonds in prior years to finance various projects. The bonds pay 7 percent per annum and interest is payable January 1 and July 1.
2. Earnings on investments for 19x1 amounted to $50,000. Collections amounted to $55,000.
3. Cash received from the General Fund was as follows:

Date	Interest	Sinking Fund
June 25	$105,000	$50,000
December 23	105,000	50,000

4. Investments with a cost of $100,000 were sold at a gain of $40,000.
5. Investments were purchased during the year for $100,000.
6. Bonds in the amount of $100,000 matured during 19x2 and were paid.

Required:

a. Prepare all of the necessary journal entries for the Debt Service Fund.

b. Prepare a balance sheet at December 31, 19x2, and a statement of revenues, expenditures, and changes in fund balance. (*Hint:* Use the format of Illustration 22–3 for the preparation of the statement of revenues, expenditures, and changes in fund balance.)

Problem 22–13 (Special Assessment Fund). The town of Hilltop authorized the establishment of a $930,000 Special Assessment Fund for the construction of a waste disposal center. To finance the construction, 10 percent, 20-year bonds for $600,000 were issued and sold at a premium of $5,000. A special property tax levy of $635,000 was levied. The first installment of $35,000 became due. The following transactions occurred in the first year 19x1:

1. Remittances of $30,000 of the current assessment were received.
2. The town paid $300,000, its share of the cost.

3. Deferred assessments of $32,000 became due.
4. Current assessments of $3,000 became delinquent.
5. Foreclosure proceedings on delinquent taxpayers was initiated. The uncollectible balance was $2,500, of which $400 was current, $400 was delinquent, and $1,700 was deferred. Interest of $200 was due.
6. $31,000 of accrued interest on assessments receivable became due, of which $30,500 was collected. Interest on bonds of $30,000 was paid.
7. The improvements are to be done by both town agencies and outside contractors. A contract of $500,000 was awarded to the principal contractor.
8. A contractor's bill of $200,000 for work completed was received.
9. Expenditures incurred by the town amounting to $80,000 were paid in addition to the contractor's invoice of $200,000.
10. $500 of bond premium was amortized.

Required:

a. Prepare all of the necessary entries in the Special Assessment Fund for 19x1.

b. Prepare the closing entries for 19x1.

c. Prepare:

(1) A balance sheet at December 31, 19x1.

(2) A statement of revenues, expenditures, and changes in fund balance.

Problem 22–14 (Internal Service Fund). The town of Hillcrest established a central purchasing and warehouse facility. The General Fund advanced $100,000 to set up the facility. During the year 19x2, the following transactions occurred:

1. Equipment was purchased on account for $60,000.
2. Materials and supplies were purchased on account for $200,000.
3. Heat, light and power invoices amounting to $6,000 were paid; rent of $30,000 was paid.
4. Office expenses of $500 were paid.
5. Salaries and wages that were paid amounted to $55,000 as follows:

Manager's salary	$30,000
Stockroom salaries	15,000
Office salaries	10,000

6. Depreciation expense was $10,000.
7. Vouchers payable of $180,000 were paid.

8. Gas, oil, and other materials and supplies used during the year were $10,000.
9. Billings for the year were: General Fund, $250,000; Enterprise Fund, $70,000; payments were $230,000 from the General Fund and $60,000 from the Enterprise Fund.
10. The inventory of materials and supplies on December 31, 19x2, amounted to $20,000.

Required:

a. Prepare the journal entries to record above transactions.

b. Prepare a balance sheet, statement of revenues, expenses, and changes in retained earnings for 19x2.

c. Prepare a statement of changes in financial position for 19x2.

Problem 22–15 (Nonexpendable Trust Fund— Endowment). The town of Mountainville received a donation of $500,000 for the establishment of a scholarship fund. Only the income is to be used in granting scholarships for the training of hotel employees. Earnings and expenditures are recorded in an expendable Endowment Earnings Fund, and principal transactions are recorded in an Endowment Principal Fund. During 19x1, the following transactions occurred:

1. Investments of $490,000 were purchased.
2. Interest earned on investments was $50,000.
3. Interest receivable of $48,000 was collected.
4. Payments of $90,000 were made for scholarships.

Required:

a. Prepare all appropriate entries in both funds.

b. Prepare closing entries.

c. For the Earnings Fund, prepare a—

(1) Balance sheet at December 31, 19x1.

(2) Statement of revenues, expenses, and changes in fund balance for 19x1.

(3) Statement of changes in financial position for 19x1.

Problem 22–16 (Enterprise Fund). The city of Larkspur provides electric energy for its citizens through an operating department. All transactions of the electric department are recorded in a self-sustaining fund supported by revenue from the sales of energy. Plant expansion is financed by the issuance of bonds which are repaid out of revenues.

All cash of the electric department is held by the city treasurer. Receipts from customers and others are deposited in the treasurer's account. Disbursements are made by drawing warrants on the treasurer.

The following is the post-closing trial balance of the department as of June 30, 19x4:

Cash on deposit with city treasurer	$ 2,250,000	
Due from customers	2,120,000	
Other current assets	130,000	
Construction work in progress	500,000	
Land	5,000,000	
Electric plant	50,000,000*	
Accumulated depreciation— electric plant		$10,000,000
Accounts payable and accrued liabilities		3,270,000
5% electric revenue bonds .		20,000,000
Retained earnings		26,730,000
	$60,000,000	$60,000,000

*The plant is being depreciated on the basis of a 50-year composite life.

During the year ended June 30, 19x5, the department had the following transactions:

1. Sales of electric energy, $10,700,000.
2. Purchases of fuel and operating supplies, $2,950,000.
3. Construction of miscellaneous system improvements (financed from operations), $750,000.
4. Fuel consumed, $2,790,000.
5. Miscellaneous plant additions and improvements placed in service, $1,000,000.
6. Wages and salaries paid, $4,280,000.
7. Sale on December 31, 19x4, of 20-year, 5 percent electric revenue bonds, with interest payable semiannually, $5,000,000.
8. Expenditures out of bond proceeds for construction of Larkspur Steam Plant Unit 1 and control house, $2,800,000.
9. Operating materials and supplies consumed, $150,000.
10. Payments received from customers, $10,500,000.
11. Expenditures out of bond proceeds for construction of Larkspur Steam Plant Unit 2, $2,200,000.
12. Warrants drawn on city treasurer in settlement of accounts payable, $3,045,000.
13. Larkspur Steam Plant placed in service on June 30, 19x5.

Required:

A worksheet of the Revenue Fund of the electric department, showing:—

a. The balance sheet amounts at June 30, 19x4.

b. The transactions for the year. (*Note:* Journal entries supporting your transactions are not required.)

c. The balance sheet amounts at June 30, 19x5.

d. Detail required for preparation of a statement of changes in financial position for the year.

(AICPA adapted)

Problem 22–17. Your examination of the accounts of your new client, the city of Delmas, as of June 30, 19x1, revealed the following:

1. On December 31, 19x0, the city paid $115,000 out of General Fund revenues for a central garage to service its vehicles, with $67,500 being applicable to the building which has an estimated life of 25 years, $14,500 to land, and $33,000 to machinery and equipment which has an estimated life of 15 years. A $12,200 cash contribution was received by the garage from the General Fund on the same date.
2. The garage maintains no records, but a review of deposit slips and canceled checks revealed the following:

Collections for services to city departments financed from the General Fund	$30,000
Office salaries	6,000
Utilities	700
Mechanics' wages	11,000
Materials and supplies	9,000

3. The garage had uncollected billings of $2,000, accounts payable for materials and supplies of $500 and an inventory of materials and supplies of $1,500 at June 30, 19x1.
4. On June 30, 19x1, the city issued $200,000 in special assessment bonds at par to finance a street improvement project estimated to cost $225,000. The project is to be paid by a $15,000 levy against the city (payable in fiscal year 19x1–2) and $210,000 against property owners (payable in five equal annual installments beginning October 1, 19x1). The levy was made on June 30. A $215,000 contract was let for the project on July 2, 19x1, but work has not begun.
5. On July 1, 19w9 (two years ago) the city issued $400,000 in 30-year, 6 percent general obligation

term bonds of the same date at par to finance the construction of a public health center. Construction was completed and the contractors fully paid a total of $397,500 in fiscal year 19x0–1.

6. For the health center bonds the city sets aside General Fund revenues sufficient to cover interest (payable semiannually on July 1 and January 1 of each year) and $5,060 to provide for the retirement of bond principal, the latter transfer being made at the end of each fiscal year and invested at the beginning of the next. Your investigation reveals that such investments earned $304 during fiscal year 19x0–1, the exact amount budgeted. This $304 was received in cash and will be invested at the beginning of the next year.

Required:

The above information disclosed by your examination was recorded only in the General Fund. Prepare the formal entries as of June 30, 19x1, to adjust the funds other than the General Fund. Entries should be classified into clearly labeled groups for each fund, and fund titles should be selected from the following list:

Special Revenue Fund
Capital Projects Fund
Debt Service Fund
Trust Fund
Agency Fund
Internal Service Fund
Special Assessment Fund
Enterprise Fund
General Fixed Assets Account Group
General Long-Term Debt Account Group

(AICPA adapted)

Problem 22–18. The following transactions represent practical situations frequently encountered in accounting for municipal governments. Each transaction is independent of the others.

1. The city council of Bernardville adopted a budget for the general operations of the government during the new fiscal year. Revenues were estimated at $695,000. Legal authorizations for budgeted expenditures were $650,000.

2. Taxes of $160,000 were levied for the Special Revenue Fund of Millstown. One percent was estimated to be uncollectible.

3. *a.* On July 25, 19x3, office supplies estimated to cost $2,390 were ordered for the city manager's office of Bullersville. Bullersville, which operates on the calendar year, does not maintain an inventory of such supplies.

   b. The supplies ordered July 25 were received on August 9, 19x3, accompanied by an invoice for $2,500.

4. On October 10, 19x3, the General Fund of Washingtonville repaid to the Utility Fund a loan of $1,000 plus $40 interest. The loan had been made earlier in the fiscal year.

5. A prominent citizen died and left 10 acres of undeveloped land to Harper City for a future school site. The donor's cost of the land was $55,000. The fair value of the land was $85,000.

6. *a.* On March 6, 19x3, Dahlstrom City issued 4 percent special assessment bonds payable March 6, 19x8, at face value of $90,000. Interest is payable annually. Dahlstrom City, which operates on the calendar year, will use the proceeds to finance a curbing project.

   b. On October 29, 19x3, the full $84,000 cost of the completed curbing project was accrued. Also, appropriate closing entries were made with regard to the project.

7. *a.* Conrad Thamm, a citizen of Basking Knoll, donated common stock valued at $22,000 to the city under a trust agreement. Under the terms of the agreement, the principal amount is to be kept intact; use of revenue from the stock is restricted to financing academic college scholarships for needy students.

   b. On December 14, 19x3, dividends of $1,100 were received on the stock donated by Mr. Thamm.

8. *a.* On February 23, 19x3, the town of Lincoln, which operates on the calendar year, issued 4 percent general obligation bonds with a face value of $300,000 payable ten years hence on February 23, 19y3, to finance the construction of an addition to the city hall. Total proceeds were $308,000.

   b. On December 31, 19x3, the addition to the city hall was officially approved, the full cost of $297,000 was paid to the contractor, and appropriate closing entries were made with regard to the project. (Assume that no entries have been made with regard to the project since February 23, 19x3.)

Required:

For each transaction, prepare the necessary journal entries for *all* of the funds and groups of accounts involved. *No explanation of the journal entries is required.* Use the following headings for your working paper:

Trans- action number	Journal entries	Dr.	Cr.	Fund or group of accounts

In the far right column, indicate in which fund or group of accounts each entry is to be made, using the coding below:

Funds:

General	G
Special Revenue	SR
Capital Projects	CP
Debt Service	DS
Special Assessments	SA
Enterprise	E
Internal Service	IS
Trust and Agency	TA

Groups of accounts:

General Fixed Assets	GFA
General Long-Term Debt	LTD

(AICPA adapted)

Problem 22–19. The city of Happy Hollow has engaged you to examine its financial statements for the year ended December 31, 19x1. The city was incorporated as a municipality and began operations on January 1, 19x1. You find that a budget was approved by the city council and was recorded, but that all transactions have been recorded on the cash basis. The bookkeeper has provided an Operating Fund trial balance. Additional information is given below:

1. Examination of the appropriation expenditure ledger revealed the following information:

	Budgeted	Actual
Personal services	$ 45,000	$38,500
Supplies	19,000	11,000
Equipment	38,000	23,000
Totals	$102,000	$72,500

2. Supplies and equipment in the amounts of $4,000 and $10,000, respectively, had been received, but the vouchers had not been paid at December 31.

3. At December 31, outstanding purchase orders for supplies and equipment not yet received were $1,200 and $3,800, respectively.

4. The inventory of supplies on December 31 was $1,700 by physical count. The decision was made to record the inventory of supplies. A city ordinance requires that expenditures are to be based on purchases, not on the basis of usage.

5. Examination of the revenue subsidiary ledger revealed the following information:

	Budgeted	Actual
Property taxes	$102,600	$ 96,000
Licenses	7,400	7,900
Fines	4,100	4,500
Totals	$114,100	$108,400

It was estimated that 5 percent of the property taxes would not be collected. Accordingly, property taxes were levied in an amount so that collections would yield the budgeted amount of $102,600.

6. On November 1, 19x1, Happy Hollow issued 8 percent general obligation term bonds with $200,000 face value for a premium of $3,000. Interest is payable each May 1 and November 1 until the maturity date of November 1, 19y5. The city council ordered that the cash from the bond premium be set aside and restricted for the eventual retirement of the debt principal. The bonds were issued to finance the construction of a city hall, but no contracts had been let as of December 31.

Required:

a. Complete the worksheet, showing adjustments and distributions to the proper funds or groups of accounts in conformity with generally accepted accounting principles applicable to governmental entities. (Formal adjusting entries are not required.)

b. Identify the financial statements that should be prepared for the General Fund. (You are not required to prepare these statements.)

c. Draft formal closing entries for the General Fund.

Problem 22–20. You were engaged to examine the financial statements of the city of Homer for the year ended June 30, 19x9, and found that the bookkeeper had recorded all transactions in the General Fund. You were furnished the General Fund trial balance, which appears opposite:

[Relates to Problem 22–19]

CITY OF HAPPY HOLLOW
Worksheet to Correct Trial Balance
December 31, 19x1

	Operating Fund Trial Balance	Adjustments		General Fund	Debt Service Fund	Capital Projects Fund	General Fixed Assets	General Long-Term Debt
		Debit	Credit					
Debits								
Cash	$238,900							
Expenditures	72,500							
Estimated revenues	114,100							
Equipment								
Encumbrances								
Inventory of supplies								
Taxes receivable—current								
Amount to be provided for the payment of term bonds								
Amount available in debt service fund—for term bonds								
	$425,500							
Credits								
Appropriations	$102,000							
Revenues	108,400							
Proceeds of bonds								
Bonds payable	200,000							
Premium on bonds payable	3,000							
Fund balance	12,100							
Vouchers payable								
Investment in fixed assets— General Fund revenue								
Reserve for encumbrances								
Reserve for inventory of supplies								
Estimated uncollectible current taxes								
	$425,500							

(AICPA adapted)

CITY OF HOMER
General Fund Trial Balance
June 30, 19x9

Debits

Cash	$ 125,180
Cash for construction	174,000
Taxes receivable—current	8,000
Assessments receivable—deferred	300,000
Inventory of materials and supplies	38,000
Improvements authorized	15,000
Estimated revenues	4,135,000
Interest expense	18,000
Encumbrances	360,000
Expenditures	4,310,000
Total debits	$9,483,180

Credits

Allowance for uncollectible current taxes . . .	$	7,000
Vouchers payable		62,090
Interest payable		18,000
Liability under street improvement project .		10,000
Bonds payable		300,000
Premium on bonds		3,000
Reserve for inventory		36,000
Reserve for encumbrances		360,000
Appropriations		4,450,000
Interest revenue		21,000
Fund balance		106,090
Revenues		4,110,000
Total credits		$9,483,180

Your audit disclosed the following:

1. Years ago the city council authorized the recording of inventories, and a physical inventory taken on June 30, 19x9, showed that materials and supplies with a cost of $37,750 were on hand at that date. The inventory is recorded on a perpetual basis.

2. Current taxes are now considered delinquent, and it is estimated that $5,500 of such taxes will be uncollectible.

3. Discounts of $32,000 were taken on property taxes. An appropriation is not required for discounts, but an allowance for them was not made at the time the tax levy was recorded. Discounts taken were charged to Expenditures.

4. On June 25, 19x9, the state revenue department informed the city that its share of a state-collected, locally shared tax would be $75,000.

5. New equipment for the police department was acquired at a cost of $90,000 and was properly recorded in the General Fund.

6. During the year, 100 acres of land were donated to the city for use as an industrial park. The land had a value of $250,000. No recording has been made.

7. The city council authorized the paving and widening of certain streets at an estimated cost of $365,000, which included an estimated $5,000 cost for planning and engineering to be paid from the General Fund. The remaining $360,000 was to be financed by a $10,000 contribution from the city and $350,000 by assessments against property owners payable in seven equal annual installments. A $15,000 appropriation was made for the city's share at the time the annual budget was recorded, and the total $365,000 was also recorded as an appropriation. The following information is also relevant to the street improvement project:

a. Property owners paid their annual installment plus a $21,000 interest charge in full.

b. Special assessment bonds of $300,000 were authorized and sold at a premium of $3,000. An $18,000 liability for interest was properly recorded. The city does not amortize bond premium or discount.

c. The city's $15,000 share was recorded as an expenditure during the year. The $5,000 for planning and engineering fees was paid. Construction began July 5, 19x8, and the contractor has been paid $200,000 under the contract for construction which calls for performance of the work at a total cost of

$360,000. This $360,000 makes up the balance in the Reserve for Encumbrances.

d. The Cash for Construction account was used for all receipts and disbursements relative to the project. It is made up of the proceeds of the bond issue and collection of assessment installments and interest minus payments to the contractor.

Required:

Prepare a 14-column worksheet to adjust the account balances at June 30, 19x9, and to distribute them to the appropriate funds or groups of accounts. It is recommended that the worksheet be in the order of the General Fund trial balance and have the following column headings:

a. Balance per books.

b. Adjustments—debit.

c. Adjustments—credit.

d. General Fund.

e. Special Assessment Fund.

f. General fixed assets.

(Number all adjusting entries. Formal journal entries or financial statements are not required. Supporting computations should be in good form.)

(AICPA adapted)

Problem 22–21. The village of Dexter was recently incorporated and began financial operations on July 1, 19x8, the beginning of its fiscal year.

The following transactions occurred during this first fiscal year, July 1, 19x8, to June 30, 19x9:

1. The village council adopted a budget for general operations during the fiscal year ending June 30, 19x9. Revenues were estimated at $400,000. Legal authorizations for budgeted expenditures were $394,000.

2. Property taxes were levied in the amount of $390,000; it was estimated that 2 percent of this amount would prove to be uncollectible. These taxes are available as of the date of levy to finance current expenditures.

3. During the year, a resident of the village donated marketable securities valued at $50,000 to the village under the terms of a trust agreement. The terms of the trust agreement stipulated that the principal amount is to be kept intact; use of revenue generated by the securities is restricted to financing college scholarships for needy students. Revenue earned and re-

ceived on these marketable securities amounted to $5,500 through June 30, 19x9.

4. A General Fund transfer of $5,000 was made to establish an Internal Service Fund to provide for a permanent investment in inventory.

5. The village decided to install lighting in the village park and a special assessment project was authorized to install the lighting at a cost of $75,000. The appropriation was formally recorded.

6. The assessments were levied for $72,000 with the village contributing $3,000 out of the General Fund. All assessments were collected during the year including the village's contribution.

7. A contract for $75,000 was let for the installation of the lighting. At June 30, 19x9, the contract was completed but not approved. The contractor was paid all but 5 percent, which was retained to insure compliance with the terms of the contract. Encumbrances and other budgetary accounts are maintained.

8. During the year the Internal Service Fund purchased various supplies at a cost of $1,900.

9. Cash collections recorded by the General Fund during the year were as follows:

Property taxes $386,000
Licenses and permits   7,000

10. The village council decided to build a village hall at an estimated cost of $500,000 to replace space occupied in rented facilities. The village does not record project authorizations. It was decided that general obligation bonds bearing interest at 6 percent would be issued. On June 30, 19x9, the bonds were issued at their face value of $500,000, payable June 30, 19z9 (20-year bonds).

No contracts have been signed for this project and no expenditures have been made.

11. A fire truck was purchased for $15,000 and the voucher approved and paid by the General Fund. This expenditure was previously encumbered for $15,000.

Required:

Prepare journal entries to properly record each of the above transactions in the appropriate fund(s) or group of accounts of Dexter village for the fiscal year ended June 30, 19x9. Use the following funds and groups of accounts:

General Fund
Capital Projects Fund
Special Assessment Fund
Internal Service Fund
Trust Fund
General Long-Term Debt Account Group
General Fixed Assets Account Group

Each journal entry should be numbered to correspond with the transactions described above. Do *not* prepare closing entries for any fund.

Your answer sheet should be organized as follows:

Trans-action no.	Fund or group of accounts	Account title and explanation	Amounts	
			Debit	Credit

(AICPA adapted)

Problem 22–22. In a special election held on May 1, 19x7, the voters of the city of Nicknar approved a $10,000,000 issue of 6 percent general obligation bonds maturing in 20 years. The proceeds of this sale will be used to help finance the construction of a new civic center. The total cost of the project was estimated at $15,000,000. The remaining $5,000,000 will be financed by an irrevocable state grant which has been awarded. A Capital Projects Fund was established to account for this project and was designated the Civic Center Construction Fund. The formal project authorization was appropriately recorded in a memorandum entry.

The following transactions occurred during the fiscal year beginning July 1, 19x7, and ending June 30, 19x8:

1. On July 1, the General Fund loaned $500,000 to the Civic Center Construction Fund for defraying engineering and other expenses.

2. Preliminary engineering and planning costs of $320,000 were paid to Akron Engineering Company. There had been no encumbrance for this cost.

3. On December 1, the bonds were sold at 101. The premium on bonds was transferred to the Debt Service Fund.

4. On March 15, a contract for $12,000,000 was entered into with the Candu Construction Company for the major part of the project.

5. Orders were placed for materials estimated to cost $55,000.

6. On April 1, a partial payment of $2,500,000 was received from the state.

7. The materials that were previously ordered were received at a cost of $51,000 and paid.

8. On June 15, a progress billing of $2,000,000 was received from Candu Construction for work done on the project. As per the terms of the contract, the city will withhold 6 percent of any billing until the project is completed.

9. The General Fund was repaid the $500,000 previously loaned.

Required:

Based upon the transactions presented above:

a. Prepare journal entries to record the transactions in the Civic Center Construction Fund for the period July 1, 19x7, through June 30, 19x8, and the appropriate closing entries at June 30, 19x8.

b. Prepare a balance sheet of the Civic Center Construction Fund as of June 30, 19x8.

(AICPA adapted)

Problem 22–23. You have been engaged by the town of Rego to examine its June 30, 19x8, balance sheet. You are the first CPA to be engaged by the town and find that acceptable methods of municipal accounting have not been employed. The town clerk stated that the books had not been closed and presented the following pre-closing trial balance of the General Fund as at June 30, 19x8:

	Debit	Credit
Cash	$150,000	
Taxes receivable—current year	59,200	
Estimated losses—current year taxes receivable		$ 18,000
Taxes receivable—prior year	8,000	
Estimated losses—prior year taxes receivable		10,200
Estimated revenues	310,000	
Appropriations		348,000
Donated land	27,000	
Expenditures—building addition constructed	50,000	
Expenditures—serial bonds paid	16,000	
Other expenditures	280,000	
Special assessment bonds payable		100,000
Revenues		354,000
Accounts payable		26,000
Fund balance		44,000
	$900,200	$900,200

Additional information:

1. The estimated losses of $18,000 for current year taxes receivable were determined to be a reasonable estimate.

2. Included in the Revenues account is a credit of $27,000 representing the value of land donated

by the state as a grant-in-aid for construction of a municipal park.

3. The Building Addition Constructed account balance is the cost of an addition to the town hall building. This addition was constructed and completed in June 19x8. The General Fund recorded the payment as authorized.

4. The Serial Bonds Paid account reflects the annual retirement of general obligation bonds issued to finance the construction of the town hall. Interest payments of $7,000 for this bond issue are included in expenditures.

5. Operating supplies ordered in the prior fiscal year and chargeable to that year were received, recorded and consumed in July 19x7. The outstanding purchase orders for these supplies, which were not recorded in the accounts at June 30, 19x7, amounted to $8,800. The vendors' invoices for these supplies totaled $9,400. Appropriations lapse one year after the end of the fiscal year for which they are made.

6. Outstanding purchase orders at June 30, 19x8, for operating supplies totaled $2,100. These purchase orders were not recorded on the books.

7. The special assessment bonds were sold in June 19x8 to finance a street paving project. No contracts have been signed for this project and no expenditures have been made.

8. The balance in the Revenues account includes credits for $20,000 for a note issued to a bank to obtain cash in anticipation of tax collections and for $1,000 for the sale of scrap iron from the town's water plant. The note was still outstanding at June 30, 19x8. The operations of the water plant are accounted for in the Water Fund.

Required:

a. Prepare the formal adjusting and closing journal entries for the General Fund for the fiscal year ended June 30, 19x8.

b. The foregoing information disclosed by your examination was recorded only in the General Fund even though other funds or groups of accounts were involved. Prepare the formal adjusting journal entries for any other funds or groups of accounts involved.

(AICPA adapted)

Problem 22–24. You have been engaged to examine the financial statements of the town of Workville for the year ended June 30, 19x7. Your examination disclosed that due to the inexperience of the town's bookkeeper all transactions were recorded in the General Fund. The following General Fund trial balance as of June 30, 19x7, was furnished to you.

TOWN OF WORKVILLE
General Fund Trial Balance
June 30, 19x7

	Debit	Credit
Cash	$ 16,800	
Short-term investments	40,000	
Accounts receivable	11,500	
Taxes receivable—current year . .	30,000	
Tax anticipation notes payable . . .		$ 50,000
Appropriations		400,000
Expenditures	382,000	
Estimated revenue	320,000	
Revenues		360,000
General property	85,400	
Bonds payable	52,000	
Fund balance		127,700
	$937,700	$937,700

Your audit disclosed the following additional information:

1. The accounts receivable of $11,500 includes $1,500 due from the town's water utility for the sale of scrap sold on its behalf. Accounts for the municipal water utility operated by the town are maintained in a separate fund.

2. The balance in Taxes Receivable—Current Year is now considered delinquent, and the town estimates that $24,000 will be uncollectible.

3. On June 30, 19x7, the town retired, at face value, 6 percent general obligation serial bonds totaling $40,000. The bonds were issued on July 1, 19x2, at face value of $200,000. Interest paid during the year ended June 30, 19x7, was charged to Bonds Payable.

4. In order to service other municipal departments, the town at the beginning of the year authorized the establishment of a central supplies warehouse. During the year supplies totaling $128,000 were purchased and charged to Expenditures. The town chose to conduct a physical inventory of supplies on hand at June 30, 19x7, and this physical count disclosed that supplies totaling $84,000 were used.

5. Expenditures for the year ended June 30, 19x7, included $11,200 applicable to purchase orders issued in the prior year. Outstanding purchase orders at June 30, 19x7, not recorded in the accounts amounted to $17,500.

6. On June 28, 19x7, the state revenue department informed the town that its share of a state-collected, locally shared tax would be $34,000.

7. During the year equipment with a book value of $7,900 was removed from service and sold for $4,600. In addition new equipment costing $90,000 was purchased. The transactions were recorded in General Property.

8. During the year, 100 acres of land were donated to the town for use as an industrial park. The land had a value of $125,000. No recording of this donation has been made.

Required:

a. Prepare the formal reclassification, adjusting, and closing journal entries for the General Fund as of June 30, 19x7.

b. Prepare the formal adjusting journal entries for any other funds or groups of accounts as of June 30, 19x7. (AICPA adapted)

Problem 22–25. In compliance with a newly enacted state law, Dial County assumed the responsibility of collecting all property taxes levied within its boundaries as of July 1, 19x5. A composite property tax rate per $100 of net assessed valuation was developed for the fiscal year ending June 30, 19x6, and is presented below:

Dial County General Fund	$ 6
Eton City General Fund	3
Bart Township General Fund	1
	$10

All property taxes are due in quarterly installments and when collected are then distributed to the governmental units represented in the composite rate.

In order to administer collection and distribution of such taxes, the county has established a Tax Agency Fund.

Additional information:

1. In order to reimburse the county for estimated administrative expenses of operating the Tax Agency Fund, the Tax Agency Fund is to deduct 2 percent from the tax collections each quarter for Eton City and Bart Township. The total amount deducted is to be remitted to the Dial County General Fund.

2. Current year tax levies to be collected by the Tax Agency Fund are as follows:

	Gross levy	Estimated amount to be collected
Dial County	$3,600,000	$3,500,000
Eton City	1,800,000	1,740,000
Bart Township	600,000	560,000
	$6,000,000	$5,800,000

3. $10,000 was charged back to Bart Township because of an error in the original computation of its current gross tax levy and the estimated amount to be collected.

4. As of September 30, 19x5, the Tax Agency Fund has received $1,440,000 in first quarter payments. On October 1, this fund made a distribution to the three governmental units.

Required:

For the period July 1, 19x5, through October 1, 19x5, prepare journal entries to record the transactions described above for the following funds:

Dial County Tax Agency Fund
Dial County General Fund
Eton City General Fund
Bart Township General Fund

Your answer sheet should be organized as follows:

[Relates to Problem 22–25]

	Dial Country Tax Agency Fund		Dial County General Fund		Eton City General Fund		Bart Township General Fund	
Accounts	Debit	Credit	Debit	Credit	Debit	Credit	Debit	Credit

Problem 22–26. You were engaged as auditor of the city of Druid as of July 1, 19x2. You found the following accounts, among others, in the General Fund for the fiscal year ending June 30, 19x2:

Special Cash

Date	Reference	Dr.	Cr.	Balance
8/1/x1	CR 58	301,000		301,000
9/1/x1	CR 60	80,000		381,000
12/1/x1	CD 41		185,000	196,000
2/1/x2	CD 45		4,500	191,500
6/1/x2	CR 64	50,500		242,000
6/30/x2	CD 65		167,000	75,000

Bonds Payable

Date	Reference	Dr.	Cr.	Balance
8/1/x1	CR 58		300,000	300,000
6/1/x2	CR 64		50,000	350,000

Construction in Progress—Main Street Sewer

Date	Reference	Dr.	Cr.	Balance
12/1/x1	CD 41	185,000		185,000
6/30/x2	CD 65	167,000		352,000

Interest Expense

Date	Reference	Dr.	Cr.	Balance
2/1/x2	CD 45	4,500		4,500
6/1/x2	CR 64		500	4,000

Assessment Income

Date	Reference	Dr.	Cr.	Balance
9/1/x1	CR 60		80,000	80,000

Premium on Bonds

Date	Reference	Dr.	Cr.	Balance
8/1/x1	CR 58		1,000	1,000

The accounts resulted from the project described below:

The city council authorized the Main Street Sewer Project and a bond issue of $350,000 to permit deferral of assessment payments. According to the terms of the authorization the property owners were to be assessed 80 percent of the estimated cost of construction and the balance was made available by the city during October 19x1. On September 1, 19x1, the first of five equal annual assessment installments was collected from the property owners. The deferred assessments were to bear interest at 5⅝ percent from September 1, 19x1.

The project was expected to be completed by October 31, 19x2.

Required:

a. Prepare a Special Assessment Fund worksheet in which you record the transactions of the Main Street Sewer Project as they should have been made by the client. Show the closing entries at June 30, 19x2, and show the account balances at that date. (Formal journal entries are not required.)

b. Prepare the formal journal entries that should be made in funds other than the Special Assessment Fund to record properly therein the results of transactions of the Main Street Sewer Project.

(AICPA adapted)

Problem 22–27. The Cobleskill city council passed a resolution requiring a yearly cash budget by fund for the city beginning with its fiscal year ending September 30, 19x3. The city's financial director has prepared a list of expected cash receipts and disbursements, but he is having difficulty subdividing them by fund. The list follows:

Cash Receipts

Taxes:

General property	$ 685,000
School	421,000
Franchise	223,000
	1,329,000

Licenses and permits:

Business licenses	41,000
Automobile inspection permits	24,000
Building permits	18,000
	83,000

Intergovernmental revenue:

Sales tax	1,012,000
Federal grants	128,000
State motor vehicle tax	83,500
State gasoline tax	52,000
State alcoholic beverage licenses	16,000
	1,291,500

Charges for services:

Sanitation fees	121,000
Sewer connection fees	71,000
Library revenues	13,000
Park revenues	2,500
	207,500

Bond issues:

Civic center	347,000
General obligation	200,000
Sewer	153,000
Library	120,000
	820,000

Other:

Proceeds from the sale of investments	312,000
Sewer assessments	50,000
Rental revenue	48,000
Interest revenue	15,000
	425,000
	$4,156,000

Cash Disbursements

General government	$ 671,000
Public safety	516,000
Schools	458,000
Sanitation	131,000
Library	28,000
Rental property	17,500
Parks	17,000
	1,838,500

Debt service:

General obligation bonds	618,000
Street construction bonds	327,000
School bonds	119,000
Sewage disposal plant bonds	37,200
	1,101,200

Investments	358,000
State portion of sales tax	860,200

Capital expenditures:

Sewer construction (assessed area)	114,100
Civic center construction	73,000
Library construction	36,000
	223,100
	$4,381,000

The financial director provides you with the following additional information:

1. A bond issue was authorized in 19x2 for the construction of a civic center. The debt is to be paid from future civic center revenues and general property taxes.

2. A bond issue was authorized in 19x2 for additions to the library. The debt is to be paid from general property taxes.

3. General obligation bonds are paid from general property taxes collected by the general fund.

4. Ten percent (10 percent) of the total annual school taxes represents an individually voted tax for payment of bonds the proceeds of which were used for school construction.

5. In 19x0, a wealthy citizen donated rental property to the city. Net income from the property is to be used to assist in operating the library. The net cash increase attributable to the property is transferred to the library on September 30 of each year.

6. All sales taxes are collected by the city; the state receives 85 percent of these taxes. The state's portion is remitted at the end of each month.

7. Payment of the street construction bonds is to be made from assessments previously collected from the respective property owners. The proceeds from the assessments were invested and the principal of $312,000 will earn $15,000 interest during the coming year.

8. In 19x2, a special assessment in the amount of $203,000 was made on certain property owners for sewer construction. During fiscal 19x3, $50,000 of this assessment is expected to be collected. The remainder of the sewer cost is to be paid from a $153,000 bond issue to be sold in fiscal 19x3. Future special assessment collections will be used to pay principal and interest on the bonds.

9. All sewer and sanitation services are provided by a separate enterprise fund.

10. The federal grant is for fiscal 19x3 school operations.

11. The proceeds remaining at the end of the year

from the sale of civic center and library bonds are to be invested.

Required:

Prepare a budget of cash receipts and disbursements by fund for the year ending September 30, 19x3. All interfund transfers of cash are to be included.   (AICPA adapted)

Problem 22–28. The city of Westgate's fiscal year ends on June 30. During the fiscal year ended June 30, 19x8, the city authorized the construction of a new library and sale of general obligation term bonds to finance the construction of the library. The authorization imposed the following restrictions:

Construction cost was not to exceed $5,000,000.

Annual interest rate was not to exceed 8½ percent.

The city does not record project authorizations, but other budgetary accounts are maintained. The following transactions relating to the financing and constructing of the library occurred during the fiscal year ended June 30, 19x9:

1. On July 1, 19x8, the city issued $5,000,000 of 30-year, 8 percent general obligation bonds for $5,100,000. The semiannual interest dates are December 31 and June 30. The premium of $100,000 was transferred to the Library Debt Service Fund.
2. On July 3, 19x8, the Library Capital Projects Fund invested $4,900,000 in short-term commercial paper. These purchases were at face value with no accrued interest. Interest on cash invested by the Library Capital Projects Fund must be transferred to the Library Debt Service Fund. During the fiscal year ending June 30, 19x9, estimated interest to be earned is $140,000.
3. On July 5, 19x8, the city signed a contract with F&A Construction Company to build the library for $4,980,000.
4. On January 15, 19x9, the Library Capital Projects Fund received $3,040,000, from the maturity of short-term notes purchased on July 3. The cost of these notes was $3,000,000. The interest of $40,000 was transferred to the Library Debt Service Fund.
5. On January 20, 19x9, F&A Construction Company properly billed the city $3,000,000 for work performed on the new library. The contract calls for 10 percent retention until final inspection and acceptance of the building. The Library Capital Projects Fund paid F&A $2,700,000.
6. On June 30, 19x9, the Library Capital Projects Fund made the proper adjusting entries (including accrued interest receivable of $103,000) and closing entries.

Required:

a. Prepare in good form journal entries to record the six preceding sets of facts in the Library Capital Projects Fund. List the transaction numbers (1 to 6) and give the necessary entry or entries. Do not record journal entries in any other fund or group of accounts.

b. Prepare in good form a balance sheet for the city of Westgate—Library Capital Projects Fund as of June 30, 19x9.   (AICPA adapted)

23

Accounting for colleges, hospitals, and welfare organizations

OVERVIEW

Although colleges, hospitals, and welfare organizations use forms of fund accounting, there are significant differences between these organizations and state and local governments. The amount of regulation and restrictions for these institutions is usually far less than that for state and local governments.

The funds used for accounting purposes by these organizations have a certain commonality, yet differences do exist for each of these types of organizations. However, despite the similarities that exist for each of those organization's form of fund accounting used, they are markedly different from the type of fund accounting used by state and local governments.

Colleges and hospitals depend to a significant degree on tuition and patient fees respectively to cover operating costs. Shortfalls usually occur and governmental subsidies, donations, and endowments usually make up the shortfall. The financial statements of these organizations are similar to those used by state and local governments, but they are somewhat closer to those used by business organizations.

Although colleges, hospitals, and welfare organizations make use of fund accounting, the accounting procedures used by these organizations are different from those used by state and local governments. The objectives and regulation of these organizations are somewhat different from that of state and local governments. For example, private colleges and hospitals are usually unable to cover operating expenses from tuition and patient fees, and the resulting shortfall is usually made up from governmental subsidies, donor grants, and endowments instead of from tax levies available to state and local governments. Although hospitals and colleges are subject to some regulation, the amount of regulation is far less than that for state and local governments.

As is the case in commercial enterprises, nonbusiness organizations prepare financial statements that disclose funds flows, liquidity, and solvency. However, the nature of these funds flows receives greater emphasis than is given to them in commercial financial statements. The reason for this is stated by Professor Robert N. Anthony as follows:

> An important distinction in some organizations is between hard money (e.g., revenues from services rendered) and soft money (e.g., annual gifts); the higher the proportion of hard money, the firmer the financial foundation.[1]

COLLEGES AND UNIVERSITIES

The overall classification of self-balancing funds used by colleges will usually fall into six types:

1. Current Fund (unrestricted and restricted).
2. Loan Funds.
3. Endowment and similar funds.
4. Annuity and Life Funds.
5. Plant Funds.
6. Agency Funds.

Fund Operations—Unrestricted Current Funds are the main operating funds of colleges and universities. As the name implies, this fund is used for the day-to-day operations of the college and is free from restrictions. *Restricted Current Funds* can also be used for operations, but they must be used within the framework of the specified purposes imposed by the grantor. *Loan Funds* are used for making loans to students, faculty, and staff. *Endowment and Similar Funds* are funds that are created by grantors and usually contain provisions that permit the income to be expended for current operations with the principal kept intact. *Term Endowment Funds* are similar to Endowment Funds except that after a specified time period the principal (corpus) becomes available for current operations. *Quasi-Endowment Funds* differ from Endowment Funds in that the restrictions are imposed by the institution's board of directors and not by an outside grantor. *Annuity and Life Income Funds* provide for payments to the grantor during the grantor's lifetime with the balance in the fund released to a current or

---

[1]Robert N. Anthony, *Financial Accounting in Nonbusiness Organizations* (Stamford: FASB, 1978), p. 49.

endowment fund at the death of the grantor. Annuity Funds provide for a *fixed payment during the grantor's lifetime* while a Life Income Fund provides for the *payment of all income* to the grantor for life. *Plant Funds* are subdivided into:

1. The unexpended portion for future acquisitions.
2. Amounts set aside for renewals and replacements.
3. Amounts set aside for retirement of indebtedness.
4. Funds already spent and thus representing the investment in plant assets.

Agency Funds are funds held by the institution for others. Examples might be funds of student governments or of faculty organizations established for their benefit. Since these funds belong to others, the fund has no Fund Balance as such and all of the assets of the fund are represented by corresponding liabilities.

Although not usually required to do so, colleges and universities almost universally use budgets for control purposes. Budgetary accounting—as used in the General Fund of a state or local government—is optional for colleges. However, colleges which receive governmental assistance for operating costs are usually required to use budgetary accounting. When used, the terminology is slightly different from that or a state or local government.

Illustrative entries

The entry to record the budget, if one is used, would be:

Unrealized Revenues	10,000,000	
Estimated Expenditures		9,500,000
Unallocated Budget Balance		500,000

Typical entries to record revenues and the source of the revenues in the unrestricted current fund are:

Current Fund—Unrestricted

(1)

Cash	6,000,000	
Accounts Receivable	500,000	
Revenue—Student Tuition and Fees		6,500,000

(2)

Expenditures—Instruction	50,000	
Allowance for Doubtful Accounts		50,000

(3)

Cash	3,000,000	
Revenues—Federal Appropriations		1,500,000
Revenues—State Appropriations		1,000,000
Revenues—Local Appropriations		500,000

(4)

Cash	100,000	
Revenues—Private Gifts		100,000

(5)

Cash	200,000	
Revenues—Endowment Income		200,000

(6)

Cash	1,200,000	
Sales and Services—Auxiliary Enterprises		1,200,000

Examples of this type of revenue would be sales from the college book store, the cafeteria, and student dormitories.

(7)

Expenditures—Instruction	6,000,000	
Expenditures—Research	300,000	
Expenditures—Public Service	450,000	
Expenditures—Academic Support	300,000	
Expenditures—Student Services	200,000	
Expenditures—Institutional Support	500,000	
Expenditures—Operation of Plant	400,000	
Expenditures—Scholarships and Fellowships	100,000	
Vouchers Payable (or Cash)		8,250,000

(8)

Expenditures—Auxiliary Enterprises	1,000,000	
Vouchers Payable (or Cash)		1,000,000

A transfer from the Current Fund—Unrestricted to the Unexpended Plant Fund for the purchase of plant assets would be recorded as follows:

Current Fund—Unrestricted

(9a)

Transfers to Unexpended Plant Funds	300,000	
Cash		300,000

Unexpended Plant Fund

(9b)

Cash	300,000	
Unexpended Plant Funds Balance—Restricted		300,000

The purchase of equipment by the Unexpended Plant Fund would require the following entries:

Unexpended Plant Fund

(10a)

Unexpended Plant Funds Balance—Restricted	200,000	
Cash		200,000

Investment in Plant

(10b)

Equipment	200,000	
Net Investment in Plant		200,000

If a gift were received with a stipulation that it must be used for the purchase of plant assets, the funds would then be considered *restricted* and the following entry would be made to record the gift:

Unexpended Plant Fund

(11)

Cash	500,000	
Unexpended Plant Funds Balance—Restricted		500,000

If the construction of a building is to be (partially) financed by the sale of bonds, the following entry would be required:

Unexpended Plant Fund
(12)

Cash	2,000,000	
Bonds Payable		2,000,000

During the construction period, entries similar to the following would be made:

Unexpended Plant Fund
(13)

Construction in Progress	1,000,000	
Cash		1,000,000

At the conclusion of the construction, the following entries would be recorded:

Unexpended Plant Fund
(14a)

Bonds Payable	2,000,000	
Construction in Progress		2,000,000

Investment in Plant Fund
(14b)

Building	2,000,000	
Bonds Payable		2,000,000

A transfer from the Current Fund—Unrestricted for the retirement of indebtedness would be recorded as follows:

Current Fund—Unrestricted
(15a)

Transfers to Funds for Retirement of Indebtedness	100,000	
Cash		100,000

Fund for Retirement of Indebtedness
(15b)

Cash	100,000	
Retirement of Indebtedness Fund Balance		100,000

A transfer of funds for renewals and replacements could be handled as follows:

Current Fund—Unrestricted
(16a)

Transfers to Funds for Renewals and Replacements	60,000	
Cash		60,000

Fund for Renewals and Replacements
(16b)

Cash	60,000	
Renewals and Replacements Fund Balance		60,000

When the bonds are retired, the appropriate entries would be:

Fund for Retirement of Indebtedness
(17a)

Retirement of Indebtedness Fund Balance	200,000	
Cash		200,000

Investment in Plant Fund

(17*b*)

Bonds Payable	200,000	
Net Investment in Plant		200,000

Current Fund—Restricted

If a federal grant were received to provide remedial reading and mathematical instruction for entering students who cannot pass placement examinations, the receipt of the funds would be recorded as follows:

(1)

Cash	500,000	
Fund Balance		500,000

Expenditures incurred could be reflected as follows:

(2)

Expenditures—Instruction	400,000	
Cash		400,000

After the expenditure, the revenues are now earned and could be recorded as:

(3)

Fund Balance	400,000	
Revenue—Instruction		400,000

Of course, the remaining $100,000 in the restricted current fund must be used for the purpose for which it was intended.

Closing entries

Since the revenues and expenditures are closed, usually as one entry, into the Fund Balance account, the closing entry (entries) are not shown because of the simplistic, mechanical procedure involved.

Depreciation

Depreciation expense is not reported as an expenditure in the statement of current fund's revenues and expenditures or as a change in the statement of changes in unrestricted current funds balance. These statements present outlays, *not* operating expenses. However, the accumulated depreciation may be shown in the balance sheet and the provision for depreciation would be shown in the statement of changes in the balance of the Investment in Plant Fund.[2]

Loan Funds

Loans Funds are created either by gifts and bequests or by board-designated transfers from the Unrestricted Current Fund. Both the principal and interest (earnings) are available for loans to faculty, staff, and students. Illustrative entries are:

[2]AICPA, *Audits of Colleges and Universities* (New York, 1973), p. 15.

1. The college received a bequest of $200,000 from an alumnus to establish a Loan Fund.

Cash	200,000	
Fund Balance—Loan Fund		200,000

2. The board of trustees authorized the transfer of $100,000 to the Loan Fund.

Cash	100,000	
Fund Balance—Loan Fund		100,000

3. Loans were made to students, faculty, and staff for $250,000. It is estimated that $10,000 may not be collected.

Notes Receivable	250,000	
Cash		250,000
Fund Balance—Loan Fund	10,000	
Allowance for Uncollectible Loans		10,000

4. Excess cash is invested.

Investments	40,000	
Cash		40,000

5. Income from loans and investments amounts to $12,000 from loans and 4,000 from investments.

Cash	16,000	
Fund Balance—Loan Fund		16,000

6. Investments that cost $15,000 were sold for $20,000.

Cash	20,000	
Investments		15,000
Fund Balance—Loan Fund		5,000

7. Loans of $100,000 became due, but only $95,000 could be collected. The remaining $5,000 is considered uncollectible.

Cash	95,000	
Allowance for Uncollectible Loans	5,000	
Notes Receivable		100,000

Endowment and similar funds

As noted earlier in this chapter, Endowment Funds can be either nonexpendable where only the income may be used, or Term Funds where the income is used for a period of time and after a specified event, the principal may be expended. In addition, Board-Designated Funds are called Quasi-Endowment Funds. The fund balance for each fund is kept separately, but investments are usually pooled. Income from pooled investments would be allocated on the basis of net asset market values in a manner similar to that used by Mutual Funds sold to investors.

Illustrative entries for the operation of these funds are:

1. The board of trustees directed that a transfer of $300,000 be made from the Unrestricted Current Fund to a Quasi-Endowment Fund for the maintenance of a rare book and manuscripts division of the library. The

income of the fund is to be used for the specified purpose and the principal is to be maintained.

Cash	300,000	
Fund Balance—Quasi Endowment		300,000

2. A wealthy alumnus donated $500,000 to the college. For three years, the income from the fund is to be used to defray the rental costs of computer terminals in the College of Business Adminstration. At the end of the three years, the principal is to be used to purchase a computer.

Cash	500,000	
Fund Balance—Term Endowment		500,000

3. A Fortune-500 Corporation endowed a chair in financial management with a contribution of $400,000. The income is to be used as an additional stipend to attract distinguished professors to the college. The principal is to be maintained intact.

Cash	400,000	
Fund Balance—Endowment		400,000

4. Each fund contributed all of its cash, except for $50,000 each, into an investment pool.

Investments	1,050,000	
Cash		1,050,000

5. Income on investments amounted to $105,000.

Cash	105,000	
Fund Balance—Quasi Endowment		25,000
Fund Balance—Term Endowment		45,000
Fund Balance—Endowment		35,000

6. Payments were made to the Unrestricted Current Fund in accordance with the terms of the endowments.

Fund Balance—Quasi Endowment	25,000	
Fund Balance—Term Endowment	45,000	
Fund Balance—Endowment	35,000	
Cash		105,000

7. Investments with a cost of $100,000 are sold for $121,000.

Cash	121,000	
Investments		100,000
Fund Balance—Quasi Endowment		5,000
Fund Balance—Term Endowment		9,000
Fund Balance—Endowment		7,000
To distribute the gain on sale of investments in the ratio of each fund's investment in the pool.		

Annuity and Life Income Funds

The distinction between these funds was noted earlier in this chapter. Accordingly, entries are now used to illustrate the operation of these funds.

1. An alumnus of the college donated $300,000 to the college with the stipulation that the income from the fund is to be paid to the donor for life. Upon the donor's death, the fund is to be transferred to an Endowment Fund to provide scholarships to needy students.

Cash—Life Income	300,000	
Fund Balance—Life Income		300,000

2. The funds were invested.

Investments	300,000	
Cash—Life Income		300,000

3. Investment income amounted to $30,000.

Cash—Life Income	30,000	
Life Income Payable		30,000

4. Payment is made to the donor.

Life Income Payable	30,000	
Cash—Life Income		30,000

5. An alumna of the college donated $200,000 to the college with the stipulation that the donor is to receive $18,000 for life at which time the fund is to be transferred to the Unrestricted Current Fund without any restrictions. The actuarial present value of the $18,000 annuity is $125,000.

Cash—Annuity	200,000	
Annuity Payable		125,000
Fund Balance—Annuity		75,000
Investments	190,000	
Cash—Annuity		190,000

6. Investment income amounted to $25,000.

Cash—Annuity	25,000	
Annuity Payable		25,000

7. The payment is made to the annuitant.

Annuity Payable	18,000	
Cash—Annuity		18,000

8. A new mortality table is issued, and the annuity is adjusted for the revised life expectancy.

Fund Balance—Annuity	30,000	
Annuity Payable		30,000

9. On the death of the annuitant an entry would be made as follows:

Annuity Payable	xxxx	
Fund Balance—Annuity	xxxx	
Cash—Annuity		xxxx

Financial statements

A comprehensive sample set of financial statements are presented as Illustrations 23–1 through 23–3. They should be reviewed carefully in the context of the journal entries used for illustrative purposes. The Agency Fund was not illustrated with entries since this fund has no fund balance and merely holds funds for others until the disbursements are due.

Illustration 23–1

SAMPLE EDUCATIONAL INSTITUTION
Balance Sheet
June 30, 19—
(with comparative figures at June 30, 19—)

Assets

	Current year	Prior year
Current Funds:		
Unrestricted:		
Cash	$ 210,000	$ 110,000
Investments	450,000	360,000
Accounts receivable, less allowance of $18,000 both years	228,000	175,000
Inventories, at lower of cost (first-in, first-out basis) or market	90,000	80,000
Prepaid expenses and deferred charges	28,000	20,000
Total Unrestricted	1,006,000	745,000
Restricted:		
Cash	145,000	101,000
Investments	175,000	165,000
Accounts receivable, less allowance of $8,000 both years	68,000	160,000
Unbilled charges	72,000	—
Total Restricted	460,000	426,000
Total Current Funds	$ 1,466,000	$ 1,171,000
Loan Funds:		
Cash	$ 30,000	$ 20,000
Investments	100,000	100,000
Loans to students, faculty, and staff, less allowance of $10,000 current year and $9,000 prior year	550,000	382,000
Due from unrestricted funds	3,000	—
Total Loan Funds	$ 683,000	$ 502,000
Endowment and Similar Funds:		
Cash	$ 100,000	$ 101,000
Investments	13,900,000	11,800,000
Total Endowment and Similar Funds	$14,000,000	$11,901,000

Liabilities and Fund Balances

	Current year	Prior year
Current Funds:		
Unrestricted:		
Accounts payable	$ 125,000	$ 100,000
Accrued liabilities	20,000	15,000
Students' deposits	30,000	35,000
Due to other funds	158,000	120,000
Deferred credits	30,000	20,000
Fund balance	643,000	455,000
Total Unrestricted	1,006,000	745,000
Restricted:		
Accounts payable	14,000	5,000
Fund balances	446,000	421,000
Total Restricted	460,000	426,000
Total Current Funds	$ 1,466,000	$ 1,171,000
Loan Funds:		
Fund balances		
U.S. government grants refundable	$ 50,000	$ 33,000
University funds:		
Restricted	483,000	369,000
Unrestricted	150,000	100,000
Total Loan Funds	$ 683,000	$ 502,000
Endowment and Similar Funds:		
Fund balances:		
Endowment	$ 7,800,000	$ 6,740,000
Term endowment	3,840,000	3,420,000
Quasi-endowment—unrestricted	1,000,000	800,000
Quasi-endowment—restricted	1,360,000	941,000
Total Endowment and Similar Funds	$14,000,000	$11,901,000

Annuity and Life Income Funds, Plant Funds, and Agency Funds

Assets

Annuity and Life Income Funds:		
Annuity Funds:		
Cash	$ 55,000	$ 45,000
Investments	3,260,000	3,010,000
Total Annuity Funds	3,315,000	3,055,000
Life Income Funds:		
Cash	15,000	15,000
Investments	2,045,000	1,740,000
Total Life Income Funds	2,060,000	1,755,000
Total Annuity and Life Income Funds	$ 5,375,000	$ 4,810,000
Plant Funds:		
Unexpended:		
Cash	$ 275,000	$ 410,000
Investments	1,285,000	1,590,000
Due from Unrestricted Current Funds	150,000	120,000
Total Unexpended	1,710,000	2,120,000
Renewals and replacements:		
Cash	5,000	4,000
Investments	150,000	286,000
Deposits with trustees	100,000	90,000
Due from Unrestricted Current Funds	5,000	—
Total renewals and replacements	260,000	380,000
Retirement of indebtedness:		
Cash	50,000	40,000
Deposits with trustees	250,000	253,000
Total retirement of indebtedness	300,000	293,000
Investment in plant:		
Land	500,000	500,000
Land improvements	1,000,000	1,110,000
Buildings	25,000,000	24,060,000
Equipment	15,000,000	14,200,000
Library books	100,000	80,000
Total investment in plant	41,600,000	39,950,000
Total Plant Funds	$43,870,000	$42,743,000
Agency Funds:		
Cash	$ 50,000	$ 70,000
Investments	60,000	20,000
Total Agency Funds	$ 110,000	$ 90,000

Liabilities and Fund Balances

Annuity and Life Income Funds:		
Annuity Funds:		
Annuities payable	$ 2,150,000	$ 2,300,000
Fund balances	1,165,000	755,000
Total Annuity Funds	3,315,000	3,055,000
Life Income Funds:		
Income payable	5,000	5,000
Fund balances	2,055,000	1,750,000
Total Life Income Funds	2,060,000	1,755,000
Total Annuity and Life Income Funds	$ 5,375,000	$ 4,810,000
Plant Funds:		
Unexpended:		
Accounts payable	$ 10,000	—
Notes payable	100,000	—
Bonds payable	400,000	—
Fund Balances:		
Restricted	1,000,000	1,860,000
Unrestricted	200,000	260,000
Total Unexpended	1,710,000	2,120,000
Renewals and replacements:		
Fund balances:		
Restricted	25,000	180,000
Unrestricted	235,000	200,000
Total renewals and replacements	260,000	380,000
Retirement of indebtedness:		
Fund balances:		
Restricted	185,000	125,000
Unrestricted	115,000	168,000
Total retirement of indebtedness	300,000	293,000
Investment in plant:		
Notes payable	790,000	810,000
Bonds payable	2,200,000	2,400,000
Mortgages payable	400,000	200,000
Net investment in plant	38,210,000	36,540,000
Total investment in plant	41,600,000	39,950,000
Total Plant Funds	$43,870,000	$42,743,000
Agency Funds:		
Deposits held in custody for others	$ 110,000	$ 90,000
Total Agency Funds	$ 110,000	$ 90,000

Source: *College and University Business Administration Administrative Service*, Part 5:7, pp. 2–3. Reprinted by permission of the National Association of College and University Business Officers.

Illustration 23–2

SAMPLE EDUCATIONAL INSTITUTION
Statement of Current Funds Revenues, Expenditures, and Other Changes
Year Ended June 30, 19—

	Current year			Prior
	Unrestricted	Restricted	Total	year total
Revenues:				
Tuition and fees	$2,600,000		$2,600,000	$2,300,000
Federal appropriations	500,000		500,000	500,000
State appropriations	700,000		700,000	700,000
Local appropriations	100,000		100,000	100,000
Federal grants and contracts	200,000	$ 375,000	395,000	350,000
State grants and contracts	10,000	25,000	35,000	200,000
Local grants and contracts	5,000	25,000	30,000	45,000
Private gifts, grants, and contracts	850,000	380,000	1,230,000	1,190,000
Endowment income	325,000	209,000	534,000	500,000
Sales and services of educational activities	190,000		190,000	195,000
Sales and services of auxiliary enterprises	2,200,000		2,200,000	2,100,000
Expired term endowment	40,000		40,000	
Other sources (if any)				
Total current revenues	7,540,000	1,014,000	8,554,000	8,180,000
Expenditures and mandatory transfers:				
Educational and general:				
Instruction	2,960,000	489,000	3,449,000	3,300,000
Research	100,000	400,000	500,000	650,000
Public service	130,000	25,000	155,000	175,000
Academic support	250,000		250,000	225,000
Student services	200,000		200,000	195,000
Institutional support	450,000		450,000	445,000
Operation and maintenance of plant	220,000		220,000	200,000
Scholarships and fellowships	90,000	100,000	190,000	180,000

Educational and general expenditures	4,400,000	1,014,000	5,414,000	5,370,000
Mandatory transfers for:				
Principal and interest	90,000		90,000	50,000
Renewals and replacements	100,000		100,000	80,000
Loan fund matching grant	2,000		2,000	
Total educational and general	4,592,000	1,014,000	5,606,000	5,500,000
Auxiliary enterprises:				
Expenditures	1,830,000		1,830,000	1,730,000
Mandatory transfers for:				
Principal and interest	250,000		250,000	250,000
Renewals and replacements	70,000		70,000	70,000
Total auxiliary enterprises	2,150,000		2,150,000	2,050,000
Total expenditures and mandatory transfers	6,742,000	1,014,000	7,756,000	7,550,000
Other transfers and additions/(deductions):				
Excess of restricted receipts over transfers to revenues		45,000	45,000	40,000
Refunded to grantors		(20,000)	(20,000)	
Unrestricted gifts allocated to other funds	(650,000)		(650,000)	(510,000)
Portion of quasi-endowment gains appropriated	40,000		40,000	
Net increase in fund balances	$ 188,000	$ 25,000	$ 213,000	$ 160,000

Source: College and University Business Administration, Administrative Service, Part 5:7, pp. 6–7. Reprinted by permission of the National Association of College and University Business Officers.

Illustration 23–3

SAMPLE EDUCATIONAL INSTITUTION
Statement of Changes in Fund Balances
Year Ended June 30, 19—

	Current Funds		Loan Funds	Endowment and Similar Funds	Annuity and Life Income Funds	Plant Funds			
	Unrestricted	Restricted				Unexpended	Renewals and replacements	Retirement of indebtedness	Investment in plant
Revenues and other additions:									
Unrestricted current fund revenues	$7,540,000								
Expired term endowment—restricted						$ 50,000			
State appropriations—restricted						50,000			
Federal grants and contracts—restricted		$ 500,000							
Private gifts, grants, and contracts—restricted		370,000	$100,000	$ 1,500,000	$ 800,000	115,000		$ 65,000	$ 15,000
Investment income—restricted		224,000	12,000	10,000		5,000	$ 5,000	5,000	
Realized gains on investments—unrestricted				109,000					
Realized gains on investments—restricted			4,000	50,000		10,000	5,000	5,000	
Interest on loans receivable			7,000						
U.S. government advances			18,000						
Expended for plant facilities (including $100,000 charged to current funds expenditures)									1,550,000
Retirement of indebtedness									220,000
Accrued interest on sale of bonds								3,000	
Matured annuity and life income restricted to endowment				10,000					
Total revenues and other additions	7,540,000	1,094,000	141,000	1,679,000	800,000	230,000	10,000	78,000	1,785,000

Expenditures and other deductions:

	(1)	(2)	(3)	(4)	(5)	(6)	(7)	(8)	(9)
Educational and general expenditures	4,400,000	1,014,000							
Auxiliary enterprises expenditures	1,830,000								
Indirect costs recovered		35,000							
Refunded to grantors		20,000							
Loan cancellations and write-offs			10,000						1,000
Administrative and collection costs			1,000						
Adjustment of actuarial liability for annuities payable					75,000				
Expended for plant facilities (including noncapitalized expenditures of $50,000)						1,200,000	300,000		
Retirement of indebtedness								220,000	
Interest on indebtedness								190,000	
Disposal of plant facilities								1,000	115,000
Expired term endowments ($40,000 unrestricted, $50,000 restricted to plant)				90,000					
Matured annuity and life income funds restricted to endowment					10,000				
Total expenditures and other deductions	6,230,000	1,069,000	12,000	90,000	85,000	1,200,000	300,000	411,000	115,000

Transfers among funds—additions (deductions):

	(1)	(2)	(3)	(4)	(5)	(6)	(7)	(8)	(9)
Mandatory:									
Principal and interest	(340,000)							340,000	
Renewals and replacements	(170,000)						170,000		
Loan fund matching grant	(2,000)		2,000						
Unrestricted gifts allocated	(650,000)		50,000	550,000		50,000			
Portion of unrestricted quasi-endowment funds investment gains appropriated	40,000			(40,000)					
Total transfers	(1,122,000)		52,000	510,000		50,000	170,000	340,000	
Net increase/(decrease) for the year	188,000	25,000	181,000	2,099,000	715,000	(920,000)	(120,000)	7,000	1,670,000
Fund balance at beginning of year	455,000	421,000	502,000	11,901,000	2,505,000	2,120,000	380,000	293,000	36,540,000
Fund balance at end of year	$ 643,000	$ 446,000	$ 683,000	$14,000,000	$3,220,000	$1,200,000	$ 260,000	$ 300,000	$38,210,000

Source: *College and University Business Administration Administrative Service*, Part 5:7, pp. 4–5. Reprinted by permission of the National Association of College and University Business Officers.

HOSPITAL ACCOUNTING

The funds used by hospitals for accounting purposes are slightly different from those used by colleges and universities. The AICPA Audit Guide recommends that the following funds be used:

1. Operating Fund—an unrestricted fund used to account for the day-to-day operations.
2. Specific Purpose Fund—a restricted fund used to account for expendable assets in accordance with a donor's restrictions.
3. Endowment Fund—a fund used to account for a trust where the principal (corpus) must be kept intact and the income can be expended for either current operations or a specific purpose in accordance with the grantor's wishes.
4. Plant Replacement and Expansion Fund—a fund used to account for land, buildings, and equipment; assets held for purposes of replacements and additions; accumulated depreciation on depreciable assets; and long-term debt associated with plant assets.

Revenues

Revenues are subdivided into Daily Patient Services (a further subdivision might be from the department rendering the service, such as Surgical, Pediatric, Obstetric, etc.); other Nursing Services; other Professional Services (laboratory, radiology, pharmacy, etc.); and other Revenues (nonmedical services, grants, endowments, etc.).

Adjustments to revenues.   Deductions from gross revenues to arrive at net revenues consist of:

1. Charity cases—these are considered deductions from revenues rather than expenses.
2. Contractual adjustments—usually from Blue Cross–Blue Shield, Medicare, and other insurance carriers.
3. Staff discounts—reductions are normally given to staff.
4. Uncollectible accounts.

Expenses

Expenses are usually subdivided into (1) Nursing Services, (2) Other Professional Services, (3) General Services, (4) Administrative Services, and (5) Fiscal Services.

Depreciation

Since depreciation is cost recoverable, depreciation expense is recorded as in commercial accounts.

Journal entries

Although fund accounting is used by hospitals, the entries used generally follow those used by commercial establishments which include accruals, deferrals, amortization, and closing entries. Typical journal entries would appear as follows:

Operating Fund. The summary entry to record revenues would be:

(1)

Accounts Receivable	4,400,000	
Revenue—Daily Patient Services		3,000,000
Revenue—Other Nursing Services		900,000
Revenue—Other Professional Services		500,000

It is customary for a hospital to show as deductions from revenue, instead of expenses, the following: (1) provision for doubtful accounts; (2) contractual allowances to third-party payers, such as Medicare, Medicaid, and Blue Cross; (3) charity services; and (4) discounts to employees. The summary entry to record these items might appear as follows:

(2)

Provision for Doubtful Accounts	200,000	
Contractual Allowances	150,000	
Charity Services	100,000	
Discounts and Allowances	50,000	
Accounts Receivable		300,000
Allowance for Doubtful Accounts		200,000

Summary entries to record the operating expenses for the year 19x1 would be:

(3)

Nursing Services	1,800,000	
Other Professional Services	800,000	
General Services	600,000	
Administrative Services	400,000	
Fiscal Services	200,000	
Cash		3,750,000
Accounts payable		50,000

(4)

Depreciation Expense	200,000	
Accumulated Depreciation—Buildings		100,000
Accumulated Depreciation—Equipment		100,000

(5)

Interest Expense	40,000	
Cash		25,000
Accrued Expenses Payable		15,000

The entries to record unrestricted gifts and bequests and a transfer from the Plant Replacement and Expansion Fund would appear as:

(6)

Cash	300,000	
Nonoperating Revenue		100,000
Transfer from Restricted Plant Replacement and Expansion Fund		200,000

The summary entry to record the write-off of uncollectible accounts and the collection of receivables would be:

(7)

Cash	4,000,000	
Allowance for Doubtful Accounts	240,000	
Accounts Receivable		4,240,000

The entry to record the purchase of equipment would be:

(8)

Equipment—Movable	250,000	
Equipment—Fixed (from Plant Replacement Fund)	200,000	
Cash		450,000

Plant Replacement and Expansion Fund—Restricted. Summary entries in this fund might appear as follows:

(1)

Cash	150,000	
Pledges Receivable		150,000

Interest earned during the year would be reflected as:

(2)

Cash	20,000	
Fund Balance		20,000

The sale of securities at a gain would appear as:

(3)

Cash	180,000	
Fund Balance		100,000
Investment in Marketable Securities		80,000

If marketable securities were purchased during 19x1, the entry to record their purchase would be:

(4)

Investments in Marketable Securities	200,000	
Cash		200,000

The transfer to the Operating Fund would be recorded as:

(5)

Fund Balance	200,000	
Cash		200,000

New pledges were received and uncollectible pledges were written off as follows:

(6)

Pledges Receivable	100,000	
Allowance for Uncollectible Pledges	30,000	
Pledges Receivable		30,000
Fund Balance		100,000

An adjustment of the Allowance for the Uncollectible Pledges account would appear as:

(7)

Fund Balance	15,000	
Allowance for Uncollectible Pledges		15,000

Specific Purpose Funds—Restricted. The entry to record the receipt of pledges would be:

(1)

Pledges Receivable	20,000	
Fund Balance		20,000

Funds transferred to other funds for the purpose specified are handled as any other transfer. An example would be:

Transfer to Operating Fund	xxx	
Cash		xxx

Endowment Fund—Restricted.

The receipt of marketable securities as part of a restricted endowment would be recorded as:

(1)

Marketable Securities	25,000	
Fund Balance—Restricted		25,000

Income earned on investments where the income is to be used for a designated purpose would be journalized as follows:

(2a)

Cash	20,000	
Due to Other Funds		20,000

(2b)

Due to Other Funds	20,000	
Cash		20,000

It is possible for endowments to be unrestricted as well as restricted. If a hospital has both types, separate funds should be used. Alternatively, one fund could be used provided separate fund balances—restricted and unrestricted—are maintained in the fund.

Closing entries.

Closing entries are not shown since all revenues and expenses are merely closed into the operating fund balance.

Financial statements

The financial statements used by hospitals include:

1. Balance sheet.
2. Statement of revenues and expenses (income statement).
3. Statement of changes in fund balances.
4. Statement of changes in financial position (for the current unrestricted fund only).

Except for the last statement, examples of these statements after incorporating the above illustrative entries appear as Illustrations 23–4 through 23–6. The statement of changes in financial position is the same format as that used by businesses.

Illustration 23–4
BAXTER HOSPITAL
Balance Sheet
December 31, 19x1
Operating Fund

Assets			*Liabilities and Fund Balances*		
Current assets:			Current liabilities:		
Cash		$ 140,000	Accounts payable	$90,000	
Accounts receivable	$ 100,000		Accrued expenses		
Less allowance for uncollectible receivables	10,000	90,000	payable	15,000	
Inventory of supplies		10,000			
Prepaid expenses		5,000			
Total current assets		$ 245,000	Total current liabilities		$ 105,000
Property, plant and equipment:			Long-term debt:		
Land		800,000	Mortage bonds payable		400,000
Buildings	1,500,000		Total liabilities		505,000
Less: Accumulated depreciation	400,000	1,100,000	Fund balance		2,140,000
Equipment	800,000				
Less: Accumulated depreciation	300,000	500,000			
Total property, plant, and equipment		2,400,000			
Total Operating Fund		$2,645,000	Total Operating Fund		$2,645,000

Plant Replacement and Expansion Fund

Restricted funds:				
Cash		$ 200,000	Fund balance	$1,180,000
Investments in marketable securities		800,000		
Pledges receivable	$ 200,000			
Less allowance for uncollectibles	20,000	180,000		
Total Plant Replacement and Expansion Fund		$1,180,000	Total Plant Replacement and Expansion Fund	$1,180,000

Specific Purpose Funds

Cash	$ 15,000	Fund balance	$ 55,000
Pledges receivable	40,000		
Total Specific Purpose Funds	$ 55,000	Total Specific Purpose Funds	$ 55,000

Endowment Funds

Cash	10,000	Fund balance	$ 240,000
Marketable securities	230,000		
Total Endowment Funds	$ 240,000	Total Endowment Funds	$ 240,000

Illustration 23–5
BAXTER HOSPITAL
Statement of Revenues and Expenses
Year Ended December 31, 19x1

Patient service revenues:

Daily patient services	$3,000,000	
Other nursing services	900,000	
Other professional services .	500,000	$4,400,000

Deductions from patient services revenues:

Provision for doubtful accounts	200,000	
Contractual allowances	150,000	
Charity services	100,000	
Discounts and allowances . .	50,000	500,000
Net patient service revenues . .		3,900,000

Operating expenses:

Nursing services	1,800,000	
Other professional services .	800,000	
General services	600,000	
Administrative services	400,000	
Fiscal services	200,000	
Depreciation	200,000	
Interest	40,000	
Total operating expenses		4,040,000
Loss from operations		(140,000)

Nonoperating revenue:

Bequests and gifts	100,000	
Transfers from plant replacement and expansion fund	200,000	300,000
Excess of revenues over expenses		$ 160,000

Illustration 23–6
BAXTER HOSPITAL
Statement of Changes in Fund Balances
Year Ended December 31, 19x1

Operating Fund:

Balance at beginning of year .		$1,980,000
Increase in fund balance for year (see Illustration 22–19)		160,000
Balance at end of year		$2,140,000

Plant Replacement and Expansion Fund:

Balance at beginning of year .		$1,175,000
Transfer to operating fund for capital outlays	$(200,000)	
Gain on sale of securities . . .	100,000	
Interest earnings for year . . .	20,000	
Increase in allowance for uncollectible pledges	(15,000)	
Restricted pledges received during the year	100,000	5,000
Balance at end of year		$1,180,000

Specific Purpose Funds:

Balance at beginning of year .		$ 35,000
Restricted gifts and pledges during year		20,000
Balance at end of year		$ 55,000

Endowment Funds:

Balance at beginning of year .		$ 215,000
Restricted gifts during the year		25,000
Balance at end of year		$ 240,000

ACCOUNTING FOR VOLUNTARY HEALTH AND WELFARE ORGANIZATIONS

Organizations that fall into this grouping are those deriving their principal funding from the general public in the form of voluntary contributions which are then used to support health, welfare, and community service projects. As mentioned in the preceding chapter, the principal pronouncement covering this group of organizations is the Audit Guide[3] issued by the AICPA in 1974. An additional pronouncement, a Statement of Position,[4] was also issued by the AICPA in 1978, but it has no effective date.

Funds

The funds used by the voluntary health and welfare organizations are similar to those illustrated previously. They include:

1. Current Fund—Unrestricted. This fund is used for operations that require only the approval of the board of directors.

---

[3]AICPA, *Audits of Voluntary Health and Welfare Organizations* (New York, 1974).
[4]AICPA, *Statement of Position 78–10, Accounting Principles and Reporting Practices for Certain Nonprofit Organizations* (New York, 1978).

2. Current Fund—Restricted. This fund is used for operations in accordance with a grantor's specifications.
3. Land, Buildings, and Equipment Fund. This fund is used to account for:
    a. Land, buildings, and equipment acquired by the organization.
    b. Liabilities arising from the acquisition or improvement of the plant assets.
    c. Current assets or investments awaiting disposition for the future acquisition or improvement of plant assets.
4. Endowment Funds. These funds are used to account for grantor-bequests which require the principal (corpus) to be maintained intact.

These four funds are similar to the same funds discussed previously for colleges and universities. A possible fifth fund is a Custodial Fund which is similar to an Agency Fund. The assets in this fund really belong to a donor and, therefore, are not really that of the organization.

Revenues

Since the terminology for recording revenue for these organizations is somewhat different from that of commercial organizations, selected entries are now presented to illustrate the procedures for recording revenue.

Current Fund—Unrestricted

(1)

Pledges Receivable	200,000	
Allowance for Uncollectible Pledges		20,000
Contribution Revenue		90,000
Deferred Contribution Revenue		90,000

To record pledges payable, 50 percent in 19x1 and 50 percent in 19x2.

Collections are handled as in commercial accounting. In 19x2, the Deferred Contribution Revenue is transferred to Contribution Revenue as follows:

(2)

Deferred Contribution Revenue	90,000	
Contribution Revenue		90,000

Current Fund—Restricted

(3)

Pledges Receivable	100,000	
Allowance for Uncollectible Pledges		10,000
Contribution Revenue		90,000

To record a pledge from Mr. and Mrs. Ames who directed that these funds be used to foster the adoption of handicapped children.

Other revenues from legacies and bequests, membership dues, program service fees, sales to the public, investment revenues, and miscellaneous revenues are treated in a similar manner as illustrated in entries (1) and (3), except that Cash and/or Accounts Receivable are debited as dictated by the circumstances.

If revenues are received from a building fund campaign, the entry to record the pledge is the same as entry (1) except that it appears in the Land,

Building, and Equipment Fund. Cash Collections are treated the same as in commercial accounting.

Donated services

On many occasions, donors donate services rather than money or goods. For instance, a physician may donate his services that would have cost $5,000 if the service were contracted for. The entry to record this transaction would be:

Current Fund—Unrestricted

(4)

Contributed Service Expense	5,000	
Contributed Service Revenue		5,000

Entries are normally *not* made for casual volunteer services. The AICPA recommends that volunteer services be recorded only when *all* of the following conditions are present:

1. The services are normally performed by salaried personnel.
2. The organization exercises control over the donor's services.
3. The value of the services are clearly measurable in dollar value.[5]

Expenses

Expenses are recorded in a manner similar to that used by business organizations. A sample entry would be:

Current Fund—Unrestricted

(5)

Professional fees	5,000	
Supplies	500	
Telephone	1,500	
Postage and Shipping	800	
Occupancy	4,000	
Printing and Publications	2,000	
Travel	1,500	
Conferences, Conventions, and Meetings	3,000	
Specific Assistance to Individuals	5,000	
Cost of Sales to Public	1,000	
Miscellaneous	1,200	
Accounts Payable		25,500

If a special project were undertaken with the use of funds from the Current Fund—Restricted, the entry would be similar to (5) above, except that the entry would appear in the restricted fund.

Depreciation

Commercial depreciation entries are made, except that the entries are made in the Land, Building, and Equipment Fund by function. An example of this can be seen as line 19 in Illustration 23–8. The total depreciation expense for 19x2 amounts to $4,200, and this same amount appears as the total expenses of the Land, Building, and Equipment Fund column in Illustration 23–7.

However, since the depreciation reduces the carrying value of the fixed

---

[5]*Audits of Voluntary Health and Welfare Organizations,* p. 21.

assets, it is necessary to transfer an amount equal to the annual depreciation charge from Fund Balance—Expended to Fund Balance—Unexpended.

Land, Building, and Equipment Fund

(6a)

Depreciation of Buildings and Equipment	4,200	
Accumulated Depreciation of Buildings and Equipment		4,200

(6b)

Fund Balance—Expended	4,200	
Fund Balances—Unexpended		4,200

Closing entries

Closing entries for these organizations' funds are no different from those discussed previously, and, therefore, are not illustrated.

Financial statements

The financial statements for these organization are:

1. Balance sheet.
2. Statement of support, revenue, and expenses and changes in fund balances.
3. Statement of functional expenses.

Sample statements appear as Illustrations 23–7 through 23–12. For a better understanding of this subject, these illustrations should be reviewed carefully.

Illustration 23–7

FAMILY SERVICE AGENCY OF UTOPIA, INC.
Statement of Support, Revenue, and Expenses and Changes in Fund Balances
Year Ended December 31, 19x2, with Comparative Totals for 19x1

	Current Funds		Land, Building, and Equipment Fund	Endowment Fund	Total all funds	
	Unrestricted	Restricted			19x2	19x1
1. Public support and revenue:						
2. Public support—						
3. Received directly—						
4. Contributions (net of estimated uncollectible pledges of $3,545 in 19x2 and $3,415 in 19x1)	$ 70,925	$16,200	—	$ 200	$ 87,325	$ 84,700
5. Contributions to building fund		—	$ 7,200	—	7,200	6,800
6. Special events (net of direct benefit costs of $28,100 in 19x2 and $26,200 in 19x1)	25,400	—	—	—	25,400	19,200
7. Legacies and bequests	9,200	—	—	400	9,600	12,000
8. Total received directly	105,525	16,200	7,200	600	129,525	122,700
9. Received indirectly—						
10. Contributed by associated organizations (net of their related fund-raising expenses estimated at $500 in 19x2 and $575 in 19x1)	2,000	—	—	—	2,000	2,000
11. Allocated by United Way of Fairshare Bay (net of their related fund-raising expenses estimated at $12,000 in 19x2 and $11,160 in 19x1)	300,000	—	—	—	300,000	279,000
12. Total received indirectly	302,000	—	—	—	302,000	281,000
13. Total support from the public	407,525	16,200	7,200	600	431,525	403,700
14. Fees and grants from governmental agencies	—	9,300	—	—	9,300	8,000

15.	Other revenue—					
16.	Membership dues—individual	500	—	—	—	500	400
17.	Program service fees (and net incidental revenue of $180)	51,000	—	—	—	51,000	47,400
18.	Sales to public (net of direct expenses of $800 in 19x2 and $700 in 19x1)	100	—	—	—	100	100
19.	Investment income	9,800	700	—	—	10,500	9,100
20.	Gain (or loss) on investment transactions	2,000	—	—	2,500	4,500	1,500
21.	Miscellaneous revenue	2,800	—	—	—	2,800	3,600
22.	Total other revenue	66,200	700	—	2,500	69,400	62,100
23.	Total public support and revenue	473,725	26,200	7,200	3,100	$510,225	$473,800
24.	Expenses:						
25.	Program services—						
26.	Counseling	168,500	24,500	1,630	—	$194,630	$182,836
27.	Adoption	72,200	—	620	—	72,820	81,260
28.	Foster home care	160,454	—	1,410	—	161,864	142,206
29.	Total program services	401,154	24,500	3,660	—	429,314	406,302
30.	Supporting services—						
31.	Management and general	50,195	—	420	—	50,615	45,069
32.	Fund raising	11,843	—	120	—	11,963	12,198
33.	Total supporting services	62,038	—	540	—	62,578	57,267
34.	Payments to affiliated organizations (Note 7)	7,168	—	—	—	7,168	6,656
35.	Total expenses	470,360	24,500	4,200	—	$499,060	$470,225
36.	Excess of public support and revenue over expenses	3,365	1,700	3,000	3,100		
37.	Other changes in fund balances:						
38.	Property and equipment acquisitions from unrestricted funds	(1,700)	—	1,700	—		
39.	Transfer of realized endowment fund appreciation	2,500	—	—	(2,500)		
40.	Returned to donor	—	(800)	—	—		
41.	Fund balances, beginning of year	80,280	2,300	64,900	201,700		
42.	Fund balances, end of year	$ 84,445	$ 3,200	$69,600	$202,300		

(See accompanying notes to financial statements)

Source: United Way of America, *Accounting and Financial Reporting, A Guide for United Ways and Not-For-Profit Human Service Organizations,* (Alexandria, Va., 1974), p. 118.

Illustration 23–8

FAMILY SERVICE AGENCY OF UTOPIA, INC.
Statement of Functional Expenses
Year Ended December 31, 19x2,
with Comparative Totals for 19x1

	Program services				Supporting services			Total programs and supporting services expenses	
	Counseling	Adoption	Foster-home care	Total	Management and general	Fund raising	Total	19x2	19x1
1. Salaries	$ 86,068	$33,776	$ 72,306	$192,150	$32,517	$ 7,503	$40,020	$232,170	$223,086
2. Employee benefits	16,625	6,846	15,453	38,924	6,591	1,520	8,111	47,035	44,360
3. Payroll taxes, etc.	4,283	1,657	3,497	9,437	1,595	368	1,963	11,400	10,768
4. Total salaries and related expenses	106,976	42,279	91,256	240,511	40,703	9,391	50,094	290,605	278,214
5. Professional fees	29,105	9,905	12,090	51,100	3,500	—	3,500	54,600	50,459
6. Supplies	3,391	1,281	2,864	7,536	758	206	964	8,500	8,006
7. Telephone	3,965	1,498	3,349	8,812	565	233	798	9,610	9,065
8. Postage and shipping	2,701	1,020	2,282	6,003	583	164	747	6,750	7,350
9. Occupancy	9,658	3,649	8,155	21,462	2,540	598	3,138	24,600	23,192
10. Rental and maintenance of equipment	3,937	1,488	3,325	8,750	—	—	—	8,750	9,237
11. Printing and publications	2,563	1,245	1,291	5,099	850	1,251	2,101	7,200	6,903
12. Travel	11,301	2,015	10,504	23,820	180	—	180	24,000	22,640
13. Conferences, conventions, meetings	7,447	755	5,178	13,380	320	—	320	13,700	12,930
14. Specific assistance to individuals	9,371	1,000	18,129	28,500	—	—	—	28,500	21,573
15. Membership dues	300	202	100	602	75	—	75	677	677
16. Awards and grants—to National Headquarters	—	5,000	—	5,000	—	—	—	5,000	5,000
17. Miscellaneous	2,285	863	1,931	5,079	121	—	121	5,200	4,923
18. Total before depreciation	193,000	72,200	160,454	425,654	50,195	11,843	62,038	487,692	460,169
19. Depreciation of buildings and equipment	1,630	620	1,410	3,660	420	120	540	4,200	3,400
20. Total expenses	$194,630	$72,820	$161,864	$429,314	$50,615	$11,963	$62,578	$491,892	$463,569

(See accompanying notes to financial statements)
Source: United Way of America, *Accounting and Financial Reporting*, p. 119.

Illustration 23-9

FAMILY SERVICE AGENCY OF UTOPIA, INC.
Balance Sheets
December 31, 19x2, and 19x1

Current Funds—Unrestricted

Assets	19x2	19x1	Liabilities and Fund Balances	19x2	19x1
Cash	$ 45,747	$ 52,667	Accounts payable and accrued expenses	$ 24,611	$ 18,702
Short-term investments—at cost which is approximately market value	20,000	10,000	Support and revenue designated for future periods	5,215	4,190
Accounts receivable less allowance for uncollectibles of $130 and $186	2,165	3,087	Total liabilities and deferred revenues	29,826	22,892
Pledges receivable less allowance for uncollectibles of $249 and $197	4,968	3,724	Fund balances:		
Supplies for use, at cost or market, whichever is lower	22,875	14,925	Designated by the governing board for—		
Prepaid expenses and deferred charges	3,516	3,769	Long-term investments	15,000	15,000
Board-designated long-term investments	15,000	15,000	Purchases of new equipment	8,300	10,000
			Special Outreach Project	25,000	—
			Undesignated, available for general activities	36,145	55,280
			Total fund balances	84,445	80,280
	$114,271	$103,172		$114,271	$103,172

Restricted

Assets	19x2	19x1		19x2	19x1
Cash	$ 3,200	$ 2,300	Fund balance: Professional education	$ 3,200	$ 2,300

Land, Building and Equipment Fund

Assets	19x2	19x1		19x2	19x1
Cash	$ 1,123	$ 700	8¼% mortgage payable, due 19z5	$ 52,370	$ 54,194
Short-term investments—at cost which is approximately market value	15,000	—			
Pledges receivable less allowance for uncollectibles of $336 and $638	11,203	21,250	Fund balances:		
Land, building, and equipment at cost less accumulated depreciation of $12,565 and $8,365	94,644	97,144	Expended	42,274	42,950
			Unexpended restricted	27,326	21,950
			Total fund balance	69,600	64,900
	$121,970	$119,094		$121,970	$119,094

Endowment Fund

Assets	19x2	19x1		19x2	19x1
Cash	$ 300	$ 700	Fund balance	$202,300	$201,700
Investments	202,000	201,000			
	$202,300	$201,700		$202,300	$201,700

(See accompanying notes to financial statements)
Source: United Way of America, *Accounting and Financial Reporting*, p. 120.

Illustration 23–10

SAMPLE LIBRARY

Statement of Support, Revenue, and Expenses, and Changes in Fund Balances

Year Ended December 31, 19x1, (with Comparative Totals for 19x0)

| | Year ended December 31, 19x1 | | | | | | | Year ended December 31, 19x0 |
| | Unrestricted | | | Current restricted | Plant | Endowment | Total | Total |
	Operating	Investment	Total					
Support and revenue:								
Support:								
Grants (Note 1):								
Governments	$ 150,000	—	$ 150,000	—	—	—	$ 150,000	$ 150,000
Other	25,000	—	25,000	—	—	—	25,000	—
Contributions, legacies, and bequests (Note 1)	350,000	$ 90,000	440,000	$75,000	—	—	515,000	490,000
Contributed services of volunteers (Note 1)	75,000	—	75,000	—	—	—	75,000	50,000
Use of contributed facilities (Note 1)	47,000	—	47,000	—	—	—	47,000	50,000
Total support	647,000	90,000	737,000	75,000	—	—	812,000	740,000
Revenue:								
Fees for services	50,000	—	50,000	—	—	—	50,000	45,000
Book rentals and fines	320,000	—	320,000	—	—	—	320,000	250,000
Investment income including net gains	25,000	93,000	118,000	10,000	—	—	128,000	103,000
Total revenue	395,000	93,000	488,000	10,000	—	—	498,000	398,000
Total support and revenue	1,042,000	183,000	1,225,000	85,000	—	—	1,310,000	1,138,000
Expenses (Note 7):								
Program services:								
Circulating library	390,000	—	390,000	75,000	$ 5,000	—	470,000	430,000
Research library	169,000	—	169,000	—	1,000	—	170,000	155,000
Collections and exhibits	49,000	—	49,000	10,000	1,000	—	60,000	50,000
Educational services	49,000	—	49,000	—	1,000	—	50,000	55,000
Community services	29,500	—	29,500	—	500	—	30,000	20,000
Total program services	686,500	—	686,500	85,000	8,500	—	780,000	710,000

Supporting services:								
General administration	315,500	3,000	318,500	—	21,500	—	340,000	290,000
Fund raising	200,000	—	200,000	—	5,000	—	205,000	200,000
Total supporting services	515,500	3,000	518,500	—	26,500	—	545,000	490,000
Total expenses	1,202,000	3,000	1,205,000	85,000	35,000	—	1,325,000	1,200,000
Excess (deficiency) of support and revenue over expenses before capital additions	(160,000)	180,000	20,000	—	(35,000)	—	(15,000)	(62,000)
Capital additions:								
Contributions	—	—	—	—	40,000	—	40,000	95,000
Investment income including net gains	—	—	—	—	5,000	—	5,000	17,000
Contributed materials, equipment, etc. (Note 1)	—	—	—	—	10,000	—	10,000	10,000
	—	—	—	—	55,000	—	55,000	112,000
Excess (deficiency) of support and revenue over expenses after capital additions	(160,000)	180,000	20,000	—	20,000	—	40,000	50,000
Fund balances at beginning of year	1,270,000	740,000	2,010,000	—	1,480,000	$985,000	4,475,000	4,425,000
Mandatory transfers— principal of indebtedness	(10,000)	—	(10,000)	—	10,000	—	—	—
Fund balances at end of year	$1,100,000	$920,000	$2,020,000	—	$1,510,000	$985,000	$4,515,000	$4,475,000

Illustration 23–11
SAMPLE LIBRARY
Statement of Changes in Financial Position
Year Ended December 31, 19x1,
with Comparative Totals for 19x0

| | Year ended December 31, 19x1 | | | | | | December 31, 19x0 |
| | Unrestricted | | | Current restricted | Plant | Total | Total |
	Operating	Investment	Total				
Sources of working capital:							
Excess (deficiency) of support and revenue over expenses before capital additions	$(160,000)	$180,000	$ 20,000	—	$ (35,000)	$(15,000)	$(62,000)
Capital additions	—	—	—	—	55,000	55,000	112,000
Excess (deficiency) of support and revenue over expenses after capital additions	(160,000)	180,000	20,000	—	20,000	40,000	50,000
Add (deduct) items not using (providing) working capital:							
Depreciation	—	—	—	—	11,000	11,000	11,000
Contributed equipment	—	—	—	—	(10,000)	(10,000)	—
Working capital provided by operations	(160,000)	180,000	20,000	—	21,000	41,000	61,000
Deferred restricted contributions and investment income received	—	—	—	$85,000	—	85,000	100,000
Sale of investments	22,000	245,000	267,000	—	—	267,000	110,000
	(138,000)	425,000	287,000	85,000	21,000	393,000	271,000

Uses of working capital:							
Purchase of investments	—	—	—	—	165,000	165,000	—
Purchase of fixed assets	—	—	—	—	35,000	35,000	35,000
Reduction of long-term debt	—	—	—	—	10,000	10,000	10,000
Deferred restricted contributions and investment income recognized as support	—	—	—	85,000	—	85,000	—
Transfers between funds	10,000	—	10,000	—	(10,000)	—	100,000
	10,000	—	10,000	85,000	200,000	295,000	145,000
Increase (decrease) in working capital	$(148,000)	$425,000	$277,000	$—	$(179,000)	$ 98,000	$126,000
Changes in working capital components:							
Increase (decrease) in current assets:							
Cash	$(129,000)	$425,000	$296,000	$ (7,000)	—	$289,000	$ (5,000)
Certificates of deposit	22,000	—	22,000	20,000	$(117,000)	(75,000)	61,000
Grants receivable	54,000	—	54,000	(8,000)	(57,000)	(11,000)	60,000
Pledges receivable	—	—	—	—	—	—	—
Prepaid expenses and other current assets	(15,000)	—	(15,000)	—	—	(15,000)	(5,000)
	(68,000)	425,000	357,000	5,000	(174,000)	188,000	111,000
(Increase) decrease in current liabilities:							
Accounts payable, accrued expenses, and current portion of long-term debt	(80,000)	—	(80,000)	—	—	(80,000)	15,000
Deferred restricted contributions, etc	—	—	—	(5,000)	(5,000)	(10,000)	—
Increase (decrease) in working capital	$(148,000)	$425,000	$277,000	$—	$(179,000)	$ 98,000	$126,000

Source: AICPA, *Statement of Position 78–10*, pp. 68–69. Copyright © 1978 by the American Institute of Certified Public Accounts, Inc.

Illustration 23–12
SAMPLE LIBRARY
Balance Sheet
December 31, 19x1, with Comparative Totals for 19x0
December 31, 19x1

Assets	Unrestricted			Current restricted	Plant	Endowment	Total	December 31, 19x0 Total
	Operating	Investment	Total					
Current assets:								
Cash, including interest-bearing accounts of $600,000 in 19x1, and $400,000 in 19x0	$ 690,000	—	$ 690,000	$ 3,000	$ 7,000	—	$ 700,000	$ 411,000
Certificates of deposit	375,000	—	375,000	75,000	—	—	450,000	525,000
Grants receivable (Note 1):								
Governments	120,000	—	120,000	—	—	—	120,000	161,000
Other	30,000	—	30,000	27,000	8,000	—	65,000	35,000
Pledges receivable, at estimated net realizable value (Note 1)	15,000	—	15,000	—	—	—	15,000	15,000
Prepaid expenses and other current assets	70,000	—	70,000	—	—	—	70,000	85,000
Total current assets	1,300,000	—	1,300,000	105,000	15,000	—	1,420,000	1,232,000
Investments—at market (Note 2)	—	920,000	920,000	—	165,000	985,000	2,070,000	2,172,000
Land, buildings, and equipment—at cost, less accumulated depreciation of $90,000 and $79,000, respectively (Note 3)	—	—	—	—	1,525,000	—	1,525,000	1,491,000
Inexhaustible collections and books (Note 1)	—	—	—	—	—	—	—	—
Total assets	$1,300,000	$920,000	$2,220,000	$105,000	$1,705,000	$985,000	$5,015,000	$4,895,000

Liabilities and Fund Balances

Current liabilities:							
Accounts payable, accrued expenses, and current portion of long-term debt	$ 200,000	—	200,000	—	$ 10,000	—	$ 210,000	130,000
Deferred restricted contributions, etc. (Note 6)	—	—	—	$105,000	5,000	—	110,000	100,000
Total current liabilities	200,000	—	200,000	105,000	15,000	—	320,000	230,000
Long-term debt (Note 4)	—	—	—	—	180,000	—	180,000	190,000
Total liabilities	200,000	—	200,000	105,000	195,000	—	500,000	420,000
Fund balances:							
Unrestricted:							
Designated by the board for:							
Investment	—	$920,000	920,000	—	—	—	920,000	740,000
Purchase of equipment	50,000	—	50,000	—	—	—	50,000	35,000
Undesignated	1,050,000	—	1,050,000	—	1,510,000	—	2,560,000	2,725,000
Restricted	—	—	—	—	—	$985,000	985,000	975,000
Total fund balances	1,100,000	920,000	2,020,000	—	1,510,000	985,000	4,515,000	4,475,000
Total liabilities and fund balances	$1,300,000	$920,000	$2,220,000	$105,000	$1,705,000	$985,000	$5,015,000	$4,895,000

Source: AICPA, *Statement of Position 78–10*, pp. 64–65. Copyright © 1978 by the American Institute of Certified Public Accountants, Inc.

QUESTIONS

1. What is the difference between "hard money" and "soft money"? What is the significance of this distinction?

2. What funds do colleges and universities generally use? Give a brief explanation of each one.

3. What types of entries are recorded in the Current Fund—Unrestricted used by colleges and universities?

4. What is the significance of the difference between restricted funds and unrestricted funds?

5. What funds do hospitals generally use? Give a brief explanation of each one.

6. Is there a difference in treatment for depreciation between colleges and hospitals? Explain.

7. In which fund is the property plant and equipment carried for hospital accounting? For college accounting? Explain the differences in treatment.

8. What funds do voluntary health and welfare organizations generally use? Give a brief explanation of each one.

9. Are donated services generally recorded in the accounts of voluntary health and welfare organizations? When should they be recorded?

10. In which fund is depreciation recorded for voluntary health and welfare organizations? Is more that one entry required to record depreciation expenses? Explain.

EXERCISES

Exercise 23–1.

1. How should charity service, contractual adjustments, and bad debts be classified in the statement of revenues and expenses for the hospital?

a. All three should be treated as expenses.

b. All three should be treated as deductions from patient-service revenues.

c. Charity service and contractual adjustments should be treated as revenue deductions while bad debts should be treated as an expense.

d. Charity service and bad debts should be treated as expenses while contractual adjustments should be treated as a revenue deduction.

2. Depreciation on some hospital fixed assets, referred to as "minor equipment," is *not* accounted for in the conventional manner. How is depreciation with respect to these assets accounted for?

a. Ignored on the basis of immateriality.

b. Handled in essentially the same manner as would be the case if the assets were assigned to the activities of a city and were accounted for in its general fund.

c. Determined periodically be inventorying minor equipment and writing the assets down to their value at the inventory date.

d. Recognized only when minor equipment is replaced.

3. To assure the availability of money for improvements, replacement, and expansion of plant, it would be most desirable for the hospital to—

a. Use accelerated depreciation to provide adequate funds for eventual replacement.

b. Use the retirement or replacement system of depreciation to provide adequate funds.

c. Sell assets at the earliest opportunity.

d. Transfer cash from the operating fund to the plant fund in amounts at least equal to the periodic depreciation charges.

4. A reason for a voluntary health and welfare organization to adopt fund accounting is that—

a. Restrictions have been placed on certain of its assets by donors.

b. It provides more than one type of program service.

c. Fixed assets are significant.

d. Donated services are significant.

5. In the loan fund of a college or university, each of the following types of loans would be found except—

a. Student.

b. Staff.

c. Building.

d. Faculty.

6. What is the recommended method of accounting to be used by colleges and universities?

a. Cash.

b. Modified cash.

c. Restricted accrual.

d. Accrual.

7. Why do voluntary health and welfare organizations, unlike some not-for-profit organizations, record and recognize depreciation of fixed assets?

a. Fixed assets are more likely to be material in amount in a voluntary health and welfare organization than in other not-for-profit organizations.

b. Voluntary health and welfare organizations purchase their fixed assets, and therefore have a historical cost basis from which to determine amounts to be depreciated.

c. A fixed asset used by a voluntary health and welfare organization has alternative uses in private industry and this opportunity cost should be reflected in the organization's financial statements.

d. Contributors look for the most efficient use of funds, and since depreciation represents a cost of employing fixed assets, it is appropriate that a voluntary health and welfare organization reflect it as a cost of providing services.

8. Which of the following receipts is properly recorded as restricted current funds on the books of a university?

a. Tuition.

b. Student laboratory fees.

c. Housing fees.

d. Research grants.

9. Which of the following funds of a voluntary health and welfare organization does *not* have a counterpart fund in governmental accounting?

a. Current unrestricted.

b. Land, building, and equipment.

c. Custodian.

d. Endowment.　　　(AICPA adapted)

Exercise 23–2 (Unrestricted Current Fund of a college). During 19x3, the Bender College had the following transactions:

1. Student tuition invoices amounting to $2,000,000 were issued. Past experience indicates that $100,000 of this amount will not be collected.
2. Various government subsidies were received amounting to $1,000,000.
3. Collections from students in the amount of $1,800,000 were received.
4. An unrestricted gift for $100,000 was received.
5. The college bookstore and cafeteria had revenues (all collected) of $500,000.
6. Expenditures incurred amounted to:

a.	Instruction,	$1,800,000.
b.	Research,	$200,000.
c.	Academic support,	$100,000.
d.	Institutional support,	$100,000.
e.	Student services,	$50,000.
f.	Public service,	$75,000.
g.	Operation of plant,	$400,000.
h.	Bookstore and cafeteria,	$300,000.

All but $300,000 of the above expenditures have been paid.

7. A transfer of $300,000 was made to the Unexpended Plant Fund.

Required:

a. Prepare the journal entries to record the above transactions.

b. Prepare closing entries.

Exercise 23–3 (Unrestricted Current Fund of a College). Using the information provided in Exercise 23–2, prepare the following:

a. A balance sheet at December 31, 19x3, for the Unrestricted Current Fund. (Assume that 19x3 is the first year of operations.)

b. A statement of revenues and expenditures for 19x3.

c. A statement of changes in fund balance for 19x3.

Exercise 23–4 (Operating Fund for a hospital). During 19x4, the Good Samaritan Hospital had the following transactions:

1. Revenues were billed as follows:
   a. Daily patient services, $2,800,000.
   b. Other nursing services, $1,000,000.
   c. Other professional services, $800,000.
2. The following adjustments were made:
   a. Provision for doubtful accounts, $300,000.
   b. Contractual allowances, $200,000.
   c. Charity services, $300,000.
   d. Employee discounts, $100,000.
3. Expenditures were incurred for:
   a. Nursing services, $2,000,000.
   b. Other professional services, $600,000.
   c. General services, $500,000.
   d. Administrative services, $300,000.
   e. Fiscal services, $200,000.
4. Depreciation for the year was:
   a. Buildings, $200,000.
   b. Equipment, $300,000.
5. Interest expense amounted to $100,000 of which $80,000 was paid.

6. Cash collections were:
   a. Patients and third-party payers, $3,000,000.
   b. Unrestricted gifts and bequests, $800,000.
   c. Transfer from Restricted Plant and Replacement Fund, $400,000.
7. Cash payments were:
   a. Vouchers payable, $3,000,000.
   b. Equipment—fixed, $400,000.
   c. Equipment—movable, $100,000.
8. Bad debts written off amounted to $200,000.

Required:

a. Prepare the journal entries to record the above transactions.

Exercise 23–5 (Operating Fund for a hospital). Using the information provided in Exercise 23–4, prepare a statement of revenues and expenses.

Exercise 23–6 (Voluntary Health and Welfare Unrestricted Current Fund). During 19x5, the Family Counseling Center had the following transactions:

1. Deferred pledges from 19x4 in the amount of $500,000 became due.
2. Unrestricted pledges were received during 19x5 in the amount of $1,000,000 of which 60 percent are payable in 19x5. Experience indicates that 10 percent of these pledges will not be collected.
3. A psychologist who normally works on the staff has agreed to work 1,000 additional hours without charging for them. The psychologist normally receives $25 per hour.
4. The following expenses were incurred:
   a. Professional fees for counseling, $800,000.
   b. Occupancy costs, $50,000.
   c. Printing and publications, $30,000.
   d. Conferences, conventions, and meetings, $20,000.
   e. Travel, $10,000.
   f. Telephone, $5,000.

g. Supplies, $5,000.
h. Miscellaneous, $10,000.

Required:

a. Prepare the journal entries to record the above transactions.

b. Prepare closing entries.

Exercise 23–7. The Professional Persons Association of Middleton is a nonprofit organization which is subject to the provisions of AICPA SOP 78–10. The dues for members are $40 per year; the fiscal year ends on August 31. Prior to September 1, 19x0, 410 members had paid their dues for the year ended August 31, 19x1. Prior to September 1, 19x1, 457 members had paid their dues for the year ended August 31, 19x2; one of these died suddenly on August 30, 19x1, and the governing board decided to return his check to his widow. During the fiscal year ended on August 31, 19x1, 36 other members dies; 15 members were dropped for nonpayment of dues; and one member was expelled—no dues refunds were made to the estates of the 36 decedents; a $20 refund was made to the person expelled. Offsetting these membership decreases, 123 new members joined in fiscal 19x1; membership as of September 1, 19x0, had been 2,980 persons. Members admitted during the year are charged dues for the full year.

The Association has reported membership dues revenue on the cash basis in prior years. You bring to the attention of the governing board the requirement that financial statements should be on the accrual basis, unless cash basis statements are not materially different. Since you are so knowledgeable, the board asks you to compute membership dues revenue for fiscal 19x1 on both the cash basis and on the accrual basis and to report to them the amount on each basis *and* your conclusion as to whether the difference between the two is material.

(AICPA adapted)

PROBLEMS

Problem 23–8. Presented below is the current funds balance sheet of Burnsville University as of the end of its fiscal year ended June 30, 19x7:

BURNSVILLE UNIVERSITY
Current Funds Balance Sheet
June 30, 19x7

Assets

Current Funds:
Unrestricted:

Cash	$210,000	
Accounts receivable—student tuition and fees, less allowance for doubtful accounts of $9,000	341,000	
State appropriations receivable	75,000	$626,000

Restricted:

Cash	7,000	
Investments	60,000	67,000
Total Current Funds		$693,000

Liabilities and Fund Balances

Current Funds:
Unrestricted:

Accounts payable	45,000	
Deferred revenues	66,000	
Fund balances	515,000	$626,000

Restricted:

Fund balances		67,000
Total Current Funds		$693,000

The following transactions presented below occurred during the fiscal year ended June 30, 19x8:

1. On July 7, 19x7, a gift of $100,000 was received from an alumnus. The alumnus requested that one half of the gift be used for the purchase of books for the university library and the remainder be used for the establishment of a Scholarship Fund. The alumnus further requested that the income generated by the Scholarship Fund be used annually to award a scholarship to a qualified disadvantaged student. On July 20, 19x7, the board of trustees resolved that the funds of the newly established Scholarship Fund would be invested in savings certificates. On July 21, 19x7, the savings certificates were purchased.

2. Revenue from student tuition and fees applicable to the year ended June 30, 19x8, amounted to $1,900,000. Of this amount, $66,000 was collected in the prior year and $1,686,000 was collected during the year ended June 30, 19x8. In addition, at June 30, 19x8, the university had re-

ceived cash of $158,000 representing fees for the session beginning July 1, 19x8.

3. During the year ended June 30, 19x8, the university had collected $349,000 of the outstanding accounts receivable at the beginning of the year. The balance was determined to be uncollectible and was written off against the allowance account. At June 30, 19x8, the allowance account was increased by $3,000.

4. During the year interest charges of $6,000 were earned and collected on late student fee payments.

5. During the year the state appropriation was received. An additional unrestricted appropriation of $50,000 was made by the state, but had not been paid to the university as of June 30, 19x8.

6. An unrestricted gift of $25,000 cash was received from alumni of the university.

7. During the year investments of $21,000 were sold for $26,000. Investment income amounting to $1,900 was received.

8. During the year unrestricted operating expenses of $1,777,000 were recorded. At June 30, 19x8, $59,000 of these expenses remained unpaid.

9. Restricted current funds of $13,000 were spent for authorized purposes during the year.

10. The accounts payable at June 30, 19x7, were paid during the year.

11. During the year, $7,000 interest was earned and received on the savings certificates purchased in accordance with the board of trustees' resolution, as discussed in item 1.

Required:

a. Prepare journal entries to record in summary the above transactions for the year ended June 30, 19x8. Each journal entry should be numbered to correspond with the transaction described above.

Your answer sheet should be organized as follows:

	Current Funds					
	Unrestricted		Restricted		Endowment Fund	
Accounts	Dr.	Cr.	Dr.	Cr.	Dr.	Cr.

b. Prepare a statement of changes in fund balances for the year ended June 30, 19x8.

(AICPA adapted)

Problem 23–9. From the following trial balance of the accounts of Watson College and the additional information given, prepare a balance sheet in the proper form for colleges and universities.

June 30, 19x1

	Debit	Credit
Cash	$ 43,500	
Students' deposits		$ 2,500
Income from endowment investments		85,500
Income from college operations		100,000
College operating expenses . . .	195,000	
Interest accrued on securities purchased	500	
Inventories:		
School supplies	5,000	
General	3,000	
Investments:		
Bonds	875,500	
Mortgages	270,000	
Stocks	990,000	
Real estate	100,000	
Mortgages payable, secured by college plant		250,000
College plant:		
Land	95,000	
Buildings	1,000,000	
Land improvements	50,000	
Equipment	160,000	
Gain on sale of Endowment Fund investments		4,000
Prepaid college expenses	2,000	
Accounts receivable:		
Students	3,000	
Miscellaneous	1,000	
Notes receivable	20,000	
Notes payable		2,000
Accounts payable		3,000
Allowance for doubtful accounts receivable		500
Allowance for depreciation of buildings held as Endowment Fund investment		10,500
Excess of assets over liabilities .		3,355,500
	$3,813,500	$3,813,500

1. An analysis of the Cash account shows that the cash should be divided as follows:

Current Funds:	
Imprest cash	$ 1,000
On deposit	35,000
Loan funds	2,000
Endowment Funds	4,000
Funds subject to annuity agreements	1,500
	$43,500

2. Investments were all made from Endowment Funds, with the exception of $25,500 in bonds, purchased from funds subject to annuity agree-

ments. The income and principal of the latter funds are to be used to make certain definite payments during the life of the annuitants. The excess of annuity payments over income has been charged to the principal of the fund.

3. Notes receivable represent loans made to students from funds that are restricted to that purpose.

4. Memorandum records show that $11,500 of Endowment Funds are loaned temporarily to the current fund.

5. These records also show that $50,000 of Endowment Funds are invested in the college plant, in full accord with the endowment terms.

6. The income from $895,000 of Endowment Fund balance is restricted.

7. It was decided that the allowance for depreciation of real estate carried among the investments be funded.

Note: In your solution you may make the following assumptions:

a. Notes payable are liabilities of the Current Fund.

b. Interest Accrued on Securities Purchased is a Current Fund account.

c. Gain on Sale of Endowment Fund Investments is to be accounted for as an addition to Endowment Fund balance.

d. The property referred to in 5 above is included in the Plant Fund asset accounts. The amount of $50,000 should be added to Endowment Fund assets as a separate item, "Amount Invested in Institutional Property."   (AICPA adapted)

Problem 23–10. Presented below is the combined balance sheet of Dexter Hospital as of December 31, 19x5:

[Relates to Problem 23–10]

DEXTER HOSPITAL
Balance Sheet
As of December 31, 19x5
Operating Fund

Assets			Liabilities and Fund Balances		
Cash		$ 20,000	Accounts payable		$ 16,000
Accounts receivable	$ 37,000		Accrued expenses		6,000
Less allowance for uncollectible					
accounts	7,000	30,000	Total liabilities		22,000
Inventory of supplies		14,000	Fund balance		42,000
Total		$ 64,000	Total		$ 64,000

Plant Replacement and Expansion Fund

Cash		$ 53,800	Morgage bonds payable		$ 150,000
Investments		71,200			
Land		400,000			
Buildings	$1,750,000		Fund balance:		
Less accumulated depreciation	430,000	1,320,000	Investment in plant		2,021,000
Equipment	680,000		Reserved for plant improvement		
			and replacement		220,000
Less accumulated depreciation	134,000	546,000			2,241,000
Total		$2,391,000	Total		$2,391,000

Endowment Fund

Cash		$ 6,000	Fund balance		$ 266,000
Investments		260,000			
Total		$ 266,000	Total		$ 266,000

During 19x6 the following transactions occurred:

1. Gross charges for hospital services, all charged to accounts receivable, were as follows:

Revenues from nursing services	$780,000
Revenues from other professional services	321,000

2. Deductions from revenues were as follows:

Provision for uncollectible receivables	$30,000
Charity services	15,000

3. The Operating Fund paid $18,000 to retire mortgage bonds payable with an equivalent fair value.

4. During the year the Operating Fund received general contributions of $50,000 and income from Endowment Fund investments of $6,500.

5. New equipment costing $26,000 was acquired. An x-ray machine which originally cost $24,000 and which had an undepreciated cost of $2,400 was sold for $500.

6. Vouchers totaling $1,191,000 were issued for the following items:

Administrative service expenses	$120,000
Fiscal service expense	95,000
General service expense	225,000
Nursing service expense	520,000
Other professional service expense	165,000
Supplies	60,000
Expenses accrued at December 31, 19x5	6,000

7. Collections on accounts receivable totaled $985,000. Accounts written off as uncollectible amounted to $11,000.

8. Cash payments on vouchers payable during the year were $825,000.

9. Supplies of $37,000 were issued to nursing services.

10. On December 31, 19x6, accrued interest income on Plant Replacement and Expansion Fund investments was $800.

11. Depreciation of buildings and equipment was as follows:

Buildings	$44,000
Equipment	73,000

12. On December 31, 19x6, an accrual of $6,100 was made for interest on mortgage bonds payable.

Required:

For the period January 1, 19x6, through December 31, 19x6, prepare journal entries to record the transactions described above for the following funds of Dexter Hospital:

Operating Fund
Plant Replacement and Expansion Fund
Endowment Fund

Each journal entry should be numbered to correspond with the transaction described above.

Your answer sheet should be organized as follows:

[Relates to Problem 23–10]

Accounts	Operating Fund Debit	Operating Fund Credit	Plant Replacement and Expansion Fund Debit	Plant Replacement and Expansion Fund Credit	Endowment Fund Debit	Endowment Fund Credit

(AICPA adapted)

The following additional information is available:

1. Under the terms of the will of John Central, founder of the hospital, "the principal of the bequest is to be fully invested in trust forevermore in mortgages secured by productive real estate in Central City and/or in U.S. government securities . . . and the income therefrom is to be used to defray current expenses."

2. The John Central Endowment Fund account balance consists of the following:

Cash received in 18x1 by bequest from John Central	$ 81,500
Net gains realized from 19t6 through 19w9 from the sale of real estate acquired in mortgage foreclosures . . .	23,500
Income received from 19x0 through 19x7 from 90-day U.S. Treasury bill investments	14,500
Balance per general ledger on January 1, 19x8	$119,500

Problem 23–11. A newly elected board of directors of Central Hospital, a nonprofit corporation, decided that effective January 1, 19x8:

a. The existing general ledger balances are to be properly adjusted and allocated to three separate funds (Operating Fund, John Central Endowment Fund, and Plant Replacement and Expansion Fund),

b. The totals of the John Central Endowment Fund and the Allowance for Accumulated Depreciation are to be fully invested in securities.

The balances in the general ledger at January 1, 19x8, were:

	Debit	Credit
Cash	$ 50,000	
Investment in U.S. Treasury bills	105,000	
Investment in common stock .	417,000	
Interest receivable	4,000	
Accounts receivable	40,000	
Inventory	25,000	
Land	407,000	
Building	245,000	
Equipment	283,000	
Allowance for depreciation . . .		$ 376,000
Accounts payable		70,000
Bank loan		150,000
John Central Endowment Fund		119,500
Fund balance		860,500
Totals	$1,576,000	$1,576,000

3. The Land account balance was composed of:

18x0 appraisal of land at $10,000 and building at $5,000 received by donation at that time. (The building was demolished 50 years ago.	$ 15,000
Appraisal increase based on insured value in land title policies issued in 19t7 . . .	380,000
Landscaping costs for trees planted	12,000
Balance per general ledger on January 1, 19x8	$407,000

4. The Building account balance was composed of:

Cost of present hospital building completed in January 19t7 when the hospital commenced operations	$300,000
Adjustment to record appraised value of building in 19u7	(100,000)
Cost of elevator installed in hospital building in January 19w3	45,000
Balance per general ledger on January 1, 19x8	$245,000

The estimated useful lives of the hospital building and the elevator when new were 50 years and 20 years, respectively.

5. The hospital's equipment was inventoried on January 1, 19x8. The cost of the inventory agreed with the Equipment account balance in the general ledger. The Allowance for Accumulated Depreciation account at January 1, 19x8, included $158,250 applicable to equipment and that amount was approved by the board of directors as being accurate. All depreciation is computed on a straight-line basis.

6. A bank loan was obtained to finance the cost of new operating room equipment purchased in 19x4. Interest on the loan was paid to December 31, 19x7.

Required:

Prepare a worksheet to present the adjustments necessary to restate the general ledger account balances properly and to distribute the adjusted balances to establish the required fund accounts. Formal journal entries are not required. Computations should be in good form and should be referenced to the worksheet adjustments which they support. In addition to trial balance columns, the following columnar headings are recommended for your worksheet:

Problem 23–12. The bookkeeper for the Jacob Vocational School resigned on March 1, 19x8, after he prepared the following general ledger trial balance and analysis of cash as of February 29, 19x8:

JACOB VOCATIONAL SCHOOL
General Ledger Trial Balance
February 29, 19x8

Cash for general current operations	$258,000
Cash for restricted current uses	30,900
Stock donated by D. E. Marcy	11,000
Bonds donated by E. T. Pearce	150,000
Building	33,000
Land	22,000
Educational and general expenditures	38,000
Faculty recruitment expenses	4,100
Total	$547,000

Credits

Morgage payable on fixed assets	$ 30,000
Private gifts, grants, and contracts— unrestricted	210,000
Private gifts, grants, and contracts—restricted	196,000
Revenue from tuition and fees	31,000
Fund balance	80,000
Total	$547,000

[Relates to Problem 23–11]

Adjustments		Operating Fund		John Central Endowment Fund		Plant Replacement and Expansion Fund	
Debit	Credit	Debit	Credit	Debit	Credit	Debit	Credit

Note: $X = n$.
$W = n - 10$.
$V = n - 20$.
$U = n - 30$.
$T = n - 40$.

(AICPA adapted)

Analysis of Cash
For the Six Months Ended February 29, 19x8

Cash for general current operations:			
Balance, September 1, 19x7		$ 80,000	
Add: Student fees . .	$ 31,000		
Gift of W. L. Jacob	210,000	241,000	
		321,000	
Deduct: Educational and general expenditures . .	38,000		
Payment of mortgage on land and building	25,000	63,000	$258,000
Cash for restricted uses:			
Gift of W. L. Jacob for faculty recruitment		35,000	
Less faculty recruitment expenses		4,100	30,900
Checking account balance, February 29, 19x8			$288,900

You were engaged to determine the proper account balances for the school as of August 31, 19x8, at the close of the school's fiscal year. Your examination disclosed the following information:

1. D. E. Marcy donated 100 shares of Trans, Inc. stock in September 19x7 with the market value of $110 per share at the date of donation. The terms of the gift provide that the stock and any income thereon are to be retained intact. At any date designated by the board of directors the assets are to be liquidated and the proceeds used to assist the school's director in acquiring a personal residence. The school will not retain any financial interest in the residence.

2. E. T. Pearce donated 6 percent bonds in September 19x7 with par and market values of $150,000 at the date of donation. Annual payments of $3,500 are to be made to the donor during his lifetime. Earnings in excess of annual payments are to be used for current operations in the following fiscal year. Upon the donor's death, the fund is to be used to construct a school cafeteria. The present value of the aggregate liability for payments to Pearce is $60,000, based on standard life expectancy tables.

3. No transactions have been recorded on the school's books since February 29, 19x8. An employee of the school prepared the following analysis of the checking account for the period from March 1 through August 31, 19x8:

[Relates to Problem 23–12]

Balance, March 1, 19x8			$288,900
Deduct: Educational and general expenditures	$14,000		
Purchase of equipment	47,000	$61,000	
Less student fees		8,000	
Net expenses		53,000	
Payment for director's residence	11,200		
Less sale of 100 shares of Trans, Inc., stock .	10,600	600	53,600
Total			235,300
Add: Interest on 6% bonds		9,000	
Less payments to E. T. Pearce		3,500	5,500
Balance, August 31, 19x8			$240,800

Required:

Assuming that all the accounts listed in the February 29 trial balance belong in the Current Fund—Unrestricted category, (1) prepare journal entries to remove items and amounts from that category which belong in other funds, (2) prepare journal entries to establish each fund, as of February 29, 19x8, and (3) record the transactions for the period March 1–August 31, 19x8. Closing entries are not required.

(AICPA adapted)

Problem 23–13. The characteristics of voluntary health and welfare organizations differ in certain respects from the characteristics of state or local governmental units. As an example, voluntary health and welfare organizations derive their revenues primarily from voluntary contributions from the general public while governmental units derive their revenues from taxes and services provided to their jurisdictions.

Required:

a. Describe fund accounting and discuss whether its use is consistent with the concept that an accounting entity is an economic unit which has control over resources, accepts responsibilities for making and carrying out commitments, and conducts economic activity.

b. Distinguish between accrual accounting and modified accrual accounting and indicate which method should be used for a voluntary health and welfare organization.

c. Discuss how methods used to account for fixed assets differ between voluntary health and welfare organizations and governmental units.

(AICPA adapted)

Problem 23–14. DeMars College has asked your assistance in developing its budget for the coming 19x1–x2 academic year. You are supplied with the following data for the current year:

1.

	Lower division (freshman– sophomore)	Upper division (junior– senior)
Average number of students per class . .	25	20
Average salary of faculty member . . .	$10,000	$10,000
Average number of credit hours carried each year per student	33	30
Enrollment including scholarship students	2,500	1,700
Average faculty teaching load in credit hours per year (10 classes of 3 credit hours)	30	30

For 19x1–x2 lower division enrollment is expected to increase by 10 percent, while the upper division's enrollment is expected to remain stable. Faculty salaries will be increased by a standard 5 percent, and additional merit increases to be awarded to individual faculty members will be $90,750 for the lower division and $85,000 for the upper division.

2. The current budget is $210,000 for operation and maintenance of plant and equipment; this includes $90,000 for salaries and wages. Experience of the past three months suggests that the current budget is realistic, but that expected increases for 19x1–x2 are 5 percent in salaries and wages and $9,000 in other expenditures for operation and maintenance of plant and equipment.

3. The budget for the remaining expenditures for 19x1–x2 is as follows:

Administrative and general	$240,000
Library	160,000
Health and recreation	75,000
Athletics	120,000
Insurance and retirement	265,000
Interest	48,000
Capital outlay	300,000

4. The college expects to award 25 tuition-free scholarships to lower division students and 15 to upper division students. Tuition is $22 per credit hour and no other fees are charged.

5. Budgeted revenues for 19x1–x2 are as follows:

Endowments	$114,000
Net income from auxiliary services	235,000
Athletics	180,000

The college's remaining source of revenue is an annual support campaign held during the spring.

Required:

a. Prepare a schedule computing for 19x1–x2 by division (1) the expected enrollment, (2) the total credit hours to be carried, and (3) the number of faculty members needed.

b. Prepare a schedule computing the budget for faculty salaries by division for 19x1–x2.

c. Prepare a schedule computing the tuition revenue budget by division for 19x1–x2.

d. Assuming that the faculty salaries budget computed in (b) above was $2,400,000 and that the tuition revenue budget computed in (c) above was $3,000,000, prepare a schedule computing the amount which must be raised during the annual support campaign in order to cover the 19x1–x2 expenditures budget.

(AICPA adapted)

24

Regulation of accounting by the SEC

OVERVIEW

Present-day accounting standards and practices, the accounting of the 1980s as reflected in this work, are the result of an evolutionary process spanning most of the decades of this century. While the external influences on the development of U.S. accounting are many, including the congress, the courts, the stock exchanges, investment bankers, and other parties at interest, nobody has had, since its inception, a more powerful or more decisive influence on accounting practice than the Securities and Exchange Commission (SEC). For this reason, no study of contemporary financial accounting can be complete without at least a basic understanding of the mandate, and the working of the SEC as well as its influence on our discipline.

Origins of the SEC

Most students of the development of accounting standards in this country would agree that by comparison to today's quality and level of accounting practices, those prevailing in the period preceding the Great Depression of the 1930s were crude indeed. While the New York Stock Exchange, in cooperation with the American Institute of Accountants did attempt during that period to upgrade the accounting principles in use and the degree of informative disclosure required of corporations, these efforts fell far short of effecting improvements in accounting sufficient in scope to save this discipline from major blame for some of the abuses which led to the collapse of the financial markets in the 1929–33 era. Indeed, a study of the evolution of accounting standards will clearly reveal that most positive improvements in this field have come about not as a result of preventive measures but rather as a result of experience and of pressures resulting from a variety of exposed failures in the performance of the accounting function.

Among the early perceptive observers who pointed to, among other weaknesses, misleading and deceptive financial reporting practices, was Harvard economist William Z. Ripley who in articles as well as in his book, *Main Street and Wall Street,* detailed the abuses and the dangers which these practices held for the investing public.

The stock market crash which started in 1929 as well as the economic disaster which followed, including the financial collapse of major enterprises, such as the Kreuger and Toll empire, heightened the clamor for an investigation into what went wrong with the operations of the security markets. Several investigations were mounted, prominent among which were those of Ferdinand Pecora for the U.S. Senate Committee on Banking and Currency which inquired into practices of investment bankers and of the banking system, as well as that of a Senate committee investigating the Kreuger and Toll collapse. The revelations which were brought to light by these investigations and by the press led to demands for reform and regulation. The promise of capital market reforms was also included in the "New Deal platform of President F. D. Roosevelt who had among his advisors Professor Adolph A. Berle. Berle, who had been influenced by Ripley's writings, published together with Gardiner Means "The Modern Corporation and Private Property," a seminal work which analyzed the structure of the modern corporation and the separation of management from ownership which it brought about. It was Berle's influence in the Roosevelt administration that is credited with the structuring of securities legislation designed to address the problems brought about by this separation of management control from ownership.

The composite of these influences led President Roosevelt to request Congress to enact a federal securities bill which would add in his words, "to the ancient rule of *caveat emptor,* the further doctrine of let the seller beware." Thus, in May 1933 the Securities Act was signed into law "to provide full and fair disclosure of the character of the securities sold in interstate and foreign commerce."

The Securities Act, originally administered by the Federal Trade Commission was amended in 1934 to provide for the creation of the Securities and Exchange Commission whose task it became to regulate the degree of disclosure, financial and nonfinancial, associated with new public security offerings as well as to require reports from those companies whose securities were already traded on the public security markets. Moreover, the Commission was given broad statutory authority to state accounting rules for registered companies and to enforce them.

Organization of the SEC

The SEC (also referred to as the Commission) is an independent regulatory agency of the U.S. government which exercises a quasi-judicial role in controlling the functions of distribution and trading in securities. The Commission is composed of five members appointed by the president with the consent of the Senate. Commissioners are appointed for a term of five years, no more than three commissioners may be members of the same political party, and one of them is designated by the president to serve as chairman.

Illustration 24–1 presents the basic organizational structure of the SEC.

The SEC also maintains nine regional offices. The following is a brief description of the functions of two SEC subdivisions which are of greatest interest to practicing accountants:

Office of the Chief Accountant provides the Commission with expert advice on matters of accounting and auditing. Having been given statutory power to develop accounting principles, the SEC, through the Office of the Chief Accountant, attends to this responsibility by the development of administrative policy, by keeping in close contact with government agencies,

**Illustration 24–1:
Organizational structure
of the SEC**

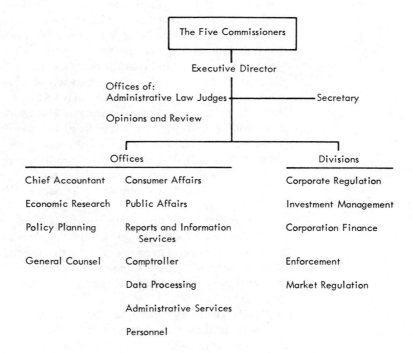

accounting organizations such as the AICPA and the FASB and other interested bodies or individuals.

The well-trained professionals on the Chief Accountant's staff stand ready to confer with and give advice on accounting matters to registrants and their accountants and also review on an on-going basis the financial data filed by firms with the Commission. The Office of the Chief Accountant also advises other divisions on accounting and auditing aspects of administrative and criminal cases handled by them.

The Division of Corporation Finance has major review and processing functions for all filings under the Securities Acts, Securities Exchange Act, the Trust Indenture Act, and the Investment Companies Act. It also has responsibility for examination of registration statements, periodic reports of corporate registrants, proxy statements, and other filings. In addition the division establishes standards of narrative and financial reporting, enforces compliance with them and sets standards for the disclosure requirements of proxy solicitations and administers disclosure requirements under various acts. The division is also responsible for the design of registration and reporting forms as well as for the drafting of rules and regulations. Moreover, through conferences, letters of comment, and other means it offers guidance and advice in the interpretation and application of a variety of regulations, rules, statutes, and forms.

PRINCIPAL ACTS ADMINISTERED BY THE SEC

The Acts administered by the SEC which are of greatest interest to accountants are the Securities Act of 1933 and the Securities Exchange Act of 1934.

The Securities Act of 1933 is the first of a series of laws designed to protect the public from manipulation, misrepresentation, and other fraudulent practices in the buying and selling of securities. This law provides for registration of securities (subject to specified exemptions) before they may be sold to the public.

The 1933 Act is a disclosure statute and the principal instruments of disclosure are a registration statement and a prospectus, each of which must contain specified financial and other information. The prospectus must be furnished to the buyer of a registered security while the registration statement, with minor exceptions, is a public document available for inspection by any person.

It is not the purpose of the registration process to judge the merits of securities offered for sale and every prospectus in fact proclaims in bold letters that the registered securities have been neither approved nor disapproved by the SEC. The SEC staff does, however, through a process of review and conferences, as needed, enforce the disclosure and reporting requirements of the 1933 Act by requiring additional information if a filing is deficient. While the registration process does not guarantee the accuracy of the registration statement (or the prospectus of which it is a part), the severe penalties which are imposed for providing false or misleading information encourage issuers to comply with the disclosure provisions of the Act.

The Securities Exchange Act of 1934

The basic purpose of the 1934 Act is to regulate the trading of securities. Thus, while the 1933 Act is concerned with the *initial* offering of securities, the 1934 Act is concerned with the *subsequent* trading of corporate securities.

The 1934 Act deals with related areas as well. Among these are the conduct of stock exchanges and their members, the conduct of brokers, of traders and particularly those of insiders as well as the use of credit for the purchase of securities (i.e., the use of margin). Important as they are, these areas affect accountants only to a limited extent and consequently our major focus here will be on those aspects of the 1934 Act which seek to make available to the public reliable information on publicly traded securities.

Accountant involvement

A key process under the 1933 Act in which accountants are significantly involved is the registration process which involves the development and the filing of a registration statement with the SEC. The 1933 Act requires registration for all initial offerings of securities for public sale except small or interstate issues. Under the act, registration is for a specific security to be issued in a specific amount.

Many of the forms which must be filed with the SEC in compliance with the 1933 Act, and other acts to be discussed later, contain financial statements. A number of SEC publications are concerned particularly with the form, the content, and the standards to be applied in the preparation of financial statements filed with the Commission. The following are the most important sources of directions and guidance in this area:

Regulation S-X is designed to integrate all the requirements governing the form and content of financial statements filed with the Commission as well as accounting requirements not covered by GAAP. Its importance is such that accountants preparing financial statements which are included or incorporated in any filing under the Securities Acts, except those for railroads and foreign issues, must constantly refer to it.

While the S-X requirements are extensive, they do not prescribe the accounting practices to be followed under every circumstance. Instead, the SEC relies on the requirement that generally accepted accounting principles as established by the FASB, be followed in preparing financial statements filed with it.

Regulation S-X is frequently amended. In September of 1980 substantially all instructions as to financial statements were centralized in Regulation S-X and the SEC required for the first time that primary financial statements in annual reports to shareholders by public companies under its jurisdiction must essentially conform with the requirements of this regulation. This was one step in achieving the SEC's objective of forging a link between the communications of the company to its shareholders and the company's similar communication to the SEC.

Regulation S-K codifies the principal regulations applicable to those portions of filings with the SEC which are outside the basic financial statements. For example, it sets forth standards of disclosure of information on nature of business, properties, segments of a business enterprise, and management's discussion and analysis of financial condition and results of operations.

Accounting Series Releases

The SEC publishes many official rulings and directives which concern the administration of the Securities Acts. Those that pertain to accounting and auditing matters are usually identified as *Accounting Series Releases (ASRs)* *ASRs* that concern accounting principles and disclosure rules represent modifications of existing regulations as well as interpretations of the regulations under which registrants file with the SEC. Pertinent *ASRs* are incorporated in Regulation S-X whenever it is updated. The frequency with which *ASRs* have been issued has accelerated. Since their inception in 1937 and until 1970, 144 were issued; by now their number is around 300.

Staff Accounting Bulletins are a more recent innovation of the SEC aimed at clarifying specific problems encountered in practice. While they are not rules of the Commission, and consequently do not enjoy official status, they represent interpretations of rules and practices followed by the Division of Corporation Finance and the Chief Accountant in administering the disclosure requirements of the federal securities laws.

The 1933 Act provides a choice of more than 20 forms that can be used depending on circumstances and on the type of company involved. We shall focus here on the most widely used registration form under the act—Form S-1.

The principal registration statement—Form S-1

The registration statement is composed of two parts, the first of which contains the information included in a prospectus. The prospectus is the document which includes all the information which must be presented to prospective investors in an enterprise which issues securities covered by it.

Generally, the prospectus includes information on:

1. The nature of the issuer's business and its history.
2. Description of securities being registered, plan of distribution, and use of proceeds.
3. Capital structure.
4. Organization of registrant and description of its property.
5. Details on directors and officers, on the remuneration of top officers, options to purchase securities, as well as interest of management in certain transactions.
6. Audited financial statements and summarized operating and financial data.

The second part of the registration statement includes schedules supporting financial statements and such information as marketing arrangements, expenses of issuance, sales to special parties, subsidiaries of registrant, franchises, and concessions as well as other details.

The preparation of a registration statement is a complex and time-consuming operation involving the management of the registering company, counsel for the company and for the underwriters, the underwriters, independent public accountants and, as needed, other experts such as engineers and appraisers.

Appendix 24–A of this chapter presents selected pages from a Joint Proxy Statement of Mattel, Inc., and Western Publishing Company, Inc., for consideration by their respective shareholders incident to a merger proposal. The selected pages represent an example of financial statements and other materials which are specified by SEC disclosure requirements as discussed in this chapter and elsewhere in this text.

Most of the financial statements and supporting footnote disclosures as well as schedules must be attested to by an independent public accountant. In helping with the preparation of the financial statements in accordance with the requirements of the SEC and in attesting to these statements, the accountant makes a major contribution to the registration process.

Accountants perform other services incident to an issuance of securities under the 1933 Act. Even though not required by the act, underwriters require, because of the special risks they bear, a "comfort letter" from the independent accountant which in effect provides "negative assurance" that the accountant found no indication that the unaudited (interim) financial statements of the issuer are false or misleading. In issuing this comfort letter the auditor does not generally perform an audit of the interim statements but does instead undertake a limited review of the financial statements and supporting information. A comfort letter will generally conclude with a statement indicating that it is for use solely by the underwriters and is not to be filed as part of the registration statement.

Reporting and disclosure requirements

A security listed on a national exchange must be registered with the SEC under the 1934 Act, while over the counter equity securities meeting certain size tests, must also be so registered. Unlike the registration of a specific issue of securities, as required under the 1933 Act, the registration under the 1934 Act is of a *class* of a corporation's securities. Once a class of securities (e.g., common stock, class A preferred) is registered all subsequent issues of the same class are considered covered by the registration. By contrast, the 1933 Act requires a separate filing for each offer of securities.

The 1934 Act contains extensive reporting requirements. This is so because securities listed under the 1934 Act may be traded over many years and the statute provides for continuing disclosure over long periods of time through initial, annual, quarterly, and periodic reports. Some of the most important of these forms will be described below:

Form 10.   When a company lists its securities for the first time on a national security exchange, or is required to register with the SEC because it just met the size test of $1 million in assets and 500 stockholders, it must file a registration statement on Form 10. Form 10 is comparable to, but not quite as extensive a document as, a prospectus under the 1933 Act. It requires, among other information, audited financial statements as well as textual disclosures.

Form 10-K is an annual report which must be filed with the SEC within 90 days after the close of the fiscal year. Its basic purpose is to update annually the information contained in the company's initial registration statement on Form 10.

Involved in the preparation of Form 10-K are the company's management, counsel, and particularly its accountants. Its preparation must comply with instructions and regulations outlined in the 1934 Act as well as with the current Regulation S-X which governs the form and content of financial statements filed with the SEC.

In late 1980, as part of its sweeping revision of the mandatory business and financial disclosure requirements applicable to most publicly held companies, the SEC made significant revisions in a number of regulations including the requirements of Form 10-K. These revisions were a major step in the SEC's objective of creating a uniform and integrated disclosure system under the securities laws.

The new regulations require that certain information in annual reports to shareholders be the same as information to be included in part II of Form 10-K. Moreover, it required for the first time that the primary financial statements in annual reports to shareholders of companies under its jurisdiction conform substantially with the requirements of Regulation S-X.

The comprehensive amount of information which must be supplied in the revised Form 10-K is contained in five parts as follows:

Part I:

  Item 1—Business.
  Item 2—Properties.
  Item 3—Legal Proceedings.
  Item 4—Security Ownership of Certain Beneficial Owners and Management.

Part II:

  Item 5—Market for the Registrant's Common Stock and Related Security Holder Matters.
  Item 6—Selected Financial Data.
  Item 7—Management's discussion and Analysis of Financial Condition and Results of Operations.
  Item 8—Financial Statements and Supplementary Data.

Part III:

  Item 9—Directors and Executive Officers of Registrant.
  Item 10—Management Remuneration and Transactions.

Part IV:

  Item 11—Exhibits, Financial Statement Schedules, and Reports on Form 8-K.

The information required by Parts I and II may, at the registrant's option, be incorporated by reference from the annual report to shareholders, provided the portions so incorporated meet the disclosure requirements of Form 10-K. The information required by Part III must be incorporated by reference from the proxy or information statement (if it was filed within 120 days of year-end).

The revised Form 10-K must be signed by the registrant's principal officer(s), principal financial officer, comptroller or principal accounting officer, and at least a majority of the board of directors.

Registrants must make a conscientious effort to supply all the information required in all forms including Form 10-K, but information need be given only insofar as it is known or reasonably available to the registrant. Nor is the requirement for information limited to that specifically required; it is necessary to disclose any material information that is necessary to keep the required information from being misleading.

Form 10-Q—Quarterly Report. Most companies which are subject to the reporting requirements of the 1934 Act must file a quarterly report on Form 10-Q within 45 days after the end of each of the first three quarters of each fiscal year. This report generally includes condensed unaudited financial statements, management's discussion and analysis of financial condition and results of operations, as well as other financial and current data.

Form 8-K—Current Report. The Current Report on Form 8-K was devised in recognition of the fact that certain significant corporate events can have an important effect on the value of securities and should be brought to the attention of the public as expeditiously as possible. Form 8-K must be filed no later than 15 days after the date on which specified events such as (1) changes in control of the company, (2) acquisition or disposition of assets, (3) bankruptcy petitions or trustee appointments, or (4) changes in the company's independent accountant, occur. Companies may also report, within 10 days after the month of occurrence, or discovery, any events that they deem to be of material importance to security holders—such as illegal or improper payments.

THE SEC'S INFLUENCE ON ACCOUNTING THEORY AND PRACTICE

Whatever doubts about the extent of the actual influence of the SEC on accounting may have been justified in the past, most objective observers of the accounting scene of the 1980s will agree that the contemporary influence of the SEC on accounting is as decisive as it is pervasive.

The Commission has broad statutory authority and rule-making powers in relation to financial reporting and disclosure. It has, however, from its inception allowed the private sector, that is, the accounting profession and bodies established by it, the first opportunity to resolve accounting issues. Generally, it was only in cases when the professional bodies have failed to act or have been too slow to act in a way that the SEC considered necessary, that the Commission has taken the initiative by promulgating rules with respect to accounting standards and practices.

While the reasons for and the circumstances surrounding such individual initiatives by the SEC differ from case to case, it is a useful generalization to say that one broad category of reasons concerns impatience by the Commission with progress in areas where progress was deemed to be needed while another broad category of reasons is concerned with the SEC's desire to furnish users with better and more meaningful tools with which to analyze and interpret published financial statements.

In order to enhance the reader's understanding of the SEC's influence on accounting, there follows a description of selected aspects of the Commission's position and actions in these two important areas of concern:

The SEC's position on the promulgation of accounting standards

Since its inception, it has been the SEC's official position that it will encourage the accounting profession to lead in the development of generally accepted accounting principles. Thus, in one of its earliest *ASRs* (*No. 4* issued in 1938), the Commission stated that in order to be accepted by it, financial statements must be prepared in accordance with accounting principles which have "substantial authoritative support," and that mere disclosure will not remedy the lack of such "support." The Commission, moreover, took the position that where it disagrees with a registrant's use of accounting principles which have authoritative support, it will accept footnote description instead of a correction of the statements to conform with the SEC's view, provided that it has not previously published an opinion on the matter at issue. The SEC explicitly reserved the right to determine what principles have substantial authoritative support as well as the right to overrule the use of a principle even if it had such support.

Thirty-five years after publication of *ASR 4*, the Commission (in *ASR 150* issued in 1973), in a renewed show of support for private sector rule making, adopted the policy that "principles, standards and policies promulgated by the FASB in its statements and interpretations will be considered by the Commission as having substantial authoritative support, and those contrary to such FASB promulgation will be considered to have no such support." This policy was not intended to negate the SEC's statutory rule-making powers and moreover, the Commission expressed its intention to continue to identify areas where investor information needs exist and to determine the appropriate methods of disclosure to meet these needs. As the discussion which follows will show, the Commission has in recent years indeed exercised these functions with vigor and determination.

Finally, *ASR 279* (1980) contains the explicit statement that financial statements filed with the Commission, which are not prepared in accordance with GAAP, will be presumed to be misleading or inaccurate, unless the SEC has provided otherwise.

Leadership in promoting change in financial accounting and reporting

Over the years, and especially in the more recent past, the SEC, whenever it felt that needed progress was too slow in coming, has taken the initiative in promoting change in accounting in various ways and particularly by means of expanded disclosure requirements.

Reporting of leases.

Over many years, as the use of leasing grew, the rule-making bodies established by the accounting profession issued a variety of pronouncements on the subject of accounting for leases. In 1973, in the obvious belief that these pronouncements did not go far enough, the SEC issued *ASR 147* which required lease disclosures that included the impact on net income as if leases which at the time did not need to be capitalized were in fact capitalized. The Commission issued these requirements with the understanding that the FASB was also reconsidering the topic of lease accounting. Thus, the Commission stated that while it did not intend to pre-judge the issues under consideration, it was prepared to reconsider its own disclosure requirements when the FASB develops improved standards of ac-counting for leases.

In 1976 the FASB did issue *SFAS 13*, "Accounting for Leases," which called for the capitalization of leases which, by meeting certain tests, were deemed to be the equivalent of long-term debt. In the following year, in *ASR 225*, the Commission conformed its disclosure requirements to the standards of *SFAS 13*, but required a more accelerated timetable for the disclosure of all financing leases on the balance sheet.

Interest capitalization.   Before the 1970s it was general practice among most companies, with the principal exception of certain utilities, to expense interest costs in the period incurred. Because there were no accounting standards on the subject and certainly no generally accepted rationale to justify interest capitalization only by utilities and some savings and loan and retail land sales companies, the number of companies in other industries which started to capitalize interest costs, and thus benefit income at least in the short term, began to increase.

The SEC, ever alert to emerging or potential abuses, in 1974 issued *ASR 163* declaring a moratorium on the adoption of interest capitalization by companies which had not practiced this procedure before. The moratorium was to be in effect until such time as the FASB would develop *Standards* governing the capitalization of interest. The SEC thus, in effect, telegraphed to the profession the need for action in this area. In 1979 the FASB, after following its usual process of public exposure and consideration, issued *SFAS 34* entitled "Capitalization of Interest Cost" which established standards for the capitalization of interest costs in certain circumstances.

Effects of price-level changes.   The problem of what to do about and how to disclose the effects of price-level changes on conventional financial state-ments has been a continuing and growing one for the accounting profes-sion. Consideration of the problem has extended over a long period of time. In 1963 *Accounting Research Study 6* "Reporting the Financial Effects of Price-Level Changes" was published and in 1969 the APB issued its *Statement 3* entitled "Financial Statements Restated for General Price-Level Changes." While an APB *Statement* does not represent a requirement of adherence as does an *Opinion*, it nevertheless represented another slow step and the com-pletion of a standby framework for use in the future. Further inflation and further pressures on the profession to act led to the issuance in 1974 of an Exposure Draft of an FASB *Statement* that would have required the inclusion with conventional financial statements of general purchasing power data patterned after concepts embodies in the above-mentioned *APB Statement No. 3*.

By 1976, however, the SEC was sufficiently impatient with the slow prog-ress in this area and sufficiently dissatisfied with the direction of the efforts towards inflation accounting that it amended Regulation S-X via *ASR 190* so as to require the disclosure of replacement cost data by certain large registrants. The stated objective of the SEC was "to provide information to investors which will assist them in obtaining an understanding of the current costs of operating the business which cannot be obtained from historical cost financial statements taken alone. . . ."

This action by the SEC was widely criticized because it called for providing only fragmentary information which included hypothetical replacement costs and which did not lead to the meaningful measurement of income or to a redetermination of the capital invested in the enterprise. But, here again, the SEC flexed its considerable muscle and caused the FASB to defer further consideration of its exposure draft on the subject. This process of reconsideration ultimately culminated in 1979 with issuance of *SFAS 33* on "Financial Reporting and Changing Prices" which is an experimental approach requiring disclosure by large enterprises of both current cost and constant dollar information. *SFAS 33* went significantly beyond the SEC initiative by requiring the reporting of restated earning figures. Having served the SEC's purpose the data required by *ASR 190* will now be gradually replaced by that required by *SFAS 33*.

Accounting for oil and gas.   Finally, in our consideration of examples of the influence of the SEC on accounting theory and practice, let us consider the evolution of the accounting for oil and gas.

The accounting for oil and gas, a controversial topic for many years, has in practice resulted in the application of two basically differing concepts. One is the full-cost method which holds that all costs, productive and nonproductive, incurred in the search for oil and gas reserves should be capitalized and amortized to income as the total oil and gas reserves are produced and sold. The other is the successful efforts method under which all costs that do not result directly in the discovery of oil and gas reserves should be expensed as incurred.

The SEC became particularly interested in the resolution of the problem of accounting for oil and gas because of the passage in 1975 of The Energy Policy and Conservation Act (EPCA). This act required that the SEC prescribe adquate accounting practices for use by oil and gas producers so as to assure the development of a reliable energy data base but also authorized the SEC to rely on the FASB for the development of appropriate accounting standards.

After a process of exposure and discussion, the FASB issued in 1977 *SFAS 19* entitled "Financial Accounting and Reporting by Oil and Gas Producing Companies" which required use of the "successful efforts" method of accounting. This was strongly opposed by many smaller oil and gas companies which claimed that the lower reported earnings which would result from the application of *SFAS 19* would impair their ability to obtain financing.

In this case the SEC intervention proved to be among the strongest. After holding hearings in 1978, it concluded that none of the existing methods of oil and gas accounting were adequate and that a new method, "Reserve Recognition Accounting," should be tried. Under this method, oil and gas producers would present on a supplementary basis the current year's additions and revisions to proved reserves of oil and gas as well as the costs associated with the discovery and development of proved reserves and all nonproductive costs. The experience gathered will determine whether reserve recognition accounting should become the required method of accounting. It was another step by the SEC in preferring inexact data that is relevant to decision making over more exactly determinable data that is irrelevant.

Having clearly been overruled, the FASB issued *SFAS 25* which suspended certain of the requirements as well as the effective data of *SFAS 19.* The controversial nature of this area of accounting as well as the SEC's position on it was further emphasized in early 1981 when the SEC, in a reversal of position, decided not to require reserve recognition accounting in the primary financial statements. Instead, the Commission indicated that it would "support an undertaking by the FASB to develop a comprehensive package of disclosures for those engaged in oil and gas producing activities." Consistent with a revised orientation the SEC was, in taking this action, motivated by a desire to reduce the complexities of its disclosure standards.

Leadership of the SEC in requiring analytically oriented data

While the profession was debating the question of the function of accounting, the SEC has firmly held the view that financial statements must be useful to investors and other decision makers. With this objective in mind, the Commission has, particularly in recent years, exercised leadership in this area by requiring more elaborate analytically oriented disclosures in financial statements. The following are some examples:

Disclosure of unusual risks and uncertainties. In the 1973–74 recession environment the SEC sensed that certain significant business uncertainties may not have been fully reflected in the financial statements of registrants. In *ASR 166* it called for alertness to situations where conditions of major uncertainty may not have been adequately conveyed to readers. In such cases registrants must consider the need for specified disclosure of such uncertainties and, in extreme cases, deviations from the conventional reporting model. Examples cited in the release included loan loss reserves, declines in marketable securities, and recovery of deferred fuel costs by utilities.

Income tax disclosures. In order to enable users of financial statements to gain a better understanding of the tax accounting of an enterprise, *ASR 149* issued in 1973 called for disclosure of a reconciliation between the effective income tax rate and the statutory federal income tax rate as well as the components of deferred tax expense. Thus, the requirements for an explanation of why the effective tax expense percentage differs from the statutory tax rate give the reader the means to judge, for example, whether the present tax benefits which the enterprise enjoys are likely to continue in the future.

In the 1980 revision of Regulation S-X and Form 10-K the SEC added a requirement for disclosure of domestic and foreign components of income taxes.

Appendix 24–A at the end of this chapter contains an example of the SEC mandated expanded income tax disclosure.

Management's discussion and analysis of financial condition and results of operation. With the issuance of *ASR 159* in 1974 the SEC introduced a very significant concept of disclosure. This concept was amended and broadened in 1980 with the specification of a new item (No. 11) in Regulation S-K.

In its revised form, Management's Discussion and Analysis of Financial Condition and Results of Operation focuses on the financial statements as a whole rather than on the summary of operations (the previous focus) and calls for discussion of at least three aspects of an enterprise's business—liquidity, capital resources, and results of operations. Within each area of discussion, favorable and unfavorable trends and the identification of significant events or uncertainties are to be emphasized. This discussion should also include a narrative discussion of the effects of inflation and changing prices on an enterprise's net sales and revenues and on income from continuing operation.

Appendix 24–B at the end of this chapter presents "Management's Discussion section of the Galveston Houston Company.

Other examples of significant disclosures.   There are, of course, other examples of SEC leadership in mandating disclosures aimed at providing the user of financial statements with data relevant to decision making. Among these are: (1) *ASR 148* which mandates disclosure of compensating balances, short-term borrowing arrangements, average interest rate, and general terms of current borrowing; (2) a requirement for the disclosure of Supplementary Income Statement Information comprising details of such important discretionary costs as maintenance and repairs, advertising, and research and development; and (3) guidelines for the computation and disclosure of the ratio of earnings to fixed charges (now under reconsideration). As to the latter see page 778 of Appendix 24–A at the end of this chapter.

The SEC's work—controversy and contribution   The work of the SEC, affecting as it does, so many different segments of society has always been a subject of controversy. There are those, like Professor George Benston, who believe that free-market forces can better ensure the interest of investors than can regulation by the SEC. And there are those, like Professor Homer Kripke, who believe that SEC filings have become routine, meaningless documents which, while providing a lucrative source of income to the professionals involved in their preparation, do not provide information that is of real relevance to investors.

The arguments about the SEC's function and utility will, of course, go on, and they do serve a very useful purpose. The evidence, as partly summarized in this chapter, clearly shows that the SEC's work has been beneficial to financial statement users as well as to the accounting profession. In fact, the SEC and the accounting profession need each other badly. Without the SEC, the accounting profession may have had difficulty in withstanding the severe public and congressional criticism of shortcomings in its performance to which it was recently exposed and, as a result, the accounting standard-setting function may not have remained in the private sector. On the other hand, without the efforts of the profession's standard-setting bodies, like the APB and the FASB, the SEC would have had to tackle the very demanding and intricate job of standard setting by itself, a job to which it could clearly not have brought resources in skilled manpower and ingenuity anywhere nearly comparable to those which have been expended by the private sector in this effort. The net results would have had to be a lower level of quality in accounting standards.

Overall, in recent years, the SEC has demonstrated creativity in its regulatory and oversight function. It has introduced such novel concepts as "differential disclosure," "continuous disclosure," and "peer review." It has, moreover, been ready to change, modify, and simplify its requirements as witness the newly promulgated integrated disclosure system in 1980. Creative chief accountants of the SEC have successfully employed a blend of prodding and supporting initiatives which have kept up a degree of "creative tension" between the SEC and the profession. In this regulatory environment real progress has been achieved, and we can look forward to further cooperation and progress in the future.

QUESTIONS

1. What is the SEC? What is its role? How is it organized?

2. Give a brief description of the major functions of the Office of the Chief Accountant of the SEC.

3. What are the major functions and responsibilities of the Division of Corporation Finance of the SEC?

4. What is a key process under the 1933 Act in which accountants are significantly involved?

5. Distinguish between the purpose of SEC Regulation S-X and that of SEC Regulation S-K.

6. Differentiate between the function of the SEC *Accounting Series Releases* and that of the SEC *Staff Accounting Bulletins.*

7. What are the basic items of information included in a prospectus?

8. Briefly describe the comfort letter which the underwriters of a newly issued security require from an independent accountant.

9. What is the basic purpose of the Securities and Exchange Act of 1934?

10. Distinguish between registration under the 1933 Act and the 1934 Act.

11. Differentiate between the requirements of Form 10-Q and those of Form 10-K.

12. What are the basic items of information which must be supplied in the recently revised Form 10-K?

13. What is the purpose of Form 10-Q?

14. What is the function of reports on Form 8-K?

15. Generally, what are the two major categories of reasons for the SEC's initiatives in influencing accounting theory and practice?

16. Are FASB pronouncements considered by the SEC as constituting substantial authoritative support for accounting principles? Discuss.

17. Briefly describe the leadership role of the SEC in promoting change in financial accounting and reporting.

18. What are some examples of significant disclosures required by the SEC beside those discussed in question 17 above?

19. The SEC's work has been the subject of controversy but it has also been beneficial to the accounting profession and to users of financial statements. Discuss.

Appendix 24–A: Selected pages from joint proxy statement of Mattel, Inc., and Western Publishing Company, Inc.

Comparative per share data

The following tabulations reflect the historical per share amounts of Mattel and subsidiaries, the historical per share amounts of Western and subsidiaries, and pro forma amounts as though the proposed Merger had been effective as of the beginning of the year ended February 3, 1979. Such data have been derived from the financial statements of Mattel and Western and the related pro forma financial statements appearing elsewhere in this Joint Proxy Statement. Such financial statements and notes thereto should be read in conjunction with this tabulation.

Mattel—Fiscal year ended on or about					
January 31	1975	1976	1977	1978	1979
Western—Calendar year	1974	1975	1976	1977	1978
Mattel:					
Historical[a]:					
Income from continuing operations . .	$ 0.10	$ 0.86	$ 0.97	$ 1.19	$ 1.23
Loss from discontinued operations . .	(0.33)	—	—	—	—
Income (loss) before extraordinary items	(0.23)	0.86	0.97	1.19	1.23
Extraordinary items	(0.97)	0.64	0.41	0.37	0.31
Net income (loss)	$ (1.20)	$ 1.50	$ 1.38	$ 1.56	$ 1.54
Cash dividends declared on common stock	—	—	—	—	$0.225
Common shareholders' equity	$ 0.84	$ 2.35	$ 3.72	$ 4.99	$ 6.21
Pro forma[b]:					
Income before extraordinary item . .					$ 1.21
Extraordinary income tax credits . . .					0.31
Net income					$ 1.52
Common shareholders' equity assuming issuance of preferred stock					$ 6.02
Common shareholders' equity assuming conversion of preferred stock[c]					$ 7.36

Mattel—Fiscal year ended on or about					
January 31	*1975*	*1976*	*1977*	*1978*	*1979*
Western—Calendar year	*1974*	*1975*	*1976*	*1977*	*1978*
Western:					
Historical[d]:					
Income before cumulative effect of accounting change	$ 2.48	$ 2.50	$ 2.64	$ 1.77	$ 2.30
Cumulative effect of accounting change	—	—	—	0.30	—
Net income	$ 2.48	$ 2.50	$ 2.64	$ 2.07	$ 2.30
Cash dividends declared on common stock	$ 0.72	$ 0.76	$ 0.79	$ 0.88	$ 0.88
Common shareholders' equity	$22.35	$24.08	$25.92	$27.10	$28.52
Pro forma[e]:					
Income before extraordinary item . . .					$ 2.88
Extraordinary income tax credits . . .					0.58
Net income					$ 3.46
Common shareholders' equity					$17.53

(a) Note E to Mattel's Consolidated Statements of Operations describes Mattel's earnings per share computation.

(b) Pro forma combines results of operations for the fiscal year ended February 3, 1979, of Mattel with the results of operations for the calendar year ended December 31, 1978, of Western. See Notes to the Pro Forma Statement of Operations for a description of the manner in which per share amounts have been calculated.

(c) The pro forma amounts assume conversion of each Mattel Preferred share into 2.10 shares of Mattel Common Stock. However, the Merger Agreement stipulates that Mattel Preferred will be convertible into from 2.10 to 2.38 shares of Mattel Common Stock, depending on the market price of Mattel Common Stock during a period of time preceding the Western Meeting. If a conversion rate of 2.38 had been used in the computation, pro forma common shareholders' equity assuming conversion of preferred stock would be $7.17.

(d) Note 6 to Western's Consolidated Statements of Earnings and Retained Earnings describes Western's earnings per share computation.

(e) The pro forma amounts assume conversion of each share of Western Common Stock into 1.134 shares of Mattel Preferred and subsequent conversion of each share of Mattel Preferred into 2.10 shares of Mattel Common Stock (equivalent of 2.4 times the pro forma fully diluted income per common share of Mattel). However, the Merger Agreement stipulates that Mattel Preferred will be convertible into from 2.10 to 2.38 shares of Mattel Common Stock, depending on the market price of Mattel Common Stock during a period of time preceding the Western Meeting. If a conversion rate of 2.38 had been used in the computations, pro forma amounts per share of Western Common Stock (equivalent of 2.6 times the pro forma fully diluted income per common share of Mattel) would be as follows:

Income before extraordinary item	$ 3.18
Extraordinary income tax credits	0.64
Net income	$ 3.82
Common shareholders' equity	$19.35

Capitalization

The capitalization of Mattel and subsidiaries as of February 3, 1979, and of Western and subsidiaries as of December 31, 1978, and the pro forma combined capitalization after giving effect to the proposed Merger are as follows:

($000)

	Mattel, February 3, 1979	Western, December 31, 1978	Pro forma adjustments[e]	Pro forma combined
Short-term debt:				
Notes payable to banks	$ 4,758[a]	$ 2,649[b]		$ 7,407
Current portion of long-term liabilities[c]	826	1,600		2,426
Total short-term debit . . .	$ 5,584	$ 4,249	—	$ 9,833
Long-term liabilities[c]:				
9½% bank secured loan	$ 20,000			$ 20,000
6¾% mortgage loan	985			985
9½% notes payable		$ 20,000		20,000
9⅝% notes payable		20,000		20,000
8⅝% note payable		8,200	$ (170)	8,030
5¾% notes payable		3,000	(100)	2,900
Capitalized lease obligations . .	17,782			17,782
Subordinated debentures	12,072			12,072
Bank term loan to acquire Western's Preferred and Common stock			60,400	60,400
Total long-term liabilities . .	$ 50,839	$ 51,200	$60,130	$162,169
Shareholders' equity:				
$25 Series A convertible preferred stock, $1 par value, authorized 3,000,000 shares; to be issued 2,416,376 shares .			$ 2,416	$ 2,416
Common stock, $1 par value, authorized 50,000,000 shares; outstanding 15,803,647 shares	$ 15,804[d]			15,804
Preferred stock, $100 par value, authorized 60,000 shares; outstanding 23, 424 shares . .		$ 2,343	(2,343)	—
Second preferred stock, $100 par value, authorized 300,000 shares; outstanding 90,611 shares		9,061	(9,061)	—
Common stock, $1 par value, $2.50 stated value, authorized 10,000,000 shares; outstanding 3,930,114 shares		9,825	(9,825)	—
Additional paid-in capital	29,947	28,351	{ (28,351) 57,984	87,931
Common stock warrants	4,968			4,968
Retained earnings	72,852	73,378	(73,378)	72,852
	123,571	122,958	(62,558)	183,971
Less: Treasury stock 111,224 common shares		(2,641)	2,641	—
Total shareholders' equity .	$123,571	$120,317	$(59,917)	$183,971

See accompanying notes.

Notes:

(a) Notes payable to banks balance at February 3, 1979, represents foreign bank borrowings. See Note 4 to Mattel's Consolidated Financial Statements included elsewhere in the Joint Proxy Statement.

(b) Notes payable to banks balance at December 31, 1978, includes domestic short-term bank loans of $2,500,000 and foreign short-term bank loans of approximately $149,000. See Note C to Western's Consolidated Financial Statements included elsewhere in this Joint Proxy Statement.

(c) For further information with respect to long-term liabilities, see Note 4 to Mattel's Consolidated Financial Statements and Note D to Western's Consolidated Financial Statements included elsewhere in this Joint Proxy Statement.

(d) Excludes 995,025 shares reserved for issuance upon exercise of stock options granted and to be granted. See Note 7 to Mattel's Consolidated Financial Statements included elsewhere in this Joint Proxy Statement.

(e) The pro forma adjustments treat the Merger as a purchase and reflect issuance of 2,416,376 shares of Mattel Preferred in exchange for 2,130,843 shares of Western Common Stock, conversion of the remaining shares of Western Common Stock into the right to receive $28.35 in cash per share, the conversion of all shares of Western Preferred and Second Preferred into the right to receive $110 in cash per share, and additional long-term bank loans of $60,400,000 expected to be used by Mattel for the acquisition of Western. The adjustments also include a revaluation to fair market value of certain Western long-term liabilities.

MATTEL, INC. AND SUBSIDIARIES
Pro Forma Balance Sheet and Statement of Operations
(unaudited)

The following unaudited Pro Forma Balance Sheet represents a compilation, adjusted as described in the accompanying notes, of the Consolidated Balance Sheet of Mattel at February 3, 1979, and the Consolidated Balance Sheet of Western at December 31, 1978, as if the Merger, accounted for as a purchase by Mattel, had been effective as of February 3, 1979.

The following unaudited Pro Forma Statement of Operations represents a compilation, adjusted as described in the accompanying notes, of the Consolidated Statement of Operations of Mattel for the year ended February 3, 1979, and the Consolidated Statement of Earnings and Retained Earnings of Western for the year ended December 31, 1978, as if the Merger, accounted for as a purchase by Mattel, had been effective as of the beginning of the year ended February 3, 1979. This statement does not purport to be indicative of the results that actually would have been obtained if the operations had been conducted on a combined basis during the period.

These statements should be read in conjunction with the individual consolidated financial statements and related notes of Mattel and Western appearing elsewhere in this Joint Proxy Statement.

MATTEL, INC. AND SUBSIDIARIES
Pro Forma Balance Sheet
(unaudited)
($000)

	Mattel February 3, 1979	Western December 31, 1978	Pro forma adjustments	Pro forma combined
Assets				
Current assets:				
Cash	$ 25,822	$ 2,907		$ 28,729
Accounts receivable, net	71,795	77,013		148,808
Inventories	80,004	55,157	$ 2,060 [(3)]	137,221
Prepaid expenses	9,401	8,963		18,364
Deferred income tax benefits . .	10,628	979	(979) [(1)]	10,628
Total current assets	197,650	145,019	1,081	343,750
Property, plant, and equipment, net	66,414	54,630	949 [(12)]	121,993
Cost in excess of net assets of purchased subsidiaries, net . .	8,960	—		8,960
Prepaid and deferred items	—	5,618		5,618
Sundry other assets	6,380	4,376	{ (520) [(2)] (300) [(7)]	9,936
	$279,404	$209,643	$ 1,210	$490,257

Liabilities and Shareholders' Equity

Current liabilities:				
Notes payable to banks	$ 4,758	$ 2,649		$ 7,407
Current portion of long-term liabilities	826	1,600		2,426
Accounts payable	21,480	14,941		36,421
Accrued liabilities	44,285	11,069	$ 1,000 [5] (1,680) [13]	54,674
Income taxes payable	30,063	2,262		32,325
Total current liabilities	101,412	32,521	(680)	133,253
Long-term liabilities	50,839	51,200	(270) [8] 60,400 [10]	162,169
Deferred income taxes	—	4,123	(4,123) [1] 2,660 [6]	2,660
Minority interest and deferred liabilities	3,582	1,482	3,200 [4] (60) [9]	8,204
Shareholders' equity:				
Capital stock:				
Preferred stock—$25 Series A .	—	—	2,416 [10]	2,416
Preferred stock	—	2,343	(2,343) [11]	—
Second preferred stock	—	9,061	(9,061) [11]	—
Common stock	15,804	9,825	(9,825) [11]	15,804
Paid-in capital	29,947	28,351	57,984 [10] (28,351) [11]	87,931
Common stock warrants	4,968	—		4,968
Retained earnings	72,852	73,378	(73,378) [11]	72,852
	123,571	122,958	(62,558)	183,971
Less: Treasury stock	—	(2,641)	2,641 [11]	—
Total shareholders' equity	123,571	120,317	(59,917)	183,971
	$279,404	$209,643	$ 1,210	$490,257

See accompanying notes to pro forma balance sheet.

MATTEL, INC. AND SUBSIDIARIES
Notes to Pro Forma Balance Sheet
(unaudited)
Adjustments to reflect the proposed Merger of Mattel and Western as a purchase by Mattel

The pro forma balance sheet reflects the proposed acquisition of Western by Mattel for cash and Mattel Preferred, together with adjustments to certain assets and liabilities of Western to reflect their fair values.

The adjustments reflected in the pro forma balance sheet are described below:

(1) Elimination of Western deferred income taxes.
(2) Adjustment of Western's investment in unconsolidated affiliate to fair value.
(3) Adjustment of Western inventories to fair value.
(4) Adjustment of Western pension liabilities for fair value of unfunded vested benefits at January 1, 1979, less related tax benefits.
(5) Recognition of estimated expenses and other accruals related to the Merger.
(6) Adjustment of Western income taxes payable (estimated taxes on undistributed foreign earnings).
(7) Adjustment of Western long-term notes receivable to fair value.
(8) Adjustment of Western long-term debt to reflect estimated current borrowing rate of combined entity.
(9) Adjustment to fair value (as required by the Merger Agreement) of amounts which will be paid for Western Stock Equivalents, less related tax benefits.

(10) Recording of long-term bank loan and issuance of Mattel Preferred as consideration for outstanding shares of Western Common Stock and Western Preferred. Amount credited to paid-in capital represents excess of fair value over par value of Mattel Preferred shares.

(11) Adjustment to reflect elimination of Western shareholders' equity accounts.

(12) Adjustment of Western property, plant, and equipment to fair value.

(13) Adjustment of other Western accrued expenses.

MATTEL, INC. AND SUBSIDIARIES
Pro Forma Statement of Operations
(unaudited)
($000 except per share amounts)

	Mattel, year ended February 3, 1979	Western, year ended December 31, 1978	Pro forma adjustments	Pro forma combined
Net sales	$493,563	$275,355		$768,918
Costs and expenses:				
Cost of sales	301,218	156,339	$ 100 (e)	457,657
Selling and administrative expenses	134,057	98,647		232,704
Interest expense, net	12,775	5,127	{ 6,250 (a) 200 (c)	24,352
Currency translation gain	(1,051)	—	(200)(d)	(1,251)
Other (income) expense, net	(1,097)	(1,942)	200 (d)	(2,839)
	445,902	258,171	6,550	710,623
Income before taxes	47,661	17,184	(6,550)	58,295
Provision for income taxes	23,700	7,700	{ 450 (b) (3,150)(f)	28,700
Income before extraordinary item . .	23,961	9,484	(3,850)	29,595
Extraordinary income tax credits . . .	6,100	—	6,100	
Net Income	30,061	9,484	(3,850)	35,695
Preferred stock dividends	—	684	5,357	6,041
Net income applicable to common shares	$ 30,061	$ 8,800	$ (9,207)	$ 29,654
Income per common and common equivalent share:				
Primary:				
Income before extraordinary item	$1.23	$2.30		$1.21
Extraordinary income tax credits	0.31	—		0.31
Net income	$1.54	$2.30		$1.52
Average common and common equivalent shares outstanding	19,910	3,819		19,910
Fully diluted:				
Income before extraordinary item				$1.21
Extraordinary income tax credits				0.24
Net income				$1.45
Average shares assuming full dilution				24,984
Pro forma ratio of earnings to fixed charges and preferred dividends				2.13

See accompanying notes to pro forma statement of operations.

MATTEL, INC. AND SUBSIDIARIES
Notes to Pro Forma Statement of Operations
(unaudited)
Adjustments to reflect the proposed Merger of Mattel
and Western as a purchase by Mattel

The adjustments to the pro forma statement of operations are:

(a) Interest expense relating to long-term debt used to purchase Western common and preferred stock. Interest expense has been computed based on 115% of the fiscal 1979 average prime rate (9%).

(b) Additional income taxes on Western undistributed foreign earnings.

(c) Imputed interest expense on revalued long-term liabilities of Western.

(e) Reclassification of Western currency translation gain.

(e) Depreciation expense pertaining to fair value adjustments made to Western property, plant and equipment.

(f) Reduction of income tax provision related to the interest expense on long-term debt.

Income per share

Primary income per common and common equivalent share, on a pro forma basis, is computed using pro forma income after reduction for the annual dividend requirement of the Mattel Preferred. The number of common and common equivalent shares is based upon the weighted average number of common and common equivalent shares outstanding during the year. Common equivalent shares represent the net number of shares which would be issued assuming the exercise of dilutive stock options and common stock warrants, reduced by the number of shares which could be purchased with certain proceeds from the exercise of those options and warrants. Under the terms of the subordinated debt indenture, the proceeds obtained from exercise of the common stock warrants must be used to retire outstanding subordinated debentures. To determine earnings for the purpose of income per share computation, net income has been increased by estimated net interest savings relating to debt assumed to have been retired with the proceeds from the exercise of the warrants.

Income per share assuming full dilution, on a pro forma basis, is computed based on the further assumption that 2,416,376 shares of the Mattel Preferred (which are not common stock equivalents) were converted at the beginning of the year into 5,074,000 shares of Mattel Common Stock using a conversion rate of 2.10; accordingly, dividends on Mattel Preferred are not deducted from pro forma income for the purpose of computing income per share assuming full dilution.

The Merger Agreement stipulates that Mattel Preferred will be convertible into from 2.10 to 2.38 shares of Mattel Common Stock, depending on the market price of Mattel Common Stock during a period of time preceeding the Western Meeting. If a conversion rate of 2.38 had been used in the computations assuming full dilution, fully diluted amounts per share, on a pro forma basis, would be as follows:

Income before extraordinary item	$1.18
Extraordinary income tax credits	0.24
Net income	$1.42

Ratio of earnings to fixed charges and preferred dividends

The ratio of earnings to fixed charges and preferred dividends, on a pro forma basis, is computed by dividing the sum of pro forma preferred dividends (adjusted to reflect such dividends on a pretax basis), interest expense and one third of rental expense into the sum of earnings before income taxes (excluding minority interest charges and equity in the earnings of an unconsolidated affiliate) and fixed charges.

MATTEL, INC. AND SUBSIDIARIES
Consolidated Statements of Operations
($000 except per share amounts)

The following Consolidated Statements of Operations of Mattel, Inc. and Subsidiaries, insofar as they relate to the three fiscal years ended February 3, 1979, have been examined by Price Waterhouse & Co., independent accountants, whose report thereon appears elsewhere in this Joint Proxy Statement (Prospectus). The statements and accompanying notes below should be read in conjunction with the other consolidated financial statements of Mattel, Inc. and Subsidiaries and notes thereto included elsewhere in this Joint Proxy Statement (Prospectus).

	Fiscal year ended				
	February 1, 1975*	January 31, 1976*	January 29, 1977	January 28, 1978	February 3, 1979
Net sales	$329,306	$340,881	$386,273	$436,645	$493,563
Cost and expenses:					
Cost of sales	210,969	270,879	237,908	266,638	301,218
Selling and administrative expenses	77,703	86,611	101,644	118,569	134,057
Interest expense, net	20,767	13,751	11,065	11,820	12,775
Currency translation (gain) loss	3,042	491	623	100	(1,051)
Nonrecurring charges	9,340	—	1,350	—	—
Other (income) expense, net	1,745	784	(996)	(1,719)	(1,097)
	323,566	309,516	351,594	395,408	445,902
Income from continuing operations before income taxes	5,740	31,365	34,679	41,237	47,661
provision for income taxes	4,117	16,829	18,260	19,400	23,700
Income from continuing operations	1,623	14,536	16,419	21,837	23,961
Loss from discontinued operations	(5,544)	—	—	—	—
Income (loss) before extraordinary items	(3,921)	14,536	16,419	21,837	23,961
Extraordinary items:					
Income tax credits	640	10,772	8,342	7,700	6,100
Provision for estimated settlement costs	(17,000)	—	(1,500)	(700)	—
	(16,360)	10,772	6,842	7,000	6,100
Net income (loss)	$ (20,281)	$ 25,308	$ 23,261	$ 28,837	$ 30,061
Income (loss) per common and common equivalent share:					
Continuing operations	$0.10	$0.86	$0.97	$1.19	$1.23
Discontinued operations	(0.33)	—	—	—	—
Income (loss) before extraordinary items	(0.23)	0.86	0.97	1.19	1.23
Extraordinary items	(0.97)	0.64	0.41	0.37	0.31
Net income (loss)	$(1.20)	$1.50	$1.38	$1.56	$1.54
Cash dividends per common share	—	—	—	—	$0.225
Average common and common equivalent shares outstanding	16,862	16,862	16,862	18,744	19,910

The accompanying notes to consolidated statements of operations and the notes to the Mattel consolidated financial statements are an integral part of these statements.

*Not covered by Accountants' Report.

MATTEL, INC. AND SUBSIDIARIES
Notes to Consolidated Statements of Operations

Note A: Financial statements for the year ended February 1, 1975

For the reasons stated below the Company's consolidated statement of operations for the fiscal year ended February 1, 1975, is not covered by an accountants' report.

In connection with the events leading to settlement of the class actions (Note 3 to Mattel's Consolidated Financial Statements), Arthur Andersen & Co., the Company's former independent accountants, resigned on September 30, 1974, and since that time have not permitted association of their auditors' reports on the Company's financial statements for fiscal 1974 and earlier years.

Because the Company's successor independent accountants, Price Waterhouse & Co., were engaged subsequent to February 2, 1974, they did not observe the physical inventory or confirm accounts receivable at that date. Price Waterhouse & Co. have not satisfied themselves by means of other procedures as to inventory and accounts receivable balances as of February 2, 1974. Because opening inventory and accounts receivable balances enter materially into the determination of results of operations and changes in financial position for the year ended February 1, 1975, Price Waterhouse & Co. are not able to express an opinion on the consolidated statements of operations, shareholders' equity, and changes in financial position or the supporting schedules for the year ended February 1, 1975.

Note B: Nonrecurring charges

Nonrecurring charges consisted of the following (in thousands):

	Fiscal year ended	
	February 1, 1975	January 29, 1977
Provision for estimated additional duty (Note 5)	$2,500	—
Write-off of Circus Theme Park pre-opening costs (Note 2)	3,440	—
Provision for termination of Mexican operation	2,200	—
Provision for insurance claim receivable	1,200	$1,350
	$9,340	$1,350

Note C: Discontinued operations

The loss on disposal of discontinued businesses in fiscal 1975 includes a provision of $6,047,000 relating to the valuation of noncurrent receivables (arising primarily from the disposal of Audio Magnetics Corporation) reduced by elimination of approximately $1,000,000 of certain accrued liabilities for discontinued operations which were no longer required. In fiscal 1977, the Company eliminated approximately $700,000 of the remaining accrued liabilities for discontinued operations due to the final resolution of these matters.

Note D: Purchase of certain minority interests

In fiscal 1975, the Company acquired the remaining interests in Radnitz/Mattel Productions, Inc. (49%), a producer of family motion pictures; Mattel Japan Ltd. (50%), a toy distributor; and the remaining 5% interest in the Circus Theme Park for an aggregate purchase price of approximately $1,283,000. These acquisitions, accounted for under the purchase method, resulted in approximately $1,164,000 of cost in excess of net assets purchased. Had these purchases been consummated at the beginning of fiscal 1975, income before income taxes from continuing operations would have been reduced by approximately $620,000 in fiscal 1975.

Note E: Income (loss) per common and common equivalent share

Income (loss) per common and common equivalent share is based upon the weighted average number of common and common equivalent shares outstanding during each fiscal year. Common equivalent shares represent the net number of shares which would be issued assuming the exercise of dilutive stock options and common stock warrants, reduced by the number of shares which could be purchased with certain proceeds from the exercise of those options and warrants. Under the terms of the subordinated debt indenture, the proceeds obtained from the exercise of the common stock warrants must be used to retire outstanding subordinated debentures. To determine earnings for the purpose of income per share computation, net income has been increased by estimated net interest savings relating to the debt assumed to have been retired with the proceeds from the exercise of the warrants. The common stock warrants were not deemed outstanding prior to fiscal 1978 and, accordingly, computations for earlier periods do not include any common equivalent shares. Computation of income (loss) per common and common equivalent share is as follows:

| | ($000 except per share amounts) | | | | |
| | Fiscal year ended | | | | |
	February 1, 1975	January 31, 1976	January 29, 1977	January 28, 1978	February 3, 1979
Income (loss) before extraordinary items	$ (3,921)	$14,536	$16,419	$21,837	$23,961
Reduction of interest expense (net of income taxes) resulting from assumed retirement of debt	—	—	—	400	615
	(3,921)	14,536	16,419	22,237	24,576
Extraordinary items	(16,360)	10,772	6,842	7,000	6,100
Net income (loss)	$(20,281)	$25,308	$23,261	$29,237	$30,676
Applicable shares:					
Weighted average shares outstanding	16,862	16,862	16,862	15,526	15,550
Weighted average common equivalent shares arising from:					
Stock options	8	—[1]	211	408	269
Warrants	—	—	—	2,810	4,091
	16,870[2]	16,862	17,073[2]	18,744	19,910
Income (loss) per common and common equivalent share:					
Income (loss) before extraordinary items	$(0.23)	$0.86	$0.97	$1.19	$1.23
Extraordinary items	(0.97)	0.64	0.41	0.37	0.31
Net income (loss)	$(1.20)	$1.50	$1.38	$1.56	$1.54

(1) Not available because of suspension of trading between September 6, 1974, through June 15, 1976.

(2) Weighted average shares were used in earnings per share computation because the dilutive effect of common equivalent shares was either not significant or antidilutive.

WESTERN PUBLISHING COMPANY, INC., AND SUBSIDIARIES
Consolidated Statements of Earnings and Retained Earnings

The following consolidated statements of earnings and retained earnings of Western Publishing Company, Inc., and Subsidiaries for the three years ended December 31, 1978, have been examined by Coopers & Lybrand, independent certified public accountants, whose report thereon appears elsewhere in this Joint Proxy Statement (Prospectus). The statements and related notes thereto should be read in conjunction with the other consolidated financial statements of Western Publishing Company, Inc. and Subsidiaries and related notes thereto, appearing elsewhere in this Joint Proxy Statement (Prospectus).

| | ($000 except per share amounts) | | | | |
| | Years ended December 31, | | | | |
	1974*	1975*	1976	1977	1978
Net sales (Note 1)	$215,568	$224,809	$237,277	$263,487	$275,355
Cost of sales (Notes 2B and 3)	125,540	130,250	134,006	153,399	156,339
Publishing, selling and administrative expenses .	64,614	66,843	72,831	83,175	88,662
Provision for doubtful accounts	4,932	6,642	8,051	8,491	9,985
	195,086	203,735	214,888	245,065	254,986
	20,482	21,074	22,389	18,422	20,369

	($000 except per share amounts)				
	Years ended December 31,				
	1974*	1975*	1976	1977	1978
Other expenses (income):					
Interest expense on long-term debt	1,335	1,886	2,729	3,078	3,460
Other interest expense	1,053	1,034	159	685	1,667
Provision for loss on closed facility (Note 4)	—	—	—	1,200	—
Gain on sale of fixed assets, net	(219)	(69)	(285)	(67)	(670)
Other, net	(1,111)	(1,070)	(616)	(514)	(1,272)
	1,058	1,781	1,987	4,382	3,185
Earnings before income taxes and cumulative effect of accounting change	19,424	19,293	20,402	14,040	17,184
Provision for income taxes (Note 5)	9,293	9,090	9,650	6,590	7,700
Earnings before cumulative effect of accounting change	10,131	10,203	10,752	7,450	9,484
Cumulative effect of accounting change (Note 2A)	—	—	—	1,143	—
Net earnings	10,131	10,203	10,752	8,593	9,484
Retained earnings at the beginning of the year	46,107	52,790	59,403	63,389	67,939
	56,238	62,993	70,155	71,982	77,423
Cash dividends (Note 6):					
Preferred stock, $6 per share	141	140	140	140	140
Second preferred stock, $6 per share	546	544	544	544	544
Common stock— $0.72 per share, 1974; $0.76 per share, 1975; $0.79 per share, 1976; $0.88 per share, 1977 and 1978	2,761	2,906	3,015	3,359	3,361
	3,448	3,590	3,699	4,043	4,045
5% common stock dividend	—	—	3,067	—	—
Retained earnings at the end of the year	$ 52,790	$ 59,403	$ 63,389	$ 67,939	$ 73,378
Earnings per share of common stock (Note 6):					
Earnings before cumulative effect of accounting change	$2.48	$2.50	$2.64	$1.77	$2.30
Cumulative effect of accounting change	—	—	—	0.30	—
Net earnings	$2.48	$2.50	$2.64	$2.07	$2.30
Weighted average common shares outstanding	$ 3,813	$ 3,813	$ 3,814	$ 3,817	$ 3,819
Pro forma amounts assuming the new method of accounting for investment tax credits is applied retroactively:					
Net earnings	$ 10,203	$ 10,817	$ 10,711		
Net earnings per common share	$2.50	$2.66	$2.63		

*Not covered by Accountants' Report.

Unaudited summary of operating data for the three month periods ended March 31, 1978, and 1979, is as follows (dollar amounts in thousands, except per share data):

	1978	1979
Net sales	$56,294	$54,563
Net earnings (loss)	(116)	119
Net loss applicable to common stock (after dividends on preferred stock of $171)	(287)	(52)
Net loss per share of common stock	(0.08)	(0.01)

WESTERN PUBLISHING COMPANY, INC. AND SUBSIDIARIES
Notes to Consolidated Statements of Earnings and Retained Earnings

1. Net sales.

Consolidated net sales include the following amounts of sales to minority-owned foreign affiliates:

1974	$1,385,000
1975	1,372,000
1976	1,760,000
1977	1,780,000
1978	2,266,000

2. Changes in accounting principles.

A. Effective January 1, 1977, Western changed its method of accounting for investment tax credits whereby investment tax credits are included in earnings as a reduction of the provision for federal income taxes in the year the related assets are placed in service rather than amortized over the estimated useful lives of the related assets. The effect of this change was to increase 1977 earnings before cumulative effect of accounting change by $149,000 ($.04 per share) and net earnings by $1,292,000 ($.34 per share).

B. Effective with the year ended December 31, 1976, Western and its domestic subsidiaries adopted the last-in, first-out (LIFO) method of inventory cost valuation. Prior to 1976, inventory cost was determined by the first-in, first-out (FIFO) method, except for inventories of work-in process for which cost was determined on an average cost method. The effect of this change was to reduce inventories by $1,360,000 and net earnings by $673,000 ($.18 per share). There is no cumulative effect of the change on prior periods since the December 31, 1975 inventory, as previously reported, is the opening inventory under the LIFO method.

3. Inventories.

Inventories used in the computation of cost of sales were as follows:

1975	$42,900,000
1976	47,759,000
1977	49,022,000
1978	55,157,000

4. Provision for loss on closed facility.

In October 1977 Western announced its decision to close its St. Louis, Missouri manufacturing facility. A provision of $1,200,000 was made in 1977 to cover operating losses during the phase-out period, equipment moving costs and expected losses on disposition of assets. The closing was completed during 1978 with the actual costs incurred approximating the amount so provided.

5. Income taxes.

A summary of the provision for income taxes is as follows:

	1976	1977	1978
Currently payable:			
Federal	$6,842,000	$3,732,000	$5,483,000
Foreign	1,579,000	902,000	1,092,000
State	835,000	804,000	796,000
	9,256,000	5,438,000	7,371,000
Deferred current:			
Federal	447,000	1,015,000	(43,000)
Foreign	(86,000)	28,000	(217,000)
State	39,000	(96,000)	132,000
	400,000	947,000	(128,000)
Deferred noncurrent:			
Federal	(30,000)	218,000	448,000
Foreign	(5,000)		(57,000)
State	29,000	(13,000)	66,000
	(6,000)	205,000	457,000
	$9,650,000	$6,590,000	$7,700,000

The provision for deferred income taxes results from the following differences in timing of deductions and income for financial statement and tax purposes:

	1976	1977	1978
Installment sales		$2,186,000	$(1,325,000)
Accrued expenses	$(312,000)	(1,126,000)	726,000
Depreciation	475,000	546,000	424,000
Allowance against receivables	225,000	(75,000)	524,000
Charge equivalent to reduction in currently payable income taxes resulting from investment tax credits	239,000		
Amortization of investment tax credits	(315,000)		
Other, net	82,000	(379,000)	(20,000)
Provision for deferred income taxes	$ 394,000	$1,152,000	$ 329,000

In 1976, 1977, and 1978 the effective tax rates were 47.3%, 46.9%, and 44.8%, respectively, as compared to the statutory federal rate of 48%. These differences are reconciled as follows:

	1976	1977	1978
Expected provision for income taxes	$9,793,000	$6,739,000	$8,248,000
State taxes, net of federal benefit	543,000	361,000	517,000
Investment tax credits	(315,000)	(525,000)	(643,000)
Other, net	(371,000)	15,000	(422,000)
Provision for income taxes	$9,650,000	$6,590,000	$7,700,000

6. Earnings and dividends per share of common stock.

Earnings per share computations are based on the weighted average number of shares of common stock outstanding during the respective years and after net earnings are reduced for preferred dividend requirements. Shares issuable under the management stock plan are excluded from the weighted average number of shares because their effect is not material.

Cash dividends per share of common stock are based on the actual number of shares outstanding on the dividend record dates, adjusted retroactively for the 5% common stock dividend in 1976.

7. Supplementary income statement information.

Supplementary income statement information is as follows:

	1976	1977	1978
Maintenance and repairs	$4,068,000	$ 4,365,000	$ 4,513,000
Depreciation and amortization of property, plant and equipment	5,394,000	5,801,000	6,233,000
Taxes, other than income taxes	6,191,000	6,608,000	7,346,000
Rents	2,824,000	2,956,000	3,101,000
Royalties	6,328,000	6,370,000	7,173,000
Advertising costs	9,865,000	15,646,000	16,298,000
Retirement plan expense	2,630,000	2,760,000	2,960,000
Deferred compensation expense (stock equivalent program)	616,000	596,000	

8. Industry segment information.

The following industry segment information as of December 31, 1978, and 1977, and for the years then ended is prepared in accordance with Financial Accounting Standards Board *Statement No. 14:*

				($000)		
1978	Net sales	Operating profit (expenses)	Identifiable assets	Depreciation and amortization expense	Capital expenditures
Consumer products	$187,337	$22,277	$147,746	$2,998	$ 4,769
Commercial products	88,018	5,831	55,368	3,185	3,107
	275,355	28,108	203,114	6,183	7,876
General corporate .		(5,797)	6,529	65	9
Interest expense . .		(5,127)			
	$275,355	$17,184	$209,643	$6,248	$ 7,885
1977					
Consumer products	$182,431	$22,790	$140,507	$2,683	$10,212
Commercial products	81,05	3,136	51,413	3,067	4,860
	263,487	25,926	191,920	5,750	15,072
Provision for loss on closed facility		(1,200)			
General corporate .		(6,923)	4,854	66	35
Interest expense . .		(3,763)			
	$263,487	$14,040	$196,774	$5,816	$15,107

Consumer products represent the manufacture, distribution and sale of adult and juvenile books, and games, toys and hobby and craft activity products. Commercial products represent commercial printing of all types.

Operating profit is total sales and revenues less operating expenses of the segments, excluding provision for loss on closed facility, general corporate expenses and interest expense. There were no significant intersegment sales. Identifiable assets by segment include all assets directly identified with those operations. Corporate assets consist primarily of cash, investment in an unconsolidated foreign affiliate and certain property, plant and equipment.

No customer accounts for 10 percent or more of total net sales.

9. **Unaudited interim financial information.**

($000 except for per share data)

	First quarter	Second quarter	Third quarter	Fourth quarter	Year
1978					
Net sales	$56,294	$65,093	$74,697	$79,271	$275,355
Gross profit	22,900	28,638	31,979	35,500	119,017
Net earnings (loss)	(116)	1,664	3,908	4,028	9,484
Net earnings (loss) per common share	(0.08)	0.39	0.98	1.01	2.30
1977					
Net sales	$53,136	$58,745	$73,538	$78,068	$263,487
Gross profit	21,977	24,463	30,021	33,627	110,088
Earnings before cumulative effect of accounting change . .	1,151	1,380	3,190	1,729	7,450
Net earnings	2,294	1,380	3,190	1,729	8,593
Earnings per common share:					
Earnings before cumulative effect of accounting change	0.26	0.31	0.79	0.41	1.77
Net earnings	0.56	0.31	0.79	0.41	2.07
1976					
Net sales	$50,420	$55,002	$65,283	$66,572	$237,277
Gross profit	22,078	24,009	28,829	28,355	103,271
Net earnings	1,460	1,856	3,896	3,540	10,752
Net earnings per common share	0.34	0.44	0.97	0.89	2.64

Information by industry segment and geographic area for fiscal 1979, 1978, and 1977 is set forth below:

By industry segment
($000)

	Toy Products	Hobby Products	Entertain-ment	Adjustments and eliminations	Consoli-dated total
Fiscal 1979:					
Sales to unaffiliated customers	$399,835	$44,204	$49,524	—	$493,563
Intersegment sales and transfers	396	1,530	25	$(1,951)	—
Total net sales	$400,231	$45,734	$49,549	$(1,951)	$493,563
Operating profit	$ 63,106	$ 838	$ 5,292		$ 69,236
Identifiable assets	$175,020	$36,479	$42,677		$254,176
Depreciation and amortization	$ 3,484	$ 1,431	$ 1,780		$ 6,695
Capital expenditures . . .	$ 3,489	$ 2,033	$ 7,696		$ 13,218
Fiscal 1978:					
Sales to unaffiliated customers	$351,119	$42,033	$43,493	—	$436,645
Intersegment sales and transfers	501	1,103	—	$(1,604)	—
Total net sales	$351,620	$43,136	$43,493	$(1,604)	$436,645
Operating profit (loss) . .	$ 56,507	$ (383)	$ 4,604		$ 60,728
Identifiable assets	$147,782	$31,874	$37,716		$217,372
Depreciation and amortization	$ 3,529	$ 1,769	$ 1,334		$ 6,632
Capital expenditures . . .	$ 5,995	$ 1,448	$ 2,883		$ 10,326
Fiscal 1977:					
Sales to unaffiliated customers	$303,103	$44,840	$38,330	—	$386,273
Intersegment sales and transfers	594	1,411	—	$(2,005)	—
Total net sales	$303,697	$46,251	$38,330	$(2,005)	$386,273
Operating profit (loss) . .	$ 54,064	$ (3,263)	$ 1,792		$ 52,593
Identifiable assets	$127,265	$33,347	$34,474		$195,086
Depreciation and amortization	$ 2,762	$ 1,396	$ 1,167		$ 5,325
Capital expenditures . . .	$ 4,092	$ 1,838	$ 2,627		$ 8,557

	United States	Western Europe	Other foreign operations	Adjustments and eliminations	Consolidated total
By geographic area ($000)					
Fiscal 1979:					
Sales to unaffiliated customers	$386,838	$75,910	$30,815	—	$493,563
Sales and transfers between geographic areas	5,776	127	34,394	$(40,297)	—
Total net sales	$392,614	$76,037	$65,209	$(40,207)	$493,563
Operating profit	$ 46,323	$14,624	$ 8,289		$ 69,236
Identifiable assets	$184,844	$35,511	$33,821		$254,176
Fiscal 1978:					
Sales to unaffiliated customers	$350,249	$60,471	$25,925	—	$436,645
Sales and transfers between geographic areas	5,178	64	30,158	$(35,400)	—
Total net sales	$355,427	$60,535	$56,083	$(35,400)	$436,645
Operating profit	$ 43,550	$13,212	$ 3,966		$ 60,728
Identifiable assets	$149,806	$42,284	$25,282		$217,372
Fiscal 1977:					
Sales to unaffiliated customers	$309,343	$52,555	$24,375	—	$386,273
Sales and transfers between geographic areas	6,497	10	26,321	$(32,828)	—
Total net sales	$315,840	$52,565	$50,696	$(32,828)	$386,273
Operating profit	$ 35,690	$12,645	$ 4,258		$ 52,593
Identifiable assets	$139,560	$29,918	$25,608		$195,086

Consolidated operating profit for fiscal 1979 of $69,236,000 ($60,728,000 for fiscal 1978 and $52,593,000 for fiscal 1977) is reduced by general corporate expenses and interest expense of $21,575,000 ($19,491,000 for fiscal 1978 and $17,914,000 for fiscal 1977) to arrive at consolidated income before income taxes and extraordinary items of $47,661,000 ($41,237,000 for fiscal 1978 and $34,679,000 for fiscal 1977).

Corporate assets of $25,228,000, principally cash, are added to identifiable assets of $254,176,000 to reconcile to consolidated assets of $279,404,000 at February 3, 1979.

The Company's foreign operations consist of marketing and manufacturing subsidiaries located principally in Western Europe, Canada, and the Orient. These subsidiaries accounted for approximately $19,900,000 of consolidated income before income taxes in fiscal 1979, approximately $16,000,000 in fiscal 1978, and approximately $15,900,000 in fiscal 1977.

Consolidated liabilities relating to foreign operations at February 3, 1979 were approximately $46,000,000.

Note 14: Quarterly financial information (unaudited)

Fiscal year ended February 3, 1979

($000 except per share amounts)

	First quarter	Second quarter	Third quarter	Fourth quarter	Fiscal year
Net sales	$94,320	$125,129	$170,204	$103,910	$493,563
Gross profit	$35,303	$ 47,884	$ 73,754	$ 35,404	$192,345
Income before extraordinary items	$ 1,802	$ 4,792	$ 16,133	$ 1,234	$ 23,961
Extraordinary items	1,100	2,900	800	1,300	6,100
Net income	$ 2,902	$ 7,692	$ 16,933	$ 2,534	$ 30,061
Income per share:					
Income before extraordinary items	$0.10	$0.25	$0.81	$0.07	$1.23
Extraordinary items	0.06	0.15	0.04	0.06	0.31
Net income	$0.16	$0.40	$0.85	$0.13	$1.54
Average common and common equivalent shares outstanding .	19,625	20,053	20,073	19,891	19,910

Fiscal year ended February 3, 1979
($000 except per share amounts)

	First quarter	Second quarter	Third quarter	Fourth quarter	Fiscal year
Net sales	$84,748	$103,053	$166,871	$81,973	$436,645
Gross profit	$31,110	$ 40,468	$ 73,889	$24,540	$170,007
Income (loss) before extraordinary items	$ 1,111	$ 4,438	$ 17,801	$(1,513)	$ 21,837
Extraordinary items	800	2,300	5,200	(1,300)	7,000
Net income (loss)	$ 1,911	$ 6,738	$ 23,001	$(2,813)	$ 28,837
Income (loss) per share:					
Income (loss) before extraordinary items	$0.06	$0.24	$0.92	$(0.09)	$1.19
Extraordinary items	0.05	0.13	0.26	(0.09)	0.37
Net income (loss)	$0.11	$0.37	$1.18	$(0.18)	$1.56
Average common and common equivalent shares outstanding .	16,862	18,766	19,609	14,951	18,744

Because of significant seasonal variations in the Toy Products segment of the Company's business, results for interim periods are not comparable.

The sum of quarterly earnings per share as reported for fiscal 1978 does not equal earnings per share for the fiscal year because the separate quarterly computations are influenced primarily by fluctuations in the Company's common stock price and the related exclusion of anti-dilutive common stock equivalents for the fourth quarter.

Note 15: Proposed acquisition

On January 9, 1979, the Company announced an agreement in principle for the merger of Western Publishing Company, Inc. (Western) into the Company.

Under the proposed terms of the agreement, the holders of Western common stock may elect to receive either $28.35 in cash or 1.134 shares of Mattel Preferred or a combination thereof. The preferred stock ($25 Series A) will be voting, cumulative, convertible and pay an annual dividend of $2.50 per share. The preferred stock is convertible into not more than 2.38 but not less than 2.1 shares of the Company's common stock.

Appendix 24–B: Galveston Houston Company— management's discussion and analysis of financial condition and results of operation

Summary of operations

The following table sets forth the periods indicated condensed statement of earnings and the relationship of the items included therein to net revenues of the company:

	($000)					
	1980		*1979*		*1978*	
Net revenues	$145,916	100.0%	$110,855	100.0%	$52,455	100.0%
Manufacturing and direct costs	83,975	57.5	67,187	60.6	28,315	54.0
Gross margin	61,941	42.5	43,668	39.4	24,140	46.0
Selling, general, and administrative	41,863	28.7	29,876	27.0	13,895	26.5
Operating income . . .	20,078	13.8	13,792	12.4	10,245	19.5
Other income (expense)	(4,101)	(2.8)	(4,843)	(4.3)	304	.6
Earnings before provision for income taxes and extraordinary item .	15,977	11.0	8,949	8.1	10,549	20.1
Provision for income taxes	5,395	3.7	2,835	2.6	4,612	8.8
Net earnings before extraordinary item .	10,582	7.3	6,114	5.5	5,937	11.3
Extraordinary item . . .					255	.5
Net earnings	$ 10,582	7.3%	$ 6,114	5.5%	$ 6,192	11.8%

The table below sets forth for the periods indicated, the percentage increase (decrease) of certain financial data as compared to the indicated prior period:

	1979–80	1978–79
Net revenues	31.6%	111.3%
Manufacturing and direct costs . . .	25.0%	137.3%
Selling, general, and administrative .	40.1%	115.0%
Operating income	45.6%	34.6%
Other income (expense)	(15.3)	*
Earnings before provision for income taxes and extraordinary item	78.5%	(15.2)
Provision for income taxes	90.3%	(38.5)
Net earnings before extraordinary item	73.1%	3.0%
Net earnings	73.1%	(1.3)%

*Income in 1978, expense in 1979.

Results of operations.

Net revenues. Net revenues for the period ended December 31, 1980, as compared to the same period ended 1978 increased $93.5 million or 178 percent. This large percentage increase was due primarily to inclusion of a full year's operation in 1980 of businesses acquired in 1978 and 1979. The results of operations of these businesses are included in the company's results from their respective dates of acquisition. Revenues from existing operations increased $35.8 million or 72 percent over the two-year period.

Of the 178 percent increase in revenues, $55 million or 105 percent resulted principally from the acquisition of three companies (the services division of the drilling segment) in November 1978 and in January 1979. In addition, equipment, spare parts and repair work revenues of the drilling and production segments accounted for a 36 percent, $18.8 million, and a 37 percent, $19.6 million, increase respectively, of which 7 percent or $3.9 million was attributable to drilling equipment business acquired. Increased revenues attributable to existing products resulted from improved production effiiciencies, additional capacity and higher levels of incoming orders due to continued high demand for the Company's products. In each of the years covered herein, the company increased prices of products sold and services performed approximately 7–10 percent.

Gross margins. Gross margins as a percentage of revenues decreased in 1979 principally as a result of the services division mentioned above. These companies attained margins lower than those historically experienced by the company due to low volumes and high costs associated with the expansion of these operations. In addition, in 1979 the company changed its method of valuing certain domestic inventories to the last-in, first-out (LIFO) method of determining cost which resulted in greater charges to manufacturing and direct costs.

In 1980, the continued high demand for oilfield products, including those of the services division, resulted in increased volumes and improved profits margins. Gross margins in 1980 for both the drilling and the production segments increased, as compared to 1979, as a result of improved manufacturing efficiencies and sales volumes.

Selling, general, and administrative expenses. Selling, general, and administrative expenses generally remained in line with sales. Increases in each of the three years were due primarily to an increase in overall operating activity and general inflationary trends. Additionally, during 1979 and 1980, the company continued expansion of the marketing, exploration and distribution facilities associated with the services portion of the drilling segment.

Other income (expense). These costs principally represent interest expense. However, in the year 1978, a nonrecurring gain from the sale of a subsidiary more than offset interest expense.

Provision for income taxes. The effective income tax rates for the years ended December 31, 1978, 1979, and 1980 were 44 percent, 32 percent, and 34 percent, respectively. The reduction in the effective tax rates in 1979 and 1980 was due to significantly higher investment tax credits in 1979 and 1980 than in prior years principally as a result of the company's increased capital expenditure program; increased income of the company's domestic international sales corporations, on a portion of which taxes were not required to be provided; and certain assets having a greater tax basis than book basis which resulted in greater depreciation in both years and greater costs of sales in 1979 for tax purposes than for book purposes.

Liquidity and financial condition

Working capital. These ratios measure the company's ability to meet its short-term obligations.

	December 31,		
	1980	1979	1978
Current assets (in thousands)	$64,028	$41,927	$24,791
Current liabilities (in thousands)	24,660	18,534	10,615
Working capital (in thousands)	$39,368	$23,393	$14,176
Current ratio	2.6 to 1	2.3 to 1	2.3 to 1
Quick ratio	1.3 to1	1.2 to 1	1.1 to 1

In order to maintain liquidity and finance the large increase in the company's business, working capital was increased substantially (178 percent) over the two year period from December 31, 1978, to December 31, 1980. As a result, current assets have covered current liabilities (current ratio) by 2.3 times or better each year and cash and accounts receivable have also exceeded current liabilities (quick ratio) by 1.1 times to 1.3 times.

Capital expenditures and long-term financing. Capital expenditures of approximately $46.5 million for the two years ended December 31, 1980, and the acquisition of businesses during 1979 were financed through a combination of internally generated funds, debt financing and the sale of common stock. In 1979, the company sold $30 million of Convertible Subordinated Guaranteed Debentures and approximately $19 million of common stock. During 1980, the company sold approximately $7 million of Industrial Development Revenue Bonds as well as borrowed under existing bank lines to finance the capital expenditures. Subsequent to December 31, 1980, the company entered into a $50 million bank revolving credit agreement which was partially used to retire short-term bank debt. In February 1981, proceeds received from the sale of assets of GH Fluid Services, Inc., were used to reduce borrowings under the credit agreement and, at that time, the commitment under the credit was reduced to $27 million. The company's capital expenditure program for 1981 is expected to be approximately $35 million. These expenditures will be financed from a combination of internally generated funds, the sale of Industrial Development Revenue Bonds, and borrowings under the bank credit agreement.

Capitalization. The following table summarizes the company's capital structure at December 31:

	December 31,		
	1980	1979	1978
Senior debt	29%	12%	32%
Convertible subordinated debentures	6	33	—
Total long-term debt	35	45	32
Deferred income taxes	3	2	1
Stockholders' equity	62	53	67
Total capitalization	110%	100%	100%

Between the year ended 1978 and the year ended 1980, stockholders' equity increased 221 percent as a result of retained profits from the company's operations, the sale of approximately $19 million of common stock in 1979, and the conversion into equity during 1980 of approximately $22 million of subordinated debentures. Total long-term debt as a percentage of total capitalization increased from 32 percent in 1978 to 45 percent in 1979 as a result of debt incurred to finance acquisitions and capital expenditures which more than offset the 96 percent increase in stockholders' equity through retained earnings and the sale of common stock. In 1980, total long-term debt declined to 35 percent of total capitalization as a result of an increase in stockholders' equity from retained earnings plus the conversion of the convertible debentures. These increases were partially offset by the increase in bank debt and other long-term financing used to partially fund the company's capital expenditure program. The company had no short-term bank debt outstanding at the end of 1979 or 1980.

Subsequent events

In January 1981, the company purchased for cash and notes Hensley Industries, Inc., and Texas Reamer Company and related entities. In February 1981, the company sold substantially all of the assets of the drilling fluids operations, other than the barite producing properties located in Missouri. Since the operations acquired and disposed of are of different sizes and involve different products, services and methods of financing, the company's historical consolidated results of operations may not necessarily be indicative of future results.

The company's unaudited pro forma results of operations for 1980 and 1979 assuming the above transactions had occurred on January 1, 1979, are included in Note 2 to the Consolidated Financial Statements. An unaudited condensed pro forma balance sheet giving effect to the above acquisitions and disposition as if they had occurred on January 1, 1981, is also shown in Note 2.

Index

A

Accountability, and estate accounting, 593–94
Accounting Principles Board (APB)
  Opinion No. 3, 768
  Opinion No. 6, 420–21
  Opinion No. 9, 32, 487
  Opinion No. 10, 31
  Opinion NO. 11, 474
  Opinion No. 15, 32, 487–89
  Opinion No. 16, 31–32, 36–37, 48
  Opinion No. 17, 32, 37
  Opinion No. 18, 95, 286, 370,
  Opinion No. 20, 477
  Opinion No. 22, 157
  Opinion No. 23, 108–9, 474
  Opinion No. 24, 474
  Opinion No. 28, 472, 474–75, 477–78
Accounting Research Bulletin (ARB)
  No. 40, 31
  No. 43, 31, 420
  No. 48, 31
  No. 49, 487
  No. 51, 95–96, 105, 140, 145, 147, 285, 291
Accounting Research Study No. 6, 768
Accounting Series Release (ASR), 763
  No. 4, 767
  No. 51, 95
  No. 147, 767
  No. 148, 771
  No. 150, 767
  No. 159, 770–71
  No. 163, 768
  No. 166, 770
  No. 190, 768–69
  No. 279, 767
Accounting Standards Executive Committee (AcSEC) of the AICPA, 396
Acquisition, definition of, 27–28
Administrator/administrix, 589
Advance cash distribution plans, of partnership liquidation, 578–80
Agencies, definition of, 3–4
Agency funds, 669–70

Allocation of retained earnings, and preferred stock, 252
Amortization, straight-line method of, 38
Antidilution, 493, 495–98
Antitrust statues, and business combinations, 28–29
Appraisal rights, 44
Asset test, of segment reporting, 457–58
Assets, guidelines for valuation of, 37

B

Balance sheet only working papers, 209–10
Bankruptcy
  distribution of estate in, 615
  involuntary, 609
  trustee in, 614–15
  voluntary, 608–9
Bankruptcy Reform Act (1978), 607, 609, 614
Bargain purchase credit, 70
Beneficiary or cestuique trust, 598
Benston, George, 771
Berle, Adolph A., 759
Billed price, shipments by home office to branch at, 5–9
Billed price in excess of cost, 5, 9–16
Billing above cost, 139
Black-market rate of exchange, 414
Blocked accounts, 414
Book value
  purchase of partially owned subsidiary at, 72–77
  purchase of partially owned subsidiary at other than, 78–80
  purchase of wholly owned subsidiary at, 63
  purchase of wholly owned subsidiary at other than, 63–69
  use of, in pooling accounting, 29
Boot, 48
Branch operations, 4–5
  and financial statements, 16
  interbranch freight charges, 17–18

Branch operations—*Cont.*
  reconciliation of reciprocal accounts, 16–17
  shipments to, at cost, 5–9
  shipments to, in excess of cost, 5, 9–16
Briloff, Abraham J., 31
Brown Shoe Company, 28
Business combinations, 26–27
  application of 90 percent rule, 45–46
  costs and expenses of consummating, 38–39
  directional and antitrust considerations
    circular combinations, 28–29
    conglomerate combinations, 28–29
    horizontal combinations, 28–29
    vertical combinations, 28–29
  and dissenting shareholders, 44–45
  legal forms of, 27–28
    acquisition, 27–28
    statutory consolidation, 27
    statutory merger, 27
  methods of accounting for, 29–48
  operating results, 46
  and pooling accounting, 30–35
  and purchase accounting, 29–30, 35–38
  purchase versus pooling accounting, 39–44
  reasons for, 27
  tax aspects of, 47–48
  taxable versus nontaxable exchanges, 39

C

Capital projects funds, 631, 657–60
Capital transaction, 324
Carrying value, 326
Caveat emptor, rule of, 759
Celanese Corporation, merger of, with Tubize Rayon Corp., 31
Cestuique or beneficiary trust, 598

Chandler Act (1938), 609
Changes in financial position, consolidated statement of, 393–95
Chapter XI, 609–10
Circular business combinations, 28–29
Clayton Act (1914), 28
Colleges and universities
  accounting for, 713–17
  annuity and life income funds, 719–20
  closing entries, 717
  current fund—restricted, 717
  depreciation, 717
  endowment and similar funds, 718–19
  financial statements, 720–27
  loan funds, 717–18
Common stock equivalents (CSE), 489–90
Complete equity method
  intercompany bond transactions, 258–60
  for partially owned subsidiary subsequent to date of acquisition, 96–104
Complex affiliation structures, 350–52
  equity approach, 359–63
  legal structures, 352–58
  mutual holdings, 358–64
  reciprocal holdings, 358, 365–74
Composition agreement option, 608
Conglomerate business combinations, 28
Consolidated financial statements
  cost method, 90, 94, 114–17
  equity method, 91–94, 96–104
  income tax considerations, 158–61
  incomplete equity method, 90, 110–13
  intercompany transactions, 105–7
  and minority interest, 105
  negative goodwill, 69–72
  purchase of partially owned subsidiary
    at book value, 72–77
    at other than book value, 78–80
  purchase of wholly owned subsidiary
    at book value, 63
    at other than book value, 63–69
  reasons for, 61–62
  for unconsolidated subsidiaries, 95–96
Consolidated retained earnings, and consolidated statements, 392
Consolidated statements, 350–52
  and changes in financial position, 393–95
  complex affiliation structures, 350–64
  consolidation theories, 382–96

Consolidated statements—Cont.
  date of acquisition, 60–80
  decreases in parent's share of ownership, 322–35
  equity method, 384–89
  increases in parent's percentages of ownership by purchases of stock, 284–99
  indirect holdings of less than 50 percent, 363–64
  intercompany profit on plant asset transactions, 192–210
  intercompany profits on inventories, 138–57
    income tax provisions on consolidated income tax returns involving profits on asset transfers, 211–18
  limitations of, 389–92
  lineal structures, 352–58
  mutual holdings, 358–64
  push-down theory, 396
  subsequent to date of acquisition, 90–107
  transactions in intercompany bonds and preferred stock, 234–57
  treasury stock approach, 359–63
Continuity of interest requirement, 48
Convertible currency, 414
Corporate reorganizations and liquidations, 609–11, 614
  accounting for, 611–16
  available options for, 607–9
    judicial route, 608–9
    nonjudicial route, 608
  Bankruptcy Reform Act (1978), 609
  distribution of estate in bankruptcy, 615
  enterprises in financial difficulty, 607
  insolvency, 607
  statement of affairs, 616–19
  statement of realization and liquidation, 619–20
  trustee in bankruptcy, 614
Corpus, 591
Cost Accounting Standards Board, 463
Cost method
  and accounting for investments in subsidiaries, 90, 94, 114–17
  conversion of, to equity method, 287–89
  intercompany bond transactions, 261–65
  intercompany profit on inventories, 173–77
  preacquisition income, 301
Creditor committee option, 608
Creditors of parent company, and consolidated statements, 392

Creditors of subsidiary companies, and consolidated statements, 391–92
Currency exchange rates, 414
Current-noncurrent method of translation, 421
Current rate method of translation, 421

D

Debt service fund(s), 631, 660–61
Debtor in possession, 610
Decreases in parent's share of ownership
  cost method, 334–35
  equity method, 326
  sale of shares by subsidiary to third parties, 323–26, 334
  sale of a subsidiary's shares by parent, 334–35
  sales by an investor of part of investment, 326–31
  sales by investors of investee's stock, 326
  stock dividends, 332–33
  subsidiary's purchase of shares from third parties, 331–32
  treasury stock transactions, 331–32, 334
Demonstrative legacy, 591
Depletion, and estate accounting, 593
Depreciation, 593
  of fixed assets, 633–34
Devise, 591
Disclosure, of consolidation policies, 157
Discrete period approach, to interim financial reporting, 471–72
Dividend rate of exchange, 414
Downstream sales
  of plant assets, 195–200
  and unconfirmed profits, 139–45

E

Earnings per share, 486
  and additional disclosures, 504
  alleged weaknesses of, 504–5
  and APB Opinion 15, 487–89
  changing conversion rates or exercise prices, 500–501
  classification of contingently issuable shares, 498–99
  complex capital structure, 489–91
  evolution of computation, 487
  and investor companies with affiliates, 502–3
  option agreements, 499–500
  options and warrants, 491–98
  in period of business combination, 501–2
  restatement of prior period, 503–4
Economic Recovery Tax Act (1981), 589

Energy Policy and Conservation Act (EPCA), 769
Enterprise funds, 631–32, 668
Enterprises in financial difficulty, 607
  available options, 607–9
  and insolvency, 607
Entity method, 384–86
  and allocation of purchase price, 78
  and date of acquisition, 386–88
  subsequent to date of acquisition, 388–89
Entity theory versus proprietorship theory, 518–19
Equity method; see also Complete equity method; Incomplete equity method
  and accounting for subsidiaries, 91–94
  conversion to, from cost method, 286–89
  sales by investors of investee's stock, 326
Estate accounting, 594–98
  accountability in, 593
  accounts relating to income, 594
  accounts relating to principal, 593–94
  claims against estate, 590
  classifications of legacies, 591
  depreciation and depletion, 593
  distinction between principle and income, 591–92
  and estate planning, 589
  inventory of assets, 590
  legal aspects of estate administration, 589–91
  reporting by fiduciary, 594
  settlement of estate, 591
Exchange ratio, 45
Executor/executrix, 589
Exempt property, 590
Exxon Oil, 28

F

Fair market values, use of, in pooling accounting, 29
Family allowance, 590
FASB Interpretation No. 18, 474, 477
Federal Bankruptcy Act (1898), 609
Federal Trade Commission, 759
Fiduciary funds, 632, 634, 668–69
Financial statement ratios, and consolidated statements, 392
Financial statement(s)
  for nonbusiness organizations, 645
  in partnerships, 527
  preparation of separate set for branch, 16
  for a state or local government, 680–90
  translation of foreign currency, 420–21

Fixed assets
  accounting for, 632–33
  depreciation of, 633–34
  valuation of, 633
Foreign currency transactions, 412
  accounting for, 414–21
  conducting foreign operations, 413
  conversion versus translation, 413–14
  currency exchange rates, 414
  forward exchange contracts, 416–18
  gains/losses to be excluded from determination of net income, 420
  hedge on foreign currency net asset/liability position, 418–19
  imports and exports, 413
  measured versus denominated, 413
  translation of foreign currency financial statements, 420–21
  unsettled, 415–16
Foreign operations
  efforts to develop worldwide standards, 411–12
  foreign accounting practices, 411
  June 1981 revised exposure draft on, 422
  segment reporting, 460–63
    disclosure requirements, 461–62
    export sales, 462
    major customers, 462
    problem areas, 462–63
    SEC's position on, 462
  transactions in foreign currencies, 412–14
    accounting for, 414–21
Form S-1, 763–64
Form 10, 764
Form 8-K, 766
Form 10-K, 764–66
Form 10-Q, 766
Forward exchange contracts, 416–17
  accounting for, 417–18
  accounting for gains and losses on speculative, 420
Forward rate of exchange, 414
Fractional (partial) elimination method, intercompany profit on inventories, 140
Free rate of exchange, 414
Freight charges, interbranch, 17
Fund accounting, 630–31
  basis of, 634–35
  budgeting, account classification, terminology and financial reporting, 635–37
  definition and types of funds, 631–32
  depreciation of fixed assets, 633–34
  encumbrances and expenditures, 637–38
  financial statements, 645

Fund accounting—Cont.
  for fixed assets and long-term liabilities, 632–33
  general fund, 638–43
  inventory of supplies, 644
  number of funds, 632
  valuation of fixed assets, 633

G

General fixed assets account group, 673–76
General fund, 631, 638–43
General legacy, 591
General long-term debt account group, 676–79
Generally accepted accounting principles, 10, 29, 63
Goodwill, treatment of, 37–38, 93–94
Goodwill approach, to admission of a partner, 551–553
Governmental accounting
  accrual basis of, 634–35
  agency funds, 669–70
  budgeting, account classification, terminology, and financial reporting, 635–36
  budgeting, control, and reporting, 636–43
  capital projects fund, 657–60
  conceptual matters, 627–29
  debt service fund, 660–61
  definition and types of funds, 631–32
  depreciation of fixed assets, 633–34
  dichotomy of, 629–30
  enterprise funds, 668
  fiduciary funds, 668–69
  financial statements, 645, 680–90
  for fixed assets and long-term liabilities, 632–33
  general fixed assets account group, 673–76
  general long-term debt account group, 676–79
  internal service funds, 665–68
  inventory of supplies, 644
  number of funds, 632
  special assessment funds, 661–65
  special revenue funds, 657
  trust funds, 670–73
  valuation of fixed assets, 633
Governmental funds, 631, 634

H

Hart-Scott-Rodino amendments (1976), 28
Health and welfare organization accounting, 733
  closing entries, 736
  depreciation, 735–36
  donated services, 735
  expenses, 735
  financial statements, 736–47

Health and welfare organization
        accounting—*Cont.*
    funds, 733
    revenues, 734–35
Hedge
    accounting for, of identifiable
        foreign currency commitment,
        419
    accounting for, on foreign
        currency net asset or liability
        position, 418–19
Homestead allowance, 590
Horizontally integrated business, 3,
    28
Hospital accounting, 728
    depreciation, 728
    expenses, 728
    financial statements, 731–33
    journal entries, 728–31
    revenues, 728

I

Income, distinction between
    principal and, 591–92
Income apportionment, and
    preferred stock, 252–57
Income beneficiary, 592, 598
Income tax disclosures, 770
Incomplete equity method
    of consolidation, 97, 110–13
    intercompany profit on
        inventories, 166–72
    for investments in subsidiaries, 90
Integral period approach, to interim
    financial reporting, 472
Inter vivos trust, 598
Interbranch freight charges, 17
Intercompany bond transactions
    complete equity method, 258–60
    cost method, 261–65
    and gain or loss on consolidated
        statements, 236–37
    gain or loss on purchase of, 258–60
    parent purchase of subsidiary,
        250–51
    purchase between interest dates,
        251
    purchase of, 236
    subsidiary purchase of parent,
        237–50
Intercompany profits on inventories
    billing above cost, 139
    cost methods, 173–77
    disclosure of consolidation
        policies, 157
    gross profit versus net profit, 157
    income tax considerations, 158–61
    incomplete equity method, 166–72
    lateral sales, 156
    lower of cost or market write-
        downs, 156–57
    partial (fractional) elimination of,
        162–65

Intercompany profits on
        inventories—*Cont.*
    sales by parent company
        (downstream), 139–45
    sales by subsidiaries (upstream),
        145–52
    unconfirmed profits, 139–56
Intercompany profits on plant asset
    transfers
    intercompany sale of
        manufacturing equipment, 201
    intercompany sales of plant assets,
        195
    sale of equipment prior to
        expiration of useful life, 201–3
    sale by parent of nondepreciable
        assets, 203
    sale by subsidiaries (upstream),
        204–6
    sales by parent company
        (downstream), 195–200
    sales by subsidiaries subsequent to
        the date of acquisition, 193–95
Intercompany transactions, 105–7
    and use of pooling accounting,
        298–99
Interest capitalization, 768
Interim dates
    purchase of preferred stock on,
        292–94
    purchase of stock on, 290–92
Interim financial reporting, 470
    APB Opinion 28, 472
    discrete period approach to,
        471–72
    income taxes, 474–79
    integral period approach, 472
    need for, 471
    problem areas in, 471
    standards for reporting revenues,
        costs, and expenses, 472–74
Internal service funds, 632, 665–68
International Accounting Standards
    Committee (IASC), 411–12
International Telephone and
    Telegraph Company (ITT), 28
Intestate, 589
Intestate distribution, 591
Inventories
    reductions of, 156–57
    unconfirmed profits on, 138–56
Investors
    sales by, of investee's stock, 326
    sales by, as part of its investment
        in a subsidiary or affiliate,
        326–31
Involuntary petition for bankruptcy,
    609

J–K–L

Joint proxy statement, of Mattel, Inc.,
    and Western Publishing Co., Inc.
    773–92

Kinney, G. R., Company, 28
Kripke, Homer, 771
Lateral sales, 156
Leases, reporting of, 767–68
Legacies, classification of, 591
Letters of administration, 590
Letters testamentary, 589
Liabilities, guidelines for valuation of,
    37
Liquidation; *see* Corporate
    reorganizations and liquidations
Lower of cost or market write-
    downs, 156

M

Management's discussion and
    analysis of financial condition
    and results of operation, 770–71
Manufacturing equipment
    intercompany sale of, 201
    sale of, prior to expiration of
        useful life, 201–3
Market write-downs, 156–57
Marshaling of assets, 571–75
Mattel, Inc., joint proxy statement of,
    and Western Publishing, Inc.,
    773–95
Maturity date extension option, 608
Mautz, R. K., 453
May, George C., 31
Minority interests
    accounting for, in consolidated
        statement, 103, 105, 391
    definition of, 3
    showing of, on consolidated
        balance sheet, 74
    verification of, 103
Mobil Oil, 28
Monetary-nonmonetary method of
    translation, 421
Multiple exchange rate, 414
Municipal Finance Officers
    Association (MFOA), 630
Mutual or reciprocal holdings, 3

N

National Conference of
    Commissioners on Uniform
    State Laws, 589
National Council of Governmental
    Accounting (NCGA), 630
NCGA *Statement No. 1*, 630–31, 635,
    643
Negative goodwill, 69–72
Nonbusiness organizations
    accounting for, 626–27
    agency funds, 669–70
    and budgeting, 636–37
    capital projects fund, 657–60
    conceptual matters, 627–29
    debt service fund, 660–61
    dichotomy of, 629–30

Nonbusiness organizations—*Cont.*
  and encumbrances and
      expenditures, 637–38
  enterprise funds, 668
  fiduciary funds, 668–69
  financial statements, 645, 680–90
  and fund accounting, 630–36
  general fixed assets account
      group, 673–76
  general fund, 638–43
  general long-term debt account
      group, 676–79
  internal service funds, 665–68
  inventory of supplies, 644
  special assessment funds, 661–65
  special revenue funds, 657
  trust funds, 670–73
Nondepreciable assets, sale by
    parent, 203
Nontaxable reorganizations, 47–48
  and judicial doctrines, 48
  types of, 47–48
  and use of boot, 48
North American Philips Corporation,
    36–37

O

Oil and gas, accounting for, 769–70
One-line consolidation, 103
One-transaction perspective, 415
Operating profit test, of segment
    reporting, 456–57
Operating transfers, 635

P

Parent company
  definition of, 3
  income tax implications between
      subsidiaries and, 108–9
  increases in percentages of
      ownership by purchases of
      stock, 284–300
  plant asset sale by, 195–200
  purchase of shares from a
      subsidiary, 289–90
  sale of subsidiary's shares by,
      334–35
  sales by, in unconfirmed profits,
      139–45
Parent method of allocating purchase
    price, 78
Parent-subsidiary relationship, 3
Part purchase/part pooling, 31
Partial (fractional) elimination of
    intercompany profits, 162–65
Partnerships, 516
  admission of partner
      investment into the partnership,
          551
      profit and loss ratio and capital
          ratio coincide, 551–55
      profit and loss ratios are
          different, 555

Partnerships—*Cont.*
      purchase from existing partners,
          548–51
  assignment of partner's interest,
      517
  bonus to partners, 525–26
  changes in profit and loss ratios,
      547–48
  death of partner, 556–57
  division of income in capital ratio,
      524–25
  division of operating results,
      521–27
  equity versus proprietorship
      theories, 518–19
  financial statements, 527
  incorporation of, 557–58
  initial contributions to capital,
      519–20
  interest on capital and loan
      accounts, 523–24
  limited life, 517–18
  liquidation in installments, 575–80
  liquidation in one transaction,
      569–75
  mutual agency, 517
  retirement of partner, 555–56
  rights of partners in liquidation,
      569
  salaries to partners, 521–22
  tax basis of partner's interest, 529
  tax basis of property in, 528
  taxation of, 518
  taxation of income, 528
  unlimited liability, 517
  written agreements, 520
Pecora, Ferdinand, 759
Penalty rate of exchange, 414
Personal property, and estate
    settlement, 591
Piecemeal acquisitions, of stock,
    285–86
Plant assets
  downstream sale of, 195–200
  intercompany sales of, 195
  sales of, by subsidiaries subsequent
      to the date of acquisition,
      193–95
  upstream sale at other than end of
      year, 207–9
  upstream sale by subsidiaries,
      204–6
Pooling accounting, 29–30, 294–96
  acquisition on interim date, 296–98
  application of 90 percent rule,
      45–46
  conditions for use of, 32–35
  consummation of combination,
      38–39
  differences between purchase
      accounting, 30
  and dissenting shareholders, 44–45
  historical development of, 30–32

Pooling accounting—*Cont.*
  intercompany transactions, 298–99
  methodology for, 41–44
  operating result, 46
  taxable versus nontaxable
      exchanges, 39
Pooling of interests, 501–2
Preacquisition income, cost method,
    301
Preferential rate of exchange, 414
Preferred stock
  allocation of retained earnings, 252
  income apportionment, 252–57
  investments in, 252
  purchase of, on interim dates,
      292–94
Price-level changes, effects of, 768–69
Principal, distinction between
    income and, 591–92
Pro forma supplementary disclosure,
    38
Probate, 589
Profit, gross versus net, 157
Profit and loss ratios, changes in, for
    partnerships, 547–48
Proprietary funds, 631–32, 634
Proprietorship theory versus entity
    theory, 518–19
Purchase accounting, 29–30
  application of, 35–38
  and costs of consummating
      combination, 38–39
  differences between pooling
      accounting, 30
  methodology for, 40–41
  operating results, 46
  pro forma supplementary
      disclosure, 38
  and purchase of stock at interim
      dates, 290–91
  and taxable versus nontaxable
      exchanges, 39
Push-down theory, 396

Q–R

Quasi-reorganizations, 611
Real property, and estate settlement,
    591
Reciprocal accounts, reconciliation
    of, 16–17
Reciprocal holdings
  indirect holdings and mutual
      relationships, 373–74
  investment in subsidiary carried at
      equity
  and investment in parent carried
      at cost, 365–70
  and investment in parent carried
      at equity, 370–73
Regulation S-K, 762
Regulation S-X, 762
Remainderman, 592, 598

Reorganizations; *see* Corporate
  reorganizations and liquidations
Reserve recognition accounting, 769
Residual equity transfers, 635
Residual legacy, 591
Retroactive adjustment, 326
Retrospective pooling, 31
Revenue test, of segment reporting,
  456
Revised exposure draft (June 1981),
  422
Revised Uniform Principal and
  Income Act (1978), 592
Right of offset, 569
Ripley, William Z., 759
Roosevelt, Franklin D., 759

S

Securities Exchange Act (1933), 453,
  759, 761–62, 764
Securities Exchange Act (1934), 453,
  761, 762
Security and Exchange Commission
  (SEC)
  disclosure requirements, 478–79
  influence on accounting theory/
    practice, 766–72
  organization of, 760–61
  origins of, 759–60
  position of, on segment reporting,
    462
  principal acts administered by,
    761–66
Segment reporting, 392, 452
  applicable accounting standards,
    454
  areas covered by segmental
    disclosures, 454–55
  asset test, 457–58
  dominant segments, 459
  evaluation of reportable segments,
    458–59
  evolving interest in, 453
  foreign operations, 461–63
  objectives of segment disclosure,
    454
  operating profit test, 456–57
  operations in different industries,
    455–60
  revenue test, 456
  SEC reporting requirements, 453
  SFAS 14, 454
  unconsolidated investments, 454
Selling price, shipments by home
  office to branch at, 5
Sherman Act (1890), 28
Special assessment funds, 631,
  661–65
Special revenue funds, 631, 657
Specific legacy, 591
Spot rate of exchange, 414
Staff Accounting Bulletins, 763

Statement of affairs, 616–19
  format, 616
*Statement of Financial Accounting
  Standards (SFAS)*
  3, 477
  8, 422, 430–34
  13, 768
  14, 392, 453–55, 458–60, 462–63
  19, 454, 769–70
  21, 454
  25, 770
  33, 769
  52, 422–30, 432
Statement of realization and
  liquidation, 619–20
Statutory consolidation, 27
Statutory merger, 27
Step transaction, 32, 48
Stock dividends, 332–33
Subsidiaries
  income tax implications between
    parents and, 108–9
  purchase of bonds, by parent
    company, 250–51
  purchase of parent's bonds, 237–50
  purchase of partially owned, at
    book value, 72–77
  purchase of partially owned, at
    other than book value, 78–79
  purchase of shares by, from third
    party, 331–32, 334
  purchase of shares from, 289–90
  purchase of wholly owned at book
    value, 63
  purchase of wholly owned at other
    than book value, 63–69
  sale of shares by, to third parties,
    323–26, 334
  sales by, in unconfirmed profits,
    145–52
  sales by investors as part of its
    investment in, or affiliate,
    326–31
  unconsolidated, 95–96
  using complete equity method,
    96–104
  using cost method, 94, 114–17
  using equity method, 91–94
  using incomplete equity method,
    110–13
Supply inventory, for nonbusiness
  organizations, 644

T

Tax Reform Act (1976), 589
Taxes
  for business combinations, 39,
    47–48
  implications between parents and
    subsidiaries, 108–9
  on intercompany profits on
    inventories, 158–61

Taxes—*Cont.*
  for partnerships, 518, 528–29
Temporal method of translation, 421
Testate distribution, 591
Third party
  purchase of shares from, by
    subsidiary, 331–32, 334
  sale of shares by subsidiary to,
    323–26, 334
Transactions in intercompany bonds
  and preferred stock
  accounting for retirement of
    treasury bonds, 235
  parent purchase of subsidiary's
    bonds, 250–51
  purchase between interest dates,
    251
  purchase of intercompany bonds,
    236–37
  subsidiary purchase of parent's
    bonds, 237–50
Treasury bonds, retirement of,
  235–36
Treasury stock method, of
  computing earnings per share,
  491–94
Treasury stock transactions,
  subsidiary's purchase of shares
  from third party, 331–32, 334
Trial balance working papers, 118–19
Trust and agency funds, 632
Trust funds, 670–73
Trusts, legal and accounting aspects
  of, 598–99
Tubize Rayon Corporation, merger
  of, with Celanese Corporation, 31
Two-transaction perspective, 415

U

Unconfirmed (unrealized) profits
  illustration of, 152–56
  sales by parent company
    (downstream), 139–45
  sales by subsidiaries (upstream),
    145–52
Uniform Partnership Act (UPA),
  516–17, 530–40, 569
Uniform Probate Code, 589
Uniform Trustees Accounting Act,
  598–99
Universities; *see* Colleges and
  universities
Unsolidated subsidiaries, accounting
  for, 95–96, 113
Unusual risks and uncertainties,
  disclosure of, 770
Upstream sale
  of plant assets, 204–6
  of plant assets at other than end of
    year, 207–9
  and unconfirmed profits, 145–52

V–W

Vertically integrated business, 3, 28
Voluntary assignment option, 608
Voluntary bankruptcy, 608–9
Voluntary petition for bankruptcy,
609

Weighted average of common shares
outstanding, computation of
earnings per share, 488–89
Welfare organization accounting; *see*
Health and welfare organization
accounting

Western Publishing Co., Inc., joint
proxy statement of, and Mattel,
Inc., 773–95

*This book has been set Linotron 202, in 10 and
9 point Zapf Book Medium, leaded 2 points.
Chapter numbers are 72 point Zapf Book Demi
and chapter titles are 30 point Zapf Book Light.
The size of the type page is 37 by 49$^{1}/_{2}$ picas.*